A Complete Greek and English Lexicon for the Poems of Homer and the Homeridæ: Illustrating the Domestic, Religious, Political, and Military Condition of the Heroic Age and Explaining the Most Difficult Passages

Thomas Kerchever Arnold, Henry Smith, Gottlieb Christian Crusius

their felicitous precision by being turned into Engli
have also added, here and there, the explanations of th
recent editors, *Dübner* on the Iliad, *Fäsi* on the Od
In carrying the work through the press, I have rem(
very considerable number of false references (some of
still remain in the third German edition), and several
neous interpretations, occasioned by a misapprehens
the German original, which a reference to the passag(
stands in the poet himself, would have enabled the]
translator to avoid. Upon the whole, however,]
executed a difficult task successfully; and well deser·
thanks of English, as well as of American students.

T.

AUTHOR'S PREFACE.

NOTWITHSTANDING the great number of excellent helps which have been published, for a series of years past, in illustration of the Homeric poems, there has still, so far as my acquaintance extends, appeared no complete Lexicon, presenting within a moderate compass, to the numerous readers, and especially to the young readers of these poems, every thing necessary for understanding them. In my apprehension, a Lexicon of a particular author, although designed only for schools, should not contain simply an alphabetic series of words with their definitions, but should also particularly notice peculiarities of expression, and those passages which in point of construction or the signification of words, are difficult to be understood, or admit of different interpretations; it should also embrace, in connexion with the words, and especially with the proper names, the requisite explanations from mythology, geography, antiquities, and other auxiliary sciences, and thus form, as it were, a repertory of every thing needful for understanding the author. To what extent I have attempted to attain this object, will be seen by noticing the contents of this Lexicon. First, then, it contains all the words found in the Iliad and Odyssey, in the hymns, and other small poems. Secondly, especial attention is paid to the explanation of difficult passages; and, as far as space permitted, differing views, when existing, have been noticed. Thirdly, it contains all the proper names, accompanied by the necessary mythological and geographical explanations.

Before speaking further of the plan of this work, it is proper, perhaps, that I should justify myself in applying to it the expression, "A complete Lexicon."

The most copious Lexicon of Homer we possess, is the work of *Damm*, which appeared in 1765, under the title: "Novum Lexicon Græcum etymologicum et reale, cui pro basi substratæ sunt concordantiæ Homericæ et Pindaricæ." It embraces, as is well known, in addition to the Pindaric vocabulary, all the words to be found in the Iliad and Odyssey, with a careful citation of the passages in which they occur. In the last edition it has been improved, in point of convenience, by an alphabetical arrangement; and by the copious additions of Prof. Rost of Gotha, it has been brought nearer to the present

▲ 3

standard of Greek scholarship. Although that carefully-execut
is not to be brought into comparison with the present, in re,
its extent and peculiar design, yet it does not contain the
wealth of the Homeric language, since all the words and
names peculiar to the hymns are wanting. That we shoɪ
in it omissions of single words, even in the Iliad and Ody:
ἄμαθος, ἀμπείρω, ἀναπείρω, Δύμη, Ἑλικάων, ἑκτάδιος, ἐ᾽
πολύτρητος, ῥυσός, φώκη, etc. was certainly, considering the ↄ
of the work, to be expected. A still older work, " W. Seber
Homericus s. Index Vocabulorum in omnia Homeri Poëmata," iₛ
catalogue of the Homeric forms of words, without explanatio:
portant as this work is for the study of Homer, it has contrib
advantage to my undertaking, except that of enabling me by
parison, to determine whether any word had been omitted. Aɪ
this comparison it was necessary to make with great cautioɪ
the text of Homer has undergone many alterations since the ᵣ
tion of the work. Among the remaining Lexicons, I may ₐ
that of Koës, which has appeared however only in the sampl
letter A ; and the separately-published Lexicons of the Iɭ
Odyssey, by *Lünemann.* How defective these books are, is kɪ
every scholar who has examined them. In the definitions
words, little more is to be found than in any general Lexico
small attention is paid to the explanation of difficult passages,
the proper names of mythology and geography. That, finally,
Lexicons do not possess this completeness, is obvious from t
that proper names are for the most part excluded, and whe
duced, commonly lack particular explanation. The Lexicon of
however, forms an exception to these remarks *, because thiₛ
guished Greek scholar directed his particular attention to the ɪ
vocabulary. With a deep conviction of the value of the servic
its lamented author has rendered to the poems of Homer, I gᵣ
acknowledge the solid information I have often derived from hi
lent work. That, however, in many difficult passages of these
a satisfactory explanation is wanting, and that many mytholog᾽
geographical articles are either not introduced, or lack an exp.
sufficient for understanding the poet, will have been remaɪ
those who have used the work.

With these remarks, it is proper I should indicate more spₑ
the plan which I have followed in the composition of this Lexiↄ

The demand which may properly be made in a Lexicon of
author, in regard to Grammar, I hope, in accordance with thↄ
the work, to have met. In the case of substantives and ad
the Epic and poetic forms of the cases are annexed, commonly
reference to the ordinary forms. The verb demanded partiↄ
tention. Here, I have given not only the main tenses, buɪ

---

* I need not say, that this applies in a still higher degree to the admirabl
of Liddell and Scott.—T. K. A.

addition the Epic and poetical forms.   Difficult forms of persons and
tenses, which the younger student would not easily trace, I have, after
the example of other Lexicons, introduced into the alphabetic series,
and referred to their ground form.   For the further information of
students, I have referred to the large Grammar of Thiersch, to the
intermediate one of Buttmann, which is commonly used in the schools,
and to that of Rost, as well as to the recently-published Grammar of
my valued colleague, Dr. Kühner [in the 3rd Ed. to his School
Grammar].   The large Grammar of Buttmann is rarely quoted, and
only when the intermediate one affords no information on the topic
in hand.   In connexion with the common forms, the poetical forms
are also given.   Finally, I have thought it expedient, according to
the derivation of the Grammars, to place the different forms of a root
under the form which is in use as the Present, cf. ἀκακίζω, ἀραρίσκω,
ἱατέομαι, &c.

In addition to the Etymology, in the case of derivative words, those
which occur only in the poets are designated as poetic, and if found
only in Epic writers, as Epic.   For these references, I gratefully
acknowledge my obligation to the Lexicon of Rost.   To quantity,
sufficient attention has, as a general principle, been paid, to mark the
long syllables.   A more extended explanation is given when the quantity admits of a doubt.

In regard to the definition of words, and to the numbering of the
significations, a careful examination will show, that I have endeavoured
to follow a natural arrangement.   That I should, in a majority of
words, agree with other Lexicons, results from the nature of the case ;
and I gratefully acknowledge, that in this point I am much indebted to
the labours of Passow and Rost.   It has been an especial aim, in the
arrangement of the significations, to render the examination of them
easy.   For this reason, the main definitions, as well as those modifica-
tions of signification which a word receives in various connexions, are
printed in spaced type [in this Ed. in Italics] ; and the peculiar significations of the middle voice are distinguished from those of the active.
In difficult words, I have not only compared the modern commentators
and translators, but have also consulted the Scholia of the old Grammarians, the Commentary of Eustathius, and the Lexicon of Apollonius.
Not unfrequently has the translation of Voss been cited verbatim,
when it appeared important in the explanation of a word or passage.   What degree of attention has been paid to the illustration of
the domestic, religious, political, and military condition of the heroic
age, will be seen by an examination of individual words, as βασιλεύς,
δῆμος, of the mythological articles, of the names of clothes, weapons, &c.
Finally, an equal degree of care has been bestowed upon the syntactic
use of verbs in reference to cases and prepositions, and upon the explanation of the particles.   In this connexion, justice requires that I
should acknowledge my indebtedness to the Grammar of Dr. Kühner,
which in this respect is so complete and copious.

In a Lexicon of a particular author, designed at the same time to

supply the place of a commentary, it appears to me necessary, not
to indicate the passages explained, but also to indicate those in wh
word occurs in a peculiar signification or connexion. This desider
I have endeavoured to supply, and have also marked the so-
ἅπαξ εἰρημένα with +. In order to distinguish the language o
hymns from that of the Iliad and Odyssey, an asterisk (*) is pre
to the words which occur only in the hymns and other small p
If to an article *Il. or *Od. is annexed, it shows that the word o
only in the Iliad or Odyssey

As I have mentioned, as a second peculiarity of this Lexicon
explanation of difficult passages, I may add a word upon this poin
careful examination of the book will show that not many difficult
sages occur, for which there is not offered at least one translatio
passages which admit of different explanations, the opposing view
always cited, with the grounds upon which they rest. The pas
which have received a more detailed explanation, have been arr;
in a special register, at the end of the preface, with a reference t
word under which the explanation is given, because, in many pas.
it might be sought under different words.

The mythological and geographical proper names have been
duced into the alphabetical series, partly because the verbal exp
tion of them is found in appellatives in use ; and partly becaus
different accentuation of the proper name and appellative, is ren
more distinct by juxtaposition.

In the case of proper names which do not occur as appellative
definitions are given, for which I am indebted principally to Her
Diss. de Mythol. Græcorum Antiquissima, and De Historiæ G
Primordiis (Opus. II. 1827). I have thus endeavoured to rem
ground of complaint which has reached me from various respe
quarters, in regard to my Lexicon of Greek proper names *.
the mythological and geographical explanations have not beer
rowed from that work, but have been for the most part writt
the purpose of illustrating the Homeric poems, will be seen by a
parison of the two works. For the mythological articles, I have
sulted especially M. G. Hermann's Handbuch der Mythologi
Homer und Hesiod, E. L. Cammann's Vorschule zu der Iliade
D. E. Jacobi's Handwörterbuch der griechischen und röm
Mythologie. Upon the principal works which have appeared c
Homeric Geography, as those of Schönemann, Voss, Uckert,
Grotefend, Völcker, as well as upon other writings which treat c
subject, as Mannert's Geographie der Griechen und Römer, O
Müller's Geschichte hellen. Stämme, I. Bd., etc., I have besto
careful attention, although the plan of the work allowed only the
important points to be noticed.

* Griechisch-Deutches Wörterbuch der mythologischen und geograph
Eigennamen, nebst beigefügter kurzer Erklärung und Angabe der Sylbenlän
Hanover, 1832.

From what has been said, it will be inferred, that I have spared no pains in consulting all the helps for the explanation of Homer, within the compass of my acquaintance. The text which I have had principally in my eye is that of Wolf; in connexion with which, however, I have referred to the editions of Heyne, Bothe, and Spitzner; and in the hymns to Ilgen, Hermann, and Franke. For definitions and explanations, materials have been drawn, not merely from the above sources, but also from the observations of Köppen, Heinrichs, Nitzsch, Nägelsbach, and from particular works on the Homeric language, as Buttmann's Lexilogus, Lehrs de Aristarchi Studiis Homericis, etc.; and I acknowledge with sincere gratitude the information I have derived from them. The work of Dr. Gräfenhan, Grammat. Dialectici Epicæ, Vol. I. L. 1, which will present an accurate and fundamental view of the phenomena of the Epic dialect, came into my hands whilst the last sheet was in the press; some more important matters from this work I have given in an appendix.

To what extent, in the execution of the work, I have succeeded in filling out the plan, which has been sketched, must be left to the candid decision of those who are qualified to judge. The more deep my conviction is of having often fallen short of my aim, the more thankful shall I be to receive any corrections or hints for improvement.

Finally, it will be the highest reward I can receive for the labour bestowed upon it, should intelligent teachers judge as favorably in regard to the utility of the book, as one sharp-sighted student of the Homeric poems has already expressed himself. I refer to Dr. Grotefend, the director of the Lyceum in this city, to whose inspection the plan of the undertaking, and a part of the work itself, was submitted.

G. CH. CRUSIUS.

Hanover, Nov. 1835.

INDEX OF DIFFICULT PASSAGES

(VID. PREFACE.)

ABBREVIATIONS.

absol. signifies absolute.
accus. ,, accusative.
act. ,, active.
adj. ,, adjective
adv. ,, adverb.
Æol. ,, Æolic.
aor. ,, aorist.
Apd. ,, Apollodorus.
Apoll. or Ap Apollonii Lex. Homeri-
  cum.
Att. ,, Attic.
Batr. ,, Batrachomyomachia.
comm. ,, common, commonly.
compar. ,, comparative.
conj. ,, conjunction.
dat. ,, dative.
depon. ,, deponent.
Dor. ,, Doric.
Ep. ,, Epic.
epith. ,, epithet.
fem. ,, feminine.
fut. ,, future.
gen. ,, genitive.
h. ,, hymn.
Il. ,, Iliad.
imperat. ,, imperative.
imperf. ,, imperfect.
infin. ,, infinitive.
intrans. ,, intransitive.

Ion. signifies Ionic.
iterat. ,, iterative.
κ. τ. λ. ,, καὶ τὰ λοιπά = etc
Lex. ,, Lexicon.
Buttm. Lex. Buttmann's Lexil(
metaph. ,, metaphorical.
mid. ,, middle.
neut. ,, neuter.
Od. ,, Odyssey.
optat. ,, optative.
partcp. ,, participle.
pass. ,, passive.
perf. ,, perfect.
plupf. ,, pluperfect.
plur. ,, plural.
poet. ,, poetic.
signif. ,, signification, signi
sing. ,, singular.
subj. ,, subjunctive.
V. ,, Vater or Voss.
= ,, equivalent to.
† ,, ἅπαξ εἰρημένον.
? ,, doubtful.
• ,, only in the hymns
•Il. ,, only in the Iliad.
•Od. ,, only in the Odyss(
[ ] ,, additions by the
  lator, or by the
  Editor.

Cp. = Cowper.
Db. = Dübner.
Död. = Döderlein.
Fäs. = Fäsi.

Note.—To save space "Il." has been omitted; so that references to which
is not prefixed, are all of them from the *Iliad.*

HOMERIC LEXICON.

A.

A, the first letter of the Gr. alphabet; as a numeral *one*; in Homer therefore the sign of the first Rhapsody. The 24 Rhapsodies (or *books*), both of the Iliad and Odyssey, are distinguished by the 24 letters of the Gr. alphabet.

a, in composition, is 1) *a privative* (before a vowel commonly ἀν), the English *in-* or *un-*, denoting a *negation* of the idea; sometimes also giving it a *bad sense*; ἄδηλος, *in*-visible, ἄπαις, child-*less*, ἄβουλος, *ill*-advised, ἀναίτιος, *in*-nocent. 2) a *copulative* [answering to the adv. ἅμα], indicates primarily a connexion of two objects, also mly conveying the notion of *equality, collection,* and *intensity*; ἄλοχος (λέχος), *bedfellow, wife*; ἀτάλαντος, *equiponderant*; ἀθρόος (θρέω), *assembled, crowded together*. 3) a *intensive*, strengthening the adj. with which it is compounded and answering to the adv. ἄγαν, ἄβρομος, *loud-roaring*; ἀσπερχής, *very impetuous*. This *intensive* a is found in but very few compounds [if at all] and is denied by many Gram. 4) a *euphonic* is prefixed for mere sound's sake to many words beginning with two consonants; ἀβληχρός for βληχρός; ἀστεροπή for στεροπή.

ἆ, interj., an exclamation denoting *displeasure, pity, astonishment*; oh! ah! ἆ δειλέ, ah *wretch!* 11, 441.

ἄδατος, ον, poet. (ἀάω), 1) *inviolable* = *what one does not dare to violate*; epith. of the waters of the Styx, 14, 271. 2) = *what one cannot violate, cannot injure*, &c.; as an ep. of a contest, Od. 21, 91. 22, 5. According to Buttm. Lexil. p. 4, the waters of the Styx are called *inviolable*, because the gods swore by them an oath *not to be broken*; and in the Od. the contest is called *inviolable*, i. e. *that which may not be spoken against*, hence *honorable, distinguished*; but Passow translates the word *irrevocable*, i. e. a contest whose result is decisive. The old Gram. suppose either a double a privative, or an a intensive, and explain ἄδατος by πολυβλαβής, *very injurious*.

ἀαγής, ές (ἄγνυμι), *not to be broken, difficult to break, strong*, ῥόπαλον, Od. 11, 575.†

ἀάομαι, depon. mid. see ἀάω.

ἄαπτος, ον, poet. (ἅπτομαι), *not to be touched, unapproachable, invincible*, epith. of the strong hands of the gods and heroes, 1, 567. 7, 309.

ἄασχετος, ον, Ep. for ἄσχετος.

ἀάω, poet. (‿ ‿ _), aor. 1. act. ἄασα, contr. ἆσα, aor. mid. ἀασάμην, 3. sing. ἄσατο, aor. pass. ἀάσθην. Of pres. only 3 sing. mid. ἀᾶται. I) Act. trans. *to injure, to harm*, with acc. ἦ ῥά τιν' ἤδη βασιλήων τῇδ' ἄτῃ ἄασας; hast thou ever before injured any king by such misfortune? i. e. brought him into such misfortune? 8, 236. *b*) Especially *to injure in the understanding, to infatuate, to befool, to mislead, to delude*, with and without φρένας: οἴνῳ, to stupify his mind with wine, Od. 21, 297. ἄασαν μ' ἕταροι, my companions befooled me, Od. 10, 68 [in this passage it is, *have wronged* or *injured* me]; and δαίμονος αἶσα, Od. 11, 61; hence pass. *to be deluded, infatuated, blinded, to fall into disaster*, 16, 685. Ἄτη, ᾗ πρῶτον ἀάσθην, Ate, by whom I was first infatuated, 19, 136. ἀασθεὶς φρεσίν, Od. 21, 301. II) Mid. [exclusively in ref. to the *mind*] *to delude oneself, to let oneself be deceived, to mistake, to err, to act foolishly*, 9, 116; also ἀάσατο μέγα θυμῷ, he was utterly infatuated in mind, 11, 340. *b*) As dep. mid. with acc. *to lead astray*, 19, 91.

Ἀβακέω (βάζω), poet. aor. ἀβάκησα, properly, *to be without speech*; gener. *to be uninformed, to be ignorant, to be unsuspicious*, Od. 4, 249.†

Ἄβαντες, οἱ, *the Abantes*, the earliest inhabitants of the island of Euboea, who went to Troy under Elephenor the son of Chalcodon; probably a colony from the Pelop. Argos which emigrated to Euboea under king Abas; according to Strabo they came from Thrace, 2, 536.

Ἀβαρβαρέη, ἡ (from ἀ and βάρβαρος native), a fountain nymph, mother of Æsepus and Pedasus by Bucolion, 6, 22.

Ἀβᾶς, αντος, ὁ (from ἀ and βαίνω not going away, Nabito, Herm.), a Trojan, son of *Eurydamas*, killed by Diomedes, 5, 148.

Ἄβιοι, οἱ, *the Abii*, nomadic Scythians in the north of Europe, accord. to Strabo, VII. p. 360, on the Ister, 13. 6. † (prop. *poor, needy*, from a and βίος: Wolf and Heyne have marked it as a proper name; it was previously explained as an adjective.)

[ἄβιος, ον, see Ἄβιοι.]

* ἀβλαβέως, poet. for ἀβλαβῶς, adv. (ἀβλαβής), *harmlessly, without harm*, h. Merc. 83.

* ἀβλαβίη, ἡ, poet. for ἀβλάβεια (βλά-

B

πτω), *inviolability.* 2) *harmlessness, innocence;* in the plur. ἀβλαβίαι νόοιο, h. Merc. 393.

Ἄβληρος, ὁ, a Trojan, killed by Antilochus, son of Nestor, 6, 32.

ἀβλής, ῆτος, ὁ, ἡ, poet. (βάλλω), *not discharged, unshot,* epith. of an unused arrow, 4, 117.†

ἄβλητος, ον, poet. (βάλλω), *not hit, unhurt,* 4, 540.†

ἀβληχρός, ή, όν (a euphon. and βληχρός), *weak, powerless, gentle;* χείρ, the feeble hand of Venus, 5, 337; τεῖχος, a weak wall, 8, 178; θάνατος, a gentle death, Od. 11, 135. [Cf. ἀμαλός and μαλακός. Buttm. Lex. 194.]

ἄβρομος, ον (a intens. and βρόμος according to Apoll. Lex.), *loud-shouting, very clamorous.* Epith of the Trojans, 13, 41.† Passow with Eustath. makes a euphon. and translates *clamorous.* Buttm. makes a copulative, and translates *shouting together.*

ἀβροτάζω, poet. (prob. from aor. 2 ἀμβροτεῖν, Epic for ἁμαρτεῖν), *to miss,* τινός any one: found only in aor. 1 subj. μήπως ἀβροτάξομεν (ep. for ἀβροτάξωμεν) ἀλλήλοιϊν, lest we miss one another. 10, 65.† See Thiersch. § 232. Buttm. Lex. p. 82.

ἄβροτος, η, ον, later ος, ον, poet. (βροτός) =ἄμβροτος, *immortal, divine, holy.* νὺξ ἀβρότη, *sacred night,* because it is a gift of the gods, 14, 78. (The meaning *without men* is doubtful. See Buttm. Lex. p. 83.)

Ἄβυδος, ἡ, *Abydos,* a city in the Trojan dominion on the Hellespont, opposite Sestos, now *Avido,* 2, 836. Hence the adv. Ἀβυδόθεν, *from A.,* and Ἀβυδόθι, *in* or *at A.*

ἀγάασθαι, see ἄγαμαι.

ἄγαγον, see ἄγω.

ἀγάζομαι, pres. not used by Homer, but supplies the tenses assigned to ἄγαμαι.

ἀγαθός, ή, όν, *good, excellent, strong,* distinguished of its kind. a) Spoken of persons, espec. of physical force and bravery; often with accus. of the limiting word, βοὴν ἀγαθός, good in the battle-cry (see βοή), epith. of leaders. β) Of birth, *noble, high-born* (opposed to χέρηες), Od. 15, 324. b) Of things and states, εἰς ἀγαθὰ εἰπεῖν, μυθεῖσθαι, to speak for good, 9, 102. 23. 305. (cf. φρονέω) πείθεσθαι εἰς ἀγαθόν, 11, 789. ἀγαθὰ φρονεῖν, to be *well-intentioned, right-minded,* 6, 162. Neut. pl. subst. ἀγαθά, Od. 14, 441. Irreg. comp. ἀμείνων, βελτίων, κρείσσων, λωΐων, superl. ἄριστος, βέλτιστος, κράτιστος, λώϊστος, etc. [Lobeck doubts the relationship between ἀγαθός and ἄγαμαι, which Buttm. approves of. Path. Serm. Græc. p. 363.]

Ἀγάθων, ωνος, ὁ (amplif. of ἀγαθός), son of Priam and Hecuba, 24, 249.

ἀγαίομαι, Ep. form of ἄγαμαι, only in pres. in the sing., *to be indignant, to be angry,* Od. 20, 16.†

ἀγακλεής, ές, poet. (ἄγαν, κλέος), gen. έος, *very illustrious, famous, glorious,*

generally of men; once of Hep (Vulcan), *Il. 21, 379.

Ἀγακλεής, contr. ῆς, ῆος, ὁ, a don, father of Epigeus, *Il. 16, 57

ἀγακλειτός, ή, όν=ἀγακλεής, po *celebrated, famous, glorious,* gener men. b) Of things: only ἀγ ἑκατόμβη, a glorious hecatomb, O

ἀγακλυτός, όν, poet. (κλυτός), which one hears much, *far-fame glorious,* generally of men. b) Of only ἀγακλυτὰ δώματα, Od. 3, 388

* ἀγαλλίς, ίδος, ἡ, a bulbous flower *of the Iris tribe,* perhaps the *lily,* h. Cer. 7. 226.

ἀγάλλομαι, mid. only pres. *to g exult in,* to be proud of any with the dat. generally in the spoken of men: ἵπποισιν κ σφιν, proud of horses and chari 114. Of gods: of the Thriæ, h. 553. Of Pan: φρένα μολπαῖς, to be in heart of the songs, h. 18, 2 mares: πώλοισιν, exulting in the 20, 222. Of birds: πτερύγεσσι, ε in their wings, 2, 462. Of ships Διὸς οὔρῳ, to exult in the fair Zeus, i. e. to be favoured with wind, Od. 5. 176. b) With a pa Hector: ἀνάλλεται ἔχων τεύχεα, he in arms, 17, 473.

ἄγαλμα, ατος, τό (ἀγάλλω), proj contributes to splendour, or ser ornament [= καλλώπισμα, πᾶν ἐφ ἀγάλλεται], *an ornament, a jewel,* Od. 4, 602. Spoken especially of offerings to the gods, *a glorious* or *able offering.* Of the Trojan horse, θεῶν, Od. 8, 509. Of a bullock a as a victim, Od. 3. 438. [The m *image,* etc. is post-Homeric.]

ἄγαμαι, dep. mid. a collateral E of ἀγάομαι and ἀγαίομαι, fut. ἀγ (Wolf νεμεσήσεαι, Od. 1, 389). aor. ἠγασάμην, ἠγασσάμην. (Fr. ἄγαμ 1 sing. pres. fr. ἀγάομαι 2 pl ἀγάασθε Ep. for ἄγασθε. Inf ἀγάασθαι for ἀγᾶσθαι, 2 pl.impf. ἠ for ἠγᾶσθε.) 1) *to esteem,* in a good *to admire, to venerate,* with acc. μῦθον, 7, 404; without acc. *to* Od. 23, 175; with partcp. 3. 224 *consider as too great;* in a bad s *envy, to grudge* (in which signif. uses the pres. ἀγάομαι and ἀγ with the dat. of pers. spoken of cially of the gods, 17, 71), and the thing: τὰ μέν που μέλλεν ὸ σθαι θεὸς αὐτός, but this must eve have envied [if it had happene therefore it did not happen. F.], 181; and with inf. νῦν μοι ἀγασθ βροτὸν ἄνδρα παρεῖναι, now ye en ye gods, that a mortal man is wi Od. 5, 119. 8, 565. 3) *to be offend to be angry at,* with acc. κακὰ ἔργα 67; κότῳ to be offended, to regar anger, 14, 111.

Ἀγαμεμνονίδης, ου, ὁ, son of Ag non =Orestes, Od. 1, 32.

Ἀγαμέμνων, ονος, ὁ (fr. ἄγαν and μένω most constant), son of Atreus, grandson of Pelops, king of Mycenæ. the most powerful of the Grecian kings before Troy. He was, it is true, commander in chief; still his power was not so great that he could issue unconditional commands. He was also distinguished by his bodily stature, 2, 478; and personal bravery, 11; but was sometimes wanting in decision and circumspection. Hurried away by passion, he insulted the priest Chrysês, and when obliged to restore his daughter, he caused Brisêis to be taken by violence from the tent of Achilles, whose anger he was able to appease only by personal apology, 9. According to Od. 1, 300, and 11, 410 sq., Ægisthus, who had seduced his wife Clytæmnêstra, in conjunction with his paramour murdered him when he returned from Troy. His daughters are named in 9, 287. Hence adj. Ἀγαμεμνόνεος, έη, έον, belonging to A.

Ἀγαμήδη, ἡ, daughter of Augêas, king of Elis, wife of Mulius. She was acquainted with all the medicinal herbs which the earth produces, 11, 740.

Ἀγαμήδης, ους, ὁ (fr. ἄγαν and μῆδος counsel, son of Erginus king of Orchomenus and brother of Trophonius, architect of the temple of Apollo at Delphi, h. in Ap. 296.

ἄγαμος, ον (γάμος), unmarried, 3. 40.†

ἀγάννιφος, ον, poet. (νίφω) very snowy, covered with snow, epith. of Oiympus, whose summit according to the statement of travellers is never free from snow, *1, 426. 18, 186.

ἀγανός, ή, όν, poet. (γάνος, γάνυμαι), 1) gentle, mild, lovely, ἔπεα, 2, 180; βασιλεύς, Od. 2, 230. ἀγανὰ βέλεα, the gentle arrows of Apollo and Artemis (Diana), since sudden, gentle death (in opposition to death produced by long sickness) was ascribed in the case of men to Apollo, and of women to Artemis, Od. 3, 280. 15, 411. See Apollo and Artemis. 2) Active, rendering mild, propitiatory, agreeable, welcome, δῶρα, 9, 113; εὐχωλή, a grateful vow, 9, 499. Od. 13, 357.

ἀγανοφροσύνη, ἡ (φρήν), mildness, gentleness, 24, 772. Od. 11, 203.

ἀγανόφρων, ον, gen. ονος, poet. (φρήν), of a gentle disposition, mildly disposed, 20, 467.

ἀγάομαι, Ep. form of ἄγαμαι, q. v.

ἀγαπάζω and ἀγαπάζομαι as dep. mid. = ἀγαπάω, only in the pres. 24, 464. Od. 7, 33. 16, 17.

ἀγαπάω (akin to ἄγαμαι), aor. ἠγάπησα, poet. ἀγάπησα, 1) to receive kindly, to treat with kindness or attention, with acc. spoken generally of men, Od. 16, 17. 23, 214; of a god: θεὸν ὧδε βροτοὺς ἀγαπαζέμεν ἀντην, that a god should thus openly favour mortals, 24, 464. 2) to be content, to be satisfied, οὐκ ἀγαπᾷς, ὁ (= ὅτι) ἐκηλος δαίνυσαι; art thou not content, that thou feastest in quiet? Od. 21, 289. 3)

ἀγαπάζομαι, dep. mid.: its partcp. stands in an absolute sense with φιλέω and κυνέω. οὐκ ἀγαπαζόμενοι φιλέουσ', do not cordially entertain, Od. 7, 33. welcome, 21, 224.

ἀγαπήνωρ, ορος, ὁ (ἀνήρ), manhood-loving, manly, bold, brave, epith. of heroes, 8, 114, Od. 7. 170.

Ἀγαπήνωρ, ορος, ὁ, son of Ancæus, grandson of Lycurgus, king and commander of the Arcadians. According to a later tradition, he was carried by a storm to Cyprus upon his return, 2, 610. Comp. Apd. 3, 10. 8.

ἀγαπητός, ή, όν (ἀγαπάω), beloved, dear, epitn. of an only son, Od. 2, 365. Il. 6, 401; thence ἀγαπητῶς, with love, cheerfully, willingly, Batr.

ἀγάρροος, ον, poet. (ῥέω), strong-flowing, rapid, epith. of the Hellespont, 2, 845; of the sea, h. Cer. 34.

Ἀγασθένης, εος, ὁ (adj. ἀγασθενής, very strong), son of Augeas, king of Elis, father of Polyxenus, 2, 624.

ἀγάστονος, ον, poet. (στένω), properly, strong-sighing; then loud-roaring, deep-roaring; epith. of Amphitrîtê, Od. 12, 97. h. Ap. 94.

Ἀγάστροφος, ὁ (from στρέφω turning himself often), son of Pæon, a Trojan, killed by Diomedes, 11, 338.

* ἀγατός, όν, poet. for ἀγαστός, admired, neut. as adv. h. Ap. 515.

Ἀγαύη, ἡ, daughter of Nereus and Doris, 18, 42; (in Wolf and Spitzner Ἀγαυή, cf. A. Gräfenhan Gr. dial. Ep. p. 58.)

ἀγανός, ή, όν (ἄγαμαι), admirable, wonderful, glorious, excellent, noble, generally epith. of kings and heroes; also of the Hippomolgi, 13, 5; of birth, μνηστῆρες ἀγανοί, noble suitors; of the Phæaces: πομπῆες ἀγανοί, excellent conductors, Od. 13, 71; and of Proserpine, Od. 11, 213. Superl. ἀγανότατος, Od. 15, 229.

ἀγγελίη, ἡ (ἄγγελος), a message, an embassy, news, tidings. ἀγγελίη τινός, a message from or about any one, 15, 640; and ἀγγελίην πατρὸς φέρειν, to bring tidings of the father, Od. 1, 408. ἀγγελίην ἐλθεῖν, to come on an embassy, i. e. to bring a message, as an ambassador, 11, 140. In the last passage and some others, the old grammarians incorrectly suppose a subst. ὁ ἀγγελίης = ἄγγελος; but the best modern critics suppose an accus. or a gen. sing. of the fem. ἀγγελίη, cf. Buttm. Lex. (in voc.) Thiersch § 268, 2. Spitzner Il. 13, 252. ἀγγελίην ἐπὶ (Wolf. ἐπὶ) Τυδῆ στεῖλαν, they sent Tydeus on an embassy, 4, 384. ἤλυθε σεῦ ἕνεκ' ἀγγελίης (gen. caus.), connect thus, ἠλ. ἀγγ. σεῦ ἕνεκα, he came on account of a message on your behalf, 3, 205. ἠέ τευ ἀγγελίης μετ' ἐμ' ἤλυθες; or comest thou to me on account of some message? 13, 252. ἀγγελίης οἴχνεσκε, he was wont to go on account of a message, i. e. to carry messages, 15, 640.

ἀγγελίης, ὁ, Ion. for ἀγγελίας, ου, ὁ, according to the ancients a form of ἄγγελος.

see ἀγγελίη; cf. Rost. ausf. Lex. who defends the view of the ancients, a messenger, an ambassador. ἠλ. σεῦ ἕνεκ'ἀγγ. he came as an ambassador on thine account, 3, 206; cf. 13, 252. 11, 640. 15, 640. 4, 384.

* ἀγγελιώτης, ου, ὁ=ἄγγελος, a messenger, h. in Merc. 296. Comp. ἔριθος.

ἀγγέλλω (ἄγω), fut. ἀγγελέω, Ep. for ἀγγελῶ, aor. ἤγγειλα, aor. mid. ἠγγειλάμην, to bear a message, to give information, to bear tidings; often absol. 8, 398. 409; with the dat. of the pers. Od. 4, 24. 2) to announce, recount, report; with accus. of the thing, ἐσθλά, 10, 448; ἔπος, 17, 701; θέμιστας, h. Ap. 391; also of the person, τινά, to give intelligence of any one, Od. 14, 120. 122; and with inf. κήρυκες ἀγγελλόντων παῖδας πρωθήβας λέξασθαι, let the heralds proclaim that the adult youth are to post themselves for their watch, &c. 8, 517; comp. Od. 16, 350.

ἄγγελος, ὁ, ἡ, a messenger, an ambassador, whether male or female: heralds are called Διὸς ἄγγελοι, messengers of Zeus, 1, 334; Ὄσσα, 2, 93; also birds by whose flight divination was performed, 24, 292. 296.

ἄγγος, εος, τό, a vessel for wine, milk, etc. 2, 471. Od. 2, 289; a jar, pail, &c.

ἄγε, ἄγετε, properly imperat. fr. ἄγω, bear; then, as interject. up! on! come on! quick! Often strengthened: ἀλλ' ἄγε, ἄγε δή, up, then! on, then! comm. with imperat. also with the 1 and 2 pl. subj. ἄγε δὴ τραπείομεν, 3, 441. ἄγε δὴ στέωμεν, 11, 348: and ἄγετε περιφραζώμεθα, Od. 1, 76; and with the 1 sing. Od. 20, 296; once only with imperat. 3 plur. 2, 437 ἀλλ' ἄγε—ἀγειρόντων. On εἰ δ' ἄγε, up, then! see εἰ.

ἀγείρω (ἄγω), aor. ἤγειρα, Ep. ἄγειρα, perf. pass. ἀγήγερμαι, aor. 1. pass. ἠγέρθην. Peculiar Ep. forms: 3 pl. plupf. ἀγηγέρατο, 3 pl. aor. ἤγερθεν for ἠγέρθησαν, aor. sync. 2 mid. ἀγερόμην, part. ἀγρόμενος. 1) Active, to collect, to assemble; spoken of men, with accus. λαόν, 2, 438; ἀγορήν, to call an assembly, Od. 2, 28. b) Of things: to collect, δημόθεν ἄλφιτα καὶ οἶνον, Od. 19, 197; πύρνα, to collect by begging pieces of wheaten bread, Od. 17, 362. II) Mid. with the sync. aor. 2 and aor. 1 pass. to assemble, to come together; περὶ αὐτόν, 4, 211. ἐς ἀγορὴν ἀγέροντο, they came to the assembly, 18, 245. b) Trop. in the aor. pass. ὅτε δὴ ἄμπνυτο καὶ ἐς φρένα θυμὸς ἀγέρθη, when now he respired and life was collected into the heart, i. e. when he came to himself, 22, 475. Od. 5, 458. ἄψορρόν οἱ θυμὸς ἐνὶ στήθεσσιν ἀγέρθη, courage (hope) returned to his breast, 4, 152. μάχην ἤγειρας, 13, 778, belongs to ἐγείρω, q. v. Of like import are the poet. forms ἠγερέθονται, ἠγερέθοντο, and ἠγερέθεσθαι accord. to Arist. for ἠγερέεσθαι.

ἀγελαῖος, αίη, αῖον (ἀγέλη), belonging to a herd, grazing in herds. Il. and Od. epith. of cattle.

Ἀγέλαος, Ion. Ἀγέλεως, ὁ (fr. ἄγω and

λαός leader of the people), 1) son of [mon], a Trojan, whom Diomēdēs [be]fore Troy, 8, 257. 2) a Greek s[lain by] Hector, 11, 302. 3) son of Dam[..] suitor of Penelopê, slain by Ulyss[es] 22, 293.

* ἀγέλαστος, ον (γελάω), without [laugh]ing, sad, h. Cer. 200; hence ἡ Ἀγ[έλαστος] πέτρη, the mourning rock at Ele[usis in] Attica; Apd. In Od. 8, 307, i[n some] editions ἀγέλαστα stands for γελα[σ]

Ἀγελείη, ἡ, poet. (ἄγω, λεία), [col]lector of booty, epith. of Minerva protectress of heroes, Il. and Od.

ἀγέλη, ἡ (ἄγω), herd, crowd, wi[thout] βοῶν and ἵππων, 19, 281.

ἀγεληδόν, adv. (ἀγέλη), in he[rds,] crowds, 16, 160.†

ἀγέληφι, poet. dat. for ἀγέλη, herd. Further see Thiersch Gr. §[..] [See also Buttm. § 56, note 9.]

ἀγέμεν, poet. for ἄγειν.

ἄγεν, Ep. for ἐάγησαν, see ἄγνυμ[ι]

ἀγέραστος, ον (γέρας), without a [gift,] as a token of honour, unrewarded,

ἀγερέθομαι, Ep. form, fr. ἀγείρω correctly ἠγερέθομαι, which see.

ἄγερθεν, poet. for ἠγέρθησαν, see ἀ[γείρω]

ἀγέρωχος, ον, proud, honour-lovin[g, am]bitious, noble-minded, epith. of th[e Tro]jans, Mysians, and Rhodians, 2, 6[54?] 430; and of Periclymenus, Od. 1[1] Used, according to the Gram., by [Hom.] in a good sense; later, insolent, ov[erbear]ing; further, see Buttm. Lex. [The] derivation is uncertain; prob. fr. γέρας, ἔχω (hence = richly-gifted[,]) τιμάοχος.

ἄγη, ἡ (ἄγαμαι), awe, admiration ration, 21, 221. Od. 3, 227.

ἄγη, Ep. = ἐάγη, see ἄγνυμι.

ἀγηγέραθ' = ἀγηγέρατο, see ἀγείρ[ω]

ἀγηνορίη, ἡ (ἀγήνωρ), manlines[s] courage, bravery; spoken gener[ally of] men; of beasts, boldness, strength, 2) arrogance, pride, insolence; h[ence] ἀγηνορίησιν ἐνιέναι τινά, to inspi[re] one with arrogance, *Il. 9, 700.

ἀγήνωρ, ορος, ὁ, ἡ, poet. (ἄγαν[,] very brave, courageous, bold, epith. [of he]roes; also θυμός, 9, 398. 2) In [bad] sense, arrogant, proud, insolent, μ[..] ρες, Od. 1, 144; and spoken of A[lo]; 9, 699; θυμός, 2, 276.

Ἀγήνωρ, ορος, ὁ, son of Anten[or and] Theanô, one of the bravest Trojan[s,] who contended even with Achillês[.]

ἀγήραος, ον, contr. ἀγήρως, ων ([..] not growing old, ever young; o[ften in] connexion with ἀθάνατος, 8, 539; i[m]able, eternal; spoken of the s[hield of] Zeus, 2, 447. Hom. has both form[s] contr. 12, 323. 17, 444. Od. 5, 218.

ἀγήρως, ων=ἀγήραος, ον, see ἀγ[..]

ἀγητός, ή, όν (ἄγαμαι), admired [admi]rable, distinguished, glorious; wit[h] εἶδος ἀγητός, glorious in form, 5, [..] 376; φρένας, Od. 14, 177.

ἀγινέω (a protracted form of ἄγ[ω,] ἀγινήσω, h. Ap. 57; to lead, to d[rive] *bring, to fetch*; spoken of things, like ἄγω: ὕλην, 24. 784. Od. 17, 294.

ἀγκάζομαι, depon. mid. (ἀγκάς), *to take up in the arms*; with accus. νεκρὸν ἀπὸ χθονός, to take up a dead body from the earth, 17, 722. †

Ἀγκαῖος, ὁ (lit. embracing with the arms, fr. ἀγκαί), 1) son of *Lycurgus* and *Eurynome*, father of Agapēnor, king of Arcadia, 2, 609. 2) an Ætolian from Pleurðn, a powerful wrestler who was vanquished by Nestor in the funeral games in honour of Amarynceus, 23, 635.

* ἀγκαλέω, Ep. for ἀνακαλέω, *to call upon, to invoke*; hence ἀγκαλέουσιν, as Herm. reads for καλέουσιν, h. in Ap. 373.

ἀγκαλίς, ίδος, ἡ, prop. a dimin. of ἀγκάλη, *the arm*; only in the plur. *the arms*; dat. ἐν ἀγκαλίδεσσι φέρειν, to bear in the arms, *Il. 18, 555. 22, 503.

* ἄγκαλος, ὁ = ἀγκαλίς, h. Merc. 82.

ἀγκάς, adv. (prop. accus. from the obsolete ἀγκή), *with* or *in the arms*, in connexion with ἔχειν, λάζεσθαι, μάρπτειν, 5, 371. 23, 711. Od. 7, 252.

ἄγκιστρον, τό (ἄγκος), *a barb, a fish-hook*, *Od. 4, 369. 12, 322.

ἀγκλίνας, poet. for ἀνακλίνας, part. aor. from ἀνακλίνω.

ἀγκοίνη, ἡ, poet. (ἀγκών), *the elbow*; plur. *the arms*, only in the dat. ἐν ἀγκοίνῃσί τινος ἰαύειν, to rest in the arms of any one, 14, 213. Od. 11, 261.

ἄγκος, εος, τό, prop. a curve, hence *the elbow, the arm*. λαβεῖν τινα κατ᾿ ἄγκεα, to take any body in one's arms, h. in Merc. 159. Comp. Herm. Commonly, 2) a *mountain-glen*; a *glen, dale*, 20, 490. Od. 4, 337.

ἀγκρεμάσασα, see ἀνακρεμάννυμι.

ἀγκυλομήτης, εω, ὁ, ἡ, poet. (μῆτις), *that has crafty* (lit. *crooked*) *designs, wily, politic, artful*, epith. of Κρόνος (Saturn), because he overreached his father Uranus, 2, 205. 319. h. in Ven. 22.

ἀγκύλος, η, ον (ἄγκη), *bent, curved, crooked*, epith. of the bow, 5, 209; and of the round-wheeled chariot, 6, 39.

ἀγκυλότοξος, ον, poet. (τόξον), *furnished or armed with bent bow*, epith. of the Pæonians, *Il. 2, 848.

ἀγκυλοχείλης, ου, ὁ, poet. (χεῖλος), *having a hooked bill* or *beak*, epith. of birds of prey, 16, 428. Od. 19, 538.

ἀγκυλοχήλης, ου, ὁ, poet. (χηλή), *having crooked claws*, Batr. 296.

ἀγκών, ῶνος, ὁ, prop. the angle formed by bending the arm, *the elbow*, 5, 582. 2) ἀγκῶν τείχεος, the salient (or jutting) angle of the wall, 16, 702.

* ἀγλαέθειρος, ον, poet. (ἔθειρα), *having beautiful hair, bright-haired*, epith. of Pan, h. in Pan. 5.

ἀγλαΐζω, poet. (ἀγλαὸς), *to make splendid* or *glittering*; in Hom. only in mid. fut. infin. ἀγλαϊεῖσθαι, *to exult in, to be proud of* a thing; with the dat. σέ φημι διαμπερὲς ἀγλαϊεῖσθαι, I declare that thou shalt glory in them perpetually (i. e. all thy life long), 10, 331. †

ἀγλαίη, ἡ, poet. (ἀγλαός), 1) every thing possessing external splendour, *beauty, blooming appearance, ornament*; a) in a good sense, spoken of Penelope : ἀγλαΐην ἐμοὶ θεοὶ ὤλεσαν, the gods have destroyed my bloom, Od. 18, 180. Ἀμφότερον, κῦδός τε καὶ ἀγλαΐη καὶ ὄνειαρ δειπνήσαντας ἵμεν, sc. ἐστί. [Here it seems to denote the *joyous look* opp. to an *exhausted jaded one* : κῦδος καὶ ἀγλαΐη form *one* complex notion.] Both strength with a joyous countenance and refreshment are ensured to those who travel after taking food. They feel both more of spirit and joyous alacrity and more refreshment, etc. Voss. Od. 15, 78; of a spirited horse, ἀγλαΐῃφ. πεποιθώς, trusting to his beauty, 6, 510 ; therefore *b*) In a bad sense, *ostentation, pride, vanity*; also in the plur. of the goatherd, Melantheus : ἀγλαΐας φορέειν, to exhibit pride, Od. 17, 244; and of a dog kept for display, Od. 17, 310. 2) In the plur. *festive joy, festivity*, h. Merc. 476.

Ἀγλαΐη, ἡ, Aglaia, wife of Charopus, mother of Nireus, 2, 672.

ἀγλαΐηφι, poet. dat. from ἀγλαΐη.

* ἀγλαόδωρος, ον, poet. (δῶρον), *with splendid gifts*, or *splendid in gifts*, epith. of Ceres, h. in Cer. 54. 192.

ἀγλαόκαρπος, ον, poet. (καρπός), *with splendid fruits, fruit-distributing*; δένδρεα, Od. 7, 155 ; epith. of Cer., h. Cer. 4. 2) *having beautiful hands* [lit. *wrists*]; ἑταίραι, h. in Cer. 23.

ἀγλαός, ή, όν, poet. (ἀγάλλω), *glittering, splendid, beautiful*; in a literal sense : ὕδωρ, sparkling water, Od. 3, 424; metaph. ἄποινα, splendid ransom, 1, 23 ; εὖχος, 7, 203. Often spoken of men : *distinguished, excellent, glorious*; of Paris : κέρᾳ ἀγλαέ, who makest a display with the bow, 11, 385; in a bad sense. See also κέρας.

ἀγνοιέω, poet. for ἀγνοέω (νοέω), aor. ἠγνοίησα, Ep. iterative form, ἀγνώσασκε, Ion. for ἀγνοήσασκε, (incorrectly written ἀγνώσασκε, Od. 23, 95,) *not to know, not to perceive*, mly with a negative, οὐκ ἠγνοίησε, she did not fail to observe, 1, 537. In Od. 24, 218, for αἴ κέ μ᾿ ἐπιγνοίη —ἦε κεν ἀγνοίῃσι, we should undoubtedly • read with Thiersch. § 216, 49. the subj. ἀγνοίῃσι. The subj. is required by πειρήσω. and φράσσω.; hence we must also read ἐπιγνώῃ for ἐπιγνοίη.

ἀγνός, ή, όν, *pure, chaste, holy*, epith. of Artemis and Proserpine, Od. 5, 123. 11, 386; once ἀγνὴ ἑορτή, a holy feast, Od. 21, 259 ; ἄλσος, h. in Merc. 187. Hence adv. ἀγνῶς, Ap. 121.

* ἄγνος, ἡ and ὁ, a kind of willow-tree, the *chaste-tree* [vitex agnuscastus], h. Merc. 410.

ἄγνῡμι, fut. ἄξω, aor. 1. ἦξα, Ep. ἔαξα, aor. 2 pass. ἐάγην, Ep. ἄγην (ᾰ once ᾱ), *to break, to break in pieces*, with accus. πολλοὶ ἵπποι ἄξαντ᾿ λίπον ἅρματ᾿ ἀνάκτων, many horses having broken left behind the chariots of their masters, 16, 371 (ἄξαντε, dual. with plur. since the poet thinks of the horses as in pairs, see Buttm. § 33. note 8. Kühner II, § 427); ὕλην, to break or dash down the forest, spoken of a rushing boar, 12, 148. 2) Pass. to be broken, to break, ἐάγη ξίφος, the sword broke, 16, 769. τοῦ δ᾽ ἐξελκομένοιο πάλιν, ἄγεν (poet for ἐάγησαν) ὀξέες ὄγκοι, when he drew it back (Machaon, the arrow), the sharp barbs were broken: others,—the barbs were bent back. The meaning to bend cannot be sustained; and the Scholia explain it: κατεάγησαν, ἐκλάσθησαν. The connexion also requires this translation. (Machaon comes to the wounded Menelaus, and draws the arrow out of his girdle; the barbs break off and remain behind; he therefore takes off his belt in order to extract the broken points.).

ἀγνώς, ῶτος, ὁ, ἡ (γνῶμι), unknown, Od. 5, 79.

* ἀγνῶς, adv. from ἀγνός, purely, h. Ap.

ἀγνώσασκε, iterative form of the aor. 1 from ἀγνοέω, Od. 23, 95. The orthography ἀγνώσσασκε is false. (See Thiersch. Gr. § 210, 22.)

ἄγνωστος, ον (γνωστός), 1) unknown, unrecognized, τινί, Od. 2, 175. 2) unknowable, not to be recognized: σ᾽ ... ἄγνωστον τεύξω πάντεσσι, I will make thee incapable of being known by any man (disguise thee), * Od. 13, 191. 397.

ἄγονος, ον (γόνος), unborn, 3, 40.†

ἀγοράασθε, see ἀγοράομαι.

ἀγοράομαι, depon. med. (ἀγορή), aor. ἠγορησάμην, 3 pl. impf. ἠγορόωντο, Ep. for ἠγορῶντο, 1) to meet in assembly, to hold an assembly, to deliberate, 4, 1. 2) to speak in an assembly, to speak in general, τινί with any one; often in connexion with μετέειπεν, 1, 73.

ἀγορεύω (ἀγορή), fut. εύσω, aor. 1 ἠγόρευσα, properly to hold an assembly. ἀγορὰς ἀγορεύειν, to deliberate, 2, 787; then, to speak in an assembly, to harangue, ἐν Δαναοῖσι, ἐνὶ Τρώεσσι, 1, 109. 7, 361. 8, 525. 2) Generally, to speak, to announce, τί τινι: θεοπροπίας, the will of the gods, 1, 385. ἔπεα πρὸς ἀλλήλους, to speak words one to another, 3, 155. μῆτι φόβονδ᾽ ἀγόρευε, advise not to flight, 5, 252. πρῆξιν ἀγορεύειν, to speak of an enterprise, Od. 3, 82.

ἀγορή, ἡ (ἀγείρω), 1) an assembly, especially a popular assembly, in distinction to βουλή an assembly of the princes, 2, 51—53. Od. 3, 127. ἀγορὴν ποιεῖσθαι, τίθεσθαι, to hold an assembly, 8, 2. Od. 9, 171; καθίζειν, Od. 2, 69; λύειν, to dismiss an assembly, 1, 305. Od. 2, 69. 2) the business in an assembly, discourse, deliberation, counsel; espec. in the plur. ἔχειν τινὰ ἀγοράων, to restrain any one from speaking, 2, 275. εἰδὼς ἀγορέων, skilled in speaking (debate), 9, 441. 3) the place of holding an assembly, marketplace, a certain place in towns where the higher classes sat upon stone seats, Od.

6, 266. Il. 18, 504; in the camp Greeks it was close by Agame tent: in Troy it was upon the citadel, παρὰ Πριάμοιο θύρησιν, 2 545. 4) market, the place of sale, 5.

ἀγορῆθεν, adv. from the assembly Od.

ἀγορήνδε, adv. to the assembly, Od.

ἀγορητής, οῦ, ὁ (ἀγορή), an speaker, connected with βουληφό and Od.

ἀγορητύς, ύος, ἡ (ἀγορή), the speaking, eloquence, Od. 8, 168.†

* ἄγος, εος, τό, Ion. for ἄγος (ἄ verence, awe, pious fear, θεῶν, 479. So Wolf. and Herm. for ἄχο ἀγός, οῦ, ὁ (ἄγω), Ep. leader, Il.

ἀγοστός, ὁ (ἄγνυμι), prop. the hence the bent-hand; the palm or of the hand, always ἕλε γαῖαν ἀγος grasped the earth with his han 425. 13, 508. [∾ ἄγκος, ἀγκάλη. S.]

ἄγραυλος, ον (αὐλή), dwelling, s or lying in the fields or country, m 18, 162; βόες, πόριες, cattle, calve in pastures, 24, 81. Od. 10, 410.

ἄγρει, pl. ἀγρεῖτε, prop. imperat ἀγρέω, Aeolic for αἱρέω, liter. seize like ἄγε, up! on! quick! pl. Od.

ἄγρη, η, the chase, the act of ca of fish, Od. 12, 330. 2) what is the game taken, prey, Od. 22, 306.

ἄγριος, η, ον (ἀγρός), in Hom. on -ος fem. Od. 9, 119; elsewhere endings, 3, 24. 19, 88; living in the (in opposition to a town), wild, strained: αἶξ, σῦς: and neut. p ἄγρια, every thing wild, game, 5. Spoken often of men: wild, rude cruel; ἄγριος Κύκλωψ, Od. 2, 19; passions: χόλος ἄγριος, fierce ange θυμός, 9, 629. ἄγρια εἰδέναι, to be savage.

Ἄγριος, ὁ, son of Porthaon and in Calydon, brother of Œneus and thous. His sons wrested the roy thority from Œneus and gave it t father; they were however slain medes, 14, 117. According to Ap 6. he was the father of Thersites.

ἀγριόφωνος, ον (φωνή), having a rough, uncouth voice or pronun ['men of barbarous speech,' Cp.] of the Sinties of Lemnos, Od. 8, 29

ἀγρόθεν and ἀγρόθε, adv. from th try, *Od. 13, 268.

ἀγροιώτης, ου, ὁ, poet. a man f country, inhabiting the country. ἀγροιῶται, rustic men, 11, 549; βο rural herdsmen, Od. 11, 293.

ἀγρόμενος, see ἀγείρω.

ἀγρόνδε, adv. to the fields, to th try. *Od.

ἀγρονόμος, ον (νέμω), prop. pastu dwelling in the country. ἀγρονόμ φαι, rural nymphs, Od. 6, 106.†

ἀγρός, οῦ, ὁ, cultivated land, *a field*, pl. possessions of lands, fields, as opposed to houses, Od. 4, 757. Il. 23, 832; *country*, as opposed to town, also a *country villa* or *estate*, Od. 24, 205. πολύδενδρος ἀγρός, an estate abounding in trees, a *well-wooded estate*, Od. 23, 139. ἐπ' ἀγροῦ, in the fields, Od. 5, 489, in opposition to the town; in the country, Od. 1, 185.

ἀγρότερος, η, ον, poet. for ἄγριος, living in the fields, *wild*, as ἡμίονοι, ἔλαφοι, 2, 852. 21, 486. 2) *field-loving*, the *huntress* = ἀγραία, epith. of Artemis (Diana), 21, 471. (The verse is doubtful.)

ἀγρότης, ου, ὁ (ἀγρός), *countryman, an inhabitant of the country*, Od. 16, 218.†

ἀγρώσσω (ἄγρη), a collat. form fr. ἀγρεύω, *to hunt, to catch*, ἰχθύς, Od. 5, 53.†

ἄγρωστις, ιος, ἡ (ἀγρός), that which grows in the fields, *grass, pasturage*, Od. 6, 90 † [Intpp. ad Theoph. make the *agrostis = triticum repens*.]

ἀγυιά, ἡ (ἄγω), once ἄγυια, 20, 254, a *way*, a *street* in towns, 6, 391. b) *road, path*, σκιόωντο πᾶσαι ἀγυιαί, all the paths or roads were darkened (growing dark): a picture descriptive of nightfall, Od. (Hom. never has the nom. sing. see Rost. Gr. § 32. p. 86.)

ἄγυρις, ιος, ἡ, Æol. for ἀγορά, an *assembly*, a *multitude*, ἀνδρῶν, Od. 3, 31; νεκύων, the multitude of the dead, 16, 661. ἐν νηῶν ἀγύρει, among the multitude of ships, 24, 141.

ἀγυρτάζω (ἀγύρτης), *to collect by begging*, χρήματα, Od. 19, 284.†

ἀγχέμαχος, ον (μάχομαι), *fighting in close combat, close-fighting*, epith. of brave warriors who fight with the lance or sword, *13, 5. 16, 248.

ἄγχι, adv. 1) *near*, in place; often with a following gen. ἄγχι θαλάσσης, 9, 43; also with gen. preceding Ἕκτορος ἄγχι, 8, 117. b) With dat. which however is generally better taken as dependent on the verb; ἄγχι παρίστατο ποιμένι λαῶν, 5, 570. 6, 405. 2) in time: *soon, forthwith*. ἄγχι μάλα, very soon, Od. 19, 301: (comp. ἆσσον, superl. ἄγχιστα and ἀγχοτάτω.)

ἀγχίαλος, ον (ἅλς), also ἀγχιάλη, h. Ap. 32, *near the sea, situated on the coast*, epith. of a maritime town, 2, 640. 697.

Ἀγχίαλος, ὁ, 1) a Greek, whom Hector slew, 5, 609. 2) father of Mentes, friend of Ulysses and king of the Taphians, Od. 1, 180. 3) a noble Phæacian, Od. 8, 112.

ἀγχιβαθής, ές (βάθος), gen. έος, *near the deep*, genr. *deep*; θάλασσα, Od. 5, 413; † [deep to the very shore, L. and S.]

ἀγχίθεος, ον (θεός), *near to the gods, similar to* them, epith. of the Phæacians, on account of their happy mode of life, or accord. to Nitzsch *nearly related to the gods*, *Od. 5, 35; cf. h. Ven. 201.

ἀγχιμαχητής, οῦ, ὁ = ἀγχέμαχος, *who fights in close combat, a close-fighting warrior*, 2, 604. 8, 173.

ἀγχίμολος, ον (μολεῖν), prop. *coming near*; only in neut. as adv. of place.

ἀγχίμολόν οἱ ἦλθε, he came near to him, 4, 529. ἐξ ἀγχιμόλοιο (sc. τόπου) 'εῖν, to see from near, 24, 352. ?) Of time, *soon*. ἀγχίμολον μετ' αὐτόν, soon after him, Od. 17, 336; or perhaps of place: close behind him.

ἀγχίνοος, ον (νόος), prop. having a mind that is always ready: quickly apprehending, *intelligent, acute*, Od. 13, 331.†

Ἀγχίσης, εω, ὁ (very similar fr. ἄγχι and ἴσος, Parilinus Herm.), 1) son of Capys and the nymph *Themis*, father of Æneas and king of Dardanus on Ida. Aphroditē (Venus) loved him and bore Æneas to him, 2. 819. 20, 239. h. in Ven. 45. Hom. mentions Hippodameia as his eldest daughter, 13, 429. 2) father of Echepolos, which see.

Ἀγχισιάδης, ου, ὁ, son of Anchises = Æneas, 17, 754.

ἄγχιστα, see ἄγχιστος.

ἀγχιστῖνος, ίνη, ῖνον (lengthened fr. ἄγχιστος), *near, crowded together*. ἀγχιστῖνοι ἔπιπτον νεκροί, 17, 361. Od. αἱ ἀγχιστῖναι ἐπ' ἀλλήλῃσι κέχυνται, 5, 141. This passage is differently explained. Heyne and Voss understand it of the slain sheep; cf. Schol. Vill. and Od. 22, 389. Damm, of the sheep huddling together from fear of the lion.

ἄγχιστος, η, ον (superl. from ἄγχι), *the nearest*; in Hom. only neut. sing. ἄγχιστον, *very near*. ὅθι τ' ἄγχιστον πέλεν αὐτῷ, where it was nearest to him [i. e. on the side that was next to him], Od. 5, 280. Often the neut. ἄγχιστα, with gen. 20, 18; tropically, spoken of a great similarity, ἄγχιστα αὐτῷ ἐῴκει, he very closely resembled him, 2, 58. Od. 6, 152. ἄγχιστα εἴσκειν τινά τινι, Od. 6, 151.

ἀγχόθι adv. = ἀγχοῦ, *near*, with gen. ἀγχόθι δειρῆς, 14, 412. Od. 13, 103.

* ἀγχοτάτω, superl. of ἀγχοῦ, *very near*; with gen. h. Apol. 18.

ἀγχοῦ, adv. (prop. gen. from the obsolete ἀγχός), *near*. ἀγχοῦ ἵστασθαι, to approach, 2, 172. 2) With gen. ἀγχοῦ δὲ ξύμβληντο πυλάων νεκρὸν ἄγοντι, near the gates they met, etc. 24. 709 Od. 6, 5.

ἄγχω, *to choke, to strangle*; with accus. ἄγχε μιν ἱμὰς ὑπὸ δειρήν, the thong under his neck choked him, 3, 371.†

ἄγω, fut. ἄξω, aor. 2 ἤγαγον, aor. 2 mid. ἠγαγόμην, Ep. ἀγαγόμην (rarely aor. 1 ἦξα, part. ἄξας, Batr. 115. 119. Ep. imper. aor. 2. ἄξετε and inf. ἀξέμεν, 24, 663; aor. 1. mid. ἠξάμην, 8, 505. 545; ἄξασθε, ἄξαντο), 1) Primary meaning, *to lead, to convey, to carry*; spoken for the most part of things living (as φέρειν, of lifeless things, Od. 4, 622); therefore 1) Of living objects, both men and brutes, *to lead, to carry away, to bring*; according to the accompanying prep. and adv. with the accus., also τινά τινι, to conduct any one to any one, Od. 14, 386; also in a chariot, ἦγον (ἵπποι) Μαχάονα, 11, 598; also of brutes: βοῦν, to bring or convey an ox, and ἑκατόμβην, a hecatomb (because it consisted of (cattle, 1, 99). Especially a) Spoken of

carrying away by violence, τέκνα, γυναῖκας, 9, 594; also τινὰ ἐν νήεσσιν, 4,
239. b) More rarely of inanimate things,
οἶνον (by ship), 7, 467; ὅστεα οἴκαδε, 7,
335; λαίλαπα, to bring a tempest, 4, 278;
φόρτον, Od. 14, 296. c) Trop. κλέος τινὸς
ἄγειν, to carry, i. e. to spread any one's
fame, Od. 5, 311; πένθος τινί, to occasion grief to any one, Batr. 49. 2) to
lead, to conduct; spoken of the commander: λαόν, 10, 79; λόχον, to lay
or set an ambuscade, 4, 392. Od. 14, 469;
of gods: τὸν δ' ἄγε Μοῖρα κακὴ θανάτοιο
τέλοσδε, Fate led him to death, 13, 602.
ἄγε νεῖκος Ἀθήνη, Minerva led the battle,
11, 721; also absolute, κῆρες ἄγον μέλανος
θανάτοιο, the Fates of black death led,
2, 834. 11, 332. 3) Trop. πολλῇσιν μ'
ἄτῃσι παρὲκ νόον ἤγαγεν Ἕκτωρ, Hector
led me foolishly into great misfortun⁓,
10, 391. So Heyne. Others (Köppen)
construe, νόον παρεξήγαγε, and take the
dative as dat. of the means: by forceful
delusion Hector misled my mind, 10, 391.
The part. ἄγων often stands with verbs of
motion. στῆσε δ' ἄγων, 2, 558. ἔβαν
ἄγοντες, 1, 391. II) Mid. to lead, carry,
or take away for oneself; with accus. λαὸν
ὑπὸ τεῖχος. the people to the wall, 4, 407;
γυναῖκα οἴκαδε, 3, 93; Trop. διὰ στόμα
τι. to carry any thing in the mouth, 14,
91. 2) to conduct home; γυναῖκα πρὸς
δώματα, to conduct a wife home, 16, 189;
without δώματα, Od. 14, 211; to marry a
wife, 2, 659. Also spoken of the father
who brings the son a wife, Od. 4, 59: and
of the bridemen, Od. 8, 28.

ἀγών, ῶνος, ὁ (ἄγω), 1) assembly, place
of assembly, a) the assembly, the circle
of spectators, 24, 1. θεῖος ἀγών, assembly
of the gods, 18, 376; where it may also
mean the place of assembling, as αἴτε μοι
εὐχόμεναι θεῖον δύσονται ἀγῶνα, who supplicating for me shall go into the divine
assembly, or (according to V.) into the
sacred place, 7, 298; (prob. the company
of female suppliants, or according to
others the temple itself as the abode of the
gods.) b) place of collection, rendezvous,
station; νεῶν, of the ships, 15, 428. 2)
the place of combat in public games, both
for the combatants and spectators, 23,
258. 448. 685. Od. 8, 200.

ἀδαημονίη, ἡ (δαήμων), ignorance, inexperience, Od. 24, 244.† [For the reading
ἀδαημοσύνη, see Bothe in loc. and Buttm.
Lexil. p. 31. Am. Ed.]

ἀδαήμων, ον, gen. ονος, poet. (δαήμων),
ignorant; inexperienced; with gen. μάχης,
Il. πληγῶν, unacquainted with blows, Od.
17, 283.

ἀδάκρυτος, ον (δακρύω), without tears,
tearless, not weeping, 1, 415. Od. 24, 61;
ὄσσε, Od. 4, 186.

Ἀδάμας. αντος, ὁ (= ἀδάμαστος), son of
the Trojan Asius, killed by Meriones, 12,
140.

ἀδάμαστος, ον (δαμάω), unconquerable,
inflexible, unyielding; epith. of Pluto, 9,
158.†

ἀδδεής, ές, poet. for ἀδεής,
always κύον ἀδδεές, 8, 423.

ἀδδηκώς, poet. for ἀδηκώς, see
ἄδδην, poet. for ἄδην.

ἀδεής, ές, poet. ἀδειής and ἀδε
fearless, bold, insolent, impuden⁓
7, 117; κύον ἀδδεές, a term of rep
423. Od. 19, 91.

ἀδελφειός and ἀδελφεός, ὁ,
ἀδελφός (δελφύς), brother ἀδελφε⁓
6, 61.

ἀδευκής, ές, gen. έος, Ep. (δευκ⁓
not sweet, bitter, sour; metaph
disagreeable prating, Od. 6, 273. [
famam, malum rumorem; so Ba
Bothe. Am. Ed. ὄλεθρος, πότμο⁓
489. 10, 245.

ἀδέψητος, ον (δεψέω), undresse⁓
*Od. 20, 2. 142.

ΑΔΕΩ, pres. obsolete; only th⁓
aor. ἀδδήσειε, and part. perf. ἀδδη⁓
also ἀδήσειε and ἀδηκότες (from ⁓
be satiated, to be disgusted. μ⁓
δείπνῳ ἀδδήσειεν, that the strange⁓
not be disgusted (incommoded)
meal, Od. 1, 134; twice, καμά⁓
κότες ἠδὲ καὶ ὕπνῳ, oppressed b⁓
and sleep, 10, 98. Od. 12, 281. κα⁓
δηκότες αἰνῷ, fatigued with severe
10, 312. 399. Some of the Schol.
from ἄδος (ἄ), and therefore doubl⁓
according to several ancient Gr⁓
Buttm. Lexil. p. 24, a is long in ἀ⁓
the doubling not necessary; but
has proved that the α is short: ad
Ausf. Gr. 2, 99. Spitzn. return⁓
double δ.

ἄδην, poet. ἄδδην. adv., prop. a⁓
an old subst. ἄδη, sufficiently, en⁓
satiety, as ἔδμεναι, 5, 203. 2) ⁓
with gen. οἵ μιν ἄδην ἐλόωσι π⁓
who shall pursue him to satiety
(to make him feel wearied and d⁓
with war), 13, 315; cf. 19, 423. ⁓
μίν φημι ἄδην ἐλάαν κακότητος, I
shall yet reduce him to misery ⁓
Od. 5, 290. The gen. is correc⁓
plained as a gen. of place; Buttm⁓
p. 27, rejects the orthography ἄδδ⁓
the notion of its being an ac⁓
ἐλαύνειν = probe exercitare: to g⁓
enough of war.]

ἀδήριτος, ον (δηρίω), uncontest⁓
fought. ἀλλ' οὐ μὰν ἔτι δηρὸν ἀ⁓
πόνος ἔσται, οὐδέ τ' ἀδήριτος. ἤτ⁓
ἤτε φόβοιο, but this labour (battl⁓
not much longer be unattempted, ⁓
fought, whether it be for victory
flight, 17, 42.† (The gen. accord⁓
tath. and Schol. A. depends upon ἀ⁓
by hyperbaton, the governing v⁓
Greek being frequently separated f⁓
governed by intervening words, cf. S
and Schol. A. τὸ δὲ ἑξῆς ἀπείρητο
ἔσται ἤτ' ἀλκῆς ἤτε φόβοιο, οἷον
σόμεθα ἤτοι ἀνδρείας ἢ φυγῆς. He⁓
Köppen incorrectly construe: πόνο⁓
ἤτε φόβοιο, the contest of force or ⁓

*ἀδίκως, adv. (from ἄδικος), u⁓
unrighteously, h. Merc. 316.

* ἀδικέω (ἄδικος), fut. ήσω, to do wrong, to insult, h. Cer. 367; part. ἀδικήσας.

ἀδινός, ή, όν. poet. (ἄδην), abundant, hence 1) closely pressing, thronged, crowded; spoken of sheep and goats, 1, 92. 4, 320; of bees, 2, 87. 2) thick, closely encompassed, κῆρ, prop. the heart, closely encompassed by the entrails or thick flesh, 16, 481. Od. 19, 516. 3) strong, vehement, loud, γόος, 18, 316; ὄψ, h. Cer. 67; Σειρῆνες, the loud-voiced Sirens, Od. 23, 326. The neut. plur. and sing. often as adv., as ἀδινὸν στοναχῆσαι, to groan aloud, 18, 124. ἀδινὰ κλαίειν, to weep passionately or aloud, 24, 510. Comp. ἀδινώτερον κλαίειν, Od. 16, 216.

ἀδινῶς, adv. strongly, heavily, deeply; ἀνενείκασθαι, to sigh deeply, or groan heavily (with deep-drawn breath), [Lexil. p. 105.] 19, 314.†

ἀδμής, ῆτος, ὁ, ἡ, poet. (δαμάω), 1) unbroken, untamed; of animals which have not yet come under the yoke, ἡμίονοι, Od. 4, 637. 2) single, unmarried, παρθένος, *Od. 6, 109. 228.

* Ἀδμήτη, ἡ, daughter of Oceanus and Tethys, h. in Cer. 421.

ἄδμητος, η, ον = ἀδμής no. 1, untamed, βοῦς, 10, 292. Od. 3, 383. 2) παρθένος, h. Ven. 82.

Ἄδμητος, ὁ, son of Pheres, king of Pherae in Thessalia, husband of Alcestis, father of Eumēlus, 2, 713.

ἄδον, see ἁνδάνω.

ἄδος, εος, τό (ἄδην), satiety; and then the consequent weariness, dislike to what one is doing, disgust. ἄδος τέ μιν ἵκετο θυμόν, weariness (or disgust) has come upon his soul, 11, 88.†

* ἄδοτος, ον (δίδωμι), ungifted, h. in Merc. 573.

Ἀδρήστεια, ἡ, Adrastēa, a city in Mysia on the Propontis, named from its founder Adrastus. The region round the town was afterwards called τὸ τῆς Ἀδραστείας πεδίον, 2, 828.

Ἀδρήστη, ἡ, Ion. for Ἀδράστη (from ἀ and διδράσκω: not to be escaped), a noble handmaid of Helen, Od. 4, 123.

Ἀδρηστίνη, ἡ, daughter of Adrastus = Ægialēa, 5, 412.

Ἄδρηστος, ὁ, Ion. or Ἄδραστος, Adrastus, 1) son of Talaus, king of Argos, father of Argea, Hippodamea, Deipyle, and Ægialeus. Driven from this city by Amphiaräus, he fled to Sicyon, where he succeeded his grandfather Polybus in the government. He received the fugitive Polynices, gave him in marriage his daughter Argea, and put in motion the expedition against Thebes, 2, 572. 14, 121. He also received the exiled Tydeus and gave him a daughter in marriage, 14, 121. 2) son of the soothsayer Merops and brother of Amphius, leader of the Trojan allies from Adrastea and Apæsus, 2, 830; slain with his brother by Diomedes, 11, 328 seq. 3) a Trojan conquered by Menelaus in battle, who was

about to yield to his prayers and spare his life, when Agamemnon killed him, 6, 37 seq. 4) a Trojan slain by Patroclus, 16, 694.

ἀδροτής, ῆτος, ἡ, perfect maturity, the perfection of the adult body, physical strength, manly vigour; connected with ἥβη, *16, 857. 22, 363; and with μένος, 24, 6. (The reading ἀνδροτῆτα is properly rejected by Wolf.)

ἄδυτος, ον (δύω), adj. unapproachable, that may not be entered; hence as subst. τὸ ἄδυτον, and in h. Merc. 247, also ὁ ἄδυτος (sc. χῶρος), the innermost part of a temple, which only priests could enter, the sanctuary; and mly the holy place, temple, 5, 448. 512.

* ᾄδω, Att. for ἀείδω; hence fut. ᾄσομαι, h. 5. 2.

* ἀδώρητος, ον (δωρέομαι), ungifted, without receiving any present, h. Merc. 168.

ἀεθλεύω, Ep. and Ion. form for ἀθλεύω (ἆθλος), only pres., which form Spitzn. has adopted in 24, 734, to contend for a prize, to combat ['to cope with him in manly games' Cp.], 4, 389; ἐπί τινι, in honour of some one, 23, 274. 2) to labour, to suffer, to endure; πρὸ ἄνακτος ἀμειλίχου, labouring for a cruel master, or in the sight of, etc. 24, 734. In the last signif. Homer generally uses ἀθλέω, q. v. *Il.

ἀέθλιον, τό, Ep. for ἆθλιον (ἆθλος), 1) a prize. ἀέθλια ποσσὶ ἀρέσθαι, to bear away the prizes in the race, 9, 124. 266. ἀέθλια ἀνελέσθαι, 23, 823; also ἀνελεῖν, 23, 736. 2) = ἄεθλος, prize-fight, contest, combat, Od. 24, 169. 3) the armour of combat, weapons, Od. 21, 62; (only in the Ep. form.)

ἄεθλον, το, Ep. and Ion. for ἆθλον, 1) a prize, reward of a combat, 22, 163; plur. 23, 259; to go for the prizes, to be sent to the race, 11, 700; mly a reward, present, 23, 620. 2) In the plur. = ἄεθλος, a combat. ἐπεντύνεσθαι ἄεθλα, Od. 24, 89.

ἄεθλος, ὁ, Ep. and Ion. for ἆθλος, 1) a contest, combat, 16, 590. Od. 8, 131. 2) combat in war, every thing one suffers, fatigue, labour, want. μογεῖν ἀέθλους, to endure troubles, Od. 4, 170. (Hom. uses only the Ep. form, except ἆθλος, Od. 8. 160.)

ἀεθλοφόρος, ον, Ep. and Ion. for ἀθλοφόρος (φέρω), prize-bringing, victorious (in the race); ἵπποι, 9, 124. The Ep. form only in *Il. 22, 22. 162.

ἀεί, adv. Ion. and poet. αἰεί and αἰέν, always, continually, for ever, ever. θεοὶ αἰὲν ἐόντες, the eternal gods, 1, 290. It stands often for emphasis' sake with other words of equivalent import, as ἀσκελὲς αἰεί, etc. The com. form occurs but seldom in Hom. 12, 211: in other cases always αἰεί, and αἰέν when a short ultimate is required, 1, 520; hence Od. 1, 341 must be read αἰέν; see Herm. h. Ven. 202.

ἀείδω, Ep. and Ion. for ᾄδω, fut. ἀείσομαι, Att. ᾄσομαι, 5, 2. 1) Intrans

B 5

to sing, absol. 2, 598 ; τινί, to any one, Od. 1, 325; παρά τινι, before any one, Od. 1, 154. b) Spoken of birds, Od. 19, 519 ; of the bowstring, to twang, Od. 21, 411. 2) Trans. to celebrate, to sing, μῆνιν, 1, 1 ; κλέα ἀνδρῶν, 9, 189; παιήονα, 1, 473. Mid. as dep. to cel-brate in song, to hymn, Ἥφαιστον, h. 17, 1. 20, 1; a prop. short, but long at the beginning of a verse, and when it occurs in a quadrisyllabic form at its close. Herm. reads ἀείσεο as Ep. imperat. aor. 2, for ἀείδεο, in h. 17. 1. Buttm. ausfür. Sprachl. § 96. Anm. 10. rejects the form ἀείδεο also in h. 20. 1.

ἀεικείη, poet. for αἰκία (εἰκός), abuse, insult, indignity, outrage, 24, 19 ; plur. ἀεικείας φαίνειν, to exhibit insolence, Od. 20, 309.

ἀεικέλιος, η, ον, also ος, ον, poet. for αἰκέλιος (εἰκός), 1) unseemly, improper, unjust, shameful, contemptible; ἀλωτὸς, Od. 9, 503; ἄλγος, horrible pain, Od. 14, 32 ; στρατός, a contemptible, i. e. small troop, 14, 82. 2) In reference to external form, mean, ugly, disgusting, Od. 6, 142 ; πήρη, δίφρος, Od. 17, 357. 20, 259 ; = ἀεικής, q. v.

ἀεικελίως, adv. poet. for αἰκελίως, unsuitably, disgracefully, horribly. *Od. 8, 231. 16, 109.

ἀεικής, ές, gen. έος, poet. for αἰκής = ἀεικέλιος, unseemly, shameful, contemptible; νόος, Od. 20, 366 ; λοιγός, πότμος, cruel suffering, end, 1, 341 ; ἔργον, an unseemly deed ; often in the plur. μισθός, pitiful wages, 12, 435. The neut. with the inf. οὐ οἱ ἀεικές—τεθνάμεν, it is not disgraceful for him to die defending his country, 15, 496 ; and absolute, ἀεικέα μερμηρίζειν, to meditate mischief, Od. 4, 533. 2) Spoken of external form, ugly, disgusting, πήρη, Od. 13, 437. The neut. plur. as adv. ἀεικέα ἕσσο, thou wert shamefully clad, Od. 16, 199.

ἀεικίζω, poet. for αἰκίζω (ἀεικής), fut. ἀεικίσω, Ep. and Att. ἀεικιῶ, ἀεικισσα, poet. ἀείκισσα, aor. mid. ἀεικισάμην, aor. 1 pass. ἀεικίσθην, to treat unbecomingly, to abuse, to insult, or dishonour ; with accus. νεκρόν, a dead body, by leaving it unburied, or in any other way, 16, 545. 22, 256 ; ξεῖνον, to treat a stranger improperly, 18, 222. 2) Mid. = act. 16, 559. ──, ─94.

ἀειράσας, see ἀείρω.

ἀείρω, poet. for αἴρω, aor. ἤειρα and Ep. ἄειρα, aor. mid. ἀειράμην and ἠράμην (ἤρατο, ἠράμεθα), with moods from aor. 2 ἀρόμην, subj. ἄρωμαι, optat. ἀροίμην, inf. ἀρέσθαι, aor. 1 pass. ἀέρθην, Ep. for ἤρθην, poet. 3 pl. ἄερθεν for ἀέρθησαν, ἀρθείς, and ἀρθείς, 3 sing. plupf. pass. ἄωρτο, Ep. form ἠερεθόνται. 1) Active, 1) to lift up, to elevate, to raise aloft; with an accus. λᾶαν, a stone, 7, 268 ; ἔγχος ἄντα τινός, to raise a spear against any one, 8, 424 ; also with ὑψόσε, to lift up high, 10, 465 ; hence aor. pass. to be lifted, κῆρες πρὸς οὐρανὸν ἄερθεν, 8, 74. ἐφύπερθεν ἀερθείς δίφρον (being raised up=) raising myself

up above him, I turned it rou round, Od. 9, 383 (of Ulysses bof the eye of Polyphemus) : spoken eagle : ἐς αἰθέρα ἀέρθη, was bor mounted to the sky, Od. 19, 540 the plupf. pass. μάχαιρα ἄωρτο, t. was suspended, hung, 3, 272. 2 i. e. to take up, to bring, δέπας, οἱ 6, 264. 3) to lift, i. e. to take a carry away, σῖτον ἐκ κανέου, Od. νεκρὸν ὑπὲκ Τρώων, 17, 589 ; ἐκ 16, 678; spoken of ships : ἄχθος, away a cargo, Od. 3, 312. II) M rise, to raise oneself; spoken of 1 horses : ὑψόσ' ἀειρέσθην, 23, 50 ship : πρύμνη ἀείρετο, the stern r 13, 85. 2) to take up for oneself bear away, to take, to receive, to πέπλον, ἕλκος ; ἀέθλια πόσσιν, prizes in the race, 9, 124 ; so κῦδοι νίκην; and strengthened, οἱ αὐτὰ to acquire glory for himself, 10, 30 dat. expresses, for another (his ad) or disadvantage), Od. 1, 240 ; but γάρ κέ σφι μάλα μέγα κῦδος ἄροιο thou wouldst acquire with ther great glory, 9, 303; [cf. 4, 95;] Τρώεσσι, 16, 84 ; πρὸς Δαναῶν, 16, to take upon oneself, to bear, τί, 107. 1, 390.

ἀεκαζόμενος, η, ον (ἀέκων), act luctantly, constrained, forced, strengthened by πολλά, 6, 458. 277. (Only partcp.)

ἀεκήλιος, ον, Ep. for ἀεικέλιος. ἔργα, unseemly deeds, 18, 77.†

ἀέκητι, adv. (ἀέκων), in spite of, the will of; often with the gen. 'A ἀέκητι, against the will of the Gree 666. θεῶν ἀέκητι, in spite of the 12, 8. Od. 8, 663.

ἀέκων, ουσα, ον (ἔκων), Ep. for not willing, reluctant, against one without design. ἀέκοντος ἐμεῖο, i my will, 1, 301. σε βίῃ ἀέκοντος νῆα, he took the ship from thee by against thy will, Od. 4, 646; see an The other form occurs only in, οὐκ πετέσθην, viz. ἵππω, not reluctant fl steeds, 5, 366, and often.

ἄελλα, ἡ (ἕλλω, εἴλω), [less pr ἄω], a tempest, whirlwind, hur when several winds meet; often plur. χειμέριαι ἄελλαι, winter stor 293. ἄελλαι παντοίων ἀνέμων, ter of all the winds, Od. 5, 292. 304; comparison : he battled ἴσος δέλλ the hurricane, 12, 40.

ἀελλής, ές (ἄελλα), excited by the tempest-driven, impetuous, κονίσα. 13.† (According to Buttm. ausf. 41, 9. 15, more correctly ἀελλῆς fo λήεις, like τιμῆς).

ἀελλόπους, οδος, ὁ, ἡ, Ep. ἀελλόπος (storm-footed, rapid as the wind, ep Iris, only in the Ep. form, *Il. 8, 4 77. 159 ; of steeds, h. Ven. 218.

[ἀελπής, see ἀελπτής.]

ἀελπτέω (ἄελπτος), not to hope, spair, ἀελπτέοντες, 7, 310 ;† which be read with the Synizesis (before Wolf, falsely written ἀέλποντες; Eustath. read ἀελπέοντες, which, according to Lobeck on Phrynicus, p. 575, is correct.)

ἀελπτής, ές (ἔλπομαι), gen. ος, *unhoped, unexpected*, Od. 5. 408. † Before Wolf, ἀελπέα, which Lobeck defends. Phryn. p. 570.

* ἄελπτος, ον (ἔλπομαι), *unhoped, unexpected*, h. Ap. 91.

ἀενάων, ουσα, ον (ἀεί, νάω), *ever-flowing.* ἀενάοντο ὕδατα, perennial waters, Od. 13, 109; † (the first a long.)

ἀέξω, orig. form, later contr. αὔξω, Epig. 13, 3; prop. ἀϜέξω with the digamma; only in the pres. and imperf. without augment. I) Act. 1) *to increase, to nourish, to bring up, to augment*; οἶνον, to cause wine to grow (the rain), Od. 9, 111; κράτος, μένος, θυμόν, to augment power, courage, 12, 214; πένθος ἐνὶ στήθεσσι, to nourish grief in the heart, 7, 139; υἱόν, to rear a son, Od. 13, 360. Spoken of the gods: ἔργον, to bless the work, to give it success, Od. 15, 372. II) Mid. *to increase, to grow, to grow up*; Τηλέμαχος ἀέξετο, Telemachus grew up, Od. 22, 426. h. Merc. 408. κῦμα ἀέξετο, the wave arose, Od. 10, 93. χόλος ἐν στήθεσσιν ἀέξεται, anger waxes in the breast, 18, 110. Metaph. ἧμαρ ἀέξεται, *the day waxes* ['till the morning brightened into noon' Cp.], 8, 66. Od. 9, 56.

ἀεργίη, ἡ (ἀεργός), *inactivity, idleness*, only Od. 24, 251. †

ἀεργός, όν, contr. ἀργός (ἔργον), *inactive, lazy, idle.* The antithesis of πολλὰ ἑορτός, 9, 320. Od. 19, 27.

ἀερέθομαι, see ἠερέθομαι.

ἀερθείς, see ἀείρω.

ἄερθεν, see ἀείρω.

ἀερσίπους, ὁ, ἡ, gen. οδος, contr. ἀρσίπους, h. Ven. 212; (πούς) [in Hom. only plur.], *foot-raising, high-stepping*, epith. of ἵπποι, • Il. 3, 327.

ἄεσα and ἆσα (ἀέσαμεν, ἄσαμεν, ἄεσαν), infin. ἀέσαι, aor. 1, from obsol. ᾽ΑΕΏ, related to ἄημι, properly to breathe in sleep, *to sleep*, Od. 3, 490; νύκτας, Od. 19, 342; (the first ἄ. but by augment ἆ.) • Od. [satiandi notionem habet ἆσαι, dormiendi vero ἀέσαι. Lob. Techn. 153.]

ἀεσιφροσύνη, ἡ, Ep. (ἀεσίφρων), *levity, thoughtlessness, folly*, in the pl. Od. 15, 470. †

ἀεσίφρων, ον, gen. ονος (ἀάω, φρήν), *disordered in mind, silly, thoughtless, simple.* The antithesis is ἔμπεδος, 20, 183; θυμός. Od. 21, 303; (prop. for ἀασίφρων. Buttm. Lexil. p. 7.) [Gr Syn. 111.]

᾽ΑΕΏ, see ἄεσα.

ἀζαλέος, η, ον (ἄζω), poet. *dried, dry, arid*, δρῦς, 11, 494; ὕλη, dry wood, Od. 9, 234. ἀζαλέη βῶς, dried bull's hide, i. e. a shield prepared of bull's hide, 7, 239; ὄρος, a dry mountain, i. e. upon which there is much dry wood, that is easily set on fire, 20, 491.

* ἀζάνω, poet. for ἀζαίνω, *to dry up*; mid. *to wither* ἀζάνεται δένδρεα, h. in Ven. 271.

* Ἀζανίς, ίδος, ἡ, *Azanian*, ἤ—κούρη, the Azanian maiden=*Corōnis*, mother of Æsculapius by Apollo, because the family of her lover was from Azania, i. e. Arcadia, h. in Ap. 209; Wolf and Ilgen. But the Ep. and Ion. form is Ἀζηνίς; hence Herm. substitutes Ἀτλαντίδα for the common reading Ἀζαντίδα; the explanation is however obscure. See Herm. and Franke in loc.

Ἀζείδης, αο, ὁ, son of Azeus=*Actor*, 2, 513.

Ἀζεύς, έως, ὁ, son of *Clymenus*, brother of Erginus, Stratius, and father of *Actor*, Pausan. 9. 37. 2.

ἄζη, ἡ (ἄζω), prop. *dryness, aridity;* then soil contracted by drought. σάκος πεπαλαγμένον ἄζη, a shield discoloured by dirt, Od. 22, 184. †.

ἀζηχής, ές, gen. έος, *continual, unceasing, incessant*, ὀδύνη, 15, 25; ὀρυμαγδός, 17, 741. The neut. ἀζηχές as adv. *unceasingly*, μεμακυῖαι, 4, 435; φαγεῖν, Od. 18, 3. (The Gram. derive it from ἀ and διέχω, so that ἀζηχής stands for ἀδιεχής by a change of δ into ζ; accord. to Rost, prop. dry, then solid, perpetual, from ἄζα. [Lob. Path. 336, prefers the former der.)]

ἄζομαι, mid. (act. ἄζω, Hes. op.), *to dry, to wither.* αἴγειρος ἀζομένη κεῖται, the poplar lies withering, ['exposed to parching airs,' Cp.] 4. 487. †

ἄζομαι, poet. depon. only pres. and impf. 1) *to stand in awe* of any one, with an accus. espy of gods and venerable personages, *to reverence, venerate, honour* any one, Ἀπόλλωνα, 1, 21; μητέρα, Od. 17, 401. 2) Intrans. *to fear, to dread*, with an infin. ἄζετο Διῒ λείβειν οἶνον, he feared to pour a libation of wine to Jupiter, 6, 266; and with μή: ἄζετο μὴ Νυκτὶ ἀποθύμια ἕρδοι, he dreaded to do any thing displeasing to Night, 14, 261.

Ἀηδών, όνος, ἡ (prop. Ep. for ἀείδων, the songstress, the nightingale). *Aëdōn*, daughter of *Pandareus*, wife of *Zethus* king of Thebes, mother of Itylus. From envy towards her sister-in-law Niobe, she meditated the murder of her eldest son, but by mistake slew her own son. Having been changed into a nightingale by Zeus, she thenceforth bewailed him, Od. 19, 518. According to a later fable she was the wife of the artist Polytechnus in Colophon, cf. Anton. Lib. 11.

* ἀήθεια, ἡ (ἦθος), *unusualness, strangeness, novel condition* or *circumstances*, Batr. 72.

ἀηθέσσω, poet. for ἀηθέω (ἀηθής), *to be unaccustomed*, with gen., spoken of horses: ἀηθεσσον ἔτι νεκρῶν, they were as yet unaccustomed to the [sight of] dead bodies, 10, 493. †

ἄημι, Ep. (ἄεω), infin. ἀῆναι, poet. ἀήμεναι, partcp. ἀείς, impf. 3 sing. ἄη, partcp. pass. ἀήμενος, imperf. mid. ἄητο (retaining always the η), *to breathe, to blow, to storm;* spoken of wind: Θρήκηθεν ἄητον, 9, 5. ἄη Ζέφυρος, Od. 14, 458. Pres. partcp. λέων νόμενος καὶ ἀήμενος, a lion which goes through rain and wind, Od. 6, 131.

Π) Mid. only in a trop. signif. δίχα δέ σφιν ἐνὶ φρεσὶ θυμὸς ἄητο, the heart within their breasts was agitated in two different directions, i. e. they were irresolute, [Bothe, "the heart in their bosom breathed discord ;" and Cowper, "each breathing discord,"] 21, 386; but also: περί τ᾽ ἀμφίτε κάλλος ἄητο, beauty breathed around, h. in Cer. 277.

ἀήρ, ἠέρος, Ion. and Ep for ἀέρος, ἡ, the lower, thick air, in distinction from the pure upper air, αἰθήρ, the atmosphere, 14. 288. 2) vapour, fog, clouds, mist, by which any thing thing is hidden from the view. ἐκάλυψε ἠέρι πολλῇ, 3, 381. 8, 50; and περὶ δ᾽ ἠέρα πουλὺν ἔχευεν, she poured much mist around, 5, 776. 3) obscurity, darkness, 5, 864. Od. 8, 562. [Lexil. p.37.]

ἀήσυλος, ον, poet. for αἴσυλος. ἀήσυλα ἔργα, impious deeds, 5, 876. †

ἀήτης, ον, ὁ (ἄημι), a blowing, a blast, spoken of vehement wind, often in connexion with ἀνέμοιο, ἀνέμων, 15, 626; also plur. ἀῆται ἀργαλέων ἀνέμων, blasts of dreadful winds, 14, 254. Od. 4, 567. b) Absol. for ἄνεμος, Od. 9, 139.

ἄητος, ον, poet. (ἄημι), stormy, boisterous. θάρσος ἄητον ἔχουσα, full of stormy boldness, used of Minerva, 21, 395. † (The derivation from ἄημι i. q. πνέω, according to Eustath. appears most natural, when we compare this with v. 386, θυμὸς ἄητο; the other explanations of the Schol. ἀκόρεστος from᾽ΑΩ to satiate, or μέγιστος, have less weight; the last is approved by Buttm. Lex. p. 45. He regards it as identical with αἴητος, and from its supposed relationship to αἰνός, gives it the idea, prodigious, astonishing.)

ἀθάνατος, ον, also ος, η, ον, 10, 404. (θάνατος and ā), 1) immortal, spoken particularly of the gods, who alone are called ἀθάνατοι, 4, 394; also of what belongs to the gods, eternal, imperishable, αἰγίς, 2, 447; δόμοι, Od. 4, 79. 2) endless, enduring, in reference to men; κακόν, Od. 12, 118.

ἄθαπτος, ον (θάπτω), unburied, 22, 386. Od. 11, 54.

ἀθεεί, adv., poet. (θεός), without god, without the will or direction of god, Od. 18, 352.†

ἀθεμίστιος, ον (θέμις), lawless, unjust, impious, Od. 18, 141; spoken of the Cyclops Polyphēmus: ἀθεμίστια εἰδέναι, to be versed in impiety, •Od. 9, 189. 428.

ἀθέμιστος, ον (θέμις [pl. θέμιστες]), prop. knowing no laws or civil institutions, lawless, uncivilized; spoken of the Cyclopes, Od. 9, 106. cf. v. 112; mly unrighteous, unjust, 9, 63. Od. 17, 363.

ἀθερίζω, only pres. and imperf. to slight, to despise, to disdain; with accus. 1, 261; connected with ἀναίνομαι, Od. 8, 212; (fr. θέρω, θεραπεύω; according to Ap. fr. ἀθήρ, ἔρος, chaff.)

ἀθέσφατος, ον (θέσφατος), prop. not to be expressed even by a god, ineffable, immeasurable, unspeakably great; θάλασσα, Od. 7, 273; γαῖα, h. 14, 4; ὄμβρος, im-

mense rain, 3, 4; νύξ, endless 11, 372. 15, 392.

Ἀθῆναι, αἱ, Ep. also ἡ Ἀθήνη Athenæ, capital of Attica, origi a fortress established by Ce called Κεκροπία; afterwards e Theseus and called by the n tutelary goddess Athenæ 2, 5 30.

Ἀθηναίη, ἡ = Ἀθήνη

Ἀθηναῖος, ὁ, an Athenian, 2,

Ἀθήνη, ἡ, Ep. also Ἀθηναίη the Roman] Minerva, daughter according to Hom. without m calls her Τριτογένεια, q. v.; ac a later fable, sprung from th Zeus, h. in Ap. 308; in Mi (hence Ἀθήνη, according to H lacia, the unsuckled.) She is th of wisdom united with power, thing stands under her prote performance of which requires and spirit. Especially is she, l lary divinity of cities at peace; e which gives prosperity to citi work; she therefore equally with tus (Vulcan) presides over every 23, 160; and especially over femal Od. 2, 116. 6, 233. 2) she als cities in war against external foe fortresses and walls are under tection, and she is called ἐρυ Ἀλαλκομενηίς. Thus she beco the goddess of war, but only of which is conducted with wisc profit, comp. Ἄρης; hence she λῆΐτις, ἀγέλεια, λαοσσόος, etc. character she conducts battles, heroes who in war unite brav discretion, 5, 333. 837. 21, 406. also she is called Παλλάς, th brandisher, and Hom. often wri λὰς Ἀθηναίη or Ἀθήνη, 1, 200. 4,

ἀθηρηλοιγός, ὁ (ἀθήρ, λοιγός), ἀθερηλοιγός, the destroyer of corn Tiresias so calls the winnowing-s which the grain is separated f beards or chaff, in the oracle future fate of Ulysses, •Od. 11, 23, 275.

ἀθλέω (ἄθλος), aor. 1. ἄθλησα, ἀθλεύω, to contend for a prize; toil, to endure, to suffer; only partcp. aor. ἀθλήσαντε πολίσσαμε we built with much labour, 7, 45:

ἀθλητήρ, ῆρος, ὁ (ἀθλέω). Ep. f τής, a combatant, a prize-fighter 164.†

ἄθλος, ὁ, prose form for ἄεθλος test, a prize-combat, Od. 8, 160.†

ἀθλοφόρος, ον, com. form for E φόρος, q. v.

Ἀθόως, Ep. for Ἄθως, q. v.

ἀθρέω, Ep. and Ion. for ἀθρέω, a σα, to regard with fixed look, t look, to gaze at, Od. 12, 232; εἰς τ and with accus. τινά, to behold, to any one, 12, 391. [Wyttenb. a d quodam θρέω traductum puta Techn. 153.]

ἀθρόος, όη, ύον, *collected, multitudinous, together, crowded.* ἀθρόοι ἴομεν, let us go together, 2, 439; also strengthened by πᾶς: ἀθρόοι ἦλθον ἅπαντες, they came all together in a body, Od. 3, 34. ἀθρόα πάντ' ἀπέτισε, he atoned for all at once, Od. 1, 43; comp. 22, 271. Hom. has only the plur.

ἄθυμος, ον (θυμός), *spiritless, dejected,* Od. 10, 463. †

ἄθυρμα, ατος, τό (ἀθύρω), *play, amusement, a plaything, a toy,* Od. 18, 323. ποιεῖν ἀθύρματα, to make playthings ['to build plaything-walls,' Cp.]; spoken of a boy making sand-heaps, 15, 363; mly *sport, amusement,* spoken of the lyre, h. Merc. 32; *trinket, ornament,* Od. 15, 415. 18, 323.

ἀθύρω, only pres. *to play, to amuse oneself;* spoken of children, 15, 364; like *ludere,* of a song, h. 18, 15; with accus. λαίφος ἀθύρων, playing with the covering, h. in Merc. 152. 2) Mid. on the lyre, h. in Merc. 485.

Ἄθως, ω, ὁ, Ep. Ἀθόως, όω, a very high mountain, or rather point, of the promontory *Actê,* on the south-west coast of the Strymonic gulf, now *Monte Santo,* or *Agios Oros,* 14, 229. h. Ap. 33.

αἰ, conjunct. Æol. and Ep. for εἰ, always in connexion with κέ, αἴ κε and αἴ κεν, for the Att. ἐάν, *if, in case, if perchance, if perhaps.* It stands 1) In the protasis of conditional sentences with the *subjunctive,* but only when a hope, wish, anxious desire, etc. is expressed, *if perchance, in case.* αἴ κέν μοι—Ἀθήνη κῦδος ὀρέξῃ ἀμφοτέρω κτεῖναι, κ. τ. λ., if perchance Minerva should accord me the glory, etc., 5, 260; so likewise 11, 797. Od. 8, 496. 12, 53. b) With the *optative,* more rarely and for the most in dependent discourse: ἠνώγεα Πρίαμος—εἰπεῖν, αἴ κέ περ ὔμμι φίλον καὶ ἡδὺ γένοιτο, μῦθον Ἀλεξάνδροιο, if perchance it might be agreeable to you, 7, 337. In other places Wolf and Thiersch read instead of the optat. the subjunct., as 5, 279. 24, 687: in Od. 13, 349. Thiersch [without reason] would read αἴθε for αἴ κε. 2) In indirect questions, after verbs of seeing, trying, proving, etc., with subjunct. *whether perchance, if perhaps.* ὄφρα ἴδητ', αἴ κ' ὔμμιν ὑπέρσχῃ χεῖρα Κρονίων, whether Kronos will protect you with his hand, 4, 249. 1, 207. Often before αἴ κε some such word as σκοπῶν, πειρώμενος, may be supplied, ὀτρυνέω ἀνστήμεναι (πειρώμενος), αἴ κ' ἐθέλῃσιν ἐλθεῖν, 10, 55; cf. 11, 796. Od. 1, 379. 2, 144. 3) In *a wish* (where for emphasis' sake it is always written αἲ) it never stands alone, but always in connexion with γάρ and γὰρ δή, *if but, would that,* always with the *optative,* which leaves it undetermined whether the wish is possible or impossible. αἲ γὰρ τοῦτο γένοιτο, would that this might be so, Od. 8, 339. αἲ γὰρ αὔτως εἴη, would that it might but be so, 4, 189; hence also of a wish whose fulfilment is impossible: αἲ

γάρ——ἡβώμι, ὡς, would that I were but still so young as, etc. 7, 132; rarely with infin. αἲ γὰρ—ἐχέμεν, Od. 7, 312, where according to the ancients ἐθέλοις is to be supplied (comp. however Rost, Gr. § 125. Anm. 3. Kühner, Gr. § 306, Rem 11, d.). In like manner Od. 24, 380.

αἶα, ἡ (properly γαῖα with the soft pronunciation), used only in the nom. gen. and accus. sing. *the earth, the land.* πᾶσαν ἐπ' αἶαν, over the whole earth; often πατρὶς αἶα, one's country; one's fatherland, 2, 162.

Αἶα, ἡ, pr. n. *Æa,* a mythic country, which is placed in the east, as the abode of *Æetes* in the Argonautic expedition (in the earliest fable prob. the Taurica Chersonesus, later Colchis, where was found a town Æa), and as the abode of Circê in the west; see Αἰαίη. Hom. has not this word as pr. n.

Αἰαίη, ἡ (Αἶα), 1) The *Ææan,* an appellation of Circe as an inhabitant of the *Ææan* island, Od. 9, 32. 2) νῆσος, the *Ææan* island, the abode of *Circe,* a mythic island, which, according to the most current and probable view, lies in the west, north of the Læstrygonians, above Sicily, whither Ulysses sailed from Æa with a north wind. According to another view the island of Circe lay in the far-north-east, and is identical with the abode of Æetes, Strabo, I. p. 45. The older Scholiasts understand by it the promontory of *Circeii* in Italy, and suppose that it was formerly an island, Od. 10, 135. It is difficult to explain the remark of Homer, Od. 12, 3, that here is the abode of Eos and the rising of Helios. The most probable explanation is, that Ulysses, after his return from the gloomy underworld, has here arrived at regions illuminated by day-light. According to Völcker, Hom. Geog. p 31, and Weidasch, Eos and Helios are to be here regarded as gods; as such, like other deities, they have several abodes, cf. 14, 259—61.

Αἰακίδης, ου, ὁ, son of Æacus=*Peleus,* 16, 15. 2) grandson of Æacus=*Achilles,* 11, 805.

Αἰᾰκός, ὁ (according to Herm. *Malivortus, averter of evil,* from αἶ and ἄκος), son of *Zeus* and *Ægina,* the just king of the island of Ægina, father of Peleus and Telamon by Endeïs, and of Phocus by the nymph Psammathe, 21, 189.

Αἴας, αντος, ὁ (according to Herm. *Vulturnus, the impetuous,* from αἴσσω, but, according to Eustath, *the pitiable,* from αἴ, αἰάζω), *Ajax* 1) ὁ Οϊλῆος and ὁ Λοκρός, son of *Oileus,* leader of the Locrians, smaller of stature than the Telamonian Ajax, but a good lancer, 2, 530. His impudent boasting against Poseidôn he expiated by his death, Od. 4, 449. He was also hated by Athênê, because, according to a later fable, he had violated Cassandra in her temple in Troy. 2) ὁ Τελαμώνιος, son of *Telamon,* king of Salamis, brother of Teucer, next to Achilles the bravest of the Greeks; he even ventured upon a single combat with Hector, 7, 182. He contended with Ulysses for the arms of Achilles, and slew himself in a fit of madness, when he failed to obtain them, Od. 11, 544.

Αἰγαγέη, ἡ, Hom. h. in Ap. 40, a conjectural reading of Ilgene's for Αἰσαγέη. He derives it from αἴξ and γῆ, and understands by it the promontory Αἰγᾶν in Æolis; according to Hermann the change is unnecessary.

Αἰγαί. αἱ, 1) αἱ Ἀχαϊκαί, a little town in Achaia, on the Crathis, with a temple of Poseidôn, not far from Helicē, 8, 203. h. Ap. 32. 2) a city on the island Eubœa, on the west coast, also having a temple of Poseidôn, 13, 21. Od. 5, 381; or an island near Eubœa, according to Strabo, p. 386, and Steph. B.; or, according to Voss, a rocky island between Tenos and Chios; comp. Eustath. 13, 21. Plin. IV. 12. Other ancient commentators understood in this place also the Achaian Ægæ. (Αἰγαί plur. fr. αἰγά=αἴξ, the dashing of the waves.)

Αἰγαίων, ωνος, ὁ (the stormy, fr. αἴξ a storm), a hundred-handed sea-giant, so called among men, but among the gods Briareus. According to Apd. 1, 1, son of Uranus and Gæa. Thetis called him to the help of Zeus when the gods threatened to bind him, 1, 403.

αἰγανέη, ἡ (αἴξ), a javelin, a hunting-spear, prop. that used for hunting wild goats. [Coraes, on Plut. T. V. 343, derives it from ἀκή. Lob. Path. 186.]

Αἰγείδης, ου, son of Ægeus=Theseus, 1, 265.

αἴγειος, είη, ειον, poet. also αἴγεος (αἴξ), of goats, relating to goats; hence τυρός, goat's-milk cheese, 11, 639. 2) made of goat's skin; ἀσκός, a goat-skin bottle. 3, 247. κυνέη αἰγείη, a helmet of goat-skin, Od. 24, 231.

αἴγειρος, ἡ, the poplar, perhaps black-poplar, aspen, populus nigra, Linn., 4, 482; as a tree of the under-world, Od. 10, 510.

αἴγεος, έη, εον, poet. for αἴγειος, Od, 9, 196.†

Αἰγιάλεια, ἡ, daughter of Adrastus, wife of Diomēdes, king of Argos, 5, 412; according to others, daughter of Ægialeus, grand-daughter of Adrastus. According to later fable she lived in adulterous intercourse with Comētes son of Sthenĕlus, and caused her husband on his return to be expelled with violence; vid. Diomedes.

αἰγιαλός, ὁ (prob. from αἴξ and ἅλς a place where the sea beats), a coast, a shore, beach, Il. and Od.

Αἰγιαλός, ὁ (the coast-land), the part of the Peloponnesus from the Corinthian isthmus to the borders of Elis, or the later Achaia, according to the fable named from Ægialeus, son of Inachus, 2, 575; cf. Apd. 2, 11.

Αἰγίαλος, a little town and territory of the Henĕti, in Paphlagonia, 2, 855.

αἰγίβοτος, ον (αἴξ, βόσκω) goat-pastur-

ing, goat-nourishing; epith. of the Ithaca, Od. 4, 606. As subst. goc ture, Od. 13, 246.

αἰγίλιψ, ιπος, ὁ ἡ (λείπω), prop. doned of goats, high, steep, inacces epith. of πέτρη, *Il. 9, 15.

Αἰγίλιψ, ιπος, ἡ, pr. n. of a pla Acarnania, built upon a rock, acco to Strabo, IX. p. 452; according to in Ithaca, or a little island near E 2, 633.

Αἴγινα, ἡ (according to Herm. Q. τια), Ægina, an island of the Saronic originally Œnōne and Œnopia, whic ceived its name from Ægina the dau of Asopus; now Engia; 2, 562. (A h. in Ap. 31.)

Αἴγιον, τό, Ægium, one of the towns in Achaia, later the rendezv the Achaian league; now Vostizza, 2

αἰγίοχος, ὁ (ἔχω), the ægis-bearer, brandisher; epith. of Zeus, Il. and (

*αἰγιπόδης, ου, ὁ (πούς), goat-fo epith. of Pan. h. 18, 2.

αἰγίς, ίδος, ἡ (either fr. αἴξ, goa cause in ancient times goat-skin was in constructing armour, or, in more accordance with Homeric usage, fr a storm, because the brandishing excited confusion), the ægis, the shi Zeus, emblem of powerful protec Hephæstûs made it of metal, 15, 30 was similar to other shields of heroes upon it were terrific images, the G surrounded by Eris, Alcē, and Iōcē, its movement Zeus excited terrou confusion. Apollo and Athēnē (Min also sometimes bore it, 15, 308. 2, 448 ægis however served not only to e terrour, but also for protection, 21 18, 204. 24, 40. It is described 5, 73 2, 448.

Αἴγισθος, ὁ, Ægisthus, son of Thy by his daughter Pelopea. He sec Clytæmnestra the wife of Agamen and slew him on his return from ' Od. 11, 409. He reigned twelve over the wealthy Mycenæ, till at le he was slain by Orestes, Od. 1, 35. cording to mythology he was suckled goat: hence his name: αἴξ θάω, θ Æl. V. H. 12, 42.)

αἴγλη, ἡ (akin to ἀγάλλω), splen brightness, of the sun and moon, C 45; of brass, 2, 458; and generally, Od. 6, 45.

αἰγλήεις, εσσα, εν (αἴγλην), glitte brilliant, shining, bright; epith. of C pus, Il. and Od. The neut. as adv. 1 11.

αἰγυπιός, ὁ, a large bird of prey, the Lammergeyer, a vulture, fr. αἴ γύψ, 17, 466. Od. 16, 217.

Αἰγύπτιος, ίη, ιον, Egyptian (al to be pronounced in Hom. as a trisyll 9, 382). 2) Subst. an Egyptian, Od.

Αἰγύπτιος, ὁ, father of Antiphus Eurynomus, an old man in Ithaca, opened the assembly convened by machus, Od. 2, 15.

Αἴγυπτος, ἡ, 1) As fem. *Egypt*, a country in North Africa, Od. 17, 448. 2) ὁ ποταμός, *the Nile*, which had in Hom. the same name with the country, Od. 4, 351. 355. 14, 257. 258.

αἰδεῖο for αἰδέο, see αἰδέομαι.

αἰδέομαι, poet. αἴδομαι, dep. fut. -έσομαι, poet. -σσ, aor. 1. mid. Ep. ᾐδεσάμην and αἰδεσσάμην, and aor. pass. with like signif. *to be abashed, to dread, to be ashamed;* only in a moral sense, in reference to gods and venerable persons, etc. 1) Absol. with infin. αἰδεσθεν ἀνήνασθαι, they were ashamed to refuse it, 7, 93; also with μήπως, 17, 95. 2) With accus. of the pers. *to stand in awe* of any one, *to venerate, to reverence, to honour,* 1, 23; spoken also of things, μέλαθρον, to honour the roof, i. e. to respect the rites of hospitality, 9, 640. (αἴδομαι only in the pres.)

αἴδηλος, ον (α and ἰδεῖν), prop. making invisible, hence *devouring, destructive;* epith. of fire, of Ares, and of Athēnē, Il. of the suitors, Od. 16, 29. (cf. Buttm. Lex. p. 50.

αἰδήλως, adv. *in a destructive manner,* 21, 220.†

Ἀΐδης (˘ ˉ), αο, ὁ, Ep. for Ἅιδης, Ep. gen. Ἀΐδεω trisyllabic, Od. 10, 512; (from α and ἰδεῖν, *Nelucus,* the invisible.) In Hom. always the name of a person, except in Il. 23, 244; *Hades, Pluto,* son of Kronos (Saturn) and Rhea, third brother of Zeus, received, at the division, the under-world, 15, 187. He was ruler of the realm of shades and of the dead, hence Ζεὺς καταχθόνιος; his wife was Persephŏnē. He was a powerful, inexorable god, yet Herăclēs (Hercules) bore off his dog Cerberus from the lower world, and even wounded the god, 5, 395. His abode was *Hades* (δῶμ' Ἀΐδαο, Ἀΐδος δόμος). According to the universal imagination of later antiquity, Hades was beneath the earth, or in the interior of it. Even in Hom. we find unquestionable traces of this notion, cf. 20, 63 seq. Od. 5, 185. 20, 81. In other passages however the fancy of the poet places it only on the other side of the ocean, which separates it from the illuminated portion of the earth, Od. 10. 509. 11, 156; without distinctly fixing it beneath the earth as he does Tartarus, 8, 16. He describes it as a region spacious and dark, with mountains, woods, and waters, like the earth, Od. 10, 509 seq. Il. 8, 16. The entrance to the nether world was furnished with strong gates, which Cerberus watched, 8, 366. Od. 11, 622. Four rivers flowed through the realm of shades: the Achĕron, Pyriphlegĕthon, Cocўtus, and Styx, Od. 10, 513. All men after death were obliged to enter the lower world; still before burial they could not pass the river, but flitted about as shadows, see ψυχή. The shades have no memory, and only recollect after they have drunk blood (Od. 11, 50. 153); with which, however, the representation in Od. 24, 10 seq. seems at

variance. The entrance to the underworld Hom. places in the west. near the gloom of the Cimmerians. Here, with him, the entrance to Hades is northward and Elysium southward (Od. 11, init.), comp. Völcker, Hom. Geogr. § 70. p. 136 seq. Concerning the situation of the lower world C. F. Grotefend has the following remark, in the Allgem. Geogr. Ephemer. B. XLVIII. 3 St. 1815, p. 258. As the earth's circuit on its upper surface had the form of a gradually declining shell, the same was imagined also to be true on the side turned from heaven, and that it was covered with a vaulted arch in a manner similar to the upper world. This nether and shade-inhabited surface was called ἀΐδης, because it had no communication with the upper world. Cf., in regard to the vaulted roof, the dreadful abode of the Titans, Τάρταρος, 8, 13. 481, and 14, 279. Kindred forms of Ἀΐδης are, by metaplasm: gen. Ἄϊδος, dat. Ἄϊδι; and the lengthened form Ἀϊδωνεύς, dat. Ἀϊδωνῆϊ. To go into the lower world is expressed by: πύλας Ἀΐδαο περήσειν, 23, 71; εἰς Ἀΐδαο δόμους or δόμον (also Ἀΐδαο δῶμα, Od. 12, 21), ἰέναι, καταδῦναι, etc.; and εἰς Ἀΐδαο alone [sc. δῶμα, etc.], 8, 367; also simply Ἀΐδόσδε. To be in the lower world: εἶναι εἰν Ἀΐδαο δόμοισιν, 22, 52; and without δόμοις Od. 11, 211.

* ἀΐδιος, ίη, ιον, for ἀείδιος (ἀεί), *eternal, everlasting,* h. 29, 3.

αἰδοῖα, τά, *the pudenda,* 13, 568.† prop. plur. from

αἰδοῖος, η, ον (αἰδώς), 1) Act. having shame, *modest, bashful, discreet, chaste;* ἄλοχος, 6, 250; ἀλήτης, a bashful beggar, Od. 17, 578. 2) Pass. inspiring shame, etc.; hence *estimable, venerable, honorable, reverend;* often united with δεινός; often ἄλοχος, 6, 250; παρθένος, 2, 514; ἑκυρός, 3, 172: and spoken only of persons, βασιλεύς, 4, 402; ξεῖνος, 19, 254. Compar. αἰδοιότερος.

αἰδοίως, adv. *honorably,* ἀποπέμπειν, Od. 19, 243.†

αἴδομαι. poet. for αἰδέομαι, q. v.

Ἄϊδος, Ἄϊδι, Ep. gen. and dat. by a metaplasm, vid. Thiersch § 181, 45. Buttm. § 56. note 8. Rost § 47. c. Often in the construction Ἄϊδος εἴσω, 6, 284; sc. δόμον, and εἰς Ἄϊδος, 13, 415; in full, 19, 322; εἰν Ἄϊδος, sc. δόμῳ, 24, 593; hence the adv. Ἀΐδόσδε, to Hades, 7, 330; (the formula εἰς Ἀΐδόσδε, Od. 10, 502, is changed by Wolf into εἰς Ἄϊδος δέ.)

ἀϊδρείη, ἡ (ἄϊδρις), *ignorance. inexperience, imprudence;* only in plur. Od. 10, 231. 11, 272. *Od.

ἄϊδρις, ιος, ι. Ep. dat. ἀΐδρεϊ (ἴδρις), *ignorant, unintelligent, inexperienced,* 3, 219; with gen. χώρου, Od. 10, 282.

Ἀϊδωνεύς, ῆος, ὁ, poet. lengthened form of Ἀΐδης, nom. 20, 61; dat. 5, 190.

αἰδώς, όος, contr. οῦς, ἡ, 1) *the feeling of shame* which one has in view of doing any thing wrong, *shame;* αἰδοῖ εἴκων, from [yielding to] shame, 10, 238 ἰσ αἰδὼς καὶ δέος, shame and fear restrained, 15, 657. αἰδῶ θέσθ' ἐνὶ θυμῷ, have shame in (your) mind, 15, 561. *b*) the *diffidence, respect, awe, reverence* of the younger before the elder, the inferior before the superior. οὐ μέν σε χρὴ αἰδοῦς, there is no need of diffidence, Od. 3, 14. 24. 8, 480. 17, 347. 2) that which inspires shame; hence *a*) *shame, disgrace*; αἰδώς, 'Αργεῖοι, it is a shame, a disgrace, 5, 787. 8, 228. 13, 122. *b*) the *pudendum*; τὰ δ' αἰδῶ ἀμφικαλύπτει, sc. εἵματα, 2, 262.

αἰεί and αἰέν, Ion. and poet. for ἀεί, q. v.

αἰειγενέτης, αο, ὁ (γιγνόμαι), *eternal, everlasting, immortal*; epith. of the gods, Il. and Od.

αἰετός, ὁ (ἄημι), Ep. for ἀετός, *eagle*, so called from his rustling flight, Linn. *falco aquila*. The eagle is of a black or brown colour and the strongest and most rapid of birds, 21, 253; for this reason especially the messenger of Zeus, 24, 310. 292. As a prophetic bird, the eagle, on account of his lofty flight and his symbolical acts, was peculiarly significant, 12, 200. Od. 19, 545; vid. Nitzsch on Od. 2, 146.

αἰζήιος, lengthened Ep. form fr. αἰζηός, 17, 520. Od. 12, 83.

ἀίζηλος, ον, according to Hesych. and Etym. Magn.=ἀίδηλος, *invisible*, with a change of the δ into ζ after the Æolic mode; prob. the correct reading in 2, 318, for ἀρίζηλος, according to Buttm. Lexil. p. 52, but see Nägelsbach Anm. p. 134. τὸν μὲν ἀίζηλον θῆκεν θεός, the god made him again invisible, according to Cic. de Div. 2, 30, *idem abdidit et duro firmavit tegmina saxo*. The connexion certainly favours this reading, since it demands an antithesis to ὅσπερ ἔφηνεν, but Spitzner has retained ἀρίζηλον, as the only reading of the Cdd.

αἰζηός, ὁ, lengthened αἰζήιος (perhaps from α intens. and ζέω, ζάω [Död. from αἴθω)], prop. to bubble up, *lively, active, hot, vigorous*, 16, 716. h. Ap. 449. As subst. in the pl. *youth, men*, with idea of strength and activity; αἰζηοὶ θαλεροί, 3, 26.

Αἰήτης, αο, ο, fr. αἶα, *Tellurinus*, according to Herm.), son of Helios (Sol) and Perse, brother of Circe, father of Medēa, the crafty king of Æa to whom Jason went in his expedition after the golden fleece, Od. 10, 137. 12, 70.

αἴητος, ον (ἄημι), Ep. for ἆητος (like αἰετός); hence πέλωρ αἴητον, the noisy monster; πνευστικός Hesych., 18, 410.† This epith. seems suitable for Hephæstus from the great noise connected with his occupation, cf. v. 409. The other explanations: (μέγας Eustath.) *great* of Buttm. and (πυρώδης Hesych.) *sooty* of Voss, seem less satisfactory; see Buttm. Lex. p. 47.

αἰθαλόεις, εσσα, εν (αἴθαλος), *sooty, black from smoke, soot-black, μέλαθρον*, 2, 415; μέγαρον, Od. 22, 239. αἰθαλόεσσα κόνις, sooty dust, i. e. ashes united with dust, or generally, dust, 18, 23.

αἴθε, Dor. and Ep. for εἴθε, a expressing a wish, *would that, oh* 1) With the optat. when it is u whether the wish is of possible o sible accomplishment: αἴθε σέο είην, oh that I were stronger th 16, 722. αἴθε τελευτήσειεν ἅπαντο that he might accomplish it all 331. 2) In connexion with ὤφελ with an infin. following, to inc wish which cannot be accomplisl Spoken of the present: αἴθ' ὄφελ νηυσὶν ἀδάκρυτος ἧσθαι, would th mightest sit here at the ships tea 415. *b*) Of the past: αἴθ' ἅμα ὤφελετε πεφάσθαι, would that ye been slain together, 24, 253. Tl εἴθε is rare in Hom. Od. 2, 32.

Αἴθη, ἡ, *Bay*, name of a steed memnon, 23, 295; adj. αἰθός, ἡ, coloured.

αἰθήρ, έρος, ὁ, in Hom. also ἡ, 1) the *pure, upper air*, in distincti the lower, ἀήρ, 14, 288; and which hidden from our eyes by clouds οὐρανόθεν ὑπερράγη ἄσπετος αἰθή heaven the infinite ether do bursts, or opens [breaks up, cle Am. Ed], 8, 558; cf. 15, 20. I Olympus extends its summit in ether, it is represented as the al the gods; hence of Zeus it i αἰθέρι ναίων, dwelling in ether, Od. 15, 523. 2) In general, *clear, weather, serenity of the sky*, =αἰθ 365. ὡς δ' ὅτ' ἀπ' Οὐλύμπου νέφος οὐρανὸν εἴσω αἰθέρος ἐκ δίης, as from Olympus a cloud comes over after a serene sky; where ἐκ is tra by *after*, signifying time, cf. Spi loc.

Αἴθικες, *Æthikes*, a people of Th dwelling on Pindus, but afterwards borders of Epirus, 2, 744. Strabo, 429.

Αἰθιοπεύς, ῆος, ὁ, an assumed e of Αἰθίοψ, for the accus. plur. Αἰθ 1, 423.

Αἰθίοπες, οἱ, sing. Αἰθίοψ, οπος form Αἰθιοπεύς (prop. *the imbr* from αἴθω and ὤψ), the *Æthiopi* Hom. they are represented as dwe Oceanus, 1, 423. 23, 206; as be remotest people of the earth (ἐ and as being separated into two di dwelling partly in the east and part west, Od. 1, 23, 24. They are nei of the Egyptians and Erembians, C The manifold opinions of comme cannot be all cited here. The old phers place them in the south, an der the Nile or the Red Sea as the line, Strabo, II. p. 103. Two cl Æthiopians are mentioned by Her 7, 70. Voss supposes the Æthiop cupied the entire margin of the li (south). The poet imagined the pians to be in the south, without ing any very accurate knowledg considers them as dwelling east *westerly*, because on account of the great heat (as Nitzsch on Od. 1, 22, remarks) they could not live in the direct south itself. He regards them therefore as being partly in Lybia and partly in the remoter parts of Asia, perhaps as far as Phœnicia, cf. Od. 4. 84. G. F. Grotefend, Geogr. Ephem. B. 48. St. 3, correctly remarks:— The Æthiopians dwelling in the remotest south belong to both hemispheres. As far as historical geography extends dwell busy, active men, Od 6, 8. Nearer the margin of the earth dwell the fabulous nations, the Æthiopians, the Phæeaces, the Pygmies, etc. In regard to the epith. ἀμύμονες, the blameless, and in regard to the journeys of the gods to them, I will only cite a remark from Völcker, Hom. Geog. § 47:— The Æthiopians are with Hom. a general name for the last inhabitants of the earth, the most remote people he knew of; to whom he might send the gods, in order to gain time for events which according to his plan must occur. The epithet ἀμύμονες rests perhaps on a similar ground with that on which certain Scythians are elsewhere denominated the most just among men (the Abii), viz., a confused notion of the innocence and justice of semi-savage nations that are but little known, which has in all ages been cherished, when an opposite opinion, a belief in their utter ferocity and wildness, has not yet been formed. See Völck. Hom. Geogr. § 46, 47.

αἰθόμενος, η, ον, prop. partcp. mid. (αἴθω), *burning, flaming*, with πῦρ, 6, 182; δαλός, 13, 320; δαΐς, Od. 1, 428.

αἴθουσα, ἡ (prop. partcp. act. from αἴθω, sc. στοά, because the sun shone into it), *porch, gallery, piazza, portico*, which extended along the house on both sides of the door, Od. 4, 297. Il. 6, 243. Above, the portico was covered by the projecting roof of the house, which was supported by pillars; towards the court it was open, so that the sun could shine in; through this porch was the passage from the court to the vestibule πρόδομος. Such porches were also attached to the out-buildings, 9, 468. Od. 8, 57. Their main design was to afford a place in which to enjoy the sun; the chariots were placed in them, Od. 4, 24; strangers were allowed to sleep in them, Od. 3, 399. In Od. 4, 302 [cf. 15, 5], the αἴθουσα is included in the πρόδομος δόμου, see Cammann Hom. Vorsch. p. 325.

αἴθοψ, οπος, ὁ ἡ (αἴθω, ὤψ), prop. of fiery look; then, *sparkling, shining, gleaming, beaming*; χαλκός; οἶνος, the sparkling wine, 4, 259; not ruddy, see Od. 12, 19, where it stands connected with ἐρυθρός; καπνός, the dark smoke, Od. 10, 152.

αἴθρη, ἡ (αἰθήρ [for tne same r. as ἀήρ, αἰθήρ, αὔρα. Lob. Path. 58]), *pure, clear air, fair weather*, 17, 646. Od. 6, 44.

Αἴθρη, ἡ, Ion. for Αἴθρα, Æthra, daughter of Pittheus, wife of Ægeus, to whom she bore Theseus. Castor and Pollux, when they rescued Helen from Theseus, made her prisoner; she followed Helen to Troy, 3, 144.

αἰθρηγενέτης, ου, ὁ, Od. 5, 296; and αἰθρηγενής, ές (γίγνομαι), epith. of Boreas, 15, 171. 19, 356; *ether-born, produced in pure* or *cold air;* correctly passive Eustath., for compounds in γενής have always such a signification. The other explanation *cold-producing*, or, according to Voss, *clear-blowing* ['cloud-dispelling,' Cp.] is against the analogy of the language.

* αἴθριος, ον (αἰθήρ), *clear, fair, serene;* epith. of Zephyr, h. in Ap. 433.

αἶθρος, ὁ (αἴθρη), *morning-cold, frost, rime*, Od. 14, 318.†

αἴθυια, ἡ, *a water-fowl* (V. Diver), *fulica mergus* ['sea-mew,' Cp.], *Od. 5, 337 and 353.

αἴθω, whence comes αἰθόμενος, q. v.

αἴθων, ωνος, ὁ (αἴθω), prop. *burning, fiery*, 1) Of colour, *shining, sparkling, flashing, gleaming, beaming;* of iron, 4, 485. 7, 473; spoken of brass and vessels made of it, 9, 123. 2) Metaph. spoken of larger animals; *fiery, fierce, spirited;* as λέων, 10, 24; ἵππος, 2, 839; ταῦρος, 16, 488. Od. 18, 371, and αἰετός, 15, 690. The old grammarians referred it to the disposition; modern commentators, *fiery-red, red*, but it cannot well denote a common and regular colour, but describes rather the *shining hide*, plumage, &c. of smooth-coated or well-fed animals: the shining steeds, the sparkling lion, eagles, the fiery bull.

Αἴθων, ωνος, ὁ, 1) the name which *Ulysses* adopted before he discovered himself to Penelope, Od. 19, 183. 2) the steed of Hector, = *Bay* or *Fiery*, 8, 185.

αἴκ' for αἴκε, see αἰ.

ἀϊκή, ἡ (ˉ ˘ ˘ from ἀΐσσω), an Ep. form of ᾆξ, *a vehement rush. an attack, impetus;* only in the plur. τόξων ἀϊκαί, a discharge of bows, V. Il. 15, 709.†

* ἄϊκτος, ον (ἱκνέομαι), *inaccessible, unapproachable*, h. Merc. 346; accord. to Herm. conject. for ὅδ᾽ ἐκτός.

ἀϊκῶς, Ep. for ἀεικῶς, *in an unseemly manner*, 22, 336.†

αἷμα, ατος, τό, 1) *blood*, with Hom. the seat of life, Od. 3, 455; hence the shades were obliged to drink blood before they could recover the power of recollection, Od. 11, 50. 97 seq. γαστὴρ ἐμπλείη κνίσσης τε καὶ αἵματος, a stomach filled with fat and blood, as food, Od. 18, 118; cf. v. 45. 2) *bloodshed, slaughter*, with ἀνδροκτασίη and κυδοιμός, 11, 164. φόνος τε καὶ αἷμα, 19, 214. 3) Like *sanguis; blood, consanguinity, race*, 6, 211. εἶναι αἵματος ἀγαθοῖο, to be of noble blood, Od. 4, 611 (perhaps from αἴω = ἄημι).

αἱμασία, ἡ [usually explained]: *thornbush*, for hedging a field or garden; mly a fence [prob. a *dry-wall* loosely put together: αἱμασίας λέγειν = to *collect* and pile up stones, etc. to make a *dry-wall*, a fence.] *Od. 18, 359. 24, 224; see Buttm. Lex. p. 76, 8. [der. from αἶμος, point, doubtful.]

αἱματόεις, εσσα, εν (αἷμα), bloody, sprinkled with blood, blood-red, blood-stained, 5, 82. Od. 22, 405; σμῶδιξ, a bloody wheal ['whelk,' Cp.], 2, 267. 2) Transl. bloody, of days, wars, etc. [ἤματα, πόλεμος, 9, 326. 650.

Αἱμονίδης, ου, ὁ, Hæmonides, son of Hæmon=Mæon, 4, 394.

Αἱμονίδης, ου, ὁ, son of Æmon=Laerkês of Thessalia, 17, 467.

αἱμοφόρυκτος, ον (φορύσσω), stained or sprinkled with blood, κρέα. Od. 20, 348.†

αἱμύλιος, ον (αἱμύλος), Ep. prop. stealing into the soul, flattering, wheedling, deceptive, λόγοι. Od. 1, 56. †h. Merc. 317; (prob. from αἷμος, a point; hence, pointed, penetrating. [Lob. thinks that αἱμύλος itself came from αἱμύλλω, which the ancients derived from ἅμα or αἵμων, scitus.])

* αἱμυλομήτης, ου, ὁ (μῆτις), flattering, cunning, h. in Merc. 13.

αἵμων, ονος, ὁ, Ep. = δαίμων, δάημων, acquainted with, experienced; with gen. θήρης, 5, 49.† Geist dispp. Hom. IV. 1, derives it from ἀΐω, audio, sentio, and therefore writes αἵμων.

Αἵμων, ονος, ὁ, 1) a hero of Pylus, 4, 296. 2) father of Mæon, q. v.

αἰνά, neut. plur. from αἰνός, q. v.

αἰναρέτης, ου, ὁ (ἀρετή) [male fortis], brave to others' harm (fearfully or hurtfully brave); only in voc. αἰναρέτη, of Achilles, 16, 31.†

Αἰνείας, αο, and Αἰνείω, 5, 334; (the praised, from αἰνέω, but acc. to h. in Ven. 198, from αἰνός), Æneas, son of Anchises and Aphroditê, a descendant of Tros, consequently related to Priam, king of the Dardanians, 2, 280 seq. 20, 215. He was, it is true, a brave hero; still he does not mingle much in the war. In the battle with Diomedes, Aphroditê (Venus) saved him, 5, 311; and in that with Achilles, Poseidôn, 20, 178. According to Hom. Æneas remains in Troy, 20, 307; later traditions speak of him as having migrated to Italy.

αἰνέω (αἶνος), fut. αἰνήσω, Ep. for αἰνέσω, aor. 1. ᾔνησα, for ἤνεσα, to praise, to commend, to approve; spoken of persons and things, with accus. Il. and Od. μή με μάλα αἶνεε μήτε νείκεε, neither praise nor blame me, ι. e. be silent about it, 10, 249.

αἰνίζομαι, depon. Ep. form fr. αἰνέω, to praise, 13, 374. Od. 8, 487.

Αἶνος, ὁ, a Pæonian slain by Achilles, 21, 210.

αἰνόθεν, adv. poet. (αἰνός), ι. e. ἐκ τοῦ αἰνοῦ; only αἰνόθεν αἰνῶς, most horribly, from bad to worse; a periphrastic superl. like οἰόθεν οἶος, 7, 97.†

αἰνόμορος, ον, poet. (μόρος), ill-fated, miserable, unfortunate, 22, 480. Od. 9, 53.

αἰνοπαθής, ές, gen. έος (πάσχω), dreadfully suffering, deeply afflicted ['sad mourner as I am.' Cp.] Od. 18, 201.†

αἶνος, ὁ, Ep. 1) discourse, na elsewhere μῦθος, Od. 14, 508. 2) mendatory discourse, praise, appr 23, 795. τί με χρὴ μητέρος αἰνα need is there of my mother's pra that I should praise her. Buttn p. 59, thinks it is distinguishe μῦθος, discourse generally, by in a speech full of meaning, skilfully [Lob. says B. was too hasty in i the existence of αἰνέω, laudo, Tecl

*Αἶνος, ἡ, Ænus, a town in Th the mouth of the Hebrus, pr Πολτυοβρία, i. e. the town of according to Strabo, VII.; hen Αἰνόθεν, from Ænus, 4, 520.

αἰνός, ή, όν, Ep. and Ion. fo dreadful, frightful, terrific, great of every thing which by its gr producing fearful and especia effects, excites our astonishme terrour; of the gods: terrible, i. stern; Zeus, 4, 25; Athênê, 8, other objects; of battle: 3, 20. Od of passions: 4, 169, 7, 215. α λόχος, a most dreadful ambuscad 441. ἐν αἰνῇσιν νεκάδεσσιν, in the heaps of the dead, 5, 885. Net αἰνὰ πάσχειν, to suffer dreadful 22, 431. Often as adv. αἰνὰ ὀλοφ to lament greatly, Od. 22, 447 τεκοῦσα, bearing for misfortune Schol. ἐπὶ κακῷ. Superl. αἰνότατ 4, 25. (The derivation is obscure. derives it from the interjection α from αἰανός; Buttm. Lexil. de from a root ἀΐω, from which by m the ending νός (as δεινός from αἰνός is formed.)

αἴνυμαι, dep. Ep. (for ἄρνυμαι [Lob. supposes a radical verb αἴν whence αἴνυμαι and ἀναίνομαι, re Techn. 124]), only pres. and imp out augm. to take, to take away, with accus. τεύχεα ἀπ' ὤμων, ὀϊστόν, 15, 459; with gen. τυρῶν αἱ taking some of the cheeses, Od metaph. πόθος αἴνυταί με, longin seizes me, Od. 14, 144.

αἰνῶς, adv. (αἰνός), terribly, fri τείρεσθαι, 5, 352; and mly exceedingly, φιλεῖν, ἐοικέναι, τέ also of wretchedness, miserably, 24.

αἴξ, αἰγός, ἡ (ἀΐσσω), dat. plur. 10, 486, goat; ἄγριος, wild goat and Od.

ἀΐξασκον, ες, ε, iter. aor. 1. fr.

Αἰολίδης, ου, ὁ, son of Æolu phus, 6, 154; Cretheus, Od. 11, 2

Αἰολίη νῆσος, ὁ, the Æolian isl abode of Æolus, son of Hippot of the winds; a mythic islar rounded by a brazen, impregnable the west of the Hom. Geog., Od The ancients made it one of the islands, and Strabo Strongyle, th of them, now Stromboli, former for its volcanic eruptions. Sin ever, Ulysses sailed without obs with a west wind to Ithaca in the east, and was driven directly back by the tempest, the moderns have, with greater probability, placed it immediately beyond the southern point of Sicily, between Sicily and Africa. Völcker, Hom. Geog. finds it in one of the Argades; Voss, on the other hand, explains the epithet πλωτή to mean *floating*, and gives it a double location, once east of Trinacria, and once west of Atlas; see πλωτός.

* Αἰολίς, ἰδος, ἡ, *Æolian*, Ep. 4.

Αἰολίων, ωνος, ὁ, son of Æolus=*Macar*, h. in Ap. 37.

Αἰόλλω, poet. (αἰόλος), *to move rapidly hither and thither, to turn often*; e. g. γαστέρα, *to turn* the stomach (breast) of an animal in roasting it, Od. 20, 27.†

αἰολοθώρηξ, κος, ὁ (θώραξ), *having a flexible cuirass* or *coat of mail* (rapid or active in his cuirass, V.); or, having a variegated, richly adorned cuirass, Köp., 4. 489.† see αἰόλος [and Buttm. Lex. 12].

αἰολομίτρης, ου, ὁ (μίτρα), *having a flexible belt* (active in the belt, V.); or, with a variegated belt, 5, 707.† see αἰόλος.

αἰολόπωλος (πῶλος), *with rapid steeds*, 3, 185.† and h. 3, 138; or, with piebald steeds, see αἰόλος.

αἰόλος, η, ον (prob. related to ἄελλα, fr. ἴλλω, εἴλω), moving or turning rapidly, *moveable, active*; spoken of animals: πόδας αἰόλος ἵππος, the light-footed courser, 19, 404. αἰόλος ὄφις, the lithe or writhing serpent, 12, 208. σφῆκες μέσον αἰόλοι, wasps moveable in the middle, 12, 161. ('Ring-streaked' cannot be reconciled with μέσον). αἰόλος οἶστρος, the flitting gad-fly, Od. 22. 300. αἰόλαι εὐλαί, swarming worms, 22, 509; spoken of arms, *easily moved, rapid*; τεύχεα, arms which can be easily handled (*light, wieldy*), 5, 295; σάκος, 7. 222. This is the true meaning in the Hom. poems, as the derivation shows, see Buttm. Lexil. p. 63. 3.) later it had the signif. *changeful of hue, gleaming, variegated*, since rapid motion gives objects this appearance; αἰόλον ὄστρακον, the variegated shell of the turtle, h. Merc. 33. (Some annotators accept this signif. in the case of the wasps, arms, etc. but Hom. for this uses ποικίλος.)

Αἰόλος, ὁ (*the rapid*, adj. αἰόλος), 1) son of Hellen and the nymph Osreis, or of Zeus; king of Thessaly, father of Cretieus, Sisyphus, Athamas, etc. 6, 154. 2) son of Hippotes and Melanippe, according to Homer; or, according to Diod. 4, 311, son of Poseidôn and Arne, great-grandson of Hippotes, king of the Æolian island. He is represented as a friend of the gods and as the disperser of the winds. He lived with his twelve children, six sons and six daughters, in blissful abundance. Od. 10, 5—9. He entertained hospitably the wandering Ulysses, and even gave him the winds enclosed in a bag; and sent after him only the gentle Zephyr,

Od. 10, 25 seq. (see Völck. Hom. Geogr. p. 115.)

Αἴπεια, ἡ, *Æpēa*. a maritime town in Messenia; according to Strabo, the later *Thuria*; or, according to Paus., *Corone*, 9, 152.

αἰπεινός, ή, όν, poet. (a form of αἰπύς), *high, loftily situated, eminent*; espec. epith. of towns situated upon mountains, Γονόεσσα, 2, 573; Ἴλιος, 13, 773; κάρηνα, lofty summits, 2, 869. Od. 6, 123.

αἰπήεις, εσσα, εν (poet. form of αἰπύς), *lying high, lofty*, Πήδασος, 21, 87.†

αἰπόλιον, τό (αἰπόλος), *a herd of goats*; mly αἰπόλια αἰγῶν, 2, 474; alone, Od. 17, 213. 20, 174.

αἰπόλος, ὁ (αἴξ and πολέω), prop. *goat-pasturing, ἀνήρ*, 2, 474. As subst. *goatherd*, generally with αἰγῶν, Od. 17, 247.

αἰπός, ή, όν, Ep. form of αἰπύς, e. g. πόλις, 13, 625. Od. 3, 130. αἰπὰ ῥέεθρα, 8, 369.

Αἶπυ, τό (adj. αἰπύ), *Æpy*, a town in Elis on the borders of Messenia, prob. the later Αἰπιόν; according to Strab. VIII. p. 349, *Margalia* on the Selleis, 2, 592. h. in Ap. 423.

αἰπύς, εῖα, ύ, poet. forms are αἰπεινός, αἰπήεις, αἰπός, 1) *high, loftily situated, eminent*; spoken of mountains and towns, ὄρος, πτολίεθρον, Ἴλιον αἰπύ, τεῖχος, Il.; βρόχος, a high depending cord, 11, 278. 2) Metaph. *deep, dreadful, difficult*, ὄλεθρος, dreadful destruction, 6, 57. According to Nitzsch, Od. 1, 11, αἰπ. ὄλεθ. is 'deep destruction in which it is easy to plunge;' [an epith. of death, where the discourse relates to escape from great danger, Nitzsch in loc.;] φόνος, dreadful slaughter, 17, 365. Od. 4, 843; χόλος, 15. 223. αἰπὺς πόνος, 11, 601. αἰπύ οἱ ἐσσεῖται, hard will it be for him, 13, 317.

Αἴπυτος, ὁ, *Æpytus*, son of Elatus, king of Phæsana in Arcadia. His monument was on the declivity of the Cyllenian mountain; from this, Αἰπύτιος, the Æpytian; τύμβος, 2, 604. cf. Paus. 8, 16, 2. [Αἰπύτιος, ον, see Αἴπυτος.]

αἱρέω, fut. αἱρήσω, aor. 2. act. εἶλον, Ep. ἕλον and ἕλεσκον, fut. mid. αἱρήσομαι, aor. mid. εἱλόμην, Ep. ἑλόμην, 1) *to take, to catch, to grasp, to seize*; with accus.. e. g. ζωόν τινα, to take one alive, 6, 38; *by what*, with gen. τινὰ κόμης, to take one by the hair, 1, 197; χειρός, by the hand, 1, 323. 4, 542; *with what*, with dat. χαλκόν ὀδοῦσιν, to hold the brass with the teeth; χερσὶ δόρυ, γαῖαν ἀγοστῷ; but, καθαρὰ χροῒ εἵμαθ' ἑλοῦσα, having taken or put clean attire upon her body, Od. 17, 58; metaph. χόλος αἵρει με, anger seizes me, 4, 23. In like manner ἵμερος, δέος, λήθη, ὕπνος. 2) *to take away, τι ἀπ' ἀπήνης*, from the carriage, 24, 579; ἀχλὺν ἀπ' ὀφθαλμῶν, the cloud from the eyes, 5, 127; with two accus. τὸν ἄτη φρένας εἷλε, confusion took away his senses, 16, 805. b) Espec. in war, α) Of things, *to take, to capture*, πόλιν, νῆας, 2, 12. β) Of persons, *to overpower, to slay*, τινά, 4, 457, and often [spoken of enemies meeting in battle, it has always this meaning, unless accompanied by ζωόν or something equivalent in the context]; Am. Ed. *to take, to seize*, ζωόν τινα, 6, 38, II) Mid. 1) *to take for oneself, to seize*, ἔγχος, δόρυ, 3, 338. 10, 31; the connected preposition to govern the translation τόξα ἀπὸ πασσάλου, to take down the bow from the hook or peg, 5, 210; ἀπ' ὤμων τεύχεα, 7, 122; ἐκ δίφροιο, to take out of the chariot, 10, 501. 2) *to take, to obtain, to procure, to receive*; τί, 18, 500; δόρπον, Od. 14, 347. Metaph. ὕπνου δῶρον, to enjoy the gift of sleep, 7, 482; ἄλκιμον ἦτορ, to take bold heart, 5, 529; ὅρκον τινός, to take an oath from any one, Od. 4, 746; also τινί, 22, 119. 3) *to select, to choose*, τέμενος, γυναῖκας, 9. 578. Od. 9, 334.

Αἴρος, ὁ (ῑ) from *a* and Ἴρος, a sportive play upon the name Irus: *not-Irus, un-happy Irus*, Od. 18, 73.†

αἴρω, contr. for ἀείρω, q. v. Hom. has of the common form only the pres. act. in εἴδοντο νέκυν αἴροντας, 17, 724; the aor. 1. mid. ἠράμεθα, ἤρατο; of the aor. 2. the indic. without augm. ἀρόμην, the other moods ἄρωμαι, ἀροίμην, ἀρέσθαι, see ἀείρω.

Ἀΐς, obsolete nom. of Ἀΐδος, q. v.

αἶσα, ἡ, Ep. (from αἴω, akin to δαίω) 1) *share*, in general, which one has of a thing; ληΐδος, a share of the booty, 18, 327. Od. 5, 40. Hence, *that which is fitting, justice, propriety*. κατ' αἶσαν, according to right, or propriety with justice (= good reason); often with εἰπεῖν. ἐν καρὸς αἴση, see κάρ. 2) the assigned *lot of life, fate, destiny*, which the gods accord to men, *fortune* or *misfortune*, 1, 416. Often in Hom. αἶσά μοι, with infin. following, εἰ δέ μοι αἶσα τεθνάμεναι, if it is my lot to die, 24, 224. cf. 16, 707. Od. 5, 113. ἔτι γάρ μοι ἐλπίδος αἶσα, I have still some hope, Od. 16, 101. 19, 84; κακὴ αἶσα, evil fate, 5, 209; com. in a bad signif. 3) *the fateful decree of a god*; Διὸς, of Zeus, 9, 608. ὑπὲρ Διὸς αἶσαν, against the decree of Zeus, 17, 321. δαίμονος αἶσα κακή, Od. 11, 61.

Αἶσα, ἡ, the goddess of *Fate*, like Μοῖρα, who at birth assigns to every one his lot, 20, 127. Od. 7, 197. The poet thus personifies *eternal, unchangeable, governing fate*, the inviolable law of nature, without however giving a form to the deity.

Αἰσαγέης ὄρος, τό, an unknown mountain in Asia Minor, near Clarus, h. Ap. 40; see Αἰγαγέη.

Αἴσηπος, ὁ, Æsepus, 1) a river in Asia Minor, which falls into the Propontis near Cyzicus, 2, 825. 12, 21. 2) son of Bucollon, a Trojan, slain by Euryalus, 6, 21.

αἴσθω, Ep. (ἄημι), only pres. part. and imperf. *to breathe out* (=ἀποπνέω), θυμόν, •16, 468. 20, 403.

αἴσιμος, ον, Ep. (αἶσα), and ος, η, ον, 1) *fitting, right, proper, just*. φρένας αἴσιμη ἦσθα, thou wert sound in mind, Od.

23, 14. αἴσιμα ἔργα ἀνθρώπων, works of men, piety, Od. 14, 84 the neut. αἴσιμα with παρειπεῖ vise that which is suitable, 6, 62 πίνειν, to drink moderately, Od. φρεσὶν αἴσιμα εἰδέναι, to know that which is right, i. e. *to be ju disposed*, 15, 207. αἴσιμα πάντα pay every thing just, to make amends, Od. 8, 348. 2) *destined* only αἴσιμον ἦμαρ, the day of f. in the construction, αἴσιμον ἦε destined by fate, 9, 245. Od. 15,

αἴσιος, ον, Ep. (αἶσα), *sent by j picious*; only in a good sense: *a* πόρος, a traveller sent for good,

αἴσσω (ᾰ and ῑ), aor. 1. act. ἤϊ ἀΐξω. partcp. ἀΐξας, aor. pass. ἠΐχθ ἀϊχθῆναι, 1) Intrans. *to move ra hasten, to run, to rush, to spring*. of things animate and inanimate; of Athênê, ἤϊξεν ἐπὶ χθόνα, sh to the earth, 4, 78; often βῆ ἀΐξα ing she went, 2, 167; of men, m hostile sense: *to rush upon, to a petuously*, ἔγχεϊ, with the lance; νῳ, ἵπποις, the sword, the chario flitting motion of the shades in t world: τοὶ δὲ σκιαὶ ἀΐσσουσιν, 495; of animals: οἱ ἵπποι μάλ' ω πεδίονδε, swiftly rushed the stee plain, Od. 15, 183; of wild boars, of birds: *to fly, to soar*, πρὸς οὐρ 868; ὑπὲρ ἄστεος, 24, 320. Od. 15 Spoken of inanimate things; of i δούρατα ἐκ χειρῶν ἤϊξαν, the spe from the hands, 5, 657; of smo χθονός, to rise from the earth. of the soul: ὡς δ' ὅτ' ἂν (ὅταν) (ἀνέρος, as when darts a man's 15, 80. 2) Pass. as depon. ἐκ χει ἠΐχθησαν, the reins flew from hi 16, 404.

ἄϊστος, ον, Ep. (ἰδεῖν), prop. which nothing is known, *uns known, vanished, annihilated*, ἄϊστον ποιεῖν τινα, to make one i used of Ulysses, because it known whether he would retur 235.

ἀϊστόω, poet. (ἄϊστος), fut. ω optat. ἀϊστώσειαν, and aor. pass. ἀ *to make invisible, to destroy*, O Hence pass. *to be destroyed, to van 10, 259.

αἰσυητήρ, ῆρος, ὁ, poet. (relate μνήτης), *princely, regal, royal*, κο 347.† Instead of this word, who and derivation were unknown the ancients, the edition of Spit αἰσυμνητήρ.

Αἰσυήτης, ὁ (αἰσυητηρ), a father of Alcathous, 2, 793. 13, 4

αἰσυλοεργός, όν, *practising wi 5, 403.† (Thus Spitzner, as the of Aristarchus for ὀβριμοεργός.)

αἴσυλος, ον (prob. from αἶσα), F *impious, improper*. αἴσυλα ῥέζειν tise impiety, 5, 403; μυθήσασθαι, *implious things*, Il.; εἰδέναι, h. N

Αἰσύμη, ἡ, a city in Thrace, 8, 304. Αἰσύμηθεν, from Æsymê.

αἰσυμνητήρ, ῆρος, ὁ=αἰσυμνήτης, 24, 347; and the ancients explain it here by βασιλικός, royal. Cf. αἰσυητήρ.

αἰσυμνήτης, ου, ὁ, poet. (αἰσυμνάω), he who adjudges to persons what is due; the arbiter or judge of a contest, Od. 3, 258.†

Αἴσυμνος, ὁ, a Greek, 11, 303.

αἴσχιστος, η, ον, superl. and αἰσχίων, compar. of αἰσχρός.

αἶσχος, εος, τό, shame, indignity, insult; in the plur. τὰ αἴσχεα, shameful deeds, 3, 342. Od. 1, 229. ὃς ἤδη νέμεσίν τε καὶ αἴσχεα πόλλ' ἀνθρώπων, one who felt the shame and many taunts of men, i. e. so that them as to give no occasion for them, 6, 351.

αἰσχρός, ή, όν (αἶσχος), compar. αἰσχίων, ον, superl. αἴσχιστος, η, ον, 1) ugly, deformed; in a physical sense, αἴσχιστος ἀνὴρ ὑπὸ Ἴλιον ἦλθεν, the ugliest man who came to Troy (under its walls), 2, 216. h. Ap. 197. 2) shameful, disgraceful, insulting; αἰσχρὰ ἔπεα, abusive, insulting words, 3, 38. The neut. followed by inlin. 2, 119.

αἰσχρῶς, adv., shamefully, insultingly, 23, 473 Od. 18, 321.

αἰσχύνω (αἶσχος), aor. 1 ᾔσχῦνα, perf. pass. ῄσχυμμαι, 1) Act. 1) to make ugly, to deform, to disfigure; with accus. πρόσωπον, 18, 24. νέκυς ᾐσχυμμένος, a corpse, i. e. treated with indignity, dishonoured (mutilated), 18, 180. 2) Metaph. to insult, to dishonour, to disgrace, γένος. λέχος, to dishonour a man's bed, Od. 8, 269. 11) Mid. to be ashamed; absolute, Od. 18, 12; τι, to shrink from any thing with shame; to fear any thing, Od. 21, 323.

Αἴσων, ονος, ὁ, (according to Herm. Opuscunnns, from· αἶσα,) son of Cretheus and Tyro, grandson of Æolus I., father of Jason, king of Iolcus, in Thessaly. According to a later tradition Medea renewed his youth, Od. 11, 259.

αἰτέω, fut. αἰτήσω, aor. infin. αἰτῆσαι, h. Ven. 225, to ask, to beg, to demand; absol. Od. 18, 49: with accus. of the pers. and thing, αἰτεῖν τι, 5, 358; τινά, Od. 17, 365; also both, τινὰ δόρυ, to ask any one for a spear, 22, 295; τινί, for any one, κούρη αἰτήσουσα τέλος θαλεροῖο γάμοιο, to solicit youthful nuptials for the damsels, Od. 20, 74. b) With infin. following, 6, 176.

αἰτιάασθαι, Ep. form for αἰτιᾶσθαι, see αἰτιάομαι.

αἰτιάομαι (αἰτία), depon. mid. 3 sing., optat. αἰτιόῳτο, Ep. for αἰτιῷτο, 3 pl. impf. ᾐτιόωντο, Ep. for ᾐτιῶντο, to blame, to accuse; with accus. 11, 78. Od. 20, 135; also with two accus. when the thing is expressed by a neut. pron., Od. 1, 32.

αἰτίζω, Ep. (αἰτέω), to ask earnestly, to beg; absol. Od. 4, 651. 17, 228; with accus. of the thing, Od. 17, 222, and of the person, Od. 17, 346.

αἴτιος, ίη, ιον (αἰτία), having the blame of any thing, guilty, blameworthy; used in Hom. only in a bad sense. οὔτι μοι αἴτιοί εἰσιν, they have in no respect wronged me, 1, 153. Od. 1, 348.

αἰτιόῳτο, Ep. for αἰτιῷτο, 3 sing. optat. pres. from αἰτιάομαι.

Αἰτώλιος, ίη, ιον, Ætolian, 4, 399.

Αἰτωλοί, οἱ, the Ætolians, inhabitants of Ætolia, in Greece, between Acarnania and Thessaly, which received its name from Ætolus, son of Endymion, 2, 638.

αἰχμάζω (αἰχμή), fut. άσω, Ep. άσσω, to brandish the lance; constr. with αἰχμάς, 4, 324.†

αἰχμή, ἡ (ἀκμή or ἀΐσσω), prop. the point of the lance, χαλκείη, 4, 461; mly the lance, the spear.

αἰχμητά, ὁ, Ep. and Æol. for αἰχμητής, 5, 197.

αἰχμητής, οῦ, ὁ, a lancer, a spearman, hence g. t. for warrior, 1, 152, and often, 2) As adj. warlike, 1, 846; ἀνήρ, 3, 49.

αἶψα, adv. quickly, directly, immediately. αἶψα δ' ἔπειτα, immediately thereupon; αἶψα δέ in the narration of a fact, 2, 664. Od. 2, 6; and αἶψά τε in general propositions, 19, 221; see Herm. ad Hymn. in Cer. 485.

αἰψηρός, ή, όν (αἶψα), hasty, quick. αἰψηρὸς κόρος γόοιο, quick is the satiety of grief (one is quickly sated with grief, V.) λῦσεν ἀγορὴν αἰψηρήν for αἶψα, he quickly dispersed the assembly; or with V. the busy council, 19, 276. Od. 2, 257. Nitzsch ad loc. translates: the stirring, the quickly moving assembly.

αἴω, poet. only pres. and impf. without augm. ἄϊον, to observe, to perceive, like sentire; mly to hear, with gen., seldom with accus. φθογγῆς, to hear the voice, 16, 508; πληγῆς, to feel the blow, 11, 532; or, rather, to hear the lash (i. e. the crack of the whip); φίλον ἄϊον ἦτορ, 15, 252, I felt my heart, (viz. its pulsation, because ἦτορ occurs for the most part in a physical sense.) Others: I knew it in my mind. Voss and Bothe: for I was breathing out my life, (with the Schol. ἀπέπνεον, so that ἀΐω=ἄω, ἄημι.)

αἰών, ῶνος, ὁ, comm. ἡ, 1) duration, long time. 2) an age, life, connected with ψυχή: αἰῶνος ἀμέρδεσθαι, to be bereaved of life, 22, 58; ἀπ' αἰῶνος ὀλέσθαι, to perish from life, 24, 725. b) Spoken of animals: αἰῶνα ἐκτορεῖν, to pierce the life, h. Merc. 42; (according to Ruhnken, the spinal marrow,) also plur. δι' αἰῶνας τορεῖν, spoken of cattle, h. Merc. 119.

ἀκάκητα, Ep. for ἀκακήτης, ου, ὁ=ἄκακος (κακός), who is free from evil, from guile, &c. the bearer of happiness, the deliverer from evil, epith. of Mercury, 16, 185. Od. 24, 10.

ἀκαλαρρείτης, αο, ὁ (ἀκαλός =ἤκαλος, still, ῥέω), gently-flowing, softly flowing, epith. of Oceanus, 7, 422, and Od.

ἄκάμας, αντος, ὁ, ἡ (κάμνω), unwearied, untiring, epith. of Sol, of the Sperchius, and of the wild boar, 18, 239. 434. 16, 176. *Il.

Ἀκάμας, αντος, ὁ, 1) son of Antênor

and Theānô, leader of the Dardanians, slain by Meriŏnes, 2, 823. 16, 342. 2) son of Eussôrus, leader of the Thracians, slain by the Telamonian Ajax, 2, 844. 6, 8. 3) son of Asius, 12, 140.

ἀκάματος, ον=ἀκάμας, untiring, never-resting, epithet of fire, 5, 4. Od 20, 123.

ἄκανθα, ἡ (ἀκή), thorn, thistle, Od. 5, 328.†

*'Ἀκάστη, ἡ (greatly distinguished, from a intens. and κέκασμαι), daughter of Oceanus and Thetis, h. Cer. 421.

Ἄκαστος, king of Dulichium, Od. 14, 336.

ἀκαχείατο, see ἀκαχίζω.
ἀκαχεῖν, see ἀκαχίζω.
ἀκαχήμενος, see ἀκαχίζω.
ἀκαχήσω, see ἀκαχίζω.

ἀκαχίζω, Ep. and Ion. ('ΑΧΩ) aor. 2 ἤκαχον, whence again fut. ἀκαχήσω, aor. 1 ἠκάχησα, mid. ἀκαχίζομαι, kindred form of ἄχομαι or ἄχνυμαι, aor. ἠκαχόμην, perf. ἀκάχημαι and ἀκήχεμαι, 3 pl. ἀκηχέδαται (perhaps ἀκηχέαται is preferable), 17, 637 ; 3 pl. plupf. ἀκαχείατο for ἀκάχηντο ; infin. perf. ἀκάχησθαι, partcp. ἀκαχημένος, fem. ἀκηχεμένη (the accent on perf. ind. and partcp. is drawn back : see Buttm. § 111, note 2; also a partcp. pres. ἀχέων, ουσα. 1) Act. to trouble, to afflict ; with accus. Od. 16, 432. 2) Mid. to trouble oneself, to grieve, to be grieved, θυμῷ, 6, 486 ; τῷ μήτι θανὼν ἀκαχίζευ, grieve not that thou art dead, Od. 11, 486 ; in the perf. to be troubled, sad, often absolute with θυμόν and ἦτορ: θεοὶ δ' ἀκαχείατο θυμόν, were troubled at heart, 12, 179. b) With gen. and dat. of the object ; ἵππων, about the steeds, 11, 702. ὅ μοι πυκινῶς ἀκάχηται, who is deeply troubled about me, Od. 23, 360.

ἀκαχμένος, η, ον, Ep. sharpened, pointed, epith of the lance, 11. ; of the axe, Od. 5, 235 ; of the sword, Od. 22, 80 ; (prop. partcp. perf. pass. from theme 'ΑΚΩ, acuo, for ἀκαχμένος with Att. redupl.)

ἀκάχοιτο, see ἀκαχίζω.

ἀκείομαι, Ep. for ἀκέομαι; but ἀκειάμενοι, a false reading for ἀκειόμενοι, from ἀκέομαι.

ἀκέομαι, Depon. Ep. mid. ἀκείομαι (ἀκήν [hence originally=to quiet]), aor. 1 ἠκεσάμην, imper. ἀκέσσαι, 1) to heal, to cure ; with acc. ἕλκεα, wounds, 16, 29 ; also τινά, any one, 5, 448 ; metaph. to calm, to allay, to help, δίψαν, to allay thirst, 22, 2 ; absol. 13, 115. Od. 10, 69. 2) to repair, to restore, νῆας, Od. 14, 383.

ἀκερσεκόμης, ου, ὁ (κείρω, κόμη), un-shorn, having long hair, epith. of Apollo, 20, 39.†

'Ἀκεσσαμενός, ὁ (partcp. ἀκεσάμενος), father of Peribœa, king of Thrace, founder of the city Akesamenæ, 21, 142.

ἀκεστός, ή, όν (ἀκέομαι), curable, that may be calmed, φρένες, 13, 115.†

ἀκέων, έουσα, dual ἀκέοντε, silent, still, quiet [cf. ἀκήν]. ἀκέων is for the most part used as an adv. without distinction of gender or number, 4, 22. 8, 459. Od.

21, 89 ; the feminine however occurs 1, 565, and once the dual Od. 14, 195 (prob. from a and ἄκαος, Ion. ἀκέων, Buttm. Lex [Cf. Död. Hom. Gloss. 130]).

ἀκήδεστος, ον (κηδέω), unca[re] neglected ; spoken of the dead [u] 6, 60.†

ἀκηδέστως, adv. in a cruel, piti[...] ner, remorselessly, *Il. 22, 465. 2

ἀκηδέω (κῆδος), aor. 1 ἀκήδεσα lect, to slight, to disregard ; with 14, 427. 23, 70.

ἀκηδής, ές, gen. έος (κηδέω), care, 1) Act. free from care, at 123; spoken of the gods, 24, 52 geni, Od. 17, 319. 2) Pass. unc[...] neglected, disregarded, as Od. 6 18. 20, 130. Il. 21, 123; of a cor[...] buried, 24, 554. Od. 24, 187.

ἀκήλητος, ον (κηλέω), not to be [...] stubborn, unbending, νόος, Od. 1

ἄκημα, ατος, τό (ἀκέομαι), a re[...] alleviation, relief, ὀδυνάων, 15, 3[...]

ἀκήν, adv. (prop. acc. from [=ἡσυχία, Hesych. ἀκᾶ, calm[...] Död. 130. According to Buttm. [...] acc. ἀκάαν, Ion. ἀκέην· ἄκαος (hiscens]), quietly, silently, stil[l] πάντες ἀκὴν ἐγένοντο σιωπῇ, [...] quiet and silent, 3, 95 ; ἀκὴν ἐσα[...] 82.

ἀκηράσιος, ον, poet. (κεράννυ[...] mixed, unadulterated, pure, οἶνο[...] 205 ; † untouched, unmown, λ[...] Merc. 72.

ἀκήρατος, ον (κεράννυμι), [...] pure, ὕδωρ, 24, 300. 2) Metap[...] jured, unwasted, κλῆρος, 15, 49[...] 532.

ἀκήριος, ον (κήρ), without mi[...] uninjured, unharmed, *Od. 12 328. b) Act. innocuous, ῥάβδος, 530.

ἀκήριος, ον (κήρ), without hea[...] physical signif. lifeless, dead, 11 Metaph. heartless, spiritless, cou 100 ; δέος (heartless fear, Cp.), 5

ἀκηχέδαται, see ἀκαχίζω.
ἀκηχεμένη, see ἀκαχίζω.

ἀκιδνός, η, ον, only compar. ἀκ[...] weak, inferior, insignificant, Od with εἶδος, in appearance, *Od.5,2

ἄκῑκυς, υος, ὁ, ἡ, Ep. (κίκυς) power, weak, feeble, *Od. 9, 515 (according to Thiersch, § 199, [...] and κίω, unable to go.)

ἀκίχητος, ον, poet. (κιχάνω), attained, unattainable. ἀκίχητ[...] to pursue what is unattainable,

ἄκλαυστος, ον, later form for [...] Od. 11, 54, 72; [in some edition

ἄκλαυτος, ον (κλαίω), 1) un lamented ; spoken of one [d]ead, 2) Act. without tears, te[a]rless 494. Voss : unwept.

ἀκλεής, έος, ὁ, ἡ, poet. ([κ]λέος[...] and ἀκλής, without fame, fam[...] glorious ; accus. sing. ἀκλέ[α, fo[...] Od. 4, 728; plur. nom. [ἀκλη[...]

strengthened for ἀκλεεῖς, 12, 318. In ἀκλεὲς αὔτως, the neut. prob. is as adv. 7, 100: Buttm. [who allows that ἀκλεές may =ἀκλεεῖς], Lex. p. 296.

ἀκλειής, see ἀκλεής.

ἀκλειῶς, adv. *ingloriously*, 22, 304. Od. i, 241.

ἀκληεῖς, poet. for ἀκλεεῖς, see ἀκλεής.

ἄκληρος, ον (κλῆρος), *without lot, without possessions*, hence 1) *poor, needy*, Od. 11, 489.† 2) *unallotted, undivided*, wild, γαῖα, h. Ven. 123.

ἀκμή, ἡ (ἀκή), *edge*. ἐπὶ ξυροῦ ἀκμῆς, on a razor's edge, ~ἵσταται [" in balance hangs, pois'd on a razor's edge," Cp.], i. e. it is on the point of decision (an adage), 10, 173.†

ἄκμηνος, ον, *fasting*, with σίτοιο or πόσιος, *without meat, or drink*, *19, 163, -16. (ἀκμή [ἄκμη Lob. Path. 193] is said to be Æol.=νηστεία.)

ἀκμηνός, όν ([=ὁ ἀκμάζων] ἀκμή), *full grown, grown up*, Od. 23, 191.†

ἀκμής, ῆτος, ὁ, ἡ (κάμνω), *unwearied, vigorous, fresh*, *11, 802. 15, 697.

* ἀκμόθετον, ον=ἀκμής, h. Ap. 520.

ἀκμόθετον, τό (τίθημι), the place where the anvil is placed, *anvil-block, stithy*, 18, 410. Od. 8, 274.

ἄκμων, ονος, ὁ (κάμνω), *an anvil*, 15, 19. Od. 8, 274.

ἄκνηστις, ιος, ἡ (ἄκανος), *the back-bone, the spine*, Od. 10, 161.†

ἀκοίτης, ου, ὁ (a copulat. and κοίτη), *bed-fellow, husband*, Il. and Od.

ἄκοιτις, ιος, ἡ, *bed-fellow, wife*, Il. ἀκοίτις, accus. plur. Od. 10, 7.

ἄκολος, ὁ (κόλον), *a morsel, a crumb*, Od. 17, 222.†

* ἀκόλυμβος, ον (κόλυμβος), *who cannot swim*, Batr. 157.

ἀκομιστίη, ἡ (κομίζω), *want of tending or care, privation*, Od. 21, 284.†

ἀκοντίζω (ἄκων), aor. ἀκόντισα and ἀκόντισσα, prop. *to hurl the javelin*, but only *to cast*, δουρί, ἔγχεϊ; also with accus. αἰχμάς, to hurl lances. The object aimed at stands in the gen. τινός, at any one; also κατά τι, ἐπί τινι, and εἰς τινα, 4, 490. 16, 358. Od. 22, 282; later also, τινά, *to hit or pierce any one with a lance*, Batr. 209.

* ἀκόντιον, τό (dimin. of ἄκων), *a dart, a javelin*, h. Merc. 460.

ἀκοντιστής, οῦ, ὁ, poet. (ἀκοντίζω), *lancer, dartman, spearman*, Il. and Od.

ἀκοντιστύς, ύος, ἡ, Ep. for ἀκόντισις (ἀκοντίζω), *the act of casting spears*, a contest with spears (i. e. as a martial game). οὐδέ τ' ἀκοντιστὺν ἐσδύσεαι, thou shalt not enter the contest of spears, 23, 622.†

ἀκόρητος, ον (κορέννυμι), *unsated, insatiable*; with gen. μόθου, πολέμου, ἀπειλάων, *7, 117. 12, 335. 14, 479; also h. Ven.

ἄκος, εος, τό (ἀκέομαι), *cure, remedy, relief, alleviation*. κακῶν ἄκος, Od. 22, 481. οὐδέ τι μῆχος ῥεχθέντος κακοῦ ἔστ' ἄκος εὑρεῖν, it will be impossible to find a remedy when the evil is done, 9, 250.

ἄκοσμος, ον (κόσμος), *without order, indecent, unbecoming*, ἔπεα, 2, 213.†

ἀκοστάω or ἀκοστέω, aor. 1 ἀκόστησα, 6, 506. 15, 263; in the phrase: ἵππος ἀκοστήσας ἐπὶ φάτνῃ, *full fed at the manger*. The best derivation is from ἀκοστή, =κριθή, barley [as being bearded, ἀκή]; hence, to consume barley, to be fed with barley, cf. Buttm. Lex. p. 72.

ἀκονάζω, h. Merc. 423; and ἀκονάζομαι, dep. mid. Ep. form of ἀκούω, *to hear*; with gen. Od. 9, 7. πρῶτοι γὰρ καὶ δαιτὸς ἀκονάζεσθον ἐμεῖο, for ye are the first to hear from me of a feast, i. e. are first invited, 4, 343.

ἀκουή, ἡ (ἀκούω). Ep. for ἀκοή, properly, *hearing*; a sound (as heard), spoken of the crash of a tree when felled: ἔκαθεν δέ τε γίγνετ' ἀκουή, there is hearing from afar, i. e. the *sound*, or *crash* of it is heard at a distance, 16, 634; others give here the signif. *echo, noise*. 2) *that which is heard*, information, μετὰ πατρὸς ἀκουὴν ἱκέσθαι, to go in quest of intelligence of his father, Od. 2, 308; βῆναι, Od. 4, 701. 5, 19.

ἄκουρος, ον (κοῦρος), *without son, childless*, Od. 7, 64.†

* ἀκουστός, ή, όν, *heard, audible*, h. Merc. 512.

ἀκούω, fut. ἀκούσομαι, aor. 1 ἤκουσα, 1) *to hear*, with the gen. of the person heard; ἀοιδοῦ; the *thing* generally in accus. μῦθον, the discourse, and τί τινος, any thing from any one (*ex aliquo*), Od. 12, 389; but also in gen. μυκηθμοῦ ἤκουσα, I heard the roar or bellowing, 12, 265. The person *about* whom any thing is heard is mly put in the gen. Od. 1, 287. 289, rarely in accus. and with περί τινος, Od. 19, 204. 2) *to hearken to* any one, *to listen*, spoken of the gods; comm. with gen., rarely with dat., which is prop. dat. commod. ἀνέρι κηδομένῳ, to hearken to a suffering man; of subjects, *to obey*, Od. 7, 11. 3) The pres. in the signif. of the past, *have heard, know* (cf. Gr. p. 766, g), Od. 3, 193. 4, 688. The mid. as depon. τινός, *to hear*, 4, 331.

ἀκράαντος, ον, poet. (κραιαίνω), *unfinished, unaccomplished*, ἔργον, 2, 138; spoken of a prophecy: *unfulfilled, not to be fulfilled*, Od. 2, 202. 19, 565.

ἀκραής, ές, gen. έος (ἄκρος, ἄημι), prop. *high-blowing, strong-blowing, brisk, fresh*, epith. of a favorable wind, *Od. 2, 421. 14, 253.

ἄκρη, ἡ (prop. fem. from ἄκρος), the *extreme*, esply *height, summit, citadel or fortress, promontory*, 14, 36. 4, 425. κατ' ἄκρης, *downwards, from above*, Od. 5, 313; and hence *utterly, from the summit*, =from the foundation, 15, 557. Cf. Virg. Æn. ii. 290.

ἄκρητος, ον, Ion. for ἄκρατος (κεράννυμι), *unmixed, pure*, οἶνος, spoken of wine unmixed with water, Od. 2, 341; γάλα, Od. 9, 297. 2) σπονδαὶ ἄκρητοι, llbation of pure wine, because, in compacts, unmixed wine was offered to the gods, 2, 341. 4, 159.

ἄκρις, ιδος, ἡ, a locust, 21, 12.†

ἄκρις, ιος, ἡ, Ion. and Ep. for ἄκρη, point, summit, peak; always in the plur. accus. δι᾽ ἄκριας, through (amongst) the mountain tops, Od. 10, 281; nom. plur. h. Cer. 383.

᾿Ακρίσιος, ὁ (unjudged, from α and κρίνω, Inseparatinus, Herm.), son of Abas and Ocelia, great grandson of Danaus, father of Danaê. He expelled his brother Prœtus; after his return they divided the kingdom, so that Acrisius reigned in Argos, and Prœtus in Tiryns, Apd. 2, 21.

᾿Ακρισιώνη, ἡ, daughter of Acrisius = Danae, 14, 319.

ἀκριτόμῦθος, ον (μῦθος), speaking in a confused manner, prating or babbling foolishly, ὄνειροι, senseless dreams, or hard of explanation, Od. 19, 560. Il. 2, 246.

ἄκριτος, ον (κριτός), 1) not separated, confused, τύμβος, a common grave, in which the multitude were thrown indiscriminately, 7, 337; μῦθοι, confused discourse, prating, 2, 796. ἄκριτα πόλλ᾽ ἀγορεύειν, Od. 8, 505. 2) undecided, unadjusted, νείκεα, unadjusted contentions, 14, 205. 304. 3) not to be decided, enduring, perpetual; ἄχος, 3, 412; adv. ἄκριτον, endlessly. πενθήμεναι, Od. 18, 174.

ἀκριτόφυλλος, ον (φύλλον), thickly leaved, covered with foliage, thickly wooded, ὄρος, 2, 868.†

ἀκροκελαινιάω, Ep. (κελαινός), only partcp. ἀκροκελαινιόων, Ep. for ἀκροκελαινῶν, becoming black on the surface, dark-flowing, epith. of a river, 21, 249.†

ἀκρόκομος, ον, poet. (κόμη), having hair on the crown, crown-haired, epith. of the Thracians, because they wore the hair bound in a knot on the crown, or wore hair on the crown only, 4, 533.†

ἄκρον, τό (neut. from ἄκρος), the extreme, the summit, the point; ᾿Ίδης, the summit of Ida, 16, 292: ᾿Αθηνέων, the promontory [head-land, Cp.] of Athens, *Od. 3, 278; ποδός, Batr. 253.

᾿Ακρόνεως, ὁ, a Phæacian, Od. 8, 111.

ἀκρόπολις, ιος, ἡ (πόλις), the upper city, a citadel, a fortress, *Od. 8, 494. 505; in the Il. ἄκρη πόλις, 6, 88.

ἀκροπόλος, ον, Ep. (πολέω), being high, high-soaring, lofty, epith. of mountains, 5, 523. Od. 19, 205.

ἀκρόπορος, ον, Ep. (πείρω), penetrating with the point, sharp-pointed, ὀβελοί, Od. 3, 463.†

ἄκρος, η, ον (ἀκή), superl. ἀκρότατος, η, ον, extreme, highest, ending in a point; in Hom. only in a physical sense: ἐπ᾽ ἄκρῳ χείλει ἐφεσταότες, standing on the extreme brink, 12, 51; ἄκρη χείρ, the end of the hand, 5, 336. ἐς πόδας ἄκρους, to the extremities (toes) of the feet, 16, 640. The neut. ἄκρον, as adv. 20, 229.

ἀκρωτήριον, τό (ἄκρος), the extremity of

a thing; hence ἀκρωτήρια πρύ top of a ship's poop, h. 33, 10.

᾿Ακταίη, ἡ (ἀκτή), prop. she w on the coast, a Nereid, 18, 41.

ἀκτή, ἡ (ἄγνυμι, prop. fem. broken, crushed), 1) Poet. cor or ground in the mill, comm. v ἀλφίτου or Δημητέρος, 13, 32; 355; see ἄλφιτον. 2) the pla the waves break, shore, coast, 11

ἀκτήμων, ονος, ὁ, ἡ (κτῆμα), possessions, poor, needy; with σοῖο, in gold, *9, 126. 268.

*ἀκτήρ, ῆρος=ἀκτίν, a now reading, h. 32, 6.

ἀκτίς, ῖνος, ἡ, dat. ἀκτίνεσσιν τῖσιν, Od. 5, 479. 11, 16; a ray with ᾿Ηελίοιο.

*ἄκτιτος, ον (κτίζω), poet. for untilled, waste, h. Ven. 123.

᾿Ακτορίδης, ου, ὁ, a descendant =Echecles, 16, 189.

᾿Ακτορίς, ίδος, ἡ, a female s Penelopê, Od. 23, 228.

᾿Ακτορίων, ωνος, ὁ, son of A ᾿Ακτορίωνε, the sons of Actôr, and Cteatus, who from their mo also called the Moliönes, 2, Μολίων.

᾿Άκτωρ, ορος, ὁ (from ἄγω lea son of Deion, in Phocis, and D husband of Ægina, father of M grandfather of Patroclus, 11, 7 1, 9. 4. 2) son of Phorbas and H brother of Augeas, husband of father of Eurytus and Cteatus Apd. 3) son of Azens, father tyochê, grandfather of Ascalap lalmenus of Orchomenus, 2, 51:

ἄκῦλος, ἡ, the edible acorn, fr evergreen-oak (ilex), Od. 10, 241

ἀκωκή, ἡ (ἀκή), point, edge δουρός, Il. and Od.

ἄκων, οντος, ὁ, a javelin, a dari ἕρκος ἀκόντων, see ἕρκος.

ἄκων, ουσα, ον (ᾱ contr. fro q. v.) only in τὼ δ᾽ οὐκ ἀέκοντε 1 Il. and Od.

ἅλαδε, adv. into the sea, to the εἰς ἅλαδε.

ἀλάλημαι, Ep. perf. with pre: from ἀλάομαι, q. v.

ἀλαλητός, ὁ (ἀλαλή), mly cry, a battle-cry, a shout of v 436. Od. 24, 463; but also a cr tress, 21, 10.

ἄλαλκε, ἀλαλκών, ἀλαλκεῖν, se ᾿Αλαλκομενηΐς, ίδος, epith. of probably from the town Alalco Bœotia, where she had a temple ing to others, from ἀλαλκεῖν, th tress, 4, 8. 5, 908.

ἀλαλύκτημαι, to toss onesel restlessly, to be agitated with a: be in anguish, 94† (prop. perf. f κτέω, with pres. signif.).

*ἀλάμπετος, ον (λάμπω), witho ness, dark, h. 32, 5.

ἀλάομαι, depon. mid. impf. aor. I ἠλήθην, Ep. ἀλήθην, peri

μαι, infin. ἀλάλησθαι, part. ἀλαλήμενος, *to wander about without aim, to rove, to stray, to roam*; with the prep. κατά, ἐπί, περί τι, 6, 201. Od. 4, 91. The perfect infin. and partcp. ἀλαλήμενος have the accent retracted on account of its pres. signif. 23, 74. Od. 11, 167. 14, 122.

ἀλαός, ον (λάω), *not seeing, blind,* prop. ˘ ˘ ˘, Od. 8, 195; but in μάντιος ἀλαοῦ, Od. 10, 493. 12, 267, ‾ ‾ ‾;) cf. Thiersch. Gram. § 190, 22. *Od.

ἀλαοσκοπιή, ἡ (σκοπίη), lit. *a blind look-out; a useless watch,* ∞-ἡν ἔχειν, ['to look in vain,' Cp.] 13, 10. ἀλαοσκοπίη is an incorrect reading 10, 515.

ἀλαόω, poet. (ἀλαός), aor. ἀλάωσα, *to make blind, to blind.* τινὰ ὀφθαλμοῦ, to blind one's eye, *Od. 1, 69. 9, 516.

ἀλαπαδνός, ή, όν (ἀλαπάζω), poet. compar. ἀλαπαδνότερος, 4, 305; *easy to vanquish.* σθένος οὐκ ἀλαπαδνόν, insuperable strength, 5, 783; spoken of cattle, Od. 18, 373. 2) *powerless, weak, unwarlike,* 2, 675; μῦθος, h. Merc. 334.

ἀλαπάζω, poet. (λαπάζω), fut. ἀλαπάξω, aor. ἀλάπαξα without augm.; prop. *to empty, to exhaust; πόλιν*, to plunder a city, to sack, 2, 367, and often. 2) *to overpower, to vanquish, to destroy,* φάλαγγας, στίχας, a Od. 17, 424. 19, 80; absol. Il. 12, 67:—then *to ruin, to reduce to distress,* Od. 17, 424.

ἀλαστέω, poet. (ἄλαστος), partcp. aor. ἀλαστήσας, prop. *not to forget a thing;* but mly, *to be displeased, to be angry,* *12, 163. 15. 21.

Ἀλαστορίδης, ον, ὁ, son of Alastor = Tros.

ἄλαστος, ον (λήθω or λάζομαι), *not to be forgotten, intolerable, immeasurable,* πένθος, 24. 105; ἄχος, Od. 4, 108. ἄλαστον ὀδύρεσθαι, to lament unceasingly, Od. 2) *not to be forgotten or forgiven, abominable, accursed,* 22, 261. Achilles applies the term to Hector: thou whose treatment of Patroclus I can never forget, 22, 261.

Ἀλάστωρ, ορος, ὁ (one burdened with the guilt of blood, or who does not forget to take vengeance) 1) father of Tros, 20, 463. 2) a companion of Sarpêdôn from Lycia, slain by Ulysses, 5, 677. 3) a Greek, who bore the wounded Teucer from the battle, 8, 333. 13, 422. 4) an Epean, 4, 295. 7, 333.

ἀλαωτύς, ύος, ἡ, poet. (ἀλαόω), a *blinding, a bereaving of sight,* Od. 9, 503.†

ἀλγέω (ἄλγος), fut. ἀλγήσω, 1) *to feel pain, to be distressed by pain,* primarily of the body; ὀδύνῃσι, 12, 206; with accus. κεφαλήν, Batr. 193. 2) Spoken of the mind: *to be troubled, to be pained,* Od. 12, 27.

ἀλγίων, ον, compar., ἄλγιστος, superl. of ἀλγεινός, q. v.

ἄλγος, εος, τό, *pain, suffering,* primarily of the body; then of the mind, *trouble, distress;* comm. in plur. ἄλγεα πάσχειν, to endure sufferings, pain, distress; spoken of the sufferings of war, 2, 667. 9, 321; by sea, Od. 1, 4.

ἀλδαίνω, poet. (ἀλδω). aor. 2 ἤλδανον, *to nourish, to make great, to enlarge,* τί τινι. μέλε' ἤλδανε ποιμένι λαῶν, she dilated the limbs of the shepherd of the people, Od. 18, 70. 24, 768.

ἀλδήσκω, Ep. (ἀλδαίνω), *to grow, to grow up;* spoken of a harvest, 23, 599.†

ἀλέασθαι, see ἀλέομαι.

ἀλεγεινός, ή, όν, poet. for ἀλγεινός (ἄλγος), irreg. compar. ἀλγίων, ον, superl. ἄλγιστος, η, ον, *painful, sad, oppressive, burdensome,* 2, 787. Od. 3. 206. 2) *difficult, hard;* with infin. ἵπποι ἀλεγεινοὶ δαμῆναι, hard to break, to be subdued, 10, 402; spoken of a mule: ἀλγίστη δαμάσασθαι, 23, 655. The compar. occurs only in the neut. ἄλγιον, mly in the signif. *the worse, so much the worse.* 18, 278. Od. 4, 292; where some [without reason] regard it as used for the positive.

Ἀλεγηνορίδης, ον, ὁ, son of Alegênôr = Promachus, [14, 503.]

ἀλεγίζω, poet. (ἀλέγω), only in pres. and imperf. *to trouble oneself about a thing, to care for;* with gen. and always with a negat. οὐκ ἀλεγίζειν τινός, 1, 160. 8, 477; once absol. *15, 106.

ἀλεγύνω (=ἀλέγω), *to trouble oneself about;* with accus. always with δαῖτα, to prepare a meal, *Od. 1, 374. 2, 139; δολοφροσύνην, to practise deceit, h. Merc. 361; ἀγλαΐας, h. Merc. 476; absol. h. Merc. 557.

ἀλέγω, poet. (α, λέγω), only pres.; kindred forms ἀλεγίζω and ἀλεγύνω, prop. to compute, to reckon together; hence, *to value, to esteem, to be careful;* comm. with negat. absol. 11, 389; absol. κύνες οὐκ ἀλέγουσαι, careless sluts, spoken of Penelopê's maidens [but without the coarse meaning that the words would have in English], Od. 19, 154. a) With gen. of the person: *to trouble oneself about one, to care for him,* 8, 483. Od. 9, 115. 275. b) With accus. of the thing: ὄπιν θεῶν, to regard the vengeance of the gods, 16, 388; νηῶν ὅπλα, to keep, to secure the tackle of ships, Od. 6, 268. c) With a partcp. spoken of the *Lilæ* (Prayers): αἱ—μετόπισθ' Ἄτης ἀλέγουσι κιοῦσαι, who walk behind Atê carefully, steadily, 9, 504.

ἀλεείνω, Ep. form of ἀλέομαι (ἀλέη), only pres. and imperf. *to escape, to shun, to flee;* with accus. absol. κερδοσύνῃ ἀλέεινεν, with craft (craftily) he turned away, avoided me, Od. 4, 251. b) With infin. κτείνειν, ἀλεξέμεναι ἀλέεινεν, 6, 167. 13, 356.

ἀλέη, ἡ, poet. (ἄλη), *the act of avoiding, escaping,* 22, 301.†

ἀλέη, ἡ (ἄλω), *warmth, the heat of the sun,* Od. 17, 23.

ἄλειαρ, ατος, τό, poet. (ἀλέω), prop. that which has been ground, *flour, wheaten flour;* in plur. Od. 20, 108.†

ἀλείς, εῖσα, έν, partcp. aor. pass. from εἴλω.

Ἀλείσιον, τό (λεῖος), *Aleisium,* a place in Elis, no longer in existence in the time of Strabo, who however mentions a region near Olympia called τὸ 'Αλεσιαῖον, 2, 617.

'Αλεισίου κολώνη, ἡ, either a hill near Alesium, or a monument of Alesius, who according to Eustath. on 2, 617, was a son of Scillus, suitor of Hippodameia, 11, 757.

ἄλεισον, τό (prob. from λεῖος, not smoothly wrought, wrought *in relief; embossed), a goblet, alwayٯ costly, and mostly of gold, 11, 774 ; and Od. 3, 53.

ἀλείτης, ου, ὁ, poet. (ἀλιταίνω), *a sinner, a seducer, a vile wretch;* spoken of Paris, and of the suitors of Penelopê, 3, 28. Od. 20, 121.

ἄλειφαρ, ατος, τό (ἀλείφω), *salve, unguent, balsam,* with which the dead were anointed before burning, 18, 351. Od. 3, 408.

ἀλείφω (λίπος), aor. ἤλειψα, aor. mid. ἠλειψάμην, 1) Act. *to anoint,* for the most part with λίπ' ἐλαίῳ, olive oil, 18, 350; also λίπ' alone, Od. 6, 227, see λίπα; spoken particularly of anointing after the bath, Od. 19, 505; κηρὸν ἐπ' ὠσίν, to rub wax upon the ears, Od. 12, 2CO　2) Mid. *to anoint oneself,* with λίπ' ἐλαίῳ, and with accus. χρόα, to anoint one's body, 14, 175.

'Αλεκτρυών, όνος, ὁ (=ἀλέκτωρ), father of the Argonaut Leïtus, 17, 602; 'Αλέκτωρ, Apd. 1, 9. 16.

*ἀλέκτωρ, ορος, ὁ (α, λέγω), prop. the sleepless, *the cock,* Batr. 193.

'Αλέκτωρ, ορος, ὁ, son of Pelops and Hegesandra, whose daughter Iphilochê married Megapenthes, son of Menelaus, Od. 4, 10.

ἀλέκω, assumed theme of ἀλέξω.

ἄλεν, Dor. and Ep. for ἐάλησαν, see εἴλω.

ἀλέν, neut. partcp. aor. pass. from εἴλω.

'Αλέξανδρος, ὁ (man-repelling, from ἀλέξω and ἀνήρ), an honorary name of *Paris* son of Priam, because according to the Schol. when a shepherd, he often bravely defended himself against robbers, 3, 16 [this is improbable].

ἀλεξάνεμος, ον (ἄνεμος), *wind-repelling,* epith. of a thick mantle, Od. 14, 529.†

ἀλέξασθαι, ἀλεξάμενος, see ἀλέξω.

ἀλεξέω furnishes tenses to ἀλέξω.

ἀλεξητήρ, ῆρος, ὁ (ἀλέξω), *repeller, defender, helper,* μάχης, a repeller of the battle (from others), protector in battle, 20, 396.†

ἀλεξίκακοςᵣ ον (κακός), *averting evil, repelling misfortune,* epith. of Nestor, 10, 20.†

ἀλέξω, (theme ΑΛΕΚ), infin. ἀλεξέμεναι, fut. ἀλεξήσω, aor. 1 optat. ἀλεξήσειεν, Od. 3, 346 ; Ep. aor. 2 ἤλαλκον, infin. ἀλαλκεῖν, partcp. ἀλαλκών (from theme ΑΛΚΩ), whence an Ep. fut. ἀλαλκήσει, Od. 10, 288, where Wolf reads ἀλάλκῃσι : mid. aor. subj. ἀλεξώμεσθα, infin. ἀλέξασθαι, 1) Act. *to ward off, to avert,* τί τινι, any thing from any one; κακὸν ἦμαρ Δαναοῖσιν, the evil day from the Greeks, 9, 251 ; νήεσσι πῦρ, 9, 347.

b) With dat. only : *to defend* an help, 3, 9. 5. 779.　2) Mid. *to re* oneself, τινά, any one, 13, 475. 62; absol. *to defend oneself,* 11, 9, 57.

ἀλέομαι and ἀλεύομαι, Ep. a (ἄλη), kindred form ἀλεείνω, ἠλευάμην and ἀλενάμην, subj. optat. ἀλέαιτο, imper. ἀλέασθ ἀλεύασθαι and ἀλέασθαι, partcp μενος, *to shun, avoid, flee ;* wit ἔγχεα, μῆνιν, and absol. 5, With infin. ὄφρα καὶ ἄλλος (Ep. for ἀλεύηται), ἠπεροπεύε another also may shrink from de Od. 14, 400. Il. 23, 340.

ἄλεται, Ep. with shortened moc for ἄληται; subj. aor. where el we find ἄλεται, 11, 192; see ἄλλο

ἀλετρεύω (ἄλετος), *to grind ;* wit καρπόν, Od. 7, 104.†

ἀλετρίς, ίδος, ἡ (ἀλέω), *grinding* grinding woman, the female slá grinds the corn, Od. 20, 105.†

ἀλεύομαι=ἀλέομαι, q. v.

ἀλέω. aor. 1 ἤλεσα, Ep. ἄλε *grind,* Od. 20, 109. † in Tmesis.

ἀλεωρή, ἡ (ἀλέομαι), poet. *th avoiding. retreating, flight,* 24, *defence, protection ;* spoken of the 12, 57. 15, 533.

ἄλη, ἡ, *the act of wandering* or about, *Od. 10, 464. 21, 284.

ἀληθείη, ἡ (ἀληθής), *truth ;* on θείην μυθεῖσθαι, καταλέγειν, 24, 4 11, 507.

ἀληθείς, see ἀλάομαι.

*ἀληθεύω (ἀληθής), fut. σω, *to s truth, to be sincere.* Batr. 14.

ἀληθής, ές (λήθω). *undisguised, true, upright,* γυνή, 12, 433. : often neut. plur. ἀληθέα εἰπεῖν, Il.

'Αλήϊον πεδίον, τό, the Aleïan Asia Minor, where Bellerophontê by the gods, wandered solitarily a 201.　According to a later tr proud of having slain Chimæra, attempted to soar upon Pegasus abode of the gods; he was thrown, and perished from grie cording to Herod. it was near Mallus in Cilicia, between the riv ramus and Sinarus, Hdt. 6, 85 nif. prob. from ἄλη, the field of ing, or from λήϊον, harvestless, tivated.)

ἀλήϊος, ον (λήϊον), without posse *poor, destitute of an estate,* *9, 12!

ἄληκτος, ον, Ep. ἄλληκτος (λήγ *ceasing, endless, incessant,* θυμός, νότος, Od. 12, 325. The neut. ε adv. incessantly, πολεμίζειν, 1 Hom. has only the Ep. form.

ἀλήμεναι, Ep for ἀλῆναι, see εἴ

ἀλήμων, ονος, ὁ (ἀλάομαι), *war about,* Od. 19, 74 ; subst. *a vagran* 17, 376.

ἀλῆναι, see εἴλω.

ἄληται (ἄληται ed. Wolf), 3 sing. subj. from ἄλλομαι, 21, 536.

ἀλητεύω (ἀλήτης), only pres. *to wander about, to roam;* often in Od., comm. spoken of vagrants, *to beg,* Od. 14, 126. 16, 101; but also of hunters, Od. 12, 338.

ἀλήτης, ου, ὁ, *a vagrant, a beggar,* *Od. 14, 124.

Ἀλθαία, ἡ, daughter of Thestius and Erythemis, sister of Læda, wife of Œnius of Calydon, who bore to him Meleager, Deīanira, etc. The post-Homeric legends state that she slew Meleager by burning the fire-brand upon which, according to the prediction of the Parcæ his life depended, because in a contest concerning the prize in the Calydonian chase, he slew her two brothers, 9, 555.

ἄλθομαι, Ep. mid. *to heal* (intrans.), *to be healed, to get well,* 5, 417.† (ἄλθω, akin to ἀλδ, to make grow.)

ἀλιαής, ές (ἄημι), gen. έος, *blowing over* ος *on the sea,* epith. of a favorable wind, Od. 4, 361.†

Ἀλίαρτος, ὁ (situated on the sea, from ἅλς and ἄρω), *Haliartus,* a town in Bœotia, on the shore of the lake Copaīs, now *Mazi,* 2, 503; also ἡ, Diod.

ἀλίαστος, ον, poet. (λιάζομαι), *unbending, not to be stayed, incessant, immense,* μάχη, πόλεμος, ὅμαδος. The neut. as adv. ἀλίαστον ὀδύρεσθαι, to lament incessantly. 24, 549. *II.

*ἀλιγείτων, ον, poet. (γείτων), *near the sea,* Ep. 4.

ἀλέγκιος, ον (ἦλιξ), prop. of equal age, but generally, *like, equal, similar,* τινί, 6, 401. Od. 8, 174.

ἁλιεύς, ῆος, ὁ (ἅλς), *a fisherman,* Od. 12, 251. 22, 384, and mly, 1) *a seaman, a sailor,* Od. 24, 418; as adj. ἐρέται ἁλιῆες, rowers on the sea, Od. 16, 349. *Od.

Ἀλιζῶνες, οἱ, sing. Ἀλιζών, ῶνος, ὁ (encircled by the sea, from ἅλς and ζώνη), the *Halizones,* a people on the Euxine, in Bithynia, neighbours of the Paphlagonians, 2, 856. Steph. According to Strabo, prob. the later Chalybians, who in his time were called Chaldæi. Eusath. and Strabo also cite the nom. Ἀλίζωνος. (They must not be confounded with Ἀλαζῶνες, a nomadic people in Scythia.)

Ἁλίη, ἡ (fem. of ἅλιος), daughter of Nereus and Doris, 18, 40.

Ἀλιθέρσης, ου, ὁ, son of Mastôr, a faithful friend of Ulysses in Ithaca, Od. 2, 157. 17, 68.

ἁλιμυρήεις, εσσα, εν, poet. (μύρω), *flowing into the sea, rushing seaward,* ποταμός, 21, 190. Od. 5, 460.

ἅλιος, ίη, ιον (ἅλς), *belonging to the sea, dwelling in the sea;* γέρων ἅλιος, the old man of the sea=*Nereus,* 1, 556; ἅλιαι θεαί, sea-goddesses, 24, 84: ἀθάναται ἅλιαι, 18, 84; also ἅλιαι alone, 18, 432. 2) *fruitless, idle, vain,* βέλος, μῦθος, ὁδός, ὅρκιον, 11. and Od. (The second signif. is comm. derived from ἅλη, but unnecessarily[?], since the earliest language connected with the sea the idea of unfruit-

fulness.) [Related to ἅλη, ἀλαός (*blind,* lit. *bereaved*), ἠλός Död.]

Ἅλιος, ὁ, 1) a Lycian, 5, 678. 2) son of Alcinous, Od. 8, 119.

ἁλιοτρεφής, ές, poet. (τρέφω), gen. έος, *nourished in the sea, sea-fattened;* epith. of seals, Od. 4, 442.†

ἁλιόω (ἅλιος), aor. ἁλίωσα, *without augm. to make vain, to frustrate, to render void,* νόον Διός, Od. 5, 104; βέλος, to shoot an arrow without effect, 16, 737.

ἁλίπλοος, ον (πλέω), *whelmed in the sea,* τείχεα ἁλίπλοα θεῖναι, to sink the walls into the sea, 12, 26.†

ἁλιπόρφυρος, ον (πορφύρα), *coloured with the purple of the murex, sea-purple, dark-purple,* ἠλάκατα, φάρεα, *Od. 6, 53. 13, 108.

ἅλις, adv. (ἀλής), 1) *in heaps, in multitudes, in crowds, in swarms,* 2, 90. Od. 13, 136. Hom. never has a seq. gen. 2) *sufficiently, enough,* 14, 121. ἦ οὐχ ἅλις, is it not enough? with a seq. ὅτι or ὡς, 5, 349. 23, 670. ὅθι ἔκειτο ἅλις εὐῶδες ἔλαιον, where there was fragrant oil in abundance, Od. 2, 339.

ἁλίσκομαι (in the act. obsol. theme Ἁλο-), fut. ἁλώσομαι only Batr. 286, aor. 2 ἑάλων, ἥλων only Od. 22, 230, subj. ἁλώω Ep. for ἁλῶ, optat. ἁλοίην, Ep. ἁλώην, 9, 592, infin. ἁλῶναι, partcp. ἁλούς (ἁλόντε with ᾰ, 5, 487), 1) *to be caught, taken, captured;* spoken of men and cities, 2) Metaph. θανάτῳ ἁλῶναι, to be snatched away by death, 21, 281. Od. 5, 312; hence also alone *to be killed,* 12, 172. 14, 81. 17, 506. Od. 18, 265. *μήπως, ὡς ἀψῖσι λίνου ἁλόντε πανάγρου—κύρμα γένησθε, lest ye, as if caught in the meshes of a net, should become a prey, 5, 487. (According to Buttm. Gr. Gram. § 33, 3, 1, the dual stands here as an abbreviated form of the plur.; it is more satisfactorily explained on the ground that the discourse relates to two objects, viz.: Hector, and the remainder of the people (see v. 485); or with the Schol.: ye and the women.) [To avoid the anomalous ᾱ in ἁλόντε, Bothe proposes to read ἁλύοντε, from ἀλύω, *trepide erro.*]

ἀλιταίνω, poet. aor. 2 ἤλιτον once, 9, 375; aor. mid. ἀλιτόμην, infin. ἀλιτέσθαι, with like signif. *to do wrong, to sin;* always with accus. τινά, to sin against any one, 9, 375. 19, 265; ἀθανάτους, Od. 4, 378; Διὸς ἐφετμάς, to violate the commands of Zeus, 24, 570.

ἀλιτήμενος, η, ον, an Ep. perf. partcp. with accent of pres. for ἠλιτημένος from ἀλιταίνω with active signif. *doing wrong, sinning;* with dat. θεοῖς, against the gods, Od. 4, 807.† According to Rost Vollst. Lexik. under ἀλιταίνω, the dat. in this passage indicates the person in whose estimation the predicate is not true of the subject: 'for he is no sinner in the eyes of the gods.'

ἀλιτήμων, ονος, ὁ (ἀλιταίνω), *sinning, wicked,* *24, 157. 186.

C 2

ἀλιτρός, ὁ, contr. for ἀλιτηρός, *a wicked man, a sinner*, 8, 361; δαίμοσιν, against the gods, 23, 595; also in a softer signif. *knave, rogue*, Od. 5, 182.

Ἀλκάθοος, ὁ (quick in defence, from ἀλκή and θόος), son of Asyêtês; he was the husband of Hippodameia the sister of Æneas, and had brought him up; Idomeneus slew him, 12, 93. 13. [427.] 465.

Ἀλκάνδρη, ἡ, wife of Polybus, in the Egyptian Thebæ, with whom Menelaus lodged, Od. 4, 126.

Ἀλκανδρος, ὁ (man-repelling, from ἀλκή and ἀνήρ), a Lycian, slain by Ulysses, 5, 678.

ἄλκαρ, τό (ἀλκή), gen. and dat. obsol. *defence, protection, bulwark;* with gen. Ἀχαιῶν, of the Achaians, 11, 823; and dat. Τρώεσσι, for the Trojans, 5, 644: but γήραος ἄλκαρ, a protection against age, h. Ap. 193. *Il.

ἀλκή, ἡ, with metaplast. dat. ἀλκί, also ἀλκῇ, Od. 24, 509. 1) *strength, physical power*, 3, 45. 6, 263. Od. 22, 237. 2) *defence, protection, help*, ὅ τοι ἐκ Διὸς οὐχ ἕπετ' ἀλκή, that help from Zeus follows thee not, 8, 140 14, 786. Od. 12, 120. 3) the power to defend, whether of body or mind, *strength, courage, boldness*, 2, 234. ἐπιειμένος ἀλκήν, clothed with courage, 7, 164. μέδεσθαι θουρίδος ἀλκῆς, to remember, think of impetuous courage, 5, 718. 4) Personified as a goddess and represented on the ægis, 5, 740.

*ἀλκήεις, εσσα, εν, poet. (ἀλκή), *defending, courageous, brave, bold*, h. 28, 3.

Ἄλκηστις, ιος, ἡ, *Alcestis*, daughter of Pelias and Anaxibia, wife of Admêtus, king of Pheræ in Thessaly. By a decree of the Fates, according to later mythology, Admetus was to be delivered from death, if some one should die for him. Alcestis laid down her life for him, but Persephônê sent her back, 2, 715.

ἀλκί, Ep. dat. of ἀλκή, from the obsol. root, ἄλξ: always ἀλκὶ πεποιθώς, trusting to his strength, 5, 299.

Ἀλκιμέδων, οντος, ὁ (meditating defence, from ἀλκή and μέδων), son of Laerces, leader of the Myrmidons under Achilles, after the death of Patroclus, his charioteer, 16, 197.

Ἀλκιμίδης, ου, ὁ, son of Alcimus = Mentor, Od. 21, 235.

ἄλκιμος, ον (ἀλκή), *strong*, ἔγχος, δόρυ. 2) Spoken of warriors, *courageous, brave;* also of animals, 20, 169.

Ἄλκιμος, ὁ, 1) father of Mentor. 2) a Myrmidon, friend of Achilles, 19, 392.

Ἀλκίνοος, ὁ (of a spirited disposition, from νόος), son of Nausithous, grandson of Poseidôn, king of the Phæeaces in Scheria, by whom Ulysses, having suffered shipwreck, was hospitably received, Od. 6, 12 seq. 8, 118.

Ἀλκίππη, ἡ, a female slave of Helen in Sparta, Od. 4, 124.

Ἀλκμαίων, ονος, ὁ (from ἀλκή and μαίομαι striving for defence), son of Amphiaraus and Eriphÿlê, brother of Am-

philŏchus, and leader of the [...] against Thebes, Od. 15, 248. [...] to later mythology, when Am [...] betrayed by his wife, was o [...] go to the Theban war, he direc [...] in case of his death, to slay his [...] He did it, and was on this acc [...] secuted by the Furies, till at last [...] rest in an island of the Achelôu [...]

Ἀλκμάων, ονος, ὁ, Ep. for Ἀ [...] son of Thestôr, a Greek, slain [...] dôn before Troy, 12, 394.

Ἀλκμήνη, ἡ, daughter of E [...] king of Mycenæ, wife of Amph [...] Thebes, mother of Heracles by Ζ [...] of Iphicles by Amphitryon. Hε [...] her, delayed the birth of Hera [...] accelerated that of Eurystheus, [...] latter might have the dominion [...] former, 14, 323. 19, 119. Od. 11, [...]

ἀλιτήρ, ηρος, ὁ (ἀλκή), *defende,* [...] ἀρῆς, averter of a curse, i. e. of [...] injury, death, 14, 485. 18, 100; [...] of a javelin: κυνῶν καὶ ἀνδρῶν, [...] against dogs and men, Od. 14, [...] 340.

Ἀλκυόνη, ἡ, a name of Cleopa [...] of Meleager; so named from [...] daughter of Æolus, who after tl [...] of her husband Ceÿx, plunged [...] sea, and was changed by Theti [...] kingfisher. The point of cor [...] would then consist only in tl [...] Marpessa, like Alcyonê, separat [...] her husband wept. More natur [...] probably, Heyne and Spitzner un [...] by ἀλκυών the kingfisher (see ἀλ [...] 562.

Ἀλκυών, όνος, ἡ, as prop. nar [...] κυόνη, 9, 563, ed. Wolf.

ἀλκυών, όνος, ἡ, Ion. for ἀλκ [...] *sea-kingfisher*, alcedo (from ἅλς a [...] because it was thought to broo [...] sea). Heyne and Spitzner wri [...] ἀλκυόνος instead of Ἀλκ. becau [...] knew nothing of the transform [...] Alcyone. They therefore refer t [...] πολυπενθέος οἶτος ἔχουσα to th [...] wailings of the kingfisher, whicl [...] mentioned by the poets. Thes [...] good point of comparison for [...] voice and tender complaints of Ν [...] separated by Apollo from her be [...] ἄλκω, obsol. for ἀλαλκεῖν, [...]

ἀλλά, conj. (prop. neut. fron [...] *but, still, yet, however, notwith* [...] it indicates in general a greate [...] opposition in the thought. It [...] 1) For connecting with the fore [...] entirely opposite idea, the fi [...] quite set aside. It then often [...] negative proposition, = *but*, 1 [...] indicates the antithesis after οὐ [...] 2) For annexing a different tl [...] such a character, that the for [...] preceding clause is but par [...] moved. This takes place b [...] affirmative and negative clau [...] is translated by *but, however,* [...] and the antithesis is prepare [...]

ἤτοι, γέ, etc. 1, 24. 16, 240. The antithesis also often consists in a hypothetic protasis, εἰ—ἀλλά, 1, 281; εἴπερ—ἀλλά, 8, 154; εἴπερ τε,—ἀλλά τε, 1, 82. 3) To mark an exception, after a negative clause. After οὔτις ἄλλος, ἀλλά is translated than, 21, 275. Od. 3, 377; also after οὔτι ἄλλος, Od. 8, 311 seq. cf. 12, 403 seq. 4) It stands at the beginning of a clause adverbially, to indicate the transition to a different thought; hence in exhortations, exclamations, etc. ἀλλ' ἄγε, ἀλλ' ἄγε δή, but come on! but up now! 5) It is often connected with other particles: ἀλλ' ἄρα, but indeed, after a negative; ἀλλὰ γάρ, but certainly, still indeed (prop. each particle retains its original signif., the first marking the antithesis, the second the reason; still the antithesis must often be supplied from the connexion); ἀλλ' οὐ γάρ, but—not, Od. 14, 334. 19, 591; ἀλλ' ἦτοι, but yet [at profecto: at videlicet. Klotz]; ἀλλὰ καὶ ὧς, but even thus; ἀλλ' οὐδ' ὧς, but not even thus.

ἄλλεγεν, ἀλλέξαι, Ep. for ἀνέλεγεν, ἀναλέξαι from ἀναλέγω.

ἄλλη, adv. (prop. dat. sing. from ἄλλος), 1) in another way, elsewhere, 13, 49; in another manner, φρονεῖν, h. Ap. 469. 2) away to some other place, elsewhere; that my reward is going away, i. e. to another, 1, 120; τρέπειν τι, 5, 187. 3) otherwise, 15, 51.

ἄλληκτος, ον, Ep. for ἄληκτος, q. v.

ἀλλήλων (from ἄλλοι, ἄλλων, prop. ἀλλάλλων), only in gen. dat. accus. of plur. and dual (the nom. is from the signif impossible). one another, mutually, reciprocally. ἴδμεν δ' ἀλλήλων γενεήν, we know each other's race, 20, 203; ἀλλήλοιϊν Ep. for ἀλλήλοιν as gen. 10, 65.

ἀλλόγνωτος. ον (γιγνώσκω), known to others, hence strange to us, foreign, δῆμος, Od. 2, 366.†

ἀλλοδαπός, ή, όν (either lengthened from ἄλλος, or contracted with ἔδαφος [no Cf. Lexil. under ἐχθοδοπῆσαι]), from another land, strange, foreign, Od. 14, 231. 2) Subst. a stranger, 3, 48.

ἀλλοειδής, ές (εἶδος), of a different form, of different appearance, Od. 13, 194.† (ἀλλοειδέα is to be read as trisyllabic.)

ἄλλοθεν, adv. (ἄλλος), from another place, from a different place, Od. 3, 318; often ἄλλοθεν ἄλλος, which, like the Latin alius aliunde, expresses a double clause, see ἄλλος; one from one place, another from another, 2, 75. Od. 9, 401.

ἄλλοθι, adv. (ἄλλος), elsewhere, sometimes with gen. ἄλλοθι γαίης, elsewhere upon earth, i. e. in a strange land, Od. 2, 131; πάτρης (elsewhere than in one's country=), far from one's country, *Od. 17, 318.

ἀλλόθροος. ον (θρόος), sounding differently, speaking in a foreign tongue, *Od. 1, 183. 3, 302.

ἀλλοῖος. η. ον (ἄλλος), of different quality, differently formed, 4, 258; always

with the idea of comparison, ἀλλοῖός μοι ἐφάνης ἠὲ πάροιθεν, thou appearest to me now a different person from what thou didst before, Od. 16, 181.

ἄλλομαι, aor 1 ἡλάμην, only Batr. 252, comm. aor. 2 ἡλόμην, of which only subj. ἅληται, Ep. ἅλεται (ἅλεται Wolf, cf. Spitz. on 11, 192), Ep. 2 and 3 sing. of sync. aor. 2 ἅλσο, ἅλτο, partcp. ἅλμενος, 1) to leap, ἐξ ὀχέων, from the chariot, Il. εἰς ἵππους. 2) Spoken of any vehement motion, to rush, to run, ἐπί τινι, upon any one, 13, 611; to fly, spoken of an arrow, 4, 125.

ἀλλοπρόσαλλος (πρός, ἄλλος), turning from one to another, alternately with both parties, fickle, inconstant, epith. of Arês, 5, 831. 889. *Il.

ἄλλος, η, ον, 1) another, with gen. ἄλλος Ἀχαιῶν; it seems to stand pleonastically with πλήσιος, ἕκαστος, 4, 81. 16, 697; ἄλλος μέν, ἄλλος δέ, the one, the other. 2) οἱ ἄλλοι and ἄλλοι, the rest, 2, 1. 17, 280. τὰ ἄλλα, contr. τἄλλα, better τἆλλα (cf. Buttm. Gram. § 29. note 2), the rest, cætera, 1, 465. 3) another, i. e. different, not like the preceding, 13, 64. Od. 2, 93; with ἀλλά following, 21, 275; or εἰ μή, h. Cer. 78; hence 4) Poet.= ἀλλότριος, strange, foreign, Od. 23, 274. 5) τὰ ἄλλα, and τὸ ἄλλο, in other respects, besides, 23, 454. 6) Hom. often connects ἄλλος with another case, or with an adv. of the same root, so that, like the Lat. alius, it contains a double clause: ἄλλος δ' ἄλλῳ ἔρεζε θεῶν, one sacrificed to one, another to another of the immortal gods, 2, 400. cf. 2, 804. Od. 14, 228. 7) Sometimes ἄλλος, like the French autre, is apparently superfluous, marking something diverse from the thing mentioned. It may often be translated, on the other hand, 21, 22. Od. 1, 132. 2, 412.

ἄλλοσε, adv. (ἄλλος), to another place, in another place, *Od. 23, 184. 204.

ἄλλοτε. adv. (ὅτε), 1) another time, once, formerly. 2) Often ἄλλοτε—ἄλλοτε, or ὅτε μὲν—ἄλλοτε δέ, 11, 566; at one time—at another, now—then, now—now. 3) In connexion with ἄλλος: ἄλλοτε ἄλλῳ Ζεὺς ἀγαθόν τε κακόν τε διδοῖ, Zeus gives good and evil now to one, now to another, Od. 4, 237.

ἀλλότριος. η, ον (ἄλλος), 1) strange, i. e. belonging to another, βίοτος, ἀλλότριον χαρίσασθαι, to be liberal with others' property, Od. 17, 452; οἱ δ' ἤδη γναθμοῖσι γελοίων ἀλλοτρίοισι, they laughed now with strange jaws, i. e. either immoderately (sparing their jaws in laughing as little as if they belonged to others), or with distorted countenance, i. e. with a forced, unnatural laugh, Od. 20, 347. 2) strange, i. e. from another land, φώς, a foreigner, Od. 18, 218;=hostile, 5, 214. Od. 16, 102.

ἄλλοφος, ον, Ep. for ἄλοφος.

ἀλλοφρονέω (φρονέω), prop. to be of another opinion, hence 1) to be thinking of something else, to be in thought, Od. 10, 374. 2) to lose one's wits or one's senses, to be senseless, 23, 698, only partcp.

ἄλλυδις, Ep. adv. (ἄλλος), to another place: with ἄλλος added, διά τ' ἔτρεσεν ἄλλυδις ἄλλος, they fled one to one place, another to another, 11, 486. 17, 729. ἄλλυδις ἄλλῃ, one in this way, another in that, Od. 5, 71. τοῦ κακοῦ τρέπεται χρὼς ἄλλυδις ἄλλῃ, the colour of the dastard changes now in this way, now in that, 13, 279.

ἀλλύεσκεν, poet. for ἀνελύεσκεν, iterat. imperf. fr. ἀναλύω.

ἄλλως, adv. (ἄλλος), 1) otherwise, in another manner, 5, 218; sometimes in a good sense, otherwise, i. e. better, 11, 391. 14, 53. 19, 401. Od. 8, 176. 20, 211. 2) otherwise (than we believe [than as it should be]), i. e. vainly, in vain, 23, 144. 3) without aim, without object, Od. 14, 124. 4) in another view, in other respects, for the rest, besides, ὁ δ' ἀγήνωρ ἐστὶ καὶ ἄλλως, 9, 695. Od. 17, 577. 21, 87.

ἅλμα, ατος, τό (ἅλλομαι), the act of leaping, springing, *Od. 8, 103. 129.

ἅλμη, ἡ (ἅλς), 1) salt water, brine, esply of the sea, Od. 5, 53. 2) the dirt from dried spray, *Od. 6, 137.

ἁλμυρός, ή, όν (ἅλμη), salt, briny; only with ὕδωρ, salt water, the briny flood, *Od. 4, 511.

ἀλογέω (λόγος), without care, to take no heed, to disregard, to despise, 15, 162.†

ἁλόθεν, adv. ἅλς, from the sea; ἐξ ἁλόθεν, from the sea, 21, 335.

ἀλοιάω, poet. for ἀλοάω (ἀλωή), to beat, to strike; with acc. γαῖαν χερσίν, 9, 568.†

ἀλοιφή, ἡ (ἀλείφω), what is used for anointing, fat, ointment, to make any thing supple, 17, 390; also oil for the human body, Od. 6, 220. 2) fat, esply hog's fat, connected with the flesh, 9, 208. Od. 8, 476.

Ἀλόπη, ἡ, a town in Phthiotis (Thessaly), near Larissa, under the dominion of Achilles, 2, 682 (otherwise unknown).

Ἅλος, ἡ, a town in Achaia Phthiotis (Thessaly) on mount Othrys, not far from Pharsālus, belonging to Achilles' realm, 2, 682. (Better Ἅλος, as Dem. Strab. from ἅλς, named from the salt-pits.)

ἁλοσύδνη, ἡ, one living in the sea, name of Thetis, 10, 607. 2) pr. n. appellation of Amphitrītē, Od. 4, 404 (from ἅλς and ὕδης, nourished from the sea: or poet. for ἁλοσύνη, from ἅλς and σύω=σεύομαι, with epenthetic δ, moving in the sea).

ἄλοφος, ον, Ep. ἄλλοφος (λόφος), without crest, 10, 258.†

ἄλοχος, ἡ (λέχος), bed-fellow, wife. 2) concubine, 9, 336. Od. 4, 623.

ἀλόων, Ep. for ἀλάον, imper. pres from ἰλάομαι, Od.

ἀλόωνται, see ἀλάομαι, Od.

ἅλς, ἁλός, ὁ, salt, sing. only Ion. and poet. 9, 214; comm. plur. ἅλες; εἰδὰρ ἅλεσσι μεμιγμένον, food seasoned with salt, Od. 11, 123. 23, 270. οὐδ' ἅλα δοίης. prov., thou wouldst not give even a grain of salt, i. e. not the smallest portion, Od.

17, 455. 2) ἡ ἅλς, poet. the briny sea, 1, 141; and often opposed t [The latter is the primary idea 11, 122. 123. Am. Ed.]

ἄλσο, Ep. syncop. 2 sing. ἅλλομαι.

ἄλσος, εος, τό (ἀλδω), a sacred wood, and mly a region conse a deity, 2, 506.

Ἄλτης, αο and εω, ὁ, a king o leges of Pedasus, father of Lae 85. 86. 22, 51.

ἆλτο, Ep. syncop. 3 sing. ao ἅλλομαι.

Ἀλύβας, αντος, ἡ, a town of t situation, according to Eustath. Metapontum, in Lower Italy, t to others=Ἀλύβη, Od. 24, 304.

Ἀλύβη, ἡ, a town on the Euxinus, whence silver comes, According to Strabo the later dwelt here, from whom the Gre procured their metals.

ἀλυσκάζω, only pres. and imp lengthened form fr. ἀλύσκω, 1) to flee; with accus. ὕβριν, Od. 17, Absol. to flee, νόσφιν πολέμοιο, 1 war, 5, 253. 6, 443.

ἀλυσκάνω, poet. form of ἀλύσκ imperf. Od. 22, 330.†

ἀλύσκω (ἀλεύομαι), poet. for ἀλύξω, aor. ἤλυξα, to avoid, to e shun; with accus. ὄλεθρον, to es struction, 10, 371; θάνατον, Od ἤλυξα ἑταίρους, I had withdraw from my companions, Od. 12, Absol. to fly, to escape, προτὶ ἄστ city, 10, 348. Od. 22, 460.

*ἀλύσσω (Ep. form from ἀλύ beside oneself, only of dogs whi tasted blood, to be fierce, 22, 70.†

ἄλυτος, ον (λύω), indissoluble 13, 37; πεῖραρ, 13, 360; δεσμοί 275.

ἀλύω, poet. (akin to ἄλη, to oneself, a) from pain, to be gre tressed, 5, 352. 24, 12. Od. 9, 398. joy: ἢ ἀλύεις, ὅτι Ἶρον ἐνίκησας, beside thyself, that thou hast co Irus, Od. 18, 333 (ῠ, once ῡ, Od.

ἀλφαίνω, poet. ἤλφον, optat. prop. to find; in Hom. to gain, to τινί τι, as μυρίον ὦνον. a prodigio Od. 15, 453; βίοτον πολύν, Od. 20, 383: ἑκατόμβοιον, 21, 79.

Ἀλφειός, ὁ, Alpheus, a river which rises in Arcadia, and flows Ionian sea near Pitanē, now Alfe 2) the river-god, 5, 545. Od. 3, 48

ἀλφεσίβοιος, η, ον (ἀλφεῖν, βοῦ cattle finding, epith. of virgins w many suitors that bring cattle as (ἔδνα), to purchase them fro parents; hence much-wooed, 18, 5

ἀλφηστής, οῦ, ὁ (ἀλφεῖν), the i the finder; adj. in the Od. ἄνδρι σταί, inventive, gainful men (ac Eustath. epith. of man, who thu guishes himself from the bea better with Nitzsch on Od. 1, 349 trious, intent upon gain, and therefore also inventive), *Od. 1, 349, h. Ap. 458.

ἄλφι, τό, indeclin. poet. shorter form for ἄλφιτον, h. Cer. 208.

ἄλφιτον, τό (ἀλφεῖν), *uncooked* or *parched barley*, because this was the earliest general food, reduced by a hand-mill to meal or a coarse powder; hence sing. ἀλφίτου ἱεροῦ ἀκτή, the ground or crushed meal of the sacred barley [a periphrasis for ἄλφιτα or ἄρτον, Schol.], Od. 14, 429. 11, 631, and μυλήφατον ἀλφ., Od. 2, 355. Oftener in the plur. ἄλφιτα, *barley-flour*, from which bread, cakes, porridge, etc. were prepared, 11, 631. Od. 10, 234. Also in sacrifices it was sprinkled on the flesh, Od. 2, 290.

ἄλφοι, see ἀλφαίνω.

Ἀλωεύς, ῆος, ὁ (thresher, from ἀλωή), son of Poseidōn and Canacē, husband of Iphimedeia, father of the Aloïdēs, Otus, and Ephialtes, 5, 386.

ἀλωή, ἡ (ἀλοάω), poet. *a threshing-floor*, a level place in the field for threshing grain, 5, 499. 20, 496. 2) a cultivated piece of ground, sown with grain or planted with trees, *fruit-garden, vineyard, corn-field*, 9, 534. Od, 1, 193.

ἀλώῃ, Ep. for ἀλῷ, 3 sing. subj. aor. 2, but ἀλώῃ, Ep. for ἀλοίη, 3 sing optat. from ἁλίσκομαι.

ἀλώμενος, partcp. pres. from ἀλάομαι.
ἀλώμεναι, Ep. for ἀλῶναι, see ἁλίσκομαι.
ἀλώω, Ep. for ἀλῶ, see ἁλίσκομαι.

ἀμ, abbrev. for ἀνά, before β, π, φ: ἀμ πεδίον, ἀμ φόνον.

ἅμα, 1) adv. *at once*: with τε—καί. *at once—and*; *both—and*, 1, 417. 8, 64, &c. 2) prep. with dat. a) of time; *at the same time with*; *together with*, ἅμα δ᾽ ἠελίῳ καταδύντι, together with the setting sun, 1, 592. b) of persons: *together with, in company with, along with*; ἅμα λαῷ θωρηχθῆναι, to arm with the people. c) Of equality, or similarity, prop. *together with*; then, *like*. ἅμα πνοιῇς ἀνέμοιο, like the blasts of wind (i. e. keeping pace with them), 16, 149. Od. 1, 98.

Ἀμαζόνες, αἱ (from ἀ and μάζος, breastless), *the Amazons*, warlike women of mythic antiquity, who allowed no man among them, and amputated the right breast in infancy, to allow a freer use of the bow. Their abode, according to most poets, was on the river Thermōdon, in Cappadocia, or in Scythia, on the Palus Mæotis. According to 6, 186, they invaded Lycia, but were destroyed by Bellerophontēs, and according to 3, 189, they also attacked Phrygia in the kingdom of Priam. Obscure traditions of armed Scythian women were probably the origin of this fable.

Ἀμάθεια, ἡ (living in the downs, from ἄμαθος), daughter of Nereus and Doris, 18, 48.

ἄμαθος, ἡ, poet.=ψάμαθος, *sand, dust*, 5, 586.† Plur. the dunes on the seacoast, h. in Ap. 439.

ἀμαθύνω (ἄμαθος), *to reduce to dust, to*

destroy, πόλιν, 9, 593. 2) *to conceal* [in the sand], κόνιν, h. Merc. 140.

ἀμαιμάκετος, η, ον, *very great, monstrous, prodigious*, epith. of Chimæra, and of a mast, 6, 179. Od. 14, 311 (of uncertain derivation, comm. from α and μῆκος, or, according to Passow, from ἄμαχος, μαίμαχος, with reduplic. *invincible*, cf. δαίδαλος.)

ἀμαλδύνω (ἀμαλός), aor. ἠμάλδυνα, prop. to render soft; hence *to destroy, to demolish*; τεῖχος, to tear down a wall, *7, 463. 12, 18.

ἀμαλλοδετήρ, ῆρος, ὁ (ἄμαλλα, δέω), *the sheaf-binder*, *18, 553, 554.

ἀμαλός, ά, όν, Ep. for ἀπαλός, *tender, weak*, 22, 310. Od. 20, 14.

ἄμαξα, ἡ, Ep. and Ion. for ἅμαξα (ἄγω), *wagon*, in distinction from the two-wheeled war-chariot, ἅρμα, 7, 426. Od. 9, 241. 2) The *Wagon*, a constellation in the northern sky, a name of the Great Bear in the heavens [compare the name Charles's Wain]; see Ἄρκτος, 18, 487. Od. 5, 273.

ἀμαξιτός, ἡ (ἅμαξα), sc. ὁδός, *a wagon-road, a street*, 22, 146. †h. Cer. 177.

ἀμάρη, ἡ, *a channel for water, a ditch*, 21, 259.†

ἀμαρτάνω, fut. ἁμαρτήσομαι, aor. ἥμαρτον, Ep. also ἤμβροτον (by metathesis, changing α into ο, with β epenthetic, and a change of the breathing,) 1) *to fail, to miss*, not to hit the mark, τινός, any one; spoken e-ply of missiles, 10, 372; hence 2) metaph. *to fail, to err, to deviate*; νοήματος ἐσθλοῦ. she swerved not from a noble mind, Od. 7, 292. οὐχ ἡμάρτανε μύθων, he mistook not the words, i. e. he always selected the right words, Od. 11, 511; also absol. *to fail, err, mistake*, 9, 501. Od. 21, 155. 3) *to fail of what one has, to lose, to be deprived of*, ὁπωπῆς, Od. 9, 512. 4) *to make a failure in any thing*; δώρων, failed not to bring gifts, 24, 68.

ἁμαρτῇ or ἁμαρτῆ, adv. (ἅμα, ἀρτάω), *together, at the same time*, 5, 656. Od. 22, 81. Others write ἀμαρτή or ὁμαρτῇ.

ἁμαρτοεπής, ές, Ep. (ἔπος), *missing the proper words, idly prating*, 13, 824.†

*ἀμαρυγή, ἡ (μαίρω), poet. for μαρμαρυγή, *the glimmering, flashing, gleaming* of the eyes, h. Merc. 45.

Ἀμαρυγκείδης, ου, ὁ, son of Amarynceus=*Diores*, 2, 622. 4, 517.

Ἀμαρυγκεύς, ῆος, ὁ (ἀμαρύσσω), son of Alector, a brave warrior who went from Thessaly to Elias, and aided Augeas against Heraclēs. As a reward, Augeas shared with him the throne. His funeral is mentioned 23, 631.

*ἀμαρύσσω, fut. ξω, *to shine, to gleam*, ἀπὸ βλεφάρων, h. Merc. 278. 415.

ἀματροχάω, poet. (τρέχω), only partcp. pres. ἀματροχόων, Ep. for ἀματροχῶν, *running with*, Od. 15, 451.†

ἀματροχίη, ἡ, Ep. (τρέχω), *the running together of chariots* [a clash of chariots, Cp.], 23, 422.†

C 4

ἀμαυρός, ή, όν, poet. (μαίρω), not shining, *dark, indistinct*, εἴδωλον, *Od. 4, 824. 835.

ἀμάχητι, adv. (μάχη), *without battle, without contest*, 21, 437.†

ἀμάω (ἅμα), aor. ἄμησα, Ep. for ἤμησα, aor. mid. ἀμησάμενος, prop. to gather; hence 1) Act. *to mow, to reap;* absol. 18, 551; with accus. 24, 451. Od. 9, 135. 2) *to collect for oneself;* with accus. γάλα ἐν ταλάροισι, the milk curd in baskets, Od. 9, 247.

ἀμβαίνω, ἀμβάλλω, and other words with ἀμβ; see ἀναβαίνω, ἀναβάλλω, etc.

ἀμβατός, όν, poet. for ἀναβατός.

ἀμβλήδην, see ἀναβλήδην.

ἀμβολάδην. adv. see ἀναβολάδην.

ἀμβροσίη, ἡ (prop. fem. from ἀμβρόσιος, sc. according to the ancients ἐδωδή), *ambrosia,* 1) *the food of the gods,* which was agreeable in taste, and secured immortality, Od. 5, 93. 199. 9, 359. 2) *the oil of the gods,* with which the immortals anointed themselves, 14, 170; cf. 172. 3) used as food for the horses of Hêrê, 5, 777, and Od. 4, 445. Eidothea gives ambrosia to Menelaus to remove a disagreeable smell. According to Buttm. Lexil. 79, it is a subst. and signifies *immortality,* for the gods eat immortality, they anoint themselves with it, and it is also the food of their steeds.

ἀμβρόσιος, η, ον, (βροτός) *immortal, of divine nature,* νύμφη, h. Merc. 230. 2) Spoken of what belongs to the gods; *ambrosial, divine,* as χαῖται, πέδιλα, ἔλαιον, 1, 529. 3) Of what comes from the gods: *divine, sacred,* as νύξ, ὕπνος, 2, 19. 57.

ἄμβροτος, ον (βροτός) =ἀμβρόσιος, *immortal, divine,* θεός, 20, 358; and spoken of whatever belongs to the gods: *ambrosial,* αἷμα, 5, 539; κρήδεμνον. Od. 5, 347. 2) *divine, sacred,* and generally *excellent, lovely;* spoken of whatever comes from the gods, νύξ, Od. 11, 330.

ἀμέγαρτος, ον (μεγαίρω), prop. not to be envied; hence 1) Spoken of things: *sad, dreadful, severe,* πόνος, 2, 420; ἀϋτμή ἀνέμων, Od. 11, 400. 2) Of persons, as epith. of contempt; *wicked, vile, miserable,* Od. 17, 219 (cf. Buttm. Lexil. p. 407).

ἀμείβοντες, see ἀμείβω.

ἀμείβω, fut. ἀμείψω, fut. mid. ἀμείψομαι, aor. 1 ἠμειψάμην, I) Act. *to alternate, to change, to exchange,* a) Intrans. only in partcp. οἱ ἀμείβοντες, *the alternating,* i. e. *the rafters,* 23, 712. b) Comm. trans. *to change, to exchange;* with accus. ἔντεα, 17, 192; τί τινος, one thing for another; τεύχεα χρύσεα χαλκέων πρός τινα, to exchange golden weapons for brazen with any one, 6, 235; γόνυ γουνός, one knee with the other, i. e. to walk slowly 11, 547. II) Mid. *to change for oneself, to exchange;* hence 1) *to interchange, to alternate;* in partcp. ἀμειβόμενος, alternating, 1, 604. 9, 471. ἀμείβεσθαι κατὰ οἴκους, to change by houses, i.e. to go from house to house, Od. 1, 375.

b) Often ἐπέεσσι, μύθοισι τινά, to alte with words with any one, i. e. to rep Spoken of place: *to exchange, to l* with accus. ψυχὴ ἀμείβεται ἕρκος ὀδό the soul passes over the wall of teeth, i. e. the lips, 9, 409; and spok drink, which goes over the lips in mouth, Od. 10, 328. 3) *to requite, to pensate;* δώροισι, to requite with sents. i. e. to make compensatory Od. 24, 285.

ἀμείλικτος, ον (μειλίσσω), *not g harsh, inexorable,* ὄψ, *11, 137; al Cer. 260.

ἀμείλιχος, ον=ἀμείλικτος, Ἀΐδη 159; ἦτορ, v. 572.

ἀμείνων, ον, gen. ονος, irreg. cor of ἀγαθός; spoken of persons: *br more valiant;* of things: *better, mor fitable,* 1, 116 (prob. originally *more sant,* from a root related to the l posit. *amanus;* see Kühner I. § 325

ἀμέλγω, only pres and imperf. *to* μῆλα, Od. 9, 238. Mid. ὄϊες ἀμελγόμ γάλα, sheep yielding milk, 4, 434.

ἀμελέω (μέλει), aor. ἀμέλησα, Ep ἠμέλ. *to be free from trouble, to neg to forget,* with gen. always with κασιγνήτοιο, not to forget a brother 330 13, 419.

ἄμεναι, Ep. for ἀέμεναι, infin. pres Ἀ.

ἀμενηνός, όν (μένος), *without po weak, feeble,* epith. of the wounded dead, 5, 887. Od. 10, 521; of dreams, 19, 562. h. Ven. 189.

ἀμενηνόω (ἀμενηνός), aor. ἀμενήνωσ *render weak, inefficacious;* with ac αἰχμήν, to make the lance inefficaci 13, 562.†

ἀμέρδω (fr. ἀμείρω, cf. κείρω, κέρ aor. act. ἤμερσα, Ep. ἄμερσα, aor. p ἀμέρθην, prop. to deprive of a share; mly, *to deprive, to bereave*: with accu the person: τὸν ὁμοῖον ἀμέρσαι, to rol equal, i. e. one having equal claims, 53. b) With accus. of the person gen. of the thing: τινὰ ὀφθαλμῶν, to prive any one of eyes, Od. 8, 64; p αἰῶνος, 22, 58; δαιτός, Od. 21, 290. 2 *blind, to obscure;* with accus. a ἄμερδεν ὄσσε, the brightness blinded tl eyes, 13, 340. καπνὸς ἀμέρδει καλὰ ἔν the smoke injured the beautiful weapo Od. 19, 18.

ἀμέτρητος, ον (μετρέω), *immeasura prodigious,* πόνος, *Od. 19, 512. 23, 24

ἀμετροεπής, ές, *immoderate in wo endlessly prating, loquacious,* 2, 212.†

ἀμητήρ, ῆρος, ὁ (ἀμάω), *mower, rea* 11, 67.†

ἄμητος, ὁ (ἀμάω), *the act of mowin reaping, the harvest,* 19, 223. †(ᾱ).

*ἀμηχανής, ές, poet. for ἀμήχανος, Merc. 447.

ἀμηχανίη, ἡ (ἀμήχανος), *embarrassme hesitation, perplexity, despair* [inopia c silii], Od. 9, 295.†

ἀμήχανος, ον (μηχανή), *without mea i. e.* 1) *helpless, unfortunate, at a l* τινός, about any one, Od. 19, 363. 2) Pass. against which there is no expedient; spoken of things: *difficult, impossible;* ὄνειροι, inexplicable dreams, Od. 19, 560; ἔργα, deeds not to be averted, *irremediable evils* (Eustath. δεινά), 8, 130. b) Of persons: *not to be subdued, impracticable, unyielding, hard-hearted,* absol. 16, 29; but ἀμήχανός ἐσσι παραρρητοῖσι πιθέσθαι, *thou art not easily brought* to obey exhortations, 13, 726.

'Αμισώδαρος, ὁ, king of Caria, father of Ατymnius, 16, 328.

ἀμιτροχίτωνες, οἱ, poet. epith. of the Lycians, 16, 419†; either, *without a girdle* [' *uncinctured,*' Cp.], (from a priv. μίτρα and χιτών, those who wear no girdle under the cuirass, cf. μίτρα,) or *having the girdle joined to the cuirass* (from a copulat. μιτ. and χιτ.).

ἀμιχθαλόεις, εσσα, εν, poet. (μίγνυμι), *inaccessible, inhospitable,* epith. of Lemnos, 24, 753. †h. Ap. 36 (prob. lengthened from ἄμικτος, and not from μίγνυμι and ἅλς).

ἄμμε, ἄμμες, ἄμμι, Æol. and Ep. for ἡμᾶς, ἡμεῖς, etc.

ἀμμῖξας, poet. for ἀναμίξας.

ἀμμορίη, ἡ, Ep. for ἀμορία (μόρος), *misfortune, misery,* Od. 20, 76.†

ἄμμορος, ον, Ep. for ἄμορος (μόρος), 1) *not participating, not enjoying,* with gen. λοετρῶν Ὠκεανοῖο, excluded from bathing in the ocean; spoken of the Great Bear, which is always visible to the Greeks. 18, 489. Od. 5, 275. 2) From μόρος, i. q. μοίρη, *unfortunate, miserable,* 6, 408. 24, 773.

ἀμνίον or ἄμνιον, τό (αἷμα), *a vessel* for receiving the blood of victims, a *sacrificial bowl,* Od. 3, 444.†

'Αμνισός, ὁ, a haven in Crete, at the river *Amnisus,* north from Cnosus, founded by Minos, Od. 19, 188.

ἀμογητί, adv. (μογέω), *without trouble, easily,* 11, 637.†

*ἀμόγητος, ον (μογέω), *unwearied,* h. 7, 8.

ἀμόθεν, adv. Ep. (ἀμός, poet. =τίς) *from some place or other, from some part or other.* τῶν ἀμόθεν εἰπὲ καὶ ἡμῖν, begin where you please and tell to us also something of them, Od. 1, 10.† Schol. Τῶν περὶ τὸν Ὀδυσσέα ὁπόθεν θέλεις πράξεων ἀπό τινος μέρους ἀρξαμένη διηγοῦ ἡμῖν.

ἀμοιβάς, άδος, ἡ, poet. fem. of ἀμοιβαῖος (ἀμοιβή), *serving for a change.* χλαῖνα, ἥ οἱ παρεκέσκετ' (=παρέκειτ') ἀμοιβάς, a mantle which lay by him (*was laid by*) for a change, Od. 14, 521.† Others read παρεχέσκετ' ἀμοιβάς, and explain it as accus. plur. of ἀμοιβή.

ἀμοιβή, ἡ (ἀμείβω), *return, recompense, compensation* or *indemnity, restitution, requital;* in a good and bad signif. χαρίεσσα ἀμοιβὴ ἑκατόμβης, a gracious return for the hecatomb, Od. 3, 59. τίειν βοῶν ἀμοιβήν, to make restitution (compensation) for the cattle, Od. 12, 382. *Od.

ἀμοιβηδίς, adv. Ep. (ἀμοιβή), *changing*

alternately, successively, 18, 506. Od. 18, 310.

ἀμοιβός, ὁ (ἀμείβω), *that exchanges with* another that relieves him, a substitute. οἱ ἦλθον ἀμοιβοί, who came to relieve others, 13, 793 †[in requital of former aid from Priam, Eustath.].

ἀμολγός, ὁ (ἀμέλγω=turgeo), *milking, milking-time;* with Hom. always νυκτὸς ἀμολγῷ, at the hour of milking. The milking-time of the night is twofold, one at evening, as 22, 317; the other in the morning, as Od. 4, 841; therefore: *evening* and *morning twilight;* and mly, *the darkness of the night,* 11, 173. Buttm. in Lex. p. 89, with Eustath. 15, 324, with great probability regards ἀμολγός as an old Achaian word meaning ἀκμή, and translates it, *in the dead* or *depth of the night.* [D. makes μολγός with prothetic a related to μολύνειν, μελαίνειν, p. 244.]

'Αμοπάων, ονος, ὁ (ἅμα, ὀπάων, companion), son of Polyæmôn, a Trojan slain by Teucer, 8, 276.

ἀμός (al. ἁμός), ή, όν, Æol. and Ep.= ἡμέτερος, our. ἀμός, ή, όν is adopted by Spitzner on the authority of Apoll. de pron. and Etym. Mag. cf. Spitzner ad 6, 414.

ἄμοτον, adv. (from ἄμεναι, ᾺΩ), *insatiably, incessantly, restlessly, continually, unceasingly,* 4, 440 (μέμαα). 13, 46. Od. 6, 83 (ταννέσθαι). [The ancients derived it from μότον, lint.]

ἀμπ. Ep. abbrev. for ἀναπ.; as ἀμπείρας for ἀναπείρας.

ἀμπελόεις, εσσα, εν (ἄμπελος), once ἀμπελόεις, as fem. 2, 561, *full of vines, abounding in grapes, vine-clad;* epith. of countries and towns, 3, 184.

ἄμπελος, ἡ, a vine, *Od. 9, 110. h. 6, 39.

ἀμπεπαλών, Ep. for ἀναπεπαλών, see ἀναπάλλω.

ἀμπερές, adv. only in tmesis, διὰ δ' ἀμπερές, Od. 21, 422; for διαμπερές, q. v.

ἀμπέχω (ἀμφί, ἔχω), impf. ἄμπεχον, *to embrace, to surround, to cover;* only ἅλμη, ἥ οἱ νῶτα καὶ εὐρέας ἄμπεχεν ὤμους, the brine, which covered his back and broad shoulders, Od. 6, 225.†

ἀμπήδησε, see ἀναπηδάω.
ἀμπνεῦσαι, see ἀναπνέω.
ἄμπνυε, see ἀναπνέω.
ἀμπνύνθη, see ἀναπνέω.
ἄμπνυτο, see ἀπνύω.

ἄμπυξ, υκος, ἡ (ἀμπέχω), *a head-band* or *fillet,* a female ornament, 22, 469.†

ἄμυδις, adv. Æol. from ἅμα, *together;* spoken of time, Od. 12, 415. 2) *together,* in a crowd, of place, 10, 300; καθίζειν, to sit down together, Od. 4, 659.

'Αμυδών, ῶνος, ἡ, a town in Pæonia, on the Axius, 2, 849.

'Αμυθάων, ονος, ὁ, 1) son of Cretheus and Tyro, brother of Æson, husband of Idomenê, father of Bias and Melampus; he is said to have founded Pylus in Messenia, Od. 11, 259. 2) 17, 348, the reading of Bothe for 'Απισάων e Cdd.

'Αμύκλαι, αἱ, a town in Laconia, on the

Eurōtas, residence of Tyndareus, famed for the worship of Apollo, now *Slavo-Chorion*, 2, 584.

ἀμύμων [͞ ͝], gen. ονος (μῶμος, censure, with a change of ω into υ; after Æol. dial.), *blameless, irreproachable*, an honorary epith. of persons in reference to birth, rank, or form, without regard to moral worth: *noble, high-born*, and thus even the adulterer Ægisthus is called, Od. 1, 29. *b*) Spoken also of things, = *excellent, glorious*, οἶκος, μῆτις, 10, 19; νῆσος, Od. 1, 232. 9, 414. 12, 261.

ἀμύντωρ, ορος, ὁ (ἀμύνω), *defender, helper, protector*, 13, 284. Od. 2, 326.

Ἀμύντωρ, ορος, ὁ, 1) son of Ormenus, 10, 266. 2) Probably another, 9, 447. 10, 266.

ἀμύνω (μύνη), ἀμυνῶ, aor. ἤμυνα, ἠμυνάμην, Ep. infin. pres. ἀμυνέμεναι for ἀμύνειν. 1) Act. *to avert, to ward off*; mly τί τινος, something from some one, λοιγὸν Δαναοῖσιν, destruction from the Greeks, 1, 341; ἄστεϊ νηλεὲς ἦμαρ, to remove the day of destruction from the city, 11, 588. *b*) More rarely τί τινος; Κῆράς τινος, to repel the Fates from any one, 4, 11; Τρῶας νεῶν, the Trojans from the ships, 15, 731; also the gen. alone, νηῶν, to defend the ships, 13, 109: περί τινος, to fight for any one, i. e. avenge him, 17, 182; sometimes without dat. of person, φόνον κακόν, 9, 599. 13, 783. Od. 22, 208; absol. 13, 312. 678. *c*) Oftener the dat. stands alone: to fight for any one, i. e. *to help, to assist* him, 5, 486. 6, 262. 2) Mid. *to avert, to remove* from oneself, with accus. νηλεὲς ἦμαρ, 11, 484. *b*) *to defend oneself, to fight for oneself*, often absol. and with gen. τινός, and with περί τινος. to fight for any one, to defend him; νηῶν, to defend the ships, 12, 179; σφῶν αὐτῶν, 12, 155, or περὶ πάτρης, to fight for one's country, 12, 243.

ἀμύσσω, fut. ἀμύξω, *to scratch, to tear, to lacerate*; c. accus. στήθεα χερσίν, to tear the skin from the breast with the hands, i. e. nails, 19, 284; metaph. θυμὸν ἀμύξεις, thou wilt tear (distress) thy heart, spoken of one in anger, 1, 243. *II.

ἀμφαγαπάζω (ἀγαπάζω), poet. form, *to embrace with love, to treat with affection, to receive hospitably*; with accus. Od. 14, 381. 2) Mid. as depon. 16, 192; h. Cer. 291.

* ἀμφαγαπάω = ἀμφαγαπάζω; whence ἀμφαγάπησα, h. Cer. 439.

ἀμφαγερέθομαι, better ἀμφηγερέθομαι, q. v.

ἀμφαγείρομαι (ἀγείρω), aor. 2 ἀμφαγέροντο, *to collect, to gather* (intrans.), τινά, about any one, 18, 37.†

ἀμφαδά, adv. see ἀμφαδός.

ἀμφαδίην, adv. see ἀμφάδιος.

ἀμφάδιος, η, ον, Ep. for ἀναφάδιος (ἀναφαίνω), *open, manifest, public*, γάμος, a real marriage, Od. 6, 288; comm. accus. ἀμφαδίην, as adv. *publicly, unconcealed*, 7, 196. 13, 356.

ἀμφαδός, όν, Ep. for ἀναφαδός (ἀνα-

φαίνω), *open, public, notorious*. ἀμφ ἔργα γένοιτο, the thing should be m fest [i. e. his secret be disclosed], Od. 391; comm. neut. sing. ἀμφαδόν, as in opposit. to λάθρῃ, 7, 243; to δόλῳ, 1, 296. 11, 120; to κρυφηδόν, Od. 14, 19, 299.

ἀμφαΐσσομαι (ἀΐσσω), *to rush up f all sides*; spoken of the mane of ho with dat. ἀμφὶ δὲ χαῖται ὤμοις ἀΐσσον the mane floated about their should *6, 510. 15, 267, only in tmesis.

ἀμφαλείφω (ἀλείφω), infin. aor. ἀλεί only in tmesis, *to anoint round about*, 582.†

ἀμφαραβέω (ἀραβέω), aor. ἀράβησα *rattle, to resound round about*; spoke arms, 21, 408.†

* ἀμφανέειν, poet. for ἀναφανεῖν, ἀναφαίνω.

ἀμφασίη, ἡ, Ep. for ἀφασίη, *speechl ness*, comm. with ἐπέων, prob. a p nasm. Δὴν δέ μιν ἀμφασίη ἐπέων λ for a long time speechlessness held h 17, 695. Od. 4, 704.

ἀμφαϋτέω (ἀϋτέω), *to resound around*, only in tmesis, 12, 160.† (ῡ).

ἀμφαφάω (ἀφάω), partcp. pres. ἀμ φόων, Ep. for ἀμφαφῶν, infin. pres. n ἀμφαφάασθαι for ἀμφαφᾶσθαι, *to handl about, to feel all over*; with accus. λό spoken of the Troj. horse, Od. 4, 277 196; τόξον, to handle the bow, Od. 586. 2) Mid. as depon. ἦ μάλα δὴ μα κώτερος ἀμφαφάασθαι, indeed, far ea is Hector now to handle, 22, 373.

ἀμφεποτᾶτο, see ἀμφιποτάομαι.

ἀμφέπω = ἀμφιέπω.

ἀμφέρχομαι, depon. (ἔρχομαι), ἀμφήλυθον, *to go around*, with ac any thing; metaph. only in Hom. με ἤλυθ' αὐτή, a cry surrounded me, 6, 122, and κνίσσης αὐτμή, the fume the fat surrounded me, Od. 12, 369. *

ἀμφέχανε, from ἀμφιχαίνω.

ἀμφέχυτ' for ἀμφέχυτο, see ἀμφιχέα

ἀμφήκης, ές (ἀκή), gen. έος, *sharp both sides, double-edged*, epith. of sword, 10, 256. Od. 16, 80.

ἀμφήλυθε, see ἀμφέρχομαι.

ἀμφήμαι (ἧμαι), *to sit round about*, in tmesis, ἀμφὶ δ' ἑταῖροι εἴατο, 15, 1

ἀμφηρεφής, ές (ἐρέφω), gen. έος, cov *all around* (or, *at both ends*), *well cove* epith. of the quiver, 1, 45.†

ἀμφήριστος, ον (ἐρίζω), *contested both sides, undecided*. 2) *equal in f* ἀμφ. τιθέναι τινά, to place one upon equality (in the race), 23, 382.†

ἀμφί, A) Adv. *round about, arou* 4, 328. Od. 2, 153; it is often separ from the verb in compos. by a particle, is to be taken in tmesis: ἀμφὶ περ adv. 21, 10. B) Prepos. with three ca *round about, around*, like περί, ex that ἀμφί, rather Ion. and poet., expre prop. enclosing on two sides: 1) gen. *about, on account of, for the sak* to indicate the object about which action is performed. ἀμφὶ πίδακος χεσθαι, to fight for a fountain, 16, 825; metaph. ἀμφὶ φιλότητος ἀείδειν, to sing about (of) love, Od. 8, 267. 2) With dat. a) Of place, around, upon, about, with the idea of rest: τελαμὼν ἀμφὶ στήθεσσιν, 2, 388. 3, 328. ἤριπε δ' ἀμφ' αὐτῷ, he sank upon it, 4, 493; also mly spoken of nearness in place, 12, 175. τὴν κτεῖνε ἀμφ' ἐμοί, at my side, near me, Od. 11, 422. Il. 9, 470. ἀμφ' ὀβελοῖσιν ἐπέα πείρειν, in the construct. praegn. to pierce the flesh with the spits, so that it is on them round about, 2, 427; in like manner, στῆσαι τρίποδα ἀμφὶ πυρί, Od. 8, 434. ἀμφ' ὀχέεσσι βαλεῖν κύκλα, to put the wheels upon the chariots, 5, 722. b) Indicating the cause; about, on account of, ἀμφὶ νέκυϊ μάχεσθαι, 16, 565. ἀμφὶ γυναικὶ ἄλγεα πάσχειν, 3, 157. 3) With accus. a) Of place, with the idea of motion about, to, or into; about, to, along, around in; ἀμφὶ ῥέεθρα, along the waves, 2, 461. ἀμφὶ ἄστυ ἔρδειν ἱρά, round about in the city, 11, 706. Of persons: οἱ ἀμφ' Ἀτρείωνα βασιλῆες, the princes about Atrides. 2, 445. cf. 5, 781. In Hom., however, the chief person is included in the sense; οἱ ἀμφὶ Πρίαμον, Priam and his followers, 3, 146. b) Indicating cause, occupation, about an object, μνήσασθαι ἀμφί τινα, to mention about any one, h. 6, 1. In Hom. ἀμφί sometimes stands after the dependent cases. In composition with verbs it has the same signif. and sometimes also, on both sides.

ἀμφίαλος, ον (ἅλς), surrounded by the sea, sea-girt, epith. of Ithaca, *Od. 1, 386. 395.

Ἀμφίαλος, ὁ, a Phaeacian, Od. 8, 114. 128.

Ἀμφιάρηος, ὁ (from ἀμφί and ἀράομαι, prayed for by both sides), son of Oïclês or of Apollo, husband of Eriphÿlê, father of Alcmæôn and Amphilôchus, a noted prophet and king of Argos. He took part in the Calydonian chase, in the Argonautic expedition, and in the Theban war. Because, as prophet, he knew that he should perish before Thebes, he concealed himself; but was betrayed by his wife for a necklace. He was swallowed with his chariot, in the Theban war, by the earth. Subsequently he had a temple at Oïōpus, Od. 15, 244.

ἀμφιάχω (ἰάχω), partcp. perf. ἀμφιαχυῖα, to cry round about, to scream, v. a. 2, 316.†

ἀμφιβαίνω (βαίνω), perf. ἀμφιβέβηκα, 1) to go around, to travel around; with accus. ἠέλιος μέσον οὐρανὸν ἀμφιβεβήκει, but when the sun had travelled round the midst of heaven, i. e. had reached the midst of heaven, 8, 68; spoken of gods: Χρύσην, to walk about Chrysê as tutelary god, i. e. to protect, 1, 37. Od. 9, 198. 2) Mly to surround, to encircle, esply in the perf. νεφέλη μιν ἀμφιβέβηκεν, Od. 12, 74; with dat. 16, 66; metaph. πύκος φρένας ἀμφιβέβηκεν, trouble has occupied thy heart, 6, 355.

ἀμφιβάλλω (βάλλω), aor. 2 ἀμφέβαλον, fut. mid. ἀμφιβαλεῦμαι, Ep. for ἀμφιβαλοῦμαι, aor. 2 ἀμφεβαλόμην, 1) Act. to cast about, to put on, one thing upon another, τί τινι: ὤμοισι αἰγίδα, to cast the aegis over the shoulders, 18, 204. b) Spoken of putting on clothing, it takes two accus., but in this case the prepos. is always separated from the verb; φάρός τινα. 24, 588; χιτῶνά τινα, Od. 3, 467; with dat. of person only in ἀμφὶ δέ μοι ῥάκος βάλον, Od. 14, 342; metaph. κρατερὸν μένος ἀμφιβάλλειν, to equip oneself with great strength, 17, 742. c) to embrace, to clasp, to throw around, in full χεῖρας γούνασι, throw the hands (arms) about any one's knees, Od. 7, 142; ἀλλήλους, 23, 97. ὡς οἱ χεῖρες ἐχάνδανον ἀμφιβαλόντι, as much as the hands of him grasping held, i. e. as much as he could hold with both hands, Od. 17, 344; hence mly, to surround, to enclose. 2) Mid. to cast about oneself, to put on, with reference to the subject, τί τινα: ὤμοισι ξίφος, to hang the sword over one's shoulders, 2, 45; πήρην, Od. 17, 197.

ἀμφίβασις, ιος, ἡ (βαίνω), the act of going around, of encircling [espec. for a defence, as of a corpse, cf. Passow, s. v. and ἀμφιβαίνω], 5, 623.†

*ἀμφίβιος, ον (βίος), living both in water and on land, amphibious; νομή, a double abode, Batr. 59.

ἀμφίβροτος, η, ον (βροτός), encompassing the man, protecting the man, always ἀμφιβρότη ἀσπίς, *2, 389. 11, 32.

ἀμφιβρύχω, see βρυχάομαι.

Ἀμφιγένεια, ἡ, a town in Messenia, prob. the later Ἀμφεια, 2, 593. Steph. after Strab. in Elis.

*ἀμφιγηθέω (γηθέω), partcp. perf. ἀμφιγεγηθώς, to rejoice around, i. e. greatly, h. Ap. 273.

Ἀμφιγυήεις, ὁ (γυιός), lame in both feet, halting, epith. of Hephæstus, 1, 607. 14, 239.

ἀμφίγυος, ον, Ep. (γυῖον), prop. having limbs on both sides, epith. of the spear, probably furnished with iron at both ends for fighting and sticking in the earth. According to others, double-cutting, wounding with both ends, or to be handled with both hands, 13, 147. Od. 16, 474. [But Herm. (with Död.) supposes it a pike for cutting and thrusting, its head being furnished, at about the middle of each side, with a sharp curved blade.]

ἀμφιδαίω, Ep. (δαίω), perf. ἀμφιδέδηα, to kindle around, in the perf. intrans. to burn around; only metaph. πόλεμος ἄστυ ἀμφιδέδηε, the contest burned around the city, *6, 329; μάχη, 12, 35.

Ἀμφιδάμας, αντος, ὁ (from ἀμφί and δαμάω), subduing round about), a hero from Scandia in Cythêra, table-friend of Molus, 10, 269. 2) father of Clysonômus from Opus, 23, 87.

ἀμφίδασυς, εια, υ (δασύς), rough round about, roughly bordered, epith. of the

C 6

ægis surrounded with tassels, θύσανοι. [Others, *woolly, shaggy all over, impenetrable*, cf. Schol. and Passow.] 15, 309.†

ἀμφιδινέω (δινέω), perf. pass. ἀμφιδεδίνημαι, *to turn* or *put around*, κολεὸν νεοπρίστου ἐλέφαντος ἀμφιδεδίνηται, the scabbard is encompassed with polished ivory [rather a scabbard *of polished ivory encloses it*], Od. 8, 405; also spoken of metal: ᾧ πέρι χεῦμα κασσιτέρου ἀμφιδεδίνηται, around which there runs a (casting=) plate of tin, 23, 562.

ἀμφιδρυφής, ές, poet. (δρύπτω), gen. έος, *lacerated all around*, ἄλοχος, a wife who tears the skin from her cheeks from grief at the death of her husband, 2, 700 †

ἀμφίδρυφος, ον=ἀμφιδρυφής, 11, 393.†

ἀμφίδυμος, ον (δύω [the verb: rather from δύο, *two*: cf. δίδυμος, τρίδυμος, *tergeminus*, &c. Lob. Path. 165]), *accessible all around*, or *having a double entrance*, epith. of a haven, Od. 4, 847.

ἀμφιελαύνω (ἐλαύνω), only in tmesis, *to draw* or *trace round about*, Il. τεῖχος πόλει, a wall about a city, Od. 6, 9.

ἀμφιέλισσος, ον, poet. (ἑλίσσω), *impelled onward on both sides, double-oared*, epith. of ships, 2, 165. It occurs only in the fem. ἀμφιέλισσα; for which reason, according to Rost Vollst. Lex., the Gramm. falsely assumed an adj. ἀμφιέλισσος, η, ον. Rost also prefers, after the use of the later Epic writers, the signif. *swaying from this side to that, unsteady*.

ἀμφιέννυμι (ἕννυμι), fut. ἀμφιέσω, aor. Ep. ἀμφίεσα (σσ), aor. mid. ἀμφιεσάμην (σσ), 1) Act. *to put around, to put on*, εἴματα, clothes (upon another), Od. 5, 167. 264. 2) Mid. *to put upon oneself*, anything, with accus. χιτῶνας, Od. 23, 142. cf. 14, 178.

ἀμφιέπω and ἀμφέπω (ἕπω), only impf. poet. *to be around* any thing, *to surround;* with accus. τὴν πρύμνην πῦρ ἀμφέπεν, the flame surrounded the stern, 16, 124. Od. 8, 437. 2) *to be engaged about* any thing, *to prepare, to attend to;* with accus. τινά, 5, 667; βοὸς κρέα, to dress ox-flesh, 17, 776; στίχας, to arrange the ranks, 2, 525. The partcp. is often absol. in the sense of an adv.: *earnestly, carefully, busily*, 19, 392. Od. 3, 118.

ἀμφιεύω (εὔω), *to singe round about*, only in tmesis, Od. 9, 389.†

ἀμφιζάνω (ἰζάνω), *to sit round about [to settle upon];* χιτῶνι, upon his tunic, 18, 25.†

ἀμφιθαλής, ές, poet. (θάλλω), gen. έος, *blooming, flourishing on both sides;* spoken of a child whose parents are both living (a child of blooming parents, V.), 22, 496.†

'Αμφιθέη, ἡ (on both sides of divine origin), mother of Anticlea, wife of Autolycus, and grandmother of Ulysses, Od. 19, 416.

ἀμφίθετος, ον, poet. (τίθημι), *that may be placed on either end;* φιάλη, either,

with Aristarchus, a goblet that c placed on either end, or having ha on both sides; *a double goblet*, •23 616.

ἀμφιθέω (θέω), *to run around;* accus. μητέρα, about the mother, O 413.†

'Αμφιθόη (θοός), daughter of N and of Doris, 18, 42.

ἀμφικαλύπτω (καλύπτω), fut. ἀμ λύψω, ἀμφεκάλυψα, 1) Act. *to round about, to conceal;* with ι prim. spoken of clothes, 2, 262: ο arm: ὄστεα, 23, 91. δόμος ἀμφεκά με, the house concealed me, receive Od. 4, 618; πόλις ἵππον, Od. 8, 51 Metaph. ἔρως φρένας ἀμφεκάλυψε, obscured my mind, 3, 442. θά μιν ἀμφ., death embraced him, 5, 68 *to surround, to put around*, to cov with a veil; τί τινι, to put any around one, to cover him with it: κεφαλῇ, Od. 14, 349; σάκος τινί, to a shield before any one (for protec 8, 331; ὄρος πόλει, to put a mou over the city, Od. 8, 569; νύκτα μά draw the veil of night around the b 5, 507.

ἀμφικεάζω (κεάζω), αορ. ἐκέασα, Ep *to hew on all sides, to split;* τὸ ι δρυός, Od. 14, 12.†

'Αμφικλος, ὁ (famed round abou κλέος), a Trojan, slain by Achilles 313.

ἀμφίκομος, ον (κόμη), *having ha around, thick-leaved*, epith. of a tre 677.†

ἀμφικοναβέω, only by tmesis, see βέω.

ἀμφικύπελλος. ον (κύπελλον), α with τὸ δέπας, the *double goblet*, ac ing to Aristot. Hist. An. 9, 40; a g which formed a cup on both enc 584; see Eustath. and Buttm. Le: 93.

ἀμφιλαχαίνω (λαχαίνω), *to dig ι about*, φυτόν, Od. 24, 242.†

'Αμφίλοχος, ὁ, son of Amphiarau Eriphýlê, a prophet of Argos, who part in the expedition of the Ep against Thebes, and then in the T war. After his return, he founded Mopsus the town of Mallus in Cilicia was killed in a duel with Mopsus 15, 248.

ἀμφιλύκη, ἡ (from the obsol. λύξ, to λευκός), only in connexion with *the twilight, the gray of the mornis* 433.†

ἀμφιμαίομαι, depon. (μαίομαι), impf. ἀμφιμάσασθε, *to touch round c to wipe off;* τραπέζας σπόγγοις, Ο 152.†

ἀμφιμάσασθε, see ἀμφιμαίομαι.

ἀμφιμάχομαι, depon. mid. (μάχ *to fight about* a place, *to assail;* accus. Ἴλιον, πόλιν, to attack, 6, 9, 412. 2) With gen. *to fight* for an] to defend him, νέκυος, 18, 20; τ 15, 391. •Il.

Ἀμφίμαχος, ὁ (from μάχομαι, fighting round about), 1) son of Cteatus, grandson of Actor, leader of the Epeans from Elis, 2, 260. Hector slew him, 13, 187. 2) son of Nomion, leader of the Carians, slain by Achilles, 2, 870.

Ἀμφιμέδων, οντος, ὁ (from μέδων, ruling round about), son of Melaneus, suitor of Penelope, whom Telemachus slew, Od. 24, 103.

ἀμφιμέλας, αινα, αν (μέλας), black round about, always with φρένες, prob. from the nature of the diaphragm, which is situated in the inmost darkness of the body; the darkly-enveloped diaphragm (the black diaphragm, heart). Others explain it, angry, gloomy, 1, 103. Od. 4, 661.

ἀμφιμέμυκε, from the following.

ἀμφιμυκάομαι, depon. (μυκάομαι), aor. ἀμφέμυκον, perf. ἀμφιμέμυκα, to bellow all around, to low, to resound, to echo. δάπεδον ἀμφιμέμυκεν, Od. 10, 227; in tmesis spoken of the gates: to creak, 12, 460.

ἀμφινέμομαι, mid. (νέμω), prop. to pasture round about, to dwell; to inhabit; with accus. 2, 521. Od. 19, 132.

Ἀμφινόμη, ἡ (pasturing round about), daughter of Nereus and Doris, 18, 44.

Ἀμφίνομος, ὁ, son of Nisus from Dulichium, a suitor of Penelope, slain by Telemachus, Od. 16, 394.

Ἀμφίος, ὁ (from ἀμφί going about), 1) son of Selagus of Pæsus, an ally of the Trojans, slain by the Telamonian Ajax, 5, 612. 2) son of Merops, brother of Adrastus, leader of the Trojans, 2, 830 (with lengthened ι).

ἀμφιξέω (ξέω), aor. ἀμφέξεσα, to scrape round about, to polish, Od. 23, 196 †

ἀμφιπέλομαι, depon. mid. poet (πέλω), to move around any one, to surround him; with dat. ἀοιδὴ ἀκουόντεσσι ἀμφιπέλεται, the song resounded around the hearers, Od. 1, 352.†

ἀμφιπένομαι, depon. mid. (πένομαι), to be occupied about any one; with accus. Od. 15, 467; hence comm. in a good signif. to tend [e. g. a wounded man], to take care of, to wait upon, 4, 220 [to take charge of]; in a bad sense to assail, to fall upon [of dogs setting to work to devour a corpse], 23, 184.

ἀμφιπεριστέφω (στέφω), to wreathe round; only in mid. with dat. metaph. χάρις οὐκ ἀμφιπεριστέφεται ἐπέεσσιν, grace is not entwined with his words, i. e. his words are not crowned with grace, Od. 8, 175.†

ἀμφιπεριστρωφάω, poet. (στρωφάω a collateral form of στρέφω), to turn round about; with accus. ἵππους, to drive the horses about, or round and round, 8, 348.†

ἀμφιπεριφθινύθω, poet. (φθινύθω), to perish round about, to dry up (of bark), h. Ven. 272.

ἀμφιπεσοῦσα, see ἀμφιπίπτω.

ἀμφιπίπτω, poet. (πίπτω), aor. 2 ἀμφέπεσον, to fall round = to fall or throw oneself upon, to embrace, τινά, any one; of a wife who in anguish throws herself upon her dead husband, Od. 8, 523.†

ἀμφιπολεύω (ἀμφίπολος), to be occupied about an object, to support, to attend to, to tend, to take care of; to wait upon; with accus. ὄρχατον (an orchard), Od. 24, 244; βίον, to protect my life [spoken by Penelope of Ulysses], Od. 18, 254. 19, 127. ʼ2) Intrans. to be about any one, to serve him, Od. 20, 78. *Od.

ἀμφίπολος, ἡ (πέλω), prop. an adj. busied about any one; with Hom. always subst. fem. handmaid, maiden, female companion, in distinction from a female slave; also ἀμφίπολος ταμίη, 24, 302.

ἀμφιπονέομαι, Ep.=ἀμφιπένομαι, fut. ἀμφιπονήσομαι, to be busy about any one, τινά, 23, 681; spoken of things, to take care or charge of, τί, 23, 159; τάφον, Od. 20, 307.

ἀμφιποτάομαι, depon. mid. (ποτάομαι). poet. form, to fly round about; with accus. τέκνα, to flutter round the young, 2, 315.†

ἀμφίρρυτος, η, ον, Ep. ἀμφίρυτος (ῥέω), having a current all around, sea-girt, epith. of islands, *Od. 1, 50. 98. only in Ep. form.

ἀμφίς (ἀμφί), poet. I) Adv. 1) about. round about, on both sides. βαθὺς δέ τε Τάρταρος ἀμφίς, 8, 481. ἀμφὶς εἶναι, to be (stand, dwell, &c.) about (a person), to dwell, 9, 464. 24, 488. ἀμφὶς ἔχειν, to clasp about, spoken of bonds, Od. 8, 340. 2) upon, on both sides. ζυγὸν ἀμφὶς ἔχειν, to have the yoke on both sides, to have it on, Od. 3, 486. ὀλίγη ἦν ἀμφὶς ἄρουρα, a little ground was on both sides (of the armies), i. e. between, 3, 115. 3) apart. γαῖαν καὶ οὐρανὸν ἀμφὶς ἔχειν, to hold earth and heaven apart, Od. 1, 54. τὼ μὲν ζυγὸν ἀμφὶς ἐέργει, them (the cattle) the yoke keeps apart, 13, 706. ἀμφὶς ἀγῆναι, to break in two, 11, 559. 4) separate, remote. ἀμφὶς εἶναι, Od. 19, 221; hence often=each for himself, Od. 22, 57. ἀμφὶς φρονέειν, φράζεσθαι, to think differently, to be of different sentiments, 2, 13. II) Prepos. like ἀμφί, comm. after its dependent case, 1) With gen. about. ἅρματος ἀμφὶς ἰδεῖν, to look over a chariot [ι. e. to see whether it is fit for use], 2, 384. b) far from. ἀμφὶς φυλόπιδος, Od. 16, 267. ἀμφὶς ὁδοῦ, out of the road, Od. 19, 221. 2) With dat. ἄξονι ἀμφίς, about the axle-tree, 5, 723. 3) With accus. Κρόνον ἀμφίς, about Cronos (Saturn), 14, 203. εἴρεσθαι ἀμφὶς ἕκαστα, to ask about every thing, i. e. each thing separately, one thing after another, Od. 19, 46.

ἀμφιστεφανόω (στέφανος), to wreathe around, like winding a garland; pass. to be wound round, like a garland; trop. ὅμιλος ἀμφιστεφάνωτο, the crowd had collected in a circle, h. Ven. 120.

ἀμφιστεφής, ές, placed about in a

circle, 11, 40, an old reading for ἀμφιστρεφής, q. v.

[ἀμφιστέφω, 18, 205, explained by Damm as a case of tmesis; see στέφω.]

ἀμφίστημι (ἵστημι), aor. 2 ἀμφέστην, trans. to place around. 2) Intrans. in mid. and aor. 2 act. to stand around; absol. 18, 233. 24, 712; with accus. ἀμφίστασθαι ἄστυ, to invest the city, 18, 233. Od. 8, 5. (Hom. only intrans.)

ἀμφιστρατάομαι (στρατός), to invest with an army, to beleaguer; with accus. πόλιν, 11, 713.†

ἀμφιστρεφής, ές, poet. (στρέφω), gen. έος, turned to different sides [of the three heads of a dragon, Schol. ἀλλήλαις περιπεπλεγμέναι=] interlaced, intertwined, 11, 40.†

ἀμφιτίθημι (τίθημι), aor. 1 ἀφέθηκα, aor. 2 mid. ἀμφεθέμην, aor. pass. partcp. ἀμφιτεθείς, 1) Act. to place around, to put around or on; κεφαλῇ κυνέην, to put a helmet on the head; hence pass. κυνέη ἀμφιτεθεῖσα, 10, 271. 2) Mid. to put upon oneself; with accus. ξίφος, Od. 21, 431.

ἀμφιτρέμω (τρέμω), to tremble all over, 21, 507. †in tmesis.

Ἀμφιτρίτη, ἡ (according to Herm. Amfractua, broken in every part), daughter of Nereus, [and accord. to later mythology] wife of Poseidōn, who ruled with him the Mediterranean sea. She bore to him Tritōn, Od. 5, 422. 12, 60.

Ἀμφιτρύων, ωνος (molesting all around, from τρύω), son of Alcæus and Hipponoë, husband of Alcmēnē, father of Iphiclēs and foster father of Heraclēs. He reigned first in Tiryns and later in Thebes, 5, 392. (ι comm. without position.)

*ἀμφιτρομέω, Ep.=ἀμφιτρέμω, to tremble all over, to be very much afraid, τινός, on account of any one, Od. 4, 820.†

*ἀμφιφαείνω, Ep. form for ἀμφιφαίνω, to shine about, τινά, h. Ap. 202.

ἀμφίφαλος, ον (φάλος), furnished with knobs or studs round about, according to the comm. explanation; accord. to Köppen, having a strong crest; or accord. to Buttm. Lexil. 523, whose φάλος stretched from the crest backwards as well as forwards; epith. of the helmet, *5, 743. 7, 41; see φάλος.

ἀμφιφοβέω (φοβέω), aor. pass. ἀμφεφοβήθην, to terrify all round. 2) Pass. to be terrified all round, to fly from, τινά, 16, 290.†

ἀμφιφορεύς, ῆος, ὁ (φέρω), a large vessel which is carried by both sides, a two-handled vase for wine, honey, Od. 2, 290. 2) an urn, 23, 99.

ἀμφιφράζεσθαι, mid. (φράζω), to consider on both sides, to weigh well, 18, 254.†

ἀμφιχαίνω (χαίνω), aor. 2 ἀμφέχανον, to yawn around, to swallow with greediness, τινά, 23, 79.†

ἀμφιχέω (χέω), aor. 1 act. Ep. ἀμφέχευα, Ep. syncop. aor. 2 mid. ἀμφεχύμην (3 sing. ἀμφέχυτο), aor. 1 pass. ἀμφεχύθην. 1) Act. prop. to pour around; metaph. to spread around; ἠέρα τινί, obscurity, mist

around any one, 17, 270. 2) Mid. aor. 1 pass. to be diffused or shed roun be poured about, to surround; with a trop. θείη μιν ἀμφέχυτο ὀμφή, a di voice sounded around him, 2, 41. ἄχος ἀμφεχύθη, distress poured itself her, Od. 4, 716. 2) Spoken of per to embrace; with accus. Od. 16, 214 sol. Od. 22, 498.

ἀμφιχυθείς, see ἀμφιχέω.

ἀμφίχυτος, ον, (χέω) poured aro τεῖχος, a wall cast up all around earth mound, 20, 145.

Ἀμφίων, ίονος (part. ἀμφιών wal around), 1) son of Jasius and Persep (according to Eustath.), father of Ch king of Orchomenus in Bœotia, Oc 285. 2) son of Zeus and Ant brother of Zethus, distinguished fc skill in song and in performing on harp. When he was surrounding Th with a wall, the stones joined thems together at the sound of his lyre. wife Niobē bore him several children 11, 262. Homer distinguishes the though later tradition often confo them, cf. O. Müller, Gesch. hell. Stä I. S. 231. 3) a leader of the Epean 692.

ἀμφότερος, η, ον (ἄμφω), both. O sing in Hom. only the neut. as adv. ὁ τερον βασιλεύς τ᾽ ἀγαθὸς κρατερός τ᾽ α τῆς, both at once, a good king and a l spearman, 3, 179; often in the dua plur. 5, 156. 17, 395.

Ἀμφοτερός, ὁ, a Trojan slain by F cles, 16, 415.

ἀμφοτέρωθεν, adv. from both side both sides. 5, 726. Od. 7, 113.

ἀμφοτέρωσε, adv. towards both in both directions, γεγωνέμεν, *8, 22

ἀμφουδίς, adv. (prob. from ἀμφίς οὔδας), from the ground; κάρη ἀείρε raise the head from the ground, Ο 237.†

ἀμφράσσαιτο, see ἀναφράζομαι.

ἄμφω, τώ, τά, τώ, gen. ἀμφοῖν, spoken of single persons, and also o parties, as 2, 124. Hom. has onl nom. and accus. Sometimes inde Cer. 15.

ἄμφωτος, ον (οὖς), two-eared, handled, ἄλεισον, Od. 22, 10.†

ἀμῷεν, Ep. for ἀμάοιεν, see ἀμάω.

ἀμώμητος, ον (μωμέομαι), irrepr able, blameless, 12, 109.†

ἄν, a particle, Ep. and enclit. κέ, t a vowel κέν (κέ is prop. only a dia variation of ἄν, and in use gen agrees with it, although it does indicate the conditional relation s tinctly, and hence admits a more quent use.—These particles indic conditional proposition or sentence they show that the predicate of th tence is not true absolutely, but is considered as depending upon ce circumstances or conditions. The E language has no word perfectly equiv to ἄν (though it may sometimes be t lated by *perhaps, possibly*, Lat. *forte*), but expresses its meaning by the mood of the verb (*may, can, might, could*, etc. write). It cannot therefore stand in sentences which express an unconditional affirmation, but only in the following cases: I) With the indicat. 1) With the indicat. pres. and perf. ἄν cannot stand, because that which is represented as actually passing or past can be subjected to no condition. The same, according to Herm. de partic. ἄν holds true of κέ; and the passages in which κέ is connected with these tenses are changed by him, e. g. τῷ καί κέ τις εὔχεται ἀνήρ—λιπέσθαι, where, according to Cod. Vrat., τέ is to be read for κέ, 14, 484; δῶρον δ᾽, ὅ ττι κέ μοι δοῦναι φίλον ἦτορ ἀνώγει, where we must read ἀνώγῃ, Od. 1, 316; τάδε κ᾽ αὐτὸς οἴεαι, where Herm. reads γ᾽ αὐτός, Od. 3, 255; ὅτε κέν ποτ᾽—ζώννυνταί τε νέοι, καὶ ἐπεντύνωσαι ἄεθλα, Od. 24, 87, where we must with Thiersch, Gr. Gram. § 322, 11, read ὅτε περ, or take ζώννυνται as subjunct. and read ἐπεντύνωνται. According to Rost, however, κέ may accompany the indicat. pres. wherever the discourse relates to things which are to be derived from others as natural consequences, as 14, 484. Od. 3, 255. 2) With the fut. indicat. we frequently find the Ep. κέ (rarely ἄν), when the proposition expressed in the fut. is dependent upon a condition; εἰ δ᾽ Ὀδυσσεὺς ἔλθοι—αἶψά κε—βίας ἀποτίσεται ἀνδρῶν, Od. 17, 540. cf. 22, 66. Commonly, however, the conditional clause is wanting; εἴρεαι, ὁππόθεν εἰμέν· ἐγὼ δέ κέ τοι καταλέξω, I will (if thou wilt hear) tell thee, Od. 3, 80, cf. 4, 176. 7, 273. 22, 42. 3) It stands with the indicat. of the histor. tenses (impf. plupf. and aor.), *a*) to indicate that the proposition would prove true, or would have proved true, only on a certain condition; but as that condition has not been, or cannot be fulfilled, so the proposition has not proved, or will not prove true; καί νύ κ᾽ ἔτι πλείονας Λυκίων κτάνε—Ὀδυσσεύς, εἰ μὴ ἄρ᾽ ὀξὺ νόησε Ἕκτωρ, and now would Ulysses have slain still more Lycians, if Hector had not immediately observed it, 5, 679. The condition is often wanting, and must be supplied from the context. ἦ τέ κεν ἤδη λάϊνον ἔσσο χιτῶνα, indeed, thou wouldst be already clothed with a tunic of stone, 3, 56. *b*) To denote repetition in past time, the action being represented by ἄν as conditional, viz. as repeated only in certain cases. In Hom., however, this use is exceedingly rare, Od. 2, 104 (19, 149. 24, 139); ἔνθα κ ε ν ἠματίη ὑφαίνεσκεν μέγαν ἱστόν, she was wont to weave (because we believed her, cf. v. 103), where Wolf needlessly reads καί. μάλιστα δέ κ᾽ αὐτὸς ἐνόησε, 13, 734, chiefly himself is wont to experience it, where some take κ᾽ as καί above. and Herm. de part. ἄν, for δέ κ᾽ proposes δέ τ᾽. Likewise οἵ κε τάχιστα ἵκμυαν, Ο 1. 18, 263, where Herm. would

read οἵ τε. A peculiar case is Od. 4, 546. ἦ γάρ μιν ζωόν γε κιχήσεαι ἦ κεν Ὀρέστης κτείνεν ὑποφθάμενος. Nitzsch on this passage says: This aor. with κέν is to be compared with no other sentence of this form; ἦ κεν are closely connected, and the whole is equivalent to κιχήσεαι· εἰ δὲ μή, κτείνεν, or otherwise Orestes has slain him, cf. Rost, Gram. p. 587, and Thiersch, § 353, 1. II) With the subjunct. ἄν serves to define more closely the idea expressed by it. The subj. expresses a *supposed notion* (*res cogitata*), but with reference to a future *decision*; the ἄν indicates the external circumstances and relations upon which the decision depends. 1) In the Epic language the subjunct. with ἄν stands instead of the fut. indicat.; with a certain difference, however, the indicat. fut. representing the future event as already decided; the subjunct. on the other hand representing the future event as one which it is possible may sooner or later occur. τάχ᾽ ἄν ποτε θυμὸν ὀλέσσῃ, he will, it is probable, soon lose his life, 1, 205. οὐκ ἄν τοι χραίσμῃ κίθαρις, thy harp would not [I deem] then avail thee, 3, 54. 2) In dependent clauses, in connexion with conjunctions and pronouns, to represent the event as conditional, i. e. as depending upon circumstances; ὄφρα ἴῃτ᾽ αἴ κ᾽ ὕμμιν ὑπέρσχῃ χεῖρα Κρονίων, whether—would protect you, 4, 249. In like manner, εἴ κε, ἤ κε; ἐπεί κε, ἐπεὶ ἄν; ὅτε κεν, ὅτ᾽ ἄν, ὁπότε κεν, etc., ὃς ἄν or κε, οἷος ἄν; comp. the several conjunctions and the relative. III) With the optative, ἄν expresses the fact that the s u p p o s i t i o n expressed by this mood is conditional; εἰ καὶ ἐγώ σε βάλοιμι—αἶψά κε—εὖχος ἐμοὶ δοίης, thou wouldst confer renown upon me, 16, 625; hence it stands, 1) To express an undetermined possibility. κείνοισι δ᾽ ἄν οὔτις—μαχέοιτο, no one would be able to contend, 1, 271. 2) The ἄν with the optat. often stands as a softer mode of expressing a command or entreaty, 2, 250, and with οὐ in the question οὐκ ἄν ἐρύσαιο; couldst thou not hold him back? instead of hold him back, restrain him, 5, 456. 3) In interrogative sentences, where the optative can be generally translated by *can* or *could*. On the optat. with ἄν in dependent clauses, e. g. with relative pronouns, see under the relative and conjunctions. IV) ἄν with the infin. and partcp. expresses also a condition, which will be clearly seen by resolving these forms of the verb into clauses expressed by the finite verb, 9, 684. V) Repetition of ἄν and κε. Hom. never repeats ἄν, but he unites 1) ἄν with κε to give greater stress to the condition, 11, 187. 13, 127. In other cases the reading is doubtful, as Od. 6, 259, where Nitzsch would read καί for κέν. 2) The repetition of κε is rare, Od. 4, 733. VI) ἄν is properly short; however, it seems long in 8, 21. 406.

ἄν, 1) Poet. abbrev. for ἀνά (better ἀν), before ν, τ; becomes before labials ἀμ, before palatals ἀγ. 2) Poet. abbrev. for ἄνα, i. e. ἀνέστη, he arose, 3, 268. cf. ἄνα.

ἀνά, abbrev. ἀν, ἀμ, ἀγ, 1) Preposition. *up, upon, on,* opposed to κατά, comm. with accus. Ep. also with gen. and dat. 1) With gen. only in the phrase ἀνὰ νηὸς βαίνειν, to go on shipboard, Od. 2, 416. 9, 177. 15, 284; where, however, according to Rost, Gr. p. 495, it is better to assume a tmesis, so that the gen. appears to depend upon ἀναβαίνειν. 2) With dat., *on, upon,* ἀνὰ σκήπτρῳ, upon the sceptre, 1, 15. ἀνὰ ὤμῳ, Od. 11, 128. ἀνὰ χερσίν, on the hands, h. Cer. 286. 3) With accus. a) Of place: to indicate a direction to a higher object, *up, upon;* τιθέναι τι ἀνὰ μυρίκην, 10, 466, ἀναβαίνειν ἀνὰ ῥωγᾶς, to ascend the steps, Od. 22, 143; to denote extension, *through, throughout, along.* ἀνὰ νῶτα, along the back, 13, 547. ἀνὰ δῶμα, through the house, 4, 670; in like manner, ἀνὰ στρατόν, μάχην, ὅμιλον: ἀνὰ στόμα ἔχειν, to have in the mouth, 2, 250. φρονεειν ἀνὰ θυμόν, to revolve in the mind, 2, 36. πᾶσαν ἀν' ἰθύν, in every undertaking, Od. 4, 434. ἀν' ἰθύν, upwards, Od. 8, 377. b) Of time, only ἀνὰ νύκτα, through the night, 14, 80. c) Of number, *to, up to.* ἀνὰ εικοσι μέτρα χεῦεν, Od. 9, 209. II) Adv. *thereon, thereupon.* ἀνὰ βότρυες ἦσαν, grapes were thereon, 18. 562. It stands pleonastically with a verb compounded with ἀνά, 23, 709. In composition it has the same signification, and besides it indicates direction towards the point of starting, *back again* [the Lat. *re-* denoting repetition, e. g. ἀναφράζομαι.

ἄνα is 1) A prepos. with retracted accent, and stands as interj. for ἀνάστηθι: *up then;* comm. ἀλλ' ἄνα, 6, 331. 2) A vocat. from ἄναξ, only in the construct. ὦ ἄνα, Ζεῦ ἄνα.

ἀναβαίνω, Ep. ἀμβαίνω (βαίνω), aor. 1 ἀνέβησα, aor. 2 ἀνέβην, aor. 1 mid. ἀνεβησάμην (once partcp. ἀναβησάμενοι, transit. Od. 15, 475), 1) Trans. in aor. 1 act. *to lead up, to cause to ascend*=τινά, any one (into a ship, to *put* a person *on board,* &c. 1, 144), once in the mid. νὼ ἀναβησάμενοι, *after* they had *put* us on board, Od. 15, 475. II) Intrans. in the aor. 2 act. *to ascend, to go up;* with accus. οὐρανόν, to mount to heaven, 1, 497; ὑπερῴα, to ascend to the upper apartments, Od. 23, 1; more frequently with εἰς, ἐπί τι; once with dat. νεκροῖς, to pass over the dead bodies, 10, 493; most generally, a) *to ascend the ship* (*go on board,* embark), often with the omission of νῆα (twice with gen. νηός, Od. 2, 416. 9, 177; see ἀνά. β) *to ascend upon land, to land,* Od. 14, 353. γ) *to put to sea, to go from the shore to sea, to sail away,* ἀπὸ Κρήτης, Od. 14, 252; esply ἐς Τροίην, to sail from Greece to Troy, Od. 1, 210. b) Metaph. φάτις ἀνθρώπους ἀναβαίνει, *fame spreads among* men, Od. 6, 29.

ἀναβάλλω, Ep. ἀμβάλλω (βάλλ prop. to throw up. 2) to throw hence *to put off, to delay,* ἄεθλον, (584. II) Mid. to lift oneself, he *begin;* with infinit. ἀείδειν, to be sing, Od. 1, 155. 8, 256 (according old Gramm. from the strong eleva the voice). 2) *to put off, defer, dela* reference to the subject). μηδ' ἔτι ἀμβαλλώμεθα, let us no longer del: work, 2, 436.

ἀνάβατος, ον, Ep. ἄμβατος (ἀναβ *that may be ascended, easy of asc* 434. Od 11, 316.

ἀναβέβρῦχε, 3 sing. perf., the pre: not occur, 17, 54.† in connex. with *the water gushes* or *spouts forth.* Gramm. assume in the pres. ἀναβρ ἀναβρῦζω; others, as Buttm. Le: trace it by comparison with ὑπο (*under water*) to ἀναβρέχω, when reading ἀναβέβροχεν; others again root βρυχάομαι, from which occu perf. βέβρῦχα, but with ῦ.

ʼΑναβησίνεως, ὁ (that travels by a Phæacian, Od. 8, 113.

ἀναβληδήν, Ep. ἀμβληδήν (ἀναβά 1), *rising* with a sudden impulse *mently,* γοᾶν, 22, 476.† [to lamen vehement outcry, Passow; *alie suspiriis,* Heyne; cf. ἀναβολάδην].

ἀνάβλησις, ιος, ἡ (βάλλω), *a del procrastination,* κακοῦ, *2, 380. 24,

ἀναβολάδην, Ep. ἀμβολάδην (ἀναβ *throwing up, boiling up.* λέβης (βολάδην, the cauldron boils bubbli 21, 364.†

ἀναβράχω (βράχω), only Ep. a ἔβραχον, *to rattle, to crash, to* spoken of arms, 19, 13; of door 21, 48.

ἀναβρόχω, occurring only in the aor. 1 ἀναβρόξειε, and in the partc 2 pass. ἀναβροχέν, *to swallow up a* *absorb;* of Charybdis: ὅτε ἀνα θαλάσσης ὕδωρ, when she swallo again the sea-water, Od. 12, 240 ὕδωρ ἀπολέσκετ' ἀναβροχέν, the being absorbed and swallowed up disappeared, Od. 11, 586. cf. Buttm 201. *Od.

ἀναβρύχω, see ἀναβέβρυχε.

ἀναγιγνώσκω (γιγνώσκω), only ἀνέγνων, *to know accurately, to p clearly,* with accus. τινά, Od. γόνον, Od. 1, 216. Il. 13, 734; σῆμα 19, 250. 23, 206; absol. *to perceive c 13, 734.

ἀναγκαίη, ἡ (prop. fem. from ἀνα Ep. *compulsion, necessity,* dat. ἀν by force, 4, 300. Od. 19, 73.

ἀναγκαῖος, αίη, αῖον (ἀνάγκη), c *sory, urgent, coercive,* necessary; a compulsory word, i. e. a dec authoritative sentence, Od. 17, 399 ἀναγκαῖον, the day of force, of slav 836,=δούλιον ἦμαρ. 2) *of necess compulsion, by compulsion,* πολε Od. 24, 499.

ἀνάγκη, ἡ (ἀνάγω), *force, com*

violence, necessity, often in the dat. ἀνάγκῃ, from necessity, *on compulsion, forced*, ἀείδειν, πολεμίζειν; also act. *with violence, vehemently* : ἰσχειν, κελεύειν, ὑπ' ἀνάγκης, by force. Od. 19, 156.

ἀναγνάμπτω (γνάμπτω), aor. 1 ἀνέγναμψα, aor. 1 pass. ἀνεγνάμφθην, *to bend back*; δεσμόν, to loose the bond, Od. 14, 348; pass. αἰχμὴ ἀνεγνάμφθη, the point was bent back, 3, 348. 7, 259.

ἀνάγω (ἄγω) fut. ἀνάξω, aor. 2 act. ἀνήγαγον, 1) *to lead up, to lead to a high place*, from the sea-coast into the country, τινά, Od. 4, 534, or into the high seas, thus often spoken of the voyage to Troy; to take any one to sea, γυναῖκα ἐξ ἀπίης γαίης, 3, 48; Ἑλένην, 6, 292; λαὸν ἐνθάδε (to Troy), 9, 338; also mly of sea-voyages, 13, 627. b) *to conduct home*, γυναῖκα δόμονδε, Od. 3, 272; often, mly, *to conduct to, to bring*, spoken of persons and things: δῶρα, to bring presents, 8, 203; τινὰ ἐς μέσσον, Od. 18, 89. 2) Mid. prop. to conduct oneself up. *to put out to sea, to sail away.* τοὶ δ' ἀνάγοντο, they sailed back, 1, 478. Od. 19, 202.

ἀναδέδρομα, see ἀνατρέχω.

ἀναδέρκω, Ep. (δέρκω), aor. 2 ἀνέδρακον, *to look up, to look upwards*; ὀφθαλμοῖσιν, to open the eyes again, (14, 436.†

ἀναδέσμη, ἡ (δέω), *a fillet, a head-band*, of females, 22, 469.†

ἀναδέχομαι, depon. mid. (δέχομαι), aor. 1 ἀνεδεξάμην, aor. sync. ἀνεδέγμην, *to take up*, σάκος, 5, 619. 2) *to take upon oneself, to bear, to endure*, ὀϊζύν, Od. 17, 563.

*ἀναδίδωμι (δίδωμι), aor. 1 ἀνέδωκα, *to proffer, to present, to give*, with accus. h. Merc. 111.

*ἀναδύνω (δύνω)=ἀναδύομαι, Batr. 90.

ἀναδύω (δύω), only mid. and aor. 2 ἀνέδυν, infinit. ἀναδῦναι, aor. 1 mid. ἀνεδυσάμην [ἀνεδύσετο or ἀνεδύσατο, Buttm. § 96. note 9], intrans. *to emerge, to come forth out of*; with gen. ἁλός, from the sea, 1, 359; and with accus. κῦμα, v. 496, to emerge from the wave. 2) *to withdraw* [towards the interior of a crowd]; ἐς ὅμιλον, to retreat into the crowd, 7, 218; and with accus. πόλεμον, to avoid the war, 13, 225; absol. Od. 9, 377. (ἀνδύεται poet. for ἀναδύεται.)

ἀνάεδνος, ον (ἔδνον), 1) *ungifted*, i. e. for whom the bridegroom presents no gifts to the parents, 9, 146. 2) *without dowry*, with whom the bridegroom receives nothing from the parents, 13, 366. This explanation is, however, justly rejected by Spitzner on 9, 146. *11.

ἀναείρω (ἀείρω), aor. 1 ἀνάειρα Ep. for ἀνήειρα. 1) *to raise, to lift up*; with accus. χεῖρας ἀθανάτοισι, to lift up the hands to the gods, 7, 130; τινά=to *throw a man*, spoken of wrestlers striving to lift up and throw each other. 2) *to lift, to bear away* (as a prize), δύω τάλαντα, 23, 614; κρητῆρα, 23, 882.

ἀναθηλέω, Ep. (θηλή), fut. ἀναθηλήσω, *to become verdant again, to bloom, bud or sprout out again*, 1, 236.†

ἀνάθημα, τό (τίθημι), that which is put up, esply *a votive offering to a deity* which is put up in a temple [not Homeric]. 2) *any present of value*; hence, *ornament, decoration.* Thus H. calls dancing and singing ἀναθήματα δαιτός, embellishments of the feast or table ['*enlivening sequel of the banquet's joys*,' Cp.], Od. 1, 152. 21, 430.

ἀναθρώσκω (θρώσκω), *to spring or leap up, to bound off.* ὕψι ἀναθρώσκειν, to bound up into the air, spoken of a descending rock, 13, 140.†

ἀναιδείη, ἡ (ἀναιδής), *shamelessness, impudence, effrontery.* ἀναιδείην ἐπιειμένος, clothed in impudence, 1, 149. ἐπιβῆναι ἀναιδείης, to have given oneself up to wantonness ['*to have overpassed the bounds of modesty.*' Cp.], Od. 22, 424.

ἀναιδής, ές (αἰδέομαι), *shameless, impudent*, as the suitors of Penelope. 2) *ungovernable, dreadful*, as κυδοιμός, 5, 593; λᾶας, the terrible or monstrous stone, 14, 521. Od. 11, 597.

ἀναίμων, ον (αἶμα), gen. ονος, *bloodless, without blood*, spoken of the gods, 5, 342.†

ἀναιμωτί, adv. *without bloodshed*, 17, 363. Od. 18, 149.

ἀναίνομαι, aor. 1 ἠνηνάμην, Ep. ἀνηνάμην, (fm ἀνά and αἶνος, Död.) [according to Buttm. r. ἀν or ἀνα (=no) with termin. αίνω], *to deny, to refuse, to reject*; with accus. δῶρα, to spurn gifts, 9, 679; ἔργον ἀεικές, a shameful act, Od. 3, 265; δόσιν, Od. 4, 651. 10, 18; τινά, to reject any one. Od. 8, 212; with infin. *to deny*, ὁ δ' ἀναίνετο μηδὲν ἑλέσθαι, said that he had not received any thing, 18, 500, also to *refuse* to do [λοιγὸν ἀμῦναι], cf. 450; absol. 7, 93. 9, 510.

ἀναιρέω (αἱρέω), aor. 2 ἀνεῖλον, and its partcp. ἀνελών, fut. mid. ἀναιρήσομαι, aor. 2 ἀνειλόμην, Ep. ἀνελ-. 1) *to lift up, to take away, to remove*; βοῦν ἀπὸ χθονός, to lift an ox from the earth, Od. 3, 453; ἄεθλια, to bear off prizes, 23, 736; πολλά, to receive much, said of a beggar, Od. 18, 16. 2) Mid. oftener, *to take up for oneself, to receive, to bear away*; κοῦρον, to take a child in the arms, 16, 8; οὐλοχύτας, to take the sacred barley, 2, 410; ἐπιφροσύνας, to assume reason, to become prudent, Od. 19, 22. [εἴ σ' ἀνελοίμην=if I were to *take* you (*hire* you), of a day-labourer, Od. 18, 357.]

ἀναΐσσω (ἀΐσσω), aor. 1 ἀνήϊξα, *to leap up, to rise suddenly* from a sitting posture, 3, 216. Od. 1, 410. πηγαὶ ἀναΐσσουσι, the fountains gush forth, 22, 148; once with accus. ἅρμα, to leap (upon =) into the chariot, 24, 440.

ἀναίτιος, ον (αἰτία), *without guilt, blameless.* ἀναίτιον αἰτιᾶσθαι, to impeach a guiltless individual, 11, 653. Od. 20, 135.

ἀνακαίω (καίω), *to kindle*, πῦρ, *Od. 7, 13. 9, 251.

*ἀνακεκλόμεναι, see ἀνακέλομαι.

*ἀνακέλομαι, poet. (κέλομαι), aor. 2 with redupl. ἀνεκεκλόμην, *to call upon, to invoke*, τινά, h. Pan. 18, 5.

ἀνακεράννυμι (κεράω), aor. ἀνεκέρασα, Ep. σσ, *to mix again*; κρητῆρα οἴνου, to mix the mingling vessel again full of wine, Od. 3, 390† [*to mingle wine again in the replenished bowl*, cf. 339].

ἀνακηκίω (κηκίω), *to spout* or *bubble up*; *to gush forth*, of sweat [*oozing* forth] and blood, •7, 262. 13, 705.

ἀνακλῑ́νω (κλίνω), aor. 1 ἀνέκλῑνα, partcp. ἀγκλίνας Ep. for ἀνακλίνας, aor. 1 pass. ἀνεκλίνθην, 1) *to incline, to lean back, to cause to rest*; τόξον ποτὶ γαίῃ, to let the bow rest (against =) upon the earth, 4, 113. The Schol. refers the action of ἀγκ. in 4, 113, to the subject, ἐπήρεισεν ἑαυτόν. Am. Ed.] πρός τι, Od. 18, 103; pass. aor. *to lean oneself back*, spoken of persons rowing and of persons sleeping. ἀνακλινθεὶς πέσεν ὕπτιος, leaning back he sank supine, Od. 9, 371. 2) *to lean back* = *to push back, to open*, opposed to ἐπιθεῖναι; θύρην, to open the door, Od. 22, 156; so also νέφος, 5, 571; λόχον [i. e. the *wooden horse*, filled with concealed warriors], Od. 11, 525.

•ἀνακλύζω (κλύζω), *to wash*, or *dash up*, Ep. 3.

ἀνακοντίζω (ἀκοντίζω), *to spout out, to dart forth, to gush out*, spoken of blood, 5, 113.†

ἀνακόπτω (κόπτω), *to strike (dash* or *drive) back, to undo*, ὀχῆας, the bolts, Od. 21, 47.†

ἀνακράζω (κράζω), aor. 2 ἀνέκραγον, *to cry out, to speak* (my thoughts) *aloud, to prate garrulously*, Od. 14, 467.†

ἀνακρεμάννυμι (κρεμάννυμι), aor. 1 ἀνεκρέμασα, partcp. ἀγκρεμάσας, *to hang up*; τί πασσάλῳ, to hang up any thing upon a hook or peg, Od. 1, 440. h. Ap. 8.

*ἀνακτορίη, ἡ (ἀνάκτωρ), *rule, command*, the direction of steeds, h. Ap. 234.

ἀνακτόριος, ίη, ιον (ἀνάκτωρ), *belonging to the master*, Od. 15, 397.†

ἀνακυμβαλιάζω (κύμβαλον), *to be overturned with a rattling noise*. δίφροι ἀνακυμβαλίαζον, the o'ertumbled chariots rang [Cp.], 16, 379.†

ἀναλέγω and ἀλλέγω (λέγω), aor. 1 ἀνέλεξα, infin. ἀλλέξαι, Ep. for ἀναλέξαι, to gather, to collect, ἔντεα, 11, 755; ὀστέα, 21, 321. •Il.

ἀναλκείη, ἡ (ἀλκή), *feebleness, weakness, cowardice*, always in the plur. 6, 74, •Il.

ἄναλκις, ιδος, ὁ ἡ (ἀλκή), *powerless, weak, cowardly*, comm. connected with ἀπτόλεμος, accus. ἀνάλκιδα and ἄναλκιν once, Od. 3, 375.

ἄναλτος, ον (ἄλθω) [ἄλδω = αὐξάνω; whence ἀλτόν = τὸ πολύ. Hes. Cf. adulter, Lob. Techn. 74], not to be satiated, *insatiable*, γαστήρ, Od. 17, 228. 18, 114. •Od.

ἀναλύω and ἀλλύω (λύω), Ep. iterative impf. ἀλλύεσκεν, aor. 1 ἀνέλυσα, *to loose, to unravel*; ἱστόν, to unravel or undo the web, Od. 2, 109. 19, 150; τινὰ ἐκ δεσμῶν, to deliver any one from bonds, Od. 11, 100; πρυμνήσια, Od. 9, 178. 2) Mid. *to*

loose for oneself; τινὰ ἐς φάος, to bring one to the light, h. Merc. 258. (ι where short in the pres, but in 110, long through the accent.)

ἀναμαιμάω (μαιμάω), *to rage thr* with accus. πῦρ ἀναμαιμάει ἄγκεα, t rages through the valleys, 20, 490.4

ἀναμάσσω (μάσσω), fut. ξω, pr *rub on, to anoint*, hence ὁ (viz. ἔργον) σῇ κεφαλῇ ἀναμάξεις, accord Damm: *facinus, quod capiti tuo ut maculam mortiferam*, i. e. whic shalt expiate with thy head, Od. 1! Eustath. derives the metaph. fro wiping of the sword upon the hea slain warrior, to show that he de death. Several modern annotators ever, suppose that the word ἀναμ properly signifies, *to wipe off*, to c and thus stands simply for *to expi* in English, to wash away a crime (ε ing to Bothe), or in French, *se lave crime* (Dugas Montbel).

ἀναμένω, poet. ἀναμίμνω (μένω), ἀνέμεινα, *to expect, to await*, τί, 'H Od. 19, 342.†

ἀναμετρέω (μετρέω), *to re-meas measure back*; Χάρυβδιν, to measu my course again to Charybdis, C 428.†

•ἀναμηλόω (μηλόω), partcp. aor. λώσας, prop. to examine with the according to Ruhnken's conjec. fo πηλήσας, h. Merc. 41.

ἀναμίγνυμι, poet. ἀναμίσγω (μί aor. 1 ἀνέμιξα, partcp. ἀμμίξας, to r *to mingle together*; κρῖ λευκόν, t therewith white barley, Od. 4, τινι, 24, 529. Od. 10, 536.

ἀναμιμνήσκω (μιμνήσκω), aor. ἐμνησα, *to remind*, τινά τι, any any thing, Od. 3, 211.†

ἀναμίμνω (μίμνω), poet. for ἀναμ await, with the accus. 2) Abso wait, to persist, •16, 363.

ἀναμίσγω = ἀναμίγνυμι, Od.

ἀναμορμύρω (μορμύρω), Ep. it impf. ἀνεμορμύρεσκε, *to roar, to re* spoken of Charybdis, Od. 12, 238.†

ἀνανέομαι, Ep. ἀννέομαι, depon (νέομαι), *to rise, to ascend*, spoken sun, Od. 10, 192.†

ἀνανεύω (νεύω), aor. ἀνένευσα, p throw the head up and move it ba token amongst the Greeks of ι opposed to κατανεύω; hence, *to ref* a nod, *to deny, to refuse*, absol. 6, 31 accus. 16, 250; with infin. 16, 252; t to shake my brows [Cp.], *to forbi* sign with the eye-brows, Od. 9, 468.

•ἀνανέω (νέω), aor. ἀνένευσα, tε up, *to recover*, like emergere, Batr.

ἄναντα, adv. *upwards, up hill*, 2!

ἄναξ, ακτος, ὁ (from ἀνά, as πέρι περί), dat. plur. Ep. ἀνάκτεσιν, 1! voc. ἄνα, spoken only of gods. l every *ruler, master, lord*, the mast family, οἴκοιο, Od. 1, 397; ma slaves, 24, 734. Od. 4, 87. 10, 5 esply, *sovereign, king*. a) Spoke *gods*; esply of Apollo, 1. 36. 75. *b*) Of *earthly princes and kings*, prop. the chief of a nation (cf. βασιλεύς). Thus Hom. calls all heroes; but Agamemnon, as commander-in-chief, he calls ἄναξ ἀνδρῶν, Il. once spoken of Orsilochus, ἄναξ ἀνδρεσσιν, 5, 546. [But also Euphētēs, 15, 532; Eumēius, 23, 288 (Am. Ed.).] *c*) Of other noble and principal men, as Tiresias, Od. 11, 143; of the sons of kings, Od. 17, 186.

ἀναξηραίνω (ξηραίνω), aor. 1 ἀνεξήρανα, whence Ep. subj. ἀνξηράνῃ for ἀνεξηρήνῃ, *to dry up*, ἀλωήν, a *seed-plot* (garden, orchard), 21, 347.†

ἀνοίγεσκον, see ἀνοίγω.

ἀναπάλλω (πάλλω), partcp. aor. 2 ἀμπεπαλών, Ep. for ἀναπεπαλών, Ep. aor. sync. 3 sing. ἀνέπαλτο, 1) *to swing upward* or *backward*; often ἔγχος ἀμπεπαλών προΐει, prop. having swung back the spear (to give it more force), he hurled it; *he hurled the uplifted spear*, 3, 355 and often. 2) Pass. mid. together with the Ep. aor. sync. mid. *to leap up, to spring up*, ἀναπάλλεται ἰχθύς, 23, 692; of Achilles, to leap up (for joy), 20, 424; spoken of a wounded horse, ἀλγήσας ἀνέπαλτο, he sprang up for pain, 8, 85. That the form ἀνέπαλτο belongs to ἀναπάλλω, and not to ἀναφάλλομαι, is proved by Spitzner in Excurs. XVI. z. Il.

ἀναπαύω (παύω), aor. 1 ἀνέπαυσα, *to cause to cease, to let rest*, τινά τινος, any one from a thing; ἔργων, from labour, 17, 550.†

*ἀναπείθω (πείθω), aor. ἀνέπεισα, *to persuade, to prevail upon*; with accus. Batr. 122.

ἀναπείρω, Ep. ἀμπείρω (πείρω), aor. 1 partcp. ἀμπείρας, *to pierce with a spit, to transpierce* or *transfix, to spit*, σπλάγχνα, the entrails, 2, 426.†

ἀναπεπταμένος, η, ον, see ἀναπετάννυμι.

ἀναπετάννυμι (πετάω), aor. 1 ἀνεπέτασα, Ep. σσ, perf. pass. ἀναπέπταμαι, *to spread out, to unfold, to expand*, ἱστία, the sails, 1, 480. Od. 4, 783; pass. said of folding-doors: ἀναπεπταμένας σανίδας ἔχον, they held open the folding-doors, 12, 122.

ἀναπηδάω (πεδάω), aor. 1 ἀνεπήδησα, Ep. ἀμπήδησα, *to leap up, to stand up*, ἐκ λόχου, from ambuscade, 11, 379.†

*ἀναπηλέω = ἀναπάλλω, aor. partcp. ἀναπηλήσας, *to swing upwards*, Hom. h. in Merc. 41, where Wolf after Ruhnken has ἀναμηλώσας, q. v.

ἀναπίμπλημι (πίμπλημι), fut. ἀναπλήσω, aor. 1 ἀνέπλησα, *to fill to the brim, to fill up*; metaph. μοῖραν βιότοιο, to fill the measure of life, 4, 170; πότμον, 11, 263; κακὰ πολλά, prop. to fill up the measure of evils, i. e. to suffer many evils, 15, 132; οἶτον, 8, 34; ἄλγεα, Od. 5, 302; κήδεα, Od. 5, 207.

ἀναπλέω (πλέω), infin. fut. ἀναπλεύσεσθαι, *to sail up, to sail out*; στεινωπόν, we sailed up the strait, Od. 12, 234; out of port into the open sea, esply spoken of the voyage to Troy, ἐς Τροίην, 11, 22.

ἀνάπνευσις, ιος, ἡ, *respiration, the re-*

covering breath, respite (breathing-time). πολέμοιο, rest from war, *11, 801.

ἀναπνέω (πνέω), aor. 1 ἀνέπνευσα, infin. ἀμπνεῦσαι, Ep. for ἀναπνεῦσαι, imper. aor. syncop. 2 ἄμπνυε, aor. 1 pass. ἀμπνύνθη, and aor. syncop. mid. ἄμπνυτο, Ep. for ἀνέπνυτο, *to respire, to take breath, to rest, to recover oneself*; κακότητος from suffering, 11, 382; πόνοιο, 15, 235. In like signif. the aor. 1 pass. and aor. sync. mid. ὁ δ' ἀμπνύνθη καὶ ἀνέδρακεν ὀφθαλμοῖσιν, he breathed again, and opened his eyes, 14, 436. ὅτε δή ῥ' ἄμπνυτο καὶ ἐς φρένα θυμὸς ἀγέρθη, when he breathed again, and life returned to his breast, Od. 5, 458. cf. 11, 359.

ἀνάποινος, ον (ποίνη), *without ransom, unransomed*, 1, 99.†

ἀναπρήθω (πρήθω), aor. ἀνέπρησα, prop. to light up; to cause to blaze up; *to burst out* [orig. = *to spirtle, to fizz*, Buttm.]; in Hom. only δάκρυα, to shed a flood of tears (cf. Buttm. Lex. p. 484), 9, 433. Od. 2, 81. Others: to shed hot tears. Död. considers it a syncopated form of ἀναπεράω, p. 8.

ἀνάπτω (ἅπτω), aor. ἀνῆψα, perf. pass. and imperat. ἀνήφθω, *to hang up, to attach, to affix*; πείρατα, to attach the ropes to the mast, Od. 9, 137; ἐξ αὐτοῦ sc. ἱστοῦ, which according to the Schol. is to be supplied from ἱστοπέδῃ, Od. 12, 51. 162; ἀγάλματα, to hang up, suspend, votive offerings (in a temple) Od. 3, 274. Metaph. μῶμον, to impute fault, blame, Od. 2, 84. *Od.

ἀνάπυστος, ον (ἀναπυνθάνομαι), *sought out, known*, Od. 11, 274.†

ἀναρπάζω (ἁρπάζω), aor. 1 ἀνήρπασα, partcp. ἀναρπάξας, *to snatch up, to bear away upwards, to pull out*, ἔγχος, 22, 276; hence, *to hurry away*; τινὰ ἀπὸ μάχης, to drag a man out of the battle, 16, 438; spoken esply of a tempest, Od. 4, 515. 5, 419.

ἀναρρήγνυμι (ῥήγνυμι), aor. 1 ἀνέρρηξα, *to tear up, to tear in pieces*, with accus. βοὸς βοείην, the skin of the ox; spoken of a lion which seizes an ox, 18, 582; γαῖαν, 20, 63. 2) *to break through, to destroy*, τεῖχος, 7, 461. *Il.

ἀναρριπτέω = ἀναρρίπτω, only pres. and impf. Od. 13, 78.†

ἀναρρίπτω, also ἀναρριπτέω (ῥίπτω), aor. ἀνέρριψα, *to throw up, to cast upward*; ἅλα πηδῷ, to fling up the brine with the oar (to indicate hard rowing), Od. 7, 328; and without πηδῷ, Od. 10, 30.

ἀναρροιβδέω (ῥοιβδέω), aor. ἀνερροίβδησα, *to swallow up again, to absorb again*. Χάρυβδις ἀναρροιβδεῖ ὕδωρ, Charybdis sucks back again the water, *Od. 12, 104. 236.

ἀνάρσιος, ον (ἄρω), *not fitting, irreconcileable*; hence, *hostile, inimical*, 24, 365. Od. 10, 459.

ἄναρχος, ον (ἄρχω), *without leader*, *Il. 2, 703. 726.

*ἀνασείω, poet. ἀνασσείω (σείω), *to brandish aloft*, δοῦρα, h. in Ap. 403.

ἀνασεύω (σεύω), Ep. syncop. aor. mid. ἀνέσσυτο, *to spring up*; αἷμα ἀνέσσυτο, the blood spouted up, 11, 458.†

ἀνασπάω, (σπάω), aor. mid. ἀνεσπά-σάμην, *to draw up*. Mid. to draw up for oneself, *to draw out*; ἔγχος ἐκ χροός, to draw out the spear from the body, 13, 274.†

ἄνασσα, ἡ (ἄναξ), *queen, mistress*, only three times; spoken of Dêmêtêr, 14, 326; of Athênê, Od. 3, 380; and of a mortal, Od. 6, 149.

ἀνάσσω (ἄναξ), fut. ἀνάξω, infin. aor. 1 mid. ἀνάξασθαι, 1) *to rule, to reign, to be sovereign*; spoken both of men and gods, comm. with dat. 1, 180; less often with gen. Τενέδοιο, Ἀργείων, 1, 38; with prep. μετ’ ἀθανάτοισιν, to rule among the immortals, 4, 61;—ἐν Βουδείῳ, to reign in Budêum, to have the royal power, 16, 572; with gen. and dat. together: Τρώεσσιν τιμῆς τῆς Πριάμου, to rule the Trojans with the power of Priam, 20, 180. Od. 24, 30. Pass. *to be ruled*, τινί, by any one, Od. 4, 177; once in the mid. τρὶς ἀνάξασθαι γένε’ ἀνδρῶν, to reign through three generations, Od. 3, 245. The accus. does not depend upon ἀνάξασθαι, but is accus. denoting the length of time, cf. Nitzsch ad loc.

ἀνασταδόν, adv. (ἵστημι), *standing upright*, *9, 671. 23, 469.

ἀναστεναχίζω = ἀνασтενάχω, poet. *to groan aloud*, νειόθεν ἐκ κραδίης, deeply from the breast, 10, 9.† ed. Wolf, where others read ἀνεστονάχιζε.

ἀνασтενάχω (στενάχω), *to sigh out, to groan aloud, to lament*, τινά, for any one, 23, 211. Mid. to sigh aloud; intrans. *18, 315.

ἀναστοναχίζω=ἀνασтεναχίζω, the earlier reading, cf. Spitzner Excurs. III.

ἀναστρέφω (στρέφω), aor. 1 ἀνέστρεψα, prop. *to turn about, to turn around, to overturn*, 23, 436. 2) Mid. *to turn oneself around, to ramble about, versari*. γαῖαν ἀναστρέφομαι, I tarry, or dwell, in a land, Od. 13, 326.

ἀναστρωφάω, poet. form of ἀναστρέφω, e. g. τόξον πάντῃ, to turn the bow in every direction, Od. 21, 394.†

(ἀνασχέθω), assumed pres. for the Ep. aor. 2 ἀνέσχεθον, see ἀνέχω.

ἀνεσχέμεν, see ἀνέχω.

ἀνάσχεο, for ἀνάσχου, see ἀνέχω.

ἀνάσχετος, ον, Ep. ἄνσχετος (ἀνέχω), *that may be endured, to be borne, tolerable*, Od. 2, 63.†

ἀνασχών, see ἀνέχω.

ἀνατέλλω (τέλλω), aor. 1 ἀνέτειλα, *to cause to come up*; ἀμβροσίην ἵπποις, to cause ambrosia to spring up for the steeds, 5, 777.†

ἀνατίθημι (τίθημι), fut. ἀναθήσω, *to place or set up, to hang up*; only metaph. ἐλεγχείην τινί, to make a charge upon or against any one, 22, 100.†

ἀνατλῆμι (ΤΛΑ’Ω), pres. obsolete aor. 2 ἀνέτλην, *to take upon oneself, to bear, to endure*, κήδεα, Od. 14, 47; φάρμακον, to

endure the magic draught, viz. to stand its strength, *Od. 10, 327; h. 14, 6.

ἀνατολή, ἡ (ἀνατέλλω), poet. *the rising* of the sun; in the plur. 4.†

ἀνατρέπω (τρέπω), *to overturn*; the mid. aor. 2 ἀνετραπόμην, *to fall to fall backwards*, *6, 64. 14, 447.

ἀνατρέχω (τρέχω), aor. 2 ἀνέδ perf. ἀναδέδρομα, 1) *to run up, to up, to rise up*; ἐγκέφαλος παρ’ ἀνέδραμεν ἐξ ὠτειλῆς, the brain from the wound upon the haft-h the spear), i. e. the socket of the head (L. and S.), 17, 297 [see also πυκναὶ σμώδιγγες ἀνέδραμον, fr weals rose up from blows, 23, 717 ἀναδέδρομε πέτρη, the rock *run rises up*, Od. 5, 412. 10. 4; and of Achilles: ἀνέδραμεν ἔρνεϊ ἶσος, up (shot up) like a shoot, 18, 56. *run back*, with αὖθις, ὀπίσω, 5, 59 ἀπέλεθρον, 11, 354.

ἄναυδος, ον (αὐδή), *without voice, less*, *Od. 5, 466. 10, 378.

ἀναφαίνω (φαίνω), aor. 1 ἀνέφην *to cause to shine, to make bright* or ἀμοιβηδὶς δ’ ἀνέφαινον δμωαί, the kindled the fire by turns (viz. to p light), Od. 18, 310; comm. meta *cause to appear, to disclose, to disco show*, θεοπропίας, divine mysteries, ποδῶν ἀρετήν, 20, 411; τινά, to di any one, to make him known, Od. ἐπεσβολίας, to show loquacity, Od. II) Mid. and pass. *to shine forth, to oneself*. ἀναφαίνεται ἀστὴρ ἐκ νεφ constellation, a star, shines forth the clouds, 11, 62; also metaph. ὅ ἀναφ., destruction appears, 11, 174; ἄρουρα, Od. 10, 29.

ἀναφαδά, adv. = ἀναφανδόν, * 221.

ἀναφανδόν (ἀναφαίνω), *visibly, o *16, 178.

ἀναφέρω (φέρω), aor. 1 ἀνένεικο mid. ἀνενεικάμην. 1) *to bring up, t up*; Κέρβερον ἐξ Ἀΐδαο, Od. 11, 6 Mid. *to fetch up from oneself*, sc. t ἀδινῶς ἀνενείκατο, he drew a deep t a deep sigh, 19, 314 (according Schol. he groaned out deeply; wh plies the ellipsis with στεναγμό Buttm. Lex. p. 105.

ἀναφλύω (φλύω), *to gush up, to up, to boil*, as boiling water, 21, 36

ἀναφράζομαι (φράζομαι), aor. 1 ἀ σάμην, optat. ἀμφράσσαιτο, Ε ἀνεφρ., *to observe again, or to ro* οὐλήν, the scar, Od. 19, 391.†

ἀναχάζομαι, mid. (χάζομαι), aor. χασάμην, partcp. Ep. ἀναχασσάμε *retreat, to retire*, Od. 7, 280. 11, the Il. mly. out of the battle; comm ἄψ, ὀπίσω, 11, 461.

ἀναχωρέω (χωρέω), fut. ήσω, *way, to retire*, often absol. with ἄψ 4, 305; πόλινδε, 10, 210; ἐκ μεγάρ 17, 461. ἀνεχώρησαν μεγάροιο μ they withdrew to a recess of the palace, Od. 22, 270.

ἀναψῦχω (ψύχω). aor. 1 pass. ἀνεψύχθην, to revive by a cool breeze, to refresh, ἀνθρώπους, the men (by Zephyrus), Od. 4, 568; φίλον ἦτορ, to refresh themselves, 13, 84; ἕλκος, to cool a (chafed and burning) wound, 5, 795. Pass. to be refreshed, to revive. ἀνέψυχθεν φίλον ἦτορ, 10, 575.

ἀνδάνω, Ion. and poet. imperf. ἥνδανον and ἐήνδανον, aor. 2 ἅδον for ἕαδον, and εὔαδον with the digamma, perf. 2 ἕαδε, to please, to gratify, to be agreeable; with dat. of the pers. ἅδε Ἕκτορι μῦθος, the word pleased Hector, 12, 80. 18, 510. Od. 3, 150: with two datives, 1, 24; with infin. οὐδ᾿ Αἴαντι ἥνδανε θυμῷ ἐστάμεν, it pleased not Ajax in his heart [θυμῷ, local dat.] to stand, 15, 674; ἑαδὼς μῦθος, a pleasing, agreeable address, 9, 173. Od. 18, 422.

ἄνδιχα, adv. (ἀνά and δίχα), in two parts, in twain, asunder; κεάζειν, to split asunder, 16, 412; δάσασθαι, 18, 511.

ἀνδράγρια, τά (ἀνήρ, ἄγρα), spoils taken from an enemy slain, βροτόεντ᾿, the gory spoils [Cp.], 14, 509.†

Ἀνδραιμονίδης, ου, ὁ, son of Andræmon = Thoas, 7, 168.

Ἀνδραίμων, ονος, ὁ, husband of Gorgô daughter of Œneus, and father of Thoas, who after Œneus reigned in Calydôn in Ætolia, 2, 638.

ἀνδραχάς, adv. (ἀνήρ), i. q. κατ᾿ ἄνδρας, man by man. Od, 13, 14.†

ἀνδραπόδεσσι, metaplastic dat. plur. from ἀνδράποδον.

ἀνδράποδον, τό, a slave; only in dat. ἀνδραπόδεσσι, as if from ἀνδράπους, 7, 475.† cf. Thiersch, Gram. § 197, 60. [According to Doederl. from ἀνήρ and ἀποδόσθαι to sell, al. ἀνήρ, πούς.]

ἀνδραχθής, ές (ἀνήρ, ἄχθος), poet. gen. έος, man-burdening, as heavy as a man can carry: χερμάδια, huge stones [a strong man's burden each, Cp.], Od. 10, 121.†

ἀνδρειφόντης, ου, ὁ (φονεύω), man-slaying, epith. of Arês, *2, 651.

ἀνδρεσσι, Ep. for ἀνδράσι.

ἀνδρόκμητος, ον (κάμνω), made or wrought by men; τύμβος, 11, 371.†

ἀνδροκτασίη, ἡ, Ep. (κτείνω), homicide, slaughter, carnage, esply in battle; comm. in the plur. the slaughter of a single man, 23, 86.

Ἀνδρομάχη. daughter of Eëtiôn, king of the Cilician Thebæ, wife of Hector, 6, 422. Her father and seven brothers were slain by Achilles. She was tenderly attached to her husband. According to a later tradition, she became, after Hector's death, the wife of Neoptolemus.

ἀνδρόμεος, έη, εον (ἀνήρ), belonging to a man, manly, human; κρέας, αἷμα, χρώς, human flesh, blood, skin; ὅμιλος, the crowd of men, 11, 538.

ἀνδρότης, ἡ, a false reading for ἀδροτής.

ἀνδροφάγος, ον (φαγεῖν), man-devouring, cannibal, epith. of Polyphêmus, Od. 10, 200.†

ἀνδροφόνος, ον, poet. (φονεύω), man-slaying, epith. of Arês and Hector, 4, 441. 1, 242; φάρμακον, a destructive drug, a deadly poison, Od. 1, 261.

ἀνδύεται, poet. for ἀναδύεται.

ἀνεγείρω (ἐγείρω), aor. 1 ἀνέγειρα, to awaken, τινὰ ἐξ ὕπνου, any one from sleep, 10, 138. Trop. to arouse, to cheer, τινὰ μειλιχίοις ἐπέεσσι, any one with soothing words, Od. 10, 172.

ἀνέγνων, see ἀναγινώσκω.

ἀνεδέγμεθα, see ἀναδέχομαι.

ἀνέδραμον, see ἀνατρέχω.

ἀνεέργω, Ep. for ἀνείργω (εἴργω), imperf. ἀνέεργον, to press back, to restrain, φάλαγγας, μάχην. *3, 77. 7, 55; with ἐξορίσω, h. Merc. 211.

ἀνέζω, a pres. assumed by the Gramm. for the aor. forms ἀνέσαντες and ἀνέσαιμι; but see ἀνεῖσα.

ἄνειμι (εἶμι), partcp. ἀνιών, imperf. ἀνήιον 1) to ascend, to arise, ἐς περιωπήν, Od. 10, 146. ἠελίου ἀνιόντος, the sun arising, 8, 538. Od. 1, 24 [here = the east]. 2) to return, ἐκ πολέμου, 6, 480; ἐξ Αἰθιόπων, Od. 5, 282; to return home by ship, Od. 10, 332. 3) Mly ἐς τινά, to approach any one, adire aliquem, to ask a favour, 22, 492.

ἀνείμων, ον (εἷμα), gen. ονος, without clothing, destitute of clothing. Od. 3, 348.†

ἀνείρομαι (εἴρομαι), poet. for ἀνέρομαι, only pres. and imperf. to ask, to inquire, to interrogate; with accus. of person, also with double accus. ὅ μ᾿ ἀνείρεαι, ἠδὲ μεταλλᾷς, about which thou questionest me and inquirest, 3, 177.

ἀνεῖσα (εἷσα), a defective aor. 1, of which only the 1 sing. optat. ἀνέσαιμι and partcp. ἀνέσαντες occur: to place upon. ἐς δίφρον ἀνέσαντες ἄγον, they placed him upon the chariot and bore him, 13, 657. εἰ κείνω γε—εἰς εὐνὴν ἀνέσαιμι, if I could but bring them to the marriage-bed, 14, 209. (The Gramm. derive these forms from the obsol. pres. ἀνέζω. Eustath. ad Il. 14, 209, explains both by ἀναθεῖναι; hence with Thiersch, Gram. § 226. Anm., it must be derived from the defective aor. εἷσα. The derivation of the aor. ἀνέσαιμι from ἀνίημι, according to Buttm., Gram. § 108, 4, is inadmissible, as no where else does an aor. 1 optat. of this form occur. [See, however, Krüger Zweiter Theil, § 38, 1, 6. p. 97, and under εἷσα.]

ἀνεκτός, όν (ἔχω), to be borne, sufferable, endurable; in H. mly with negat. ἔργα. οὐδ᾿ ἔτι ἀνεκτά, 1, 573. Od. 20, 223. οὐκέτ᾿ ἀνεκτῶς, no longer tolerable, 8, 355.

ἀνελθών, partcp. aor. 2 from ἀνέρχομαι.

ἀνέλκω (ἕλκω), to draw upward, to draw up; τόξου πῆχυν, to draw up the curve of the bow, in order to shoot [cf. τόξον], 11, 375. 13, 583; but also νευρήν, to draw the bow-string, Od. 21, 128. 150; σταθμόν, 12, 434. 2) Mid. to draw out for oneself; τρίχας, to tear one's hair, 22, 77; ἔγχος, to draw forth the lance from the body of an enemy, Od. 22, 97.

ἀνελών, see ἀναιρέω.

ἄνεμος, ὁ (ἄημι). *a blowing, a breeze, wind.* H. mentions only four winds: Eurus, Notus, Zephyrus, and Boreas, Od. 5, 295.

ἀνεμοσκεπής, ές, poet. (σκέπας), gen. έος, *guarding against the wind, warding off the wind,* epith. of the mantle, 16, 224.†

ἀνεμοτρεφής, ές, poet. (τρέφω), gen. έος, *nourished by wind, storm-nursed.* It occurs twice: κῦμα, a wave excited by the wind, 15, 625; ἔγχος, a spear whose handle is taken from a tree which has been exposed to the wind, and thus become firm in fibre, 11, 256.

Ἀνεμώλεια, ἡ, see Ἀνεμώρεια.

ἀνεμώλιος, ιον (ἄνεμος), *windy;* only trop. *useless. idle, unprofitable, vain.* ἀνεμώλια βάζειν, to prate idle words, 4, 355. Od. 4, 837.

Ἀνεμώρεια, ἡ, later Ἀνεμώλεια, a town in Phocis near Delphi, that derived its name from the strong winds which swept it from Parnassus, 2, 521.

ἀνενείκατο, see ἀναφέρω.

ἀνέπαλτο, see ἀναπάλλω.

ἀνερείπομαι, depon. mid. (ἐρείπω [ut— σφάλλειν, *ad casum dare,* ἀνασφάλλειν, *resurgere,* eodem modo ἐρεῖψαι est *dejicere,* ἀνερεῖψαι, *sustollere, et in altum levare.* Lob. Tech. 44]), aor. 1 ἀνερειψάμην, *to snatch up, to bear away, upwards, to carry off;* with accus. spoken esply of the Harpies and of a tempest, Od. 1, 241. 4, 727; once of the gods, 20, 234 (to assume a pres. ἀνερείπτω is not necessary, cf. Buttm., Gr. Gram. p. 131).

ἀνερύω (ἐρύω), *to draw up, to hoist,* ἱστία, the sails, Od. 9, 77, in tmesis.

ἀνέρχομαι (ἔρχομαι), aor. 2 ἀνήλυθον, *to go up, to ascend,* ἐς σκοπιήν, a watchtower, a place of observation, Od. 10, 97; trop. spoken of a young tree: *to grow up, to shoot up,* Od. 6, 163. 167. 2) *to come back, to return,* with which ἄψ and αὖθις stand, 4, 392. 6, 187.

ἀνερωτάω (ἐρωτάω), imperf. ἀνηρώτων, *to question, to ask again,* Od. 4, 251.†

ἀνέσαιμι, see ἀνεῖσα.

ἄνεσαν, see ἀνίημι.

ἀνέσαντες, see ἀνεῖσα.

ἀνέσει, Ep. for ἀνήσει, see ἀνίημι.

ἀνέσσυτο, see ἀνασεύω.

ἀνέστιος, ον (ἑστία), *without a hearth, without a home,* 9, 63.†

ἄνευ, adv. with gen. *without, apart from;* spoken of persons and things. ἄνευ θεοῦ, without god, without the will or influence of a god, Od. 2, 372. ἄνευ ἐμέθεν, without my wish and knowledge, 15, 232. 2) *far from, remote from.* ἄνευ δηΐων, far from the enemy, 16, 239.

ἄνευθε, and before a vowel ἄνευθεν (ἄνευ), *far, remote, far off,* absol. often with partcp. ὤν, οὖσα, ὄν, *far-distant;* κιών, *going away,* 1, 35; according to Plat. ἀποχωρῶν. 2) With gen. like ἄνευ, *without, apart, from.* ἄνευθε θεοῦ, without god, without divine co-operation, 5, 185. ἄνευθεν ἐμεῖο, 16, 80. *b) remote,*

far from. ἄνευθε πατρός τε φίλων 78. Od. 10, 554.

ἀνέφελος, ον (νεφέλη), *unclouded, less,* Od. 6, 44.† (ᾰ)

ἀνέχω (ἔχω), 3 sing. indicat. pr ἔχῃσι, Od. 19, 111; fut. ἀνέξω, ἄνεσχον, poet. ἀνέσχεθον, fut. mi ἕξομαι and ἀνασχήσομαι, Ep. infi σχήσεσθαι, aor. 2 mid. ἀνεσχόμη imperat. ἄνσχεο and ἀνάσχεο. I) *hold up, to raise, to lift up,* with κεφαλήν, Od. 17, 291; often χεῖρα ἀνέχ., to raise the hands to the g prayer; once to lift the hands for listic combat, Od. 18, 89; comi mid. σκῆπτρον θεοῖσι, to raise the to the gods (in swearing), 7, 412, trop. *to maintain;* εὐδικίας, to m righteousness, justice, Od. 19, 111. *hold back, to check, to restrain,* 23, 426. 3) Intrans. *to project, to emerge.* αἰχμὴ ἀνέσχεν, the spea projected, 17, 310; *to emerge fr water,* Od. 5, 320. II) Mid. 1) *to hold oneself up, to keep erect,* fall, esply spoken of the wound 285; hence metaph., *a) to bear, dure,* comm. with accus. κήδεα once with gen. δουλοσύνης ἀνέχε endure slavery, Od. 22, 423; in pendent clause stands for the mo a partcp. as with verbs of sufferin ἀνέξομαί σε ἄλγε' ἔχοντα for ἔχειν not suffer thee to endure, etc. παρὰ σοίγ' ἀνεχοίμην ἥμενος, I cou to sit by thee, Od. 4, 595. ξείνο χεσθαι, to suffer strangers among, 32; hence, to receive hospitably, 13. *b)* Absol. *to hold out, to restra self;* often τέτλαθι καὶ ἀνάσχεο, b and command thyself, 1, 586. 5, 382 *hold up, to elevate,* like ἀνέχειν (wh discourse relates to things belong us), with accus. σκῆπτρον, the sce swear, 10, 321; δούρατα, to raise th for hurling, 11, 593. 12, 138; χε raise the hands to smite oneself fo 22, 34; and for joy, Od. 18, 100 partcp. pres. ἀνασχόμενος stands absol. *to rise, to raise oneself* (for str where from the preceding somethi be sometimes supplied, as ξίφος, It is not necessary, however, witl tath., to supply χεῖρα at 23, 666. (25. 18, 95. (In Od. 24, 8. ἀνά τ' ἀλλ ἔχονται, ἀνά is a prepos. with the they hold one by another, i. e. h gether.

ἀνεψιός, ὁ, *a sister's son;* and kinsman by blood, *a cousin,* •9, 46 ι lengthened 15, 554).

ἀνέω, obsol. theme of ἀνίημι.

ἄνεω, usually written ἄνεῳ, as i an obsol. adj. ἄνανος, ἄναος, ἄνεως ἄω, αὖω), and regarded as a nom Att. decl. *noiseless, still, silent:* use with the *sing.* (and with ref to a *fem.* noun) in Od. 23, 93, ἡ δην ἧστο is against this suppositi occurs usually only with the plu νεσθα, ἐγένοντο, ἦσαν. According to Buttm. Lex. p. 107, it is, as even Aristarchus supposed, an adv. like οὕτω, and should therefore be written ἄνεω without ι.

ἀνήγαγον, see ἀνάγω.

ἀνῇη, Ep. for ἀνῇ, see ἀνίημι.

ἀνήκεστος, ον (ἀκέομαι), not to be healed, incurable, intolerable, χόλος, ἄλγος, *5, 394. 15, 217.

ἀνηκουστέω (ἀκούω), aor. ἀνηκούστησα, not to hearken to, not to obey, τινός, any one, *15, 230.

ἀνήμελκτος, ον, poet. (ἀμέλγω), unmilked, Od. 9, 439.†

ἀνήνοθε, Ep. ('ΑΝΕΘΩ), 3 sing. perf. 2, which occurs partly in the signif. of the present to mark a concluded action, and partly in narration as a preterite, to issue forth, to spring up. αἷμ' ἔτι θερμὸν ἀνήνοθεν ἐξ ὠτειλῆς, the blood still warm gushed from the wound, 11, 266; and κνίσση ἀνήνοθεν, the smoke of the fat rolls upward, Od. 17, 270. (It is comm. referred to ἀνθέω, see Thiersch, Gram. § 232, 20, but, according to Buttm. Lex. p. 134, the theme is ἄνθω, ἀνέθω, lengthened by redupl.)

ἀνήνυστος, ον (ἀνύω), not to be accomplished, unaccomplished, ἔργον, Od. 16, 111.

ἀνήνωρ, ορος, ὁ (ἀνήρ), not a man, unmanly, cowardly, *Od. 10, 340, 341.

ἀνήρ, gen. ἀνέρος and ἀνδρός, dat. pl. ἀνδράσι and ἄνδρεσσι, a man, as opposed to a woman, 17, 435; also with the idea of bravery, ἀνέρες ἔστε, φίλοι, be men, 5, 529, cf. ἄναξ ἀνδρῶν. 2) man, in opposition to a god, πατὴρ ἀνδρῶν τε θεῶν τε. 3) man, in opposition to a youth; and, 4) a husband, 19, 291. Od. 11, 327. Very common is the junction of this word with another subst. or adj. as ἀνὴρ βασιλεύς, ἀνὴρ ἥρως, ἀνὴρ Ἀργεῖος, by which the expression becomes more honorable. (α is prop. short, but in the arsis and in the trisyllabic cases always long.)

ἀνήροτος, ον (ἀρόω), unploughed, uncultivated, *Od. 9, 109. 123.

ἀνῆφθω, see ἀνάπτω.

Ἄνθεια, ἡ, a town in Messenia, according to Strab. the later Thuria, 9, 151.

Ἀνθεμίδης, ου, ὁ, Ep. for Ἀνθεμωνιάδης, son of Anthemiōn, 4, 488.

Ἀνθεμίων, ωνος, ὁ, father of Simoeisius in Troy, 4, 473.

ἀνθεμόεις, εσσα, εν (ἄνθεμον), flowery, blooming, epith. of meadows, 2, 467. 2) adorned with flowers; in connexion with λέβης, κρητήρ, metal vessels probably adorned with figures of flowers. Others understand it as meaning enamelled, 23, 885. Od. 3, 440.

*ἄνθεμον, τό, poet. = ἄνθος, flower, blossom; prop. ornament, decoration, h. 5, 9.

ἀνθερεών, ῶνος, ὁ (prob. from ἀνθέω), the chin. χειρὶ ὑπ' ἀνθερεῶνος ἑλεῖν, to take hold of the chin with the hand (the sign of supplication), *1, 501.

ἀνθέριξ, ικος, ὁ (ἀθήρ), the beard on the ear of corn; an ear of corn, 20, 227.†

ἀνθέω, aor. 1 ἤνθησα, infin. ἀνθῆσαι, to shoot up, to grow up; in this prob. prim. signif. it is found in Od. 11, 320. †h. Ap. 139.

Ἀνθηδών, όνος, ἡ, a town in Bœotia, on the coast, with a port, 2, 508.

ἄνθινος, ή, όν (ἄνθος), of flowers, flowery. εἶδαρ ἄνθινον, food from flowers, Od. 9, 84.† Thus Hom. calls the fruit of the lotus, which the Lotophagi ate; prob. merely a poet. designation of a vegetable diet formed from blossoms; others explain it metaph. delicate.

ἀνθίστημι (ἵστημι), aor. 2 ἀντέστην, trans. to place opposite. 2) Intrans. aor. 2 and mid. to oppose oneself to, to resist, τινί, any one, 20, 70; absol. 16, 305. *Il.

ἄνθος, εος, τό (ἀνά), prop. the shooting bud, τέρεν' ἄνθεα, Od. 9, 449; comm. a blossom, a flower, 2, 89. 9, 542; trop. ἥβης ἄνθος, the bloom of youth, 13, 484; κουρήιον, h. Cer. 108.

ἀνθρακιή, ἡ (ἄνθραξ [which Lob. thinks may be related to αἴθω: he compares candeo, carbo]), a heap of coals, 9, 213.†

ἄνθρωπος, ὁ, man, as a race, and as an individual, in distinction from gods and brutes; also the dead are called ἄνθρωποι, Od. 4, 565.

'ΑΝΘΩ, assumed theme of ἀνήνοθε.

ἀνιάζω (ἀνία), trans. to excite disgust, to weary, with accus. 23, 721; to distress, to afflict, Od. 19, 323. 2) Intrans. to be displeased, to be weary, to be tired, of a thing, Od. 4, 460. 598; then to be grieved, to grieve oneself, with dat. κτεάτεσσιν, about his possessions, 18, 300. (ι either long or short in H.)

ἀνιάω (ἀνία), Ion. and Ep. ἀνιήσω, partcp. aor. pass. ἀνιηθείς = ἀνιάζω, to weary, to vex, with accus. Od. 2, 115. Pass. to be burdened. οὐ γάρ τίς τοι ἀνιᾶται παρεόντι, no one is burdened by thy presence, Od. 15, 335; esply and often, ἀνιηθείς, absol. dejected, disgusted, troubled. [Ἦ μὴν καὶ πόνος ἐστὶν ἀνιηθ. κ.τ.λ. (1) nimirum laboribus fungimur, ut moleste ferentes redire velimus. Lehrs. The toil is undoubtedly one for returning home, from weariness and disgust; or (as Felton translates it) truly the labour is such that one might justly wish to return, being worn out by the long-continued fatigue of the war, 2, 291. (2) N. presses the aor. partcp. perpessos diuturnæ mansionis ærumnas tum demum reverti: i. e. not to return home till they had endured (borne to the end) the hardships of so protracted a stay: but had they not endured them already during the nine years?] (ι always long in Hom.)

ἀνιδρωτί, adv. (ἱδρόω), without sweat, without toil, 15, 228.

ἀνίη, ἡ, Ion. for ἀνία, grief, trouble, pest, plague. δαιτὸς ἀνίη, the plague of the feast, Od. 17, 446. ἄπρηκτος ἀνίη, a desperate evil ['that woe without a cure.' Cp.] : thus Scylla is called, *Od. 12, 221. (ι always long.)

ἀνιηθείς. see ἀνιάω.

ἀνίημι (ἵημι), fut. ἀνιήσω, once ἀνέσει, Od. 18, 265, aor. 1 ἀνῆκα and ἀνέηκα, aor. 2 only 3 plur. ἄνεσαν, subj. ἀνήῃ for ἀνῇ, optat. ἀνείην, partcp. plur. ἀνέντες. I) Act. *to send up, to let ascend*. ἀήτας Ὠκεανὸς ἀνίησιν, Oceanus sends up the blasts of Zephyr, Od. 4, 568; ὕδωρ, *to cast up water*, opposed to ἀναροιβδεῖν, spoken of Charybdis, Od. 12, 105. (Here also have been cited ἀνέσαντες, ἀνέσαιμι, to place upon, see ἀνεῖσα.) 2) Comm. *to let loose*, hence *a) to let go, to leave*. ὕπνος ἀνῆκεν ἐμέ, sleep left me, 2, 71. δεσμῶν τινὰ ἀν., to free any one from bonds, Od. 8, 359; to liberate, as opposed to ἁλῶναι, Od. 18, 265; according to others, *to send home. b) to loosen, to open*, πύλας, the gates, 21, 537 (i. e. by undoing the bars of the gates which secured them on the inside). *c)* Esply, *to let loose upon any one, to send upon, to set upon*. σοὶ δ' ἐπὶ τοῦτον ἀνῆκεν 'Αθήνη, *tibi hunc immisit*, 5, 405; and ἄφρονα τοῦτον, v. 761; hence mly *to excite, to urge, to incite*, Ζεὺς—ἀνῆκεν, 16, 691; τοῖσιν (for them, for their aid) Θρασυμήδεα δῖον ἀνῆκεν, 17, 705; often with infin. Μοῦσα ἀοιδὸν ἀνῆκεν ἀείδειν, the muse excited the bard to sing, Od. 8, 73. σὲ δ' ἐνθάδε θυμὸς ἀνῆκεν ἀνασχεῖν, 6, 236. 7, 25. II) Mid. *to loosen for oneself, to open*; with accus. κόλπον, to bare the bosom, 22, 80; αἶγας, to draw the skin from the goats, to flay them, Od. 2, 300. (ι short, but used long if the metre requires it.)

ἀνιηρός, ή, όν (ἀνία), *burdensome, troublesome, sad;* πτωχός, a troublesome beggar; compar. ἀνιηρέστερος, Od. 2, 190.

ἀνιπτόπους, ποδός, ὁ, ἡ (νίπτω, πούς), *with unwashed feet*, 16, 235. †epith. of the Σελλοί, the priests of Zeus at Dodona, to indicate their rough mode of life; as they probably lived like a kind of monks, destitute of every convenience.

ἄνιπτος, ον (νίπτω), *unwashed*, 6, 266.†

ἀνίστημι (ἵστημι), fut. ἀναστήσω, Ep. ἀνστήσω, aor. 1 ἀνέστησα, imper. ἄνστησον, Ep. for ἀνάστησον, aor. 2 ἀνέστην; dual ἀνστήτην, Ep. for ἀναστήτην, partcp. ἀνστάς, for ἀναστάς. I) Trans. in the pres. imperf. and aor. 1 act. *to cause to rise*, with accus. of the person sitting, *to chase away, to scatter*, 1, 191; γέροντα χειρός, to raise the old man by the hand, 24, 515; *to wake* out of sleep, κήρυκα the herald, 24, 689; to wake to life the dead, 24, 551. 756; from an abode, i. e. *to cause to emigrate*, Od. 6, 7; metaph. *to excite, to instigate*, esply to combat, τινί, against any one, 7, 116. 10, 176. II) Intrans. in the aor. 2 perf. act. and mid. *to get up, to arise*, from a seat, in order to speak, τινί, to any one, 1, 58. v. 205; ἐξ ἐδέων, 1, 533; from an encampment, 10, 55. 2) *to rise* from rest for combat, 2, 694; τινί, against any one, 23, 635. Od. 18, 334; *to

arise again*, spoken of the woun dead, 15, 287. 21, 56.

ἀνίσχω (ἴσχω), a form of ἀνέχ up, χεῖρας θεοῖσι, 8, 347; mid. *mand oneself, to endure*, 7, 110.

ἀνιχνεύω (ἰχνεύω), *to trace out*, 20, 192.†

ἀννεῖται, poet. for ἀνανεῖται, νέομαι. Od.

ἀνξηραίνω, poet. for ἀναξηραίνω ἀνόημων, ον (νόημων), *without senseless, imprudent*, *Od. 2, 270.

ἀνόητος, ον (νοέω), *unobserved ceived [not to be comprehended, ful]*, h. Merc. 80.

ἀνοίγνυμι, poet. ἀνοίγω and (οἴγνυμι), imperf. ἀνέῳγεν and and Ep. iterative ἀναοίγεσκον, 2 *to open, to unlock, to undo*, θύ doors, Od.; κλη¯δα, to open, thru the bolt, 24, 455, see κληίς; ἀπ πῶμα, to remove the cover from 16, 221.

ἀνόλεθρος, ον (ὄλεθρος), *not de snatched from destruction, unsl* 761.†

ἄνομαι, see ἄνω.

ἄνοος, ον (νόος), *thoughtless, se devoid of mind*, 21, 441.†

ἀνοπαῖα, or ἀνόπαια according t tarchus, Od. 1, 320; ὄρνις ὡς ὁ διέπτατο, an ancient word about meaning the Gramm. are at va Most probably ἀνοπαῖα is an = ἀνωφερές, *she flew away upwa* Empedocles, according to Eust employed it (καρπαλίμως δ' ἀνό Herodian likewise explains it adverb, for ἀοράτως, *invisibly (* and ὄπω = ὄπτομαι). Others, a tarchus, write ἀνόπαια, and regard kind of eagle, like the sea-eagle; again write ἀν' ὀπαῖα, from ὀπαῖ aperture for smoke; hence Voss, through the aperture for smoke sh So also Nitzsch.

ἀνορούω (ὀρούω), aor. 1 ἀνόρουσα out augm. *to arise suddenly, to spr to ascend*, ἐκ θρόνων and ἐξ ὕπνου the seats, from sleep; ἐς δίφρον, to upon the chariot, 11, 273† and sp the sun: 'Ηέλιος ἀνόρουσεν ἐς ου the sun mounted quickly up the sl 3, 1.

ἀνόστιμος, ον (νόστιμος), *with turn, who cannot return; ἀσ τιθέναι*, to prevent a person's retu 4, 182.†

ἄνοστος, ον (νόστος), *without retu returning*, Od. 24, 528.†

ἄνουσος, ον (νοῦσος), *without s in health, well*, Od. 14, 255.†

ἀνούτατος, ον (οὐτάω), *not wo distinguished from ἄβλητος; esp wounded with the sword, unclo* 540.†

ἀνουτητί, adv. *unwounded*, 22, 3 ἀνστάς, ἄνστησον, ἀνστήσων, την, abbrev. Ep. for ἀναστάς, ετ ἀνίστημι.

ἀνστρέψειαν, poet. for ἀναστρέψειαν, Il. ἀνσχεθέειν, ἄνσχεο, poet. for ἀνασχεθεῖν, ἀνάσχου, from ἀνέχω.

ἄνσχετος, poet. for ἀνάσχετος. Od.

ἄντα (ἀντί), 1) *against, opposite*, face to face, esply with μάχεσθαι. στῆ ἄντα σχομένη, she stood, with her face turned towards him, Od. 6, 141; metaph. θεοῖσι ἄντα ἐῴκει, he resembled the gods, face to face, i. e. plainly, 24, 630. ἄντα τιτυσκόμενος, straight before him *at* the object, Od. 21, 48. II) Prep. with gen. *opposite, before.* Ἤλιδος ἄντα, opposite Elis, 2, 626. ἄντ᾽ Αἴαντος ἐείσατο, against Ajax, 15, 415. ἄντα παρειάων σχέσθαι κρήδεμνα, to hold a veil before the cheeks, Od. 1, 334. ἄντα σέθεν, *before thee*, in thy presence, Od. 4, 115. b) Esply in a hostile sense, *against*; ἄντα Διὸς πολεμίζειν, to fight against Zeus, 8, 428. cf. v. 424.

ἀντάξιος, ον (ἄξιος), prop. standing in equipoise, *equal in worth, equivalent;* with the gen. ἰητρὸς ἀνὴρ πολλῶν ἀντάξιος ἄλλων. worth as much as many others, 11, 514; hence the neut. οὐκ ἐμοὶ ψυχῆς ἀντάξιον, not an equivalent to me for life, 9, 401. *Il.

*ἀνταποδίδωμι (δίδωμι), aor. 2 ἀνταποδοῦναι, to give again, to give back, to restore, Batr. 187.

ἀντάω (ἄντα), imperf. ἤντεον, fut. ἀντήσω, aor. ἤντησα. The pres. ἀντάω does not occur in H.=ἀντιάω, 1) With gen. *to meet* any one (designedly), 16, 423; spoken of things: *to happen upon, to engage in*, to partake of; as μάχης, δαίτης, ἐνωπῆς, to meet the sight, to see, Od. 3, 97. 2) With dat. *to meet* any one (by chance), to fall in with any one, 6, 339; absol. 4, 375.

Ἄντεια, ἡ, *Antēa*, daughter of king Iobates in Lycia, wife of Prœtus; in the tragic poets *Sthenobœa*, 6, 160.

ἀντέχω (ἔχω), imper. aor. 2 mid. ἀντίσχεσθε, *to hold against, to hold before;* mid. *to hold before oneself*, τί τινος, something against any thing; τραπέζας ἰών, to oppose the table to the arrows, Od. 22, 74.†

ἄντην, adv. (ἀντί [*Lob.* thinks it an *adverbial acc.* like πέραν, fm ἄντη: which Hermann reads in Soph. El. 175 in the sense of a *prayer*]), 1) *opposite, against.* ἄντην ἵστασθαι, to place oneself in opposition, 11, 590. 2) *directly forwards, ex adverso;* ἔρχεσθαι, to go forward, 8, 399. ἄντην βαλλόμενος, hit, wounded in the breast, 12, 152. 3) *in the face of, openly, visibly.* ἄντην εἰσιδεῖν, to look in the face. ἄντην ἀγαπάζειν, to love visibly, 24, 464. ὁμοιωθήμεναι ἄντην, visibly to compare, to vie, with any one, 1, 187. Od. 3, 120. In the last phrase some give it the signif. *placed before,* i. e. in direct comparison with others [as Passow, with reason]; δέμας ἐναλίγκιος ἄντην, very similar, Od. 2, 5.

Ἀντηνορίδης, αο, ὁ, son of Antenor, 3, 121.

Ἀντήνωρ, ορος, ὁ (contending with a man, conf. ἀντιάνειρα), son of Æsyetes

and Cleomestra, husband of Theano, father of Agēnor, Acamas, etc.; one of the wisest of the Trojan princes, who advised in vain the surrender of Helen and the restoration of her effects. According to a later tradition, he emigrated, after the destruction of Troy, to Italy, and built there Padua, 3, 184. 7, 347.

ἀντί, prepos. with gen. 1) Of place: *opposite, against.* ἀντὶ ὀφθαλμοῖιν, before the eyes, Od. 4, 115. Wolf, however, has ἄντα, as in 15, 415, and in other places ἀντί for ἀντία, cf. 8, 233. 21, 481. 2) Commonly spoken of an equivalent, a comparison: *in place of, instead, for.* ἀντὶ πολλῶν λαῶν ἐστιν ἀνήρ. one man is equal to many, 9, 116. ἀντὶ κασιγνήτου ξεῖνος τέτυκται, a guest is instead of, i. e. equal to, like a brother, Od. 8, 546. τῶνδ᾽ ἀντί, 23, 650; separated from the word governed, 21, 75.

ἀντία, adv. prop. neut. plur. from ἀντίος.

ἀντιάνειρα, ἡ (ἀνήρ), fem. occurring only in the nom. and accus. plur.: *manlike, masculine*, epith. of the Amazons, *Il. (Masc. ἀντιάνωρ is not used.)

ἀντιάω, Ep. ἀντιόω, for ἀντιῶ (ἀντί), aor. 1 ἠντίασα; poet. form ἀντάω and ἄντομαι, *to go against, to meet.* 1) With gen. of the person: *to meet* any one, chiefly from design, both with a good intention, as Od. 24, 56, and with a bad: *to go against in battle, to attack*, 7, 231. b) Spoken of things. πολέμοιο, μάχης, to go against the war, the battle, to engage in it, 13, 215. 20, 125; of the gods: *to accept, to receive, to enjoy*, the gods being regarded as present and participating; ἑκατόμβης, ἱρῶν, to accept of a hecatomb, of victims, 1, 67. Od. 1, 25. 3, 436. 2) With the dat. *to meet any one by accident, to fall in with*, Od. 18, 147; ἐμῷ μένει, 6, 127. 3) With accus. *to go to,* in order to prepare; ἐμὸν λέχος ἀντιόωσα, preparing my couch, only 1, 31. II) Mid. as depon. *to take part,* with gen. γάμου, in the wedding, 24, 62.

ἀντιβίην, adv. (βίη), prop. accus. fem. from ἀντίβιος, *contending against, face to face, in a hostile manner;* ἐρίζειν τινί, to contend perversely with any one. 1, 278; ἐπέρχεσθαί τινι, to rush upon any one, 5, 220. *Il.

ἀντίβιος, η, ον (βίος), prop. using force against any one, *contentious, hostile;* only dat. ἀντιβίοισιν ἐπέεσσι, Il. and Od. The neut. ἀντίβιον as adv. *against;* μάχεσθαί τινι, to fight against any one, 3, 435.

ἀντιβολέω (ἀντιβολή), aor. ἀντεβόλησα, 11, 809, *to go against, to approach.* a) With gen. of the thing: *purposely to approach, to take part in;* μάχης, τάφου, the battle, the funeral solemnity, 4, 342. Od. 4, 547. b) With the dat. *to meet by chance*, to fall in with; comm. spoken of the pers. 7, 114; rarely of things; φόνῳ, to be present at the slaughter, Od. 11, 416. 24, 87. (Buttm. Lex. p. 122, rejects ἀντεβόλησα.)

D

ἀντίθεος, η, ον (θεός), godlike, divine, mly distinguished, comm. epith. of heroes, in reference to descent, strength, and physical advantages; also of the companions of Ulysses, Od. 4, 571; sometimes of nations, 12, 408. Od. 6, 241; rarely of women. ἀντιθέη ἄλοχος, Od. 11, 117. 13, 378; of Polyphemus, Od. 1, 70; and of the suitors, Od. 14, 18.

ἀντίθυρος, ον (θύρα), opposite the door; hence, κατ' ἀντίθυρον κλισίης, Od. 16,159.†

'Ἀντίκλεια, ἡ, daughter of Autolycus, wife of Laertes, mother of Ulysses and Ctimĕnē; she died from grief for her absent son, 11, 85. 15, 362.

'Ἀντῖκλος, ὁ, a Greek who was with Ulysses in the wooden horse before Troy, Od. 4, 286.

ἀντικρύ, adv. (prob. from ἀντικρούω), 1) directly opposite, against; like ἄντην, e. g. μάχεσθαι, 5, 130. 819; ἀπόφημι, to say face to face, to one's face, openly, 7, 362; with gen. 8, 301. 2) directly through, straight forward; ἀντικρὺ δι' ὤμου, straight through the shoulder, 4, 481; hence also throughout, entirely, διαμᾶν, 3, 359. (ἀντικρύς is not Homeric, ν is origin. anceps, but in H. always long, except 5, 130.)

'Ἀντίλοχος, ὁ (opposing the ambuscade), eldest son of Nestor and Eurydĭcē; according to Od. 3, 452 (of Anaxibia, Apd). He accompanied his father to Troy, distinguished himself by brave deeds, and was beloved by Achilles, 23, 556. At the funeral games of Patroclus he received, in chariot-racing, the second prize; in running, the last, 18, 623 sqq. He was killed before Troy by Memnon, king of the Æthiopians, Od. 4, 188.

'Ἀντίμαχος, ὁ (fighting against), a Trojan, father of Hippolochus, Pisander, and Hippomachus, who insisted most strenuously that Helen should not be surrendered, 11, 122 sqq.

'Ἀντίνοος, ὁ, son of Eupīthes, the most impudent among the suitors. He hurled the stool at Ulysses, excited Irus against him, and was slain by him, Od. 4, 660. 18. 46. 22, 15 sqq.

ἀντίον, adv. see ἀντίος.

'Ἀντιόπη, ἡ, daughter of Asōpus, mother of Amphion and Zethus, Od. 11, 260. According to Apd. daughter of Nycteus.

ἀντίος, η, ον (ἀντί), against, opposite, towards, in both a good and bad signif. ἀντίος ἔστη, he stood opposite, i. e. over him; ἦλθεν, he came towards. Il. b) Comm. with gen. ὅστις τοὖγ' ἀντίος ἔλθοι, whoever should come towards it, 5, 301; rarely with dat. 7, 20. 20, 22. 2) The neut. sing. ἀντίον, and plur. ἀντία. often stand as adv., 1) towards, against, before, with gen. ἀντίον ἰέναι τινός, to go against any one. 5, 256; ἀντί 'Αλεξάνδροιο, 3, 425; ἀντία (before) δεσποίνης φάσθαι, Od. 15, 377. 2) In a hostile signif. against. ἀντίον εἰπεῖν, to contradict, 1, 230. στήμεναι ἀντία τινός, to withstand any one, 22, 253. μάχεσθαι ἀντία τινός,

20, 88. Od. 1, 79, with gen. (Ir αὐδᾶν τινά, to speak against, answer any one. the accus. depen αὐδᾶν; in like manner with εἰπεῖι

ἀντιόω, Ep. for ἀντιῶ, see ἀντιά ἀντιπεραῖος, η, ον (ἀντιπεράς opposite, esply beyond the sea. περαῖα, the opposite coast, 2, 635.

ἀντιάχεσθε, see ἀντέχω.

*ἀντίτομος, ον (τέμνω), cut the neut. τὸ ἀντίτομον, an a chiefly from roots, h. Cer. 229.

ἀντιτορέω (τορέω), aor. 1 ἀντετό perforate, to pierce through; spok spear: with gen. χροός, 5, 337. 2) through, with accus. δόμον, 10, Merc. 178. (ἀντιτορήσων is the of Herm. for αὐτοπρεπὴς ὥς, v. 86 to accomplish the way.)

ἄντιτος. ον, poet. for ἀνάτιτος (quited again. ἄντιτα ἔργα, deeds compense or vengeance, Od. 17, 5 ἄντιτα ἔργα γένοιτο παιδὸς ἐμο would there be deeds of venge my son, 24, 213.

'Ἀντιφάτης, αο, ὁ, in the accus φατῆα, Od. 10, 116. [1] a Troja by Leonteus, 12, 191.] 2) son lampus, father of Oïcles, Od. 15, king of the savage, gigantic Læstr who devoured one of the sc Ulysses. According to the Schol of Poseidōn, Od. 10, 111 sqq.

ἀντιφερίζω (φέρω), to put oneself to compare oneself, τινί, with a *21, 357; τί, in any thing, 488.

ἀντιφέρω (φέρω), only in the put oneself against, to oppose ones sol. μάχῃ, 5, 701. Od. 16, 238; pr Il. and Od. by a common Græcis γαλέος 'Ολύμπιος ἀντιφέρεσθαι, it to oppose Olympian [Zeus], 1, 58 accus. of the thing and dat. of tl μένος τινί, one's strength to any o to measure strength with any 482.

'Ἀντίφονος (reciprocally slay younger son of Priam, 24, 250.

'Ἀντιφος, ὁ, 1) son of Priam cuba, whom, together with Isus, bore off, and liberated for a ra 490. Agamemnon slew him, 11, son of Pylæmĕnes and the nymph a Mæonian and ally of the Tro 864. 3) son of Thessalus, leade Greeks from Nisyrus and the Cε islands, 2, 678. 4) a friend of Ul Ithaca, Od. 17, 68. [5) son of Æ in Ithaca. He accompanied Ul Troy, and was devoured by the Od. 2, 19 seq.]

ἄντλος, ὁ, the bilge-water in hold; also, the ship's hold itself, 411. 15, 479.

ἀντολή, ἡ, see ἀνατολή.

ἄντομαι, poet. form fr. ἀντάω, the mid. pres. and imperf.; prop. ἀλλήλοισιν ἐν πολέμῳ, to meet other in battle, 15, 698. Trop. ἤντετο θώρηξ, the double cuirass was fastened together [the edges of the cuirass met, so as to lie double one over the other, Döderl.] ; according to others, stood in the way, 4, 133. 2) Mly, *to meet, to fall in with*, 2, 595; and with dat. 11, 237.

ἄντρον, τό, *a cave, grotto, cavern*, *Od. 9, 216, and often.

Ἀντρών. ῶνος, ὁ (Ἄντρων, h. Cer. 491), a town in Thessaly on Œta, prob. a place full of caves, 2, 697.

ἄντυξ. υγος, ἡ, prop. any *curve* or *circle*; hence, 1) *the rim* or *margin of the shield*, a metallic hoop covered with leather, 6, 118; also *the shield* itself, 14, 412. 2) *the seat-rim*, a margin which extended around upon the two semicircles of the chariot-seat, and terminated in a knob to which the reins were fastened, 5, 262. H. mentions two ἄντυγες, 20, 500. 5, 728; either because the chariot-seat consisted of two semicircles, or because a rim extended around above and below. 3) *a circle*, the path of the planets, h. 7, 8.

ἄνυσις, ιος, ἡ (ἀνύω), *accomplishment, fulfilment, end, completion*. ἄνυσις δ᾽ οὐκ ἔσσεται αὐτῶν, there will be no accomplishment of them, i. e. they will not attain it, 2, 347. οὐκ ἄνυσίν τινα δήομεν, we shall find no end, i. e. we shall effect nothing, Od. 4, 544.

ἀνύω (ἄνω), fut. ἀνύσω, aor. 1 ἤνυσα, fut. mid. ἀνύσομαι, Ep. σσ, 1) *to accomplish, to bring to an end*; with accus., a) ἔργον, to finish a work, Od. 5, 243. b) to make way. ὅσσον τε νηῦς ἤνυσεν, as much as a ship traversed, sc. ὁδοῦ, Od. 4, 357. cf. 15, 294. c) *to destroy, to consume*, spoken of fire, Od. 24, 71. 2) With particp. [and negat.] *to achieve nothing*. οὐκ ἄνύω φθονέουσα, by envious resistance I effect nothing, 4, 56. In Od. 16, 373, οὐ γὰρ ὀΐω, ἀνύσσεσθαι τάδε ἔργα, the Schol. explain the fut. mid. by ἀνυσθῆναι, I do not think these things will be effected. Passow regards it as mid., in which case we must supply ἡμᾶς (α and υ always short).

ἄνω (ᾱ), imperf. ἦνον, akin to ἀνύω, *to finish, to accomplish* ; ὁδόν, to accomplish a journey, Od. 3, 496. Pass. *to be accomplished*, spoken of time ; νὺξ ἄνεται, the night is coming to an end, 10, 251. (Related to the adv. ἄνω, and theme of ἀνύω ; α long, except 18, 473.)

ἄνω, adv. (ἀνά), *up, upwards, above, over*, Od. 11, 596 ; spoken of the cardinal points: *northward*, 24, 544.

ἄνωγα, Ep. old perf. without augm. with the signif. of a pres., *I command, bid, order, incite, prompt*; often in connexion with ἐποτρύνω, κέλομαι, very often θυμὸς ἀνώγει or ἄνωγέ με, my mind prompts me, i. e. I desire, with accus. of the pers. and infin. pres. or aor., 2, 280; with dat. only, 10, 531. 18, 339. 20, 139. Of this perf. occur only : ἄνωγας, ἄνωγε, ἄνωγμεν, subj. ἀνώγῃ, optat. ἀνώγοις, imper. ἄνωγε (comm. ἄνωχθι, ἀνωγέτω and ἀνώχθω), ἀνώγετε and ἄνωχθε, infin.

ἀνωγέμεν for ἀνωγέναι, plupf. ἠνώγει, ἠνώγει, ἠνώγειν. This perf. passes over into the flexion of the pres.; hence, 3 pres. ἀνώγει, ἀνώγετον [a pres. ἀνώγω defended by Spitzn. ad 18, 90]; 3 perf. ἄνωγε or ἄνωγεν, imperf. ἤνωγον and ἄνωγον, hence fut. ἀνώξω, aor. 1 ἤνωξα, Od. 10, 531. (Buttm. Lex. p. 185, assigns it to an old theme ἄγω, related to ἀγγέλλω ; according to others, an old perf. from ἀνάσσω.)

ἀνῶγεν, see ἀνοίγνυμι.

(ἀνωγέω), obsol. pres. from which is derived the imperf. ἠνώγεον, 7, 394, for which Bentley reads ἤνωγον : Sptz. ἠνώγειν.

ἀνώγω, Ep. fut. ἀνώξω, *to command, to bid*, a new pres. formed from ἄνωγα, q. v.

ἀνωθέω (ὠθέω), aor. part. ἀνώσας, *to push up* or *off*, sc. ναῦν, impelling the ship from land into the high sea, Od. 15, 552.†

ἀνωϊστί, adv. (οἴομαι), *unexpectedly*, Od. 4, 92.†

ἀνώϊστος, ον (οἴομαι), *unexpected, unapprehended, unsuspected*, 21, 39. †Epigr. 14, 1.

ἀνώνυμος, ον (ὄνομα), *nameless, unnamed*, Od. 8, 552.†

ἀνώομαι=ἀνίομαι, a senseless reading in h. Ap. 209, for which μινυόμενος has been proposed, and for which Herm. proposes ἀγαιόμενος.

ἄνωχθι, ἄνωχθε, see ἄνωγα.

ἄξασθε, ἄξαντο, see ἄγω.

ἄξετε, see ἄγω.

ἀξίνη, ἡ (perhaps from ἄγνυμι), *an axe, the battle-axe*, of which the Hom. heroes made use only in exigencies, 13, 612. 15, 711. (ῑ)

ἄξιος, ίη, ιον (ἄγω), prop. equiponderant ; hence, 1) *of equal value*; with gen. λέβης βοὸς ἄξιος, a cauldron equal in value to an ox, 23, 885. οὐδ᾽ ἑνὸς ἄξιοί εἰμεν Ἕκτορος, we are not equal to the single Hector, 8, 234. σοὶ δ᾽ ἄξιον ἔσται ἀμοιβῆς, viz. δῶρον, it will be to thee worth a recompense, i. e. will bring thee a like present, Od. 1, 318. 2) absol. *worthy, suitable, agreeable*. ἄξια ἄποινα, suitable ransom, 6, 46; ὦνος, Od. 15, 429.

Ἀξιός, ὁ, a river in Macedonia, which flows into the Thermaic gulf, now *Vistrizza*, 2, 849.

ἄξυλος, ον (ξύλον), *without wood*. 2) *not deprived of wood*; ὕλη, an uncut, dense forest, 11, 155.†

Ἄξυλος, ὁ, son of Teuthras from Arisbe in Thrace, slain by Diomedes, 6, 12. (υ is here long.)

ἄξων, ονος, ἡ (ἄγω), *the axle-tree* in a chariot, of iron, brass, or ash-wood ; also the entire *wheel*: ὑπὸ δ᾽ ἄξοσι φῶτες ἔπιπτον, the men fell under the wheels, *16, 378.

ἀοιδή, ἡ, later contr. ᾠδή h. Cer. (ἀείδω), 1) *song*, primarily, the gift of song, the art of song, 2, 595. Od. 1, 328. b) the act of *singing*, which was comm. accompanied by the harp, Od. 1, 421. 17, 605

2) *song, poem* which was sung. στονόεσσα ἀοιδή, an elegy, 24, 721. 3) the subject of the song: *story, report, tradition*, Od. 8, 580. 24, 200.

ἀοιδιάω (ἀοιδή), Ep. form fr. ἀείδω, *to sing*, *Od. 5, 61. 10, 227.

ἀοίδιμος, ον (ἀοιδή), *sung, celebrated in song*; in a good sense, h. Ap. 299; in a bad sense, hence *infamous*. 6, 358.†

ἀοιδός, ὁ (ἀείδω), *a singer* and *poet, a bard*; prop. an adj., hence ἀοιδὸς ἀνήρ. The Epic minstrel, in the heroic age, was highly honoured, and kings and sovereigns derived pleasure from his art. Indeed he was often their friend, as one was commissioned by Agamemnon to guard his wife, Od. 3, 267. He was, like the μάντις, inspired by a deity, and hence holy and inviolable; he was αὐτοδίδακτος: no one taught him his art (Od. 22, 347), but a god bestowed upon him the gift. It was the Muses chiefly who inspired him and aided his memory, Od. 8, 73.

ἀολλής, ές (related to εἴλω and ἄλλω), *gathered together, all together, crowded*; always in the plur. οἱ δ᾽ ἅμα ἀϊστώθησαν ἀολλέες, they all disappeared together, Od. 10, 259; spoken esply of armies: ἀολλέες ὑπέμειναν, in thick array they maintained their ground, 5, 498.

ἀολλίζω (ἀολλής), aor. ἀόλλισα, aor. 1 pass. ἀολλίσθην, *to bring together, to assemble*; with accus. 6, 287. Pass. *to be assembled, to assemble*, 15, 588. *11.

ἄορ, ἄορος, τό (ἀείρω), prop. any weapon which one bears: *the sword*, which was suspended from a belt; with ξίφ, 21, 173. Od. 11, 24; ταννήκες, 14, 385. cf. ξίφος. (a in the dissyllabic cases is always long; in the trisyllabic, long in the arsis and short in the thesis.)

ἄορες, οἱ, only in accus. plur. ἄορας, Od. 17, 222.† of doubtful signification. This word is mentioned among several presents. Eustath. and Apollod. explain it to mean *women* [γυναῖκας], considering it a metathesis for ὄαρας; others explain it to mean *tripods*, or *cauldrons*, λέβητες (with handles for hanging). Prob. it is, with Hesych., to be regarded as only a heterogeneous form for ἄορα, *swords*; as some of the Gramm. also read; cf. Thiersch, Gram. § 197, 60.

ἀορτήρ, ῆρος, ὁ (ἀείρω), prop. a belt of any kind from which something hangs, but esply *a sword-belt* = τελαμών, the band from which the sword was suspended, 11, 31. Od. 11, 609. 2) *a thong* from which the wallet hung, Od. 17, 198.

ἀοσσητήρ, ῆρος, ὁ (ἀοσσέω), *a helper, deliverer, defender, protector*, 15, 254. Od. 4, 165.

ἄουτος, ον (οὐτάω), *unwounded, uninjured*, 18, 536.†

ἀπαγγέλλω (ἀγγέλλω), iterat. impf. ἀπαγγέλλεσκον, aor. 1 ἀπήγγειλα, *to bear a message, to announce, to relate*, τινί τι, any thing to any one; with πάλιν, *to report, to bring back information*, Od. 9, 95.

ἀπάγχω (ἄγχω), *to throttle, to st* with accus. Od. 19, 230.†

ἀπάγω (ἄγω), fut. ἀπάξω, aor. 2 γον, *to bear away, to carry away, away, to conduct*, with accus. Od. often with οἴκαδε, Od. 16, 370 αὖτις, πατρίδα γαῖαν, *to take back, vey home*, 15, 706; υἱὸν εἰς Ὀπόεν 326. 2) *to bring*, βοῦς, Od. 18, 27ε

ἀπαείρω (ἀείρω), Ep. for ἀπαίρω *up, to bear away*. 2) *to take onesel to go away, to depart*, with gen. · from the city, 21, 563.†

ἀπαί, poet. for ἀπό.

ἀπαίνυμαι, depon. (αἴνυμαι), Ep ἀποαίνυτο, *to take away, to take* accus. τεύχεα, κῦδος, Il.; νόστον, 419. τί τινος, ἥμισύ τ᾽ ἀρετῆς ἀπο Ζεὺς ἀνέρος, Zeus takes half strength from a man, Od. 17, 322.

Ἀπαισός, ἡ (Παισός, ἡ, 5, 612), in Asia Minor, 2, 828.

ἀπαΐσσω (ἀΐσσω), aor. partcp. ἀι *to spring* or *leap down, to hasten* with gen. κρημνοῦ, from the ro 234.†

ἀπαιτίζω (αἰτίζω), poet. form οι τέω, *to demand back, to reclaim*, χρ Od. 2, 78.†

ἀπάλαλκε, ἀπαλάλκοι, see ἀπαλέ.

ἀπάλαμνος, ον, poet. (παλάμη), fc λαμος, prop. without a hand, henc *less, awkward*; ἀνήρ, an irresolute 5, 597.†

ἀπαλέξω (ἀλέξω), fut. ξήσω, αοι tat. ἀπαλεξήσαιμι and Ep. aor. 2 ο κον, *to ward off, to repel, to hold* τινά, Od. 4, 766; τινά τινος, any on another, 24, 371; with the gen. thing, κακότητος, to hold back a from destruction, to spare him, 1 κύνας κεφαλῆς, 22, 348.

ἀπάλθομαι, Ep. (ἀλθέω), fut. ἀπο μαι, *to heal entirely*, ἕλκεα, woun 405. 419.

ἀπαλοιάω (ἀλοάω), Ep. aor. λοίησα, prop. to thresh out, then *in pieces, to crush*; with accus. ὀ 522.†

ἀπαλός, ή, όν (prob. from ἅπτω), t^{he} touch, *tender*; spoken chiefly of the human body, δειρή, αὐχήι 11, 115. Neut. as adv. ἁπαλὸν γε laugh gently, Od. 14, 465.

ἀπαλοτρεφής, ές (τρέφω), gen. ἑο *nursed, well-fattened*, σίαλος, 21,

*ἁπαλόχρως, ὁ, ἡ (χρώς), accu ἁπαλόχροας, *having tender skin*, 14.

ἀπαμάω (ἀμάω), aor. 1 ἀπήμ *mow down, to cut off*; with acc. 301. †in tmesis.

*ἀπαμβλύνω (ἀμβλύνω), peri ἀπήμβλυμαι, *to blunt*. Pass. *to blunt, to perish*, Ep. 12, 4.

ἀπαμβροτεῖν, see ἀφαμαρτάνω.

ἀπαμείβομαι (ἀμείβω), *to r answer*; chiefly in partcp. ἀπαμε προσέφη, Il. and Od.; τινά, Od. 347.

ἀπαμΰνω (ἀμύνω), aor. ἀπήμΰνα, to ward off, to hold back, to avert, τί τινι, any thing from any one; λοιγὸν ἡμῖν, to avert destruction from us, 1, 67; κακὸν ἦμαρ Αἰτωλοῖσιν, 9, 597. 2) Mid. a) to defend oneself; πόλις ᾗ ἀπαμυναίμεσθα, in which we may defend ourselves, 15, 738. b) to repel from oneself, τινά, 24, 369. Od. 16, 72.

ἀπαναίνομαι, dep. mid. (ἀναίνομαι), aor. 1 ἀπηνηνάμην, to deny utterly, to refuse, to reject, 7, 183; with acc. Od. 10, 297.

ἀπάνευθε, only before a vowel ἀπάνευθεν (ἄνευθε), 1) Adv. far off or away, apart, ἀπάνευθε κιών, going away, 1, 35 [Nägelsbach shows that κιών is to be taken as aor., 'having withdrawn.' ἀποχωρήσας Plat.]; φεύγειν, 9, 478. 2) As prep. with gen. far from, away from, ἀπάνευθε νεῶν, 1, 45; τοκήων, Od. 9, 36; metaph. ἀπάνευθε θεῶν, without the knowledge or agst the will of the gods, 1, 549.

ἀπάντῃ or ἀπάντη, adv. (ἅπας), in every direction, Il.; κύκλῳ ἀπάντῃ, all around; on every side, Od. 8, 278.

ἀπανύω (ἀνύω), aor. 1 ἀπήνυσα, to finish entirely; οἴκαδε, sc. τὴν ὁδόν, to accomplish the journey home, Od. 7, 326.†

ἄπαξ, adv. once, *Od. 12, 22.[once for all, at once, Od. 12, 350].

ἀπαράσσω (ἀράσσω), aor. 1 ἀπήραξα, to smite off (κάρη, 14, 497), to strike off or down, with the spear or sword; with accus. τρυφάλειαν, 13, 577; δόρυ ἀντικρύ, 16, 116; χαμᾶζε, to the earth, 14, 497. *Il.

ἀπαρέσκω (ἀρέσκω), only in the mid. to conciliate entirely, to gain over again. οὐ νεμεσητὸν, βασιλῆα ἄνδρ' ἀπαρέσσασθαι, it cannot be a just subject of censure, to conciliate again a royal personage, when one has been the first to act with passion [or, injustice], 19, 183.† Thus the ancients explained this clause, in harmony with the position of Achilles and Agamemnon (Sch. ἀπαρέσσασθαι, τουτέστι τῆς βλάβης ἀπαλλάξασθαι καὶ ἐξιλάσασθαι). So Damm and Voss. Heyne, considering this opposed to both the sense of the passage and the meaning of ἀπαρέσασθαι=to be displeased, angry, as it occurs in later writers, refers βασιλῆα ἄνδρα to Achilles: "one must not take it ill if a royal personage is displeased." So Passow and Bothe. But (1) the testimony of Eustath. and the Schol. is adverse to this view; (2) ἀπό in composition often indicates only a strengthening, cf. ἀπειπών, 9, 309; and (3) the apodosis, "we cannot censure a royal personage who is insulted, if he is angry at the insult," does not accord with the protasis, which exhorts Agamemnon to greater moderation. [Surely moderation is recommended, if the want of it justly offends.]

ἀπάρχομαι, depon. mid. (ἄρχω), aor. 1 ἀπηρξάμην, to begin, to commence; used only of the sacred act preceding a sacrifice, which consisted in cutting off some of the hairs from the forehead of the victim and casting them into the fire; hence

τρίχας ἀπάρχεσθαι, to cut off the hair, and commence the sacrifice, by throwing it into the fire ['to give the forelock to the flames,' Cp.], 19, 254. Od. 14, 422; and absol. ἀπαρχόμενος, beginning the sacrifice, Od. 3, 446.

ἅπας, ἅπασα, ἅπαν (πᾶς), entire, all, whole, plur. all together. οἶκος ἅπας, the whole house, Od. 4, 616.

ἄπαστος, ον (πάομαι), that has not eaten, fasting, 19, 346. b) With gen. ἐδητύος ἠδὲ ποτῆτος, without taking meat (and=) or drink, Od. 4, 788.

ἀπατάω (ἀπάτη), fut. ἀπατήσω, aor. Ep. ἀπάτησα, to deceive, to mislead, to cheat, to defraud, τινά, any one, 9, 344. Od. 4, 348.

ἀπάτερθε, before a vowel ἀπάτερθεν, adv. (ἄτερ), separated, apart. 2) Prep. with gen. far from, far away from, 5, 445. *Il.

ἀπάτη, ἡ (ἀπαφεῖν [cf. ἀπαφίσκω]), deceit, deception, fraud, mly in a bad sense, connect. with κακή, 2, 114; also without a bad signif. an artifice, plur. Od. 13, 294.

ἀπατήλιος, ον (ἀπάτη), deceitful, deceptive, wily: -α βάζει [fallacia loquitur], *Od. 14, 127. 157; εἰδώς, practised in deceit, in wiles.

ἀπάτηλος, ον=ἀπατήλιος, 1, 526.† and h. 7, 13.

ἀπατιμάω (ἀτιμάω), aor. ἀπητίμησα, to dishonour, to insult grossly, τινά, 13, 113.†

(ἀπαυράω), Ep. in the pres. obsol. impf. sing. ἀπηύρων, ας, α, as aor. (ἀπηύρατο. Od 4, 646, is an anomalous reading) and partcp. aor. 1 ἀπούρας, to take away, to seize and bear away, to despoil, to rob. a) With double accus. τινὰ θυμόν, to take away a man's life; in like manner τεύχεα. b) With dat. of the pers. τινί τι, 17, 236. Od. 3, 192. Note.—That it is construed with gen. of pers. seems to be doubtful: 1, 430, τήν ῥα βίῃ ἀέκοντος ἀπηύρων, whom they took away by violence against his will. Here the gen. is absol. or dependent upon βίῃ (by violence offered one unwilling, cf. Od. 4, 646); and in Od. 18, 273, it is governed by ὄλβον. [Cf. however the passages cited by Spitzner ad Il. 15, 186; also Od. 19, 405, and 19, 89; ὅτ' Ἀχιλλῆος γέρας αὐτὸς ἀπηύρων. Am. Ed.] The aor. originally prob. sounded ἀπέϝραν (as ἀπέδραν); partcp. ἀπόϝρας, hence ἀπούρας; and the pres. ἀποϝράω, ἀπαυράω. According to Buttm. (Lex. p. 144) it is related to εὑρεῖν: according to others to αἱρέω. [So Lob., "non multum abest, quin ἀπαυρᾶν τί τινος latino auferre præmium ab aliquo, auferre aliquid inultum, par et simile esse putem." Lob. Techn. 136.]

(ἀπαφάω), obsol. pres., whence comes ἀπαφίσκω, q. v.

ἀπαφίσκω, Ep. (ΑΦΩ [cf. ἀκαχίζομαι fm ἄχομαι, Lucus, and as to the meaning the Lat. palpare. Hence the notion is that of stroking down. To this ἀπάτη, -άω are related]), aor. ἤπαφον, infin. ἀπαφεῖν,

D 3

mid. 3 sing aor. optat. ἀπάφοιτο 1) *to deceive, to cheat, to delude*, τινά, any one, Od. 11, 217. 2) Mid. same signif. with act. μήτις με βροτῶν ἀπάφοιτ᾽ ἐπέεσσιν, lest some one of mortals should deceive me with words, *Od. 23, 216.

ἀπέειπε, see ἀπεῖπον.

ἀπέεργε, see ἀποέργω.

ἀπειλέω (related to the Dor. ἀπελλαί [Doric name for the *popular* assembly; whence ἀπελλάζειν. Of the same family as ἠπ-ύω, ἔπ-ος, ὄψ, Buttm., p. 177]), fut. ἀπειλήσω, prop. *to speak loud, to boast*, cf. 8, 150; hence 1) Mly in a bad sense, *to threaten, to menace*, τινί τι, any thing to any one; and instead of the accus. the infin. 1, 161. Od. 11, 313; ἀπειλάς, to utter threats, 16, 201. 2) In a good signif. *to boast, to vaunt* oneself, Od. 8, 383. b) *to vow, to promise*, 2, 863. 872. (Impf. dual ἀπειλήτην, Od. 11, 313. Cf. Thiersch, § 221, 83. Buttm., § 105, note 16.)

ἀπειλή, ἡ, always plur. [in H.] *boasting* (as the verb), *threatening*, 9, 244. Od. 13, 126. b) *vaunting*, a boastful promise, in a good sense, 20, 83.

ἀπειλητήρ, ῆρος, ὁ, *a boaster, a threatener*, 7, 96.†

ἄπειμι (εἰμί), fut. ἀπέσομαι, poet. σσ, impf. ἀπῆν, Ep. ἀπέην, plur. ἄπεσαν, *to be absent, to be distant*; absol. with gen. τινός, from any one, 17, 278. Od. 19, 169.

ἄπειμι (εἶμι), imper. ἄπιθι, partcp. ἀπιών, *to go forth, to go away, to depart*, chiefly in the partcp. The pres. in the signif. of the fut. Od. 17, 593.

ἀπεῖπον (εἰπεῖν), a defect. aor. 2, a supplement to ἀπόφημι; 3 sing. Ep. ἀπέειπε and ἀπόειπε, subj. ἀποείπω, optat. ἀποεί ποιμι, imper. ἀπέειπε and ἀπόειπε, infin. ἀποειπεῖν, ἀπειπέμεν. 1) In H. only, *to speak out, to utter, to announce*, κρατερῶς, 9, 432; with accus. μῦθον, ἀγγελίην, 7, 416. 9, 309; ἐφημοσύνην, Od. 16, 340. 2) *to refuse, to deny*, τί, any thing, 1, 515; hence also 3) *to denounce*, Od. 1, 91; and *to renounce*, μῆνιν, anger, 19, 35 (ἀπόειπε with gen 3, 406, where now stands, accord. to Aristarchus correctly, ἀπόειπε, q. v.).

Ἀπειραίη, ἡ, the Apiraean, γρηΰς, Od. 7, 8. Eustath. derives it as Dor. from Ἤπειρος from the continent, or from Epirus, but against the quantity of the first syllable; cf. Ἀπείρηθεν.

ἀπειρέσιος, ον, and ἀπερείσιος, poet. lengthened for ἄπειρος, *boundless, unbounded*, γαῖα. 2) Mly *infinite, immeasurably great* or *numerous*, ἄποινα, 1, 13; ὀϊζύς, ἄνθρωποι.

Ἀπείρηθεν, adv. either *from the continent*, or *from Epirus*, Od. 7, 9; cf. Nitzsch in loc. The poet. intends perhaps by ἡ ἄπειρος or Ἄπειρη the unbounded region towards the north.

ἀπείρητος, η, ον, Ion. and Ep. for ἀπείρατος (πειράω), 1) *unattempted, untried, unessayed*, spoken of things, πόνος,

17, 41; cf. ἀδήριτος. 2) *unprot tried*, said of persons. where one knowledge, Od. 2, 170; hence rienced, *unacquainted with*, φιλό Ven. 133.

ἀπείριτος, ον, poet. for ἀπ *boundless*, πόντος, Od. 10, 195. 120.

ἀπείρων, ονος, ὁ ἡ (πεῖρας), *illi immeasurable*, γαῖα, δῆμος, δεσμο 340; ὕπνος, an infinitely long sl 776. Od. 7, 286.

ἀπεκλανθάνω (λανθάνω), imp mid. ἀπεκλελάθεσθε; *to cause t entirely*. 2) Mid. *to forget entire* gen. θάμβευς, forget astonishme cease to wonder, Od. 24, 394.†

ἀπέλεθρος, ον (πέλεθρον), prop be measured by a πέλεθρον (=π *immeasurable*, ἴς, Il. Od. 9, 538. as adv. ἀπέλεθρον, *immeasurably* a great distance, 11, 354.

ἀπεμέω (ἐμέω), aor. 1 ἀπέμεσα, *to expectorate, to vomit forth*, wit αἷμα, 14, 437.†

ἀπεμνήσαντο, see ἀπομιμνήσκω

ἀπεναρίζω, poet. (ἐναρίζω), pro spoil a corpse of arms; but mly t with double accus. ἔντεα τινά, 15, 343; only in tmesis.

ἀπένεικα, see ἀποφέρω.

ἀπέπλω, see ἀποπλώω.

ἀπερείσιος, ον=ἀπειρέσιος, poe

ἀπερύκω (ἐρύκω), fut. ἀπερύξ *strain, to keep back, to repel*; wit 4, 542. Od. 18, 105.

ἀπέρχομαι (ἔρχομαι), aor. 2 a perf. ἀπελήλυθα, *to go away, to* with prep. and with gen. alone, οἴκου, 24, 766. Od. 2, 136.

ἀπερωεύς, έως, ὁ (ἐρωέω), one strains, *a hinderer, a baffler*, ἐμῶν 8, 361.†

ἀπερωέω (ἐρωέω), aor. ἀπερώησ *to flow back*, but mly *to hasten retire*; with gen. πολέμου, to ret the conflict, 17, 723.†

ἄπεσαν, see ἄπειμι.

ἀπευθής, ές (πεύθομαι), 1) which one has heard nothing, u *unascertainable*, Od. 3, 88. 2) A has heard nothing, *ignorant, uni* Od. 3, 184.

ἀπεχθαίρω (ἐχθαίρω), aor. 1 ἀ 1) *to hate bitterly*, with accus. 3, Trans. *to render odious, to make* ing. ὕπνον καὶ ἐδωδήν τινι, Od. 4.

ἀπεχθάνομαι, mid. (ἐχθάνομαι) ἀπηχθόμην, *to become odious, to t* τινι, 6, 140. 24, 27. (The pres. veat, Od. 2, 202, has likewise an signif.; ἀπηχθόμην is aor. A pr χθομαι is not known to H. Cf. Gram. § 114. Rost. p. 288.

ἀπέχω (ἔχω), fut. ἀφέξω and ἀπ Od. 19, 572; aor. 2 ἀπέσχον, f ἀφέξομαι, aor. 2 mid. ἀπεσχό Act. *to repel, remove, avert. a*) something from any thing, χεῖρας 1, 97; νῆα νήσων, Od. 15, 33. b) τί τινι; πᾶσαν ἀεικείην χροΐ, every indignity from the body, i. e. to protect it against, 24, 19; χεῖρας μνηστήρων, Od. 20, 263. II) Mid. to restrain oneself, to abstain from a thing; with gen. πολέμου, from the war, 8, 35; ἀλλήλων, 14, 206; βοῶν, Od. 12, 321: to spare any one, Od. 19, 489. b) With accus. and gen. χεῖρας κακῶν, to restrain the hands from evil, Od. 22, 316.

ἀπηλεγέως. adv. (ἀλέγω), recklessly, openly, μῦθον ἀποειπεῖν, 9, 309. Od. 1, 373.

ἀσήμαντος, ον (σημαίνω), uninjured, unharmed, Od 19, 282.†

ἀσήμων, ον, gen. ονος (σῆμα), without injury. 1) Pass. uninjured, unharmed, 1, 415. 13, 761. 2) Act. innocuous, harmless, ὥρος, πομποί; hence ὕπνος, propitious sleep, 14, 164; μῦθος, 12, 80.

ἀπήνη, ἡ, a carriage, a wagon, a four-wheeled vehicle, different from ἅρμα, chiefly for transporting freight, =ἅμαξα, 24, 324. Od. 6, 72. ["Synonyma sunt plurima: πήνα, Hes. Gallicumque benna. Γάτος, ὄχημα Τυῤῥηνοί, Hes. καπάνη (media longa), ἀμάνη, ἅμαξα, ἅγαννα: nec sciri potest unane horum omnium stirps fuerit, an specie similis re diversa." Lob. Path. 194.]

ἀπηνήναντο, see ἀπαναίνομαι.

ἀπηνής, ές, gen. έος (antithet. to ἐνηής) ["opp. προσήνης: nonnulli a praepositionibus deflexa putant, ut ab ὑπό, ὑπήνη διὰ τὸ ὑποκάτω εἶναι ἢ ὡς εἰρήνη, γαλήνη." Lob. Path. 194], harsh, cruel, unfriendly, unyielding, θυμός, μῦθος, νόος, 15, 94. Od. 18, 381.

ἀπήραξεν, see ἀπαράσσω.

ἀπηύρων, ας, α, see ἀπαυράω.

ἀπήωρος, ον (αἰωρέω), hanging down, far-waving, ἀπήωροι δ᾽ ἔσαν ὄζοι, Od. 12, 435.†

ἀπιθέω (πείθω), fut. ἀπιθήσω, aor. ἀπίθησα, not to obey, to be disobedient, τινί, always with a neg. οὐδ᾽ ἀπίθησε μύθῳ, he was not disobedient, i. e. he obeyed the word, 1, 220; with gen. h. Cer. 448.

ἀπινύσσω (πινυτός), to be without sense, without consciousness, κῆρ, 15, 10. b) to be silly, foolish, Od. 6, 258.

ἄπιος, η, ον (from ἀπό, as ἀντίος from ἀντί), remote, distant. τηλόθεν ἐξ ἀπίης γαίης, from far, from the distant land, 1, 270. Od. 7, 25. (The old Gramm. take it incorrectly as a proper name, and derive it from Ápis, the name of an old king who reigned in Peloponnesus. They understood by it Peloponnesus. This appellation is however post-Homeric, and the two words are moreover distinguished by the quantity; ἄπιος has ᾰ, and Ἆπιος has ᾱ; see Buttm., Lex. p. 154.

Ἀπισάων, ονος, ὁ, 1) son of Phausius, a Trojan, 11, 578. 2) son of Hippasus, a Paeonian, 17, 348.

ἀπιστέω (ἄπιστος), to disbelieve, to distrust, with accus. Od. 13, 357.†

ἄπιστος, ον (πίστις), 1) perfidious,

faithless. *3, 106. 24, 63. 2) incredulous, mistrustful, κῆρ, Od. 14, 150. 391.

ἀπίσχω, poet.=ἀπέχω, Od. 11, 95.†

*ἄπληστος, ον (πίμπλημι), insatiable, immense, χόλος, h. Cer. 83; thus correctly with Herm. for ἄπλητος.

ἁπλοΐς, ΐδος, ἡ, simple, single, χλαῖνα, 24, 230. Od. 24, 276. (The opposite of διπλοΐς, it being wrapped but once round the body; cf. διπλοΐς.)

*ἁπλόω (ἁπλοῦς), aor. ἥπλωσα, to spread, to unfold, οὐρήν, Batr. 74 (86).

ἄπνευστος, ον (πνέω), without breath, breathless, swooning, Od. 5, 456.†

ἀπό, Ep. ἀπαί, 1) Prep. with gen. from. 1) Spoken of space, a) To indicate distance from a place or object, with verbs of motion, often with the subordinate idea of elevation: down from. ἀφ᾽ ἵππων ἆλτο χαμᾶζε, down from the chariot, Il. ἀφ᾽ ἵππων, ἀπὸ νεῶν μάχεσθαι, to attack from the chariots, from the ships, 15, 386; ἅψασθαι βρόχον ἀπὸ μελάθρου, to suspend the cord from a beam, Od. 11, 278; pleonast. ἀπ᾽ οὐρανόθεν. b) To denote departure or origin from a place without regard to distance, from. ἵπποι ποταμοῦ ἀπὸ Σελλήεντος, horses from the river Selleis, 12, 97. ἀπὸ πύργου, 22, 447. c) To denote distance from a place or object with verbs of rest. μένειν ἀπὸ ἧς ἀλόχοιο, to remain far from his spouse, 2, 292; ἀπ᾽ Ἄργεος, 12, 70; and pleonast. ἀπὸ Τροίηθεν, 24, 492; metaph. ἀπὸ σκοποῦ καὶ ἀπὸ δόξης μυθεῖσθαι, to speak wide from the mark and expectation, i. e. against them, Od. 11, 344. ἀπὸ θυμοῦ εἶναι, to be far from the heart, i. e. hated, 1, 562. 2) Of time, to indicate departure from a given point, after, since; ἀπὸ δείπνου, 8, 54. 3) In other relations in which a departure from something is conceivable; a) Of origin. οὐκ ἀπὸ δρυὸς οὐδ᾽ ἀπὸ πέτρης ἐστί, he springs neither from the oak nor the rock, i. e. proverbial, he is not of uncertain origin, Od. 19, 163. b) Of the whole, in reference to its parts, or that which belongs to them. κάλλος ἀπὸ Χαρίτων, Od. αἶσα ἀπὸ ληΐδος, a share in the spoil, Od. 5, 40. ἄνδρες ἀπὸ νηός, h. 12, 6. c) Of the cause. ἀπὸ σπουδῆς, from seriousness, seriously, 12, 233. d) Of the means and instrument. ἀπὸ βιοῖο πέφνεν, with the bow, 24, 605. II) As adv. without case, poet. from, away, far, without, when it is for the most part to be connected with the verb. πάλιν δ᾽ ἀπὸ χαλκὸς ὄρουσε βλημένου, 21, 594; in like manner, Il. 845. Od. 16, 40. III) In composition with verbs it signifies dis-, de-, re-, un-, in-, etc., away, off, etc., and indicates separation, departure, cessation, completion, requital, want.

ἄπο (with retracted accent), thus written when it stands after the subst. it governs. θεῶν ἄπο κάλλος ἔχουσα, h. Ven. 77. Further, many Gramm. accent thus the word in the signif. far from; this accentuation was, however, rejected

D 4

by Aristarchus and Herodian as needless, cf. Schol. Ven. Il. 18, 64. In Wolf's H. it is found only Od. 15, 517.

ἀποαίνυμαι, poet. for ἀπαίνυμαι.

ἀποαιρέομαι, poet. for ἀφαιρέομαι.

ἀποβαίνω (βαίνω), fut. ἀποβήσομαι, aor. 2 ἀπέβην, Ep. aor. 1 mid. ἀπεβήσατο, and ἀπεβήσετο = ἀπέβη. 1) to go away, to depart, ἐκ πολέμοιο, 17, 189; also μετ' ἀθανάτους, 21, 298; πρὸς Ὄλυμπον, Od. 1, 319. 2) to descend, to alight, ἐξ ἵππων, from the chariot, 3, 263; and gen. alone, 17, 480; ἐπὶ χθόνα, 11, 619.

ἀποβάλλω (βάλλω), only in tmesis, aor. 2 ἀπέβαλον, to cast away; with accus. χλαῖναν, to throw away the cloak. 2) to let fall, δάκρυ παρειῶν, tears from the cheeks, Od. 4, 198; νῆας ἐς πόντον, to cause the ships to run into the sea, Od. 4, 358.

ἀπόβλητος, ον (βάλλω), to be cast away, despicable, worthless, ἔπεα, δῶρα, 2, 361. 3, 65.

ἀποβλύζω (βλύζω), to belch, to eructate, to vomit forth, οἶνον, 9, 491.†

ἀποβρίζω, poet. (βρίζω), partcp. aor. ἀποβρίξας, to sleep one's fill, Od. 9, 151. 12, 7.

ἀπογυιόω (γυιόω), subj. aor. ἀπογυιώσω, to lame entirely, and mly to weaken, to enfeeble, 6, 265.†

ἀπογυμνόω (γυμνόω), partcp. aor. pass. ἀπογυμνωθείς, to lay bare, esply to despoil of arms, Od. 10, 301.†

ἀποδάζομαι, obsol. pres. which furnishes the tenses to ἀποδαίομαι.

ἀποδαίομαι, poet. (δαίω), fut. ἀποδάσομαι, Ep. σσ, aor. ἀπεδασάμην, to share with others; τινί τι, to divide any thing with any one, 17, 231. 24, 595.

ἀποδειδίσσομαι, poet. (δειδίσσομαι), to frighten away or back; with accus. 12, 52.†

ἀποδειροτομέω (δειροτομέω), fut. ήσω, to cut the throat, to cut off the head, to kill, τινά, 18, 336. Od. 14, 35.

ἀποδέχομαι, depon. mid. (δέχομαι), aor. 1 ἀπεδεξάμην, to take, to receive, with accus. ἄποινα, 1, 95.†

ἀποδιδράσκω (διδράσκω), aor. 2 ἀπέδραν, to run away, to fly; ἐκ νηός, Od. 16, 65; νηός, 17, 516.

ἀποδίδωμι (δίδωμι), fut. ἀποδώσω, aor. 1 ἀπέδωκα, aor. 2 optat. ἀποδοίην, infin. ἀποδοῦναι, 1) to give out, to restore, to return, τί τινι, something to any one; spoken chiefly of things which one is under obligation to give back; hence, 2) to repay, to requite; θρέπτρα τοκεῦσιν, to repay to parents their dues for rearing, i. e. to make returns of gratitude and duty, 4, 478. 17, 302; πᾶσαν λώβην, to expiate the whole insult, 9, 387.

ἀποδίεμαι, poet. (δίημι), to drive back, to drive away; τινὰ ἐκ μάχης, to drive any one from the fight, 5, 763.† (ἀποδ. with ᾱ), cf. δίεμαι.

ἀποδοχμόω (δοχμόω), aor. 1 ἀπεδόχμωσα, to bend sidewise, to bend to one side; αὐχένα, the neck, Od. 9, 372.†

ἀποδράς, see ἀποδιδράσκω.

ἀποδρύπτω (δρύπτω), aor. 1 ἀπέ... aor. 1 pass. ἀπεδρύφθην, to tear scratch, to excoriate, to lacerate; accus. Od. 17, 480; ἔνθα κ' ἀπὸ δρύφθη, here would his skin have lacerated, Od. 5, 426.

ἀποδρύφω = ἀποδρύπτω, in ἵνα μ ἀποδρύφοι ἑλκυστάζων, lest by dra he should lacerate him, 23, 187.† optat. accord. to Buttm., Gram. Anm. 13; or, according to Passow, aor. 2 from ἀποδρύπτω.)

ἀποδύνω, poet. for ἀποδύομαι; σ the impf. ἀπέδυνε βοείην, he put o ox-hide, Od. 22, 364.†

ἀποδύω (δύω), fut. ἀποδύσω, ἀπέδυσα, aor. 2 ἀπέδυν, aor. 1 mid. σάμην, 1) Trans. pres. act., also fu aor. to pull off, to strip off, with f εἵματα, the clothes from any one; spoken of stripping off the arms of warriors, τεύχεα, 4, 532. 2) Intrans and aor. 2 to put off from oneself, off; εἵματα, to put off one's clothe 5, 343. 349.

ἀποείκω, poet. for ἀπείκω (εἴκι retire from, to leave; with gen. ἀπόεικε κελεύθου, leave the way immortals; adopted by Wolf, 3, 40 ἀπόεικε, after Aristarchus [cf. ἀπε The ancients understood by κέ θεῶν, the path by which the gods Olympus (Schol. Ven. A. τῆς εἰς τὰ ὁδοῦ εἴκε καὶ παρεχώρει μὴ βαδίζουα αὐτούς). The following verse doe accord with the metaph. signif. com intercourse of the gods, as translat Voss.

ἀποεῖπον = ἀπεῖπον.

ἀποεργάθω, poet. for ἀπείργω; impf. ἀπόεργαθεν, to separate, to div remove, τινά τινος, 21, 599; ῥάκεα ᾱ he removed the rags from the w Od. 21, 221.

ἀπόεργω, Ep. for ἀπείργω, in ἀπόεργον, to keep off, to separate, to d τί τινος. ὅθι κληῗς ἀπόεργει αὐχέ στῆθός τε, where the clavicle sep the neck and breast, 8, 326; τινά to drive one from a thing, 24, 238; accus. alone, Od. 8, 296. ἀποεργμέ Ven. 47, is a perf. pass. partcp. wi redupl.; cf. Buttm., Gram. under ε

ἀπόερσα, a defect. Ep. aor. 1 i subj. ἀποέρση, optat. ἀποέρσειε, 6, 21, 283. 329, to tear away, to hurry sweep off; with accus. (It is mly de from ἀπέρρω, with a causative s Buttm., in Lex. p. 156, with more p bility derives it from ἀπέρδω) [to away, to sweep away, 21, 283: con ing ἔρδω a causative of ῥέω, and re to ἄρδω. ὅν ῥά τ' ἔναυλος ἀποέρση, the torrent has washed away, 21, 329 μιν ἀποέρσειε ... ... ποταμός, lea flood should wash him away. So 6, ἔνθα με κῦμ' ἀπόερσε, there the wave have washed me away. So Lob.].

ἀποθαυμάζω (θαυμάζω), aor. ἀπ

μασα, _to be greatly astonished at;_ with accus. Od. 6, 49.†

ἀπόθεστος, ον, poet. (ἀποτίθημι), _abjectus, despised,_ κύων [' _a poor unheeded cast-off,'_ Cp.], Od. 17, 296.† Some derive it from θέσσασθαι, to wish; hence: not wished for, disregarded.

ἀποθνήσκω (θνήσκω), partcp. perf. ἀποτεθνηώς, _to die away, to die;_ in the perf. _to be dead,_ 22, 432.

ἀποθρῴων, see ἀποθρῴσκω.

ἀποθρῴσκω (θρῴσκω), aor. 2 ἀπόθορον, _to leap down, to spring away;_ with gen. νηός, to leap down from the ship, 2, 702. 16, 748. 2) _to rise,_ or _ascend (lightly)_ from any thing; of smoke, γαίης, Od. 1, 58.

ἀπόθυμιος, ον (θυμός), prop. remote from the heart, _disagreeable, odious._ ἀπόθυμια ἔρδειν τινί, to displease any one, 14, 261.†

ἀποικίζω (οἰκίζω), aor. 1 ἀπῴκισα, _to cause to emigrate, to settle, to transplant, to another abode,_ τινὰ ἐς νῆσον, Od. 12, 135.†

ἄποινα, τά (from α and ποίνη), _the ransom,_ by which freedom is purchased for a prisoner, 1, 13. 111; or the price a prisoner gives for life and liberty, 2, 230. 6, 46. 2) mly _requital, compensation,_ 9, 120. (Used only in the plur.)

ἀποίσω, see ἀποφέρω.

ἀποίχομαι, depon. mid. (οἴχομαι), _to be absent, to be at a distance,_ Od. 4, 109; πολέμοιο, to keep aloof from the war, 11, 408. 2) _to remove oneself, to go away,_ τινός, 19, 342.

ἀποκαίνυμαι, depon. mid. poet. (καίνυμαι), _to surpass, to vanquish;_ τινά τινι, any one in something, *Od. 8, 127. 219.

ἀποκαίω (καίω), optat. aor. ἀποκήαι, _to burn up, to consume;_ with accus. 21, 336.† (In tmesis.)

ἀποκαπύω (καπύω), aor. ἀπεκάπυσα, _to breathe out, to gasp away,_ ψυχήν, 22, 467.† (In tmesis.)

ἀποκείρω (κείρω), Ep. aor. 1 ἀπέκερσα, aor. 1 mid. ἀπεκειράμην, prop. _to shear off;_ then _to cut off, to cut through,_ with accus. τένοντε, the sinews, 10, 456. 14, 466. 2) Mid. _to cut off_ for oneself; χαίτην, to cut off one's hair, as a token of grief, 23, 141. *Il.

ἀποκηδέω (κηδέω), partcp. aor. ἀποκηδήσας, _to be negligent, to be careless, inattentive._ αἴ κ' ἀποκηδήσαντε φερώμεθα χεῖρον ἄεθλον, if we from being negligent should carry off a smaller prize, 23, 413.† The dual is here used with the plur. because the speaker (Antilochus) has in mind himself and his steeds.

ἀποκινέω (κινέω), aor. 1 ἀπεκίνησα, Ep. iterative, ἀποκινήσασκε, _to remove, to drive away, to take away;_ with accus. δέπας τραπέζης, to remove the goblet from the table. 11, 636; τινὰ θυράων, to drive any one from the door, Od. 22, 107.

*ἀποκλέπτω (κλέπτω), fut. κλέψω, _to steal away, to purloin,_ h. Merc. 522.

ἀποκλίνω (κλίνω), _to bend away, to turn_ aside, _to drive back;_ with accus. βοῦς εἰς αὖλιν, h. Ven. 169; trop. ἄλλῃ ἀποκλίνειν, to turn in another direction, i. e. to give the dream another _turn_ (=interpretation), Od. 19, 556.†

ἀποκόπτω (κόπτω), fut. ἀποκόψω, aor. 1 ἀπέκοψα, _to cut away, to cut off;_ with accus. αὐχένα, τένοντας, 11, 146. Od. 3, 449; παρήορον, to separate a mate-horse by severing the thong with which it was attached [' _the side-rein,'_ Cp.], 16, 474.

ἀποκοσμέω (κοσμέω), _to put in order by taking away;_ hence, _to clear away,_ ἔντεα δαιτός, the furniture of a feast, Od. 7, 232.†

ἀποκρεμάννυμι (κρεμάω), aor. 1 ἀπεκρέμασα, _to let any thing hang down, to droop_ (trans.); ἡ ὄρνις αὐχέν' ἀπεκρέμασεν, the bird ' _her head reclined_' [Cp.], 23, 879.†

ἀποκρίνω (κρίνω), ἐn the partcp. aor. 1 ἀποκρινθείς, _to separate, to sunder._ τὼ οἱ ἀποκρινθέντε ἐναντίω ὁρμηθήτην, these, separated (from their friends), rushed against him. 5, 12.†

ἀποκρύπτω (κρύπτω), aor. 1 ἀπέκρυψα, _to conceal, to hide,_ τινί τι, any thing from any one; τινὰ νόσφι θανάτοιο, to hide any one from death, i. e. to rescue him from death, 18, 465.

ἀποκτάμεν, ἀποκτάμεναι, see ἀποκτείνω.

ἀποκτείνω (κτείνω), aor. 1 ἀπέκτεινα, aor. 2 ἀπέκτανον, Ep. ἀπέκταν, ας, α, infin. ἀποκτάμεν for ἀποκτάναι, aor. 2 mid. with pass. signif. ἀπεκτάμην, partcp. ἀποκτάμενος, _to kill, to slaughter, to slay,_ τινὰ χαλκῷ, any one with the brass [weapon], Il. and Od. ἀπέκτατο πιστὸς ἑταῖρος, his faithful companion was slain, 15, 435. (On ἀπεκτάμην, see Buttm., § 110, 7.)

ἀπολάμπω (λάμπω), _to shine forth, to flash back, to be reflected,_ τινός, from a thing: ὡς αἰχμῆς ἀπέλαμπε, so flashed back [the splendour] from the spear, 22, 319. 2) Mid. χάρις δ' ἀπελάμπετο πολλή, grace was reflected afar, 14, 183. Od. 18, 298. h. Ven. 175.

ἀπολείβω (λείβω), _to let drop,_ mid. _to drop, to distil,_ τινός, from any thing. ὀθονέων ἀπολείβεται ὑγρὸν ἔλαιον, the liquid oil trickled from the close-woven linen, i. e. it was so thick that the oil did not penetrate it; or, according to Voss, it was so glossy that oil seemed to be flowing down [so Cp., ' _bright as with oil,'_ &c.], Od. 7, 107.† πλοκάμων, h. 23, 3.

ἀπολείπω (λείπω), 1) _to leave behind, to leave remaining,_ οὐδ' ἀπέλειπεν ἔγκατα, he left not the entrails remaining, Od. 9, 292. 2) _to abandon;_ spoken of place, δόμον, 12, 169. 3) Intrans. _to go from, to go out, to fail,_ Od. 7, 117.

ἀπολέσκετο, see ἀπόλλυμι.

ἀπολήγω (λήγω), fut. ἀπολήξω, aor. 1 ἀπέληξα, _to leave off, to cease, to desist;_ with gen. μάχης, to quit the battle; εἰρεσίης, to desist from rowing, Od. 12, 224. b) With partcp. οὐδ' ἀπολήγει χαλκῷ δηϊόων, he does not cease cutting

D 5

down with his sword, 17, 565. cf. Od.
19, 166. c) Absol. *to cease, to pass away*,
6, 149.

ἀπολιχμάω (λιχμάω), *to lick off, to suck*,
in H. only in the mid. οἵ σ' ἀτειλὴν αἷμ'
ἀπολιχμήσονται, which will suck the
blood from the wound, 21, 123.†

ἀπολλήξῃς, ἀπολλήξειαν, Ep. for ἀπο-
λήξῃς, ἀπολήξειαν, see ἀπολήγω.

ἀπόλλῦμι (ὅλλυμι), fut. ἀπολέσω, Ep.
σσ, aor. 1 ἀπώλεσα and ἀπόλεσσα, mid.
aor. 2 ἀπωλόμην, 3 plur. ἀπόλοντο, perf.
2 ἀπόλωλα, 1) In the act. trans. *to
destroy, to kill, to slay*; spoken chiefly of
slaughter in battle; with accus. 1, 268.
5, 758; also of things: *to raze*, Ἴλιον, 5,
648. 2) *to lose. to suffer the loss of*; often
θυμόν, to lose life. ἀπολ. νόστιμον ἦμαρ,
to lose the day of return, Od. 1, ·354;
βίοτον, οἶκον, Od. 2, 49. 4, 95. II) Mid.
and also 2 perf. has an intrans. signif. :
to perish, to die, to be lost, undone, to fall
(in battle); often with dat. ὀλέθρῳ, Od.
3, 87; more rarely with accus. αἰπὺν
ὄλεθρον, to die a cruel death, Od. 9, 303;
κακὸν μόρον, by an evil fate, Od. 1, 166 :
ὑπό τινι, to perish by some one, Od. 3,
235. 2) *to disappear, to vanish, to fail*,
καρπὸς ἀπόλλυται, the fruit disappears,
Od. 7, 117. ὕδωρ ἀπολέσκετο, the water
vanished (Cp.), Od. 11, 586. ἀπό τέ
σφισιν ὕπνος ὄλωλεν, their sleep is lost, it
has left them, 10, 186. οὐ γὰρ σφῷν γε
γένος ἀπόλωλε τοκήων, for the race of
your fathers is not lost, i. e. you are not
of unknown descent; or, with Nitzsch,
you are not degenerate, the nobility of
your ancestry is not lost in you, Od. 4,
62. cf. 19, 163.

Ἀπόλλων, ωνος, ὁ (prob. from ἀπόλλυμι, the destroyer), *Apollo*, son of Zeus
and Latona, brother of Artĕmis; accord. to
4, 101, born in Lycia (see Λυκηγενής), or
according to later mythology, in Delos,
h. in Ap. 27; with long, flowing hair,
and of eternal beauty and youth. In H.
he is distinguished from Helios, and
appears, 1) As *a god inflicting punishment*, and as such carries a bow and
arrows (hence the epith. ἀργυρότοξος,
κλυτότοξος, ἕκατος, etc.). He slays with
his arrows men who die not by a violent,
but by a sudden natural death; just as
the sudden death of women is ascribed to
Artĕmis, Od. 11, 318. 15, 410. He slays
also in anger; he sends pestilence and
contagion upon men, 1, 42. 2) As *the
god of prophecy;* his oracle is represented
as being in the rocky Pytho, 9, 405; he
communicates the gift of foreseeing future events, 1, 72. 3) As *the god of song
and the lyre;* he communicates to bards
the knowledge of the past, Od. 8, 488;
and enlivens by the music of the lyre the
feasts of the gods, 1, 602. 4) Finally, he
is mentioned by H. as *the protector of
herds;* he fed the mares of Eumēlus, 2,
766; and pastured the herds of Laomedon, 21, 448. In the Iliad he is always
on the side of the Trojans, and is wor-

shipped as the tutelary deity in Tr
on the coast of Asia (Chrysè, Ci
509; see the appellations Σμινθεύς,
(Ἀπόλλων has prop. ᾰ; in the qu
labic cases also a.)

ἀπολούω (λούω), aor. 1 ἀπέλου
mid. ἀπολούσομαι, aor. 1 mid.
σάμην, *to wash off, to wash;* with
accus. Πάτροκλον βρότον αἱματό
wash away the clotted gore from
clus, 18, 345. 2) Mid. *to wash*
ἅλμην ὤμοιϊν, to wash the brine f
shoulders, Od. 6, 219; with double
23, 41.

ἀπολῠμαίνομαι, mid. *to purify*
chiefly in a religious sense, to
oneself by bathing before a s
when any one by some act, a
touching a dead body, had beco
clean, •1, 313, 314. 2) *to destroy*,

ἀπολῡμαντήρ, ῆρος, ὁ, *a destr
spoiler.* δαιτῶν ἀπολ., the spo
feasts, *a disturber;* the beggar
thus called, Od. 17, 220. 377. I
plained by the Schol.: ὁ τὰ καθ
ἀποφερόμενος τῶν εὐωχιῶν, one w
sumes the fragments of a feast,
licker (Voss, *fragment-eater*). T
planation agrees with the signif.
λυμαίνεσθαι occurring in H., and d
therefore the preference over the
nation of modern lexicons, viz.,
turber of feasts.

ἀπολύω (λύω), aor. 1 ἀπέλυσα, f
ἀπολύσομαι, 1) *to loose, to unl
τινος;* ἱμάντα κορώνης, to loose th
from the ring, Od. 21, 46;
τρόπιος, Od. 12, 420. 2) *to
liberate;* in the Il. to liberate
for a ransom, 1, 95. 6, 427. II)
ransom, to redeem, τινὰ χρυσοῦ,
for gold, 22, 50. (ῡ)

ἀπομηνίω (μηνίω), fut. ἀπομηνί
1 ἀπεμήνισα. *to cherish wrath, to
in anger*, τινί, 2, 772. 7, 230. Od.
(ῐ in the pres., ῑ in the fut. and a

ἀπομιμνήσκομαι, mid. (μιμνήσ
ἀπεμνησάμην, *to remember*, in
τινί is dat. commod.: to bethink
in favour of any one.

ἀπόμνῡμι and ἀπομνύω (ὄμνυ
perf. ἀπώμνυ, and 3 plur. ἀπώμν
1 ἀπώμοσα, *to swear*, to take an
something has not happened or
happen, ὅρκον. Od. 2, 377. 10,
assure on oath that one will not d
not done something, *to abjure* (a
ἐπόμνυμι), •Od. 10, 345. 18, 58.

ἀπομόργνῡμι (ὀμόργνυμι), aor.
ἀπομορξάμην, 1) *to wipe off, to
with accus. αἷμα, blood, 5, 798.
2) Mid. *to wipe oneself;* παρειὰς
wipe the cheeks with the hands
200; δάκρυ, 2, 269. Od. 17, 304.

ἀπομυθέομαι, depon. mid. (μ
to dissuade, to warn against, τ
109.†

ἀπονάω, poet. (νάω = ναίω), ob
aor. 1 ἀπένασα, Ep. σσ (aor. 1 ι
νασάμην, prop. *to cause any one*

in another place, *to transplant, to cause to emigrate,* and mly, *to send away,* with the accus. κούρην ἄψ, to send back the camsel, 16, 86. 2) Mid. *to change one's residence, to emigrate;* Δουλίχιόνδε, to remove to Dulichium, 2, 629; Ὑπερησίηνδε, Od. 15, 254.

ἀπονέομαι, depon. (νέομαι), only pres. and imperf. *to go away, to return, to go back;* ἐκ μάχης, 16, 252; προτὶ ἄστυ, to the city, 12, 74; ἐπὶ νῆας, to the ships, 15, 305; ἐς πατρός, sc. δόμον, Od. 2, 195. (ᾱ)

ἀπόνηθ', ἀπονήμενος, see ἀπονίνημι.

ἀπονίζω (νίζω), in the pres. and imperf. used for ἀπονίπτω. 1) *to wash off* or *away;* with accus. Od. 23, 75. 2) Mid. *to wash oneself from;* with accus. ἱδρῶ θαλάσσῃ, to wash oneself from sweat in the sea, 10, 572. (In ἀπενίζοντο, ε is used as long.)

ἀπονίνημι (ὀνίνημι), *to profit from;* in H. only Mid. ἀπονίναμαι, fut. ἀπονήσομαι, aor. 2 Att. ἀπωνήμην, Ep. ἀπονήμην, optat. 2 sing. ἀπόναιο, partcp. ἀπονήμενος, *to use, enjoy, to have advantage,* τινός, of any thing. οἶος τῆς ἀρετῆς ἀπονήσεται, he will enjoy his bravery alone, 11, 763. οὐδὲ—ἧς ἥβης ἀπόνηθ' (for ἀπώνητο, he had no advantage from his youth, 17, 25; also obsol. οὐδ' ἀπώνητο, he had no advantage, profit (viz., from raising the dog), Od. 17, 293; (Theseus from the seduction of Ariadne), Od. 11, 324; (Ulysses from his son), Od. 16, 120.

ἀπονίπτω (νίπτω), a later form for νίζω; the pres. mid. once Od. 18, 179; aor. 1 ἀπένιψα, aor. 1 mid. ἀπενιψάμην, *to wash away, to cleanse by washing;* with accus. βρότον ἐξ ὠτειλέων, to wash away the blood from wounds, Od. 24, 189. 2) Mid. *to wash oneself (sibi);* with accus. χρῶτα, the body, Od. 18, 172.

ἀπονοστέω (νοστέω), fut. ἀπονοστήσω, *to come back, to return home;* also with ἄψ, 1. 60. Od. 13, 6, and often.

ἀπόνοσφι, before a vowel ἀπόνοσφιν (νόσφι), adv. *separately, apart, afar,* βῆναι, 11, 555; εἶναι, 15, 548. ἀπόνοσφι καθίζεσθαι, 2, 233. ἀπόνοσφι τραπέσθαι, to turn oneself aside, Od. 5, 350. 2) Prep. *far from, remote from;* with gen. (which mly precedes), ἐμεῦ, far from me, 1, 541; φίλων ἀπόνοσφιν, Od. 5, 113.

*ἀπονοσφίζω (νοσφίζω), aor. 1 ἀπενόσφισα, Ep. σσ, *to separate, to divide,* τινὰ δόμων, h. in Cer. 158. Pass. *to be deprived of,* ἀμβροσίης ὀδωδῆς, h. Merc. 562.

ἀποξέω (ξέω), aor. 1 ἀπέξεσα, *to shave off,* hence *to cut off;* with accus. χεῖρα, =ἀποκόπτω, 5, 81.†

ἀποξύνω (ὀξύνω), aor. 1 ἀπέξυνα, *to sharpen, to point;* with accus. ἐρετμά, oars, Od. 6, 269. 9, 326. In both passages the connexion plainly requires the signif. *to smooth,* for which reason Buttm., Lexil. p. 70. would read ἀποξύνουσιν for ἀποξύνουσιν, and ἀποξῦσαι for ἀποξῦναι.

ἀποξύω (ξύω)=ἀποξέω, aor. 1 ἀπέξυσα, *to shave off, to polish;* γῆρας, to strip off old age, sc. *to become young,* a fig.

borrowed from serpents that cast their skins, 9, 446.†

ἀποπαπταίνω (παπταίνω), fut. ἀποπαπτανέω, Ep. for ἀποπαπτανῶ, *to look around* (as if to fly), *to look around fearfully,* 14, 101.†

ἀποπαύω (παύω), aor. 1 ἀπέπαυσα, fut. mid. ἀποπαύσομαι, 1) *to cause to cease, to stop, to restrain,* τινά, any one, 18, 267; τινός, from a thing; πολέμου, 11, 323; also with accus. and infin. τινὰ ἀλητεύειν, to stop one from begging, Od. 18, 114. 2) Mid. *to cease, to abstain from,* πολέμου, 1, 422. Od. 1, 340; where now ἀποπαυέ stands instead of ἀποπαύεο.

ἀποπέμπω (πέμπω), fut. ἀποπέμψω, Ep. ἀππέμψει, Od. 15, 83; aor. ἀπέπεμψα, *to send away, to send off, to let go;* with accus. 2) *to send back,* δῶρα, Od. 17, 76.

ἀποπέσῃσι, see ἀποπίπτω.

ἀποπέτομαι (πέτομαι). aor. 2 ἀπεπτάμην, partcp. ἀποπτάμενος, *to fly away, to fly back;* spoken of an arrow, 13, 857; of the god of dreams, ἀποπτάμενος ᾤχετο, he vanished in flight, 2, 71; of the soul, Od. 11, 222.

ἀποπίπτω (πίπτω), aor. 2 ἀπέπεσον, *to fall down, to sink down,* 14, 351; spoken of the bats, ἐκ πέτρης, to fall down from the rock, Od. 24, 7.

ἀποπλάζω (πλάζω), only aor. pass. ἀποπλάγχθην, partcp. ἀποπλαγχθείς, in the act. *to cause to wander* or *err.* Pass. *to wander, to be struck back* [in an object aimed at], Od. 8, 573; νῆσον, to be driven from the island, Od 12, 285; ἀπὸ θώρηκος πολλὸν ἀποπλαγχθείς, ἑκὰς ἔπτατο οἰστός. from the cuirass 'wide wand'ring' (Cp.) flew the arrow away, 13, 592. ἡ μὲν ἀποπλαγχθεῖσα (τρυφάλεια) χαμαὶ πέσε, springing far away the helmet fell to the ground, 13, 578.

ἀποπλείω, poet. for ἀποπλέω (πλέω), *to sail away, to set sail,* οἴκαδε, 9, 418. Od. 8, 501.

ἀποπλύνω (πλύνω), *to wash away* or *off;* with accus. only the iterat. imperf. λάϊγγας ποτὶ χέρσον ἀποπλύνεσκε, the sea washed the stones to the beach, Od. 6, 95.†

ἀποπλώω, Ion. for ἀποπλέω; to which the Ep. aor. 2 ἀπέπλω belongs Od. 14, 339.†

ἀποπνέω, Ep. ἀποπνείω (πνέω), *to breathe out, to exhale;* with accus. πυρὸς μένος, to breathe out the strength of fire, said of the Chimæra, 6, 182; πικρὸν ἁλὸς ὀδμήν, to exhale the disagreeable odour of the sea, Od. 4, 406. 2) *to expire;* θυμόν, to breathe forth the life, i. e., to die, 4, 524. 13, 654; and without θυμόν, Batr. 100.

*ἀποπνίγω (πνίγω), aor. 1 ἀπέπνιξα. *to choke outright, to strangle,* τινά, Batr. 119.

ἀποπρό (πρό), 1) Adv. *far away,* φέρειν, 16, 669. 2) Prep. with gen. *apart, far from,* νεῶν, 7, 343. (In composition it strengthens ἀπό.)

ἀποπροαιρέω (αἱρέω), partcp. aor. 2

ἀποπροελών, *to take away, to take off*,
τινός, any thing; σίτου, Od. 17, 457.†

ἀπόπροέηκε, see ἀποπροίημι.

ἀποπροελών, see ἀποπροαιρέω.

ἀπόπροθεν, adv. *from far, from a distance* [remote, far away], 10, 209. Od. 6, 218.

ἀπόπροθι, adv. ἀποπρό, *in the distance, far away*, 10, 410. Od. 4, 757.

ἀπόπροίημι (ἵημι), aor. 1 Ion. ἀποπροέηκα, *to send far away, to send forth, to despatch*, τινὰ πόλινδε, any one to the city, Od. 14, 26; ἰόν, to shoot an arrow, Od. 22, 82. 2) *to let fall*, ξίφος χαμᾶζε, Od. 22, 327. (‒‿‿‿‒).

ἀποπροτέμνω (τέμνω), partcp. aor. 2 ἀποπροταμών, *to cut off from, to carve from*; with gen. νώτου ['carving forth a portion from the loins of a huge brawn,' Cp.], Od. 8, 475.†

ἀποπτάμενος, see ἀποπέτομαι.

ἀποπτύω (υ in the pres. ῡ or ῠ) (πτύω), *to spit out, to vomit forth, to throw, cast up*, τί, any thing, 23, 781; said of the seawave, ἁλὸς ἄχνην ['scatter wide the spray,' Cp.], 4, 426.

ἀπόρθητος, ον (πορθέω), *not pillaged, not razed, unsacked*, πόλις, 12, 11.†

ἀπόρνυμι (ὄρνυμι), *to excite from a place*, only mid. *to rush forth from a place*; Λυκίηθεν, to come from Lycia, 5, 105.†

ἀποροὕω (ὀρούω), aor. 1 ἀπόρουσα, *to leap down, to hasten down*, from a chariot, 5, 20, 336. 2) *to recoil* [21, 593: πάλιν δ' ἀπὸ χαλκὸς ὄρουσεν, 'with a swift recoil back flew the spear,' Cp.; of a person], *to spring back*, 21, 251. Od. 22, 95.

ἀπορραίω (ῥαίω), aor. 1 ἀπόρραισα, prop. *to break off.* 2) *to tear away*, τινά τι, any thing from any one [σὲ ... κτήματα, *to rob you of your property*], Od. 1, 404; τινὰ ἦτορ, *to deprive of life*, Od. 16, 428.

ἀπορρήγνυμι (ῥήγνυμι), aor. 1 ἀπέρρηξα, *to break off, to tear away*; with accus. δεσμόν, his halter, spoken of a horse, 6, 507; κορυφὴν ὄρεος, Od. 9, 481; θαιρούς, to break [*burst*, Cp.] the hinges (of a gate), 12, 459.

ἀπορρῑγέω (ῥιγέω), perf. 2 †ἀπέρρῑγα; prop. I shudder with cold; hence fig. *I shudder to do any thing; I shrink from doing it; dare not do it*; c. infin. Od. 2, 52.† (The perf. with pres. signif.)

ἀπορρίπτω (ῥίπτω), aor. 1 ἀπέρριψα, *to throw away, to cast off*; with accus. καλύπτρην, a veil, 22, 406; metaph. μῆνιν, to lay aside anger, 9, 517; μηνιθμόν, •16, 282.

ἀπορρώξ, ῶγος, ὁ, ἡ (ῥήγνυμι), prop. adj. *torn off, steep, abrupt.* ἀκταὶ ἀπορρῶγες, the rugged shores. Od. 13, 98. 2) ἡ as subst. *a portion torn off, a fragment, a branch*; spoken of a river, Στυγὸς ὕδατος ἀπορρώξ, an arm of the Stygian water, 2, 755; of Cocýtus, Od. 10, 514; also spoken of excellent wine. ἀμβροσίης καὶ νέκταρος, an efflux of ambrosia and nectar. Od. 9, 359.

ἀποσεύομαι (σεύω), only in]
aor. 2 mid. ἀπεσσύμην, *to haste*
rush away or off; with gen.
from the house, 9, 390; ἐς μυχό
236. (υ short; σ doubled with a

ἀποσκεδάννυμι (σκεδάννυμι),
ἀπεσκέδασα, *to scatter, to dispers*
asunder; with accus. ψυχάς, Od,
βασιλῆας, 19, 309; metaph. κήδε
to dismiss cares from the mind
wide thy cares, Cp.]; *to dispel.* O

ἀποσκίδνημι, poet. form from
δάννυμι; in H. only mid. ἀπος
to disperse, 23, 4.†

ἀποσκυδμαίνω (σκυδμαίνω), (i
to be very angry, to be vehemently
τινί, against any one, 24, 65.†

ἀποσπένδω (σπένδω), *to pour ou*
to pour out wine at sacrifices, a
taking oaths, in honour of the
pour out a drink-offering, to off
tion, •Od. 3, 394. 14, 331.

· ἀποσταδά, adv. = ἀποσταδόν,
143.†

ἀποσταδόν, adv. (ἀφίστημι), a
a distance, μάρνασθαι, 15, 556.

ἀποστείχω (στείχω), aor. 2 ἀπ
to go away, to depart, Il.; οἴκαδ
turn home, Od. 11, 132; ἀνὰ νῆ
12, 143.

ἀποστίλβω (στίλβω), *to gl*
sparkle, to emit brightness. λίθ
στίλβοντες ἀλείφατος, stones, sh
with oil; ὡς must be here supp
H. uses this expression to indic
brightness), Od. 3, 408.†

ἀποστρέφω (στρέφω), fut. ἀπο
aor. 1 ἀπέστρεψα, Ep. iterat. ἀπ
ασκε, 1) Trans. *to turn away,*
back; πόδας καὶ χεῖρας (in orde
them behind), Od. 22, 173; *to*
ἰχνία, h. Merc. 76. b) *to cause to*
make to return; with accus. 15,
197; *to draw off any one from an*
τινὰ πολέμοιο, 12, 249 (where]
reads ἀποστρέψεις for ἀποτρέψεις
στρέψοντας ἑταίρους, sc. αὐτόν, fι
call him back, 10, 355. 2) [Acco
some interpreters it is] *intrans.*
11, 597, ἀποστρέψασκε=*it rolled*
a stone). [But in this sense, as
observes, we should at least exp
στρέφειν, and it is prob. trai
κραταιΐς.]

ἀποστρέψασκε, see ἀποστρέφω.

ἀποστυφελίζω (στυφελίζω), αor
στυφέλιξα, *to drive back by force,*
τινά τινος, 16, 703. τρὶς νεκροῦ ἀπ
λιξαν, thrice they drove him bε
pulsed him) from the dead bod
158.

•ἀποσυρίζω (συρίζω), *to pipe*
whistle, h. Merc. 280.

ἀποσφάλλω (σφάλλω), aor. 1 ἀπ
to lead from the right road, to ε
stray; τινά, any one, Od. 3, 320;
τινὰ πόνοιο, to cause any one tε
the object of his labour ['*to frust*
labours,' Cp.], 5, 567.

ἀποσχίζω (σχίζω), aor. 1 ἀπέσ

split off, to split asunder, to cleave ; with accus. πέτρην, Od. 4, 507.† in tmesis.

ἀποτάμνω (Ion. for ἀποτέμνω), aor. 2 ἀπέταμον, to cut off, to cut asunder, στομάχους, 3, 392 [ῥῖνα, οὔατα, &c.] ; ἵπποιο παρηορίας, 8, 87. 2) Mid. to cut off any thing for oneself, κρέα, 22, 347 ; hence to drive away, βοῦς, h. Merc. 74.

ἀποτηλοῦ, adv. (τηλοῦ), far in the distance, remote, Od. 9, 117.†

ἀποτίθημι (τίθημι), aor. 1 ἀπέθηκα, aor. 2 mid. ἀπεθέμην, subj. ἀποθείομαι Ep. for ἀποθῶμαι, infin. ἀποθέσθαι, 1) to lay aside, to lay up, to put up ; with accus. δέπας ἐπὶ χηλῷ, 16, 254. 2) Mid. to lay down or aside, to put off, τί, any thing ; φύσας ὅπλα τε πάντα, 18, 409 ; τεύχεα, to lay down one's arms, 3, 89 ; metaph. ἐνιπήν, to lay aside objurgation, 5, 492.

*ἀποτιμάω (τιμάω), fut. ἀποτιμήσω, not to honour, to slight ; with accus., h. Merc. 35.

ἀποτίνυμαι, poet. for ἀποτίνομαι. πολέων ποινήν, to take vengeance for many [a Grecian slain, Cp], 16, 398 ; τινά τινος, to cause one to atone for any thing, Od. 2, 73.

ἀποτίνω (τίω), fut. ἀποτίσω, aor. 1 ἀπέτισα, fut. mid. ἀποτίσομαι, aor. 1 ἀπετισάμην. I) Act. prop. to pay back, to requite, τὰ τριπλῇ, 1, 128 ; πολλά τινι, Od. 2, 132 ; a) Esply in a bad sense, to pay the penalty, to atone for any thing, τινί τι : τιμήν τινι, to make compensation, and satisfaction to any one, 3, 286 ; πᾶσαν ὑπερβασίην τινί. to requite [take vengeance upon] one for transgression, Od. 13, 193 : Πατρόκλοιο ἕλωρα, to pay the penalty for Patroclus slain, 18, 93. σύν τε μεγάλῳ ἀπέτισαν σὺν σφῇσιν κεφαλῇσι, and then shall they make full satisfaction, even with their own heads, etc. (aor. for fut.) 4, 161. b) In a good sense, to repay, to make good, κομιδήν τινι, 8, 186 ; εὐεργεσίας, Od. 22, 235. cf. Od. 2, 132. II) Mid. 1) to exact compensation. satisfaction. etc. ; with accus. of the thing, ποινὴν ἑτάρων, to require satisfaction, i. e., to take vengeance for his companions, Od. 23. 312 ; and mly to punish, βίας, Od. 16, 255. 3, 216 ; with accus. of the pers. τινά, to cause any one to make atonement, or to punish him, Od. 24, 480 ; absol. Od. 1, 268.

ἀποτίω=ἀποτίνω, not occurring in the pres.

ἀποτμήγω, Ep. form of ἀποτμήγω, aor. 1 ἀπότμηξα, to cut. or lop off, to cleave away ; with accus. χεῖρας ξίφει, 11, 146 ; κεφαλήν, Od. 10, 440 ; spoken of rivers κλιτῦς, to sweep away many a declivity [Cp.], 16, 390 ; metaph. τινά τινος, to cut off, or intercept any one from a thing, λαῶν, 10, 364. 22, 456.

ἄποτμος, ον (πότμος), unfortunate, wretched, 24, 388. Superl. ἀποτμότατος, Od. 1, 219.

ἀποτρέπω (τρέπω), fut. ἀποτρέψω, aor. 2 ἀπέτραπον, aor. 2 mid. ἀπετραπόμην, 1) to turn away, to turn aside, to divert, to

drive away, τινά, 15, 276 ; λαόν, 11, 758 ; πολέμοιο, to dissuade any one from war, 12, 249. 2) Mid. to turn away, to turn back ; with αὖτις, 10, 200. 12, 329.

ἀποτρίβω (τρίβω), fut. ἀποτρίψω, to rub off, to wipe off. πολλά οἱ ἀμφὶ κάρη σφέλα — πλευραὶ ἀποτρίψουσι βαλλομένοιο, i. e., the ribs of him pelted at shall drive back (lit. rub off) many stools thrown at his head, i. e., many stools thrown at his head shall at least hit his ribs, Od. 17, 232.† Some read πλευράς, and take σφέλα in the nom., less in accordance with the poetic language. [Others refer ἀμφὶ κάρη to the throwers: 'many stools whirled round the head,' &c.]

ἀπότροπος, ον (τρέπω), turned away, separated, far from men, Od 14, 372.

ἀποτρωπάω, poet. form of ἀποτρέπω, to turn away ; τινά, 20, 119 ; τί, Od. 16, 405. 2) Mid. to turn oneself away, τινός, from a thing ; τόξου τανυστύος, to withdraw or shrink from straining the bow, Od. 21, 112 ; with infin. to delay, to hesitate, δακέειν ἀπετρωπῶντο λεόντων, 18, 585.

ἀπούρας, a solitary partcp. aor. 1 from an obsol. root, which in signification belongs to ἀπαυράω, to take away, q. v. [Either an anomaly for ἀπουρήσας, as ἔχραισμον from χραισμεῖν ; or a regular or syncopated form of a barytone, ἀποαϝείρας.—ἀπαυρᾶν arising from elision, ἀπουρᾶν from contraction ; for οαυ=ωυ (as in ἑωυτοῦ) or ου, the α falling away, Död. p. 18]

ἀπουρίζω, fut. ἀπουρίσω, only 22, 489.† ἄλλοι γὰρ οἱ ἀπουρίσσουσιν ἀρούρας ; according to the common explanation, Ion. for ἀφορίζω, they will remove the boundaries of his fields, and so lessen them ; or, according to Buttm., Lexil. p. 146, related to ἀπαυράω (they will take his fields from him), who also prefers the other reading ἀπουρήσουσιν.

*ἀποφαίνω (φαίνω), aor. 1 ἀπέφηνα, to disclose, to bring to light, to make known, to manifest, Batr. 143.

ἀποφέρω (φέρω), fut. ἀποίσω, aor. 1 ἀπένεικα, to bear away, to bring away ; with accus. spoken of horses, ἀπό τινος, 5, 256. 2) to carry from one place to another, to convey ; τεύχεά τινι, Od. 16, 360 ; τινὰ Κόωνδε, of ships, 14, 255 ; μῦθον τινί, to report tidings to any one, 10, 337.

*ἀποφεύγω (φεύγω), to flee away, to escape, with accus. Batr.

ἀπόφημι (φημί), to announce ; with ἀντικρύ, to declare directly, 7, 362, Ep. 2) Mid. in like manner: ἀπόφασθε ἀγγελίην, 9, 422. To this is assigned the aor. ἀπεῖπον, q. v.

ἀποφθίω (φθίω), imperf. ἀπέφθιθον, poet.=ἀποφθίνω, to perish, Od. 5, 110. 133. 7, 251. (Buttm., Gram. § 114, rejects the reading ἀπέφθιθον, and prefers ἀπέφθιθεν for ἀπεφθίθησαν, as aor. pass. from φθίω, cf. Rost, Gram. p. 334.)

ἀποφθινύθω, poet. (φθινύθω), intrans. to perish, to die, 5, 643. 2) Trans. θυμόν, to lose life, 16, 540. *Il.

ἀποφθίνω, poet. (φθίνω), only aor. sync. mid. ἀπεφθίμην, impf. ἀποφθίσθω, 8, 429, optat. ἀποφθίμην for ἀποφθιοίμην, Od. 10, 51; partcp. ἀποφθίμενος, aor. 1 pass. ἀπεφθίθην; hence 3 plur. ἀπέφθιθεν, Od. 23, 331 [conf. also ἀποφθίθω], to perish, to die, 3, 322; λυγρῷ ὀλέθρῳ, Od. 15, 268; λυγαλέῳ θανάτῳ, Od. 15, 358; ἠὲ πεσὼν —ἀποφθίμην—ἠὲ ἀκέων τλαίην, whether I falling from the ship should perish in the sea, Od. 10, 51.

ἀποφώλιος, ον, poet. accord. to the Schol.=μάταιος, prop. idle, vain, empty, worthless. Od. 14, 212; spoken of the mind, νόον ἀποφώλιος, Od. 8, 177; οὐκ ἀποφώλια εἰδώς, not knowing worthless things, not weak of understanding, Od. 5, 182. 2) fruitless, unproductive; εὐναὶ ἀθανάτων, Od. 11, 249. (The deriv. is uncertain; according to some from φωλεός, according to others from ἀπό and ὄφελος.)

ἀποχάζομαι, depon. mid. (χάζομαι), to yield, to retire, βόθρου, Od. 11, 95.†

ἀποχέω (χέω), Ep. aor. ἀπέχευα, to pour out, to spill, εἴδατα ἔραζε, *Od. 22, 20. 85, in tmesis.

ἀποψύχω (ψύχω), partcp. aor. pass. ἀποψυχθείς, 1) to breathe out, to be breathless, to swoon, Od. 24, 348. b) to become cool. 2) Mid. to let (a thing) dry; to dry for oneself; with accus. τοὶ δ' ἱδρῶ ἀπεψύχοντο χιτώνων, they dried the sweat of the garments ['their tunics sweat-imbued—They ventilated,' Cp.], 11, 621. 22, 1; ἱδρῶ ἀποψυχθείς, 21, 561.

*ἀπρεπέως, poet. for ἀπρεπῶς, adv. (πρέπω), in an unbecoming manner, indecorously, h. Merc. 272.

ἄπρηκτος, ον (πράσσω) 1) undone, unaccomplished, vain, unproductive, fruitless; ἄπρηκτον πόλεμον πολεμίζειν, 2, 121; ἄπρηκτοι ἔριδες, idle contentions, 2, 376. 2) Pass. not to be managed, severe, incurable, unavoidable. ὀδύναι, Od. 2, 49; ἀνίη, Od. 12, 223. The neut. as adv. ἄπρηκτον νέεσθαι, to return without effecting one's purpose, 14, 221.

ἀπριάτην, adv. (πρίαμαι), unbought, unransomed, gratuitously, 1, 99. Od. 14, 317.

ἀπροτίμαστος, ον, Ep. for ἀπρόσμαστος (μάσσω), untouched, undefiled, pure, 19, 263.†

ἄπτερος. ον (πτερόν), unwinged, without wings; only in the phrase τῇ δ' ἄπτερος ἔπλετο μῦθος ['nor his words flew wing'd away,'Cp.], i. e., what he said did not escape her; she noted it, although words easily fly away (πτερόεντα), Od. 17, 57. 19, 29.

ἀπτήν, ἀπτῆνος, ὁ, ἡ (πτηνός), unfeathered, unfledged, callow, νεοσσός, 9, 323.†

ἀπτοεπής, ές (πτοέω, ἔπος), fearless or undaunted in speaking, bold, 8, 209.† According to others, ἀπτοεπής from ἅπτεσθαι, assailing with words, cf. 1, 582.

ἀπτόλεμος, ον, poet. (πόλεμος), unwarlike, cowardly, *2, 201.

ἅπτω, aor. 1 ἦψα, aor. 1 mid. ἠψάμην and ἀψάμην, aor. pass. Ep. ἑάφθη, q. v.

1) Act. to attach, to fasten, to join accus. only ἐϋστρεφὲς ἔντερον οἰ 21, 408. 11) Mid. to join for o βρόχον ἀφ' ὑψηλοῖο μελάθρου, to the noose fast to the lofty roof, (277; to attach oneself to, to stick to, τόφρα μάλ' ἀμφοτέρων βέλε' ἧπτι long the weapons hit both sides, 11, 85, and mly to touch, to grasp hold of, to clasp, to seize; wit ἅψασθαι γούνων, νηῶν, χειρῶν, κε κύων συὸς ἅπτεται κατόπισθε, ἰσ γλουτούς τε, a dog seizes the boa behind, by the hips and loins, Thus Eustath. explains the pass accordance with connexion, ass that to the genit. an accus. of definition is annexed, and sup κατὰ with ἰσχία, etc. Others co ἰσχία τε γλουτούς τε, with ἐλισσόμ δοκεύει: metaph. βρώμης ἠδὲ ποτῖ touch food and drink, Od. 10, 379.

ἅπτω, fut. mid. ἅψομαι, to infl kindle, to light; only mid. to take blaze up; ὅτε δὴ τάχ' ὁ μοχλὸς— μέλλεν ἅψεσθαι, when now the 'should soon have flamed' (Cp.) fire, Od. 9, 379.

ἀπύργωτος, ον (πυργόω), without unfortified, Θήβη, Od. 11, 263.†

ἄπυρος, ον (πῦρ), without fire, not come in contact with fire, unsoiled spoken of cauldrons and tripods new, 9, 122. 23, 267; or, with oth to be used on the fire, but e. g. for wine.

ἀπύρωτος, ον=ἄπυρος, φιάλη, a not yet touched by fire, 23, 270.†

ἄπυστος, ον (πυνθάνομαι), 1) F which nothing is heard, unknou heard of, Od. 1, 242. 2) Act. w heard of nothing, ignorant, unin Od. 5, 127; with gen. μύθων, 675.

ἀπωθέω (ὠθέω), fut. 1 ἀπώσω, ἄπωσα, Ep. ἀπέωσα, fut. mid. aor. 1 mid. ἀπωσάμην, to thrust a drive or push away; with accus. ρ abrade the skin, to break it, ὀμίχλην, to scatter the cloud, 1 τινά τινος and ἔκ τινος, to drive on ἄνδρα γέροντος, 8, 96; ἐκ Τροίης, 1 spoken of the winds and waves: from the right way, to turn aside 81. 2) Mid. to drive away from to repulse, to avert; with accus. 8, 206; κακὰ νηῶν, misfortune fr ships, 15, 503; πόλεμον νηῶν, 1 θυράων λίθον, Od. 9, 394.

ἄρα, particle Ep. also ἄρ and ερ (ΑΡΩ). [All the forms occur befo sonants; before vowels ἄρ' and may also stand before a vowel w digamma.] This particle, which stands as the first word of a se but which occupies an early plac expresses, in accordance with its tion from ΑΡΩ, to suit, to be ada close connexion, exactly, just, only, thereupon. 1) A most intim nexion between two ideas or thoughts: a) After relatives, in correlative clauses, of place, time, and manner. Ἀτρείδης δ' ἄρα χεῖρα—τὴν βάλεν, ᾗ ῥ' ἔχε τόξον, precisely the hand with which, 13, 594. τῇ ῥα, just there, just where, 14, 404. 11, 149; εὖτ' ἄρα, ὅτ' ἄρα, just as; τότ' ἄρα, exactly then. b) After a demonstrative pronoun, when by it an object previously named is referred to, or something already stated in general is repeated and more exactly explained, just, exactly, then, e. g. 4, 499—501, υἱὸν Πριάμοιο νόθον βάλε Δημοκόωντα— τόν ῥ' Ὀδυσεὺς—βάλε, him then, and v. 488. τοῖον ἄρα—ἐξενάριξεν Αἴας (as a recapitulation of the whole narration), cf. 13, 170 —177; τόν ῥα—νύξε; so ταῦτ' ἄρα, just these; with demonstrat. adv. τῷ ἄρα, just therefore, ἔνθ' ἄρα, just then or there, ὡς ἄρα, just so, and the frequent ἦ ῥα and ὡς ἄρ' ἔφη. Hence c) In sequences, οὗτοι ἄρ'—ἦσαν, these then were, 2, 760; τοὔνεκ' ἄρα, on this account then: here belongs the construction with interrogatives, τίς τ' ἄρ, τῶν—ἦν, now then, who of these, etc., 2, 761. Hence 2) It is also employed in clauses where a previous mistake is indicated, or information upon some unthought of point communicated, then, therefore. νηλέες οὐκ ἄρα σοί γε πατὴρ ἦν ἱππότα Πηλεύς, not therefore was, 16, 33. cf. 9, 316. Od. 13, 209. 17, 454; also in explanatory and illustrative clauses. ὅτι ῥα, ἐπεί ῥα, because namely, 1, 56. 13, 416. 3) It indicates the direct progress of actions and events: hence it serves a) To connect actions and states which in point of time succeed one another, and of which the one seems to proceed from the other, then, thereupon, 1, 68. 306. 464; hence frequently in connexion with αἶψα, αὐτίκα, καρπαλίμως; further, ἐπεί ῥα, ὅτε ῥα, as soon as, 14, 641; and in both protasis and apodosis, ὅτε δὴ ῥα—δὴ ῥα τότε, then forthwith, 11, 780. b) Mly in enumerating several consecutive events, 5, 592. With negat. οὐδ' ἄρα, it signifies, according to Nägelsbach, a) and not once, Od. 9, 92. b) and immediately not (no longer), Od. 4, 716; cf. Nägelsbach, Excurs. III. p. 191. Kühner, Gram. § 630.

ἀραβέω (ἄραβος), aor. 1 ἀράβησα, to rattle, to resound; spoken of the arms of a falling warrior. ἀράβησε τεύχε' ἐπ' αὐτῷ, 4, 504. 5, 42, and often.

ἄραβος, ὁ (ἀράσσω [and the other verba pulsandi, ῥάω, ῥαβάσσω. Lob. Path. 285]), noise, rattling; ὀδόντων, chattering of the teeth, 10, 375.†

Ἀραιθυρέη, ἡ, a town and territory in Argolis, accord. to Strabo the later Phlius, between Sicyon and Argos, which took its name from the daughter of Aras; or rather the signif. is from ἀραιός and θυρέα, a narrow pass, 2, 571.

ἀραιός, ή, όν, thin, small, narrow, κνῆμαι, 18, 411; γλῶσσαι, 16, 161; εἴσοδος, the narrow entrance of a port, Od. 10, 90. 2)

delicate, weak, unwarlike; spoken of the hand of Aphrodîtê, 5, 525.

ἀράομαι, depon. mid. (ἀρά), fut. ἀρήσομαι, aor. 1 ἠρησάμην, to pray, to address supplications to the gods; with dat. Ἀπόλλωνι, 1, 35. 2) to wish, yet only when one's wish is expressed aloud; with infin. 4, 143. Od. 1, 163; with ἕως and optat. Od. 19, 367. b) to wish present, to invoke; with accus. ἐπεὶ—ἀρήσετ' Ἐριννύς, when the mother shall invoke the Erinnyes, Od. 2, 135. Once ἀρήμεναι for ἀρᾶν, infin. act., but according to Buttm., Gram. § 114, aor. 2 pass. of the root ἄρομαι, in accordance with the connexion: πολλάκι που μέλλεις ἀρήμεναι, thou wilt oft have prayed, Od. 22, 322.

ἀραρίσκω, poet. (th. ΑΡΩ [cf. ἐλελίζω, ἀκαχίζω, ἀπαφίσκω]), aor. 1 act. ἦρσα, infin. ἄρσαι, aor. 2 act. ἤραρον. Ep. ἄραρον, partcp. ἀραρών, perf. ἄρηρα, partcp. ἀρηρώς, fem. ἀραρυῖα, pluperf. ἀρήρειν, aor. 1 pass. only 3 plur. ἄρθεν, 16, 211, Ep. aor. 2 mid. only partcp. ἄρμενος. (The pres. ἀραρίσκω, Od. 14, 23, has been formed from the aor. 2 act.) 1) Trans. in the aor. 1 and 2 act. (The last twice intrans. 16, 214. Od. 4, 777.) To join, hence 1) to annex, to bind, to fit to, to secure, to prepare, τί, any thing; τινί, with or of something; κέρα, to bind the horns, 4, 110. οἱ δ' ἐπεὶ ἀλλήλους ἄραρον βόεσσι, when with their shields they had locked themselves together, 12, 105; and pass. μᾶλλον δὲ στίχες ἄρθεν (Ep. for ἄρθησαν), the ranks pressed more closely together, 16, 211. b) τί τινι, to fasten or attach one thing to another; ἰκρία σταμίνεσσιν, Od. 5, 252; ἄγγεσιν ἅπαντα, to preserve, to put up every thing in vessels, Od. 2, 289; πέδιλα πόδεσσιν, Od. 14, 23; hence mly to construct, to prepare, to build, τί τινι, any thing of or from a thing; τοῖχον λίθοισι, to build a wall of stones, 16, 212 (in which sense also the perf. ἄρηρεν stands, Od. 5, 248; which is, however, according to the Schol. only a false reading for ἄρασσεν, cf. Nitzsch ad loc.). Metaph. μνηστήρσιν θάνατον, to prepare death for the suitors, Od. 16, 169. 2) to provide, to furnish, τί τινι; πώμασιν ἀμφορέας, Od. 2, 353; νῆα ἐρέτῃσιν, Od. 3, 280; metaph. ἤραρε θυμὸν ἐδωδῇ, he furnished, i. e. refreshed his heart with food, Od. 5, 95. 3) to suit any thing to any one, to make agreeable, only 1, 136. γέρας ἄρσαντες κατὰ θυμόν, suiting a present to my mind, i. e., selecting one, etc. II) Intrans. in the perf. and plupf. 1) to be joined together, to stand in close array, and mly to fit, to be suited to, to sit close. Τρῶες ἀρηρότες, the Trojans in close array, 13, 800; and so aor. 2, 16, 214. ζωστὴρ ἀρηρώς, a close-fitting girdle, 4, 134; mly with dat. θώρηξ γυάλοισι ἀρηρώς, a cuirass joined together, constructed of plates, 15, 530. cf. Od. 6, 267; to suit, τινί, any thing. δοῦρα παλάμηφιν ἀρήρει, 3, 338. κυνέη ἑκατὸν πολίων πρυλέεσσ' ἀραρυῖα, 5, 744. πύλαι πύκα στιβαρῶς ἀραρυῖαι, 12, 454 ; σανίδης, Od. 2, 344; rarely with prepos. ἐν ἁρμονίῃσιν ἀρήρῃ, the timbers hold fast in the joints, Od. 5. 361. cf. ἁρμονίη. πίθοι ποτὶ τοῖχον ἀρηρότες, vessels arranged against the wall (fitted to the wall), Od. 2, 342; metaph. οὐ φρεσὶν ᾗσιν ἀρηρώς, not firm in understanding, Od. 10, 553. 2) *fitted out, well furnished;* σκολόπεσσι, with fishes, 12, 56. ζώνη ἑκατὸν θυσάνοις ἀραρυῖα, 14, 181. cf. Od. 2, 267. 3) Metaph. *to be befitting, agreeable, pleasant.* μῦθος, ὃ—πᾶσιν ἤραρεν, which was pleasing to all, Od. 4, 777, aor. 2 here intrans. III) Mid. only the partcp. aor. 2 sync. as adj. ἄρμενος, η,·ον, *fitted to, attached to;* with dat. ἐπίκριον ἄρμενον τῷ ἱστῷ, the sail-yard attached to the mast, Od. 5, 254; with ἐν : τροχὸς ἄρμενος ἐν παλάμῃσιν, a wheel suited to the hands, 18, 600; πέλεκυς, Od. 5, 234.

ἄραρον, see ἀραρίσκω.

ἀράσσω [see ἄραβος], fut. ξω, *to strike, to knock, to beat;* in our editions of H. found only in tmesis, ἀπαράσσω and συναράσσω [and once ἐξαράσσω, Od. 12, 422], q. v. In Od. 5, 248, Bothe, instead of the reading ἄρηρεν of Eustath., has adopted the reading of the Codd. ἄρασσεν. He reads, therefore, καὶ ἥρμοσεν ἀλλήλοισιν γόμφοισιν δ' ἄρα τήνγε καὶ ἁρμονίῃσιν ἄρασσεν. Also Nitzsch, Bd. 11. p. 36, approves this as the only true reading, because ἄρηρεν is always elsewhere used intransitively, and ἤραρεν with ἥρμοσεν is tautological; cf. Apoll. Rhod. 11. 614. ʾΑρασσεν stands for συνάρασσεν, belongs prop. to γόμφοισιν, and is by zeugma to be referred to ἁρμονίῃσιν also. Bothe translates the verse : ʼ he hammered (fastened) together the raft with nails and joints.ʼ

ἀράχνιον, τό (ἀράχνη), *a spider's web,* Od. 8, 280. 16, 35. *Od.

ἀργαλέος, έη, έον, *heavy, difficult, troublesome, oppressive,* that which can hardly be borne; more rarely, which is difficult to accomplish, ἔργον, ἄνεμος, μνηστύς, Od. 2, 199; mly with dat. of pers. and infin. ἀργαλέον μοι πᾶσι μάχεσθαι, hard it is for me to contend with all, 20, 356; more rarely, ἀργαλέος γὰρ ʾΟλύμπιος ἀντιφέρεσθαι, hard is it to oppose the Olympian Zeus, 1, 589, and Od. 4, 397 (prob. from α intens. and ἔργον; or, according to some, from ἄλγος, with an exchange of λ for ρ).

ʾΑργεάδης, ου, ὁ, son of Argeus=*Polymelus,* 16, 417.

ʾΑργεῖος, είη, εῖον (ʾΑργος), *of Argos, Argive.* ʾΗρη ʾΑργείη, the Argive Hērē, 4, 8 ; ʾΕλένη, the Peloponnesian, 2, 161; cf. ʾΑργος, h. 3. 2) Subst. *a man of Argos,* primarily an inhabitant of the city of Argós. *b)* an inhabitant of the Argive territory; and, because this was the principal people before Troy, a denomination of all the Greeks, 2, 352.

ʾΑργειφόντης, ου, ὁ (ʾΑργος, φονέω), *the Argicide,* an appellation of Hermēs, because he slew the guardian of many-eyed Argus, 2, 103. Od [ʾΑργος (propter oculorum splend Micuus. See note, end of ἀργός.

ἀργεννός, ή, όν, poet. for ἀργό shining, ὄϊες, but also ὀθόναι coloured veil, 3, 141 [hence the ʾΑργεννοῦσαι and the promont γεννον=Capo Bianco, *Lob. Path.*

ἀργεστής, ᾱο, ὁ (ἀργός) epith. o prob. *rapid,* or *raising white fo albus Notus,* Hor., [=*rapidus, ve ταχύς, Apoll.,* for in H. (mist Horace) *Notus* does not *dispe collect* the clouds. *Luc.* p. 181]), 21, 334. As an adj. it is, accor the Gramm., oxytone, ἀργεστής; name, paroxytone, cf. Spitzner a 306.

ἀργέτι, ἀργέτα, poet. for ἀργῆτι, see ἀργῆς.

ἀργῆς, ῆτος, ὁ, ἡ, *white, clear,* beaming [Lucas would construe i *flashing,* to combine both *rapid brightness.* It is an epithet, ἀστεροπή (*fulgur*), but of κεραυ men), the *lightning* that *strike* spoken of lightning : but also o ἀργῆς δημός, white fat, 11, 817. (poet. shortened dat. and accus. ἀργέτα, 11, 817. 21, 127).

ἀργικέραυνος, ου, ὁ (κεραυνός), a blaze of white lightning. *darting ing lightning,* epith. of Zeus; sul hurler of lightning (Voss), *20, 16

ἀργινόεις, εσσα, εν (ἀργός), shining, epith. of the towns Cami Lycastus, from the white limestone tains, 2, 647. 656 ; οὔρεα, h. Ap. 1

ἀργιόδους, οντος, ὁ, ἡ (ὀδούς), *toothed, white-tusked,* epith. of bo dogs, 10, 264. Od. 8, 60.

ἀργίπους, ποδος, ὁ, ἡ (πούς), *footed,* epith. of dogs, 24, 211.† of h. in Ven. 212. See note on ʾΑργει

ʾΑργισσα, ἡ, a place in Thess lasgiōtis, on the Penēus, the la gura, 2, 737.

ἄργμα, τος, τό (ἄρχω), *the firs the firstlings,* the portions of the cut off and burnt in honour of th Od. 14, 446.†

ʾΑργος, ὁ, pr. name of a dog, 292 ; see adj. ἀργός.

ʾΑργος, εος, τό, 1) *Argos* (*Arg* city in Argolis, on the Inachu Argo, in the time of the Trojan residence of Diomēdēs, 2, 559. the epithets ʾΑχαιϊκόν, ʾΙασον, ʾΙπ 2) the *Argolic plain,* the realm i Agamemnon ruled, having his re in Mycenæ, 1, 30. 2, 108. 3) I also the entire *Peloponnesus,* Arg the chief city of the Achaians most powerful kingdom in the ponnesus; hence, in connexio Hellas, it stands for all Greece, 344. 4, 726. 4) τὸ Πελασγικόν, a Thessaly, under the dominion of A according to some the later Lari extant in the time of Strabo, 2, 681. (ἄργος, τό, signifies, accord. to Strab., *plain*, and is peculiarly a name of Pelasgian towns, as Λάρισσα, see Müller I. § 125.)

ἀργός, ή, όν (related to ἄργυρος [see Hermann's note in Ἀργειφόντης]), *shining, gleaming, white*, epith. of a goose, Od. 15. 161; and of victims shining with fat (*nitidus*), 23, 30. 2) *rapid, fleet*, often epith. of dogs, πόδας ἀργοί, 18, 578. Od. 2, 11; and without πόδας, 1, 50. (According to the Schol. and some modern commentators, it signifies *white dogs*, see Köppen; the connexion, however, refutes this signif., since the reference is to the entire race. The signif. *swift-footed*, some derive from ἄργον and the intens. a, ἀεργός, contr. ἀργός, *without toil, swift-running*. The true derivation is that, being primarily used of light, it signifies *glimmering, shining* (Herm. *micuus*); then of the running of dogs, *feet*, since swiftness in running produces a glimmering appearance: see Nitzsch in Anm. to Od. 2, 11.)

Ἀργόσδε, to Argos.

ἀργύρεος, έη. εον (ἄργυρος), *silver, adorned with silver*, often used of articles belonging to the gods and to the rich, 1, 49. 5, 727. Od. 4, 53.

ἀργυροδίνης, ου (δίνη), *silver-whirling, having silver eddies*, epith. of rivers, *2, 752. 21, 8.

ἀργυρόηλος, ον (ἧλος), *adorned with silver nails* or *studs*, ξίφος, θρόνος, 3, 334. Od. 7, 162.

ἀργυρόπεζα, ή (πέζα), *silver-footed*, metaph. for shining, epith. of Thetis, *1, 538.

ἄργυρος, ὁ (related to ἀργός), *silver*. H. mentions it very often, and names as its source the town Alybe in the country of the Halizones (cf. Ἀλύβη). We find mention of vessels of massive silver, e. g., a *mixing vase* (Od. 9, 203), *cauldrons, goblets, cups*, etc., Od. 1, 137. 4, 53. In other places the articles seem only plated or washed with silver, e. g., the handles of the swords, 11, 31. Od. 8, 404; the door-posts in the palace of Alcinous, Od. 8, 89; or inlaid with silver, e. g., a seat, Od. 19, 56; the bed of Ulysses, Od. 23, 200.

ἀργυρότοξος, ον (τόξον), *having a silver bow, god of the silver bow*, epith. of Apollo, 1, 706. Od. 7, 64; also as subst. 1, 37.

Ἀργυφέη, ή, an unknown town in Elis, h. Ap. 422; where Ilgen would read Ἀρηνίγενεια

ἀργύφεος, έη, εον. poet. (ἄργυρος [Vocalis (ε) extrinsecus additæ exemplum certum sed unicum praebet ἀργύφεος: quod propter consonæ mutationem cum ξυλήφιον et ξυλήριον conferri posset, nisi utrumque mendi speciem praeberet. *Lob. Path.* 299]), *silver-shining, silver-white*; σνίος, 18, 50; φᾶρος, robe, Od. 5, 230. [In Hes. Theog. 574, ἀργυφής of a garment.]

ἄργυφος, ον=ἀργύφεος, epith. of sheep, 29. 621. Od. 10, 85.

Ἀργώ, οῦς, ή. *Argo*, the ship of the Argonauts, named either from the builder Argos, or from ἀργός, swift, Od. 12, 70.

ἀρδμός, ὁ (ἄρδω), a place where cattle are watered, *a watering-place, a drinking-place*, 18, 521. Od. 13, 247.

*ἄρδω, fut. ἄρσω, *to give drink, to water*, h. 8, 3. Mid. *to water oneself, to drink*, h in Ap. 263.

ἀρειή, ή (ἀρά), *cursing, imprecation, threatening, menacing*, 17, 431; 20, 109 (ἄ).

Ἀρέθουσα, ἡ (ἄρι, θέω, that runs briskly), a fountain on the west side of the island Ithaca, Od. 13, 408.

Ἄρειος, ον (Ἄρης), mly Ἀρήιος in H., *devoted to Arês*. τεῖχος Ἄρειον, the wall of Arês, i. e., Thebes.

ἀρείων, ἄρειον, *better, stronger, superior, braver*; a compar. which from the meaning is assigned to ἀγαθός, related to ἄρι or Ἄρης; accus. sing. ἀρείω, for ἀρείονα, Od. 3, 250; nom. plur. ἀρείους, for ἀρείονες, Od. 2, 477.

Ἀρείων, ονος, ὁ, the steed of Adrastus, to which he owed his deliverance before Thebes, 23, 346. Ἀρίων, Apd.

ἄρεκτος, ον, Ep. for ἄρρεκτος (ῥέζω), *not done, unaccomplished*, 19, 150.†

ἀρέσαι, ἀρέσασθαι, see ἀρέσκω.

ἀρέσκω (th. ἀρέω), fut. ἀρέσω, aor. 1 act. ἤρεσα, mid. fut. ἀρέσομαι, Ep. σσ, aor. 1 ἠρεσάμην, Ep. σσ, 1) Act. in H. trans. *to make good, to compensate, to requite, to make satisfaction*, 9, 120. 2) Mid. oftener, *to make good for oneself, to compensate* or *requite for oneself*. ταῦτα ἀρεσσόμεθα, these things will we settle, 4, 362. 6, 526. Od. 22, 55; said of persons: *to propitiate, to conciliate, to appease*, τινά, Od. 8, 402; τινί, by a thing; τινὰ δώροισιν, to propitiate any one by presents, 9, 112. Od. 8, 396, 415.

ἀρετάω (ἀρετή), *to prosper, to flourish, to succeed*, Od. 8, 329. λαοὶ ἀρετῶσι, the people flourish, Od. 19, 144.

Ἀρετάων, ονος, ὁ, a Trojan who was slain by Teucer, 6, 31.

ἀρετή, ἡ, *worth, ability, excellence*, any thing by which one distinguishes himself. In H. it means esply, 1) In gods, *glory*, 9, 498. 2) In men, *strength, courage, bravery, activity of body*; also external advantages, *fortune, beauty, honour*, etc. ἀμείνων παντοίας ἀρετὰς, ἠμὲν πόδας, ἠδὲ μάχεσθαι, superior in every virtue, both in running and fighting, 15, 642; *fortune*, spoken of Ulysses, Od. 13, 44; *strength*, Od. 18, 133. 3) In women, *excellence, beauty, fortune*, Od. 2, 206. 18, 350. (The moral idea of virtue is not known to H. It is derived from ἄρω or from Ἄρης, or, accord. to Nitzsch on Od. 3, 57, from ἀρέω, any thing which is pleasing.)

ἀρή, ἡ, Ion. for ἀρά, *prayer, supplication, petition*, 15, 378. 23, 199, ἀράων ἀίουσα. Od. 4, 767; mly in a bad sense, *imprecation, malediction*. ἐξαίσιος ἀρή, cruel imprecation, 15, 598; hence 2) the *destruction*, *evil*, or *misfortune* imprecated, 12, 334. Od. 2, 59. 24, 489, ἀρὴν καὶ λοιγὸν ἀμῦναι. [14, 485, ἀρῆς ἀλκτῆρα γενέσθαι (cædis vindicem, *Heyne*), *one who averts from himself the curse of unrevenged blood*, i. e., by killing the slayer of his near relation. *Lob.*] (According to Heyne, 12, 334, the word in the first signif. has a, in the second, ἄ; but, according to Passow, the quantity depends upon the position in the verse.)

ἀρήγω (related to ἀρκέω), fut. ἀρήξω, *to help*, *to assist*, *to come to aid*, τινί, any one; often in the Il. also with dat. instrum.: ἔπεσιν καὶ χερσίν, to help with word and deed. 1, 77. 2) *to repel*, with accus. ὄλεθρον, Batr. 280.

ἀρηγών, όνος, ὁ, ἡ, *a helper*; as fem. *4, 7.

Ἀρηΐθοος, ον (θοός), *fleet as Arês*, *rapid in the battle*, *4, 280.

Ἀρηΐθοος, ὁ, pr. n. 1) husband of Philomelê. grandfather of Menesthius, king of Arnê in Bœotia, with the appellation of club-bearer, 7, 9. cf. v. 137 seq. Lycurgus surprised him on his return from Arcadia in an ambuscade, and slew him, 9, 141 seq. His grave was shown in Arcadia, Paus. 2) father of Menesthius, 7. 8; for the ὅν, v. 9, relates to Ἀρηΐθόοιο ἄνακτος, see Heyne. 3) a Thracian, charioteer of Rhigmus, slain by Achilles, 20, 486.

Ἀρήϊος, ον, Ion. for ἄρειος, *devoted to Arês*, *warlike*, *brave*, *martial*; spoken often of persons; more rarely of things: τεύχεα, ἔντεα, weapons of Arês, 6, 340. Od. 16, 284.

Ἀρηϊκτάμενος, η, ον (κτείνω), *slain by Arês*, *fallen in battle*, 22, 72.†

Ἀρηΐλυκος, ὁ (λύκος, a wolf like Arês), 1) father of Prothoênôr, q. v. 2) a Trojan, slain by Panthous, 26, 308.

Ἀρηΐφατος, ον (ΦΕΝΩ, πέφαμαι). *slain by Arês*, *killed in battle*, 19, 31. Od. 11, 41.

Ἀρηΐφῐλος, *beloved by Arês*, *warlike*, *brave*, epith. of the Achaians, 6, 73.

ἀρήμεναι, see ἀράομαι.

ἀρημένος, η, ον (ᾰ), an Ep. partcp. perf. pass. of doubtful derivation; explained by the Schol. by βεβλαμμένος, *burdened*, *oppressed*, *tormented*. γήραϊ λυγρῷ ἀρημένος, 18, 435: oftener in the Od. ὕπνῳ καὶ καμάτῳ ἀρημένος, oppressed with sleep and fatigue, Od. 6, 2. (Accord. to Thiersch, Gram. § 232, p. 385, from ἀρέω, related to βαρύς; according to others, to ἀραιός.)

(ἄρήν, ὁ,) in nom. obsol.; from this the syncop. cases ἀρνός, ἀρνί, ἄρνα, plur. ἄρνες, dat. ἀρνάσι, Ep. ἀρνέσσι, prop. *a male sheep*, *a ram*, Od. 4, 85; but particularly *a young sheep*, *a lamb* (from ῥήν, with euphon. prefix α, hence ἀρήν, ἀρρήν, ἀρσήν).

ἀρηρομένος, η, ον, see ἀρόω.

Ἀρήνη, ἡ, a town in Elis, on the river Minyeius, according to Strabo, VIII. 346,

prob the later *Samicon*, which, pe[rhaps] was the fortress of Arene; but acc[ording to] another passage of Strabo, VIII. 34[...] later *Erana*, in Messenia: cf. Paus[...] 3 2, 591. 11, 723.

Ἄρης, gen. Ἄρεος, Ep. Ἄρηος, Ἄρεϊ, Ἄρει, Ep. Ἄρηϊ, accus. Ep. Ἄρην, Ἄρηα, 5, 909, vocat. Ἄρες, son of Zeus and Hêrê, god of w[ar,] of the fierce tumult of battle; the s[on] of stormy, impetuous bravery, in c[ontra]distinction from Athênê. He is [repre]sented as the brother of Eris (Di[scord,] Deimos (Terror) and Phobos (Flig[ht] his sons, 4. 440. 13, 280. 15, 11[...] delights only in war and bloodshe[d,] πολέμοιο, μιαιφόνος, βροτολοιγος, he knows in his bravery neither pl[...] moderation (θοός, θοῦρος, ὄβριμος) has his abode chiefly among the warlike nations, the Thracia[ns] Phlegyes, and the Ephyri, 13, 30[...] in the Il. is sometimes on the side [of the] Trojans, sometimes on that of the [Greeks] (ἀλλοπρόσαλλος). Arês is large and [awe]some in appearance; his body co[vers ...] plethra; he cries as loudly as [...] men, upon being wounded by Dio[medes] 5, 860. Of his earlier fortunes, th[e con]finement in which he was held b[y Otos] and Ephialtês, and from which h[e was] delivered by Hermês, and his in[trigue] with Aphroditê, are mentioned by [...] 385. Od. 8, 267 seq. 2) As an app[ell.] stands for *war*, *battle*, *slaughter*, *d[estruc]tion*, *arms*, when, however, the per[soni] cation is not entirely lost sight of [...] ἄγειν Ἄρηα, *to begin the battle*, [...] and ἔριδα Ἄρηος, 14, 149: ἐγείρει[ν] Ἄρηα, 2, 440; *weapons*, for ἔγχος, [...] (The first syllable short; in the [...] however, it is long, cf. 5, 31.)

ἀρητήρ, ῆρος, ὁ (ἀράομαι), pro[phet] who prays; then *a priest*, since h[e prays] for the people, *1, 11. 5, 78.

Ἀρήτη, ἡ (ᾱ), daughter of Rhe[xenor,] wife of Alcinous in Phæacia, Od. [...] 77.

Ἀρητιάδης, ου, ὁ (ᾰ), son of . [...] Od. 16, 395. (The first α short.)

ἀρητός, ή, όν, Ion. for ἀρατός (ᾰρ[...] *wished for*, *prayed for*. 2) In [a] bad sense, *imprecated*, *accursed*, *ful*, γόος, 17, 37.

Ἄρητος, ὁ, 1) son of Nestor, 41[...] 2) son of Priam, slain by [Auto]medon, 17, 494.

ἄρθεν, Ep. for ἤρθησαν, see ἀρα[ρίσκω] ἀρθμέω (ἀρθμός), aor. 1 partcp. [...] σας, *to join*. 2) Intrans. *to be* [...] *together*. διέτμαγεν ἐν φιλότητι σαντε, they parted from each othe[r] in friendship [' *they parted friend[ly]* 7, 302.†

ἄρθμιος, η, ον (ἀρθμός), *united i[n]* *ship*, *friendly*; *at peace with a[ny]* τινί, Od. 16, 427.†

*ἀρθμός, ὁ (ἄρω), *union*, *i[n]* *friendship*, h. Merc. 524.

ἀρι-, an inseparable particle, [...]

which heightens the meaning, prob. related to ἀρείων.

Ἀριάδνη, ἡ (Herm. *Roborina*), daughter of Minos and Pasiphaê, who helped Theseus out of the labyrinth. She followed him, but was slain on the island Dia (Naxos) by Artĕmis. By '*the testimony of Dionysus*' (Διονύσου μαρτυρίησιν), commentators understand that Ariadnē received the embraces of Theseus in a grove of the island which was sacred to that god, and was therefore slain, Od. 11, 321 seq. 11. 18, 592.

ἀρίγνωτος, η, ον (γνωτός), *much distinguished, easily known*, ἀρίγνωτοί τε θεοί, 13, 72. Od. 6, 108. 2) In the iron. sense, *well known*, noted, *notorious*, Od. 17, 375. (ˇ ˉ ˉ ˇ and ˇ ˉ ˇ, Od. 17.)

ἀριδείκετος, ον (δείκνυμι), much pointed out, hence, *greatly distinguished, very famous*; chiefly as superl. with gen. ἀνδρῶν, λαῶν, 11, 248. Od. 8. 382.

ἀρίζηλος, ον, also ἀριζήλη, 18, 219 (from ἄρι and ζῆλος=δῆλος, with the digamma, which prob. before δ passed over into σ); *very clear, very manifest, very brilliant*, αὐγή, 22, 25; φωνή, a clear voice; spoken of a miraculous phenomenon: τὸν (sc. δράκοντα) ἀρίζηλον θῆκε θεός, the god made him visible, or, according to others, *significant*, i. e., a prodigy, 2, 319. cf. Buttm. Lex. p. 53 sqq., and ἀίζηλος.

ἀριζήλως, *clearly, entirely*, Od. 12, 453.†

ἀριθμέω (ἀριθμός), fut. ήσω, infin. aor. 1 pass. ἀριθμηθήμεναι for ἀριθμηθῆναι, *to count, to reckon up, to count together, to enumerate*; with accus. Od. 4, 411. 10, 204. εἴπερ γάρ κ' ἐθέλοιμεν—ἀριθμηθήμεναι ἄμφω, if we both, Achaians and Trojans, should be counted, 2, 124.

ἀριθμός, ὁ (ἄρω), *number, amount, multitude*, *Od. 4, 451. 11, 449.

Ἄριμα, τά, sc. ὄρη, *the mountains of the Arimi*; or, as a people, Ἄριμοι οἱ, *the Arimi*, 2, 783. εἰν Ἀρίμοις most commentators take as mountains, see Τυφωεύς. This chain of mountains has been located in Mysia, Lydia, Cilicia, and Syria: since, in the imagination of the poets, a giant inspired by Zeus lies buried where there are earthquakes and volcanic fire. Strab., XIII. p. 606, prefers Mysia; here, at any rate, was a region exhibiting traces of volcanic fire, and which was therefore called ἡ Κατακεκαυμένη.

ἀριπρεπής, ές, gen. έος (πρέπω), *exceedingly prominent, very distinguished, magnificent, glorious, splendid*, spoken of men, beasts, and things; with dat. ἀριπρεπὴς Τρώεσσιν, distinguished among the Trojans, 6, 477.

Ἀρίσβας, αντος, ὁ, father of Liocritus, perhaps a Theban, 17, 345.

Ἀρίσβη, ἡ, a town in Troas, not far from Abydos, 2, 836. Adv. Ἀρίσβηθεν, from Arisbê, 11, 96.

*ἀρίσημος, ον (σῆμα), *very distinguished*, noted, h. in Merc. 12.

ἀριστερός, ή, όν, *left*; ὦμος, the left shoulder. ἐπ' ἀριστερά, upon the left; μάχης, 5, 355; στρατοῦ, 13, 326; χειρός, on the left hand. 2) Metaph. spoken of omens, *sinister, inauspicious*, because to the Greek diviner, who looked towards the north, the left hand indicated misfortune, 12, 240. Od. 20, 242. [σκαιός is not used in this sense. Död.]

ἀριστερόφιν, adv. or Ep. accus. with suffix φιν (cf. Rost, Dial. § 23, b), ἀριστερός, *upon the left side, left*; only with prepos. ἐπ' ἀριστερόφιν, 13, 309. 17, 116.

ἀριστεύς, ῆος, ὁ (ἄριστος), *the best, the most excellent*, sing. 17, 203; in H. chiefly plur., οἱ ἀριστῆες, the chiefs, chieftains, leaders, 2, 404.

ἀριστεύω (ἀριστεύς), *to be first, to be most excellent, to distinguish oneself, to excel*, τινός, any one, 6, 461; τινί, in a thing, βουλῇ, in counsel, 11, 627; also ἐν μάχῃ, 11, 409; and with the infin. 6, 460.

ἄριστον, τό, *breakfast, prandium*, taken in H. soon after sunrise, 24, 124. Od. 16, 2 (ἄ).

ἄριστος, η, ον (superl. of ἀγαθός from ἀρείων), *the best, most excellent, most distinguished*, in H. spoken only of external advantages, and esply of warlike power. Ἀργείων οἱ ἄριστοι, the noblest of the Argives; often connected with the accus., εἶδος ἀρίστη, most excellent in form, 2, 715. ἵπποι ἄριστοι, 2, 763 (contr. with article ὥριστος for ὁ ἄριστος, 11, 288; see Thiersch, Gram. § 165, 1.)

ἀρισφαλής, ές, gen. έος (σφάλλω), *very slippery*, οὐδός. Od. 17, 196 †

ἀμφραδέως, adv. *very clearly*, Od. 23, 225.†

ἀμφραδής, ές, gen. έος (φράζομαι), *easily distinguishable, very plain or clear, very observable*, 23, 240; σῆμα, Od. 11, 126. 23, 73.

Ἀρκαδίη, ἡ (prop. fem. from ἀρκάδιος), *Arcadia*, a district in the middle of the Peloponnesus, 2, 603.

Ἀρκάς, άδος, ὁ (ἄ), *an Arcadian*, an inhabitant of Arcadia, 2, 611.

Ἀρκεισιάδης, ου, ὁ (ἄ), son of Arcesius =*Laertes*, Od. 4, 755.

Ἀρκείσιος, ὁ, *Arcesius*, son of Zeus and Euryodia, husband of Chalcomedūsa, father of Laertēs, Od. 16, 118. 120. (According to Eustath. ad loc. he received the name because he was suckled by a bear.)

Ἀρκεσίλαος, ὁ (from ἀρκέω and λαός, *defender of the people*), son of Lycus, leader of the Bœotians in the Trojan war, sailed to Troy with ten ships, and was slain by Hector, 2, 495. 15, 329.

ἀρκέω, fut. ἀρκέσω, aor. 1 ἤρκεσα, 1) *to avert, to hold back, to remove*, τινί τι, something from any one; ὄλεθρον τινί, 6, 16, and ἀπό τινος, 13, 440. 2) With dat. only, *to defend, protect, help* any one, 15, 529. Od. 16, 261; and without cases, *to profit, to avail, to be of use*; οὐδ' ἤρκεσε θώρηξ, the cuirass did no good, 13, 371.

ἄρκιος, η, ον (ἀρκέω), helping, advantageous, sufficient, μισθός, 10, 304. 2) on which one may depend, sure, certain, safe (Ap ἕτοιμον), οὐ οἱ ἄρκιον ἐσσεῖται, with infin. 2, 393 [there shall be nothing on which he can rely (which can give him a well-grounded hope of escaping the dogs and birds). νῦν ἄρκιον ἢ ἀπολέσθαι ἠὲ σαωθῆναι, now we may rely upon it (i. e., it is certain) that we shall either perish or be saved. Buttm., Lex. p. 163]. 15, 502. (Accord. to Buttm. the last is the primary meaning, and the only one in H.; hence μισθὸς ἄρκιος, a sure, definite reward.)

ἄρκτος, ὁ. ἡ. 1) a bear, Od. 11, 611. h. Ven. 71. 2) Ἄρκτος, pr. n. the Great Bear or the Wain, a constellation in the northern heavens, which embraces seven stars, and towards which Ulysses directed his course, Od. 5, 273. It is very near the polar star, and to the inhabitants of the northern hemisphere never sets, 18, 485 seq. Od. 5, 273. According to a later fable, it was Callisto metamorphosed to a bear.

ἅρμα, ατος, τό (ἄρω), a chariot, esply the war-chariot; the plur. often stands for the sing. 2) the chariot and team, 4, 306. 10, 322. Often ἵπποι καὶ ἅρματα, 5, 199. The war-chariots of the Hom. heroes had but one axle-tree (ἄξων) and two wheels (τροχοί), 5, 838. 6, 42. From the middle of the chariot and out of the axle-tree proceeded the pole (ὁ ῥυμός), which was single. The felloes (ἡ ἴτυς) of the wheels, 4, 486, were surrounded by iron or brazen tires (ἐπίσσωτρα). The hole of the nave, and the nave itself (αἱ πλῆμναι), were guarded with metal, and to this the spokes (κνῆμαι) were attached. Upon the axle-tree was placed a body or seat (ὁ δίφρος), which was circular before and behind, and had an opening for the convenience of ascending and alighting. At the fore-end of the pole was a hole, in which a pin (ὁ ἕστωρ) was inserted to keep the yoke from slipping (cf. τὸ ζυγόν). Two horses were commonly attached to one chariot; sometimes a third was added, which was bound to one of the pole-horses with a thong, and was called παρήορος. In single passages mention is made of a chariot with four horses, 8, 185. In the chariot were always two warriors, one who fought with the spear, ὁ παραιβάτης, and another acting as charioteer (ὁ ἡνίοχος). The chariot was chiefly used in the first onset, in order to force the enemy to sudden flight, 11, 711. 761. This, of course, could happen only on level ground. In battle itself, the warriors leapt from the chariot and fought on foot: cf. the several words, and esply ἵππος, παραιβάτης, ἡνίοχος.

Ἅρμα, ατος, τό, a village in Bœotia, not far from Tanagra, where Amphiarāus

and his chariot were swallowed up t earth, 2, 499.

ἁρματοπηγός, όν (πήγνυμι), that : chariots; ἀνήρ, chariot-maker, 4, 48

ἁρματροχιή, ἡ (τροχός), a wheel-ru 505.†

ἅρμενος, ον, see ἀραρίσκω.

ἁρμόζω [ἄρω], aor. 1 ἥρμοσα, I) t together, to fit together, to unite, τί spoken of naval architecture. ἥρμ ἀλλήλοισιν &c. πάντα, he joined toge Od. 5, 247. 2) Intrans. to fit, to su the cuirass. ἥρμοσε αὐτῷ, it fitted 3, 333. 17, 210. II) Mid. to join tog for oneself, to construct, σχεδίην χ Od. 5, 162.

Ἁρμονίδης, ου, ὁ (ῑ), a Trojan a father of Phereclus, 5, 60.

ἁρμονίη, ἡ (ἁρμόζω), prop. a jo together, a joint, or cramp, Od. 5, 361. 2) Trop. an alliance between compact, agreement, 22, 255.

* Ἁρμονίη, ἡ, daughter of Arês Aphroditê, wife of Cadmus, h. Ap.

Ἀρναῖος, ὁ, name of the beggar which he had received from his mc Od. 18, 5.

ἀρνειός, ὁ (prop. adj. from ἀ ἀρνειὸς ὄις, the male sheep; subst. a 2, 550. Od. 1, 25.

ἀρνέομαι, depon. mid. aor. 1 ἠρ μην, to deny, to refuse, to reject; accus. ἔπος, to refuse a request, 14, γάμον, Od. 1, 249. 2) Absol. to sa io refuse, to deny, 14, 191; ἀμφί τι Merc. 390.

ἀρνευτήρ, ῆρος, ὁ, a tumbler, 16, 2) a diver, who plunges head firsi the water, 12, 385. Od. 12, 413 (prob. ἀρήν). [The distinction in signi without ground, and, whether the co rison is with a diver (δύτης), or w tumbler (κυβιστήρ), it is always the s

Ἄρνη, ἡ, a town in Bœotia, 2, abode of the mace-bearer Areīthou 8. According to Strabo, it is the Acræphiôn; according to Paus Chæroneia; others think it was lowed by the lake Copais, Strabo, I 413. Thucydides, 1, 60, makes it 60 years after the taking of Troy, t Bœotians, who, having before bee pelled by the Pelasgians, fled to Ar Thessaly, and then again expelle Pelasgians. Perhaps they only r the Bœotian town.

ἀρνός, ἀρνί, etc., from the obsol. q. v.

ἄρνυμαι, depon. mid. (from αἴρω only pres. and imperf., to seek to what one does not yet possess, to for oneself, to procure, to acqui gain; with the accus. of the thin dat. of the pers., τιμήν τινι, to satisfaction for any one, 1, 159; β to gain an ox-hide as a prize, 22, 1 to strive to retain what one has servare, to defend, to maintain, 1 κλέος, 6, 446; ψυχήν, to deliver hi Od. 1, 5.

ἀροίμην, ἄροιο, ἄροιτο, see ἀραίω.

ἄροσις, ιος, ἡ (ἀμόω), arable ground, plough-land, 9, 580. Od. 9, 134.

ἀροτήρ, ῆρος, ὁ (ἀρόω), a ploughman, an agriculturist, 18, 542.

ἄροτος, ὁ (ἀρόω), ploughing, tilling, in the plur. tillage, Od. 9, 122.†

ἄροτρον, τό (ἀρόω), a plough, aratrum, 10, 553. Od. 13, 32.

ἄρουρα, ἡ (ἀρόω), arable land, seeded land, land under tillage, 6, 195. 2) land in general, 3, 115. πατρὶς ἄρουρα, country. Od. 1, 407. 3) the whole earth, ἐπὶ ζείδωρον ἄρουραν, 8, 486. Od. 3, 3.

Ἄρουρα ἡ, as pr. n.=Γαῖα, 2, 548 [and in Wolf, in Od. 11, 309].

ἀρόω, 3 plur. pres. ἀρόωσι, Ep. for ἀροῦσι, fut. ἀρόσω, partcp. perf. pass. ἀρηρομένος, to plough, to till, to cultivate, Od. 9, 108. νειὸς ἀρηρομένη, a ploughed fallow, a well-tilled fallow, 18, 548.

ἁρπάζω, fut. ἁρπάξω, aor. 1 ἥρπαξα and ἥρπασα, to tear away, to carry away, to plunder, to rob, said often of animals of prey, 9, 556; τινά, to ravish or bear off any one, 3, 444; πήληκα ἀπό τινος, to wrest or seize away one's helmet, 13, 528. 2) to grasp suddenly, to seize, λᾶαν, 12, 445 (prob. from the th. ἅρπω).

ἁρπακτήρ, ῆρος, ὁ (ἁρπάζω), a robber, a ravisher, 24, 262.†

ἁρπαλέος, η, ον, seizing, rapacious; trop. enticing, attractive; accord. to others, pass. eagerly sought, κέρδεα ἁρπαλέα (hoarded gains, V.), Od. 8, 164.

ἁρπαλέως, adv. eagerly, greedily, ἦσθε, Od. 6, 250. 14, 110.

Ἁρπαλίων, ωνος, ὁ, son of Pylæmĕnēs, king of the Paphlagonians, slain by Meriones, 13, 641 seq.

ἅρπη (ἅρπω [cf. sarpo and ὅρπη, which Hesych. says was an instrumentum falcatum. Lob. Techn. 259]), a swift bird of prey, with a clear voice, prob. the sea-eagle, falco ossifragus, Linn.; according to V., an eagle, 19, 350.†

Ἅρπυια, ἡ (ἅρπω), plur. αἱ Ἅρπυιαι, prop. which robs, which seizes away; H. mentions first the harpy Podargē, 16, 150, which bore the steeds of Achilles to Zephyr. In the Od. they appear in the plur. as spirits of the tempest (personified storms), as indistinct mythic rapacious beings. When any one disappeared, so that it was not known what was become of him, it was said the harpies had borne him off, Od. 1, 241. 20, 77. Accord. to Hes., h. 267, they are the daughters of Thaumas and Electra. Later writers gave them the body of a bird with the face of a maiden, Apd. 1, 2, 6.

ἄρρηκτος, ον (ῥήγνυμι), not to be broken, indissoluble, τεῖχος, δεσμοί, πεῖραρ, 13, 360. Od. 8, 275. 2) Metaph. indestructible, 2, 490.

ἄρρητος, ον (ῥέω), unspoken, not uttered, ἔπος, Od. 14, 466.†

ἄρσην, εν, gen. ενος, Ion. for ἄρρην, masculine, vigorous, strong, θεός, 8, 7; βοῦς, 7, 315; ὄϊες, Od. 9, 425.

Ἀρσίνοος, ὁ (kindly disposed), father of Hecamēdē, a distinguished citizen of Tenedos, 11, 626.

ἀρσίπους, οδος, ὁ ἡ, see ἀερσίπους.

Ἀρτακίη, ἡ, a fountain in the country of the Læstrygŏnes, Od. 10, 108. A fountain of the same name is mentioned in the Argonautic story, near Cyzicus.

ἀρτεμής, ές (ἄρτιος), uninjured, unharmed, sound, 5, 515. Od. 13, 43.

Ἄρτεμις, ιδος, ἡ (accord. to Herm. Sospita, or =ἀρτεμής, the inviolate), Artemis (Diana), daughter of Zeus and Latona, sister of Apollo, goddess of the chase; spoken of in connexion with the island Ortygia, Od. 5, 123. She is the symbol of immaculate virginity, of youthful beauty, and excels in height and elegance of stature all the nymphs, Od. 6, 102. Her love for the chase led her continually to the mountains and forests. She slew women with her arrows, as Apollo did men; hence the sudden and easy death of women was ascribed to her, 6, 205. She is always on the side of the Trojans. Her appellations are, ἰοχέαιρα, κελαδεινή, ἀγροτέρη, q. v.

* Ἀρτεπίβουλος, ὁ (ἄρτος and ἐπιβουλεύω), one that lies in wait for bread, Artepibūlus, name of a mouse, Batr. 264.

ἄρτι, 1) In H., in compos., it signifies perfectly, exactly, as if from ἄρτιος. 2) now, at once, at this moment, 19, 56. 21, 288, where Wolf more correctly reads ἄρ τι.

ἀρτιεπής, ές, gen. έος (ἄρτιος, ἔπος), speaking excellently, skilled in speaking, 22, 281.†

ἄρτιος, η, ον (ἄρω), suiting, fitting, exactly agreeing, coinciding; only neut. plur. ἄρτια βάζειν, to speak to the point, 14, 92. οἱ φρεσὶν ἄρτια ᾔδη, he thought things agreeing with him, i. e., he was of like sentiments, 5, 326. This appears to be a more correct explanation than 'he found him wise of mind,' cf. Od. 19, 248.

ἀρτίπος, Ep. for ἀρτίπους, ποδος, ὁ ἡ (πούς), having straight, well-formed feet, swift of foot, epith. of Arēs and of Ate, 9, 505.

ἀρτίφρων, ονος, ὁ ἡ (φρήν), perfect in understanding, very intelligent, Od. 24, 260.†

ἄρτος, ὁ, bread, esply wheaten bread, *Od. 17, 343. Batr. 35.

* Ἀρτοφάγος, ὁ (φαγεῖν), Bread-eater, name of a mouse, Batr. 214.

† ἄρτυμα, ατος, τό (ἀρτύω), which serves to prepare food, seasoning, a condiment, Batr. 41.

ἀρτύνω and ἀρτῦνω (ἄρω), fut. ἀρτυνέω, aor. 1 ἤρτυνα, aor. 1 pass. ἀρτύνθην, aor. 1 mid. ἠρτυνάμην, 1) to join together, κ annex, to arrange; σφέας αὐτούς, to form themselves in close array, 12, 86; σφέας αὐτοὺς πυργηδόν, to arrange themselves in the form of a tower, i. e., in a parallelogram, 12, 43. 2) Mly to prepare, to make ready, to put in order, to dress (a line, phalanx, &c.), ὑσμίνην, 15, 303; λόχον,

Od. 14, 469. ἀρτύνθη μάχη, the fight began, 11, 216; esply spoken of every thing for which craft and cunning are requisite, *to devise, contrive, &c., δόλον, ψεύδεα, θάνατόν τινι*, Od. 24, 153. II) *to join, to prepare, to arrange for oneself.* ἐρετμὰ τροποῖς ἐν δερματίνοισιν, to fasten the oars in leathern thongs, Od. 4, 782; metaph. βουλήν, to arrange, to deliver counsel or advice, 2, 55; according to others, to cause to assemble in council.

ἀρτύω = ἀρτύνω, only pres. and imperf., 18, 379. Od. 11, 439.

Ἀρύβας, αντος, ὁ, a Phœnician from Sidon, Od. 15, 326.

ἀρχέκακος, ον (κακός), *beginning evil;* νῆες, the woe-commencing ships of Paris, 5, 63.†

Ἀρχέλοχος, ὁ, son of Antenor, a Trojan, slain by Ajax, 2, 823. 14, 465.

Ἀρχεπτόλεμος, ὁ, son of Iphitus, cha-rioteer of Hector, 8, 128.

ἀρχεύω, poet. (ἄρχω), *to lead, to com-mand,* with dat. 5, 200.

ἀρχή, ἡ, *commencement, beginning, cause, occasion.* εἴνεκ' ἐμῆς ἔριδος καὶ Ἀλεξάν-δρου ἔνεκ' ἀρχῆς, i. e., ἕνεκα ἐμῆς καὶ ἕνεκα Ἀλ. ἀρχῆς ἔριδος, on account of my quarrel, and on account of Paris the cause of it; or, accord. to the Venet. Schol , on account of the beginning of Paris, 3, 100; hence it is said of him, ἥτ' ἔπλετο νείκεος ἀρχή, 22, 116; of Patroclus, 11, 604. φόνου ἀρχή, Od. 21, 4. 2) the point of commencement, ἐξ ἀρχῆς, from the beginning, i. e., *always, of old,* Od. 2, 254.

ἀρχός, ὁ, *leader, commander, chief,* also ἀρχὸς ἀνήρ. ἀρχοὶ μνηστήρων, Od. 4, 653; a commander of the ship, h. 6, 25.

ἄρχω, fut. ἄρξω, aor. 1 ἦρξα, 1) Active, *to be first,* to do any thing first, when an-other is to follow; esply, *to precede, to lead the way,* rarely with partcp., ἦρχε κιών, 3, 447; hence, a) Mly *to com-mence, to begin, to prepare;* with gen. μάχης, μύθοιο, δαιτὸς θεοῖς, to regulate a banquet for the gods, 15, 95; with infin. ἦρχε νέεσθαι, he went forth first, 2, 84; and with the partcp. ἦρχον χαλεπαίνων, I was first angry, 2, 378. 2) to be first, as leader, *to lead, to command, to rule;* mly with gen., rarely with dat. 2, 805. Od. 14, 230; or with ἐν, 13, 690; once intrans. according to Schol. like κρατεῖν: *to have the advantage, to conquer.* σέο ἔξεται ὅττι κεν ἄρχῃ, it will depend upon thee what prevails (in counsel): Voss, however, what he proposes (Bothe, *quodcunque prior dixerit*), 9, 102. II) Mid. *to com-mence, to begin,* without reference to others; with gen. μύθων, Od. 7, 233. Il. 9, 97; μολπῆς, Od. 6, 101; also, ἔκ τινος, Od. 23, 199; also with infin. 7, 324. 2) In religious acts, see ἀπάρχεσθαι, *to offer any thing as a sacrifice,* πάντοθεν μελέων, i. e., to begin by cutting off the limbs on all sides, Od. 14, 428.

ἈΡΩ, poet., an obsol. pres.; see ἀρα-ρίσκω.

ἀρωγή, ἡ (ἀρήγω), *help, aid, prot [favour],* 4, 408. ἐπ' ἀρωγῇ τινι, favour to either party [with parti 23, 574.

ἀρωγός, όν, *helping,* in H. only a *helper, a defender, a favourer,* 205. Od. and ἐπὶ ψευδέσσιν, a hel liars [cf. ψευδής], 4, 235; in an asse 18, 502 [=*patronus,* in judicio. H.

ἆσαι, contr. for ἀάσαι, from ἀά Infin. aor. 1, from ἄω, *to satia* 574.

ἄσαιμι, see ἄω.

Ἀσαῖος, ὁ, a Greek slain by Hect 301.

ἄσαμεν, see ἄεσα.

ἀσάμινθος, ἡ, Ep. *a bathing-t* 576, and Od. [∽σμήχειν, *to wash* Benfey. *Död.* " Multa pro desper linquenda.—ἀσάμινθος, quo non *labrum* sed *cista* et πᾶν τὸ κοῖλο ficatur." *Lob. Path.* 369.]

ἄσατο, see ἀάω.

ἄσασθαι, see ἄω.

ἄσβεστος, ον, also ἀσβέστη 1 (σβέννυμι); *unquenchable, inexti able,* φλόξ, mly metaph. *unceasi mense, infinite;* γέλως, βοή, κλέος, 584.

[Ἄσβεστος, ὁ, a demon, καμίνω δ Epig. 14, 9; in Barnes Ἀσβολος.]

ἆσε, contr. for ἄασε, see ἀάω.

ἀσήμαντος, ον (σημαίνω), *pro marked,* then, *without a keepe watched,* μῆλα, 10, 485.†

ἄσθμα, ατος, τό (ἄω), *difficult tion, a gasping, painful breathing* ἀργαλέῳ ἔχετ' ἄσθματι, he was op with a dreadful difficulty of bre •16, 109.

ἀσθμαίνω (ἄσθμα), *to breathe wi cully, to respire heavily,* spoken dreaming, 10, 496; *to gasp for* spoken of one running. 10, 377; *t in the throat,* spoken of the dying, 21, 182.

Ἀσιάδης, ου, ὁ, son of Asius, 1 (The first a long.)

Ἀσίης, Ion. for Ἀσίας, gen. αο, son of Cotys, grandson of Manes, Lydia, 2, 461. Ἀσίω ἐν λείμω Wolf, upon the meadow of Asias. according to the Schol. and Etymo Steph., gen. for Ἀσίου, from Ἀσία according to Herod., 4, 45, gave n a district in Lydia. It was a fruit gion on the Caÿstrus, which by em was called λειμών and Ἀσία. (In XIV. p. 650, Ἀσίῳ stands as a Herm., on h. Ap. 250, and Spitzne this alone correct; so that this takes its name from ἄσις (slim Mannert's Geograph. VI. 2, p. 15. the necessity of the metre, Ἀσίω

Ἀσίνη, ἡ, a town in Argolis, we Hermionê, under the dominion mêdês, 2, 560.

ἀσινής, ές (σίνομαι), *uninjure harmed,* Od. 11, 110. 12, 137.

Ἄσιος, ὁ, 1) son of Dymas, bro

Hecuba, a Phrygian, slain by Ajax, 16, 717. 2) son of Hyrtacus from Arisbe, an ally of the Trojans, slain by Idomeneus, 2. 835. 13, 384. 17, 582.

Ἄσιος, η, ον, of Asia, hence Ἀσίῳ ἐν λειμῶνι, ed. Spitzner; see Ἀσίης.

ἄσις, ιος, ἡ, slime, filth, 21, 321.†

ἄσιτος, ον (σῖτος), without eating, fasting, spoken of Penelopê, Od. 4, 788.†

Ἀσκάλαφος, ὁ, son of Arês and Astyŏchê, brother of Ialmenus, king of the Minyæ in Orchomenus, an Argonaut and a hero in the Trojan war; he was slain by Deïphŏbus, 2, 511; and 15, 110. (ἀσκάλαφος, the night-owl.)

Ἀσκανίη, ἡ, a town and territory on the Ascanian lake, on the borders of Phrygia and Mysia, upon the authority of Strabo. He understands therefore 2, 862, of the borders of Phrygia, and 13, 792, of the borders of Mysia. Steph. calls it incorrectly a town of Troas.

Ἀσκάνιος, ὁ, 1) a Phrygian, an ally of the Trojans from Ascania, 2, 862. 2) son of Hippotion, a Mysian and ally of the Trojans, 13, 793.

ἀσκεθής, poet. for ἀσκηθής. a false reading, Od. 14, 255 [defended by Bothe].

ἀσκελέως, adv. from ἀσκελής, continually, unceasingly. ἀσκ. ἀεὶ μενεαίνειν, 19, 68.†

ἀσκελής, ές (from a intens. and σκέλλω to dry up, Schol. σκληρός), very dry, withered, lean, powerless, Od. 10, 463. 2) Metaph. hard, obstinate, perpetual, pertinacious. So the neut. ἀσκελές as adv. ἐχόλωται, Od. 1, 68. κλαίειν, Od. 4, 543. (According to others, better no. 1. from ἀ and σκέλος, without legs, powerless.)

ἀσκέω, imperf. ἤσκουν, 3 sing. before a vowel ἤσκειν for ἤσκεεν, aor. 1 ἤσκησα, perf. pass. ἤσκημαι, 1) In H. in the orig. signif.: to work skilfully, to elaborate; with accus. εἴρια, 3, 388; esply to work or do any thing professionally; κέρα, 4, 110. ἅρμα χρυσῷ εὖ ἤσκηται, the chariot is well adorned with gold, 10, 438; very often in the partcp. with another verb: θρόνον τεύξει ἀσκήσας, working as an artist he will make a seat, 14, 240. Batr. 125. 2) to put in order, to arrange skilfully, to clean; χιτῶνα, Od. 1, 439. χορὸν Δαίδαλος ἤσκησεν Ἀριάδνῃ, Daedalus composed or invented a dance for Ariadnê, 18, 592. Thus Voss, Damm, and Köppen. It is explained by διδάσκειν χορόν. But ἀσκεῖν always indicates professional work; hence better, to construct a dance. The allusion is to an artificial work of Dædalus; and, at a later day, a relief of white marble, called the choral dance of Ariadne, was shown in Gnossus. So Heinrichs in loc., Siebel on Paus. 9, 40 2.

ἀσκηθής, ές (ἀσκέω [ἀσκηθής fm ἀσκάσιός (the στ being softened into θ, as in ἀγαθός fm ἀγαστός), σκάζω, σκαιός. Död. Pott compares the Ga-l, sgad.—(scatheless!)]), prop. taken care of; hence, un-

harmed, uninjured, 16, 247; often spoken of a happy return, Od. 5, 26. 144. (For ἀσκεθέες, Od. 14, 255, Wolf has correctly adopted ἀσκηθέες, to be pronounced ἀσκηθεῖς.)

ἀσκητός, όν (ἀσκέω), carefully wrought, skilfully prepared; νῆμα, fine-spun yarn, Od. 4, 134; artificially wrought, λεχος, *Od. 23, 189.

Ἀσκληπιάδης, ου, ὁ, son of Æsculapius = Machaon, 4, 204.

Ἀσκληπιός, ὁ, Æsculapius, in the Il. not yet a divinity, but an excellent physician, father of Podalirius and Machaŏn, prince of Trikka and Ithômê in Thessaly, 2, 732. It is not determined whether he is meant in the Od. 4, 232, under the name Παιήων; in the Il. he is distinguished from the physician of the gods. In later writers, son of Apollo and Corŏnis or Arsinoê, god of the healing art, Hom. h. 15. (ῐ by poet. licence, 2, 731.)

ἄσκοπος, ον (σκοπός), prop. not hitting the mark; hence, inconsiderate, thoughtless, careless, 24, 157. 186.

ἀσκός, ὁ, a skin-bottle, for holding wine, 3, 247. Od. 9, 196; a skin-sack of Æolus, Od. 10, 19.

ἄσμενος, ον (prop. for ἠσμένος [for ἠσάμενος (cf. ἤσατο δ' αἰνῶς, κ.τ.λ., he rejoiced, Od. 9, 353), ἀδέω new theme fm ἀδεῖν. Syncope (1) aspirates an initial spiritus lenis, ἡέλιος, ἥλιος; (2) softens an initial spiritus asper. Thus ἤλατο, ἁλόμενος become ἆλτο, ἄλμενος. Död.], fr. ἥδομαι), pleased, joyful, glad. φύγεν ἄσμενος ἐκ θανάτοιο, glad to have escaped death, 20, 350. Od. 9, 63. ἐμοὶ δέ κεν ἀσμένῳ εἴη, it would be pleasing to me, 14. 108.

ἀσπάζομαι, depon. mid. (σπάω), prop. to welcome any one, by extending him the hand and drawing him towards oneself, to receive kindly, to embrace. to salute, τινὰ χερσίν, with the hands, Od. 3, 35; δεξιῇ ἐπέεσσί τε, 10, 542.

ἀσπαίρω (σπαίρω), to palpitate, to struggle, chiefly spoken of dying men and beasts, 3, 293. 12, 203; ποδεσσί, with the feet, Od. 22. 473; once spoken of the heart, 13, 443.

ἄσπαρτος, ον (σπείρω), unsown, not sown, *Od. 9, 109. 123.

ἀσπάσιος, η, ον (ἀσπάζομαι), also ος, ον, Od. 23, 233. 1) welcome, desired, dear, agreeable. τῷ δ' ἀσπάσιος γένετ' ἐλθών, 10, 36. Od. 5, 394, ἀσπάσιον τόνγε θεοὶ κακότητος ἔλυσαν, to his joy the gods delivered him, Od. 5, 397. 2) joyful, glad, content, Od. 23, 238 [here more properly belongs Od. 5, 397; cf. Passow, and Crusius, ed. 1, s. v.].

ἀσπασίως, adv. gladly, willingly, joyfully; γόνυ κάμψειν, gladly to bow the knee, i. e., to supplicate, 7, 118. 11, 327; ἰδεῖν, Od. 4, 523.

ἀσπαστός, όν=ἀσπάσιος, welcome, desired, Od. 23, 239. The neut. ἀσπαστόν, as adv. ὡς Ὀδυσῆ (i. e., Ὀδυσῆϊ) ἀσπαστὸν ἐείσατο γαῖα καὶ ὕλη, so desirable to Ulysses appeared the land and the forest, Od. 5, 398. 8, 295.

ἄσπερμος, ον (σπέρμα), without seed, *without offspring, childless,* 20, 303.†

ἀσπερχές (σπέρχω and a intens.), *hastily, very warmly, vehemently, impetuously;* esply μενεαίνειν, 4, 32. Od. 1, 20; κεχολῶσθαι, 16, 61.

ἄσπετος, ον (ἀσπεῖν, i. q., εἰπεῖν), prop. *unspeakable, ineffable.* ἄσπετα πολλά, unspeakably many, 11, 704. ὅσσα τάδ' ἄσπετα πολλά, how manifold are these immense numbers. Od. 4, 75: hence, 2) Mly, *unspeakably great, infinite, immense;* ὕλη, also οὖδας, ῥόος, κλέος, ἀλκή. The neut. ἄσπετον, adv. τρεῖτε ἄσπετον, you tremble greatly, 17, 322. 3) φωνὴ ἄσπετος, h. Ven. 238, Passow explains as 'a noiseless voice,' contrary to the Gr. *usus loquendi;* the emendation of Hermann is excellent: φωνὴ τρεῖ ἄσπετον, cf. Herm. ad loc.

ἀσπιδιώτης, ου, ὁ (ἀσπίς), a *shield-bearer, armed with a shield,* always with ἀνήρ, *2, 554.

ἀσπίς, ίδος, ἡ (prob. from σπίζω), the *round shield,* cf. σάκος and λαισήιον. The shield was commonly prepared of bull's hide, having several coats of it one over another (βοείη and ταυρείη). The shield of the Telamonian Ajax had seven layers of leather, and over them an eighth of brass, 7, 222. 12, 294. Other shields again had merely metal plates, as that of Achilles, 20, 270. It was perfectly round (εὔκυκλος), and so large that it covered almost the entire body (ἀμφιβρότη). In the middle it had an arched elevation, 20, 275; in the middle of this is a boss (ὀμφαλός), hence ὀμφαλόεσσα, 6, 118. Inwardly there were handles (κάνόνες) and a leathern strap (τελαμών), by which, out of battle, it was carried on the back.

ἀσπιστής, οῦ, ὁ (ἀσπίς), *bearing a shield, armed with a shield,* only in gen. plur. ἀσπιστάων, *4 90. 5, 577.

Ἀσπληδών, όνος, ἡ, a town in Bœotia, on the river Melas, in the realm of the Minyæ, 2, 511; also Σπληδών, Strabo.

ἀσπουδί, adv (σπουδή), *without zeal, without pains, without toil,* 8, 112; without spirited resistance, in a *cowardly* way, 22, 304.

ἄσσα, Ion. for ἅτινα, see ὅστις.

ἄσσα, Ion. for τινά, ὁπποῖ ἄσσα, Od. 19, 218.† (ἄσσα for ἄσσα, 10, 409, is doubtful: cf. Spitzner.)

Ἀσσάρακος. ὁ, son of Tros and Callirrhöë, grandson of Ericthonius, father of Capys, grandfather of Anchises, 20, 232 seq.

ἆσσον adv. compar. to ἄγχι, *nearer;* often with ἰέναι, ἱκέσθαι, to approach; sometimes with gen. 14, 247; αἵματος, Od. 11, 39.

ἀσσοτέρω, adv., a later compar. from ἆσσον, *nearer;* with gen., and also with prep. καθίζειν παραὶ πυρί, to seat oneself nearer the fire, *Od. 17, 572.

ἄσταχυς, υος, ὁ=στάχυς, wi phon., *an ear of corn,* 2, 148.†

ἀστεμφέως, adv. (ἀστεμφής), ably, *firmly;* ἔχειν, to hold fas 419. 459.

ἀστεμφής, ές (στέμβω [=κινῶ· ἀ ἀκίνητος. Lob. thinks στέμβειν care, proterere, fin στείβειν ἀστεμφής (c. a pleonast.)=στιππ calus, spissus, compactus; ther immobilis. Cf. στιβαρός: et apud veteres firmum dicebatur. F Techn. 33]), *immoveable, firm, u* βουλή. *2, 344. † Neut. ἀστε adv., ἔχειν τι, to hold any th moveable, 3, 219.

Ἀστέριον, τό, a place near M not far from the mountain Tit Thessaly, 2, 735.

Ἀστερίς, ίδος, ὁ (star-island), island in the Ionian sea, on th east entrance of the sound betw phallenia and Ithaca, Od. 4, 846. ρία, ἡ, Strabo, X. p. 457. It h sought in vain by the moderns; to Dodwell the island Dascalio, to W. Gell the promontory Che Nitzsch ad loc.

ἀστερόεις, εσσα, εν, Ep. (ἀστ *starry, abounding in stars,* οὐρα *star-like, sparkling, shining;* θω 134; δόμος, 18, 370.

Ἀστεροπαῖος, ὁ (ἀστεροπή), son gon, grandson of the river-god leader of the Pæonians, slain by A 12, 102. 21, 137 seq.

ἀστεροπή, poet. for ἀστραπή [∿ Hesych. explains στροπή, στροφή, by ἀστραπή, *igneus vortex, quem* facit. Lucret. 6, 297. Lob. Te *lightning, a flash of lightning,* *10

ἀστεροπητής, οῦ, ὁ, the *hurler of li the thunderer,* appellat. of Zeus,

ἀστήρ, έρος, ὁ, dat. plur. ἀστ ἄστρασι (Buttm. approves th Gram., § 47, N. 3.), a *star, a const* 22, 307. Od. 13, 93. ἀστὴρ ὀπωρ *autumnal star* [the dog-star], 5, 5 *meteor,* 4, 75 (a *fire-ball,* Köp.).

ἀστός, ὁ (ἄστυ), a *citizen,* 11, 2 13, 192.

ἀστράγαλος, ὁ [οἷον ἀστρά ἐναλλαγῇ τοῦ β. Eust. 1289, 59. γεσθαι=στρέφεσθαι. Et. Magn. . στράγξ, στραγγουρία (urina t Plin.). στραγγαλίζειν (= συσ Hesych.). στραβός, ἀστραπή fm Lob. Techn. 54], 1) *the neck-vertebra,* 14, 466; also plur. a ji δέ οἱ αὐχὴν ἀστραγάλων ἐάγη, his n luxed from the joint, Od. 10, 560. *ankle-bone,* the bone at the ankl from which dice were made; he a kind of die, in the plur. the *dice,* 23, 88.

ἀστράπτω (στράπτω), partcp. στράψας, to *lighten,* to *hurl li* ἐπιδέξια, *2, 353.

ἄστρον, τό, a *constellation; as* in plur. 8, 555. Od. 12, 312.

ᾶστυ, εος, τό, a town, a city, in H. spoken both of large and small towns, with the name in the gen. Ζελείης, Ἰλίου πόλις καὶ ᾶστυ, 17, 144 (where, accord. to the Schol., by πόλις is to be understood the social union of citizens, πολίτεια; and by ᾶστυ, the walls and houses. τεῖχος καὶ δόμοι); plur. abodes, habitations in general, Od. 1, 3. Adv. ᾶστυδε, to the city, 18, 255.

Ἀστύαλος, ὁ (ᾶλς), a Trojan, slain by Polypœtes, 6, 29.

Ἀστυάναξ, ακτος, ὁ (ᾶναξ, defender of the city), appellat. of Scamandrius, son of Hector, which the Trojans gave him, 6, 403.

ἀστυβοώτης, ου, ὁ (βοάω), crying through the city, epith. of the herald, 24, 701.†

Ἀστυνόμη, ἡ (νέμω, city-swaying), daughter of Chryses (Χρυσηΐς), born at Chrysa. Achilles took her captive in the Hypoplacian Thebes, whither her father had sent her for protection from the enemy. Agamemnon received her as his share of the booty, but was obliged to restore her to her father to avert the wrath of Apollo, 1, 370. [The name, however, is not found in the text of H.]

Ἀστύνοος, ἡ (νόος), a leader of the Trojans, slain by Diomêdês, 5, 144. 2) son of Protiaon, a Trojan, slain by Neoptolemus, 15, 455.

Ἀστυόχεια, Ep. for Ἀστυόχη (ἔχω, protecting the city), 1) daughter of Actor, mother of Ascalaphus and Ialmenus by Arês, 2, 513. 2) daughter of Phylas of Ephyra, mother of Tleptolemus by Heraclês, 2, 658. According to Pindar, Od. 7, 41, Astydamia.

[Ἀστυόχη, 2, 513; see Ἀστυόχεια, no. 1.]

Ἀστύπυλος, ὁ (πύλη), a Pæonian, slain by Achilles, 21, 209.

ἀσύφηλος, ον, unworthy, vile, insulting. ὥς μ' ἀσύφηλον ἔρεξεν, that he treated me shamefully, 9, 697. (Eustath., however, ἀσύφηλον αὐτὸν ἐν Ἀργ. ῥέξαι, ὅ ἐστι, θεῖναι, ποιῆσαι, to make any one vile; but in H. ῥέζειν always means, 'to do, to do to, to perform.') οὔπω σεῦ ἄκουσα κακὸν ἔπος οὐδ' ἀσύφηλον, I have not yet heard from thee' an evil or unworthy word, 24, 767. *Il. (The derivation is uncertain, according to Eustath., prob from ἄσοφος, lengthened ἀσόφηλος, Æol. ἀσύφηλος, accord. to others from αἴσυλος).

ἀσφαλέως, adv. (ἀσφαλής), continually, unceasingly, 13, 145; metaph. securely, safely, prudently, ἀγορεύειν, Od. 8, 171. (V. speaking to the point.)

ἀσφαλής, ές (σφάλλω), not tottering, immoveable, standing firm, Od. 6, 42 [θεῶν ἕδος ἀσφαλές, the immoveable seat of the gods; elsewhere only] the neut. ἀσφαλές, as adv. perpetually, continually, 15, 683.

Ἀσφαλίων, ονος, ὁ, a servant of Menelaus, Od. 4, 216.

ἀσφάραγος, ὁ (φάρυγξ), the throat, the gullet, 22, 328.†

ἀσφοδελός, όν (ἀσφόδελος, the asphodel), producing asphodel. ἀσφοδελὸς λειμών, the asphodel-meadow in the nether world, where the shades of heroes abide, Od. 11, 539. h. Merc. 221. (The asphodel is a lily-form plant, the bulb on whose roots was used as food by poor people, Hes. Op. 4.)

ἀσχαλάω, 3 sing pres. ἀσχαλάᾳ for ἀσχαλᾷ, to be vexed, sad, dejected, indignant, τινος, about any thing, Od. 19, 159. 534; with partcp. 2, 293. 24, 403. οἵ πού με μάλ' ἀσχαλόωσι μένοντες, who are probably waiting for me very unwillingly; are much vexed at having to wait for me so long, Od. 1, 304 (according to Doederl. related to ἄχος, as ἴσχω with ἔχω).

ἀσχαλόω, see ἀσχαλάω.

ἀσχάλλω=ἀσχαλάω. Od. 2, 193.†

ἄσχετος, ον (σχεῖν), Ep. ἀάσχετος, 1) not to be held in, ungovernable, irresistible, μένος, 5, 892; but μένος ἄσχετος, ungovernable in strength or anger, Od. 2, 85. 2) not to be endured, insupportable, πένθος, 16, 549.

Ἀσωπός (ᾶσις, slime-river), a river in Bœotia which falls into the Euripus, now Asopo, 2, 572. 2) the river-god, son of Oceanus and Tethys, father of Ægina, Antiŏpê, Od. 11, 260.

ἀτάλαντος, ον (τάλαντον), prop. like in weight, equal to, like, τινί, 2, 627; Διὶ μῆτιν, equal in wisdom to Zeus, 2, 169; θεόφιν, Od. 3, 110.

ἀταλάφρων, ονος, ὁ, ἡ (φρονέω), having a child-like mind, hence mly tender, παῖς, 6, 400.†

ἀτάλλω (ἀταλός), to skip like a child, hence 1) to leap joyfully, to gambol; spoken of sea animals, ἐκ κευθμῶν, leaping from the clefts, 13, 27. 2) Trans. ἀτιτάλλω, to nourish, to bring up, to foster, Ep. Hom. 4, 2. Pass. to increase, to grow up, h. in Merc. 400.

ἀταλός, ή, όν (related to ἀπαλός), child-like, tender, juvenile, παρθενικαί, Od. 11, 39. Il. 20, 222. ἀταλὰ φρονεῖν, to cherish youthful, joyful feelings, to be blithe or gay of heart, 18, 567. cf. h. Cer. 24.

ἀτάρ, conjunct. chiefly poet.=αὐτάρ, but, yet, however, like δέ; it always begins the clause: 1) It denotes mly an unexpected, a surprising antithesis, 3, 268. 270; often with the voc. 6, 429; Ἕκτορ, ἀτάρ που ἔφης, Hector, but thou saidst, 22, 331; after an antecedent μέν, 6, 84. 86. 2) It expresses a sudden transition, chiefly in the apodosis after ἐπειδή. αὐτὰρ ἐπειδὴ Τρῶας ἐνόησαν, ἀτὰρ ἐγένετο ἰαχή, but when they perceived the Trojans, then arose a cry, 12, 144. 3) It is often connected with other particles: ἀτάρ τε, 4, 484; ἀτὰρ δή, 23, 871; ἀτὰρ μὲν νῦν γε, Od. 18, 123.

ἀταρβής, ές (τάρβος), undismayed, fearless, appellat. of Phobos, 13, 299.†

ἀτάρβητος, ον (ταρβέω)=ἀταρβής· νόος, 3, 63.†

ἀταρπιτός, ἡ, Ion. for ἀτραπιτός, a path, 18, 565. Od. 17, 234.

E

ἀταρπός, ή, Ion. for ἀτραπός (fr. τρέπω) prop. ὁδός, a way from which one cannot wander; a path, a footway, 17, 743. Od. 14, 1.

ἀταρτηρός, ή, όν (prob. from ἀτηρός, with a repetition of the first letters), injurious, hostile, ἔπεα 1, 223; Μέντωρ, Od. 2, 243.

ἀτασθαλία, ή (ἀτάσθαλος), indiscretion, impiety, insolence. arrogance; always in the plur. 4, 409. Od. 1. 7.

ἀτασθάλλω (ἀτάσθαλος), to be indiscreet, insolent, arrogant; only partcp. *Od. 18, 57. 19, 88.

ἀτάσθαλος, ον (ἄτη), indiscreet, insolent, arrogant, presumptuous, infatuated; spoken of men and actions, 22, 418. Od. 16, 86; often in the neut. plur. ἀτάσθαλα μηχανᾶσθαι, ῥέζειν, to practise wickedness, 11, 695; and esply spoken of the suitors in the Odyss., Od. 3, 207. 17, 588. (According to Etym. Mag. from ἄτη and θάλλω [fm ἀταστός, verbal of a form ἀτάζειν, fm ἀτέω († ἄω, noceo), Död. who thinks ἀτασθλός was syncopated fm ἀτασταλός, as ἱμάσθλη fm ἱμαστάλη, θύσθλα fm θύσταλα,. &c. p. 163]).

ἄτε (prop. accus. plur. from ὅστε). as, like, like as, 11, 779. 22, 127.† Thus Damm. According to Lehrs de Aristarch. stud. p. 162 seq. it never stands thus in H., but is to be taken as neut. plur.

ἀτειρής, ές (τείρω), not to be worn out, indestructible, firm, lasting; spoken of brass and iron, 5, 292. 2) Metaph. indefatigable, unconquerable; of men, 15, 697; μένος, Od. 11, 270; of the voice, 17, 555; and of the heart, κραδίη, πέλεκυς ὥς ἐστιν ἀτειρής, thy heart is unyielding, like an axe, 3, 60.

ἀτέλεστος, ον (τελέω), unfinished, unended, unaccomplished, Od. 8, 571. ἀτ. τιθέναι πόνον (in connexion with ἅλιος), to make the labour unaccomplished, i. e., to render nugatory, 4, 57; hence vain, fruitless, ὁδός, Od. 2. 273. 2) without ending, without ceasing, ἔδειν, Od. 16, 111.

ἀτελεύτητος, ον (τελευτάω), unaccomplished, unfulfilled, 1, 527; ἔργον, *4, 175.

ἀτελής, ές (τέλος), without end; pass. unfinished, Od. 17, 546.† 2) uninitiated; with gen. ἱερῶν, h. in Cer. 481.

ἀτέμβω, to injure, to violate; with accus. ξείνους, Od. 20, 294. 21, 311: metaph. to deceive, θυμόν, Od. 2, 90. Pass. to be deprived of, to be bereft, τινός, of any thing; ἴσης, of an equal share, 11, 705. Od. 9, 42. ἀτέμβονται νεότητος, they are bereft of youthful vigour, 23, 445.

ἀτέοντες, see ἀτέω.

ἄτερ, poet. prep. with gen. without, πολέμου, 4, 376. 2) apart, far from ἄλλων, 1, 498.

ἀτέραμνος, ον (τείρω). unsoftened, hard, stern, inexorable, κῆρ, Od. 23, 127† [opp. of τέρην, Lob.].

ἀτερπής, ές (τέρπω), joyless, sad, dis-

agreeable, λιμός, 19, 354; χῶρος, 279.

ἄτερπος, ον=ἀτερπής, 6, 285.†

ἀτέω (ἄτη), to act blindly, fool-ha only in partcp. 20, 332† [ἀτέων o partcp. in Hdt. infatuated].

ἄτη, ή (ἀάω [ἄειν, to hurt, harm; ἀατός, ἀάτη, ἀϝάτα, Pind. Pyth. 4, 24 αὐάτα]), 1) My injury, d tion, evil, 2, 111. 8, 237; partic. disturbance, confusion, 16, 805; a discretion, 1, 412; blindness, fo which crime is perpetrated, 19, 8 15, 233. 2) wickedness, the base act Ἀλεξάνδρου, 6, 356. Od. 12, 37; misfortune, punishment, which one by crime, Od. 4, 261; with the s nate idea of guilt, blood-guiltin 480.

Ἄτη, ή, Atê, as a goddess, daug Zeus, who seduces men to in actions, and thereby brings evi them. She has soft feet, with wh does not touch the earth (ἀπαλοὶ but rushes rapidly (ἀρτίπος) ov heads of men, and accomplishes t lutions of Zeus and Fate; she lea himself into an illusion, and is hurled from heaven, 19, 91—130, 505.

ἀτίζω (τίω), to value little, no gard, to be careless; only partcp. 2

ἀτῑμάζω=ἀτῑμάω, only pres. an Od. In the Il. only Ep. iterativ ἀτῑμάζεσκον, 9, 450.

ἀτῑμάω (τῑμάω), Ep. fut. (ἀ aor. 1 ἠτῑμησα, not to honour, value, to disregard, to despise; wit mly of persons; also ἔργον μάχης μῦθον, 14, 127; chiefly in the Il.

ἀτῑμητος, ον (τῑμή), not valued, garded, despised, 9, 648.†

ἀτῑμίη, ή (τῑμή), dishonour, in: famy, contempt; in plur. ἀτῑμίη λειν τινά, to bring any one into co Od. 13, 142.†

ἄτῑμος, ον (τῑμή), compar. ἀτ 16, 90; superl. ἀτῑμότατος, l noured, dishonoured, despised, 1, not valued, without payment. οἶκον ἄτιμον ἔδεις, thou consur possessions without recompense, 451. (Accord. to Eustath. eithe ῥητον, unavenged, or adv. ἀτίμ δωρεάν.)

ἀτιτάλλω, Ep. (ἀταλός), aor. 1 to rear, to nourish, to bring accus. spoken of children, 14, 20; and of brutes, to feed, 5, 271. Od

ἄτιτος. ον (τίω), unpaid, un unavenged, 13, 414. ἵνα μήτι τοιο ποινὴ δηρὸν ἄτιτος ἔη, punishment for my brother ma long unpaid, 14, 484. Becau: has here ῑ, Clark proposes δηρὸν ἀ cf. Spitzner ad loc.

Ἄτλας, αντος, ὁ (from τλῆνα intens. the supporter), a g "knows the depths of the sea, a the pillars which keep heaven a

apart (ἀμφίς)," Od. 1, 52. His origin is
not mentioned by H.; he is the father
of Calypso [and of Maia. h. 17, ‹].
Perhaps the original idea is that of a
mountain upon whose summits the heavens rest. Whether H. intended the
mountain in Libya, or another in the
west, is uncertain. Accord. to Hesiod,
Th. 507—519. he is a doomed Titan, who
as a punishment bears up the vault of
heaven.

ἄτλητος, ον (τλῆμι), not to be borne, insupportable, ἄχος, πένθος, *9, 3. 19, 367.

ἄτος, ον, contr. for ἄατος, poet. (ἀω),
insatiable; with gen πολέμοιο, in battle,
μάχης, δόλων ἠδὲ πόνοιο, 11, 430. Od. 13,
293.

ἀτραπιτός, ἡ (τρέπω)=ἀταρπός, a path,
Od. 13. 195.†

Ἀτρείδης, ου, ὁ, son of Atreus, often
plur. οἱ Ἀτρεῖδαι, the Atridæ, Agamemnon
and Menelaus.

Ἀτρείων, ωνος, ὁ=Ἀτρείδης.

ἀτρεκέως, adv. (ἀτρεκής). exactly, truly,
agreeably to truth, ἀγορεύειν, καταλέγειν;
once with μαντεύσθαι, Od. 17, 154.

ἀτρεκής, ές, exact, correct, true; the
neut. ἀτρεκές, as adv. truly, strictly, 5,
208. δεκὰς ἀτρεκές, exactly a decade,
Od. 16, 245 (prob. from τρέω, not trembling, not from τρέχω [the insertion of
the k sound is found in spe-c-us=σπέος:
Hesych. gives ἀα συστροφὴ ὕδατος. Cf.
aqua. Lob.]).

ἀτρέμα, before a vowel ἀτρέμας, adv.
(τρέμω), without trembling, immoveable,
quiet, still. ἀτρέμας ἧσο, 2, 200. ἔχειν
ἀτρέμα τι, to hold any thing still, 15, 318
(without σ only in this place); Od. 13,
42.

Ἀτρεύς, ῆος, ὁ, son of Pelops and Hippodamia, brother of Thyestes, king of
Mycenæ, accord. to H. father of Agamemnon and Menelaus by Aeropē (accord. to Æschyl. grandfather and foster-
father). [A later tradition represents
that] he quarrelled with his brother
Thyestes, and placed his sons before him
to eat. His famous sceptre Thyestes in-
herited, 6, 106 (from ἀ and τρέω, the unterrified).

ἄτριπτος, ον (τρίβω), prop. unworn;
spoken of hands, not hardened, unexer-
cised, Od. 21, 151.†

ἄτρομος, ον (τρέμω), not trembling, fearless, unterrified, μένος, θυμός, *5, 125. 16,
163.

ἀτρύγετος. ον (τρυγάω), where is nothing to be harvested, unfruitful, barren;
epith. of the sea in distinction from the
earth, which is called πολυφόρβος, 1, 316;
and once of the ether, 17, 425. h. Cer. 67.
[Herodianus, E. M. 167, 29: ἀπὸ τοῦ
ἀτρύγετος ἀτρύγετος (ut ἀτίετος) καὶ πλεο-
νασμῷ τοῦ γ ἀτρύγετος. ap. Lob. Path.
145]

Ἀτρυτώνη (τρύω), the unwearied, the
indefatigable, the invincible, epith. of
Athênê (lengthened from ἀτρύτη), 2, 157.

ἄττα, a term of affection used by a

younger in addressing an older person,
good father (related to ἄππα, πάππα), 9,
607. Od. 16, 31.

ἀτύζομαι (related to ἀτέω [and so to
ἄειν, nocere, Död., who, however, derives it from ἀτύειν, a collateral form of
ἀτέειν, as ἀχεύειν, ἀχέειν]), aor. 1 pass.
ἀτυχθείς, to be amazed, to be confounded,
to be terrified, bewildered, 1) Absol. ἀτυζομένη δὲ ἔοικας, you appear like one
confounded, 15, 96. ἀτυζομένη (sc. ὥστε)
ἀπολέσθαι, shocked to death, 22, 474 [præ
dolore mente captam ut periculum mortis
esset. Heyne]. 2) With accus. πατρὸς
ὄψιν, to be terrified at the sight of, 6,
463. 3) Often to fly terrified, πεδίοιο,
through the plain, 18, 7 ; spoken of steeds,
6, 38. (The act. ἀτύζω, to confound, is
first found in Ap. Rh.)

Ἀτυμνιάδης, ου, ὁ, son of Atymnius=
Mydôn, 5, 581.

Ἀτύμνιος, ὁ, 1) father of Mydôn, a
Trojan, 5, 581. 2) son of Amisodarus of
Caria, who was slain by Antilŏchus, 16,
317 seq.

αὖ, adv. the original signif. relates to
place : back, backwards, as still in the
verb, αὐερύειν; then metaph. 1) Of
time : again, once more, νῦν αὖ, δεύτερον
αὖ; also to indicate a repetition, 1, 540.
2) on the other hand, on the contrary, but,
to indicate an antithesis to the preceding,
mly connected with δέ (δ᾽ αὖ), 4, 417. Od.
3, 485. αὖ often=δέ, 11, 367; hence
often after a preceding μέν, 11, 17. 19,
108 seq. 3) likewise, further, moreover,
to facilitate the progress of the narration,
3, 200. Od. 4, 211.

αὐαίνω (αὖος), Ep. for αὐαίνω, to dry, to
dry up, to wither, partcp. aor. 1 αὐανθέν,
dried, seasoned, Od. 9, 321.†

αὐγάζομαι, mid. (αὐγή), prop. I am en-
lightened ; hence, to see clearly, to perceive, to distinguish, τί, any thing, 23,
458.† (The act. αὐγάζω, to enlighten.)

Αὐγειαί, αἱ, 1) a town in Laconia,
near Gythium ; later, accord. to Strabo,
Αἴγειαι, 2, 583. 2) a town in Locris, 2,
532.

Αὐγείας, ου, ὁ (the shining), epith. for
Αὐγέας, son of Phorbas and Hyrminê, or
of Elius or Hellus, king of Ephyra in
Elis, an Argonaut, father of Agasthênês,
Phyleus, and Agamêdê, 11, 740. H.
mentions him in a contest with Neleus;
he is chiefly known by his herd of three
thousand cattle, whose stall was not
cleaned in thirty years; Heraclês accomplished this labour in one day, Apd. 2, 5.
5.

αὐγή. ἡ, light, a beam of light, splendour, brilliancy; spoken chiefly of the
sun. ὑπ᾽ αὐγὰς Ἠελίοιο φοιτᾶν, ζώειν,
to walk, to live under the beams of the
sun, Od. 2, 181. 15, 349; also spoken of
lightning and of fire, 13, 244. Od. 6, 308.

Αὐγηιάδης, ου, ὁ, Ep. for Αὐγειάδης, son
of Augeas=Agasthênês, 2, 624.

αὐδάω, impf. ηὔδων, aor. 1 ηὔδησα, to
discourse, to speak; τινά, to address any

E 2

one; often ἀντίον αὐδᾶν τινά, to answer any one; with double accus. ἔπος τινὰ ἀντίον αὐδᾶν, 5, 170. μεγάλα αὐδᾶν, to utter impious words, Od. 4, 505.

αὐδή, ἡ (ἄω), speech, language, voice; spoken of men, and prop. of the sound and strength of the voice; once of the twittering of a swallow, Od. 21, 411.

αὐδήεις, εσσα, εν (αὐδή), endowed with human voice, speaking, melodious; spoken prop. of men, Od. 5, 334. cf. Il. 19, 407. If a deity receives this appellation, it is thereby indicated that he employs a human voice. Thus Circê, Od. 10, 136; Calypso, Od. 12, 449.

αὐερύω (ἐρύω), aor. 1 αὐέρυσα, to draw back; with accus. νευρήν (in order to shoot), 8, 325; chiefly absol. to draw back the neck of the victim whose throat is to be cut, 1, 459 seq. 2) to draw out again, στήλας, 12, 261.

αὐθ', i. e. αὔτε, before a spiritus asper, 2, 540.

αὖθι. adv. contr. for αὐτόθι, 1) Of place [=ἐν τῇ αὐτῇ χώρᾳ, in the same place where one already is (even, just, precisely), there]: on the spot, there, here, 1, 492. 3, 244. 7, 100. ἐζόμενος κατ' αὖθι, 13, 653 (where κατά belongs to ἔζεσθαι), cf. Od. 21, 55; in like manner κατ' αὖθι λίπεν, 24, 470. 2) Of time: at once, instantly, Od. 18, 339.

αὐίαχος, ον, crying together, shouting aloud, epith. of the Trojans, 13, 41.† (Eustath. makes it from ἀ intens. and ἰαχή, between which an Æol. digamma, for euphony's sake, is inserted, whence arose υ; others say, not crying, contrary to the custom of the Trojans; since H. represents the Greeks as advancing to battle in silence, the Trojans shouting).

αὔλειος, η, ον (αὐλή), belonging to the court or yard before a house. αἱ αὔλειαι θύραι, the doors of the court; either the doors which lead from the street into the front yard, or from the vestibule into the front yard. οὖδος αὔλειος, the threshold of the court door, *Od. 1, 104.

αὐλή, ἡ (ἄω), the court, an open, airy place which surrounded the house. It was encircled by a wall, paved, and furnished with a double door, Od. 9, 184. In the court were situated the stables for cattle, and in the centre stood the altar of Zeus ἑρκεῖος. From the court one entered the πρόδομος. In the αὐλή was often the place for family meeting, and also the court for the cattle, 4, 344. Achilles had a similar court about his tent, 24, 452. 2) the fence encircling the court, 5, 138. Od. 14, 5. 3) Sometimes the entire dwelling, Od. 4, 72. cf. Od. 1, 425.

αὐλίζομαι, depon. (αὖλις), prop. to spend the night in the court; to be enclosed, spoken of cattle and swine, Od. 12, 265. 14, 412. *Od.

*αὔλιον, τό (αὐλή), a fold, a grotto, a hut, a dwelling, h. Merc. 103.

αὖλις, ιδος, ἡ, a place of stopping,

esply to spend the night, a can h. Merc. 71. αὖλιν θέσθαι, camp, 9, 232; spoken of bir ἐσιέμεναι, betaking themselv Od. 22, 473.

Αὐλίς, ίδος, ἡ, a village in Bο a large and small haven, wher of the Greeks assembled to s Troy, now Vathi, 2. 496.

αὐλός, ὁ (ἄω, to blow), a wi ment, which, partly from th piece necessary to it, and partl strong, deep tone, we may co have been similar to our h clarionet, a flute, a pipe. It w cane, wood, bone, or metal, l 495. h. Merc. 451. Voss, Od. 10 αὐλῷ for αὐλῇ. There were m cf. Eustath. on Il. 18, 495, and eı ger in Wieland's Attic Museum 1. 8. 330 seq. 2) any hollow forated to admit something: t the spear, into which the sha troduced. ἐγκέφαλος παρ' α ἔδραμεν ἐξ ὠτειλῆς, then gushe brain by the socket (others, mo bably, in a stream). περόν αὐλοῖσιν διδύμοισι, the clasp w spear) from the wound, 17, 2 with double holes; in which t caught, Od. 19, 227; metap παχύς, a thick jet of blood (ἡ ἀν αἵματος, Eustath.), Od. 22, 18.

αὐλών, ῶνος, ὁ (αὐλός), a ι defile, a valley, h. in Merc. 95.

αὐλῶπις, ιδος. ἡ (ὤψ), epith. met, τρυφάλεια, accord. to Heς nished with a visor, 5, 182. J to the Schol., having a socket the crest was inserted. *Il.

αὖος, η, ον, Att. αὖος (ἄω, αὔ dry, hardened. ξύλα, βοέη [δeı πάλαι, περίκηλα. The neut. sinϛ adv. hollow; spoken of a dull, de as if it were produced by dι [opp. to the ringing sound o 12. 160; αὖον ἄϋσεν, 13, 44. [Cι ἐβρόντησεν, Hes. Th. 839; arid Lucr. 6, 119. "Epitheton iu c siccis mutuatum, quæ collisa fragorem edunt." Lob.]

ἄϋπνος, ον (ὕπνος), without sl less, νύκτες, ἀνήρ, 9, 325. Od. 1ϳ

αὔρη, ἡ, Ion. for αὔρα (ἄω, aϛ a breath, a breeze, air, ὀπωρίνϛ 147; esply the cool air from wι the morning, Od. 5, 469.

αὔριον, adv. (αὔρη, prop. αὔριος [αὔριον, sync. fm ἀέερ early in the morning. Cf. d mane: and Germ. Morgen, Död.]), the morrow, 8, 538. 351.

αὐσταλέος, η, ον, poet. (αὐ prop. dried up, withered, dirty 19, 327.†

αὐτάγρετος, ον (ἀργέω), poet. ρετος, self-chosen, at one's o luntary, Od. 16, 148;† witϳ Merc. 474.

αὔταρ, conj. (from αὖτ' ἄρ'),=ἀτάρ, but, still, however, furthermore; like ἀτάρ used at the beginning of a sentence, to indicate an antithesis, 1, 133; or to mark a sudden transition, 1, 488. 3, 315. 20. 38. αὔταρ ἄρα, 2, 103.

αὖτε, adv. poet. (from αὖ and τε)=αὖ, again, 1, 202. 578. 2) but, on the other hand, also used to mark an antithesis or a transition, or instead of δέ after μέν, 3, 241. Od. 22, 6.

αὐτέω (ἀΰω), to cry, to shout, 20, 50; spoken of things: to resound, to sound, 12, 160. [Cf. αὖον ἀΰτειν in αὖος.] 2) With accus. τινά, to call any one, *11, 258.

αὐτή, ἡ (ἀΰω), a cry, a loud shout, esply the battle-cry, with πτόλεμος, 6, 328; and the battle itself, 11, 802. ἵκετ' ἀϋτή, 11, 466; ed. Spitz. (where Wolf reads ἵκετο φωνή).

αὐτῆμαρ, adv. (ἦμαρ), on the same day, 1, 81. Od. 3, 311.

αὐτίκα, adv. (αὐτός), at once, instantly, on the spot; often αὐτίκα νῦν and μάλ' αὐτίκα, also αὐτίκ' ἄρα, αὐτίκ' ἐπεί, as soon as; αὐτίκ' ἔπειτα, then directly; with partcp. αὐτίκ' ἰόντι, the moment thou art gone, Od. 2, 367. 17, 327.

αὖτις, adv. Ion. for αὖθις (lengthened fr. αὖ), again, back. πάλιν αὖτις φέρειν, to carry back again, 5, 257; often with verbs: αὖτις ἰέναι, to go again. 2) hereafter, at a subsequent time, 1, 140. 3, 440.

αὐτμή, ἡ (ἄω), a breath, air, wind, spoken of the breath of men, 9, 609; of the wind of the bellows, 18. 471; of the wind, Od. 11, 400, 407. 2) fume, vapour, smoke, 14, 174. Od. 12. 369; heat, flame, Od. 9, 389.

αὐτμήν, ένος, ὁ, poet.=αὐτμή, 23, 765. Od. 3, 289.

αὐτοδίδακτος, ον (διδάσκω), self-taught, self-educated, Od. 22, 347.†

αὐτόδιον, adv. (lit. on the same way), on the spot, at once. Od. 8, 449.† (Either fm ὁδός, or only lengthened fm αὐτός, as μαψίδιως fm μάψ.)

αὐτόετες, adv. (ἔτος), in the same year, in one year, Od. 3, 322.†

αὐτόθεν, adv. (αὐτός), from the same place, from here, from there; mly with prep.: αὐτόθεν ἐξ ἑδρέων, directly from the seats, 20, 77. Od. 13, 56.

αὐτόθι, adv. poet. and Ion. (αὐτός), in the same place, here, there, 3, 428. Od. 4, 302.

*Αὐτοκάνης ὄρος, τό, a promontory in Æolis near Phocæa in Asia, h. in Ap. 35. Ilgen would read Ἀκροκάνης, and refers it to the promontory Κάνη of Strabo. Herm. thinks the reading is not to be changed, and that perhaps we are to understand by it a part of the promontory.

αὐτοκασιγνήτη, ἡ, an own sister, Od. 10, 137.†

αὐτοκασίγνητος, ὁ, an own brother, *Il. 3, 238.

Αὐτόλυκος, ὁ (λύκος), son of Hermês (Mercury) and Chiônê or Philônis, father of Anticlêa, grandfather of Ulysses. He had his residence on Parnassus, and was noted for dissimulation and cunning, Od. 19, 394 seq. He bore off the famous helmet of Amyntôr from Eleôn, 10, 267; and gave to his grandson the name of Ulysses, Od. 19, 439.

αὐτόματος, η, ον (μέμαα), acting from one's own motion, spontaneous, self-moved, of his (its) own accord; αὐτόματος ἦλθε, 2. 408. 5, 749; spoken esply of the wonderful tripods of Hêphæstus (Vulcan), which moved themselves, *18, 376.

Αὐτομέδων, οντος, ὁ (μέδων), son of Diôrês, charioteer of Achilles from Scyrus, 9, 209. 17, 429.

Αὐτονόη, ἡ, a handmaid of Penelŏpê, Od. 18, 182.

Αὐτόνοος, ὁ, 1) A Greek slain by Hector, 11, 301. 2) a Trojan whom Patroclus slew, 16, 694.

αὐτονυχί, adv. (νύξ), in the same night, 8, 197.†

*αὐτοπρεπής, ές (πρέπω), a doubtful reading in h. Merc. 86. This word yields here no sense. Wolf adopts the reading of the Cdd. Paris and Mosc.: ὁδὸν αὐτοτροπήσας, which is equally unsatisfactory. The conjecture of Hermann accords best with the connexion: ὁδὸν ἀντιτορήσων, about to pass over a way.

αὐτός, ή, ό (from αὖ—τος), prop. again he, then the same; he, she, it. I) the same, self, and spoken of all three persons which are indicated by the verb; the personal pronouns are, however, often connected with it; in the third person it stands alone. It gives prominence and distinctness to an object, and occurs in many senses: 1) In the Hom. language, αὐτός frequently indicates an antithesis to a person or thing. Thus the body, in distinction from the soul, is called αὐτός; αὐτούς, bodies, in opposition to souls, 1, 4; αὐτός, the prince, in distinction from his subjects, 8, 4; αὐτοί, men, in distinction from the ships, 7, 338. b) even, to render the connected noun emphatic, 6, 451; in designations of place, precisely, exactly, 13, 614; esply with σύν: αὐτῇ σὺν φόρμιγγι, together with the lyre, 9, 194; and without σύν: αὐτῇ γαίη αὐτῇ τε θαλάσσῃ, 8, 24. 2) self, of oneself, of one's own accord, 17, 254. οἱ δὲ καὶ αὐτοὶ πανέσθων, Od. 2, 168. b) self, i. e. without another, alone, 2, 233. 8, 99. 13, 729. Od. 1, 53. 15, 310. 3) Often in connexion with the personal pronouns, but always separated in the oblique cases: ἐμέθεν αὐτῆς, οἱ αὐτῷ, σὲ αὐτόν, etc.; the pron. once stands after, as αὐτόν μιν, Od. 4. 244. Also αὐτός alone stands for the pron. of the first and second persons: αὐτός for ἐγὼ αὐτός, 13, 252; περὶ αὐτοῦ, i e. ἐμαυτοῦ, Od. 21, 249. 4) Often in the gen. αὐτοῦ, αὐτῶν, etc. is put for emphasis' sake with the possessive pronoun. τὰ σ' αὐτῆς ἔργα, thine own works, 6, 490; αὐτῶν σφετέρῃσιν ἀτασθαλίῃσιν ὄλοντο, by their own folly Od. 1, 7. 5) the same, the very *same,* for ὁ αὐτός, often in H., 12, 225. Od. 8, 107. II) *he, she, it,* esply in the oblique cases. αὐτόν is regarded by the Grammarians as enclitic when it signifies barely *him.* In 12, 204, the Schol. retain the *enclisis* [and read κόψε γάρ αὐτον]; the moderns reject it: cf. Thiersch, § 205, 11. Anm. III) With the article, ὁ αὐτός, ἡ αὐτή, τὸ αὐτό, *the same, the very same;* still rare in H. τὼ δ᾽ αὐτώ, 1, 338; τὴν αὐτὴν ὁδόν, 6, 391. IV) In composition it signifies 1) *self-originated,* not formed by human instrumentality. 2) *mixed with nothing;* αὐτόξυλος, merely of wood. 3) *personally, of one's own power.*

αὐτοσταδίη. ἡ (ἴστημι), *close combat,* where man fights with man (with the sword or spear), 13, 325.†

αὐτοσχεδά, adv. =αὐτοσχεδόν, 16, 319 †

αὐτοσχεδίη. ἡ (prop. fem. from αὐτοσχέδιος, *very near*), in H., a combat where man contends with man, =αὐτοσταδίη, *a close combat, mêlée* [*mingled battle, hand to hand,* Cp.]; only in the dat. and accus. αὐτοσχεδίην μίξαι χεῖράς τε μένος τε, to mingle hands and strength in close fight, to mingle battle, 15, 510. αὐτοσχεδίην πλήττειν τινά, to strike any one close at hand, i. e. with the sword, 12, 192. 2) ἐξ αὐτοσχεδίης, *suddenly, without premeditation,* h. Merc. 55.

αὐτοσχεδόν, adv. once αὐτοσχεδά (σχεδόν), *very near, close at hand, cominus;* μάχεσθαι, to fight man to man; οὐτάζεσθαί τινα, to wound any one in close fight, i. e. with the sword, 7, 273.

αὐτοτροπήσας, see αὐτοπρεπής.

αὐτοῦ, adv. (prop. gen. from αὐτός), *in the same place, there, here;* often with another word: αὐτοῦ ἐνὶ Τροίη, 2, 237; αὐτοῦ ἔνθα, just there, 8, 207; κεῖθι αὐτοῦ. h. Ap. 374; αὐτοῦ ἀγρῶν, Od. 4, 639. 2) *on the spot, directly,* 15, 349.

αὐτόφι, αὐτόφιν, Ep. gen. and dat. sing. and plur. from αὐτός, always with prep. ἀπ᾽ αὐτόφιν, ἐπ᾽ αὐτόφιν, παρ᾽ αὐτόφιν, 11, 44. 12, 302.

Αὐτόφονος, ὁ, a Theban, father of Polyphontes, 4, 395.

αὐτοχόωνος, ον, Ep. for αὐτόχωνος contr. from αὐτόχοανος (χοάνη), *barely cast, rough cast,* not smoothed by filing and polishing, epith. of the discus, 23, 826. † (Others: whole cast, not hollow.)

αὔτως or αὕτως (the old Gramm. distinguish αὔτως, *idly,* and αὕτως for οὕτως, *thus;* cf. Schol. on Il. 1, 133; Etym. Mag. Buttmann, Lex. would take αὕτως every where as a form of οὕτως. Herm. de pron. αὐτός, Opusc. I. p. 338, and Thiersch, Gram. § 198, 5, consider αὔτως more as the true form, and as an adv. from αὐτός, with the Æol. accent, which last we may regard as most correct. Wolf follows them in the Il., but αὕτως stands still in the Od.) It signifies prop., 1) *even so, just so, thus; hoc ipso modo.* αὔτως ὥστε γυναῖκα, 22, 125. Od. 14, 143; hence, Ep. ὡς δ᾽ αὔτως,

later ὡσαύτως, in the same way Od. 3, 64. 2) *even thus still,* a reference to a past state, 18, 338 λευκὸς ἔτ᾽ αὔτως, 23, 267; or, *even thus,* in reference to a prese ἀλλὰ καὶ αὔτως ἀντίον εἶμ᾽ αὐτ even thus I will go against them 18, 198; often καὶ αὔτως, *ev nevertheless,* i. e. without reward hence, 3) *only thus, nothing m nisi.* ἀλλ᾽ αὔτως ἄχθος ἀρούρης mere burden of the earth. Od. often in connexion with adv., μὰ ἀκλεὲς αὔτως, etc.; hence also, *to no purpose.* αὔτως ῥ᾽ ἐπέεσσ᾽ μεν, we contend with words to pose, 2, 342; without reason, 6,

αὐχένιος, η, ον, *belonging to* τένοντες αὐχένιοι, the sinews of t Od. 3, 450.†

*αὐχέω (from αὐχή, related to vaunt oneself, to boast, ἐπί τινι, I

αὐχήν, ένος, ὁ, *the neck,* sp men, 5, 147. 161; of brutes, 5, 6

αὐχμέω (αὐχμής [Död. derive fm αὐστός, αὐκτός; as αἰχμή fm δραχμή fm δράσσειν]), prop. *to withered; to look squalid, rough;* γῆρας λυγρὸν ἔχεις αὐχμεῖς τε κα 24, 250.†

*αὐχμήεις, εσσα, εν (αὐχμή), dr *dirty, squalidus,* h. 18, 6.

I. αὔω, Ep. for αὔω, prob. dry; hence, *to kindle, to light,* Od.

II. αὔω, aor. 1 ἤϋσα and ἄϋσ *cry, to shout aloud;* often with μακρόν, μέγα, δεινόν. b) Spoke animate things: *to sound, to* 13, 409; ἄϋον, 441. 2) Trans. τινά, any one, rarely, 11, 461. (αὔω, dissyllabic in pres. and but in the further flexion with ῡ

ἀφαιρέω, and poet. ἀποαιρέω (αἱρέω), fut. ἀφαιρήσω, aor. partcp. ἀφελών, fut. mid. ἀφαι aor. 2 mid. ἀφειλόμην and ἀφελό *to take away, to take from,* τινί τ 455. 2) Mid. more frequent, *away any thing for oneself, to* always with the idea of one's vantage, τι, any thing, νόστο 16, 82. 690. The pers. from who thing is taken stands in the dat and rarely gen.: *to take away from any one, to deprive him of* τινὰ κούρην, 1, 275; τινὶ γέρας Od. 1, 9; πολλῶν θυμόν, to depri of life, 5, 673. Od. 22, 290.

ἄφαλος, ον, *without a crest-co metal boss* or *socket,* into which is inserted, 10, 258.†

ἀφαμαρτάνω (ἁμαρτάνω), aor. τον and ἀπήμβροτον, 16, 466, *to to hit,* τινός, any one, said esply spears, etc., 8, 119. 2) *to lose* possessed, *to be bereft* or *depr* thing, with gen. 6, 411.

ἀφαμαρτοεπής, ές (ἔπος), =ἁμ who misses his point in speakin *cious,* 3, 215 † ἀφανδάνω (ἀνδάνω), *not to please, to displease,* Od. 16, 387.

ἄφαντος, ον (φαίνω), *invisible, not seen, vanished, destroyed, forgotten,* *6, 60. 20, 303.

ἄφαρ, adv. poet. (either from ἄπτω, or from ἀπό and ἄρα: cf. Thiersch, § 198, 3. Anm.): originally it signified an immediate consequence; hence, 1) *directly, immediately, quickly, suddenly,* 19, 405. In certain phrases, as ' it is better,' it means *directly, forthwith, in promptu,* i. e. the advantage accrues immediately after the act, Od. 2, 169. Il. 17, 417. 2) Often without the idea of immediate consequence, *then, thereupon,* 11, 418. Od. 2, 95; ἄφαρ αὐτίκα, then immediately, 23, 593. 3) *continually, constantly,* according to Damm, only 23, 375.

'Αφαρεύς, ῆος, ὁ, son of Calêtôr, slain by Æneas, 13, 541.

ἀφαρπάζω (ἀρπάζω), αορ. 1 ἀφάρπαξα, *to tear away,* κόρυθα κρατός, the helmet from the head, 13, 189.†

ἀφάρτερος, η. ον (compar. fr. adv. ἄφαρ), *quicker, fleeter,* ἵπποι, 23, 311.†

ἀφαυρός. ή. όν, *weak, powerless, feeble,* παῖς. 7, 235; oftener in compar. ἀφαυρότερος, and superl. ἀφαυρότατος (fr. αὔω, ἀφαύω, or fr. παῦρος with a intens.).

ἀφάω (ἀφή), *to feel, to touch, to examine,* ἀσπίδα, 6, 322; † only partcp. pres. ἀφόωντα, Ep. from ἀφάωντα; ἀφόωντα, ed. Wolf; ἀφόωντα, Spitzn., which last, according to Cd. Venet. and Apoll. Lexic. alone is correct: cf. Spitzner ad loc.

'Αφείδας, αντος, ὁ (from ἀ and φείδω, *unsparing*), son of Polyphêmôn from Alybas, father of Eperitus, for whom Ulysses gave himself out, Od. 24, 305.

ἀφείς, see ἀφίημι.

ἄφενος, τό, *abundance, wealth, riches,* in connexion with πλοῦτος, 1, 171. Od. 14, 99. (Apoll. and Schol. think it from ἀπό and ἑνός, prop. ἡ ἀφ' ἑνὸς ἐνιαυτοῦ περίουσα, the products of a year.)

ἀφέξω and ἀφέξομαι, see ἀπέχω.

* ἄφηλιξ, ικος (ἧλιξ), *beyond the years of youth, growing old,* h. in Cer. 140.

ἄφημαι (ἧμαι), *to sit apart, separate,* only partcp. pres., 15, 106.†

ἀφήτωρ, ορος. ὁ (ἀφίημι), *the hurler, he that shoots arrows,* appellat. of Apollo, 9. 404.† (Some derive it from φάω, and regard it as=ὁμοφήτωρ, the diviner.)

ἄφθιτος, ον (φθίω), *not destroyed, imperishable, everlasting,* mly spoken of what belongs to the gods, 2, 46. Od. 9, 133.

* ἄφθογγος, ον (φθόγγος), *soundless, voiceless, dumb,* h Cer. 198.

ἄφθονος, ον, without envy, 1) Act. *not envious, benevolent, giving freely,* h. 30, 16. 2) Pass. *not penurious, abundant, in abundance,* h. in Ap. 536.

ἀφίημι (ἵημι), 3 plur. imperf. ἀφίουν, as if from ἀφιέω, fut. ἀφήσω, αορ. 1 ἀφέηκα and ἀφῆκα, αορ. 2 dual and plur. subj. ἀφέη Ep. for ἀφῇ, optat. ἀφείην, I) *to*

send away, to dismiss, to let go, τινά, any one, in a good and bad signif., 1, 25; ζωόν τινα, *to let one go alive,* 20, 464: spoken chiefly of missile weapons: *to cast, to discharge, to hurl,* as δόρυ, ἔγχος and κεραυνόν, 8, 133; mly *to cast away;* ἄνθος, *to cast the flower,* said of grape-vines just setting for fruit, Od. 7, 126; metaph. δίψαν, *to remove thirst,* 11, 642; μένος, *to lose the strength,* 13, 444. 16. 613, etc.; in Pass.: τοῦ δέ τε πολλοὶ ἀπὸ σπινθῆρες ἵενται, from it (the star) many sparks were emitted, 4, 77. II) Mid. *to send oneself away from any thing;* hence, *to let go off, to let loose;* with gen. δειρῆς οὔπω ἀφίετο πήχεε, she did not loosen her arms from his neck, Od. 23, 240. (ι prop. short, long only by augm.; once, however, without this reason, Od. 22, 231.)

ἀφικάνω, poet. (ἱκάνω), only pres. and imperf.=ἀφικνέομαι, *to go to, to come to, to reach;* mly with accus., once with πρός, 6, 386.

ἀφικνέομαι, depon. mid. (ἱκνέομαι), fut. ἀφίξομαι, αορ. ἀφικόμην, perf. ἀφῖγμαι, Od. 6, 297; *to go to, to come to, to reach, to go to a person or a place;* mly with accus. νῆας, *to the ships,* more rarely with εἰς, ἐπί, κατά, and ὑπό and πρός τι, Od. 6, 297; metaph. *to overtake, to affect,* ἄλγος ἀφίκετό με, 18, 395.

ἀφίστημι (ἵστημι), αορ. 2 ἀπέστην, perf. ἀφέστηκα, syncop. form in dual and plur. ἀφεστᾶσι, partcp. ἀφεσταώς, 3 plur. pluperf. ἀφέστασαν, αορ. mid. ἀπεστησάμην. 1) Trans. *to put away,* not used in H. 2) Intrans. in aor. 2, perf. and pluperf., like the mid. *to stand apart, to stand aloof, to remove,* 4, 340. Od. 11, 544; *to be removed,* τινός, from a thing, 23, 517. b) In the mid. *to weigh out for oneself,* in order to pay; once, δείδω, μὴ τὸ χθιζὸν ἀποστήσωνται χρέος, I fear, lest they should pay back to us the debt of yesterday, i. e. requite evil for evil, 13, 745.

ἄφλαστον, τό, *the curved stern of a vessel,* with its decorations, 15, 716.† (In the Schol. on Ap. Rh., σανίδιον κατὰ τὴν πρύμνην.)

ἀφλοισμός, ὁ (related to ἀφρός), *foam, the froth of one enraged,* 15, 607.† (Others more improb. ψόφος ὀδόντων, gnashing of teeth.)

ἀφνειός, όν (ἄφενος), *rich, wealthy, opulent,* with gen. βιότοιο, in the means of living, 5, 544; χρυσοῖο, Od. 1, 165. The compar. ἀφνειότερος and superl. ἀφνειότατος, 20, 220.

ἀφοπλίζω (ὁπλίζω), *to disarm,* only mid. *to disarm oneself,* with ἔντεα, *to lay aside one's arms,* 23, 26.†

ἀφορμάω (ὁρμάω), in H. only depon. pass. ἀφορμάομαι, in aor. pass. ἀφωρμήθην, *to rush away, to hasten away,* ναῦφιν, 2, 794; hence absolute, *to go away, to depart,* Od. 2, 376.

ἀφόωντα, or ἀφόωντα, see ἀφάω.

ἀφραδέω (ἀφραδής), *to be imprudent,*

indiscreet, to speak or *act inconsiderately*, Od. 8, 294. Il. 9, 32.

ἀφραδής, ές (φράζομαι), *inconsiderate, irrational, imprudent*, μνηστῆρες. Od. 2, 282. νεκροὶ ἀφραδέες, the unreflecting, senseless dead, Od. 11, 476; adv. ἀφραδέως, *thoughtlessly, indiscreetly*, 3, 436.

ἀφραδίη, ἡ (φράζομαι), *inconsideration, imprudence, carelessness, folly;* often in the plur. 5, 649; νόοιο, 10, 122. 16, 354. 2) *ignorance, inexperience*, πολέμοιο, 2, 368.

*ἀφράδμων, ον = ἀφραδής, h. in Cer. 257.

ἀφραίνω, poet. (φρήν), *to be irrational, indiscreet, foolish*, 2, 257. Od. 20, 360.

*ἄφραστος, ον (φράζομαι), *not observed, unknown*. ἔργα, h. Merc. 80; *not to be discovered, invisible*, στίβος, h. Merc. 353. Compar. ἀφραστότερος, Epigr. 14.

ἀφρέω (ἀφρός), *to foam, to froth*. ἵπποι ἄφρεον στήθεα, upon the breast, 11, 282.† (ἄφρεον with synizesis.)

ἀφρήτωρ, ορος. ὁ (φρήτρη), *without society, without tribe, without connexions, unsocial*, 9, 63.†

'Αφροδῑ́τη, ἡ, daughter of Zeus and Diône, 5, 348; or, according to a later tradition, born from the foam of the sea (ἀφρός), h. in Ven., wife of Hêphæstus (*Vulcan*), and paramour of Arês (*Mars*) (Od. 8, 276), goddess of sensual love and of marriage, of pleasure and of beauty, 5, 429. Od. 20, 74. She is represented as exceedingly attractive and beautiful, 3, 396; distinguished by her smiling look (φιλομμειδής), but tender and unfitted 'or war. She is beautifully adorned (χρυσείη), the Graces themselves having furnished her clothing, 5, 338, and these constitute her society. She always carries a magic girdle, with which she subdues both gods and men, 14, 214 seq. With this girdle Hêrê inspires Zeus with great love for herself. Aphroditê was on the side of the Trojans; she had given occasion to the war. 5, 349 seq. Æneas was her son. 5, 313. She had splendid temples in Cyprus and in Cythêrê. 2) Metaph. like Ἄρης, it signifies *love, the enjoyments of love*, Od. 22, 444.

ἀφρονέω (ἄφρων), *to be foolish*, or *to act irrationally, foolishly*, only partcp. pres., 15, 104.†

ἀφρός, ὁ, *foam*, of water, 5, 599; of a raging lion, *20, 168.

ἀφροσύνη, ἡ (ἄφρων), *want of reason, senselessness, indiscretion, folly*, Il. in plur. Od. 16, 278. 24, 457.

ἄφρων, ον (φρήν), *irrational, senseless, indiscreet, inconsiderate, foolish* (antith. to ἐπίφρων), Od. 23, 12; *rash, raging*, spoken of Arês and Athênê, 5, 761. 875.

ἄφυλλος, ον (φύλλον), *leafless, deprived of leaves*. 2, 425.†

ἀφυσγετός, ὁ (ἀφύω), *slime, mud, filth*, which a river bears with it, 11, 495.†

ἀφύσσω, fut. ἀφύξω, aor. 1 ἤφυσα and poet. σσ, aor. mid. ἀφυσάμην, Ep. σσ, 1) *to draw off*, esply from a larger vessel to

a smaller, οἶνον ἀπό and ἐκ κρητῆ 598. Od. 9, 9; ἐν ἀμφιφορεῦσιν 349; with gen. alone, pass. πὸ πίθων ἠφύσσετο οἶνος, much w drawn from the vessels, Od. 23, ̣ Metaph. πλοῦτον, to accumulate as if to draw up in full draughts passage 1, 170, οὐδέ σ' ὀΐω ἐνθάδ' ἐών. ἄφενος καὶ πλοῦτον ἀφύξειν, plained in different ways; 1) In cients we find a twofold expla Some (Eustath. and Schol. Venet posed an hyberbaton, and cor ἐνθάδ' ἄτιμος ἐών with εἰμι ɛ v. 169, so that the former words Achilles. Others (Schol. Venet posed the nom. stands for gen., ̣ ferred these words to Agamemno In the modern annotators we threefold explanation: a) The connected with that of Eustath differs in constructing ἐνθάδε wit ξειν, viz. 'I do not believe, since dishonoured (without reward), th will here accumulate riches.' R and Stadelmann p. 62, prefer this, because the nom. ἄτιμος ἐών sta close connexion with ὀΐω, partly b it agrees with the connexion, Achilles thinks that Agamemno make little progress without his h The second explanation (Clark Köppen) refers ἄτιμος ἐών, on acc v. 175, to Agamemnon, and cons οὐκ ὀΐω σε, ὅτιμος ἐών (for ἄτιμον ἐ ἀφύξειν. Reference is made to for a similar anacoluthon. 3) Bo planations, the one on account hyperbaton, and the other on acco the harsh anacoluthon, are jus jected by almost all modern critics. either make σ' a dat. σοί (cf. Wolf. l. p. 102, and Spitzner, Excurs. ̣ 3), or they read with Bentley σοὶ ὀ cause οι is not elided in σοί (cf Anm. p. 6. Bothe and Thiersch, 10). They read consequently, ο̇ ὀΐω ἐνθάδ', ἄτιμος ἐών, etc., i. e. ' nᵒ ᵘ ind whilst I am dishonoui gather riches for you here. With t planation the words connect far with the preceding νῦν δ' εἰμι ɛ and the reply of Agamemnon mainly on t is threat of Achille Mid. 1) *to draw off* or *out for one pour out* or *in;* with accus. οἱ κρητῆρος, 3, 259; and ἀπὸ κρητῆρ 579. 2) Metaph. *to heap up*, α φύλλα ἠφυσάμην, Od. 7, 285. Ο ἔντερα χαλκὸς ἤφυσα, see διαφύσσε

'Αχαιαί, αἱ, *Achaian* or *Achæan* ι fem. of 'Αχαιός, Od. 2, 119.

'Αχαιάς, άδος, ἡ, Ep. for 'Α *Achaian, Achæan*. 2) As sub *Achaian* or *Achæan woman*, 5, 422

'Αχαϊκός, ή, όν, Ep for 'Α *Achaian* or *Achæan;* λαός, the A or Achæan people, 13, 141; 'Αργος.

'Αχαιΐς, ΐδος, ἡ, *Achaian* or *A* with or without γαῖα, the *Achaia* esply the dominion of Achilles in Thessaly, 1, 254; see 'Αχαιοί. 2) Subaud. γυνή, an Achaian woman, 2, 235; in contempt, 9, 395.

'Αχαιοί, οἱ, nom. sing. 'Αχαιός, ὁ, the Achaians or Achæans, the most powerful of the Grecian tribes in the time of the Trojan war, whose main residence was in Thessalia, 2, 684; but who also had possessions in Peloponnesus as far as to Messene, chiefly in Argos, 5, 114. The Danai and Myrmidons were branches of this tribe. Perhaps they had spread themselves also to Ithaca, Od. 1, 90; and to Crete, Od. 19, 138. Tradition says they derived their name from Achæus, son of Xuthus, grandson of Hellen, Apd. 1, 7. 3. The entire Greeks are often so called in H. from the main tribe, 1, 2. Od. 1, 90.

ἄχαρις, ι (χάρις), disagreeable, joyless; in compar. ἀχαρίστερος, Od. 20, 392.†

ἀχάριστος, ον (χαρίζομαι), disagreeable, displeasing, Od. 8, 236† [δόρπον ἀχαριστότερον, 'a sadder feast,' Cp.].

*ἀχειρής, ές (χείρ), without hands, epith. of the crabs, Batr. 300.

'Αχελώϊος, ὁ, Ep. for 'Αχελῷος, a river between Ætolia and Acarnania, which flows into the Ionic sea; now Aspro-Potamo, 21, 194. 2) a river in Phrygia, which rises in the mountain Sipylus, 24, 616.

ἄχερδος, ἡ, more rarely ὁ, a wild, thorny bush, suitable for hedging; thorn-bush, thorn, the hawthorn, Od. 14, 10.†

ἀχερωΐς, ἴδος, ἡ, the white poplar, the silver poplar, pópulus alba, Linn.; 13, 389. 16, 482; prob. from 'Αχέρων, because it was believed that Heraclês brought it from the under-world. *Il.

'Αχέρων, οντος, ὁ (as if ὁ ἄχεα ῥέων, the river of woe), Acherôn, a river of the under-world, into which Pyriphlegethôn and Cocýtus flow, Od. 10, 513. *Od.

ἀχεύω (ἄχος), to be sad, afflicted, troubled, only partcp. with accus. θυμόν, in heart, 5, 869; τινός, about any one, Od. 16, 139; and with εἵνεκα, Od. 21, 318.

ἀχέω=ἀχεύω, also only partcp. τινός, about any one, 18, 446; and with ἕνεκα, 20, 293.

ἄχθομαι (ἄχθος), 1) to be laden, freighted, νηῦς ἤχθετο τοῖσι, the ship was laden, Od. 15, 457. b) Metaph. to be burthened or oppressed, ὀδύνῃσι, oppressed with pains, 13, 354; with accus. ἄχθομαι ἕλκος, I am pained by the wound, 5, 361. 2) Esply spoken of mental states: to be oppressed, pained, sad, indignant, vexed, grieved; with κῆρ, 11, 274. 400; ἤχθετο δαμναμένους Τρωσίν, he grieved to see them conquered by the Trojans, 13, 352 (ἤχθετο in Od. 14, 366. 19, 337, belongs to ἔχθομαι).

ἄχθος, εος, τό (related to ἄγω), load, burden. ἄχθος ἀρούρης, burden of the earth, proverbially spoken of a worthless man, 18, 104. Od. 20, 379.

'Αχιλλεύς, ῆος, ὁ, also 'Αχιλεύς (when required by the metre), son of Peleus and Thetis, king of the Myrmidons and Hellênes in Thessalia, the bravest hero before Troy. He was educated by Phœnix; son of Amyntor, who also accompanied him to Troy, 9, 448; in music and the healing art he was instructed by Chiron, 11, 832. His friend is Patroclus; his son, Neoptolemus, who resided in Scyros, 19, 326—333; and whom Ulysses brought to Troy, to engage in the contest, Od. 11, 509. Achilles is the hero of H.: great physical power, a great mind, violent passions, but also a feeling heart, are his characteristics. Insulted by Agamemnon, he forgets himself in his wrath; he finally gives ear to his mother, but does not fight for the Greeks till the death of Patroclus, 19, 321. According to H. he died in battle, Od. 24, 430. 5, 310. (The name is derived from ἄχος and λαός, the people's grief, Apd. Molestinus, Herm.)

ἀχλύς, ύος, ἡ, obscurity, darkness, cloud, esply the darkness of death, the night of death; spoken of fainting, 5, 696 [κατὰ δ' ὀφθαλμῶν κέχυτ' ἀχλ., 'sickly mists,' Cp.]; of death, Od. 22, 88 (υ is long in nom. and accus.).

ἀχλύω (ἀχλύς), aor. ἤχλυσα, to become dark, to darken or cloud, spoken of the sea, Od. 12, 405.†

ἄχνη, ἡ, Ion. for ἄχνα (related to χνόη), prop. what is abraded from the surface of a body; hence 1) chaff, 5, 499. 2) foam of the sea, 4, 426. Od. 5, 403.

ἄχνυμαι, Ep. depon. only pres. and imperf. ἄχος), to feel pain, to be afflicted, sad, troubled; often with accus. θυμόν, κῆρ ἐνὶ θυμῷ, and with gen. caus. τινός, about any one, Od. 14, 376; and περί τινι, h. Cer. 77; also θυμὸς ἄχνυτο, 14, 38; once spoken of lions, 18, 320; cf. ἀκαχίζω.

ἄχολος, ον (χολή), without bile, without anger. 2) which expels anger, anger-quelling, φάρμακον, Od. 4, 221.†

ἄχομαι, mid. to be sad, to be afflicted, Od. 18, 256. 19, 129.

ἄχος, εος, τό (a word derived from the natural ejaculation of one in pain, as ah!), pain, grief, sadness, affliction, trouble; always spoken of the mind: ἐμοὶ δ' ἄχος, it pains me, 5, 759; with gen. about any one, ἐμοὶ ἄχος σέθεν ἔσσεται, I shall have pain on thy account, 4, 169: also in plur. ἄχεα, sufferings, pains, 6, 413. Od. 19, 167.

ἀχρεῖον, adv. (prop. neut. of adj. ἀχρεῖος, ον), unprofitably, uselessly, aimlessly, only twice: 1) ἀχρεῖον ἰδών, 2, 269, looking foolish or confused, spoken of Thersites, who looked confounded or embarrassed when he received blows from Ulysses. Voss translates, 'with a wry look;' and with this agrees the explanation of Wolf in Vorles. zu Il. p. 44. "But it is uncertain," says Wolf, "whether Thersites does this from pain or

E 5

purposely, to excite the pity of the Greeks.
The latter agrees well with his character." 2) ἀχρεῖον ἐγέλασσεν, Od. 18, 163,
she laughed without cause, she uttered a
forced laugh; spoken of Penelopê, who,
notwithstanding her inward trouble,
wished to appear cheerful to the suitors.
Here again ἀχρεῖον expresses something
artificial. unnatural (ἐπίπλαστον, ὑπο
κεκριμένον. Schol. A.), Usteri.

ἀχρημοσύνη, ἡ (ἀχρήμων), poverty,
want, penury, Od. 17, 502.†

* ἄχρηστος, ον (χρηστός), profitless,
vain, neut. as adv. Batr. 70.

ἄχρι, before a vowel ἄχρις (related to
ἄκρος), adv. 1) Of place: at the extreme, on the surface, 17, 599. b) to the
extreme, entirely, 4, 522. 2) Of time:
until, with gen. ἄχρι μάλα κνέφαος, till
late at night, Od. 18, 369.

ἀχυρμιή, ἡ (ἄχυρον), prop. the place
where the chaff falls, a chaff-heap, 5,
502.†

ΑΧΩ, see ἀκαχίζω.

ἄψ, adv. of place: backwards, back,
often with a verb: ἄψ ὁρᾶν, ὠθεῖν. 2)
Of time: again, 5, 505.

Ἀψευδής (from ἀ and ψεῦδος, not deceitful), daughter of Nereus and Doris,
18, 46.

ἀψίς, ἴδος, ἡ, Ion. for ἁψίς (ἅπτω),
a knot, a mesh. ἀψῖδες λίνου, the meshes
of the net, 5, 487.†

ἀψόρρον, adv. see ἀψόρρος.

ἀψόρροος, ον (ῥέω), back-flowing, epith.
of Oceanus, which like a river encircles
the earth and flows back into itself, 18,
399. Od. 20, 65.

ἀψόρρος, ον (prop. abbreviated from
ἀψόρροος), retreating back, ἀψόρροι ἐκίο
μεν, ἀπονέοντο, 3, 313. Oftener the neut.
sing. ἀψόρρον as adv. back, with βαίνειν,
ἀπονέεσθαι. b) again, 4, 152.

ἄψος, εος, τό (ἅπτω), connexion, articulation, esply of the limbs, a joint. λύθεν
δὲ οἱ ἄψεα πάντα, all her limbs [joints]
were loosed (i. e. in slumber), Od. 4, 794.
18, 189.

ΑΩ, theme of ἄημι.

ΑΩ. theme of ἄεσα and ἄσα, q. v.

ΑΩ (ᾱ). pres. infin. ἄμεναι for ἀέμεναι,
infin. fut. ἄσειν, aor. 1 ἄσα, infin. ἄσαι,
infin. fut. ἄσεσθαι, aor. 1 ἄσασθαι; 1) to
satiate, τινά, any one; with gen. mat.
ἄσαι Ἄρηα αἵματος, Arês with blood, 5,
289; ἵππους δρόμου, 18, 281; metaph.
spoken of the spear: ἱεμένη χροός ἄμεναι
ἀνδρομέοιο, lusting to sate itself with
human flesh, 21, 70. II) Mid. to satiate
oneself; ἦτορ σίτοιο, to refresh the heart
with food, 19, 307; ἑῶμεν or ἄωμεν (19,
402) is assigned to this verb as subj. for
ἄωμεν, see ἑῶμεν.

ἄωρ. see ἄορες.

ἄωρος, ον (ὥρα), untimely, unformed;
hence ugly, deformed (Schol. ἀπρεπής),
πόδες, spoken of Scylla, Od. 12, 89.†

ἄωρτο, 2 sing. pluperf. pass. from
ἀείρω.

ἀωτέω (expanded form fr. ἄω), origin-

ally to snore; then to sleep, spokeof a deep sleep; in H. always with
10, 159. Od. 10, 548; see Buttm
p. 182.

ἄωτον, τό and ὁ ἄωτος (in H. th
is indeterminate; Pindar has only
later poets have also τὸ ἄωτον from
prop. a flock, or lock of wool. ἐύ
οἰός ἄωτος, the well-twisted wool
sheep, spoken of a sling, 13, 599.
also Od. 1, 443; spoken of the
skin of a sheep, Od. 9, 434; once
of the finest linen: λίνοιο λεπτὸν
the delicate nap or down of the li
661; metaph. the best, the most be
inasmuch as the woolly surface of
tests their beauty and newne
Buttm. Lex. p. 182. According
old Schol. it signifies a flowe
metaph. like ἄνθος, the bloom, i.
finest, the most beautiful (still the
flower is nowhere found in the po

B.

B, the second letter of the Greel
bet; hence the index of the secor
sody.

βάδην, adv. (βαίνω), step by step
antith. to running, 13, 516.†

* βαδίζω (βάδος), fut. ίσω, to ste
to travel, h. Merc. 210.

βάζω, fut. βάξω, perf. pass. βε
to prate, to speak, to talk; with
ἀνεμώλια, μεταμώνια, to prate idle
πεπνυμένα, ἄρτια, to speak discr
the point, Od. 8, 240. δίχα βε
speak diffrently, Od. 3, 127; with
accus. βάζειν τινά τι, to say any
any one, 9, 59; and pass. ἔπος β
Od. 8, 408.

βάθιστος, η, ον, superl. for βαθ

* βάθος, εος, τό (βαθύς), depth,
Batr. 86.

βαθυδινήεις, εσσα, εν (δίνη), dee
ing, having deep whirlpools, onl
21, 15. 603; elsewhere the follow

βαθυδίνης, ου, ὁ (δίνη), deep-t
deep-eddying, having deep wh
epith. of Oceanus and of rivers
Od.

βαθύζωνος, ον (ζώνη), deep-gird
girdled close under the breast, so
garment might hang in full fol
to the feet, because this took pl
on festal days; hence in genera
didly clothed, or beautifully girdle
of the Trojan women, 9, 594. Od
[According to Passow, low-gird
girdled close under the breast, b
the hips.]

* βαθύθριξ, τριχος, ὁ, ἡ (θρι
thick hair, thick-woolled, thicl
spoken of sheep, h. Ap. 412.

* *βαθύκληρος, ον* (*κλῆρος*), *rich in land, having great estates*, Ep. 16, 4.

Βαθυκλῆς, ῆος, ὁ, son of Chalcon, a Myrmidon, slain by Glaucus, 16, 594.

βαθύκολπος, ον (*κόλπος*), *deep-bosomed*, either literally from their full bosoms, or from the folds of the dress; hence, *splendidly-clothed*, epith. of the Trojan women, 18, 122; and of the nymphs, h. Ven. 258.

βαθύλειμος, ον (*λειμών*), *having rich meadows, having deep grass*, epith. of a town, 9, 151. 293.

βαθυλήϊος, ον (*λήϊον*), *having high grain, fruitful*, *τέμενος*, 18, 550.†

βαθύνω (*βαθύς*), *to make deep, to deepen, to excavate;* with accus. *χῶρον*, 23, 421.†

βαθυῤῥείτης, αο, ὁ (*ῥέω*)=*βαθύῤῥοος*, 21, 195.†

βαθύῤῥοος, ον (*ῥέω*), *deep-flowing*, epith. of Oceanus, 14, 314. Od. 11, 13.

βαθύς, εῖα, and Ep. *βαθέη*, *βαθύ*, superl. *βάθιστος*, 1) *deep* or *high*, according to the position of the speaker; *τάφρος*, *ἄμαθος*, *Τάρταρος*, *ἠϊών*, lofty coast [or, perhaps, having deep sand], 2, 92; metaph. of the soul: *φρὴν βαθεῖα*, the inmost soul, 19, 125. 2) *deep*, with the idea of *thick, dark*, *ὕλη*, 5, 555; also metaph. *ἀήρ*, the thick air, Od. 1, 144; *λαῖλαψ*, the strong tempest, 11, 306. 3) *deep* in length, or extending inward, *ἄγκος*, 20, 489; hence *αὐλή*, a deep court (V. with lofty enclosure), 5, 142.

* *βαθύσκιος, ον* (*σκιά*), *deep-shaded*, h. Merc. 229.

* *βαθύστερνος, ον* (*στέρνον*), *high-breasted, wide-arched;* and mly *broad*, *ala*, frag. Hom. 23.

βαθύσχοινος, ον (*σχοῖνος*), *deeply overgrown with rushes, rushy*, epith. of Asopus [‘*to the reedy banks of the Asopus*,’ Cp.], 4, 383. h. 8, 5.

* *βαθύτριχα*, see *βαθύθριξ*.

βαίνω, fut. *βήσομαι*, aor. 1 trans. *ἔβησα*, aor. 2 *ἔβην*, Ep. *βῆν*, 3 plur. *ἔβησαν*, Ep. *βῆσαν*, *ἔβαν*, *βάν*, subj. *βῶ*, Ep. *βείω*, optat. *βαίην*, infin. *βήμεναι* and *βῆναι*, partcp. *βάς*, *βᾶσα*, *βάν*, perf. *βέβηκα*, also the sync. forms *βεβάασι*, infin. *βεβάμεν*, partcp. *βεβαώς*, *βεβαυῖα*, pluperf. *ἐβεβήκειν*, syncop. 3 plur. *βέβασαν*, also Ep. aor. mid. *ἐβήσετο*, more rarely *ἐβήσατο* = *ἔβη*. According to Buttm., Gr. Gram., *ἐβήσατο* is correct only when used in a causative sense for *ἔβησε*. N.B. The form *βέβηκα*, rare in H., has only the signif. *to have gone;* the sync. forms *βέβαα*, that of the pres. *to go*, and the pluperf. mostly an aorist sense. (The ground form is ΒΑΩ, Ep. forms *βιβάω*, *βίβημι*, *βιβάσθω*.) I) Intrans. *to go*, and 1) *to walk, to step, to proceed*, spoken of men and beasts, the direction of the motion being indicated sometimes by the prep. *εἰς*, *ἐν*, *ἐπί*, *κατά*, *μετά*, *πρός*, etc., and sometimes by the accus. merely: *εἰς δίφρον*, 5, 837; also *δίφρον*, *νέας*, 3, 262. Od. 3, 162; *ἐπὶ νηός*, to ascend the ship, to embark, 13, 665; but *ἐπὶ νηυσίν*, to sail away in ships, 2, 351 [also *ἐν νηυσίν*, 2, 510]; *ἐπί τινα*, to go to any one, 2, 18: *ἀμφί τινι*, to go about any one (to defend him), 5, 299; *μετ' ἴχνιά τινος*, to follow one’s steps, Od. 3, 30. *b*) In a hostile sense: *to rush upon any one*, with *ἐπί*, *μετά* and accus., also *ἐπί τινι*, 16, 751. 2) With partcp. of another verb, by which the kind of motion is determined: *ἔβη φεύγων*, he fled; *ἔβη ἀΐξασα*, see *ἀΐσσω*; the partcp. fut. denotes the aim: *ἔβη ἐξεναρίξων*, he went to slay, 11, 101; *ἀγγελέων*, Od. 4, 28. 3) With infin. following: *to set out, to proceed, to begin*. *βῆ δ' ἰέναι*, he set out to go, quickly he went, 4, 199; so also *βῆ θέειν*, *ἐλάαν*. 4) Metaph. spoken of inanimate things: *ἐννέα ἐνιαυτοὶ βεβάασι*, nine years have passed away, 2, 134. *πῇ ὅρκια βήσεται ἡμῖν*, whither will our oaths go, i. e., what will become of our oaths, 2, 339. *ἰκμὰς ἔβη*, the moisture (of the bull’s hide) vanished, 17, 392. II) Trans. in aor. 1, only poet. and Ion. act. *ἔβησα*, 1) *to cause to go, to conduct, to cause to mount* or *alight*. *φῶτας βῆσεν ἀφ' ἵππων*, 16, 810; but *ἀμφοτέρους ἐξ ἵππων βῆσε κακῶς ἀέκοντας*, he hurled both down from the chariot, unwilling as they were, 5, 164. *βῆσαι ἵππους*, 11, 756.

* Βάκχειος, *είη*, *ειον*, relating to Bacchus or to his orgies, *drunken, intoxicated, frantic*, Βάκχειος Διόνυσος, hymn. 18, 46.

βάλανος, ἡ, *an acorn*, fruit of the oak, *Od. 10, 242. 13, 409.

Βαλίος, ὁ (adj. *βαλιός*, spotted [fortasse, i. q. *αἰόλος*. *Lob.*]), *Piebald*, a horse of Achilles, 16, 149.

βάλλω [primitive *βέλ-ω* in *βέλος*], fut. *βαλέω*, aor. 2 *ἔβαλον*, perf. *βέβληκα*, pluperf. *βεβλήκειν* (often in the sense of the aor., 5, 66. 73, 661), perf. pass. *βέβλημαι*, Ep. also *βεβόλημαι*, yet with the difference that the former is used literally of body, the latter metaph. of mind, 9, 3; pluperf. *βεβλήμην*, 3 plur. *βεβλήατο* for *βέβληντο*. Of an aor. sync. mid. with pass. signif. occur *ἔβλητο*, infin. *βλῆσθαι*, partcp. *βλήμενος*, subj. *βλήεται* for *βλήηται*, optat. (*βλείμην*) *βλεῖο*, etc. I) Act. *to cast, to throw, to hurl*; *λύματα εἰς ἅλα*, 1, 314; spoken of all kinds of missile weapons: *ἰόν*, Od. 20, 62; hence, *to shoot, to hit, to wound*, *τινά*, or *τί τινι*, e. g. *τινὰ δουρί*, any one with the spear, 5, 73; *ὀϊστῷ*, 5, 393; *στῆθος χερμαδίῳ*, 14, 410; *τινὰ λάεσσιν*, 3, 80; also *τινά τί τινι*, 11, 583; still the dat. is mly wanting; *τινὰ στῆθος*, to hit any one in the breast, 4, 480; also absol. *to hit*, in opposition to *ἁμαρτάνω*, to miss, 11, 351. 13, 10; as a consequense, *to prostrate, to lay* a person *low, to slay*, *τινὰ ἐν κονίῃσι*, 8, 156. cf. 4, 173. 5, 17; metaph. *ἄχεϊ*, *πένθεϊ βεβολημένος*, hit, wounded by pain, sorrow, 9, 3. Od. 10, 247. *b*) *to cast;* spoken of a strong motion: *to drive;* e. g. *ἑτέρωσε κάρη*, to cast the head to the other side, 8, 306;

ἑτέρωσε ὅμματα, to turn away the eyes, Od. 16, 179; spoken of ships, νῆας ἐς πόντον, to urge the ships into the sea, Od. 4, 359 ; νέας πρὸς πέτρας, Od. 12, 71. 2) to hit, spoken of touching a surface, to besprinkle, to bespatter, to bestrew. ῥαθά-μιγγες ἔβαλλον ἄντυγα, the drops be-sprinkled the chariot-rim, 11, 536. 20, 501; of dust, τινά, 23, 502. κτύπος οὔατα βάλλει, the noise strikes the ear, 10, 535. τόπον ἀκτῖσι βάλλει ἥέλιος, the sun irra-diates the place, Od. 5, 479. 3) to cast away, to let fall, to lose ; δάκρυ, to shed tears. 4) In a weaker sense, to put, to put on, to annex, to put off, τὶ ἐν χερσίν τινος, 5, 574 ; κύκλα ἀμφ᾽ ὀχέεσσι, 5, 722; φιλό-τητα μετ᾽ ἀμφοτέροισι, to establish friend-ship between the two, 4, 16; ὕπνον ἐπὶ βλεφάροισι, to let fall, Od. 1, 364. b) Oftener of clothing and weapons : to put on. 5) to fall, to flow, to run, spoken of a river, εἰς ἄλα, 11, 722; of steeds: περὶ τέρμα, about the goal, 23, 462. II) Mid. 1) to hit, to touch for oneself ; χρόα λουτροῖς, ᾿ο cleanse one's limbs in the bath, h. Cer. 50. 2) to cast any thing about oneself, to put on; ἀμφὶ ὤμοισιν ξίφος, to suspend, 3, 334 ; αἰγίδα, 5, 738; metaph. ἐν θυμῷ χόλον τινί, to cherish anger against any one in the heart, 14, 50 ; μετά, or ἐν φρεσίν, ἐν θυμῷ, to lay any thing to heart, to consider, to ponder, νόστόν, 9, 435. 611. Od. 11, 428; more rarely, to lay up, to preserve in the heart, 15, 566; absolute, ἑτέρωσ᾽ ἐβάλοντο ; they determined otherwise, Od. 1, 234; where Nitzsch with Spitzner prefers ἑτέρωσ᾽ ἐβάλοντο, the reading of other manu-scripts : ἐβόλοντο for ἐβούλοντο, is ap-proved by Thiersch, Gram. § 168, 12, and Buttm., Lexil. p. 199. [For the pass. signif. of the 2 aor. sync. mid. see Buttm. § 110, 7.]

βαμβαίνω (related to βάζω), to stammer, to shudder for fear, to chatter with the teeth, 10, 375.†

βάν, Ep. for ἔβαν, see βαίνω.

βάπτω, 1) to dip, to immerse, with accus. πέλεκυν εἰν ὕδατι (to harden it), Od. 9, 392.† 2) to tinge, to colour, Batr. 224.

βαρβαρόφωνος, ον (φώνη), speaking a foreign tongue, rude of speech, epith. of the Carians, 2, 867.† (Voss, ' with a bar-barous utterance,' since the Carians as Pelasgians spoke Greek, but their pro-nunciation was uncouth.)

βάρδιστος, η, ον, Ep. for βράδιστος, superl. see βραδύς.

ΒΑΡΕΩ = βαρύθω, only used in the Ep. partcp. βεβαρηώς, burdened, heavy. οἴνῳ βεβαρηότες, drunken with wine, *Od. 3, 139. 19, 122.

* βάρος, τό, weight, load, Batr. 91.

* βαρύβρομος, ον (βρέμω), heavily thun-dering, crashing, fr. 78.

βαρύθω (βαρύς), to be loaded, burdened, incommoded. βαρύθει μοι ὦμος ὑπ᾽ αὐτοῦ, my shoulder is distressed by the wound, 16, 519.†

βαρύνω (βαρύς), aor. 1 ἐβάρυνα, ; pass. ἐβαρύνθην, also Ep. perf. βεβ. (see ΒΑΡΕΩ), to load, tu burden, t press, with accus. τινά, 5, 664. βαρύνεσθαι γυῖα, χεῖρα, to be distrᵉ lame in the limbs, in the hand, 19 20, 480. κάρη πήληκι βαρυνθέν, the burdened with the helmet, *8, 308.

βαρύς, εῖα, ύ, 1) heavy, great, sᵢ βαρεῖαι χεῖρες, 1, 89. b) heavy, heavily pressing, severe, troublesom pressive ; ὀδύναι, great pains ; sᶜ ἄτη, ἔρις, etc. 2) Spoken of sᵢ φθόγγος, Od. 9, 237 ; esply the neut. and plur. βαρύ and βαρέα, as adv. στενάχειν, to groan heavily, alouᵢ 334.

βαρυστενάχων, ουσα, ον (στενάχω) ing, groaning heavily, *4, 153.

* βαρύφθογγος, ον (φθογγή), voiced, loud-roaring, λέων, h. Ven.

βασίλεια, ἡ, fem. of βασιλεύς, ᵢ princess, *Od. 7, 241.

βασιλεύς, ῆος, ὁ, I) ruler, king, reign, and mly commander, leader, In the heroic age, βασιλεύς was tᴴ signation of the chief of any comm or district, who owed his authority valour his wealth, or his intelliᵍ As all oodily and mental endowι were considered a direct gift of the so also was the regal dignity ; hen was called διογενής, διοτρεφής. duties and employments of the kiᵢ 197. Od. 1, 386 (δίκη βασιλήων), we He assembled the public council, aᵢ in debate, 2, 50. 9, 33. Od. 2, 26. was leader of the nation in war. was obliged to decide upon righ wrong, 16, 542. Od. 19, 110. 4) I his place to present the solemn fices, 2, 402. 412. [Cf. Jahrbüch. und Klotz, März 1843, p. 255.] power was limited; he could ᵢ nothing without consulting the respectable men of the nation (γερόντων), and, in important case general assembly of the people (ἀ His prerogatives (γέρας) were 1 presidency on public occasions, larger portion at feasts, 8, 162. distinct portion of land (τέμενο [Tributes or] gifts established by c (θέμιστες), 9, 156. The ensigns of dignity were the scepᵗre (σκῆπτρο the service of heralds (κήρυκες Cammann Vorschule z. Hom. p. 2 Helbig. die sittlich. Zustände des ᵢ Heldenalters, Leips. 1839, p. 27 II) a prince, a king's son ; also, all nobility who had possessions, gᵢ small, Od. 1, 394. 8, 41. 390. III master of a family, 18, 556. Frᵒ word comes the Ep. compar. βᵢ τερος, a greater king, more royᶜ superl. βασιλεύτατος, the greatesᵗ 9, 69. (Prob. from βαίνω in the sense, and λαός, that conducts the to war.) [The royal dignity, even heroic age, was hereditary : c

Humpert. de Civitat. Hom. Bonnæ, 1839, p. 4—11.]

βασιλεύω (βασιλεύς), to be king, to rule, to reign, ὑπὸ Πλάκῳ, 6, 425. 2) to rule over any one, to govern, with dat. 2, 206; [esply] once with gen. [to be queen] Πύλου, Od. 11, 285 [cf. Il. 6, 425].

βασιλήϊος, ίη, ήϊον, Ion. for βασίλειος (βασιλεύς), royal, princely, γένος, Od. 16, 401.†

βασιληΐς, ίδος, ἡ (fem. adj. to βασιλήϊος), τιμή, the royal dignity, 6, 193.†

βάσκε, only in connexion with ἴθι, βάσκ' ἴθι, go, hence away, haste, 2, 8. The imper. of an Ep. form of βαίνω, which occurs in compos. in the infin. ἐπιβάσκω, q. v.

βαστάζω, fut. σω, to lift up, to elevate, to raise, with accus. λᾶαν, τόξον, Od. 11, 503. 21, 405. 2) to bear, τὶ νώτοισι, upon the back, Batr. 78.

βάτην, for ἐβήτην, see βαίνω.

Βατίεια, ἡ (prob. from βάτος, thorn-hill), a hill before the Scæan gate of Troy, by tradition the sepulchral mound of Myrinna, q. v. 2, 813.

* βατοδρόπος, ον (δρέπω), plucking or extirpating brambles, h. Merc. 190.

βάτος, ἡ, a bramble, a thorn-bush, Od. 24, 230.†

* βατραχομυομαχία, ἡ, battle of the frogs and mice, a well-known mock-heroic poem, incorrectly ascribed to H.

* βάτραχος. ὁ, a frog, Batr.

βεβάασι, βεβάμεν, βέβασαν, βεβαώς, see βαίνω.

βεβαρηώς. see βαρεω.

βεβήκει, see βιάω.

βεβλήαται, βεβλήατο, see βάλλω.

βεβολήατο, see βάλλω.

βεβρώθω, Ep. form for βιβρώσκω (theme ΒΡΟΩ with epenth. θ), to consume, to devour, εἰ δὲ σύγ' — ὠμὸν βεβρώθοις Πρίαμον Πριάμοιό τε παῖδας, if thou couldst devour Priam and his sons raw [alive], 4, 35.† (According to Buttm., Gram., βεβρώθοις belongs to a peculiar verb with strengthened sense βεβρώθω (from ΒΡΟΩ, with epenth. θ): cf. Rost, p. 284.)

βεβρωκώς, βεβρώσεται, see βιβρώσκω.

βέη, βείομαι, see βέομαι.

βείω, Ep. for βῶ, see βαίνω.

βέλεμνον, τό, poet.=βέλος, only in the plur. a missile, arrows or spears, *15, 484. 22, 206.

Βελλεροφόντης, ου, ὁ (from Βέλλερος and φονή), the slayer of Bellerus, an appellation of Hipponous, son of Glaucus, who slew unintentionally Bellerus, prince of the Corinthians, 6, 155; see Ἱππόνοος. [The tradition in regard to Bellerus is post-Homeric.]

* βελόνη, ἡ (βέλος), a needle, a point, Batr. 130.

βέλος, εος, τό (βάλλω). 1) a missile weapon, telum, esply, a javelin, an arrow, and mly whatever is hurled at an enemy, a stone, Od. 9, 493; poet. the gentle arrows of Apollo and Artemis, to indi-

cate a sudden death, see Apollo and Artemis; but also of plague, 1, 51. 2) the direction or stroke of a missile weapon, 8, 513; hence, ἐκ βελέων τινὰ ἄλκειν, to draw any one from the track of missile weapons, 4, 465. 3) Metaph. spoken of the pangs of parturition, 11, 269.

βέλτερος, η, ον, [related to βόλεσθαι, velle, according to some], poet. irreg. compar. of ἀγαθός. better, more excellent, prob. related to βάλλω.

βελτίων, ον, irreg. compar. of ἀγαθός. Od. 17, 18. † Earlier reading for βέλτερον.

βένθος, εος, τό, Ep. for βάθος, τό, deep, depth, esply of the sea, 11. θαλάσσης πάσης βένθεα εἰδέναι, to know the depths of the sea, i. e., to possess great intelligence, in contradistinction from the physical strength of Atlas, who bore the pillars of heaven, Od. 1, 53: cf. 4, 386. βένθεα ὕλης, the depths of the forest, Od. 17, 316; βένθοσδε, Od. 9, 51.

βέομαι and βείομαι (ΒΕΙΩ), 2 sing. βέη, 1 plur. βιόμεσθα, h. Ap. 528; βεόμεσθα, an Ep. pres. with fut. signif. : 1 will go, I will walk. οὔτε Διὸς βέομαι φρεσίν, I will not walk (conduct) according to the mind of Zeus [i. e. I will not obey him], 15, 194; I will live, 16, 852. 22, 431 (either an Ep. fut. like κείω, or a subj. used as a fut. from βάω, βαίνω, Buttm., Gr. Gram. § 114. Thiersch, Gram. § 223, 88. Rost, p. 284).

βέρεθρον, τό, Ep. for βάραθρον, abyss, gulf, spoken of Tartarus, 8, 14; and of Scylla, Od. 12, 94.

βῆ, poet. for ἔβη, see βαίνω.

βηλός, ὁ (prob. from ΒΑΩ), a threshold, poet. dwelling-house, *1, 591. 15, 23.

* βῆμα, τό (βαίνω), a step, a pace, a footstep, h. Merc. 222. 345.

βήμεν, βήμεναι, see βαίνω.

Βῆσα, ἡ, a town of the Locrians, 2. 532; according to Strabo Βῆσσα, and only a forest valley.

βήσαμεν, βῆσε, see βαίνω.

βήσετο, see βαίνω.

βῆσσα, ἡ (βαίνω), a ravine, a forest valley, H. mly οὔρεος ἐν βήσσης, in the glades of the mountain; alone 18, 588. Od. 19, 435. h. Ap. 284.

βητάρμων, ονος, ὁ (ἁρμός), a dancer, prop. one who takes steps after measured time, *Od. 8, 250. 383.

βιάζω, Ep. earlier form, βιάω (βία), whence perf. act. βεβίηκα, pres. mid. 3 plur. βιόωνται for βιῶνται, Od. 11, 503: 3 plur. optat. βιῷτο Ep. for βιῶτο, 11, 467; imperf. 3 plur. βιόωντο, Ep. for ἐβιῶντο, Od. 23, 9; fut. mid. βιήσομαι, aor. mid. ἐβιησάμην (βιάζω in the act. occurs in H. as pres. only Od. 12, 297; elsewhere H. employs βιάζομαι in the pres. and imperf. as depon. mid. These tenses are pass. in 15, 727. 16, 102). 1) Act. to subdue, to overpower, to oppress, to force, τινά, Od. 12, 297; metaph. ἄχος βεβίηκεν Ἀχαιούς, pain oppressed the Achaians, 10, 145; hence pass. βιάζεσθαι βελέεσσιν, to be harassed by weapons, 11, 576. II) Mid. more freq. as dep. to overcome, to subdue, τινά, 22, 229. Od. 21, 343: τινὰ ψεύδεσι, to vanquish any one by deceit, to overreach him, 23, 576; with double accus. τινὰ μισθόν, to wrest from one his hire, 21, 451.

βίαιος, η, ον (βίη), violent, acting by violence, ἔργα, Od. 2, 236. † Κῆρες, h. 7, 17.

βιαίως, adv. violently, forcibly, *Od. 2, 237.

Βίας, αντος, ὁ, 1) son of Amythaon and Idomene from Pylos, brother of Melampus. He courted Pero, the daughter of Neleus; and, after Melampus had procured for Neleus the cattle of Iphiclus, he received her as a wife. His sons are Talous, Perialces, etc. Apd. 1, 9. 11. Whether the companion of Nestor mentioned Il. 4, 296, is brother of Melampus, accord. to Od. 15, 225 seq. is uncertain. 2) an Athenian, 13, 691. 3) a Trojan, 20, 460.

βιάω, Ep. form for βιάζω, q. v.

βιβάς, ᾶσα, άν, partcp from the obsol. βίβημι, a form of βαίνω, mly μακρὰ βιβάς, long-striding, with ὕψι, 13, 371.

βιβάσθων, ουσα, ον, partcp. from the obsol. βιβάσθω=βαίνω, always with ἀκρά, taking long strides, *Il.

βιβάω. Ep. form of βαίνω, to stride. πέλωρα βιβᾷ, he strode prodigiously, h. Merc. 225; imperf. ἐβίβασκεν, h. Ap. 133; also partcp. βιβῶν, βιβῶσα, 3, 22. Od. 11, 539.

βιβρώσκω (fut. βρώσω), aor. 2 ἔβρων, ep. h. Ap. 127; perf. βέβρωκα, fut. pass. βεβρώσομαι, to eat, to devour, to consume, with accus. 22, 94; and with gen. Od. 22, 403. χρήματα κακῶς βεβρώσεται, the property will be riotously consumed (Ep. form βεβρώθω).

βίη, ἡ, Ep. for βία, Ep. dat. βίηφι, 1) strength, force, spoken chiefly of bodily power, rarely of mental, 3, 45; also of brutes and inanimate things, ἀνέμων; H. often used it periphrastically of distinguished men, like μένος, σθένος, etc., e. g. Πριάμοιο βίη, the force of Priam= the powerful Priam, 3, 105; so Διομήδεος, and with an adj. Ἡρακληείη, the power of Heraclês, 2, 665. 11, 699. 2) violence, mly in plur. violent acts, 5, 521. Od. 15, 329.

Βιήνωρ, ορος, ὁ, Ep. for Βιάνωρ, a Trojan, slain by Agamemnon, 11, 92.

*βιοθάλμιος, ον (θάλλω), in the vigour of life, in the bloom of vigorous life, h. Ven. 190.

βίος, ὁ, life, life-time, *Od. 15, 491; and Batr.

βιός, ὁ, a bow, =τόξον, Il. and Od.

βιοτή, ἡ =βίοτος, life, Od. 4, 565.†

*βιότης, ητος, ἡ =βίοτος, h. 7, 10.

βίοτος, ὁ (βιόω), life, as μοῖρα βιότοιο, the measure of life, 4, 170. 2) the means of living, bona vitæ, property, ἀλλότριος, another's property, Od. 1, 160. 377.

βιόω (βίος), aor. 2 ἐβίων, infin. βιῶναι,

aor. 1 mid. ἐβιωσάμην. 1) to live, spo of men and beasts. 2) to restore lif save life. σὺ γάρ μ' ἐβιώσαο, thou saved my life, only Od. 8, 468. βιόμεσθα, h. Ap. 528. see βέομαι.

βιψᾶτο, βιόωνται, βιόωντο, see βιάζ

*βλαβερός, ή, όν (βλάπτω), injuri hurtful, h. Merc. 36.

βλάβω [as πείρειν is imperfectly re plicated in πρέπειν, so βέλειν, βαλεῖ βλάβειν. Död.], th. of βλάπτω, ob except in βλάβεται, see βλάπτω.

*βλαισός, ή, όν, crooked, bent wards, spoken chiefly of the f crooked-legged, Batr. 299.

βλάπτω (βλάβω), aor. 1 ἔβλαψα, p pass. βέβλαμμαι, aor. 1 pass. ἐβλάφ aor. 2 pass. ἐβλάβην, 23, 461 (from βλ only βλάβεται occurs), 1) to imped running, to obstruct, to hinder, v accus., Od. 13, 22; τινὰ κελεύθου, hinder one from returning, Od. 1, ι γούνατα, to lame any one's knees, 7, 2 hence, pass. βλάβεται γούνατα, 19, βλάβεν (for ἐβλάβησαν) ἅρματα καὶ ἱν chariots and horses were hindered, mained behind, 23, 545. βέλεμνα Δι βλαφθέντα, arrows obstructed by Ζ or rendered ineffectual, 15, 489. β φθῆναι ἐνὶ ὄζῳ, to be held in a branch be entangled, 6, 39; ἐν ἀσπίδι, 15, 6 κατὰ κλόνον, to be impeded in the tun of battle, 16, 331. 2) Metaph. to ι fuse, to astound, to mislead, φρένας, 724. Od. 14, 178; also without φρένα 507. Od. 21, 294; and βλαφθείς, 9, 5 hence: βλάβεται ἀγορητής, the orato confused, 19, 82. 2) to injure, to h Batr. 180; in H. only βεβλαμμένος ἦ wounded in heart, once 16, 660; others, more correctly, βεβλημένος. Spitzner ad loc.

βλεῖο, see βάλλω.

βλεμεαίνω, to feel one's strength, t arrogant, to be proud, always with σθε of one's strength, *8, 337. 2) In Batr. 275, to desire earnestly, to strive to threaten. [Död. connects it with roots βαλ-, βολ-, βλεφ- &c., and me it mean looking courageous, havin spirited look. Hesych. gives ζαβλεμ =μεγάλως, πεποιθώς, and Panyas, fr. has ἀβλεμέως πίνων, fortiter bib Later writers give it a neg. mean ἀβλεμέως, ἀφροντίστως.]

*βλέπω, to see; with accus. ὄρμ Batr. 67.

βλέφαρον, τό (βλέπω), the eyelid plur. 10, 26. Od. 5, 271, dual Od. 490.

βλήεται, Ep. for βλήηται, see βάλλ βλήμενος, η, ον, see βάλλω.

βλήτρον, τό (βάλλω), a cramp or ξυστὸν κολλητὸν βλήτροισι, a pike tened with cramps (rings) or nails, 678.† (less probably, joint.)

βληχή, ἡ, a word derived from sound. the bleating of sheep, ὀίων, 12, 266.†

βλοσυρός, ή, όν, honourable, ma

terrible, savage (δεινός, σεμνός, Eustath.), ὀφρύες, πρόσωπα, *7, 212. 15, 608.

βλοσυρῶπις, ἡ (ὤψ), of frightful look, epith. of Gorgo, 11, 36.†

βλωθρός, ή, όν (βλώσκω), growing up, shooting up, slender, spoken of trees, 13, 390. Od. 24, 234.

βλώσκω, poet. (for μλώσκω, from μόλω), aor. 2 ἔμολον, perf. μέμβλωκα (for μέμλωκα), to go, to come, spoken of ships, 15, 720; also metaph., chiefly of time, 24, 781. Od. 17, 190.

βοάγριον, τό (βοῦς—ἄγριος), a shield formed of the wild ox-hide, 12, 22. Od. 16, 296 [either fm βοῦς ἄγριος (Et. Magn. ἐξ ἀγρίων βοῶν γενόμενα), or fm βοῦς, ἀγρεύω. Apoll. τὰ τῶν βοῶν ἀγρεύματα, boûm exuviæ: de bove captum, i. e. scutum corio bubulo tectum.

Βοάγριος, ὁ, a stream in Locris near Thronium, which in Strabo's time was called Μάνης, the raging, 2, 533.

βοάω (βοή), fut. βοήσω, aor. 1 ἐβόησα, partcp. βοήσας, Ion. contr. βώσας, 12, 337; Ep. pres. indic. βοάᾳ for βοᾷ, βοόωσιν for βοῶσιν, partcp. βοόων for βοῶν, etc. 1) to call aloud, to cry, spoken chiefly of heroes; of animals: of the cock, to crow, Batr. 193; of inanimate things: to resound, to roar, to re-echo. κῦμα βοάᾳ ποτὶ χέρσον, the wave roared upon the land, 14, 394; ἠϊόνες βοόωσιν (poet. for βοῶσιν), 17, 265.

βοέη, fem. from the following.

βόειος, η, ον, and βόεος, η, ον (βοῦς), relating to cattle, made of ox-hide. ἡ βοείη and ἡ βοέη, subaud. δορά, ox-hide, 11, 843; then a) a shield covered with ox-hide, 5, 512 (as 10, 155, ῥινὸν βέος). b) a thong, h. Ap. 487. 503.

βοεύς, ῆος, ὁ, a thong of ox-hide attached to the sails, Od. 2, 426. 15, 291. h. Ap. 407.

βοή, ἡ, a cry, a loud call, also a cry of grief, lamentation, Od. 14, 265; esply the battle-cry, the tumult of battle. βοὴν ἀγαθός, a common epith. of distinguished heroes, in reference to their loud voice of command, good in the battle-cry [or in the battle itself, Passow]. 2) Metaph. spoken of the sound of instruments, 18, 495; of the noise, tumult of the sea, Od. 24, 48.

Βοηθοίδης, ου, ὁ, son of Boethous = Ετεωνεύς, Od. 4, 31.

βοηθόος, ον (θέω), hastening to the tumult of battle, swift in battle, spoken of heroes, 13, 477; ἅρμα, 17, 481.

βοηλασίη, ἡ (ἐλαύνω), the driving off of cattle, the plunder of cattle, the common kind of robbery in the Homeric age; and mly plundering, robbery, 11, 672.†

βοητύς, ύος, ἡ, Ion. for βόησις, the act of calling, crying, clamour, Od. 1, 369.†

βοθρός, ὁ (related to βάθος), a hole, ditch, pit, 17, 58. Od. 11, 25.

Βοίβη, ἡ, a town in Pelasgiotis, in Thessalia, not far from Pheræ; now Bio, 712; hence: Βοιβηΐς, ΐδος, ἡ, Bœbean;

ἡ λίμνη, the Bœbean lake, near the town thus called, Il. l. c.

Βοιώτιος, ίη, ιον, a Bœotian, an inhabitant of Bœotia, a district in Hellas, which derived its name from Bœotus, o from its rich pastures, 4, 294.

(βολέω), obs. theme of βεβόλημαι, see βάλλω.

βολή, ἡ, a cast, the act of throwing metaph. as βέλος, αἱ βολαὶ ὀφθαλμῶν, the glance of the eyes, *Od. 4, 150.

βόλομαι, Ep. for βούλομαι, q. v.

βομβέω (from βόμβος), fut. ήσω, to give a hollow sound, to rattle, spoken only of falling bodies, Il. and Od.

βοόων, Ep. for βοῶν, see βοάω.

*βορβοροκοίτης, mud-lier, name of a frog (from βόρβορος, slime, and κοίτη, bed), Batr. 229.

Βορέης, αο, ὁ, Ep. for Βορέας, gen. Βορέω, 23, 692; 1) the north wind, or, more exactly, the north-north-east. 2) Boreas, as a mythic personage, son of Astræus and Eos, Hes. Th. 379; he dwelt in Thrace, 9, 5. He is sire of the mares of Erichthonius, 20, 205. (Βόρέης, 9, 5.)

βόσις, ιος, ἡ (βόσκω), food, pasture, 19, 268.†

βόσκω, fut. βοσκήσω, 1) to pasture, to drive to the pasture, spoken of a herdsman, βοῦς, 15, 548 [cf. Spitzner ad 16, 150]. 2) to feed, to nourish, primarily of animals, but also of men, τινά, Od. 14, 325; and γαστέρα, to fill the stomach, Od. 17, 228. 559. II) Mid. to pasture or feed oneself, to graze, spoken of animals, κατά τι, 5, 162 [also absol. Od. 12, 355]. 2) to crop, to feed upon; with accus. ποίην, h. Merc. 232. cf. 559.

βοτάνη, ἡ (βόσκω), pasture, food, grass, 13, 493. Od. 10, 411.

βοτήρ, ῆρος, ὁ (βόσκω), a herdsman, Od. 15, 504.†

*βοτής, οῦ, ὁ = βοτήρ, Epigr. 11, 1.

βοτός, ή, όν (βόσκω), pastured, fed; τὰ βοτά. every thing which is pastured, cattle, 18, 521.†

βοτρυδόν, adv. (βότρυς), in clusters, like grapes, πέτονται, 2, 89; said of bees.†

βότρυς, υος, ἡ, the grape, a cluster of grapes, 18, 562.† h. 6, 40.

βοῦ (βοῦς), often in composition indicates that which is very great, prodigious, e. g., βούβρωστις, etc.

βούβοτος, ον (βόσκω), grazed by cattle, Od. 13, 246.†

βούβρωστις, ἡ (βοῦς, βιβρώσκω), prop. bulimy, voracious hunger, and mly hunger, poverty, want, 24, 532.†

βουβών, ῶνος, ὁ, the groin, the pudendum, the thigh, 4, 492.†

βουγάϊος, ὁ (γαῖα), one who is proud of his strength, a boaster, only as a term of reproach, 13, 824. Od. 18, 79.

Βούδειον, τό (ἡ Βούδεια, Steph.), 16, 572; a town of uncertain position, prob. a town in Magnesia, according to Steph., or in Phthiotis, according to Venet. Schol.

βουκολέω (βουκόλος), *to pasture cattle*; with accus. of βοῦς, 21, 448. 2) Mid. *to feed, to graze*, 20, 221.

Βουκολίδης. ου, ὁ, son of Bucolus = Sphelus, 15. 338.

*βουκολίη, ἡ, *a herd of cattle*, h. Merc. 498.

Βουκολίων, ωνος, ὁ, eldest son of Laomedon, husband of Abarbarea, 6, 22.

βουκόλος, ὁ, *a herdsman* (from βοῦς and the obsol. κολέω), with ἀνήρ, 13, 571. Od. 11, 293.

βουλευτής, οῦ, ὁ (βουλεύω), *counsellor, senator*; as adj. γέροντες, the old men of the council, 6, 114.†

βουλεύω (βουλή), fut. σω, aor. 1 σα, and aor. 1 mid. σάμην, 1) *to hold a council, to consult, to deliberate*, absol. 2, 347; often with βουλήν, to give counsel, 9, 75; 10, 147; to hold a council, to deliberate, 10, 415; τινί, to counsel any one, to consult for any one, 9, 94. 2) *to plot, to decide upon, to purpose*, with accus. ὄλεθρον, φύξιν, κέρδεα, ὁδὸν φρεσίν, Od. 1, 141; and with dat. of the pers. τί τινι, to purpose any thing against any one, with infin. following, 9, 458; also περί τινος, Od. 16, 234; ἐς μίαν, sc. βουλήν, to take like counsel, to be unanimous, harmonious, 2, 379. II) Mid. *to advise oneself, to form a resolution, to decide, to purpose*; with accus. ἀπάτην, 2, 114; βουλεύειν τινά, h. Merc. 167, is false Greek; hence H. connects ἐμέ and σέ with ἐπιβήσομαι, cf. Franke ad loc.

βουλή, ἡ, *counsel* which one imparts, *advice*, 2, 55. 10, 147. 2) *purpose, will, resolution*, esply of the gods, 12, 235. Od. 8, 82. 3) *a council* or *assembly*, as βουλὴ γερόντων, the assembly of the elders, in distinction from ἀγορά, q. v. 2, 143. 194.

βουληφόρος, ον (φέρω), *giving counsel, who deliberates*, epith. of sovereigns in the Il. and of the ἀγορά in Od. 9, 112.

βούλομαι, Ep. βόλομαι (only βόλεται, 11. 319; βόλεσθε, Od. 16, 387), fut. βουλήσομαι, h. Ap. 264. 1) *to will, to wish* (according to Buttmann, Lex, βούλομαι is distinguished from ἐθέλω, the latter expressing a mere wish, or proclivity, whereas the former expresses an active willing, with purpose: still in H. βούλομαι also stands for ἐθέλω); with accus. τί, any thing, 3, 41; mly with infin. or with accus. and infin. 1, 117. Od. 16, 387. Ζεὺς Τρώεσσιν ἐβούλετο κῦδος ὀρέξαι, Zeus wished to bestow glory upon the Trojans, 11, 79. cf. 319. 2) τί τινι, without infin. *to grant, to purpose, to accord* any thing to any one, Τρώεσσιν βούλετο νίκην, said only of the gods, because with them to will and to accomplish are identical, 7, 21. 2) *to wish rather, to prefer*; with ἤ or ἤπερ following: βούλομ' ἐγὼ λαὸν σόον ἔμμεναι ἢ ἀπολέσθαι, I would rather that the people should be safe than that they should perish, 1, 117. 11, 319. Od. 3, 232; sometimes also without ἤ, 1, 112.

βουλυτός, ἡ (λύω), subaudit. καιρός, the time when the cattle are unyo this took place at sunset; in H. adv. βουλυτόνδε, *at evening*, 6, 779. 9, 58.

βουπλήξ, ῆγος ἡ (πλήσσω), prop. goading the oxen; in H. subst. *an goad*, stimulus, 16, 135.†

Βουπράσιον, τό, a town in Elis, on borders of Achaia; in the time of St a territory in addition had this n (perhaps from πράσον, a leek), 2, 61!

βοῦς, βοός, ὁ and ἡ, dat. plur. βουσί, βόεσσι, *a bull, an ox, a cow*; also ἄρσην and ταῦρος βοῦς, 17, 389. subaud. ἀσπίς, a shield covered with hide, 7, 238 (where the Dor. accus. is found), 12, 105.

βουφονέω (βουφόνος), *to slaughter c* 7, 466.†

*βουφόνος, ον (φονεύω), *slaughteri sacrificing cattle*. h. Merc. 436.

βοῶπις, ιδος, ἡ (βοῦς, ὤψ), *ox-eyed, large-eyed* ['*ample-eyed*,' Cp.], epit distinguished women, 3, 144, and of majestic Hêrê, 1, 551.

Βοώτης, ου, ὁ = βούτης, *the herdsma* H. the constellation of *Arcturus*, the Great Bear; so named by the Ion who made the Great Bear a wagon, 5, 272.

βραδύς, εῖα, ύ. compar. βραδύτερος βράσσων, superl. βράδιστος, and by tathesis βάρδιστος, 23, 310. 530; *sluggish*; spoken also of the mind, *stupid*, νοός, 10, 226.

βραδυτής, ῆτος, ἡ (βραδύς), *slow sluggishness*, 19. 411. [†]

βράσσων, ον, compar. of βραδύς 226.

βραχίων, ίονος, ὁ, *the arm*; πρυ the upper part of the arm, *the shou* plur. Od. 18, 69.

βράχω, a word derived from the s it describes, *to crash, to rattle, to c to resound*, spoken chiefly of inani things; of the rattling of armour, 4, of the creaking of a chariot, 5, 835; o resounding of the earth, 21, 387; a the roaring of a river, 21, 9. 2) Of l beings: *to cry, to roar*; of the wou Arês, 5, 863; of a horse, 16, 468 (w Spitzner, however with probability, derstands the noise of his fall).

* βρέγμα, ατος, τό, *the upper part head, the skull*, Batr. 231.

βρέμω, *fremo, to murmur, to roa resound*, spoken of the sea, 4, 42! like manner the mid. βρέμομαι, 2, and of the wind, 14. 399.

βρέφος, τό, *the embryo in the wom* 266.† later an infant (related to τρέφ

βρεχμός, ὁ = βρέγμα, *the upper pa the head*, 5, 586.†

Βριάρεως, ὁ, a hundred-handed g see Αἰγαίων (*the strong*).

βριαρός. ή, όν (βριάω), *strong*, epith. of the helmet, *11, 375.

βρίζω, poet. (related to βρίθω), *t heavy*; mly *to be drowsy, to be ina* 4, 223.†

βριήπῠος, ον (ἀπύω), crying aloud, loud-voiced [' brazen-throated,' Cp.], epith. of Arês, 13, 521.†

βρῑθοσύνη, ἡ (βριθύς), heaviness, burden, load, weight, 5, 839. 12, 460.

βρῑθύς, εῖα, ύ (βρίθω), heavy, weighty, always epith. of the spear, ἔγχος, Il. and Od.

βρίθω, fut. βρίσω, h. Cer. 456; aor. 1 ἔβρισα, perf. 2 βέβριθα, with pres. signif. and mid. 1) to be heavy, to be burdened, weighed down, τινί and τινός, σταφυλῇσι μέγα βρίθουσα ἀλωή, a vineyard heavily laden with grapes, 18, 561. βεβρίθει (subaud. ναῦς) σάκεσσι καὶ ἔγχεσιν, Od. 16, 474, cf. 19, 112. ταρσοὶ μὲν τυρῶν βρῖθον, Od. 9, 219. 15, 334; also mid. μήκων καρπῷ βριθομένη, a poppy loaded with fruit, 8, 307; and with the idea of an oppressive surcharge, ὑπὸ λαίλαπι πᾶσα βέβριθε χθών, the whole earth is burdened with the tempestuous rain, 16, 384; metaph. ἔρις βεβριθυῖα (for βαρεῖα), 21, 385. 2) to have preponderance, to be superior, to surpass, in aor. 1 ἐέδνοις βρίσας (prevailing by bridal gifts), Od. 6, 159; spoken of an overpowering multitude: to press hard, to prevail, 12, 346. 17, 233. 512.

* βρῐ́μη, ἡ. rage, anger, noise, h. 28, 10.

* βρῑσάρματος, ον (ἅρμα), chariot-loading, epith. of Arês, h. 7, 1. cf. 5, 839.

Βρῑσηίς, ῐ́δος, ἡ, daughter of Brises, Hippodamia, a female slave of Achilles, who had slain her husband Mynes and her brothers, 19, 291—300. Agamemnon took her from him, 2, 689 sqq.

Βρῑ́σης, εος, Ep. ῆος, ὁ, son of Ardys, king of the Lelëges in Pedasus, or a priest in Lyrnessus, 2, 689. 1, 392.

βρομέω (βρόμος), to hum, spoken of gnats, 16, 642.†

βρόμος, ὁ (βρέμω), roaring, crackling, spoken of fire, 14, 396.† 2) Of the loud sound of flutes, h. Merc. 452. h. 26, 10.

βροντάω (βροντή), aor. 1 ἐβρόντησα, to thunder, always spoken of Zeus, 8, 133. Od. 12, 415.

βροντή, ἡ, thunder, Διός, 13, 796; Ζηνός, Od. 20, 121.

βρότεος, ον, Ep. for βρότειος (βροτός), mortal, human, φωνή, Od. 19, 545.† h. Ven. 47.

βροτόεις, εσσα, εν (βρότος), sprinkled with blood, bloody; ἔναρα, bloody spoils, 6, 484; once βροτόεντ ἀνδράγρια, *14, 509.

βροτολοιγός, όν (λοιγός), man-destroying, man-slaying, epith. of Arês [' homicidal Mars,' Cp.], often in Il.; once Od. 8, 115.

βροτός, ὁ, ἡ, mortal, prop. adj. βροτὸς ἀνήρ, 5, 604; often as subst. a mortal, a man, and ἡ βροτός, a mortal woman, Od. 5, 334 (related to μόρος).

βρότος, ὁ, the blood which is flowing from a wound, or which has already coagulated, gore, always with αἱματόεις; 7, 425; μέλας, Od. 24, 189 (Æol. from ῥέω, ῥότος).

βροτόω, to make bloody; βεβροτωμένα τεύχεα, arms defiled with blood [' armour gore-distained,' Cp.]. Od. 11, 41.†

βρόχος, ὁ, a noose, a knot, for suspending, *Od. 11, 278. 22, 472.

* βρύκω, ξω, to bite, to tear by biting, prop. to gnash with the teeth, Epigr. 14, 13.

Βρύσειαί, Ep. for Βρύσεαί, an old town in Laconia, south of Sparta, 2, 583 (perhaps from βρύσις, ἡ, welling up).

βρυχάομαι, depon. mid. perf. βέβρυχα, to roar to howl; H. has only the perf. and pluperf. with pres. signif.; spoken of the shriek of one falling with a mortal wound, 13, 393. 16, 486 (not 'gnashing the teeth'); and of the noise of waves, 17, 264. Od. 5, 412. 12, 242.

βρύω, to overflow, with reference to an internal force swelling and bursting; to be swollen, distended. ἔρνος ἄνθεϊ βρύει, bursts into flower, 17, 56.†

βρώμη, ἡ, poet. for βρῶμα, food, connected with ποτής, *Od. 10, 177. h. Cer. 394.

βρῶσις, ιος, ἡ (βιβρώσκω), the act of eating food, in distinction from πόσις, 19, 210. Od. 1, 191.

* βρωτός, ή, όν, adj. verb. (βιβρώσκω), eaten, edible, Batr. 30.

βρωτύς, ύος, ἡ=βρῶσις, 19, 205. Od. 18, 407.

βύβλινος, η, ον, made of papyrus, ὅπλον νεός, Od. 21, 391.† According to Eustath. not here the Egyptian paper-plant, from the inner bark of which ropes were made, but either hemp or tree-bark. Voss translates 'from the bark of the byblus.'

* βῠθός, ὁ, depth, abyss, Batr. 119.

βύκτης, ου, ὁ (βύω: or, more probably, βύζω), blowing, blustering, roaring, rude, ἄνεμοι, Od. 10, 20.† (ἠχητικοί, Schol.)

* βύρσα, ἡ, skin, hide, Batr. 127.

βυσσοδομεύω (δομέω), prim. to build in the depths; hence metaph. to meditate, to purpose any thing secretly; only in a bad sense, κακὰ φρεσί, to purpose evil secretly in the heart, Od. 8, 273. 17, 66; μύθους ἐνὶ φρεσί, Od. 4, 676. *Od.

βυσσός, ὁ=βυθός, depth, 24, 80.†

βύω, fut. βύσω, perf. pass. βέβυσμαι, to stop up, to fill up, τινός, with any thing; τάλαρος νήματος βεβυσμένος, a basket filled with yarn, Od. 4, 134.†

βῶλος, ἡ (prob. from βάλλω), a clod, a lump of earth, Od. 18, 374. †

βωμός, ὁ (βαίνω), an elevation, a support upon which something is placed, a pedestal, a base of a statue, Od. 7, 100; a stand for a chariot, 8, 441. 2) Esply an altar, often ἱεροί or θεῶν βωμοί. βωμός is distinguished from ἐσχάρα by having steps or an ἀνάβασις. Cf. Nitzsch on Od. 2, p. 15.

[βῶν, 7, 228, see βοῦς, and cf. Buttm., Gram. § 50, note 2.]

Βῶρος, ὁ, 1) son of Perieres, husband of Polydora, daughter of Peleus, 16, 177;

rf. Apd. 3, 13. 2) father of Phæstus, from Tarne in Lydia, 5, 44

βώσαντι, see βοάω.

βωστρέω, to call, to call to, for help, τινά, Od. 12, 124.† [from βοάω lengthened, like ἐλαστρέω].

βωτιάνειρα, ἡ (βόσκω, ἀνήρ), man-nourishing, nurse of heroes, epith. of Phthia. 1, 155 †

βώτωρ, ορος, ὁ, Ep (βόσκω), herdsman, connected with ἀνήρ, 12, 302. Od. 14, 102.

Γ.

Γ, the third letter of the Greek alphabet, and hence the sign of the third rhapsody.

γαῖα, ἡ, like αἶα, poet. for γῆ (which form rarely occurs in H., 21, 63. Od. 11, 67, etc.), 1) the earth, the ground, the land, in distinction from the heavens or the sea, 8, 16. 46, 479. 2) land, region, often with πατρίς, father-land, country; in the plur. also often spoken of islands, Od. 8, 284. 3) earth, ground, 2, 699. 15, 715; also dust. ὑμεῖς πάντες ὕδωρ καὶ γαῖα γένοισθε, may you become earth, dust [' rot where ye sit,' Cp.], 7, 99; hence also κωφὴ γαῖα, spoken of Hector's corpse, 24, 54.

Γαῖα, ἡ, pr. n. Gæa (Tellus), wife of Uranus (Cœlus), mother of the Cyclôpes, Titans, etc. h. 30, 17; μήτηρ πάντων.

Γαιήϊος, η, ον (γαῖα), springing from Gæa. Γαιήϊος υἱός, son of Gæa=Tityus, Od. 7, 324.

γαιήοχος, ον (ἔχω), earth-holding, earth-embracing, epith. of Poseidôn; earth-quakes being, on the one hand, ascribed to him (see ἐνοσίχθων), and he could, on the other, hold together and secure the earth (Voss. earth-girdling, not, however, with perfect propriety, since ἔχειν is in H. never equivalent to cingere, and Poseidôn is god only of the Mediterranean sea); later, earth-defending. Cf. Cammanns, Vorsch. p. 173. Il. 9, 183. Od. 1, 68.

γαίω, only partcp. pres. to be proud of any thing, to exult in, always with κύδεϊ, one's strength: spoken of Zeus, Arês, etc. *1, 405 (an old theme, to be seen in many derivatives, as γάνυμαι, γηθέω, etc.).

γάλα, γάλακτος, τό, milk, λευκόν, 4, 434. Od. 4, 88

γαλαθηνός, όν (θῆσθαι), milk-sucking; hence young, tender, νεβροί, *Od. 4, 336.

*Γαλαξαύρη, ἡ, a nymph, companion of Persephonê, h. Cer. 423.

Γαλάτεια, ἡ, daughter of Nereus and Doris, 18, 45.

* γαλῆ, ἡ, a weasel, a marten, Batr. 5.

γαλήνη, ἡ, quiet, rest, serenity, a calm, esply spoken of the sea. γαλήνη νηνεμίη,

a windless calm, Od. 5, 392. 2) the surface of the sea. ἐλαύνειν γαλήνην brush the placid flood,' Cp.; to sail calm seas], *Od. 7, 319.

γάλοως, gen. γάλοω, ἡ, nom. pl. γα sister-in-law, husband's sister, *3, 12

γαμβρός, ὁ (γαμός), any one relate marriage; hence 1) son-in-law, freq. 2) brother-in-law, sister's husl 5, 474. 13, 464.

γαμέω (γάμος), fut. γαμέσω and γα 9, 391; aor. 1 ἔγημα, fut. mid. γαμέσ poet. σσ, 3, 394; aor. 1 ἐγημάμην Spoken of the man, to take a wi marry, τινά, also ἄλοχον, 9, 399; al a mere physical signif., Od. 1, 36 Mid. spoken of the woman, to get ried, to marry, τινί, Od. 18, 269. the parents, to give in marriage, to m γυναῖκα τινί, 9, 394.

γάμος, ὁ, a marriage, 1) As a day, a wedding. γάμον τεύχειν, ἀρ: to prepare the nuptial solemnity, O 277. 4, 770; exply nuptial feast, 19, Od. 1, 226 (in distinction from εἰλα Od. 4, 3. 3) nuptials, wedlock, Oc 272. Il. 13, 382.

γαμφηλαί, αἱ (related to γνάμπτω jaw-bones, the cheeks, only plur. *13,

γαμψῶνυξ, υχος, ὁ, ἡ (ὄνυξ), crooked claws, epith. of birds of αἰγυπιοί, 16, 428. Od. 16, 217.

γανάω (γάνος), to gleam, to glitt shine, only partcp. pres. γανόω γανόωσαι. Ep. for γανῶντες, γαν prim. spoken of polished metals, 13, of garden-beds: πρασιαὶ γανόωσαι, did beds, Od. 7, 128; of a flower. h 10.

γάνυμαι, depon. mid. (γαίω), fut. σομαι, Ep. σσ, to be glad. to be delig to rejoice in, with dat. ἀνδρὶ οὐ γαν ται, 14, 504; a'so γάνυται φρένα, glad at heart, 13, 493. Od. 12, 43.

Γανυμήδης, εος, ὁ, accus. εα and η of king Tros in Troy, great-grands Dardanus, the most beautiful you his time; he was borne off by through the instrumentality of an and chosen by him as cup-bearer in of Hebe, 5, 266; and 20, 232 (of che disposition).

γάρ, conj. (γέ, ἄρα), for, since, bec employed in assigning a rea-on. particle, which never stands at th ginning of a sentence, unites properl signif. of γέ and ἄρα, and is used i troducing a proof, an explanation, plement, and a consequence. It car be translated for, although, with th ception of the Hom. γάρ τε, it annexes a clause so closely to th ceding. 1) In introducing a proof explanations: for, because, namely. explanatory signif. is esply preponde when a demonstrative pronoun or a precedes, 1, 9. 12, 55. 8, 148. As a liarity of the Greek language, note following : a) Very common is it fo explanatory clause with γάρ to pro the clause to be explained, in which case it must be translated *indeed*, or *since*, 1, 423. 7, 73. The following clause is introduced by τῷ: πολλοὶ γὰρ τεθνᾶσιν Ἀχαιοὶ — τῷ σε χρὴ — παῦσαι, 7, 328. Most frequently it follows an address, Od. 1, 337. 10, 174. 190. 226. *b*) Often the clause to be proved must be supplied from the connexion, 11, 408. Od. 10, 501. 2) In introducing a supplement or consequence; here belongs γάρ, *a*) In exclamatory and optative clauses: αἲ γάρ, εἰ γάρ, q. v. *b*) In questions: τίς γάρ, for who; πῶς γάρ, 1, 122. 10, 424. 18, 182. 3) In connexion with other particles: ἀλλὰ γάρ, *at enim, sed enim*, in which use the proving clause sometimes follows, but is mly omitted, 7, 242. Od. 14, 355; γὰρ δή, for indeed, 2, 301. Od. 5, 23; γὰρ οὖν, for now; γάρ ῥα, for certainly; γάρ τε, for, 1, 81; γάρ τοι, for certainly; οὐ μὲν γάρ, for certainly not, 24, 66. cf. Rost, p. 706. Kühner, § 692. [καὶ γάρ, for indeed, 3, 188. 4, 43; καὶ γάρ ῥα, for indeed now, 1, 113.]

Γάργαρον, τό, the southern point of Mount Ida in Troas, on which stood a temple of Zeus, 8, 48. 14, 292. (As appellat. *multitude, fulness*.)

γαστήρ, έρος, contr. γαστρός, ἡ, *the belly, the paunch*, v e n t e r; *the womb*, 6, 58. 2) Chiefly *the stomach*; hence, *appetite, greediness*. βόσκειν γαστέρα, to fill the stomach, Od. 17, 228. Batr. 57; but γαστέρι νέκυν πενθῆσαι, to mourn for one dead with the stomach, i. e., by fasting, 19, 223. 3) *stomach, a stomach-sausage*, a stomach filled with minced meat, Od. 18, 44.

γάστρη, ἡ, the belly, a round belly of a vessel, 18, 348. Od. 8, 437.

γαυλός, ὁ [but γαῦλος, ship], *a milkpail, a pail*, Od. 9, 223.†

* γαυρόω (related to γαίω), *to make proud*. mid. *to conduct proudly, to pride oneself*, Batr. 267.

(γάω), obsol. theme fr. which the Ep. perf. γέγαα for γέγονα is derived, see γίγνομαι.

γδουπέω, poet. for δουπέω=δουπέω.

γέ, an enclitic particle, marking the emphatic character of an idea, and giving it prominence. It stands always after the word to which it gives force. It can sometimes be translated by *truly, indeed, still, at least*; but can mly be expressed only by emphasis of voice. γέ serves consequently 1) To give prominence to a idea, whether in amplification or limitation. In this case it cannot mly be translated, but is to be indicated by stress of voice: χόλον γε, 1, 81; ὄφρ' εὖ εἰδῶ, εἰ ἐτεόν γ' Ἰθάκην τήνδ' ἱκόμεθα, Od. 24, 259. Very frequently it stands with personal and demonstrative pronouns: ἔγωγε, σύγε. Also twice in one sentence, 5, 288. 21, 266. εἰ σύγε σῷ θυμῷ ἐθέλοις κέλομαι γάρ ἔγωγε, 23, 894. cf. 15, 48. On the use of γέ with the pronoun, the following is to be noted: *a*) When in disjunctive

clauses the pronoun is placed in antithesis to itself, or to a substantive separated from it, γέ is found in the second member: εἰπέ μοι, ἠὲ ἑκὼν ὑποδάμνασαι, ἦ σέ γε λαοὶ ἐχθαίρουσ', whether *thou* of thine own accord art overcome (dost willingly suffer it), or whether *thee* the people hate, etc. Od. 3, 214. cf. Il. 2, 237. 10, 481. 12, 239. In this case the pronoun is for us often superfluous. *b*) γέ is attached to a pronoun in order to recall with emphasis a preceding idea. For us in this case the pronoun is often superfluous: πατὴρ δ' ἐμὸς ἄλλοθι γαίης, ζώει ὅγ' ἢ τέθνηκεν, Od. 2, 131. cf. 3, 89. Il. 10, 504. The last is true also in adversative sentences. 2) γέ assumes rather the character of a conjunction, and serves to give prominence to the proof or supplement of a clause, and has either an adversative or concessive signif., Od. 19, 86. It is then often connected with relatives and conjunctions, and can be translated by *indeed, at least, certainly, namely*. *a*) With relatives, as ὅς γε, ὅστις γε, οἷός γε, 5, 303. Od. 1, 229. *b*) With conjunctions, εἴγε, *if indeed, since, si quidem*, Od. 9, 529. Il. 1, 393; εἰ μή γε, Od. 10, 343; ὅτε—γε, Od. 2, 31; ὅτε—μή—γε, Il. 13, 319; πρίν γε, οὐ πρίν γε, namely not before; also repeated, πρίν γε, πρίν γε, 5, 288; ἐπεί—γε, *quandoquidem*, 1, 299. 3) οὐδέ —γε, μηδέ—γε, at least not, 14, 221. γέ with a preceding negat. can mly be translated *never*, 1, 261. Od. 4, 291. γὲ μέν has an adversat. signif.: *but*, a t, Il. 2, 703. Od. 5, 206. Cf. Kühner, § 596. Thiersch, § 303.

γέγαα, γεγάασι, γεγαώς. See γίγνομαι.

γέγηθα, perf. of γηθέω.

γέγωνα, poet. perf. with pres. signif. of which the 3 sing. is also imperf. with aor. signif., partcp. γεγωνώς, infin. γεγωνέμεν, plupf. ἐγεγώνει. From a pres. γεγωνέω, derived from this perf., the following forms occur: infin. γεγωνεῖν, imperf. ἐγεγώνευν, Od. 9, 47; *to call audibly, to cry, to proclaim*. ὅσον τε γέγωνε βοήσας, as far as he crying called audibly, i. e. as far as his voice reached, Od. 5, 400. Il. 12, 337; τινί, to call to any one, 8, 227; also μετὰ θεοῖς, Od. 12, 370.

γεγωνέω. See γέγωνα.

γείνομαι (obsol. theme ΓΕΝΩ), aor. I ἐγεινάμην, 1) In the pres. only Ep. and pass. *to be born, to be begotten*. οἱ γεινόμενοι, those who are born, 10, 71. Od. 4, 208. 2) Aor. 1 mid. *to bear, to beget*, spoken both of mother and father, 5, 800. ἐπὴν γείνεαι αὐτός, when thou hast begotten them (men), Od. 20, 202 (this is subj. aor. 1, with shortened mood-vowel, γείνηαι).

γείτων, ονος, ὁ, *neighbour*, Od. 4, 16; as adj. *neighbouring*, Od. 9, 48. Batr. 67.

γελαστός, ή, όν (γελάω), *laughed at, laughable, ridiculous*, ἔργα, Od. 8, 307.† Cf. ἀγέλαστος.

γελάω, contr. γελῶ, and Ep. γελόω,

partcp. γελοωντες and γελώοντες, Od. 18, 111; Ep. form γελοιάω, aor. 1 ἐγέλασα, poet. σσ, 1) *to laugh*, ἐπί τινι, at any think, 2, 270; μάλα ἡδύ, very heartily, 11, 378; δακρυόεν, tearfully, 6, 484; χείλεσιν, with the lips, i. e. apparently, 15, 102; see ἀχρεῖον, ἀλλοτρίοις γναθμοῖς, see the adj. 2) Spoken of inanimate things; ἐγέλασσε δὲ πᾶσα περὶ χθὼν χαλκοῦ ὑπὸ στεροπῆς, laughed round about, i. e. the whole earth gleamed with the brightness of the brass, 19, 362. Cf. h. in Cer. 14.

γελοιάω, Ep. form from γελάω, aor. 1 ἐγελοίησα, h. Ven. 49; whence γελοίων, 3 plur. imperf. and partcp. γελοίωντες (γελοιῶντες), Od. 20, 390.

γελοῖος, η, ον, Ep. for γέλοιος (γέλως), *laughable, ridiculous*, 2, 215.†

γελοίωντες, Od. 20, 390; either poet. for γελόωντες, or read with Buttm. γελοιῶντες, and derive from γελοιάω.

γέλος, ὁ, Æ 1. for γέλος; γέλον for γέλω stood before Wolf, Od. 20, 346.

γελώ, γελόωντες, see γελάω.

γελόωντες, see γελάω.

γέλως, ωτος, ὁ, dat. γέλῳ for γέλωτι, Od. 18, 100; accus. γέλω or γέλωτα and γέλων, Od. 18, 350. 20, 346; *a laugh, laughter* (more correctly in the dat. γέλῳ; Buttm. Gram. § 56, note 6. Thiersch Gram. § 188. Kühner Gram. I. § 295, 1).

γενεή, ἡ, Ion. for γενεά, 1) *birth, family, race, descent*, 6, 145. 151. 21, 153. γενεῆς καὶ αἵματος, of race and blood, 6, 211. γενεῇ τινος and ἔκ τινος, 21, 157. γενεὴν Διὸς εὔχομαι εἶναι, 21, 187. Of steeds: *race, stock, breed*, 5, 208. 265; hence with τόκος, race and birth, 7, 128. 15, 141; hence, *a) birth-place*, 20, 340; and with πατρὶς ἄρουρα, Od. 1, 407; also of the eagle's eyrie, Od. 15, 175. *b) race, stock, family*, esply *noble descent*, 20, 306. Od. 4, 27. αὐτῷ γὰρ γενεὴν ἄγχιστα ἐῴκειν, 14, 474. *c) offspring, descendant*, as with Spitzner it is perhaps to be understood in 21, 191. 2) *race*, i. e. all who belong to a species, spoken of men, esply those who are contemporary (*æquales*), 6, 146; and in like manner, φύλλων γενεή, the race (crop) of leaves (*folia uno eodemque vere prognata*); hence also, *a) the age of man, a generation*, which accord. to Hdt. was 33 years, so that three generations amounted to 100 years, 1, 250. Od. 14, 325. *b) age* in general: γενεῇ ὁπλότερος, 2. 707; ὁπλότατος, 9, 38; πρότερος, 15, 166. Cf. Spitzner, Excurs. IX. § 2, p. 7.

γενέθλη, ἡ (γένος), 1) *birth, generation, race, stock*, of men: εἶναι γενέθλης or ἐκ γενέθλης, Od. 4. 232; of horses: *stock*, 5, 270. 2) *place of origin, origin*, ἀργύρου, 2, 657. 3) *offspring, descendant*, h. Ap. 135. Cf. Spitzner Excurs. IX. § 3. p. 12.

γενειάς, άδος, ἡ, *beard*, Od. 16, 176.†

γένειον, τό (prob. from γένος), *the chin.* γενείου ἅπτεσθαι, 10, 454. Od.

γενειάω (γένειον), aor. ἐγενείησα, *to become bearded, to obtain a beard, to arrive at manhood*, •Od. 18, 176. 269.

γένεσις, ιος, ἡ (ΓΕΝΩ), *generation*,

creation, origin, spoken only of Ocea θεῶν γένεσις, •14, 201.

γενετή, ἡ, poet. for γενεή, *birth* γενετῆς, from birth, 24, 535. Od. 18, Merc. 440.

γενναῖος, η, ον (from γέννα, ἡ, Ε[γένος), suit d *to one's descent, in natural*. οὔ μοι γενναῖον, 5, 253.†

γένος, τό (ΓΕΝΩ), 1) *race, birtl. scent*, 6, 209; hence γένος (accus. a εἶναι ἔκ τινος, to spring from any 5, 544. γένος βασιλήων εἶναι, to s from kings, Od. 4, 63; hence also *of birth, country*, Od. 15, 267. 24. Esply, *a) race, family, kindred*, (583. 15, 533. *b) offspring, descen* 19, 122; so also with adj. θεῖον γέν 180. 9, 538. 2) *race*, as the coll body of individuals in a species: ἡμ ἀνδρῶν, race of demi-gods, 12, 23, ἱ 18; also βοῶν γένος, Od. 20, 212. 3) in reference to time, *the age of man* 3. 248; mly *age*; γένει ὕστερος, yo in age, 3, 215.

γέντο, 3 sing. aor. of a theme elsev absol.; accord. to some, Æol. for ἕλτο, as κέντο for κέλετο, *he seiz* grasped, with accus. 5, 25. 8, 43 Buttm. Gram. § 114. Rost Gram. IV. 6.

γένυς, υος, ἡ, accus. plur. γένυας, γένῦς. Od. 11, 320; *the cheek-bon jaw*, both of men and brutes, 11, 41

ΓΕΝΩ, theme of γίγνομαι.

γεραιός, ή, όν (γηραιός, not fou H.), *old, aged*, esply *venerable* by subst. ὁ γεραιός, *an old man, a ven sage*; αἱ γεραιαί, *the aged women trons*, 6. 87. Comp. γεραίτερος, η.

γεραίρω (γέρας), prop. to distingu a gift: and generally, *to honour, i tinguish. τινὰ νώτοισιν*, any one back-pieces, 7, 321. Od. 14, 441.

Γεραιστός, ὁ, *Geræstus* a prom and port in Eubœa, orig. a temp grove of Poseidôn, now *Cabo Man Lion*, the town is called *Gerestro*, 177.

γερανός, ή, *a crane*, •2, 460. 3, 3

γεραρός, ή, όν (γεραίρω), hon venerable, epith. of heroes. C γεραρώτερος, η, ον, •3, 170. 211.

γέρας, αος, τό, plur. Ep. γέρα for gen. γεράων, related to γῆρας, 1) *sent, a reward, a)* a gift to disti any one, e. g. a larger portion o and wine, Od. 4, 66; or a part spoil, Od. 7, 10. Cf. Il. 1, 118 spoken of gods, 4, 49. *b)* any a formed to honour any one, as to hair in honour of [or mourning f dead. Od. 4, 197. Il. 16, 457. 2 *prerogative, dignity, power*, as γέρας γερόντων, this is the office aged men (viz. to sit in council), Od. 11, 184.

•γεράσμιος, ον (γέρας), *honouri ferring honour*, h. Merc. 122.

Γερήνιος, ὁ, *the Gerenian*, ep Nestor, from the town *Gerenia* (I

Paus. 3. 21), or *Gerenon* (Γέρηνον, τό, Eust.), in Messenia, where Nestor was educated, whilst Heracles destroyed Pylus, 2, 336.

γέρον, see γέρων.

γερούσιος, η, ον, *belonging to old men, appertaining to old men* as members of the council : ὅρκος, an oath which they swore, 22, 119. γερούσιος οἶνος, wine of honour, a larger portion of wine by which the eldest were honoured at the table of the king. 4, 259. Od. 13, 7—9.

γέρων, οντος, ὁ, voc. γέρον, *an old man, an elder ;* οἱ γέροντες, the eldest of the nation, who were distinguished by their experience and respectability of character, and whose counsel was first asked by the king, 2, 83. 4, 344. Cf. βουλή and βασιλεύς. 2) As adj. in neut. γέρον σάκος, an old shield, Od. 22, 184.

γεύω, *to cause to taste,* in H. only mid. γεύομαι, fut. γεύσομαι, aor. 1 ἐγευσάμην, *to taste,* τινός : προικὸς Ἀχαιῶν, Od. 17, 413. 2) Metaph. *to make a trial, to try, to taste, to feel,* mly spoken of fighting ; χειρῶν, to try the fists, Od. 20, 181 ; so also ὀιστοῦ, ἀκωκῆς. γευσόμεθα ἀλλήλων ἐγχείῃσιν, we will try one another with spears, 20, 258.

γέφῡρα, ἡ, *a dam, a dyke, a levee, a wall of earth,* to prevent the overflowing of a river : τὸν δ' οὔτ' ἄρ τε γέφυραι ἐεργμέναι ἰσχανόωσι, the well-fortified dykes do not r-strain it, 5, 88, 89. (Voss and Köppen, *bridges,* a signif. not found in H. : see ἔργω and 17, 797.) 2) the interval between two armies, which like a dyke separates them : *battle-field.* Thus modern critics explain πολέμοιο γέφυρα and γέφυραι, 4, 371. The sing. is found only 8, 553. The ancients more correctly understood by it the spaces between the ranks, in which one could best flee. Between the hostile armies there was no space. Cf. Wolf's Vorles. II. p. 269.

γεφυρόω (γέφυρα), aor. 1 γεφύρωσα, *to make a dam, to dam up,* with accus. ποταμόν, to dam up a river, in that a fallen tree checks the current, 21, 245 ; κέλευθον, to make a way or passage, *15, 357.

γῆ, ἡ, contr. γέα=γαῖα, in H. as pr. n. 3, Od. 4. 15, 36.

* γηγενής, έος. ὁ, ἡ (γένος), *earth-born, son of the earth,* epith. of the giants, Batr. 7.

γηθέω (γαίω), fut. ήσω, aor. γήθησα, perf. γέγηθα. with pres. signif. *to rejoice, to be glad, joyful,* with φρένα, θυμῷ, absol. often with partcp. τῷγε ἰδὼν γήθησεν, 1, 330. νῦν δή που Ἀχιλλῆος κῆρ γηθεῖ, φόνον—Ἀχαιῶν δερκομένῳ for δερκομένου, now indeed the heart of Achilles rejoices, as he beholds the slaughter of the Achaians, 14, 140 (cf. Rost, p. 643, Anm. 3. Kühner, § 587, c. Anm. 1). b) With accus of that at which one rejoices, 9, 77 : εἰ νῶϊ—Ἕκτωρ γηθήσει προφανεῖσα, whether Hector will rejoice over us when we appear, etc. 8, 377, 378. (προφανεῖσα

is dual fem. gen. according to the reading of Aristarch. ; others read προφανεῖσα and refer it to ἰδώμαι.) Cf. Spitzner.

γηθοσύνη, ἡ (γηθέω), *joy, gladness,* *13, 29. 21, 390 ; plur. h. Cer. 437.

γηθόσυνος. η, ον (γηθέω), *joyful, glad, cheerful,* τινί, about any thing, 13, 82. Od. 5, 269.

(γήθω), obsol. theme of γηθέω.

γηράς, see γηράω.

. γῆρας, αος, τό, dat. γήραϊ and γήρᾳ (Thier., § 189, 18), *age, old age,* 5, 183 Od. 2, 16.

γηράω and γηράσκω, aor. 2 ἐγήρα (like ἔδρα), 7, 148 ; partcp. γηράς, 17, 197. 1) *to grow old, to become aged.* 2) Metaph. spoken of fruits, *to become old, to ripen,* Od. 7, 120.

γῆρυς. υος, ἡ, *a voice, a call,* 4, 437 †

*γηρύω (γῆρυς [Död. supposes it allied to γέρω, resembling, but not related to, κέρω (=to cry, queri). Hence intens. γράζειν, γρύζειν, grunnire (grunt): hence γηρύεσθαι =fabulari, opp. to the earnest and important ἀγορεύειν, ἀγοράασθαι, p. 197]), *to utter a sound* or *voice.* 2) Mid. *to sing,* h. in Merc. 426.

Γίγαντες, οἱ, sing. Γίγας, αντος, ὁ (from ΓΑΩ *Genitales,* Herm.), a savage race and odious to the gods, in the region of Hyperia, hence in the neighbourhood of Trinacria, or perhaps in Epirus, which Zeus destroyed on account of their crimes, Od. 7, 59. 206. 10, 120. According to Od. 7, 206, they were related to the Phæaces, and sprung from Poseidôn. 2) According to Hes. Th. 105, monstrous giants with serpent-legs, sons of Uranus and Gæa, who endeavoured to storm Olympus, but were vanquished by the lightnings of Zeus, Batr. 7. Apd. 1, 6. 1.

γίγνομαι (γένω), fut. γενήσομαι, aor. 2 ἐγενόμην, perf. γέγονα, Ep. (γέγαα), 3 plur. γεγάασι (anomal. 2 plur. γεγάατε, Batr. 143, for which Thiersch, § 217, reads γεγάασι), partcp. γεγαώς, infin. γεγάμεν, *to be born, to come into being, to become, to happen.* The aor. 2, *I came,* takes the place of the aor. of εἰμί. I was ; in the perf. *to be by birth,* and mly *to be.* 1) Spoken of men : *to be born, to become.* ἐξ ἐμέθεν γεγαῶτα, sprung from me, 9, 456. Od. 4, 112. In the aor. 2, *to be,* Od. 6, 201. The perf. often with pres. signif. ὁπλότεροι γεγάασι, they are younger, 4, 325. Od. 13, 160. 2) Of inanimate things : *to arise, to come into being, to happen.* γίγνεται ἄνθεα, the flowers arise, come into being, 2, 468. τάδε οὐκ ἐγένοντο, this did not happen, 3, 176. b) Of mental states : ἄχος γένετο αὐτῷ, he was pained. ποθὴ Δαναοῖσι γένετο, desire seized the Greeks, 11, 471. 3) With predicate following : a) Subst. *to become something* ; χάρμα τινί, a rejoicing to any one, 6, 82. φόως τινὶ γίγνεσθαι, to become a light to, 8, 282 ; μέλπηθρά τινι, 18, 179 ; proverbial, ὕδωρ καὶ γαῖαν, to become water and earth, i. e., to be destroyed, 7, 99. πάντα γίγνεσθαι, to be-

:ome every thing, Od. 4, 418.; cf. 458. *b*) With adj. τοῖσι πόλεμος γλυκίων γένετο, 2, 453. 4) With prep. and adv. ἐπὶ νηυσίν, to be at the ships, 8, 180. ὅπως ὄχ' ἄριστα γένοιτο, 3, 110.

γιγνώσκω, fut. γνώσομαι, aor. 2 ἔγνων, partcp. γνούς, subj. γνῶ and γνώω, optar. γνοίην, imper. γνῶθι, infin. γνῶναι and γνώμεναι,. 1) *to observe, to perceive, to apprehend, to discover, to recognize, to become acquainted with*, τινά, 5, 815; ἀσπίδι, by the shield, 5, 182; in a bad sense: εὖ νύ τις αὐτὸν γνώσεται, many a one will then become well acquainted with him [i. e., will fall by his hands], 18, 270; sometimes with gen. γνῶ χωομένοιο, he observed that he was angry, 4, 357. Od. 21, 36. 23, 109. 2) *to know, to understand*, βουλήν, 20, 20. ὄρνιθας γνῶναι, to understand the flight of birds, Od. 2, 159. It is followed by ὅτι, also ὅ, *quod*, 8, 140; ὡς and εἰ, 21, 266.

γλάγος, εος, τό, Ep. for γάλα, *milk*, *2, 471. 16, 643.

γλακτοφάγος, ον (φαγεῖν), contr. for γαλακτοφάγος, *milk-eating*, epith. of the Hippomolgi, 13, 6; later, name of a Scythian tribe.

Γλαύκη, ἡ, daughter of Nereus and Doris, 18, 39.

γλαυκιάω (γλαυκός), *to look about with sparkling eyes*, spoken of lions, only partcp. pres. γλαυκιόων, of fiery look, 20, 172.†

γλαυκός, ἡ. όν (λάω, γλαύσσω [in Ap. Rhod. 1, 1281. δια-γλαύσσουσι] = γελαΰσσω; whence γλαυκός, as λευκός fm λεύσσω, Död.: who makes to *shine* the primary meaning of γελᾶν], prop *shining, bright*, accord. to the derivat.; epith. of the eyes of lions, cats, hence *bluish-grey, blue, clear* ('dark,' Voss), only of the sea, 16, 34.† [Vox γλαυκός splendoris vim qualicunque colori adjunctam notat, *Luc.*]

Γλαῦκος, ὁ, *Glaucus*, 1) son of Sisyphus and Meropē, father of Bellerophontes, with the appellation Ποτνιεύς, because he dwelt in Potniæ in Bœotia. Aphroditē inspired his mares with such fury that they tore him in pieces, 6, 154. 2) son of Hippolochus and grandson of Bellerophontes, leader of the Lycians, friend of Diomēdēs, 2, 876. Cf. 6, 119 seq.

γλαυκῶπις, ιδος, ἡ (ὤψ), accus. γλαυκώπιδα and γλαυκῶπιν, Od. 1, 156; epith. of Athēnē, either *with sparkling eyes*, as cats and owls, *bright-eyed, with beaming or fiery eyes*, cf. 1, 200: or *having lightbrown, hazel eyes, clear-eyed*, having special reference, however, to her piercing look (Schol. Venet. ἀπὸ τῆς πρὸς τὴν πρόσοψιν τῶν ὀφθαλμῶν καταπλήξεως), ('blue-eyed,' Voss), 2, 166. 2) Substantive, *the clear-eyed*, 5, 406. Cf. Nitzsch on Od. 1, 44; and Cammann, p. 187.

Γλαφύραι, αἱ, a town in Thessalia, otherwise unknown, 2, 712.

γλαφυρός, ή, όν (γλάφω), *excava hollow, arched*, epith. of grottoes, a and of the φόρμιγξ, πέτρη, 2, 88; λιμήν, a deep, spacious harbour, Od 305.

γλήνη, ἡ (λάω [accord. to Död. fu λαίνειν, inus., whence γελανής. I Cf. τρανής, πρηνής, &c., fm τετραθ περαίνειν]), 1) *the sight of the eye pupil of the eye*, 14, 494. Od. 2) *a pu* (maiden), from the diminished ima the pupil of the eye; in contempt, γλήνη, timorous puppet! 8, 164.

γλῆνος, εος, τό (λάω [also refern inus. γελαίνειν, Död.]), *an ornamen thing precious*, 24, 192.†

* γληχών, ῶνος, ἡ, Ion. for βλη *penny-royal*, h. in Cer 209.

Γλῖσας, αντος, ἡ (Γλίσσας and Γλια Paus.), an old town in Bœotia Thebes, on Mount Hypaton, in rui the time of Pausanias, 2, 504.

γλουτός, ὁ, *the buttock, the seat*, *1 plur. 8, 340.

γλυκερός, ή, όν = γλυκύς, compar. κερώτερος, *sweet*, Il. Od.

γλυκύθυμος, ον (θυμός), *of mild d sition, sweet-tempered*, 20, 467.†

* γλυκυμείλιχος, ον (μείλιχος), *su flattering, sweetly caressing*, h. 5, 19.

γλυκύς, εῖα, ύ, compar. γλυκίων, *s having an agreeable taste*, νέκταρ 598; metaph. *lovely, agreeable, sn* πόλεμος, ἵμερος, αἰών, Od. 5, 152.

* γλύφανον, τό (γλύφω), *a carver's k a chisel, an auger*, h. Merc. 41.

γλυφίς, ίδος, ἡ (γλύφω), *a notch ci* the arrow to fit it to the bow-strin 122. Od. 21, 419.

* γλύφω, fut. ψω, *to excavate, to he out*, Batr.

γλῶσσα, ἡ, *the tongue* of men animals; γλώσσας τάμνειν, to cut u tongues of victims, Od. 3, 332. 341. tongues at the end of the sacrificial were offered esply to Hermês, i. e., were cut up, laid on the fire, burned: cf. Athen. I. 14.) 2) *di language*, 2, 804. γλῶσσ' ἐμέμικτο language was mixed, 4, 438. h. 113.

γλωχίς or γλωχίν, ῖνος, ἡ (γλώξ), 1 any projecting, tongue-formed p the end of the yoke-strap, 24, (On the ending, see Buttm., Gra 41, 2.)

γναθμός, ὁ (γνάω, κνάω), *the jaw* of and beasts; proverbial: πάντας ὀδ γναθμῶν ἐξελαύνειν, to knock all teeth from the jaws, Od. 18, 29; ἀλλοτρίοις γναθμοῖς γελᾶν, Od.; se λότριος.

* γνάθος, ἡ = γναθμός, Ep. 14, 13 common prose form.

γναμπτός, ή, όν (γνάμπτω), *cu crooked*, ἄγκιστρον, Od. 4, 369; γέντι 416. 2) *flexible, supple*, spoken o limbs of animate beings; me γναμπτὸν νόημα, a placable disposi 24, 41.

γνάμπτω, aor. 1 γνάμψα, to bend, to curve. ἐν γόνυ γνάμψῃ, 23, 731.†

γνήσιος, η, ον (sync. from γενήσιος), belonging to the race, genuine, pure, regular; υἱός in opposition to νόθος, 11, 102. Od. 14, 202.

γνύξ, adv. (γόνυ), with bent knee, always γνὺξ ἐριπεῖν, to sink upon the knees, •5, 68.

γνῶ, γνώμεναι, γνώομεν, see γιγνώσκω.

γνώριμος, ον (γιγνώσκω), known, an acquaintance, Od. 16, 9.†

γνωτός, ή, όν (γνῶναι), known, noted. γνωτὸν δέ, καὶ ὃς μάλα νήπιός ἐστιν, it is known even to him, who is very simple, for ἐκείνῳ, ὅς, 7, 401. 2) related, a relative by blood, of any degree, 3, 174; hence also for brother, 15, 336. 17, 35.

γνώω, γνώωσι, see γιγνώσκω.

γοάω, Ep. γοόω, infin. pres. Ep. γοήμεναι, fut. γοήσομαι, aor. 2 γόον, 6, 500; γοάασκεν, iterat. imperf., 1) to lament, to mourn, to complain, often in partcp. 2) With accus. to bewail, to mourn, πότμον τινός. Of the mid. only the fut. occurs, 21, 124. (γοήμεναι is, Buttm. Gram., § 105, note 16, an infin. pres.)

γόμφος, ὁ, a peg of wood, a nail, a pin, Od. 5, 248. † Here, nails with which Ulysses fastened the vessel or raft together.

• γονεύς, έως, ὁ, a procreator, a father, plur. parents, h. Cer. 241.

γονή, ἡ (γένω), that which is begotten, a child, offspring, progeny, 24, 539. Od. 4, 755.

γόνος, ὁ (γένω), 1) race, origin=γένος, Od. 1, 216. 4, 207. h. Ven. 104. 2) What is begotten, child, descendant, 5, 635; and often.

Γονόεσσα, ἡ, Ep. for Γονοῦσα, Gonoesa, a fortified village, or a promontory between Pellēnē and Ægira in Achaia, 2, 573. Cf. Paus. 5, 18. 2.

γόνυ, τό, gen. γούνατος and γουνός, nom. plur. γούνατα and γοῦνα, gen. γούνων, dat. γούνασι (γούνασσι) and γούνεσσι, 9, 488. 1) the knee. γόνυ κάμπτειν, to bend the knee, i. e., to rest, to sit, 7, 118. ἐπὶ γοῦνα ἕζεσθαι, to seat oneself upon the knees, 14, 437. The ancients considered the knees as the chief seat of physical power, hence γούνατα τινὸς λύειν, to loose one's knees, to lame him, to prostrate him, to slay him, 5, 176. εἰσόκε μοι φίλα γούνατα ὀρώρῃ, whilst my knees move, i. e., as long as I am strong, 9, 610. Od. 18, 133. ὥς τοι γούναθ' ἕποιτο, that your knees might obey you, 4, 314. 2) In humble supplication. it was customary to embrace the knees; hence ἅπτεσθαι γούνων, 1, 512; γοῦνα λαβεῖν, Od. 6, 147; γούνατα τινὸς ἱκάνεσθαι, Od. 3, 92; also γοῦνα κύειν, 8, 371. Hence also, ἐν γούνασι θεῶν κεῖται, it lies in the lap of the gods, it depends on their will, 17, 514. Od. 1, 267; accord. to Nitzsch, 'in the power of the gods,' since the early language indicated this by the term knee.

γόον, Ep. for ἔγοον, see γοάω.

γόος, ὁ (γοάω), wailing, lamentation, complaint, always connected with weeping, τινός. for any one, Od. 4, 113; chiefly lamentation for one dead, 18, 316.

γοόω, see γοάω.

Γόργειος, η, ον (Γοργώ), of Gorgo, belonging to Gorgo, Gorgon. Γοργείη κεφαλή, the Gorgon head, 5, 741. Od. 11, 634.

Γοργυθίων, ωνος, ὁ, son of Priam and Castianira from Æsyme; Teucer slew him, 8, 302.

Γοργώ, ἡ, gen. Γοργοῦς (the terrible, related to ὀργή). Gorgo, a frightful monster, whose head is mentioned chiefly as exciting terrour. Medusa is mly understood by it, one of the three Gorgones mentioned by Hesiod, whose look was petrifying, 8, 349. 11, 36. H. places her in the lower world, Od. 11, 634. Hesiod and later writers mention three: Stheno, Euryale, and Medusa, daughters of Phorcys and Ceto, who had serpents for hair. According to Hesiod, they dwell far west on Oceanus; accord. to later writers, in the Gorgon isles.

Γόρτυς, υνος, ἡ (Γόρτυνα, ἡ, Strab.), Gortyna, chief city of the island of Crete, near its centre, on the river Lethæus, subsequently famed for its splendid edifices and two ports; the ruins are near the modern Messara, 2, 646. Od. 3, 294. (On the nom. Γόρτυν, see Buttm., Gram. § 41.)

γοῦν (γε, οὖν), at least, hence, only twice, in the Il. 5, 258. 16, 30. Accord. to Thiersch, § 329, 1. Anm. and Spitzner on 5, 258, γοῦν is not Homeric; hence the latter has adopted γ' οὖν after the Cod. Venet.

γουνάζομαι, depon. mid. (γόνυ), fut. γουνάσομαι, prop. to embrace any one's knees; hence, to supplicate at one's feet, to supplicate earnestly, τινά, 1, 427; ὑπέρ τινος, for any one, 15, 665; πρός τινος and τινός, to conjure by any one, Od. 11, 68. 13, 324; but γούνων γουνάζεσθαι, to embrace one's knees, 22, 345 (Ep. form γουνόομαι).

γούνατα, γούνασι and γούνασσι, see γόνυ.

Γουνεύς, ὁ (field-man. γουνός), leader of the Arcadians before Troy, 2, 747.

γουνόομαι, Ep. for γουνάζομαι, 1) to supplicate, with accus. 9, 583. πολλὰ θεοὺς γουνούμενος, Od. 4, 443. 2) to vow in supplicating, Od. 10, 521. Cf. v. 526.

γουνός, ὁ (γόνος), a cultivated field, a fruitful field, a fertile place, rarely alone, Od. 11, 193; mly γουνὸς ἀλωῆς, a fertile field, 18, 97. Od. 1, 193; also Ἀθηνάων. Od. 11, 323. (Others say the signif. fruitful field conflicts with γουνὸς Ἀθηνάων: for Attica was stony and not fertile. They cite as akin to it γόνυ, γωνός, according to which it would signify prop. projecting angle; and then mly elevation.)

γραῖα, ἡ (γραῖος), *an aged female, an old woman*, Od. 1, 438.†

Γραῖα, ἡ, a very ancient town in Bœotia, near Orôpus; accord. to Pausan. the later *Tanagra*, 2, 498.

γραπτύς, ύος, ἡ, *a scratch, an injury,* e. g., by thorns. γραπτῦς for γραπτύας, Od. 24, 229.†

γράφω, aor. 1 ἔγραψα, *to scratch, to engrave,* with accus. γράψας ἐν πίνακι θυμοφθόρα πολλά, after he had inscribed upon the tablet many fatal signs, 6, 168 (a kind of picture-writing or hieroglyphics; for H.'s heroes were not acquainted with alphabetic writing, cf. Wolf, Proleg. p. lxxxi; and also σήματα); spoken of the spear's head: *to graze, to injure,* ὀστέον, 17, 599.

Γρήνικος, ὁ, Ion. for Γράνικος, a river in the Lesser Mysia, now *Ustwola*, 12, 31; afterwards famed by the battle of Alexander the Great (from Γρᾶς, the conductor of a colony, and νίκη, Strab. xiii. 582).

γρηῦς, ἡ, Ep. also γρηΰς, Ion. for γραῦς. dat. γρηΐ, voc. γρηΰ and γρηΰ, *an aged female, an old woman.* (γρηῢς is incorrect; see Thiersch, Gram. § 181, 46, c.)

* γρουνός, ὁ = γρυνός, *fire-brand,* Fr. 67.

γύαλον, τό (prob. related to κοῖλος), *a hollow, an arch;* θώρηκος, the swell of the cuirass, 5, 99. This piece of armour consisted of two curved plates, one of which covered the breast, the other the back; these were joined at the sides by hooks or thongs, see Pausan. 10, 26. 2; hence, θώρηξ γυάλοισιν ἀρηρώς, a cuirass fitted together from convex plates, *15, 530. 2) *ravine, valley,* h. Ap. 336. h. 25, 5.

Γυγαίη λίμνη, ἡ, 1) the *Gygæan lake,* a lake in Lydia. at Mount Tmolus, not far from the Caÿstrus, later Κολόη, 20, 391. 2) the nymph of the lake, mother of Mesthles and Antiphus, 2, 865 (from γύγης, a water-fowl).

* γυιάτιδος, Epig. 15, 13; a corrupt word, for which Herm proposes ἀγυιάτη.

γυῖον, τό, *a limb,* chiefly *a hand, foot, knee;* always in the plur. τὰ γυῖα, limbs; ποδῶν γυῖα, the feet, 13, 512; hence, γυῖα λύειν, to loose the limbs, 7, 6; ἐλαφρὰ θεῖναι, to render the limbs light, 5, 122; ἐκ δέος εἴλετο γυίων, Od. 6, 140. 2) *the body, the lap.* h. Merc. 20.

γυιόω (γυιός), γυιώσω, *to lame, to enfeeble,* ἵππους, 8, 402. 416.†

γυμνός, ή, όν. *naked, bare;* mly *without arms, unarmed,* 16, 815; also spoken of things: γυμνὸν τόξον, the bared bow, i. e. the bow taken from its case, Od. 11, 607; γυμνὸς ὀϊστός, the bared arrow (taken from the quiver), Od. 21, 417.

γυμνόω (γυμνός), fut. ώσω, only aor. 1 pass. ἐγυμνώθην, 1) *to lay bare, to uncover;* in the pass. *to strip oneself, to deprive oneself,* with gen. ῥακέων, to free oneself from the rags, Od. 22, 1. 2) Chiefly spoken of warriors, who are spoiled of their arms, 12, 428; and τεῖχος

ἐγυμνώθη, the wall was laid bare open to attack, 12, 399.

γυναικεῖος, είη, εἶον (γυνή), *femi longing to women.* γυναικείαι βουλ 11, 437.†

γυναιμανής, ές, gen. έος (μαί *woman-mad, extravagantly fond of* (amorous, V.), epith. of Paris, *3, 769.

γύναιος, α, ον = γυναικεῖος. δῶρα, presents to a woman, *Od. 15, 247.

γυνή, ἡ, gen. γυναικός, 1) *a wo female,* in distinction from a m. 683, without reference to rank o therefore often in Od. *a maid;* als contemptuous signif.: γυναικὸς ἀ τέτυξο, thou art become a woman, Often in connexion with subst. have the force of adj. γυνὴ ταμίη, ὁ etc. 2) *a wife, a cons.rt,* 6, 160. 3) *a mistress of a family, a mistre 4) a mortal woman,* in distinction goddess, 14, 315. Od. 10, 228. In θήσατο μαζόν, 24, 58, according Schol. γυναῖκα stands for γυναικ this construction can be explained fig. καθ᾽ ὅλον καὶ μέρος. Cf. Th Gram. § 273.

Γύραι, αἱ (sc. πέτραι, the *Gyræan* where the Locrian Ajax sufferec wreck; accord. to Eustath. near nus, or, more correctly, near th montory Caphareus of Eubœa, 500; cf. Quint. Sm. 570 (from whence adj. Γυραῖος, αίη, αιον, Gy hence Γυραίη πέτρη, Od. 4, 507.

γυρός, ή, όν, *round, curved,* c γυρὸς ἐν ὤμοισιν, *round-shou hump-backed,* Od. 19, 246.†

Γυρτιάδης, ου, ὁ, son of Gyrtius tius, 14, 512.

Γυρτώνη, ἡ (Γυρτών, ῶνος, 8t town in Pela᛫giôtis (Thessalia), declivity of Olympus, on the Penê *Salambria,* 2, 738.

γύψ, γυπός, ἡ, dat. plur. γύπεσ *vulture,* Il. and Od. 11, 578.

γωρυτός, ὁ, *bow-case,* Od. 21, 54 (to χωρέω, equivalent to θήκη, ὡς χ τὸ ῥυτόν, Eustath.).

Δ.

Δ, the fourth letter of the alphabet the sign of the fourth rhapsody.

δα, an inseparable prefix, strengthens the signif., according derived from διά, *very, exceedingl δαείω,* Ep. for δαῶ, see ΔΑΩ.

(δάζομαι), obsol. theme, from are formed the fut. and aor. of δα δαήμεναι, Ep. for δαῆναι, see Δ δαήμων, ον, gen. ονος (δαῆναι), *ing. intelligent, acquainted with, expert,* *skilful,* with gen. ἄθλων, Od. 8, 159; ὀρχηθμοῖο, v. 263; ἐν πάντεσσ' ἔργοισι, Il. 23, 671.

δαῆναι, see ΔΑΩ.

δαήρ, έρος, ὁ, voc. δᾶερ, *brother-in-law,* husband's brother. (On the word see Buttm., Gram. § 45, 5. note 1, and gen. plur δαέρων, dissyllabic, 24, 769.) *Il.

δάηται, see δαίω.

δαΐ, Ep. dat. see δαΐς, 13, 286.

δαιδάλεος, η, ον (δαίδαλος), *artfully,* *skilfully made; beautifully wrought; artfully adorned;* spoken of weapons or furniture which are inlaid or adorned with metal or wood: ἔντεα, θρόνος, ζωστήρ, and other productions of art; in Od. 1. 131, δαιδάλεον belongs to θρόνον. Cf. Nitzsch on the verse, p. 99.

δαιδάλλω (δαίδαλος), *to work artfully,* *to adorn skilfully, to ornament, to inlay;* to adorn with gold, silver, and ivory, λέχος χρυσῷ, ἀργύρῳ, Od. 23, 200; σάκος, Il. 18, 479.

δαίδαλον, τό, subst. *a work of art, embroidery,* sing. Od. 19, 227; plur. τὰ δαίδαλα, *works of art,* Il. 5, 60; pictures inwrought with metal-work and embroidery, 14, 179 (prob. from δάω, δάλλω, δαιδάλλω).

Δαίδαλος, ὁ, prop. *the artist,* is a collective name, and indicates a series of Attic and Cretan artists, who, at the beginning of the arts, gave life and motion to statues. H. calls him ὁ Κνώσσιος, from Knosos (Gnossus) in Crete, and as the inventor of an artificial dance which he wrought for Ariadnê, 18, 592; cf. ἀσκέω and χορός. Accord. to Attic tradition, he was the son of Eupalamus in Athens, father of Icarus. He fled on account of the murder of his nephew Talus to Crete, and built there the labyrinth; thence he went to Sicily, Apd. 3, 15, 8.

δαΐζω, poet. (δαίω), fut. ξω, aor. ἐδάϊξα, perf. pass. δεδαϊγμένος, 1) *to divide, to share, to separate into parts,* Od. 14, 434; with accus. often *to tear in pieces, to split, to cut in pieces.* χιτῶνα χαλκῷ, 2, 416; κόμην, to tear out the hair, 18, 27; hence δεδαϊγμένος ἦτορ, pierced through at the heart, 17, 535. *b)* Metaph. ἐδαΐζετο θυμὸς ἐνὶ στήθεσσιν, the heart in their breast was torn (by disquiet and pain), 9, 8: but ὥρμαινε δαϊζόμενος κατὰ θυμὸν διχθάδι', with ἦ, ἤ following, he deliberated upon it doubly divided in mind, i. e., he was balancing between two purposes, 14, 20. ἔχων δεδαϊγμένον ἦτορ, having a torn (troubled) heart, Od. 13, 320. 2) *to cut or hew down; to cleave, to slay,* ἵππους τε καὶ ἄνέρας, 11, 497. Pass. often χαλκῷ δεδαϊγμένος, hewn down with the sword, 18, 236 22, 72.

δαϊκτάμενος, η, ον (δαΐς, κτείνω), *slain in battle,* *21, 146. 301.

δαιμόνιος, ίη, ον (δαίμων), prop. proceeding from a demon or divinity, *divine,* νίξ, h. Merc. 98. 2) Spoken of every thing which according to the belief of the

old world indicated a higher power, which excited astonishment, and thus fear; *astonishing, admirable.* H. uses it only in the vocative as a word of address to men, to express astonishment, horrour, etc. at a strange action or speech; *strange, wonderful,* sometimes in a good sense, *my (good) friend,* as 2, 190. 6, 407. Od. 14, 443; sometimes in reproach, *wretch, wretched (cruel, wicked) man,* 1, 561. 4, 31.

δαίμων, ονος, ὁ, ἡ, 1) any *divine being,* believed to be efficient in the production of events which were regarded as above ordinary human capability and power, and which yet could be ascribed to no particular divinity, 5, 438; we are not, however, to associate the later demons with those of H.; *a demon, a divinity.* The demon guides the fate of men, Od. 16, 64; he sends them happiness, is their tutelary spirit, Od. 21, 201; but he also allots misfortunes, sends sickness, Od. 5. 396. κακὸς δαίμων, Od. 10, 64. δαίμονος αἶσα κακή, Od. 11, 61; hence often used for *fate, happiness, misfortune.* τοὶ δαίμονα δώσω, I will give the demon to thee, i. e., death, 8, 166. πρὸς δαίμονα, against destiny, 17, 98. σὺν δαίμονι, with divine aid, 11, 792. 2) *deity, god, goddess,* spoken of definitely named divine persons, Aphroditê, 3, 420. h. 18, 22; and in the plur. *gods,* 1, 122. 6, 115.

δαίνυ' for ἐδαίνυσο, see δαίνυμι.

δαίνυμι, Ep. (δαίω), fut. δαίσω, aor. 1 mid. ἐδαισάμην, Ep. forms: 3 sing. optat. mid. δαίνυτο (for νιτο), 24, 665; 3 plur. δαινύατο, Od. 18, 248; imperf. mid. 2 sing. δαίνυ' for ἐδαίνυσο, 24, 63; 1) Act. prop. *to distribute, to give one his portion,* spoken only of a host: δαῖτά τινι, to give any one food, 9, 70; τάφον, γάμον, a funeral feast, a marriage feast, Od. 3, 309 4, 3. Il. 19, 299. 2) Mid. *to eat, to feast,* spoken of the guests; often absolutely, but also with accus. δαῖτα, to consume a feast; in like manner εἰλαπίνην, κρέα; and of the gods, ἑκατόμβας, 9, 535.

δαΐς, ἴδος, ἡ (δάω), 1) *a brand, a torch, a flambeau,* only plur. Od. 1, 428. 2) *war, battle,* only in the apocopat. dat. δαΐ, 13, 286. 14, 387.

δαίς, τός, ἡ (δαίω), *a meal, a feast, an entertainment, a sacrificial feast,* often in H. spoken of men and gods. δαὶς ἐΐση, an equally distributed feast, πίειρα 19, 179. 2) Of the *food* of wild beasts, 24, 43, but not often [Aristarchus, according to Lehrs, p. 96, placed the comma before βροτῶν, so as to connect it with δαῖτα, which would bring the signif. to no. 1].

δαίτη, ἡ, poet. for δαίς, 10, 217. Od. 3, 44. 7, 50.

δαίτηθεν, adv. *from the feast,* Od. 10, 216.

δαιτρεύω (δαιτρός), fut. σω, prop. *to divide into equal portions, to distribute,* spoken of booty, 11, 688. 2) *to cut off, to carve,* Od. 14, 433.

δαιτρόν, τό (δαίω), *that which is dis-*

F

tributed, a portion; πίνειν, to drink a given portion, 4, 262.†

δαιτρός, ὁ (δαίω), *one who distributes, a carver, a distributer,* chiefly of meat at a feast in small pieces, because the hands were used in eating, *Od. 4, 57. 17, 331.

δαιτροσύνη, ἡ, *carving, helping or distributing meat at table,* Od. 16, 253.†

δαιτυμών, όνος, ἡ (δαιτύς), mly *a companion at table.* 1) one who is invited, *a guest, a feaster,* Od. 8, 66. 2) an ordinary *companion at table,* once, *Od. 4, 621; see Nitzsch on the verse.

δαιτύς, ύος, ἡ, Ep. for δαίς, *a meal, an entertainment,* 22, 496.†

Δαίτωρ, ορος, ὁ, a Trojan slain by Teucer, 8, 275.

δαίφρων, ονος, ὁ, ἡ, signifies 1) (from δαίς, φρήν), *thinking of battle, eager for battle, warlike,* 2, 23; thus in the Iliad, except 24, 325 (a book mly regarded as of later date). 2) (from δαῆναι), *wise, intelligent, experienced;* so always in the Od. 15, 356. 8, 373: according to Buttm., Lex. p. 209. Nitzsch, on Od. 1, 48, derives it simply from δαῆναι in the signif. *to have proved, tried;* consequently spoken of a warrior: *proved, tried;* and of one in peace: *experienced, intelligent* [cf. G. Hermann, Opusc. VII. p. 250].

δαίω, the ground meaning of the root ΔΑ is perhaps *to divide, to cut up, to destroy.* There occur:

1) δαίω, poet., in the act. only pres. and imperf., perf. 2 δέδηα, aor. 2 mid. 3 sing. subj. δάηται=καίω. 1) Trans. in the act. = καίω [δαίειν = to *set on fire;* καίειν to *destroy by fire, to burn.* Död.], *to kindle, to inflame, to set on fire;* with accus. πῦρ, φλόγα, 9, 211; also δαῖέ οἱ ἐκ κόρυθος—πῦρ, she (Athênê) kindled a flame upon his helmet, 5, 4. cf. v. 7. 2) Mid. perf. 2 δέδηα. intransit. *to burn, to burst into flames, to flame,* as δαιόμενον σέλας, 8, 75; metaph. ὄσσε δαίεται, his eyes sparkle, spoken of the lion, Od. 6, 132; of Hector, 12, 466. πόλεμος δέδηε, the war is enkindled, rages, 20, 18. ἔρις, στέφανος πολέμοιο; ὄσσα δεδήει, the report was enkindled, i. e. spread rapidly, 2, 93; οἰμωγὴ δέδηε, arose, Od. 20, 353.

2) δαίομαι, poet. (only mid. in H. in the signif. *to divide,* act. δαίζω), fut. δάσομαι, Ep. σσ, aor. 1 ἐδασάμην, Ep. σσ, perf. δέδασμαι (δεδαίαται, Od. 1, 23), also a form δατέομαι. 1) Reflex. (for oneself), *to divide, to distribute, to share,* τί τινι; in the pres. κρέα μνηστῆρσι, Od. 17, 332. 15, 140; often in the fut. and aor. πάντα ἄνδιχα, to divide all into two parts, 18, 511; also κτήματα, μοίρας, πατρώϊα; likewise, *b) to tear in pieces,* 23, 21. Od. 18, 87. 2) Pass. *to be divided,* in the perf. 1, 125; spoken of the Ethiopians: διχθὰ δεδαίαται, Od. 1, 23. δαίεται ἦτορ, my heart is torn, Od. 1, 48.

δάκνω, aor. 2 ἔδακον, infin. Ep. δακέειν, *to bite, to sting,* spoken of dogs and gnats, 7, 572; of a mouse, Batr. 47; metaph.

δάκε φρένας Ἕκτορι μῦθος, the dis[course] wounded Hector's heart, 5, 493 (! aor. 2 in Il.; pres. in Batr.).

δάκρυ, τό, poet. for δάκρυον, *tea[r]* nom. and accus. sing. and dat. δάκρυσι.

δακρυόεις, εσσα, εν (δάκρυον), le[...] 1) Act. *weeping abundantly, sh[...] tears,* 6, 455. The neut. as adv. δα[...] γελᾶν, to laugh with tears in the e[...] 484. 2) *worthy of tears, lamentab[...]* λεμος, μάχη, 5, 737.

δάκρυον, τό (poet. δάκρυ), *a [...]* δακρυόφιν, Ep. gen. 17, 696. Od. 4 often δάκρυα, χέειν. λείβειν, βάλλει[...]

δακρυπλώω (πλέω), *to flow in* spoken of an intoxicated man, [...] eyes overflow, Od. 19, 122.†

δακρυχέω, *shedding tears, weeping* in partcp. pres., Il. and Od.

δακρύω, aor. 1 ἐδάκρυσα, perf. δεδάκρυμαι, intrans. *to weep, to shed* in perf. pass. *to be in tears,* 16, 7[...] δάκρυνται ὄσσε, eyes were full of Od 20, 204; παρειαί, v. 353.

* δάκτυλος, ὁ, *a finger, a toe,* Bat δᾱλός, ὁ (δαίω), [titio] *a brand, [...] brand,* 13, 320, and Od. 5, 488.

δαμάζω=δαμάω, as pres. not u[...] H.; but aor. 1 pass. ἐδαμάσθην, 16, 316.

δάμαρ, αρτος, ἡ, poet. (δαμάω), *a a consort;* prop. *domita,* in disti from ἀδμής, 3, 122. Od. 4, 126.

Δάμασος, ὁ, a Trojan, 12, 183.

Δαμαστορίδης, ου, ὁ, son of Dar =the Lydian *Tlepolemus,* 16, 416. suitor *Agelaus,* Od. 22, 293.

Δαμάστωρ, ορος, ὁ (the tamer), of Agelaus in Ithaca, Od.

δαμάω, fut. δαμάσω, poet. σσ δαμάω, thus δαμάᾳ, δαμόωσιν, aor. μασα, perf. σσ, fut. mid. δαμά poet. σσ, aor. 1 mid. ἐδαμασάμην σσ, subj. 3 sing. δαμάσσεται for σηται, 11, 478; perf. pass. δέδμημα[...] 1 pass. ἐδμήθην and ἐδαμάσθην, pass. ἐδάμην, 3 plur. δάμεν for ἐδά[...] subj. δαμείω, Ep. for δαμῶ, δαμείην, infin. δαμῆναι, Ep. δαμ[...] fut. 3 pass. δεδμήσομαι, h. Ap ground signif. 1) *to subdue,* her Spoken of animals: *to tame, to under the yoke,* for travelling or [...] ture, 10, 403. 2) Of maidens: *to* under the yoke of wedlock, *to m[...] espouse,* subigere, τινὰ ἀνδρί, [...] On Od. 3, 269, see πεδάω; also reference to marriage: *to violate, ile,* 3, 301. 3) Mly *to subdue, to c[...] to vanquish,* spoken of fate, Od. [...] Il. 16, 434. 816. 18, 119; τινὰ πλ[...] Od. 4, 244. 18, 54; also by prayen θήτω (cf. *vinci precibus),* 9, 158. a) *to conquer* in battle, στίχας, [...] pass. τινί, ὑπό τινι, or χεροίν τ[...] 429. 2, 860; hence also *to kill,* 1, 98, and often. b) *to bring into sub[...] to subject,* τί τινι, 6, 159: an[...] often: ἦ τοι πολλοὶ δεδμήατο κούρ[...]

many youths are subject to thee, 3, 183. 5, 878. Od. 3, 304. *c*) Metaph. spoken of states and inanimate objects : *to subdue, to overpower, to exhaust;* of sleep, 10, 2 ; of wine, Od. 9, 454 ; of passions, 6, 74. 14. 316 ; of the waves of the sea : to be exhausted, Od. 8, 231. II) Mid. like the act. except with a reference to the subject, 5, 278. 10, 210. δαμάσασθαι φρένας οἴνῳ, to stupify the mind with wine, Od. 9, 454. (Other forms are δαμνάω, δάμνημι.)

δαμείω, δάμεν, δαμήμεναι, see δαμάω.

δαμνάω = δαμάω, of which occurs only 3 sing. pres. δαμνᾷ, Od. 11, 221 ; 3 sing. impf. ἔδαμνα and δάμνα, iterat. fr. δάμνασκε, h. Ven. 252 ; and 2 sing. pres. mid. δαμνᾷ for δάμνασαι, 14, 199; cf. Spitzner.

δάμνημι, pass. δάμναμαι, Ep. (like ἵστημι) = δαμνάω, to subdue, to overpower. Besides the pres. act. H. uses the pres. and imperf. pass. The mid. only Od. 14, 488. h. Ven. 17.

δαμόωσιν, Ep. for δαμῶσιν, see δαμάω.

Δανάη, ἡ. daughter of Acrisius, mother of Perseus by Zeus. 14, 319 ; see Περσεύς.

Δαναοί, οἱ, the *Danai*, prop. the subjects of king Danaus of Argos; in H., 1) the inhabitants of the kingdom of Argos = Ἀργεῖοι, the subjects of king Agamemnon. 2) Often the Hellênes in general, because Agamemnon was the principal leader, 1, 42. 56, and Od. (Danaus, son of Belus, father of fifty daughters, contended with his brother Ægypt concerning the kingdom of Egypt, fled to Greece, and founded Argos, about 1500 B.C. Apd. 2, 1. 4. According to Ottfr. Müller, Gesch. hell. St. 1. p. 109, Danaus is only a mythic personification of the stock. He derives the name from δανός, dry, and thinks that originally τὸ δανάον Ἄργος was used in the same sense as τὸ δίψιον.)

δανός, ή, όν (δαίω) dried, dry, withered, ξύλα, Od. 15, 322.† δανὰ ξύλα, fire-wood, [δανός combustible ; fit for burning. Död.]

δάος, τό (δαίω) = δαλός, a pine torch, a fire-brand, a torch, 24, 647. Od. 4, 300, and often.

δάπεδον, τό (δα, Dor. for γῆ or for διά), ground, earth, Od. 11, 577. 2) Mly the floor of a chamber, the house-floor, 4, 2 ; chiefly Od.

δάπτω, and with reduplicat. δαρδάπτω, fut. δάψω, to tear in pieces, to lacerate, spoken of wild beasts, 11, 481 ; metaph. of a spear : χρόα, to tear the skin, 13, 831 ; and of fire : to consume, *23, 183.

Δαρδανίδης, ου, ὁ, a son or descendant of Dardanus = *Priam.* 3, 303 ; *Anchises,* h. in Ven. 178. [2) = *Ilus,* 11, 166.]

Δαρδανίη, ἡ, *Dardania,* 1) an old city in Asia Minor, on the Hellespont, at the foot of Ida, which was founded by the old king Dardanus, and whose residence it was, 20, 216; distinct from Ilium of Strab., XIII. p. 590; and from the Æol.

town ἡ Δάρδανος, which lay further south, 110 stadia from the mouth of the Rhodius, which falls into the Hellespont, Strab., XIII. 595. 2).sc. γῆ, a small district above Troas on the Hellespont which Æneas ruled. H. mentions only the inhabitants, the Dardanians, i. e., Δάρδανοι, q. v.; according to Strab., XIII. v. 561, p. 596, from Zeleia to Scepsis.

Δαρδάνιος, ίη, ιον, *Dardanian,* proceeding or named from Dardanus. αἱ Δαρδάνιαι πύλαι, the Dardanian gate, 5, 789 = αἱ Σκαιαί, q. v. 2) Subst. the *Dardani,* i. q. Δάρδανοι, q. v.

Δαρδανίς, ίδος, ἡ, *Dardanian,* also *Trojan,* as subst. a *Trojan woman,* 18, 122. 339.

Δαρδανίων, ωνος, ὁ, prop. a descendant of Dardanus, in the plur. = Δάρδανοι, e. g. Τρῶες καὶ Δαρδανίωνες. 7, 414.

Δάρδανοι, οἱ, sing. 2, 701, the *Dardanians,* prop. the inhabitants of Dardania, the subjects of Æneas ; they were the more ancient stock, hence the poet joins Τρῶες καὶ Δαρδανίωνες, 3, 456. 7, 348.

Δάρδανος, ὁ, son of Zeus and Electra, brother of Jasius from Arcadia; he emigrated to Samothrace, and thence to Asia Minor, where he founded the town Dardania. His wife Batia, daughter of Teucer, bore him Ilus and Ericthonius, 20, 215. 303. Apd. 3, 12. 1. 2) son of Bias, a Trojan, whom Achilles slew, 20, 460. 3) Adj. = Δαρδάνιος : Δάρδανος ἀνήρ, 16, 807.

δαρδάπτω, a strengthened form of δάπτω, to tear in pieces, 11, 479 ; metaph. κτήματα, Od. 14, 92 ; χρήματα, to squander property, Od. 16, 315.

Δάρης, ητος, ὁ, a priest of Hêphæstus in Troy, father of Phegeus and Idæus, 5, 9. seq.

δαρθάνω, aor. ἔδαρθον, Ep. ἔδραθον, to sleep, only aor. Od. 20, 143.†

δασασκέτω, δάσασθαι, δάσομαι, see δαίω.

δάσκιος, ον, poet. (δα, σκιά), very shady, deeply shaded, ὕλη, Il. Od. and h.

δασμός, ὁ (δαίω), division, distribution, 1, 166. + h. in Cer. 86.

δασπλῆτις, ἡ, difficult of approach, dreadful, terrible, epith. of the furies. Od. 15, 234.† (From δα and πελάω, not πλήσσω. Thiersch, Gram. § 199, 5. Cf. τειχεσιπλήτης.) [= δαιδο πελάτις, δαισπελάτις (cf. κραταίπεδον, κράσπεδον), that brings a torch near ; approaching with a torch ; torch-bearing. Död.].

δασύμαλλος, ον (μαλλός), having thick wool, thick-woolled, Od. 9, 425.†

δασύς, εῖα, ύ, rough, thickly planted, hairy, ῥῶπες. δέρμα, *Od. 14, 49. 51.

δατέομαι (δαίω), Ep. form in pres. and impf. for δαίομαι, 1) to divide, to distribute, ληΐδα, 9, 138 ; metaph. μένος Ἄρηος δατέονται, they divided among one another the fury of Arês, i. e., they fought on both sides with equal rage, 18. 264. χθόνα ποσσὶ δατεῦντο, they divided the ground with their feet, i. e., passed over it in steps, 23, 121. *b*) to allot to oneself, i. e., to receive, spoken of the gods, who are pleased with the savour of sacrifices, 8. 550. c) Mly to distribute, κρέα, Od. 1, 112. 2) to lacerate, to crush, 20, 394.

Δαυλίς, ίδος, ή, a town in Phocis, upon an elevation not far from Delphi, the scene of the old fable of Têreus, Prognê, and Philomêlê, 2, 520 (from δαυλός, thickly overgrown).

δάφνη, ή, laurel, Od. 9, 183. †h. Ap. 396.

δαφοινεός, όν=δαφοινός. εἷμα δαφοινεόν αἵματι, 18, 538.†

δαφοινός, όν (δα, φοινός), blood red, very red, dark-red, fire-coloured, spoken of lions, serpents, and jackals, *Il. h. Ap. 304.

ΔΑΩ, Ep. th. of διδάσκω, with the signif. to teach and to learn; from this theme the following forms occur in H.: aor: 2 act. δέδαε, perf. partcp. δεδαώς, aor. 2 pass. ἐδάην, subj δαῶ, Ep. δαείω, infin. δαῆναι, Ep. δαήμεναι, whence fut. δαήσομαι, perf. act. δεδάηκα, and perf. pass. partcp. δεδαημένος, h. Merc. 483; and an infin. pres. (as if fr. δέδαα) δεδάασθαι. 1) The signif. to teach has only the aor. 2 act. δέδαε, with double accus. τινά τι, Od. 6, 233. 8, 448; and with infin. Od. 20, 72. 2) To the signif. to learn, to know, to experience, belong the remaining forms Thus aor. 2 pass. with accus. 6, 150; once with gen. πολέμοιο δαήμεναι, to be acquainted with war, 21, 487; τινός, to become acquainted with, Od. 19, 325; partcp. perf. act. δεδαώς, having learned, instructed, ἐκ θεῶν, Od. 17, 519; and δεδάηκε ἄεθλον, has learned [is acquainted with] a combat, Od. 8, 134. οὐ δεδαηκότες ἀλκήν, not acquainted with conflict, defence, Od. 2, 61. Pres. mid. to teach oneself, to become acquainted with. δεδάασθαι γυναῖκας, to inform oneself about the women, Od. 16, 316. (To the same theme belong also the Ep. forms δνω and δέατο.)

δέ, conj. but, on the other hand, on the contrary. This conj., which, like the Lat. autem, may indicate every kind of opposition, has either an adversative or conjunctive force. I) Adversative, 1) Most commonly in the case of opposed notions, of which the first has μέν, see μέν; also μέν, μέν, and δέ, δέ, succeed each other. b) δέ often stands also without a preceding μέν, when the speaker would not give a pre-intimation of the antithesis, or where the first member forms but a weak antithesis. In the last case it is found also with the repetition of the same or of an equivalent word, ὡς Ἀχιλεὺς θάμβησεν—θάμβησαν δὲ καὶ ἄλλοι, 24, 484; οἱ δὲ καὶ αὐτοὶ— ἄλγε' ἔχουσιν, Od. 1, 33. Il. 14, 9. 12. From the last use of δέ without μέν has 2) the conjunctive force of this particle developed itself. Here it can mly be translated by and, but must often be omitted in translating. This takes place

a) When a transition is made from subject to another: cf. 1, 43—49 When it connects sentences of whic latter may be regarded as standin subordinate relation, in which ca often expresses a reason, and stan γάρ. It can then be translated by for, because [or omitted]: ἀλλὰ πύ ἄμφω δὲ νεωτέρω ἐστὸν ἐμεῖο, 1, 259 cf. 2, 26. 9, 496. 3) It often stands i apodosis, and has both an adversativ conjunctive force. a) The adversati on the other hand, on my part, agai After a hypothetical protasis: εἰ δε δώωσιν, ἐγὼ δέ κεν αὐτὸς ἕλωμαι. self on the other hand, etc. 1. 13: 215. β) After a comparative or re protasis: οἵη περ φύλλων γενεή, τ καὶ ἀνδρῶν, 6, 146. Od. 7, 108. b conjunctive δέ annexes the apodos the protasis as if a relation, not of s dination but of equality, existed be tnem; thus, after a temporal pr with ἐπεί, ἐπειδή, ὄφρα, ὁπότε, ἕως, 16, 199. 21, 53. 4) In connexion other particles: a) καὶ δέ, also o other hand, but also, in H. 23, 8(16, 418. b) δὲ δή, but still, but n 94. c) δέ τε, and also 1, 404: but Od. 1, 53. 4, 379 [also separated, 519]. δέ never stands at the begi of a sentence, but takes the secone often the third place.

δέ, inseparable enclitic particle. is annexed 1) To nouns, to indica direction whither. It stands mly the accus. κλισίηνδε, Θρήκηνδε, οἰ In Ἀϊδόσδε it is connected with th because the accus. is to be supplie Ἀϊδής. More rarely we find it wit as ὄνδε δόμονδε, to his house. 2) T nouns, to strengthen their demonst force: as ὅδε, τοιόσδε, etc. (Th probably originated from δή.)

δέατ' for δέατο. Ep. the only forn obsol. verb δέαμαι, Od. 6. 242.† π μοι ἀεικέλιος δέατ' εἶναι, before l peared ugly to me. (Accordi Buttm., Lex. p. 216, from aor. 2 δαī see, whence pass. δέαμαι for δάαμ appear. Before Wolf the readin was δόατ', and was referred to δοε q. v.)

δέγμενος, see δέχομαι.

δέδαα, δεδάατι, δεδάηκα, δεδα δεδαώς, see ΔΑΩ.

δεδαίαται, see δαίω 2.

δεδαϊγμένος, see δαΐζω.

δέδασται, see δαίω 2.

δέδηε, δεδήει, see δαίω.

δέδια, Ep. δείδια, in the plur. a[analogy of verbs in μι, without vowel, δείδιμεν, δείδιτε, δεδίασι, ι δείδιθι, etc. Perf. from the old with pres. signif. I fear, instead later pres. δείδω, see δίω.

1) δεδίσκομαι and δειδίσκομα pres. and impf. Ep. form (from δε to greet, to welcome, τινά, δεξιτερ Od. 20, 197; δέτται, to greet w

cup, i. e., to drink to, Od. 18, 121 ; absol. Od. 3, 41 (from δέκομαι, δίσκομαι, with reduplicat. δεδίσκομαι).

II) *δεδίσκομαι, a form of δεδίσσομαι, h. Merc. 103.

δεδίσσομαι, poet. δειδίσσομαι, q. v.

δεδμήατο, see δαμάω.

δεδμημένος, 1) Perf. partcp. from δαμάω, 10, 2. 2) From δέμω, to build, 6, 245.

δεδοκημένος, Ep. partcp. perf. pass. from the Ion. δέκομαι for δέχομαι, watching, lying in wait, 15, 730.†

δέδορκα, see δέρκομαι.

δεδραγμένος, see δράσσω.

δέελος, η, ον, Ep. for δῆλος, 10, 466.†

δεῖ (from δέω), it is necessary, it is fitting ; in H. Il. 9, 337 ; † elsewhere always χρή : see δέω.

δείδεκτο and δειδέχατο, Ep. strengthened form for δέδεκτο, δεδέχατο : see δείκνυμι.

δειδήμων, ον, gen. ονος (δείδω), fearful, cowardly, timid, 3, 56.†

δείδια, etc., see δείδω and δίω.

δειδίσκομαι, see δεδίσκομαι II.

δειδίσσομαι, Ep. and δεδίσκομαι, only h. Merc. 163 ; depon. mid. (δείδω), fut. δειδίξομαι, infin. aor. 1 δειδίξασθαι, 1) Trans. to terrify, to frighten, to frighten away, τινά, any one, 4, 184 ; τινὰ ἀπὸ νεκροῦ, any one from a corpse, 18, 164. 2) Intrans. to fear, to be dismayed, 2, 190.

δείδοικα, see δείδω.

δείδω, only 1 sing. pres. (formed from the Ep. perf. δείδια), fut δείσομαι, aor. 1 ἔδεισα, Ep. ἔδδεισα, partcp. δείσας, perf. δέδοικα, Ep. δείδοικα (also the Ep. δέδια, δείδια, etc.), with pres. signif. 1) Intrans. to fear, to be anxious, to be alarmed, often absol. ; only περί τινι, for any one, 10, 240. h. Cer. 246 ; also with μή, that, following, δείδω, μή τι πάθῃσιν, 11, 470 ; rarely with infin. δείσαν ὑποδέχθαι, 7, 93. 2) Trans. to fear, to dread, τινά or τί, very often θεούς, Od. 14, 389 On the orthography ἔδδεισα, more correctly ἔδεισα, see Buttm., Gram. p. 274, margin. note. Kühner, p. 120.

δειελιάω (δείελος), only aor. 1 partcp. δειελιήσας, to await the evening, to wait till evening. σὺ δ᾽ ἔρχεο δειελιήσας, Od. 17, 599.† (Accord. to Clarke and Buttm. Lex. p. 229, to take an afternoon's repast, which, however, the ancient Gramm., oi παλαιοι, according to Eustath. rejected. The latter explains it, ἕως δείλης διατρίψας ἐνταῦθα.)

δείελος, ον (δείλη), belonging to the declining day, relating to afternoon and evening. δείελον ἦμαρ. evening, Od. 17, 606. ὁ δείελος ὀψὲ δύων, sc. ἥέλιος, the late evening: the late-setting sun of evening, 21, 232.

δεικανάομαι, depon. mid. only pres. and imperf. δεικανόωντο (δείκνυμι), to offer the hand in greeting; and mly to welcome, to salute, to receive, ἐπέεσσι, δέπασσιν, Od. 18, 111. Il. 15, 86.

δείκνυμι, th. ΔΕΚΩ, aor. 1 δεῖξα, aor.

mid. ἐδειξάμην, h. Merc. 367; perf. mid. δείδεγμαι, Ep. for δέδεγμαι, 3 plur. δειδέχαται, 3 sing. pluperf. δείδεκτο, and 3 plur. δειδέχατο, 1) Prop. to present the hand ; hence a) to show, to point out, to indicate, τί τινι, spoken of the gods : σῆμα, τέρας, to let a sign or prodigy be seen, Od. 3, 174. Il. 13, 244 ; ἔργα, h. 31, 19. b) to advertise, to inform, 19, 332. 2) Mid. a) to point to, εἴς τι, h. Merc. 367. b) to show, τί τινι, 23, 701. c) to greet, to welcome, 9, 196. Od. 4, 59 ; perf. and pluperf. mid. with pres. signif. δεπάεσσιν (dat. instrum.) δειδέχατ᾽ ἀλλήλους, they greeted one another with cups, i. e., they drank to one another, 4, 4 ; κυπέλλοις, 9, 671. cf. 9, 224 ; μύθοισι, Od. 7, 72 ; see Buttm., Gramm., under δείκνυμι, p. 274.

δείλη, ἡ (contr. from δειέλη, sc. ὥρα), the declining day, the latter part of the afternoon, and the early part of the evening, 21, 111.† as the connexion with ἠώς and μέσον ἦμαρ shows. (According to Buttm., Lexil. p. 225, from εἴλη, heat, prop. the time in which the heat extends itself, afternoon ; δείλη has the same relation to εἴλη, as διώκω to ἰώκω.)

δείλομαι (δείλη), to incline towards evening, accord. to Aristarch. δείλετο for δύσετο, Od. 7, 289.†

δειλός, ή, όν (δείδω), fearful, cowardly, timid, opposed to ἄλκιμος, 13, 278 ; hence in H. weak, contemptible, miserable, bad, 1, 293 ; δειλαὶ δειλῶν ἐγγύαι, Od. 8, 351. On this passage cf. ἐγγυάω. 2) wretched, unfortunate, miserable, poor, in the address : ἆ δειλέ, ἆ δειλοί, Od. 14, 361. Il. 11, 816.

δεῖμα, ατος, τό (δείδω), fear, terrour, fright, 5, 682.†

*δειμαίνω, ανῶ, to be afraid, h. in Ap. 404.

*δειμαλέος, η, ον, frightful, dreadful, ὅπλον, Batr. 289.

δείματο, see δέμω.

δείμωμεν, Ep. for δείμωμεν, see δέμω.

Δεῖμος, ὁ (app. δειμός), Terrour, in the Il. as a personified, mythic being, servant and charioteer of Ἄρης, like Phobos, 4, 440. 11, 37. 15, 119. According to Hes. the son of Ἄρης.

δεινός, ή, όν (δείδω), frightful, terrible, awful, terrific, αἰγίς, πέλωρον, chiefly neut. as adv. δεινὸν ἀῦτεῖν, to shout terribly, 11, 10 ; δέρκεσθαι, 3, 342. 2) In a milder signif. applied to that which by its greatness and power inspires awe and admiration: aweful, sublime, venerable, in connexion with αἰδοῖος, 3, 172. 18, 394. Od. 8, 22.

δεῖος, ους, τό, poet. for δέος, 15, 4 ; only in gen.

δειπνέω (δεῖπνον), aor. ἐδείπνησα, pluperf. δεδειπνήκει, Od. 17, 359 ; to breakfast, to take the morning meal, 19, 334. and often Od. ; later, to take the principal meal; so even in h. Ap. 497.

δείπνηστος, ὁ (δειπνέω), the time of breakfast, meal-time, Od. 17, 170. (According to the Schol. the Gramm. make a distinction: δείπνηστος, *meal-time;* δειπνηστός, the meal itself.

δειπνίζω (δειπνέω), aor. 1 ἐδείπνισα, only partcp. δειπνίσσας, *to entertain, to give a meal to any one,* with accus. *Od. 4, 535. 11, 411.

δείπνον, τό. in H. *breakfast,* or, more correctly, the principal meal, which was taken by those not in service about noon; in distinction from δόρπος, 8, 53. 10, 578. Od. 15, 316. An army going to battle took this meal at day-break, 2, 381; mly *meal, repast, entertainment,* Od. 17, 176; spoken of horses: *food,* 2, 383. (According to Nitzsch on Od. 1, 124, it is in H. everywhere the *principal meal;* according to Voss on h. Cer. 128, it is prop. *an early meal,* which as a feast indeed might last till towards evening; in H. it seems every where to signify *meal* in general.)

* δειράς, άδος, ἡ (δειρή), *the ridge of a mountain,* a mountain-chain, h. Ap. 281.

δειρή, ἡ, *the neck,* of men and beasts, 3, 396.

δειροτομέω (τέμνω), fut. ήσω, *to cut off the neck, to behead,* 21, 89. Od. 22, 349.

δείρας, see δέρω.

Δεισήνωρ, ορος, ὁ, a Lycian, 17, 217.

(δείω), assumed th. of δείδω.

δέκα, οἱ, αἱ, τά, indecl. *ten* (from δέκω, δείκνυμι, the ten fingers), often for an indefinite number.

δεκάκις, adv. *ten times,* 9, 379.†

δεκάς, άδος, ἡ, *a decade,* the number ten, 2, 128. Od. 16, 245.

δέκατος, η, ον (δέκα), *tenth;* often as a round number, 1, 54.

δεκάχιλοι, αι, α, *ten thousand* (only in H.), 5, 860.†

δέκτης, ου, ὁ (δέχομαι), prop. a receiver; then *a beggar,* Od. 4, 248.†

δέκτο, see δέχομαι.

* δέλτος, ἡ, *a writing-tablet,* a table, Batr. 2, in the plur.

* Δέλφειος, η, ον (Δελφοί), *Delphian,* βωμός, h. in Ap. 496; doubtful. Herm. conjectures αὐτίκ᾽ ἄρ᾽ ἀφνειός for αὐτὸς Δέλφειος.

δελφίν, see δελφίς.

* Δελφίνιος, ὁ, the *Delphian,* appell. of Apollo, either from the name of the serpent slain by him, or because he, upon a dolphin, or changed into a dolphin, led the Cretan colony which emigrated to Delphi, h. in Ap. 493, see Paus. 1, 19, 1.

δελφίς, ῖνος, ὁ, more correctly δελφίν, *a dolphin* (see Buttm., Gram. § 41, note 1), 21, 22. Od. 12, 96.

* Δελφοί, ῶν, οἱ, *Delphi,* a famous oracle in Phocis, first found h. 27, 14; in H. elsewhere Πυθώ, q. v.

δέμας, τό, defect. (δέμω), *the form of the body, the stature, a body, the external shape,* mly spoken of men with φυή, 1, 115; and with εἶδος, 24. 376; twice of animals, Od. 10, 240. 17, 307; and mly *body,* νεκρόν, Batr. 106. 2) As adv. like *instar, in form, in the likeness of.* δέμας πυρός, 'ike fire, 11, 596. 13, 673. (In

H. only in accus., e. g. μικρός, ἄρισ δέμας.)

δέμνιον, τό (δέμω), always in the pl *a bedstead,* Od. 4, 297. 1, 277, and oft in Il. only 24, 644; and mly *a bed, a cou*

δέμω, aor. 1 ἔδειμα, perf. pass. δέδμην aor. 1 mid. ἐδειμάμην, 1) *to build, construct;* with accus. πύργον, τείχ ἕρκος ἀλωῆς, h. Merc. 87. θάλα πλησίοι ἀλλήλων δεδμημένοι, 6, 245. 2 2) Mid. *to build for oneself,* οἴκους, Od 9 (the imperf. only Od. 23, 192; pres. Merc. 87).

δενδίλλω, only partcp. *to wink with* eyes: accord. to the Schol. *to give* understand by a side look; mly *to g the wink,* εἴς τινα, 9, 180.†

δένδρεον, τό, Ion. for δένδρον, a *tr* in H. always the Ion. form (δένδρε δενδρέων, 3, 152. Od. 19, 520, are d syllabic).

δενδρήεις, εσσα, εν (δένδρον), *wood woody, covered with trees,* *Od. 1, 51. Ap. 221.

Δεξαμένη, ἡ, daughter of Nereus a Doris, 18, 44 (on the contrary, δεξαμε *the fish-pool*).

Δεξιάδης, ου, ὁ, son of Dexius=*Ip nous,* 7, 15.

* δεξιάομαι, depon. mid. (δεξιά), *welcome with the right hand,* h. 5, 16.

δεξιή, ἡ (sc. χείρ, origin. fem. of δεξι *the right hand,* as a mark of salutation promise, 10, 542. 2) *a promise, an agr ment,* a contract, 2, 341. 4. 159.

δεξιός, ή, όν. 1) *right, on the ri hand;* μαζός, the right breast, 4. 4 ὦμος, Od.; ἐπὶ δεξιά, *on the right,* to *right,* opposed to ἐπὶ ἀριστερά, 7, 238. *propitious, auspicious, lucky,* chie spoken of the flight of birds and of ot omens in divination. To the Gr diviner, who faced the north, auspici omens came on the right from the e inauspicious on the left from the w 12, 239; hence ὄρνις δεξιός=αἴσιος, 821. Od. 15, 160; see ἐνδέξιος, ἐπιδέξ According to Buttm., Lex. p. 291 never signifies in H. *ingenious, dexter* (δεξιός, from δέκω, related to δέχομαι δείκνυμι.)

δεξιόφιν, adv. (δεξιός), ἐπὶ δεξιόφιν, *the right, at the right,* 13, 308.†

δεξιτερός, ή, όν, poet. (lengthened f δεξιός), Ep. dat. δεξιτερῆφι, *at* or *o right.* δεξιτερὴ χείρ, 7, 108. Od. 1, 1 and δεξιτερή alone, the right hand, 1,

δέξο, see δέχομαι.

δέος. ους, τό. Ep. δεῖος, of which gen. δείους (δείω), *fear, alarm,* often χλωρόν, ἀκήριον. 2) *cause of fear.* τοι ἔπι δέος, thou hast no cause of i. e., thou hast nothing here to fear Nägelsbach), 1, 515; and with infin. οὔ δέος ἔστ᾽ ἀπολέσθαι, 12, 246.

δέπας, αος, τό. plur. nom. δέπα, plur. δεπάεσσι, δέπασσιν. *a goblet, a* nily of gold, or silver with a golden Od. 15, 116. Also connected with ἀ κύπελλον. q. v. Mly it is a drinking-

Δέρκομαι. 103 Δέχομαι.

yet sometimes a larger cup in which the mixing took place, 11, 632.

δέρκομαι. depon. iterat. imperf. δερκέσκετο, perf. δέδορκα, aor. 2 ἔδρακον, 1) to look, to see, to look on; often ἐμεῦ δερκομένου ἐπὶ χθονί, so long as I see the light on the earth, i. e., as long as I live, 1, 88; δεινόν, to look terribly. The perf. with pres. signif. πῦρ ὀφθαλμοῖσι δεδορκώς, flashing fire from the eyes, Od. 1., 446. 2) Trans. to see, to perceive, to behold, with accus. 14, 141.

δέρμα, ατος, τό (δέρω), the pelt, the skin, a hide, mly of beasts, once of men, 16, 341. 2) a prepared skin, leather, a skinbottle, Od. 2, 291.

δερμάτινος, η, ον, leathern, τροποί, *Od. 4, 782 8, 53.

δέρον, for ἔδερον, see δέρω.

δέρτρον, τό (δέρω), the peritoneum or omentum, a membrane covering the bowels. δέρτρον ἔσω δύνειν, i. e. εἰς δέρτρον. to penetrate to the caul, spoken of the vultures of Tityus, Od. 11, 579.†

δέρω, aor. 1 ἔδειρα, to draw off the skin, to flay, with accus. βοῦν, 2, 422; μῆλα, Od. 10, 533.

δέσμα. ατος, τό, poet. for δεσμός (δέω). only in the plur. δέσματα, bonds, fetters, Od. 1, 204. 8, 278. 2) the band with which the hair of the higher classes of women was confined, a fillet, 22, 468.

* δεσμεύω (δέσμη), to bind, to fetter, h. 6. 17.

δεσμός, ὁ (δέω). in the plur. δεσμοί, Il. and Od.; also δεσμά, τά, h. Ap. 129. h. 7, 13; fetter, bond, 5, 391; of a horse: the halter, 6, 507; a cable, Od. 13, 100; the door-thong, Od. 21, 241.

* δεσπόζω (related to δεσμός), fut. σω, to rule, to command, τινός, h. Cer. 366.

δέσποινα, ἡ, a female sovereign, a mistress, also ἄλοχος, γυνὴ δέσποινα, *Od. 3, 403. 7, 347.

* δεσπόσυνος, ον, belonging to the master of a family, λέχος. h. Cer. 144.

δετή, ἡ (prop. fem. from δετός, sc. λαμπάς), a bundle of pine-sticks tied together, a torch, 11, 554. 17, 663.

δευήσεσθαι, see δεύω.

Δευκαλίδης, ον, ὁ, Ep. for Δευκαλιωνίδης, son of Deucalion = Idomeneus, 12. 117.

Δευκαλίων, ωνος, ὁ, son of Minos and Pasiphaë, father of Idomeneus, an Argonaut and Calydonian hunter, 13, 452. Ulysses (Odysseus) names him to Penelope as his father, Od. 19, 180. 2) a Trojan, slain by Achilles, 20, 478.

δεῦρο. adv. of place, here, hither, mly with verbs of motion, 1, 153. Od. 4, 384. 2) As a particle of exhortation, up! on! here! δεῦ' ἄγε, come on! δεῦρ' ἴθι. come hither! 3, 130. (With the plur. δεῦτε.) Instead of δεῦρο, 3, 240, Spitzner and Dindorf have adopted δεύρω, after Herodian and the Schol. Cf. Thiersch, Gram. § 147, 5.

δεύτατος, η, ον, the last, superl. of δεύτερος, 19, 51. Od. 1, 286.

δεῦτε, adv. here, hither, etc., like δεῦρο, always with the plur.: δεῦτε φίλοι, δεῦτ' ἄγετε, 7, 350; ἴομεν, 14, 128. (From δεῦρ' ἴτε, contr.: so Buttm.)

δεύτερος, η, ον, superl. δεύτατος, η, ον, the second, 1) In respect of rank and order, spoken of one inferior in combat, 23, 265. 498. 2) In respect to time: δεύτερος ἦλθε, he came as the second, i. e., later, 10, 368; with gen. ἐμεῖο δεύτερος, later than I, after me, outliving me, 23, 248. The neut. often as adv. δεύτερον, for the second time, secondly, again, connected with αὖ and αὖτε, and plur. δεύτερα, 23, 538.

I) δεύω (only pres. and imperf. act. and pass.), to moisten, to wet, with accus. γαῖαν, παρειάς, 13, 655. Od. 8, 522; dat. δάκρυσι, with tears, Od. 7, 260. Pass. Il. 9, 570. 2) to fill, ἄγγεα, the vessels, 2, 471.

II) δεύω, prop. δεϝ, with digamma, Ep. for δέω (cf. δεῖ), of the act. only aor. 1 ἐδεύησε and δῆσε for ἐδέησε, to want, to fail. ἐδεύησεν δ' οἰήϊον ἄκρον ἱκέσθαι, it failed to reach the extremity of the rudder, Od. 9, 540. (483.) δῆσεν ἐμεῖο (without digamma), he lacked me, 18, 100. More mly, 2) Mid. δεύομαι, fut. δευήσομαι, to want, to be destitute, to need, τινός, 2, 128. Od. 6, 192; θυμοῦ, to be deprived of life, 3, 294. οὐ δεύεσθαι πολέμοιο, not to lack battle, i. e., to have enough to combat, [οὐδαμοῦ οἶμαι ἀπολεμήτους εἶναι Eust.] 13, 310. Others, as Heyne, explain it without necessity, 'to be inferior' ['no where so much to need battle, i. e., aid, as upon the left;' so Clarke and Bothe]. 3) to be wanting in a thing, to be inferior. μάχης πολλὸν ἐδεύεο, thou wert far inferior in battle, with gen. of person. ἄλλα πάντα δεύεαι 'Αργείων, in all other things thou art inferior to the Argives, 23, 484.

δέχαται, see δέχομαι.
δέχθαι, see δέχομαι.

δέχομαι, depon. mid. fut. δέξομαι, aor. 1 ἐδεξάμην, perf. δέδεγμαι, pluperf. ἐδεδέγμην or ἐδέγμην, partcp. δεδεγμένος or δέγμενος, fut. 3 δεδέξομαι = δέξομαι, Ep. sync. aor. ἐδέγμην; from this ἔδεκτο and δέκτο. imper. δέξο, infin. δέχθαι. Thiersch, § 218, 59, 60. Rost, Gram. p. 291, and Dial. 51. (Here belongs as an Ep. perf. δεδοκημένος from δέκομαι, 15, 730, watching, lurking.) 1) to take, to receive, to accept, what is presented, with accus. ἄποινα, δέπας, and in various regards. a) Spoken of the gods: ἱρά, to receive the victims, 2, 420. b) to receive hospitably, to entertain, τινά, 18, 331. Od. 19, 316. c) to receive as an infliction, to bear, to suffer, μῦθον, Od. 20, 271; κῆρα, to suffer fate, 18, 115. Mly παρά τινος, to receive from one, 24, 429; oftener τινός alone, 7, 400; and with dat. δέχεσθαί τι τινί, to take any thing from any one, 2, 186. Od. 15, 282; but χρυσὸν ἀνδρὸς ἐδέξατο, she received gold for her husband [i. e. she betrayed him], Od. 11,

F 4

327. 2) to receive, τινά, a) In a hostile sense, to await, to expect. In H. in this signif. only the perf. δέδεγμαι or δέγμαι, with pres. signif. and pluperf. as imperf. ἐδεδέγμην or ἐδέγμην, partcp. δεδεγμένος and δέγμενος, fut. δεδέξομαι; often with dat. instrum.: ἔγχεϊ, δουρί, τόξοισι: τόνδε—δεδέξομαι δουρί, 5, 238; spoken of a hunter standing at his station, 4, 107; also of the boar: ἀνδρῶν καὶ κυνῶν κολοσυρτόν δέχαται, they await the tumult of the men and dogs, 12, 147. b) Mly to wait, to await, with ὁππότε, εἰσόκε, 2, 794. 10, 62; with accus. and infin. only Od. 9. 513. 12, 230. 3) Intrans. or pass. once to follow, like excipere: ὥς μοι δέχεται κακὸν ἐκ κακοῦ, thus one misfortune after another follows me, 19, 290.

δεψέω (δέφω), fut. ήσω. partcp. aor. 1 δεψήσας, prop. to prepare hides, to soften, κηρόν, Od. 12, 48.†

δέω, infin. pres. δεῖν, h 6. in Dion. 12, fut. δήσω, aor. ἔδησα and δῆσα, aor. 1 mid. ἐδησάμην. Ep. iterat. δησάσκετο, 24, 15, perf. pass. δέδεμαι, Ep. form δίδημι, from this δίδη, 11, 105. 1) to bind, to fetter, to fasten, τινὰ δεσμῷ, or ἐν δεσμῷ. to bind one with fetters, 10, 443. 5, 386. χαλκέῳ ἐν κεράμῳ δέδετο, he lay bound in a brazen prison, 5, 387; with ἔκ τινος, παρά τινι and τι, to fasten to any thing: metaph. πῶς ἂν ἐγώ σε δέοιμι, how could I bind thee, i. e. hold thee to thy word, Od. 8, 352 (Nitzsch, however, takes it in lit. signif.). 2) to restrain, to hinder; μένος καὶ χεῖρας δῆσαι, 14. 73; τινὰ κελεύθον, to hinder any one from a journey, Od. 4, 380. 469. II) to bind on any thing for oneself (sibi), ὑπὸ ποσσὶ πέδιλα, 2, 44; περί and παρά τι. 8, 26. 17, 290; ὅπλα ἀνὰ νῆα, Od. 2, 430.

δέω, aor. 1 δῆσα, see δεύω.

δή, adv. (prop. abbrev. from ἤδη). already, now, just, certainly, indeed. It is never found at the beginning of a clause, except in the Ep. constructions δὴ τότε, δὴ γάρ, but as subordinate gives strength to another word. The orig. signif. is I) temporal, 1) already, just, now, spoken of the immediate present in distinction from the past or the future, καὶ δή, and now, 1, 161; δὴ νῦν, just now. Od. 2, 25; μὴ δή, ne jam, after verbs of fearing, 14, 44. 2) already, at last, still, in numbering, 2, 134. 24, 107; καὶ δή, and already, 1, 161. 15, 251; ὡς δή, as already, 17, 328; γὰρ δή, for already, 17, 546. 3) Esply is δή connected with adv. of time, to express that now something becomes a reality, as νῦν δή, now then, Ep. δὴ νῦν, esply in the apodosis τότε δή, then at last, or δὴ τότε, ὀψὲ δή; in the protasis ὅτε δή, ὁπότε δή, when now, etc. From this last use has arisen II) The determinative signif. [its conclusive and therefore exclusive force] by which δή defines precisely the degree and measure of an idea: just, exactly, only, now. 1) With verbs, esply with the imper. ἄγε δή, come then, 3, 441; φράζεσθον δή, consider only,

6, 306. Often with μή: μὴ δή—ἐλ only do not hope [= hoc tantum te ne—], 20, 200. 2) With adj. ὠκύμορο μοι ἔσσεαι, 18, 95; esply with sup κράτιστοι δή, 1, 266. 3) With pronot it either marks the prominence of word: ἐκεῖνος δή, he now [exclus he and no other]; or recalls a forego subject, τοῦπερ δὴ θυγάτηρ, his daugl now, 6, 398. 4) With indefinite nouns, it heightens the indefiniten ἄλλοι δή, others, whoever they be [whom you please], 1, 295. 5) V particles, a) just, exactly, now, a) V conjunctions: ὡς δή, ἵνα δή, t that now: ὡς δή, that however [v ὄφελον, utinam]. Od. 1, 217. β) V particles of explanation: γὰρ δή, Ep γάρ, mly with temporal signif δή, mostly ironical, 1, 110. γ) ἀλλὰ but now. δ) With interrogative parti [= modo, the speaker wishing that question, if nothing else, may be ansv ed. N.]: πῇ δή, 2, 339; ποῦ δή. b) tainly, truly, assuredly; ἢ δή, ἢ μάλα καὶ δή, δή που, assuredly indeed; δή α now again, which also by crasis f δῆΰτε; incorrect therefore is δ' αὐτι 340. 7, 448.

δηθά=δήν, abbrev. δήθ', 2, 435; long, a long time; δηθὰ μάλα, very l δηθύνω (δηθά), to delay, to loitei linger, 1, 27, and Od. 12, 121.

Δηϊκόων, ωντος. ὁ, son of Pergasu Trojan, slain by Agamemnon, 5, 534 from Δηϊκόων for Δηϊκάων, from δι δαΐς and κάω=κτείνω, slaying in bat

Δηϊοπίτης. ον, son of Priam, by Ulysses (Odysseus), 11, 420.

δήϊος, η, ον, Ion. for δάϊος (δαΐς), tile. destructive, ἀνήρ, πόλεμος; consuming fire. 6, 331. 2) Subst enemy. 2, 544. (ῐ; sometimes dissyll ηι with synizesis, 2, 415. 544. cf. Spi Pros § 6, 5, d.) *II.

δηϊοτής. ῆτος. ἡ (δήϊος), the tumu war, battle, contention; often Il. slaughter, massacre, Od. 12, 257.

Δηΐοχος, ὁ, a Greek. 15, 341.

δηϊόω, contr. δηόω (δήϊος), fut. δη aor. ἐδήωσα, aor pass. ἐδηώθην, pro treat in a hostile manner; to desola destroy, to cut down, to slaughter, to in pieces, with accus. and dat. inst ἔγχεϊ, χαλκῷ; ἀλλήλων ἀμφὶ στή ἀσπίδας, to destroy the shields each other's breasts, 5, 452; ἔλαφο tear in pieces a stag, 16, 158; περί to fight about any one, 18, 195, (δηϊ often resolved like verbs in αω: δη δηϊόψεν, etc.; the contr. form is f according to the necessity of the n δηΐουν δηϊώωσιν.)

Δηΐπυλος, ὁ, a companion of Sthen 5, 325.

Δηΐπυρος, ὁ, a Grecian hero, sla Helenus, 13 576.

Δηΐφοβος, ὁ, son of Priam and He one of the first heroes among the Tr 12, 94. 13, 413. In Od. 4, 276, h companied Helen to the hollow horse, and according to a late tradition became her husband after the death of Paris.

δηλέομαι, depon. mid. (δαίω), fut. δηλήσομαι, aor. 1 ἐδηλησάμην, 1) to destroy, in opposition to ὀνινάναι, h. Merc. 541; to harm, to injure, with accus. ῥινὸν, Od. 22, 278; Ἀχαιοὺς ὑπὲρ ὅρκια, to injure the Achaians contrary to the oaths, 4, 67. 72; to slay, Od. 11, 401. b) Of inanimate things: to destroy, to lay waste, καρπόν, 1, 156; ὅρκια ὑπερβασίῃ, to violate the oaths by transgression, 3, 107. 2) Intrans. to do injury, to do wrong, 14, 102; ὑπὲρ ὅρκια, to do wrong contrary to treaty, 4, 236. 271 (it is unnecessary to supply Ἀχαιούς, as 4, 67).

δήλημα, τό (δηλέομαι), injury, destruction, δηλήματα νηῶν, said of the winds (abstr. for concr.), Od. 12, 286.†

δηλήμων, ον, (δηλέομαι), gen. ονος, injurious, destructive, 24, 33. Subst. destroyer. βροτῶν δηλήμων, the destroyer of mortals, Od. 18, 85. 116.

*δηλητήρ, ῆρος, ὁ (δηλέομαι), destroyer, Ep. 15, 8.

*Δηλιάς, άδος, ἡ, Delian, belonging to the island Delos, h. Ap. 157.

Δῆλος, ἡ, Delos, a little island of the Ægean sea, which belonged to the Cyclades, with a town of the same name, birth-place of Apollo and Artĕmis, originally Ὀρτυγία, Od. 6, 162. h. in Ap. 16, 61 (prob. from δῆλος, visible, because Zeus caused it suddenly to emerge, when Latona was persecuted by Hērē).

δῆλος, η, ον (Ep. δέελος, 10, 466.†), visible, plain, manifest, Od. 20, 333.†

Δημήτηρ, gen. τερος and τρος, accus. μήτρα and Δήμητρα (prob. γῆ and μήτηρ, mother earth). Dēmētêr (Ceres), daughter of Kronus and Gæa (Tellus), sister of Zeus, mother of Persephŏnē by Zeus, the symbol of productive fruitfulness; hence, the tutelary deity of agriculture, and through this of civil order and law, 5, 500. She had a temple in Pyrasus in Thessalia, 2, 696. She loved Iasion, and by him bore Plutus, Od. 5, 125. Esply h. in Cer.

δημιοεργός, όν, Ep. for δημιουργός (ἔργον), prop. working for the public benefit; holding a public office; profitable to the commonwealth. Thus H., Od. 17, 383, characterizes seers, physicians, architects, bards, and Od. 19, 135, public heralds; metaph. ὄρθρος, the morning that calls forth the population to work, h. Merc. 98.

δήμιος, ον (δῆμος), relating to the people, pertaining to the commonwealth, public, οἶκος, Od. 20, 264; πρῆξις, a public affair, opposed to ἰδίη, Od. 3, 82; αἰσυμνῆται, Od. 8, 259. δήμιόν τι ἀγορεύειν, to speak any thing for the public good, Od. 2, 32; the neut. plur. δήμια πίνειν, adv. to drink at the public cost, 17, 250. According to Nitzsch on Od. 1, 226, wine which stood as a common stock in the tent of the chief leader, cf. 9, 71.

δημιουργός, see δημιοεργός.

δημοβόρος, ον (βορά), devouring the people, i. e. that consumes the property of the people, βασιλεύς, 1, 231.†

δημογέρων, οντος, ὁ (γέρων), an elder, one who for age and birth is honoured by the people, 3, 149; [Död. considers it a sort of popular tribune, or counsellor] the prince himself, 11, 372. *II.

Δημόδοκος, ὁ, the blind bard in the house of the king of the Phæaces, Alcinous in Scheria; the muse took away his sight and bestowed upon him the gift of song, Od. 8, 44 seq.

δημόθεν, adv. from the people, at the public expense, Od. 19, 197.†

Δημοκόων, ωντος, ὁ. son of Priam and of a female slave from Abydos, slain by Odysseus (Ulysses), 4, 499.

Δημολέων, οντος, ὁ, son of Antenor and Theānō, slain by Achilles, 20, 395.

Δημοπτόλεμος, ὁ, a suitor of Penelŏpē, Od. 22, 242.

δῆμος, ὁ, 1) the people, a community, 2, 547. Od. 1, 237, governed by one king or by several chiefs. In the heroic age, every community or district was independent; states, properly so called, did not exist; at the extent, smaller communities only attached themselves to a larger. Thus, among the Phæaces there were twelve princes; Alcinous was the thirteenth. As divisions of the people, H. mentions tribes and families (φῦλα and φρῆτραι). Further, he distinguishes 1) kings (ἄνακτες, βασιλῆες), 2) the chief men (γέροντες), and 3) the free citizens (δῆμος), who were by no means proper subjects of the king, but only obeyed him when the public good required it. Hence δήμου ἀνήρ, a man of the people, 2, 198; and as adj. δῆμος ἐών, perhaps for δήμιος, a man of the people, 12, 213. 2) the country, the territory, which a people occupied, often with gen. ἐν δήμῳ Ἰθάκης, Λυκίης, Φαιήκων; metaph. Ὀνείρων, the land of dreams, Od. 24, 12. κατὰ δῆμον, in the land, Od. 4, 167 [also (3) the country opp. the city, Od. 11, 14, Κιμμερίων ἀνδρῶν δῆμός τε πόλις τε. Död.] (prob. from δέμω, culture; according to Rost from th. ΔΑΜ, δαμάω, the subject folk. And so Död. cf. δέδμητο δὲ λαὸς ὑπ' αὐτῷ).

δημός, ὁ, fat, grease (prop. of the caul) of beasts, Il. and Od.; and of men, 8, 380.

Δημοῦχος, ὁ, son of Philêtôr, a Trojan slain by Achilles, 20, 457.

*Δημοφόων, ωντος, ὁ, Ep. for Δημοφῶν (from φάω, brightest of the people, cf. Etym. Mag.), son of Keleus and Metanīra, whom Dēmêtêr educated in Eleusis, h. in Cer. 234.

δήν (related to δή), long, a long time οὐδὲ δὴν ἦν, he lived not long, 6, 131 (before the δ the vowel always becomes long).

δηναιός, ή, όν (δήν), long-lasting, long-lived, 5, 407.†

δήνεα, τά (related to δήω), resolutions,

purposes, designs, thoughts; ἤπια, gentle thoughts, 4, 361; in a bad signif., artifices, plans, wiles, ὀλοφώϊα, Od. 10, 289 (Hesych. assumes τὸ δῆνος as sing.).

δήποτε, δήπου, in H. only separated see δή.

δηριάομαι, depon. mid. poet. (δῆρις), pres. infin. δηριάασθαι, Ep. for δηριᾶσθαι, imperf. 3 plur. δηριόωντο, Ep. for ἐδηριώντο (also aor. from δηρίομαι), to contend, to fight, with arms, Od. 8, 78; περὶ νεκροῦ, about a dead body, 17, 134; with words: ἀμφί τινι, 12, 421.

δηρίομαι, depon. aor. 1 mid. δηρισάμην, and aor. pass. ἐδηρίνθην, only in aor. in H. to contend, to fight, δηρίσαντο ἐπέεσσι, Od. 8, 76.† τὼ περὶ Κεβριόναο δηρινθήτην, they fought about Kebriones, 16, 756.†

δῆρις, ιος, ἡ, contention, fighting, combat, battle, 17, 158. Od. 24, 515.

δηρός, ή, όν (δήν) = δηναιός, long, long-lived. δηρὸν χρόνον, a long time, 14, 206. h. Cer. 282; the neut. δηρόν as adv. long, ἐπὶ δηρόν, for a long time, 9, 415.

δῆσε, Ep. for ἔδησε from δέω, but also for ἐδήησε from δέω, to want, see δεύω.

δήω, Ep. fut. without the tense characteristic, from ΔΑΩ, there occur δήεις, δήομεν, δήετε, I shall find; with accus. οὐκέτι δήετε τέκμωρ Ἰλίου, you will not accomplish the destruction of Troy, 9, 418. 685; ἄλσος, Od. 6, 291. (According to others, pres. with fut. signif.)

*Δηώ, οῦς, ἡ, a name of Démêtér (Ceres), h. in Cer. 492. (The deriv. uncertain; prob. from δήω, to find; see Spanhem. Call. in Cer. 133.)

Δία, see Ζεύς.

Δία, ἡ, the island Naxos, near Crete; ἐν Δίῃ, Od. 11, 325. It was called divine, because it was sacred to Dionysus (Bacchus.) See Ἀριάδνη.

διά, 1) Prepos. with gen. and dat., ground signif. through. 1) With gen. a) Of place: a) To indicate a motion which goes through an object and out again, διὰ ὤμου ἦλθεν ἔγχος, through the shoulder. ἔθυσεν διὰ προμάχων, 17, 281. For greater exactness of idea, H. connects διά with ἐκ and πρό, see διέκ and διαπρό. β) Of motion in place, without the connected idea of emerging: through, διὰ νήσου ἰών, Od. 12, 335. b) Of the manner, prop. post-Homeric: only ἔπρεπε καὶ διὰ πάντων, before all, 12, 104. 2) With accus. a) Of place, to denote extension through an object; only poet. διὰ δώματα, διὰ βήσσας, Il. b) Of time, to indicate extension through a period: διὰ νύκτα, through the night [by night], 2, 57 [in some passages, as here, the two ideas of time and place are combined, see Passow]. c) Of cause, means, etc. a) The cause: through, on account of, δι' ἀτασθαλίας, Od. 23, 67. β) The means: through, διὰ μαντοσύνην, 1, 72; Ἀθηναίης διὰ βουλάς, 15, 71. II) Adv. without case: through, esply in the compounds διαπρό, διέκ, q. v. III) In compos. it

denotes 1) A motion through any th 2) Completion and intenseness: t entirely. 3) Separation [often like in English]: apart, asunder. 4) Mu operation: with one another. 5) A r gling in colours and materials: διάλει mixed with white (διά prop. ` `, but so times long in the beginning of a ve 3, 357. 4, 135. 11, 436).

διαβαίνω (βαίνω), aor. 2 διέβην, par διαβάς, 1) Intrans. to place the apart, to stride, εὖ διαβάς ['par wide his feet for vantage' sake. Cp.] 458. 2) Trans. to go through, to cr to pass over; with accus. τάφρον, cross the ditch, 10, 198; and absol. Ἤλιδα, to cross to Elis, Od. 4, 635.

διαγιγνώσκω (γιγνώσκω), aor. 2 ii διαγνῶναι, to distinguish, to discrimi to inspect closely, τινά, 7, 124; ὀστέα 240. *Il.

διαγλάφω (γλάφω), aor. 1 partcp. γλάψας, to dig out, to hollow out, εὖ Od. 4, 438.†

διάγω (ἄγω), aor. 2 διήγαγον, 1) to duct through, to transport, τινά (by sl Od. 20, 187.† 2) to spend a perio time, to live, αἰῶνα, h. 19, 7.

διαδαίομαι (δαίω), Ion. to divide distribute, διὰ παῦρα δασάσκετο, 9, 3: see διαδατέομαι.

διαδάπτω (δάπτω), aor. 1 ἔδαψα, to in pieces, to lacerate, χρόα, *5, 858. 398.

διαδατέομαι, Ep. (δατέομαι), to tribute, διὰ κτῆσιν δατέοντο, 5, 158 †

διαδέρκομαι, depon. (δέρκομαι), ac διέδρακον, to look through, to see thro with accus. 14, 344.†

διαδηλέομαι, depon. mid. (δηλέομαι injure severely, to lacerate. ὀλίγοι κύνες διεδηλήσαντο, the dogs had ne torn thee to pieces, Od. 14, 37.†

διάει, see διάημι.

διαείδομαι, Ep. mid. (εἴδω), fut. είσομαι, 1) to let be seen, to show clee ἀρετήν, 8, 535. 2) to show oneself clee ἀρετῇ διαείδεται, 13, 277.

διαειπεῖν, poet. for διειπεῖν, q. v.

διάημι, Ep. (ἄημι), from the form δι 3 sing. imperf. διάει. to blow thro with accus. *Od. 5, 478. 19, 440.

διαθειόω (θειόω), to fumigate with b stone, Od. 22, 494.†

διαθρύπτω (θρύπτω), aor. 2 pass. ετρύφην, to break in pieces. ξίφος τρυφέν, 3, 363.†

διαίνω, aor. 1 ἐδίηνα, to moisten, to with accus., 21, 202. 22, 495. I διαίνετο ἄξων, *13, 30.

διαιρέω (αἱρέω), aor. 2 διεῖλον, 1 διέλον, to take apart, to separate, accus. only in tmesis, 20, 280.†

διακεάζω (κεάζω), aor. ἐκέασα, poet. to split apart, to split, ξύλα, in tm Od. 15, 322.†

διακείρω (κείρω), aor. 1 infin. διακέρ prop. to cut apart or in pieces; met to destroy, to render void, ἔπος, 8, 8.†

διακλάω (κλάω), aor. 1 διέκλασα,]

σσ, to break in pieces, with accus. τόξον, 5, 216.†

διακοιρανέω, formerly πολέας διακοιρανέοντο, 4, 230; now, more correctly, πολέας διὰ κοιρανέοντα, see κοιρανέω.

διακοσμέω (κοσμέω), fut. ήσω, to arrange separately, to divide, to place, τινά, 2, 476; διακοσμηθῆναι ἐς δεκάδας, to be divided into decades, 2, 126. διὰ τρίχα κοσμηθέντες. distributed into three parts, 2, 665. 2) Mid. to arrange throughout, to adorn, with accus. μέγαρον, Od. 22, 457.

διακριδόν, adv. (διακρίνω), distinctly, clearly, decidedly, ἄριστος, 12, 103. 15, 108.

διακρΐνω (κρίνω). fut. Ep. διακρινέω, for διακρῐνῶ, aor διέκρῑνα, aor. 1 pass. διεκρίθην and διεκρίνθην, optat. 2 plur. διακρινθεῖτε, infin. Ep. διακρινθήμεναι, partcp. διακρινθείς, 1) to separate from one another, to put asunder, with accus. αἰπόλια, 2, 475; to part, spoken esply of combatants: μένος ἀνδρῶν, 2, 387. cf. 7, 292; metaph. to distinguish, σῆμα, Od. 8, 195; hence pass. with fut. infin. mid., Od. 18, 149, to be separated, to separate, 2, 815; of combatants: to separate, to withdraw from each other, i. e. to end the contest, to become reconciled, 3, 98. οὐ γὰρ ἀναιμωτί γε διακρινέεσθαι ὀΐω μνηστῆρας καὶ κεῖνον, I do not think the suitors and he will separate without blood, Od. 18, 149. 20, 180.

διάκτορος, ὁ, a messenger, appell. of Hermês as messenger of the gods (in the Iliad this office is commonly discharged by Iris, cf. 2, 786), connected with Ἀργειφόντης, 2, 103; with Ἑρμῆς, Od. 12, 390. 15, 319; and often alone in the hymns. (Mly derived from διάγω: ὃς διάγει τὰς ἀγγελίας τῶν θεῶν, cf. Eustath. on 2, 103. Buttm. Lex., p. 230, derives it from an old theme διάκω, διώκω, intrans. I run, so that it is = διάκονος. Nitzsch, on Od. 1, 84, prefers the derivation from διάγω, and explains it: the conductor: [and so Död. cf. Ἑρμ. ἡγεμόνιος, πομπαῖος, ἐνόδιος, &c.: qui erranti comiter monstrat viam. His conducting the shades across the Styx is post-Homeric.]

διαλέγομαι (λέγω), Ep. aor. 1 διελεξάμην, to separate (in thought), to revolve, to ponder any thing, to reflect upon. τίη μοι ταῦτα διελέξατο θυμός; why did my heart ponder these things? •11, 407. 17, 97.

διαμάω (ἀμάω), fut. ήσω, to mow through, to cut through, with accus., χιτῶνα [ripp'd wide his vest. Cp.], •3, 359. 7, 253.

διαμελεῖστί, adv. (μελεϊστί), limb from limb, piecemeal, τάμνειν, •Od. 9, 291. 18, 339.

διαμετρέω (μετρέω), to measure through, to measure off, χῶρον, 3, 315.†

διαμετρητός, ή, όν (μετρέω), measured off. measured, χῶρος, 3, 344.†

•διαμήδομαι = μήδομαι, Ep. 4, 12, doubtf.

διαμοιράομαι, dep. mid. (μοιράω), to divide into parts, to separate. ἔπταχα πάντα διεμοιρᾶτο, divided them all into seven pieces, Od. 14, 434;† in the following, τὴν ἴαν—θῆκεν, supply μοῖραν.

διαμπερές, adv. 1) through and through, entirely through, 5, 284. Od. 5, 480; with gen. 12, 429. 20, 362. κλήρῳ νῦν πεπάλαχθε διαμπερές, cast lots throughout, 7, 171. 2) Spoken of time: continually, uncessingly. αἰεὶ διαμπερές, ἤματα πάντα διαμπερές, 15, 70. 16, 99 (from διά, ἀνά, and πέρας, with epenthetic μ).

διάνδιχα, adv. (διά, ἀνά, δίχα), in two ways, in two parts; μερμηρίζειν, to be of two opinions, to hesitate, to ponder anxiously, 1, 198. 13, 455; with ἤ, ἤ following: σοὶ διάνδιχα δῶκε, he hath given to you in a divided manner, i. e. but one of two things, 9, 37. Schol. διῃρημένως.

διανύω (ἀνύω), fut. ύ'σω, aor. διήνυσα, to complete entirely, to finish; ὁδόν, to finish a way or journey, h. Cer. 380. κακότητα διήνυσεν ἀγορεύων, he finished narrating his sufferings, i. e. he recounted his sufferings to the end, •Od. 17, 517.†

διαπείρω (πείρω), to pierce through, 16, 405.† in tmesis.

διαπέρθω (πέρθω), fut. διαπέρσω, aor. 1 διέπερσα, aor. 2 διέπραθον, infin. διαπραθέειν, Ep. for διεπραθεῖν, aor. 2 mid. διεπραθόμην, to destroy utterly, to lay waste, to ravage, with accus. πόλιν, ἄστυ. 2) Mid. only aor. 2, to perish, Od. 15, 384.

διαπέταμαι, depon. mid. (πέταμαι), aor. 2 διεπτάμην, to fly through, spoken of missiles, 5, 99; absol. to fly away, 15, 83. Od. 1, 320.

•διαπλέκω, (πλέκω), fut. ξω, to interweave, to entangle, to weave together, h. in Merc. 80.

διαπλήσσω (πλήσσω), to break in pieces, to split, with accus. δρῦς, 23, 120.† Thus Wolf; where others read διαῤῥήσσοντες or διαπλίσσοντες.

διαπορθέω, poet. = διαπέρθω, from which partcp. aor. 1 διαπορθήσας, 2, 691.†

διαπραθέειν, see διαπέρθω.

•διαπρέπω (πρέπω), to be prominent, to be visible, h. Merc. 351.

διαπρήσσω (πρήσσω, Ion. for πράσσω), to bring to an end, to accomplish, to finish, with accus. κέλευθον, Od. 2, 213; also without κέλευθον, they marched through the plain, 2, 785; with partcp. ἤματα διέπρησσον πολεμίζων, I spent days in fighting, 9, 326. ἄπαντα οὔτι διαπρήξαιμι λέγων ἐμὰ κήδεα, if I were to recount to you my sufferings for a year, I should not get through them all, Od. 14, 197.

διαπρό (πρό), through and out, entirely through, Wolf in the Il. διαπρό, in the Od. διὰ πρό, 5, 66. Od. 22, 295; cf. Spitzner, Excurs. XIV. on Il.

•διαπρύσιον, adv. passing through, spoken of place: πρὶν πεδίοιο διαπρύσιον τετυχηκώς, a hill extending far into the

F 6

plain, 17, 748. 2) *piercing, loud* of sound, ἤϋσεν, 8, 227. h. Ven. 80; prop. neut. from

*διαπρύσιος, ον, *passing through, penetrating, piercing*, h. Ven. 19; κεραϊστής, h. Merc. 336 (prob. Æol. from περάω).

διαπτοιέω (πτοέω), *to frighten away, to scare*, with accus. γυναῖκας, Od. 18, 340.†

*διαπυρπαλαμάω, see πυρπαλαμάω.

διαρπάζω (ἀρπάζω), *to tear in pieces, to lacerate*, spoken of wolves: μῆλα, 16, 355.

διαρραίω (ῥαίω), fut. σω, aor. 1 infin. διαρραῖσαι, *to break in pieces entirely, to destroy utterly;* with accus. of inanimate things: πόλιν, οἶκον, *to destroy;* of men, 9, 78. 2) Mid. fut. διαρραίσομαι, with pass. signif. τάχα δ᾽ ἄμμε διαρραίσεσθαι ὀΐω, quickly I think, we shall both be destroyed, 24, 355. (So the Schol. διαφθαρήσεσθαι; Damm and Voss take the infin. fut. in an act. signif. and supply αὐτόν.)

διαρρήγνυμι (ῥήγνυμι), *to break through, to break in pieces;* with accus. only mid. διαρρήξασθαι ἐπάλξεις *to break through* the breastworks, 12, 308.†

*διαρρήδην, adv. (διαρρηθῆναι), *with clear words, distinctly*, h. Merc. 313.

διαρρίπτω (ῥίπτω), *to throw through, to shoot through,* only Ep. imperf. 3 sing. διαρρίπτασκεν ὀϊστόν, Od. 19, 575.†

διασεύω (σεύω), only 3 sing. Ep. aor. 2 mid. διέσσυτο, with accus. λαόν, *to hurry through the people,* 2, 450; often with gen. τάφροιο, *through the ditch,* 10, 194; spoken of missiles, with gen. στέρνοιο, 15, 542; ἐκ μεγάροιο, Od. 4, 37.

διασκεδάννυμι (σκεδάννυμι), fut. σκεδάσω (ἄ), aor. διεσκέδασα, *to scatter,* with accus. δούρατα, Od. 5, 370; *to destroy,* νῆα, Od. 7, 275; metaph. ἀγλαΐας τινί, *to dissipate one's arrogance,* Od. 17, 244.

διασκίδνημι (σκίδνημι), poet. form from διασκεδάννυμι, *to scatter,* νέφεα, 5, 526.†

διασκοπιάομαι, depon. mid. (σκοπιάζω), *to look down around from an elevation, to watch, to observe,* with accus. ἕκαστα, *10, 388. 17, 252.

διασχίζω (σχίζω), aor. 1 διέσχισα, aor. 1 pass. διεσχίσθην, *to split asunder, to tear in pieces,* with accus. ἱστία, Od. 9, 71. Pass. 16, 316.

διατάμνω, Ep. for διατέμνω, and aor. 2 διέταμον, *to cut through,* 17, 522. 618, in tmesis; Ep. form διατμήγω.

διατελευτάω (τελευτάω), *to finish entirely,* to accomplish fully, with accus. 19, 90.†

*διατίθημι (τίθημι), aor. 1 διέθηκε, *to place apart, to put, to place, to lay,* θεμείλια, h. Ap. 254. 294.

διατινάσσω (τινάσσω), aor. 1 διετίναξα, *to shake apart, to dash in pieces,* with accus. σχεδίην, Od. 5, 363.† in tmesis.

διατμήγω (τμήγω), Ep. for διατέμνω, aor. 1 διέτμηξα, aor. 2 διέτμαγον, aor. 2 pass. διετμάγην, 1) *to cut through, to cut in pieces;* κηροῖο τροχὸν τυτθά, Od. 12, 174; δόρυ χαλκῷ, Od. 8, 507; metaph.

νηχόμενος λαῖτμα διέτμαγον, swimm I cut through the deep, Od. 7, 276. 5, 409. 2) Mly, *to separate, to sca* Ἀχαιούς, 21, 3; νῆας, Od. 3, 291. P 1) *to be cut in pieces, to be divi* σανίδες διέτμαγεν, Ep. for διετμάγη 12. 462. 2) *to separate, to scatter,* 354; *to part,* 1, 531. 7, 302. cf. ἀρθμέ

διατρέχω (τρέχω), aor. 2 διέδραμον *run through,* with accus. κέλευθα, ὕδ *Od. 3, 177. 5, 100.

διατρέω (τρέω), aor. 1 διέτρεσα, *to away from fear, to scatter,* *11, 481.

διατρίβω (τρίβω), aor. 1 διέτριψα *rub or bruise in pieces,* with accus. ῥί 11. 847. 2) Spoken of time: prop. suba χρόνον, *to spend time,* and as intrans *linger, to delay,* τινός, about any thi ὁδοῖο, a journey, Od. 2, 404; hence, *to procrastinate, to check, to hinder,* w accus. Od. 2, 265; χόλον, 4, 42; so μητ γάμον, Od. 20, 341; with double acc διατρίβει Ἀχαιοὺς γάμον, *to put off* Achaians about the marriage, Od. 2, 2

διάτριχα, adv. *in three ways, in th parts;* Wolf always writes διὰ τρί it is only in h. Cer. 86, that διάτριχα found; cf. Spitz. on Il. 2, 655.

διατρύγιος, ον (τρύγη), ὄρχος, Od. 342,† a vineyard whose grapes ripen different times (διά), Eustath., or who grain is sown between the rows of vin The first is correct.

διατρυφέν, see διαθρύπτω.

διαφαίνομαι (φαίνω), only mid. *to sh through, to be visible, to appear,* with g νεκύων, between the dead, 8, 491; spok of a glowing body, *to sparkle, to shi brightly,* Od. 9, 379.

*διαφέρω (φέρω), only fut. mid. δι σομαι, *to bear apart;* mid. *to differ, contend, to be at variance,* h. Merc. 25

διαφθείρω (φθείρω), fut. διαφθέρο perf. 2 διέφθορα, 1) *to destroy utterly, desolate,* with accus. πόλιν, 13, 625. The second perf. intrans. *to perish,* li perii: μαινόμενε — διέφθορας, thou rushing to destruction, 15, 128. (Sch διέφθαρσαι.)

διαφορέω (φορέω), a form of φέρω, disperse, to spread abroad,* κλέος, Od. 333.†

διαφράζω (φράζω), only Ep. aor. διεπέφραδον, *to speak clearly, to show d tinctly,* τινί τι, 18, 9. Od. 6, 47.

διαφύσσω (φύσσω), aor. 1 διήφυσα, E διάφυσσα, 1) Prop. *to draw through, draw out* any thing from a vessel to bottom, with accus. οἶνον, Od. 16, 1 2) Metaph. *to pierce, to cut through, lacerate,* cf. Virg. Æn. II. 600, hauri διήφυσε σαρκός, he (the boar) tore t flesh, Od. 19. 450: so also in tmesis, b τ᾽ ἔντερα χαλκὸς ἤφυσε, the brass [we pon] cut through the entrails, 13, 507.

διαχέω, Ep. διαχεύω (χέω), only aor. 3 plur. διέχευαν, *to pour out, to diffu* 2) In H. only: *to divide, to carve, to d tribute,* spoken of slain victims, wl accus. 7, 316. Od. 3, 456.

διάω, more correctly διαέω, see διάημι.

*διδάσκαλος, ὁ, ἡ, a teacher, a female teacher, h. Merc. 556.

διδάσκω (δάω), aor. 1 act. ἐδίδαξα, Ep. ἐδιδάσκησα, h. Cer. 144; perf. pass. δεδίδαγμαι, to teach, to instruct. a) With accus. of the thing: πάντα, 9, 442. b) With accus. of the pers. τινά, 11, 832. c) With double accus. τινά τι, to teach a man any thing, 23, 307. Od. 8, 481; for accus. the infin. δμῶας ἔργα ἐργάζεσθαι, to teach the maids to perform work, Od. 1, 384. 22, 422; hence, pass. to be instructed, to learn, τὶ πρός τινος, to learn any thing from any one, 11, 831; and partcp. with gen. διδασκόμενος πολέμοιο [a learner yet of martial feats. Cp.], 16, 811.

δίδημι, Ep. form, from δέω, to bind; from which, δίδη, 3 imperf. for ἐδίδη, 11, 105.†

διδοῖ, διδοῖσθα, see δίδωμι.

διδυμάων, ονος, ὁ (δίδυμος), a twin-brother, only in dual and plur. connected with παῖς, and alone, 5, 548.

δίδυμος, η, ον, double, twofold, αὐλοί, Od. 19, 227. 2) twins, in plur. 23, 641. (prob. from δίς.)

δίδωμι, fut. δώσω, aor. 1 ἔδωκα, and δῶκα, only in indicat. sing. aor. 2 act. (ἔδων), only in plur. indicat. ἔδομεν, etc. and in the subj., optat., imperat., perf. pass. δέδομαι. H. has: 1) Also forms from διδόω, pres. διδοῖς and διδοῖσθα, 19, 270; (incorrectly διδοῖσθα, διδοῖ, imperf. ἐδίδου for ἐδίδου, and fut. διδώσομεν, Od. 13, 358; infin. διδώσειν, Od. 24, 314. 2) Forms with lengthened stem-vowel: pres. imperat. δίδωθι, Od. 3, 380; infin. διδοῦναι for διδόναι (not aor. 2, 24, 425. 3) The iterat. forms of aor. 2, δόσκον, δόσκε, Od. 19, 76. 1) to give, to present, to bestow, τινί τι, 1, 123; in reference to the gods, to offer to devote, θεοῖσι ἑκατόμβας, 7, 450; spoken of the gods, to grant, to accord, εὖχος, νίκην, κῦδος, often of evils: to decree, to inflict, ἄλγεα, κήδεα, 1, 96. Od. 7, 242. b) With accus. "the pers. τινά τινι, to give over, to deliver, νέκυν πυρί, κυσίν, 17, 127; τινα ὀδύνῃσιν, ἀχέεσσι, 5, 397; esply of parents, who give their daughters in marriage to a man: θυγατέρα ἀνδρί, 6, 192. 11, 226. c) An infin. is often added, which serves as a further limitation of the sentence: δῶκε τεύχεα Ἐρευθαλίωνι φορῆναι, he gave arms to Ereuthalion to bear, 7, 149; and with the infin. pass. πολεμόνδε φέρεσθαι, 11, 798. cf. 23, 183. 2) With accus. and infin. to give, to grant, to let, to permit, αὐτὸν πρηνέα δὸς πεσέειν, let him fall prone, 6, 307. 3) Pass. only once: σύ τοι δέδοται πολεμήϊα ἔργα, the works of war are not accorded to thee, 5, 428.

δίε, see δίω.

διέργω, Ep. for διείργω (ἔργω), to separate, to keep apart, with accus. τοὺς διέεργον ἐπάλξιες, 12, 424.†

διέδραμον, see διατρέχω.

διειπον (εἶπον), a defect. aor. 2, of which occur only imper. διειπε, infin. διαειπέμεν, Ep. for διειπεῖν, prop. to speak through, to finish speaking; then, to speak clearly, distinctly, with dat. of the person, 10, 425. διαειπέμεν ἀλλήλοισιν, to converse fully with each other, Od. 4, 215.

διείρομαι, poet. and Ion. (ἔρομαι), only pres. to question strictly, to interrogate strictly, τί, 1, 550; and τινά τι, any one about any thing, 15, 93. Od. 4, 292.

διέκ (διά, ἐκ), entirely, through; Wolf in the Il. correctly, διέκ, 15, 124; but in Od. δι᾽ ἐκ. Od. 17, 61. 10, 388. cf. Spitzner Excurs. XVIII.

διελαύνω (ἐλαύνω), aor. 1 διήλασα, 1) Trans. to drive through, τί τινος; ἵππους τάφροιο, 10, 564; to thrust through, ἔγχος λαπάρης, a spear through the loins, 16, 318; δόρυ ἀσπίδος, 13, 161. 2) Intrans. to pass through, to hurry through, with accus. ὄρη, h. Merc. 96.

διελθέμεν, see διέρχομαι.

δίεμαι, mid. (ΔΙΗΜΙ), like τίθεμαι, in H. there occur of the pres. 3 plur. δίενται, subj. δίηται, δίωνται, optat. δίοιτο (cf. τίθοιτο), infin. δίεσθαι, 1) Intrans. to become terrified, to fly, spoken of horses: δίενται πεδίοιο, they fly through the plain, 23, 475; of lions: σταθμοῖο δίεσθαι, to let himself be driven from the enclosure, 12, 304. 2) Oftener trans. [as causative] to terrify, to chase away, to drive, with accus. 7, 197; δηίους, 12, 276; ξεῖνον ἀπὸ μεγάροιο, Od. 20, 343; ἵππους προτὶ ἄστυ, to drive the steeds to the city, 15, 681; spoken of a dog: κνώδαλον, ὅ, ττι δίοιτο, Od. 17, 317. (Rem. δίεμαι together with the above cited forms belongs to the act. ΔΙΗΜΙ, which has the trans. signif. to chase, to terrify, of which the 3 plur. imperf. ἐνδίεσαν still occurs. The mid. means either to let oneself be driven, or it has the signif. of the act. with a weak reflexive sense; δίω on the contrary is always intrans. and signifies to fear [but Il. 22, 251 τρὶς περὶ ἄστυ . . . δίον, fled, with var. lect. δίες. Död.].

διέξειμι (ἔξειμι), to pass through any thing. τῇ ἔμελλε διεξίμεναι πεδίονδε, there he was about to pass out into the plain, 6, 393.†

διεξερέομαι (ἐρέομαι, Ep. form, from εἴρομαι), to question closely, to scrutinize, τινά τι, 10, 432.†

διεπέφραδε, see διαφράζω.

διέπραθον, see διαπέρθω.

διέπτατο, see διαπέταμαι.

διέπω (ἔπω), imperf. δίειπον and δίεπον, 1) to manage, to direct, to administer, τί, e. g. πόλεμον, to prosecute the war, 1, 166. Od. 12, 16. 2) to arrange, to put in order, to command, στρατόν, 2, 207; ἀνέρας σκηπανίῳ, to drive away the men with a staff, 24, 247.

διερέσσω (ἐρέσσω), aor. διήρεσα, poet. σσ, to row through, χερσί, with the hands, *Od. 12, 444. 14, 351.

διερός, ή, όν, only twice in the Od. and a word of doubtful signif. The ancients explained it, *wet, moist*; metaph. *fresh, lively, living.* (Eustath. after Aristarch. ζώς, σπουδαῖος, and derived it from διαίνω); hence, διερὸς βροτός, a vigorous (living) mortal, Od. 6, 201. (Others read here δνερός from δνή, unhappy.) διερῶ ποδὶ φευγέμεν, tο fly with swift foot, Od. 9, 43. Nitzsch on Od. 6, 201, takes as the prop. signif. *liquid, flowing,* liquidus; metaph. *active, moveable.* He construes the sentence thus: οὗτος ἀνήρ, ὅς κεν ἵκηται φέρων δηϊότητα, οὐκ ἔστι διερὸς βρ. οὐδὲ γένηται, and paraphrases it, 'neither now nor ever shall that man move actively and well, who penetrates with hostile force into the land of the Phæaces.' Voss, 'there moves not yet a mortal man, nor shall there ever be one, who,' etc. Lehrs de Aristarch. stud. p. 59 [and so Död.], derives διερός from δίεμαι (cf. στυγερός), and explains it, Od. 9, 43, by *fugax*; but Od. 6, 201, act. *fugator.* ' *Non est iste vir fugator homo,* i. e. *non is est, quem fugere opus sit.*'

διέρχομαι (ἔρχομαι), fut. διελεύσομαι, aor. 2 διῆλθον, infin. Ep. διαλθέμεν, *to go through, to pass through, to traverse,* with accus. πῶϋ, the flock, 3, 198; ἄστυ, 6, 392; with gen. μεγάροιο, Od. 6. 304. 2) *to pass through, to pierce,* spoken of missiles, with gen. χροός, to pierce through the skin, 20, 100; absol. 23, 876. 3) Metaph. *to go over, to reflect upon,* μετὰ φρεσί τι, h. Ven. 277.

διέσσυτο, see διασεύω.

διέτμαγεν, see διατμήγω.

διέχω (ἔχω), aor. 2 διέσχον, only intrans. *to go through, to penetrate, to pierce,* to pass through a body and come forth on the opposite side, spoken of an arrow: διὰ δ' ἔπτατο ὀϊστός, ἀντικρὺ δὲ διέσχε, the arrow flew through and came forth on the other side, 5, 100; so also 11, 253. 20, 416. In like manner δι' ὤμου ἔγχος ἔσχεν, 13, 520.

δίζημαι, Ep. depon. mid., fut. διζήσομαι, Od. 16, 239 (from δίζω), *to seek out, to search for,* τινά, 4, 88; or with εἴπου. 2) *to seek to procure, to be at pains, to strive;* absol. ἔκαστος μνάσθω ἐέδνοισιν διζήμενος, let each one woo, striving with presents, Od. 16, 391; νόστον τινί, to seek to accomplish one's return, Od. 23, 253; and with accus. alone, Od. 11, 100. (An Ion. word, with η retained.)

δίζυξ, υγος, ὁ, ἡ (ζυγόν), pl. δίζυγες, *harnessed in pairs,* or *two abreast,* ἵπποι, *5, 195. 10, 473.

δίζω, only imperf. δίζε, *to doubt, to be doubtful, to be uncertain,* with ἤ, 16, 713.†

διηκόσιοι, αι, α, Ep. for διακόσιοι, *two hundred,* Il.

διηνεκής, ές (διανέκω, i. q. διαφέρω), *continuous, uninterrupted,* continuus, the adj. spoken only of place: *far-extending, long, great,* ῥάβδος, 12, 297; νῶτος, 7, 321; ῥίζαι διηνεκέες, 12, 134; ἀτραπιτοί, far-extending ways, Od. 13, 195; ὦλξ, the continuous or long furrow, Od. 18, 375. The adv. διηνεκέως with

ἀγορεύειν, *to recount at large,* in natural order, Od. 7, 241. 12, 56.

διήρεσα, see διερέσσω.

δίηται, see δίεμαι.

δίημι (ἵημι), *to send through, to th* *through, to discharge,* with gen. only tmesis. διὰ δ' ἧκε σιδήρου, *Od. 21,*

δϊκνέομαι, depon. mid. (ἱκνέομαι), διΐξομαι, aor. διϊκόμην, *to go thro* only metaph. *to narrate at length,* πά *9, 61. 19, 186.

Διϊπετής, ές (Διὸς, πίπτω), fallen f Zeus, i. e. from the air, *descending* *heaven,* an appell. of rivers, because are swollen by rain, 17, 263; an Αἴγυπτος (Nile), Od. 4, 477. Later οἰωνοί, h. in Ven. 4 (the second ι lon

διΐστημι (ἵστημι), only intrans. a διέστην, dual διαστήτην, and pres. διΐσταμαι, 1) *to open, to divide itsel* *separate,* 12, 86; θάλασσα, the sea vided, 13, 29. 2) Metaph. *to diffe* *quarrel.* ἐξ οὗ—διαστήτην ἐρίσαντε, quarrelled and were alienated, *1, 6.

[Δίφιλος = Διῒ φίλος, thus Fre and others, 1, 74. cf. Jahr. J. und p. 258]

δικάζω (δίκη), fut. δικάσω, aο ἐδίκασα, Ep. σσ, 1) Act. spoken judge: *to judge, to pronounce sent* *to decide* between two parties, with τινί; Τρωσί τε καὶ Δαναοῖσι δικάζέτ him decide the controversy bet the Trojans and Greeks, 8, 431. τ (σκήπτροις) ἔπειτ' ἤϊσσον ἀμοιβηδ δίκαζον, with these they (γέροντες) and in turn delivered their sentenc 506. ἐς μέσον ἀμφοτέροισι δικάσ decide (ye princes), between the according to equity. Thus speaks Ν laus, 23, 574, when Antilochus, a games of Patroclus, received the s prize, which was prop. due to Eum Menelaus now also lays claim because Antilochus had artfully im his chariot, v. 579. εἰ δ' ἄγε, ἐγὼν δικάσω, come on, said he at last, self will deliver a judgement; he proposes that Antilochus should that he did not intentionally imped chariot, Od. 11, 547; spoken of κρυπτάδια, to take secret resolutio 542. 2) Mid. of the parties: *to* *law, to bring a matter before a cour* 11, 545. 12, 440.

δίκαιος, η, ον (δίκη), *just, righ* *practising justice,* one who fulfils right demands towards gods and thus Chirôn, 11, 832; the Abii, 13, 181; on the other hand, the suit οὐδὲ δίκαιοι, Od. 2, 282, as al Cyclôps, Od. 8, 575 (because they vi the universally sacred rites of hospi Compar. δικαιότερος, and superl. τατος.

δικαίως, adv. *justly, in a be* *manner,* μνάσθαι, Od. 14, 90.†

δικασπόλος, ὁ (πολέω), *a judge, o* *dispenses justice,* 1, 238; with ἀν 11, 186.

*δικάρηνος, ον (κάρηνον), two-headed, Batr. 300.

*δικέρως, ωτος, ὁ (κέρας), two-horned, epith. of Pan, h. 18. 2.

δίκη, ἡ, 1) Originally, usage, custom. right, that which is introduced by custom, ἥ᾽ ἐστὶ δίκη βασιλήων, Od. 4, 691; θεῶν, Od. 19, 43. αὕτη δίκη ἐστὶ βροτῶν, this is the lot of mortals, Od. 11, 218; δμώων, Od. 14, 59. 2) right, justice, a cause or suit. δίκης ἐπιδευὲς ἔχειν, to lack justice, 19, 180. δίκην ἐξελαύνειν, to expel. to pervert justice, 16, 388; τίειν, Od. 14, 84. εἰπεῖν δίκην, to speak justice, to pronounce (spoken of a judge), 18, 508. b) In the plur. δίκαι, the administration of justice, 16, 542. Od. 11, 570. 3) cause, suit; διδόναι καὶ λαμβάνειν, to give and receive right, i. e. to submit a cause and receive a decision, h. Merc. 312.

δικλίς, ίδος, ἡ (κλίνω), bent double, double, folding, epith. of [two-leaved] doors, πύλαι, θύραι, 12, 455. Od. 2, 345.

δίκτυον, τό, a fishing-net, Od. 22, 386.†

δινεύω and δινέω (δίνη), (δινεύω only pres. and imperf. iterat. δινεύεσκεν), from δινέω also aor. 1 pass. δινηθείς, 1) Act. to turn in a circle or vortex, to whirl, to move around, σόλον, 23, 840; ζεύγεα, to drive around. 18, 543; μοχλόν, to twirl the stake, Od. 9, 388. 2) Intrans. to turn oneself in a circle, spoken of dancers, 18, 494; metaph. to wander about, to move around, κατὰ μέσσον, 4, 541; παρὰ ὄνα, 24, 12; κατὰ οἶκον, Od. 19, 67; in like manner in pass. ὄσσε δινείσθην, the eyes rolled around, 17, 680; to walk about, Od. 9, 153. ἐπὶ ἄστεα δινηθῆναι, Od. 16, 63.

δίνη, ἡ, a vortex, a whirlpool, in a river, *21, 11. 132.

δινήεις, εσσα, εν (δίνη), whirling, full of whirlpools, epith. of a river, 2, 877. Od. 11, 242.

δινωτός, ή, όν (δινόω), prop. turned in a circle; in H. turned round, formed round (well-turned), λέχεα, 3, 391; κλισίη, Od. 19, 56. ἀσπὶς ῥινοῖσι βοῶν καὶ νώροπι χαλκῷ δινωτή, a curved or arched shield made of bull's hide and glittering brass, 13, 407.

Διογενής. έος, ὁ, ἡ (γένος). sprung from Zeus, Jove-born, a common epith. of heroes and kings, because they receive their dignity from Zeus, the king of kings, cf. 1, 337. Od. 2, 352.

Διόθεν, adv. (Διός), from Zeus, according to the will of Zeus, 15, 489. 24, 194.

διοϊστεύω (ὀϊστεύω), fut. σω, to shoot an arrow through, τινός, any thing, Od. 19, 573. 21, 76. 97. 2) Absol. to shoot an arrow, Od. 12, 102.

διοίσομαι, see διαφέρω.

δίοιτο, see δίεμαι.

*διοιχνέω (οἰχνέω), to go through, to walk about, h. 3, 10.

Διοκλῆς, ῆος, ὁ, 1) son of Orsilochus, grandson of Alpheus, father of Crethon and Orsilochus, king of Pheræ in Messenia, 5, 542. Telemachus spent the night with him, Od. 3, 488; prob. a

vassal of Agamemnon, cf. 9, 151. 2) one of the princes of Eleusis, whom Dêmêtêr taught the ceremonies of the sacred service, h. Cer. 473 (but v. 153 Διόκλου).

διόλλυμι (ὄλλυμι), perf. II. διόλωλα, trans. to destroy utterly. 2) Mid. and perf. II. intrans. to perish utterly. οὐδ᾽ ἔτι καλὸς οἶκος ἐμὸς διόλωλε, and my house is no longer ruined with any show of decency, i e. formerly ye did it with moderation, but now without any regard to decency, Od. 2, 64.†

Διομήδη, ἡ, daughter of Phorbus, slave of Achilles, 9, 665.

Διομήδης, εος, ὁ, accus. η, and εα, son of Tydeus and Deipýlê, husband of Ægialea, king of Argos, 5, 412. He took part in the second expedition against Thebes, 4, 406; and went to Troy with 80 ships, 2, 568. He was among the bravest in the army, and performed many exploits, which H. celebrates in the fifth book (Διομήδους ἀριστεία). He exchanged armour with the Lycian Glaucus, an hereditary guest, 6, 230. According to H., he returned happily to Argos, Od. 3, 180; according to later tradition, he directed his course, after his return, to lower Italy, where he built the town Arpi.

Δῖον, τό, a town in Eubœa, on the promontory Kenæon, 2, 538.

Διόνυσος, Ep. Διώνυσος, ὁ, son of Zeus and Semelê, god of wine and joy, 14, 325; h. 6, 56. H. was acquainted with the insult offered him in Thrace. Him, the drunken divinity, the Thracian Lycurgus would not tolerate, so that he fled to Thetis into the sea, 6, 132, seq. According to Od. 11, 325, the poet was also acquainted with his love for Ariadnê. (The word according to Voss, signifies the god of Nysa, or, according to Herm., Torculus, from διά and an old verb, from wꞁich ὄνυξ is derived.)

διοπτεύω (ὀπτεύω), to observe closely, to look about, 10, 451.†

διοπτήρ, ῆρος, ὁ, a spy, a scout, 10, 562.†

διορύσσω (ὀρύσσω), partcp. aor. 1 διορύξας, to dig through; τάφρον, to open a ditch or furrow, Od. 21, 120.†

δῖος, δῖα, δῖον (from Διὸς for δῖιος), prop. sprung from Zeus, prob. 9, 538; then generally. divine, exalted, great, glorious, excellent. 1) As epith. of the gods, only in fem. δῖα θεά, glorious goddess, 10, 290; often δῖα θεάων, most exalted of goddesses, δῖα Χάρυβδις, Od. 12, 104. 2) Of distinguished men, not heroes merely, but others: noble. excellent, δῖος ὑφορβός, Od. 14, 48 : of entire people : δῖοι Ἀχαιοί, δῖοι ἑταῖροι (Σαρπηδόνος), 5, 692. 3) Of noble animals : ot horses; ἵππος, 8, 185. 4) Of inanimate things, as the earth, sea, cities (cf. ἱερός), since they are under the divine influence or derive their origin from gods, Od. 5, 261. Il. 16, 365.

Δῖος, ὁ, son of Priam, 24, 251.

*Διόσκουροι, οἱ, sons of Zeus, chiefly

Castôr and Polydeukês (*Pollux*), only divided, Διὸς κοῦροι, h. 16, and 33, 1. 9.

Διοτρεφής, ές (τρέφω), *nourished by Zeus*, epith. of kings, see Διογενής, and of Scamandrus, 21, 223; ἄνθρωποι, Od. 5, 378.

δίπλαξ, ακος, ἡ, *laid double, laid twofold, in double layers*, δημός, 23, 243. 2) As subst. ἡ, *a double mantle*, a mantle that can be wrapt around double. cf. Od. 13, 224. Il. 10, 134; others say, a garment of double texture, the ground being white, the figures purple, or generally. of double texture, 3, 126. 22, 441; in Il. ἡ δίπλαξ χιτών, Od. 19, 241.

διπλόος, η, ον, contr. only in fem. διπλῆ, *double, two-fold*, θώρηξ, 4, 133; χλαῖνα, a double mantle, 10, 134. Od. 19, 226.

δίπτυχος, ον (πτύσσω), *double-folded, laid double*, λώπη, a double garment, Od. 13, 224. Also neut. plur. δίπτυχα ποιεῖν, to lay double, i. e. to lay the flesh or thigh pieces of the victims upon a layer of fat, and upon this to place still another, 1, 461. Od. 3, 458.

Δίς, ὁ, obs. nom. of the oblique cases Διός, Διΐ, Δία, of Ζεύς, q. v.

δίς, adv. *twice, double*, Od. 9, 491.†

δισθανής, ές (θανεῖν), *twice dead*, Od. 12, 22.†

δισκέω (δίσκος), *to cast the discus*. δίσκῳ ἐδίσκεον ἀλλήλοισιν, among one another, Od. 8, 188.†

δίσκος, ὁ (δικεῖν), *the discus, the quoit*, a round flat stone, with a hole and thong in the middle with which to hurl it. It was as early as H.'s time a common sport, to cast this, 2, 774. Od. 4, 626; he who cast it furthest receiving the prize, esply Od. 8, 186; δίσκου οὖρα, 23, 431. It is distinct from the σόλος, q. v.

δίσκουρα, τά (οὖρον), *the distance to which the discus was cast*. ἐς δίσκουρα λέλειπτο, he was left a quoit's cast behind, 23, 523.† cf. οὖρον.

*διττός, ή, όν (Ep. δισσός), *two-fold, double*, Batr. 61.

διφάω, *to seek out, to trace*; τήθεα, to seek oysters, spoken of a diver, 16, 747.†

δίφρος, ὁ (for διφόρος), 1) Prop. the *chariot-seat*, for two persons, the *double seat* in the war-chariot for the charioteer and the warrior, 5, 160. 23, 132. It was round, partly open for mounting, and hung upon straps, 5, 727; sometimes in the Il. it signifies the *war-chariot* itself; a *travelling-carriage* with two seats, Od. 3, 324. 2) Mly, *a seat, a chair*, and, as it seems, a low one, 3, 424. Od. 4, 717.

δίχα, adv. 1) *divided into two parts: double*. δίχα πάντα ἀρίθμεον, in two bands, Od. 10, 203. 2) Metaph. *of two sorts, in two ways, different*, 18, 510; θυμὸν ἔχειν, to have different sentiments, 20, 32; βάζειν, Od. 3, 127.

διχθά, adv. poet. for δίχα, *two-fold*, etc. τοὶ διχθὰ δεδαίαται, Od. 1, 23. διχθὰ κραδίη μέμονε, my heart is divided, 16, 435.

διχθάδιος, η, ον, *two-fold, double*, Κῆρες, 9, 411; neut. as adv. 14, 21.

*διχόμηνος, ον (μήν), *in the middl[e] the month*, at the time of the full m[oon] h. 32, 11.

δίψα, ἡ, *thirst*, 11, 642.

*διψαλέος, η, ον, poet. (δίψα), thi[rsty] Batr. 9.

διψάω (δίψα), *to thirst, to be thi[rsty]* Od. 11, 584.†

δίω, Ep. ground form of δείδω. F[rom] this occur: imperf. ἔδιον, Ep. δίο[ν] sing. δίε, perf. δέδια and δείδια, with [plur.] signif. pl δέδιμεν, δέδιτε, δεδίασι, in[fin.] δέδιθι, infin. δέδιμεν, partcp. δεδιώ[ς] plur. pluperf. ἐδέδισαν, and from thi[s] imperf. δείδιε, 18, 34. [24, 358.] 1) tran[s]. *to fear, to be fearful*, περὶ γὰ[ρ] νηυσὶν Ἀχαιῶν, he feared greatly fo[r] ships of the Achaians, 9, 433. 11, ποιμένι λαῶν, in like manner in the [ ] δέδια = δείδοικα, see δείδω. 2) *to fle[e] run*, περὶ ἄστυ, only at 22, 251 [with lect. δίες. Död.]. The middle f[orm] δίενται, δίηται, etc. belong to δίεμαι,

διωθέω (ὠθέω), aor. δίωσα, *to [ ] apart, to tear asunder*, 21, 244.†

διώκω (δίω), only pres. and impe[rf.] Active, *to cause to run*; hence, *drive away, to drive forward, to e[tc.]* with accus, διώκω δ' οὔτιν' ἔγωγε, I [ ] no one forth, Od. 18, 409; ἅρμα ἵππους, 8, 439; sometimes absol. to d[rive] 23, 344. 424; spoken of a ship driv[en by] winds or oars, Od. 5, 332; hence ἡ δὲ νηῦς ἤλυθε, ῥίμφα διωκομένη, [the] ship approached rapidly propelled, 13, 162. 2) *to pursue, to follow*, in [op]position to φεύγω; τινά, 5, 672; [ ] 5, 223. 8, 107; metaph. *to strive aft[er] seek to obtain*, ἀκίχητα, 17, 175. 3[ ] trans. *to run swiftly, to hasten*, h. [ ] 350. cf. 5, 213. 23, 344. II) Mid. *to [ ] before me*, τινὰ πεδίοιο, through the [ ] 21, 602; δόμοιο, Od. 18, 8.

Διώνη, ἡ, mother of Aphrodīt[e by] Zeus, 5, 370. h. Ap 93. Accord. to Th. 353, daughter of Oceanus [and] Tethys; or, Apd. 1. 3, daught[er of] Uranus (Cœlus).

Διώνῡσος, ὁ, Ep. for Διόνυσος.

Διώρης, εος, ὁ, 1) son of Amaryn[ceus] leader of the Epēi, slain before Tr[oy by] Peirus, 2, 622. 4, 518. 2) father o[f Au]tomedôn companion in arms of Acl[ ] 17, 429.

δμηθείς, δμηθήτω, see δαμάω.

δμῆσις, ιος, ἡ (δαμάω), *the act o[f sub]duing, taming, curbing*. ἵππων [ ] δμῆσίν τε μένος τε, to hold the c[ ] and the force of steeds [L e. to be [ ] restrain or to urge on against the en[emy] 17, 476.

δμήτειρα, ἡ, *a female subduer, [con]queror*, epith. of Night [*resistles[s] queror of all*. Cp.], 14, 259;† prop

*δμητήρ, ῆρος, ὁ, *a subduer, con[q]* victor, h. 21, 5.

Δμήτωρ, ορος, ὁ, a fictitious cha[racter] feigned by Odysseus (Ulysses), [son of] Jason, king of Cyprus, Od. 17, 443.

δμωή, ἡ, prop. one subdued; he[nce]

slave (female), spoken primarily of those free-born and reduced to slavery by war (distinct from δούλη), 18, 28. cf. 9, 658. b) Mly. *a female slave, a maid-servant*, only plur. also δμωαὶ γυναῖκες, 6, 323. They were employed at all kinds of house-work. They were obliged to clean the house, grind the corn, bake, weave, etc.

δμώς, ωός, ὁ (δαμάω), [from δμής (L.). Dōd. supposes a dialectic δομάν᾽ δμώς by metath. fm δομητός, domi us,] prop. one conquered; hence, *a slave*, primarily by capture in war (see δοῦλος), Od. 1, 398. b) Mly. *a slave, a servant, a bond-man*, often in the plur. δμῶες ἄνδρες. The male slaves were obliged to do the heavier house-work, to split wood, to look to the cattle, to take care of the flocks, and to till the ground. In the Iliad only 19, 333; often in Od. Accord. to Nitzsch on Od. 4, 10, δμώς, a slave in general, whether born such, purchased, or taken in war.

δνοπαλίζω (δονέω), fut. ξω, *to shake hither and thither, to hurl down*, with accus. ἀνὴρ ἄνδρ᾽ ἐδνοπάλιζεν, 4, 472; ῥάκεα, *to fling* (cast, wrap) *his tatters* round him, Od. 14, 512.

δνοφερός, ή. όν (δνόφος = νέφος), *dusky, dark, black*, νύξ, Od. 13, 269; ὕδωρ, 9, 15. 16, 4.

δοάσσατο, defect. aor. 1 mid., of which the 3 sing. subj. occurs δοάσσεται (for δοάσσηται), *to appear, to seem*. ὧδε δέ οἱ φρονέοντι δοάσσατο κέρδιον εἶναι, thus it appeared to him, on reflection, to be better, 13. 458. Od. 5, 474. ὡς ἄν τοι πλήμνη γε δοάσσεται ἄκρον ἱκέσθαι κύκλου, that the nave of the wheel may seem to graze the surface (the exterior part of the goal), 23, 339. (A shortened form fr. δοιάζω; it is according to Buttman, Lex., p. 212, more correctly derived from δέαται, it seems (with vowel-change of ο for ε) (q. v.).

δοιή. ή. *doubt, uncertainty*. ἐν δοιῇ (εἶναι), to be in doubt, 9, 230.†

δοιός, ή. όν, *two-fold* [in later poets (δ. γάμος, Call.), but in H. always *two*. Död.], only dual δοιώ, and plur. δοιοί, αί, ά = δύω, *two, both*, 5, 7. 28. The neut. plur. δοιά as adv. *in two ways, of two kinds*, Od. 2, 46. The dual δοιώ is indecl., 24, 648.

δοκεύω (δέκομαι), *to endeavour to seize*, with accus. spoken of a dog following a wild animal: ἰσχία γλουτούς τε [close-threatening flank or haunch. Cp.], 8, 340; hence *to watch, to lie in wait for*, τινά, 13, 545. 16, 313; mly *to observe*. Ὠρίωνα. of the Great Bear, 18, 488. Od. 5, 274; δεδοκημένος, see δέχομαι.

δοκέω, aor. 1 ἐδόκησα Ep. for ἔδοξα, h. Merc. 208. 1) Trans. *to be of opinion, to think, to believe*, δοκέω νικήσειν Ἕκτορα, I believe I shall conquer Hector, 7, 192. 2) Intrans. *to appear. to seem*; with dat. of the pers. πέπλος οἱ δοκέει χαριέστατος εἶναι, 6, 90; ὥς μοι δοκεῖ εἶναι ἄριστα, as it seems to me to be best, 9, 103;

more rarely with infin. fut. 6, 338; δόκησε σφίσι θυμὸς ὡς ἔμεναι, their feelings seemed to be such, Od. 10, 415.

δοκός, ἡ, *a beam*, esp. of the roof, 17, 744. Od. 19, 38.

δόλιος, η, ον (δόλος), *crafty, deceitful, sly, artful*, spoken only of things, ἔπεα, τέχνη; κύκλος, the crafty circle which the hunters draw around a wild animal, *Od. 4, 792. Adv. δολίως, *craftily*, Batr. 93.

Δολίος, ὁ, *a slave of Laertês in Ithaca*, father of Melanthius and Melanthô, Od. 4, 735.

δολίχαυλος, ον (αὐλός), *having a long tube, long-tubed*; αἰγανέη, a hunting-spear with a long tube into which the iron head of the spear was introduced, or simply *long-shafted*, Od. 9, 156.†

δολιχεγχής, ές (ἔγχος). *armed with a long spear*, Παίονες. 21, 155.†

δολιχήρετμος; ον (ἐρετμός), *having long oars, long-oared*, νῆες, Od. 4, 499; spoken of people: *using long oars, sea-faring*, maritime, Φαίηκες, *Od. 8, 191

δολιχόδειρος, ον, Ep. δουλιχόδειρος.

δολιχός, ή, όν, *long*, spoken of space: ἔγχεα, δόρυ. 2) Of time: *long, lasting*, νόσος, νύξ; of space and time together: πλόος, Od. 3, 169. Neut. as adv. δολιχόν, 10, 52.

*Δολιχός, ὁ (accord. to Voss l. c. to be written Δόλιχος), pr. n. of a prince in Eleusis, h. in Cer. 155.

δολιχόσκιος, ον (σκιά), *long-shadowing, casting a long shadow*, epith. of a spear, Il. and Od.

δολόεις, εσσα, εν, poet. (δόλος), *crafty, cunning, insidious, artful*, Κίρκη, Od. 9, 32; metaph. spoken of bonds, δέσματα, Od. 8, 281.

δολομήτης, ου, ὁ = δολόμητις, only in voc. δολομῆτα. 1, 540.†

δολόμητις, ι (μῆτις), *full of artful plots, perfidious, artful*, epith. of Ægisthus and Clytemnestra, *Od. 1, 300. 11, 422.

Δόλοπες, οἱ, see Δόλοψ.

Δολοπίων, ίονος, ὁ, father of Hypsênôr, a Trojan, priest of Scamander, 5, 77. (fr. δόλοψ.)

δόλος, ὁ (δέλεαρ), 1) Prop. *a bait*, to take fish, Od. 12, 252: hence, any *trap* or *stratagem*, to take or deceive any one, spoken of the Trojan horse, Od. 8, 494; and of the net-work in which Hêphæstus confined Arês, Od. 8, 276. δόλος ξύλινος, a mouse-trap, Batr. 116. 2) In general: *cunning, deceit, an artful plot, a stratagem*, often in the plur. δόλοι, tricks, wiles, 6, 187.

*δολοφραδής. ές (φράζω), *of crafty mind, cunning*, h. Merc. 282.

δολοφρονέων, ουσα, ον (φρονέω), *devising deception, plotting fraud, crafty-minded*, only partcp. Il. and Od.

δολοφροσύνη, ή, *thought of treachery, meditated deception, fraud*, plur. *artifices*, 19, 97. 112. h. Merc. 361.

Δόλοψ, οπος, ὁ, 1) *a Dolopian*. The Dolopes were a powerful tribe in Thessalia, on the river Enīpeus, 9, 484; later on Pindus. II) As masc. prop. nom. 1) son of Lampus, grandson of Laomedôn, a Trojan slain by Menelaus, 15, 525 seq. (δόλοψ, a spy.) 2) son of Clytius, a Greek, 11, 302.

Δόλων, ωνος, ὁ, son of Eumêdês, a Trojan, who attempted to penetrate, as a spy, the camp of the Greeks, but was taken and slain by Diomêdês and Odysseus (Ulysses), 10, 314 seq. (from δόλος, cunning).

δόμονδε, adv. to one's home, homeward; also ὅνδε δόμονδε, 16, 445; † often Od.

δόμος, ὁ (δέμω), prop. what is built, a building; hence, 1) a house, dwelling, spoken of the temples of the gods, 6, 242 [Ἐρεχθῆος πυκινὸν δόμον, the firm house of Erectheus = the temple of Athênê, Od. 7, 81, cf. Nitzsch ad loc.]; of the dwellings of men; also the compass of all the buildings, 6, 242; in this case mly plur.; also of brutes, as pens of sheep, and nests of bees, 12, 301. 169. 2) a chamber, an apartment, esply that of the men, 1, 255. 22, 291.

δονακεύς, ῆος, ὁ (δόναξ), a reed-bed, a place full of rushes, 18, 576.†

δόναξ, ακος, ὁ (δονέω), 1) a reed, δόνακες, reed-stalks, Od. 14, 474. h. Merc. 47. 2) that which is made of reed, an arrow, 11, 584.

δονέω, aor. 1 ἐδόνησα, fut. mid. δονήσεται, to put in motion, to agitate, to drive hither and thither, with accus. spoken of the wind which agitates the trees, 17, 55; and drives the clouds, 12, 157; of the gad-fly: οἶστρος βόας ἐδόνησεν, it drove about the cattle, Od. 22, 300. Mid. fut. with pass. signif. h. Ap. 270.

δόξα, ἡ (δοκέω), opinion, notion, expectation. ἀπὸ δόξης, contrary to expectation, 10, 324. Od. 11, 344.

δορός, ὁ (δέρω), a leathern bottle, *Od. 2, 354. 380.

δορπέω (δόρπον), fut. δορπήσω, to sup, to take the evening meal, Od. 15, 302.

δόρπον, τό, the evening meal, supper, ἅμα ἠελίῳ καταδύντι, 19, 207. 24, 2; and mly, a meal; in plur. δόρπα, 8, 503. Od. 4, 213.

δόρυ, τό, gen. Ep. δούρατος and δουρός, dat. δούρατι, δουρί, accus. δόρυ, dual δοῦρε, plur. δούρατα, δοῦρα, gen. δούρων, dat. δούρασι and δούρεσσι (H. never uses the common form δόρατος), 1) wood, the trunk of a tree, Od. 6, 167. 2) Mly a beam, timber; δόρυ νήιον and δοῦρα νεῶν, ship-timber, 2, 135. 3) every thing made of wood, a spear-handle. δόρυ μέλινον, an ashen spear-handle, cf. ἔγχος, mly a spear, lance, javelin; the Hom. heroes bore in battle and generally elsewhere two spears, 11, 43. Od. 1, 256; and hence poet. war, battle, δουρὶ πόλιν πέρθαι, to ravage a city by war, 16, 708.

Δόρυκλος, ὁ, son of Priam, slain by the Telamonian Ajax, 11, 489.

*δορυσθενής, ές (σθένος), powerful with the spear, h. Mart. 3.

δόσις, ιος, ἡ (δίδωμι), a present, a 10, 213. Od. 6, 208.

*δότειρα, ἡ, a giver (female), a d Ep. 7, 1; fem. from

δοτήρ, ῆρος, ὁ, poet. (δίδωμι), a giv donor, bestower, σίτοιο, 19, 44. +h. ?

δαύλειος, η, ον (δοῦλος), slavish, se Od. 24, 252.†

δούλη, ἡ, a female slave, a maid-ser prop. one born in slavery, fem. of δο 3, 409. Od. 4, 12.

δοῦλος, η, ον (δοῦλος), slavish, se only δούλιον ἦμαρ, the day of slave 463.

Δουλίχιον, τό, an island in the Ic sea, south-east from Ithaca, whic cording to H. belonged to the Echin and was inhabited by Epeans; fro the warrior Meges went to Troy; cording to Strabo, the island Dol according to a tradition of the mo Greeks, a sunken island Cacaba, 2, Δουλιχιόνδε, adv. to Dulichium. Od 397. Δουλιχιεύς, ῆος, ὁ, an inhabita Dulichium.

δουλιχόδειρος, ον, Ep for δολιχόδ (δειρή), having a long neck, long-ne epith. of the swan, 2, 460. 15, 692.

δουλοσύνη, ἡ, slavery, servitude, b age, Od. 22, 423.†

δουπέω, poet. (δοῦπος), aor. 1 ἐδού and ἐγδούπησα, perf. 2 δέδουπα, make a noise, to make a heavy so esply spoken of falling in battle, δούπησε πεσών, he gave a hollow so in falling. 2) absol. to sound, to 13, 426. 23, 679.

δοῦπος, ὁ, noise, a dull or heavy so δούπος ἀκόντων, the clash of spe ποδῶν, the sound of feet, Od. 16, spoken of the noise of the sea, O 401; of the rushing of mountain torr 4, 455.

δουράτεος, η, ον (δόρυ), wooden, ma wood, ἵππος, Od. 8, 493. 512. h. Merc.

δουρηνεκής, ές (ἐνεγκεῖν), only neu adv. as far as a spear is cast, a sp cast off, 10, 357.†

δουρικλειτός, όν (κλειτός), fame hurling the spear, famed with the s epith. of heroes, δ, 578. Od. 15, 52.

δουρικλυτός, όν (κλυτός) = δουρικλ 2, 645. Od. 17, 71; and often.

δουρικτητός, ή, όν (κτάομαι), capt with the spear, taken in war, 9, 343.†

δουρός, δουρί, see δόρυ.

δουροδόκη, ἡ (δέχομαι), a place for k ing spears, an armoury for spears, O 128.†

δόχμιος, η, ον (δοχμή), trans across, oblique, neut. plur. as πάραντά τε δόχμιά τ' ἦλθον, side and obliquely through, 23, 116.†

δοχμός, ή, όν, oblique, sidewise; ἀΐσσοντε, 12, 148.†

*δοχμόω, to bend, to incline to the in the pass. h. Merc. 146.

δράγμα, ατος, τό (δράσσω), wha can grasp with the hand, a hand bundle of corn, as much as the r grasps in cutting. δράγματα ταρφέα πίπτει, handful after handful falls, 11, 69; or as much as the labourer embraces to bind, a sheaf, 18, 552.

δραγμεύω (δράγμα), to collect the ears of grain into sheaves, to bind in bundles, 18, 555.†

δραίνω (δράω), to wish to do any thing, 10, 96.†

*δράκαινα, ἡ. a female dragon, fem. of δράκων, h. in Ap. 300.

*Δράκανον, τό, a town and promontory on the island Icaria, h. 26, 1.

Δρακίος, ὁ, a leader of the Epēi, 13, 692.

δράκων, οντος, ὁ, a dragon, a large serpent, 2, 308; in H., as with us, dragons belong to the class of fabulous animals, cf. 11, 39. Od. 4, 457 (prob. from δέρκομαι).

*δράξ, ακός, ὁ (δράσσω), a handful, Batr. 240.

δράσσω, depon. mid. δράσσομαι, perf. δέδραγμαι, to grasp, to seize, to collect, with gen. only partcp. δεδραγμένος κόνιος, grasping the dust with the hand, *13, 393. 16, 486. (The act. only in later writers.)

δρατός, ή, όν, metathesis for δαρτός (δέρω), flayed, skinned, σώματα, 23, 169.†

δράω, pres. subj. δρώωσι, optat. δρώοιμι, to be active; esply to serve, to wait upon, *Od. 15, 317. 324.

ΔΡΑΩ, obsol. theme of διδράσκω.

ΔΡΕΜΩ, obsol. theme; see τρέχω.

δρεπάνη, ἡ (δρέπω), a sickle, 18, 551.†

δρέπανον, τό = δρεπάνη, Od. 18, 368.†

δρέπω, to break off, to pluck, with accus. ἄνθεα, h. Cer. 425; mly Od. 12, 357. h. Cer. 429.

*δρησμοσύνη, ἡ, service, worship, ἱερῶν, h. Cer. 476.

Δρῆσος, ὁ, a Trojan, slain by Euryalus, 6, 20.

δρηστήρ, ῆρος, ὁ, Ion. for δραστήρ (δράω), a servant; fem. δρήστειρα, ἡ, a female servant, *Od. 10, 349. 16, 248.

δρηστοσύνη, ἡ, activity, assiduity in serving, Od. 15, 321.†

δριμύς, εῖα, ύ, sharp, biting, pungent, prop. spoken of taste, then metaph. βέλος, the piercing arrow (spoken of the shooting pangs of parturition), 11, 270; fierce, violent, κόλος, 18, 322; δριμεῖα μάχη, the fierce battle, 15, 696; μένος, Od. 24, 319.

δρίος [= δρυΐος. D.], in the plur. τὰ δρία, Hes. underwood, thicket, forest. δρίος ὕλης, Od. 14, 353.† (The gender in the sing. is uncertain, since besides the nom. sing. in H. and the plur. in Hes. no cases occur.)

δρόμος, ὁ (ΔΡΕΜΩ, δέδρομα), 1) the act of running, a roce, 18, 281. 23, 758. 2) a race-course, a race-ground, Od. 4, 605; and, in general, level surface, Batr. 96.

Δρυάς, άδος, ἡ (δρῦς), a Dryad, a woodnymph, who lived and died with her own peculiar tree.

Δρύας, αντος, ὁ, 1) one of the Lapithæ, a friend of Peirithous, 1, 263. 2) father of king Lycurgus, 6, 130.

δρύϊνος, 'η, ον, of oak, of oaken wood, Od. 21, 43.†

δρυμός, ὁ, plur. τὰ δρυμά, an oak wood, and mly, a wood, a forest, only in plur. 11, 118. Od. 10, 150. 197.

δρύοχος, ὁ (ἔχω), plur. δρύοχοι, according to Eustath. and the Schol. the oaken props or stays, standing in two rows, on which the ship rested, whilst being built, that it might not be injured by the wet sand. Damm and Passow incorrectly define it to be the oaken ribs fastened in the keel of a ship to which the remaining wood-work is attached, Od. 19, 574.† Odysseus (Ulysses) compares the axes placed in a row to them.

Δρύοψ, πος, ὁ, 1) son of Priam, slain by Achilles, 20, 455. 2) son of Apollo, father of Dryopē, h. in Pan. 34.

δρύπτω, aor. 1 ἔδρυψα, aor. mid. ἐδρυψάμην, 1) to scratch, to tear off, to lacerate; βραχίονα ἀπὸ μυιώνων, to tear the arm from the muscles, 16, 324. 2) Mid. to tear oneself, παρειάς, Od. 2, 153.

δρῦς, δρυός, ἡ, an oak, it was sacred to Zeus, Od. 14, 328. As an adage: οὐ πως νῦν ἔστιν ἀπὸ δρυὸς οὐδ᾽ ἀπὸ πέτρης ὀαρίζειν, it behoves not now to chat together (as) from an oak or a rock, i. e. to talk familiarly about indifferent things, 22, 126; οὐκ ἀπὸ δρυὸς οὐδ᾽ ἀπὸ πέτρης ἐσσί, thou art neither from the oak nor from the rock, i. e. thou art not of doubtful descent, Od. 19, 163.

δρυτόμος, ον, poet. for δρυοτόμος (τέμνω), felling oaks, cutting oaks, *11, 86. 16, 633.

δρώοιμι, δρώωσι, see δράω.

δῦ, Ep. for ἔδυ, see δύω.

δυάω (δύη), to render unhappy, to plunge into wretchedness, ἀνθρώπους, Od. 20, 195.† (δυάομαι, Ep. for δύνασι.)

δύη, ἡ, wretchedness, misery, misfortune. δύης ἐπὶ πῆμα γενέσθαι, to sink in the depths of misery, *Od. 14, 338. (Prop. from δύω, immersion.)

*δυήπαθος, ον (πάσχω), suffering misery, miserable, h Merc. 468.

Δύμας, αντος, ὁ, 1) father of Asius and Hecuba in Phrygia, 16, 718. a) a Phæacian, Od. 6, 22.

δύμεναι, see δύω.

Δύμη, ἡ, Dyma, a town in Achaia, on the sea, at an earlier period, Στράτος, 11.; now Caminitza, h. in Ap. 425.

(δῦμι), obsol. form from δύω.

δύναμαι, depon. mid. fut. δυνήσομαι, aor. 1 ἐδυνησάμην and ἐδυνάσθην, to be able, to have power, to be in a condition to do any thing, absol. and often with infin. b) With accus. Ζεὺς δύναται ἅπαντα, Zeus has all power, can do all things, Od. 4, 237. c) μέγα δύνασθαι, to be very powerful, Od. 1, 275. (υ is long in the partcp. by the arsis, Od. 1, 275.)

Δυναμένη, ἡ (the mighty), a Nereid, 18, 43.

δύναμις, ιος, ἡ, power, ability, might, force; esply bodily power. ὅση δύναμις πάρεστιν, as far as my power extends,

8, 294; πὰρ δύναμιν, beyond my power, 13, 787.

δύνω, a form of δύω, only in the indicat. pres. and imperf. mid. δύομαι, 8, 43; see δύω.

δύο or δύω, with dual and plur., *two*, in H. indecl. τῶν δύο μοιράων, 10, 253. δύω κανόνεσσ᾽ ἀραρυῖα, 13, 407. δύω δ᾽ ἄνδρες ἐνείκεον, 18, 498. σὺν δύο, *two together*, 10, 224.

δυοκαίδεκα and δυώδεκα, poet. for δώδεκα, indecl. *twelve*, Il. and Od.

δυς, an inseparable particle denoting *aversion, difficulty, weariness, misfortune*, etc. like the English *in-, un-, mis-,* etc.; to words having a good signif. it gives an opposite sense, and [sometimes] in words of a bad signif. it strengthens the sense.

δυσαής, ές, poet. (ἄημι), *blowing adversely, blowing violently, blustering*, epith of the wind and chiefly of Zephyr, 23, 200; gen. δυσαῶν for δυσαέων, Od. 13, 99.

δυσάμμορος, ον (ἄμμορος), *very unfortunate, ill-fated*, *22. 428. 485.

δυσαριστοτόκεια (ἄριστος, τίκτω), one who had borne, to her misfortune, a most brave son, *an unhappy mother of a hero*, so Thetis calls herself, 18, 54.

δύσβωλος, ον (βῶλος), *having a bad soil, unfruitful*, Ep. 7.

δύσεο, δύσετο, see δύω.

δύσζηλος ον (ζῆλος), *irascible, choleric*. Od. 7, 307. 2) *dangerously rivalling*, τινί, Ep. 8, 2.

δυσηλεγής, ές (λέγω), *laying in a hard bed* [= ἀλεγεινός (fm. ἀλγεινω, ἀλέγειν), *afflictire, causing grief*], epith. of war and of death, 20, 154. Od. 22, 325 (others say from ἀλέγω. regarding no one).

δυσηχής, ές (ἠχέω), *sounding dreadfully, terribly*, epith. of war, prop. spoken of the clash of arms, 2, 686. 2) *having an evil sound*, in whose very name lies an evil foreboding, *frightful, abominable*, epith. of death, *16, 442. 18, 464; τινί, h. Ap. 64.

δυσθαλπής, ές (θάλπω) *ill at warming, badly warming, cold*, χειμών, 17, 549.†

δυσθύμαίνω (θυμός), *to be vexed, to be angry*, h. Cer. 363.

δυσκέλαδος, ον (κέλαδος), *sounding dreadfully, resounding*, φόβος, 16, 357.†

δυσκηδής, ές (κῆδος), *anxious, melancholy, sad*, νύξ, Od. 5, 466.†

δυσκλεής, ές (κλέος), *without fame, inglorious*, poet. accus. δυσκλέα for δυσκλεία, 2, 115. 9, 22.

δύσκον. see δίω.

δυσμενέων, ουσα, ον (μένος), *ill-disposed*, in partcp. masc. sing. and plur. *Od.

δυσμενής, ές (μένος), *adverse, hostile, evil-disposed*, 3, 51, and often; and subst. *an enemy*, 10, 193.

δυσμήτηρ, ερος, ἡ (μήτηρ), *an evil mother, a bad mother*, Od. 23, 97.†

δύσμορος, ον (μόρος), *having an evil lot, unfortunate, wretched*, Il. and Od.

Δύσπαρις, ιος, ὁ, *unfortunate Paris, odious Paris* [*curst Paris* Cp.], *3, 39. 13, 769.

δυσπέμφελος, ον (πέμπω), *dang[erous], cross, boisterous, stormy*, πόντος, [

δυσπονής, ές (πόνος), *laborio[us], some, wearisome*, Od. 5, 493.†

δύστηνος, ον (στένω), *groaning, sighing deeply, wretched, miserabl[e]*, δυστήνων παῖδες, the children of w[retched] parents, 6, 127.

*δυστλήμων, ον (τλήμων), *muc[h suffer]ing, wretched*, h. Ap. 53l.

δυσχείμερος, ον (χεῖμα), *having winter, wintry, stormy*, epith of [2, 750. 16, 234.

δυσώνυμος, ον (ὄνυμα, Æol. for *having a bad name*; hence, *odiou[s], abominable*, as μοῖρα, 12, 116; 7 19, 571.

δυσωρέομαι, depon. mid. (fr. ι οὖρος), fut. ήσομαι, *to have an night-watch, to watch without rest*, of dogs which watch the shee[p] μῆλα, 10, 183.† Spi[t]zner, instea[d] mid. δυσωρήσονται (for which T § 346, 10, requires δυσωρήσων[τ] restored from Apoll. Lex. the a ωρήσωσι, which also analogy (cf. recommends.

δυσωρέω, act. ed. Spitz. cf. δυσω (the final remark).

- δύω, aor. 2 ἔδυν, sing. 3 δῦ for ι iterat. δύσκον, subj. δύω, intin Ep. δύμεναι, partcp. δύς, perf. mid. pres. δύομαι, fut. δύσομαι ἐδυσάμην, with the Ep. forms ἐδύσετο, imper. δύσεο (characte[r] aor. 1, and termination of aor. 2 partcp. δυσόμενος Od. 1, 24, is commentators considered future the Epic poets the fut. is used dicate that also which common place, but it is better to consider it of aor. 2, cf. Rost. Gr. p. 408. Krüg. Flexionslehre, p. 115, t the pres. only the partcp. δύων 21, 232. The form δύνω = δύομ these forms have the intrans. si *go in*, hence, 1) Spoken of the r of place: a) Of places and regi *go into, to enter, to penetrate plunge into*, with accus. πόλιν, t the city; τεῖχος, 15, 345. δῦνα[ι] Od. 13, 366; πόντον, to plunge sea, 15, 19; γαῖαν, to go under th 6, 19; δόμον ᾿Αΐδος εἴσω, 3, 322 δῦναι (spoken of the stars), 11. 6[3] πόλεμον, μάχην, ὅμιλον, to go war, the battle, the crowd; δύεσθ ἀγῶνα, to enter an assembly of th 18, 376; with prep. βέλος εἰς ἐγ δῦ, the arrow penetrated into th 8, 85; ἐς πόντον; uncommon: εἰς Αἴαντα, he pressed upon A shelter himself under his shield) b) Metaph of human conditions: γυῖα δέδυκεν, fatigue entered th 5, 811. ὀδύναι δῦνον μένος ᾿Ατρεί 268. δῦ μιν ᾿Άρης Arês, i. e. mart entered him, 17, 210; also with accus. Od. 20, 286. 2) Spoken o and arms, with accus. apparentl to put on, to clothe oneself in ; δύνειν and δύεσθαι, δῦναι, δύσασθαι τεύχεα, ἔντεα, κυνέην, to put on a helmet, 5, 845; χιτῶνα, to put on a tunic, 18, 416. 23, 61. δ) Also with added dat. τεύχεα ὤμοιϊν, to put the arms about one's shoulders, 16, 64. ἔντεα χροΐ, 9, 596; and with prepos. ἐν: ὅπλοισιν ἐνὶ ἐδύτην, 10, 254; ἐν τεύχεσσι δύοντο, Od. 24, 496; also εἰς τεύχεα, Od. 22, 201; metaph. δύεσθαι ἀλκήν, to gird oneself with strength [to put on one's might, Cp.], 9. 231. 3) Absol. to penetrate, to soak into, δύνει ἀλοιφή, 17, 392; πᾶν δ' εἴσω ξίφος, 16, 340. Esply spoken of the sun and stars: to set, to go down, often ἠέλιος δ' ἄρ ἔδυ, δύσετο δ'. ἠέλιος, and Βοώτης ὀψὲ δύων, and δυσομένου Ὑπερίονος beginning to set, Od. 1, 24. (δύω is short in the pres and imperf. act. and mid. in the remaining tenses long, as also in δύνω; hence δύω is long only in subj. aor. 2, as 6, 340. 7, 193. etc.)

δύω, see δύο.

δυώδεκα, poet. for δώδεκα, q. v.

δυωδεκάβοιος, ον, poet. (βοῦς), worth twelve oxen, 23. 703.†

δυωδέκατος, η, ον, Ep. for δωδέκατος, the twelfth, ἠώς, 1, 493.

δυωκαιεικοσίμετρος, ον (μέτρον), containing two-and-twenty measures, τρίπους [of twenty and two measures. Cp.], 23, 264.†

δυωκαιεικοσίπηχυς, υ (πῆχυς), two-and-twenty cubits long, ξυστόν, 15, 678.†

δῶ, τό, abbrev. Ep. form for δῶμα, a house, used only in the nom. and accus. 1, 426. Od. 1, 176 [prob. the primitive word, Buttm. Gram. § 57, note 3.—See note on κρῖ].

δώδεκα, indecl. twelve, poet. also δυοκαίδεκα and δυώδεκα, Il. and Od. The number 12. like 9, used often in H. as a round number.

δωδέκατος. η. ον, the twelfth, poet. δυοδέκατος and δυωδέκατος, 24, 781.

Δωδωναῖος, αίη, αῖον, Dodonian, an appellation of Zeus, from the celebrated oracle at Dôdôna. Achilles called upon him as god of the Pelasgians, to whom also the Myrmidons belonged, 16, 233.

Δωδώνη, ἡ, according to Schol. Ven. a town in Molossis, in Epirus, on mount Tomarus. At an earlier day it belonged to Thesprôtia; and according to H. Il. 2, 750. the Perrhæbi came from its vicinity, Hdt. also was acquainted with it, 7, 185. It was the oldest and most noted oracle of Greece. Tradition says that Deucaliôn first built here a temple to Zeus, to which subsequently, according to Hdt. 2, 55, a pigeon flew from the oracle at Thebes in Egypt, which spoke with a human voice and commanded the inhabitants to establish here an oracle of Zeus. Strabo, more correctly, denies its Egyptian origin, and calls it an establishment of the Pelasgians, cf. Πελασγικέ, 16, 233. The temple was situated on mount Tomarus.

The priests (Σελλοί) communicated oracles sometimes from the rustling of the sacred oak (cf. Od. 14, 327), sometimes from the sound of a brazen caldron moved by the wind. It was, according to Pouqueville, near the place now called Proskynisis. (According to Strabo, there was a second Dôdôna in Perrhæbia, near Scotussa.) The name is said to have been derived from the sound of the caldron Δώδω.

δώῃ and δώῃσι, Ep. for δῷ, see δίδωμι.

δῶμα, ατος, τό (δέμω)?, 1) a house, a dwelling, often in plur. δώματα; spoken of men and gods, δῶμ' 'Αΐδαο, 15, 251.' 2) a single apartment of a house, a room, an apartment, esply that of the men, i. q. μέγαρον, often in the Od.

δωρέομαι, depon. mid. (δῶρον), aor. ἐδωρησάμην, to bestow, to present, with accus. ἵππους, 10, 557.†

δωρητός, ή, όν (δωρέομαι), presented with gifts, that may be propitiated with presents, 9, 526.†

Δωριεύς, έος, ὁ, plur. Δωριέες, the Dorians, one of the main branches of the Hellênes, deriving their name from Dorus, son of Helen. They resided at first about the Olympus, but removed subsequently to the district of Dôris, and after the Trojan war to Peloponnesus and Asia Minor. Hom. Od. 19, 177, speaks of Dorians in Crete, and calls them τριχάϊκες, the trebly-divided [with waving locks. Dôd. vid.], according to the Schol. because they dwelt in Euboea, Crete, and Peloponnesus, or, more correctly, because they inhabited three cities.

Δώριον, τό, Dôrium, a place in western Messênia or Elis, where the bard Thamyris in a contest with the Muses lost his sight, 2, 594. According to Strab. VIII. p. 350, it is unknown; some think it a district or a mountain; others suppose it to be Oluris in Messenia. According to Pausan. 8, 33, 7, who says its ruins were a fountain, it was situated on the Neda near Andania; according to Gell it was in the vicinity of the modern Sidero Castro.

Δωρίς, ίδος, ἡ, daughter of Nêreus and Dôris, 18, 45.

δῶρον, τό, a gift, a present, a) δῶρα θεῶν, either presents which are made to them, votive offerings, 3, 54. 8, 203; or which are received from them, 20, 268. δῶρα 'Αφροδίτης, the gifts of Aphroditê, i. e. beauty, and the pleasures of love, 3, 54. Ὕπνου δῶρον, the gift of sleep, 7, 482. b) In reference to men, 17, 225. Od. 1, 311: esply gifts of hospitality, which friends mutually gave, Od. 4, 589. 600.

*Δώς, ἡ (the giver), a name of Dêmêtêr, h. Cer. 122, ed. Herm.; Δηώ, Wolf.

δωτήρ, ῆρος, ὁ, a giver; δωτῆρες ἐάων, Od. 8, 325.†

δωτίνη, ἡ, a gift, a present = δῶρον, Il. and Od.

*Δώτιον πεδίον, τό, the Dotian plain.

A

a plain surrounded by mountains between Magnêsia, Phthiôtis, and the Pelasgian plain near Ossa, h. 15, 5.

Δωτώ, οὖς, ἡ, a Nereid, 18, 43.

δώτωρ, ορος, ὁ, a giver, a bestower. Hermês is called δώτωρ ἐάων, Od. 9, 335. h. 16, 12.

δώωσι, see δίδωμι.

E.

E, the fifth letter of the Greek alphabet, and therefore the sign of the fifth book or rhapsody.

ἔᾱ, 1) Ep. for ἦν, see εἰμί. 2) For εἶα, see ἐάω.

ἐᾶ, see ἐάω.

ἐάγην, see ἄγνυμι.

ἔαδα, see ἀνδάνω.

ἐάλη, see εἴλω.

1) ἐανός, ή, όν, Ep. (prob. from ἕω, ἕννυμι, as στέφανος from στέφω), 1) As adj. with ᾱ, prop. that may easily be put on, flexible, soft (fine, V.); πέπλος, a light, soft robe, 5, 734. 8, 385. ἐανῷ λιτί, 18, 352; and κασσίτερος, thin-beaten, flexible tin, 18, 613.

II) ἐανός, as subst. always with ᾰ, once εἰανός, 16, 9; a robe, a garment, of goddesses and distinguished women: νεκτάρεος ἑανός, 3, 389. 14, 178. 21, 507. This word, which occurs only in the Il., varies in the quantity of its penultima. As an adj. it has ᾱ, and Buttm. would derive it from ἐάω, so that originally it signifies yielding, pliant. As subst. it has always ᾰ and is masc., cf. 21, 507. (Later ἐανόν.) The significations fine, thin, shining, splendid, are derived by mere conjecture from the Hom. passages.

ἔαξα, see ἄγνυμι.

ἔαρ, ἔαρος, τό, poet. gen. εἴαρος, h. Cer. 174; and ἦρος, h. Cer. 455; spring, 6, 148. ἔαρ νέον ἱστάμενον, the newly beginning spring, Od. 19, 519.

ἐαρινός, ή, όν, poet. εἰαρινός, q. v.

ἔασιν, Ep. for εἰσί, 3 plur. pres. from ἦμαι

ἐάφθη (Wolf), more correctly, ἐάφθη (Spitz. aft. Aristarch. and Tyrann.), Ep. 3 sing. aor. 1 pass. only twice, ἐπὶ δ' ἀσπὶς ἐάφθη καὶ κόρυς, 13, 543; and ἐπ' αὐτῷ δ' ἀσπὶς ἑ. κ. κ. 14, 419, prob. from ἅπτω for ἥφθη, with the syllab. augm. ἐάφθη = ἤφθη (al. inflictum erat; al. aptum, alligatum erat). I substitute Spitzner's explanation: "loco priore gutture Apharei Æneæ cuspide perrupto caput in alteram partem reclinatum fuisse tradit, galea ergo et clypeus, utpote loro subnexo retenti, ei sunt juncti et in eandem vergunt partem. Quare non adjicit αὐτῷ ... Hector vero Ajacis saxo percussus resupinus cadit, eique adjuncti tenentur clypeus et galea." Excurs. xxiv. Buttm., Lex., p. 242, would, with the old

Grammarians, without probah | it from ἔνομαι, as an aor. | pa

ἐάω, Ep. εἰάω, fut. ἐάσω, a | Ep. ἐάσα, 1) to let, i. e. to allow, to suffer, absol. 17, 449 : and accus. τούσδε δ' ἔα φθ | those perish, 2, 346. τὰ n ἐάσομεν, we will let that be gone [will renounce vain mus past. Cp.], 18, 112. οὐκ ἐᾶ suffer, i. e. to hinder, to forb 25. 2) to let go, to let depar to give up, with accus. χόλο ἵππους, to lead steeds, 4, 220 let any one go, 4, 42; also, to one, 5, 148; and often. 3) t to forbear, to cease, with infi 24, 71; also with accus. Od. is short in the pres. and imp σ long: H. uses in the pres. a partly the contract. forms ἐῷ, and partly the Ep. forms ἐάᾳ, monosyllabic, 5, 256).

ἐάων, gen. plur. from ἐύς, q.

ἑβδόματος, η, ον, poet for ἕβδο

ἕβδομος, η, ον (ἑπτά), the s and Od.

ἔβλητο, Ep. see βάλλω.

ἐγγεγάασι, see ἐγγίγνομαι.

ἐγγείνομαι (γείνομαι), in t obsol., only aor. 1 ἐνεγεινάμη gender within, with accus. γείνωνται, 3 plur. subj. aor. 1, |

ἐγγίγνομαι (γίγνομαι), Ep. pe plur. ἐγγεγάασιν, to be born i be in, to live in; with dat. τοὶ ἐ Ἰλίῳ, who dwell in Troy, 4, 41.

ἐγγυαλίζω (γύαλον), fut. ἐ aor. 1 ἐγγυάλιξα, prop. to give hand, hence to give up, to com to bestow, τί τινι; σκῆπτρόν τι τιμήν, κῦδος, κέρδος; τινά τιν any one to one, Od. 16, 66.

ἐγγυάω (ἐγγύη), fut. ήσω, to any thing as a pledge, hence t security, mid. to be bail. to b δειλαί τοι δειλῶν γε καὶ ἐγγύ ασθαι, Od. 8, 351.† Among th explanations of this passage Schol.), the connexion seems b by the following construction τῶν δειλῶν (i. e. ὑπὲρ τῶν δειλῶν, καὶ δειλαί εἰσ' ἐγγυάασθαι, i. e. for the worthless give a wort curity. Or, with Passow, 'for t less it is of no avail to become So, in effect, Baumgarten-Crusiu büch für Philol. IX. 4, p. 43 sureties,' says he, 'are gene bad as the persons for whom undertaken.' Nitzsch [observ δειλός is weak, powerless] refers Hêphæstus, and explains: δειλ ἐγγύαται ὁ πρὸς δειλὸν ἐγγυ who gives security to a wea gives a weak security [the reason thus how could I (Hêphæstus) (Poseidôn) responsible, if Ar refuse to pay? lame suitor, lam Cp.].

ἐγγύη, ἡ (γυῖον), *surely* by delivering a pledge; and mly *security, surety*, τινός, for any one, Od. 8. 351.†

ἐγγύθεν, adv. (ἐγγύς), 1) Of place: *from near, near*, e. g. ἔρχεσθαι, ἴστασθαι; with dat. ὁ γάρ οἱ ἐγγύθεν ἦεν, he was near him, 17, 554. 2) Of time: *near, soon*, 18, 133.

ἐγγύθι, adv. (ἐγγύς), 1) Of place: *near*, sometimes with gen. Πριάμοιο, 6, 317. 2) Of time: *near, soon*, 10, 251; with dat. 22, 300.

ἐγγύς, adv. 1) of place: *near, near by*, either without a case or with gen.; also with infin. following, 11, 340. 2) Of time: *near, soon*, 22, 453. Od. 10, 86.

ἐγδούπησαν, see δουπέω.

ἐγείρω, aor. 1 ἤγειρα, mid. aor. sync. ἠγρόμην, Ep. ἐγρόμην, infin. ἐγρέσθαι, and with pres. accent ἔγρεσθαι, Od. 13, 124, perf. 2 ἐγρήγορα: here belong the forms ἐγρήγορθε, ἐγρηγόρθαι, ἐγρηγόρθασι, 1) Act. 1) *to wake, to awaken*, τινὰ ἐξ ὕπνου, 5, 413; and alone, 10, 146. 2) *to arouse, to excite, to animate, to encourage*, τινά, 5, 208. 15, 242; often Ἄρηα, to excite Arês, i. e. the battle, Il.; and πόλεμον, φύλοπιν, πόνον, μάχην, also θυμόν, μένος, to excite the spirit. 11) Mid. together with the sync. aor 2 and perf. 2, *to be awake, to watch*, 2, 41; ἀμφὶ πυρήν, 7, 434. The perf. 2, *I am awake* (imper. ἐγρήγορθε for ἐγρηγόρατε, infin. ἐγρηγόρθαι for ἐγρήγορθαι), 10, 67 (as if from ἐγρήγορμαι), and 3 plur. perf. ἐγρηγόρθασι, 10, 419; which extraordinary form either comes through ἐγρηγόρθαι, or has sprung from a theme ἐγρήγω abbrev. ἐγέρθω, and from this ἐγρήγορθαι); see Buttm. Gram. p. 277. Bost Dial. 75. D. Anm. 1.

ἔγκατα, τά, the interior, *the entrails*; only plur. 11, 176. Od.; dat. plur. ἔγκασι, 11, 438.

ἐγκατεπήγνῡμι (πήγνυμι), aor. 1 ἐγκατέπηξα, *to infix, to fasten* in; ξίφος κουλεῷ, to thrust the sword into the scabbard, Od. 11, 98.†

ἐγκατατίθημι (τίθημι), only mid. aor. 2 3 sing. ἐγκάτθετο, and imperat. ἐγκάτθεο, *to lay down upon for oneself, to place in, to conceal*; ἱμάντα κόλπῳ, to hide the girdle in the bosom, as an amulet (not 'to put on around'), 14, 219. 223; thus Voss and the Schol.; metaph. τὴν ἄτην θυμῷ, to weigh the punishment in one's heart, Od. 23, 223. Extraordinary is τελαμῶνα ᾗ ἐγκάτθετο τέχνῃ, Od. 11, 614; prop. he laid the sword-belt upon his art, i. e. he applied to it his art. According to Eustath. a periphrasis for ἐτεχνήσατο, because it was not prepared easily and quickly, but with toil. Others explain it [better], ἐποίησεν, he invented, devised [conceived, Fäsi] it, etc. This explanation is preferred by Nitzsch. The reading of the Schol. Harl. is easier: ὃς κείνῳ τελαμῶνι ἣν ἐγκάτθετο τέχνην, he laid out [ex-

pended all the resources of] his art upon it. So Schneider in Lex.

ἔγκειμαι (κεῖμαι), fut. ἐγκείσομαι, *to lie in*, with dat. ἱματίοις, to lie in garments, spoken of one dead, 22, 513.†

*Ἐγκέλαδος, ὁ (the roaring), one of the hundred-handed giants who stormed heaven, Batr. 285.

ἐγκεράννῡμι (κεράννυμι), aor. 1 ἐνεκέρασα, *to mix in, to mingle, to dilute*, οἶνον, 8, 189. Od. 20, 223.

ἐγκέφαλος, ὁ (κεφαλή), prop. adj., which is in the head; subst. *the brain* (subaud. μυελός, marrow), Il. and Od. χόλος δ' εἰς ἐγκέφαλον δῦ, Il. 8, 85.

ἐγκιθαρίζω (κιθαρίζω), *to play to any one on the guitar* or harp, h. Ap. 201. Merc. 17.

*ἐγκλιδόν, adv. (κλίνω), *bending, inclining*, h. 23.

ἐγκλίνω (κλίνω), perf. pass. ἐγκέκλιμαι, *to bend, to incline to.* 2) *to lean upon*, hence metaph. πόνος ὔμμι ἐγκέκλιται, the labour rests upon you, 6, 77.†

ἐγκονέω (κονέω), *to be diligent, quick*, esply in service, only partcp. στόρεσαν λέχος ἐγκονέουσαι, they quickly prepared the bed, 24, 648. Od. 7, 340.

ἐγκοσμέω (κοσμέω), *to arrange in*, τί τινι; τεύχεα νηΐ, to arrange the tackling and furniture in a ship, Od. 15, 218.†

ἐγκρύπτω (κρύπτω), aor. 1 ἐνέκρυψα, *to hide in, to conceal*; δαλὸν σποδιῇ, Od. 5, 488.† (Buttm. for the sake of position would read here ἐγκρύψε for ἐνέκρυψε, cf Ausf. Gr. § 7, p. 38.), h. Merc. 416.

ἐγκυκάω, see κυκάω.

ἐγκυρέω, Ion. and poet. (κυρέω), aor. 1 ἐνέκυρσα, *to fall into, to fall upon* any thing, with dat. φάλαγξι, upon the phalanxes, 13, 145.†

*ἐγρέμαχος, ον (μάχη), *exciting battle* [battle-rousing]; fem. ἐγρεμάχη, epith. of Athênê, h. Cer. 424.

ἔγρεο, see ἐγείρω.

ἐγρηγόρθαι, ἐγρηγόρθασι, ἐγρήγορθε, Ep. perf. forms; see ἐγείρω.

ἐγρηγορόων, Ep. for ἐγρηγορῶν, from ἐγρηγοράω, *watching, waking*, a newly formed pres. from the perf. ἐγρήγορα, Od. 20, 6.†

ἐγρηγορτί, adv. (ἐγρήγορα), *awake*, 10, 182.†

ἐγρήσσω (from ἐγέρω, ἐγείρω), *to watch, to be awake*, only pres. 11, 551. Od. 20, 33.

ἔγρομαι, a pres. form assumed without reason for the infin. ἐγρέσθαι, Od. 13, 124, which the Gramm. and Wolf accent ἔγρεσθαι, see ἐγείρω.

ἐγχείη, ἡ, Ep. for ἔγχος, *a spear, a lance*, 3, 345. [The signif. 'battle with spears,' is unnecessary, cf. Jahrb. J. und K., p. 259, Am. Ed.]

ἐγχείῃ, Ep. for ἐγχέῃ, see ἐγχέω.

ἔγχελυς, υος, ἡ, *an eel*, plur. ἐγχέλυες, Ep. for ἐγχέλεις, 21, 203. 353.

ἐγχεσίμωρος, ον, *skilled in the use of the spear*, epith. of brave warriors, 2, 692. Od. 3, 188. (The ancients themselves did not know the derivation.

They explain it: οἱ περὶ τὰ δόρατα μεμορημένοι, and derive it from μόρος, μοίρα, whose fate it is to bear the spear; others from μῶλος, battle, changing λ into ρ; others from μωρός, raging with the spear. If we compare ἰόμωροι and ὑλακόμωροι, we may infer that the word indicates skill.)

ἐγχέσπαλος, ον (πάλλω), wielding the spear, epith. of warriors, *2, 131.

ἐγχέω (χέω), 3 sing. subj. ἐγχείη, Ep. for ἐγχέῃ, aor. 1 act ἐνέχευα, 3 plur. ἐνέχεαν, mid. ἐνεχευάμην, 1) to pour in, with accus. ὕδωρ, οἶνον, 18, 347. οἶνον δεπάεσσι, to pour wine into the goblets, Od. 9, 10. b) to pour in, spoken of things dry; ἄλφιτα δοροῖσιν, Od. 2, 354. 2) Mid. to pour in for oneself (sibi), ὕδωρ), Od. 19, 387: often in tmesis.

ἔγχος, εος, τό, a spear, a javelin. The spear consisted of a long wooden shaft (δόρυ), which was pointed with brass (αἰχμή), 6, 319. Commonly it was six feet and more long; that of Hector was eleven cubits (ἑνδεκάπηχυ). The shaft was commonly made of ash, cf. μελίη. The lower end of the shaft (σαυρωτήρ) was also pointed with brass, that, when the bearer wished to rest, it might easily penetrate the earth, 10, 152. 22, 224. The spear was used both in thrusting and hurling. Hence warriors went into battle with two, that they might have a second when the first had been fruitlessly hurled or been broken, 3, 18. 12, 298. cf. Köpke Kriegswes. der Griechen, p. 115.

ἐγχρίμπτω (χρίμπτω), aor. 1 act. ἐγχρίμψα, aor. 1 pass. only partcp. ἐγχριμφθείς, 1) to force on, to push on, to drive on; once intrans. to press on. τῷ σὺ μάλ᾽ ἐγχρίμψας ἐλάαν σχεδὸν ἅρμα καὶ ἵππους, pressing on to this (the goal) drive the chariot and horses near, 23, 334. Mly pass., 1) αἰχμὴ ὀστέῳ ἐγχριμφθεῖσα, the point driven to the bone, 5, 662. ἀσπίδ᾽ ἐνιχριμφθείς, dashed down with the shield, 7, 272. 2) Absol. to crowd in, to push close on. νωλεμὲς ἐγχρίμπτοντο, 17, 413; with dat. πύλῃσιν, to the gates, *17, 405.

ἐγώ, and Ep. before a vowel ἐγών, gen. Ep. ἐμέο, ἐμεῖο, ἐμεῦ, μευ, ἐμέθεν, I, gen. of me; also strengthened ἔγωγε; μ᾽ for μοι in μ᾽ οἴῳ, Od. 4, 367; cf. Gram. and on the plur. see ἡμεῖς.

ἐδάην, see ΔΑΩ.

ἐδανός, ή, όν, pleasing, agreeable, delicious, an epith. of oil in 14, 172.† h. Ven. 63. (The ancients derived it from ἐδύς, ἥδομαι.)

ἔδαφος, τό (ἕδος), a seat, basis, bottom, upon which any thing rests, νηός, Od. 5, 249.†

ἔδεισα, Ep. for ἔδεισα, see δείδω.

ἐδέδμητο, see δέμω.

ἐδείδιμεν, ἐδείδισαν, see δείδω, δίω.

ἔδεκτο, see δέχομαι.

*ἔδεσμα, ατος, τό (ἔδω), food, victuals; Batr. 31.

ἐδήδοται, ἐδηδώς, see ἔδω

ἐδητύς, ύος, ἡ (ἔδω), food, victuals, oft with πόσις, 9, 92. Od. 1, 150. 3, 67.

ἐδμεναι, Ep. for ἐδέμεναι, from ἔδω.

ἔδνον, τό, only in the plur. τὰ ἔδνα, Ion. ἔεδνα, bridal presents, in differe senses: 1) presents which the su gives the bride: the common use. presents which the suitor gives to t father of the bride, and with which he a manner purchases her, 16, 178. Od 318. 2) the dowry or outfit which father gives the bride; according Nitzsch, a part of the bridal preser Od. 1, 277. 2, 196 (in the Il. always ἔ in the Od. also ἔεδνα).

ἐδνοπάλιζεν, see ὀνοπαλίζω.

ἐδνόω, Ep. ἐεδνόω (ἔδνα), to promise presents, only in mid. aor. 1 ἐεδνωσάμ to betroth a daughter, θύγατρα, spol of a father who marries his daugh Od 2, 53.†

ἐδνωτής, Ep. ἐεδνωτής, οῦ, ὁ (ἔδνα), one who affiances, the bride's fathe father-in-law, 13, 382;† only in the form.

ἔδομαι, see ἔδω, ἐσθίω.

ἔδος, εος, τό (ἔζομαι), 1) the ac sitting. οὐχ ἕδος ἐστί, it is no tim sit, 11, 648. 23. 205. 2) a seat, 1, 581. 3) a residence, an abode, spoke Olympus: ἀθανάτων ἕδος, the abode the immortals, 8, 456; and metaph. place on which any thing rests, gro hasis. ἕδος Θήβης, and periphrastic ἕδος Οὐλύμποιο, 24, 144; situation, 13, 344.

ἐδράθον, Ep. for ἔδαρθον, see δαρθά ἐδράμον, see τρέχω.

ἕδρη, ἡ, Ion. and Ep. for ἕδρα (ἕδ 1) a seat, 19, 77. 2) the place where sits, the seat of honour. τίειν τινὰ ἕ to honour one with a chief seat, 8, cf. 13, 311.

ἑδριάομαι, depon mid. (ἕδρα,) in ἑδριάασθαι Ep. for ἑδριᾶσθαι, imp ἑδριόωντο Ep. resol. for ἑδριῶντο, to oneself, to sit down, 10, 198. Od. 3, 3 ἐδύν and ἔδυν. see δύω.

ἔδω (Ep. for ἐσθίω), Ep. infin. ἔδμε fut. ἔδομαι, 4, 237; perf. act. ἔδ partcp. ἐδηδώς, perf. pass. ἐδήδοται aor. ἔφαγον), iterat. imperf. ἔδεσκε to eat, with accus. Δημήτερος ἀκτήν 322; with gen. Od. 9, 102; also spo of brutes: to eat, to devour. 2) Ἰσ᾽ικε to consume, οἶκον, κτήματα. Od. met καμάτῳ καὶ ἄλγεσι θυμόν, the heart labour and care, Od. 9, 75. cf. 24, (For ἔδω in the pres. ἐσθίω, ἐσθω occurs.)

ἐδωδή, ἡ (ἔδω), food, nourishment, for horses, 8, 504. Od. 3, 70.

ἑέ, poet. for ἕ, himself, herself, it see οὗ.

ἔεδνα, τά, ἐεδνόω, ἐεδνωτής, Ep. ἔδνα, ἐδνόω, ἐδνωτής. q v.

ἐεικοσάβοιος, ον, Ep. for εἰκοσ. (β worth twenty oxen. τιμὴν ἐεικοσάβ ἄγειν, to bring a recompense of tw oxen, Od. 22, 57. Neut. plur. *Od. 1.

ἐείκοσι, and before a vowel ἐείκοσιν, Ep. for εἰκοσι.

ἐεικόσορος, ον. Ep. for εἰκόσ., *having twenty ranks of rowers*, Od. 9, 322,† a rare form for εἰκοσήρης like τριήρης.

ἐεικοστός, ή, όν, Ep. for εἰκοστός, *the twentieth*.

ἐείλεον, Ep. for εἴλεον, see εἰλέω.

ἐεισάμενος, ἐεισάμην, see ΕΙΔΩ.

ἐεισάσθην, 15, 544, see εἶμι.

ἐέλδομαι, ἐέλδωρ, see ἔλδομαι, ἔλδωρ.

ἐέλμεθα, ἐελμένος, see εἴλω.

ἐέλπομαι, see ἔλπομαι.

ἐέλσαι, see εἴλω.

ἐεργάθω, see ἐργάθω.

ἐέργνυμι, Ep. form of ἐέργω, *to shut up*, κατὰ σνφεοῖσιν ἐέργνυ, Od. 10, 238;† see ἐέργω.

ἐέργω, see ἔργω.

ἐερμένος, see εἴρω.

ἔρση, ἐερσήεις, Ep. for ἔρση, ἐρσήεις.

ἔερτο, see εἴρω.

ἔερχατο, see ἔργω.

ἐέσσατο, see ἔννυμι.

ἐέσσατο, see εἶσα.

ἔεστο, see ἔννυμι.

ἕζομαι, depon. mid. (ΈΔΩ, ΕΩ), only pres. and imperf. without augm. *to seat oneself, to sit*, mly with ἔν τινι, rarely ἔς τι, Od. 4. 51; with ἐπί τινι and τι; metaph. κῆρες ἐπὶ χθονὶ—ἐζέσθην. the fates [of the Achaians] (in the balance) settled to the earth [*sunk low; subsided.* Cp.], 8, 74. (There is no act. ἕζω, from which it is common to derive the tenses εἷσα, εἰσάμην, ἐέσσομαι, see εἶσα.)

ἔηκε, Ep. for ἧκε, see ἵημι.

ἔην, Ep. for ἦν, see εἰμί.

ἐήνδανε, see ἀνδάνω.

ἔηος, gen. masc. as if from ἐεύς, see ἐΰς.

ἔης, gen. Ep. for ἦς, but ἑῆς from ἑός.

ἦσθα see εἰμί.

ἦσι, see εἰμί.

ἴθ', abbrev. for ἔτι.

ἔθειρα, ἡ, prop. *the hair of the head*, h. 7, 4, in the Il. only plur.; spoken of the mane of horses, 8, 42; or of the horsehair crest, *16, 795 (related to ἐθείρω).

ἐθείρω (θέρω), *to attend, to take care of, to cultivate*, ἀλωήν, 21. 347.†

ἐθελοντήρ, ῆρος, ὁ, Ep. for ἐθελοντής (ἐθέλω), *one who acts voluntarily, a volunteer*, Od. 2. 292.†

ἐθέλω. fut. ἐθελήσω, imperf. ἤθελον and ἔθελον, iterative ἐθέλεσκον, 1) *to will* (see βούλομαι). *to wish*, often with infin., or accus. with infin.; the imperat. with negat. serves the purpose of the Lat. *noli*, 2, 247; also absol. chiefly in the partcp. where it may be translated *willingly, gladly*, 10, 556. 2) Sometimes with negat. it is equivalent to *to be able, to be wont*, with infin. 13, 106. 21, 366. Od. 3, 120 (ἐθέλω always in H., never θέλω).

ἔθεν, Ep. for οὗ, q. v.

ἐθήσομαι, see θηέομαι.

ἔθνος, εος, τό (ἔθω), *any multitude living or dwelling together, a troop, a multitude, a nation*, ἑταίρων, Ἀχαιῶν;

spoken of animals: *a swarm, a flock, a herd*, of bees, geese, pigs, 2, 469. 459.

ἔθορον, see θρώσκω.

*ἔθος, ους, τό, Att. for ἦθος, *habit, custom*, Batr. 34.

ἔθρεψα, see τρέφω.

ἔθω, from which we have the Ep. partcp. ἔθων, *accustomed*, 9, 540. 16, 260; mly perf. 2 εἴωθα, Ion. ἔωθα, partcp. εἰωθώς, *to be wont, to be accustomed*, with infin. The partcp. perf. is used absol. for *accustomed, customary*. μᾶλλον ὑφ' ἡνιόχῳ εἰωθότι ἅρμα οἴσετον, they will draw the chariot better under the accustomed charioteer, 5, 231.

εἰ, conj. Ep. and Dor., also αἰ, I) *if*, in the protasis of a conditional sentence. According to the relation of the condition to the conviction of the speaker, it stands 1) With the indicat. in all tenses when the condition is represented as something certain or without doubt, with pres., 1, 178; preter., 1, 290; fut., 1, 294. The apodosis is either in the indicat. of all tenses (also imperat. 1, 173), or in the optat. with ἄν, 1, 293. 6, 129. 2) With the subjunct. when the condition is represented as a mere supposition to be decided, *in case that, allow that*, mly εἴ κε, αἴ κε and εἰ—ἄν, in prose ἐάν. With the subjunct. εἰ also stands in the Ep. language alone, esply εἴπερ, εἴ γ' οὖν, καὶ εἰ, Od. 12, 96. 14, 373. Il. 12, 223. The apodosis is either in the indicat. with one of the principal tenses (or imperat.), or in the subjunct. aor. and pres., 1. 137; or in the optat. with ἄν, 4, 97. 3) With the optat. when the condition is represented as a mere supposition without regard to reality, a simple conjecture. Τρῶες μέγα κεν κεχαροίατο, εἰ τάδε πάντα πυθοίατο, the Trojans would rejoice, if they should learn all this, 1, 257. The apodosis stands in the optat. with ἄν, and sometimes also in the indicat., 10, 223. 4) With the indicat. of the historical tenses, when the reality of the condition is denied or rejected. The apodosis then stands, *a*) Mly in the indicat. hist. tenses with ἄν, so that the reality of the conclusion is also denied. καί νύ κ' ἔτι πλέονας—κτάνε Ὀδυσσεύς, εἰ μὴ ἄρ' ὀξὺ νόησε Ἕκτωρ, and Odysseus (Ulysses) would have slain still more, if Hector had not quickly perceived it, 5, 679. Od. 4, 363. *b*) Or in the optat. with ἄν, the apodosis being merely indicated as possible, 2, 80. 5, 311. II) *if but, would that*, a particle of wishing, prop. a hypothetic protasis without apodosis, with optat., 16, 559. 24, 74; mly εἴθε, εἰ γάρ, αἲ γάρ, q. v. III) *whether*, in indirect questions, after verbs of considering, seeking, asking, knowing, saying, etc., with indicat., 1, 83. 5, 183. If the discourse relates to events expected and yet to be ascertained, εἴ κε or ἤν is employed with the subjunct., 15, 32. Also εἰ, *whether*, is found with other verbs, in which case σκοπεῖν or πειρᾶσθαι must be

G

supplied. The subjunct. or optat. may follow, 11, 797. 10, 55; on the general construction of εἰ, cf. Gr. 1281, sqq. 1361, sqq. [§ 851, sqq. § 877, sqq.]. IV) εἰ mly begins the sentence, so that other particles follow, as εἰ γάρ, εἰ δέ, εἰ καί, εἰ μή, etc., which see under their own articles. It follows in καὶ εἰ, even if; οὐδ' εἰ, not(even) if; ὡς εἰ, as if, see ὡσεί.

εἰαμενή or εἱαμενή, ἡ, a low moist place about rivers and swamps, a low ground, a marsh, meadow, pasture, *4, 483. 15, 631. It is mly derived from ἧμαι, sedere, hence εἰαμενή (εἴαται) for ἡμένη. Spitzner writes εἱαμενή, because both the deriv. and the best Gramm. require the spiritus asper.

εἰ—ἄν stands in H. for the Ep. αἴ κε, αἴ κε, when it is separated by particles, as εἰ δ' ἄν, εἴπερ ἄν, 3, 288. Of the contracted forms ἐάν and ἤν, only the last is found in H., cf. εἰ, I. 2.

εἰανός. Ep. for ἐανός, 16, 9.†

εἶαρ, ρος, τό, poet. for ἔαρ, q. v.

εἰαρινός, ή, όν, Ep. for ἐαρινός (ἔαρ), relating to spring, vernal. ὥρη εἰαρινή, spring-time. ἄνθεα εἰαρινά, vernal flowers, 2. 89. Od. 18, 367.

εἴασα, εἴασκον, see ἐάω.

εἴαται, εἴατο, Ep. for ἧνται, ἧντο, see ἧμαι.

εἴατο, Ep for ἧντο, see εἰμί, I am.

εἴβω, Ep. for λείβω, to drop, always εἴβειν δάκρυον, to shed tears. *Od. 4, 153.

εἰ γάρ, 1) for if, in hypothet. sentences, 13, 276. 17, 156. Od. 18, 366. 2) O that, if but, a particle of wishing, with optat., 8, 538. 17, 561; more mly αἴ γάρ, q. v.

εἴγε, conj. 1) if at least, if indeed, si quidem, spoken of things which one may reasonably suppose; mly it is separated by other words. εἰ δύνασαί γε, 1, 393. 18, 427. It is found only once united: εἴγε μὲν εἰδείης, Od. 5, 206.

εἰ γοῦν, even if, although, 5, 258 † Thiersch, § 329. 1, rejects γοῦν as unhomeric, and reads εἰ γ' οὖν, which Spitzner adopts, see γέ.

εἰ δ' ἄγε, come on then! up then! in connexion with νῦν, δή, μήν, with imperat. and with δεῦρο, 17, 685; also with subj. or fut., Od. 9, 37; also with plur. following. 6, 376; and itself in the plur. εἰ δ' ἄγετ'—πειρηθῶμεν, 17, 381. There is a partial ellipsis of the protasis: εἰ δὲ βούλει, ἄγε.

εἰδάλιμος, η, ον (εἶδος), handsome, beautiful in form, comely. Od. 24, 279.†

εἶδαρ, ατος, τό, Ep. for ἔδαρ (ἔδω), food, food for horses, 5, 369; bait for fish, Od. 12, 252.

εἰ δέ, 1) but if, and if, in complete sentences, see εἰ. 2) εἰ δέ is sometimes used elliptically as an antithesis, in which case the verb must be supplied from the connexion. εἰ δὲ καὶ αὐτοὶ (sc. φεύξονται), φευγόντων, but if they will fly, let them fly, 9, 46. cf. 262. Il. 21, 487.

εἰδέω, 1) For εἰδῶ, subj. of οἶδα. 2)

An assumed theme for some forms εἴδω and οἶδα, see ΕΙΔΩ.

εἰδησέμεν, Ep. for εἰδήσειν, see ΕΙΔ

εἰ δή, of a thing assumed to be gra[n] or undoubted, with indic.: seldom v subj. as 1, 293 (where some make ε̣ ξομαι, subj.), cf. 21, 463. 1) if indee[d] quidem jam; if now truly, if really, 111. 18, 120. 24, 57. Od. 22, 359. whether really, in questions, Od. 1, ; 17, 484.

Εἰδοθέη, ἡ, Ep. for Εἰδοθέα, daug[h]l of Prôteus, who instructed Menelau[s] the island of Pharos, how he could s her father and compel him to proph Od. 4, 365 seq. (from εἶδος and θε[ά] divine form: in Eurip. Θεονόη.)

εἴδομαι, εἶδον, see ΕΙΔΩ

εἶδος, εος, τό (ΕΙΔΩ), the appeara[nce] the form, mien, spoken often of the hu[man] form in connexion with φυή, δέμα[ς] 58. 24, 376; of a dog, Od. 17, 308.

ΕΙΔΩ, ΙΔΩ, to see, to know, in pres. act. obsol. The tenses in use a

A) The aor. act. εἶδον, Ep. ἴδον, i[n] ἰδεῖν, Ep. ἰδέειν, partcp. ἰδών, subj. and Ep. ἴδωμι, optat. ἴδοιμι, and the mid. εἰδόμην and Ep. ἰδόμην, imp ἰδοῦ, infin. ἰδέσθαι, subj. ἴδωμαι, they nify to see, to perceive, to behold, to obs[erve] and belong as aor. to ὁράω and ὁράο q. v. Remarkable is: οὐκ ἴδε χάριν α (sc. ἀλόχου), he did not enjoy her g or favour; spoken of a warrior shortly after his marriage, 11, 243. Eustath. explains it: οὐκ ἐχάρη ἐπ συμβιώσει αὐτῆς οὐδ' ἐπὶ τῇ τεκνοποι Others, 'he saw not her loveliness;' Köppen understands by χάρις, tha gratitude, in reference to πολλὰ δ' ἐδ Here belong the Ep. and Ion. mid. pass. εἴδομαι, aor. 1 εἰσάμην, ἐεισάμην, partcp. εἰσάμενος, and ε μενος, 1) to be seen; hence, to ap[pear] to seem, 8, 558; εἴδεται ἦμαρ, 13, 98 τοι κῆρ εἴδεται εἶναι, that seems d to thee, 1, 228. 2, 215. 2) to be li[ke] resemble, with dat. ἐείσατο φθο Πολίτῃ, he resembled Polītēs in v 2, 791. 20, 81.

B) Perf. οἶδα, 2 οἶσθα, and οἶδας, 1, 337:† plur. ἴδμεν, ἴστε, ἴσασι. εἰδῶ, Ep. ἰδέω, 14, 235: plur. εἴδομε εἰδῶμεν, εἴδετε, Ep. for εἰδῆτε, εἰ optat. εἰδείην, imperat. ἴσθι, infin. ἰδ and ἴδμεν, Ep. for εἰδέναι, partcp. υἶα, ός: from this always the ἰδυίῃσιν πραπίδεσσιν, plup-rf. ἤδε[α] for ἤδειν, 2 Ep. ἠείδης. ἠείδεις, ἠ[ε] for ᾔδεις. 3 ᾔείδη, ᾔείδει, Od. 9, ᾔδεεν, ᾔδεα. ᾔδε, Ep. for ᾔδει, 3 ἴσαν for ᾖσαν, 18, 405; fut. εἰ[σ] more rarely poet. εἰδήσω, infin. εἰδή[σ]ειν Od. 6, 257. 7, 327; all with the to know (prop. to have perceive[d] understand, to recognize, to becom quainted with, often connected wi σάφα, also with φρεσί, ἐνὶ φρεσί, φρένα, κατὰ θυμόν, in mind; pri[m] with accus. or infin. οἶδε νοῆσα[ι].

τινὶ εἰδέναι, to feel gratitude (to be grateful) to any one, 14, 235. The dependent clause follows with the partcp. or with ὡς, ὅτι, ὅπως, more rarely the relat. ὅ, for ὅτι, 18, 197; in cases of doubt with εἰ, whether, or with ἤ, ἤ, 10, 342; also with only one ἤ, Od. 4, 109. 2) to understand, to be conversant with, πολεμήϊα ἔργα, 11, 719; also μήδεα, in like manner ἤπια δήνεα, to cherish gentle thoughts or sentiments, 4, 361; hence mly, to be disposed, as, ἄρτια, αἴσιμα, etc. 3) The partcp. often as adj.: γυναῖκες ἀμύμονα ἔργα εἰδυῖαι, women skilled in excellent works, 9, 270, cf. 3, 202. As adj. mly the partcp. with gen. εὖ εἰδὼς τόξων, well skilled (expert) in the bow (= archery), 2, 718; in like manner μάχης, πολέμου, etc. The gen. however is also found with the finite verb, 12, 229. 15, 412. The fut. εἰδησέμεν signifies also, to become acquainted with, Od. 6, 257.

εἴδωλον, τό (εἶδος), a form, an image. 2) a shadowy form, an illusive image or phantom, which has the exact form of the object (person) it is to represent, 5, 449; esply in pl. the shades of the dead, 23, 72. Od. 1, 476.

εἴεν, see εἰμί.

εἶθαρ, adv. poet. (εὐθύς), immediately, forthwith, *5, 337.

αἴθε, adv. if but, oh that, with optat. Od. 2, 33; more mly αἴθε, q. v.

εἰ καί, 1) if even, with indic. and optat. si etiam; in most cases καί refers to a word standing near, 16, 623. Od. 6, 310. 7, 194. 2) although, where it may be compared with the Lat. etiamsi, etsi, in so far as it refers to the whole concessive clause, 23, 832. Od. 11, 356. 18, 376. 3) whether also, in indirect questions, 2, 367. From this is to be distinguished καὶ εἰ. q. v. cf. Spitzner Excurs. XXIII. on Il. p. 7.

αἴ κε, εἰ κεν, if, Ep. = ἐάν, see εἰ I. 2. and αἴ κε.

εἴκελος, η, ον (εἴκω), like, similar, τινί, H. oftener ἴκελος.

εἰκοσάκις, adv. twenty times, 9, 379.†

εἴκοσι, indecl. Ep. ἐείκοσι, before a vowel ἐείκοσιν, twenty. In H. εἴκοσι never except in composition takes ν, but ι before a vowel is elided, εἴκοσ', Od. 2, 212. [εἰκοσίμετρος, containing twenty measures, so Villoison and Clarke. 23, 264.]

εἰκοσινήριτος, ον (νήριτος), full twenty-fold. The derivation is doubtful: according to Damm, the second factor is νήριτος, without dispute: but it is far better to explain the word with Eustath and the Schol. = πρὸς εἴκοσιν ἐριστὰ ἤτοι ἐρίζοντα καὶ ἰσάζοντα. ἄποινα, a twenty-fold ransom, 22, 349, a ransom competing with twenty (others), or equal to them [εἰκοσπλασίονα, εἰκοσάκις ἐξισούμενα τῇ τοῦ σώματος σωτηρίᾳ. Schol. A.].

εἰκοστός, ή, όν, Ep. ἐεικοστός, the twentieth.

εἶκτα, εἶκτον, εἴκτην, see ἔοικα.

εἰκυῖα, see ἔοικα.

ΕΙΚΩ, as pres. obsol.: from which only the 3 sing. imperf. occurs: σφίσιν εἶκε, it seemed good to them, 18, 520;† on the contrary, the perf ἔοικα, q. v.

εἴκω, fut εἴξω, aor. εἶξα, Ep. iterat. 3 sing. εἴξασκε, 1) to yield, to retreat, also with ὀπίσσω, backwards, τινί, from any one; with gen. of place: εἴκειν πολέμου, to retreat from the battle, 5, 348; and with both: χάρμης Ἀργείοις, to retreat out of the battle from the Greeks, 4, 509; also from civility, 24, 100. Od. 2, 14; hence b) Metaph. to yield, to be inferior, τινί τι, to any one in any thing, 22, 459: also with dat. εἴκειν πόδεσσι, to be inferior in swiftness of foot, in running, Od. 14, 221. c) Also of the body: to yield, ὅπῃ εἴξειε μάλιστα, where it could not withstand (the lance), i. e. might be wounded, 22, 321. 2) to yield, to give way to, to follow, with dat. ὕβρει, arrogance, αἰδοῖ, ὄκνῳ: ᾧ θυμῷ εἴξας, following his inclination, 9, 598. 3) Apparently trans. εἶξαι ἡνία ἵππῳ, prop. to yield to the horse in respect to the reins, i. e. to give him loose reins, 23, 337, cf. 1. b.

εἰλαπινάζω (εἰλαπίνη), to feast, to be present at a feast, only pres. Il. and Od. from which

εἰλαπιναστής, οῦ, ὁ, a guest, one who feasts, 17, 577.†

εἰλαπίνη, ἡ, a splendid feast, a banquet, a sacrificial feast, Od. 11, 415. 1, 226 (prob. from πίνειν κατ' εἴλας).

εἶλαρ, ατος, τό (εἴλω), prop. covering, then a protection, a defence, spoken of a wall: νεῶν τε καὶ αὐτῶν, a protection for the ships and for ourselves, 7, 338; of a rudder: κύματος εἶλαρ, against the waves, Od. 5, 257.

εἰλάτινος, η, ον, Ep. for ἐλάτινος, of fir, of fir-wood; Il. and Od.

εἷλε, see αἱρέω.

Εἰλείθυιαι, αἱ, the goddesses who preside over child birth, according to 11, 270, daughters of Hêrê goddess of marriage, who send indeed bitter pangs, but also help women in labour, and aid the birth; plur. 19, 119; but sing. 19, 103. 16, 187. The discourse is clearly of one, Od. 19, 188, who had a temple at Amnisus in Crete. According to Hes. Th. 922, there is but one, daughter of Zeus and Hêrê, Apd. 1, 3. 1. In later writers she is the same with Artĕmis (from ἐλεύθω, she who comes, Venilia Herm.).

Εἰλέσιον, τό, a place in Bœotia, near Tanagra, 2, 499. (According to Strabo, Εἰλέσιον, from ἕλος, swamp.)

εἰλέω, see εἴλω.

εἰλήλουθα. εἰλήλουθμεν, see ἔρχομαι.

εἰλίπους, οδος, ὁ, ἡ (εἴλω), dragging or trailing heavily the feet, with a trailing or lumbering gait, epith. of cattle, from their unsteady gait, esply with the hinder feet: only dat. and accus. plur. (Buttmann, Lex. p. 266, would translate it 'stampffüssig,' having feet suited for threshing (heavy-footed).)

εἰλίσσω, Ep. for ἐλίσσω.

εἶλον and εἰλόμην, see αἱρέω.

εἰλύαται, see εἰλύω.

εἰλῦμα, τό (εἰλύω), a veil, covering, clothing, Od. 6, 179.†

εἰλυφάζω, to whirl, to roll, with accus. φλόγα, 20, 492.†

εἰλυφάω = εἰλυφάζω, partcp. pres. εἰλυφόων for εἰλυφῶν, whirling, rolling, 11, 156.†

εἰλύω, Ep. for εἰλύω, perf. pass. εἰλῦμαι, 3 plur. εἰλύαται for εἰλύνται, partcp. pass. εἰλυμένος, to wind about, to envelope, to veil, to wrap up, to cover, with accus. τινὰ ψαμάθοισιν, any one with sand, 21, 319 :† or prop. the compound κατειλύω. Of the pass. only the perf. αἵματι καὶ κονίῃσιν εἰλῦτο, he was covered with blood and dust, 16, 640. Mly partcp. εἰλυμένος ὤμους νεφέλῃ, the shoulders enveloped in cloud, 5, 186; χαλκῷ, 18, 522; σάκεσι, Od. 14, 479. (ν always long, except in εἰλύαται.)

εἴλω in the pass., εἰλέω in the act. Ep. for εἰλέω (th. ϜΕΛΩ), aor. 1 infin. ἔλσαι and ἐέλσαι, partcp. ἔλσας, perf. pass. ἔελμαι, partcp. ἐελμένος, aor. 2 pass. ἐάλην (like ἐστάλην from στέλλω), 3 plur. ἄλεν for ἄλησαν, infin. ἀλῆναι and ἀλήμεναι, partcp. ἀλείς, εἶσα, ἕν, all purely Epic forms. 1) Act. 1) to press, to thrust, to drive to straits, esply an enemy in war; with an accus. and the prep. κατά, ἐπί, or simply the dat. obsol., 8, 215; κατὰ πρύμνας ἔλσαι, 1, 409; Τρῶας κατὰ ἄστυ, 21, 225; and with the mere dat. θαλάσσῃ ἔλσαι Ἀχαιούς, to drive the Achaians to the sea, 18, 294; also θῆρας ὁμοῦ εἰλεῦντα κατὰ λειμῶνα, driving the wild beasts over the meadow, Od. 11, 573; hence metaph. of a storm: τινά, to drive any one along, Od. 19, 200; in the Od. also to strike: ἐπεί οἱ νῆα κεραυνῷ Ζεὺς ἔλσας ἐκέασσε, when Zeus striking with lightning dashed in pieces his ship, Od. 5, 131. 7, 250. 2) to drive together, to shut up. Ἀχαιοὺς Τρῶες ἐπὶ πρύμνῃσιν, 18, 447; ἐν μέσσοισι, 11, 413; ἐνὶ σπῆϊ, to shut up in a cave, Od. 12, 210; ἐν στείνει, Od. 22, 460. Pass. to be pressed, to be driven. κατὰ ἄστυ ἐέλμεθα, 24, 662. cf. 18, 287; hence, of Ares: Διὸς βουλῇσιν ἐελμένος, pressed by the counsels of Zeus, 13, 524; hence also, b) to hold back, to check, τινά, 2, 294. II) Mid. and aor. pass. to be crowded together, to be shut in, to crowd together. ἀμφὶ Διομήδεα, 5, 782; spoken esply of persons beleaguered: ἀνδρῶν εἰλομένων, when men are besieged, 5, 203; esply in the aor. pass. οἳ δὴ εἰς ἄστυ ἄλεν, they crowded together into the city, 22, 12; Ἀργείους ἐκέλευσα ἀλήμεναι ἐνθάδε, to assemble, 5, 823; ἐς ἄστυ, 16, 714; ἐπὶ πρύμνῃσιν, 18, 76. 286. Hence also μὲν ὕδωρ, collected water, 23, 420. b) to bend oneself together, to gather oneself (bodily) up. τῇ ὕπο πᾶς ἐάλη, under this (the shield) he drew himself entirely up, i. e. he concealed himself, 3, 408. 20, 278.

ἧστο ἀλείς, he sat bent together, 16, 40; also of a lion gathering himself to spring on the prey, 20, 168; so also a warrior Ἀχιλῆα ἀλεὶς μένεν, he awaited Achilles on the alert, 21, 571. cf. 22, 308. Od. 2 538.

εἷμα, ατος, τό (ἕννυμι), a garment, clothing, dress in general, spoken of kinds of clothes; hence often plu αἵματα, the entire dress, Od. 2, 3. 6, 2

εἷμαι, see ἕννυμι.

εἵμαρται, εἵμαρτο, see μείρομαι.

εἰ μέν, with εἰ δέ, often serves to ma an antithetic relation between two c ditions. Sometimes the apodosis wanting. e. g. εἰ μὲν δώσουσι γέρας (καλῶς ἕξει, well and good), εἰ δέ κε δώωσιν, 1, 135.

εἰμέν, Ep. and Ion. for ἐσμέν, see εἰ εἱμένος, see ἕννυμι.

εἰ μή, 1) if not, unless, nisi, in c ditional clauses, where the whole cla is intended to be denied, see μή, 2, 1 261. 2) except, without a verb, after ἄλλος. Od. 12, 326. 17, 383.

εἰμί (th. ἔω), H. forms: pres. 2 si ἐσσί and εἶς, 1 plur. εἰμέν, 3 plur. ἐ subj. ἔω and εἴω (εἴῃς, εἴῃ, not in Wolf), optat. εἴην, also ἔοις, ἔοι, in ἔμεναι, ἔμμεναι, ἔμεν, ἔμμεν, partcp. (ὄντας, ὄντες, Od.), imperf. 1 sing. ἔα, ἔην, ἔον, ἔσκον, 2 ἔησθα, ἦσθα, 3 ἔην, ἦεν, ἔσκε, 2 dual ἤστην, 3 plur. (εἴατο, Od. 20, 106, where others εἴατο), fut. ἔσομαι, Ep. ἔσσομαι, 3 ἐσσεῖται, etc. On the inclination of accent. see Thiersch Gram. § 62. [Gr 82. Jelf. i. § 62, 63. Buttm. § 14, 2]. As a verb of existence (in which case inclination takes place), 1) to be exist, to have being. τὰ ἐόντα τά τ' ἐ μέσα, the present and the future, 1, chiefly in the signif. to live. οὐ δὴ he did not long live, 6, 131. ἔτι they are still alive, Od. 15, 433. Hence gods are often denominated αἰὲν ἐό the ever-living, and οἱ ἐσσόμενοι, terity; with an adv. Κουρήτεσσι κ ἦν, it fared badly, went ill with, 9, διαγνῶναι χαλεπῶς ἦν, it was hard t tinguish, 7, 424. 2) ἐστι with a follo infin., it is possible, it is permitted can; often even with negat. πὰρ δύναμιν ἔστι πολεμίζειν, a man cannot fig yond his strength, 13, 787. οὔπως καταβῆμεναι, it is not possible to des 12, 65. cf. 357. The person is in the still also with accus. and infin., 1 Od. 2, 316. 3) ἐστι with the dat. pers, it is to me, i. e. I have, I po εἰσίν μοι παῖδες, I have sons, 10, II) As copula: 1) to be, mly conn with the subst. and adj.; also wit verbs, ἀκέων, ἀκήν, ἐγγύς, etc. 2) gen. it indicates possession, pro descent. αἵματος εἰς ἀγαθοῖο, thou good blood. Od. 4, 611; material: ἔσαν μέλανος κυάνοιο, the stripes w dark steel, 11, 24. 3) With dat κατηφείη καὶ ὄνειδος ἔσσεται, 17, also in the constr. ἐμοὶ δέ κεν ἀσμένῳ εἴη, it would be grateful to me, 14, 108. 4) Freq. with prepos. ἐκ πατρὸς ἀγαθοῦ, to spring from a noble father, 14, 113. 5) εἶναι is frequently omitted, e. g. 3, 391. 10, 437. 113. On εἴην in 15, 82, see εἶμι, at the close.

εἶμι (th. ἴω), pres. subj. ἴω, ἴησθα and ἴῃς, 3 ἴῃσι. ἴῃ, 1 plur. ἴομεν, Ep. for ἴωμεν, 3 ἴωσι, optat. 1 sing. εἴην, 15, 82 ; 3 ἴοι, εἴη and ἰείη, 19, 209 ; infin. ἴμεναι, ἰμέναι, 20, 365 ; cf. Thiersch § 229 ; ἴμεν, ἰέναι, partcp. ἰών. imperf. Ep. ἤϊα, ἤϊον, 2 ἤϊες and ἴες, 3 ἤϊεν, ἤϊε, ἤεν, ἤε, ἴεν, ἴε, 3 ἴτην, 1 plur. ᾔομεν, Od. 3, ἤϊον and ἤϊσαν, ἴσαν. Finally, in Ep. fut. mid. εἴσομαι, and aor. 1 εἰσάμην, to which may be added the pres. ἴεμαι. The pres is even in H. used as a fut., 10, 55, though it is found in him as a pres. also. 1) to go, to come, to travel, to journey; frequently, according to the connexion, a) to go away, to return; often limited by adverbs: ἆσσον, αὖτις, ἐπί, ἐς, ἀνά, μετά, ἰέναι, ἀντία and ἀντίον τινός, to go against any one, 5, 256 ; ἐπί τινα, to go to any one, 10, 55. b) With accus. ὁδὸν ἰέναι, to go a journey, Od. 10, 103 ; with gen. of the place, ἰὼν πεδίοιο, going through the plain, 5, 597. c) With partcp. fut. it expresses an action which one is going or intending to perform. εἶσι μαχησόμενος, he goes to fight, 17, 147; also with infin., 15, 544. 2) Metaph. a) to fly, spoken of birds and insects, 17, 756. 2, 87. b) Of inanimate things : to go, to travel ; ἐπὶ νηὸς ἰέναι, in a ship, Od. ; spoken of an axe and spear: πέλεκυς εἶσι διὰ δουρός, the axe goes through the plank, 3, 61. Spoken of food, 19, 209 ; of clouds, smoke, tempest, 4, 278. 21, 522; and of time: (ἔτος) εἶσι τέταρτον, the fourth year will come to an end, Od 2, 89. so Eustath., Voss; but Nitzsch, ' the fourth year will come,' in which case, in v. 106, τρίετες is to be changed into διετες, and in v. 107, τέτρατον into δὴ τρίτον. II) Mid. in the same signif. ἐς περιωπήν, to ascend to a place of observation, 14, 8. διαπρὸ δὲ εἴσατο καὶ τῆς, it went entirely through this also (μίτρῃ), 4, 138. 13, 191 (iota is short, but in ἴομεν sometimes long for metre's sake), see ἴεμαι.—N. B. 15, 80 seq. ὡς δ᾽ ὅτ᾽ ἂν ἀΐξῃ νόος ἀνέρος, ὅστ᾽ ἐπὶ πολλὴν γαῖαν ἐληλουθὼς—νοήσῃ ἔνθ᾽ εἴην ἢ ἔνθα, cf. εἴσσω. Some of the ancients take εἴην, or, by another reading, ἤην, as 1 sing. imperf. of εἰμί (I was); others read ἤϊα or ᾔειν as 3 sing. imperf. of εἶμι (ibam): others again, εἴη as 3 sing. optat. from εἰμί or εἶμί: Voss leaves it undecided from which verb he takes it. Hermann, in the essay de leg. quibusd. subtilicrib. serm. Hom. (Op. II. 57), prefers the reading ἤην (hic fui et illic), which certainly suits ἐληλουθὼς well. Still as ἤην occurs nowhere else as 1 pers., and as ἔνθα ἢ ἔνθα mly indicates motion, it is most probably to be regarded

with Spitzner as optat. of εἶμι, εἴην (cf. 24, 130. Od. 14, 496), should I go here or there [secum cogitat, huc iverim an illuc] ? The last mentioned critic, since the first pers. does not accord well with the Epic diction, thinks the reading εἴη more agreeable to the Hom. form of speech. Cf. Spitzner on the passage.

εἰν, poet. for ἐν, in.

εἰνάετες, adv. (ἐννέα, ἔτος), nine years long, from adj. εἰναετής, of nine years, Il., and Od. 3, 118.

εἰνάκις, adv., poet. for ἐννάκις, nine times, Od. 14, 230.

εἰνάλιος, η, ον, Ep. for ἐνάλιος, in the sea, of the sea ; κῆτος, a monster of the sea. Od. 443; κορώνη, the sea-crow, *Od. 5, 67.

εἰνάνυχες, adv. (ἐννέα νύξ), nine nights long, 9, 470.†

εἰνατέρες, αἱ, wives of brothers, sisters-in-law, *6, 378. 22, 473. (Sing. obsolete.)

εἴνατος, η, ον, Ep. for ἔννατος, q. v.

εἴνεκα, Ep. for ἕνεκα, q. v.

εἰνί, Ep. for ἐν.

εἰνόδιος, η, ον, Ep. for ἐνόδιος (ὁδός), on the way, 16, 260.†

εἰνοσίφυλλος, ον (ἔνοσις, φύλλον), leaf-shaking, clothed with foliage ; forest-clad [Cp.], epith. of mountains [there stands, his boughs waving, the mountain Neritus sublime. Cp.], 2, 632. Od. 9, 22.

εἴξασκε, see εἴκω.

εἷο, Ep. gen. for οὗ, his.

εἰοικυῖαι, see ἔοικα.

εἶσα, i. q. εἶπον, q. v.

εἰπέμεναι, εἰπέμεν, see εἶπον.

εἴπερ, 1) if indeed, if really ; if, in hypothetical sentences, when the two members are harmonious. The indic. subj. and optat. follow (see εἰ). εἰ τελέει περ, 8, 415. 16, 118. 24, 667. Od. 1, 188. εἴπερ γάρ κ᾽ ἐθέλῃσιν Ὀλύμπιος—ἐξ ἑδέων στυφελίξαι, 1, 580. In this passage, the apodosis is wanting. according to the interpretation of Wolf and Spitzner, viz. ' he is able to do so.' Voss, on the other hand, places the comma after Ὀλύμπιος ἀστεροπητής. and takes the words ἐξ ἑδέων στυφελίξαι (optat.), as apodosis, for ' if the Olymp. thunderer should will. he could hurl us,' etc. 2) even if, although, when the members are antith., 1, 81. 4, 38, 261. 8, 153.

εἴποθεν, more correctly εἴ ποθεν, if from any where, whether from any where, Od. 1. 115. ll. 9, 380.

εἴ ποθι, if any where, *Od. 12, 96.

εἶπον, Ep. ἔειπον, iterat. εἴπεσκον, subj εἴπω, 2 sing. εἴπῃσθα, optat. εἴποιμι, infin. εἰπεῖν, partcp. εἰπών. The imperat. εἰπέ, εἴπατε, Od. 3, 407; also the poet. form ἔσπετε, to say, to speak, τί τινι, any thing to any one : also, εἰπεῖν τινα, to address any one, 12, 210. 17, 237; εὖ εἰπεῖν τινα, to speak well of one, Od. 1, 302 ; (from ἔπω, prop. to recount ; in use, it is the aor. of φημί.)

εἴποτε, more correctly εἴ ποτε, 1) if ever, if at any time, with indicat., 1, 39.

394; with subj., 1, 340. 2) *whether ever,
if ever*, in indirect questions with optat.,
2, 97. 3) The Hom. formula εἴποτ᾽ ἔην
γε is variously explained. Most critics
take it as an expression of a sad remembrance of what formerly existed; δαὴρ
αὖτε ἐμος ἔσκε, εἰ ποτ᾽ ἔην γε, 3, 180.
Thiersch § 329, 3, 'he was also my
brother-in-law, if indeed he ever was so'
[which is hardly credible]. Wolf likewise
remarks in Vorles. zu Il. II. p. 202: "It
expresses tender sensibility connected
with dejection and regret: 'once he
was.'" So Eustath. understands it; he
says, 'it is as if she would say, οὐκ ἔστι,
ἀλλὰ ποτὲ ἦν,' cf. Herm. ad Viger. p.
946: "*Cujus formulæ, quæ perdifficilis
explicatu est, hic videtur sensus esse; si
unquam fuit, quod nunc est non amplius,
i. e. si recte dici potest fuisse, quod ita sui
factum est dissimile, ut fuisse unquam vix
credas. Est enim hæc loquutio dolentium,
non esse quid amplius; ut vim ejus
Germanice [Anglice] sic exprimas,*" but,
alas! no longer so. Schütz in Hoogeveen
Doct. Part. in Epit. red. p. 630, incorrectly considers it as an optat. 'ah would
he were so still.' Besides 3, 180, this
formula stands in 11, 761. 24, 426. Od.
15, 268. 19, 315.
   εἴ που, *if perhaps (perchance, haply),
if by any means*, Od. 4, 193.
   εἴ πως, *if perchance, if in any way*, 13,
807.
   Εἰραφιώτης, ου, ὁ, voc. Εἰραφιῶτα,
appellat. of Dionÿsos. Hom. h. 26, 2.
(The derivation is uncertain; perhaps
from ἐν and ῥάπτω, sowed into the thigh.
Schwenk in Zeitschr. für Alterthumsw.
No. 151, 1835, derives it from ἔαρ and
φίω = φύω, and translates, *spring-born*.)
   εἴργω = ἔεργω, see ἔργω.
   εἴρερος, ὁ (εἴρω, to bind), *captivity,
servitude, or a female slave*, cf. Nitzsch,
Od. 8, 529.†
   *Εἰρεσίαι, αἱ, a town in Hestiæôtis
(Thessalia), h. in Apoll. 32. Others read,
Πειφεσίαι; Ilgen understands by Εἰρεσίαι, the island *Irrhesia* of Pliny.
   εἰρεσίη, ἡ (ἐρέσσω), *the act of rowing*,
*Od. 10, 78. 11, 640.
   Εἰρεσιώνη, ἡ (εἶρος), 1) An olive
branch wound with wool and hung with
fruits, a kind of harvest garland, which
on the festivals Πυανέψια and Θαργήλια
was carried around by boys with singing
and then hung upon the house-door.
2) the *song* on such an occasion; and
then only a *song*, to solicit charity, Ep. 15.
   Εἰρέτρια, ἡ, Ion. for Ἐρέτρια; an important town in the island of Eubœa,
near Palæo Castro, 2, 537.
   εἴρη, ἡ, *an assembly, a place of assembling*, plur., 18, 531.† (According to
Schol. = ἀγορά, from ἐρεῖν) or from εἴρω,
sero, keeping locked (the sacred gates, V.).
   εἴρημαι, see εἴρω.
   εἰρήνη, ἡ, *peace*, Od. 24, 486. ἐπ᾽
εἰρήνης. *in peace*, 2, 797. Od. 24, 486
(prob. from εἴρω, *sero*).

εἴριον, τό. Ep. for ἔριον, q. v.
   εἰροκόμος, ον (κομέω), *working wo-
carding wool*, 3, 387.†
   εἴρομαι, Ion. and Ep. depon. m
infin. εἴρεσθαι, imperf. εἰρόμην, f
εἰρήσομαι, 1) *to ask*, τινά, any one
after any one, 1, 553. 6, 239; τί, a
any thing, 0, 416; and τινά τι, any
about any thing, Od. 7, 237; also α
τι, Od. 11, 570. 2) *to say*, cf. εἴρω. (
forms ἐρέω, ἐρέομαι, ἔρομαι, q. v.)
   εἰροπόκος, ον (πόκος), *woolly, core
with wool*, epith. of sheep, 5, 337. Od
443.
   εἶρος, τό, Ep. for ἔρος, *wool*, *Od
135. 9, 226.
   εἴρυαται, see ἐρύομαι.
   εἰρύομαι and εἰρύω, Ep. for ἐρύομ
and ἐρύω, q. v.
   εἴρω, poet. (theme FEP, *sero*), o
partcp. perf. ἐερμένος, pluperf. ἔερ
*to arrange in a row, to fasten togeth
to bind*; ὅρμος ἠλέκτροισιν ἐερμένος
necklace joined or strung with amb
Od. 18, 296. h. Ap. 104; and ἔερτο, (
15, 460.
   εἴρω, fut. ἐρέω, Ep. for ἐρῶ, perf. pa
εἴρημαι, 3 pluperf. pass. εἴρητο, fut.
εἰρήσομαι (aor. 1 pass. ῥηθείς, from t
theme ΡΕΩ). The pres. is Ep. a
occurs only in the 1 sing., Od. 2, 1
The common form of the fut. h Cer. 4
1) *to speak, to say, to tell*, τί, 4, 363;
μέν τοι μέλεος εἰρήσεται αἶνος, not em
praise shall be spoken to thee, 23, 7
τινί τι, any thing to any one, 1, 297.
*to speak to, to communicate, to announ
ἔπος*, 1, 419; φόως ἐρέουσα, (about)
announce the light, 2, 49. II) Mid.
say, like the act., 1, 513. Od. 11, 5
mly *to ask*, prop. 'I cause to be told n
conf. εἴρομαι. (These forms from εἰ
belong in use to φημί, q. v. The J
fut. ἐρέω, *I will say*, must not be co
founded with the pres. ἐρέω, *I ask*)
   εἰρωτάω, Ion. and Ep. for ἐρωτάω, o
pres. *to ask, to interrogate*, τινά τι, (
about any thing, *Od. 4, 347. 17, 138.
   εἰς, Ion. and Ep. ἐς, 1) Prep. w
accus., ground signif. *into, to whithe
(cf. ἐν), to indicate a motion into
interior of an object, 1) Spoken
space: a) Of a local object, *into*,
οἴχεσθαι ἐς Θήβην, 1, 366; εἰς ἅλα; ἐς
of persons, with the implied idea of r
dence, εἰς Ἀγαμέμνονα, 7, 312; ἐς Μ
λαον. Od. 3, 317; with verbs of seein
εἰς ὦπα ἰδέσθαι, to look (into) in the fa
b) Of quantity: εἰς δεκάδας ἀριθμεῖσι
to be counted into decades, 2, 124.
Of time: a) In assigning a limit, t
until: ἐς ἠέλιον καταδύντα; in l
manner ἐς τί ἔτι, till how long, 5, 4
b) In indicating continuance of tu
for: ἐς ἐνιαυτόν, for a year, a year to
Od. 4, 86; ἐς θέρος, in the summer, t
14, 384. 3) Of cause, manner, e
a) The aim, εἰπεῖν εἰς ἀγαθόν, for m
9, 102. b) Way and manner, ἐς μ
βουλεύειν, harmoniously, 2, 379. c

reference, εἰς φύσιν, Batr. 52. Remark 1) εἰς is often found with verbs signifying rest, instead of the prep. ἐν with the dat. It is a constructio prægnans by which the verb at the same time embraces the idea of motion: ἐφάνη λῖς εἰς ὁδόν, 15, 276; ἐς θρόνους ἕζοντο, Od. 4, 51. Rem. 2) εἰς stands apparently with the gen. by an ellipsis: εἰς Ἀίδαο, subaud. δόμον; εἰς Αἰγύπτοιο (ὕδωρ), Od. 4, 581. II) Adv.; in this signif. it occurs but rarely. τὼ δ᾽ εἰς ἀμφοτέρω Διομήδεος ἄρματα βήτην, 5, 115. III) In compos. it has the general signif. into, to.

εἷς, μία, ἕν, gen. ἑνός. μιᾶς, ἑνός, one; with super., 12, 243, also with art. ἡ μία, 21, 272; an Ep. form of εἷς is ἰός. q. v.

εἴσα (theme ΕΩ), an Ep. defect. imperf. εἷσον, partcp. ἕσας, ἕσασα, aor. 1 mid. ἑσάμην and ἑέσσατο, 1) to seat, to cause to sit, ἐν κλισμοῖσι, ἐς θρόνον, ἐπὶ θρόνον, 2) to place, to lay, to bring into a place, δῆμον ἐν Σχερίῃ, Od. 6, 8; σκοπόν. to place a watcher, 23, 359; λόχον, to lay an ambuscade, 4, 392. Od. 4, 531: τινὰ ἐπὶ νηός, h. 7, 10; and so mid. ἑέσσατο, Od. 14, 295; (what is wanting is supplied by ἱδρύω, see Buttm. Gram. § 108.)

εἰσαγείρω, poet. ἐσαγείρω (ἀγείρω), 1) to collect into, with accus. ἐρέτας ἐς νῆα, 1, 142. 2) Mid. to assemble (themselves) in, Od. 14, 248. b) Metaph. with accus. θυμόν, to recover spirit, 15, 240. 21, 417.

εἰσάγω, poet. ἐσάγω (ἄγω), aor. 2 εἰσήγαγον, to lead into, to introduce, with accus. Λαοδίκην ἐσάγουσα. leading in Laodikē, 6, 252. (The Schol. takes ἐσάγουσα intrans. and Voss. renders 'going to Laodike'), with double accus. ἑταίρους Κρήτην, to conduct his companions to Crete, Od. 3, 191; conf. Od. 4. 43; metaph. ποταμῶν μένος, 12, 18.

εἰσαθρέω, poet. ἐσαθρ. (ἀθρέω), to behold, to discern in the midst, τινά, 3, 450.†

εἰσακούω, poet. ἐσακούω (ἀκούω), aor. ἐσάκουσα, without augm. to hearken to, to understand, absol. 8, 97.† φωνήν, h. in Cer. 243

εἰσάλλομαι, depon. mid. (ἄλλομαι), aor. 1 ἐσήλατο, and aor. 2 ἐσᾶλτο, to spring upon, to leap upon, with accus. τεῖχος, πύλας, to storm a wall, the gates, *12, 438. 466.

εἰσάμην, Ep. 1) Aor. 1 mid. of εἴδω. 2) Aor. 1 mid. of εἶμι.

εἰσαναβαίνω (βαίνω), aor. 2 εἰσανέβην, infin. εἰσαναβῆναι, to mount up, to ascend, to go up to, with accus. Ἴλιον, λέχος. and εἰς ὑπερῷα, Od. 19, 602.

εἰσανάγω (ἄγω), to lead into; τινὰ εἴρερον. any one into slavery, Od. 8, 529; cf. εἴρερος.

εἰσανεῖδον, def. aor. (ΕΙΔΩ), to look up to any thing, with accus. οὐρανόν, *16, 232. 24, 307.

εἰσάνειμι (εἶμι), to ascend upon, to mount. with accus. spoken of the sun, οὐρανόν, 7, 423.†

εἰσάντα, Ep. ἔσαντα (ἄντα), opposite,

over against. ἔσαντα ἰδεῖν, to look into the face, 17, 334; εἴσαντα only Od. 5, 217.

εἰσαφικάνω, poet. form of εἰσαφικνέομαι, 14. 230. Od. 22, 99.

εἰσαφικνέομαι. depon. mid. (ἱκνέομαι), only aor. εἰσαφικόμην, to go to a place, to arrive at, with accus. Ἴλιον, Il.; also τινά, Od. 13. 404.

εἰσβαίνω, poet. ἐσβαίνω (βαίνω), aor. 1 ἐσέβησα, aor. 2 ἐσέβην, 1) Trans. to introduce, to bring in, ἑκατόμβην, 1, 310.† 2) Intrans. to enter, to go on board, esply of a ship, Od. 9, 103. 179.

εἰσδέρκομαι, depon. (δέρκομαι), aor. ἐσέδρακον, to look at, to perceive, to behold. with accus.. Il. and Od. only aor.

εἰσδύω, poet. ἐσδύω (δύω), only mid. εἰσδύομαι, to go into, to enter. ἀκοντιστὺν ἐσδύσεαι, thou wilt enter the battle fought with spears, 23, 622.†

εἰσεῖδον (ΕΙΔΩ). Ep. εἴσιδον, defect. aor. of εἰσοράω, to look upon, to behold.

εἴσειμι (εἶμι), to go in, to come to, μετ᾽ ἀνέρας. Od 18, 184; with accus. οὐκ Ἀχιλῆος ὀφθαλμοὺς εἴσειμι. I will not come before the eyes of Achilles, 24, 463.

εἰσελαύνω, Ep εἰσελάω (ἐλαύνω), aor. 1 εἰσέλασα, to drive into, ἵππους, 15, 385; absol. εἰσελάων, the herdsman driving in, Od. 10, 83. 2) Intrans. to steer into, prop. subaud. ναῦν, Od. 13, 113.

εἰσερύω (ἐρύω), to draw into; with accus. νῆα σπέος, to draw the ship into a grotto, Od. 12, 317.†

εἰσέρχομαι, poet. ἐσέρχομαι (ἔρχομαι), fut. ἐσελεύσομαι, aor. 2 εἰσῆλθον, poet. εἰσήλυθον, to go into, to come into, to enter, with accus. Μυκήνας, πόλιν. also οἶκόνδε, 6, 305; metaph. μένος ἄνδρας ἐσέρχεται, strength enters the men, 17, 157. Od. 15, 407.

εἶσθα, Ep for εἶς, see εἶμι.

εἰσθρώσκω (θρώσκω), aor. 2 ἔσθορον, Ep. for εἰσέθορον, to leap into, only absol., *12, 462. 21, 18.

εἰσιέμεναι, see εἰσίημι.

εἰσίζομαι, poet. ἐσίζομαι (ἵζομαι), to seat oneself in; λόχον, to place oneself in an ambuscade, 13, 285.†

εἰσίημι (ἵημι), to send in, mid. to betake ones if to. αὖλιν ἐσιέμεναι, partcp. pres. betaking oneself to a resting-place, Od. 22, 470.† Others take it as partcp. pres. mid. of εἴσειμι (εἶμι): and this is probably the more correct view.

εἰσίθμη, ἡ (εἴσειμι), entrance, Od. 6, 264.

εἰσκαλέω, poet. ἐσκαλέω, to call in, mid. to call to oneself; only in tmesis, ἐς δ᾽ ἄλοχον ἐκαλέσσατο, 24, 193.†

εἰσκαταβαίνω, Ep. ἐσκαταβαίνω (βαίνω), to descend into any thing, with accus. ὄρχατον, Od. 24, 222.†

ἐΐσκω, Ep. lengthened from ἴσκω (εἴσος), 1) to make similar, to render like. αὐτὸν ἤϊσκεν δέκτῃ. he made himself like a beggar, Od 4, 247. 13, 313. 2) to esteem like, to compare to, τινά τινι, 3, 197. Τυδεΐδη αὐτὸν πάντα ἐΐσκω, I consider him in all respects like Tydides, 5, 181. τάδε νυκτὶ ἔίσκει, Od. 26. 362; to compare, τινά τινι, 3, 197. Od. 6, 152. 8, 159. 3) to regard as, to judge, to suppose, absol. Od. 4, 148, and with accus. and infin., Od. 11, 363. ἢ ἄρα δή τι ἔίσκομεν ἄξιον εἶναι τρεῖς ἑνὸς ἀντὶ πεφάσθαι, we judge it now sufficient that three have been slain instead of one, 13, 446. 21, 332.

εἰσμαίομαι (μαίομαι), aor. 1 ἐσεμασάμην, Ep. σσ, to affect, to distress, only metaph. μάλα με ἐσεμάσσατο θυμόν, he greatly distressed my heart, *17, 564. 20, 425.

εἰσνοέω (νοέω). aor. 1 εἰσενόησα, to remark, to perceive, τινά, Il. and Od.; ἴχνια, h. Merc. 218.

εἴσοδος. ἡ (ὁδός), entrance, access, Od. 10, 90.†

εἰσοιχνέω (οἰχνέω), to go into, with accus. νῆσον, *Od. 6, 157. 9, 120.

εἰσόκε, before a vowel εἰσόκεν (εἰς ὅ κε). 1) till, until, mly with the subjunc. which expresses an expected end, 2, 332. 446. b) With indicat. fut. 21, 134. Od. 8, 318. Il. 3, 409 (in this passage better subjunc. aor. with shortened mood vowel). c) With optat. 15, 70. Od. 22, 444. 2) as long as, with subjunc., 9, 609. 10, 89.

εἴσομαι, 1) Ep. fut. mid. of οἶδα, see ΕΙΔΩ. 2) Ep. fut mid. of εἶμι.

*εἰσοπίσω, adv. (ὀπίσω), for the future, in future, h. Ven. 104.

εἰσοράω (ὁράω), partcp. εἰσορόων, Ep. for εἰσορῶν, fut. εἰσόψομαι. aor. 2 εἰσεῖδον, mid. infin. pres. εἰσοράασθαι, Ep. for εἰσορᾶσθαι. to look upon, to behold, to regard, with accus. 1) With the idea of veneration. εἰσορᾶν τινα ὡς θεόν, to look upon any one as a god, i. e. to venerate, 12, 312; or ἶσα θεῷ, Od. 15, 520. 2) Mid. like the act., Od. 3, 246.

εἶσος, εἴση, εἶσον (ἰ), Ep. lengthened from ἴσος, used however only in the fem., like, æqualis. in the following constructions: 1) δαὶς ἐίση, an evenly divided feast, a common feast, spoken esply of sacrificial feasts in which each one receives an equal portion, 1, 468, and often. 2) νῆες ἐῖσαι, the even-floating ships. i. e. built alike strong on both sides, so as to preserve their equipoise in sailing, 1, 306. 3) ἀσπὶς πάντοσ' ἐίση, the every where equal shield, i. e. extending alike from the centre to all sides, hence entirely round, 3, 347. 4) φρένες ἔνδον ἐῖσαι, an equable mind, a mind remaining the same in all circumstances, Od. 11, 337. 14, 178. [5) ἵπποι ἐῖσαι (σταφύλῃ ἐπὶ νῶτον), 2, 765.]

εἰσόψομαι, fut. of εἰσοράω.

εἰσπέτομαι (πέτομαι), aor. εἰσεπτάμην, to fly into, with accus. πέτρην. 21, 494.†

εἰσφέρω (φέρω). 1) to bring in, to carry in, with accus. ἐσθῆτα, Od. 7, 6. 2) Mid. to bear away with oneself, to sweep away. spoken of a river; with accus. πεύκας, 11, 495.

εἰσφορέω, a form of εἰσφέρω, *Od. 91. 19, 32

εἰσχέω (χέω), to pour in, 2) Mid. pour oneself in, to rush into; only sync. mid. ἐσέχυντο κατὰ πύλας, t rushed into the gates, *12, 470. 610

εἴσω, Ep. ἔσω. 24, 155. 184. 199. 7. 58; adv. (from εἰς). 1) to, into, wards, εἰπεῖν, Od 3. 47. εἴσω ἀσπιδ' ἔ he broke in the shield, 7, 270; a) o with accus, which mly follows depends upon the verb: Ἴλιον εἰ Οὐρανὸν εἴσω, etc. Only 24, 155. 199, ἔσω precedes. b) With gen. Od. 8, 290. 2) within, inside, perh Od. 7. 13.

εἰσωπός, όν (ὤψ), in the sight of, hat in view; with gen. εἰσωποὶ ἐγένι νεῶν, they were in sight of the ships, 653.†

εἶται, see ἕννυμι.

εἴτε—εἴτε, conj whether—or, be it —or that. in indirect double interr tion: a) With indic., 1, 65. Od. 3, b) With subj.. 12, 239; εἴτε is also lowed by ἢ καί, 2, 349.

εἴτε for εἴητε, see εἰμί.

εἰῶ, Ep. for ἐάω, 4, 55; but εἰω, εἰμί.

εἰώθα, see ἔθω.

εἴων, see ἐάω.

εἴως, Ep. for ἕως, q. v.

ἐκ, before a vowel ἐξ, prepos. with g General signif. is from, out of, in cor distinction from ἐν. 1) Of place: denoting removal from the interior immediate vicinity of a place, out, of. away from, esply with verbs motion, ἰέναι, ἔρχεσθαι, etc. ἐκ νη from the ships. 8, 213. b) In denoi distance with verbs of rest, without, c Ep. ἐκ βελέων. without the reach weapons, 11. 163. With verbs of sta ing, sitting, hanging, etc., ἐκ standi indicate the idea of consequent mot or distance contained in the verb. δίφρον γουνάζεσθαι, down from chariot. 11. 130. αὐτόθεν ἐκ δίφρ καθήμενος, Od. 21, 420. ἐκ πασσαλ κρέμασεν φόρμιγγα, he hung from (u the hook, Od. 8, 67. 2) Of time: Spoken of direct departure from a pe of time, from, esply ἐξ οὗ, from wl time, since; and ἐκ τοῦ or ἐκ τo from this time, 1. 493 ἐξ ἀρχῆς. fi the beginning, at first. b) Spoken of direct consequence, after. ἐξ αἰδ 16, 365. 3) Spoken of cause, mann etc.: a) Of origin. εἶναι, γίγνεσθαι τινος, to spring from any one, 15, b) Of the whole in reference to its pa ἐκ πολέων πίσυρες, 15, 680. c) Of author or agent, with pass and intra verbs, Ep. and Ion. like ὑπό, by. λῆθεν ἐκ Διός, 2, 669. ἀπολέσθαι τινος, 18. 107. d) Of the cause. θεόφιν πολεμίζειν, to fight at the inst tion of the gods, 17, 101. cf. 5, ἐκ θυμοῦ φιλεῖν, to love from the he

9, 486. e) Of suitableness, after, accord-ing to. ὀνομάζειν ἐκ γενεῆς, (=) by the name of, after his family [by his here-ditary name. Cp.], 10, 68. 4) ἐκ is often separated by some words from its gen., 11, 109; it is also in Epic writers placed after the gen., 1, 125; ἐκ after the subst. receives the accent; also when it is emphatic, 5, 865. See also the articles, διέκ, παρέκ, ὑπέκ. II) Adv. ἐκ is also used in its orig. signif. as an adv. of place: ἐκ δ' ἀρ-γύρεον τελαμῶνα, and thereon (attach-ed to it), 18, 480; and often in tmesis, 1, 436. 13, 394. III) In compos. ἐκ = out (of), away from, utterly; express-ing separation, origin, completion.

Ἑκάβη, ἡ, Hecuba, daughter of Dymas, king of Phrygia, sister of Asius and wife of Priam, 16, 718; in later writers, daughter of Kisseus.

Ἑκάεργος, ὁ (ἔργον), working at a dis-tance, far shooting; according to Nitzsch, throwing from a distance, epith. of Apollo, because he slew with arrows, = ἑκηβόλος, as adj. 5, 439. 2) As subst. the far-shooter, 1, 147, and Od. 8, 323.

ἐκάην, aor. 2 pass. of καίω.

ἔκαθεν, adv. (ἑκάς), from far, from a distance, also = ἑκάς, Od. 17, 25.

ἐκάθιζον, see καθίζω, Od. 16, 408.

Ἑκαμήδη, ἡ, daughter of Arsinous of Tenedos, whom Nestor received as a slave, 11, 624.

ἑκάς, adv. (ἐκ), far, at a distance, far from; often as prep. with gen. 5, 791; and often with ἀπό, 18, 256. Compar. ἑκαστέρω, superl. ἑκαστάτω, at the far-thest, 10, 113.†

ἑκαστέρω, adv. compar. of ἑκάς, Od. 7, 321.†

ἑκαστόθι, to each or every, Od. 3, 8.†

ἕκαστος, η, ον, each (one), every one, as a collective adj. frequently with the plur. 1, 606. 10, 215; more rarely in the plur. Od. 9, 164. 24, 417. It also stands in the sing. in apposition, after a noun or pronoun plur. for the purpose of more exact definition, when the latter might rather stand in the relation of a gen. οἱ δὲ κλῆρον ἐσημήναντο ἕκαστος, each one of them, 7, 175. πᾶσιν ἐπίστιόν ἐστιν ἑκάστῳ, Od. 6, 265.

ἑκάτερθε, before a vowel ἑκάτερθεν (ἑκάτερος), on both sides; also with gen. φίλων, 3, 340.

Ἑκάτη, ἡ, Hecate, daughter of Perses or Peræus and Asteria, grand-daughter of Koius and Phœbē, to whom Zeus gave the power to operate every where. She presided over purifications, wealth, honour, and all prosperity, h. in Cer. 25. 52. Hes. Th. 409. There was a cave sacred to her in Zerinthus in Samo-thrace, Steph. At a later day she was confounded with Artĕmis, and worshipt as presiding over the magic art (prob. from ἕκατος, the far-working).

ἑκατηβελέτης, αο, ὁ, Ep. for ἑκηβόλος, 1, 75. †h. Ap. 157.

ἑκατηβόλος, ον (βάλλω), far-throwing, far shooting, or, hitting from a distance, epith. of Apollo, 5, 444; of Artĕmis, h. 8, 6. As subst. 15, 231.

ἑκατόγχειρος, ον (χείρ), hundred-handed, epith. of Briareus, 1, 402.†

ἑκατόζυγος, ον, Ep. for ἑκατόνζυγος (ζυγόν), having a hundred benches of rowers, hundred-oared, 20, 247.†

ἑκατόμβη, ἡ (βοῦς), a hetacomb. prop. a sacrifice of an hundred oxen; but mly, a solemn sacrifice, a festal sacrifice, e. g. of twelve oxen, 6, 93. 115; of eighty-one oxen, Od. 3, 59; also of other animals, Od. 1, 25.

ἑκατόμβοιος, ον (βοῦς), worth a hundred oxen, τεύχεα, *2, 449. 6, 236.

ἑκατόμπεδος, ον (πούς), a hundred feet long, 23, 164.† (Others ἑκατόμποδος).

ἑκατόμπολις, ι (πόλις), having a hundred cities, Κρήτη, 2, 649.†

ἑκατόμπυλος, ον (πύλη), having a hun-dred gates, hundred-gated, epith. of the Egyptian Thebes, 9, 383 †

ἑκατόν, indecl. a hundred, Il. and Od.

ἕκατος, ὁ (ἑκάς), far-shooting, epith. of Apollo, 7, 83. 2) As subst. the far-shooter, 1, 385; cf. ἑκάεργος, ἑκατηβόλος.

ἐκβαίνω (βαίνω), aor. 1 ἐξέβησα, aor. 2 ἐξέβην, 1) Intrans. to descend, to alight, to disembark, from a ship, 3, 113; πέτρης, to descend from a rock, 4, 107. 2) Trans. in the aor. 1 and fut. act. to disembark, to put out, with accus. Od. 24, 301. Il. 1, 438.

ἐκβάλλω (βάλλω), aor. 2 ἐξέβαλον, Ep. ἔκβαλλον, 1) to cast out of the ship, Od. 15, 481; τινα δίφρου, to hurl or dash a man down from his chariot, 5, 39. 2) to strike or knock out, i. e. to cause any thing to fall, τί τινι, and with gen. βιὸν χειρός, to strike the bow from the hand, 14, 419. 15, 468; also ἔκτοσε χειρός, Od. 14, 277; δοῦρα, to fell trees, Od. 5, 243. 3) to let fall; δάκρυα, Od. 19, 362; metaph. ἔπος, 18, 324. Od. 4, 503.

ἔκβασις, ιος, ἡ (βαίνω), an exit, the act of coming from or out of, a landing-place; ἁλός, a landing-place from the sea, Od. 5, 410.

ἐκβλώσκω, poet. (βλώσκω), aor. 2 ἐξ-έμολον, poet. ἔκμολον, to go out, 11, 604.†

ἐκγεγάμεν, see ἐκγίγνομαι.

ἐκγεγάονται, see ἐκγίγνομαι.

ἐκγεγαώς, ἐκγεγαυία, see ἐκγίγνομαι.

ἐκγελάω (γελάω), aor. ἐξεγέλασα, poet. σσ, to laugh out, to laugh aloud, Od. 16, 354. Il. 6, 471.

ἐκγίγνομαι, depon. mid. (γίγνομαι), aor. 2 ἐξεγενόμην, Ep. perf. ἐκγέγαα, from this the infin. Ep. ἐκγεγάμεν, partcp. Ep. ἐκγεγαώς, υἶα, from which comes an Ep. fut. ἐκγεγάονται, without σ, h. Ven. 198. Buttm. p. 272, note. 1) to be born or begotten of, τινός, any one, 5, 637. 20, 231; with dat. Πορθεῖ, 14, 115. 2) In the perf. to spring from, to descend from, τινός, any one, 5, 248. Od. 10, 138.

ἔκγονος, ον (ἐκγίγνομαι), begotten or

born of any one, as subst. *a descendant, progeny*, Il. and Od. ἡ ἔκγονος, *a daughter*, Od. 11, 235. ·

ἐκδέχομαι, depon. mid. (δέχομαι), *to take from, to receive in succession*, τί τινι, any thing from one, 13. 710.†

ἐκδέω (δέω), aor. ἐξέδησα. *to bind, to fasten*, with the accus. σανίδας, to fasten the door (with the thong), i. e. to lock it, Od. 22, 174; with gen. δρῦς ἡμιόνων, to attach the (felled) oaks to the mules (for them to drag home). [Not, *bound them on the mules*. Cp.], 23, 121.

ἔκδηλος, ον (δῆλος), *very clear, very manifest, distinguished*, μετὰ πᾶσιν, amongst all, 5, 2.†

ἐκδιαβαίνω (βαίνω), partcp. aor. 2 ἐκδιαβάντες, *to go entirely through* any thing, with accus. τάφρον, a trench, 10, 198.†

ἐκδίδωμι (δίδωμι), aor. 2 imperf. ἔκδοτε, *to give out, to give up, to deliver again*, with accus. κτήματα, 3, 159.†

*ἔνδικος, ον (δίκη), administering justice, *taking vengeance, punishing*, Batr. 96.

ἐκδύνω, Ep. for ἐκδύομαι, Od. 1, 437.

ἐκδύω (δύω), aor. 1 ἐξέδυσα, aor. 2 ἐξέδυν, partcp. ἐκδύς, 1) Trans. in the fut. and aor. 1, *to strip off*, τινὰ χιτῶνα, the tunic from any one. Od. 14, 341. 2) Mid. with aor. 2 intrans. *to put off, to lay aside*, τεύχεα, 3, 114. b) *to go out*, with gen. μεγάροιο, of the house, Od. 22, 234; metaph. *to escape*, with accus. ὄλεθρον, 16, 99; for ἐκδύμεν (Ep. infin. aor. 2, accord. to Wolf), read ἐκδῦμεν, i. e. ἐκδύῃμεν, optat. aor. 2; conf. Buttm. Lex. p. 424. Thiersch § 231, 101.

ἐκεῖθι, adv. *there, in that very place*, Od. 17, 10.†

ἐκεῖνος, η, ο, Ep. κεῖνος (ἐκεῖ), *he, she, it, that person*, with pron. κεῖνος ὅγε, that person there, 3, 391; with subst. without art. κεῖνος ἀνήρ. b) Also δεικτικῶς, for adv. there; κεῖνος Ἄρης, 5, 604. Od. 18, 239; the dative κείνῃ as adv., Od. 13, 111. Voss on Aratus 75, decides that it must be ᾽κεῖνος when the preceding word is most important, 7, 77; on the other hand ἐκεῖνος, 9, 646. and var. lec.] 24, 90.

ἐκέκαστο, see καίνυμαι.

ἐκέκλετο, see κέλομαι.

ἐκέκλιτο, see κλίνω.

ἔκηα, see καίω.

ἐκηβολίη, ἡ (βάλλω), *skill in shooting*, or *hitting at a distance*; plur. 5, 54.†

ἐκηβόλος, ον (βάλλω), *far-shooting, far-hitting*, as ἑκατηβόλος, epith. of Apollo, 1, 14. 2) As subst. *the far-shooter*, 1, 96. 110.

ἔκηλος, ον, 5, 759; and εὔκηλος, prop. ἔϝκηλος, 1, 554. Od. 3, 263. 1) *quiet*, Od. 21, 259; *free from care, at ease*, 5, 759. h. Merc. 480. 2) *unmolested, unhindered*. ἔκηλος ἐρρέτω. let him go unhindered to ruin, 9, 376. cf. 6, 70. 17, 340. 3) Metaph. spoken of a *resting, fruitless* field, h. Cer. 431. (According

to Buttm. Lex. p. 284, prob. related ἑκών, ἕκητι, with the adj. ending ηλ [related to ἀκήν, ἀκᾶ, ἀκαλός (= ἥσυχο Hesych.), ἧκα. Lob. Path. 109. Död. 134

ἕκητι, prep. with gen. *on account o by means of*; esply of the gods: *by t will of, by the favour of* Ἑρμείαο, *O 15, 319. 19, 86.

ἐκθνήσκω (θνήσκω), only aor. 2, *to di γέλῳ ἔκθανον, they died with laughte i. e ̓laughed long and loud, Od. 18, 100

ἔκθορον, see ἐκθρώσκω.

ἐκθρώσκω (θρώσκω), aor. 2 ἐξέθορον, E ἔκθορον, *to leap from, to spring out*, wit gen. προμάχων, 15, 573. Od. 10, 20; metaph. κραδίη μοι ἔξω στηθέων ὶ θρώσκει, my heart leaps from my breas i. e. beats violently, 10, 95.

ἐκκαθαίρω (καθαίρω), *to purify, to cle out*, with accus. οὔρους, 2, 153.†

ἐκκαιδεκάδωρος, ον (δῶρον), *sixtee palms long*, κέρα, 4, 109.†

ἐκκαλέω (καλέω), aor. 1 act. partc ἐκκαλέσας, 24, 582. aor. 1 mid. ἐκκαλε σάμενος, *to call forth*, τινά. Mid. *to ca to oneself*, Od. 24, 1.

ἐκκαλύπτω (καλύπτω), partcp. aor. m ἐκκαλυψάμενος, *to uncover, to unvei mid. *to uncover oneself*, Od. 10, 279, tmesis.

ἐκκατιδών, old reading for ἐκ κατιδὼ 4, 508.

ἐκκίω (κίω), *to go out*, Od. 24, 492 ;† tmesis.

ἐκκλέπτω (κλέπτω), *to steal away, take away privately*, with accus. to le off privately, Ἀρῆα, 5, 390.†

ἐκκυλίω (κυλίω), only aor. pass. ὲ ἐκυλίσθην, *to roll out, to fling off*; pas *to be rolled from, to tumble from*, δίφροιο. *6, 42. 23, 394.

ἐκλανθάνω, ἐκλήθω (λήθω), Ep. aor. act. ἐκλέλαθον, and aor. 2 mid. ἐξελ θόμην, Ep. ἐκλελαθόμην with redupl. Act. *to cause to forget*. τινά τι: Μοῦσ αὐτὸν ἐκλέλαθον κιθαριστύν, they caus him to forget his harp-playing. i. e. th took away from him the art of playii on the harp, 2, 600; also τινά τιν Ἥρης ἐκλελαθοῦσα, h. Ven. 40. 2) Mi *to forget*. with gen. ἀλκῆς, 16, 602; a with the infin. Od. 10, 557.

ἐκλέλαθον, see ἐκλανθάνω.

ἐκληθάνω, poet. for ἐκλανθάνω, Od. 221.†

ἔκλησις, ιος, ἡ (λήθω), *the act of f getting, forgetfulness*, Od. 24, 485.†

ἐκλύω (λύω), fut. mid. ἐκλύσομαι, *loose, to release*. 2) Mid. = act. τ κακῶν, to release any one from toils, O 10, 286 †

ἐκμάσσατο, see ἐκμαίομαι.

*ἐκμαίομαι, depon. mid. (μαίομαι), a 1 ἐκμάσσατο for ἐξεμάσ. *to invent, discover*, with accus. τέχνην, h. Me 511.

ἐκμείρομαι (μείρομαι), perf. ἐξέμμορ *to participate chiefly in, to obtain chief share of*, with gen. θεῶν τιμῆς, O 5, 335.†

ἐκμολεῖν, see ἐκβλώσκω.

ἐκμυζάω (μυζάω), partcp. aor. 1 ἐκμυζήσας, to suck out, with accus. αἷμα, 4, 218.†

ἔκπαγλος, ον (ἐκπλήσσω), exciting astonishment or terrour; terrific, frightful, awful, spoken of men, 18, 170; of things: χειμών, Od. 14, 522; ἔπεα, 15, 198. The accus. neut. ἔκπαγλον and ἔκπαγλα, as adv. dreadfully, terribly, as κοτεῖσθαι, and mly, vehemently, exceedingly, φιλεῖν.

ἐκπάγλως, adv. = ἔκπαγλον, Il. and Od.

ἐκπαιφάσσω, poet. (παιφάσσω), to leap furiously forth, 5. 803.†

ἔκπαλθ for ἔκπαλτο, see ἐκπάλλω.

ἐκπάλλω (πάλλω), only sync aor. 2 mid. ἔκπαλτο, to gush out. μυελὸς σφονδυλίων ἔκπαλτο, the marrow gushed forth from the vertebræ, 20, 483.†

ἐκπατάσσω (πατάσσω), partcp. perf. pass. ἐκπεπαταγμένος, to push out, metaph. = ἐκπλήσσω, to terrify, to astound, pass., Od. 18, 327.†

ἐκπέμπω (πέμπω), 1) to send out or forth, 24, 681; κειμήλια ἄνδρας ἐς ἀλλοδαπούς, 24, 381; τινά. Od. 16, 3. b) to bring away, spoken of things: θεμείλια φιτρῶν καὶ λάων, removed the foundation of blocks and stones, 12, 28. 2) Mid. to send away from oneself, to dismiss, τινὰ δόμου, any one from the house. Od. 20, 361.

ἐκπέσοται, see ἐκπίνω.

ἐκπεράω (περάω), aor. 1 ἐξεπέρησα, to go through, to pierce through, with accus. λαῖτμα μέγα, to pass through the great deep, Od. 7. 35. 9, 323; absol. spoken of arrows and spears, 13, 652.

ἐκπέρθω (πέρθω), fut. ἐκπέρσω, aor. ἐξέπερσα, Ep. ἔκπερσα, to sack, to destroy, with accus. πόλιν, Ἴλιον, *1, 164; and often.

ἐκπεσέειν, see ἐκπίπτω.

ἐκπέτομαι. depon. mid. (πέτομαι), aor. 2 ἐξέπτην (from the form ἴπταμαι), to fly out, Batr. 223.

ἐκπεύθομαι, Ep. for ἐκπυνθάνομαι.

ἐκπεφυνῖαι. see ἐκφύω.

ἐκπίνω (πίνω), aor. 2 ἔκπιον, Ep. for ἐξέπιον, perf. pass. ἐκπέπομαι, to empty, to exhaust, *Od. 9, 353. 22, 56.

ἐκπίπτω (πίπτω), aor 2 ἐξέπεσον, Ep. ἔκπεσον, infin. Ep. ἐκπεσέειν, to fall out, with gen. δίφρου, of the chariot, ἵππων, and with the dat. of pers. τόξον οἱ ἔκπεσε χειρός, from the hand, 8, 329. δάκρυ οἱ ἔκπεσε, 2, 266.

ἐκπλήσσω (πλήσσω), aor. pass. ἐξεπλήγην and ἐκπλήγην, Ep. for ἐξεπλάγην. 1) Act. to strike out, to cast out, metaph. any one (as by a blow), to stun, to terrify or amaze, τινά, Od. 18, 231. 2) Pass. intrans. to be amazed or confounded, to be stunned, to be awe-struck, 18, 225, with accus. ἐκ γὰρ πλήγη φρένας, he was amazed in mind, 16, 403.

ἐκποτέομαι, Ep. for ἐκπέτομαι (πέτομαι), to fly away, to fly down, spoken of snow, with gen. Διός, from Zeus, 19, 357.†

ἐκπρεπής, ές, gen. έος (πρέπω), distinguished, excellent, eminent, ἐν πολλοῖσι, 2, 483.†

ἐκπροκαλέω (καλέω), aor. ἐκπρούκαλεσάμην, Ep. σσ, to call out or forth, mid. to call to oneself, τινὰ μεγάρων, from the house, Od. 2, 400 † h. Ap. 111.

ἐκπρολείπω (λείπω), partcp. aor. 2 ἐκπρολιπών, to leave (by going forth), with accus. λόχον, their ambush (the cavity of the wooden horse), Od. 8, 515.†

ἐκπτύω (πτύω), aor. 1 ἐξέπτυσα, to spit out, στόματος ἅλμην, Od. 5, 322.†

ἐκπυνθάνομαι (πυνθάνομαι), aor. 2 ἐξεπυθόμην, only infin. to seek. to ascertain, to enquire, with ἦ, ἤ following. *10, 308. 320, in tmesis.

ἐκρέμω, imperf from κρέμαμαι.

ἐκρέω (ῥέω), to flow out, only in tmesis, 13, 655. Od. 9. 290.

ἐκρήγνυμι (ῥήγνυμι), aor. 1 ἐξέρρηξα, to break out, to tear out or up, with accus. νευρήν. 15, 469; with gen. ὕδωρ ἀλὲν ἐξέρρηξεν ὁδοῖο, the pent up water had torn away a part of the road, *23, 421.

ἐκσαόω (σαόω, Ep. for σώζω), aor. 1 ἐξεσάωσα, to rescue, to deliver, τινά, 4, 12; τινὰ θαλάσσης, from the sea, Od. 4, 501.

ἐκσεύω (σεύω), to drive out, only mid. ἐκσεύομαι, aor. sync. 3 sing. ἐξέσσυτο, aor. 1 pass. ἐξεσύθην to hasten out, to hurry away, with gen. πυλέων, out of the gates, 7, 1. φάρυγος ἐξέσσυτο οἶνος, the wine gushed from his throat, Od. 9, 373; metaph. βλεφάρων ἐξέσσυτο ὕπνος, sleep fled away from the eyes, Od. 12, 366. 2) Spoken of the spear's head: to come out, to emerge, in the aor. pass. 5, 293.

ἐκσπάω (σπάω), aor. 1 mid. ἐξεσπασάμην, poet. σσ, 1) Act. to draw out, with accus., 5, 859. 2) Mid. to draw out (with reference to the subject), ἔγχος στέρνοιο, his spear from his breast, *4, 530. 7, 255.

ἐκστρέφω (στρέφω), aor. 1 ἐξέστρεψα, to turn out, to tear out, with accus. ἔρνος βόθρου, the plant from the trench, 17, 58.†

ἔκτα, see κτείνω.

ἐκτάδιος, ίη, ιον (ἐκτείνω), extended, spread out, wide, χλαῖνα, 10, 134.†

ἔκταθεν, see κτείνω.

ἔκταμε, see ἐκτάμνω.

ἐκτάμνω, Ep. for ἐκτέμνω (τάμνω), aor. 2 ἐξέταμον, Ep. ἔκταμον, 1) to cut out, with accus. μηρούς, the thigh-bones (of the victims), 2, 123; ὀιστὸν μηροῦ, an arrow from the thigh (spoken of the physician), 11, 515. 829. 2) to cut down, to fell; of trees, timbers, αἴγειρον, 4, 486; ῥόπαλον, Od. 9, 320; and of the boar, ὕλην, 12, 149.

ἔκταν, Ep. for ἔκτασαν, see κτείνω.

ἐκτανύω (τανύω, Ep. for τείνω), aor. 1 ἐξετάνυσσα, Ep. σσ, aor. 1 pass. ἐξετανύσθην. 1) to stretch out. to extend on the ground, τινά. 11, 844; ἐν κόνι, 24, 18. Spoken of the wind: ἐπὶ γαίῃ, to cast to the ground, 17, 58; pass. to be stretched out, to be prostrated, to lie, 7, 271.

G 6

ἐκτελείω, Ep. for ἐκτελέω.

ἐκτελέω, Ep. ἐκτελείω (τελέω), fut. ἐκτελῶ, Ep. ἐκτελείω, aor. 1 ἐξετέλεσα, Ep. σσ, perf. pass. ἐκτετέλεσμαι, aor. pass. ἐξετελέσθην. 1) to finish, to complete, with accus. ἔργον, ἄεθλον, φᾶρος, Od. 2, 98; in the pass. spoken of time, Od. 11, 294. 2) to finish, to fulfil, to perform, spoken of the gods. γάμον, Od. 4, 7; τινὶ γόνον, to give offspring to any one, 9, 493; to perform, to fulfil, ὑπόσχεσιν, ἀπειλάς, ἐέλδωρ. Il. and Od.

ἐκτίθημι (τίθημι), aor. 2 partcp. ἐκθείς, to put out, to place out, λέχος, Od. 23, 179.†

ἐκτινάσσω (τινάσσω), to thrust out, to dash out, only aor. 1 pass. ἐκ δ' ἐτίναχθεν ὀδόντες, 16, 348.†

ἔκτοθεν, adv. Ep. for ἔκτοθεν, from without, without, apart from, *Od. 1. 132; but ἔκτοθεν αὐλῆς, Od. 9, 338, is without in the court.

ἔκτοθι, adv. (ἐκτός), out of, without, with gen. *15, 391. 22, 439.

*ἐκτορέω (τορέω), to thrust out, with accus. αἰῶνα, to take away life, h. Merc. 42.

Ἑκτορίδης, ου, ὁ, son of Hector = Astyanax, 6, 401.

ἐκτός, adv. (ἐκ), out of, without, εἶναι, 4, 151; ἐκτὸς ἀπὸ κλισίης, 10, 151; mly with gen. out of, far from, τείχεος, Il. and Od.

ἕκτος, η. ον (ἕξ), the sixth, Il. and Od.

ἔκτοσε, adv. out of, without, with gen. Od. 14, 277.†

ἔκτοσθε, before a vowel ἔκτοσθεν, Ep. ἔκτοθεν (ἐκτός), from without, without, also as prep. on the outside of, with gen. 9, 552, conf. ἔκτοθεν.

*ἐκτρέφω (τρέφω), aor. 1 mid. ἐξεθρεψάμην, to bring up, to nourish; mid. to rear for oneself, τινά, h. Cer. 221. Batr. 30

ἔκτυπε, see κτυπέω.

*ἐκτυφλόω (τυφλόω), to blind utterly, Batr. 241.

Ἕκτωρ, ορος, ὁ, Hector, son of Priam and Hecuba, husband of Andromachê and father of Astyanax, the bravest amongst the Trojan leaders and heroes, 2, 816. He bravely defended his country, and at last fell by Achilles, 24, 553. From this the adj. Ἑκτόρεος, έη, εον, appertaining to Hector, χιτών (from ἔχω, who held fast, who protected; Plat. Cratyl. p. 393 = ἄναξ).

ἑκυρή, ἡ, a mother-in-law, *22, 451. 24, 770.

ἑκυρός, ὁ, poet. a father-in-law, *3, 172. 24, 770.

ἐκφαίνω (φαίνω), fut. ἐκφανῶ, aor. 1 pass. ἐξεφαάνθην, Ep. for. ἐξεφάνθην, aor. 2 pass. ἐξεφάνην, 1) to expose, to bring to view, φόωςδε, to bring to light (spoken of the goddess of birth), 19, 104. 2) Mid. with aor. 1 and 2 pass. to shine out, to appear, to gleam, to become visible, 4, 468; ὅσσε δεινὸν ἐξεφάανθεν, terribly gleamed the eyes, 19, 17; with gen.

Χαρύβδιος, from Charybdis, Od. 441.

ἐκφέρω (φέρω), fut. ἐξοίσω, 1) to bring out, to bring out, τινά and τί τινος, 23†. 23, 259; a) to bear out, esply spoken of the dead. 24, 786. b) to bear away of a prize, ἄεθλον, 23, 785. c) to bear away, to carry out, κτῆμα, Od. 15, 4 2) to bring on, μισθοῖο τέλος, the time reward, 21, 450. 3) Intrans. sc. ἑαυτ to outrun, to run before, spoken of a ra of men, and also of horses, 23, 3 759.

ἐκφεύγω (φεύγω), aor. 2 ἐξέφυγον, ἐκφυγόν, to flee away, to escape. 1) W gen. of place, ἁλός, out of the sea, (23, 236; esply spoken of missile weapor to fly away, 11. 380; χειρός, from t hand, 5, 18. 2) With accus. when denotes escape from danger: to avoid, escape, ὁρμήν, 9, 355; θάνατον, κῆρα, and Od.

ἔκφημι (φημί), fut. ἐξερέω, aor. 2 εἶπον, to speak out, to communicate, announce, τί τινι. Of φημί H. has or infin. pres. mid. ἐκφάσθαι ἔπος, *Od. 246. 13, 308.

ἐκφθίνω (φθίνω), to consume entire to destroy; only 3 pluperf. pass. νη ἐξέφθιτο οἶνος, the wine was consum out of the ships, *Od. 9, 163. 12, 329.

ἐκφορέω (a form of ἐκφέρω), to bear o Od. 22, 451. 24, 417. Mid. poet. press forth, νηῶν, out of the ships, 360.

ἔκφυγε, see ἐκφεύγω.

ἐκφύω (φύω), perf. ἐκπέφυκα, partc fem. ἐκπεφυυῖαι, to beget, to cause grow. 2) Intrans. mid. aor. 2 and pe act. to spring or grow from, with ge ἑνὸς αὐχένος, from one neck, 11, 40.†

ἐκχέω, Ep. ἐκχεύω (χέω), aor. 1 mi Ep. ἐκχευάμην, pluperf. pass. ἐξεκεχύμη Ep. aor. sync. 2, ἐξέχυτο, and ἔκχυτ partcp. ἐκχύμενος. 1) to pour out, ol (for sacrifice), 3, 295. II) Mid. 1) A 1 to pour out for oneself, to shoot or ὀϊστούς. Od. 22, 3. 2) With Ep. a sync. 2 to pour itself out, to stream for 21, 300; metaph. spoken of things, 526; of numerous men and anim streaming forth, 16. 259. ἱππόθεν, ο of the horse, Od. 8, 515.

ἐκχύμενος, ἔκχυτο, see ἐκχέω.

ἑκών, ἑκοῦσα, ἑκόν, voluntary, willi without force. 2) purposely, of design, set purpose, 10, 372. Od. 4, 372.

ἐλάαν, see ἐλαύνω.

ἐλαίη, ἡ. the olive-tree, the olive, e͒ply in the Od. sacred to Athênê, heu ἱερή. Od. 13, 372.

ἐλαΐνεος, η, ον, = ἐλαϊνός, *Od. 9, 32 394.

ἐλαϊνός, ἡ, όν, made of the olive-tree, olive-wood, 13, 612. Od. 5, 236.

ἔλαιον. τό (ἐλαίη), oil, olive-oil, m anointing oil, used after bathing and ofte perfumed, Od. 2, 339. Il. 23, 186; ofte λίπ' ἐλαίῳ, see λίπα.

ἔλασα, ἐλάσασκε, see ἐλαύνω.

Ἔλασος, ὁ, a Trojan slain by Patroclus, 16, 696 (= the driver; from ἔλασις).

ἔλασσα, see ἐλαύνω.

ἐλάσσων, ον, gen. ονος (compar. of the poet. ἐλαχύς, and used as compar. of μικρός). smaller, less, worse, 10, 357.

ἐλαστρέω. Ion. for ἐλαύνω, to drive, with accus. ζεύγεα, teams, 18, 543.†

ἐλάτη, ἡ, the pine, or red-fir, pinus abies, Linn.: 5, 560. 2) that which is made of pine-wood: an oar, 7, 5. Od. 12, 172.

ἐλατήρ, ῆρος, ὁ (ἐλαύνω), a driver, esply of horses, a charioteer, *4, 145. 23, 369. 2) one who drives away, βοῶν, h. Merc. 14.

*Ἐλατιωνίδης, ao. ὁ, poet. for Ἐλατίδης, son of Elatius = Ischys, h. Apoll. 210.

Ἔλατος, ὁ, 1) sovereign of the Lapithæ at Larissa in Thessaly, father of Kæneus (Cæneus) and Polyphēmus, also of Ischys. 2) An ally of the Trojans, slain by Agamemnōn, 6, 33. 3) a suitor of Pēnelopē, Od. 22, 267.

Ἐλατρεύς, έως, a Phæacian, Od. 8, 111 (the rower).

ἐλαύνω, poet. ἐλάω (Ep. ἐλόω), poet. imperf. ἔλων for ἔλαον, 24, 696; fut. ἐλάσω, Att. ἐλῶ (whence Ep. ἐλόωσι for ἐλῶσι, Od. 7, 319: infin. ἐλάαν for ἐλᾶν), aor. 1 ἤλασε, poet. ἔλασα, σσ, Ep. iterat. aor. ἐλάσασκε, subj. Ep 2 sing. ἐλάσησθα, aor. 1 mid. ἠλασάμην, Ep. σσ, perf. pass. ἐλήλαμαι, pluperf. ἠληλάμην and ἐληλά-μην, 3 sing. ἐληλάδατο, Od. 7, 86: or more correctly ἐληλέατο, for the ἐρηρέδατ' of Wolf; conf. Thiersch 212, 35. Buttm. § 103, p. 197. I) Act. 1) to drive, to put in motion, spoken of men, brutes, and inanimate things, with accus. τινὰ ἐς μέσσον, 4, 299; of flocks: μῆλα ὑπὸ σπέος, 4, 279; εἰς σπέος, Od. 9, 337; particularly a) Of horses, chariots, ships, ἵππους, ἅρματα, νῆα, 5, 236. Od. 7, 109; hence: νηῦς ἐλαυνομένη, a sailing ship, Od. 13, 155. b) to drive off, of cattle seized as plunder, βοῦς, 1, 154. c) to press, to urge as an enemy: οἱ δέ μιν ἅδην ἐλόωσι, καὶ ἐσσύμενον πολέμοιο, 13, 315 (cf. ἄδην, Spitzner ad loc. places a comma after ἐλόωσι, and connects consequently καὶ ἐσσύμενον with πολέμοιο). ἔτι μίν φημι ἄδην ἐλάαν κακότητος, Od. 5, 290 (cf. ἄδην). Metaph. χεὶρ ὀξείης ὀδύνῃσιν ἐλήλαται (Voss. 'my hand is tortured with sharp pangs'), 16, 518. 2) to strike, to thrust, esply spoken of missile weapons: διὰ στήθεσφιν δόρυ, 8, 259; and pass. ὀϊστὸς διὰ ζωστῆρος ἐλήλατο, the arrow was driven through the girdle, 4, 135; ὤμῳ ἔνι, 5, 400: hence: to strike, to smite, to cleave, of other weapons: ἐλαύνειν τινὰ ξίφει, 11, 109; with double accus. τινὰ ξίφει κόρσην, to smite one with a sword on the temple, 13, 576. cf. 614: also οὐλήν, Od. 21, 219; mly b) to strike, τινὰ σκήπτρῳ, 2, 199; πέτρην, Od. 4, 507; χθόνα μετώπῳ, the earth with the forehead, Od. 22, 94. c) πόντον ἐλάτρσιν, to strike the sea with oars, 7, 5; hence ἐλαύνοντες,

those rowing, Od. 13, 22. 3) to drive, metaph. a) Spoken of the working of brass, which is driven or beaten out by hammers: to beat, to forge, ἀσπίδα, 12, 296; πτύχας, 20, 270. b) to draw or trace out, τάφρον, 9, 349; hence: χάλκεοι τοῖχοι ἐληλάδατ', brazen walls were traced, Od. 7, 86 (where Wolf reads ἐρηρέδατο); ὄγμον, to mow a swath, 11, 68. c) κολφὸν ἐλαύνειν, to excite a tumult, 1, 575. d) ἐλαύνειν δίκην, see ἐξελαύνω. 4) Intrans. to travel, to go, to proceed, spoken of chariots: μάστιξεν ἐλάαν, βῆ δ' ἐλάαν, 11; of ships, Od. 3, 157. 12, 124. II) Mid. with reference to the subject, chiefly in the signif. number 1, to drive away for oneself. with accus. Od. 4, 637; ἵππους ἐκ Τρώων, 10, 537; ῥύσια, 11, 674.

ἐλαφηβόλος, ον (βάλλω). stag-slaying; ἀνήρ, a stag-hunter, a deer-shooter, 18, 319.†

ἔλαφος, ὁ, ἡ, a stag, a hind. ἐλάφοιο κραδίην ἔχων, having the heart of a stag, i. e. cowardly, 1, 225. cf 13, 102.

ἐλαφρός, ή, όν, compar. ἐλαφρότερος, superl. ἐλαφρότατος (kindred to ἔλαφος), 1) light in motion, agile, swift, γυῖα, 5, 122. 13, 61; spoken of men, with accus. πόδας, Od. 1, 164; and with the infin. of horses: θείειν, swift (of a horse), Od. 3, 370. 2) light in weight, λᾶας, 12, 450: metaph. light, i. e. not burdensome or distressing, πόλεμος, 22, 287.

ἐλαφρῶς, adv. lightly, πλώειν, Od. 5, 240.†

*ἐλάχιστος, η, ον, superl. of ἐλαχύς, the smallest, the least, h. Merc. 573.

ἔλαχον, see λαγχάνω.

ἐλαχύς, εῖα, ύ, small, short, insignificant, worthless; the positive occurs only in the fem. ἐλάχεια, as proparoxyt. Od. 9, 116. 10, 509. h. Ap. 197; and (as the reading of Zenodotus) Od. 9, 116, 10, 509, instead of λάχεια. Voss in his translation follows Zenodotus, and Bothe has adopted the same reading. See λάχεια.

ἐλάω, an old form for ἐλαύνω.

ἔλδομαι and oftener ἐέλδομαι, prop. ἐϜέλδομαι, poet. depon. only pres. and imperf. to wish, to desire, to long for, with gen. τινός, 14, 269. Od. 5, 210; and with accus. 5, 481; and with infin. τῶν τις καὶ μᾶλλον ἐέλδεται ἐξ ἔρον εἶναι (ἵημι). [things] of which men are more eager to satisfy their desire [things sought with keener appetite by most Than bloody war. Cp.], 13, 638. Od. 4, 162. 5, 219; once in pass. signif.: νῦν τοι ἐελδέσθω πόλεμος, κακός, now let evil war be desired by thee, 16, 494.

ἔλδωρ and ἐέλδωρ, τό, poet. wish, desire, longing (only in the Ep. form), 1, 41. Od. 17, 242.

ἔλε, Ep. for εἷλε, see αἱρέω.

ἐλεαίρω, a lengthened Ep. form of ἐλεέω, Ep. iterat. imper. ἐλεαίρεσκον, to have compassion, to pity, with accus. παῖδα, 6, 407; with κήδομαι, 2, 27. 11, 665,

ἐλεγχείη, ἡ, Ep. (ἐλέγχω), reproach, blame, shame, ignominy, Il. and Od.

ἐλεγχής, ές, gen. έος, poet. (ἐλέγχω), superl. ἐλέγχιστος, covered with reproach, reprehensible, infamous, despised, 4, 242; superl. 2, 285. Od. 10, 72.

ἔλεγχος, τό. reproach, blame, ignominy, shame; ἔλεγχος ἔσσεται, 11, 315 ἡμῖν δ' ἂν ἐλέγχεα ταῦτα γένοιτο, to us this would be a reproach, Od. 21, 329; esply in personal audresses, to denote disgraceful cowardice; abstract for concrete, κάκ' ἐλέγχεα, cowardly dastards, 2, 235. 5, 787 (as in Lat. opprobria).

ἐλέγχω, aor. 1 ἤλεξα (prob. from λέγω), to put to shame; to disgrace, to dishonour, with accus. τινά, Od. 21, 424; hence to despise. μὴ σύγε μῦθον ἐλέγξῃς μηδὲ πόδας, despise not their address, nor their journey, i. e. their mission [slight not their embassy, nor put to shame Their intercession. Cp.], 9, 522.

ἐλάειν, i. e. ἐλεῖν, see αἱρέω.

ἐλεεινός, ή, όν (ἔλεος), pitiable, deserving compassion, exciting pity, 24, 309. 2) pitiful, woeful, δάκρυον, 8, 331. 16, 219; compar. ἐλεεινότερος, 24, 504; superl. ἐλεεινότατος, Od 8, 530. The neut. sing. and plur. as adv. ἐλεεινά, pitiably, 2, 314.

ἐλεάω (ἔλεος), fut. ἐλεήσω, aor. ἠλέησα, poet. ἐλέησα, 1) to compassionate, to pity any one, τινά, and absol. to feel pity, 6, 484. 16, 431. 2) to regret, to lament, 17, 346. 352.

ἐλεήμων, ον, gen. ονος (ἐλεάω), compassionate, merciful, Od. 5, 191.†

ἐλεινός, ή, όν, Att. for ἐλεεινός, also h. Cer. 285.

ἐλεητύς, ύος, ἡ, Ep. for ἔλεος, compassion, pity, *Od. 14, 82. 17, 451.

ἔλεκτο, see λέγω.

ἐλελίζω, poet. (a strengthened form from ἐλίσσω), aor. 1 act. ἐλέλιξα, aor. 1 mid. ἐλελιξάμην, aor. 1 pass. ἐλελίχθην, Ep. sync. aor. 2 mid. 3 sing. ἐλέλικτο, 13, 558. 1) to put in a tremulous motion, to whirl, to roll, with accus. σχεδίην, Od. 5, 314; pass. Od. 12, 416; hence mly to cause to tremble, to shake, to agitate, Ὄλυμπον, 1, 530. 8, 199. Pass. to tremble, to shake, 12, 448; ἐλελίχθη γαῖα, 22, 448; ἐλελίζετο πέπλος, h. Cer. 183. 2) to turn suddenly, without the notion of repetition, spoken always of the sudden turning of warriors from flight against the enemy, 17, 278. Pass. 5, 497. 6, 106. 11, 588. II) Mid. to dart forward in spiral folds, winding in spiry volumes, spoken of a serpent, in aor. 1, 2, 316. 11, 39. 2) Like pass. to tremble, to shake, ἔγχος ἐλέλικτο, 13, 558.

Ἑλένη, ἡ, Helena, daughter of Zeus and Leda, sister of Kastôr and Polydeukês (Castor, Pollux), and Klytæmnêstra (Clytemnestra), wife of Menelaus, mother of Hermionê, famed for her beauty. She was seduced by Paris son of Priam and conveyed to Troy, and thus became the cause of the Trojan war, 2,

161. 3, 91. 121, seq. After the destruc tion of Troy, she returned with Menelau to Sparta, Od. 4, 184, seq. (prob. = ἐλάιν the torch, i. e. cause of war.)

Ἕλενος, ὁ, Helenus, 1) son of Priam an Hekabê (Hecuba), a noted prophet, 6, 7(According to a later tradition, he alon of the sons of Priam survived; he wer to Epirus, and after the death of Ne ptolemus married Andromachê, Pau 2) son of Œnopiôn, 5, 707.†

ἐλεόθρεπτος. ον (τρέφω), marsh-nou rished, marsh-born, growing in marshe σέλινον, 2, 776.†

ἔλεος, ὁ, pity, compassion, 24, 44.†

ἐλεός, ὁ, the table upon which the coo carved the meat, a kitchen table, 9, 21. Od. 14, 432.

ἔλεσκον. see αἱρέω.

ἑλετός, ή, όν, that which one can seize that may be taken. ἀνδρὸς ψυχὴ πάλι ἐλθεῖν, οὔτε λεϊστή, οὔθ' ἑλετή, for οὔι λεϊστόν, οὔθ' ἑλετὸν ψυχὴν πάλιν ἐλθεῖι it is not to be obtained by booty or ga that the soul of a man should retur again, 9, 409.†

ἕλευ, Ep. for ἕλου, see αἱρέω.

ἐλεύθερος, η, ον (from ἐλεύθω), free only ἐλεύθερον ἦμαρ, the day of freedom i. e. freedom itself: opposed to δούλιο ἦμαρ, 6, 455. ἐλεύθερος κρητήρ, th mixing-cup of freedom, i. e. which mingled in joy at regaining freedon *6, 528.

Ἐλευσινίδης, αο, ὁ, son of Eleusis = Keleos (Celeus).h. in Cer. 105 (with short

[Ἐλευσίνιος, ία, ιον, Eleusinian,] Cer. 267.]

Ἐλευσίς, ῖνος, ἡ (ἔλευσις, arrival), town and borough in Attica, belongin to the tribe Hippothoontis, having temple of Dêmêtêr, famed for the Eleu sinian mysteries, which were celebrate by yearly processions from Athens; no Lepsina, h. in Cer. 97; Ἐλευσῖνα δῆμος, v. 490.

Ἐλευσίς, ῖνος, ὁ, father of Kelec (Celeus) and Triptolemus, founder Eleusis. Apd. 1, 5. 2.

ἐλεφαίρομαι, depon. mid. (kindr. wit ἔλπω), aor. 1 partcp. ἐλεφηράμενος, deceive by empty hopes, and mly to d ceive, to delude; spoken of dreams, O 19, 565 (with reference to ἐλέφας, q. v v. 564, as a paronomasia), with accu 23, 338.

ἐλέφας, αντος, ὁ, ivory, the tooth of a elephant; in H. only in this signi Elephants themselves are not mentione ivory, however, was procured by con merce, and was valued as an ornamen 5, 583, together with gold and silve Od. 4, 73. Deceitful dreams con through a gate of ivory, since ivory l its shining promises light, but deceiv by its impenetrable opacity, cf. Scho Od. 19, 560; see ἐλεφαίρομαι and ὄνειρο

Ἐλεφήνωρ, ορος. ὁ, son of Chalcôdô sovereign of the Abantes before Troy, 540. 4, 463.

[ἔλεψα, aor. 1 of λέπω. q. v.]

Ἐλεών, ῶνος, ὁ, 1) a village in Bœotia, north-west of Tanagra, 2, 500. 10, 266; the Gramm. fix upon it as the residence of Amyntor, see Strab. IX. p. 439, upon Parnassus; others take it for Ἡλώνη. (Ἐλεών, see ἕλος, a marshy place.)

ἐληλάδατο see ἐλαύνω.

ἐλήλαται, ἐλήλατο, see ἐλαύνω.

ἐληλουθώς, see ἔρχομαι.

ἐλθέμεν, ἐλθέμεναι, see ἔρχομαι.

Ἑλικάων, ονος, ὁ, son of Antênôr and husband of Laodikê (Laodice), daughter of Priam, 3, 123.

Ἑλίκη, ἡ, a considerable town in Achaia, founded by Iôn, with a splendid temple of Poseidôn. It was destroyed by an earthquake Olym. 101, 4. Il. 2, 575. 8, 203.

*ἑλικοβλέφαρος, ον (βλέφαρον), having moving eye-lashes, shooting lively glances, h. 5, 19.

*ἑλικτός, ή, όν (ἑλίσσω), wound, tortuous, curled, h. Merc. 192.

*Ἑλικών, ῶνος, ὁ, Helikôn (Helicon), a noted mountain in Bœotia, sacred to Apollo and the Muses, now, according to Wheeler, Lιcona. In H. h. in Nep. this mountain was also sacred to Poseidôn, Batr. 1.

Ἑλικώνιος, η, ον, Heliconian, of Helicon. 2) Subst. ὁ Ἑλικώνιος, an appellation of Poseidôn. Some commentators, 20, 404, derive it from the town Helicê in Achaia, where Poseidôn was worshipt, see Ἑλίκη, cf. Hdt. 1, 148. According to its form, more correctly derived from the mountain Helicon in Bœotia; see Ilgen, ad h. in Pos. 21, 3, and Paus. 9 29, 1.

ἑλικῶπις, ιδος, ἡ, see ἑλίκωψ.

ἑλίκωψ, ωπος, ὁ (ἑλίσσω), having glancing eyes, having rolling eyes, fiery-eyed; a mark of spirit and youthful fire. Voss: having gay, joyful looks, epith. of the Achaians, *1. 389. 3, 190; and a pecul. fem. ἑλικῶπις, 1, 98;† an epith. of the Muses, h. 33, 1. Wolf and Köppen prefer the deriv. from ἕλιξ, ἕλικος (ἑλικτός), with round arched eyes, Apoll. Lex. cf. (βοῶπις).

ἕλιξ, ικος, ὁ, ἡ, adj. twisted, bent, curved, as epith. of cattle, like camurus, crooked-horned. It is incorrectly referred to the legs: for it is mly connected with εἱλίποδες, 21, 448. Od. 1, 92.

ἕλιξ, ικος, ἡ, subst. prob. any thing twisted; particularly a bracelet, 18, 401.† h. in Ven. 87.

ἑλίσσετο, see λίσσομαι.

ἑλίσσω, poet. (ἕλιξ), imperf. εἱλισσόμην, 12, 49; aor. 1 act. ἕλιξα, aor. 1 mid. ἑλιξάμην, aor partcp. pass. ἑλιχθείς, 1) to roll, to twist, to whirl, to turn around, mid. ἑλισσόμενον περὶ δίνας, 21, 11. Esply a) Subaud. ἵππους: περὶ τέρματα, to guide round the goal, 23, 309. 466; in the aor. partcp. turned again, viz. from flight, 12, 74. II) Mid. 1) to wind oneself, to turn oneself, ἀμφί τι, h. 5, 40, and

with accus. h. 32, 3, spoken of the serpent, περὶ χειρ̣, 22, 95; of the fume of fat, to roll up in volumes, 1, 317; hence also to turn hither and thither, to run hither and thither, of Hêphæstus: περὶ φύσας, about his bellows, 18, 372; of a wild boar: διὰ βήσσας, 17, 283. cf. 8, 340. 12, 49. 2) Like the act. to roll, to whirl around, with accus. κεφαλὴν σφαιρηδόν, 13, 204.

ἑλκεσίπεπλος, ον (πέπλος), having a long trailing robe, epith. of the Trojan women, 6, 442. 22, 105.

ἑλκεχίτων, ον (χιτών), having a long chitôn or tunic, having a trailing tunic, epith. of the Iônians, 13, 665.†

ἑλκέω, poet form of ἕλκω, from which, besides the imperf. εἵλκεον, 17. 395, the fut. ἑλκήσω, aor. 1 act. ἥλκησα, aor. 1 partcp. pass. ἑλκηθείς, accus. with the strengthened signif., 1) to drag, to draw along, with accus. νέκυν, 17, 395; as prisoners: ἑλκηθεῖσαι θύγατρες, 22, 62. Esply a) to tear, τινά (spoken of dogs, which tear a corpse), 17, 558. 22, 556. b) Mly to abuse, to dishonour, γυναῖκα, Od. 11, 580.

ἑλκηθμός, ὁ (ἑλκέω), a dragging, a drawing along, capture, 6, 465.†

ἕλκητον, see ἕλκω.

ἕλκος, εος, τό, a wound. ἕλκος ὕδρου, a wound from a serpent, *2, 723; often plur.

ἑλκυστάζω, poet. form of ἕλκω, to draw, to drag along, only partcp. pres. *23, 187. 24, 21.

*ἑλκύω, a later form of ἕλκω, aor. Ep. ἕλκυσα, Batr. 235.

ἕλκω, poet. ἑλκέω, infin. pres. ἑλκέμεναι and ἑλκέμεν, poet. for ἕλκειν, only pres. and imperf. the last without augment in Il. and Od.; εἷλκον, only h. Cer. 308. 1) to draw, to drag, to trail; to draw along, to drag along; spoken of things animate and inanimate, τινὰ ποδός, any one by the foot, 13, 383. Od. 16, 276; ἐκ δίφροιο, 16, 409; ὀιστὸν ἐκ ζωστῆρος, 4, 213; also βέλος, ἔγχος; ἄροτρον νειοῖο, to draw the plough through the field, 10, 353; of mules, 17, 743. ὥστε—νειὸν ἀν' ἕλκητον βόε οἴνοπε πηκτὸν ἄροτρον, Od. 13, 32 (the subj. after ὥστε is prop. to be resolved by ἐάν, Rost, Gr. § 123, 2). Esply a) to draw, to pull; νευρὴν γλυφίδας τε, to draw the bow-string and arrow-notch (for shooting an arrow), Od. 21, 419. Il. 4, 122; conf. ἀνέλκω. b) to draw up, for weighing. ἕλκειν τάλαντα, to draw up the scales, 8, 72. 22, 212; ἱστία βοεῦσιν, to draw up the sails, Od. 2, 246. 15, 291. c) to draw, to draw down; νῆας ἅλαδε, to launch the ships, 2, 152. 163; pass. 14, 100. d) Metaph. to draw after, to let follow, νύκτα, 8, 486. 2) to drag, Ἕκτορα περὶ σῆμα, 24, 52. 417. Mid. to draw (with reference to the subject), ξίφος, a sword, 1, 194; χαίτας ἐκ κεφαλῆς προθελύμνους, to draw out the hairs from the head with the roots, 10, 15; τόξον ἐπί τινι, to draw

the bow at any one (viz. τόξου πῆχυν). 11, 583. ἐπισκύνιον, see the word, spoken of lions, 17, 136. Il. and Od.

ἔλλαβε, Ep. for ἔλαβε, see λαμβάνω.

Ἑλλάς, άδος, ἡ, 1) Originally, a town in Phthiôtis (Thessaly), according to tradition founded by Helenus. Its situation is unknown. It belonged, together with Phthia, to the dominion of Achilles, and was the capital of the realm of the Æacidæ, 2, 683. 2) the territory of the town Hellas, between the Asôpus and Enîpeus, and, in connexion with Phthia, the realm of Peleus, 9, 395. Od. 11, 496. 3) It indicates, in connexion with Argos, as there were the extremities of the country, all Greece, Od. 1, 344; cf. Nitzsch ad loc.

ἑλλεδανός, ὁ (ἐλλάς), a straw band, for binding sheaves, 18, 553.† h. Cer. 456.

*ἐλλείπω (ἐν, λείπω), imperf. ἐλλειπον to leave behind in. 2) Intrans. to be behind, to remain behind. h. Ap. 213.

Ἕλλην, ηνος, ὁ, plur. οἱ Ἕλληνες, the Hellênes, the main stock of the original inhabitants of Greece, who derived their name, according to tradition, from Hellên, son of Deukalíôn (Deucalion); they dwelt first about Parnassus in Phocis, and subsequently emigrated into Thessaly, Apd. 1, 7. 3. In H. prop. the inhabitants of the city and territory of Hellas in Thessaly, who had become powerful by the spread of the Pelasgians. As the Hellênes, together with the Achaians, were the most powerful tribes before Troy, H. embraces all the Greeks under the name Πανέλληνες, 2, 530.

Ἑλλήσποντος, ὁ, the sea of Hellê, so called from Hellê, daughter of Athamas, who was drowned here: now the straits of the Dardanelles, or of Gallipoli, 2, 845.

ἐλλισάμην, see λίσσομαι.

ἐλλίσσετο, see λίσσομαι.

ἐλλιτάνευε, see λιτανεύω.

ἑλλός, ὁ, a young stag, a fawn, ποικίλος, Od. 19, 228.†

ἔλοιμι, see αἱρέω.

ἕλον, ἑλόμην, see αἱρέω.

ἕλος, εος, τό, a marsh, a swamp, a meadow, a moist place fit for pasturage. εἰαμενὴ ἕλεος, a low pasture, 4, 483. Od. 14, 474.

Ἕλος, ους, τό, 1) a town on the sea in Laconia, above Gythion, founded, according to tradition, by Hêlius son of Perseus, or rather named from its swamps. At a later period it was destroyed by the Spartans, and its inhabitants reduced to slavery, 2, 584. 2) a village or region in Elis on the river Alphêus, not known in the time of Strabo, 2, 594.

ἑλόωσι, see ἐλαύνω.

ἐλπίς, ίδος, ἡ, hope. ἔτι ἐλπίδος αἶσα, there is still some hope, Od. 16, 101. 19, 84. h. Cer. 37.

Ἐλπήνωρ, ορος, ὁ, voc. Ἐλπῆνορ, a companion of Odysseus (Ulysses), who was transformed by Kirkê (Circe). Intoxi-

cated with wine, he fell asleep on Circê's roof, and during his sleep falling down broke his neck, Od. 10, 552. Odysseus (Ulysses) saw him in Hadês, Od. 11, 51.

ἔλπω, poet. 1) Act. to excite hope, to cause to hope, to let hope, τινά, any one Od. 2, 91 13, 380. Oftener 2) Mid. ἔλπομαι, Ep. ἐέλπομαι, perf. ἔολπα, plup. perf. ἐώλπειν, with signif. of the pres. and imperf. to hope, and mly, to expect to think, to suppose, 7, 199; and, in a bad sense, to apprehend, to fear, 13, 8; also absol. ἔλπομαι. 18, 194. It has a) Accus. νίκην, 13, 609. 15, 539. b) More mly an infin. 3, 112; or an accus. with an infin. οὐδ᾽ ἐμὲ νηίδα γ᾽ οὕτως ἔλπομαι γενέσθαι. I do not think I am born so simple, 7, 198; chiefly with an adjunct clause having a distinct subject, Od. 6, 297. According to the difference in sense we find the infin. pres., perf., fut. and aor., 9, 40. Od. 3, 375. 6, 297. Il. 13, 288. Often the pleon. θυμῷ, κατὰ θυμὸν ἐν στήθεσσιν, also θυμὸς ἔλπεται (imperf. without augm. with exception of Od. 8, 419).

ἐλπωρή, ἡ, poet. for ἐλπίς, hope, with infin., *Od. 2, 280. 6, 314.

ἔλσαι, infin. ἔλσας, see εἴλω.

ἐλύω, Att. ἐλύω, only aor. 1 pass. ἐλύσθην, to wind up. to crook, to coil pass. to roll oneself, to crook or coil oneself up, to prostrate oneself; προτάρου ποδῶν. 24, 510. ὑπὸ γαστέρ᾽ ἐλύσθεν curled up under the belly, Od. 9, 433. but ῥυμὸς ἐπὶ γαῖαν ἐλύσθη, the pole fell to the ground, 23, 393

ἔλχ᾽ for ἕλκε, see ἕλκω.

ΕΔΩ, ἔλδω, obsol theme of εἴλω.

ΕΔΩ, obsol. root of the aor. εἶλον, see αἱρέω.

ἔλων, Ep. for ἔλαον, see ἐλαύνω.

ἔλωρ, ωρος, τό (ἑλεῖν), booty, spoil, prey spoken esply of unburied corpses, the prey (ἔλωρ καὶ κύρμα) of enemies, 5, 488. 684; or of birds and dogs, Od. 3, 271. 2) ἔλωρα (τὰ) Πατρόκλοιο, the prey of Patroclus, i. e. the penalty for his slaughter, 18, 93.

ἑλώριον, τό = ἔλωρ, booty, prey, plur 1, 4.†

ἐμβαδόν, adv. (ἐμβαίνω), on foot, by land, 15, 505.†

ἐμβαίνω (βαίνω), aor. 2 ἐνέβην or ἔμβην subj. ἐμβέῃ, ἐμβήῃ for ἐμβῇ, perf. ἐμβέβηκα, 3 plur. ἐμβεβάασαν, partcp. ἐμβεβαώς, 1) Intrans. to enter, to step into to go into, to mount, νηὶ into the ship, Il., and absol. 2, 619 ἵπποις καὶ ἅρμασι, into the chariot, 5, 199; metaph. μολυβδαίνη κατὰ βοὸς κέρας ἐμβεβαυῖα, a leaden ball fixed upon the horn of the ox, 24, 81. 2) to tread on trample upon, τινί, Od. 10, 164; absol. ἔμβητον, dash on! in the address of Antilochus to his horses, 23, 403 (upon the race-ground) 3) to intervene, to approach; ἀπ᾽ Οὐλύμποιο, 16, 94. 4) Trans. aor. 1 ἐνέβησα, to bring in, to put in, with accus. Od. 11, 4, in tmesis.

ἐμβάλλω (βάλλω), aor. 2 ἐνέβαλον, Ep. ἔμβαλον, infin. ἐμβαλέειν, 1) *to cast in.* according to the context *to hurl in, to lay on, to bring, to give,* mly τί τινι, rarely ἔν τινι, πῦρ νηί, to cast fire into the ship, 15, 598; τινὰ πόντῳ, 14, 258; τὶ χερσίν,† to give any thing into the hand, 14, 218; in a bad sense, 21, 47; τινὰ εὐνῇ, to conduct any one to the couch, 18, 85; κώπης, to lay hands on the oars [to row with all their might; *incumbere remis*]. subaud. χεῖρας, Od. 9, 489. 10. 129. 2) Metaph. of the soul: ἵμερον θυμῷ, to infuse a longing into the mind, 3, 139; μένος τινί, 10, 366; also with double dat. σθένος τινὶ καρδίῃ, θυμῷ, to inspire any one's heart with strength, with courage, 14, 151. II) Mid. *to cast in for oneself,* κλήρους, 23, 352; metaph. τὶ θυμῷ, to lay any thing to heart, to expect, 10, 447. 23, 313.

ἐμβασιλεύω (βασιλεύω), *to be king, to reign,* τινί, over any one, 2, 572. Od. 15, 413.

Ἐμβασίχυτρος, ὁ (χύτρα), Pot-explorer, name of a mouse, Batr. 137.

ἐμβέβασαν, see ἐμβαίνω.

ἐμβεβαώς, s–e ἐμβαίνω.

ἐμβέῃ and ἐμβήῃ, see ἐμβαίνω.

ἐμβῇ, Ep. for ἐνέβη. see ἐμβαίνω.

ἐμβλάττω, formerly 6, 39, now divided.

ἐμβρέμομαι, depon. mid. (βρέμω), to *murmur, to roar in,* with dat. ἱστίῳ, 15, 627.†

ἔμβρυον, τό (βρύω), prop. the unborn fruit of the womb, *an embryo,* 2) *a new-born lamb,* *Od. 9, 215. 309. 342.

ἔμεθεν, poet. for ἐμοῦ. see ἐγώ.

ἐμεῖο, Ep. for ἐμοῦ, see ἐγώ.

ἐμεμήκον, see μηκάομαι.

ἔμεν and ἔμεναι, see εἰμί.

ἔμεν and ἔμεναι, Ep. for εἶναι, see ἵημι.

ἐμέο, ἐμοῦ, Ep. for ἐμοῦ, see ἐγώ.

ἐμέω, *to spit out,* αἷμα. 15, 11.†

[ἐμήσατο, aor. 1 mid. of μήδομαι.]

ἔμικτο, see μίγνυμι.

ἔμμαθε, see μανθάνω.

ἐμμαπέως, poet. adv. *immediately, directly, quickly,* with ἀπόρουσε, 5, 836, and ὑπάκουσε, Od. 14, 485 (prob. from μαπέειν = μάρπτειν, to grasp, *to clutch;* others improb. from ἅμα τῷ ἔπει, with the word).

ἐμμεμαώς, υῖα, ός, Ep. μεμαώς, vehe-mently desirous, *ardently striving, eager, vehement,* *5, 142. 330. 240. 838 (see μέμαα).

ἔμμεν and ἔμμεναι, Ep. for εἶναι, see εἰμί.

ἐμμενές, adv. (neut. from ἐμμενής), *steadfast, constant, perpetual,* always ἐμμενὲς αἰεί, 10, 361. Od. 9, 386.

ἔμμορα. see μείρομαι.

ἔμμορος, ον (μόρος), *partaking of, sharing in,* with gen. τιμῆς, Od. 8, 480.† h. Cer. 481.

ἐμός, ἐμή, ἐμόν, adj. possess. (ἐμοῦ), *mine, my,* more rarely compounded with the article, τοὐμός, 8, 360. Strengthened by the gen. of αὐτός: ἐμὸν αὐτοῦ χρεῖος,

my own need. Od. 2, 45. h. Ap. 328. Often also objective: ἐμὴ ἀγγελίη, an embassy which concerns me, 20, 205.

ἐμπάζομαι, Ep. depon. only pres. and imperf. *to trouble oneself about* any thing, *to care for* any thing, with gen. θεοπροπίης, 16, 50;† often in the Od.: once with accus. ἱκέτας, Od. 16, 422 (prob. from ἔμπαιος).

ἔμπαιος, ον, Ep. adj. = ἔμπειρος, *acquainted with, experienced in,* *Od. 20, 379. 21, 400 (with shortened diphthong in Od. 20. 379).

*ἔμπαλιν, adv. (πάλιν), *backwards, back,* h. Merc. 78.

ἐμπάσσω (πάσσω), aor. 1 ἐνέπασα, Ep. σσ, *to sprinkle upon;* in H. *to inweave,* with accus. 3, 126,† and in tmesis, 22, 441.

ἔμπεδος, ον (ἐν, πέδον), prop. *standing in the earth;* hence *firm, immoveable, not to be shaken,* τεῖχος, βίη, ἴς, μένος. τοῖσι ἔμπεδα κεῖται, sc. γέρα, their gifts lie still secure, 9, 335. 2) Of time: *perpetual, constant, lasting,* φυλακή, 8, 521; κομιδή, Od. 8, 453. 3) Metaph. *firm, steadfast, constant,* ἧτορ, φρένας, 6, 352. Od. 18, 215; spoken of Priam, 20, 183. The neut. sing. and plur. ἔμπεδον and ἔμπεδα, with the same signif., 1, *firmly, steadfastly, μένειν.* 2) *perpetually, constantly,* θέειν (to go on running), 13, 141. Od. 18, 113.

*ἐμπελάζω (πελάζω), fut. σω, intrans. *to approach,* δόμῳ, h. Merc. 523.

ἐμπεσεῖν, see ἐμπίπτω.

ἐμπήγνυμι, fut. πήξω, *to stick* or *thrust into, to strike* (only in tmesis), 5, 40. Od. 22, 83.

ἔμπης, Ep. and Ion. for ἔμπας (prop. ἐν πᾶσι), *at all events, for all that* (cf. *toutefois*). i. e. *although, still, yet;* hence often ἀλλ᾽ ἔμπης, but still, 1, 562. Od. 4, 100; or with δέ preceding, Od. 3, 209; and following, 5, 191; strengthened, ἀλλὰ καὶ ἔμπης, but even so; but never-theless, 2, 297. 19, 422; καὶ ἔμπης, Od. 5, 205; and so also in the passages, where according to some it signifies *entirely, totally, at all,* 14, 174. 19, 308. Od. 19, 302. Sometimes it stands also when, of two cases, one is indicated as preponderating. τόφρ᾽ ὑμεῖς εὔχεσθε —σιγῇ ἐφ᾽ ὑμείων, ἵνα μὴ Τρῶές γε πύθωνται, ἠὲ καὶ ἀμφαδίην, ἐπεὶ οὔτινα δείδιμεν ἔμπης, since, *for all that* [or, *be that as it may*], we fear no one (i. e. though they *should* hear), 7, 195; also in other cases; see 12, 236. 17, 632; hence with ref. to something unexpected: ἔμπης, μοι τοῖχοι, κτλ., why surely [strange as it is, the walls of the house] seem to me to shine like fire [= *tamen ita est, quanquam non putabam* initio], Herm. ad Vig. p. 782. So also Od. 18, 334. 2) Often connected with πέρ with a partcp. (*tmetsi*). Νέστορα δ᾽ οὐκ ἔλαθεν ἰαχή, πίνοντά περ ἔμπης, 14, 1. Properly ἔμπης belongs in sense to what precedes, as ὅμως is also constructed; the sense is: the cry still did not escape

Nestor, although occupied with drinking, see 17, 229. Od. 11, 351. 15, 361. According to the Gramm., in 14, 174, and Od 18, 395, it signifies ὁμοίως, but incorrectly, see Spitzner ad loc.

ἐμπίμπλημι and ἐμπίπλημι (πίμπλημι), aor. 1 ἐνέπλησα, aor. 1 mid ἐνεπλησάμην, aor. 1 pass. ἐνεπλήσθην, infin. ἐνιπλησθῆναι, Ep. sync. aor. 2 mid. ἔμπληντο, 21, 607, and ἔμπληντο, Od. 8, 16. 1) to fill up, to fill full, τί τινος, any thing with any thing; ῥέεθρα ὕδατος, 21, 311; θυμὸν ὀδυνάων, Od. 19, 117. 2) τινά, to satiate any one, Od. 17, 503; hence pass. aor. 1. υἱὸς ἐνιπλησθῆναι ὀφθαλμοῖς, to satiate myself with looking on my son; to gaze my fill, Od. 11, 452. Mid. to fill oneself, τινός, with any thing, 21, 607. Od. 7, 221; esply Ep. aor. 2 mid., Od. 8, 16. 2) to fill for oneself, τι; spoken of the Cyclôpes. μεγάλην νηδύν, Od. 9, 296· and with gen. μένεος θυμόν, 22, 312.

ἐμπίπτω (πίπτω), aor. ἐνέπεσον and ἔμπεσον, 1) to fall in, to fall upon, to hit; with dat. πῦρ ἔμπεσε νηυσίν, the fire fell into the ships, 16, 113, and ἐν ὕλῃ, 11, 155. ἐνέπεσε ζωστῆρι ὀϊστός, the arrow pierced into the girdle, 4, 134. 2) Metaph. spoken of men: to rush in, to press in; with dat. ὑσμίνῃ, into the battle, 11, 297; προμάχοις, Od. 24, 526. b) Of the mind: χόλος ἔμπεσε θυμῷ, anger has entered the soul, 9, 436. 14, 207; and with double dat., 16, 206.

ἔμπλειος and ἐνίπλειος, η, ον, Ep. for ἔμπλεος (πλέος), filled, full, with gen. *Od. 14, 113; only in the Ep. form.

ἐμπληγδήν, adv. (ἐμπλήσσω), rashly, inconsiderately, Od. 20, 132.†

ἔμπλην, adv. (πλάω, πελάζω), near, in the neighbourhood. with gen., 2, 526.†

ἐμπλήσατο, see ἐμπίπλημι.

ἔμπληντο, ἔμπληντο, see ἐμπίμπλημι.

ἐμπλήσσω, see ἐνιπλήσσω.

ἐμπνέω, Ep. ἐμπνείω, aor. 1 ἐνέπνευσα and ἔμπνευσα, 1) to breathe into or upon, to blow upon, with dat.: μάλ' ἐμπνείοντε μεταφρένῳ, breathing on my back [of horses held immediately behind a person], 17, 502; with accus. ἱστίον, into the sail, spoken of wind, h. 6, 33. 2) Metaph. to inspire, to give, τί τινι, any thing to any one. spoken of the gods: μένος, θάρσος τινί, 10, 482. Od. 9, 381; with infin.. Od. 19, 138.

ἐμποιέω (ποιέω), fut. ήσω. to make ... in, with accus. 18, 490; ἐν πύργοις πύλας, gates in towers, 7, 438. 18, 450. 2) Mid. like act. h. Merc. 527.

ἐμπολάω (ἐμπολή), Ep. imperat. mid. ἐμπολόωντο, to purchase; mid. to purchase for oneself, with accus. βίοτον, Od. 15, 456.†

ἔμπορος (πόρος), any one who travels in another person's ship, a sea-passenger, a traveller, later ἐμβάτης, *Od. 2, 319. 24, 300.

ἐμπρήθω = ἐνιπρήθω, q. v.

ἐμπυριβήτης, ὁ (πῦρ, βαίνω), going on the fire, pre-bestriding, τρίπους, 23, 702.†

ἐμφορέω, poet. form of ἐμφέρω (φορέω), to bring in, only pass. to be brought in, with dat. κύμασιν ἀμφορέοντο, they were borne in upon the waves, *Od. 12, 419. 14, 309.

ἔμφυλος, ον (φῦλον), belonging to the same race or tribe, native, ἀνήρ, Od. 15, 273 †

ἐμφύω (φύω), aor. 1 ἐνέφυσα, aor. 2 ἐνέφυν, perf. (ἐμπέφυκα), only 3 plur. ἐμπεφύασι, partcp. fem. ἐμπεφυῖα, 1) Trans pres. act. fut. and aor. 1 act. to implant, to inspire, to infuse into, τί τινι. θεός μοι ἐν φρεσὶν οἴμας παντοίας ἐνέφυσεν, a deity has breathed many melodies into my soul, Od. 22, 348. 2) Intrans. mid. and aor. 2 and perf. act. to be produced in, to grow in; with dat. τρίχες κρανίῳ ἐμπεφύασι, the hairs grow upon the skull of the horses, 8, 84: hence metaph to cling to, to fasten oneself to. ὡς ἔχετ' ἐμπεφυῖα, thus she held clinging fast, 1, 513; with double dat. ἐν τ' ἄρα οἱ φῦ χειρί for ἐνέφυ, held fast his hand, 6, 253, and often.

ἐν, poet., Ep. ἐνί or εἰνί, I) Prep. with dat. ground signif. in. on, upon, at. 1) Used of place, ἐν signifies a) being in a place. ἐν γαίῃ. ἐν δώμασι; in like manner in geography, ἐν Ἄργεϊ, ἐν Τροίῃ. b) being surrounded by any thing. οὐρανὸς ἐν αἰθέρι καὶ νεφέλῃσι, 15, 192; often spoken of persons: between, amidst. among st, of being in a crowd, ἐν ἀθανάτοις; hence before, coram (surrounded by a crowd of hearers). ἐν πᾶσιν, Od. 2, 194. 16, 378; metaph. of external and internal conditions in which one may be. ἐνὶ πτολέμῳ, ἐν φιλότητι, 4, 258. 7, 302. So also of persons in whose power any thing lies. δύναμις γὰρ ἐν ὑμῖν, the power is in you, Od. 10, 69. cf. 11. 7, 102. c) being upon another thing. ἕστη ἐν οὔρεσιν, upon the mountains. ἐν ἵπποις. d) being in or by another thing. ἐν οὐρανῷ, 8, 555. ἐν ποταμῷ, 18, 521. 2) Used as cause, instrument, means, it signifies a) before, with. ὁρᾶν, ἰδεῖν ἐν ὀφθαλμοῖς, to see before or with the eyes, 1, 587. Again: ἐν χερσὶ λαβεῖν, to take with the hands, 15, 229. cf. Od. 9, 164. b) Suitableness: according to. ἐν μοίρῃ, i. e. κατὰ μοῖραν. Od. 22, 54. ἐν καιροῦ αἴσῃ, 9, 378. 3) Apparently ἐν often stands for εἰς with verbs of motion, since it includes at the same time the idea of the subsequent rest; thus ἐν γούνασι πίπτειν, to fall (and remain) upon the knees, 5, 370 Often βάλλειν ἐν κονίῃσι. ἐν τεύχεσσιν ἔδυνον, 23, 131. 4) Sometimes it stands with a gen., in which case a subst. is to be supplied. ἐν Ἀλκινόοιο, subaud. οἴκῳ, Od 10, 282; particularly εἰν Ἀΐδαο, 22, 389. 5) ἐν also stands after a subst., 18, 218; esply ἐνί, which then has t e accent on the first syllable, 7, 221. II) Adverb: ἐν is often an adv. of place without case: therein, thereby, thereon, Od. 1, 51. 2, 340, where it is sometimes explained as in tmesis

[mly connected with δέ, thus ἐν δέ; it then takes the adv. signif. *besides, moreover, together, with*, etc., Od. 5, 260]. III) In composition it has an adv. signif. and indicates the *resting* or *being* in or upon something.

ἐν, neut. of εἷς, *one*.

ἐναίρω, infin. pres. ἐναιρέμεν, aor. 1 mid. ἐνηράμην, 1) *to destroy, to kill,* τινά, in the Il. always in battle with the adjunct τόξῳ, χαλκῷ; πολλοὶ δ' αὖ σοὶ Ἀχαιοὶ ἐναιρέμεν, many Achaians hast thou to slay, 6, 229. Mid. in the signif. of act. with reference to the subject with accus., 5, 43. 6, 32. Od. 24, 424, and metaph. μηκέτι χρόα καλὸν ἐναίρεο, destroy not thy beautiful skin, Od. 19, 263. (Buttm. Lexil. p. 109. Rem. derives it, not from ἐν and αἴρω, but from ἕτερος, related to ἔναρα, ἐναρίζω, hence, prop. to send to the nether world.)

ἐναίσιμος, ον (αἴσιμος), prop. that which is in fate, 1) *indicating fate, prophetic, ominous, auspicious, fatalis, portentous,* 2, 353. ἐναίσιμα μυθήσασθαι, to utter words of fate (spoken of a soothsayer). Od. 2, 159; neut. sing. as adv. ἐναίσιμον ἐλθεῖν, to come seasonably, 6, 519. 2) *befitting, just, equitable,* δῶρον, ἀνήρ, φρένες.

ἐναλίγκιος, ον (ἀλίγκιος), *similar, like,* τινί, 5, 5; and τί, in any respect, θεοῖς, αὐτήν, Od. 1, 371; and often.

ἐνάλιος, Ep. εἰνάλιος, q. v.

ἔναλος, ον (ἅλς) = ἐνάλιος, *in the sea,* h. Ap. 180.

ἐναμέλγω (ἀμέλγω), *to milk into,* with dat. Od. 9, 223.

ἔναντα, adv. (ἄντα), *over against, opposite,* with gen. 20, 67.†

ἐναντίβιον, adv. from ἐναντίβιος (βία), *striving forcibly against,* and mly *against,* with μάχεσθαι, στῆναι, μεῖναι, Il. and Od.

ἐναντίος, η, ον (ἀντίος), 1) *opposite, in front of,* 6, 247; with dat., 9, 190. Od. 10, 89; hence, *visible,* Od. 6, 329. 2) *against, in opposition to,* in a hostile sense, mly with gen. Ἀχαιῶν, 5, 497; [but sometimes in a friendly sense with gen. and vice versa in a hostile sense with dat. cf. 1, 534. (Nägelsb.), 15, 304. 20, 252. Od. 14, 278.] Frequently the accus. neut. ἐναντίον, adv. as with μάχεσθαι, μίμνειν, ἐλθεῖν, etc.

ἔναξε, aor. ⸆ from νάσσω.

ἔναρα, τά (ἐναίρω), *the arms* taken from a slain enemy, *spolia;* and mly *war-spoils, booty.* ἔναρα βροτόεντα, bloody arms, 6, 68. 480. (Sing. not used.)

ἐναργής, ές, *visible, clear, manifest, plain,* spoken esply of the gods who appear to men in their real form: χαλεποὶ θεοὶ φαίνεσθαι ἐναργεῖς, terrible are the gods when they appear manifest, 20, 131. cf. Od. 7, 201. ἐναργὲς ὄνειρον, a plain dream, Od. 4, 841; (some derive it from ἀργός, ἀργής, *white, clear,* others from ἐν ἔργῳ.)

..αρηρώς, υῖα, ός (partcp. perf. from

ἐνάρω), only as an adj., *fitted in, fastened in,* Od. 5, 236.†

ἐναρίζω (ἔναρα), fut. ἐναρίξω, aor. 1 ἐνάριξα, prop. to strip a slain enemy, in H. with double accus. τινὰ ἔντεα, to despoil any one of his arms, 17, 187. 22, 323. 2) *to slay in battle,* 5, 155; and mly *to slay,* •1, 191.

ἐναρίθμιος, ον (ἀριθμός), *reckoned with, counted among, numbered with,* Od. 12, 65. 2) *esteemed,* ἐν βουλῇ, 2, 202.

ἔνατος, η, ον, and εἴνατος, *the ninth,* 2, 295. 313.

ἔνασσαν, Ep. for ἔνασαν, see ναίω.

ἔναυλος, ὁ, poet. (αὐλός), 1) *a ravine,* formed by winter torrents, 16, 71; *the torrent* itself, 21, 283. 312. 2) *a valley,* h. Ven. 74, 124.

ἐνδείκνυμι (δείκνυμι), *to show, to manifest,* only mid. *to shew oneself to any one,* Πηλείδῃ ἐνδείξομαι, either with Voss: 'I will explain myself to Peleides,' or with the Schol.: 'I will defend myself,' (ἀπολογήσομαι), 19, 83.†

ἕνδεκα, indecl. (δέκα), *eleven,* Il. and Od.

ἑνδεκάπηχυς, υ (πῆχυς), *eleven cubits long,* ἔγχος, •8, 494.

ἑνδέκατος, η, ον, *the eleventh,* ἡ ἑνδεκάτη, absol. subaud. ἡμέρα, Od. 2, 374.

ἐνδέξιος, η, ον (δεξιός), *on the right, on the right hand.* ἐνδέξια σήματα, omens on the right, i. e. auspicious, 9, 236; see δεξιός. Often as adv. ἐνδέξια, *on the right, to the right:* this direction was in all important cases observed as auspicious, 1, 597; in lots, 7, 184. Thus also Odysseus (Ulysses) begging, Od. 17, 365. 2) Later: *dexterous, skilful,* h. in Merc. 454.

ἐνδέω (δέω), aor. 1 ἐνέδησα, *to bind in* or *upon, to fasten, to fetter,* with accus. νευρήν, 15, 469; τὶ ἔν τινι, Od. 5, 260; metaph. Ζεὺς ἐνέδησέ με ἄτῃ, Zeus has entangled me in misfortune, 2, 111. 9, 18. (Conf. ἐφάπτω.)

ἐνδιάομαι, dépon. (ἔνδιος), *to be in the open air,* h. 32, 6.

ἐνδίημι, Ep. (δίημι), 3 plur. imperf. ἐνδίεσαν, for ἐνεδίεσαν, *to drive away, to pursue,* 18, 584 † conf δίεμαι.

ἔνδινα, τά, *the entrails, the intestines,* 23, 806.† (from ἔνδον), or, the parts concealed under the armour, a doubtful passage.

ἔνδιος, ον, *at mid-day;* ἔνδιος ἦλθε, Od. 4, 450. Il. 11, 725. (From Δίς, obsol. root of Διός, the bright sun; hence in reference to mid-day, the brightest part of the day, morning and evening being comparatively dusky, cf. εὔδιος, ἤέρι, ἠέριος.)

ἔνδοθεν, adv. (ἔνδον), *from within,* ὑπακούειν, Od. 4, 283. 20, 101. 2) *within, inside of,* with gen. αὐλῆς, 6, 247.

ἔνδοθι, adv. (ἔνδον), *within,* 6, 498, with θυμός, 1, 243. Od. 2, 315. 2) *within, inside of,* with gen. πύργων, 31, 18, 287.

ἔνδον, adv. (ἐν), *within, in, at home,* ἔνδον εἶναι, mly spoken of a dwelling,

10, 378. 13, 368. 2) With gen. Διὸς ἔνδον, in the abode of Zeus, 20, 13. 23, 200.

ἐνδουπέω (δουπέω), aor. 1 ἐνδούπησα, without augm. *to fall in with a noise, to make a heavy sound in.* μέσσῳ ἐνδούπησα, I dashed into the midst [of the waves]. *Od. 12, 443. 15, 479.

ἐνδυκέως, adv. *carefully, zealously, assiduously, faithfully, cordially,* in the Il. rarely δέχεσθαι, 23, 90. Often in the Od. with πέμπειν, λούειν; ἐνδ. ἐσθίειν, to eat eagerly, Od. 14, 109; (prob. fr. ἐν and δύω, conf. ἀτρεκής from τρέω.)

ἐνδύω = ἐνδύομαι, only imperf. ἐν δυνε, 2, 42. 10, 21.

ἐνδύω (δύω), aor. 1 ἐνέδυσα, aor. 2 ἐνέδῦν, partcp. ἐνδύς, aor. 1 mid. ἐνεδυσάμην. 1) Trans. *to dress, to clothe,* τινά. Batr. 160. 2) Mid. with aor. 2 and perf. act. intrans. *to go in,* then, *to put on, to dress in,* with accus. χιτῶνα, 5, 736; χαλκόν, 11, 16.

ἐνέηκα, Ep. for ἐνῆκα, see ἐνίημι.

ἔνεικαι, see φέρω.

ἔνειμι (εἰμί), imperf. ἐνῆεν, 3 plur. ἔνεσαν, *to be in, to be at, to be within,* 1, 593. Od. 9, 164; with dat. ἔνείη μοι ἦτορ, if a brazen heart were within me, 2, 490.

ἕνεκα, Ep. εἵνεκα and ἕνεκεν (Od. 17, 288. 310), prep. *on account of, for the sake of, for, by means of,* with gen. placed sometimes before and sometimes after: ἕνεκ᾿ ἀρητῆρος, 1, 94.

ΕΝΕΚΩ, obsol. root, from which several of the tenses of φέρω, are formed.

ἐνενήκοντα, Ep. ἐννήκοντα, indecl. *ninety,* 2, 602.

ἐνένιπον, see ἐνίπτω.

ἐνένιπτεν, see ἐνίπτω.

ἐνένισπον, see ἐνίσπω.

ἐνέπω and ἐννέπω, imper. ἔννεπε, optat. ἐνέποιμι, partcp. ἐνέπων, imperf. ἔνεπον and ἔννεπον, aor. ἔνισπον, infin. ἐνισπεῖν, subj. ἐνίσπω, optat. ἐνίσποιμι, fut. ἐνίψω, 7, 447. Od. 2, 137, and ἐνισπήσω, Od. 5, 98. 1) *to tell, to relate, to recount, to communicate,* τί τινι. any thing to any one, μῦθον, ὄνειρον, ὄλεθρον, 8, 412. 2, 80. ἄνδρα μοι ἔννεπε, announce to me the man, Od. 1, 1; μνηστήρων θάνατον, Od. 24, 414. 2) *to speak, to say, to talk,* absol. 2, 761. Od. 3, 93; πρὸς ἀλλήλους, 11, 643; (fr ἐν and ἔπω accord. to the old Gram.; Buttm. Lexil. p. 123, makes it only a strengthened form of εἰπεῖν, as ὄψ, ὀμφή, ἐνοπή, so ἔπω, ἔμπω, ἐνέπω.)

ἐνερείδω (ἐρείδω), aor. 1 ἐνέρεισα, *to push, thrust,* or *drive in,* μοχλὸν ὀφθαλμῷ, the stake into the eye, Od. 9, 383.†

ἔνερθε, before a vowel ἔνερθεν, also νέρθε, νέρθεν, adv. *from beneath,* 13, 75; *beneath:* οἱ ἔνερθε θεοί, the infernal gods, 14, 274. 2) With gen. *beneath,* ἔνερθε Ἀΐδεω, 8, 16; also ἀγκῶνος ἔνερθε. 11, 234.

ἔνεροι, οἱ (prop. ἐνϜεροι, *inferi*), *the inhabitants of the infernal world,* both the deities and the dead, 15, 188. h. Cer. 358. (From ἐν ἔνερ, *infer*.)

ἐνέρτερος, η, ον, compar. of ἔνεροι *deeper, farther under.* ἐνέρτερος Οὐρανιώνων, deeper than the children o Uranus, 5, 898.†

ἔνεσαν, Ep. see ἔνειμι.

ἐνεσίη, ἡ, Ep. ἐννεσίη (ἐνίημι), *sugges tion, counsel, command,* plur. 5, 894.†

ἐνεστήρικτο, see ἐνστηρίζω.

ἐνετή, ἡ (ἐνίημι), *a buckle, a clasp,* = περόνη, 14, 180 †

Ἐνετοί, οἱ, *Heneti,* a people in Paphla gonia, who however are not afterward mentioned, 2, 852. Tradition connect them with the Venetians in Italy an makes the last the descendants of th former Ἐνετοί. Strabo.

ἐνεύδω (εὕδω), *to sleep in.* with dat οἴκῳ, in the house, *Od. 3. 350. 20, 95.

ἐνεύναιος, ον (εὐνή), *lying in the bed* τὸ ἐνεύναιον, *bedding, bed,* Od. 14, 51 plur. *beds,* *Od. 16, 35.

ἐνηείη, ἡ (ἐνηής), *gentleness, mildnes benevolence.* 17, 670.†

ἐνηής, ές, *gentle, mild, benevolent,* 17 204. 23, 252. Od. 8, 200 (related to ἐύς).

ἔνημαι (ἦμαι), *to sit in,* Od. 4, 272.†

ἐνήρατο, 3 sing. aor. mid. from ἐναίρω ἔνθα, adv. (ἐν), 1) Of place: *there, i that place, here;* also for relat. ὅθι, *where* 1, 610. It more rarely expresses motion, *hither, thither,* 13, 23. Od. 3 295; with gen. h 18, 22. Often ἔνθα καὶ ἔνθα, *here and there, hither an thither,* 2, 462; *thither and back,* Od. 2 213; in the length and breadth, 7, 156 10, 264. Od. 7, 86. 2) Of time: *then, a that time, now,* 2, 155. Od. 1, 11; als ἔνθα δ᾿ ἔπειτα, Od. 7. 196.

ἐνθάδε, adv. (ἔνθα), 1) *there, here,* 2 296. Od. 2, 51. 2) *thither, hither,* 4, 179

ἔνθεν, adv. (ἐν), 1) Spoken of place *from hence, from thence.* ἔνθεν μὲν— ἔνθεν δέ, from this side—from that side Od. 12, 235. ἔνθεν, ἔνθεν with gen. h Merc. 226. *a*) Metaph. of descent: ἔνθε ἐμοὶ γένος, ὅθεν σοι, my race is derive from the same source whence thine is 4, 58. *b*) For the relat. ὅθεν: οἶνος ἔνθεν ἔπινον. of which they drank, Od. 4 220; with ἔνθα preceding, Od. 5, 195 2) Of time: *from this time, henceforth* 13, 741.

ἐνθένδε, adv. (ἔνθεν), *from hence, henc away,* *8, 527 9, 365.

ἔνθορε, see ἐνθρώσκω.

ἐνθρώσκω (θρώσκω), aor. 2 ἔνθορον Ep. for ἐνέθορον, *to leap in, to sprin among,* with dat. ὁμίλῳ, 15, 623; πόντῳ 24, 79. λὰξ ἔνθορεν ἰσχίῳ, he dashe his heel against his thigh [*smote wit his uplifted heel Ulysses' haunch.* Cp.] Od. 17 233.

ἐνθύμιος, ον (θυμός), *lying on the heart causing anxiety.* μή τοι λίην ἐνθύμιο ἔστω, let him not be a great cause o anxiety to thee, Od. 13, 421.†

ἐνί, poet. for ἐν, also in composition see ἐν.

ἐνιαύσιος, ον (ἐνιαυτός), *a year old,* σῦ Od. 16, 454.†

ἐνιαυτός, ὁ, *a year.* Διὸς ἐνιαυτοί, the years of Zeus, so far as he regulates the course of time, 2, 134. cf. Od. 14, 93. Originally it meant any complete period of time, embracing particular phenomena, a cycle, hence ἔτος ἦλθα, περιπλομένων ἐνιαυτῶν, the year came in the revolutions of time, Od. 1. 16. τελεσφόρον εἰς ἐνιαυτόν, within (i. e. up to it, as its limit) the completed year [τελεσφόρος, bringing an end, completing both other things and *itself*], Od. 4, 86.

ἐνιαύω (ἰαύω), *to sleep in, to dwell in,* *Od. 9, 187. 15, 557.

ἐνιβάλλω, poet. for ἐμβάλλω.

ἐνιβλάπτω, old reading in 6, 39. 647; see βλάπτω.

ἐνίημι (ἵημι), fut. ἐνήσω, aor. 1 ἐνῆκα, Ep. ἐνέηκα, partcp. aor. 2 ἐνείς, 1) *to send in, to let in, to drive in,* spoken of persons; τινά, any into the war, 14, 131; πέλειαν (to introduce another), Od. 12, 65; metaph. with accus. of the pers. and dat. of the thing: τινὰ μᾶλλον ἀγηνορίῃσιν, to lead one deeper into his pride, i. e. to increase his haughtiness, 9, 700; πόνοισι, to plunge into troubles, 10, 89; ὁμοφροσύνῃσιν, Od. 15, 198. 2)| *to put into,* according to the difference of the context: *to throw into, to thrust into,* mly τί τινι, rarely ἔν τινι; πῦρ νηυσίν, 12, 441; often ἐνιέναι νῆα πόντῳ, to launch, Od. 2, 295; also without νῆα, to put to sea, Od. 12, 401; metaph. of the mind: τινὶ ἀνάλκιδα θυμόν, to infuse into any one a timid spirit, 16, 656. τινὶ θάρσος ἐνὶ στήθεσσιν, 17, 579; τινὶ κότον, to excite anger in any one, 16, 449.

Ἐνιῆνες, οἱ. Ion. for Αἰνιᾶνες, sing. Ἐνιήν, the *Ænianes,* an ancient tribe, which dwelt first about Ossa, and afterwards in Epirus, between Othrys and Œta, 2, 749.

ἐνικλάω (κλάω), poet. for ἐγκλάω, *to break in pieces;* metaph. *to destroy, to make null,* with accus. *8, 408. 422.

Ἐνιπεύς, ῆος, ὁ, a river in Elis, which flowed into the Alphēus, now *Enipeo,* Od. 11, 238. Thus Strabo; but probably the river here mentioned is the *Thessalian Enipeus,* which flowed into the Apidanus, or rather the river god whose form Poseidōn assumed, cf. Nitzsch ad Od 3, 4.

ἐνῑπή, ἡ (ἐνίπτω). *a harsh address,* always in a bad signification, *blame, reproof, invective,* 4, 02; *threatening, insult,* Od. 20, 266; often strengthened by an adj., 5, 492. Od. 10, 448.

ἐνίπλειος, ον, poet. for ἔμπλειος, q. v.

ἐνιπλήσασθαι for ἐμπλήσασθαι, from ἐμπίμπλημι.

ἐνιπλήσσω (πλήσσω), Ep. for ἐμπλήσσω, aor. 1 ἐνέπληξα, partcp. ἐνιπλήξας, only intrans. *to fall into, to plunge into,* with dat. τάφρῳ, 12, 72. 15, 344; ἕρκει, to fall into a snare, see ἕρκος, Od. 22, 469.

ἐνιπρήθω (πρήθω), Ep. for ἐμπρήθω,

fut. ἐμπρήσω (9, 242) and ἐνιπρήσω, aor. 1 ἐνέπρησα, *to set on fire, to inflame, to burn up,* with accus. νῆας, νεκρούς: often strengthened with πυρί and πυρὸς αἰθομένοιο, 16, 82. 2) Spoken of wind, *to blow into, to swell out.* ἐν δ' ἄνεμος πρῆσεν ἱστίον. the wind blew into or swelled the middle of the sail, 1, 481 [πρήθω = (1) *to burn,* (2) *to spirtle, to pour out; to blow*], Buttm. Lex. 486.

ἐνίπτω, poet. aor. 2 ἐνίπον (incor. ἐνένιπον) and ἠνίπαπον (with redupl. like ἐρύκακον), prob. *to address harshly, to assail with harsh language, to chide, to blame* c. personæ accus.; not however always with the idea of abuse. κραδίην ἠνίπαπε μύθῳ, he excited his heart [of Ulysses *rousing up* his own courage: "*smiling on his breast reprov'd The mutinous inhabitant* within." Cp.]; Od. 20, 17; often with a dat. χαλεπῷ μύθῳ χαλεποῖσι ὀνείδεσιν, 2, 245. 3, 438; also simply μύθῳ τινά, to reprove any one with words, 3, 427; and without μύθῳ, 24, 768. 15, 546. (H. has two aorists; ἐνένιπτεν, 15, 546. 552, is rejected by Buttm. Lex. p. 125, as contrary to the *usus loquendi,* he would read ἐνένῑπεν, which Sptz. adopts; ἐνίσσω is a form of equivalent import. According to Ruhnken, the theme is ἶπος, a press; hence ἴπτω, ἐνίπτω, to press, to burden; see Thiersch, § 232, p. 389.)

ἐνισκίμπτω, Ep. for ἐνσκίμπτω (σκίμπτω), aor. 1 act. partcp. ἐνισκίμψας, aor. 1 pass. ἐνισκίμφθην, 1) *to fasten to, to fix,* τί τινι; οὔδει καρήατα, hanging their heads to the ground, 17, 437. Pass. *to be fastened in, to remain attached.* δόρυ οὔδει ἐνισκίμφθην, 16, 612. 17, 528.

ἐνισπε, ἐνισπεῖν, see ἐνέπω.

Ἐνίσπη, ἡ, a place in Arcadia, unknown even in the time of Strabo, 2, 606; cf. Paus. 8, 25, 7.

ἐνίσπω, poet. form of ἐνέπω, of which, however, H. has only single forms supplementary to ἐνέπω, viz. fut. ἐνίψω and ἐνισπήσω, aor. 2 ἔνισπες, etc. The aor. 2 ἐνίκισσε, 23, 473, should be changed to ἐνένῑπε, see Buttm. Lexil. p. 125; Spitzner has adopted ἐνένιπεν.

ἐνίσσω, poet. form of ἐνίπτω (as πέσσω of πέπτω) [= *to fall* on a man], *to assail, to chide.* with accus.; but absol. 15, 198. 22, 497; also partcp. pass. ἐνισσόμενος, Od. 24, 163.

ἐνιτρέφω, an old reading, 19, 326.

ἐνιχρίμπτω, poet. for ἐγχρίμπτω.

ἐννέα, indecl. *nine.* The number nine is often used by the poets as a round number, and as a triple triad; it seems to have been esteemed sacred, 2, 96. 6, 174. 16, 785.

ἐννεάβοιος, ον (βοῦς), *worth nine oxen,* τεύχεα, 6, 236.†

ἐννεακαίδεκα, indecl. *nineteen,* 24, 496.†

ἐννεάπηχυς, υ (πῆχυς), *nine cubits long,* 24, 270. Od. 11, 311.

ἐννεάχῑλοι, αι, α, poet. for ἐννεάκις χίλιοι, *nine thousand,* *5, 860. 14, 148.

ἔννεον, Ep. for ἔνεον, see νέω.

ἐννεόργυιος, ον (ὀργυιά), nine fathoms long, Od. 11, 312.† (in H. it is quadrisyllabic, and it is to be read ἐννεόργυιος).

ἐννέπω, poet. for ἐνέπω. q. v.

ἐννεσίη, ἡ, poet. for ἐνεσίη, q. v.

ἐννέωρος, ον (ὥρα), for nine years, nine years old, ἄλειφαρ, 18, 351. ἐννέωρος βασίλευε, he reigned during nine years, Od. 19, 179 (always trisyllabic, by synizesis of εω).

ἐννήκοντα, Ep. for ἐνενήκοντα, Od. 19, 174.†

ἐννῆμαρ, adv. (ἐννέα and ἦμαρ), for nine days, often in Il. and Od.

Ἔννομος, ὁ, 1) an ally of the Trojans from Mysia, mentioned as an augur, slain by Achilles, 2, 858 17, 218. 2) A Trojan, slain by Odysseus (Ulysses), 11, 422.

Ἐννοσίγαιος, ὁ, poet. for ἐνοσίγαιος (ἔνοσις), the earth-shaker, appellation of Poseidôn, because earthquakes were ascribed to him; as subst. 7, 455 and 9, 183, see Ποσειδῶν. (ἔνοσις) related to ὤθομαι, so Buttm. Lex. p. 115. [No: he considers ἔνοσις related to ἔνω, ἐνόω with the meaning of to shake.]

ἕννυμι, poet. (ΈΩ), fut. ἕσω, poet. σσ, aor. 1 act. ἕσσα. aor. 1 mid. ἑσσάμην, Ep. ἑεσσάμην, infin. ἕσασθαι, 24, 646; perf. pass. εἷμαι, partcp. εἱμένος, 3 plur. pluperf. εἵατο, 18, 596; also as if from ἕσμαι, so 2 sing. perf. ἕσσαι, and pluperf. 2 sing. ἕσσο, 3 ἕστο and ἕεστο, 12, 464; 2 dual ἕσθην. Fundamental signif. 1) to clothe, to put on; with double accus. τινὰ εἵματα, χλαῖναν, 5, 904. Od. 15, 338 2) Mid. and pass. to clothe oneself in, to attire oneself in, prop. spoken of clothes; with accus. φᾶρος, Od. 10, 543. χρύσεια εἵματα ἕσθην, they had attired themselves in golden clothing. 18, 517. χλαίνας εὖ εἱμέναι, beautifully clad in mantles. Od. 15, 331. 2) Metaph. spoken of weapons: to put upon oneself (sibi), περὶ χροΐ χαλκόν, 14, 383; τεύχεα, 4, 432; also ἀσπίδας ἑσσάμενοι, covering themselves with shields. 14, 372; also εἱμένος ὤμοιιν νεφέλην, 'his shoulders wrapt in cloud,' 15, 308; and ἦ τέ κεν ἤδη λάϊνον ἕσσο χιτῶνα, already hadst thou been clothed with a tunic of stone, i. e. wouldst have been stoned, 3, 56.

ἐννύχιος, η, ον (νύξ), by night, nightly, nocturnal, 11, 683. Od. 3, 178.

ἔννυχος, η, ον = ἐννύχιος, 11, 716.†

ἐνοινοχοέω (χέω), to pour wine into, οἶνον, in the partcp., Od. 3, 472.†

ἐνοπή, ἡ (ἐνέπω), 1) a voice, a tone, Od. 10, 147; a sound, of inanimate things, αὐλῶν, συρίγγων, 10, 13. 2) a cry, esply a battle-cry, in connexion with κλαγγή, 3, 2; μάχη, 12, 35. b) a cry of lamentation, 24, 160.

Ἐνόπη, ἡ (appell. ἐνοπή), a town in Messênia, which Agamemnon promised to Achilles for a dowry, 9, 150; according to Paus. 3, 26, = Gerênia.

ἐνόρνυμι (ὄρνυμι), aor. 1 ἐνῶρσα, aor.

συ... mid. only 3 sing. ἐνῶρτο, act. to excite in, to awaken in; with accus. re and dat. of pers. σθένος τινί, to excite strength in any one, 2, 451; γόον τινί, t 499; αὐτοῖς φύζαν, 15, 62. Mid. to b excited in or among, to arise amongst ἐνῶρτο γέλως θεοῖσιν, 1, 599. Od. 8, 32(

ἐνορούω (ὀρούω), aor. 1 ἐνόρουσα, t leap in or upon; with dat. to rush upo to attack, Τρωσί, 16, 783; spoken lions: αἴγεσιν, *10, 486.

ἔνορχος, ον (ὄρχις), not mutilated, n castrated, 23, 147.†

Ἐνοσίχθων, ονος, ὁ (ἔνοσις, χθών earth-shaker, a name of Poseidôn; as ad 7, 445. Subst. often 8, 208; see Ἐ νοσίγαιος.

ἐνοσκίμπτω, see ἐνισκίμπτω.

ἐνοστάζω (στάζω), perf. pass. ἐνέστακτα to instil; metaph. εἰ δή τοι σοῦ πατρὸς ἐ ἔστακται μένος, if the spirit of the fathe is implanted in (instilled into. Cp.) the Od. 2, 271.†

ἐνοστηρίζω (στηρίζω), to fasten in, onl pass. ἐγχείη γαίῃ ἐνεστήρικτο, the spe remained fixed in the earth, 21, 168.†

ἐνοστρέφω (στρέφω), to turn in. Mi to turn oneself in; with dat. μηρὸς ἰσχ ἐνοστρέφεται, the thigh-bone turns in th socket, 5, 306.†

ἐντανύω (τανύω) = ἐντείνω, fut. ἐ τανύω, aor. 1 ἐνετάνυσα, aor. 1 mi ἐνετανυσάμην, to stretch, to bend; wit accus. βιὸν, τόξον, νευρήν, Od. 19, 57 587; pass. Od. 21, 92; mid. τόξον, bend his bow. Od. 21, 403. *Od.

ἐνταῦθα, adv. (ἐν), hither; to this, 9, 601 ἐνταυθοῖ, adv. (ἐν), here, κεῖσο, 21, 12 ἧσο, Od. 18, 105. h. Ap. 363. Nev hither. Cf. Herm. ad Arist. Nub. 813.

ἔντεα, τά, weapons, arms, 5, 220. ἔντε Ἀρήϊα, 10, 407; chiefly the cuirass, 1 34. 2) Mly utensils, furniture; δαιτό the furniture of a feast, Od. 7, 23; νηό h. Ap. 489 (According to Buttm. Le p. 134, from ἕννυμι, prop. that which o puts on; the sing. is obsol.).

ἐντείνω (τείνω), perf. pass. ἐντέταμα 1) to stretch, to strain; perf. pass. to strained or stretched in, to hang; with d δίφρος ἱμᾶσιν ἐντέταται, the chariot bo hangs in braces, 5, 728. 2) to stret upon or over, spoken of a helmet; ἱμᾶσι 'with many a thong, well braced withi (Cp.), 10, 263.

ἔντερον, τό (ἐντός), a gut, sing. on ἔντερον οἰός, a sheep's gut, Od. 21, 4(2) Elsewhere plur. the bowels, the testines, 11.

ἐντεσιεργός, όν (ἔντεα 2, ἔργον), worki in harness, i. e. drawing, ἡμίονοι, 277.†

ἐντεῦθεν, adv. thence, hence, Od. 568.†

ἐντίθημι (τίθημι), imperf. 3 sing. ἐτίθει (τιθέω), aor. 1 ἐνέθηκα, aor. 2 inf ἐνθέμεναι, Ep. for ἐνθεῖναι, mid. aor. ἐνεθέμην, 3 sing. ἔνθετο, imperat. ἔνθε act. only in tmesis, to put in, to place to introduce, with accus, mly of i animate things : κῆρε, 8, 70 ; νῶτον ὀῖός, 9, 207. Mid. 1) *to put* or *place in, to introduce* (with reference to the subject), τί τινι : ἱστία νηΐ, to put the sails into the ship, Od. 11, 3; spoken of persons : τινὰ λεχέεσσι, to lay any one on the bed, 21, 124. *b*) Metaph μή μοι πατέρας ὁμοίῃ ἔνθεο τιμῇ, place not our fathers in equal honour, i. e. do not confer equal honour upon them, 4, 410. 2) *to put into for oneself, to assume*, τί, chiefly, metaph. ἵλαον ἔνθεο θυμόν, assume a gentle spirit, 9, 369; χόλον θυμῷ, to conceive anger in his heart, 6, 326 ; κότον, Od. 11, 102; μῦθον θυμῷ, to take the word to heart, Od. 1, 361.

ἔντο, see ἕξημι.

ἐντός, adv. (ἐν), *therein, in*, 10, 10. Od. 2, 341. 2) Prep. with gen. *within*, λιμένος ἐντός, 1, 432, and often.

ἔντοσθε, and before a vowel ἔντοσθεν, adv. = ἐντός. *in, within*, absol. 10, 262. 2) With gen. 6, 364. Od. 1, 126.

ἐντρέπω (τρέπω), *to change, to turn about*, only pres. pass. οὐδέ νύ σοί περ ἐντρέπεται ἦτορ ; even now is thy heart not changed ? i. e. art thou not brought to a different purpose,—dost thou not relent ? 15, 554. Od. 1, 60.

ἐντρέχω (τρέχω), *to turn in; metaph. to move in.* εἰ γυῖα ἐντρέχοι, 19, 385.†

ἐντροπαλίζομαι, depon. mid. Ep. (frequent. from ἐντρέπω), *to turn oneself often*, 6, 496; esply spoken of one who in a slow retreat from an enemy often looks back, *15, 547. 17, 109 ; always partcp. ἐντροπαλιζόμενος, *oft turning*, or *looking back.*

*ἐντροπίη, poet. (ἐντρέπω), *the act of turning, an artifice, a trick*, δόλιαι ἐντροπίαι, crafty artifices [slippery *turns*], h. Merc. 245.

ἐντύνω and ἐντύω (ἔντεα), aor. 1 partcp. ἐντύνας, aor. 1 mid. ἐντυνάμενος, *to equip, to prepare, to arrange, to furnish*, with accus. ἵππους, to make ready the horses, 5, 720 ; εὐνήν, to prepare the bed, Od. 23, 289 ; ἀοιδήν, to begin the song, Od. 12, 183 ; εὖ ἐντύνασα ἓ αὐτήν, having beautifully arrayed herself, 14, 162. Mid. 1) *to arm* or *prepare oneself*, Od. 6, 33; esply, *to adorn oneself*, Od. 12, 18. 2) *to prepare for oneself, to arrange for oneself*, with accus. δαῖτα, to prepare a feast for oneself, Od. 3, 83; ἄριστον, 24, 124 ; ἐντύω occurs only in the imperf. act.)

ἐντυπάς, adv. (τύπτω), *stretched upon the earth*, ἐντυπὰς ἐν χλαίνῃ κεκαλυμμένος, prostrate enveloped in a mantle, spoken of the sorrowing Priam, 24, 163.† (According to Voss ' so that only the form (of the body appeared'). [Cp.: "the *hoary king sat mantled*, muffled close."]

ἐντύω, a form of ἐντύνω, q. v.

Ἐνυάλιος, ὁ ('Ενυώ), *the warlike, the god of battle*, either as a name of Arês, only in Il. as subst. 2, 651. 7, 166 ; or as an epith. 17, 211. (Eustath. derives it from ἐνύω = φονεύω, Hesych. πολεμιστής.)

Ἐνυεύς, ῆος, ὁ, king of Scyrus, whom Achilles slew, 9, 668.

ἐνύπνιος, ον (ὕπνος), *occuring in sleer*, whence neut. as adv. ἐνύπνιον, in sleep, *in slumber*, θεῖός μοι ἐνύπνιον ἦλθεν ὄνειρος, a divine vision appeared to me in sleep, 2, 56. Od. 14, 495 ; cf. Thiersch, § 269 ; (ἐνύπνιον as a subst. a dream, a vision, in a later signif.)

Ἐνυώ, όος, ἡ, *Enyô*, the slaughtering goddess of war, companion of Arês, 5, 333. 592 ; the *Bellona* of the Romans, (from ἐνύω = φονεύω, Herm. on the other hand ὕω, *Inundona*, cf. 'Ενυάλιος).

ἐνωπαδίως, adv. (ἐνωπή), *facing, in the presence of*, Od. 23, 94, Wolf.† Others read ἐνωπιδίως.

ἐνωπή, ἡ (ὤψ), *the countenance*, only in the dat. ἐνωπῇ, as adv. *in view of, openly*, *5, 374. 21, 510.

ἐνώπια, τά, *a wall of a house*, chiefly, the front walls, on both sides of the entrance. They were in part covered by the porch, and the chariots were generally placed against them, 8, 435. Od. 4, 42 ; as well as captured arms, 13, 261. They were characterized as παμφανόωντα, because they were upon the sunny side, or because they were adorned with metallic ornaments, Od. 4, 45; (prop. neut. plur. from ἐνώπιος, that which is before the eyes).

ἐνωπιδίως, see ἐνωπαδίως.

ἐνώψ, ῶπος, Ep. for ἐνωπή, *the countenance*, hence κατ' ἐνῶπα, in the face, a reading adopted by Spitzner, after Aristarchus, for κατένωπα, 15, 320.†

ἐξ, prep. before a vowel for ἐκ.

ἕξ, indecl. *six*. In composition ξ becomes κ before κ and π.

ἐξαγγέλλω (ἀγγέλλω), aor. 1 ἐξήγγειλα, *to proclaim, to publish, to disclose*, τί τινι, 5, 390.†

ἐξαγνῦμι (ἄγνυμι), *to break out, to break in pieces*, with accus. ἐξ αὐχένα ἔαξε βοός, *5, 161. 11, 175; (occurs only in tmesis).

ἐξαγορεύω (ἀγορεύω), *to speak out, to communicate, to publish*, with accus., Od. 11, 234.†

ἐξάγω (ἄγω), aor. 2 ἐξήγαγον, poet. ἐξάγαγον, *to lead out, to lead away, to bring out*, τινά, mly with gen. of place : τινὰ μάχης, ὁμίλου. πολέμοιο, 5, 35. 353 ; ἐκ μεγάροιο, Od. 8, 106 ; metaph. spoken of Ilithyia, the goddess presiding over births: τινὰ πρὸ φόωσδε, to bring any one to light, i. e. into the world, 16, 188. 2) Neut. *to go out, to march out.* τύμβον χεύαμεν ἐξαγαγόντες, 7, 336. 435. Thus Eustath. and Voss.: ' assembled without;' others : ἐξάγειν ἐκ πεδίον, to erect out of the plain, cf. Heyne ; [so Bothe, *educentes ex campo tumulum.*]

Ἐξάδιος, ὁ, one of the Lapithæ, at the marriage of Pirithous, 1, 264.

ἐξέετες (a form of ἐξέτης), adv. *for six years*, Od. 3, 115.†

ἐξαίνυμαι, depon. (αἴνυμαι), *to take away, to despoil*, with accus. θυμόν, *to*

take away life, 4, 531, with double accus.
5, 155; and δῶρα, Od. 15, 206; (only pres.
and imperf.)

ἐξαίρετος. ον (ἐξαιρέω), taken out,
selected, chosen, distinguished, 2, 227.
Od. 4, 643.

ἐξαιρέω (αἱρέω). aor. 2 ἐξεῖλον, poet.
ἔξελον, infin. ἐξελεῖν, aor. mid. ἐξειλόμην,
poet. ἐξελόμην, to take out, esply to
choose, to select, κούρην τινί, for any one,
11, 627. 16, 56. Oftener mid. to take out
for oneself, τί τινος, ὀϊστὸν φαρέτρης,
from the quiver, 8, 323; esply, a) to
take away by force, to bereave, to despoil,
2, 690; and with ἐκ, 9, 331; frequently,
θυμόν, φρένας, either with double accus.
τινὰ θυμόν, to take away one's life, 15,
460. 17, 678; or with accus. and gen.
τινὸς φρένας, 19, 137; μελέων θυμόν, Od.
11, 201; once τί τινι, 6, 234. b) to take
out of several, i. e. to choose for oneself,
9, 272. Od. 14, 232.

ἐξαίρω (αἴρω), only mid. aor. 1. 3 sing.
ἐξήρατο, to bear off for oneself, to secure,
μισθούς, Od. 10, 84· with gen. Τροίης, to
bear off as plunder from Troy, *Od. 5, 39

ἐξαίσιος, ον (αἴσιος), contravening
right and justice, unrighteous, unjust,
indecorous, wrong, ἀρή. 15, 598. οὔτε
τινὰ ῥέξας ἐξαίσιον, nor ever wronging
any man by an unjust act, Od. 4, 690. 2)
exceeding the due measure, extraordinary.
δείσας τινά, fearing him excessively, as
adv. Od.17, 577.

ἐξαίσσω (ἀΐσσω), aor. 1 ἐξῄιξα, aor. 1
pass. ἐξηίχθην, intrans. to leap out, to
rush forth, 12, 145; likewise pass. ἐκ δέ
μοι ἔγχος ἠΐχθη παλάμηφιν, the spear
flew from my hands, 3, 368.

ἔξαιτος, ον (αἴω = αἴνυμαι), taken out,
selected, excellent οἶνος, 12, 320; ἐρέται,
Od. 2, 307.

ἐξαίφνης, adv. (αἴφνης), suddenly, unexpectedly, *17, 738. 21, 14.

ἐξακέομαι, depon. mid. (ἀκέομαι), aor.
1 optat. ἐξακεσαίμην, to cure entirely, to
heal thoroughly, to restore, 9, 507; metaph.
to appease, to reconcile, χόλον, 4, 36. Od.
3, 145.

ἐξαλαόω (ἀλαόω), fut. ώσω, to blind entirely, to render blind, τινά, Od. 11, 103;
ὀφθαλμόν, *Od. 9, 453. 504.

ἐξαλαπάζω (ἀλαπάζω), fut. ξω, aor.
ἐξαλάπαξα, to empty, to depopulate, πόλιν,
Od. 4, 176; chiefly in war: to sack,
hence, to destroy, to raze, πόλιν, τεῖχος,
νῆας, 20, 30.

ἐξαλέομαι, depon. mid. (ἀλέομαι), to
avoid, to escape, 18, 586. in tmesis.†

ἐξάλλομαι, depon. mid. (ἅλλομαι), only
part. aor. 2 sync. ἐξάλμενος, to leap out,
to spring forth, with gen. προμάχων,
from the front ranks, *17, 342. 23,
399.

*ἐξαλύω, poet. for ἐξαναλύσκω, to avoid,
to escape, with acc. μόρον, h. 6, 51.

ἐξαναδύω (δύω), aor. 2 ἐξανέδυν, partcp.
ἐξαναδύς, to come forth, to emerge, ἁλός,
from the sea, *Od. 4, 405. 5, 438; ἀφ'
ὕδατος, Batr. 183.

*ἐξαναιρέω (αἱρέω), aor. 2 ἐξανεῖλον,
take out, to take away, with gen. h.
Cer. 235.

ἐξαναλύω (λύω), infin. aor.1 ἐξαναλῦσα
to liberate completely, to set entirely fre
to deliver, ἄνδρα θανάτοιο, from deat
*16, 442 22, 180.

ἐξαναφανδόν, adv. (ἀναφανδόν), openl
plainly, Od. 20, 48.†

*ἐξάνειμι (εἶμι), to ascend from. 2)
return, with gen. ἄγρης, h. 18, 15.

ἐξανίημι (ἵημι), to emit, to send fort
spoken of the bellows: αὔτμήν, 18, 471.

ἐξανύω (ἀνύω), aor. 1 ἐξήνυσα. to finis
to accomplish, to execute, βουλάς, 8. 37
2) to slay (conficere), τινά, *11, 365. 2
452

ἐξαπατάω (ἀπατάω), fut. ήσω, aor.
ἐξαπάτησα, without augm. to deceit
with accus., 9, 371. Od. 9, 414.

ἐξαπαφίσκω, Ep. (ἀπαφίσκω), aor.
ἐξήπαφον, Od. 14, 379; aor. 1 ἐξαπάφησ
h. Ap. 376; aor. 2 mid. only optat. ἐ
ἀπάφοιτο, 9, 376. 14, 160; to deceii
cheat, τινὰ μύθῳ, Od. l. c. Mid. = ai
Διὸς νόον. to deceive the mind of Zeu
14, 160; ἐπέεσσιν, 9, 376. The parte
ἐξαπάφουσα as pres. is found in h. A
379; it should prob. be written ἐ
ἀπαφοῦσα, as aor. 2; cf. h. Ven. 38.

ἐξαπίνης, adv. = ἐξαίφνης, suddenl
unexpectedly, 9, 6; and often.

*ἐξαπλόω (ἁπλόω), to unfold, to exten
δέμας, Batr. 106.

ἐξαποβαίνω (βαίνω), aor. 2 ἐξαπέβην,
go out of, to disembark, νηός, Od. 12, 306

ἐξαποδύνω (δύνω), to strip, to take o
εἵματα, Od. 5, 372;† cf. δύνω.

ἐξαπόλλυμι (ὄλλυμι), to destroy utterl
only intrans. aor. 2 mid. ἐξαπωλόμη
and perf. 2 ἐξαπόλωλα, to perish from,
vanish from, with gen. Ἰλίου, from Tro
6, 60. ἐξαπόλωλε δόμων κειμήλια, t
stores have vanished from the house
18, 290; ἠέλιος οὐρανού, Od. 20, 357.

ἐξαπονέομαι, an old reading for
ἀπον·, separated.

ἐξαπονίζω (νίζω), to wash off, to clea
πόδας τινί, Od. 19, 387.†

ἐξαποτίνω (τίνω), to expiate entirely.
atone for, with accus. Ἐρινύας, 21, 412

ἐξάπτω (ἅπτω), aor. 1 ἐξῆψα, to appen
to attach, with accus. and gen. πείσμ
κίονος, the cable to a column or pilla
Od. 22, 466. Ἕκτορα ἵππων, 24, 51. Mi
to attach oneself to, 8, 20.

ἐξαράσσω (ἀράσσω), to strike out.
crush, ἐκ δέ οἱ ἱστὸν ἄραξε, Od. 12, 422
in tmesis. cf. ἀράσσω.

ἐξαρπάζω (ἁρπάζω), aor. 1 ἐξήρπαξα.
snatch away, to bear off, with accus. ai
gen. of the place: τινὰ νεός, from th
ship, Od. 12, 100; absol. to bear awa
3, 380. 20. 443.

ἐξαρχος. ον (ἄρχος), making a beginnin
subst. a beginner. θρήνων, 24, 721.†

ἐξάρχω (ἄρχω), to begin, to commenc
with gen. μολπής. ἐξάρχοντος (supp
from the context ἀοιδόν), 18, 606. Od.
19; γόοιο, 18, 51; with accus. βολλ

ἀγαθάς, to propose first salutary counsel, 2, 273; and χορούς, h. 27, 18. Mid. to begin, with gen. βουλῆς. Od. 12, 339.

ἐξαυδάω (αὐδάω), to speak out, to utter, connected with μὴ κεῦθε, 1, 363. 18, 74.

ἐξαῦτις, adv. (αὖτις), again, anew, 1, 223. 2) Of place: back. 5, 134. Od. 4, 213.

ἐξαφαιρέω (ἀφαιρέω), to take away, only mid. aor. 2 ἐξαφειλόμην, to take away for oneself; ψυχήν τινος, to take a man's life, Od. 22, 444.†

ἐξαφύω (ἀφύω), to draw out, to empty, to exhaust, οἶνον, Od. 14, 95.†

ἐξεῖδον (ΕΙΔΩ), Ep. ἔξιδον, defect. aor. of ἐξοράω, to see (out) μέγ᾽ ἔξιδεν ὀφθαλμοῖσιν, he saw clearly with his eyes, 20, 342.†

ἐξείης, adv. (poet. for ἑξῆς), in course, in succession, in order, 1, 448. Od. 1, 145.

ἔξειμι (εἶμι), 2 sing. pres. Ep. ἔξεισθα, infin. ἐξίμεναι, imperf. ἐξῄει, to go out, θύραζε, 18, 448; with gen. μεγάρων, Od. 1, 374. h. Ap. 28.

ἐξεῖπον (εἶπον), defect. aor. 2 of ἔκφημι, to declare, to communicate, τινί τι 9, 61. 24, 654.

ἐξείρομαι, Ion. for ἐξέρομαι (εἴρομαι), to interrogate, to seek for, with accus. τινά, 5, 756: βουλήν, to ask counsel, only imperf. ἐξείρετο, 20, 15. Od. 13, 127.

ἐξεκυλίσθην, see ἐκκυλίω.

ἔξεισθα, see ἔξειμι.

ἐξελαύνω (ἐλαύνω), fut. ἐξελάσω, infin. ἐξελάαν (8, 527), aor. 1 act. ἐξήλασα, Ep. ἐξέλασσα, 1) to drive out, to drive away, to expel, spoken of men and brutes, with accus. τινὰ γαίης, to expel any one from the land, Od. 16, 381; τάφροιο, 8, 255; μῆλα ἄντρου, Od. 9, 312; πάντας ὀδόντας γναθμῶν, to knock out every tooth from a man's jaws, Od. 18, 29; metaph. δίκην ἐξελαύνειν (subaud. ἀγορῆς), to expel or banish justice, 16, 388. 2) Intrans. to proceed, to drive, 11, 360.

ἐξελεῖν, see ἐξαιρέω.

ἐξέλκω (ἕλκω), to draw out, with gen. θαλάμης, Od. 5, 432. Pass. Il. 4, 214; see ἄγνυμι.

ἐξέμεν, Ep. for ἐξεῖναι, see ἐξίημι.

ἐξέμεν for ἔξειν, see ἔχω.

ἐξεμέω (ἐμέω), aor. 1 ἐξήμεσα, to vomit forth, to cast forth, spoken of Charybdis, *Od. 12, 237. 437.

ἐξέμμορε, see ἐκμείρομαι.

ἐξεναρίζω (ἐναρίζω), fut. ίξω, and aor. 1. to strip the armour from the dead, with accus. τινὰ τεύχεα, 5, 151. 7, 146. 13, 619. 2) to kill. to slay, 4, 488. Od. 11, 272.

ἐξερεείνω, Ep. (ἐρεείνω), to seek after, to inquire after, to explore, 9, 672; πόρους ἁλός, Od. 12, 259; metaph. to try, εἰθόραν [to elicit its tones], h. Merc. 483. Mid. like the act. τινὰ μύθῳ, 10, 81.

ἐξερείπω (ἐρείπω), aor. 2, only subj. ἐξερίπῃ and partcp. ἐξεριπών, prop. to cast down; in aor. 2 intrans. to fall, spoken of the oak, 14, 414; χαίτη ζεύγλης, the mane falling from the collar of the yoke, *17, 440. 19, 416.

ἐξερέομαι, depon. mid. Ep. form of ἐξείρομαι, to seek out, only pres. and imperf.; see ἐξερέω.

I) ἐξερέω, Ep. for ἐξερῶ, fut. of ἔκφημι, to declare, to proclaim, 1, 204. ὧδε ἐξερέω, 1, 212. 8, 286. (It must not be confounded with the following word.)

II) ἐξερέω, Ep. for ἐρεείνω (ἐρέω), only pres. 3 plur. ἐξερέουσι, subj. 3 sing. ἐξερέῃσι, optat. ἐξερέοις, partcp. ἐξερέων, to interrogate, to enquire after, to seek, with accus. ἕκαστα, Od. 14, 375; absol. Od. 3, 116; γόνον, to ask after a man's family, Od. 19, 166; to explore, to examine, κνημούς, Od. 4, 337. 17, 128 (like ἐξερεείνω, Od. 12, 259). Mid. as depon. ἐξερέομαι, to question, ἔκ τ᾽ ἐρέοντο, 9, 671; and infin. ἐξερέεσθαι, subj. ἐξερέηται, Od. 1, 416; optat. ἐξερέοιτο, Od. 4, 119.

ἐξερύω (ἐρύω), aor. 1 ἐξείρυσα, poet. σσ and ἐξέρυσσα, Ep. iterat. aor. ἐξερύσασκε, to draw out, to pull out, to tear out; with accus. and gen. βέλος ὤμου, the weapon from the shoulder, 5, 112; in like manner δόρυ μηροῦ, 5, 666; ἰχθύας θαλάσσης, Od. 22, 386; but τινὰ ποδός, to draw a man out by the foot, 10, 490; δίφρον ῥυμοῦ (by the pole), 10, 505; to tear out, μήδεα, Od. 18, 87.

ἐξέρχομαι, depon. (ἔρχομαι), only aor. 2 ἐξήλυθον and ἐξῆλθον, to go out, to come out, 9, 476. 576; with gen. κλισίης, out of the tent, 10, 140; μεγάροιο, Od. 21, 229.

ἐξερωέω (ἐρωέω), aor. 1 ἐξηρώησα, to spring out of the way, to run from the way, spoken of horses, 23, 468.†

ἐξεσίη, ἡ (ἐξίημι), embassy, mission; only ἐξεσίην ἐλθεῖν, to go on an embassy, to go any where as an ambassador, 24, 235. Od. 21, 20; see ἀγγελίην ἐλθεῖν.

ἐξέτης, ες, another form of ἐξαέτης (ἔτος), six years old, ἵππος, *23, 266. 655.

ἐξέτι (ἔτι), prep. with gen. since, from the time. ἐξέτι τοῦ ὅτε, from the time when, 9, 106. ἐξέτι τῶν πατρῶν, from the time of the fathers, Od. 8, 245. h. Merc. 508.

ἐξευρίσκω (εὑρίσκω), aor. 2 optat. ἐξεύροιμι, to find out, to discover, 18, 322.†

ἐξηγέομαι, depon. mid. (ἡγέομαι), to lead or conduct out, τινός, 2, 806.†

ἐξήκοντα, indecl. (ἕξ), sixty, 2, 584. Od. 14, 20.

ἐξήλασα, see ἐξελαύνω.

ἐξήλατος, ον (ἐξελαύνω), beaten, hammered out, ἀσπίς, 12, 295.†

ἐξῆμαρ, adv. (ἦμαρ), during six days, *Od. 10, 80.

ἐξημοιβός, όν (ἐξαμείβω), changed, for a change; εἵματα, garments for change, Od. 8, 249.†

ἐξήπαφον, see ἐξαπαφίσκω.

ἐξηράνθη, see ξηραίνω, Il.

ἐξήρατο, see ἐξαίρω.

ἐξηρώησα, see ἐξερωέω.

ἑξῆς, poet. ἐξείης (ἔχω, ἔξω), in order, one after another, *Od. 4, 449. 580.

ἐξίημι (ἵημι), only infin. aor. 2 ἐξέμεν,

H

Ep. for ἐξεῖναι, and aor. 2 mid. 3 plur. ἔξεντο in tmesis. Act. *to send out*, with accus. ἐς 'Αχαιούς, 11, 141. Mid. *to send out, to expel*, only in the common formula: ἐπεὶ πόσιος καὶ ἐδητύος ἐξ ἔρον ἕντο, after they had expelled the desire of food and drink, 1, 469. 2, 432.

ἐξιθΰνω (ἰθύνω), *to make exactly straight* [to divide it aright. Cp.], δόρυ νήϊον, 15, 410.†

ἐξικνέομαι, depon. mid. (ἰκνέομαι), only aor. 2 ἐξικόμην, *to arrive at, to reach*, with accus. θώκους, 8, 439; esply *to reach at length*, with accus., Od. 13, 206. Il. 9, 479.

ἐξίμεναι, see ἔξειμι.

ἐξίσχω (ἴσχω = ἔχω), *to hold out*; with accus. and gen. of place: ἐξίσχει κεφαλὰς βερέθρου, she *protrudes* [Cp.] her heads out of the abyss (spoken of Scylla), Od. 12, 94.†

ἐξοίσω, see ἐκφέρω.

ἐξοιχνέω, poet. (a form of οἴχομαι), *to go out*, 3 plur. pres. ἐξοιχνεῦσι, 9, 384.†

ἐξοίχομαι (οἴχομαι), *to go out, to go away, to depart*; the pres. prop. with signification of perf. ἐς 'Αθηναίης, sc. δόμον, 6, 379. Od. 4, 665.

ἐξόλλυμι (ὄλλυμι), aor. 1 ἐξώλεσα, *to annihilate, to destroy utterly*, Od. 17, 597; φρένας τινί, to destroy a man's understanding (in tmesis), 7, 360. 12, 234.

*ἐξολολύζω (ὀλολύζω), *to howl out, to wail*, Batr. 101.

ἐξονομάζω (ὀνομάζω), prop. *to call by name*; *to name, to utter*, h. Merc. 59; and frequently ἔπος τ' ἔφατ', ἐκ τ' ὀνόμαζεν, where it must be connected with ἔπος, to utter the word, like *eloqui verbum* (Voss, 'beginning he spake'), 1, 361. 3, 398, seq. [she said what she had to say and declared it fully, Nägelsb. ad Il. 1, 361].

ἐξονομαίνω (ὀνομαίνω), aor. 1 subj. ἐξονομήνῃς, and infin. ἐξονομῆναι. *to call by name*, with accus. ἄνδρα, 3, 166; γάμον, to name her marriage, Od. 6, 66. h. Ven. 253.

ἐξονομακλήδην, adv. (ὄνομα, καλέω), *mentioned by name, by name*; with ὀνομάζειν, 22, 415, and καλεῖν, Od. 4, 278.

ἐξόπιθεν, also ἐξόπιθε, adv. poet. for ἐξόπισθεν (ὄπισθεν), *from behind, on the back part, backwards*, 4, 298. 2) As prep. with gen. *behind*, κεράων, *17, 521.

ἐξοπίσω, adv. (ὀπίσω), 1) Of place: *backwards*, 11, 461; also prepos. with gen. *behind*, 17, 357. 2) Of time: *hereafter, in future*; only in Od. 4, 35. 13, 144.

*ἐξοργίζω (ὀργίζω), *to make angry, to exasperate*. Pass. *to become very angry*, Batr. 185.

ἐξορμάω (ὁρμάω), partcp. aor. 1 ἐξορμήσας, *to go forth, to rush* or *hurry forth*. μή σε λάθῃσιν κεῖσ' ἐξορμήσασα sc. νηῦς, lest it (the vessel) unperceived by you rush thither, Od. 12, 221.†

ἐξορούω (ὀρούω), *to spring out, to leap out*, only in tmesis; spoken of the lot, 3, 325; of men, Od. 10, 47.

ἐξοφέλλω (ὀφέλλω), *to increase greatl[y] to augment*, with accus. ἔεδνα, Od. 15, 18[?]

ἔξοχ' for ἔξοχα, see ἔξοχος.

ἔξοχος (ἐξέχω), origin. prominen[t] metaph. *distinguished, excellent*; spoke[n] of men, 2, 188; of brutes, 2, 480; of piece of land, τέμενος, 6, 194. 20, 18[?] often with gen. ἔξοχος 'Αργείων, eminen[t] among the Argives, 3. 227; also wi[th] dat. ἔξοχον ἡρώεσσιν for ἐν ἡρώεσσιν, 483. The neut. ἔξοχον and ἔξοχα as ad[v.] *most, among all, before all*, 5, 61; ἐμ[οὶ] δόσαν ἔξοχα, they gave it me by prefe[r]ence (before the rest), Od. 9, 551; oft[e] with gen. ἔξοχον ἄλλων, 9, 641; wi[th] superl. ἔξοχ' ἄριστοι, by far the best, 638. Od. 4, 629; also μέγ' ἔξοχα, Od. 1[,] 227.

ἐξυπανίστημι (from ἐξ, ὑπό, ἀν[ά] ἵστημι), only in aor. 2, *to arise from place under*. σμῶδιξ μεταφρένου ἐ[ξ] ὑπανέστη, a weal arose upon his back, 267.†

*ἐξυφαίνω (ὑφαίνω), *to finish a web, weave out*. Batr. 182.

ἔξω, adv. (ἐξ), *out, without*, Od. 10, 9[?] 2) *out of, away from*, 17, 265. Od. 12, 9[?] with gen. which, however, often depen[ds] at the same time upon the verb; στ[?] θέων, 10, 94. ἔξω βήτην μεγάροιο, O[d.] 22, 378.

ἔξω, see ἔχω.

ἔο. Ep. for οὗ, q. v.

ἔοι, Ep. for οἷ, see οὗ.

ἔοι, Ep. for εἴη, see εἰμί.

ἔοικα, ας, ε, perf. with pres. sign[if.] (from ΕΙΚΩ, q. v.), 3 dual Ep. εἴκτο[ν] partcp. ἐοικώς, once εἰκώς, 21, 254; fe[m.] εἰκυῖα, once plur. ἐοικυῖαι, 18, 418; pl[up.] perf. ἐῴκειν, εις, ει, dual Ep. εἴκτην, plur. ἐοίκεσαν, 13, 102. Also the [E]p. pass. form εἴκτο, was like, 23, 107, a[nd] ἤϊκτο, Od. 4, 796. 1) *to be similar, to [be] like, to resemble*, τινί, any one, τί, in a[ny] thing; Μαχάονι πάντα, in all respec[ts] 11, 613; δέμας γυναικί, Od. 4, 7[9] strengthened by ἄγκιστα [to resembl[e] closely], εἰς ὦπα, 14, 474. Od. 1, 4[1] chiefly in partcp. νυκτὶ ἐοικώς, li[ke] night, 1, 47. cf. 3, 151, etc. 2) *befit, to behove; to' be proper, becom[e] just*; always impers., except Od. [?] 348, where ἔοικα is pers., I ought, behoves me. ἔοικα δέ τοι παραειδε[ιν] ὥστε θεῷ, it behoves me to sing be[fore] thee as before a god; cf. however, no. often absol., as 1, 119; it takes the p[e.] in the dat., 9, 70. Only Od. 22, 196, [?] σε ἔοικεν, seems to form an except[ion] supply, however, from the preced[ing] passage, καταλέξασθαι; or it is c[on]structed with an accus. and infin. o[ὐ] ἔοικε, κακὸν ὥς, δειδίσσεσθαι, it does [not] become you to tremble like a coward, 190. 234; or with an infin. simply: [?] ἔοικ' ὀτρυνέμεν, 4, 286. The partcp. often used as an adj. *becoming, suit[ed] fitting, deserved*. μῦθοι ἐοικότες, s[uit-] able speech, Od. 3, 124 (Voss: s[imi]lar, i. e. to the discourse of Ulys[ses] ἐοικότα καταλέξαι, Od. 4, 239. ἐοικότι κεῖται ὀλέθρῳ, he lies in deserved death, i. e. he has his due punishment, Od. 1, 46; but εἰκυῖα ἄκοιτις, a fitting, i. e. dear spouse, 9, 399. 3) to seem, to appear; only ἔοικα δέ τοι παραείδειν, ὥστε θεῷ, I seem to thee as to a god to sing [videor (mihi) tibi tanquam deo acciners. Fäsi.], Od. 22, 348. (So Eustath.—Voss: thou listenest to my song like a god.) In this signif. ἔοικα is not elsewhere found in H., and therefore the former explanation seems preferable.

ἐοῖο, Ep. for ἐοῦ, see ἐός.
ἔοις, Ep. for εἴης, see εἰμί.
ἔολπα. perf. see ἔλπω.
ἔον, Ep. for ἦν, see εἰμί.
ἔοργα (ἔργω), see ἔρδω.
ἑορτή, ἡ, a feast, a festival, *Od. 20, 156 21, 258.
ἑός, ἑή, ἑόν, Ep. for ὅς, ἥ, ὅν, pron. possess. (from οὖ), his, her, mostly without the article; this is found but rarely connected with it to strengthen it. τὸν ἑόν τε Πόδαργον, 23, 295; τὰ ἃ δώματα, 15, 88. b) Strengthened by αὐτός: ἑὸν αὐτοῦ χρεῖος, his own need, Od. 1, 409. (The hiatus is mly found with it, cf. Od. 2, 247.)
ἐπαγάλλομαι, mid. (ἀγάλλω), to be proud of any thing, to glory in with dat. πολέμῳ, 16, 91.†
ἐπαγγέλλω (ἀγγέλλω), aor. 1 ἐπήγγειλα, to announce, to report, εἴσω, Od. 4, 775.†
ἐπαγείρω (ἀγείρω), to collect, to bring together, with accus. 1, 126.†
ἐπάγην, see πήγνυμι.
ἐπαγλαΐζομαι, depon. mid. (ἀγλαΐζω), to pride oneself in any thing, to glory in. οὐδέ ἅ φημι δηρὸν ἐπαγλαΐεῖσθαι (infin. fut.), I think he will not long exult in them, 18, 133.†
ἐπάγω (ἄγω), aor. 2 ἐπήγαγον, to lead to, to bring to, with accus. λῖν, 11, 480. ὡς ἐπάγοντες ἐπῆρσαν. subaud. κύνας, as leading them they pressed on, i. e. as they pressed on to the chase, or absol. attacking, Od. 19, 445; metaph. to induce, to cause, in connexion with πείθω, Od. 14, 392.
ἐπαείρω, Ep. for ἐπαίρω (ἀείρω), aor. 1 ἐπήειρα, to raise, with accus. κεφαλήν, 10, 80; to lift up upon, to lay upon, with accus. and gen. of place; τινὰ ἀμαξάων, upon the carriages, 7, 426; κρατευτάων, *Il. 9, 214.
ἔπαθον, see πάσχω.
ἐπαιγίζω (αἰγίς), to blow strongly upon, to rush upon, spoken of wind, 2, 148. Od. 15, 293.
ἐπαινέω (αἰνέω), fut. Ep. ἐπαινήσω (1 plur. ἐπαινήσομεν, 16, 443), aor. ἐπήνησα, to praise, to approve, to pronounce good; mly absol., but also with accus. μῦθον, 2, 335: and with dat. of the pers. Ἕκτορι, to agree with Hector, 18, 312; and μῦθόν τινι, h. Merc. 457.
ἐπαινός, ή, όν (αἰνός), very frightful, very terrible; only fem. ἐπαινή as epith. of Persephónē, 9, 457. Od. 10. 491. 534.

11, 47. According to others euphemistic for ἐπαινετή, lauded, venerable. The first explanation, as a strengthening of αἰνή (δεινή), deserves the preference; cf. Voss on h. Demet. 1. Buttm. Lex. p. 62, rejects ἐπαινή. and would read ἐπ' αἰνή, ἐπί being taken as an adv. = moreover, besides.

ἐπαΐσσω (ἀΐσσω), aor. 1 ἐπήϊξα, iterat aor. ἐπαΐξασκε, aor. 1 mid. ἐπηϊξάμην, to rush upon, to assail, often absol.: spoken of the wind, 2, 146; mly of battle. a) With gen. τινός, against any one, 5, 263. 323; never in the Od. b) With dat. τινί: Κίρκη ἐπαΐσσειν, to rush upon Kirkē (Circē), Od. 10, 295. 322; also with dat. instrum. ἔγχεϊ, δουρί, 5, 584; τινὶ μελίῃσι, Od. 14, 281. 3) With accus. transit. to attack, to fall upon, μόθον ἵππων, 7, 240. cf. 18, 159; τεῖχος, 12, 308; Ἕκτορα, 23, 64. II) Mid. to move oneself quickly; with gen. χεῖρες ὤμων, from the shoulders, 23, 628. b) With accus. ἐπαΐξασθαι ἄεθλον, to rush upon the prize, 23, 773.
ἐπαιτέω (αἰτέω), optat. aor. ἐπαιτήσειας, to ask for in addition, to demand further, with accus. 23, 593.†
ἐπαίτιος, ον (αἰτία), that is guilty, that deserves to be complained of, culpable. οὔτι μοι ὕμμες ἐπαίτιοι, I have no reason whatever to complain of you, 1, 335.†
ἐπακούω (ἀκούω), fut. ἐπακούσω and ἐπακούσομαι, h. Merc. 566; aor. ἐπήκουσα, Ep. without augm. to listen to, to hearken to, mly with accus. ἔπος, 2, 100; spoken of Hélios, πάντα, 3, 277. Od. 11, 109; but also gen. βουλῆς, to hear the counsel, 2, 143. h. Merc. 566.
ἐπακτήρ, ῆρος, ὁ (ἐπάγω), that goes upon a chase, a hunter, Od. 19, 435. ἄνδρες ἐπακτῆρες, 17, 135.
ἐπαλάομαι, depon. pass. (ἀλάομαι), aor. partcp. ἐπαληθείς, to wander over, to wander through, to reach in wandering; with accus. Κύπρον, to wander to Cyprus, Od. 4, 83. πόλλ' ἐπαληθείς, after a long wandering, *Od. 4. 81. 15. 176.
ἐπαλαστέω (ἀλαστέω), aor. 1 partcp. ἐπαλαστήσας, to be displeased at, to be angry, Od. 1, 252.
ἐπαλείφω (ἀλείφω), aor. ἐπήλειψα, to anoint, to besmear, οὔατα πᾶσιν, *Od. 12, 47. 177, 200.
ἐπαλέξω (ἀλέξω), fut. ἐπαλεξήσω, to ward off, to avert, to remove, τί τινι, any thing from any one; Τρώεσσιν κακὸν ἦμαρ, 20, 315. 2) to aid, to assist, τινί, one, 8, 365. 11, 428. *Il.
ἐπαληθείς, see ἐπαλάομαι.
ἐπαλλάσσω (ἀλλάσσω), aor. 1 ἐπαλλάξας, 1) to exchange, to alternate. 2) to entwine. to connect, 13, 359.† ἔριδος κρατερῆς καὶ ὁμοιΐου πολέμοιο πεῖραρ ἐπαλλάξαντες ἐπ' ἀμφοτέροισι τάνυσσαν, the snare or cord of terrible contention and common war they drew alternately to both sides, i. e. they gave the victory now to the Trojans, now to the Greeks. The discourse is of Zeus and Poseidón,

of whom the former aids the Trojans, the latter the Greeks. This explanation which Heyne gives, has the difficulty that Zeus, who knows nothing of the undertaking of Poseidôn, must be regarded as contending with him; cf. Spitzner and Köppen. Hence it is better with the ancients to explain ἐπαλλάξαντες by συνάψαντες, συνδήσαντες, to connect, to entwine, to bind together, and to understand it as indicating a continual, unceasing battle. Thus Damm: *pugnæ funem connectentes, ad utrosque intenderunt.* Köppen considers πείραρ πολ. = πείρατα πολ., see πείραρ, and translates: 'the issue of common war they stretched, alternating, over both,' cf. 11, 336. 14, 389. [The metaphor seems more satisfactorily taken from a cord, tied in a knot, whose two ends are drawn in opposite directions, to make the knot faster, cf. Jahrb. Jahn und Klötz, März 1843, p. 261. *Ed. Am.*]

ἐπάλμενος, see ἐφάλλομαι.

ἐπάλξις, ιος, ἡ (ἀλέξω), *a breast-work, a parapet,* esply the battlements of the city walls, behind which the besieged fight, *12, 258. 22, 3.

'Επάλτης, αο, ὁ, a Lycian slain by Patroclus, 16, 415. ('Επιάλτης.)

ἐπάλτο, see ἐφάλλομαι.

ἐπαμάομαι, depon. mid. (ἀμάω), aor. ἐπημησάμην, *to heap up, to heap together,* εὐνήν (of leaves), Od. 5, 482.†

ἐπαμείβω (ἀμείβω), fut. ἐπαμείψω, 1) *to exchange, to change,* τεύχεά τινι, arms with any one, 6, 230. 2) Mid. *to go alternately hither and thither,* with accus. νίκη ἐπαμείβεται ἄνδρας, victory alternates amongst men, 6, 339.

ἐπαμοιβαδίς, adv. (ἐπαμείβω), *alternately, mutually, reciprocally.* ἀλλήλοισιν ἔφυν ἐπαμοιβαδίς, they had grown mutually interlaced (the trees), Od. 5, 481.†

*ἐπαμοίβιος, ον = Ep. ἐπημοιβός, ἐπαμοίβια ἔργα, things of exchange, barter, h. Merc. 516.

ἐπαμύντωρ. ορος, ὁ (ἀμύντωρ), *a helper, a protector,* Od. 16, 263.†

ἐπαμύνω(ἀμύνω), aor. 1 ἐπήμυνα, infin. ἐπαμῦναι, *to come to aid, to help, to assist,* with dat. and absol. *6, 362. 8, 414.

ἐπανατίθημι (τίθημι), *to lay upon,* whence aor. 2 infin. ἐπανθέμεναι (for imperat.) σανίδας, shut the gates, 21, 535.† Wolf after Aristarchus has here introduced ἐπανθέμεναι instead of the former ἐπ' ἂψ θέμεναι.

ἐπανίστημι (ἴστημι), aor. 2 ἐπανέστην, *to cause to rise;* intrans. aor. 2 and perf. *to rise in addition,* 2, 85.†

*ἐπαντιάω (ἀντιάω), *to meet, to fall in with,* h. Ap. 152, in aor. 1.

ἐπαοιδή, ἡ, Ep. and Ion. for ἐπῳδή, prop. *a magic song;* then, *an incantation* for staunching blood, Od. 19, 457.†

ἐπαπειλέω (ἀπειλέω), aor. 1 ἐπηπείλησα, *to threaten in addition,* absol. 14, 45; τινί τι, to threaten a man with any thing, 1, 319; ἀπειλάς, Od. 13, 127.

ἐπαραρίσκω, poet. (ΑΡΩ), aor. 1 ἐ ἦρσα, perf. ἐπάρηρα, Ion. for ἐπάραρ 1) Trans. aor. 1, *to attach to, to fast to;* θύρας σταθμοῖσιν, to fix the doors the posts, 14, 167. 339. 2) Perf. a pluperf. intrans. *to be attached, to* infixed, κληῒς ἐπαρήρει, 12, 456.

ἐπάρη, ἡ, Ion. for ἐπάρα (ἀρά), an i precation, a curse, 9, 456.†

'παρήγω (ἀρήγω), infin. aor. 1 ἐπαρῆξ *to help, to aid,* τινι, 24, 39. Od. 13, 391

ἐπαρήρει, ἐπαρηρώς, see ἐπαραρίσκω.

ἐπαρκέω (ἀρκέω), aor. 1 ἐπήρκεσα, *ward off, to avert, to remove,* τινί τι, a thing from any one; ὄλεθρόν τινι, 2, 8: with accus. *to hinder* any thing, Od. 568.

ἐπάρουρος, ον (ἄρουρα), *living in country, being a rustic,* Od. 11, 489.†

ἐπαρτής, ές (ἀρτέω), *equipped, rea prepared,* *Od. 8, 151. 14, 332.

*ἐπαρτύνω = ἐπαρτύω, h. in Cer. 1 in mid.

ἐπαρτύω (ἀρτύω), *to attach to, to fast* with accus. πῶμα, Od. 8, 447; meta πῆμα κακοῖο, to prepare punishment crime, Od. 3, 152. 2) Mid. *to prej for oneself,* δεῖπνον, h. in Cer. 128.

ἐπάρχομαι, mid. (ἄρχω), aor. 2 ἐπ ἄμην, prop. *to begin in addition,* i religious signif.: to devote the firs a thing to the deity; always ἐπάρξα δεπάεσσιν, spoken of libation; accorc to Butim. Lex. p. 167, 'to pour out the goblets for the purpose of libati so that in ἐπί the approach to each i vidual guest is indicated. Voss tr lates: 'to begin anew with gobl The word δεπάεσσι may be expla more correctly, 'into the goblets;' he to pour 'the first into the goblets' libation), since the goblets were alr in the hands of the guests; cf. Nit ad Od. 7, 183; and Köppen ad Il. 1, 2) Mly, *to present, to offer,* with ac νέκταρ, h. Ap. 125.

ἐπαρωγός, ὁ (ἀρωγός), *a helper, an* Od. 11, 498.†

ἐπασκέω (ἀσκέω), perf. pass. ἐπήσκι *to labour carefully in addition, to fur* with any thing, with dat. αὐλὴ ἤσκηται τοίχῳ καὶ θριγκοῖσι, the cou surrounded with a wall and battlem Od. 17, 266.†

ἐπασσύτερος, η, ον (ἄσσον), *nea each other, close upon one anothe quick succession:* sing. κῦμα ἐπασσύ ὄρνυται, wave upon wave arose, 4, elsewhere plur., 8, 277. Od. 16, 366.

ἔπαυλος, ὁ (αὐλή), *a stall for caf pen,* for the night, Od. 23, 358.†

ἐπαυρίσκω (ΑΥΡΩ), H. has of the the pres. only, 13, 733. Of the act. aor. 2 subj. ἐπαύρῃ, infin. ἐπαυρεῖν, ἐπαυρέμεν, fut. mid. ἐπαυρήσομαι, ἐπηυρόμην, from which 2 sing. ἐπαύρηαι and ἐπαύρῃ. and 3 plur αύρωνται, I) Act. 1) *to take to on to obtain, to procure, to partake, to e* with gen. κτεάτων, 18, 302. Od. }

b) Frequently spoken of missiles; *to touch, to graze, to injure*, as it were *tasting*, with accus. χρόα, 11, 573. 13, 649. 15, 316; absol. 11, 391; and with gen. λίθον, to graze the stone (goal), 23, 340. II) Mid. 1) *to enjoy, to participate in*, in a good and bad signif. with gen. νόου, to enjoy intelligence, i. e. to enjoy the fruit of it, 13, 733; βασιλῆος, to learn to know their (bad) king [ironically: *that all may find much solace in their king*. Cp.]. 1, 410, 15, 17; and absol. οἴω μιν ἐπαυρήσεσθαι, I think he will soon feel it, or reap the fruits of it, 6, 353. *b)* With accus. *to receive*, to draw upon oneself, κακὸν καὶ μεῖζον, Od. 18, 107.

ἐπαφύσσω (ἀφύσσω), aor. ἐπήφυσα, *to pour upon* (in *addition*), Od. 19, 388 †

ἐπεγείρω (ἐγείρω), aor. sync. mid. ἐπ-έγρετο, partcp. ἐπεγρόμενος, 1) Act. *to awaken, to arouse*, with accus., Od. 22, 431. 2) Mid. *to wake up, to awake*, 10, 124. 14, 256; only aor. sync.

ἐπέγρετο, see ἐπεγείρω.

ἐπέδραμον, see ἐπιτρέχω.

ἐπέην, see ἔπειμι (εἰμί).

ἐπεί, Ep. also ἐπειή (ἐπί), conj. used to indicate time and motive. 1) Of time: *as, when, after*, always spoken of the past, *a)* With the indicat. in asserting a fact, 1, 57. 458. *b)* With the subj. when the declaration is conditional [or *indefinite*], mly with ἄν or κε (ἐπεὶ ἄν, contr. ἐπήν). ἐπεὶ ἄν σύ γε πότμον ἐπίσπῃς, when thou shalt have met thy fate. Without ἄν with subj. only 15, 363. h. Ap. 158; cf. however Thiersch, § 324, 4. *c)* With optat. when the declaration indicates a frequently.recurring case [*indefinite frequency*], 24, 14. The Ep. ἄν or κε is added when there is a condition, or the discourse is oblique, 9, 304. 19, 208. 24, 227; cf. Thiersch, § 324, 8. 2) Of a ground or motive: *as, because, since, inasmuch as, quoniam*, Ep. also ἐπειή, *a)* With indicat. ἄν is added when the clause is conditional. ἐπεὶ οὔ κεν ἀνιδρωτί γ' ἐτελέσθη, since it would not have been accomplished, 15, 228. *b)* In other cases the construction is as in no. 1. It can also often be translated by *for*, 3, 214. Sometimes, esply in address, ἐπεί stands where the protasis is wanting; we may supply, 'I will tell thee,' 3, 59. Od. 1, 231. 3, 103; or, 'let us fight,' 13, 68 (according to Voss, the apodosis is v. 73). 3) With other particles: ἐπεί ῥα, as soon as, since now. *b)* ἐπεί γε, since at least, since' (that is). *c)* ἐπεὶ οὖν, *when then* [referring a present action to the past from which it proceeds, &c.], *when once, when first* [with ref. to an action *to be related*, which depends upon this. Näg.], when therefore. *d)* ἐπεί περ, since indeed, since yet. ἐπεὶ οὔ is dissyllabic by synizesis, Od. 19, 314.

Ἐπειγεύς, ῆος, ὁ, son of Agaclês, a Myrmidon, who, on account of the slaughter of his uncle, was obliged to fly

from Budēum to Pēleus, and who went with Achilles to Troy. He was slain by Hector, 16, 571, seq.

ἐπείγω, only pres. and imperf. I) Act. *to press, to urge, to pursue closely*, with accus., 12, 452; κεμάδα, to press, to pursue a roe. 10, 361; hence pass. ἐπ-είγεσθαι βελέεσσιν, to be pressed by weapons, 5, 622. 13, 511, *b) to drive, to urge on*, spoken esply of wind, 15, 382; νῆα, h. Ap. 408; and pass. Od. 13, 115; ἐρετμα, to move the oars, Od. 12, 205; hence, *to drive, to hasten*, ὦνον, Od. 15, 445. *c)* Intrans. *to press, to oppress, to urge*. ἀνάγκη ἐπείγει. 6, 85; γῆρας, 23, 623; cf. h. Ven. 231. II) Mid. *to urge (on) for oneself, to hasten*, γάμον, Od. 2, 97. 19, 142. *b) to press oneself*, spoken of the wind; hence, *to hasten, to make haste*, with infin., 2, 354. 6, 363. Frequently the partcp. ἐπειγόμενος stands as an adj. *hastening, rapid, quick*, 5, 902. *c)* With gen., hastening after any thing, *to long for, to desire*, ὁδοῖο, Od. 1, 309. 315. Ἄρηος, 19, 142; and with accus. and infin. ἠέλιον, δῦναι ἐπειγόμενος, wishing the sun might set, Od. 13, 30. (According to Buttm. Lex. p. 118, not a compound word.)

ἐπειδάν, conj. *as soon as, when, after*, 18, 285.† Thiersch, § 324, 1, rejects the word as not Homeric; and reads ἐπὴν δή.

ἐπειδή, conj. (ἐπεὶ δή), *since, as, when, after*. 1) Mly with indicat. and with preterite: ἐπειδὴ πρῶτα, since first, when once, *b)* With subj. ἐπειδή—δαμάσσεται (for δαμάσσηται), 11, 478. cf Spitzner 2) More rarely in assigning a reason, *since, because*, with indicat., 14, 65. In addresses, without apodosis, Od. 3, 211. 14, 149, ἐπεί has ε lengthened, 22, 379.)

ἐπείδον (εἶδον), defect. aor. 2 of ἐφοράω, *to look upon, to look at*, with accus., *22, 61; see ἐφοράω.

ἐπείη, Ep. for ἐπεὶ ἤ, always in the signif. *since, because*. According to Schol. Ven. ad Il. 1, 156, ἐπεὶ ἤ, would be more correct. This Thiersch, § 324, 2, approves, and Spitzner has adopted it.

ἐπείη, optat. pres. of ἔπειμι (εἰμί).

ἐπεί κε, see ἐπεί.

(ἐπείκω), obsol. pres. of ἐπέοικε, q. v.

ἔπειμι (εἰμί), imperf. Ep. ἐπῆεν and ἐπέην, plur. ἔπεσαν, fut. Ep. ἐπέσσομαι, *to be at, to be upon, to be over*, absol. 5, 127. Od. 2, 344; with dat. loci, κάρη ὤμοισιν ἐπείη, may my head (no longer) remain on my shoulders, 2, 259; with dat. of pers. οἷσιν ἔπεστι κράτος, h. Cer. 150. 2) Of time: *to be after, to be left behind*, Od. 4, 756.

ἔπειμι (εἶμι), 3 sing. imperf. Ep. ἐπῄειν, 3 plur. ἐπῄϊσαν, Od. 11, 233, and ἐπῇσαν, Od. 19, 445; fut. ἐπείσομαι, aor. 1 mid. ἐπεισαμένη, 21, 424. 1) *to go to, to come upon, to approach*, with accus. ἀγρόν, to go to the field, Od. 23, 359; metaph. πρίν μιν καὶ γῆρας ἔπεισιν, before old age comes upon her, 1, 29. 2) Esply in a hostile signif. *to rush upon, to attack*, *to fall upon*, with accus., 11, 367; with dat. 13, 482. 17, 741; and often without cases: ὁ ἐπιών, the one attacking, 5, 238; often ἐπ' ἀλλοισιν ἰόντες, marching against each other, 11.

Ἐπειοί, ὁ, *the Epēans*, the oldest inhabitants of Elis, who derived their name from Epēus, the son of Endymiôn, 2, 619; cf. Paus. 5, 1. 2.

Ἐπειός, ὁ, *Epēus*, son of Panôpeus, who, with the aid of Athênê, constructed the wooden horse, Od. 8, 493. He vanquished Euryalus in boxing, at the funeral games of Patroclus, but in casting the iron ball was conquered by Polypœtes, 23, 664, seq. 839.

ἐπεί—περ, conj. *since at least*, with indicat. always separated, see ἐπεί.

ἔπειτα, adv. (ἐπί, εἶτα), *thereafter, hereafter, afterwards, hereupon, thereupon, then*, marks 1) Primarily, the progress from one action to another in the narration. In future actions it signifies, *directly after*, Od. 2, 60; καὶ τότ' ἔπειτα, and then at once, 1, 426. It often follows πρῶτον, is connected with αὐτίκα, αἶψα; also ἔνθα, ἔπειτα Sometimes it stands pleonastically, after a participle with a finite verb, 14, 223. 2) It often forms in the Epic language the apodosis, to render it emphatic: *a*) After a particle of time: ἐπειδὴ σφαίρῃ πειρήσαντο, ὠρχείσθην δὴ ἔπειτα, then they danced, Od. 8, 378; cf. 18. 545. *b*) After a particle of doubt or condition: εἰ μὲν δὴ νῦν τοῦτο φίλον,— Ἑρμείαν μὲν ἔπειτα — ὀτρύνομεν, then will we send, Od. 1, 84. 2, 273; so also in hypothetical clauses with ὅς κε, 1, 547. 2, 392. 3) *therefore*, (according to what you say), *then*, *a*) In a question, 9, 437. Od. 1, 65. *b*) In other clauses, 15, 49. 18, 357.

ἐπεκέκλετο, see ἐπικέλομαι.

ἐπέκερσε, see ἐπικείρω.

ἐπελαύνω (ἐλαύνω), aor. 1 ἐπήλασα, perf. pass. ἐπελήλαμαι, *to drive upon, to hammer out over*, spoken only of the working of metals, χαλκόν, 7, 223; of a shield: πολὺς ἐπελήλατο χαλκός, much brass was beaten out over it, 13, 804. 17, 493.

ἐπελήλατο, see ἐπελαύνω.

ἐπέλησε, see ἐπιλανθάνω.

ἐπεμβαίνω (βαίνω), partcp. perf. Ep. ἐπεμβεβαώς, *to go upon*, perf. *to stand upon*, with gen. οὐδοῦ, upon the threshold, 9, 582.†

ἐπενείκαι, see ἐπιφέρω.

ἐπένειμε, see ἐπινέμω.

ἐπενήνεον, see ἐπινηνέω.

ἐπενήνοθε (ἐνήνοθε), 3 sing. of an old Ep. perf. with pres. signif. which is also used as imperf. *to be* or *lie upon, to sit upon*, only four times; spoken of the head of Thersîtês, as imperf. ψεδνὴ ἐπενήνοθε λάχνη, thin woolly hair was upon it, 2, 219; of a mantle: ἐπενήνοθε λάχνη, 10, 134; as pres. with accus. οἷα θεοὺς ἐπενήνοθεν αἰὲν ἐόντας, such as adheres to the gods, Od. 8, 365. h. Ven. 62. (Buttm.

Lex. p. 111, from ἔνθω or ἐνέθω, per with Att. redupl. ἐνήνοθα, see Thiersch § 232.)

ἐπεντανύω, Ep. form of ἐπεντείνω, *stretch upon, to extend upon*, Od. 2 467 †

ἐπεντύνω and ἐπεντύω (ἐντύω), *to equi to put in order*, ἵππους, to harness th horses, 8, 374. Mid. *to put oneself i order, to prepare oneself*, ἄεθλα, for th contests, Od. 24, 89.

ἐπέοικα (ἔοικε), *it is becoming, it befitting, it is proper*, with dat. pers. an infin. 4, 341; or accus. with infin., 1, 12 10, 146. Ellipt. with accus. ὧν ἐπέοι ἱκέτην ἀντιάσαντα (subaud. from th foregoing οὐ δεύεσθαι), which it is n becoming that an approaching suppliar should lack, Od. 6, 193. 14, 511. 2) *is agreeable, it pleases*, 9, 392.

ἐπέπιθμεν, see πείθω.

ἐπέπληγον, see πλήσσω.

ἐπέπλως, see ἐπιπλώω.

ἐπεποίθει, see πείθω.

ἐπεπόνθει, see πάσχω.

ἐπέπταρε, see ἐπιπταίρω.

ἐπέπτατο, see ἐπιπέταμαι.

ἐπέπυστο, see πυνθάνομαι.

ἐπερείδω (ἐρείδω), aor. 1 ἐπέρεισα, *stay upon, to lean upon, to thrust agains* with accus. ἔγχος ἐς κενεῶνα, 5, 856 absol., 11, 235; metaph. ὑ' ἀπέλεθρο to apply prodigious power, 7, 269. O 9, 538.

ἐπερέφω (ἐρέφω), *to roof over*, ar hence, generally, *to build*, in tmesis, ε νηὸν ἔρεψα, 1, 39.†

ἐπερρώσαντο, see ἐπιρρώομαι.

ἐπερύω (ἐρύω), aor. ἐπέρυσα, Ep. σ *to draw to, to draw towards*, θύρην κορών (with the ring), Od. 1, 144 (see κορώνη ἐπὶ στήλην ἐρύσαντες, *Od. 12, 46.

ἐπέρχομαι (ἔρχομαι), fut. ἐπελεύσομα aor. 2 ἐπῆλθον, Ep. ἐπήλυθον, perf. ε ἐλήλυθα, 1) *to come to, to come on, come near, to approach*, with dat. 1 200; and absol. often indicating wh was unexpected, Od. 9, 214; metap ἐπὶ κνέφας ἦλθε, darkness came on, 1 194. Ἀχαιοῖς ἐπήλυθε νύξ, 8, 488. 474; τοῖσιν ἐπήλυθε ὕπνος, sleep can upon them, Od. 5, 472. 12, 311; wi the accus. esply when it contains th idea of *surprising* or *creeping upon i sensibly*; ἐπήλυθέ μιν ὕπνος, Od. 4, 79 10, 31; and of the spears: cutting th spear pressed upon the neck, 7, 262. In a hostile signif. *to rush against ai one, to fall upon, to attack*; witho case, and with dat. 5, 220. Spoken lions: βουσίν, 10, 485. 15, 630. 3) places: *to pass through, to go throug like obire*, with accus. ἄγκεα, *to through the valleys, 18, 321. Od. 16, 2

ἐπεσβολίη, ἡ (ἔπος, βάλλω), wor which one drops inconsiderately, pratt *loquaciousness, idle discourse*. ἐπεσβολί ἀναφαίνειν, to exhibit idle prattle seem loquacious. Cp.], Od. 4, 159† (n from ἔπεσι, but from ἔπεα and βάλλειν ἐπεσβόλος, ον (βάλλω), *uttering idle, foolish words*, *loquacious* (qui verba jacit); λωβητήρ (V. a troublesome prater), 2, 275.† According to Döderlein it is not to be explained by ἔπεα ἐκβάλλων, but by ἔπεσι βάλλων, i. e. ἰάπτων, *verbis lacessens* or *feriens*.

ἔπεσον, see πίπτω.

ἐπέσπον, see ἐφέπω.

ἐπέσσεται, see ἔπειμι (εἰμί).

ἐπέσσυνται, see ἐπισεύω.

ἐπέστη, see ἐφίστημι.

ἐπέσχον, see ἐπέχω.

ἐπετήσιος, ον (ἔτος), *annual, lasting a year*, καρπός, Od. 7, 118.†

ἔπευ, Ion. for ἔπου, see ἔπομαι.

ἐπευφημέω (εὐφημέω), αορ. ἐπευφήμησα, *to assent, to speak approvingly*. ἐπευφήμησαν αἰδεῖσθαι, κ.τ.λ., [*their voice was to respect* (him). Cp.], 1, 22.†

ἐπεύχομαι, depon. mid. (εὔχομαι), fut. ἐπεύξομαι, αορ. 1 ἐπευξάμην, *to pray, to supplicate* a divinity, θεοῖς, Διΐ, 3, 350. Od. 14, 423. 2) *to vaunt oneself, to boast*, absol. and τινί, over any one, 11, 431.

ἔπεφνον, see ΦΕΝΩ.

ἐπέφραδον, see φράζω.

ἐπέχω (ἔχω), αορ. 2 ἐπέσχον, partcp. ἐπισχών, αορ. 2 mid. ἐπεσχόμην, Ep. 3 plur. pluperf. ἐπώχατο, q. v. 1) *to hold on, to, upon*, with dat. πόδας θρήνυϊ, to put the feet upon the stool, 14, 241. Od. 17, 410; hence : *to hold out, to reach, to present*, οἶνον, 9, 489; μαζὸν παιδί, 22, 83. 2) Intrans. *to rush upon, to assail*, τινί, Od. 19, 71. cf. Od. 22, 75. 3) *to check, to restrain, to withhold*, with accus. ῥέεθρα, 21, 244; and θυμὸν ἐνιπῆς, *to restrain the mind from rebuke*, Od. 20, 266; hence absol. *to restrain oneself, to delay*, Ἀντίνοος δ᾽ ἔτ᾽ ἐπεῖχε, Od. 21, 186. 4) *to embrace, to occupy, to extend*, with accus. ἑπτὰ πέλεθρα, 21, 407. ὁπόσσον ἐπέσχε πῦρ, as far as the fire extended, 23, 238. II) Mid. 1) *to direct oneself to, to assail*, like act. 2. Spoken of shooting with the bow, ἐπισχόμενος, aiming, Od. 22, 15. 2) Like act. 3, *to restrain, to withhold, to hold up*, with accus. ἑανῶν πτύχας. h. Cer. 176.

ἐπήβολος, ον (βάλλω), *that has attained any thing, partaking, possessing*, with gen. νηός, ἐρετάων, Od. 2, 319.†

ἐπήγαγον, see ἐπάγω.

ἐπηγκενίδες, αἱ [*long planks*. Cp.], the *long planks* on the sides of a ship, which served to cover the ribs of the sides (σταμῖνες) and extended from stem to stern. To prevent the pressure of water, Odysseus (Ulysses) covers these planks with osier hurdles (ῥίπεσσι οἰσυΐῃσιν), Od. 5, 253, seq † (prob. from ἐνεγκεῖν = φέρειν, to extend oneself), see Nitzsch ad loc. and σταμίν.

ἐπῆεν, Ep. for ἐπῆν, see ἔπειμι (εἰμί).

ἐπηετανός, όν (ἔτος), 1) *lasting a whole year*, παρέχειν γάλα ἐπηετανόν, to give milk the whole year, Od. 4, 89; πλυνοί, Od. 6, 86. 2) *sufficient for a whole year, abundant, superfluous*, Od.

18, 360. 8, 233. The neut. ἐπηετανόν as adv. always in the year, Od. 7, 128 ; *abundantly, in abundance*, *Od. 7, 99. 10, 427.

ἐπήϊεν, see ἔπειμι (εἶμι).

ἐπῆλθον, and ἐπήλυθον, see ἐπέρχομαι.

*ἐπηλυσίη, ἡ, *enchantment, fascination*, h. Cer. 218, 220. Merc. 37.

ἐπημοιβός, όν (ἀμείβω), *alternating, exchanging, corresponding*; ὀχῆες, two bolts meeting each other, which one from each side of the door were fitted together, and held by a lock, see κληΐς, 12, 456 ; χιτῶνες, clothes for a change, Od. 14, 513.

ἐπημύω, see ἠμύω.

ἐπήν, conj. Hom. for ἐπάν, see ἐπεί.

ἐπήνεον, see ἐπαινέω.

ἐπῆξα, see πήγνυμι.

ἐπηπύω (ἠπύω), *to call to joyfully, to applaud*, with dat., 18, 502.†

ἐπήρατος, ον (ἐράω), *beloved, lovely, charming, agreeable*, spoken only of inanimate objects: δαίς, 9, 228 ; εἴματα, Od. 8, 366 ; mly of regions of Ithaca, Od. 4, 606.

ἐπήρετμος, ον (ἐρετμός), *at the oar, rowing*, ἑταῖροι, Od. 2, 403. 2) *furnished with oars*, νῆες, *Od. 4, 559.

ἐπηρεφής (ἐρέφω), *covering over, standing over, overhanging*, πέτραι, Od. 10, 131. 12, 59, κρημνοί, 12, 54 [overhanging precipices].

Ἐπήριτος, ὁ (*disputed*), son of Aphidas, from Alybas, whom Odysseus (Ulysses) pretended to be, Od. 24, 306.

ἐπῆρσε, see ἐπαραρίσκω.

ἐπῆρσαν, see ἔπειμι (εἶμι).

ἐπητής, οῦ, ὁ (ἔπος), *affable, humane, kind, benevolent*, *Od. 13, 122. 18, 128.

ἐπήτριμος, ον (ἤτριον), prop. close-woven, hence; *thickly over, close together, compact*, πυρσοί, 18, 211; δράγματα ἐπήτριμα πῖπτον, the sheaves fell close together, fell thick, 18, 552. 2) Of time : *in quick succession*, *19, 226.

ἐπητύς, ύος, ἡ (ἐπητής), friendly address, and mly *kindness, benevolence*, Od. 21, 306.†

ἐπί, I) Prepos. with gen., dat., and accus. Ground signif. *at, upon*, in manifold relations. A) With gen. a) To mark rest in a place: *on, upon, in, at, near*, esply with verbs of existence, rest, etc. : ἐπὶ μελίης ἐρεισθείς, 22, 225 ; and without a verb: ἐπὶ ὤμων, ἐπ᾽ ἀγροῦ, ἐπὶ κρατὸς λιμένος, *at the head of*, Od. 13, 102; metaph. ἐπὶ ξυροῦ ἀκμῆς, 10, 173 ; see ἀκμή. b) To mark motion to an object, with verbs of motion : ἐρύειν νῆα ἐπ᾽ ἠπείροιο, upon the land, 1, 485; βαίνειν ἐπὶ νηός. 2) Spoken of the time *in* or *during* which any thing happens. ἐπ᾽ εἰρήνης, in time of peace, 2, 797 ; ἐπὶ προτέρων ἀνθρώπων, 5, 637. 3) To mark manner, cause, etc. : only σιγῇ ἐφ᾽ ὑμείων, in silence by yourselves, i. e. for yourselves, 7, 195. B) With dative, 1) Spoken of place: a) To mark rest *upon, at*, or *by* an object: ἐπὶ χθονί, on the

H 4

earth. 1, 88: ἐπί τινι καθῆσθαι. to sit by any one, Od. 2, 369; ἐπ' ἔργῳ, at the work. Od. 16, 111; also spoken of a conjunction, or concomitancy of things: ἐφ' ἕλκεϊ ἕλκος ἀρέσθαι, wound upon wound, 14, 130. cf. Od. 7, 120; ἐπὶ τῇσι, in addition to these, 9, 639; ἐπὶ τοῖς, to this, i. e. besides this, Od. 3, 113; ταχὺς ἔσκε θέειν ἐπὶ εἴδεϊ, together with, i. e. besides his beauty, Od. 7, 126. 17, 308. Hence also spoken of succession in time and place. ἐπὶ τῷδε ἀνέστη, with, i. e. after him, 7, 163. *b)* To mark motion to any thing, with verbs of motion, and that in a hostile signif. : *upon, against*, 1, 382. 3, 15. 2) Of time: ἐπὶ νυκτί, by night, 8, 529; ἐπ' ἤματι τῷδε, on this day, 13, 234; but ἐπ' ἤματι, by day, Od. 2, 284, and as adv. *daily*, Od. 14, 105. 3) Of manner, cause, etc.: *a)* To mark design, purpose : ἐπὶ δόρπῳ, for supper, Od. 18, 44; ἐπὶ χάρμη, 13, 104; ἐπὶ Πατρόκλῳ, for Patroclus, 23, 776; υἱὸν ἐπὶ κτεάτεσσι λιπέσθαι, to leave a son for his treasures [i. e. to inherit them], 5, 154. *b)* To mark the ground or motive: *about, at, for, on account of*; γελᾶν ἐπί τινι, 2, 270; μογεῖν, πάσχειν ἐπί τινι, 1, 162. 9, 492. *c)* To mark the price, or only, the condition : *for*; ἐπί τινι ἀθλεύειν. 23, 274; ἐπὶ μισθῷ for hire. ἐπὶ δώροις, for presents, 9, 162. *C)* With accus. 1) Of place: *a)* To mark direction or motion to an object : *to, towards, against*; ἐπὶ νῆας ἔρχεσθαι, ἔξεσθαι ἐπ' ἐρετμα, Od. 12, 171. *b)* To mark motion *upon or over*, or an extension, or spreading out upon : πλεῖν ἐπὶ οἴνοπα πόντον, Od. 1, 183. cf. 2, 370; ἐπ' ἐννέα κεῖτο πέλεθρα, Od. 11, 577; ἐπὶ γαῖαν, *per terram*, Od. 4, 417. cf. Od. 1, 299; ἐπὶ δεξιά, ἐπ' ἀριστερά, to the right, to the left. 2) Of time: *a)* In marking the limit : ἐπ' ἠῶ, till morning, Od. 7, 288. *b)* To mark continuance: *for, during*; ἐφ' ἡμέραν, 2, 299; ἐπὶ δηρόν, for a long time, 9, 415. In like manner to mark the measure: ὅσον ἐπι, as far as, 2, 616; ἐπὶ ἥμισυ πάσης, to the half of the entire ship, Od. 13, 114. 3) Of manner, cause, etc.: *a)* To mark design or purpose: ἐπὶ βοῦν ἴτω, for an ox, i. e. to fetch him, Od. 3, 421; στέλλειν ἐπ' ἀγγελίην, on an embassy, 4, 384; more rarely spoken of persons: ἐπ' Ὀδυσσῆα ἰέναι, Od. 5, 149. *b)* To mark conformity: ἐπὶ στάθμην, by the line, Od. 5, 245; ἐπ' ἴσα, 12, 436. *c)* To mark a respect in which any thing is true; ἄριστοι πᾶσαν ἐπ' ἰθύν, in every attack, 6, 79. II) As an adv. often found in H. in the signif. *then, moreover, besides, thereupon*, etc. 1, 458. 5, 705. Od. 3, 164. 285. It must often be connected with the verb. III) In composition with a verb it sometimes has the local significations of the adv. and sometimes it denotes a consequence in time, an accession, etc.

ἔπι, in anastrophe. 1) for ἔπι, when it follows the governed word. 2) for ἔπ-

εστι, *it is present, it is there, there thou art*, Od. 14, 92 ; mly with dat.. 515. Od. 11, 307. Also with inf following, οὐκ ἐπ' ἀνήρ—ἀρὴν ἀπὸ οἴκ ἀμῦναι, there is no man to avert the ε from the house, Od. 2, 59.

ἐπιάλλω (ἰάλλω), aor. 1 ἐπίηλα, *to se to, to cast upon, to lead* or *bring to*. τινι; οὖρον Κῆρας τινί, Od. 2, 31 ἐπίηλεν τάδε ἔργα, he has brought abo these things, *Od. 22, 49.

ἐπιάλμενος, see ἐφάλλομαι.

ἐπιανδάνω, poet. for ἐφανδάνω, q. v.

ἐπιαύω, another reading for ἐνίαυ Od. 15, 557.

ἐπιάχω, poet. (ἰάχω), *to call to, to shε aloud to, to cheer, to applaud with shou* 7, 403. 13, 822. 2) Mly, *to cry out*, ' 860. 14, 148 (only pres. and imperf.).

ἐπίβαθρον, τό (βαίνω), *the passaε money*. the price paid by a passeng (ἐπιβάτης) on ship-board, Od. 15, 449.†

ἐπιβαίνω (βαίνω), fut. ἐπιβήσω. aor ἐπέβησα, aor. 2 ἐπέβην, infin. Ep. ε βήμεναι, fut. mid. ἐπιβήσομαι, aor. mid. ἐπεβησάμην (only the Ep. forι ἐπεβήσετο, ἐπιβήσεο). 1) Intrans. *mount, to ascend, to step upon* or *in a)* With gen. ἵππων δίφρου, 5, 46 ; 44 ; πύργων, νεῶν, etc. again: κροσσάι to mount the battlements, 12, 444 ; γαῖ to disembark, Od. 12, 282; metaph. ο corpse, to be la d upon the funeral pi 4, 99. *b) to go to, to reach*, with ge πόληος, to the city, 16, 396; with accι rarely; Πιερίην ἐπιβᾶσα, over Pie [not *to* P.], 14, 226. Od. 5, 50; οfι metaph. ἀναιδείης, to give oneself to impudence. Od. 22, 424. εὐφ συνης, Od. 23, 52; τέχνης, to try art. Merc. 166, 465. 2) Transit. only f and aor. 1 act. *to cause to mount, to cai to ascend*; τινὰ ἵππων, upon the chari 8, 129 ; hence : *to lead to, to place upε to bring to*, πολλοὺς πυρῆς, 9, 546 ; τι πάτρης, to send one to his country, C 7, 223; metaph. εὐκλείης, σαοφροσύν to elevate any one to renown, to bri one to understanding, 8, 285. Od. 23,

ἐπιβάλλω (βάλλω), aor. 2 act. ἐπέβαλ aor. 2 mid. ἐπεβαλόμην, 1) Act. *to c upon. to lay upon*, with accus., 11, 8 ἐπιβάλλειν ἱμάσθλην, subaud. ἵπποις, give the horses the lash, Od. 6, 320. Intrans. *to cast oneself upon, to go to* δὲ Φεὰς ἐπέβαλλε, the ship sailed to Phε Od. 15, 297; h. Ap. 427. 2) Mid. *to c upon for oneself*, κλήρους, Od. 14, 2 *b) to cast oneself upon a thing, to f upon it, to seek* or *strive after*, with gε ἐνάρων, 6, 68.

ἐπιβάσκω (βάσκω), poet. form of ε βαίνω. with transit. signif.: κακῶν ε βασκέμεν υἷας Ἀχαιῶν, to bring the aε of the Achaians into misfortunes, 2, 23

ἐπιβήμεναι, see ἐπιβαίνω.

ἐπιβήτωρ, ορος, ὁ, *one that moun ἵππων*, Od. 18, 263. 2) *a leaper* (spoκ of the boar), *Od. 11, 131.

ἐπιβλής, ῆτος, ὁ (ἐπιβάλλω), prop. tl

which is thrust forward; *a bolt* or *bar*, for fastening the door, 24, 453.†

ἐπιβοάω (βοάω), only fut. mid. ἐπιβώσομαι, Ion. for ἐπιβοήσομαι, *to cry to*. 2) Mid. *to call upon*, *to call to for aid*, with accus. θεούς, 10, 463. Od. 1, 378.

°ἐπιβόσκομαι (βόσκω), *to pasture upon*, *to feed upon*, τινί, Batr. 54.

ἐπιβουκόλος, ὁ (βουκόλος), *a herdsman*, always with βοῶν, °Od. 3, 422.

ἐπιβρέμω (βρέμω), *to roar against*, *to kindle* (trans.) with a roaring sound, πῦρ [*the wind roars through the fire.* Cp.] 17, 739.†

ἐπιβρίθω (βρίθω), aor. 1 ἐπέβρῑσα, *to fall heavily upon*. ὅτ' ἐπιβρίσῃ Διὸς ὄμβρος, when the rain of Zeus falls violently, 5, 91. 2) Metaph. *to press upon*, *to press heavily*, πόλεμος Τρώων, 7, 343. 12, 414; in a good sense: ὁππότε Διὸς ὧραι ἐπιβρίσειαν ὕπερθεν, when the hours of Zeus from above load (the vines) with fruit; *weigh down their boughs*, Od. 24, 344.

ἐπιβωσόμεθα, see ἐπιβοάομαι.

ἐπιβώτωρ, ορος, ὁ (βώτωρ), *a shepherd*, perhaps *chief-shepherd*, μήλων, Od. 13, 222.†

ἐπιγδουπέω, Ep. for ἐπιδουπέω, *to utter sounds around*; to this is referred: ἐπὶ δ' ἐγδούπησαν [rolled sounds, as of thunder, around him], 11, 45.

ἐπιγίγνομαι (γίγνομαι), *to arise again*, *to come again*, spoken of time, 6, 148. 2) *to reach*: ὅσον τ' ἐπὶ δουρὸς ἐρωὴ γίγνεται, °15, 358.

ἐπιγιγνώσκω (γιγνώσκω), aor. 2 ἐπίγνων, subj. 3 plur. Ep. ἐπιγνώωσι for ἐπιγνῶσι, optat. ἐπιγνοίη. *to recognize*, *to know again*, with accus. Od. 24, 217. 2) *to become acquainted with*, *to view* (the strife), °Od. 18, 30.

°ἐπιγναμπτός, ή, όν, *bent, curved, twisted*, h. Ven. 87.

ἐπιγνάμπτω (γνάμπτω), aor ἐπέγναμψα, *to curve, to bend around, to twist*, with accus. δόρυ, 21, 178; metaph. (*to bend the mind =*) *to influence, to prevail with, to persuade*, τινά, 2, 14; κῆρ, 1, 569; νόον ἐσθλῶν, to persuade the minds of the brave, °9, 514.

ἐπιγνοίη, see ἐπιγιγνώσκω.

ἐπιγνώωσι, see ἐπιγιγνώσκω.

ἐπιγουνίς, ίδος, ἡ (γόνυ), the part above the knee, *the thigh*. μεγάλην ἐπιγουνίδα θεῖτο, [so] he would get a bulky thigh [i. e. grow stouter], °Od. 17, 225.

ἐπιγραβδήν, adv. (ἐπιγράφω), *grazing* [*lightly inscribing*] *the surface; superficially, with a scratch*, 21, 166.†

ἐπιγράφω (γράφω), aor. 1 ἐπέγραψα, *to graze* or *scratch upon the surface*, with accus. χρόα, 4, 139; with double accus. τινὰ ταρσόν, to graze one on the sole of the foot, 11, 388; hence, 2) ἐπιγράφειν κλῆρον, *to mark a lot* (by scratching upon it), 7, 187. (It is = σημαίνεσθαι, v. 175; the idea of writing is inadmissible.)

°ἐπιδαίομαι, depon. mid. (δαίω), *to communicate, to give*; ὅρκον, to take an

oath *upon it*, h. Merc. 383 [Herm. prefers ἐπιδώσομαι ὅρκον].

Ἐπίδαυρος, ἡ, a city in Argolis, on the Saronic gulf, with a temple of Æsculapius, now *Pidauro*, 2, 561.

ἐπιδέδρομε, see ἐπιτρέχω.

ἐπιδέξιος, ον (δεξιός), prop. *on the right*, only neut. plur. ἐπιδέξια, as adv. *on the right*. ὀρνυσθ' ἑξείης ἐπιδέξια, rise in order [to try the bow] from left to right, i. e. to the right beginning from him who occupies the seat of honour, at the mixing vessel, Od. 21, 141; see Buttm. Lex. p. 291. This direction was regarded as propitious, see δεξιός; hence ἀστράπτων ἐπιδέξια, lightening on the right (a sign of prosperity promised by the deity), 2, 353.

ἐπιδευής, ές, poet. for ἐπιδεής, *needing, wanting, lacking*, with gen. δαιτὸς εἴσης οὐκ ἐπιδευεῖς, sc. ἐσμέν, we lack not a common meal, 9, 225. ἄλλης λώβης οὐκ ἐπιδευεῖς, sc. ἐστέ, ye need no other wrong, 13, 622; absol. ὅς κ' ἐπιδευής, sc. ᾖ, who is needy, poor, 5, 481. 2) *inferior, deficient* (in), with gen. βίης, in power, Od. 21, 185; with double gen. βίης ἐπιδευέες εἰμὲν Ὀδυσσῆος, we are inferior in strength to Odysseus (Ulysses), Od. 21, 253; the neut as adv. ἐπιδευὲς ἔχειν δίκης, to lack justice, 19, 180.

ἐπιδεύομαι, depon. mid. (δεύομαι), *to fail in, to want, to lack*, with gen. χρυσοῦ, 2, 229; τούτων, Od. 15, 371. 2) *to be inferior, to be weaker*, with gen. μάχης, 23, 670; also with gen. of the pers.: πολλὸν κείνων ἐπιδεύεαι, thou art much inferior to them, 5, 636; and with double gen. μάχης Ἀχαιῶν, in battle to the Greeks, 24, 385.

ἐπιδημεύω (δημεύω), poet. for ἐπιδημέω, *to abide in the country, to be at home*, Od. 16, 28.†

ἐπιδήμιος, ον (δῆμος), *among the people, internal, domestic*, πόλεμος, 9, 64. b) *at home, present*, Od. 1, 194.

ἐπιδίδωμι (δίδωμι), fut. ἐπιδώσω, aor. 1 ἐπέδωκα, infin. aor. 2 ἐπιδοῦναι, *to give in addition, to add to*, τί τινι, 23, 559; to give as a dowry, θυγατρὶ μείλια, 9, 148. 290. 2) Mid. *to take thereto for oneself*, only ἐπιδώμεθα θεούς, let us take the gods to it (viz. as witnesses, supply from v. 255, μάρτυρους), 22, 254. (Schol. μάρτυρους ποιησώμεθα.) The derivation from ἰδέσθαι is improbable, although Voss. follows it: 'let us look up to the gods.'

ἐπιδινέω (δινέω), aor. partcp. ἐπιδινήσας, partcp. aor. pass. ἐπιδινηθείς, 1) Act. *to turn about, to whirl around in order to cast*, with accus. 3, 378. 7, 269. Pass. *to fly around in a circle*, spoken of an eagle, Od. 2, 151. 2) Mid. *to revolve any thing by oneself*; metaph. ἐμοὶ τόδε θυμὸς πόλλ' ἐπιδινεῖται, my mind often revolves this, i. e. the thought often occupies (haunts) my mind, Od. 20, 218.

ἐπιδιφριάς, άδος, ἡ (δίφρος), *the upper rim of the chariot-seat* = ἄντυξ, 10, 475.†

H 5

ἐπιδίφριος, ον (δίφρος), lying upon the chariot-seat, being upon the chariot seat. δῶρα ἐπιδίφρια τιθέναι, to lay the presents upon the chariot-seat, •Od. 15, 51. 75.

ἐπιδραμεῖν, ἐπιδραμέτην, see ἐπιτρέχω.

ἐπίδρομος, ον (ἐπιδραμεῖν), prop. whither one can run, accessible, exposed to attack; τεῖχος, a wall easy to storm or scale, 6, 434.†

ἐπιδύω (δύω), aor. 2 ἐπιδῦναι, to set only in tmesis. μὴ πρὶν ἐπ' ἠέλιον δῦναι, 2, 413 †

ἐπιδώμεθα, see ἐπιδίδωμι.

ἐπιείκελος, ον (εἴκελος), similar, resembling, τινί, always with ἀθανάτοισιν and θεοῖς, 4, 394, and Od. 15, 414.

ἐπιεικής, ές (ἔοικα), 1) suitable, becoming, fitting, proper. τύμβος ἐπιεικὴς τοῖος, a mound such as is fitting, 23, 246. Often the neut. either absol. ὡς ἐπιεικές, as is fitting. 8, 431; or with infin. ὅν κ' ἐπιεικὲς ἀκούειν, which (μῦθος) it is suitable to hear, 1, 547. cf. Od. 2, 207.

ἐπιεικτός, ή, όν (εἴκω), yielding, giving way; always with a negat. μένος οὐκ ἐπιεικτόι unyielding spirit, 5, 892; σθένος, invincible strength, 8, 32; πένθος, unceasing grief, 16, 549; hence, 2) With negat. intolerable, evil, like σχέτλιος. ἔργα οὐκ ἐπιεικτά (not to be endured), Od. 8, 307. The explanation ' not yielding,' i. e. having permanence, seems against the Hom. usus loquendi; cf. Nitzsch ad Od. 8. 307.

ἐπιειμένος, η, ον, see ἐπιέννυμι.

ἐπιείσομαι, see ἔπειμι (εἶμι).

ἐπιέλπομαι, depon. mid. only pres. (ἔλπω), to hope, with infin, 1, 545; with accus., Od. 21, 126.

ἐπιέννυμι, poet. for ἐφέννυμι (ἕννυμι), aor. 1 ἐπίεσσα, partcp. pass. ἐπιειμένος, 1) to put on, to clothe, to put over; with accus. χλαῖναν, to lay over, Od. 20, 143; metaph. in the partcp. perf. ἐπιειμένος, clothed with; with accus. ἐπιειμένος ἀναιδείην, clothed with impudence, 1, 149; ἀλκήν, with power, 7, 164. Od. 9, 214. 2) Mid. to clothe oneself with, νεφέλην, 14, 350; only in tmesis.

ἐπιζάφελος, ον, vehement, violent; χόλος, 9, 525; and the adv. ἐπιζαφελῶς, vehemently, exceedingly, 9, 516. Od. 6, 330. (The deriv. is uncertain; according to Apoll. from ζα and ὀφέλλειν.)

ἐπίηλε, see ἐπιάλλω.

ἐπίηρα, only twice, in the phrase ἐπίηρα φέρειν τινί, to be favorable to any one, to render oneself agreeable, to show kindness, •1, 572. 578. Wolf. (Buttm. Lex. p. 335, supposes a tmesis, and writes separately, ἐπὶ ἦρα, cf. ἦρα.)

ἐπιήρανος, ον (ἄρω), agreeable, welcome, with dat., Od. 19, 343.† [Lexil. 341, 344.]

•ἐπίηρος, ον, agreeable, grateful, Frag. h. 56 † [Lexil. 338.]

ἐπιθαρσύνω (θαρσύνω), to inspirit, to encourage, to embolden, any one, with accus., 4, 183.†

ἐπιθεῖτε, see ἐπιτίθημι.

ἐπίθημα, τό, Ep. for ἐπίθεμα, that

which is placed upon any thing, a cover a lid, 24, 228.†

ἐπιθρέξας, see ἐπιτρέχω.

ἐπιθρώσκω (θρώσκω), to leap upon; with gen. νηός, the ship, 8, 515; with the dat. τύμβῳ, upon the grave (by way of insult), 4, 177; without cases: τόσσον ἐπιθρώσκουσι, so far they leap (spoken of horses), •5, 772.

ἐπιθύω (θύω), aor. partcp. ἐπιθύσας, 1) to rush upon, to attack, 18, 175. Od. 16, 297. 2) to desire earnestly, h. Merc. 475. (Some derive it from ἰθύω, but this has always short υ; in both cases the υ is long; and ι is long by its position in the arsis.)

ἐπιίστωρ, ορος, ὁ, ἡ (ἵστωρ), acquainted with, experienced in; with gen. μεγάλων ἔργων (peritum, i. e. auctorem magnorum factorum, Damm), Od. 21, 26 †

•ἐπικαίω (καίω), to kindle upon, to light, πῦρ, h. Ap. 491; in tmesis, 22, 170.

•ἐπικαμπύλος, ον (καμπύλος), curved, bent, h. Merc. 90.

ἐπίκαρ, adv. on the head, a different reading for ἐπὶ κάρ, 16, 392; see κάρ.

ἐπικάρσιος. η, ον (ἐπικάρ), prop. head foremost, stooping forward. αἱ νῆες ἐφέροντ' ἐπικάρσιαι, the ships were borne forward with depressed prow ['their heads deep plunging.' Cp.] (Voss, 'with depressed masts'), Od. 9, 70 (according to Schol. 'careening, oblique, inclined').

Ἐπικάστη, ἡ, in the tragic poets Ἰοκάστη, daughter of Menœceus, and wife of king Laïus of Thebes, to whom she bore Œdipus. After he had ignorantly slain his father and solved the riddle of the Sphinx, he received as a prize his mother for a wife. When she discovered her relationship to him, she put an end to her life by hanging, Od. 11, 271.

ἐπίκειμαι, depon. mid. (κεῖμαι), fut. ἐπικείσομαι, to lie upon; spoken of doors, to be joined to, Od. 6, 19; metaph. ἐπικείσετ' ἀνάγκη, force will overpower 6, 458.

ἐπικείρω (κείρω), aor. 1 Ep. ἐπίκερσα, to shear off, to cut off; φάλαγγας, to cut down the squadrons, i. e. to penetrate, 16, 394. 2) Metaph. to hinder, to render void; μήδεα, •15, 467. 16, 120.

ἐπικελαδέω, poet. (κελαδέω), to cry out, to cheer, to applaud, only in tmesis. ἐπὶ δὲ Τρῶες κελάδησαν, •8, 542. 18, 310.

ἐπικέλλω, poet. (κέλλω), aor. ἐπέκελσα, 1) to impel, to run into, spoken only of ships; νῆας, to run ships to the shore, Od. 9, 148. 2) Without accus. intrans. to land, to lie on the strand; Od. 9, 138; and of the ship, ἡ ἠπείρῳ ἐπίκελσεν, the ship ran upon the land, •Od. 13, 114.

ἐπικέλομαι, depon. mid. poet. (κέλομαι). aor. 2 Ep. ἐπεκεκλόμην, to call to, with accus. Ἐρινῦς, 9, 454.†

ἐπικεράννυμι (κεράννυμι), aor. 1 infin. ἐπικρῆσαι, Ep. for ἐπικεράσαι, to mingle with. 2) to mingle again; οἶνον, to mix wine again, Od. 7, 164.†

ἐπικερτομέω (κερτομέω), to insult, to

mock, to deride; only in the partcp. with προσέφης, 16, 744. Od. 22, 194. 2) In a milder signif. to jest with, to banter, 24, 649.

ἐπικεύθω (κεύθω), fut. ἐπικεύσω, to conceal, to hide, often with the negat., 8, 321; μῦθον, Od. 4, 744.

ἐπικίδνημι, Ep. (κίδνημι, poet. form of σκεδάννυμι), pres. and imperf. mid. to strew over, to sprinkle upon. 2) to spread itself upon, to diffuse itself; with accus. ὕδωρ ἐπικίδναται αἶαν, the water spreads itself over the land, 2, 850; spoken of the morning light, *7, 451. 458.

ἐπικλείω, poet. (κλείω), to praise, to celebrate, with accus. ἀοιδήν, Od. 1, 351.† Or, with Nitzsch, to accompany with applause. The var. lec. ἐπικλύουσ' is preferred by Näg. ad Il. p. 230; and seems confirmed by Plato's ἐπιφρονέουσιν; but it wants MS. authority.

Ἐπικλῆς, ῆος, ὁ, a Lycian ally of the Trojans, slain by Telamonian Ajax, 12, 378.

ἐπίκλησις, εος, ἡ (ἐπικαλέω), an appellation, a surname; only accus. absol. with the surname. τὸν ἐπίκλησιν Κορυνήτην κίκλησκον, 7, 138. Ἀστυάναξ, ὃν Τρῶες ἐπίκλησιν καλέουσι, 22, 506. Od. 5, 273. h. Ap. 386.

ἐπικλίνω (κλίνω), perf. pass. ἐπικέκλιμαι, to lean upon; pass. to be inclined. οὐδ' εὗρ' ἐπικεκλιμένας σανίδας, he found not the doors inclined, i. e. shut, 12, 121.†

ἐπίκλοπος, ον (κλέπτω), thievish, cunning, Od. 11, 364. 13, 291; also with gen. μύθων, crafty in words, 22, 281; τόξων, dexterous with the bow [rather, join θηητὴρ καὶ ἐπίκλοπος, a right cunning examiner of the bow. Fäsi. It is ironical]. Od. 21, 397.

*ἐπικλύζω (κλύζω), to inundate, to sprinkle, pass. κύμασι, Batr. 69.

ἐπικλύω (κλύω), to listen to, to understand, with accus., 23, 652; with gen. Od. 5, 150.

ἐπικλώθω (κλώθω), fut. ἐπικλώσω, aor. 1 act ἐπέκλωσα, aor. 1 mid. ἐπεκλωσάμην, 1) to spin; only metaph.; prop. spoken of the Parcæ, who spin for every one his fate; then mly of the gods, to impart, to allot, to assign, τί τινι; τινὶ ὄλβον, Od. 3, 208. 16, 64. ᾧτε Κρονίων ὄλβον ἐπικλώσῃ γαμέοντί τε γεινομένῳ τε, to whom the son of Kronus (Saturn) in his marriage and birth shall allot happiness, Od. 4, 208 (Eustath. reads instead of the fut. ἐπικλώσῃ with more propriety). 2) Mid. as depon. spoken of the gods, to spread; ὄλεθρον ἀνθρώποις, destruction over men, Od. 8, 579; οἰζύν, Od. 20, 196; and with infin. instead of accus. to allot, to grant; οἰκόνδε νέεσθαι, Od. 1, 17. and ζώειν, 24, 525 (in the Il. only once).

ἐπικόπτω (κόπτω), fut. ἐπικόψω, to strike upon from above; βοῦν, to strike upon the neck of the ox in order to kill it, to slay the ox, Od. 3, 443.†

ἐπικουρέω (ἐπίκουρος), fut. ἐπικουρήσω, to help, to aid, absol., 5, 614.†

ἐπίκουρος, ον (κοῦρος), helping, aiding; only as subst. a helper, an assistant; spoken of Arês, βροτῶν, h. 7, 9; and as fem., 21, 431. The plur. often used of the allies of the Trojans, 2, 130. 815. H. calls them frequently τηλεκλητοί, *9, 233.

ἐπικραίνω, Ep. lengthened ἐπικραιαίνω (κραίνω), aor. 1 ἐπέκρηνα, Ep. ἐπεκρήηνα, optat. ἐπικρήνειε, imperat. ἐπικρήηνον, 1) to finish, to fulfil, to accomplish, to grant, τινί τι; ἐπικρήηνον, 1, 455; ἀρήν τινος, 15, 599; and absol. οὔ σφιν ἐπικραίαινε, he did not grant it to them, 3, 302. 2) to rule to govern, θεούς, where Herm. would substitute οἴμους, h. Merc. 531 (from ἐπικραίνω. only ἐπικρήνειε, 15, 599, and pres. h. Merc. l. c.).

ἐπικρατέω (κρατέω), to hold the rule, to command, to govern, with dat. νήεσσιν, 10, 214, and absol., Od. 17, 320. 2) to have the mastery, to be victorious, to conquer, 14, 98.

ἐπικρατέως, adv. (ἐπικρατής), with great force, with might, *16, 81. 23, 863.

*ἐπικρέμαμαι, depon. mid. (κρέμαμαι), to hang upon, to hang over, to impend. πέτρη ἐπικρέμαται, h. in Ap. 284.

ἐπικρήηνον, Ep. see ἐπικραίνω.

ἐπικρήνειε, see ἐπικραίνω.

ἐπικρῆσαι, see ἐπικεράννυμι.

ἐπίκριον, τό (ἴκριον), a sail-yard, *Od. 5, 254. 318.

ἐπικυρέω (κυρέω), aor. ἐπέκυρσα, to fall upon any thing; to this is assigned ἐπὶ σώματι κύρσας, 3, 23; see κυρέω.

ἐπιλάμπω (λάμπω), aor. 1 ἐπέλαμψα, to shine upon. ἠέλιος ἐπέλαμψε. the sun shone thereon, 17, 650.† h. Merc. 141.

ἐπιλανθάνω and ἐπιλήθω (λήθω), aor. ἐπέλησα, fut. mid. ἐπιλήσομαι, aor. 2 mid. ἐπελαθόμην, 1) Act. to cause to forget; with gen. in aor. 1: ὁ ὕπνος ἐπέλησεν ἁπάντων, sleep caused a forgetfulness of every thing, Od. 20, 85. 2) Mid. to forget thereupon, any thing, with gen. Ἰθάκης, Od. 1, 57; and, generally, to forget. 7, 452; τέχνης, Od. 4, 455. The pres. ἐπιλανθάνω is not found in H., and from ἐπιλήθω only ἐπελήθετο, Od. 5, 324.

ἐπιλέγω (λέγω), to collect to or in addition; only mid. in tmesis, ἐπὶ δὲ ξύλα πολλὰ λέγεσθε, 8, 507, and λέγοντο, v. 547.

ἐπιλείβω (λείβω), to pour upon, esply upon the flame in making libations of wine, Od. 3, 341; and in tmesis, 1, 463.

*ἐπιλέπω (λέπω), aor. ἐπέλεψα, to peel off, to strip off the bark, h. Merc. 109, where the reading is questioned [but without cause, Passow].

ἐπιλεύσσω (λεύσσω), to look upon, to see, τόσσον, 3, 12.†

ἐπιλήσομαι, see ἐπιλανθάνω.

ἐπιλήθος, ον (ἐπιλήθω), causing to forget, producing oblivion; with gen. φάρμακον κακῶν ἐπιληθον ἁπάντων, which caused an oblivion of all evils, Od. 4, 221.†

ἐπιληκέω (ληκέω), to make a noise upon, to clatter [to beat time whilst others dance, Passow, cf. Athenæus I. 13], Od. 8, 379.†

H 6

ἐπιλίγδην, adv. (λίγδην), *scratching, grazing,* 17, 599.†

ἐπιλλίζω (ἰλλίζω), *to give the wink, to make a sign with the eyes,* with dat., Od. 13, 11.† h. Merc. 387.

ἐπιλωβεύω (λωβεύω), *to insult, to offer an affront to,* Od. 2, 323.†

ἐπιμαίνομαι, depon. (μαίνομαι), aor. ἐπεμηνάμην, *to be madly desirous of any thing, to desire vehemently;* with dat. τῷ γυνὴ Προίτου ἐπεμήνατο, κρυπταδίῃ φιλότητι μιγέμεναι, for him the wife of Prœtus passionately longed, that she might enjoy illicit love (according to Voss and the Schol. for ὥστε—μιγήμεναι); Köppen and Passow, by a forced construction, connect the sentence ἐπεμήνατο τῷ μιγήμεναι, 6, 160.†

ἐπιμαίομαι, depon. mid. (μαίομαι), fut. ἐπιμάσομαι, Ep. σσ, aor. 1 ἐπεμασάμην, Ep. σσ, 1) *to touch, to handle, to feel,* with accus. μάστιγι ἵππους, 17, 430. 5, 748; τινὰ ῥάβδῳ, Od. 13, 429. 16, 172. οἰῶν ἐπεμαίετο νῶτα, Od. 9, 441; spoken of a physician, ἕλκος, *to examine a wound,* 4, 190; ξίφεος κώπην, *to grasp the hilt of the sword,* Od. 11, 530; χείρ, i. e. χειρί, not χεῖρ as ed. Wolf. [cf. Eustath. and Bothe]. ἐπιμασσάμενος, *grasping with the hand* (viz. the sword), Od. 9, 301. cf. 19, 480; metaph. πυρὸς τέχνην, *to essay the art of fire,* h. Merc. 108. 2) With gen. *to seek to attain, to desire, to strive after;* σκοπέλου, to seek the rock, Od. 12, 220; and metaph. νόστου, Od. 5, 344; δώρων, 10, 401 (μαίομαι is used only in the pres. and imperf.; the other tenses are furnished by the obsol μάομαι.

ἐπιμάρτυρος, ὁ (μάρτυρος), *a witness* on any occasion; spoken only of the gods, 7, 76. Od. 1, 273.

ἐπιμάσσομαι, see ἐπιμαίομαι.

ἐπίμαστος, ὁ (ἐπιμάομαι), prop. *sought out, picked up;* ἀλήτης, passively, a beggar picked-up on the road, Od. 20, 377.† The Schol. explains it actively, 'a beggar that picks up his living.'

ἐπιμειδάω (μειδάω), aor. partcp. ἐπιμειδήσας, *to smile at or upon;* always with προσέφη, 4, 356. 10, 400. Od. 22, 371.

*ἐπιμειδιάω = μειδάω, h. 9, 3.

ἐπιμέμφομαι, depon. mid. Ion. (μέμφομαι), *to blame about, to reprove for, to reproach with,* τινί τι, Od. 16, 97; with dat. of pers., Od. 16, 115. 2) *to trouble oneself about, to be displeased with, to be angry;* with gen. εὐχωλῆς, on account of a vow, 1, 65; and with ἕνεκα, 1, 94.

ἐπιμένω (μένω), aor. ἐπέμεινα, 1) *to remain at, to tarry, to wait,* ἐν μεγάροις, Od. 4, 587; ἐς αὔριον, Od. 11, 351; ἐπίμεινον, τεύχεα δύω, wait, that I may put on my armour, 6, 340; and with ἵνα, h. Cer. 160.

ἐπιμήδομαι, depon. mid. (μήδομαι), *to plot, to devise, to contrive;* δόλον τινί, an artifice against any one, Od. 4, 437.†

ἐπιμηνίω (μηνίω), *to be angry, to be in a rage with,* τινί, any one, 13, 460.†

ἐπιμιμνήσκω (μιμνήσκω), aor. 1 mid ἐπεμνησάμην, and aor. 1 pass.- ἐπεμνήσθην, 1) *to remind of.* 2) Mid. with aor. pass. *to remember, to think of,* with gen. παίδων, 15, 662; χάρμης, 17, 103. τοῦ ἐπιμνησθείς, remembering him, Od. 4, 189. (Only the mid. and partcp. aor. 1 pass.)

ἐπιμίμνω (μίμνω), poet. form fr. ἐπιμένω, *to remain, to wait for,* *Od. 14, 66. 15, 372.

ἐπιμίξ, adv. *mixed, mingled together, pell-mell;* spoken of warriors and horses confusedly blended together, 21, 16. 11, 525. Od. 11, 537. κτείνονται ἐπιμίξ they were slain without distinction, 14, 60

ἐπιμίσγω (μίσγω), Ep. form of ἐπιμίγνυμι, 1) Act. *to mingle with.* 2 Mid. which alone H. uses, *to have intercourse with* any one, *to have commerce or communication with;* with dat. Φαιήκεσσι, to come to the Phæacians, Od. 6, 241; in the Il. always spoken of battle *to meet, to mingle in fight;* Τρώεσσι, with the Trojans, 10, 548; absol. to mingle in the battle, 5, 505.

ἐπιμνησαίμεθα, see ἐπιμιμνήσκω.

ἐπιμύζω (μύζω), aor. 1 ἐπέμυξα, *to murmur or mutter at, to sigh from displeasure* *4, 20. 8, 251 (prop. to say μῦ to, always spoken of inarticulate sounds).

ἐπινέμω (νέμω), aor. 1 ἐπένειμα, *to impart, to share, to distribute;* with dat σῖτον τραπέζῃ, to distribute the bread to the table, i. e. upon the table, 9, 216. 24, 625; spoken of persons: to distribute among several, Od. 20, 254.

ἐπινεύω (νεύω), aor. 1 ἐπένευσα, *to give the nod to, to make a sign to,* as an indication of command or of assent to prayer, τινί, 9, 620. ὡς οἱ ὑπέστη πρῶτον, ἐμῷ δ' ἐπένευσα κάρητι, as I first promised him, and nodded with my head (to confirm the promise), 15, 75. h in Cer. 169; and by tmesis, ἐπ' ὀφρύσι νεῦσε, 1, 528. Od. 16, 164; and only nod. κόρυθι, 22, 314.

ἐπινεφρίδιος, ον (νεφρός), *at or upon the kidneys,* 21, 204.†

ἐπινέω or ἐπινήθω (νέω), aor. 1 ἐπένησα *to spin,* like ἐπικλώθω, used of the Parcæ τινί τι, *to allot* any thing to any one ἄσσα οἱ Αἶσα γεινομένῳ ἐπένησε λίνῳ what Aisa spun in a thread for him at birth, i. e. what she allotted him, 20 128; spoken of Moira, 24, 210. (H. does not use the pres.)

ἐπινήνέω, Ep. form (νηνέω, νήω), *to heap upon, to lay upon;* νεκρούς... καίης, upon the funeral pile, *7, 128. 43?

*ἐπινήχομαι, depon. mid. Ep. form (νήχομαι), *to swim upon,* Batr.

ἐπίνυσσεν, see πινύσσω.

*ἐπινώτιος, ον, *lying on the back,* Bat 80.

ἐπίξυνος, ον, poet. for ἐπίκοινος (ξυνός) *common, in common,* ἐπιξύνῳ ἐν ἀρούρῃ [= κοινοὺς ὅρους ἐχούσῃ, Schol. Villois on the common boundary of a field, 422.†

*ἐπιοινοχοεύω (οἰνοχοέω), to pour out wine, θεοῖς, h. Ven. 205.

*ἐπιόπτης, ου. ὁ. poet. for ἐπόπτης, ου, ὁ, a looker-on, a spectator, Ep. 12.

ἐπιορκέω (ἐπίορκος), fut. ἐπιορκήσω, to swear falsely, πρὸς δαίμονος, by a divinity, 19, 188.†

ἐπίορκος, ον (ὅρκος), swearing falsely, perjured. H. has only the neut. as subst. in the sing.: a false oath; as εἰ δέ τι τῶνδ' ἐπίορκον. sc. ἐστί, 19, 264; and ἐπίορκον ὀμνύναι, to swear a false oath, *10, 332. 19. 260.

ἐπιόσσομαι, depon. poet. (ὄσσομαι). to look at with the eyes; metaph. to consider, to observe; θάνατον ἐταίρων, 17, 381.†

ἐπίουρα, τά, see under οὖρον.

ἐπίουρος, ὁ (οὖρος), a spectator, a watch, an inspector, a keeper, like ἔφορος, with gen. ὑῶν ἐπίουρος, Od. 13, 405; with dat Κρήτῃ, ruler over Crete, 13, 450.

ἐπιόψομαι. see ἐφοράω.

ἐπιπάσσω (πάσσω), to strew or sprinkle upon, with accus. φάρμακα, only in tmesis, *4, 219. 5, 401.

ἐπιπείθομαι, mid. (πείθομαι), fut ἐπιπείσομαι. prop. (to allow oneself) to be persuaded; to yield to persuasion, Od. 2, 103. 10. 406; generally, to obey, to comply with, μύθῳ, 1, 565. 4, 412; with double dat. εἰ δέ μοι οὐκ ἐπέεσσ' ἐπιπείσεται, if he shall not obey my words, 15, 162. 178.

ἐπιπείλομαι, depon. mid. poet. (πέλομαι), to come to, to arrive; only the sync. partcp. ἐπιπλόμενον ἔτος, *Od. 7, 261. 14, 287; τινί, to any one, in tmesis, Od. 15, 408. 2) to reach, to extend, like ἐπιγίγνεσθαι, in tmesis, 10, 351.

ἐπιπέταμαι or ἐπιπέτομαι, depon. mid. (πέτομαι), aor. 2 ἐπέπταμην, and from ἐπεπτόμην the infin. ἐπιπτέσθαι, to fly to, with dat. εἰπόντι ἐπέπτατο δεξιὸς ὄρνις, 13, 821. Od. 15, 160; and spoken of an arrow, καθ' ὅμιλον, 4, 126.

ἐπιπίλναμαι, depon. mid. poet. (πίλναμαι), a form of ἐπιπελάζω, to draw near, to approach. χιὼν ἐπιπίλναται [snow invades. Cp.], Od. 6, 44.† (Only in the pres.)

ἐπιπλάζομαι (πλάζω), partcp. aor. 1 pass. ἐπιπλαγχθείς, to wander over, to stray about, with accus. πόντον, over the sea, Od. 8, 14.†

ἐπιπλέω (πλέω), to sail over, to navigate, with accus. ὑγρὰ κέλευθα, 1, 312; ἁλμυρὸν ὕδωρ, Od. 9, 227. (Only pres. and imperf. and in addition from the Ion. form ἐπιπλώω pres., aor. 1, and aor. 2, q. v.)

ἐπιπλήσσω (πλήσσω), fut. ἐπιπλήξω, to strike upon, with accus. τόξῳ, 10, 500; metaph. to reprove, to chide, to reproach, τινί, *12, 211. 23, 580.

ἐπιπλώω, Ion. and Ep. for ἐπιπλέω; from which partcp. pres. ἐπιπλώων, Od. 5, 284; 2 sing. aor. 2 ἐπέπλως, Od. 3, 15; partcp. ἐπιπλώς, 6, 291; and aor. 1 ἐπιπλώσας, 3, 47.

ἐπιπνέω, Ep. ἐπιπνείω (πνέω), aor. 1 ἐπέπνευσα, to blow upon, to breathe upon, to blow, absol. 5, 698; esply spoken of a favorable wind, with dat. νηΐ, to blow upon the ship, Od. 4, 357. 9, 139 (only the Ep. form ἐπιπνείω).

ἐπιποιμήν, ένος, ὁ, ἡ (ποιμήν), shepherd, shepherdess, as fem. Od. 12, 131.†

ἐπιπρέπω (πρέπω), to be prominent or conspicuous, to show or discover itself in, to appear in. οὐδέ τί τοι δούλειον ἐπιπρέπει, nothing servile appears in thee, Od. 24, 252.†

ἐπιπροέμεν, see ἐπιπροΐημι.

ἐπιπροϊάλλω (ἰάλλω), aor. 1 ἐπιπροΐηλα, to send forth to, with accus. θεούς, h. Cer. 327; spoken of things: to place before; τράπεζάν τινι. to place a table before any one, 11, 628.

ἐπιπροΐημι (προΐημι), aor. 1 3 sing. ἐπιπροέηκε, infin. aor. 2 ἐπιπροέμεν, Ep. for ἐπιπροεῖναι, to send away to, to send forth to, spoken of men, with accus. τινά, 9, 520; and dat. of the place: τινὰ νηυσίν, any one to the ships, 17, 708. 18, 58; but τινὰ νηυσὶν Ἴλιον εἴσω, to send any one in ships to Troy, 18, 439. b) Of missiles: to cast at, to throw or shoot at; ἰόν τινι, an arrow at any one, 4, 94. 2) Apparently intrans. to steer to, to sail to, sc. ναῦν: νήσοισιν, to the islands, Od. 15, 299. (ι in the middle syll. is short.)

*ἐπιπροχέω (χέω), to pour out at or upon any occasion, metaph. θρῆνον, to pour forth a lamentation, h. 18, 18.

ἐπιπταίρω (πταίρω), aor. 2 ἐπέπταρον, to sneeze at or upon; τινὶ ἐπέεσσι, at any one's words, Od. 17, 545.† This was considered a propitious omen, h. Herm. 297.

ἐπιπτέσθαι, see ἐπιπέτομαι.

ἐπιπωλέομαι, depon. mid. (πωλέομαι), obire, to go over, to walk about, with accus. mly spoken of leaders: to inspect, with accus. στίχας ἀνδρῶν [' the warrior ranks Ranges' Cp.], 3, 196. 4, 250; spoken also of warriors, in order to attack, στίχας ἔγχεΐ τε ἄορί τε, 11, 264. 540.

ἐπιρρέζω, poet. (ῥέζω), iterat. imperf. ἐπιρρέζεσκον, to sacrifice at or upon, Od. 17, 211.†

ἐπιρρέπω (ῥέπω), to incline towards. met. ἡμῖν ὄλεθρος ἐπιρρέπει, ' our own preponderating scale plunges us' (Cp.) into destruction, 14, 99.†

ἐπιρρέω (ῥέω), to flow to or upon, to run, spoken of a river: μὶν καθύπερθεν ἐπιρρέει, it flows upon it above, 2, 754; metaph. of men, to flow to, *11, 724.

ἐπιρρήσσω (ῥήσσω), to draw into, to push in, to thrust into; ἐπιβλής, τὸν τρεῖς ἐπιρρήσσεσκον (iterat. imperf.), a bar, which three were wont to thrust in (to bar the door), *24, 454. 456.

ἐπιρρίπτω (ῥίπτω), aor. ἐπίρριψα, to cast upon, to throw to or against, δοῦρά τινι, a spear at any one, Od. 5, 310.†

ἐπίρροθος, ον, Ep. ἐπιτάρροθος, hastening to aid, helping, subst. helper, assistant, with dat. 4, 390. 23, 770; see ἐπι-τάρροθος (for ἐπιρροθέω).

ἐπιρρώομαι, depon. mid. Ep. (ῥώομαι), aor. 1 ἐπερρωσάμην, 1) to move rapidly or vehemently, at or about, with dat. μύλαις δώδεκα ἐπερρώοντο γυναῖκες, twelve women moved vigorously (work-ed) at the mills, Od. 20, 107. 2) Spoken of the hair: to roll or fall upon. χαῖται ἐπερρώσαντο κρατὸς ἀπ᾽ ἀθανάτοιο, the locks rolled forwards from his immortal head, 1, 529. cf. h. 26, 14; see ῥώομαι. By ἐπί is indicated that the motion of the hair follows the nod, Nägelsb.

ἐπισείω, Ep. ἐπισσείω (σείω), to shake or brandish against, τί τινι, spoken of Zeus: αἰγίδα πᾶσιν, to brandish the ægis against all (to excite terror), *4, 167. 15, 230 (only the Ep. form).

ἐπισεύω, Ep. ἐπισσεύω, for the most part poet. (σεύω), aor. 1 ἐπέσσευα, perf. pass. ἐπέσσυμαι, with pres. signif., plu-perf. ἐπεσσύμην; which is also Ep. aor. 2. hence partcp. with retracted accent, ἐπεσσύμενος. I) Act. to drive away, to put in motion, with accus. δμῶας, to excite the servants against (me), Od. 14, 399; κῆτός τινι, to drive a sea-monster against one, Od. 5, 421. 2) Metaph. κακά τινι, to send evils upon any one, Od. 18, 256; ὀνείρατα, Od. 20, 87. II) Mid. and pass. esply perf. pass. as pres., and pluperf. as Ep. aor., prop. to be driven on. 1) to hasten to, to rush to, 2, 86; hence, ἐπεσσύμενος, hastening, ἀγορήνδε to the assembly, 2, 207; νομόνδε, 18, 575; with dat. τινί, to hasten to any one, Od. 4, 841; εἴς τινα, 13, 757; with gen. of place, πεδίοιο, through the plain, 14, 147; with accus. νῆα, to the ship, Od. 13, 19; δέμνια, Od. 6, 20; with infin. ὁ δ᾽ ἐπέσσυτο διώκειν, he made haste to pursue him, 21, 601; metaph. ἐπέσσυταί τοι θυμός, thy heart is driven, is prompted (to desire), 1, 173. 9, 42. b) In a hostile signif. to rush upon, to attack, often absol. and with dat., 5, 459. 884; with accus. τεῖχος ἐπεσσύμενος, 12, 143. 15, 395. (The gen. is unusual: τείχεος, 12, 388; depends upon βάλε: he cast him from the wall; cf. Spitzner: metaph. spoken of fire and water, 11, 737. Od. 5, 314. H. has only the Ep. form.)

ἐπίσκοπος, ὁ (σκοπέω), 1) an observer, a spy, a scout, with dat. νήεσσιν, against the ships, 10, 38. 342. 2) overseer, com-mander, protector, spoken of Hector, 24, 729. ἐπίσκοποι ἁρμονιάων, the defenders of covenants (of the gods), 22, 255; ὁδαίων, inspector of wares, Od. 8, 163.

ἐπισκύζομαι, depon. mid. (σκύζομαι), aor. 1 ἐπεσκυσάμην, to be displeased, angry at any thing, 9, 370; τινί, any one, Od. 7, 306.

ἐπισκύνιον, τό (σκύνιον), the skin of the forehead, above the cavity of the eyes, which moves in various passions, super-cilium, the brow; hence metaph. like ὀφρύς, as a sign of anger, pride, spoken of lions: πᾶν δέ τ᾽ ἐπισκύνιον κάτω ἕλ-κεται, he draws down his whole brow into frowns [Cp.], 17, 136.†

ἐπισμυγερῶς, adv. (ἐπισμυγερός), as if scorched by flames (σμύχω, uro); hence shamefully, miserably, ἀπέτισεν, Od. 3, 195; ναυτίλλεται [cum sua pernicie navi-gaverit, cf. Barnes and Bothe], *Od. 4, 672.

ἐπίσπαστος, η, ον (ἐπισπάω), drawn to oneself, attracted. ἐπίσπαστον κακὸν ἔχειν, to have drawn an evil upon one-self, *Od. 18, 73. 24. 462.

ἐπισπεῖν, see ἐφέπω.

ἐπισπέρχω (σπέρχω), to urge forward, to hasten on, Od. 22, 451; with accus. κέντρῳ, to urge or spur on, sc. the steeds. 23, 430. 2) Intrans. to urge oneself, to hurry forward rapidly, ἄελλαι ἐπισπέρ-χουσι, Od. 5, 304.

ἐπισπέσθαι, ἐπισπόμενος, see ἐφέπω.

ἐπίσπω, see ἐφέπω.

ἐπισσείω, see ἐπισείω.

ἐπισσεύω, see ἐπισεύω.

ἐπίσσωτρον, τό, Ep. for ἐπίσωτρον.

ἐπισταδόν, adv. (ἐφίστημι), proceeding to, going up to, Od. 12, 392. 13, 54. οἱ δ᾽ ἄρα δόρπον ἐπισταδὸν ὁπλίζοντο, *Od. 16, 453; ἐπισταδόν is unnecessarily ex-plained 'one after another;' Voss, 'busily.' The sense is, 'they went and prepared the evening meal.'

ἐπίσταμαι, depon. imperf. ἐπιστάμην, without augm. fut. ἐπιστήσομαι, 1) to understand, to know, to be acquainted with, with accus. ἔργα, 23, 705; ἔργα περικαλλέα, Od. 2, 117; spoken of wo-men who are skilled in feminine works. 2) to understand, to know how, to be able; spoken both of the mind, as φρεσίν, 14, 92; θυμῷ, Od. 4, 730; and of the body, as χερσίν, 5, 60; with infin., 4, 404. ἐπίστατο μείλιχος εἶναι, he knew how to be mild to all, 17, 671. The partcp. pres. ἐπιστάμενος, η, ον, prop. under-standing, mly as adj. intelligent, practised, experienced, often absol. of men and brutes, and also ἐπιστάμενοι πόδες, 18, 599. a) skilful, dexterous, mostly with infin. σάφα εἰπεῖν, 4, 404. b) With gen. ἐπιστάμενος πολέμοιο, acquainted with war, 2, 611, ed. Barnes; ἀοιδῆς, Od. 21, 406. c) With dat. ἐπιστάμενος ἄκοντι, sc. πολεμίζειν, 15, 282 (prob. Ion. for ἐφίσταμαι, to direct one's thought to any thing. cf. the Germ. verstehen and the Engl. understand). [Buttm. thinks it a simple vb.]

ἐπισταμένως, adv. intelligently, skil-fully, scientifically, dexterously, 10, 265. Od. 20, 161.

ἐπιστάτης, ου, ὁ (ἐφίστημι), origin. one who approaches; only σὸς ἐπιστάτης, who approaches thee, a beggar, Od. 17, 455.† (Hesych. ἀπὸ τοῦ ἐφίστασθαι τῇ τραπέζῃ.)

*ἐπιστεναχίζω = ἐπιστενάχομαι, Batr. 73; but ἐπιστοναχίζω, ed. Frank.

ἐπιστενάχομαι, depon. mid. (στενάχω), to groan at or over, 4, 154.†

ἐπιστεφής, ές (ἐπιστέφω), up to the brim, brimful, with gen. only κρητῆρας ἐπιστεφέας οἴνοιο, mixing-vessels brimful of wine, 8, 232. Od. 2, 431; see ἐπιστέφω.

ἐπιστέφω (στέφω), only in the mid. ἐπιστέφομαι, always κρητῆρας, ἐπεστέψαντο οἴνοιο, they filled the vessels full to the brim [they crowned the vessels with wine], 1, 470. 9, 175. Od. 1, 148, and elsewhere. The old Gramm. thus unanimously explain this, see Athen. XV. p. 674. I. 13, and also most modern, as Heyne, Voss ; and Buttm. Lex. p. 291, who explains it, 'to fill so full that the liquor rises above the brim and forms a crown.' To fill the vessel thus full was a religious custom. To a use of garlands there is here no reference, as in Virg. Æn. 1, 723. The gen. with verbs of filling is common.

ἐπιστήμων, ον (ἐπίσταμαι), intelligent, experienced, acquainted with, Od. 16, 374.†

ἐπίστιον, τό (prop. neut. of ἐπίστιος, belonging to the hearth), subst. a cover, a shed, under which the ships drawn on shore stood supported by stakes; otherwise νεώριον; πᾶσιν ἐπίστιόν ἐστιν ἑκάστῳ, each one of all (the Phæaces) has here a shed, Od. 6, 265; † cf. Nitzsch ad loc. Voss, incorrectly, 'they rest each one upon supporting props.' The masc. ἑκάστῳ cannot refer to νῆες [in like manner Cowper, inaccurately, 'each stationed in her place.' Am. Ed.].

ἐπιστοναχέω (στοναχέω) = ἐπιστενάχομαι, from which aor. 1 ἐπεστονάχησα, to roar, spoken of the sea, 24, 79.†

*ἐπιστοναχίζω = ἐπιστεναχίζω, q. v.

ἐπιστρέφω (στρέφω), to turn to, to turn towards, with accus. only aor. 1 ἐπιστρέψας, 3, 370.† 2) Mid. to turn oneself towards, to go, to penetrate, h. 27, 10.

ἐπιστροφάδην, adv. (ἐπιστρέφω), turning hither and thither, turning on all sides; κτείνειν, to slay (to smite them) on all sides, 10, 483; τύπτειν, Od. 22, 308 (others, fiercely; Voss, vigorously; Schol. ἐνεργῶς).

ἐπίστροφος, ον (ἐπιστρέφω), prop. turning oneself to, consorting with, holding intercourse with; with gen. ἀνθρώπων, with men, Od. 1, 177.†

Ἐπίστροφος, ὁ, son of Iphitus, grandson of Naubolus, leader of the Phocians before Troy, 2, 517. 2) leader of the Halizonians, an ally of the Trojans, 2, 856. 3) son of Evênos, brother of Mynes, slain by Achilles on the expedition against Lyrnessus, 2, 692.

ἐπιστρωφάω (στρωφάω), poet. form of ἐπιστρέφω, intrans. as ἐπιστρέφομαι, to turn oneself to, to go into, to visit; a cus. πόληας, to go through cities, Voss, Od. 17, 486;† metaph. of cares, h. Merc. 44.

Ἐπίστωρ, ορος, ὁ, a Trojan, slain by Patroclus, 16, 695 (signif. = ἐπιστήμων).

ἐπισφύριον, τό (σφυρόν, prop. neut. of ἐπισφύριος), an ankle-clasp, a kind of hook or buckle, by which the greaves, consisting of two plates, were fastened : κνημῖδες ἐπισφυρίοις ἀραρυίαι. According

to others, a covering for the ankle, by which the plates were fastened ; hence Voss, 'plates fastened together with silver ankle-coverings.' *3, 331. 11, 18, etc.

*ἐπισχεδόν, adv. (σχεδόν), near, almost, h. Ap. 3.

ἐπισχερώ, adv. (σχερός), prop. connected together, in a row, one after another, in order, like ἐφεξῆς, with κτείνεσθαι, ἀναβαίνειν, *11, 668. 18, 68.

ἐπισχεσίη, ἡ (ἐπέχω), a pretence, a pretext; with gen. οὐδέ τιν' ἄλλην μύθου ποιήσασθαι ἐπισχεσίην ἐδύνασθε, ἀλλ' ἐμὲ ἱέμενοι γῆμαι, you were able to make no other pretext for your resolution (or attempt) but wishing to marry me, Od. 21, 71.† (The ancients explain μῦθον here by στάσις, uproar, noise, it being Æol. for μόθος, see μῦθος).

ἐπίσχεσις, ιος, ἡ (ἐπέχω), 1) restraint, hindrance. 2) abstinence, moderation, temperance, with infin. following, Od. 17, 451.†

ἐπίσχω (ἴσχω), form of ἐπέχω, 1) to direct, to guide, ἵππους, 17, 465. 2) to hold up, to check, Od. 20, 266 (according to the Schol. who explains ἐπίσχετε by κατάσχετε, as aor. 2 from ἐπέχω, q. v.).

ἐπίσωτρον, τό, Ep. ἐπίσσωτρον, the tire, the iron band encompassing the wooden circumference of a wheel (σῶτρον); only in the Ep. form, *5, 725. 11, 537. 23, 519.

ἐπιτάρροθος, ὁ, ἡ, a helper, an assistant, spoken of the gods; μάχης, in battle, 12, 180; also fem. 5, 808. 828. (From ἐπίρροθος, as ἀταρτηρός fr. ἀτηρός, see Thiersch, § 174. 7).

ἐπιτείνω (τείνω), to stretch, to extend; only in tmesis, 17, 736. Od. 11, 19.

ἐπιτέλλω (τέλλω), aor. 1 act. ἐπέτειλα, aor. 1 mid. ἐπετειλάμην, perf. pass. ἐπιτέταλμαι. 1) Act. to end in addition (cf. τέλλω in Schneider's Lex.), to annex, to add; thus in tmesis. κρατερὸν δ' ἐπὶ μῦθον ἔτελλε [asperam ei vocem tamquam onus imposuit. Näg. Lob. 'Ρημ. 115], spoke in addition a harsh speech, 1, 25, 326. 16, 199. 2) to commission, to order, to command, to impose, to bid, τί τινι, πολλά τινι, 4, 229; μῦθόν τινι [but see above], 11, 486; often with only one of the two cases, συνθεσίας, to give commands to any one, 5, 320; often. absol. with infin. instead of accus., 4, 229. Hence pass. ἐμοὶ δ' ἐπὶ πάντ' ἐτέταλτο, every thing was entrusted to me, Od. 11, 524; with infin., 2, 643. 2) Mid. like act. to commission, to command, any one with infin., 2, 802. 10, 61; with accus. νόστος, ὃν ἐκ Τροίης ἐπετείλατο Ἀθήνη, the return which Athênê had commanded from Troy, Od. 1, 327.

*ἐπιτερπής, ές (ἐπιτέρπω), pleasurable, agreeable, h. Ap. 413.

ἐπιτέρπω (τέρπω), 1) to delight with, to charm; only 2) Mid. to delight in, to be charmed with, ἔργοις, Od. 14, 228;† and with accus. θυμόν, ἦτορ, h. Ap. 146. 204.

ἐπιτέτραπται, see ἐπιτρέπω.

ἐπιτετράφαται, see ἐπιτρέπω.

ἐπιτηδές, adv. *enough, sufficiently, adequately;* in two passages: ἐς δ' ἐρέτας ἐπιτηδὲς ἀγείρομεν, let us collect on board rowers enough, 1,.142. μνηστήρων σ' ἐπιτηδὲς ἀριστῆες λοχόωσιν, in sufficient numbers the chief of the suitors lie in wait for thee, Od. 15, 28; later, with changed accent, ἐπίτηδες. (According to Damm. from τείνω [So Död.: = μετ' ἐπιτάσεως, *intente; intently, earnestly*]: according to Buttm. Lex. p. 299, from ἐπὶ τάδε or τάδεσι; or, according to Passow, from τῆδες, a form of τῆτες).

*ἐπιτηρέω (τηρέω), aor. 1 partcp. ἐπιτηρήσας, *to wait for, to watch for,* νύκτα, h. Cer. 245.

ἐπιτίθημι (τίθημι), fut. ἐπιθήσω, aor. 1 ἐπέθηκα, aor. 2 optat. ἐπιθεῖτε, Ep. for ἐπιθείητε, infin. ἐπιθεῖναι, aor. 1 mid. ἐπιθήκατο, aor. 2 mid. ἐπέθετο, partcp. ἐπιθέμενος, *to place upon, to put upon,* 1) *to put upon, to lay upon,* mly τινί τι; κρατὶ κυνέην, Il. rarely; τινὰ λεχέων, to lay any one upon the bed, 24, 589; φάρμακα, 4, 190; εἴδατα, to place food (upon the table), Od. 1, 140; spoken of sacrifices, Ποσειδάωνι ταύρων μῆρα, to offer the thighs of oxen to Poseidōn, Od. 3, 179; Ἀπόλλωνι, Od. 21, 267. *b)* Metaph. *to lay upon, to inflict,* ἄλγεα Τρωσί, 2, 40. πολλοὶ γὰρ δὴ τλῆμεν ἐξ ἀνδρῶν, χαλέπ' ἄλγε' ἐπ' ἀλλήλοισι τιθέντες, many of us have suffered from [on account of] men, inflicting grievous pangs upon one another, says Diōnē to Aphroditē, 5, 384. The Schol. unnecessarily connects ἐξ ἀνδρῶν and τιθέντες. The sense is, 'we have already suffered much because we have taken part in the affairs of men,' cf. v. 385, seq θωήν, to inflict punishment, Od. 2, 102 2) *to put at or to, to attach, to add,* ἄλλα, 7, 364. 391; τινί τι; κορώνην, a curved end (to the bow), 4, 111; περόνην, Od. 19, 256. *b) to place before,* in order to close any thing, λίθον θύρησιν, Od. 13, 370; θύρας, to close the doors. 14, 169. Od. 22, 157; hence said of the Hours: ἠμὲν ἀνακλῖναι νέφος ἠδ' ἐπιθεῖναι, to put back the cloud and place it before, i. e. to open and shut, 5, 751. 8, 395; spoken of the Trojan horse, λόχον, Od. 11, 525. *c)* Metaph. μύθῳ τέλος ἐπιθεῖναι, to put an end to the word, i. e. to fulfil the declaration, 19, 107. 20, 369; φρένα ἱεροῖσιν, to fix his heart upon, to direct his mind to the victims, 10, 46. II) Mid. *to put upon,* τί τινι; στεφάνην κεφαλῆφιν, 10, 31; χεῖρας στήθεσσίν τινος (his hands), 18, 317.

ἐπιτιμήτωρ, ορος, ὁ (τιμάω), *an avenger, one who inflicts punishment,* epith. of Zeus, ἐπιτιμήτωρ ἱκετάων τε ξείνων τε, Od. 9, 270.†

ἐπιτλῆναι (ΤΛΑΩ), only imper. aor. ἐπιτλήτω, absol. *to continue patient at or under;* with dat. μύθοισιν ἐμοῖσιν, my words, *19, 220. 23, 591.

ἐπιτολμάω (τολμάω), *to have courage,*

to dare, to take courage, to encourage oneself,* with infin., Od. 5, 353; absol. *to remain patient,* *Od. 17, 238.

ἐπίτονος, ον (τείνω), *stretched,* whence the subst. ὁ ἐπίτονος (subaud. ἱμάς), a rope with which the sail-yard is made fast to the mast, *the yard-rope,* Od. 12, 423.†

ἐπιτοξάζομαι, depon. mid. (τοξάζω), prop. *to bend the bow at any one, to shoot, to aim at any one,* with dat., 3, 79.†

ἐπιτραπέω, Ep. for ἐπιτρέπω, ἐπιτραπέουσι, 10, 421.†

ἐπιτρέπω (τρέπω), aor. 1 act. ἐπέτρεψα, aor. 2 act. ἐπέτραπον, aor. 2 mid. ἐπετραπόμην, perf. pass. ἐπιτέτραμμαι, plur. Ion. and Ep. ἐπιτετράφαται, I Act. 1) *to turn to, to give over to, to commit to, to thrust to,* τί τινι; οἶκόν τιν (to one's care), Od. 2, 226; without accus. expressed, aor. 2, τοῖσιν ἐπετράπομει μάλιστα, to these we trusted most [sc τὸ φυλάσσειν], 10, 59; instead of the accus. we have also the infin., 10, 116 421. θεοῖς ἐπιτρέπειν τι, to leave to the gods, Od. 19, 502; hence pass. ᾧ ἐπι τετράφαται λαοί, to whom the people are entrusted, 2, 25; and spoken of the Hours: τῆς ἐπιτέτραπται οὐρανός, 5, 750 2) *to turn to, to leave to, to yield to* νίκην τινί, 21, 473; παισὶ κτήματα, t leave possessions to children, Od. 7, 149 and without accus. [expressed], οὐ ἐπέτρεπε [sc. ἑαυτόν, cf. Nägelsb. p. 313] γήραϊ, he yielded not to age, 10, 79. Il Mid. *to turn oneself to.* σοὶ θυμὸ ἐπετράπετο εἴρεσθαι, thy mind was in clined to ask, Od. 9, 12.

ἐπιτρέχω (τρέχω), aor. 2 ἐπέδραμον partcp. aor. 1 ἐπιθρέξας, 13, 409; † per ἐπιδέδρομα, *to run to,* both to render and to attack. ἅρματα ἵπποις ἐπέτρεχον the chariots rolled after the horses, 23 504. 2) *to run over, to graze,* spoken a spear, 13, 409. λευκὴ δ' ἐπιδέδρομε αἴγλη, glittering splendour glances ove it, Od. 6, 45. cf. Od. 20, 357.

ἐπιτροχάδην, adv. *running over cu sorily, hastily, briefly* (but to the point) *in a summary way,* only ἀγορεύειν, 213. Od. 18, 26.

ἐπιφέρω (φέρω), fut. ἐποίσω, *to brin to* or *upon,* only in a hostile signif. χεῖράς τινι, to lay hands upon one, i. to attack him, Od. 16, 438; and βαρεί χεῖρας, 1, 89.

*ἐπιφθάνω (φθάνω), partcp. aor. 2 ἐπ φθάς, *to be beforehand, to anticipat Batr. 217.

ἐπιφθονέω (φθονέω), *to envy, to refu enviously, to grudge, to forbid,* with da Od. 11, 149.†

ἐπιφλέγω (φλέγω), *to kindle, to set fi to, to burn up,* with accus. ὕλην, νεκρό *2, 455. 23, 52.

*ἐπιφράζομαι (φράζομαι), aor. 1 ε ἐφρασάμην, Ep. σσ, and with like sign aor. 1 pass. ἐπεφράσθην, Od. 5, 183. *to think of, to meditate upon, to conside with accus. βουλήν, 2, 282. 13, 741 absol. 21, 410; mly *to observe, to perceive, to understand*, τι, 5, 665; in connexion with νοεῖν, Od. 8, 94. 533; *to recognize*, Od. 18, 94. 2) *to devise, to plan, to excogitate*, ἀλεθρόν τινι, Od. 15, 444; absol. οἷον δὴ τὸν μῦθον ἐπεφράσθης ἀγορεῦσαι! Od. 5, 183.

ἐπιφρονέω (ἐπίφρων), *to be thoughtful, intelligent, wise, discreet*, only partcp. pass., Od. 19, 385.†

ἐπιφροσύνη, ἡ (ἐπίφρων), *discretion, prudence, thoughtful care*, Od. 5, 437; in the plur. ἀνελέσθαι ἐπιφροσύνας, to assume a thoughtful care, •Od. 19, 22.

ἐπίφρων, ον (φρήν), *considerate, thoughtful, intelligent, wise, prudent*, spoken of persons, Od. 23, 12. ἐπίφρων βουλήν, *prudent or wise in counsel*, Od. 16, 242; of things, βουλή, a *prudent counsel*, Od. 3, 128. 19, 326.

•ἐπιφωνέω (φωνέω), *to call to, to call on any occasion*, Fr. 42.

ἐπιχειρέω (χείρ), fut. ρήσω, *to lay hands upon, to seize*, with dat. δαίπνῳ, •Od. 24, 386. 395.

ἐπιχεῦαι, see ἐπιχέω.

ἐπιχέω (χέω), aor. 1 Ep. ἐπέχευα, infin. ἐπιχεῦαι, aor. 1 mid. ἐπεχευάμην, Ep. aor. sync. 2 mid. ἐπέχυντο, 1) *to pour upon or over*; χερσὶν ὕδωρ, water upon the hands, 24, 303. Od. 4, 212; χέρνιβα προχόῳ, water from the pitcher, Od, 1, 136; metaph. of sleep, in tmesis: μνηστήρεσσιν ὕπνον, Od. 2, 395; ἀνέμων ἀῦτμένα, to excite the breath of the winds, Od. 3, 289; δούρατα, to cast spears, 5, 618. *b*) Mid. *a*) *to pour upon for oneself*, spoken of things dry: *to pour upon, to heap upon*, ὕλην (as ballast), Od. 5, 257; χύσιν φύλλων, (an effusion =) a heap of leaves, Od. 5, 487. *b*) With Ep. sync. aor. 2, only metaph of a multitude of men: *to pour upon, to rush to*, τοὶ δ' ἐπέχυντο, 15, 654. 16, 295.

ἐπιχθόνιος, ον (χθών), *living on the earth, earthly*, 1) As epith. of ἀνήρ, βροτός, ἄνθρωπος, 1, 266. 2, 553. 2) As subst. *an inhabitant of the earth*, h. 14, 2.

ἐπιχράω (χράω), *to attack, to fall upon, to assail*, with dat. of men and brutes, Τρώεσσιν, ἄρνεσσιν, 16, 352. 356. μητέρι μοι μνηστῆρες ἐπέχραον, the suitors assailed my mother, i. e. pressed her with their suit, Od. 2, 50 (μοι is dat. ethicus used in the language of familiar discourse. Nitzsch.).

ἐπιχρίω (χρίω), aor. 1 ἐπέχρισα, 1) *to anoint, to besmear*, with accus. τόξον ἀλοιφῇ, Od. 21, 179: παρειάς, Od. 18, 172. 2) Mid. *to anoint oneself*, ἀλοιφῇ. •Od. 18, 179.

ἐπιψαύω (ψαύω), *to touch upon the surface, to graze, to touch*; metaph. *to feel (slightly)*. ὅστ' ὀλίγον περ ἐπιψαύῃ πραπίδεσσιν, who can feel though but a little with his heart, Od. 8, 547.†

ἐπιωγαί, αἱ (ἰωγή), *places near the shore, where ships, secure from storms, could lie at anchor, roads [sheltering coves. Cp.]*, Od. 5, 404.†

ἐπίων, see ἔπειμι (εἶμι).

' ἔπλε, Ep. for ἔπελε, see πέλω.

ἔπλεο or ἔπλευ, Ep. for ἐπέλου, and ἔπλετο, Ep. for ἐπέλετο, see πέλομαι.

ἐπλήντο, see πελάζω.

ἐποίσω, fut of ἐπιφέρω.

ἐποίχομαι (οἴχομαι), *to go to, to go, to come to*, 1) Absol., Od. 1, 143; limited, πάντοσε, 5, 508: ἀνὰ στρατόν. 1. 383. 2) With accus. of persons and inanimate things, *a*) *to go to* any one, μνηστῆρας, Od. 1, 324. *b*) *to go about, to go through, to inspect*, spoken of a leader, 6, 81; στίχας ἀνδρῶν, 15, 279. πάσας ἐπῴχετο, he (went) up to them all (the seals), Od. 4, 451. *c*) *to fall upon* any one, *to attack*, with accus. οὐρῆας, spoken of Apollo, 1, 50; Κύπριν χαλκῷ (with a weapon), 5, 330; esply spoken of Apollo and Artĕmis: ἀγανοῖς βελέεσσιν (to pierce with gentle shafts. Cp.), Od. 11, 173. 15, 411; see Ἀπόλλων. 3) Of things: *to go to any thing, to go about*, τί; νηῶν ἴκρια, 15, 676; metaph. ἐποίχεσθαι ἔργον, *to go to their work, to pursue or attend to it*, 6, 492; δόρπον, Od. 13, 34; spoken of women: ἱστὸν ἐποίχεσθαι, *to go about the loom*, see ἱστόν, 1, 31.

ἔπομαι, mid. see ἔπω.

ἐπόμνυμι and ἐπομνύω (ὄμνυμι), imperf. ἐπώμνυον, fut. ἐπομοῦμαι, aor. ἐπώμοσα, *to swear by, to take an oath* of a thing; absol., Od. 15, 437; with accus. ὅρκον, with μήποτε and infin., 9, 132. 274; ἐπίορκον, *a false oath*, 10, 332.

ἐπομφάλιος, ον (ὀμφαλός), *at, upon the navel; on the boss*, spoken of a shield: βάλεν σάκος μέσσον ἐπομφάλιον, in the centre, on the boss, 7, 267.†

ἐποπίζομαι, depon. (ὀπίζομαι), *to honour, to reverence, to dread*, with accus. Διὸς μῆνιν, Od. 5, 146.† h. Ven. 291.

ἐποπτάω (ὀπτάω), *to roast upon, to roast*, ἔγκατα, Od. 12, 363.†

ἐποπτεύω (ὀπτεύω), *to look upon*, esply *to inspect, to superintend*, with accus. ἔργα ἐποπτεύεσκε, Od. 16, 140.†

(ἐπόπτομαι), pres. obsol., fut. ἐπόψομαι, see ἐφοράω.

ἐπορέγομαι, mid. (ὀρέγω), partcp. aor. ἐπορεξάμενος, *to extend oneself towards, in order to attack, to extend the spear* for a thrust, 5, 335.† subaud. ἔγχει, see ὀρέγω.

ἐπόρνυμι and ἐπορνύω (ὄρνυμι), imperf. ἐπώρνυε, aor. 1 ἐπῶρσα, imperat. ἔπορσον, Ep. aor. sync. mid. ἐπῶρτο, 1) *to excite, to awaken*, τί τινι; μένος τινί, 20, 93. 2) *to urge on, to send to*, spoken of the gods: ὕπνον τινί, *to send sleep upon any one*, Od. 22, 429; ὀϊζύν, Od. 7, 271; μόρσιμον ἦμαρ, 15, 613. *b*) Frequently in a hostile signif. *to excite, to rouse against* any man, 5, 765; and with infin., 7, 42. 11) Mid. together with Ep. aor. 2 and pluperf. *to rush against, to assail*; with dat. Ἀχιλῆι, against Achilles, 21, 324.

ἐποροίω (ὀροίω), aor. 1 ἐπόρουσα, *to leap upon, to spring upon, to rush upon*, any man, with dat. always in a hostile signif., 3, 379. 4, 472; and ἐν πόντῳ, h.

Ap. 400; with double dat. τινὶ δουρί (with the spear), 16, 320; metaph. spoken of sleep: αὐτῷ ὕπνος ἐπόρουσε, sleep fell upon him (with the notion of haste), Od. 23, 343. b) With the accus. ἅρμα, to leap upon the chariot, 17, 481.

ἔπορσον, see ἐπόρνυμι.

ἔπος, εος, τό, a word, and generally every thing expressed by speech; hence also, speech, narration, tradition. H. ἔπος καὶ μῦθος, discourse and narration, Od. 11, 561; in the plur. Od. 8, 91. According to the connexion it signifies a) a word pledged, a promise: διακέρσαι ἔπος, 8, 8. b) counsel, command, 9, 100. c) a response or oracle of a soothsayer, Od. 12, 266. d) narration, song of a bard, Od. 8, 91. 17, 519. e) word, in opposition to deed, 15, 234; hence ἔπεσιν καὶ χερσὶν ἀρήγειν, to help any man by word and deed, 1, 77. cf. Spitz. ad Il. 15, 234. f) the contents of discourse, matter, nearly = πρᾶγμα, thing, 11, 652. Od. 22, 289, in connexion with μῦθος, where ἔπος relates more to the substance of the narration, μῦθος to its intellectual form.

ἐποτρύνω (ὀτρύνω), aor. 1 ἐπώτρυνα, to incite, to urge on. 1) Spoken of persons, with accus. to encourage, to urge, to impel, to command; often θυμὸς ἐποτρύνει, and in connexion with ἀνώγει, mly with accus. and infin. following, ἑταίρους τάφρον διαβαινέμεν, to cross the trench, 12, 50; with dat. of the pers. and infin. only, 15, 258. Od. 10, 531. 2) Of things: to excite, to press, with accus. πόλεμόν τινι, to excite a contest against any man, Od. 22, 152; πομπήν, to ask urgently an escort, Od. 8, 30; but ἀγγελίας πολίεσσιν, to send embassies to the cities, Od. 24, 355. II) Mid. to press for oneself, to urge, πομπήν, Od. 8, 31.†

ἐπουράνιος, ίη, ιον (οὐρανός), in heaven, heavenly, epith. of the gods, 6, 129. Od. 17, 484.

ἐποχέομαι, mid. (ὀχέω), fut. ἤσομαι, to ride upon, to travel, ἵπποις, 10, 380; ἵπποις καὶ ἅρμασι, to ride in chariots, *17, 449.

*ἐπόψιος, ον (ὄψις), to be looked at, conspicuous, remarkable, noted, h. Ap. 496 (old reading for ὑπόψιος, 3, 42).

ἐπόψομαι, see ἐφοράω.

ἔπραθον, see πέρθω.

ἑπτά, indecl. seven, often in Il. and Od.

ἑπταβόειος, ον (βόειος), made of seven layers of ox-hide, seven-hided, σάκος, *7, 220. 222.

ἑπταετής, ές (ἔτος), of seven years, only in neut. ἑπτάετες as adv. during seven years, *Od. 3, 305. 7, 259.

ἑπταπόδης, ον ὁ (πούς), seven feet long, θρῆνυς, 15, 729.†

*ἑπτάπορος, ον (πόρος), having seven courses, with seven paths, epith. of Pleiades, h. 7, 7.

Ἑπτάπορος, ὁ, a river of Mysia, 12, 20. According to Strab. XIII. p. 603, it is called Πολύπορος. It rises in the mountain Teunos, and falls, after manifold

windings, into the Sinus Adramyttēnus, at the village Celænæ.

ἑπτάπυλος, ον, seven-gated, having seven gates, epith. of the Bœotian Thebes, 4, 406. Od. 11, 263. cf. Apd. 3, 6, 6.

ἔπταρον, see πταίρω.

ἔπτατο, see πέτομαι.

ἔπτακα (ἑπτά), seven-fold; δαίζειν, to divide into seven parts, Od. 14, 434.†

ΕΠΩ, an obsol. theme from which come ἔπος, εἶπον, ἐνέπω and ἐννέπω, prop. to arrange; then, to speak, to say.

ἕπω, imperf. εἶπον, 1) Act. only Ep. to be about any thing, to be employed, to be busy, mly with prep. ἀμφί, μετά, περί: ἀμφ' Ὀδυσῆα Τρῶες ἕπον, the Trojans were engaged about Odysseus (Ulysses), i. e. they encompassed him, 11, 483, μετὰ Τυδέος υἱόν, to hasten to the son of Tydeus, 10, 516; περὶ τεύχεα, to busy oneself about the arms, 15, 555. In all these and other passages, a tmesis may be supposed. 2) Trans. with accus. to take care of, to clean, τεύχεα, 6, 321. II) Mid. ἕπομαι, imperf. εἱπόμην and Ep. ἑπόμην fut. ἕψομαι, aor. 2 ἑσπόμην, imperat. Ep σπεῖο, ἑσπέσθω, subj. ἕσπωμαι, optat ἑσποίμην, infin. σπέσθαι, Od. 22, 324 ἑσπέσθαι, 5, 423; partcp. ἑσπόμενος, 12 395. The first ε, in the subj., optat. infin., and partcp., is rejected by Becker Thiersch, § 232, 56. Buttm. Gram. p 280, and Spitz. Excurs. X. on Il., consider it correct and Epic, but reject the pres. ἕσπεται, Od. 4, 826; for which ἔρχεται must be read; signif. to follow 1) Spoken of living beings: to go after to accompany, with dat. chiefly of warriora who follow a leader, 2, 524. 675 seq., strengthened by ἅμα, 5, 551. Od. 11 372; again, μετά τινι, 18, 234; also μετα κτίλον ἕσπετο, the flock followed the ram, 13, 492; again, σύν τινι, Od. 7, 304 b) Metaph. spoken of inanimate things often of ships, Il.; of bridal presents ὅσσα ἔοικε φίλης ἐπὶ παιδὸς ἕπεσθαι, a many as it is suitable to give with a dea daughter, Od. 1, 278. 2, 197. τρυφάλει ἕσπετο ἅμα χειρί, the helmet followe the hand, i. e. he retained the helmet i his hand, 3, 376. ἐπάλξις ἕσπετο, th breast-work followed, i. e. fell down, 12 398; metaph. to attach to, to be connecte with, to follow, as κῦδος, τιμή, Ἄτη, 415. 9, 573; ἔκ τινος, from, by means o any man, 8, 140; to which meaning b longs h. Ven. 261. 2) to be able to follo to come forth with, τινί, 16, 154. Od. 319; metaph. spoken of the limbs and th bodily powers: γούνατα αὐτῷ ἕπεται, 314; χεῖρες, Od. 20, 237. 3) In a hosti signif. to pursue, τινί, 11, 165; ἀμ αὐτόν, 11, 474. 15, 257; only in Il. In the imperat. equivalent to, to com ἕπεο προτέρω, come nearer, 18, 387. O 5, 91.

*ἐπωλένιος, ον (ὠλένη), upon the elbow in the arms, h. Merc. 433. 510.

ἐπώνυμος, ον (ὄνομα, ὄνυμα), derivin its name from, named after, having a su

name, from any particular occasion. Ἀλκυόνην καλέεσκον ἐπώνυμον, they named her Alcyonê with a surname (in reference to the sad fate of her mother), 9, 562; the real name of a person containing a reference to character or fortune, Od. 7, 54. 19, 409. h. Ap. 373.

ἐπῶρτο, see ἐπόρνυμι.

ἐπώχατο, most probably 3 plur. pluperf. pass. from ἐπέχω, 12, 340.† πᾶσαι (πύλαι) ἐπώχατο, all the gates were closed (ἐπικεκλεισμέναι ἦσαν, Apoll. Hesych.). From ἐπέχω, perf. with change of vowel ὦχα (cf. συνόχωκα, ὀχεύς), perf. pass. ἐπώγμαι: ἐπέχειν τὰς πύλας, to shut the gates, is after the analogy of ἐπέχειν τὰ ὦτα, cf. Buttm. Gr. Gram. ἔχω; Rost, p. 308; Thiersch, § 232, 64; who however translates it: to press. Other explanations are a) 3 plur. pluperf. from ἐποίχω, with the reading ἐπώχατο, which cannot by any means signify 'to shut.' b) 3 plur. imperf. from ἐποίχομαι; with the reading πάσας ἐπώχατο, the Trojans ran to all, which does not accord with the connexion.

ἔραζα, adv. (ἔρα), on the earth, to the earth, with πίπτω and χέω, Il. and Od.

ἔραμαι, Ep. for ἐράω, depon. mid. aor. 1 ἠρασάμην, Ep. σσ, to love, to love dearly, with gen. frequently spoken of persons, 3, 446; of things: πολέμου, μάχης, 9, 64. 16, 208; δόρποιο, h. Cer. 129.

ἐραννός, ή, όν (ἐράω), lovely, charming, epith. of beautiful towns, 9, 531. Od. 7, 18.

ἔρανος, ὁ, a meal, to which each guest contributes his share, Od. 1, 226. 11, 415; a pic-nic. According to Nitzsch ad Od. 1, 226, ἔρανος, in the sense of a contribution to a common object, e. g. an entertainment, is not found in H., but it is to be taken in a general signif.: an entertainment of princes with a superior king; perhaps, a friendly entertainment.

ἐρατεινός, ή, όν (ἐράω), lovely, agreeable, charming, often spoken of countries, cities, rivers, also ἠνορέη. ὁμηλικίη, 3, 175. 6, 156; of persons, Od. 4, 13. 8, 230.

ἐρατίζω, Ep. form of ἐράω, to desire vehemently, with gen. κρειῶν ἐρατίζων, *11, 551. 17, 660.

ἐρατός, ή, όν (ἐράω), beloved, lovely, agreeable: δῶρ' Ἀφροδίτης, 3, 64.† Often in the hymns.

ἐργάζομαι, depon. mid. (ἔργον), augm. εἰργ., 1) to work, to be active, absol. Od. 14, 272. h Cer. 139; spoken of bellows, 18, 469. 2) Trans. to perform, to do, to practise, with accus. ἔργα, Od. 20, 72; ἔργα ἀεικέα, to practise shameful deeds, 24, 733; ἐναίσιμα, Od. 17, 321; also χρυσόν, to work gold, Od. 3, 435.

ἐργάθω, ἐεργάθω, poet. form of ἔργω, to separate: χρόα ἔργαθεν, 11, 437.† ἀπὸ δ' αὐχένος ὦμον ἐέργαθεν, 5, 147.†

ἐργασίη, ἡ (ἐργάζομαι), work, labour, activity, h. Merc. 486.

Ἐργῖνος, ὁ, son of Clymenus, king of Orchomenus, h. Ap. 297.

ἔργμα, τό (ΕΡΓΩ), = ἔργον, work, act, deed, h. 27, 20. 32, 19.

ἔργον, τό (ΕΡΓΩ), 1) work, deed, action, often plur. θέσκελα, ἀήσυλα ἔργα, ἔργα φιλοτήσια, the delights of love, Od. 11, 246; and in antithesis with μῦθος, βουλή, 9, 443. 2) work, labour, business, occupation, trade, limited by an adj. or subst. ἔργα γάμοιο, the works of marriage. ἔργα πολεμήϊα, works of war, 5, 428. 429. θαλάσσια ἔργα, seafaring business, 2, 614; fishing, Od. 5, 67; also spoken of animals, Od. 17, 313. Chiefly in the following special connexions: a) ἔργα ἀνδρῶν, works of men, i. e. agriculture, as the peculiar employment of men. Hence also ἔργον, labour in the field, Od. 14, 222; and ἔργα in the plur. cultivated fields, estates, 2, 751. Od. 14, 344; esply πίονα ἔργα, Od. 4, 318; and ἔργα πατρώϊα, Od. 2, 22; also ἔργα βοῶν, Od. 10, 98. b) ἔργα γυναικῶν, the works of women, i. e. partly the cares of housekeeping, but esply weaving, spinning, and other female labours of art, 9, 128. Od. 2, 117, cf. Od. 1, 356. c) In the Il. esply the labours of war, fighting, battle, war, 4, 470. cf. 539; also ἔργον μάχης, 6, 522. 3) the product of labour, work. ἔργα γυναικῶν, woven stuffs, 6, 289. ἔργα Ἡφαίστοιο, metallic products, Od. 4, 617. 4) Generally, work, thing, matter, affair, 1, 294; ἔργα δαιτός, 9, 228; ὅπως ἔσται τάδε ἔργα, how these things shall end, 4, 14; spoken of a great stone: μέγα ἔργον, a huge affair, 5, 303. 20, 286.

ἔργω, and mly ἐέργω, Ion. and Ep. for εἴργω, aor. 1 act. ἔρξα, perf. act. ἔεργμαι, 3 plur. Ep. ἔρχαται (without augm.), pluperf. 3 plur. ἐέρχατο and ἔρχατο, partcp. aor. pass. ἐρχθείς. The Attics distinguish between εἴργω, to exclude, and εἴργω, to include. H. has only the spirit. len. (εἴργω is found only 23, 72, ἐέργω prop. ἐϜέργω is most common, a form of ἐϜέργνυμι, ἐργάθω.) Primary signif. to separate; according to the connexion 1) to include, to hem in, to confine, with accus. ἔντος ἐέργειν, to include within, to limit, 2, 617. 845. 9, 404; δόμον, to shut up, Od. 7, 88; pass. with ἐν: ἐρχθέντ' ἐν ποταμῷ, confined in the river, 21, 282. Od. 10. 283. ἔνθα τε φρένες ἔρχαται, where the diaphragm is shut up, 16, 481. σάκεσσι ἔρχατο, 17, 354. γέφυραι ἐεργμέναι, confined, i. e. firmly fortified dams or dykes, 5, 89; see γέφυρα (pontes sublicis firmati, Heyne) 2) to exclude, to separate, to prohibit, to remove, 23, 72; with ἀπό: βέλος ἀπὸ χροός, 4, 130. ὅσσον ἐκ νηῶν ἀπὸ πύργου τάφρος ἔεργεν, all the space from the ships onward, which the trench separated from the wall, 8, 213; cf. Spitz. [all the space from the ships to the wall and from the wall to the ditch, cf. Schol. and Heyne, ad loc.]; with the gen. alone: παιδός, 4, 131; ἐεργόμενος πολέμοιο, restrained from war, 13, 525. 3) Generally, *to press, to crowd*, λαὸν ἐπ' ἀριστερά, pressing the people to the left, or separating the people, i. e. touching the left side of the army, 12, 201; ἐπὶ νῆας, 16, 395; with ἐκτός, and gen., Od. 12, 219.

ἘΡΓΩ, obsol. pres. which furnishes tenses to ἔρδω or ῥέζω, q. v.

ἔρδω, poet. (ἘΡΓΩ), fut. ἔρξω, aor. ἔρξα, perf. ἔοργα, pluperf. ἐώργειν, 1) *to do, to make, to perform*, often absol., 4, 29; with accus. ἔργα, 10, 51. Od. 2, 236; with the dat. pers. τί τινι, 14, 261. Od. 14, 289; but more frequently with double accus. κακόν and κακά τινα, 3, 351. 9, 540; also εὖ ἔρξαι τινά, to benefit any man, 5, 650. 2) Esply *to offer, to sacrifice*, ἑκατόμβας, ἱερὰ θεοῖς, 2, 306 (ἔοργα and ἐώργειν are used iu the signif. *to do*, cf. ῥέζω).

ἐρεβεννός, ή, όν (Ἔρεβος), *dark, gloomy*, νύξ, 5, 659; and ἀήρ, *5, 864.

Ἐρέβευσφι(ν), see Ἔρεβος.

ἐρέβινθος, ὁ, *a chick-pea*, perhaps *cicer arietinum*, Linn., 13, 589.†

Ἔρεβος, εος, τό, Ep. gen. Ἐρέβευς, Ἐρέβευσφι, *Erebus*, a gloomy place under the earth, between the upper world and the palace of Pluto, through which souls departing from the upper world pass to Pluto; *the nocturnal gloom of Hades*, but it is better to explain it, with Völcker and Nitzsch (Od. 10), the dark earth as the dwelling of the dead, and especially *the valley of death*, 8, 368. Od. 10, 528. 12, 81; Ἐρέβευσφι, 9, 572, appears corrupted from Ἐρέβεσφι, according to Thiersch, § 186, 4. Rost. Dial. 23, c.

Ἐρεβόσδε, adv. *to Erebus*, Od. 20, 356.†

ἐρεείνω, poet. (ἔρομαι), *to ask, to interrogate*, with accus. pers. τινά, 6, 176; of the thing, γενεήν, 6, 145; and with double accus. τινά τι, Od. 1, 220. 4, 137; also ἀμφί τινι, after any man, Od. 24, 263. 2) *to try*, said of the lyre, h. Merc. 487. 3) *to say, to speak*, h. Merc. 313. Herm. reads ἐρέεινον for ἐρέεινεν and translates: *quum singula accurate disceptassent*. 11) Mid. as depon., Od. 17, 305. h. Merc. 313.

ἐρεθίζω (ἐρέθω), *to irritate, to provoke*, in a good signif. only : δμωάς, μητέρα, to excite to interest and curiosity, Od. 19, 45. b) Elsewhere in a bad signif. *to excite to anger. to irritate*, 1, 32; κερτομέοις, χαλεποῖς ἐπέεσσι, 5, 419. Od. 17, 395; and spoken of lions : κύνας τ' ἄνδρας τε, 17, 658.

ἐρέθω (kindred with ἔρις), poet. form of ἐρεθίζω, *to irritate, to anger*, with accus., 1, 519; and with infin., h. 7, 4, in the Od. spoken of cares: *to disquiet, to distress*, Od. 4, 813. πυκιναὶ δέ μοι ἀμφ' ἀδινὸν κῆρ ὀξεῖαι μελεδῶναι ὀδυρομένην ἐρέθουσιν, poignant cares thronging about my enveloped heart distress me grieving, Od. 19, 517 (μοί belongs to κῆρ).

. ἐρείδω, aor. 1 ἔρεισα, aor. 1 mid. ἠρεισάμην, perf. pass. ἐρήρεισμαι, 3 plur.

Ion. ἐρηρέδαται, 3 sing. pluperf. ἠρήρειστο, aor. 1 pass. ἠρείσθην (augm. only in th' aor. mid.), 1) Act. 1) Trans. *to plac firmly on, to lean upon, to fix firmly upon* with accus. and prep. πρὸς, περί τι, ἐπ' τινι and dat. alone. δόρυ πρὸς τεῖχο 22, 112. Od. 8, 66 ; ἀσπίδ' ἐπὶ πύργω, 2: 97; pass. ἐπὶ μελίης ἐρεισθείς, leanec supported upon his spear, 22, 225. ἑ δὲ θρόνοι περὶ τοῖχον ἐρηρέδατο, withi were seats placed around the wall (other fixed), Od. 7, 97. λᾶε ἀρηρέδαται δύ 23, 329. χάλκεοι τοῖχοι ἐρηρέδατ' ἔνθ καὶ ἔνθα, brazen walls were erected o both sides, Od. 7, 86. According t Buttm. Gr. Gram. § 98, the readin ἐληλάδατ' or better ἐληλέατο, rejected b Wolf, is to be preferred, see ἐλαύνω. S also Voss: the walls extended); agai to put upon with violence, οὔδει ἐρεισθ he was stretched upon the ground, : 145. 11, 144; οὔδει δέ σφιν χαῖται ἐρηρ δαται, their manes extended to th ground, 23, 284. b) *to thrust* any thin *to press, to strike*, with the accus. sinc by pressure a moveable object is urge forward: ἀσπὶς ἀσπίδα ἔρειδε, κόρι κόρυν, ἀνέρα δ' ἀνήρ, shield presse shield, 13, 131 (said of pent-up troops) βελέεσσίν τινα, to press with missile: 16, 108; hence pass. *to be thrust*, to l pressed, with διά: διὰ θώρηκος ἠρήρειστ ἔγχος, the spear penetrated the cuiras 3, 358. 7, 252. 2) Intrans. *to lean upo to press*. ἀλλήλησιν ἐρείδουσαι, pressin one upon another, i. e. quickly; accor ing to Eustath. 'turning towards eac other, so that one maid held the hea the other the feet of the dead,' Od. 2 450; perhaps also intrans. βελέεσσιν, l 108. II) Mid. *to support oneself upon*, lean upon, with dat. σκήπτρῳ ἔγχεϊ, wi gen. ἐρείσατο χειρὶ γαίης, with the har upon the earth, 5, 309. 11, 355. 2) Absc *to press, to exert oneself*, ἐρεισάμενο βάλε, 12, 457; and generally *to strive struggle*, 16, 736, of steeds, 23, 735. C ἐρηρέδαται, see Thiersch, § 212. 35. Buttm. p. 183.

ἐρείκω, aor. 2 ἤρικον, act. *to tear* pieces, to break up; only mid. with a 2 intrans. *to tear, to break*. ἐρεικόμει περὶ δουρί, spoken of the cuirass, 13, 44 ἤρικε κόρυς. *17, 295.

ἔρειο, Ep. for ἔρου, see ἔρομαι.

ἐρείομεν, Ep. for ἐρέωμεν, see ἐρέω.

ἐρείπω, poet. aor. 2 ἤριπον, perf. pas ἐρήριμμαι, 3 sing. pluperf. ἐρέριπτο, E shortened for ἐρήρ., 1) Trans. in th act. *to cast down, to demolish*, with t: accus. τεῖχος, ἐπάλξεις, 12, 258. 15, 35 ἐρέριπτο τεῖχος Ἀχαιῶν, the wall of t: Greeks was torn down, 14, 15. 2) I trans. in aor. *to tumble down, to fall*. Mly spoken of men: ἐξ ὀχέων, ἐν κονί γνύξ; ἔστη γνὺξ ἐριπών, he sank on l knees, but still held himself up [*ste (superiore parte* corporis), *Damm*], 5, 3 ἤριπε πρηνής, 5, 58. Od. 22, 296. b) (trees: 16, 482. 13, 389. 21, 243.

Ἔρεμβοι, οἱ, *the Erembi*, a people mentioned by H. after the Sidonians, Od. 4, 84. According to Hellanicus and most of the old Geogr. Strab. 16, p. 728, they were Troglodytæ (fr. ἔρα, earth, and ἐμβαίνειν), and dwelt east of Egypt, in Arabia. Others sought them in Cyprus; others still make them a branch of the Æthiopians, as Völcker Geogr. p. 89.

ἐρεμνός, ή, όν (kindred with ἔρεβος), *dark, black. gloomy*, γαῖα, Od. 24, 106. h. Merc. 427; more cly with the idea of dreadful, as αἰγίς, λαῖλαψ, νύξ, 4, 167.

ἐρέζα, see ῥέζω.

ἐρέομαι, Ep. for εἴρομαι, whence imperf. ἐρέοντο, infin. ἐρέεσθαι, *to ask*.

ἐρέπτομαι, depon. mid. (kindred with ἐρείπω), *to graze, to eat, to feed upon, to browse*, always of brutes, λωτόν, κρῖ, πυρόν, 2, 776. 5, 196. 19, 553; δημόν (of a corpse), 21, 204; spoken of men who eat the uncooked fruit of the lotus, Od. 9. 97; always and only partcp.

ἐρέριπτο, see ἐρείπω.

ἐρεσίη, ἡ, see εἰρεσίη.

ἐρέσσω (akin to ἐρέθω), *to row*, always intrans., 9, 361. Od. 11, 78.

ἐρέτης, ου, ὁ (ἐρέσσω), *a rower*, only in the plur. Il. and Od.

Ἐρετμεύς, ῆος, ὁ (= ἐρέτης), a Phæacian, Od. 8, 112.

ἐρετμόν, τό (Ep. for ἐρετμός), *an oar*, εὔηρες, in H. always as neut., Od. 11, 121. 12, 15. 23, 268; also in the plur., Od. 11, 125.

Ἐρέτρια, ἡ, see Εἰρέτρια.

ἐρεύγομαι, depon. mid. aor. 2 ἤρυγον, 1) intrans. *to belch, to eject wind upwards from the stomach*, spoken of the Cyclops: ἐρεύγετο οἰνοβαρείων, heavy with wine, he belched, Od. 9, 374. b) Metaph. of the sea, *to dash up*, ἐρευγομένης ἁλός, 17, 265. κύματα ἐρεύγεται ἠπειρόνδε, the waves dashed (with a *roaring* sound) *roaring* upon the land, Od. 5, 403. 438. c) In the aor. 2, *to bellow*, spoken of an ox, only 20, 403. 404. 406. 2) Trans. with the accus. φόνον αἵματος, *to vomit forth the bloody gore*, 16, 162.

Ἐρευθαλίων, ωνος, ὁ, a noble Arcadian, who was slain by Nestor in a war of the Pylians and Arcadians, 7, 136. 4, 319 (= ἐρευθός).

ἐρεύθω, aor. ἔρευσα, *to redden, to dye* or *colour red*; γαῖαν αἵματα, •11, 394. 18, 329.

ἐρευνάω (kindred with ἐρέω), fut. ήσω, *to search for, to track*, spoken of dogs: ἴχνια, Od. 19, 436; of lions: μετ' ἀνέρος ἴχνια, 18, 321; τεύχεα, *to seek the weapons*, Od. 22, 180; τινά, h. Merc. 176.

ἐρέφω, aor. 1 ἔρεψα, *to cover over*, esply *to furnish with a roof, to roof*; θάλαμον καθύπερθεν, 24, 450. Od. 23, 193; *to build*, since roofing is the finishing operation: εἴποτέ τοι χαρίεντ' ἐπὶ νηὸν ἔρεψα (if I have ever built thee a well-pleasing temple, thus Voss), 1, 39; see ἐπερέφω.

Ἐρεχθεύς, ῆος, ὁ, in the earlier fables

was not distinguished from Erichthonius; according to H. he was a son of *Earth*, educated by Athênê in her temple, and, as the primitive hero of Athens, worshipt with the patron goddess of the city, 2, 547. Od. 7, 81. According to later tradition, son of Hêphæstus and *Earth* or Atthis, daughter of Cranaus, Apd. 3, 14. 6.

ἐρέχθω (kindr. with ἐρείκω), *to tear in pieces*; metaph. θυμὸν δάκρυσι καὶ στοναχῇσι, *to torture the mind with tears and sighs*, Od. 5, 83. Pass. h. Ap. 358. 2) *to hurry hither and thither*, spoken of a ship: ἐρέχθεσθαι ἀνέμοισι, *to be tossed [rocked.* Cp.] by the (tempestuous) winds, 23, 317.

ἐρέω, Ion. for ἐρῶ, see εἴρω, and φημί.

ἐρέω, Ep. pres. for εἴρομαι, *to ask, to seek*, whence partcp. ἐρέων, 7, 128; subj. ἐρείομεν, Ep. for ἐρέωμεν, 1, 62; optat. ἐρέοιμεν, Od. 4, 192.

ἔρημος, η, ον (Att. ἐρῆμος, ον, prob. from ΕΡΑ), *solitary, deserted*, spoken of places, 10, 520. Od. 3, 270; μῆλα, 5, 140.

ἐρηρέδαται, see ἐρείδω.

ἐρητύω (ἐρύω), aor. 1 ἐρήτῡσα, iterat. form ἐρητύσασκε, aor. 1 pass. ἐρητύθην, 3 plur. ἐρήτῡθεν, Ep. for ἐρητύθησαν, without augm. I) Act. *to restrain, to check, to repress*, with accus. φάλαγγας, λαόν, often with dat. instrum. ἀγανοῖς, μειλιχίοις, ἐπέεσσιν. Pass. ἐρήτυθεν καθ' ἕδρας, they were restrained (or *settled*) upon their seats, 2, 99. 211; cf. 8, 345. Od. 3, 155. b) Metaph. *to hold in check, to moderate, to restrain*, θυμόν, 1, 192. Pass. 9, 635. 462. 13, 280. II) Mid. as depon. with accus. λαόν, 15, 723 (υ long before σ when a long syllable follows, short when a short follows, cf. Spitz. Pros. § 52, 5).

ἐρι-, an inseparable particle, which, like ἀρι, is used only in composition, and strengthens the idea of the word, *very*.

ἐριαύχην, ενος, ὁ, ἡ (αὐχήν), *having a lofty neck, high-necked*, epith. of steeds, •10, 305. 11, 159.

ἐριβρεμέτης, ου, ὁ (βρέμω), *loud-thundering*, epith. of Zeus, 13, 624.†

•ἐρίβρομος, ον (βρέμω), *loud-roaring, loud-thundering*, epith. of Dionȳsos, h. Bacch. 6, 36.

ἐρίβρυχος, ον (βρύχω), *loud-bellowing*, h. Merc. 116.

ἐριβῶλαξ, ακος, ὁ, ἡ, and ἐρίβωλος, ον (βῶλαξ), *having great clods [deep-soiled.* Cp.], an epith. of fertile regions: both forms often occur in the Il.; in the Od. each once, Od. 5, 34. 13, 235.

ἐρίγδουπος, ον (δοῦπος), Ep. for ἐρίδουπος, ον, 1) *loud-thundering*, epith. of Zeus, 5, 672; and often. 2) *loud-roaring, resounding*, ποταμοί. Od. 10, 515; πόδες ἵππων, 11, 152; αἴθουσα, *the resounding porch*, 24, 323. Od. 3, 349 (ἐρίγδουπος only of Zeus and the hoofs of horses; elsewhere ἐρίδουπος).

ἐριδαίνω, Ep. (ἐρίζω), aor. 1 mid. ἐριδήσασθαι, 1) *to contend, to dispute, to quarrel*, with dat. and ἀντία τινός, Od. 1, 79 ; and μετά τινι, Od. 21, 310 : primarily spoken of a contest with words, ἐπέεσσι, 2, 342. 1, 574 ; metaph, spoken of winds, ἀλλήλοιϊν, 16, 765. 2) *to fight, to struggle*, Od. 2, 206. ἐριδαίνομεν εἵνεκα τῆς ἀρετῆς [where τῆς is *dpt* on ἀρετῆς, Fäsi], we struggle on account of the virtue, viz. of Penelopê, as Aristarchus rightly explains it, τῆς ταύτης ἀρετῆς, s. Nitzsch ad loc. who rejects the explanation of Thiersch, Gr. § 284, 20, ' for precedence,' and of Voss : ' to combat for the prize,' absol. *to combat. to contend*, ἐριδήσασθαι ποσσίν, in running, 23, 792.

ἐριδήσασθαι, see ἐριδαίνω.

ἐριδμαίνω (poet. form of ἐρίζω), *to irritate, to provoke*, with accus. σφῆκας, 16, 260.†

ἐρίδουπος, ον = ἐρίγδουπος.

ἐρίζω (ἔρις), aor. 1 mid. (ἐρίσσεται subj. aor. 1), 1) *to contend, to dispute, to quarrel*, τινί with any man, primarily spoken of a verbal contest, then generally of a hostile disposition. τινί, with any man, 1, 6. 6, 131. 13, 109 ; ἀντιβίην τινί, to contend face to face with any man, 1, 277 ; περὶ ἴσης, for justice [*suo jure*, Heyne], 12, 423. 2) *to combat, to contend, to vie*, τινί, with any man, 6, 131; the thing which the combat respects stands, *a*) In the accus. Ἀφροδίτῃ κάλλος, with Aphroditê in beauty, 9, 389. Od. 5, 213. *b*) περί τινος, as μύθων, concerning eloquence, τόξων, in archery, 15, 284. Od. 8, 225. *c*) In the dat. ποσί, δρηστοσύνῃ, 13, 325. Od. 15, 321. *d*) With infin. χερσὶ μαχήσασθαι, Od. 13, 38; absol. Νέστωρ οἷος ἔριζεν (sc. αὐτῷ), vied with him, 2, 555, Wolf. II) Mid. *to contend*, with double dat. with any man, about any thing, 5, 172. ἀνδρῶν κέν τίς μοι ἐρίσσεται (for ἐρίσηται) κτήμασιν, no one of men would vie with me in possessions, Od. 4, 80.

ἐρίηρες, οἱ, see ἐρίηρος.

ἐρίηρος, ον (ἄρω), plur., by metaplasm, ἐρίηρες, prop. very suitable, hence: *a*) (*greatly*) *attached, faithful, intimate, dear*, ἑταῖροι, 3, 47. Od. 9, 100. *b*) *pleasing, agreeable*, who pleases all, ἀοιδός, Od. 1, 346.

ἐριθηλής, ές (θάλλω), *very verdant, blooming, beautiful, luxuriant*, epith. of cultivated fields and trees, *5, 90. 10, 467. 17, 53.

ἔριθος, ὁ, *a labourer, a hired reaper*, 18, 550. 560. 2) *a servant, a companion*, hence τλήμων γαστρὸς ἔριθος = *crepitus ventris*, h. Merc. 296.

ἐρικυδής, ές (κῦδος), *very distinguished, famous, glorious*; δῶρα θεῶν, 3, 65 : ἥβη, 11, 225; and often δαίς, 24, 802. Od. 3, 66.

ἐρίμυκος, ον (μυκάομαι), *loud bellowing*, epith. of cattle, 20, 497. Od. 15, 235.

ἐρινεός, ὁ, *the wild fig-tree, caprificus*, Od. 12, 103. 2) In the Il. it is also a proper name of a particular region near Troy; *the fig-hill*, according to Voss, Strabo, XIII. p. 597, calls it a strong

place planted with fig-trees, from which the city was most accessible to the enemy, 6, 433. ἐρινεοῖ ἠνεμόεις, here was the watch-tower, 22, 145.

Ἐρινύς, and Ἐρινύς, ύος, ἡ, plur. a Ἐρινύες, contr. Ἐρινῦς. 9, 484; *the Erin nyes*, goddesses of vengeance (the Furies o the Romans), H. does not mention thei number, form or names, the sing. stand 9, 571. 19, 87; mly plur., 9, 454, seq They are the symbol of the scourging o a guilty conscience which follows every act of impiety, and especially of the curs which rests upon any wretch who vio lates the most sacred duties of humanity They punish therefore the disobedienc of children to parents, 9, 454. Od. 2, 135 11, 280; violated duties towards parents kindred, and suppliants, 15, 204. Od. 17 475; perjury, 19, 260; and every slaugh ter, 9, 571. Since they punish the impiou man here in life, they show themselve hostile to men, and prompt them also t wicked actions, 19, 87. Od. 15, 231 Thus in character they approach th Fates, and as goddesses of fate they d not permit men to learn too much o their future destiny, 19, 418. They dwe in Erebus, Od. 15, 234. Il. 9, 571; and the punish transgressors even after death 19, 270. According to Hes. Th. 18 *Earth* (Gaia) bore them from drops o the blood of Uranus, and Apd. 1, 1. mentions as their names: *Tisiphon Megæra*, and *Alectô*. 2) As appel *curses*: τῆς μητρός, 21, 412 (ῠ in the nom in the derived cases ῠ. Ἐρινύς prol derived from an Arcad. word ἐρινύω, t be angry, Paus. 8, 25. 4: or from ἐρίν ἐρευνάω, to track, hence the correct o thography is Ἐρινύς, adopted by Spitz.)

ἔριον, τό, Ion. and Ep. εἴριον (dim from εἶρος), *wool*, often in the plur. τ εἴρια, 3, 388; ἔριον only Od. 4, 124.

ἐριούνης, ου, and ἐριούνιος, ὁ, *th brings prosperity*, according to Scho from ἔρι and ὀνίνημι, *very useful*, epith of Hermês, 20, 72; ἐριούνης only 20, 3 Od. 8, 322. 2) As pr. n. for *Hermês*, 2 360. 440.

ἔρις, ιδος, ἡ, accus. ἔριν and ἔριδα (th last most common ; ἔριν only in the Od. 1) *contention, strife, discord ;* μάχεσθα to contend in strife, i. e. with words, 8 (so Wolf rightly), cf. 7, 210. 20, 66 ; i like manner ἔριδι ξυνελαύνειν, to brin into strife, 20, 134. ἔριν στῆσαι ἔν τιν Od. 16, 292; particularly in the Il. spoke of war: *contest, battle*, 3, 7. 5, 732. ἔρι ξυνάγειν Ἄρηος, 5, 861. ἔριδα προβάλλε 11, 529. 2) *combat, emulation, rivalr* hence ἐξ ἔριδος, from rivalry, 7, 111. O 4. 343. ἔρις ἔργοιο, emulation in a wor Od. 18, 366. ἔριδα προφέρειν, to sho rivalry, Od. 6, 92. ἔριδα προφέρεσθ τινὶ ἀέθλων, to propose a combat to a man, Od. 8, 210.

Ἔρις, ιδος, ἡ, *Eris*, as a goddess, t author of fighting and contention, 4, 44 sister and wife of Arês, 5, 518. 20, 4

Accord. to Hes. Th. 223, she is the daughter of Night. She is mentioned 11, 3. 4. 18, 535. Later, the goddess of strife and discord.

ἐρισθενής, ές (σθένος), very strong, all-powerful, epith. of Zeus, 13, 54. Od. 8, 289.

ἔρισμα, ατος, τό (ἐρίζω), the occasion of contention, the apple of discord, contention, 4. 38.†

ἐρισφάφυλος. ον (σταφυλή), of large grapes. οἶνος [the vinous grape, large-cluster'd. Cp.], *Od. 9, 111. 358.

*ἐρισφάραγος, ον (σφαραγέω), i. q. ἐρισμάραγος, loud-sounding, loud-thundering, epith. of Poseidôn, h. Merc. 187.

ἐρίτιμος, ον (τιμή), highly-prized, precious, splendid, highly-honoured, epith. of the ægis, 2, 447 ; and of gold, *9, 126.

ἔριφος, ὁ, ἡ, a kid, Il. and Od.

Ἐριφύλη, ἡ, daughter of Talaus and Lysimachê, wife of Amphiaräus. She suffered herself to be bribed by Polynices with the necklace of Harmonia, and persuaded her husband to take part in the expedition against Thebes, although as a prophet he foresaw his death. According to the direction of the father, her son Alcmæon put her to death, Od. 11, 326.

Ἐριχθόνιος, ὁ, son of Dardanus and Batia, father of Tros, distinguished for his wealth, as three thousand mares fed in his pastures, 20, 219, seq.

Ἐρωπις, ιδος, ἡ, wife of Oïleus, 13, 697.

*ἐρώπις, ιδος, ἡ (ὤψ), large-eyed, Ep. 1, 2.

ἑρκεῖος, ον, Att. ἕρκειος, prop. belonging to the court (ἕρκος), hence Ἑρκεῖος, ὁ, house-protecting, an epith. of Zeus, because as a tutelary deity he commonly had his altar in the front court, Od. 22, 335.†

ἑρκίον, τό (dimin. from ἕρκος), an enclosure, a hedge, a wall, αὐλῆς, 9, 476. Od. 18, 102.

ἕρκος, εος, τό (εἴργω), 1) an enclosure, a hedge, a fence, for the protection of fields and gardens, 5, 90 ; and especially about the court of the dwelling, Od. 21, 238 ; hence the court, the front court, Od. 2) a cage, a net, a trap to take birds ; perhaps a fowling-floor, Od. 22, 489. 3) Metaph. a protection, a defence, spoken of the girdle and the shield : ἕρκος ἀκόντων, against javelins, 4, 137. 15, 646 ; βελέων, 5. 316 ; spoken even of persons, of Achilles and Ajax : ἕρκος πολέμοιο, bulwark of the war, 1, 284. 3, 229 ; like πύργος. Of frequent occurrence is the formula ποῖόν σε ἔπος φύγεν ἕρκος ὀδόντων! what a word has escaped the fence of thy teeth! and ἀμείψεται ἕρκος ὀδόντων, Od. 10, 328. Il. 9, 409. The old commentators, and with them Damm and others, understand by it the protection of the teeth, as a periphrasis for the lips ; others, as Wolf, Nitzsch, better, the teeth themselves, from their simi-larity to a palisade, see Nitzsch ad Od. 1, 64.

ἕρμα, ατος, τό. I) (From the root ἔρδω, ἐρέδω, ἐρείδω), any thing which contributes to the support or strengthening of a body, a prop, a stay, a post ; esply the shores upon which ships, when drawn out upon the land, rested, to prevent their rotting ; later φάλαγγες, 1, 486. 2, 154 ; metaph. spoken a) Of men : ἕρμα πόληος, the support, the pillar of the city, 16, 549. Od. 23, 121 ; and b) Spoken of a pointed arrow : μελαινέων ἕρμ᾽ ὀδυνάων, the prop [or, as the substratum] of black pangs, upon which the pangs, as it were, rested, 4, 117 (Voss, 'the fountain of dark tortures ;' Aristarchus rejects the verse).

II) (From εἴρω, to place in a row), only in the plur. ἕρματα, τά. every thing strung in a row, an ear-ring, a pendant, 14, 182. Od. 18, 297 (ἐνώτια, Schol.), cf. Buttm. Lex.

Ἑρμαῖος, η, ον, consecrated to Hermês ; hence ὁ Ἑρμαῖος λόφος, the hill of Hermês, in Ithaca, behind the city, on the mountain Neïon, Od. 16, 471.

Ἑρμῆς, Ep. Ἑρμείας, ὁ, gen. Ἑρμείαο, Ἑρμείω, 15, 214 ; and Ἑρμέω, h. Merc. 413 ; dat. Ἑρμῇ, Ep. Ἑρμείᾳ, Ἑρμέῃ (ed. Spitz. Ἑρμέᾳ), 5, 390, and Ἑρμείῃ, h. 18, 36 ; accus. Ἑρμῆν, Ep. Ἑρμείαν, voc. Ἑρμῆ, Ep. Ἑρμεία, Hermês (Mercurius), son of Zeus and Maia, according to Od. 8, 335. 14, 435. He is a messenger of the gods, together with Iris, supporting, however, more the character of a protector and mediator, 24, 334. Od. 5, 28 ; hence διάκτορος. As ensigns, he bore the golden-winged shoes, Od. 5, 45, and the magic rod, the caduceus, with which he closed in sleep the eyes of men and opened them again, v. 47 ; whence χρυσόρραπις. He is the bestower of blessings, of prosperity, and of wealth acquired by traffic, whence ἐριούνιος, ἀκάκητα, σῶκος, 14, 491. Od. 15, 319. On account of his wisdom and cunning he is called εὔσκοπος, and he protects wise and crafty men, Od. 19, 397. He is mentioned in Od. 24, 1, as guide of departed souls into the under world. In the Hom. hymn an account is given of his birth, the invention of the seven-stringed lyre, and his first theft of cattle. (Signif. according to Damm, from εἴρω, to speak, for ἐρέας, one who communicates ; more correctly, from εἴρω, perf. pass. ἕρμαι, to join : the mediator, the negotiator.)

Ἑρμιόνη, ἡ, 1) daughter of Menelaus and Helena ; according to H. she became the wife of Neoptolemus, to whom she was promised by Menelaus when before Troy. According to a later tradition, she was first betrothed to Orestês. He accordingly slew Neoptolemus and married Hermionê, Pind. 2) a town in Argolis, with a haven and a temple of Dêmêtêr, now Castri. It was supposed that there was an entrance from here to the infernal world, 2, 560. 'Ερμιών, όνος, ή, Scyl. Polyb.

ἑρμῖς or ἑρμῖν, ῖνος, ὁ (ἕρμα), a support; esply a bed-post, foot of the bedstead, *Od. 8, 278. 23, 198.

Ερμος, ὁ, Hermus, a river in Æolis (Asia), which rises in Phrygia, flows by Smyrna, and empties itself into the gulf of Smyrna between Temnos and Leuca; now Sarabad, 20, 392.

ἕρνος, εος, τό, a young scion, a shoot, a sprout, spoken of young trees which had run up to some height, 17, 53. Od. 6, 163; as a simile of Achilles, ἀνέδραμεν ἕρνεῖ ἶσος. 18, 56; Spoken of Telemachus, Od. 14, 175.

ἕρξω, see ἕρδω.

*ἑρόεις, εσσα, εν (ἔρος), lovely, amiable, h. Ven. 264. h. Merc. 31.

EPOMAI, Ep. form εἴρομαι, ἐρέομαι and ἐρέω; H. has only of the aor. ἠρόμην, subj. ἐρώμεθα, optat. ἔροιτο, and the infin. as pres. accented ἔρεσθαι (Att. ἐρέσθαι), to ask, τινά or τί, also with double accus., Od. 3, 243; and τινὰ περί τινος, any man concerning any man, Od. 1, 135. 405; ἀμφί τι, Od. 11, 572; ἀμφί τινι, Od. 19, 95.

ἔρος, ὁ, Ep. for ἔρως, q. v.

ἑρπετόν, τό (ἕρπω), in the Ep. language not merely that which creeps, but every thing which goes on feet, generally, a beast. ὅσσ' ἐπὶ γαῖαν ἑρπετὰ γίγνονται (Voss, 'every thing that lives and moves on the earth'), Od. 4, 418;† later, a creeping thing, a snake.

ἑρπύζω (from ἕρπω), to creep, to crawl, to move with difficulty, spoken of men who from trouble or great age crawl along, Od. 1, 193. 13, 220. Il. 23, 225.

ἕρπω, to creep, to crawl. εἷρπον ῥινοί, the skins crawled, spoken of a prodigy, Od. 12, 395; elsewhere, to creep about imperceptibly, Od. 17, 158. 2) Generally to go, to walk, to move, 17, 447. Od. 18, 131. h. Cer. 366.

ἐῤῥάδαται, see ῥαίνω.

ἔῤῥιγα, see ῥιγέω.

ἔῤῥω (kindred with ῥέω), fut. ἐῤῥήσω, h. Merc. 259. 1) to walk painfully, to walk unsteadily, to halt, spoken of the gait of Hêphæstus, 18, 421. 2) to go about sad or wretched, to wander around, Od. 4, 367. h. Merc. 259; esply to go or come to misfortune or injury, 8, 239. 9, 364. b) Often, to go to one's ruin, 9, 377; esply in the imperat. an expression of disgust: ἔῤῥε, go to ruin, away with thee, begone, 8, 164. Od. 10, 72. ἔῤῥετε, 24, 239.

ἔρση, ἡ, Ep. always ἐέρση (prob. fr. ἄρδω), dew, 23, 598. Od. 13, 245; plur. ἐέρσαι αἵματι μυδαλέαι, dew-drops, impregnated with blood, 11, 53. These bloody dew-drops, which were regarded as a token of divine anger, proceed from certain butterflies, which after emerging from the chrysalis state emit a bloody fluid, which appears, often in consider-

able quantities, upon leaves, plants, an fences, see Wilms. Naturgesch. 2. 646. 2) ἔρσαι, Od. 9, 222, new-born lamb

ἐρσήεις, εσσα, εν, Ep. ἐερσήεις, dew covered with dew. ἐρσήεις λωτός, l 348. b) Metaph. of a corpse: fresh, l. uncorrupted. ἐερσήεις κεῖται, 24, 41 ἐρσήεις, v. 757.

'Ερύαλος, ὁ, a Trojan, slain by Patrocl 16, 411. (Heyne from the Cdd. h 'Ερύλαος (from ἐρύω and λαός, deliver of the people), with whom agree Spi and Buttm. Lex. p. 286, since the lo α in 'Ερύαλος contravenes analogy).

ἐρύγμηλος, η, ον (ἐρυγεῖν), loud-bellowing, epith. of an ox, 18, 580.†

ἐρυγών, see ἐρεύγομαι.

ἐρυθαίνω, poet. for ἐρυθραίνω, to redde only mid. to make oneself red, to blu *10, 484. 21, 21.

'Ερυθαῖνοι, οἱ (ὑψηλοί), a town Paphlagonia, according to Eustath.; more correctly, with Strab., XII. p. 5 two hills on the sea, which in his tin from the red colour of the soil, we called 'Ερυθῖνοι, 2, 855.

'Ερύθραι, αἱ, an old town of Bœot on Cithæron, in the region of Platæa, the south bank of the Asôpus, 2, 4 According to Eustath. the Bœotian to should be written βαρυτόνως and t Ionian ὀξυτόνως; more correctly, ho ever, should both be written βαρυτόν to distinguish them from the adj. ἐρυθρό at present, we find 'Ερυθραί in H Thuc. etc.

ἐρυθρός, ή, όν, red, prop. dark-r οἶνος, Od.; νέκταρ, 19, 38; generally ruddy, χαλκός, 9, 365.

ἐρυκακέειν, ἐρύκακον, see ἐρύκω.

ἐρυκανάω, poet. form for ἐρύκω, hold back. κεῖνον ἐρυκανόωσι, Od. 199.†

ἐρυκάνω, poet. form for ἐρύκω, Od. 429.†

ἐρύκω (poet. forms ἐρυκάνω, ἐρυκανά fut. ἐρύξω, aor. 1 ἔρυξα, aor. 2 ἤρύκακ 5, 321. 20, 458; and ἐρύκακον, int ἐρυκακέειν, I) Act. to hold back, 1) hold, to restrain, ἐνὶ μεγάροισι γυναῖκ Od. 19, 16; esply spoken of guests, τι 6, 217. Od. 1, 14; to hold fast, πόν πολλοὺς ἐρύκει, 21, 39; γῆ, 21, 62. 2 check, to hold in, to restrain, ἵππ λαόν, 6, 80 (from flight); metaph. μεῖ to check one's force, 8, 178: θυμόν, restrain one's mind, i. e. will, Od. 105. ἕτερός με θυμὸς ἐρύκει, anot thought checks me, Od. 9, 302. 3 hold back, to keep off, to repel; with case 11, 352; τινά τινος, e. g. μά from battle, 18, 126; also τινί τι, t ἀλαλκεῖν; κακόν τινι, to avert evil fr any man, 15, 450; λιμόν τινι, Od. 5, 1 4) to hold back, i. e. to hold apart separate. ὀλίγος δ' ἔτι χῶρος ἐρύκει, 161. II) to hold oneself back, to del Od. 4, 373. 17, 17. μή μοι ἐρύκεσ delay not, 23, 443. b) With accus. delay any man, 12, 285.

Ἐρύλᾶος, ὁ, a Trojan, 16, 411. ed. Spitz. ; cf. Ἐρύαλος.

ἔρυμα, τό (ἐρύομαι), protection, defence, covering, χροός, spoken of the μίτρη, 4, 137.†

Ἐρύμανθος, ὁ, a mountain in Arcadia, on the borders of Elis, where Hêraclês slew the Erymanthian boar; now Xiria, Od. 6, 103.

Ἐρύμας, αντος, ὁ, 1) a Trojan, slain by Idomeneus, 16, 345. 2) a Trojan, slain by Patroclus, 16, 415 (the protector).

ἐρυσάρματος, ον (ἄρμα), chariot-drawing, epith. of horses, 15, 354. 16, 370; only in the metaplastic plur. ἐρυσάρματες, ἐρυσάρματας.

ἐρυσίπτολις, ι (πόλις), delivering the city, protecting the city, as epith. of Athênê, 6, 305.† h. 10, 1.

ἐρυσμός, ὁ (a form of ἔρυμα), a protection, h. Cer. 230.

ἐρύω and εἰρύω, Ion. and poet. fut. act. ἐρύσω (Ep. σσ) and ἐρύω (with σ elided); whence 3 plur. ἐρύουσι, 11, 454. 15, 351; aor. 1 act. ἔρυσα (Ep. σσ) and εἴρυσα, perf. pass. εἴρυμαι, whence 3 plur. εἰρύαται, 14, 75; pluperf. 3 plur. εἴρυατο, 15, 654; mid. fut. ἐρύσομαι, Ep. ἐρύομαι, aor. 1 mid. ἐρυσάμην (Ep. σσ) and εἰρυσάμην, pluperf. εἴρυτο, he had drawn, Od. 22, 90. H. also uses 1) From the form ΕΙΡΥΜΙ the mid. εἴρυμαι, ἔρυμαι, in the signif. to deliver, to protect, in single forms: 3 plur. pres. εἰρύαται for εἴρυνται, 1, 239; εἰρύαται, Od. 16, 463; imperf. εἴρυντο, 12, 454. 2) The forms with ῡ in the pres. and imperf. infin. ἐρύσθαι, εἴρυσθαι, ἔρυσο, ἔρυτο, and ῥῦτο. are to be regarded as contracted forms from ἐρύομαι; εἰρύαται is long by the arsis, as ἐρύετο, 6, 403. In the signif. of the aor. stands ἔρυτο, 5, 23. 538; cf. Rost's Gram. p. 302. Kühner, § 235 (ἐρύω has always ῡ short; only in the contr. imperf. ῡ). (The form ῥύομαι always signifies to deliver.) 1) Act. 1) to draw, more closely defired by prepos. or adv. with accus. πάλιν ἐρύειν τινά, to draw a man back, 5, 836; ὀϊστὸν ἐξ ὤμοιο, 5, 110; νευρὴν ἐπί τινι, to draw the string (of the bow) against any man, 15, 464; esply νῆα εἰς ἅλα, 1, 141; on the other hand, ἤπειρόνδε, Od. 10, 403; ἐπ' ἠπείροιο, the ship upon land (to guard it against rotting), Od. 16, 359; pass. νῆες εἰρύαται ἐπὶ θινί, the ships are drawn up on the sea-shore, 4, 248. 14, 75. ὀδὸν εἰρύαται, according to the Schol. are drawn up upon the way, Od. 6, 265; cf. below, 3 b. 2) to draw with violence, hence a) to snatch, to tear away, ἔγχος ἐκ χειρός, 13, 598; ῥινὸν ἀπ' ὀστεόφιν, Od. 14, 134; κρόσσας πύργων, 12, 258; προκρόσσας, 14, 35; esply νεκρὸν ἐρύειν, sometimes, to snatch away the dead body, spoken of the friends of the slain, to save it from abuse, 5, 573. 17, 581; sometimes spoken of enemies, to tear away the dead body, to plunder or insult it, 17, 230. 419. 18, 450. b) to draw, to

drag, τινὰ ποδός, Od. 17, 479; περὶ σῆμα, 24, 16; hence spoken of dogs: τινὰ πρὸ ἄστεος, any man before the city, 11, 454. 15, 351. II) Mid. 1) to draw, to draw off, to draw out, always with reference to the subject, to oneself, after or for oneself; μάχαιραν, to draw one's knife, 3, 271; φάσγανον. ξίφος; δόρυ ἐξ ὠτειλῆς, 21, 200; τόξον, to stretch the bow, in order to shoot, Od. 21, 125; νῆας, 14, 79. Od. 9, 194. ἐρύσατό τε πάντα, they drew all off (from the ships, in order to eat), 1, 466, etc. 2) to draw to oneself, with violence; τινὰ μάχης, to snatch any man out of the battle, 5, 456; νεκρόν τινι, the dead, like the act., 17, 104. 18, 152. 14, 422. 18, 174; hence 3) to snatch away, viz. from danger, to deliver, to rescue, τινά, spoken of Apollo, who rescued Æneas from the enemy, 5, 344. 11, 363. Od. 22, 372. χρυσῷ ἐρύσασθαί τινα, to free for gold, to ransom, 22, 351 (the signif. of the Schol. 'to weigh,' is not necessary), hence, in general, a) to deliver, to shelter, to protect, ἔρυτο, 4, 186. ἐρύετο Ἴλιον, 6, 403. Λυκίην εἴρυντο, 16, 542. πύλας εἴρυντο, 12, 454. b) to ward off, to restrain, to repel, to obstruct; Κῆρα, 2, 859. ἥ (μίτρη) οἱ πλεῖστον ἔρυτο, which most effectually kept off from him (the spear), 4, 138. 5, 538. ὀδὸν εἰρύαται, they obstruct the way, Voss, Od. 6, 265. Metaph. Διὸς νόον, to restrain the will of Zeus, 8, 143; χόλον, to check anger, 24, 584. c) to draw any thing to oneself for preservation, protection, etc. to guard, to keep, to protect, to watch, θύρας, Od. 23, 229; ἄκοιτιν, Od. 3, 268. ἔτι μ' αὖτ' εἰρύαται, they watch me still (Telemachus, of the suitors), Od. 16, 463; metaph. φρεσὶν ἐρύεσθαί τι, to keep any thing in the heart, Od. 16, 459; to spy out, to explore, δήνεα θεῶν, Od. 23, 82. οἵτε θέμιστας πρὸς Διὸς εἰρύαται, who guard the laws from Zeus [i. e. received from Zeus], or with authority derived from Zeus], 1, 239. d) to observe, to follow, ἔπος, βουλάς, 1, 216. 21, 230.

ἔρχαται, ἔρχατο, see ἔργω.

ἐρχατάω, poet. form from εἴργω, to enclose, to hem in; only in the pass. σύες ἐρχατόωντο. Od. 14, 15.†

ἐρχθείς, see ἔργω.

ἔρχομαι, depon. defect. fut. ἐλεύσομαι, aor. ἦλθον, Ep. ἤλυθον, infin. ἐλθεῖν, Ep. ἐλθέμεναι, perf. Ep. εἰλήλουθα, 1 plur. εἰλήλουθμεν, 9, 49; partcp. εἰληλουθώς, ἐληλουθώς, 15, 81.† 1) to come, to go, and according to the context and the connected prep. and adv. to arrive, to go away, to come back, αὖτις, ἂψ, πάλιν ἐλθεῖν, 1, 425. a) Spoken of animate beings: of men and brutes; metaph. also of other motion: by ship, 13, 172. ἐπὶ πόντον ἔρχεσθαι, to go upon the sea, Od. 2, 265; to voyage, of ships, Od. 14, 334; hence, on the other hand, πεζὸς ἦλθε, he came on foot, by land, 5, 204. 17, 613; spoken of the flight of birds and bees, 2, 88. b) Spoken of inanimate

I

things : of the dead, 17, 161 ; of natural phenomena, 9, 6. 4, 276 ; of the change of time : ἦλθε κνέφας, φάος ἦλθε, 8, 500. 17, 615 ; θέρος, Od. 11, 192 ; of other objects : γέρας ἔρχεται ἄλλη, the reward goes elsewhere, 1, 120 ; esply of missiles, 7, 261 ; διὰ ἀσπίδος, 3, 357 ; metaph. of the state of the body and soul : κακὸν ἦλθε, θάνατος, 15, 450. Od. 13, 60 ; τὸν δ' αἶψα περὶ φρένας ἤλυθ' ἰωή, the voice reached his sense or intellect : made itself audible, 10, 139 ; ὀδύνη διὰ χροὸς ἦλθε, 11, 398 ; ἄχος ἀπὸ πραπίδων ἦλθε, 22, 43. 2) It is construed a) With the accus. of the place whither : κλισίην, in to the tent, 1, 322 ; εἰς κλισίην. b) With accus. of nearer specification : ὁδὸν ἐλθεῖν, to go a way, a journey, Od. 3, 316 ; and spoken of those who lie in ambuscade, 1, 151 ; according to some, "to go on a (military) expedition" (so Näg.); αὐτὰ κέλευθα, to go the same ways, 12, 225. cf. Od. 9, 262; ἀγγελίην ἐλθεῖν, to go on an embassy, 11, 140 ; see ἀγγελίη. ἐξεσίην, 24, 235. c) With gen. of place : πεδίοιο, to go through the plain, 2, 801. d) With partcp. α) Fut. which indicates the purpose : ἔρχομαι ἔγχος οἰσόμενος, I go to bring the spear, 13, 256. β) With pres. partcp. or perf. which expresses the manner of coming : ἦλθε θέουσα, she came running, 11, 715 ; ἦλθε φθάμενος, 23, 779. αἴ κεν νέκυς ῃσχυμμένος ἔλθῃ, if the corpse come back disfigured, 18, 180. γ) The partcp. ἐλθών seems to be often used pleonastically, although it serves more completely to present the action : οὐ δύναμαι— μάχεσθαι ἐλθὼν δυσμενέεσσιν, I cannot go and fight with the enemy, 16, 521.

ἔρῳ, for ἔρωτι, see ἔρως.

ἔρῳ, Ep. ἐρέω, see εἴρω.

ἐρῳδιός, ὁ, the common heron, ardea major, Linn., which builds its nest in marshes and sea-rushes. Köppen incorrectly supposes it to be the bittern, ardea stellaris, 10, 274.† It appears on the right (δεξιός), as ominous of good, and according to the Schol. was, especially for those who desired to execute some stratagem, a fortunate sign. Odysseus (Ulysses) and Diomêdês on their nocturnal visit as spies to the Trojan camp, could not see it, but only heard it, hence they concluded the enemy could not see themselves.

ἐρωέω (root ῥέω), fut. ἐρωήσω, aor. ἠρώησα, 1) to flow, to stream, to gush out. αἷμα περὶ δουρὶ ἐρωήσει, 1, 303. Od. 16, 441 ; metaph. of any violent motion, hence : 2) to leap, to run, αἱ (the steeds) δ' ἠρώησαν ὀπίσσω, they ran back, 23, 433. 3) to hasten back, to cease, with gen. πολέμοιο, χάρμης, to cease from battle, 13, 776. 14, 101. 17, 422, h. Cer. 302 ; also absol. to retire, to withdraw. νέφος οὔποτ' ἐρωεῖ, the cloud never retires, Od. 12, 75 ; to loiter, to tarry, 2, 179. 3) Once trans. to cause to retire, to repulse, τινὰ ἀπὸ νηῶν, 13, 57.

ἐρωή, ἡ, 1) any vehement motion, impulse, impetus, force, rushing, esply spoke[of missiles : βελέων ἐρωή, the invasion [the dint, Cp.] of weapons, 4, 542. 17 562 ; δούρατος, 11, 357 ; ὅσον τ' ἐπὶ δουρὸς ἐρωὴ γίνεται, as far as the cast of a spear extends, 15, 358. λείπετο δουρὸς ἐρωήν a spear's cast off, 23, 529. b) Metaph of men : ὀφέλλει ἀνδρὸς ἐρωήν, the ax augments the power of the man, 3, 62 λικμητῆρος, 13, 590. cf. 14, 488. 2) retrea cessation, rest, πολέμου, ‑16, 302. 17, 761

ἔρως. ωτος, ὁ, poet. ἔρος. Of the poet form H. has ἔρος, ἔρῳ (more correctl ἔρῳ), Od. 18, 212 ; accus. ἔρον. Th nom. ἔρως stands only in two passages where position occurs, 3, 442. 14, 94 gen. ἔρωτος, Batr. 78 ; accus. ἔρωτα, h Merc. 449 ; love, θεᾶς, to a goddess, 14 315. Od. 18, 212 ; and generally, desire longing, appetite, πόσιος καὶ ἐδητύος, 9 92 ; γόου, 24, 227.

ἐρωτάω, Ion. and Ep. εἰρωτάω, 1 ask ; hence imperf. ἠρώτα, Od. 15, 423.†

ἐς, Ep. and Ion. for εἰς, q. v. Also fo the compounds beginning with ἐς, se under εἰς.

ἐσαγείρατο, see εἰσαγείρω.

ἐσάγω, ἐσαθρέω, see εἰσάγω, etc.

ἐσᾶλτο, see εἰσάλλομαι.

ἐσάντα, see εἰσάντα.

ἔσβη, see σβέννυμι.

ἐσδύσεαι, see εἰσδύω.

ἐσέδρακον, see εἰσδέρκομαι.

ἐσελεύσομαι, see εἰσέρχομαι.

ἐσεμάσσατο, see εἰσμαίομαι.

ἐσέχυντο, see εἰσχέω.

ἐσῆλθεν, see εἰσάλλομαι.

ἐσθήν, see ἕννυμι.

ἐσθής, ῆτος, ἡ (ἕννυμι), a garment, robe, a dress, Od. 1, 165 ; mly colle clothing. 2) cloth, carpeting, used for bed, Od. 23, 290 (with digamma : restit

ἐσθίω, Ep. ἔσθω and ἔδω, only in t pres. and infin. ἤσθιε, ἤσθε, to eat, consume, with accus. metaph. πάντας π ἐσθίει (devours them all), 23, 182. οἶ ἐσθίεται, the house, i. e. the property being consumed, Od. 4, 318.

ἐσθλός, ή, όν, like ἀγαθός, good, valor ous, brave, noble, excellent in its kin a) Spoken of men and of every thi which concerns them : θηρητήρ, an e cellent hunter, 5, 51 ; ἐν τινι, 15, 2 Esply in Il. a) Spoken of excellence war, brave, in opposition to κακός, 2, 3 5, 469. β) noble, of good descent, Od. 553. b) Of things : φάρμακα, heali medicines, Od. 4, 228 ; τεύχεα, κτήμα etc. c) good, favorable, propitious, νηός, Od. 24, 311. 2) As subst. ἐσθλοί, the noble, the distinguished, ofte τὸ ἐσθλόν, good fortune, prosperity, opposition to κακόν, 24, 530 ; τὰ ἐσθ prosperity, Od. 20, 86 ; possessions, va ables, Od. 10, 523.

ἔσθος, εος, τό (poet. for ἐσθής), a g ment, cloth, 24, 94.

ἔσθω, poet form from ἐσθίω, to eat consume, mly of men, Od. 9, 479 ;

brutes, Od. 13, 409; metaph. κειμήλια, Od. 2, 73.

ἐσιδεῖν, see εἰσεῖδον.

ἐσιέμεναι, see εἰσίημι.

ἐσίζηται, see εἰσίζομαι.

ἔσκον, see εἰμί.

ἐσόψομαι, see εἰσοράω.

ἐσπέριος, η, ον (ἕσπερος), 1) Spoken of the time of day: belonging to the evening, at evening, Od. 2, 357; ἑσπέριος ἀπονεοίμην, 21, 560. 2) Of a point of the compass: western, belonging to the west, ἑσπέριοι ἄνθρωποι, Od. 8, 29.

ἕσπερος, ὁ, plur. τὰ ἕσπερα, Od. 17, 191; the evening hours, vesper, the evening, μέλας, Od. 1, 423. 4, 786. 2) Adj. belonging to evening, h. 18, 14; esply ὁ ἑσπερος ἀστήρ, the evening star, 22, 318 (with digamma).

ἔσπετε, Ep. imperat. for εἴπατε, a poet. form with epenthetic σ, four times in the Iliad, only in the constr. ἔσπετε νῦν μοι Μοῦσαι, see εἶπον.

ἑσπόμην, see ἕπομαι.

ἔσσα, ἔσσαι, ἐσσάμενος, see ἕννυμι.

ἐσσεῖται, see εἰμί.

ἐσσεύοντο, see σεύω.

ἐσσί, see εἰμί.

ἔσσο, see ἕννυμι.

ἔσσυμαι, see σεύω.

ἐσσύμενος, prop. partcp. perf. pass. from σεύω, as adj. hasty, rapid, precipitate, from which adv. ἐσσυμένως, hastily, quickly, rapidly, 3, 85; and Od. see σεύω.

ἑστάμεν, ἑστάμεναι, see ἵστημι.

ἔσταμεν, see ἵστημι.

ἕσταν, see ἵστημι.

ἕστασαν, 3 plur. pluperf., but ἔστασαν for ἕστησαν, see ἵστημι.

ἕστηκα, ἑστήκειν, see ἵστημι.

ἕστο, see ἕννυμι.

ἕστρωτο, see στρώννυμι.

ἕστωρ, ορος, ὁ, the shaft-pin, the pin or nail at the end of the pole, over which a ring (κρίκος) was put. Through this ring the yoke-straps were made fast, 24, 272.† (Prob. from ἵημι, ἀπὸ τοῦ ἕσται.)

ἐσχάρη, ἡ, Ep. ἐσχαρόφιν for ἐσχάρης, ἐσχάρῃ, Od. 5, 59. 7, 169; 1) the hearth, the house-hearth (a fire-place on the earth), primarily for affording warmth; hence Penelopē worked by it with her maidens, Od. 6, 305. b) the place for sacrificing, Od. 14, 420; hence suppliants sought refuge in it, hence: καθέζετο ἐπ᾽ ἐσχάρῃ ἐν κονίῃσι πὰρ πυρί, he seated himself on the hearth in the dust by the fire, Od. 7, 153; cf. v. 169. Dat. ἐπ᾽ ἐσχαρόφιν, Od. 19, 389. 2) any fireplace. ὅσσαι Τρώων πυρὸς ἐσχάραι, as many fire-places as are in the camp of the Trojans, 10, 418 (perhaps more correctly: as many fire-hearths as there are of Trojans, i. e. as many Trojan h⁃ads of families).

ἐσχατάω (ἔσχατος), to be last, to be at the end, only partcp. pres. ἐσχατόων, ὦσα, Ep. for ἐσχατῶν, ὦσα. δηΐων

ἐσχατόων, last man of the enemy, i. e. one in the rear, 10, 206; also spoken of cities (a frontier town), *2, 508. 616. (According to Buttm. the correct form is ἐσχατόω.)

ἐσχατιή, ἡ, 1) the extremity. a) the limit, the border, the end of a place, νήσου, λιμένος, Od. 2, 391. 5, 238; Φθίης, the borders of Phthia, 9, 484. ἐσχατιὴ πολέμοιο, the end of the battle, the extreme limb of the action, either the extremity of the wing or the rear. 11, 524. 20, 328. b) Spoken of a place remote from a town, esply lying on the sea, Od. 14. 104. 2) the most remote part, thus ἀγροῦ, Od. 4, 517. 5, 489.

ἔσχατος, η, ον (prob. from ἔχω, ἔσχον), the extreme, the last, the most remote, spoken only of place: ἔσχατοι ἄλλων, 10, 434; and ἔσχατοι ἀνδρῶν, thus H. calls the Ethiopians, because they were conceived of as dwelling at the extremity of the earth's surface, Od. 1, 23. Neut. plur. as adv. ἔσχατα, at the end, 8, 225.

ἐσχατόω, see ἐσχατάω.

ἔσχον, ἐσχόμην, see ἔχω.

ἔσω, see εἴσω.

*ἑταιρεῖος, η, ον, as a friend, belonging to friendship. 2) intimate, φιλότης, h. Merc. 58.

ἑταίρη, ἡ, Ep. and Ion. ἑτάρη, only 4, 441; a female companion, a female friend, a mistress. metaph. spoken of flight: φόβου ἑταίρη. 9, 2; and of the lyre, δαιτὶ ἑταίρη, Od. 17, 271. h. Merc. 478.

ἑταιρίζω. Ep. ἑταρίζω (ἑταῖρος), aor. 1 ἑταίρισα, Ep. σσ, aor. 1 mid only optat. ἑταρίσσαιτο, to join or associate oneself with any man, to be a companion, τινί, 24, 335. h. Ven. 46. Mid. to make any man a companion for oneself, to take as an associate, τινά, 13, 456.

ἑταῖρος, ὁ, Ep. and Ion. ἕταρος, a companion, an associate, an assistant, a helper, a comrade, spoken generally of associates in war and travel, 1, 179. Od. 1, 5; with dat., 18, 251: prop. adj. hence: ἑταῖρος ἀνήρ, Od. 8, 584; metaph. a favorable wind is called ἐσθλὸς ἑταῖρος, a good companion, Od. 11, 7. 12, 149 (both forms used according to the necessities of the metre, prob. ἕτης, akin to ἕτερος).

ἑτάρη, ἡ and ἕταρος, ὁ, see ἑταίρη, ἑταῖρος.

ἐτεθήπεα, see ΘΑΦΩ.

Ἐτεοκλῆς, έους, Ep. ῆος, son of Œdipus and Epicastē (in H. not Iocastē), who agreed with his brother Polynīces, that they should reign alternately, each a year. Eteocles did not fulfil this covenant; hence arose the Theban war. For Tydeus, who came to him as an ambassador of Polynices, he laid an ambuscade, 4, 375; whence the adj. Ἐτεοκλήειος, η, ον, Eteoclean, βίη Ἐτεοκληείη, the power of Eteocles, see βίη. 4, 386.

Ἐτεόκρητες, οἱ (from ἐτεός and Κρής, true Cretans), the Eteocretans (native

Cretans, Voss), one of the five tribes in Crete. They were the aboriginal inhabitants of the island, and not of Hellenian derivation. According to Strab. they lived in the south; their chief city was Prasus, Od. 19, 176.

ἐτεός, ή, όν, *true, real*, as adj. νεικεῖν πόλλ' ἐτεά, to utter many true reproaches 20, 255; elsewhere only the neut. sing. as adv. 1) *true, agreeable to truth*, μαντεύεσθαι. 2, 300; (Hesych. ἀληθὲς) ἀγορεύειν, 15, 53. 2) *in truth, in reality*, and often in the Od. εἰ ἐτεόν γε, if indeed really, Od. Ϟ 122.

ἐτεραλκής, ές (ἀλκή), *in which the strength or power is attached to one of two parties; decisive* (ἑτεροκλινής). Δαναοῖσι μάχης ἑτεραλκέα νίκην δοῦναι, to give a decisive victory in battle to the Greeks (Voss, 'an alternating victory;' Köppen, 'shifting'), 7, 26. 8, 171. Od. 22, 236. δῆμος ἑτεραλκής, a decisive body, a superior force, i. e. which gives new courage to the others, 15, 738 (Voss, *changeful*).

ἐτερήμερος, ον (ἡμέρη), *changing with the day*. ζώουσ' ἑτερήμεροι, they live on alternate days. spoken of Kastôr and Polydeukês (Castor and Pollux), Od. 11, 303.†

ἕτερος, η, ον, ἑτέρηφι, Ep. dat. fem. 1) *the other, one of two*, alter, 5, 258. 288; plur. ἕτεροι, *the one part*, alterutri, 20, 210. 7, 292. 378. In correlative clauses we have ἕτερος μέν, ἕτερος δέ, or ἄλλος, ἕτερος, 13, 731; also ὁ μέν, ἕτερος δέ, 22, 151; sometimes the first ἕτερος is wanting. 7, 420. 24, 528. ἑτέρῃ χειρί, with one hand, or ἑτέρῃ or ἑτέρηφιν alone, according to the connexion, with the right or left, 12, 452. 16, 734 *b*) In counting, *the second*, instead of δεύτερος. 16, 179; ἕτεροι δέ, 7, 420. 2) *the other, alius*, opposed to many, like ἄλλος; ἕτερα ἅρματα. sc. those of *the enemy*, 4, 306; ἕτερος, ἄλλος, 9, 313; ἕτεραι, ἄλλαι, Od. 9, 124.

ἑτέρσετο, see τερσαίνω.

ἑτέρωθεν, adv. *from the other side*, ἐπιάχειν, 13, 835. 2) Poet. for ἑτέραθι, *on the other side, opposite*, 3, 230. 6, 247. h. Merc. 366.

ἑτέρωθι, adv. *on the other side, elsewhere*, Od. 4, 531. Il. 5, 351; ἔνθεν—ἑτέρωθι, Od. 12, 235.

ἑτέρως. adv. *in another manner, otherwise*. νῦν δ' ἑτέρως ἐβάλοντο θεοί, Od. 1, 234.† H. has elsewhere only ἑτέρωσε, hence Spitz. de vers. heroic. p. 97 [and Observ. in Quint. Smyrn. p. 63], would read ἑτέρωσ', cf. βάλλω.

ἑτέρωσε, adv. *to another side, elsewhere, away*; νέκυν ἐρύειν, 4, 492; cf. 23, 231. ἑτέρωσε κάρη βάλλειν, 8, 306; φοβεῖσθαι, Od. 16, 163.

ἐτέταλτο, see ἐπιτέλλω.

ἐτετεύχατο, see τεύχω.

ἔτετμον, see ΤΕΜΩ.

ἐτέτυκτο, see τεύχω.

Ἐτεωνεύς, ῆος, ὁ, son of Boêthous,

servant of Menelaus (θεράπων), Od. 4 22. 15, 95. According to the Schol. h was a relative of Menelaus, his fathe being son of Argēus, and grandson o Pelops. (Eustath. signif. ὃν ἀληθεύει χρή.)

Ἐτεωνός, ὁ, a town in Bœotia, on the Ἀσθπις, afterwards called, according to Strab., Σκάρφη, 2, 497.

ἔτης, ον, ὁ, only plur. *an acquaintance a friend, a dependant*, always distin guished from relatives by blood or nea kindred (ἑταῖροι, συνήθεις, App.), m κασίγνητοί τε ἔται τε, 6, 239. Od. 15, 27 ἔται καὶ ἀνεψιοί, 9, 464. ἔται καὶ ἑταῖρο 7, 295. Nitzsch, ad Od. 4, 3, understand the *descendants* or rather *the retainer of the house* (prob. from ἔθος or ἐτό ἐτεός).

ἐτήτυμος, ον (Ep. lengthened fr. ἔτυμος *true, real, pure, genuine, μῦθος, νόστο Od. 3, 241. 23, 62. Esply the neut. adv. ἐτήτυμον, *truly, really*, κείνου ὁ υἱὸς ἐτήτυμον, he is really his son, Od. 157.

ἔτι, adv. 1) Spoken of the present *still, even*, ἔτι καὶ νῦν, even now sti 1, 455. 2) Spoken of the future: ye *still further, for the future*, 1, 96. Od. 756. Often with the negat. οὐδ' ἔτι δ ἦν, and he lived not much longer, 139. Od. 2, 63. 3) Enhancing the signi with a compar. ἔτι μᾶλλον, still more, 97. [Spoken also of past time, 2, 28 Od. 4, 736; *yet, even, when*]; (from ε εἰμί, to be, cf. Thiersch, § 198, 4; 7 the arsis, 6, 139.)

ἔτλην, see τλῆναι.

ἑτοιμάζω (ἕτοιμος), fut. άσω, Ep. σ *to make ready, to prepare, to give at on γέρας, 1, 118. 19, 197. Mid. = act. ἱ Ἀθήνη, to present a victim to Athên 10, 571; ταύρους, Od. 13, 184.

ἕτοιμος, η, ον, Att. ἕτοιμος, *ready, p pared*, hence, 1) *real, accomplish plain*. ἦ δὴ ταῦτα ἑτοῖμα τετεύχατ these things indeed have really happe ed, i. e. are accomplished, 14, 53. ἄρ' ἑτοῖμα τέτυκτο, this was plain, so, Od. 8, 384. *b*) that can be execut *suitable, salutary*, μῆτις, 9, 425. 2) *ready, prepared, in readiness*, ὀνεία 9, 91. αὐτίκα γάρ τοι ἔπειτα μεθ' Ἐκτ πότμος ἑτοῖμος, decided, appointed, 96 (prob. from ἐτός).

ἔτορον, see τορέω.

ἔτος, εος, τό, *a year, distingui* from ἐνιαυτός, Od. 1, 16; in plur. 328. 11, 691.

ἔτραπον, see τρέπω.

ἐτράφην, ἔτραφον, see τρέφω.

ἔτυμος, η, ον (ἐτεός), *true, pure, gen* only neut. plur. ἔτυμα, *truth*, in opposi to ψεύδεα, Od. 19, 203. 567. The sing. ἔτυμον, as adv. *truly, agreeab truth*, 10, 534. Od. 4, 140. 157. *truth, really*, like ἐτεόν, 23, 440. Od 26.

ἐτώσιος, ον (ἐτός, *frustra*), *vain effectual*. πάντα ἐτώσια τιθέναι, Od

256; hence: *profitless, idle*, ἄχθος, 18, 104. Esply neut. sing. as adv. *vainly*, *idly*, 3, 368. 14, 407.

εὖ and Ep. ἐΰ. before two consonants, so that υ becomes long, adv. (prop. neut. from ἐΰς), *well, rightly, properly*. εὖ ἔρδειν, 5, 650; εὖ εἰπεῖν τινα, to *speak well of*, Od. 1, 302; esply with the notion: *skilfully, dexterously*, εὖ καὶ ἐπισταμένως, 10, 265; εὖ κρίνασθαι, Od. 4, 480. 2) *happily, fortunately*. εὖ οἴκαδ᾽ ἱκέσθαι, 1, 19. Od. 3, 188. 3) Strengthening, as εὖ μάλα. *very, exceedingly*; with numerals: εὖ πάντες, *all together*, Od. 4, 294. (On the separation of the εὖ, see Thiersch, § 170, 7, 8, 9; Herm. ad h. Ap. 36.)

εὖ, Ion. and Ep. for οὗ. q. v.

εὐαγγέλιον, τό (ἄγγελος), *a present for a good message, a reward for joyful news*, *Od. 14, 152. 166.

*εὐαγέως, poet. for εὐαγῶς (εὐαγής), *purely, holily*, h. Cer. 275. 370.

εὐάδε, see ἀνδάνω.

Εὐαιμονίδης, αο, ὁ, son of Euæmon = Eurypylus, 5, 76.

Εὐαίμων, ονος, ὁ, son of Ormenus, father of Eurypylus, brother of Amyntor, and great-grandson of Æolus, 2, 736.

εὐανθής, ές (ἄνθος), *very blooming, luxuriant*, λάχνη, Od. 11, 320;† χοροί, h. 30, 14.

Εὐάνθης, εος, ὁ, father of Maron, Od. 9, 197.

Εὔβοια, ἡ, *Eubœa*, an island of the Ægean sea, separated by the Euripus from Bœotia, now *Negroponte*. H. calls its inhabitants Abantes. It derived its name, according to the mythographers, from *Eubœa*, daughter of Asôpus, or rather, from its good pastures for cattle (εὖ βοῦς), 2, 535. Od. 3, 174.

εὔβοτος, ον (βόσκω), *having good pastures, good for pasturing*, Συρίη, Od. 15, 406.†

*εὔβους, ουν (βοῦς), *abounding in cattle*, accus. εὔβουν, Herm. εὔβων, h. Ap. 54.

εὐγένειος, ον, Ep. ἠϋγένειος, *having a long beard, long maned* (Cp), λίς, λέων, only in the Ep. form, Il., Od. 4, 456.

εὐγενής, ές, Ep. ἠϋγενής and εὐηγενής (γένος), *nobly born, of good extraction*, *11, 427. 23. 81. In H. always εὐηγενής with η epenthetic, see Thiersch, § 166, 4; ἠϋγενής, only h. Ven. 94.

εὖγμα, ατος. τό (εὔχομαι), *boast*. κενὰ εὔγματα, Od. 22, 249.†

εὔγναμπτος, ον, Ep. ἐϋγναμπτος (γναμπτός), *well, beautifully bent*, in Ep. form; ἐλικαἰ δες. Od. 18, 294.†

*εὐδαιμονίη, ἡ (δαίμων), *happiness, good fortune, felicity*, h. 10, 5.†

εὐδείελος, ον, epith. of Ithaca and of islands generally, most prob. signifying: *very plain, widely visible, conspicuous* (εὐπερίορπτος, App. Schol.), from δῆλος, resolved δέελος and δείελος, because islands, being bounded by the sea, stand out clearly to view; esply spoken of Ithaca, on account of its high shores,

*Od. 2, 167. 9, 21. 13, 212; of islands, Od. 13, 234; and Κρίση, h. Ap. 438. Thus Passow and Nitzsch ad Od. 9, 21. We have also the following derivations: 1) *situated in the west, western*, from δείλη, *evening*, but in the first place this word does not occur in the signif. *west*, and in the next place it is applicable, at the most, only to Ithaca, not to all islands. 2) *Exposed to the afternoon heat, sunny* (thus Voss in several places), from εὖ and εἴλη with δ inserted, cf. Eustath. ad Od. 9, 21. 3) *beautifully lighted, lying in the evening light*, according to Schol. ad Od 9, 21, from δείελος is far-fetched, see Buttm. Lex. p. 224.

εὐδικίη, ἡ (δίκη), *uprightness, the practice of uprightness*; in the plur. εὐδικίας ἀνέχειν, *to exercise justice*, prop. acts of justice [to maintain justice. Cp.], Od. 19, 111.†

εὔδμητος, ον, Ep. ἐΰδμητος (δέμω), *well-built, beautifully built*, always in the Ep. form, except Od. 20, 302.

εὕδω, fut. εὑδήσω, aor. 1 εὕδησα, 1) to *sleep, to go to sleep*, with the accus. γλυκὺν ὕπνον εὕδειν, to enjoy sweet sleep, Od. 8, 445; spoken of death, 15, 482. 2) Metaph. *to rest, to cease*, spoken of the wind, 5, 524 (kindr. with ᾽ΑΩ, ΑΥΩ).

Εὔδωρος, ὁ, son of Hermês and Polymêlê, was educated by his grandfather Phylas, king of Ephyra in Thesprotia; one of the five leaders of the Myrmidons, 16, 179, see.: see Πολυμήλη.

εὐειδής, ές (εἶδος), *of handsome form, having a beautiful figure, beauteous*, γυνή, 3, 48.†

εὐεργεσίη, ἡ (εὐεργής), *good, noble conduct*, Od. 22, 374: in opposition to κακοεργίη. 2) *beneficence, kindness*; plur. εὐεργεσίας ἀποτίνειν, to requite benefits, *Od. 22, 235.

εὐεργής, ές (ἔργον), 1) Mly *well-wrought, beautifully built*, δίφρος, νηῦς, Il.; λώπη, Od. 13, 224; χρυσός, well-wrought gold, Od. 9, 202. 2) *well-done*, hence plur. εὐεργέα, benefits, Od. 4, 695. 22, 319.

εὐεργός, όν (ἔργον), *nobly acting, excellent*. καὶ ἢ κ᾽ εὐεργὸς ἔῃσιν, *Od. 11, 434. 15, 422.

εὐερκής, ές (ἕρκος), *well-fenced, well-enclosed, well guarded*, αὐλή, 9, 472; θύραι, Od. 17, 267.

εὔζυγος, ον, Ep. ἐΰζυγος (ζυγός), *well yoked*, in H. spoken of ships: *having beautiful rowers' seats, well-furnished with rowers* = εὐήρετμος, *Od. 13, 116. 17, 288; others interpret, *well-planked; strong-built* (only in the Ep. form).

εὔζωνος, ον, Ep. ἐΰζωνος (ζώνη), *having a beautiful girdle, well-girded*, epith. of noble women, because the girdle about the breast gave a graceful form to the robe, 1, 429, and h. Cer.

εὐηγενής, ές, Ep. for εὐγενής, q. v.

εὐηγεσίη. ἡ (ἡγέομαι), *happy rule, good government*, Od. 19, 114.†

I 3

εὐηκής, ές (ἀκή), well-pointed, very sharp, αἰχμή, 22, 319 †

Εὐηνίνη, ἡ, daughter of Evênus = Marpessa, 9, 557.

Εὐηνορίδης, ᾳυ, ὁ. son of Evenor = Leocritus, Od. 22, 294.

Εὔηνος, ὁ (= εὐήνιος, gentle), Evenus, 1) son of Arês and Dêmonīcê, king of Ætolia, father of Marpessa. When Idas, son of Aphareus, bore off his daughter, he pursued him to the river Lycormas. and, as he could not overtake them, he plunged into it, and it received from him the name Evenus. Apollo likewise loved Marpessa, and wrested her from Idas, in the city Arenê in Messenia. Idas fought with him for her; Zeus at length separated them ; and upon the free choice which he granted her, Marpessa chose Idas, 9, 557. 2) son of Selepius, king of Lyrnessus, father of Mynes and Epistrophus, 2, 693.

εὐήνωρ, ορος, ὁ, ἡ (ἀνήρ), prop. manly, in H. an epithet of wine and of iron ; strengthening the courage. or invigorating men, *Od. 4, 622. 13, 19 ; or befitting a man, heart-ennobling [Cp.] (Voss, ' the spirit-strengthening wine and the man-ennobling brass ').

Εὐήνωρ, ορος, ὁ, father of Leocritus, Od. q. v.

εὐήρης, ες (ἄρω), well-joined, well-fitted, easy to handle or use, epith of an oar, *Od. 11, 121 [smooth-shaven. Cp.] (The derivation from ἐρέσσω is incorrect.)

*εὐήρυτος, ον (ἀρύω), easy to draw, ὕδωρ, h. in Cer. 106.

*εὐθαρσής, ές (θάρσος), of good courage, resolute, bold, h. 7, 9.

*εὐθέμεθλος, ον, Ep. ηὐθέμεθλος, well-founded, γαῖα, h. 30, 1.†

*εὐθηνέω, to be in a flourishing condition, vigere ; to abound in, to be rich, with dat. κτήνεσιν, h. 30, 10 (akin to τιθήνη).

εὔθριξ. τριχος, ὁ, ἡ (θρίξ), having beautiful hair, having a beautiful mane ; with flowing mane. epith. of steeds ; only in the Ep. form ἐΰτριχας, *23, 13. 301. 351.

εὔθρονος, ον, Ep. ἐΰθρονος (θρόνος), having a beautiful seat, well-throned, epith. of Εῶς ; always Ep. form, 8, 565. Od. 6, 48.

εὔθυμος, ον (θυμός), 1) having good courage. 2) In H. benevolent, kind, Od. 14, 63.† Adv. εὐθύμως, courageously, Batr.

*εὐθύς and εὐθύ, adv. of place, straight, directly, εὐθὺ Πύλονδε, h. Merc. 342 ; εὐθύς, 355. In the Il. and Od. only the older form ἰθύς, ἰθύ.

*εὔϊππος, ον (ἵππος), having good steeds, epith. of Ischys, h. Ap. 210.

Εὔϊππος, ὁ, a Trojan, slain by Patroclus, 16. 417.

εὐκαμπής, ές (κάμπτω), well-bent, beautifully curved, δρέπανον, κληΐς, *Od. 18, 368. 21, 6 ; τόξον, h. 27, 12.

*εὔκαρπος. ον (καρπός), fruitful, abounding in fruits, γαῖα, h. 30, 5.

εὐκέατος, ον, poet. for εὐκέαστος (κεάζω) easy to split, easily cleaved, κέδρος, Od 5, 60.†

εὔκηλος, ον. Æol. lengthened from ἔκηλος, prop. ἐϝκηλος (see ἄκηλος), qui·l 1, 554. 2) undisturbed, 11, 371. Od. 14, 479

εὐκλεής, ές (κλέος), Ep. εὐκλεής. accus plur. εὐκλείας, 10, 281. Od. 21, 331 εὐκληεῖς, 12, 318 ; glorious, famous. oι μὰν ἡμιν εὐκλεές, it is not glorious for us, 17, 415 ; whence adv. εὐκλεῶς, Ep ἐϋκλειῶς, gloriously, 22, 110.

εὐκλείη, ἡ, Ep. for εὐκλεία, fame, glory Od. 14, 402. τινὰ εὐκλείης ἐπιβῆσαι, to elevate any man to fame, Voss [to mount him on glory's heights. Cp.], Il. 8, 285.

εὐκλειής, ές and adv. εὐκλειῶς, poet. fo εὐκλεής and εὐκλεῶς.

εὐκληΐς, ῖδος, ἡ (κλαΐς), well-locked θύρη. 24, 318.†

*εὔκλωστος, ον (κλώθω), well-spun well-woven, χιτών, h. Ap. 203.

εὐκνήμις, ῖδος, ὁ, ἡ, Ep. εὐκνήμιδι (κνημίς), having beautiful greaves, in the Il. epith of the Achæans ; in the Od. also of ἑταῖροι, Od. 2, 402 ; always in the plur and Ep. form, 1, 17.

εὔκομος, Ep. ἐΰκομος, having beautiful hair, fair-haired, epith. of noble women Il. Od. h. Cer. 1.

*εὐκόσμητος, ον (κοσμέω), beautifully adorned, h. Merc. 384.

εὔκοσμος, ον (κοσμός), well-arranged only adv. εὐκόσμως, in (fitting) order Od. 21, 123.†

*εὔκραιρος, ον (κραῖρα), beautifully horned. spoken of cattle, h. Merc. 209.

εὐκτίμενος, η, ον (κτίμενος), well-built well-inhabited, well-situated, nily an epith. of towns, islands, regions ; spoken of houses, streets, and gardens, Od. 4 476. Il. 6, 391. 20, 496. The common form εὐκτιμένη, h. Ap 36, Herm. has re jected.

ἐΰκτιτος, ον, Ep. and Ion. for εὔκτιστο (κτίζω), handsomely built, Αἶπυ, 2, 592. h. Ap. 423.

εὐκτός, ή, όν (εὔχομαι), wished, desirea 14, 98.†

εὔκυκλος, ον (κύκλος), well-rounded, i the Il. epith of the shield, 5, 797 ; in th Od. of the chariot, Od. 6, 58. 70 ; accor ing to Eustath. to be referred to th wheels : having beautiful wheels, Vo [strong-wheel'd. Cp.] : κάντον, Batr. 35.

εὐλείμων, ον, gen. ονος (λειμών), havin good meadows, abounding in meadows meadowy (convenient for pasturing Voss), νῆσος. Od. 4. 607.†

εὐλή, ἡ (εἰλέω), a worm, a maggot, pr duced in dead bodies, etc., plur., *Il 26. 22, 509. 24, 414.

εὔληρα, τά, Ep. for the comm. ἡνί rein, check, 23, 481 ;† (prob. from εἰλ Schol. οἱονεὶ εἴληρα, ἀπὸ τοῦ περιειλεῖσθ τοὺς ἱμάντας χερσὶ τῶν ἡνιόχων).

Εὔμαιος, the faithful swine-herd Odysseus (Ulysses), son of Ctesius, kiι of the island Syria ; he was stolen by female Phœnician slave of his fathι

and by .the Phœnician sailors sold to
Laertes, Od. 15, 402, seq. Odysseus
(Ulysses) comes to him clad like a beggar, Od. 14, 1, seq. Telemachus lodged
with him when he returned from Sparta.
He conducted Odysseus (Ulysses) to the
town, Od. 17, 201; and aided him in
slaying the suitors, Od. 22, 267, seq.
(prob. from εὖ and ΜΑΩ, the well-disposed).

*εὐμελίη, ἡ, poet. for εὐμέλεια, good
singing, the reading preferred by Herm.
for εὐμυλίη, in h. Merc. 325.

εὐμελίης, ου, ὁ, Ep. ἐϋμμελίης, q. v.

εὐμενέτης, ου, ὁ, poet. for εὐμενής, well-
disposed, kind, affectionate (in opposition
to δυσμενής), Od. 6, 185.†

εὐμενής, ές (μένος), well-disposed, benevolent, kind, ἦτορ, h. 21, 7.†

Εὐμήδης, εος, ὁ (very wise), father of
Dolon, the rich herald of the Trojans,
10, 314.

*εὐμήκης, ες (μῆκος), very long, Batr.
130.

εὔμηλος, ον (μῆλος), having good or
many sheep, abounding in sheep, Ὀρτυγίη,
Od. 15, 406.† (V. 'good for sheep').

Εὔμηλος, ὁ, son of Admêtus and
Alcestis, who in eleven ships led the
Thessalians from Pheræ, Boibê, and
Iolcus, 2, 711. He possessed excellent
horses, and would have won the prize in
the funeral games of Patroclus, had not
his chariot been broken, 23, 288, seq.
Iphthîmê, daughter of Icarius, is mentioned as his wife, Od. 4, 798.

εὐμμελίης, ὁ. Ep. for εὐμελίης, Ep. gen.
ἐϋμμελίω for ἐϋμμελίαο (μελία [by as-
similation for ἐϋσμελίης, fm. the orig.
form σμελία, cf. σμῖλαξ. σμῖλος, δένδρον·
οἱ δὲ πρῖνος. Hesych. Död.]), having a
good ashen spear, skilled in the use of
the spear, epith. of brave warriors, 17, 9;
and esply of Priam, 4, 165. (The common
form εὐμελίης does not occur in H.)

*εὐμολπέω (εὔμολπος), to sing sweetly,
h. Merc. 478.

[Εὔμολπος, Eumolpus, a masc. proper
name, h. Cer. 154, 475.]

*εὐμυλίη, ἡ, h. Merc. 325, an unknown
word, for which Herm. would read
εὐμελίη, Frank εὐελίη.

εὐνάζω = εὐνάω (εὐνή), fut. άσω, to
cause to lie down, to lay down, Od. 4,
406. Mid. to lie down, to go to sleep, Od.
20, 1; παρά τινι, and with dat. alone,
Od. 5, 119. h. Ven. 191; also spoken of
brutes, *Od. 5, 65.

εὐναιετάων, ωσα, ον, well-inhabited,
pleasant to live in, well-furnished; always
in pass. signif. with πόλις, δόμοι, and
μέγαρα, 2, 648. Od. 2, 400 (used only in
the partep.).

εὐναιόμενος, η, ον (ναίω), well-inhabited, populous; like εὐναιετάων with
πόλις, πτολίεθρον, and Βούδειον, 16, 572;
Σιδονίη, Od. 13, 285. There is no verb
εὐναίω.

εὐνάω and εὐνάζω (εὐνή), fut. εὐνήσω,
aor 1 pass. εὐνήθην 1) Act. to place in

ambush, τινά, Od. 4, 440; mly to put to
rest, to put to sleep; hence metaph. to
quiet, to soothe = παύω, γόον, Od. 4, 758.
2) Mid. with aor. pass. to go to bed, to go
to sleep, to sleep, εὐνηθῆναί τινι, with any
one, 2, 821. 16, 176; and ἐν φιλότητι
εὐνηθῆναι, 14, 360; metaph. spoken of
storms: to be hushed, to be stilled, Od. 5,
384.

εὐνή, ἡ, Ep. gen. εὐνῆφι; 1) a couch,
a bed, ἐξ εὐνῆφιν, 15, 580. Od. 2, 2, seq.;
generally a place of rest, of the army, 10,
408; a lair of a wild beast, 11, 115; of
cattle, Od. 14, 15; in the plur. εὐναί, the
couches of Typhôeus, which some explain as the grave, 2, 783. b) a bed, i. e.
a bedstead, the cushion for a bed, Od. 16,
34. c) the nuptial couch. εὐνῆς ἐπιβήμεναι, 9, 133; hence marriage, co-
habitation. φιλότητι καὶ εὐνῇ μιγῆναι,
to indulge the pleasures of love, 3, 445.
2) Plur. εὐναί, anchor-stones, i. e. stones
used for anchors, which were either let
down to hold the ship, or, as Nitzsch ad
Od. 2, 418, p. 120, thinks, stones or
masses of matter, with which the ship
was attached to the strand when the
water at the shore was too deep, see 14,
77; again, 1, 436. Od. 15, 498. 9, 137
[the above view is, however, retracted by
Nitzsch, tom. III. p. 35].

εὐνῆθεν, adv. from the bed, Od. 20, 124.

Εὔνηος, ὁ, Ion. for Εὔνεως, son of
Jason and Hypsipyle, in Lemnos, who
sent wine to the Greeks in Troy, 7, 468;
and exchanged a mixing-cup for Lycaon,
23, 747 (from νηῦς, the good sailor, so
named from his father).

εὔνητος, ον, Ep. ἐϋννητος (νέω), well-
spun, beautifully woven, χιτών, πέπλος,
18, 596. Od. 7, 97; always in the Ep.
form.

εὐνῆφι, εὐνῆφιν, see εὐνή.

εὖνις, ιος, ὁ, ἡ, bereft, deprived, with
gen. υἱῶν, 22, 44; ψυχῆς, Od. 9, 524
(According to Eustath. from εἷς, ἑνός,
whence ἕνις, εὖνις. cf. εὔκηλος).

ἐϋννητος, ον, Ep. for εὔνητος, q. v.

εὐνομίη, ἡ (νόμος), good observance of
law, good morals, loyalty, Od. 17, 487;†
in plur. good laws, h. 30, 11.

εὔξεστος, ον, Ep. ἐΰξεστος, η, ον (ξέω),
well-smoothed, well-polished; spoken especially of any thing made of wood, and
smoothed with a plane or any similar
tool, especially of chariots, tables, bath-
ing-tubs, oars, etc., 7, 5. Od. 4, 48;
sometimes with two, and sometimes with
three endings, see Thiersch, Gram. § 201,
16. In Od. 14, 225, ἄκοντες ἐϋξέστοι,
it refers to the shaft, not, as Bothe supposes, to the point.

εὔξοος, ον, Ep. ἐΰξοος (ξέω), well-
smoothed; like εὔξεστος, spoken of chariots, tables, and spear-shafts, 2, 390. 10,
373; but Od. 5, 237, σκέπαρνον ἐΰξοον,
the well-whetted axe, which is explained
by some as act. 'that hews well.'

εὔορμος, ον (ὅρμος), having good anchorage, or, with Nitzsch, 'having

I 4

level shores,' λιμήν, 21, 23. Od. 4, 358.

*εὔοχθος, ον (perhaps from ὀχή), *fertile, fruitful,* γῆ, Ep. 7, 2.

*εὔπαις, δος, ὁ, ἡ (παῖς), *abounding in children, blessed with offspring,* h. 30, 5.

εὐπατέρεια, ἡ (πατήρ), *the daughter of a noble father* (V., 'of noble descent'), epith. of Helen and Tyro, 6, 292. Od. 11, 235.

Εὐπείθης, εος, ὁ (adj. εὐπειθής), father of the suitor Antinous of Ithaca; he wished to avenge the death of his son, whom Odysseus (Ulysses) had slain among the suitors, by a combat against him, but was slain by Laertes, Od. 1, 383. 24, 469, seq.

εὔπεπλος, ον (πέπλος), *having a beautiful mantle, handsomely clad, well-dressed,* epith. of noble women, 5, 424; Ναυσικάα, Od. 6, 49.

εὐπηγής, ές (πήγνυμι), Ep. for εὐπαγής, prop. pressed together; spoken of the physical frame, *well-knit, strong, firm.* ξεῖνος μέγας ἠδ᾽ εὐπηγής, Od. 21, 334.†

εὔπηκτος, ον (πήγνυμι), *well-joined, firmly built,* epith. of buildings and tents, 2, 661. 9, 663. Od. 23, 41.

εὔπλειος, η, ον, Ep εὔπλειος (πλεῖος), *well-filled, entirely full,* πήρη, Od. 17, 467.†

εὐπλεκής, ές, Ep. εὔπλεκής (πλέκω), *well-interwoven, beautifully entwined,* = εὔπλεκτος; θύσανοι, δίφροι, *2, 449. 23, 436; only in the Ep. form.

εὔπλεκτος, ον, Ep. ἐΰπλεκτος (πλέκω), *well, beautifully interwoven. well-twisted,* δίφρος, 23, 335, Ep. form; σειραί, *strongly twisted cords,* 23, 115, comm. form.

εὐπλοίη, ἡ, Ep. for εὔπλοια (πλέω), *a prosperous voyage or navigation,* 9, 362.†

εὐπλοκαμίς, ῖδος, ἡ, Ep. form from ἐϋπλόκαμος, *having beautiful tresses; fair-hair'd,* only ἐϋπλοκαμῖδες Ἀχαιαί, *Od. 2, 119. 19, 542.

εὐπλόκαμος, ον, Ep εὐπλόκαμος (πλόκαμος), *having beautiful tresses, fair-hair'd,* epith. of goddesses and of women, 6, 380. Od. 5, 125, seq.; only Ep. form.

εὐπλυνής, ές, Ep. ἐϋπλυνής (πλύνω), *well-washed, clean,* φᾶρος, Od. 8, 392. 425; only Ep. form.

εὐποίητος, ον and η, ον (ποιέω), *well-made, beautifully wrought,* spoken of works of every kind: *well-built,* πύλη, κλισίη; the fem. εὐποιήτη, 5, 466. 16, 636; but εὐποίητος πυράγρη, Od. 3, 434; (Thiersch, § 201, 16.)

*εὐπόλεμος, ον (πόλεμος), *good in war, warlike,* h. 7, 4.

εὐπρήσσω (πρήσσω), *to make well, to arrange well;* whence ἐϋπρήσσεσκον, Od. 8, 259.† Eustath. reads, more correctly, ἐϋ πρήσσεσκον, see Thiersch, Gram. § 170, 7.

εὐπρηστος, ον (πρήθω), *strongly kindling, vehemently excited,* ἀϋτμή, from

the bellows (V. 'the glow-enkindling blast'), 18, 471.†

εὔπρυμνος, ον (πρύμνα), *having a well-built or beautifully adorned stern,* νῆες, 4, 248.†

εὔπυργος, ον (πύργος), *furnished with good towers,* epith. of fortified towns, 7, 71.†

εὔπωλος, ον (πῶλος), 'having beautiful horses, abounding in horses, famed for horses,* epith. of Ilium, 5, 551. Od. 2, 18, often.

εὐράξ, adv. (εὖρος), *sidewise,* *11, 251. 15, 541.

εὐραφής, ές, Ep. ἐϋρραφής (ῥάπτω), *well-stitched, sowed fast,* δοροί [*skins close-seamed.* Cp.], *Od. 2, 354. 380; only Ep. form.

εὐρεής, ές, Ep. ἐϋρρεής, Ep. form of εὐρείτης; only in the gen. εὐρρεῖος, ποταμοῖο, contr. from εὔρρεέος, in *6, 5ι8. 15, 265, and elsewhere; see the following.

εὐρείτης. ον, ὁ, Ep. ἐϋρρείτης, αο (ῥέω), *beautifully flowing, fair-flowing,* epith. of rivers, 6, 34. Od. 14, 257.

*Εὔριπος, ὁ, the *Euripus,* the strait between Euboea, Boeotia, and Attica: now the strait of *Egribos,* h. Ap. 222. (Prob. from εὖ and ῥίπτω.)

εὑρίσκω, fut. εὑρήσω, h. Merc. 302; aor. act. εὗρον, and aor. mid. εὑρόμην. 1) *to find* what one seeks, *to invent, to discover, to devise;* with accus. μῆχος, to devise a means, 2, 343; κακοῦ ἄκος. 9, 250 (see ἄκος); τέκμωρ Ἰλίου, *to find* the end of Ilium, i. e. accomplish its destruction, 7, 81. 9, 49; but τέκμωρ τι, *to find* an expedient, a remedy, Od. 4, 374. 2) *to find by chance, to light upon, to fall in with,* spoken of persons and things very often; with partcp. αὐτὸν ἥμενον, 5, 752. Mid. *to find out for oneself, to devise,* τέκμωρ, 16, 472; ὄνομα, Od. 19, 403; θανάτου λύσιν ἑταίροισιν, to find deliverance from death for his companions, Od. 9, 421. 2) *to find by chance* or *unawares,* οἵ τ᾽ αὐτῷ κακὸν εὗρετο, he drew evil upon himself, Od. 21, 304.

εὔροος, ον, Ep. ἐϋρροος, *beautifully flowing, rapidly flowing,* epith. of rivers, *7, 329; 21, 130; always in the Ep form.

Εὖρος, ὁ, the *Eurus,* or *south-east* wind one of the four main winds of H., Od. 5 295. 232. It is stormy, 2, 145. 16, 765 and as a warm wind it melts the snow Od. 19, 206. (According to some, from αὔρα, according to others, kindred to ἠώς, cf. Buttm. Lex. p. 43, note 4.)

εὖρος, εος, τό (εὐρύς), *breadth, width* Od. 11, 312.†

ἐϋρραφής, poet. for εὐραφής, q. v.

ἐϋρρείος, Ep. gen. see εὐρεής.

ἐϋρρείτης, ὁ, Ep. for εὐρείτης, q. v.

ἐϋρροος, Ep. for εὔροος, q. v.

εὐρυάγυιος, νια, νιον (ἀγυιά), *having broad streets, with spacious streets,* epith. of large cities, 2, 329. Od. 4, 246 230; also χθὼν εὐρυαγυία, h. Cer. 16 occurring only in the fem.

Εὐρυάδης, ου, ὁ, a suitor of Penelŏpê, slain by Telemachus, Od. 22, 267.

Εὐρύαλος, ὁ, 1) son of Mecisteus; he went with his kinsman Diomêdês to Troy, 2, 565; was one of the bravest heroes, 6, 20; he was also a powerful wrestler, but was conquered by Epeus, 23, 680. 2) a Phæacian, a victor in wrestling, who presented Odysseus (Ulysses) with a sword, Od. 8, 115.

Εὐρυβάτης, ου, ὁ, 1) a herald of Agamemnon, 1, 320. 9, 170. 2) a herald of Odysseus (Ulysses), who followed him to Troy, 2, 184. Od. 19, 247.

*εὐρυβίης, αο, ὁ, Ion. and Ep. for εὐρυβίας (βία), wide-ruling, having a wide sway. Κελεός, h. Cer. 295.

Εὐρυδάμας, αντος, ὁ, 1) a Trojan, father of Abas and Polyidus, who knew how to interpret dreams, 5, 149. 2) a suitor of Penelŏpê of Ithaca, slain by Odysseus (Ulysses), Od. 18, 297. 22, 283.

Εὐρυδίκη, ἡ, daughter of Clymenus, wife of Nestor, Od. 3, 452.

Εὐρύκλεια, ἡ, daughter of Ops son of Pisenor; Laertes had purchased her at the price of twenty cattle, Od. 1, 429. 430. She brought up Odysseus (Ulysses), Od. 19, 482; then with Eurynome discharged the office of house-keeper and had the charge of the female slaves, Od. 22, 396. 23, 289. Her fidelity, attachment, and activity are often praised.

εὐρυκρείων, οντος, ὁ (κρείων), wide-ruling, epith. of Agamemnon and of Poseidôn, *1, 102. 355.

Εὐρύλοχος, ὁ, a companion and fellow-wanderer of Odysseus (Ulysses); he conducted a part of the crew to Circê, accompanied Odysseus (Ulysses) to the under-world, occasioned the slaughter of the sacred oxen of Helius, by which he drew death upon himself and his companions, Od. 10, 205. 11, 23.

Εὐρύμαχος, ὁ, son of Polybus, according to Od. 4, 629 : he and Antinous were the most respectable amongst the suitors of Penelŏpê; he was crafty and subtle, Od. 1, 399. 2, 177. He was slain by Odysseus (Ulysses), Od. 22, 69.

Εὐρυμέδουσα, ἡ, a female slave of Alcinous, king of Phæacia, who brought up Nausicaa, Od. 7, 8.

Εὐρυμέδων, οντος, ὁ, 1) father of Periboea, leader of the giants in Epirus, Od. 7, 58; cf. Pind. Pyth. VIII. 15—19. 2) son of Ptolemæus, the noble charioteer of Agamemnon, 4, 228. 3) a servant of Nestor, 8, 114. 11, 620.

εὐρυμέτωπος, ον (μέτωπον), broad-browed, always an epith. of cattle, 10, 292. Od. 3, 282.

Εὐρυμίδης, ου, ὁ, son of Eurymus = Telemus, a Cyclops, Od. 9, 509.

Εὐρυνόμη, ἡ, 1) daughter of Oceanus and Thetis, who received Hêphæstus when hurled from heaven into the sea, 18, 398, seq. According to Hes. Th. 98, she was the mother of the Graces; before

Kronus, she with Ophian had the dominion of Olympus, Ap. Rh. 503. 2) the trusty stewardess of Odysseus (Ulysses), Od. 17, 490, seq. 19, 96.

Εὐρύνομος, ὁ, son of Ægyptius in Ithaca, a suitor of Penelŏpê, Od. 2, 22. He is also mentioned in the contest with Odysseus (Ulysses), Od. 22, 242.

εὐρύνω (εὐρύς), aor. 1 εὐρῦνα, to make broad, to widen, with ἀγῶνα, to enlarge the arena of combat, Od. 8, 260.†

εὐρυόδειος, α, ον (ὁδός), having broad roads, with wide ways (widely roamea over, V.), epith. of the earth, since it can be travelled over in all directions, only in fem. 16, 635. Od. 3, 453; and often.

εὐρύοπα, ὁ, Ep. for εὐρυόπης, as nom. 5, 265; as voc. 16, 241; a form of εὐρύωψ, whence the accus. εὐρύοπα, 1, 498. 8, 206; either (from ὤψ), wide-seeing, far-seeing, or (from ὄψ), wide-thundering, epith. of Zeus. The last signif. seems to contravene the Hom. usus loquendi, since ὄψ, though used to indicate the voices of men and beasts, is not applied to every loud noise. Eustath. and Hesych. give both explanations; Heyne, Wolf, Thiersch, § 181. 47. Anm. 2, decide in favour of the first signif. and Voss. ad h. Cer. 3, translates it the ruler of the world, see 13, 732. In h. Cer. 441, connected with βαρύκτυπος. [See Jahrb. von Jahn und Klötz. März 1843, p. 264.]

εὐρύπορος, ον (πόρος), prop. having broad ways, widely navigated, always an epith. of the sea, 15, 381. Od. 4, 432. 12, 2.

εὐρυπυλής, ές (πυλή), having wide gates, wide-gated, Ἀΐδος δῶ, 23, 71. Od. 11, 571.

Εὐρύπυλος, ὁ, son of Euæmon, grandson of Ormenus, ruler of Ormenion in Thessaly, who sailed to Troy with forty ships, 2, 736; a brave warrior; he slew many Trojans, was wounded by Paris, and healed by Patroclus, 11, 841. In Pindar he is represented as the son of Poseidôn, king of Cyrene, and received the Argonauts in Lybia, cf. Müller, Orchom, p. 466. 2) son of Poseidôn and Astypalæa, father of Chalciopê, king of Cos, 2, 676. 3) son of Telephus and Astyochê, sister of Priam, king of Mysia. He was induced, by presents which Priam sent to his mother or wife, to go to the aid of Troy. He was slain by Neoptolemus, Od. 11, 520, seq. cf. Strab. p. 587.

εὐρυρέεθρος, ον (ῥέεθρον), flowing in a broad channel, wide-flowing, epith. of the Axius, 21, 141.†

εὐρυρέων, ουσα, ον (ῥέω), wide-flowing, epith. of the Axius, 2, 849. 16, 288; of the Xanthus, *21, 304.

εὐρύς, εῖα, ύ, gen. έος, είης, έος (Ep. accus. εὐρέα for εὐρύν, 6, 291. 18, 140); broad, wide, spacious, chiefly epith. of the heavens, the sea, countries, etc. [twice of cities, 2, 575. 18, 591]. εὐρέα νῶτα θαλάσσης, 2, 159. εὐρέες ὦμοι, 3,

227. τεῖχος εὐρύ, a thick wall, 12, 5. κλέος εὐρύ, a wide-spread report, Od. 23, 137. Cf. εὐρύτερος, 3, 194.

εὐρυσθενής, ές (σθένος), having a wide dominion, wide-ruling, epith. of Poseidôn, 7, 455. Od. 13, 140.

Εὐρυσθεύς, ῆος, ὁ, son of Sthenelus, and grandson of Perseus, king of Mycenæ; he was prematurely born, for Hêrê accelerated his birth, that he, and not Hêraclês might reign, according to an oath of Zeus in relation to the descendants of Perseus, 19, 100. 123, seq. Thus Eurystheus became master of Hêraclês and imposed upon him the well-known twelve labours, 15, 639. The last of these labours was to bring up the dog from hell, 8, 363. Od. 11, 617, seq.

Εὐρυτίδης, ου, ὁ, son of Eurytus = Iphitus, Od. 21, 14.

Εὐρυτίων, ωνος, ὁ, a Centaur, Od. 21, 295. cf. Apd. 2, 5. 4.

Εὔρυτος, ὁ, 1) son of Actor and Molione, brother of Cteatus, by tradition son of Poseidôn. Both marched to aid Augeas against the Pylians and Nestor, 11, 709, seq., and also against Hêraclês. who slew him in ambush, 2, 621. They were called Ἀκτορίωνε and Μολίονε, 11, 709. According to Apd. 2, 7. 2, they had together only one body, but two heads, four hands, as many feet, and possessed great strength. 2) son of Melaneus and Stratonice, king of Œchalia (in Thessaly, 2, 730; or in Messenia, Od. see Οἰχαλίη), father of Iole, of Iphitus, of Mollon, etc., a famous archer. According to H. Apollo slew him, because he had challenged him to a contest in archery, Od. 8, 226, seq. Odysseus (Ulysses) received from his son Iphitus the bow of Eurytus, Od. 21, 32, seq. According to a late tradition Hêraclês slew him because he would not give him Iole, Apd. 2, 4. 8 (the bow-drawer, from ἐρύω).

*Εὐρυφάεσσα, ἡ (the far-seeing), sister and wife of Hyperion, mother of Helius, of Sêlêne and Eôs, h. 31, 4.

εὐρυφυής, ές (φύω), wide-growing, epith. of barley, Od. 4, 604.†

εὐρύχορος, ον (χορος), having a broad space, roomy, spacious, extensive, epith. of cities and countries, 2, 498 (according to the Schol. Ep. shortened for εὐρύχωρος, see Thiersch, § 168, 10, and Nitzsch ad Od. 6, 4; with Passow we may derive it more simply from χορός, having broad dancing-places, hence generally, having broad plains).

εὐρύωψ, οπος, ὁ, see εὐρύοπα.

εὐρώεις, εσσα, εν (εὐρώς), mouldy, musty; and, since mould is generated only in the dark, confined places, it signif. generally, dark. gloomy, epith. of the under-world, 20, 65. Od. 10, 512. 23, 322. 24, 10 (improb. with Apoll. Hesych. poet. for εὐρύς).

Εὐρώπη, ἡ, Europa. 1) daughter of

the Phœnician Agenor and of Telephas[s] according to Apd. 3, 1. 1; H. calls h[er] the daughter of Phœnix (if this is not a[n] appel.), mother of Sarpedon and Min[os] by Zeus, who bore her off to Crete, the form of a bull, 14, 321. Batr. [?] H. does not mention her name; it occu[rs] first in Hdt. 1, 2. 2) the name of a [di]vision of the world, first mentioned in Ap. 251; in which place only northe[rn] Greece seems to be intended. (Sign[if.] εὐρωπός = εὐρύς; hence εὐρώπη, s~. χω[ς] the extended, the far-stretching land; [cf.] Herm. ad h. Ap. 1. c.)

ἐΰς, ἐΰ, Ep. ἠΰς, ἠΰ, gen. ἐῆος, acc[.] ἐΰν, 8, 303. Od. 18, 127; ἠΰν, 5, 62 neut. ἠΰ, 17, 456. 20, 80; the form[s] and εΰ in neut. only adv. 1) good, exc[el]lent, beautiful, glorious, spoken of perso[ns] and things, 2, 653. μάνος ἠΰ, 17, 4[56] The gen. sing. ἐῆος, in the signif. of φῦ[s] stands now correctly instead of ἑῆος, h[as] 1, 393, and 15, 138. 24, 422. 550, wh[ere] it should even signify thine. 2) Ge[ne]rally plur. neut. ἐάων, as if from a no[m.] τὰ ἐά, good things, good, 24, 528; plai[n] neut. except θεοὶ δωτῆρες ἑάων, Od. 325. 335. h. 17, 12 (see Buttm. § 35, 3. Thiersch. Gram. § 183, 10; on the oth[er] hand, Doederlein supplies from δώ[ρον] the kindred subst. δόσεων, cf. Kühn[er] § 243, 3). [Cf. Jahrb. Jahn und Klo[tz] März 1843, pp. 264, 265.]

εὖσα, see εὔω.

εὔσελμος, ον, Ep. ἐΰσσελμος (σέλμ[α] well-furnished with oar-benches, or row[ing] epith. of ships, 2, 170, and often. does not occur in the nom., cf. Spitz[er] Il. 16, 1.)

εὔσκαρθμος, ον, Ep. ἐΰσκαρθμος (σ[καί]ρω), lightly bounding, easily leap[ing] epith. of horses, 13, 31.†

εὔσκοπος, ον, Ep. ἐΰσκοπος (σκο[πός] that takes good aim, good to hit, Ἄρτε[μις] Od. 11, 198. 2) (fr. σκοπέω,) seeing w[ell] looking out sharply, epith. of Herm[es] 24, 24. Od. 1, 38; only in the form.

ἐΰσσελμος, ον, Ep. for εὔσελμος. q.

Ἐΰσσωρος, ὁ, Ep. Εὔσωρος, fathe[r of] Acamas of Thrace, 6, 8.

εὐσταθής, ές, Ep. ἐΰσταθής (ἵστη[μι] standing firm, well-founded, μέγαρον. 374; θάλαμος, Od. 23, 178; alway[s] the Ep. form.

εὐστέφανος, ον, Ep. ἐΰστέφανος [(στέ]φανος), 1) beautifully crowned, V[enus] epith. of Artěmis, 21, 511; of Aphro[ditê] and Mycene, Od. 8, 267. 2, 120; of mêtêr, h. Cer. 224; accord. to Apol[l.] Il. 21, 511, from στεφάνη, περικεφαλ[αία] εἶδος. The back hair, to wit, wa[s] closed in a net, see ἀναδέσμη, and [was] fastened with a band (στεφάνη) b[ut] According to others it is to be [inter]preted of the girdle and = εὔζωνο[ς] strongly fortified, strongly walled, epith. of the city Thebe, 19, 99; στεφάνη (only in the Ep. form).

εὔστρεπτος, ον, Ep. ἐΰστρεπτος (στρ[έφω]

well-twined, well-twisted, spoken of leathern thongs, *Od. 2, 426. 15, 291.

εὐστρεφής, ές, Ep. ἐϋστρεφής, well-wound, well-twisted, spoken of cords, etc., Od. 9, 425. 10, 167; of a bow-string, 15, 463; of a gut-string, Od. 21, 408; always in the Ep. form.

εὐστροφος, ον, Ep. ἐϋστροφος (στρέφω), well-wound, well-twisted; οἰὸς ἄωτος, the well-twisted wool of the sheep, i. e. the string of the sling, *13, 599. 716, in the Ep. form.

*εὔστρωτος, ον (στρώννυμι), well-spread, well-made, λέχος, h. Ven. 158. Cer. 286.

εὖτε, Ep. 1) Conj. of time, for ὅτε (which arises from this by a rejection of the digamma), at the time, when, as. a) With indic. 11, 735. The apodosis begins with ἔνθα τῆμος, δὴ τότε, καὶ τότε, etc., 6, 392. Od. 13, 93. b) In connexion with ἂν εὖτ' ἄν (see ὅτ' ἄν), in case that, as soon as, as often as, 1, 242. Od. 1, 192; once without ἄν, Od. 7, 202. c) With optat. h. 17, 8. 2) Adv. of comparison, for ἠϋτε, as when, only once, 3, 10; and according to Aristarch., 19, 386; where Wolf and Spitz. write εὖτε; Buttm., Lex., would read ἠϋτε, and Bothe has adopted the reading.

εὐτειχής, ές = εὐτείχεος.

εὐτείχεος, ον (τεῖχος), having strong walls, well-walled, Τροίη, Ἴλιος, 1, 129. A metaplast. accus. πόλιν εὐτείχεα, is found in 16, 57; which on account of the accent cannot be assigned to εὐτειχής (see however Thiersch, § 200, 20).

*εὐτείχητος, ον (τεῖχος) = εὐτείχεος, h. Ven. 112.

εὔτμητος, ον, Ep. ἐϋτμητος (τέμνω), beautifully cut, well-cut, always spoken of leathern articles, *7, 304. 10, 567; always in the Ep. form.

εὐτρεφής, ές, Ep. ἐϋτρεφής (τρέφω), well-fed, fat, *Od. 9, 425. 14, 530.

εὔτρητος, ον, Ep. ἐϋτρητος, well-bored, well-pierced, λοβοί, 14, 182; † Ep. form.

Εὔτρησις, ιος, ἡ, a village in Thespiæ, in Bœotia, with a temple of Apollo, who had an oracle there, 2, 502. According to Steph. it received its name from the many roads which traversed it.

ἔϋτριχος, see ἐΰθριξ.

εὔτροχος, ον, Ep. ἐΰτροχος (τροχός), having good wheels, with beautiful wheels, ἅρμα. ἄμαξα, 8, 438. Od. 6, 72; always in the Ep form.

εὔτυκτος, ον (τεύχω), well-made, handsomely wrought, well-built, κλισίη, 10, 566. Od. 4, 123; κυνέη, 3, 336; ἱμάσθλη, 8, 44.

*εὔϋμνος, ον (ὕμνος), abounding in hymns, much-praised, h. Ap. 19, 207.

εὐφημέω (εὔφημος), fut. ήσω, to use propitious words, or words of good omen, or to refrain from all words of bad omen, especially in sacrifices and religious matters; hence generally to be still, to be silent, like favete linguis. εὐφημῆσαι κέλεσθε, command to be silent, 9, 171.†

Εὔφημος, ὁ, son of Trœzenus, an ally of the Trojans, leader of the Cicones, 2, 846.

*εὐφήμως, adv. (φήμη), of good omen, propitiously; piously, religiously, h. Ap. 171.

Εὐφήτης, ον, ὁ, king of Ephyræ, on the Selleis in Elis, 15, 532.

Εὔφορβος, ὁ, son of Panthous, one of the bravest Trojans; he wounded Patroclus, and was slain by Menelaus, 16, 806, seq. 17, 59. (Pythagoras affirmed that he was once this Euphorbus, cf. Diog. Laert. 8, 1. 4.) [Cf. also Horat. Carm. I. 28, 10.]

εὐφραδής, ές (φράζω), speaking well, eloquent. 2) clear, only adv. εὐφραδέως, distinctly, eloquently; πεπνυμένα ἀγορεύειν, Od. 19, 352.†

εὐφραίνω, Ep. ἐϋφραίνω (φρήν), fut. εὐφρανέω, aor. εὔφρανα, 1) Act. to delight, to gladden, to please, τινά, 5, 688; τινὰ ἐπέεσσι, 24, 102; νόημα ἀνδρός, Od. 20, 82. 2) Mid. to be delighted, to enjoy oneself, Od. 2, 311 (both in the comm. and in the Ep. form, 7, 297).

εὐφρονέων, ουσα, ον, Ep. ἐϋφρονέων (φρονέω), well-disposed, benevolent; it denotes at once a kind disposition and intelligence, cf. Nitzsch, Od. 2, 160; only as partcp. in the often repeated verse: ὅ σφιν ἐϋφρονέων ἀγορήσατο, etc., 1, 73, seq.

εὐφροσύνη, ἡ, Ep. ἐϋφροσύνη (εὔφρων), gladness, joy, cheerfulness, Od. 9, 6. 20, 8; in the plur. Od. 6, 156. *Od.

εὔφρων, ον, Ep. ἐϋφρων (φρήν), joyful. gladsome, gay, 15, 99; θυμός, Od. 17, 531. 2) Act. gladdening, cheering, οἶνος, 3, 246; in both forms.

εὐφυής, ές (φύω), of beautiful growth, growing well, πτελέη. 15, 243; μηροί, beautiful thighs, *4, 147.

εὔχαλκος, ον (χαλκός), made of beautiful brass, or beautifully wrought of brass, as στεφάνη, ἀξίνη, Il.; λέβης. Od., handsomely adorned with brass, μελίη. κυνέη. 13, 612.

*εὐχερής, ές (χείρ), managing any thing easily, dexterous, Batr. 62.

εὐχετάομαι, poet. form for εὔχομαι, infin. εὐχετάασθαι, Ep. for εὐχητᾶσθαι, imperf. εὐχετόωντο, Ep. for εὐχετῶντο, 1) to affirm any thing of oneself with confidence, as τίνες ἔμμεναι εὐχετόωνται, Od. 1, 172; hence, 1) to vaunt oneself, to boast, ἐπέεσσι, 12, 391. 17, 19; ἐπί τινι, about any thing, Od. 22, 412. 2) In reference to the gods: to pray, to supplicate, with dat. Κρονίωνι, to Zeus, 9, 268; θεοῖσιν, 15, 369. Od. 12, 356; and generally, to show reverence, to thank any man, spoken of men only in reference to a god, 11, 761. τῷ μέν τοι—, θεῷ ὡς, εὐχετοψμην, Od. 8, 467; see εὔχομαι.

εὐχή, ἡ, a vow, a petition, a prayer, only Od. 10, 526.†

Εὐχήνωρ, ορος, ὁ, son of the prophet Polyidus of Corinth, 13, 663; according to Paus. 1, 43. grandson of Polyidus (from εὖχος and ἀνήρ).

εὔχομαι, depon. mid. fut. εὔξομαι, aor. εὐξάμην: ground meaning, to declore aloud, to affirm confidently; hence, 1) boastingly to affirm of oneself, to announce oneself, often with infin. esply in reference to family: πατρὸς ἐξ ἀγαθοῦ γένος εὔχομαι εἶναι, 14, 113. Od. 1, 180 (in this there is contained not exactly the idea of boasting, but merely the declaration with a certain degree of complacency; since in that time every one boasted of that which he believed himself to be, see Nitzsch ad Od.); it stands elliptically: ἐκ Κρητάων γένος, εὔχομαι, viz. εἶναι. I boast descent from the Cretans, Od. 14, 199; often, to boast, to vaunt, to brag, 1, 91. 2, 597; αὔτως, 11, 388. 2) to vow, to promise, with infin., 18, 499; to vow, esply to the gods, τινί, and infin. εὔχετο Ἀπόλλωνι ῥέξειν ἑκατόμβην, 4, 119; and because benefits were in this way expected from the gods, 3) generally to implore, to supplicate, θεῷ, a god; and absol., 1, 87. 6, 240; also with dat. commod. αἴτε μοι εὐχόμεναι, praying for me, 7, 298. (H. never uses the augment.)

εὖχος, εος, τό, glory, honour, esply military glory, victory; often διδόναι εὖχός τινι, to give glory to any man, spoken both of the conquered, 5, 285. 654. 11, 445; and of the gods, 7, 81. 203; often in connexion with κλέος, νίκην; εὖχος ὀρέγειν, πορεῖν τινι, 13, 327. Od. 22, 7; cf. Spitz. ad Il. 15, 462; ἀρέσθαι, 11, 290. Passow explains it, the object of supplication, but most of the ancients fame, and this signif. is required in the Hom. use.

εὐχροής, ές, a rare poet. form for εὔχροος (χρόα), of a beautiful colour, Od. 14, 24.†

εὐχωλή, ἡ (εὔχομαι), 1) boasting, vaunting, 8, 229; exultation, the shout of victory, in opposition to οἰμωγή, 4, 450. 864. b) the object on account of which one vaunts himself (cf. Wolf Vorles.). εὐχωλήν τινι καταλείπειν, 2, 160. 4, 173. 22, 433. 2) a vow made to the gods, 1, 65. 93; prayer, supplication, 9, 499. Od. 13, 357.

εὔω (kindred with αὔω), to singe, to burn off; mostly used of swine, from which the bristles were singed before roasting, Od. 2, 300. 14, 75. 426. σύες εὐόμενοι τανύοντο διὰ φλογός, the swine were stretched for singeing over the fire. 9, 468; and spoken also of the singeing of the eyebrows of the Cyclops, Od. 9, 389 (εὔω deserves the preference over αὔω, cf. Buttm. Gram., vol. ii. p. 140).

εὐώδης, ες (ὄζω, ὄδωδα), odoriferous, sweet-scented, fragrant, θάλαμος, 3, 382; ἔλαιον, Od. 2, 339.

εὐῶπις, ιδος ἡ, having beautiful eyes, having a lovely countenance, κούρη, *Od. 6, 113. 142. h. Cer. 334.

ἔφαγον, see ἐσθίω, ἔδω.

ἐφάλλομαι, depon. mid. (ἅλλομαι), aor. sync. 2 ἐπᾶλτο, partcp. ἐπάλμενος and ἐπιάλμενος, 1) to spring upon, to leap upon; ἵππων, the chariot, 7, 15; absol. κύσσε μιν ἐπιάλμενος, Od. 24, 320; esply 2) to leap upon, in a hostile signif., to rush upon, τινί, any man, 13, 643. 21, 140; and often absol. in the partcp., 7, 260. (H. uses only 3 sing. aor. ἐπᾶλτο and the partcp. aor. sync. ἐπάλμενος and ἐπιάλμενος, Passow.)

ἔφαλος, ον (ἅλς), situated on the sea, maritime, epith. of sea-board towns, *2, 538. 584.

ἔφαν, see φημί.

ἐφανδάνω, poet. ἐπιανδάνω (ἁνδάνω), to please, to be agreeable. ἡ βουλὴ θεοῖσιν ἐφήνδανε, 7, 45; also pres ἐπιανδάνει, 7, 407; and imperf. ἐπιήνδανε in the Od. often.

ἐφάνη, see φαίνω.

ἐφάπτω (ἅπτω), fut. ἐφάψω; only 3 sing. perf. pass. ἐφῆπται, and 3 pluperf. pass. ἐφῆπτο, and aor. 1 mid. ἐφηψάμην. I) Act. to attach to, to fasten to; hence pass. to be attached to; only in a metaph. signif. with dat. of pers. Τρώεσσι κήδε' ἐφῆπται, woes are attached to the Trojans, threaten them, 2, 15. 69: ὀλέθρου πείρατα, 12, 79. Od. 22, 33 (see πεῖραρ); ἀθανάτοισιν ἔρις καὶ νεῖκος, 21, 513. II] Mid. to touch, to lay hold of, to attain; with gen. ἐπὴν χείρεσσιν ἐφάψεαι (i. e. ἐφάψῃ) ἠπείροιο, as soon as thou shalt touch the land with thine hands, Od. 5, 348.

ἐφαρμόζω (ἁρμόζω), fut. όσω, intrans to fit, to be suitable, to suit, τινι, 19, 385.†

ἐφέζομαι, depon. mid. (ἕζομαι), to si upon, to seat oneself upon, with dat δίφρῳ, δενδρέῳ, 3, 152; πατρὸς γούνασι 21, 506. 2) to seat oneself by, Od. 17 334 (only pres. and imperf.).

ἐφέηκα, see ἐφίημι.

ἐφείην, see ἐφίημι.

ἐφεῖσα (εἶσα), defect. aor. 1 infin ἐφέσσαι, Ep. for ἐφέσαι, mid ἐφεισάμην imperat. ἐφέσσαι, Ep. for ἔφεσαι, partcp ἐφεσσάμενος. Ep. for ἐφεσάμενος, infin fut. ἐφέσσεσθαι, 9, 455; I) Act. to pu upon, to lay or place upon. καταστῆσα καὶ ἐφέσσαι τινά, to convey to and pu ashore, Od. 13, 274. II) Mid. to plac any thing for oneself upon, to lay upon μήποτε γούνασιν οἷσιν ἐφέσσεσθαι φίλον υἱόν, 9, 455. ἐμὲ—γούνασιν οἷσιν ἐφεσ σάμενος. Od. 16, 443. b) With gen ἐφέσσαί με νηός, put me on board th ship, Od. 15, 277. cf. 14, 295.

ἐφέλκω (ἕλκω), I) Act. to draw to wards, to entice, to allure, hence pass. t be enticed, ῥείθροισιν ἐφελκόμενος, h. 18 9. II) Mid. to draw or drag to or afte oneself; with accus. ἐφέλκετο ἔγχος, he drew the spear along with him, 13, 597 metaph. ἐφέλκεται ἄνδρα σίδηρος, th sword attracts (excites) the hero, Od. 16 294. 2) to trail, to drag. πόδας ἐφελ κόμενοι, dragging feet, 23, 696.

ἐφέννυμι, poet. ἐπιέννυμι, q. v.

ἐφέπω (poet. ἕπω), imperf. ἔφεπον, Ep. for ἐφεῖπον, fut. ἐφέψω, aor. ἐπέσπον, infin. ἐπισπεῖν, partcp. ἐπισπών, I) Act. primary signif. *to be behind*, hence 1) *to follow, to pursue, to drive*, τινά, 11, 177; absol., 15, 742: to attack, to assault, 20, 357. 494. *b*) *to drive before one*, ἵππους, 24. 326; and ἵππους τινί, to drive or impel one's horses against any man, 16, 724. 732. *c*) *to wander over* a place, *to go through, to run through* or *over*, κορυφὰς ὀρέων, Od. 9, 121 : πεδίον, the plain, 11, 496; ὑσμίνης στόμα, to pass through the gorge of battle ('to urge the battle in the foremost ranks,' Passow], 20, 359. 2) *to follow any thing zealously, to prosecute, to pursue*, frequently : πότμον, θάνατον ἐπισπεῖν, to overtake or meet with death, i. e. to bring it on by one's own fault, 2, 359; in like manner οἶτον, ὀλέθριον ἦμαρ, Od. 3, 134. Il. 19, 294. II) Mid. ἐφέπομαι, aor. ἐφεσπόμην, infin. ἐπισπέσθαι, 1) *to follow, to pursue*, τινί, any man, 13, 495; ἐπισπέσθαι ποσίν, with the feet, i. e. to follow running, 14, 521. 2) *to obey, to hearken to*, θεοῦ ὀμφῇ, Od. 3, 215; ἐπισπόμενοι μένει σφῷ, yielding to their impulse, Od. 14, 262. (Of the mid. H. uses only the aor.)

ἐφέσσαι, see ἐφεῖσα.

ἐφέσσαι, see ἐφεῖσα.

ἐφέστιος, ον (ἑστία), 1) *that is upon* or *at the hearth.* Esply of a suppliant who sits at the hearth. ἐμὲ ἐφέστιον ἤγαγε δαίμων, a god led me to the hearth, Od. 7, 248. 2) *at one's own hearth, at home (settled, resident)*; ἐφέστιοι ὅσσοι ἔασιν, *as many as are at home (are settled; reside) in Troy*; 2, 125. Thus the Schol., ὅσοι ἑστίας (τουτέστιν, οἰκίας) αὐτόθι (i. e. in the city of Troy) διανέμουσι. So also Eustath. and Hesych. Others say, 'whoever sit about the fireplaces in the camp;' but cf. v. 130, and the other Hom. passages in which ἐφέστιος never refers to military life.—Od. 3, 224. ἦλθε—ἐφέστιος, Od. 23, 55.

ἐφετμή, ἡ (ἐφίημι), *command, commission, order, injunction*, 1, 484; esply in the plur., Il. In οἱ δ' αἰεὶ βούλοντο θεοὶ μεμνῆσθαι ἐφετμέων, Od. 4, 353, supply ἡμᾶς : the gods would that we should always remember their commands; but the preterite is unsuitable, should we even with the Schol. render ἐφετμαί prayers. Hence Wolf, after Zenodotus, has included this verse in brackets, see Nitzsch ad loc.

ἐφευρίσκω (εὑρίσκω), aor. ἐφεῦρον, 1) *to find, to meet with*, τινά, 2, 198, seq. 2) *to devise, to invent*, μῆτιν, Od. 19, 158 (where Wolf ἐθ' εὑρίσκω).

ἐφηλάομαι, depon. mid. (ἐφιάομαι), *to insult, to deride, to mock at*, τινί, *Od. 19, 331. 370.

ἐφηγέομαι, depon. mid. (ἡγέομαι), aor. ἐφηγησάμην, *to conduct any man any where, to lead on*, ἐπὶ στίχας ἡγήσατο, he led on the ranks, 2, 687.† In tmesis.

ἔφημαι, depon. (ἧμαι), *to sit upon, to sit by*, with dat. θρόνῳ, Od. 6, 309; κληΐδεσσιν, *Od. 12. 215.

ἐφημέριος, η, ον (ἡμέρα), *at a day, for a day, during the day.* οὔ κεν ἐφημέριός γε βάλοι δάκρυ, he could not shed a tear all day, i. e. through the (whole) day, Od. 4, 223. Mly at or for *the* day. ἐφημέρια φρονεῖν, to care only for the present day, not to trouble oneself about the future, *Od. 21, 85.

ἐφημοσύνη, ἡ = ἐφετμή, *commission, command*, 17, 697. Od. 16, 340.

ἔφησθα, see φημί.

ἔφθην, see φθάνω.

ἔφθιαθ' for ἐφθίατο, see φθίω.

Ἐφιάλτης (the leaper upon ; Alp), son of Alôeus and Iphimedeia, brother of Otus, and by tradition son of Poseidôn. They were giants, of enormous size and strength ; they heaped the mountains Ossa and Pelion the one upon the other, and attempted to storm heaven; Apollo slew them, Od. 11, 304—319. They held, 5, 385, Arês for thirteen months a prisoner; Hermês, however, delivered him, their step-mother Eribœa betraying the fact.

ἐφιζάνω (ἰζάνω) = ἐφίζω, *to sit upon, to sit at*, δείπνῳ, 10, 578; metaph. spoken of sleep, *10, 26.

ἐφίζω (ἴζω), only imperf. *to sit at*, esply *to sit upon*, *Od. 3, 411. 19, 55.

ἐφίημι (ἵημι), fut. ἐφήσω, aor. sing. ἐφῆκα and ἔφηκα, of the aor. 2, the subj. ἐφείω, Ep. for ἐφῶ, optat. ἐφείην, imperat. ἔφες, fut. mid. ἐφήσομαι, I) Act. 1) *to send to, to despatch to*, spoken of persons, τινά τινι, *Ἶριν Πριάμῳ, 24, 117; esply in a hostile signif. *to incite, to provoke, to instigate*, τινά, always with infin, ἐχθοδοπῆσαι, 1, 518; ἀεῖσαι, Od. 14, 464. 2) Spoken of inanimate things; *to cast against, to let fly at, to shoot against, to hurl*, of missiles, βέλεά τινι, 1, 51 ; λᾶαν, μελίην, 3, 12. 21, 170; hence also χεῖράς τινι, to lay hands on any man, 1, 567, seq. *b*) Metaph. κήδεά τινι, to send disasters upon any man, 1, 445 ; πότμον, 4, 396; νόστον τινί, to allot a (disastrous) return to any man, Od. 9, 38 ; spoken of Zeus. II) Mid. only *to command, to command, to direct*, τινί τι, only fut., 23, 82; absol., 24, 300. Od. 13, 7 (ι is poet. long; only ἐφίει has ῑ, Od. 24, 180).

ἐφικνέομαι, depon. mid. (ἱκνέομαι), aor. ἐφικόμην, *to attain, to arrive at, to hit or strike*, 13, 613.†

ἐφίστημι (ἵστημι), perf. (ἐφέστηκα), 3 plur. ἐφεστᾶσι, infin. ἐφεστάμεν, partcp. (ἐφεστηκώς) ἐφεσταότος, pluperf. ἐφεστήκειν, 3 plur. ἐφέστασαν, aor. 2 ἐφέστην, I) Trans. *to put* or *place upon*, H. only, II) Intrans. in the perf., pluperf., aor. 2, and mid. *to stand upon* or *in*, with dat. πύργῳ, 6, 373; δίφρῳ, 17, 609. 2) *to stand at* or *by*, κεφαλῆφιν, to stand at a man's head, 10, 496; θύρῃσιν, at the doors, Od. 1, 120; ἐφέστασαν ἀλλήλοισι, together, 13, 133; also παρά and ἐπί τινι, 12, 199; ἐπὶ χείλει, 12, 52; absol., Od. 22, 203. *b*) In a hostile signif. *to press upon, instare, ἀλλήλοισιν,* 15, 703. Batr. 284. Metaph. Κῆρες ἐφεστᾶσιν θανάτοιο μυρίαι, innumerable fates threaten, 12, 326. *c*) *to direct one's attention, to observe, to be busy at.* ἐπιστάντες κατέτρωξαν, Batr. 126. The pres. mid. *to place oneself at,* only once: θύρῃσιν ἐφίστατο, at the doors, 11, 644.

ἐφόλκαιον, τό (ἐφέλκω), πηδάλιον, Eust. *a helm, a rudder.* Thus Voss, Od. 14, 350; according to others, *a boat* = ἐφόλκιον.

ἐφομαρτέω (ὁμαρτέω), *to follow, to pursue,* absol., *8, 191. 12, 412. 23, 414; only imperf.

ἐφοπλίζω (ὁπλίζω), fut. ἐφοπλίσω, aor. ἐφώπλισα, partcp. ἐφοπλίσας, Ep. σσ, fut. mid. ἐφοπλίσομαι, 1) Act. *to prepare, to make ready,* with accus. δαῖτά τινι, a meal, 4, 344; ἄμαξαν καὶ ἡμιόνους, to harness the mules and carriage, Od. 6, 37; νῆα, to furnish out a ship, Od. 2, 295. 2) Mid. *to prepare any thing for oneself,* δόρπα, 8, 503. 9, 66.

ἐφοράω (ὁράω), fut. ἐπόψομαι, and Ep. ἐπιόψομαι, aor. ἐπεῖδον, 1) *to inspect closely, to look at, to survey,* with accus. spoken of the gods: ἀνθρώπους, to look upon men, Od. 13, 214; of Hêlius: πάντ' ἐφορᾷ καὶ ἐπακούει, 3, 277. Od. 11, 109. 12, 323; to visit, Κακοΐλιον, Od. 23, 19. 2) *to view,* in order to choose, *to look out, to select,* with accus. only in fut. in the Ep. form: ἐπιόψομαι, 9, 167. τάων (νεῶν) ἐγὼν ἐπιόψομαι, ἥτις ἀρίστη, from these I will select that which is best, Od. 2, 294.

ἐφορμάω (ὁρμάω), aor. ἐφώρμησα, aor. 1 pass. ἐφωρμήθην, 1) Act. *to urge against, to excite, to provoke against,* τί τινι, πόλεμόν τινι, war against any man, 3, 165; ἀνέμους, Od. 7, 272. II) Mid. with aor. pass. *to be urged on, to be excited* or *impelled,* esply with infin. ἐμοὶ αὐτῷ θυμὸς ἐφορμᾶται πολεμίζειν, my mind feels impelled (desires) to fight, 13, 74. Od. 1, 275. 4, 713; and without θυμός, Od. 21, 399; hence, 2) *to run to, to rush forth,* Od. 11, 206; esply in a hostile signif. *to rush upon, to attack, to assail,* ἔγχεϊ, 17, 465; often absol., 20, 461. Od. 22, 300. *b*) *to make an attack upon, to assault,* trans. with an accus. ἔθνος ὀρνίθων, 15, 691. cf. 20, 461.

ἐφορμή, ἡ (ἐφορμάω), *a place for attacking, a passage, an entrance,* Od. 22, 130.†

ἐφυβρίζω (ὑβρίζω), *to treat with insolence, to insult about,* in the partcp., 9, 368.†

ἔφυδρος, ον (ὕδωρ), prop. *at* or *near the water.* 2) *moist, bringing rain,* epith. of Zephyr, Od. 14, 458.†

ἐφύπερθε and ἐφύπερθεν, adv. (ὕπερθε), *upon, above,* Il. and Od. 2) *from above,* Od. 9, 383.

Ἐφύρη, ἡ, Att. Ἐφύρα, Ερἡτρα, 1)

the ancient name of Corinth, accord. to Paus. so called from Ephyra the daughter of Oceanus, see Κόρινθος, 6, 152. 2) an old Pelasgic town on the river Selleis in Elis, in the land of the Epêans, the abode of Augeias where (11, 741) many poisonous herbs grew, 2, 659; cf. Strab. VIII. p. 338, who also takes 15, 531. Od. 1, 259. 2, 328, of Ephyra in Elis, cf. Ottf. Müllers Geschr. Hell. Stämme I. p. 273. 3) a very ancient town in Thesprotia, i. e. on the main-land opposite the Phæaces; later *Cichyrus.* Mannert, Sickler, p. 42f; and Nitzsch ad Od. I. p. 45, explain Od. 1, 259. 2, 328, of the Thesprotian Ephyra, because Odysseus (Ulysses) on his return from Ephyra to Ithaca came to the Taphians who dwelt north of Ithaca. 4) a town in Thessaly, later *Crannon,* whence Ἔφυροι, q. v. (Ἐφύρα, prob. Æol. for Ἐφόρα = Ἐπωπή, a watchtower.)

Ἔφυροι, οἱ, the *Ephyri,* according to the Ven. Schol. Steph. and Strab. IX. p. 442, the inhabitants of Crannon in Thessaly (Pelasgiotis), which at an earlier period was called Ephyra, 13, 301.

ἔχαδον, see χανδάνω.

ἔχεα, see χέω.

ἐχέθυμος, ον (θυμός), *possessing intelligence,* or *checking one's desires.* οὐκ ἐχέθυμος, Od. 8, 320.†

Ἐχεκλῆς, ῆος, ὁ, son of Actor, husband of Polymêlê, ruler of the Myrmidons, 16, 189.

Ἔχεκλος, ὁ = Ἐχεκλῆς, 1) son of Agênor, slain by Achilles, 20, 474. 2) Trojan slain by Patroclus, 16, 694.

Ἐχέμων, ονος, ὁ, Ep. Ἐχέμμων (Ἐχέμμων, ed. Heyne), son of Priam, slain by Diomêdês, 5, 160, seq.

Ἐχένηος, ὁ, one of the noble Phæaces, Od. 7, 155. 11, 342.

ἐχεπευκής, ές (πεύκη), *sharp, sharp-pointed, painful,* epith. of the arrow, 1, 51. 4, 129. (According to Buttm. Lex. p. 326 the ground signif. of πεύκη is not *bitterness,* but a *point;* the first is adopted by the ancients, see Eustath. See πεύκη.)

Ἐχέπωλος, ὁ (having steeds), 1) son of Thalysius, a Trojan, slain by Antilochus, 4, 458. 2) son of Anchises from Sicyon, who presented to Agamemnon the mare Æthe, because he would not go with him to Troy, 23, 296.

ἔχεσκον, see ἔχω.

Ἔχετος, ὁ, son of Euchênor and Phlogea, a cruel king of Epirus, who cut off the noses and ears of strangers and cast them to the dogs, Od. 18, 85. According to the Schol. he blinded his daughter Metope and mutilated her lover Æchmodicus. Others make him the son of Buchetus and ruler of the Sicilian; cf. Od. 21, 308.

ἔχευα, ἐχευάμην, see χέω.

ἐχέφρων, ον, gen. ονος (φρήν), *having understanding, intelligent, prudent, wise,* 9, 341; epith. of Penelope (Voss. *chaste*), Od. 4, 111. 17, 390.

Ἐχέφρων, ονος, ὁ, son of Nestor and Anaxibia or Eurydïce, Od. 3, 413.

ἔχησθα, Ep. for ἔχῃς, see ἔχω.

ἐχθαίρω, poet. (ἔχθος), aor. ἤχθηρα, to hate, to be hostile to, with accus. opposed to φιλεῖν, Od. 4, 692. 15, 71. Il. 9, 452. 20, 306.

ἔχθιστος, η, ον, most hated, most odious, irreg. superl. of ἐχθρός, Il.

ἐχθοδοπέω (ἐχθοδοπός), aor. infin. ἐχθοδοπῆσαι, to proceed to act or to speak in a hostile manner, τινί, against any man, 1, 518.† (The derivation of ἐχθοδοπός is obscure: the grammarians derive it from ἔχθος and δοῦπος, to rush on with hostility, or = hostile-looking, ἐχθρός and ΟΠΤΩ; a derivation which Buttm. approves of: according to others it is only a lengthened form of ἐχθρός as ἀλλοδαπός.)

ἔχθομαι, poet. (ἔχθος), only pres. and imperf. to be odious, τινί, *Od. 4, 502. 756; ἤχθετο, Od..14, 366. 19, 338.

ἔχθος, εος, τό, enmity, hatred, hostility, Od. 9, 277; plur. ἔχθεα λυγρά, grievous enmity, 3, 416. (Related either to ἄχθος, or ἔξω, ἐκτός.)

ἐχθρός, ή, όν (ἔχθος), hated, odious, spoken both of persons and things, τινί, 9, 312. Od. 14, 156; δῶρα, 9, 378. (Superl. ἔχθιστος.)

Ἐχῖναι, αἱ, νῆσοι, Ep. for Ἐχῖνάδες, the Echinades, a group of little islands in the Ionian sea, near the mouth of the Achelöus, on the coast of Ætolia and Acarnania. The nearest lay, according to Strab. X. p. 459, only five stadia, the most remote fifteen stadia from the coast, now Curzolari, 2, 625. Strabo reckons Dulichium amongst them. They acquired the name Hedgehog-islands (from ἐχῖνος), from their form; because they lay about the Achelous like the quills of a hedgehog, see Buttm. Lex. p. 364. According to Völcker Hom. Georg. p. 60, H. thought them on the coast of Elis, very near Samé and Zacynthus.

Ἐχίος, ὁ, 1) father of Mēkisteus, a Hellenian, 8, 333. 2) a Greek, slain by Polites, 15, 339. 3) a Trojan, slain by Patroclus, 16, 416. (Ἐχίος, with a different accent from ἔχιον, adder's-bane.)

ἔχμα, ατος, τό (ἔχω). 1) any thing that holds back or obstructs, an obstruction, a hindrance, ἀμάρης δ᾽ ἐξ ἔχματα βάλλειν, to remove the rubbish from the channel, 21, 259; hence a) a bulwark, a defence, both for any thing: ἔχματα πύργων, 12, 260; and against any thing: ἔχμα ἐπηλυσίης. h. Merc. 37. b) a prop, a support, ἔχματα νηῶν, of stones, to hold firm the ships, according to the Schol. κρατήματα, 14, 410. (The transition from the sing. to the plur. is worthy of note.) 2) that which binds together, a bond, a chain, a fetter; ῥηγνύναι ἔχματα πέτρης, to burst the bonds of the rock, i. e. that which confined the stone to its bed of rock, 13, 139.

ἔχω, imperf. εἶχον, Ep. ἔχον, iterat. form imperf. ἔχεσκον, fut. ἔξω and oftener σχήσω, aor. act. ἔσχον, infin. σχεῖν, Ep. σχέμεν, fut. mid. ἔξομαι and σχήσομαι, aor. mid. ἐσχόμην, 3 sing. σχέτο, without augm. only 7, 248. 21, 345; imperat. σχοῦ, infin. σχέσθαι, partcp. σχόμενος. An Ep. form of the aor. is ἔσχεθον, σχέθον, and from the aor. is formed a new pres. ἴσχω. Ground signif. to hold and to have. I) Act. 1) Trans. to hold, to grasp, to hold fast, a) Primarily, to hold in the hands, χειρί or ἐν χειρί τι, 1, 14. 6, 319; μετὰ χερσίν, 11, 184. ἔχειν τινά τινος, to hold any man by any thing, χειρός, ποδός, by the hand, the foot, 4, 154. 11, 488. 16, 763. The direction is often indicated by an adv. or prep.: πρό τινος, ἐπί τινι, ἀντία ἀλλήλων, 5, 300. 569. ἔχειν τινί τι, to hold any thing to any man, 9, 209; metaph. φυλακάς, to keep watch, 9, 1; ἀλαοσκοπιήν, 13, 10; σκοπιήν, Od. 8, 302. b) to hold erect, to bear, to carry, κάρη ὑψοῦ, 6, 509: κάρη ὑπὲρ πασῶν, to erect the head above all, Od. 6, 107; κίονας, Od. 1, 53; hence metaph. to shelter, to protect, to preserve, 22, 322. 24, 730. c) to hold fast, to hold in, τινά, any man (by force or kindness), ἵππους, 4, 302; cf. 227, hence: ὀχῆες εἶχον πύλας, the bars held the doors fastened, 12, 456. 24, 453. metaph. ἔχει βέλος ὀξὺ γυναῖκα, held fast, pierced, 11, 269. ἐν φρεσίν, to retain, 2, 33. d) to hold up, to check, to restrain, to hold off (always, except 13, 51), in the fut. σχήσειν, 20, 27. 23, 720; ὀδύνας, 11, 848; τινά τινος, to repel or restrain any man from any thing, 2, 275. 13, 687. e) to hold out against, to withstand, esply an attacking enemy, 13, 51. Od. 1, 198, οὐδέ οἱ ἔσχεν ὀστέον, nor did his bone withstand, 16, 740. f) to keep towards, to direct, mly ἵππους, νῆας, 3, 263; with ἐπί τινι, or adv. as πρόσθε, Πύλονδε, 11, 760: and absol. to sail any where, Od. 3, 182. 2) to have. a) to possess, spoken of every thing which belongs to any man as property, παράκοιτιν, 3, 53. cf. 13, 173. Od. 4, 569; hence pass. τοῦπερ θυγάτηρ ἔχεθ᾽ (ἔχετο) Ἕκτορι, whose daughter was had by Hector, i. e. married to Hector, 6, 398. b) Spoken of the gods, to hold, to inhabit, οὐρανόν, Ὄλυμπον, Od. 1, 67. 4, 756. αἴθηρ ἔχει κορυφήν, Od. 12, 78; also with the idea to have in power, to take care of, πατρώϊα ἔργα, Od. 2, 22. ἵππους ἔχων ἀτίταλλε, 24, 280. c) to have, to seize, to apprehend, spoken respecting any thing that appertains to soul or body; πόνον, ἄλγεα, μένος, 6, 525. 5, 895. 516. Often the condition stands as subject and the person as object, in the accus. Δία οὐκ ἔχεν ὕπνος, sleep held not Zeus, 2, 2. Ἀχαιοὺς ἔχε φύζα, 9, 2; hence pass. ἔχεσθαι ἄσθματι, to be seized with laborious breathing, 15, 10; in like manner: κακότητι, ἄλγεσι, Od. 8, 182. d) to have with oneself, to carry, to lead, spoken of things: σάκος ὤμῳ, εἷμα ἀμφ᾽ ὤμοισιν; and according to the st bst. to cause, to *make*, spoken of a helmet; καναχὴν ἔχε, it emitted a sound, 16, 105. φόρμιγγες βοὴν εἶχον, the harps sounded, 18, 495; ὕβριν, to exhibit insolence, Od. 1, 368. The partcp. ἔχων often stands with another verb for greater exactness: τὸν ἔξαγε χειρὸς ἔχων, he led him out by the hand, 11, 488; cf. 24, 280. 2) Intrans. 1) *to hold oneself*, to be in a place or condition. εὖ ἔχει, it is well, Od. 24, 245; *to maintain oneself, to persist*; mly limited by an adv. ἔχον (sc. οὕτως), ὥστε τάλαντα γυνή (sc. ἔχει), they held themselves, as a woman holds the balance (in equipoise); the first time intrans., the second trans., 12, 433. (Köppen from v. 436, supplies unnecessarily μάχην: 'they made the fight equal'). ἔξω, ὡς λίθος, Od. 19, 494. ἔχον ὡς σφιν πρῶτον ἀπήχθετο Ἴλιος, they were disposed, as at first, when Troy was odious to them, 24, 27. ἔχεν ἦ—ἐσάλτο, he held himself where he leaped in, 13, 679. οὐδ᾽ οἱ ἔγχος ἔχ᾽ ἀτρέμας, the spear remained not quiet, 13, 557; in opposition to ἐλέλικτο. 2) *to hold oneself, to tend to, to extend*; ὑψόσε, to extend upwards, Od. 19, 38. ὀδόντες ἔχον ἔνθα καὶ ἔνθα, projected here and there, 10, 263. ἔγχος ἔσχε δι᾽ ὤμων, passed [as *we* say, *held right on*] through the shoulders. 14, 452. 3) *to be able, to be in a condition*, with infin. οὔπως ἔτι εἶχεν ὑποτρέσαι, he was no longer able to fly, 7, 217. 16, 110; without infin., 17, 354. II) Mid. *to hold oneself, to maintain oneself*, κρατερῶς, 16, 501. 17, 559; ἄντα σχομένη, holding herself opposite, i. e. opposite to him, Od. 6, 141. 2) *to hold oneself, to attach oneself, to hang on, to remain*, in a place: ἔγχος σχέτο ἐν τῇ ῥινῷ, 7, 248. πρὸς ἀλλήλοισι, ἔχονται, they hang to one another, Od. 5, 329; ἀνὰ δ᾽ ἀλλήλησιν, up upon one another, Od. 24, 8; with gen. alone: πέτρης, upon the rock, Od. 5, 429; metaph. ἔσχετο φωνή, the voice faltered, 17, 696. *b*) Esply *to depend on* any man, τινός; σέο ἔξεται, it will depend upon thee, 9, 102; with infin., h. 30, 6; and ἔκ τινος, Od. 11, 346; hence *c*) *to be in any man's power, to be in a man's possession*. ἔντεα μετὰ Τρώεσσιν ἔχονται, 18, 130. 197; metaph. πείρατα νίκης ἔχονται ἐν θεοῖσιν, the event of victory is in the power of the gods, 7, 102. 3) *to withdraw oneself, to retire* [always aor. or fut. except 14, 129], with gen. αὐτῆς, 2, 98; μάχης, 3, 84; βίης, Od. 4, 422. 4) *to hold, to bear* for oneself, or with reference to the subject; with accus. ἀσπίδα πρόσθε, the shield before oneself, 12, 294; κρήδεμνα ἄντα παρειάων, Od. 1, 334. 21, 65, μένος καὶ χεῖρας σχήσεσθαι, like act. σχήσειν, 17, 638. cf. 12, 125. The following passage is differently explained; it belongs in signif. to no. 3, mid: οὐδ᾽ ἔτι φασὶν σχήσεσθ᾽ ἀλλ᾽ ἐν νηυσὶ μελαίνησιν πεσέεσθαι, they say that they can no longer hold back, but will plunge into the dark ships, 9, 235. cf. 12,

106, 107. In both passages the Trojans are the subject. Thus Eustath. (ἤγουν ἐφέξειν ἑαυτοὺς, ἀλλὰ διώκοντας, ἐμπεσεῖσθαι ταῖς νηυσί), and Schol. Ven. and Voss. Another explanation, which Ruhkopf in Köpp. Anm. zu Il. 12, 105, gives, supplies ἡμᾶς to σχήσεσθαι, and refers it to the Greeks. They also quote Eustath. and the Schol. brev.; but the connexion does not favour the interpretation. The case is different with 12, 125. 17, 639. cf. πίπτω.

ἐψιάομαι, depon. mid. (ἐψία), prop. to play with small stones; but generally *to play, to jest, to be pleased*, Od. 17, 530; *to be charmed*, with dat. μολπῇ καὶ φόρμιγγι, *Od. 21, 429.

ἔω, see εἰμί.

ἔω, ἐῷ, see ἐάω.

ἔωθα, see ἔθω.

ἐώκει, see ἔοικα.

ἐώλπει, see ἔλπω.

ἔωμεν, 19, 402; in ἐπεί χ᾽ ἔωμεν πολέμοιο,† ed. Wolf; a rare form. Eustath. and the Gramm. explain it: πληρηθῶμεν, κορεσθῶμεν, and compare it to the formula ἐξ ἔρον ἔντο. They even derive it from a theme ἔω, i. e. πληρῶ, and consider it as subj. aor. 2 pass. Such an aor. pass. is contrary to all usus loquendi. Buttm. Lex. p. 25, and Gram. under ἄω, justly maintain that we must write either ἔωμεν or ἔωμεν. The first is the most simple. 1) ἔωμεν, Ep. for ὦμεν, 1 plur. aor. 2 subj. act. from ἵημι in the intrans. signif. *when we desist from war*, see ἵημι. 2) ἔωμεν, according to Buttm. Lex. p. 26, subj. pres. from ἈΩ, *to satiate*, prop. ἄωμεν, and Ep. for metre's sake ἔωμεν; and on account of the spir. len. he reads ἐπεί κ᾽ ἔωμεν, when we become sated with war; have had enough of the war. Spitz. Exc. 31, ad Il. defends the common deriv., and with the ancients adopts the forms ἔω, ἑάω, ἄω, ὦμεν and ἔωμεν, remarking that it is distinguished by the spir. asp. from ἑάω, ἐῶ.

ἐών, see εἰμί.

ἐῳνοχόει, see οἰνοχοέω.

ἐώργει, see ἔρδω.

ἕως, Ep. also εἵως, conj. of time. 1) To express simultaneous action, *as long as, whilst*, with indic. when the affirmation respects a reality; in the apodosis prop. τέος, often simply δέ or τόφρα, 18, 15. 1, 193. 10, 507. Od. 12, 327. 2) In introducing a consequent, *up to, until; a*) With indicat., 11, 342. Od. 5, 123. *b*) With subj. and κέ, when a contemplated end is expressed, 3, 291. 24, 185. *c*) With optat. after a historical tense, Od. 5, 386. 9, 376; and with κέ, Od. 2, 78. 3) *in order that, that*, like ὄφρα, with optat., Od. 4, 800. 6, 80. 4) As adv. for τέως, *for a time, some time, in the mean time*, 12, 141. 13, 143. Od. 3, 126; prop. it then stands with an omission of the clause belonging to it, cf. Nitzsch ad Od. 3, 126. ἕως and εἵως change with the necessities of the metre; ἕως has its natural quantity only once, Od. 2, 78 ; elsewhere it is either monosyllabic, as 17, 727 ; or to be pronounced as a trochee, like είος, as Thiersch, § 168, 10, would write it, 1, 193. 10, 507, and often.

έωσι, see είμί.

έωσι, see έάω.

έωσφόρος, ον (έως, φέρω), bringing the morning [day's harbinger, Cp.]; as a pr. n. Έωσφόρος, the morning star, 23, 226 ; † according to Hes. Th. 381, son of Astræus and Eôs (in H. to be read as a trissyllable).

Z.

Z, the sixth letter of the Greek alphabet; and hence the index of the sixth rhapsody.

ζα-, an inseparable particle, a dialectic variety of δα, which in composition strengthens the notion of the simple word, as ζάθεος, ζάκοτος. It is mly derived from διά; more correctly, Hartung considers it a collateral form of άγα (άγαν).

ζαής, ές, gen. έος (άημι), blowing violently, stormy, άνεμος, 12, 157. Od. 5, 368. The heteroclit. accus. ζαήν for ζαῆ (as Σωκράτην for Σωκράτη) is found in Od. 12, 313; see Thiersch, Gram. § 193, 35.

ζάθεος, έη, εον (θεός), divine, very sacred, holy, spoken of countries and places, inasmuch as they were supposed to be inhabited by the gods, Κίλλα [Cilla the divine. Cp.], Νίσα, Κρίσα, *1, 38. 2, 520.

ζάκοτος, ον (κότος), very angry, furious, violently enraged, 3, 220.†

Ζάκυνθος, ή, an island in the Ionian sea, south of Samê, which, with Ithaca, Samê, and two small unknown islands, Ægilips and Crokyleia, constituted the Kephallenian kingdom, which was subject to Odysseus (Ulysses); now Zante, 2, 634. Because in this place the position before ζ is neglected, Payne-Knight, in Proleg. Hom. p. 79, would read Δάκυνθος, see Thiersch, § 146. 8. ύλήεσσα Ζάκυνθος, Od. 9, 24; but ύλήεντι, agreeing with Ζάκυνθος, is feminine [see ύλήεις], Od. 1, 246. 16, 123. The fact is, the first syllable can stand no where in heroic verse but at the close of a dactyl; hence the Epic poets could not prolong the preceding vowel.

*ζαμενής, ές (μένος), very strong, very brave; only in the superl. ζαμενέστατος, h Merc. 307, as epith. of Apollo.

ζατρεφής, ές (τρέφω), gen. έος, well-fed, fat, stout, ταῦροι, 7, 223; αῖγες, Od. 14, 106; φῶκαι, Od. 4, 451.

ζαφλεγής, ές (φλέγω), gen. έος, prop. brightly burning; only metaph. very ardent, spirited, lively, spoken of men, 21, 165; and of horses, h. 7, 8.

ζαχρηής, ές, gen. έος, pressing on ar-

dently, blowing violently, impetuous, spoken of winds, 5, 525 ; and of warriors, *12, 347. 13, 684. In the last passage, it is, with Heyne, Voss, and Spitzner, to be referred to the Greeks. (Undoubtedly Ion. for ζαχραής from ζά and χράω; the reading ζαχρειής, as well as the derivation from χρειά, is unsuitable, see Thiersch, Gram. § 193. 35.)

ζάω, contract. ζῶ, I live; only partcp. pres. ζώντος, 1, 88 ;† see ζώω.

ζειά, ή, spelt, farra, according to Voss a species of wheat, cultivated like wheat, and better suited to the south than the north. It occurs only in the plur. and is spoken of as food for horses, Od. 4, 41. 604. This same spelt seems to be called όλυρα, 5, 196. Still Sprengel, Hist. rei Herbar., makes a distinction between όλυρα, triticum Spelta, and ζειά, triticum Zea, the last having grains like barley and larger ears.

ζείδωρος, ον (ζειά, δῶρον), grain-giving, producing nourishment, epith of the earth, 2, 548. Od. 3, 3. (The deriv. from ζάω, life-giving, according to Hesych. is contrary to analogy.)

Ζέλεια, ή, Zelea, a town in Troas, at the foot of Ida, later belonging to Cyzicus, 2, 824. (From the neglect of position before this word, Payne-Knight, Proleg. Hom. p. 19, would read Δέλεια.) Cf. Ζάκυνθος, extr.

ζέσσεν, see ζέω.

ζεύγλη, ή (ζεύγνυμι), in H. distinguished from ζυγόν; the part of the yoke into which the heads of the harnessed animals were introduced; each yoke had therefore two ζεύγλαι; the yoke-ring, the yoke-bow, *17, 440. 19, 406.

ζεύγνυμι (the infin. pres. ζευγνύμεναι, ζευγνύμεν) and ζευγνύω, whence the imperf. ζεύγνυον for έζεύγν., 19, 343, aor. 1 έζευξα, Ep. ζεῦξα, aor. mid. έζευξάμην, perf. pass. έζευγμαι. I) Act. 1) to yoke together, to yoke, to harness, with accus. ίππους, βόας; sometimes with ύφ άρματι, ύπ' άμάξησιν, ύπ' άπήνη or όχεσφιν, 23, 130. Od. 3, 478 6, 73. 2) to join, to unite, σανίδες έζευγμέναι, 18, 276. II) Mid. to yoke or harness for oneself, ίππους, Od. 3, 492. 15, 145. 24, 281. (The form ζευγνύμεν, 16, 145, is worthy of note, with ῠ as infin. pres., but having every where else ῠ. Buttm., Herm., and Becker would write ζευγνύμμεν, which the analogy έμεν, έμμεναι favours. Spitz., on the other hand, after the ancients, writes ζευγνύμεν'. see Thiersch, § 231. 102. Buttm. Ausf. Gram. § 107. Anm. 30. p. 535. Rost. Gram. ζεύγνυμι.)

ζεύγος, τό (ζεύγνυμι), a yoke, a pair, spoken of draught animals, 18, 543.†

Ζεύς, ό, vocat. Ζεῦ; the oblique cases are sometimes formed from ΔΙΣ, gen. Διός, dat. Διί, accus. Δία; sometimes from ΖΗΝ, gen. Ζηνός, dat. Ζηνί, accus. Ζῆνα (Ζῆν', 14, 265); Zeus (Jupiter), son of Cronus and Rhea, 15, 187; the most powerful amongst the gods, the father of

Nv

gods and men. 1) He is the ruler of the gods, who stand far below him in power and dignity. He convokes the assemblies of the gods, to deliberate on the concerns of his kingdom; yet durst no one of the gods oppose his settled resolution, 8, 12, seq. 19, 258. 2) He is, as god of the heavens, the governor of all natural phenomena. As such, he is throned in ether (αἰθέρι ναίων, ὑψίζυγος); he collects the clouds; hence, νεφεληγερέτης, κελαινεφής, gives rain and sunshine, and excites tempests. Thunder and lightning are the signs of his anger; by these he terrifies men, and gives them omens (hence τερπικέραυνος, ἀστεροπητής, ἀργικέραυνος, ἐρίγδουπος, ἐριβρεμέτης, etc.). 3) He also governs the fates of men (ταμίας); yet is he himself subject to the laws of Fate, 10, 71. Od. 6, 188. He is the author of royalty, the protector of magistrates, directs the assemblies of men, Od. 2, 69; the defender of house and hearth (ἑρκεῖος), Od. 22, 335; he is the patron of hospitality, protects guests and suppliants, hence, ξείνιος, Od. 9, 270. 6, 207; and ἱκετήσιος, Od. 13, 213. 4) His sister and wife is Hêrê, who often so opposes his will, that he threatens her with punishments, and even executes them, 15, 17, seq. 19, 95, seq. Not unfrequently he excites her just displeasure by the violation of nuptial fidelity, 14, 317, seq. 5) The form of Zeus is sublime, and inspires awe. With his head, which is surrounded with ambrosial locks, he gives assent or expresses his anger. The tokens of his power are thunderbolts and the ægis (αἰγίοχος). As the tutelary deity of the Pelasgians he is called Πελασγικός, and Δωδωναῖος, because he had an oracle at Dôdôna, see Δωδώνη. (In signif. Ζεύς is related to ζέω and ζάω, according to Herm. Fervius, live-giver, and Διός, fr. ΔΙΣ, prob. the upper air.)

Ζεφυρίη, ἡ, subaud. πνοή, the west wind, the western breeze, prop. a fem. from ζεφύριος, Od. 7, 119.† (The first syllable is here long by the arsis.)

Ζέφυρος, ὁ, 1) Zephyrus, the evening or west wind, one of the four main winds which H. mentions. It comes from the western ocean, Od. 4, 567; is opposed to Εὖρος, Od. 5, 332; still it blows with Boreas from Thrace, 9, 5; and unites with Notus on the Trojan plain. These apparent contradictions are most probably to be explained by the circumstance, that H. in the four main winds includes also the intermediate ones, cf. Nitzsch ad Od. 2, 419. It is often rough and violent (Od. 5, 295); brings snow, Od. 19, 206; and rain, Od. 14, 458; still its breath is also soft, Od. 7, 119; and breathes coolness upon the blessed in the Elysian fields. 2) It appears personified, 23, 200; and, as a deity, the wind-gods feast with him. To him the harpy Podarge bore the steeds of Achilles,

16, 150. According to Hes. Th. 379 he is the son of Astræus and Podargê.

ζέω, imperf. Ep. ζέε for ἔζει, 21, 365. aor. 1 ἔζεσα, Ep. σσ, to seethe, to boil, to bubble up, to be boiling hot, spoken of water, 18, 349. 21, 365. Od. 10, 360. and λέβης ζεῖ, the cauldron boils, 21, 362.

Ζῆθος, ὁ, son of Zeus and Antiopê, brother of Amphîon, husband of Ædon, Od. 11, 262. 19, 523.

ζηλήμων, ον (ζηλέω), gen. ονος, jealous, envious, unfavorable, θεοί, Od. 5, 118.†

*ζηλοσύνη, ἡ, poet. for ζῆλος, zeal. 2 jealousy, envy, h. Ap. 100.†

*ζηλόω (ζῆλος), fut. ώσω, aor. 3 sing optat. ζηλώσαι, 1) to emulate, to imitate 2) to be jealous, to envy, absol. h. Cer 168. 223.

(Ζήν), gen. Ζηνός, see Ζεύς.

*ζητεύω, poet. for ζητέω, to seek, with accus. h. Ap. 215. Merc. 392.

ζητέω, fut. ήσω, to seek, to seek out, to search for, to trace, τινά. 14, 258; † βόας h. Merc. 22. 2) to inquire, to ask for any thing; with γένος, Batr. 25.

ζόφος, ὁ, darkness, obscurity, hence 1) the obscurity of the lower world 'Ερεβόσδε ὑπὸ ζόφον, Od. 20, 356. b) the realm of shades itself, 15, 191. Od. 11 57. h. Cer. 482. 2) the dark, shaded side of the earth, the evening darkness, the west, evening, in opposition to ἠώς, Od 10, 190, and cf. 8, 29; πρὸς ζόφον, in antithesis to πρὸς ἠῶ τ' ἠέλιόν τε, Od. 13 241. Il. 12, 339. It is thus correctly explained by Heyne, Uckert, Grotefend Nitzsch ad Od. 2, 146. Strabo and Voss interpret it incorrectly midnight (see Völcker's Hom. Geogr. § 27, p. 42). According to Buttm. Lex. p. 378, of the same family with ὀνόφος, νέφος.

ζυγόδεσμον, τό (δεσμός), the yoke-band the leathern thong with which the yoke was bound to the pole, so that the animals did not draw by traces, but by the pole, 24, 270.† It is called ἐννεάπηχυ nine cubits long, it being bound thrice around; cf. Köpke Kriegswesen de Griech. p. 137. (In H. it is neut., late also ὁ ζυγόδεσμος.)

ζυγόν, τό (ζεύγνυμι), Ep. gen. sing ζυγόφιν, 24, 576. 1) a yoke, a transverse piece of wood attached to the pole, upon the two sides of which were two wooden bows or yokes (ζεύγλη and sometimes ζυγόν), into which the necks of the draught animals were introduced. In the middle, where it was attached to the tongue, it had an elevation (ὀμφαλός 24, 269. 273. 5, 730. Od. 3, 486. It was furnished with rings (οἴηκεσσιν ἀρηρός 24, 269, for the reins, to prevent them from slipping, cf. λέπαδνον, ἕστωρ, κρίκος esply as ζυγὸν ἵππειον or ἵππων, mentioned 5, 799. 851. 2) the bridge or cross bar, by which the two arms of the lyre were connected, and in which the pegs were inserted, 9, 187. h. Merc. 50. 3) Plur. the rowers' seats or benches, the transverse beams in the middle space of vessels, which bound together the sides and formed seats for the rowers, Od. 9, 99. 13, 21. (The ground signification of ζυγόν is uniting, and especially a body which unites two others. In H. only neut.)

ζυγός, ὁ = ζυγόν, h. Cer. 217; in a metaph. signif. a burden.

ζωάγρια, τά (ζωός, ἀγρεύω), a reward for the preservation of life, prop. the present which the prisoner gives the victor for his life: ζωάγρια τίνειν, to pay this reward, 18, 407. ζωάγρια ὀφέλλειν τινί, to owe to any man the reward for saving life, i. e. to owe one's life to him, Od. 8, 462.

ζωγρέω (ζωός, ἀγρεύω), 1) to take alive, to grant one's life, with accus. (to a prisoner in war), 6, 46. 10, 378. 2) to preserve in life, to reanimate, θυμόν, 5, 698.

ζωή, ἡ (ζάω), life. 2) In H. the support of life, sustenance, property, like βίος. *Od. 14, 96. 16, 429.

ζῶμα τό (ζώννυμι), prop. a broad band or girdle, worn about the loins. Thus, the covering of the loins worn by wrestlers, subligaculum. 23, 683. With the Hom. warriors this band which was under the ζωστήρ, was connected with the cuirass, and since it was, as it were, a part of the cuirass, the latter is also called ζῶμα, which is otherwise called θώρηξ, 4, 187. 216. Thus Aristarchus, cf. Lehrs de Aristarch. stud. p. 125, and Voss. Others, as Heyne, understand by it, with Eustath., the under garment or doublet, of the Hom. warriors, which was confined by a girdle (ζωστήρ), Od. 14, 482 [see Heyne ad Il. 4, 132].

ζώνη, ἡ (ζώννυμι), 1) a girdle, a zone, a waist-band, chiefly of females, which they wore above the hips, so that the robe might fall in ample folds, 14, 181. Od 5, 231. 10, 544; hence metaph. ζώνην λύειν, to loose the girdle, 11, 245. cf. h. Ven. 256. 2) Metaph. the part of the body where the girdle was worn, between the hips and the short ribs (ὁ περὶ τὸν γαστέρα τόπος), the smaller part of the body, the waist. Ἄρεϊ ζώνην ἴκελος, 2, 479; opposed to στέρνον; κατὰ ζώνην νύξε, he wounded him in the side or abdomen, 11, 234. Others (Wolf) interpret it in both passages of the girdle, as ζωστήρ, but this is clearly distinguished from it, 11, 236. Thus Voss, 'he wounded him in the girdle' [he pierced the broider'd zone. Cp.].

ζώννυμι, aor. ἔζωσα, aor. mid. ἐζωσάμην, iterat. imperf. ζωννύσκετο, 1) Act. to gird, esply to gird for battle, to put on armour, Od. 18, 76. II) Mid. to gird oneself, ζωστῆρι, 10, 78; ῥάκεσιν περὶ μήδεα. Od. 18, 67; absol. to gird oneself, to equip oneself, esply for battle, 11, 15. 23, 685. Od. 18, 30. b) With accus. χαλκόν, to put on the girdle, to gird on a weapon, 23, 130.

ζωός, ή, όν, living, alive, as ζωὸν ἑλεῖν τινα, 6, 50; ζώς, Ep. rare form for ζωός (from ζαός), 5, 887; accus. ζών, 16, 445.

ζωρός, όν (akin to ζωός), prob. strong; hence spoken of wine: unmixed, undiluted, strong. ζωρότερον κέραιε, mingle the wine stronger, i. e. mix less water with it, 9, 203.†

ζώς = ζωός, q. v.

[ζῶσμα = ζῶμα, but the form is rejected by Th. Magist. p. 411.]

ζωστήρ, ῆρος, ὁ (ζώννυμι), the girdle, the waist-belt of warriors, which was worn around the body above the μίτρη and ζῶμα to protect the abdomen, so that it embraced the lower part of the cuirass, 4, 132, seq. 186, 215. 11, 236. It was probably made of leather and variegated (παναίολος, φοίνικι φαεινός, 7, 305), and covered with metal plates, 11, 237. It was confined by buckles or clasps, 4, 132. 2) a girdle with which the tunic (χιτών) was confined, Od. 14, 72.

ζῶστρον, τό, a girdle, a belt, Od. 6, 38.†

ζώω, Ep. and Ion. for ζάω, to live, with accus. ζώειν ἀγαθὸν βίον, to lead a good [i. e. happy, tranquil (Cp.)] life, Od. 15, 491; and often in connexion with ὁρᾶν φάος Ἠελίοιο, 18, 61. H. has always, except ζῶντος, 1, 88, the form ζώω, arising from doubling the vowel of ζῶ, only in the pres. and imperf. ζώω, ζώεις, etc., partcp. ζώοντος, infin. ζώειν, ζωέμεναι, ζωέμεν, imperf. ἔζωον (see Thiersch, § 220. 74; Buttm. p. 284. Rost, p. 305).

H.

H, the seventh letter of the Greek alphabet, and therefore the sign of the seventh book.

ἤ, Ep. also ἠέ, a conjunction, indicating either exclusion or diversity. I) Exclusion: 1) In disjunctive sentences: ἤ, or; ἤ, ἤ, either, or; it not only expresses like aut, the necessary, but also like vel, an arbitrary exclusion, 1, 27. 138. Od. 14, 330. b) To indicate an equal weight in the opposing clauses, τέ is added: ἤτε, ἤτε = εἴτε, 11, 410. 17, 42. c) ἠμέν, ἠδέ, express not the disjunctive, but like τέ, τέ, the copulative signif.; prop. as well, as, 2, 789. 5, 128. Often to ἠδέ is annexed καί, 5, 128. Also ἠμὲν—καί, correl., 15, 664; ἠμὲν—δέ, 12, 428; or μὲν—ἠδέ, Od. 12, 168; τὲ—ἠδέ, Od. 1, 12. Often also ἠδέ is used alone, 1, 334. 2) In disjunctive questions: or, whether. a) In direct questions, either double: ἤ, ἤ, utrum, an (in which case the first is not translated), Od. 1, 175. 6, 120; or single, Od. 1, 226. If a question has already preceded, ἤ, an serves to decide or to limit it: ἦ ἵνα ὕβριν ἴδη, peradventure to see, 1, 203. 5, 466. Od. 4, 710. b) In indirect questions, either single : whether, 8, 111. Od. 16, 138; or in the double question: ἤ, ἤ, whether, or, 1, 190. Od. 6, 142. Also the first ἤ is sometimes wanting, or its place supplied by εἰ. II) Diversity : than, quam. 1) After a comparative, and after such words as express an idea of comparison, as ἄλλος, οὐδεὶς ἄλλος; after βούλομαι, 1, 117. 2) It stands between two comparatives, when two qualities in one object are compared : πάντες κ' ἀρησαίατ' ἐλαφρότεροι πόδας εἶναι, ἤ ἀφνειότεροι χρυσοῖο, all would desire rather to be swift of foot than rich, Od. 1, 164 ['would desire to be swifter of foot than they now are, rather than richer,' in order either to escape or to ransom themselves, since to be richer would avail them nothing. Fäsi] 3) ἤ stands sometimes after a comparative, with the gen. of a demonstrative pronoun, so that the following clause may be regarded as an apposition to the pron., 15, 509. Od. 6, 182; cf. Kühner, § 622, seq. Thiersch, § 312. 352, note; ἤ οὐ and ἤ οὐκ are commonly to be pronounced with synizesis, 5, 349.

ἤ, adv. occurs in a two-fold signif. 1) In positive clauses it serves for confirmation and assurance: certainly, truly, surely, verily. It stands sometimes alone, 1, 229; mly however it is strengthened by other particles: ἤ δή, verily, of a truth, 1, 518; ἤ μάλα, certainly (very), 3, 204. Od. 16, 183; ἤ μάλα δή, most certainly; assuredly, 8, 102. Od. 1. 384; ἤ που, surely; ἤ τε, certainly. In like manner, ἤ νυ, ἤ που, when the affirmation at the same time contains a doubt, 3, 43. 22, 11; esply, ἤ μήν (μέν, μάν), a strengthened affirmation, most commonly used in an oath, verily, 2, 291; also with an infin. in dependent discourse: καί μοι ὄμοσσον, ἤ μέν μοι—ἀρήξειν, that thou wilt certainly (or assuredly) protect me, 1, 77. 14, 275. 2) In interrogations : num, where it cannot be translated into English; it includes at the same time an affirmation, mly in the following connexions: ἤ ἄρα δή, ἤ ῥα, ἤ ῥά νυ, ἤ νυ, ἤ νύ που. It stands without particles only when the party proposing the question, by a question immediately following conjecturally answers the first, in which case it may be rendered perhaps, peradventure: τί με ταῦτα λιλαίεαι ἠπεροπεύειν; ἤ πή με—άξεις, wilt thou peradventure lead me away, 3, 400. Od. 9, 405. 452.

ἤ, imperf. of εἰμί. 2) Imperf. of ἠμί.

ἤ, dat. fem. of the relat. pron. ὅς, ἤ. ὅ, in H. mly as an adv. (subaud. ὁδῷ or μερίδι). 1) where, whither, with τῇ, preceding, 13, 53. 2) as, in what way, ἤ θέμις ἐστί, as is right, 2, 73. 9, 33 According to Buttm. Lex. p. 535, ἤ in H. has only a local signif. and in both passages must be written ἤ θέμις ἐστί, Od. 9, 268. 24, 286. With him agrees

Thiersch, § 343, 7. Spitz. Excurs. II. Nitzsch ad Od. 3, 45, approves the ἤ only when it stands with a gen., 9, 134. 276. Od. 9, 268.

ἤα, see εἰμί.

ἠβαιός, ή, όν, little, small, mly with negat. οὐ οἱ ἔνι φρένες οὐδ' ἠβαιαί, he has no understanding, not even a little, not the least, 14, 141. Od. 21, 288. Often the neut. ἠβαιόν as adv. little, Od. 9, 462; and with negat. οὐδ' ἠβαιόν, 2, 380.

ἠβάω (ἤβη), aor. ἤβησα, 1) to be arrived at the age of puberty, to be in the bloom of one's life, to possess the full power of a man. εἴθ' ὡς ἡβώοιμι, 7, 157. 11. 670. ἀνὴρ οὐδὲ μάλ' ἡβῶν, 12, 382. 2) Metaph. ἡμερὶς ἡβώωσα, a vigorous vine, Od. 5, 69. (H. has sometimes the contr. forms, ἡβῷμι, ἡβῶν, sometimes the forms with the vowel repeated after ω : ἡβώοντα, ἡβώοιμι,—ἡβώωσα, which Heyne would write ἡβωῶσα, is correct; it is not a contraction but a repetition of the vowel, see Thiersch, § 220, 70.) [See also Buttm. § 105, note 10.]

ἤβη, puberty, the age of manhood, which was reckoned from the eighteenth year: hence mly youth, the age of youth, the most powerful age of men, 24, 348. Od. 10, 279. ἤβης ἱκέσθαι μέτρον, to arrive at the measure of youth, 11, 225; ἤβης ἄνθος ἔχειν, 13, 484; and generally youthful vigour, manly vigour, 23, 432. Od. 8, 181. h. 7, 9.

Ἤβη, ἡ, Hebê, daughter of Zeus and Hêrê, wife of Hêraclês, Od. 11, 603. h. 14, 8; she appears as the cup-bearer of the gods, 4, 2; and as the handmaid of Hêrê, 5, 722. She bathes Arês her brother, 5, 905; later the goddess of youth.

*ἡβητής, οῦ, ὁ (ἤβη), a youth, a marriageable young man, κοῦροι ἡβηταί h. Merc. 56.

ἡβῷμι, see ἡβάω.

ἡβώοιμι, ἡβώοντα, ἡβώωσα, Ep. expanded forms from ἡβάω.

ἠγάασθε, see ἄγαμαι.

ἤγαγον, ἡγαγόμην, see ἄγω.

ἠγάθεος, η, ον (ἄγαν, θεός), very divine, sacred, holy, epith. of towns, countries mountains, since they were regarded as under particular divine protection, 1. 252. Od. 2, 308. (Prob. fr. ἄγαν and θεῖος, or according to others fr. ἀγαθός, η is a poet. lengthening of α, see Buttm. Lex. p. 323.)

ἠγάσσατο, see ἄγαμαι.

ἡγεμονεύω (ἡγεμών), 1) to go before, to point out; τινί, to go before any man Od. 3, 386; and absol., 5, 53. h. Ap. 437 Il. 15, 46; with accus. ὁδόν, to show the way, Od. 6, 261. 7, 30 : and ὁδόν τινι Od. 24, 225; metaph. ῥόον ὕδατι, to prepare a course for the water, 21, 258. 2 to lead, to conduct, to command, with gen., 2, 527. 552; once with dat., 2, 816 in this signif. mly in the Il.

ἡγεμών, όνος, 1) a guide upon the road, Od. 10, 505. 15, 310. 2) a leader a commander, a general, 2, 265. 11, 746; often also ἀνὴρ ἡγεμών, 2, 365. 11, 746.

ἡγέομαι. depon. mid. (ἄγω), fut. ἡγήσομαι, aor. ἡγησάμην, 1) to go before, to lead, to guide, opposed to ἕπομαι, often absol., 9, 192. 12, 251, with dat. of pers., 22, 101; also πρόσθεν ἡγεῖσθαι, 24, 96. νήεσσι ἡγήσατο Ἴλιον εἴσω, he conducted the ships to Ilium (spoken of the prophet Calchas), 1, 71; ὁδόν τινι, to lead the way for a man = to show him it, Od. 10, 263; hence, ἡγεῖσθαί τινι πόλιν, to conduct any man to the town, Od. 6, 114; δόμον, Od. 7, 22; a rare construction is ἡμῖν ἡγεῖσθω ὀρχηθμοῖο (of a minstrel), let him lead us in the dance [strike a dance, Cp.]. i. e. play for us, Od. 23, 134. 2) Esply in the Il.: to lead, to command. a) With dat. where the idea of going before prevails, 2, 864. 5, 211; ἐπὶ στίχας, 2, 687. (Others, for ἐφηγήσατό σφιν στίχας, who went before the ranks, Vos.) νήεσσιν ἐς Τροίην, 16, 169. b) With gen. like ἄρχειν, to lead on, to command, 2, 567. 620, 851.

ἡγερέθομαι, Ep. lengthened from ἀγείρομαι, only in the 3 plur. pres. and imperf. ἠγερέθονται and ἠγερέθοντο and infin. ἠγερέθεσθαι, 10, 127; which Spitz. after Aristarch. has adopted for ἠγερέεσθαι.

ἠγερέομαι, Ep. for ἀγείρομαι, only infin. pres. ἠγερέεσθαι, 10, 127; see ἠγερέθομαι.

ἤγερθεν, see ἀγείρω.

ἡγηλάζω (collateral Ep. form of ἡγέομαι), to lead, with accus. τινά, Od. 17, 217. κακὸν μόρον ἡγηλάζειν, to lead a wretched fate, i. e. to suffer, to endure it, *Od. 11, 618.

ἡγήτωρ, ορος, ὁ (ἡγέομαι), a conductor, ἀνείρων, epith. of Hermês, h. Merc. 14; a leader, a commander, in connexion with μέδοντες, 2, 79. Od. 7, 98.

ἠγοράασθε, see ἀγοράομαι.

ἠγορόωντο, see ἀγοράομαι.

ἠδέ. conj. poet. and; it connects, like καί, two words; sometimes τε precedes, 9. 99, σκῆπτρόν τ᾽ ἠδὲ θέμιστες and τέἠδὲ καί, 5, 822; often ἠδὲ καί, and also, 1, 334. 2) Most commonly it follows ἠμέν, see ἠ.

ἤδεα, pluperf. of οἶδα, see ΕΙΔΩ.

ἤδη, adv. (δή), already, now, jam, 1) Of the immediate present: νῦν ἤδη, or ἤδη νῦν, even now, now, 15, 110. With a preterite it may be translated by just, just now; and with a fut. by immediately, at once, Od. 1, 303. 2) Of past events: already: 1, 250. 260. ἤδη ποτὲ πάρος, already before, 1, 453. 2, 205. 3) Of unexpected, or long since expected events: now at length, 1, 456.

ἤδομαι, depon. mid. aor. ἡσάμην, to be pleased, to delight in; ἥσατο πίνων, Od. 9, 353.†

ἦδος, εος, τό, pleasure, joy, enjoyment, δαιτός, the enjoyment of a feast, 1, 576. ἡμῖον ἦδος, our joy, 11, 318. 2) profit, advantage, only Ep. τί μοι τῶν ἦδος;

what advantage have I from this? 18, 80. αὐτὰρ ἐμοὶ τί τόδ᾽ ἦδος; [only by implication: but thence what joy to me? Cp.] Od. 24, 95.

*ἡδυγέλως, ωτος, ὁ, ἡ (γέλως), laughing sweetly, laughing amiably, epith. of Pan, h. 18, 37.

ἡδυεπής, ές (ἔπος), sweetly speaking, sweet-longued, epith. of Nestor, 1, 248;† sweetly singing, ἀοιδός, Μοῦσαι, h. 20, 4. 32, 2.

*ἥδυμος, ον, poet. for ἡδύς, sweet, agreeable, epith. of sleep, h. Merc. 241. 449; see νήδυμος.

ἡδύποτος, ον (πίνω), sweet to drink, pleasant, οἶνος, *Od. 2, 340. 3, 391. h. 6, 36.

ἡδύς, εῖα, ύ (akin to ἅδω, ἀνδάνω), once an adj. of two endings: ἡδὺς αὐτμή, Od. 12, 369; superl. ἥδιστος, Od. 13, 80. 1) agreeable, sweet, delightful; spoken of objects of sense: of taste, οἶνος, Od. 2, 350. 3, 51; of smell, ὀδμή, Od. 9, 210; of hearing; ἀοιδή, Od. 8, 64; again: ὕπνος, κοῖτος, 4, 131. Od. 19, 510; and generally φίλον καὶ ἡδύ ἐστι, 4, 17. 7, 387. Od. 24, 435. 2) Metaph. of the mind, agreeable, cheerful. Often the neut. ἡδύ, as adv. esply ἡδὺ γελᾶν, to laugh pleasantly, heartily, 2, 270.

ἠέ, poet. for ἤ, or.

ἠε, see εἶμι.

ἠείδειν, ἠείδη, ἠείδης, Ep. pluperf. of οἶδα, see ΕΙΔΩ.

ἠέλιος, ὁ, poet. for ἥλιος (ἔλη), always in the poet. form: the sun. Of its rising we find mly ἀνιέναι, once ἀνορούειν, Od. 3, 1; and ἀνανεῖσθαι, Od. 10, 192; στείχειν πρὸς οὐρανόν, Od. 11, 17; of noon, μέσον οὐρανὸν ἀμφιβαίνει, 8, 68; of afternoon, μετενίσσετο βουλυτόνδε, 16, 779; or ἂψ ἐπὶ γαῖαν προτρέπεται, Od. 11, 18; of sunset, δύω, ἐπιδύω, καταδύω, and ἐμπίπτειν Ὠκεανῷ, 8, 485. φάος ἠελίοιο, the light of the sun : hence φάος ἠελίοιο ὁρᾶν = to live, 5, 120. Od. 10, 498. 2) To indicate the points of compass : the east, the west, Od. 13, 240. πρὸς Ἠῶ τ᾽ Ἠέλιόν τε, in opposition to ζόφος. towards the dawn and the sun, always indicates the east, not the east and south, since the poet recognizes only two heavenly regions, the light side, and the obscure, or the east and the west, 12, 239. Od. 9, 26; cf. ζόφος, and Völcker's Hom. Geogr. § 15—19.

Ἥλιος, ὁ, poet. for Ἧλιος (the last form, Od. 8, 271), Hêlios, god of the sun, son of Hyperîon, Od. 12, 176; and Euryphaessa, h. 31; see Ὑπερίων. His wife was Persê, and his children Αἰήτês and Kirkê (Circê), Od. 10, 136, seq. He rises in the east from the ocean, and sinks into the same in the west. The nymph Neæra bore him Phaethūsa and Lampetia, who watched the herds of their father in Trinacria, Od. 12, 132. Oaths were sworn by him, because he hears and sees every thing, 3, 277. He betrayed to Hêphæstus the amour of Aphroditê and

Arês, Od. 8, 271. With Zeus a boar is offered to him, 19, 197; and a white ram in opposition to a black one for the dark earth, 3, 104. Steeds and chariot are mentioned first in h. Merc. 69. It was only at a later period that Hêlios was confounded with Apollo and Phœbus.

ἦεν, see εἰμί.

ἠέπερ, adv. poet. for ἤπερ.

ἠέρα, see ἀήρ.

ἠερέθομαι, Ep. collat. form of ἀείρομαι, 3 plur. pres. ἠερέθονται, to hang, to hover, to flutter, spoken of tassels, 2, 448; of grasshoppers, 21, 12; metaph. ὁπλοτέρων φρένες ἠερέθονται, the minds of younger men are ever unstable [Cp.], *3, 108.

ἠέρι, see ἀήρ.

Ἠερίβοια, ἡ, Ep. for Ἐρίβοια, daughter of Eurymachus a son of Hermês, the second wife of Alôeus; step-mother of the Aloïdæ, Otus and Ephialtes. From hatred to her step-sons she discovered to Hermês the place where they held Arês imprisoned, 5, 389. (Ἐρίβοια, one who brings many cattle.)

ἠέριος, η, ον, Ion. and Ep. for ἀέριος (ἀήρ), in the darkness of the morning, dusk, in the morning, early, 1, 497. 557. 3, 7; and Od. 9, 52. Voss derives it correctly from ἀήρ, since very early in the morning every thing is wrapt in vapour; he translates therefore: in the misty dawn, 1, 497; and from the misty air, 3, 7; with which Wolf, Vorles. 4, 189, agrees. Buttm., in Lex. p. 42, derives it from ἦρι, early.

ἠεροειδής, ές (εἶδος), gen. έος, Ep. for ἀεροειδής, that which is like to the distant dusky air (ἀήρ), dusky, hazy, misty, cloudy, obscure, epith. of the sea, from its blue misty colour, 23, 744. Od. 2, 263; of grottoes, Od. 12, 80. 13, 366; and of a distant rock, Od. 12, 233; and of the prospect of a man standing upon watch: ὅσσον ἠεροειδὲς ἀνὴρ ἴδεν ὀφθαλμοῖσιν, as far as a man with his eyes beholds the dark distance, i. e. as far as a man's vision extends over the blue expanse of the sea, 5, 770. (The word should be taken as a subst.; Köppen's explanation of ἠεροειδές as an adv. like ἠεροειδέως is incorrect; for it is not equivalent to ἐν ἀέρι.)

ἠερόεις, εσσα, εν, Ion. and Ep. for ἀερόεις (ἀήρ), cloudy, dusky, gloomy, dark, murky, epith. of Tartarus, 8, 13; and of ζόφος, as the under world and dark side of the earth, 12, 240. 15, 191; hence ἠερόεντα κέλευθα, the dark paths of death, Od. 20, 64.

ἠεροφοῖτις, ιος, ἡ (φοιτάω), walking in darkness, veiled in darkness, epith. of the Furies, since they threaten death and unforeseen calamity, *9, 571. 19, 87.

ἠερόφωνος, ον (φωνή), crying through the air; clear, shrill-voiced, epith. of heralds, 18, 505.†

Ἠετίων, ωνος, ὁ, 1) king of Hypoplacian Thebê in Cilicia, father of Andro-mache, 1, 366. 6, 396. Achilles slew him together with seven sons, when he sacked Thebê, 6, 416. cf. 23, 827. 2) an Imbrian, a friend of Priam, who liberated Lycaon from slavery and sent him to Arisbe, 21, 42, seq. (According to Damm. from ἀετός.)

ἤην, ὁ, from which Ep. the oblique cases ἠέρος, ἠέρι, ἠέρα of ἀήρ, are formed.

ἠθεῖος, είη, εῖον (ἦθος), trusty, beloved, worthy, dear, in the Il. mly in voc. as subst. ἠθεῖα, 6, 518. 10, 37. 22, 229; where the young brother always addresses the elder: ἠθείη κεφαλή, dear head, like our 'dear heart;' thus Achilles addresses the shade of Patroclus, 23, 94; and Eumæus calls Odysseus (Ulysses) ἠθεῖος, Od. 14, 147. (The deriv. from ἦθος, one with whom intercourse is wont to be held, is most prob.; improb. from θεῖος, uncle, or θεῖος, divine.)

ἦθος, εος, τό (Ion. for ἔθος), an accustomed abode, hence a haunt, a dwelling, spoken only of beasts; of horses: the accustomed pasture, Voss, Il. 6, 511. 15, 268; of swine, the accustomed sty, Od. 14, 411.

ἤια, τά (εἶμι), 1) the food which one takes with him on a journey, provision for the road, pros. ἐφόδια, Od. 2, 289. 410. 4, 363. 5, 266. 9, 212. 12, 329; and generally, food, nourishment; also λύκων ἤια, the food of wolves, 13, 103. 2) chaff, husks, pods, elsewhere ἄχυρα, as the Gramm. explain, ἠίων θημῶν καρφαλέων Od. 5, 368. The Gramm. derive it from εἶμι, imperf. ἤιον, and explain it τὰ φερόμενα, what is carried (food), and that which moves easily (chaff), see Thiersch, Gram. § 166, 2. (Iota is commonly long in the arsis; twice short, Od. 4, 463. 12, 329; and at the close of the verse it is to be pronounced with synizesis, Od. 5, 266. 9, 212, where Wolf writes ἤϊα, perhaps also correctly, Od. 5, 368, ἤιων.) [Fäsi, ᾖα.]

ἤϊε, see εἰμί.

ἤϊθεος, ὁ, Ep. for ἤθεος, a youth who has arrived at manhood but who is yet unmarried, a young man. παρθένος ἠίθεός τε, 18, 593. 22, 127. νύμφαι τ' ἠίθεοί τε, Od. 11, 38.

ἤϊκτο, see ἔοικα.

ἤϊξε, see ἀΐσσω.

ἠϊόεις, εσσα, εν (ἠϊών), having banks, deep-embanked (Cp.), 5, 36;† epith. of the Scamander, to indicate its high banks (according to the common derivation of the Gramm. from ἠϊών, όνος, prop. ἠϊονόεις, and by syncope, ἠϊόεις, Etym. Mag. Buttm. Lex. p. 324, derives it from ἤϊον, akin to εἰαμένη, meadow, = 'meadowy,' 'skirted with meadowland'). [Död. makes it muddy, i.e. full of earthy matter: related to αἶα, αἶος, dry.]

ἤϊον, see εἶμι.

Ἠιόνες, αἱ, *Eiones*, a village in Argolis, in the region of the promontory Scyllæum; later a port of the Mycenians, 2, 561. Strab.

Ἠιονεύς, ῆος, ὁ (an inhabitant of the shore), 1) a Greek, slain by Hector, 7, 11. 2) a Thracian, father of Rhesus, 10, 435.

ἤιος, ὁ, an epith. of Phœbus, of uncertain derivation, 15, 365. 20, 152. h. Ap. 120; prob. the *far-shooter*, Voss; according to the Schol. for ἰήιε from ἵημι, or, more correctly, from the original form ἄω, ἤιος, Ep. ἤιος, as ἤλιος and ἠέλιος. Aristarch., on the other hand, would write it ἤιος. Others say, from ἰάομαι, the healer (but Phœbus never appears as the god of the healing art), or from the exclamation ἰή, ἰή, with which Apollo was addressed (of which traces are first found h. Ap. 500). Buttm., Lex. p. 246, regards it as a corruption of εὐς or ἠΰς.

ἤισαν, see εἶμι.

ἤχθη, see ἀΐσσω.

ἠιών, όνος, ἡ. Ep. for ᾐών, Batr. 13, the *sea-shore*, the *sea-coast*, the *coast*, the *strand*, 2, 92. ἠιόνες προύχουσαι, projecting shores, or sand-downs (*dunes*) running into the sea, Od. 6, 138.

ἦκα, adv. (ἀκή). 1) *softly, gently, low.* ἦκα ἐγορεύειν, 3, 155; spoken of a thrust or blow, *gently, softly*, 24, 508. Od. 18, 92; spoken of walking slowly, Od. 17, 254; spoken of shining: ἦκα στίλβοντες ἐλαίῳ, mildly shining with oil, 18, 596 (according to the old Gramm. to be taken as a comparison: and so Voss, 'bright as the soft lustre of oil'). 2) Generally *somewhat, a little.* ἦκ' ἐπ' ἀριστερά, 23, 336; and ἦκα παρακλίνειν κεφαλήν, to bend the head a little sidewise, Od. 20, 301. (Buttm., Lex. p. 327, correctly taking ἀκήν as the root, gives as the primary signif. *feebly*, and recognizes it as the positive of ἧσσον, ἥκιστα; cf. Thiersch, § 198. 2.) [Död., asserting the relationship to ἀκήν, denies that to ἧσσον.]

ἦκα, see ἵημι.

ἠκαχε, see ἀκαχίζω.

ἠκέσατο, see ἀκέομαι.

ἤκεστος, η, ον, Ep. for ἄκεστος (κεστός), *ungoaded*, spoken of cattle that have not yet felt the goad of the driver, *unbroken, untamed*, *6, 94. 275. 309.

ἥκιστος, η, ον (superl. from the adv. ἦκα), only in ἥκιστος δ' ἦν ἐλαυνέμεν ἵππα, he was the *slowest* to drive the chariot, 23, 531, Wolf.† Others write ἥκιστος as superl. of ἥσσων, *the worst*. Buttm., Lex. p. 327, regards ἥκιστος as correct, only because it has the signif. *the weakest, worst*, although he finds in ἦκα the true positive of ἥσσων, ἥκιστα. [Död. the *quietest*, hence *slowest*: quite unconnected with ἥκιστα.]

ἥκω, to (*have*) *come*, to *arrive*, always with the idea of the action perfected; τηλόθεν, 5, 478; εἰς Ἰθάκην, Od. 13, 325.

ἠλάκατα, τά (plur. from the obsol.

ἠλάκατον), the *wool on the distaff*, or the threads which are drawn from the distaff, Od. 6, 53; hence ἠλάκατα στρωφᾶν, to spin threads, Od. 6, 306. 7, 105; and στροφαλίζειν, †Od. 18, 315.

ἠλακάτη, ἡ, prop. *a reed*, then generally any thing made of or similar to a reed, a *spindle, a distaff*, 6, 491. Od. 1, 357. (Prob. from ἠλάσκω, to turn around.)

ἠλάκατον, τό, see ἠλάκατα.

ἤλασα, see ἐλαύνω.

ἠλασκάζω, poet. lengthened from ἠλάσκω, 1) Intrans. *to wander about*, 18, 281. 2) *to avoid, to flee.* ἐμὸν μένος ἠλασκάζει (mine anger), Od. 9, 457. It is not necessary, with Passow, to change it to ἠλυσκάζει; for ἠλασκάζει may have this different construction as well as φεύγειν, ἀτύζεσθαι, cf. Herm. ad Orph. Arg. 439.

ἠλάσκω (an Ep. form of ἀλάομαι)ͅ a poet. lengthened form is ἠλασκάζω, 1) *to wander around, to rove up and down*; spoken of animals, καθ' ὕλην, 13, 104; of bees, to swarm about, 2, 470.

ἠλᾶτο, see ἀλάομαι.

ἤλδανε, see ἀλδαίνω.

Ἠλεῖος, είη, εῖον, *Elean*, appertaining to Elis. οἱ Ἠλεῖοι, *the Eleans*, inhabitants of Elis, 11, 671.

Ἠλέκτρη, ἡ, 1) daughter of Oceanus and Tethys, wife of Thaumas, mother of Iris and the Harpies, h. in Cer. 418. 2) = Λαοδίκη, daughter of Agamemnon.

ἤλεκτρον, τό, and ἤλεκτρος, ὁ, ἡ, *electron*, either amber, or a metallic mixture of gold with perhaps a fifth of silver. Especially may the latter be understood in Od. 4, 73, where it is mentioned between gold and silver as an ornament of the walls; but in Od. 15, 460. 18, 296 (χρύσεον ὅρμον ἔχων μετὰ δ' ἠλέκτροισιν ἕερτο), we may understand a golden necklace with beads of amber, Ep. 15, 10. Eustath. ad Od. 4, 73, mentions both; he calls the first μίγμα χρυσοῦ καὶ ἀργύρου; Plin. IX. 65, calls it a mixture of three parts gold and one part silver. Voss ad Virg. Ec. 6, 62. Ottfr. Müller (Archäol. p. 35), Buttm. Schrift. der Berl. Akadem. der Wissenschaft. histor. Classe 1818, p. 38, decide in favour of amber; on the other hand, Passow, Nitzsch (Anmerk. zu Od. 1, 238), Wiedasch consider it as a metallic mixture; cf. Dilthey de Electro et Eridano. 1824. (Without doubt it is derived from ἠλέκτωρ.)

ἠλέκτωρ, ορος, ὁ, *the shining sun*, as subst., 6, 513; and adj. ἠλέκτωρ Ὑπερίων, the beaming Hyperion, *19, 398. h. Ap. 369 (prob. from the same root with ἥλιος).

ἠλεός, ή, όν (ἠλός), *infatuated, foolish*, φρένας ἠλεέ, infatuated in mind; senseless, Od. 2, 243. 2) Act. *causing folly*, οἶνος, *Od. 14, 464; cf. ἠλός.

ἠλήλατο, see ἐλαύνω.

ἠλίβατος, ον, *ascending precipitously*;

and generally *very high* ; mly as an epith.
in H. of πέτρη, 15, 273. 16, 35. Od. 9,
243. 10, 88. 13, 196. h. Merc. 404; and
of trees, h. Ven. 268. (Herm. has, however, included the verse in brackets as
spurious.) The deriv. is uncertain ; the
most common deriv. is from ἥλιος and
βαίνω (Apoll. ὑψηλή, ἐφ᾽ ῇ ὁ ἥλιος πρῶτον
βάλλει or ἧς ὁ ἥλιος μόνος ἐπιβαίνει),
passed over only by the sun, upon which
the sun rests all day : or, as others think,
from ἠλός akin to ἀλιτεῖν, and hence =
δύσβατος, *inaccessible, precipitous* ; or
from ἀλιτεῖν and βαίνω for ἀλιτόβατος,
upon which one easily makes a false step,
cf. ἠλιτόμηνος. The last deriv. is adopted
by Buttm. Lex. p. 329.

ἤλιθα, adv. (ἅλις), *sufficiently, abundantly*, always ἤλιθα πολλή, 11, 677. Od.
5,. 483.

ἡλικίη, ἡ (ἧλιξ), generally *an age, the
period of life*, æ t as, *old age*, 22, 419; but
chiefly, the *age of strength* and activity,
from perhaps eighteen to fifty years;
hence 2) Collect. *contemporaries, those
of the same age;* esply *youthful companions*, *16, 808.

ἧλιξ, ικος, ὁ, ἡ, τό, *of ripe age, adult,
full-grown, of equal age*, spoken of cattle,
Od. 18, 373.†

ἥλιος, prose form of ἠέλιος, q. v.

῝Ηλιος, ὁ, Ep. Ἡέλιος, q. v.

῝Ηλις, ιδος, ἡ, *Elis*, a country on the
western side of Peloponnesus, which was
bounded by Achaia, Arcadia, Messenia,
and the sea. H. knows nothing of the
later division into Κοίλη, Πισᾶτις, and
Τριφυλία, nor of any city of Elis. The
Epeans were the ruling tribe, perhaps of
Pelasgian origin ; the southern part
belongs to Nestor's dominions; and here
dwelt the Achæans (or Achaians), 2, 615.
626. Od. 4, 635. 13, 275. H. has only the
accus. ῝Ηλιδα in the passages quoted;
Ηλιν was used, at a later day, of the
city.

ἤλιτε, see ἀλιταίνω.

ἠλιτόμηνος, ον (ἀλιταίνω, μήν), prop.
missing the month, *untimely, born too
soon*, 19, 118.†

ἥλκησε, see ἑλκέω.

ἧλος, ὁ, *a nail, a stud;* only as an
ornament of the sceptre, sword, and
goblet. σκῆπτρον, χρυσείοις ἥλοισι πε-
παρμένον, studded with golden nails, 1,
246. cf. 11, 29. 633.

ἠλός, ἡ, όν (ἀλή), *wandering, silly, foolish*. φρένας ἠλέ, senseless, 15, 128†
(whence ἠλεός. q. v.).

ἤλυθον, see ἔρχομαι.

Ἠλύσιον πεδίον, τό, *the Elysian field,
Elysium*, a beautiful plain, situated at
the western extremity of the earth (this
is indicated by the Zephyr), on the ocean,
where, as in Olympus itself, no storm,
rain, or snow approaches, but ever-during
spring prevails. In this abode H. places
heroes and favorites of the gods, e. g.
Rhadamanthus son of Zeus, and Menelaus, and represents them as living

there with the body without seeing death.
Whether it is to be considered as an
island, or as a plain situated on the
margin of the ocean, is no where in H.
clearly expressed ; Hesiod. Op. 169, and
later writers, speak of the ' islands of the
blessed,' see Völcker. Hom. Geogr. § 78.
p. 156. Nitzsch ad Od. 4, 563 (fr. ἤλευσις,
= ἔλευσις, coming).

ἤλφον, see ἀλφαίνω.

ἤλω, see ἀλίσκομαι.

ἠλώμην, see ἀλάομαι.

Ἡλώνη, ἡ, a town of the Perrhæbians
in Thessaly (Phthiōtis), on the Eurōtas ;
later Δειμώνη, according to Strab., 2,
739.

ἧμα, ατος, τό (ἵημι), *a cast, a throw, the
act of casting a missile*. ἥμασιν ἄριστος,
very excellent in casting the spear, 23,
891. †

Ἡμαθίη, ἡ, *Emathia*, a country between the rivers Erigon and Axius, north
of Pieria, 14, 226. h. Ap. 217; later, a part
of Macedonia (perhaps from ἤμαθος =
ἄμαθος, sandy).

ἠμαθόεις, εσσα, εν (ἄμαθος), Ion. for
ἀμαθόεις, *sandy*, epith. of the city Pylos,
because it lay on the coast, 2, 77; and
also in fourteen other passages, always
Πύλος, ἀμαθόεις. The deriv. from a river
Amathos, according to Strab. is improbable, since an adj. with the ending όεις
from a river is unheard of.

ἧμαι (prob. perf. pass. from ᾽ΕΩ, ἕδω),
imperf. ἥμην. Peculiar Ion. forms are
the 3 plur. pres. ἕαται and Ep. εἵαται for
ἧνται, and 3 plur. imperf. ἕατο, Ep. εἵατο
for ἧντο, prop. *I am seated, laid, placed,*
hence 1) *to sit, to lie, to remain*, with
partcp. ὀνειδίζων, 2, 255. Od. 4, 439. 8,
505. 2) *to sit still, quietly, idle*, with
σιγῇ, 3, 134. Od. 11, 142.

ἧμαρ, ατος, τό, poet. for ἡμέρα, *a day,*
χειμέριον, and ὀπωρινόν, a winter day, an
autumn day, 11 ; again, αἴσιμον, μόρσιμον,
the day of fate = the day of death, 8, 72.
15, 613. νηλεὲς ἧμαρ, 11, 484; ὀλέθριον,
19, 409 ; κακόν, 9, 251 ; ἐλεύθερον, the day
of freedom, 6, 455 ; δούλιον, ἀναγκαῖον,
the day of slavery, the day of force, often
slavery itself, 6, 463. 16, 836 ; ὀρφανικόν,
the day of orphanage, 22, 490; and νόστιμον, the day of return. Od. 1, 9 ; ἐπ᾽
ἤματι, day by day, daily, Od. 12, 105. 14,
105; upon a day, 10, 48. Od. 2, 284; for
a day, 19, 229.

ἠμάτιος, η. ον (ἧμαρ), *by day, during
the day*, Od. 2, 104. 19, 149. 2) *on every
day, daily*, 9, 72.

ἤμβροτον, see ἁμαρτάνω

ἡμεῖς, *we*, plur. of ἐγώ. Æol. and Ep
ἄμμες, gen. ἡμέων, always dissyllabic, Ep.
ἡμείων. dat. ἡμῖν, and according to the
necessity of the metre ἥμιν or ἡμίν, as
enclitic, 11 415. Od. 11, 344 ; Æol. ἄμμι,
ἄμμιν, accus. ἡμέας, ἧμας, Od. 16, 372,
Æol. and Ep. ἄμμε, Rost. Dial. 44.
Kühner, § 301.

ἠμέν—ἠδέ (ῆ), poet. for καί—καί, *both -
and*, see ῆ.

ἡμέρη, ἡ (ἦμαρ), a day; used seven times, 8, 541. Od. 11, 294. Hom. divides the day into three parts, ἠώς, μέσον ἦμαρ, δείλη, 21, 111. cf. Od. 7, 288.

ἡμερίς, ίδος, ἡ, fem. of ἥμερος, tame, esply used of trees; subst. the cultivated vine [the garden-vine. Cp.], Od. 5, 69. †

ἥμερος, ον, tame tamed, domestic, χήν, Od 15, 162.

ἡμέτερος, η, ον (ἡμεῖς), our, belonging to us. ἐφ᾽ ἡμέτερα, sc. δώματα, νέεσθαι, to return to our homes. 9, 619. Od. 15, 88. εἰς ἡμέτερον, sc. δῶμα, Od. 2, 55. 7, 301. ἡμέτερόνδε, Od. 8, 39.

ἡμί, prop. Att. for φημί, only ἦ, 3 sing. imperf. he spake, always after a quoted speech; once with subject, 6, 390.

ἡμι-, half, in composition.

ἡμιδαής, ές (δαίω), half-burnt, νηῦς, 16, 294.

ἡμίθεος, ὁ (θεός), a demi-god; as adj. half-divine, heroic. ἡμιθέων γένος ἀνδρῶν, 12, 23. † h. 31, 19.

ἡμιόνειος, η, ον (ἡμίονος), belonging to mules, drawn by mules. ἄμαξα ἡμιόνειος, a carriage drawn by mules, 24, 189. Od. 6, 72. ζυγὸν ἡμιόνειον, a span of mules, 24, 268.

ἡμίονος, ἡ, rarely ὁ (ὄνος), a mule. 17, 742. They were difficult to tame, 23, 655; and were used particularly in mountainous regions (hence ὀρεύς, οὐρεύς), for drawing waggons, &c., and for agriculture, 10, 352. Od. 8, 124. By the wild mules in Paphlagonia (2, 852) Köppen understands the Dschiggetai, equus hemionus, Linn. 2) As adj. βρέφος ἡμίονον, a mule-foal, 23, 266.

ἡμιπέλεκκον, τό (πέλεκυς), a half-axe, an axe with an edge on only one side, *23. 851. 858. 883 (κ doubled for metre's sake).

ἡμίπνοος, ον (πνέω), half-breathing, half-dead, Batr. 255.

ἥμισυς, σεια, συ (from μέσος), half, the half or moiety; sing. only in the neut. τιμῆς βασιληΐδος ἥμισυ, the half of the royal dignity, 6, 193. 9, 579. 580; also in the plur. ἡμίσεες λαοί, 21, 7. Od. 3, 155.

ἡμιτάλαντον, τό (τάλαντον), a half-talent, χρυσοῦ, *23, 571. 796.

ἡμιτελής, ές (τελέω), half-finished. δόμος ἡμιτελής, a half-finished house, half-built, 2, 701. † The most simple explanation is: the house which Protesilaus, just married, was building for himself and his wife, was not yet completed upon his sudden departure for Troy; for it was customary, at marriage, to build a new house. Thus Heyne (an unfinished mansion. Cp.). Another explanation is, according to Etym. M. and Poseidonius Strab. VII. p. 454, 'half-abandoned,' because now occupied only by the wife; thus Damm, Wolf, Passow; and a third: 'he left his house incomplete,' i. e. without children. Thus Schol. brev. and Runhken.

ἦμος (prop. = ἦμαρ), Ep. adv. for ὅτε,

at the time when, when, after, spoken of past time, usually only of the time of day; the apodosis begins with τῆμος. 11. 86 seq.; often with δὴ τότε, δὴ τότ᾽ ἔπειτα, καὶ τότε, 1, 475. 8, 68. Od. 9, 58. It stands always with the indic., mly with the aor., rarely with the imperf. and pluperf., 1, 475. 8, 68; cf. Thiersch, § 316, 18.

ἡμύω (μύω), aor. ἤμυσα, to nod, to incline or bend, to sink. ἤμυσε κάρη, the head sank (spoken of one dying), 8, 308; and of a horse: ἤμυσε καρήατι, he drooped (with the head), 19, 405; of a harvest-field: ἐπί τ᾽ ἠμύει ἀσταχύεσσιν [the loaded ears bow before the gale. Cp.], 2, 148; ἐπί is adv. (Others incorrectly interpret it of the wind: ἐπημύει ἀσταχύεσσιν, it falls upon the ears, Hesych.): metaph. of cities: to sink, to fall, 2, 373. 4, 290. (ῠ in the pres.; ῡ in aor. 1.

ἤμων, ονος, ὁ (ἵημι), one who hurls spears, a spearman, a lancer, ἤμονες ἄνδρες, 23, 886. †

ἤν, conj. contract. from ἐάν, if, when, whether. On the construction see εἰ with ἄν. It stands with the subjunc. 9, 692. Od. 5, 120; with the optat. in the orat. obliq. Od. 13, 415.

ἠναίνετο, see ἀναίνομαι.

ἤνεικα, ἠνείκαντο, see φέρω.

ἠνεμόεις, εσσα, εν (ἄνεμος), windy, gusty, exposed to the wind, epith. of places situated in lofty positions (esply of Troy), of mountains and trees, 2, 606. 8, 499, and Od. 3, 172. 19, 432.

ἡνία, τά (ἵημι), the reins or lines of chariot-horses, which were often adorned with gold or ivory, 5, 226. 583. Od. 6, 81. Only in the plur. (the sing. ἡνίον is later, and means, a curb).

ἡνίκα, adv. when, at the time when, with indic. pres. Od. 22, 198. † (Voss, ad Arat. Phænom. 561, would read ἦν κεν ἀγινῇς.)

Ἡνιοπεύς, ῆος, ὁ (rein-maker), son of Thebaus, charioteer of Hector, 8, 120.

ἡνιοχεύς, ῆος, ὁ, poet. for ἡνίοχος, *5, 505. 8, 312.

ἡνιοχεύω (ἡνίοχος), to hold the reins, to guide the horses, to drive, absol., 11, 103 Od. 6, 319.

ἡνίοχος, ὁ (ἔχω), prop. the reins-holder, then the charioteer, the driver. In the Hom. war-chariots (see ἅρμα) were always two warriors; prob. on the left the charioteer, and on the right the παραβάτης, i. e. the hero who fought from the chariot. The charioteer is also called ἡνίοχος θεράπων, 5, 580. 8, 119. He was a warrior, as well as his companion, of noble family, as was Patroclus, the charioteer of Achilles, 16, 244. Also the bravest heroes are often called ἡνίοχοι, as Hector, 8, 89. 15, 352; cf θεράπων.

ἠνίπαπε, see ἐνίπτω.

ἦνις, ιος, ἡ (ἔνος), accus. plur. ἦνις for ἤνιας, 6, 94; a year old, a yearling, βοῦς, 10, 292. Od. 3, 382. (In the accus. sing. ἦνιν, long ι is used.)

K

Ἡνοπίδης, ου, ὁ, son of Enops = Satnius, 14, 444.

ἠνορέη, ἡ, Ep. dat. ἠνορέηφι (ἀνήρ), manhood, strength, manly courage, 4, 303. Od. 24, 509.

ἤνοψ, οπος ., ἡ (poet. for ἄνοψ from ἀ and ὄψ), which cannot be looked upon for its lustre: dazzling, blinding, sparkling; always ἤνοπι χαλκῷ, 16, 408. Od. 10, 360. [Död. gives it the strange meaning of bent. ναπ-, γναπ-, γναμπτ-.]

Ἦνοψ, οπος, ὁ, 1) a Mysian father of Satnius and Thestôr, 14, 445. 16, 401. 2) father of Clytomêdês, an Ætolian, 23, 634.

ἤνπερ, conj. even if; although, with subj. Od. 16, 276; see ἤν.

ἦντο, see ἧμαι.

ἠνώγεα, ἠνώγει, see ἀνώγα.

ἦξε, see ἄγνυμι.

ἠοῖος, η, ον (ἠώς), 1) Of time: early in the morning, matutinus; hence: ἡ ἠοίη, sc. ὥρα, morning, Od. 4, 447. 2) Of a point of the compass: east, opposed to ἑσπέριος. ἠοῖοι ἄνθρωποι, eastern men, *Od. 8, 29.

ἧπαρ, ατος, τό, the liver, 11, 579; ὅτι φρένες ἧπαρ ἔχουσιν, Od. 9, 301. 2) Plur. ἥπατα, as a dish, Batr. 37.

ἤπαφε, see ἀπαφίσκω.

ἠπεδανός, ή, όν. feeble, tottering, weak, spoken of Hêphæstus, Od. 8, 11. h. Ap. 316; and Il. 8, 104; of the servant of Nestor, because he did not drive rapidly. (The ancients explain it by ἀσθενής, and derive it from ἀ and πέδον. not standing firmly: according to Schneider it is an amplification of ἤπιος.)

ἤπειρος, ἡ, the main land, the continent. spoken of the main land in distinction from an island, and of an island in opposition to the sea, Od. 13, 114. 1) Acarnania, with Leucadia, 2, 635. Od. 24, 378; and according to some also ἤπειρος μέλαινα, Od 14, 97. 21, 109. (The ancients understood in part Samos or Ætolia.) 2) Hellas. or a part of it, h. Cer. 130; chiefly Attica, h. in Dion. 22; prob. also Od. 14, 97 seq. 3) The later Epirus, Od. 18, 84. 21, 109. (Derived from ἄπειρος, sc. γῆ.) Cf. Völcker, Hom. Geogr. p. 61.

ἤπερ, poet. ἠέπερ, than, than even, than indeed, 1, 260. Od. 4, 819; see πέρ.

ἤπερ. see ὅσπερ.

ἠπεροπεύς, ῆος. ὁ, Od. 11, 364;† and ἠπεροπευτής. οῦ, ὁ (ἠπεροπεύω), a deceiver, a seducer,* 3, 39. 13, 769. h. Merc. 282.

ἠπεροπεύω, fut. σω, to cheat, to deceive, to seduce. to lead away by crafty discourse, with accus. esply γυναῖκας and φρένας γυναιξί, 5, 349. Od. 15, 421. h. Merc. 577; τινὰ ταῦτα, i. e. διὰ ταῦτα, 3, 399. (Prob. fr. εἰπεῖν, ἠπύω. Passow.) [= ἀπροπεύειν (ἀπρεπής), to deal unhandsomely by.]

*ἠπητής, οῦ, ὁ, a cobbler, a botcher, a tailor, Batr. 184.

ἠπιόδωρος, ον (δῶρον), willingly giving, benevolent, bounteous, μήτηρ, 6, 251.†

ἤπιος, ίη, ιον, 1) gentle, mild, kind, τινί, to any one, 8, 40. Od. 10, 337. ἤπια εἰδέναι τινί, to be kindly disposed towards any one, 16, 73. Od 13, 405. 2) Act. calming, smoothing, alleviating, φάρμακα, 4, 218. 11, 515. (Prob. from ἔπος.)

ἤπου, now ἦ που, or, and than perhaps, see ἦ.

ἤπου, now, according to Wolf, ἦ που, surely, indeed, see ἦ.

ἠπύτα. ὁ, Ep. for ἠπύτης (ἠπύω), the loud crier, hence ἠπύτα κῆρυξ, the loud-crying (loud-voiced) herald, 7, 384.†

Ἠπυτίδης, ου, ὁ, son of Epytus = Periphas, a Trojan; 17, 324.

ἠπύω (akin to εἰπεῖν), 1) to cry, to cry aloud, to call to, τινά. Od. 9, 399. 10, 83. 2) Intrans. spoken of wind: to roar, to whistle, 14, 399; of the lyre: to sound, to resound, 17, 271. (ῠ in the pres., cf. Spitzner, Pros. § 52. 5.)

*ἦρ, poet. for ἔαρ, spring, in gen. ἦρος ἀειρομένοιο, h Cer. 455; see ἔαρ.

ἦρα, once in Hom. ἦρα φέρειν τινί, 14, 132; and thrice; ἦρα ἐπιφέρειν τινί, Od. 3, 164. 16, 375. 18, 56; to do a kindness to, to gratify. θυμῷ ἦρα φέροντες, gratifying their inclination, spoken of those who from love of life stood aloof from battle, 14, 162. [Cp. attentive only to their own repose.] The other explanation: gratifying their anger, with reference to Agamemnon, v. 49, is forced. (Buttm., Lexil. p. 335, properly supposes a tmesis of ἐπιφέρειν, and hence in 1, 572. 578, writes ἐπίηρα separately: cf. ἐπίηρα. With him agrees Nitzsch ad Od. 3, 164. Buttm. with Herodian considers ἦρα as an accus. sing from an obsol. word ἦρ = χάρις; Thiersch, G. § 199, 3, on the other hand with Aristarch. as an accus. plur. from an adj. ἦρος. (Root ἔραμαι, or more prob. ἄρω.)

Ἡρακλείδης, αο, ὁ, son of Heraclês = Tlepolemus, 2, 653. 5, 628. [2] = Thessalus, 2, 679.]

Ἡρακλέης, Ion. and Ep. Ἡρακλῆς, gen. Ἡρακλῆος, Heraclês, son of Zeus and Alcmênê, 14, 324. 18, 118. His birth was retarded by Hêrê, and that of Eurystheus accelerated, 19, 98—125. Of the twelve famous labours which Eurystheus imposed upon him, the command to bring the dog of Pluto is mentioned, 8. 362 seq. Od. 11, 623. When Laomedon would not give him the reward for delivering his daughter Hesionê, 20, 14? seq. he captured Troy and slew Laomedon and his sons, Priam excepted, 5, 64? On his return he was driven by Hêrê to Coe, 14, 250 seq. In order to avenge himself on Neleus on account of the purification for the murder of Iphitus being denied, he captured Pylos and wounded there Pluto himself, 11, 689 seq. On his death, see 18, 117. In the under-world Odysseus (Ulysses) met his shade, Od. 11 601 seq. although he, in connexion with Hebe, is blessed among the immortal gods, cf. v. 608. Of his wives there is mentioned Megara, Od. 11, 268; and of his sons Thessalus, 2, 679; and Tlepolemus, 2. 657. (Damm derives the name from ἥρα and κλέος, *love of glory*. Herm. *Popliclutus*.)

Ἡρακλήειος, είη. ειον, Ep. for Ἡράκλειος, *pertaining to Héraclés, Herculean*, only in the fem. βίη Ἡρακληείη, 2, 658.

ἥραρε, see ἀραρίσκω.

ἥρατο, see αἴρω.

ἥρᾶτο, see ἀράομαι.

Ἥρη. ἡ, Ion. and Ep. for Ἥρα, *Héré*, daughter of Kronus and Rhea, sister and wife of Zeus, 16, 432; the queen of heaven and the first of goddesses. She was nurtured in the house of Oceanus, when Zeus cast Kronus into Tartarus, 14. 202 seq. In character she is proud, ambitious of power, and deceitful; she often deceives her husband, cf. 14, 153; yet she often experiences on this account his anger, 15, 13—21. In the Hom. poems she appears as the enemy of the Trojans; she collects the Grecian army against Troy, 4, 28, seq. because she considered herself neglected by the Trojans. United with Poseidôn and Athênê she aids the Greeks, 5, 768 seq. 20, 33; and then commands Hêphæstus to drive back the river-god Xanthus within his banks when pursuing Achilles, 21, 377 seq. From earlier traditions, it is mentioned that she accelerated the birth of Euristheus and retarded that of Hêraclês, 19, 97; the latter on his return from Troy she drove to the coast of Cos by a storm, 14, 250; and was wounded by him in Pylos, 5, 392. To Zeus she bore Hebê, Ilithyia, Arês, and Hephæstus. Argos, Mycenæ, and Sparta are her favorite cities, 4, 51, 52. (Prob. according to Herm. from ΑΡΩ, who translates the name *Populonia*, and understands by it the union of social life; Heffter, on the other hand, nuptial union.)

ἥρηρει, see ἀραρίσκω.

ἠρήρειστο, see ἐρείδω.

ἦρι. adv. *early in the morning*, μάλ᾽ ἦρι or ἦρι μάλα, very early, 9, 360. Od. 19, 320. 29, 156. (Prob. dat. from ἦρ, contr. of ἔαρ, the spring-time, or from ἀήρ, ἠήρ.)

ἠριγένεια, ἡ (γίγνομαι), *early-born*, *rising early in the morning*, or with reference to ἀήρ, born of the morning mist, epith. of Ἡώς, Aurora (some explain it as act. *producing the morning*, which contravenes the etymol. cf. αἰθρηγενής), 1, 477. 2) As pr. n. the *goddess of the morning*, Od. 22, 197. 23, 347.

Ἡριδανός, ὁ. *Eridanus*, a fabulous stream of the ancient geogr. which rose in the north-west, coming from the Rhipæan mountains, and flowed into the ocean; first, Hesiod. Th. 338. Batr. 20. Most of the ancients referred it to the Padus, some to the Rhodanus or Rhenus.

ἤριπε, see ἐρείπω.

ἠρίον, τό (prob. from ἔρα), *a hill, a mound, a sepulchral mound*, 23, 126.†

ἤρυτε, see ἐρύω.

ἤρυγε, see ἐρεύγομαι.

ἠρῶ, see ἀράομαι.

ἠρώησαν, see ἐρωέω.

ἥρως, ὁ, gen. ἥρωος, dat. ἥρωι, Ep. ἥρῳ, accus. ἥρωα, Ep. ἥρω'. Instead of the gen. ἥρωος with the mid. syllable short, Od. 6, 303, some read ἥρως; instead of ἥρω' as accus. we should write ἥρω without apostr. 6, 63. 13, 428. Od. 11, 520; with which, however, Spitzner does not agree. 1) *a hero, a noble*, esply are kings and princes, the commanders and their companions, so called in Hom.; but also all warriors, especially when addressed: ἥρωες Δαναοί, ἥρωες Ἀχαιοί, ἄνδρες ἥρωες, 2, 110. 15, 220. Od. 1, 101; and generally. all who distinguished themselves by their strength. courage, prudence, and skill as artists; also every freeman, an honorable man, 7, 44. Od. 8. 483. 2) *a demi-god*, a middle class between gods and men, who sprung from a god on the paternal or maternal side; of which we find the first trace 12, 25.

ἥσατο, see ἥδομαι.

ἥσειν, see ἵημι.

ἦσθα, see εἰμί.

ἤσκειν, see ἀσκέω.

ἦσο. see ἧμαι.

ἥσσων, ἧσσον, gen. ονος, *inferior, worse*, especially in strength, *weaker, feebler*, 16, 722. 23, 858. The neut. as adv. ἧσσον, *worse*, Od. 15, 365. (In the gram. an irreg. compar. to κακός; according to the root it belongs to ἧκα.)

ἧσται, see ἧμαι.

ἤστην, see εἰμί.

ἡσυχίη, ἡ, *rest, peace, tranquillity, enjoyment*, Od. 18, 22; † h. Merc. 356.

ἡσύχιος, ον, poet. for ἥσυχος, *quiet, still, gentle, unobserved*, 21, 598;† whence adv. ἡσυχίως, *quietly*. h. Merc. 438.

ᾐσχυμμένος, see αἰσχύνω.

ἦτε, by the τέ added the relation of equivalence is indicated; therefore it nearly = εἶτε; doubled, ἦτε, ἦτε, *either*, or, 17, 42; or single, 19, 148. cf. ἤ.

ἦτε, or according to Wolf, ἦ τε, see ἤ.

ἠτιάασθε, see αἰτιάομαι.

ἠτιόωντο, see αἰτιάομαι.

ἦτοι, Ep. (prob. fr. ἦ and τοί), conj. *surely, certainly, verily;* it denotes 1) *an assurance*, and hence often stands with μέν, and the following correlative δέ. ἀλλά: *assuredly, verily, certainly, truly*, 7, 451. 17, 514; esply after a vocat. 7, 191. 21, 446. Od. 4, 78. 16, 309. 2) It introduces alone a sentence. like μέν, to an antithetic clause with δέ, when it may be sometimes translated *now*, 1, 68. Od. 15, 6. 24, 154; or it begins, like μήν, the antithesis to a preceding clause, *indeed, surely*, esply ἀλλ᾽ ἦτοι, *but yet*, 1, 211. Od. 15, 488. 16, 278. 3) It stands also to convey the idea of assurance, after conj. which introduce adjunct clauses: ὡς ἦτοι, ὄφρ᾽ ἦτοι, 23, 52. Od. 3, 419 5, 24. 4) ἦτοι for ἤ, *or*, after a preceding ἤ, occurs once, Od. 19, 599.

K 2

Often in Pindar ἤ—ἤτοι stands for ἤ—ἤ. (As a strengthening particle we find also ἤ τοι (Bothe: ἤτοι). Il. 6, 56.)

ἦτορ, ορος, τό, *the heart,* as a part of the human body, 22, 452; on 15, 252, see ἀέω, and in a wider signif. = στῆθος, 2, 490. 2) Metaph. *a) the powers of life, life,* of which the beating of the heart is the index, 5, 250. 11, 115. *b) heart, spirit,* as the seat of feelings, propensities, wishes, etc. 3, 31. 5, 529. 8, 437; also *soul, spirit,* as the thinking principle, 1, 188. (Prob. from ἄημι, breathing, like *animus.*)

ἠϋγένειος, ον, Ion. and Ep. for εὐγένειος.

ἠϋγενής, ές, Ion. and Ep. for εὐγενής.

ηὔδα, see αὐδάω.

*ἠΰζωνος, ον, Ep. for εὔζωνος, Fr. 54.

*ἠϋθέμεθλος, ον, Ep. for εὐθέμεθλος.

ἠΰκομος, ον, Ion. for εὔκομος.

ἠΰς, ἠΰ, Ep. for ἐΰς, q. v.

ηὔσε, see ἀΰω.

ἠΰτε, Ep. partic. 1) *as, like,* with single words, 1, 359. 2, 87. *b)* Also after a comparative for ἤ, 4, 277; according to Spitzner ἠΰτε stands in its ordinary sense and the comparison is elliptical: 'blacker than it really is.' So also Damm: *nubes magis atra veluti pix.* 2) In the signif. of ὡς ὅτε, *as when,* with indicat. 2, 87; with subj. 17, 547. (According to Buttm. Lexil. ἠΰτε sprung from ἤ εὖτε; once we find εὖτε for ἠΰτε. 3, 10.)

ʹΗφαιστος, ὁ, *Hephæstus,* son of Zeus and Hêrê (1, 577. 578), god of fire and of the mechanic arts, which need the aid of fire, especially of working metals. He and his sister Athênê are the teachers of all the arts mentioned in Hom. At his birth he was ugly in form, weak in the feet and lame, (ἠπεδανός, χωλός, ἀμφιγυήεις,) for which reason Hêrê threw him into the sea. Two sea-goddesses, Thetis and Eurynômê, received him, and he remained with them nine years, 18, 395. Zeus also once hurled him from Olympus, when he attempted to aid his mother, upon the island of Lemnos, where the kind Sintians received him, 1, 590. In 18, 382, Charis is assigned to him as a wife; in the Od. 8, 267, Aphroditê. At the request of Thetis he made new arms for Achilles, and here his workshop in Olympus and his working of metals are described to us. 18, 468 seq. Hom. mentions the infidelity of his wife Aphroditê, Od. 8, 267 seq. His common residence is Olympus, his favorite place on earth the island Lemnos, Od. 8, 283. The most noted of the productions of Hêphæstus are, 1) The arms of Achilles, and especially the shield, upon which the heavens and the earth and the most important scenes of life were depicted, 18, 478. 2) The net, in which he entangled Arês and Aphroditê, Od. 8, 274. 3) The brazen dwellings of the gods, 1, 606. 4) The sceptre and the ægis of Zeus, 2, 101. 15 309. Hom. often calls fire φλόξ

ʹΗφαίστοιο, 9, 468 [and also simply ʹΗφαιστος, 2, 426]. II) As an appellat. for *fire,* 2, 426. (According to Herm. fr. ἅπτειν and ἄϊστος, *qui ignem ex occulto excitat;* according to Heffter more prob. fr. φάω, φαῖστος, with a prosthesis of η, *the light-producer.*)

ἦφι, Ep. for ἤ, 22, 107.

*ἠχέω (ἠχή), aor. 1 ἤχησα, intrans. *to sound, to resound, to echo,* h. Cer. 38.

ἠχή, ἡ, *sound, echo, noise, roaring,* spoken of a multitude, 2, 209. 12, 252. Od. 3, 150; of battle; 8, 159. 15, 355; of wind, 16, 769.

ἠχήεις, εσσα, εν (ἠχή), *sounding, resounding, roaring,* spoken of the sea, 1, 157; δώματα, Od. 4, 72. h. 13, 5.

ἤχθετο, see ἔχθομαι

ἧχι, Ep. for ᾗ, adv. *where,* 1, 607 (not ἦχι as in the Od.).

*ἠχώ, όος, ἡ, *sound, noise,* but esply *echo, reverberation,* h. 18, 21.

ἠῶθεν, adv. (ἠώς), *from the morning, from the dawn; in the morning,* 7, 372, and often. 2) *at the dawn,* at day-break, 18, 136. Od. 1, 372. 15, 308.

ἠῶθι, adv. (ἠώς), *in the morning, at the dawn;* always ἠῶθι πρό, before day-light, 11, 50. Od. 6, 36.

*ἠῷος, η, ον (ἠώς), *in the morning, early,* h. Merc. 17.

ἠώς, gen. οῦς, dat. οῖ, accus. ἠῶ, 1) *the dawn of day, the early dawn,* 9, 618 seq. Od. 6, 48. 2) *the time of the morning dawn, morning;* accus. ἠῶ, during the morning, Od. 2, 434; the gen. ἠοῦς, on the morning (of the following day), 8, 470. 525. 3) *the rising day-light,* 8, 1 (accord. to Eustath., Voss, and others, *day-light* itself, and the *whole day,* 13, 794. Od. 19, 571); e. g. ὅτε δὴ τρίτον ἦμαρ ἐϋπλόκαμος τέλεσσ' ʹΗώς, but when Aurora brought about (not brought to an end) the third day, Od. 5, 390. 9, 76. 10, 144; hence the days were counted by the mornings, 1, 493. Od. 19, 192. 571; cf. Völck. Hom. Geog. p. 126. Nitzsch ad Od. 2, 434. 4) As a point of the compass: *morning, east,* in πρὸς ἠῶ τ' ἠέλιόν τε, see ἠέλιος (from ἀέω. ἄημι, prop. the morning-air).

ʹΗώς, ἡ, as pr. n. *Aurora,* the goddess of the dawn or of the breaking day-light. She was according to h. 31, daughter of Hyperion and Euryphaessa; according to Hesiod. Th. 372, of Theia wife of Tithônus, mother of Memnon, 11, 1. Od. 4, 188. h. Ven. 219. She bore away Orion and Clitus on account of their beauty, Od. 5, 121. 15, 250; and as a goddess had her residence in western Æa (according to Nitzsch, Od. 5, 1, prob. because an appearance similar to the dawn shows itself in the evening sky). She rises in the morning from the couch of her husband, to bring the light, 11, 1; or, according to 19, 1, 2. Od. 22, 197, from the waves of Oceanus; and the bright morning-star precedes her, 23, 226. She spreads her light over the whole earth, but the poets say nothing of her setting. According to

Od. 23, 246, she performs her journey with two horses. She is called χρυσόθρονος, εὔθρονος, κροκόπεπλος, ῥοδοδάκτυλος, ἠριγένεια, etc.

Θ.

Θ, the eighth letter in the Greek alphabet; and therefore the sign of the eighth book.

θαάσσω, Ep. for θάσσω, to sit, 9, 194. 15, 124. Od. 3, 336. h. Merc. 172; only in the pres. and imperf. (According to Buttm. Lexil. p. 350, from the root θέ- or θα- (in the sense of sit), cf. τίθημι.)

θαιρός, ὁ, the hinge of a door; the hinges were attached to the door, and not, as with us, to the door-post [the doors were so constructed as to have pivots above and below, which turned in sockets; the pivot is called στροφεύς, the sockets στρόφιγγες, cf. Bothe in loc.], 12, 459.†

θαλάμη, ἡ, the lurking-place, lair, or den of a wild-beast, Od. 5, 432.†

θαλαμηπόλος, ὁ (πολέομαι), attending in the sleeping-chamber or apartment of the women; the fem. the chamber-maid, lady's-maid, *Od. 7, 8. 23, 293.

θάλαμος, ὁ, any apartment or chamber in the interior of a house, and 1) the sleeping-apartment of married persons, the nuptial chamber, 3, 423. 6, 243—250; the bridal-chamber, 18, 492. 2) the common apartment of the mistress of a family, 3, 127. Od. 4, 121; also any other room or chamber in the inner part of the house, 23, 317. 3) Also the store-room, in which clothes, arms, and provisions were kept, 4, 143. 6, 288; and according to Od. 2, 337, it would seem to be a vault below, cf. Nitzsch ad loc. cf. Od. 8, 439. 15, 99. (Prob. from θάλπω.)

θάλασσα, ἡ (prob. from ἅλς), the sea, sea-water, the interior or Mediterranean sea, in distinction from the ocean, 1, 34. Od. 12, 1. 2.

θαλάσσιος, ον (θάλασσα), belonging to the sea; hence, nautical. θαλάσσια ἔργα (maritime affairs; mar. employs, Cp.), navigation, 2. 614: fishing, Od. 5, 67.

θάλεα, τά (θάλυς), blooming fortune, happiness, a superfluity of all delights, res floridæ. θαλέων ἐμπλησάμενος κῆρ, having filled his heart with contentment or joy [not, with delicacies, Cp.], 22, 504;† cf. θάλεια.

θαλέθω, poet. form for θάλλω, to bloom, Od. 23, 191; metaph. spoken of men: to be in the bloom of life, Od. 6, 63. 2) to flourish, to abound in any thing, with ἀλοιφῇ, 9, 467. 23, 32.

θάλεια, ἡ, as adj. used only in the fem. as an epith. of δαίς, 7, 475. Od. 3, 420. 8, 76. 99; a flourishing, i. e. rich, sumptu-

ous feast. The old Gramm. derive it incorrectly from θάλειος; it is rather the fem. of an obsol. adj. θάλυς, an Ep. form of θῆλυς, to which also τὰ θάλεα belongs, Buttm.

Θάλεια, ἡ, Thalīa, daughter of Nêreus and Dôris, 18, 39.

θαλερός, ή, όν (θάλλω), blooming, flourishing; hence, fresh, vigorous, active; only in the metaph. signif. as αἰζηοί, πόσις; γάμος, blooming marriage, i. e. marriage in the bloom of youth, Od. 6, 66; μηρώ, strong, vigorous thighs, 15, 113; χαίτη, a full mane, 17, 439. 2) gushing, strong, rich, abundant; φωνή, the gushing, rich voice, 17, 696. Od. 4, 705: δάκρυ, abundant tears; the copious tear, 2, 266; γόος, unceasing lamentation, Od. 10, 457. (According to others, θαλερός signifies, in connexion with φωνή, loud, strong.)

θαλίη, ἡ (θάλλω), prob. bloom; metaph. blooming fortune, abundance, joy. ἐν πολλῇ θαλίῃ, in full bliss, 9, 143; plur. Od. 11, 603.

θαλλός, ὁ (θάλλω), a sprout, a sprig, a branch, Od. 17, 224.†

θάλλω, only in h. Cer. 402; Ep. θηλέω, Od. 5, 73; aor. 2 ἔθαλον, Ep. θάλον, h. 18, 33; perf. 2 τέθηλα, partcp. τεθηλώς, fem. τεθαλυῖα (Ep. for τεθηλυῖα, for metre's sake), pluperf. τεθήλει, 1) to bloom, to flourish, to be verdant; spoken of the earth, ἄνθεσι, h. Cer. 402. 2) to have an abundance, to abound in, with dat. σταφυλῇσιν (spoken of a vine), Od. 5, 69; φυλλοῖσι. Od. 12, 103; metaph. ἀλοιφῇ, 9, 208. The partcp. mly absol. blooming, luxuriant, abundant, ἀλωή, εἰλαπίνη, ἀλοιφή, Od.

θάλος, εος, τό, a sprout, a sprig, a sucker, metaph. spoken of men, 22, 87. λευσσόντων τοιόνδε θάλος χορὸν εἰσοιχνεῦσαν, when they behold such a sprout (one so blooming in youthful beauty) entering the dance, Od. 6, 157. the partcp. agrees in gender with the object understood (κατὰ σύνεσιν), h. Ven. 279.

θαλπιάω (θάλπω), to become warm, to be warm; only partcp. θαλπιόων for θαλπιῶν, Od. 19, 319.†

Θάλπιος, ὁ, son of Eurȳtus, grandson of Actor, commander of the Epēans before Troy, 2, 620 (from θάλπος, that warms).

θάλπω, only pres. to make warm, to warm, with accus. στέατος, τροχόν, Od. 21, 179; τόξον, i. e. to make the bow flexible by rubbing it with fat over the fire, *Od. 21, 246.

θαλπωρή, ἡ (θάλπω), prop. warming; always metaph. the act of refreshing, recreation, resting, 10, 253. Od. 1, 167; comfort, joy, opp. ἄχεα, 6, 412.

θαλύσια, τά, subaud. ἱερά (θάλλω), the offerings of the first-fruits which were made to the gods, 9, 534. In this place it is represented as offered to all the gods; later, this offering was made only to Dêmêtêr, Theocrit. 7, 3.

Θαλυσιάδης, ου, ό, son of Thalysius = Echepôlus, 4, 458

θαμά, adv. (ᾱμα), always of time: *often, frequently, continually*, 16, 207. Od. 1, 143. θαμὰ θρώσκοντες ὀϊστοί, 15, 470; also of time; for the sense is, that the new bow-string might endure (not give way under) the arrows which should be shot in rapid succession.

*θαμβαίνω, poet. form θαμβέω, to be *amazed at, to regard with astonishment*, with accus. εἶδος, h. Ven. 84. h. Merc. 407.

θαμβέω (θάμβος), aor. ἐθάμβησα, Ep. θάμβησα, 1) *to be amazed, to be astonished*, absol. 1, 199. Od. 1, 323. 2) Trans. with accus. *to be astonished at, to behold with astonishment*, Od. 2, 155. 16, 178. 17, 367.

θάμβος, εος, τό (θάομαι), Ep. gen. θάμβευς, Od. 24, 394; *astonishment, amazement, admiration, terrour*, 3, 342. Od. 3, 372.

θαμέες (θαμά), dat. θαμέσι, accus. έας, an Ep. adj. used only in the plur. masc. = θαμειός, *frequent, thick, in great numbers, in quick succession*. As a sing. θαμής or θαμύς are assumed, 10, 264. 11, 552. Od. 14, 12; see Thiersch, § 199. 5. Buttm. Ausf. Gram. § 64. Anm. 2.

θαμειός, ή, όν (θαμά), *frequent, close together, in great numbers;* only in the fem. plur. nom. and accus, *1, 52. 14, 422. 18, 68.

θαμίζω (θαμά), *to come or go frequently*, 18, 386. 425. Od. 5, 88. 8, 161. 2) *to be common* or *frequent;* with partep. οὔτι κομιζόμενός γε θάμιζεν, he was not often attended, Od. 8, 451.

θάμνος, ό (θαμινός), *a shrub, a bush, shrubbery, a thicket,* sing. Od. 23, 190. h. Cer. 107; plur. 11, 156. Od. 5, 471. 476.

Θάμυρις, ιος, ό, accus. Θάμυριν, ὁ Θρῆιξ, a bard of the fabulous ages, of Thrace, son of Philammôn and Argiopê. He was conquered in a contest with the Muses, and deprived of his eyes and his art, 2, 595. Apd. 1, 3. 3.

θάνατόνδε, *to death,* 16, 693.

θάνατος, ὁ (θανεῖν), *death,* both natural and violent, *slaughter,* 3, 309; in the plur. *kinds of death,* Od. 12, 341. Natural death is brought by the goddess of fate (μοῖρα, μόρος), according to the universal law of nature; violent death, contrary to the common termination of life, by Κήρ (κῆρες θανάτοιο); sudden death in the bloom of life by Apollo and Artêmis, cf. μόρος and κήρ.

Θάνατος, ὁ pr. n. *the god of death,* death personified; H. calls him the twin brother of Hypnos (Sleep), 14, 231. 16, 454. 672. His form is not further described by him. According to Hes Th. 759, he is the son of Νύξ (Night), and dwells in Tartarus.

θανέειν, contr. θανεῖν, see θνήσκω.

θάομαι, prop. Dor. for θεάομαι, q. v.; depon. mid. fut. θήσομαι, *to regard with astonishment, to admire, to wonder at;*

only optat. aor. θησαίατ᾽ for θήσαιντο, Od. 18, 191.†

θάπτω, aor. 1 θάψα, Ep. for ἔθαψα, plupf. pass. ἐτέθαπτο, to perform the last offices to a corpse, i. e. 1) *to burn* it, Od. 12, 12. Il. 21, 323. 2) *to bury, to inter* the collected bones, ὑπὸ χθονός, Od. 11, 52.

θαρσαλέος, έη, έον, Att. θαρραλέος (θάρσος), *bold, courageous, confident,* in a good sense. πολεμιστής 5, 602; also in a bad, *rash, audacious,* Od. 17, 449 19, 91; compar. θαρσαλεώτερος, 10, 223. Adv. θαρσαλέως, *boldly, audaciously,* Od. 1, 382

θαρσέω, Att. θαρρέω (θάρσος), aor. ἐθάρσησα, Ep θάρσησα, perf. τεθάρσηκα, *to be bold, courageous, of good courage, resolute;* mly absol., often imperat. θάρσει, τεθαρσήκασι λαοί, the people are full of courage, 9, 420 687. 2) Trans. with accus. θάρσει τόνγ᾽ ἄεθλον, be of good courage in this contest, Od. 8, 197.

θάρσος, εος, τό, Att. θάρρος, 1) *resoluteness, good courage, confidence, boldness.* 2) In a bad sense: *rashness, imprudence,* 17, 570 21, 395.

θάρσυνος, ον (θάρσος). *courageous, confident, bold,* πόλις, 16, 70; *confiding in,* with dat. οἰωνῷ, 13, 823.

θαρσύνω, Att. θαρρύνω (θαρσύς, poet. for θρασύς), iterat. imperf. θαρσύνεσκε, *to make courageous, spirited, confident, to encourage, to inspirit,* τινά, 18, 325; ἐτόρ τινι ἐνὶ φρεσίν. 16, 242; and dat. instrum. ἐπέεσσι, μύθῳ, 4, 233. Od. 9, 377.

θάσσων, ον, *faster, swifter,* compar. of ταχύς, q. v.

θαῦμα, ατος, τό (θάομαι), 1) *an object of wonder, a miracle,* any thing which is beheld with admiration and astonishment; often with θαῦμα ἰδέσθαι and ἰδεῖν, a prodigy to behold, 5, 725. h. Ven. 206; spoken of Polyphêmus: θαῦμα πελώριον, Od. 9, 190. 2) *astonishment, amazement,* Od. 10, 326.

θαυμάζω (θαῦμα), fut. θαυμάσομαι, Ep. σσ, aor. ἐθαύμασα, 1) Intrans. *to wonder, to be astonished,* often with partep. 24, 692; with infin. οἷον δὴ θαυμάζομεν Ἕκτορα—αἰχμητήν τ᾽ ἔμεναι καὶ θαρσαλέον πολεμιστήν! how wonder we so, that Hector is both a lancer and a brave warrior! 5, 601. 2) Trans. with accus. *to wonder at* any thing, *to regard with astonishment.* 10, 12. Od. 1, 382; connected with ἀγάασθαι, Od. 16, 203; οἷον ἐτύχθη, at what happened, 2, 320.

θαυμαίνω, Ep. form of θαυμάζω, fut. ανῶ, *to wonder at,* Od. 8, 108.†

Θαυμακίη, ἡ, a city in Magnesia (Thessaly), under the dominion of Philoctêtes; according to Eustath. the later Θαυμακοί, 2, 716.

*θαυμάσιος, ίη, ιον (θαῦμα), *wonderful, astonishing,* h. Merc. 443.

*θαυμαστός, ή, όν. *wonderful, astonishing,* h. Cer. 10

*θαυματός, ή, όν. poet. for θαυμαστός h. Merc. 80. Bacch. 34.

ΘΑΦΩ, poet. obsol. root of the perf. τέθηπα, pluperf. Ep. ἐτεθήπεα for ἐτεθήπειν, and aor. 2 ἔταφον (in the perf. the second aspirate is changed into the tenuis, and in the aor. the first). The perf. has the signif. of the pres. *to wonder, to be astonished, to be amazed*, often in the partcp., 4, 243. 21, 29. 64. θυμός μοι ἐν στήθεσσι τέθηπεν, my mind in my breast is amazed (*my soul is stunn'd within me*, Cp.), Od. 23. 105; also ἐτεθήπεα θυμῷ, Od 6, 166. Of the aor. 2 only the partcp. ταφών, 9, 193. 11, 545 (see Buttm. Gram. p. 285).

ΘΑΩ, Ep. defect. of which only the infin. pres. mid θῆσθαι for θάσθαι, and 3 sing. aor. mid. θήσατο, partcp. θησάμενος, occur. 1) *to suck, to milk.* γυναικά τε θήσατο μαζόν, he sucked at a woman's breast, see γυνή, 24, 58. h. Cer. 236; spoken of sheep: αἰεὶ παρέχουσιν ἐπηετανὸν γάλα θῆσθαι, they always give milk the whole year (lit., milk *to milk* [infin.]; for a man *to milk* it), Od. 4, 89. 2) *to suckle.* Ἀπόλλωνα θήσατο μήτηρ, the mother suckled Apollo, h. Ap. 123.

θεά, ἡ, fem. of θεός, *a goddess*; in connexion with another subst. θεὰ μήτηρ, 1 280, and θεαὶ Νύμφαι, 24, 615 (θεά retains the alpha through all the cases); hence θεᾶς, θεάν, the dat. plur. θεαῖς, but θεῆς, 3, 158; θῆσιν, 8, 305. Herm. ad h. Ven. 191, would always read θεαῖς; θεά must be pronounced as a monosyllable after πότνια, Od. 5, 215. 13, 391. 20. 61. Buttm., Ausf. Sprachl. I. p. 261, reads πότνα, and then θεά is dissyllabic.

θεά, ἡ (θεάομαι), sight, view. αἰδεσσαί με θεᾶς ὕπερ, reverence me by thy countenance [by thy sweet face], h. Cer. 64; as an adjuration, a doubtful reading. Herm. would write θέης; Ilgen takes it as a pr.n. Θέη for Θεία, as Ρέα, Ρήη [see Bothe in loc.].

θέαινα, ἡ, poet. for θεά, *goddess*, 8, 5. Od. 8, 341.

Θεανώ, οῦς, ἡ, daughter of Cisseus, wife of Antēnōr, priestess of Athēnē in Troy, 5, 70. 6, 298. According to later poets, sister of Hecabē (Hecuba).

θέειον, τό, Ep. for θεῖον, q. v.

θεειόω, Ep. for θειόω.

θείεν, see τίθημι.

θειλόπεδον, τό (εἵλη, πέδον), a place exposed to the sun for drying any thing, *a drying-place*, Od. 7, 123;† viz. a space in the vineyard exposed to the rays of the sun, where grapes were dried on the stocks, in order to prepare the *vinum passum*, cf. 18, 566. τῆς (subaud. ἀλωῆς) ἕτερον (sc. πέδον) θειλόπεδον λευρῷ ἐνὶ χώρῳ τέρσεται ἠελίῳ ἑτέρας δ' ἄρα τε τρυγόωσιν, ἄλλας δὲ τραπέουσι, in this, a drying-place, on the level ground, is warmed by the sun [the arid level glows, Cp.], and they are gathering some and treading out others. Voss translates, 'some grapes, spread out on the level place, are drying in the sun' (he understands, of course, a place in which the

plucked grapes are dried), see Nitzsch ad loc.

θεῖμεν, see τίθημι.

θεῖναι, see τίθημι.

θείνω (akin to κτείνω and θάνω), aor. 1 ἔθεινα, partcp. θείνας, 20, 481; *to strike, to cut down, to goad*, with accus. 1, 588. 16, 339; and with dat. instrum. ἄορι, with the sword, βουπλῆγι, μάστιγι, 10, 484. 6, 135. On θεινομένου in Od. 9, 459, see ῥαίοιτο.

θείομεν, poet. for θῶμεν, see τίθημι.

θεῖον, τό, Ep. θέειον and once θήιον, Od. 22, 493; *sulphur*, spoken of lightning, 8, 135. 14, 415. Od. 12, 417. It was used as a sacred means of purification, 16, 228. Od. 22, 493; see θειόω.

θεῖος, η, ον (θεός), *divine*, sprung from a deity, γένος, 6, 180; or sent by a deity, ὀμφή, 2. 41. 2) *consecrated to a deity, holy, sacred*, ἀγών, χορός, 7, 298. Od. 8, 264. 3) *divine, glorious*, spoken not only of men who are distinguished by peculiar powers and qualities, but also of every thing which is great, beautiful, sublime, or excellent in nature; ἅλς, 9, 214 [sacred salt, prob. because derived from the sea, ἐξ ἁλὸς δίας]; ποτόν, Od. 2, 341. 9, 205; cf. Nitzsch ad Od. 3, 265, p. 190.

θειόω, Ep. θεειόω (θεῖον), fut. ώσω, *to fumigate with sulphur, and purify*, δῶμα, Od. 22, 482. Mid. Od. 23, 50 (both times the Ep. form).

θείω, Ep. for θέω, θῶ, see τίθημι.

θέλγω, aor. ἔθελξα, ἐθέλχθην, *to stroke with the hand, to caress*, mulcere, and to overcome any one by such charms addressed to the sense, hence: 1) *to charm, to benumb*, spoken of bodies with the accus. of the wand of Hermēs: ἀνδρῶν ὄμματα θέλγει, with which he seals the eyes of men, Od. 5, 47. 24, 3. Il. 24, 343. θέλξας ὄσσε φαεινά, sealing the bright eyes, 13, 435. (It is not to be taken of the obscurity of death.) b) *to charm*, i. e. to transform by enchantment, τινά, Od. 10, 291. 318, 326. Others explain it in a metaph. sense, to restrain, to appease; but against the context, cf. v. 432; and Nitzsch ad loc. 2) *to charm, to infatuate*, metaph. of the mind: only in a bad signif. to deprive a man utterly of his mental powers, *to overreach, to deceive, to blind, to seduce, to infatuate*, spoken of the Sirens, Od. 12, 40 : νόον, to deprive of reason, 12, 255. h. Cer. 36; θυμόν, to enfeeble the mind, 15, 594; and dat. instrum. λόγοισιν, ἐπέεσσιν, by words, Od. 1, 57. 3, 267; ψεύδεσσι, δόλῳ, 21, 276. 604; spoken of the suitors: ἔρῳ δὲ θυμὸν ἔθελχθεν, they were infatuated by love, Od. 18, 212. b) Rarely in a good signif.: *to charm, to chain* (by a narration), Od. 17, 521; pass. Od. 17, 514.

*θελκτήρ, ηρος, ὁ (θέλγω), *a soother, an assuager*, ὀδυνάων, h. 15, 4.

θελκτήριον, τό (θέλγω), any thing which has an enchanting power over the mind; *an instrument of enchantment, a charm, delight, rapture*, spoken of the girdle of

K 4

Aphroditê. 14, 215. Songs are called θελκτήρια βροτῶν, the delights of mortals, Od. 1, 337; and the Trojan horse: θεῶν θελκτήριον, the joy of the gods, Od. 8, 509. Others make θελκτήριον here an adj., and connect it with ἄγαλμα, a propitiatory offering.

θέλω, Ep. ἐθέλω, to will, to wish, whence θέλοι, h. Ap. 46; where however Herm. would read ἐθέλω.

θέμεθλον, τό (θέμα), a foundation, a bottom. ὀφθαλμοῖο θέμεθλα, the bottom, i. e. the cavities of the eye, 14, 493. στομάχοιο θέμεθλα, the bottom of the throat, *17, 47.

θεμείλιον, τό = θεμέθλιον, the foundation, τιθέναι, to lay the foundation; διατιθέναι, h. Ap. 254. Il. 12, 28; προβαλέσθαι, 23, 255; only in the plur.

θέμεν, and θέμεναι, see τίθημι.

θέμις, ιστος, Ep. for θέμιδος, ἡ (from θέω, τίθημι). in general. any thing which is introduced and sanctioned by use, that which is proper, becoming; hence 1) order, custom, right, 5, 761; often θέμις ἐστί, it is right, reasonable, with dat. of the pers. and infin. Od. 14, 56. Il. 14, 386. ἤ or ᾗ θέμις ἐστί. as is the custom, as is fitting, 2, 73. 9, 33; cf. ᾗ, and with gen. ἡ θέμις ἀνθρώπων πέλει, 9, 134. 19, 177. ἥτε ξείνων θέμις ἐστίν, Od. 9, 168; in connexion with ἀγορή, the assembly of judges, 11, 807. 2) In the plur. οἱ θέμιστες, ordinances, decrees; of the gods: Διὸς θέμιστες, the oracles of Zeus, Od. 16, 403. b) Spoken of men: laws, statutes, institutions, Od. 9, 112, 115; chiefly spoken of rulers and judges: οἴτε θέμιστας πρὸς Διὸς εἰρύαται, who guard the laws from Zeus [voluntate, auspiciis Jovis regnant, Heyn.], 1, 238. 2, 206; [cf. ἐρύω.] judicial sentences, κρίνειν θέμιστας σκολιάς, to give unjust decisions (to pervert justice), 16, 387; and of subjects: λιπαρὰς τελεῖν θέμιστας, to pay rich tributes, customs, i. e. the customary gifts to the king, 9, 156. 298.

Θέμις, ιστος, ἡ, Themis, daughter of Uranus and Gæa, Tellus (Hes. Th. 135), occurs in H. only three times. · She performs in Olympus the office of a herald, and calls the gods to an assembly, 20, 4; at a feast of the gods, she receives those who come, and preserves order in it, 15, 87; she arranges assemblies of the people and dismisses them, Od. 2, 68. In the Hymns she is called the friend of Zeus, h. 22, 2; and the companion of Nikê (Victory), h. 7, 4. Later, she appears as the protectress of legal order and the goddess of justice.

θέμιστα, θέμιστας, see θέμις.

θεμιστεύω (θέμις), to give laws, to administer justice, τινί, Od. 11, 569; spoken of the gods, βουλήν, to give an oracle, h. Ap. 253. 2) to rule, to govern, τινός, *Od 9, 114.

*θεμιστοπόλος, ον (πολέω), administering the laws, administering justice, epith. of kings, h. Cer. 103. 473.

*θεμιτός, ή, όν, poet. for θέμιστός (θε-

μίζω), according to law, just, right, h. Cer. 302.

θεμόω (τίθημι), to set, i. e. to force. νῆα θέμωσε χέρσον ἱκέσθαι, the wave forced the ship to come to the land, *Od. 9, 486. 542.

θέναρ, αρος, τό (θείνω), the palm of the hand, with which a man strikes, 5, 339.†

θέο, Ep. for θοῦ, see τίθημι.

θεόδμητος, ον (δέμω), built by a god, god-built, πύργοι, 8, 519 †

θεοειδής, ές (εἶδος), similar to a god, god-like, epith. of distinguished heroes, still only in reference to physical superiority, 2, 623; also of the suitors, Od. 21, 186. 277; see θεουδής, cf. Buttm. Lex. p. 352.

θεοείκελος, ον (εἴκελος), similar to a god, like θεοειδής, 1, 131. Od. 3, 416.

θεόθεν, adv. (θεός), from god, Od. 16, 147.†

Θεοκλύμενος, ὁ, son of Polypheides, a descendant of Melampus and a famous prophet, Od. 15, 256.

θεοπροπέω (θεοπρόπος), to prophesy, to communicate the will of the gods, to explain divine signs, only partcp. 1, 109. Od. 2, 184.

θεοπροπίη, ἡ, prop. the explanation of signs given by the deity, prophecy = μάντεια, 1, 87; cf. Eustath. Od. 1, 415. 2) = θεοπρόπιον, an oracle, a revelation, 1, 385. 11, 794. 16, 36.

θεοπρόπιον, τό, any thing which is indicated by the gods, a divine command, a divine response, an oracle, a revelation, a prophecy, *1, 85. 6, 438.

θεοπρόπος, ὁ, a prophet, a seer, a general name of those who, from signs, interpret the will of the gods, 12, 228. Od. 1, 416. (Mly derived from θεός and προειπεῖν or τὰ θεοῖς πρέποντα λέγειν; accord. to Buttm., Lex. p 350, from πρέπω, in the signif. to break forth, to sound out, hence θεὸς πρέπει, a god sends a sign. (θεοπρόπιον is the sign, and the expounder is called θεοπρόπος.)

θεός, ὁ, ἡ, Ep. θεόφιν, gen. plur. 17, 101; dat. plur. 7, 366; nom. plur. θεοί as a monosyllable, 1, 18. 1) Masc. god; indefinite = δαίμων, a god, 17, 99. Od. 3, 131. σὺν θεῷ, with god, with god's help, 9, 49. ἐκ θεόφιν, through the gods, 17, 101. ὑπὲρ θεόν, against god. against god's will, 17, 327. 2) As fem. ἡ = θεά, often in H. θήλεια θεός, 8, 7. 3) As adj. in the compar. θεώτερος, diviner. θύραι θεώτεραι, more used by the gods, Od. 13, 111. The Hom. gods have bodies with blood, and are formed like men, larger however and more handsome and far superior in their powers, 5, 859 seq. 15, 361. 24, 407. They are immortal and enjoy an eternal youth; sickness and other human infirmities they do not experience; still they are not secure from all misfortune, 5, 336. 883. 858. In intelligence and knowledge they far excel mankind, without however being omniscient, 5, 441. 2, 485. In a moral point of view they do not rise above

men; they have desires and passions,
failings and weaknesses. They govern
the world, and especially the affairs of
men; allot happiness and misfortune.
Men, however, often draw evils upon
themselves, by their own perverseness,
and then it is the allotment of fate, see
μοῖρα, Od. 1, 33, 34. They commonly
appear to men in assumed forms or enveloped in a cloud, 5, 127. 14, 343. 20,
131.150. Their dwelling is Olympus and
heaven, see Ὄλυμπος.

Θεουδής, ές. *fearing god, reverencing the
gods;* hence, *pious, upright,* νόος, θυμός,
Od. 6, 121. 19, 364; βασιλεύς, *Od. 19, 109.
(Buttm., Lex. p. 352, justly distinguishes
this word from θεοειδής, the contraction
of which rather would be θεώδης, and derives θεουδής from δείδω and θεός Hesych.
θεοσεβής, Schol. Palat. θεοδεής or δεισι-
δαίμων. So Pass. and Nitzsch. Lobeck
hesitates.)

θεούφιν, see θεός.

θεραπεύω (θεράπων), *to be a servant, to
serve,* in opposition to ἄρχω, Od. 13, 265.†
2) Mid. = act. h. in Ap. 380.

*θεράπνη, ἡ, poet. contr. fr. θεράπαινα,
a female servant, h. Ap. 157.

θεράπων, οντος, ὁ, *a servant, an attend-
ant, a companion, a helper.* It is distinct
from δοῦλος, and signif. a voluntary servant, not merely of free birth but often
of noble descent, 15, 431. seq.; thus Patroclus is θεράπων, the comrade of Achilles, 16, 244; Merionês of Idomeneus, 23,
113; all heroes are called θεράποντες
Ἀργος, 2, 110. 7, 382; and especially those
attendants of heroes who guide the horses,
charioteers, ἡνίοχοι θεράποντες, 5, 580.
So (a private) *herald* was often a θεράπ.
in the *service* of an individual, Od. 18,
424. In the Od. the θεράποντες perform
duties of various kinds in the house, Od.
1, 109; they are, however, always like
the squires of knights, of noble descent,
as Eteoneus, Od. 4, 22; (from θέρω, fo-
ure. prop. devoted to a man's service.)

θερέω, Ep. for θερῶ, see θέρομαι.

θερμαίνω (θερμός), aor. 1 ἐθέρμηνα, *to
warm, to make warm, to heat,* with accus.
λοετρά, 14, 7. Pass. *to become warm, to
be heated,* Od. 9, 376.

θερμός, ή, όν (θέρω), *warm, hot,* in different degrees; warm, 14, 6. 11, 266;
but also seething hot, Od. 19, 388; metaph. δάκρυα θερμά, hot tears, 7, 426.
Od. 4, 523.

θέρω (θέρω), *to warm, to heat,* ὕδωρ, Od.
8, 426; pass. *to become warm* or *hot, to
be warmed,* Od. 8, 437. πνοιῇ δ᾽ Εὐμήλοιο
μετάφρενον εὐρέε τ᾽ ὤμω θέρμετο, by the
breath (of the steeds close behind him)
were the back and broad shoulders of
Eumêlus warmed, 23, 381.

θέρος, εος, τό (θέρω), gen. Æol. θέρευς,
Od. 7, 118; dat. θέρει, 22, 151; prop.
warmth; esply the warm season, *summer,*
opposed to ὀπώρη, Od. 12, 76; opposed to
χεῖμα, Od. 7, 118.

θέρομαι, a defect. mid. fut. θέρσομαι,

aor. 2 pass. ἐθέρην, subj. θερέω, Ep. for
θερῶ, *to become warm, to warm oneself,
to become hot,* Od. 19, 64. 507; πυρός, by
the fire, Od. 17, 23. 2) *to glow. to be
burned,* πυρός, 6, 331. 11, 667. (The act.
θέρω is rare.)

Θερσίλοχος, ὁ, a Pæonian, an ally of
the Trojans, slain by Achilles, 17, 216.
21, 209.

Θερσίτης, αο, ὁ, the ugliest of the
Greeks before Troy in body and mind.
He was squint-eyed, lame of one foot,
and hump-backed. His slanderous tongue
found fault with every one, and in his
impudent harangues he did not spare
even the most dignified characters. Odysseus (Ulysses) compelled him to hold
his tongue by a blow of his sceptre, 2,
211—271. (From θέρσος = θέρος, the *hot,
over-loud* speaker.) According to Apd.
1, 8, 1, son of Agrius.

θές, see τίθημι.

θέσκελος, ον (θεός and εἴσκω, ἴσκω,
origin. = θεοείκελος), *god-like: similar to
the gods; divine, supernatural, wonderful,* spoken only of things, in a metaph.
signif. (θεοείκελος on the other hand in a
proper signif.), ἔργα, 3, 130. Od. 11, 374.
610: as adv. ἔικτο θέσκελον αὐτῷ, he was
wonderfully like him, 23, 107 (see Buttm.
Lex. p. 357).

θεσμός, ὁ (τίθημι), *an ordinance, law,
decree, custom.* λέκτροιο παλαιοῦ θεσμὸν
ἵκοντο, they went to the custom of their
ancient couch [i. e. to the couch they
habitually shared in years long past],
Od. 23, 295.† θεσμοὶ εἰρήνης, the laws of
peace, h. 7, 16.

θεσπέσιος, ίη, ιον (θεός, εἰπεῖν), prop.
spoken or *inspired by a god;* the signif.
from εἰπεῖν is, however, obscure in ἀοιδὴ
θεσπεσίη, 2, 600. θεσπέσιαι Σειρῆνες. Od.
12, 158; generally, 1) *divine,* βηλός, 1,
591; ἄντρον, Od. 13, 363; and dat. θε-
σπεσίῃ, subaud. βουλῇ. as adv., by the
counsel of the gods, by the divine decree,
2, 367. 2) Most commonly as an epith. of
any thing great and glorious, whether
proceeding from nature or men: *divine,
grand, sublime, glorious, wonderful,
powerful, violent,* χάρις, ὀδμή, χαλκός,
φόβος, φύζα, powerful flight, 9, 2; so
also νέφος, λαίλαψ, 15, 669. Od. 9, 68.
(As an epith. of φόβος, φύζα, etc. it has
also been interpreted *supernatural, divinely sent,* but without necessity, see
Buttm. Lex. p. 358 [a *great* and *general*
flight. B.])

Θέσπια, ἡ, or Θέσπεια, Ep. for αἱ Θε-
σπιαί, *Thespiæ,* an ancient town, at the
foot of Helicon in Bœotia, according to
Strabo a colony of Thracians, or, according to a native tradition, named from
Thespius, son of Erechtheus, famed for a
temple of Erôs (Cupid) and the Muses,
now *Rimocastri,* 2, 498. Wolf, after Herodian and Venet. has ῑ; Heyne, on the
other hand, Θέσπεια, which Spitzner has
adopted.

θεσπιδαής, ές (δαίω), gen. έος, prop.

god-kindled; generally, *violent, terrible,* always an epith. of fire, 12, 441. Od. 4, 418 (see Buttm. Lex. p. 358). In 12, 177, some take πῦρ in a metaph. signif., the heat of contest, cf. λάϊνον.

Θέσπις, ιος, ὁ, ἡ (θεός, εἰπεῖν), *inspired by god, divinely inspired,* epith. of ἀοιδή and ἀοιδός, *Od. 1, 328. 8, 498. 17, 385. 2) divine, glorious, violent,* ἄελλα, h. Ven 209.

Θεσπρωτοί, οἱ, the *Thesprotians,* inhabitants of Thesprotia, a small region in the middle of Epirus. In the Od. they dwell not only on the coast of the proper Epirus, but in the interior as far as Thessaly. They were of Pelasgic origin, and one of the main tribes of this region, Od. 14. 315. 327. 16, 65. 427.

Θεσσαλός, ὁ, Ion. for Θετταλός, son of Heraclês and Chalciopê daughter of Eurypȳlus king of Cos, father of Pheidippus and Antiphus, 2, 679. (As a national name the word does not occur.)

Θεστορίδης, ου, ὁ, son of Thestor = Calchas, 1, 89; = Alcmæon, 12, 394; [also a name found in Epigr. 5, 1.]

Θέστωρ, ορος, ὁ, 1) son of Idmon, a prophet and Argonaut, father of Calchas, of Alcmæon, of Leucippê and Theonoê, Hyg. f. 160. 2) son of Enops, a Trojan, slain by Patroclus, 16, 401.

Θέσφατος, ον (θεός, φημί), 1) *spoken or communicated by God* [never in the transferred sense of *great, vast.* Buttm. Lex. p. 358]. θέσφατόν ἐστι, it is appointed by God, 8, 477; τινί, Od. 4, 561. 10, 473. As subst. not *an oracle,* a *divine response,* as Buttm. explains it, but *the predetermination of the gods; divinely predestined fate;* hence with adj. παλαίφατα θέσφατα (= decrees of the gods declared of old=) *ancient oracles,* 5, 64. Od. 9, 507. 11, 151. 13, 172. See Nitzsch ad Od. 9, 507. 2) Generally, *procured or sent by god.* ἀήρ, Od. 7, 143.

Θέτις, ιος and ιδος, ἡ, gen. ιδος, 8, 370; dat. Θέτῑ for Θέτιι, 18, 407: daughter of Nereus and Doris, wife of Peleus and mother of Achilles, not from choice, but by an appointment of Zeus, 18. 431. 24, 62. She tenderly loves her son, and on his account supplicates Zeus to avenge the insult offered him, 1, 502, seq. Zeus is greatly moved, for once, when the gods had conspired to bind him, she had delivered him from this disgrace, 1, 397, seq. She has her dwelling in the depths of the sea, and she is therefore called ἁλοσύδνη, 20, 207. According to 24. 78. 753. cf. 1, 357. 18, 35, her dwelling is in the vicinity of the Trojan dominions.

Θέω, and θείω, fut. θεύσομαι, 1) *to run, to fly, to hasten,* spoken of men and animals with the adjunct: πόδεσσι, ποσί, 23, 623. Od. 8, 247; μετά τινα, 10, 63; πόλεος πεδίοιο, through the wide plain, 4, 244; spoken of horses: περὶ τρίποδος θέειν, to run for a tripod (in a race), 11, 701; metaph. περὶ ψυχῆς Ἕκτορος θέειν, to run for Hector's life, 22, 161. (Both

Hector and Achilles ran thus rapidly for the prize was the life of the first which he sought to save and his adversary to destroy.) 2) Spoken of inanimate things, *to run, to fly,* spoken of a ship, 1, 483; often in Od. of a fragment of rock, 13, 141; of a potter's wheel, 18 601; of a quoit, ἀπὸ χειρός, Od. 8, 193 3) Of things without motion; φλὲψ ἀνὰ νῶτα θέουσα, a vein running along the back, 13, 547; ἄντυξ πυμάτη θέεν ἀσπίδος, 6, 118. 4) It is often connected a particp. with other verbs: as ἦλθε θέων he came running, or he came quickly hastily, 6, 54; and παρέστη, 15, 619 (the extended Ep. form θείω is found in the infin., partcp., and pres. subj.; see Thiersch, § 221. 82)

ΘΕΩ, obsol. root of τίθημι, q. v.

Θεώτερος, a, ον, see θεός.

Θῆβαι, ῶν, αἱ, poet. Θήβη, ἡ, *Thebæ Thebes.* 1) the oldest city in Bœotia, on the Ismênus, built by Cadmus, from whom the citadel was called Κάδμεια and enlarged by Amphion; now Thiva H. uses the sing. 4, 378. 406. Od. 11, 265 plur. 5, 804. 6, 223. It had epith. ἑπτάπυλος, seven-gated, Od. 11, 263; see Apd. 3, 6. 6; cf. Ὑποθῆβαι. 2) the ancient capital of upper Egypt, *Thebais,* on the Nile, later called Διὸς πόλις, famed for its opulence: hence it is called ἑκατόμπυλοι, only plur. 9, 381. Od. 4, 124. 126.

Θήβασδε, poet. for Θήβαζε, *to Thebes,* 23, 279. [3) a city in Troas, 22, 479; see Θήβη.]

Θηβαῖος, αίη, αῖον. *Theban,* as subst. a Theban, an inhabitant of Thebes in Bœotia, Od. 10, 492.

Θηβαῖος, ὁ, a Trojan, father of Enio peus, 8, 120.

Θήβη, ἡ, 1) Poet. for Θῆβαι, No. 1 2) a city in Troas, on the borders of Mysia, which was inhabited by Cilicians It was situated at the foot of mount Placus (hence Ὑποπλακίη), and was the residence of Eëtion, the father of Andromache. Achilles destroyed it; according to the Schol. the later *Adramyttium* 1, 366. 6, 397; plur. Θήβῃσιν, 22, 479 once. Strab. XIII. p. 585. In later writers, only τὸ Θήβης πεδίον, a fruitful region, south of Ida, near Pergamus, is mentioned.

Θήγω, fut. ξω, aor. 1 mid. ἐθηξάμην, 1 Act *to whet, to sharpen,* spoken of the wild boar, ὀδόντας, 11, 416. 13, 475. 2 Mid. *to sharpen any thing for oneself,* δόρυ, *2. 382.

Θηέομαι, Ion. for Θεάομαι, pres. opt θηοῖο, contr. imperf. 3 plur θηεῦντο, Ep for ἐθηοῦντο, aor. 1 ἐθηησάμην, optat. plur. θησαίατο, fr. θάομαι, *to see, to behold, to look upon,* with the addition notion of wonder, hence *to regard with astonishment, to wonder, to wonder at,* with accus. 10, 524; πάντα θυμῷ, Od 5, 76; absol. with θαμβεῖν, 23, 728. 8, and often with the partcp. Od. 5, 75. 8, 1

Θήης, Ep. for θῆς, see τίθημι.

Θηητήρ, ῆρος, ὁ, Ion. for θεατής (θηέομαι), a beholder, a judge or connoisseur, one acquainted with, τόξων. Od. 21, 397.†

Θήϊον, τό, Ep. for θεῖον. q. v.

Θήλεας. accus. plur. θῆλυς.

Θηλέω, Ep. (θηλή) = θάλλω, to bloom, to be verdant, with gen. Od. 5 73;† see θάλλω.

Θῆλυς, θήλεια, θῆλυ (Ep. also θῆλυς, gen. commun., 19, 97. 5, 269. 10, 216. Od. 5, 467). 1) female, of the female sex, opposed to ἄρρην), θήλεια θεός, a female deity, 8, 7; θηλείας ἵππους, 5, 269; αὐτή, female voice, Od. 6, 122. Since with the female sex the ideas of fruitfulness, softness, and tenderness are connected, it signif. 2) fruitful, fructifying, fresh, tender. ἐέρση θῆλυς, the fresh dew, Od. 5, 467. (Others, ' the fructifying dew,' incorrectly, on account of its connexion with the cutting morning frost.) The compar. θηλύτερος, η, ον, poet. positive; only, however, θηλύτεραι θεαι and γυναῖκες, 8, 520. Od. 8, 324, and that with the idea of the fruitful or tenderer sex, as Passow remarks (' the tender woman,' V.).

Θημών, ῶνος, ὁ (τίθημι), a heap, ἡΐων, Od. 5, 368.†

Θήν, Ep. enclit. particle (primarily a dialect. form of δή); it expresses a subjective conviction; surely, certainly, 9, 394. Od. 3, 352; in H. always in an ironical signif., as δήπου (opinor), assuredly, certainly, 13, 620. 17, 29; and strengthened, ἦ θην, certainly, indeed; often οὔ θην, assuredly—not; not—I take it, 2, 276 8, 448. οὐ μέν θήν γε, not—I presume (or hope). Od. 5, 211.

Θηοῖο, see θηέομαι.

ΘΗΠΩ, obsol. root of τέθηπα, see ΘΑΦΩ.

Θήρ, θηρός, ὁ, a wild animal, esply a beast of prey, a wild beast, 10, 184. h. 18, 13; see φήρ.

Θηρευτής, οῦ, ὁ (θηρεύω), only as an adj. κύνεσσι καὶ ἀνδράσι θηρευτῇσι, dogs and hunters. *12, 41. cf. 11, 325.

Θήρη, ἡ (θήρ), the chase, the hunting of animals, 5, 49. 10, 360; prey, Od. 9, 158.

Θηρεύω (θήρη), to hunt, Od. 19, 365; in th- partcp.†

Θηρητήρ, ῆρος, ὁ, Ion. and poet. (θηράω), a hunter, Il., and ἄνδρες θηρητῆρες, 12, 170. αἰετὸς θηρητήρ, *21, 252.

Θηρήτωρ, ορος, ὁ, poet. for θηρητήρ, 9, 544.†

Θηρίον, τό (prop. dimin. of θήρ); a wild animal; a (wild) beast, without the diminutive force, spoken of a stag, μέγα θηρίον *Od. 10, 171. 180.

*Θηροσκόπος, ον (σκοπέω), lying in wait for wild animals, h. 27, 11.

Θής, θητός, ὁ, a hireling, a hired labourer, Od. 4, 644,† where θῆτες are mentioned with δμῶες; they were free, but poor house-holders, who had, it is true, family establishments of their own, but derived their support from the wealthy land-holders, by performing menial offices, see θητεύω. The interpret. 'serfs is incapable of proof. (According to Buttm. Lex. p. 350. from ΘΕΩ, τίθημι θα- [θάακος, seat], like the Germ. Sasse, Insasse.)

Θησαίατο, see θηέομαι.

Θήσατο, see ΘΑΩ.

Θησεύς, ῆος and έως, accus. Θησέα, Theseus, son of Argeus and Æthra, or, by tradition, of Poseidôn, king of Athens. Among the many exploits ascribed to him, the most remarkable are: the slaughter of the Minotaur, in Crete, by the help of Ariadnê, Od. 11, 322; his contest with the Centaurs at the marriage of Peirithous, etc. He also, by uniting the inhabitants of Attica in one place, laid the foundation of the later city of Athens, 1, 265. Od. 11, 631. This verse is, however, as borrowed from Hesiod, Sc. 182, marked as not genuine.

Θητεύω (θής), aor. ἐθήτευσα, to labour for hire, to work as a hireling, as a daylabourer. Cf. θής, 21, 444. Od. 18, 357; τινί, Od. 11, 389.

Θίς, θινός, ὁ, later θίν (from τίθημι), prop. any heap. πολὺς δ' ἀμφ' ὀστεόφιν θὶς ἀνδρῶν πυθομένων, around is a heap of bones of putrefying men, Od. 12, 45. 2) Chiefly sand-heaps on the sea-coast, dunes; and gener. the coast, the strand, θαλάσσης or ἁλός, in the dat. or accus. Od. 7, 290. 9, 46. The gender is to be recognized only in 23, 693; according to which it is masc. Later, it is masc. and fem. Incorrectly, the Gramm. distinguish ὁ θίς, a heap, and ἡ θίς, a shore.

Θίσβη, ἡ, poet. for Θίσβαι, αἱ, Thisbe, an ancient town in Bœotia at the foot of Helicon, between Creusa and Thespiæ, with a port, now Gianiki; accord. to Maynert = Σῖφαι, sing. 2, 502; cf. Strab. p. 411.

Θλάω, aor. ἔθλασα, Ep. σσ, to bruise in pieces, to dash in pieces, to grind to pieces, to crush, with accus. κοτύλην, 5, 307; κυνέην, 12, 384; ὀστέα, Od. 18, 97.

Θλίβω, fut. θλίψω, to press, to crush; mid. θλίψεται ὤμους, he will chafe his shoulders, Od. 17, 221.†

Θνήσκω (for θανήσκω, from θάνω), fut. θανοῦμαι, infin. θανέεσθαι, aor. 2 ἔθανον, perf. τέθνηκα; also the syncop. forms: plur. τέθναμεν, τέθνασι, optat. τεθναίην, imperat. τέθναθι, infin. Ep. τέθναμεν and τεθνάμεναι, partcp. τεθνεώς; only dat. τεθνεῶτι, Od. 19, 331; Comm. Ep. τεθνηώς, ῶτος; sometimes in the gen. τεθνηότος, Od. 24, 56. Il. 13, 659; as fem. once τεθνηκυῖα, Od. 4, 734. (The reading τεθνειώς, Wolf, after Aristarchus, has banished from H. Spitzner agrees with Wolf, ad Il. 6, 70. Buttm. regards it as established, at least for the gen. τεθνειῶτος, see Rem. Ausf. Gram. § 110. 10, 6.) 1) to die, to find a man's death, spoken both of natural and violent death; ὑπὸ χερσίν τινος, by the hands of any one,

15, 289. οἰκτίω τῳ θανάτῳ θανεῖν, to die a most pitiable death, Od. 11, 412. 2) In the perf. to be dead, opposed to ζάω, Od. 2, 131; partcp. τεθνηκώς one dead, a corpse, and even τεθνηὼς νεκρός, 6, 71; in like manner θανών, a dead person, 8, 476.

θνητός, ή, όν (θνήσκω), mortal, an epith. of men; subst οἱ θνητοί, mortals, in opposition to ἀθάνατοι, 12, 242. Od. 19, 593.

θοινάομαι, in H. depon. pass. (θοίνη), to feast, aor. 1 infin. θοινηθῆναι, Od. 4, 36 †

*θοίνη, ἡ, a feast, a repast, food, Batr. 40

θοαί, αἱ νῆσοι, see θοός.

Θόας, αντος, ὁ, Thoas, 1) son of Andraemon and Gorgo, king of Pleuron and Calydon in Aetolia, 2, 638. 4, 275. Od. 14, 499. 2) son of Dionȳsus and Ariadnê, king of Lemnos, father of Hypsipȳlê. He alone, in the slaughter of the men in Lemnos, was saved by his daughter, she sending him in a ship to Oenoê, 14, 230. 3) a Trojan, slain by Menelaus, 16, 311.

Θόη, ἡ (adj. θοή), Thoê, daughter of Nereus and Doris, 18, 40.

θόλος, ἡ, a dome, particularly a circular building with a dome; in the Od. an adjoining building between the house and the court, in which were kept furniture and provisions, kitchen-vault. Voss, Od. 22, 442. 459. That it rested upon pillars is evident from the fact, that Odysseus (Ulysses) attached the cord to a column in hanging the maids. Od. 22, 466.

θοός, ή, όν (prob. from θέω), swift, rapid. a) Spoken of warriors, active, prompt, vigorous, in battle; often in the Il ᾿Αρης. 5, 430; also with infin. θοὸς ἔσκε μάχεσθαι. 5. 536. νῦν θοοὶ ἐστέ, 16, 422, now be active,' i. e. alert in battle, as an exhortation to bravery, with which also the following passage agrees. Thus Heyne and Spitzner. Others, with Eustathius, think they find here a reproach for cowardice, and translate it in a sarcastic signification, 'now ye are swift!' ἄγγελος, h. 18. 29. b) Spoken of inanimate things which are moveable: βέλος, ἅρμα, μάστιξ. θοὴ δαίς, a hasty, quickly-prepared meal (take care that the meal be quickly prepared), Od. 8, 38; see αἰψηρός. θοαὶ νῆες, a constant epith. of ships, since they are swift and easily managed; the other interpretation, 'running to a point,' is less suitable, 1, 12. νὺξ θοή, swift night, either because it comes suddenly on, or, more correctly, because to men loving repose it seems to pass swiftly away (hence Voss, 'swift-flying night'). Buttm., Lex. p. 365, explains it, 'the swift night, as incessantly following the sun, and seizing on what he leaves;' with the implied notion of unfriendliness, 10, 394. 468. In Od. 12, 284, seq. Nitzsch, 'the sharp night-air.' c) Spoken of objects without motion: running to a point,

pointed; only θοαὶ νῆσοι, the pointed islands, Od. 15. 299; the little precipitous islands at the mouth of Achelous, which formed the extreme points of the Echinades, and form their cliffs or promontories projecting into the sea, were called θοαί or ὀξεῖαι, Strab. VIII. 350; now Cursolari. (The primary signif. is from θέω, running rapidly to an object; and therefore spoken of material objects running to a point, pointed; according to others. akin to θήγειν.)

θοόω (θοός, c.), aor. 1 ἐθόωσα, to point, to make pointed, to sharpen, ὁμαλόν, Od. 9, 327.†

θόρε, Ep for ἔθορε, see θρώσκω.

*Θορικός, ὁ (θόρικος. Thuc.), Thoricus, one of the twelve ancient cities in Attica, upon the east coast, founded by Cecrops; later, a place and borough (δῆμος) belonging to the Acamantian tribe; now, Porto Mandri; whence the adv. Θορικόνδε, h. in Cer. 126.

*θορυβέω (θόρυβος), to make a noise, to cry, Batr 191.

ΘΟΡΩ, obsol. root of θρώσκω, q v.

θοῦρις. ιδος, ἡ, fem. of θοῦρος, q. v.

θοῦρος, ὁ. fem. θοῦρις, ιδος, ἡ (θόρω), prop. springing upon, attacking, impetuous, violent, the masc. always an epith. of Ares, 5, 30; the fem. spoken of arms with which one presses upon an enemy, ἀσπίς, 11, 32. 20, 162; αἰγίς, 15, 308; often θοῦρις ἀλκή, impetuous strength, in attacking and defence, often in the Il.; once in Od. 4, 527.

θόωκος, ὁ. see θῶκος.

Θόων. ωνος, ὁ, 1) son of Phænops, brother of Xanthus, a Trojan, slain by Diomêdês, 5, 152. 2) a Trojan, slain by Odysseus (Ulysses), 11, 422. 3) a Trojan, who attacked the camp with Asius, 12, 140. 4) a Trojan, slain by Antilochus, 13, 545. 5) a noble Phæacian, Od. 8, 113. 6) = Θῶν.

θοῶς, adv. from θοός, swiftly, instantly, 5, 533. Od. 5, 243. h. 7, 7.

Θόωσα, ἡ, a nymph, daughter of Phorcys, mother of Polyphêmus, Od. 1, 71. 72

Θοώτης, ου, ὁ, voc. Θοῶτα, the herald of Mnestheus, 12, 342, 343.

Θράσιος, ὁ, a Pæonian, slain by Achilles, 21, 210.

θράσος, τό. prop. only θάρσος with metath. fearlessness, courage, 14, 416.†

θρασυκάρδιος, ον (καρδία,) bold hearted, spirited, decided, *10, 41. 13, 343.

θρασυμέμνων, ον, gen. ονος (μένος), boldly-enduring, ever-courageous, epith. of Hêraclês, 5, 639. Od. 11, 267.

Θρασυμήδης, ους, ὁ, son of Nestor, who went with his father to Troy; leader of the watch, 9, 81, seq. He returned prosperously with his father, Od. 3, 39. 442.

Θρασύμηλος, ὁ, the charioteer of Sarpedon, slain by Patroclus, 16, 463 (otherwise Θρασυμήδης).

θρασύς, εῖα, ύ (θράσος), bold, brave, spirited, epith. of heroes, 8, 89. 12, 60;

oftener χεῖρες, 11, 553; and πόλεμος, 6, 254. Od. 4, 146; later in a bad ·signif. (also Voss, *arrogant*.)

θρέξασκον. see τρέχω.

•Θρεπτήριος. ον, *skilled in nourishing*, *in bringing up*. τὰ θρεπτήρια, wages for nursing or bringing up (see θρέπτρα), h. Cer. 168. 223.

θρέπτρα, τά (τρέφω), prop. the present, receiv·d by the person who nurses or brings up a child when the nursling is grown, *wages for nursing or bringing up*; then, *the gratitude* and *requital* which a child gives to his parents in age, for the care he has received. οὐδὲ τοκεῦσιν θρέπτρα φίλοις ἀπέδωκε, he requited not his dear parents' care [liv'd not to requite their love, Cp.] 4, 478. 17, 302.

θρέψα, Ep. for ἔθρεψα, see τρέφω.

Θρηΐκιος, ίη, ιον (Θρήκη), *Thracian*; πόντος, the Thracian sea, the northern part of the Ægean sea. 23, 230; φάσγανον and ξίφος. see these words. Σάμος Θρηϊκίη Samothracia, see Σάμος, 13, 12.

Θρῆϊξ, ῖκος, ὁ, contr. Θρῇξ, Ion. for Θρᾷξ, *a Thracian*. The inhabitants of Thrace were auxiliaries of the Trojans, 2. 844. Sometimes in the full form, Θρήϊκα, Θρήϊκες, Θρήϊκας, 2, 595. 4, 533; sometimes contract. Θρῇκες, 24, 234; Θρῃκῶν, 4, 519 (Thiersch, Gram. § 170, 4, would write Θρηκῶν, as coming from Θρηΐκων); ι is short in H.

Θρήκη, ἡ, Ion. for Θρᾴκη, *Thracia*, *Thrace*, a region north of Greece, by which it was bounded (through the Penēus and the sea) on the south, 23, 230. Towards the north, east, and west, Thrace in H. has no definite boundaries, and embraces all countries lying above Thessaly (8, 845). As a portion of them, he mentions Pieria, Emathia, Pæonia; as nations or tribes, the Pæonians and Ciconians; as mountains, Olympus, Athos, and the Thracian mountains (Θρήϊκων ὄρη, 14, 227; prob. accord. to Eustath. the Scomius and Hæmus); and the river Axius. It produces cattle, 11, 222; and wine, 9, 72; it is the habitation of the winds, v. 4; and, on account of the rudeness and savage valour of its inhabitants, the residence of Arês, 13, 301. Od. 8, 360. From this comes the adv. Θρῄκηθεν, from Thrace, 9, 5; and Θρήκηνδε, to Thrace, Od. 8, 361.

θρηνέω (θρῆνος), *to lament, to groan, to wail*, absol. Od. 24, 61; with accus. ἀοιδήν, to sing a dirge, 24, 722. [? See note.]

θρῆνος, ὁ (θρέω), *lamentation, wailing*, esply *the wailing for the dead*, which the singers commenced and women repeated, 24, 721; and gener. *any plaintive song*, spoken of the song of the birds, h. 18, 18.

θρῆνυς, νος ὁ (θρᾶνος), *a foot-stool*, which commonly stood by the θρόνος and κλισμός, 14, 240. Od. 1, 131. 2) *a bench for rowers*, the seat of the rowers, 15, 729; cf. ζυγόν.

Θρῆξ, ηκός, ὁ, Ion. for Θοᾷξ, see Θρῆϊξ.

•Θριαί, αἱ, the *Thriæ*, nymphs of Parnassus, who brought up Apollo, and invented the art of prophesying by little stones thrown into an urn, h. Merc. 552; cf. Herm. ad loc. and Apd. 3, 10. 2.

θριγκός, ὁ, the *projecting edge* (*coping*, or *cornice*) on the upper part of an (inner or outer) wall, the projecting part of a house-wall, which served to throw off the rain, *a battlement, a cornice*, Od. 17, 267. In the passage περὶ δὲ θριγκὸς κυάνοιο, Od. 7, 87, round about was a cornice of dark brass, it is commonly understood of the interior of the house, but Nitzsch ad loc. takes it as the coping of the exterior wall, for the description of the interior of the house commences v. 97.

θριγκόω (θριγκός), aor. ἐθρίγκωσα, to furnish the upper part of a wall with a coping, *to finish off*, and gener. *to enclose* or *fence*, ἀχερδῳ, Od. 14, 10.†

Θρινακίη, ἡ, νῆσος, Ep. for Θρινακρία (θρῖναξ), *Thrinacia*, i. e. the triangular island, or having three promontories, Od. 11, 107. The old and several modern critics understand by it the island of *Sicily*, and place in it the giants, Cyclôpes, Læstrygones, Siculi, and Sicani, see Strab. VI. p. 251. So Voss and Mannert. In H. it is a desolate island, and he gives it no occupants except the herds of Hêlios, Od. 11, 108. 109. G. F. Grotefend therefore justly remarks: "Italy was but obscurely known; it was confounded with several islands, Sicania, Od. 24, 306; and the land of the Siculi, Od. 20, 383: cf. 24, 366, if Sicania does not signify Sicily. The Sicani and Siculi are also later mentioned as inhabitants of lower Italy, Thuc. 6, 2. Also the giants, Cyclôpes, and Læstrygones seem not to dwell in Thrinacia, according to H. According to Völcker's Hom. Geog. p. 110, Thrinacia is not indeed the country of the giants, Cyclôpes, Læstrygones, etc., but a little island, distinct from Sicily, sacred to Hêlios.

θρίξ, τριχός, ἡ, dat. plur. θριξί, *the hair*, both of men and brutes, Od. 13, 399. 431. Il. 8, 83; ἀρνῶν, the wool of lambs, 3, 273; κάπρου, the bristles of the wild boar. 19, 254.

Θρόνιον, τό, *Thronium*, the chief town in Locris, on the Boagrius, later the capital of the Epicnemidian Locrians; now *Paleocastra* in Marmara, 2, 533.

θρόνον, τό, only in the plur. τὰ θρόνα, *flowers*, as ornaments in weaving and embroidery, 22, 442. In Theoc. II. 59, it is used of flowers and herbs.

θρόνος, ὁ, *a seat, a chair*, esply an elevated arm-chair, before which a foot-stool (θρῆνυς) was always placed. It was commonly wrought elaborately, and of costly materials, 14, 238. 8, 442. 18, 390. To make the seat soft, λῖτα, τάπητες, χλαῖναι, ῥήγεα were spread over it, '·l. 1, 130. 10, 352. 20, 150 (from θρᾶνος).

Θρόος, ὁ (θρέω), a noise, a roar, a cry, a loud call, 4, 337.†

*θρυλλίζω (θρύλλος), to strike a discordant note on the lyre, h. Merc. 488.

θρυλλίσσω (θρύλλος), fut. ξω, to break in pieces, to crush, θρυλλίχθην μέτωπον, 23, 396.†

*θρύλλος, ὁ, and θρῦλος (akin to θρόος), noise, uproar, outcry, Batr. 135. (Several ancient Gramm. prefer the reading with one λ.)

Θρυόεσσα, ἡ, poet. for Θρύον.

*θρύον, τό, a rush, juncus, a marsh-plant, 21, 351.†

Θρύον, τό, poet. Θρυόεσσα, ἡ, 11, 711, Thryon, a town in Elis, the boundary of the Pylians and Eleans, on the Alpheus, through which there was here a ford; it was situated upon a hill; according to Strab. the later Epitalium, 2, 592. It belonged to the dominion of Nestor; the passage 5, 545, where it is said of the Alpheus, that it flows through the land of the Pylians, does not conflict with 11, 711, where Thryon is named as a frontier town; for, although the river flowed by Thryon, it might still in other places flow through the interior of the realm, see Heyne ad loc.

θρώσκω, aor. 2 ἔθορον. Ep. θόρον, 1) to spring, to leap, ἐκ δίφροιο, 8, 320; χαμᾶζε, 10, 528. 15, 684: metaph. spoken of inanimate things: to spring, to fly, spoken of the arrow, 15, 314. 16, 774: spoken of beans and vetches, 13, 589   2) to leap upon, to make an attack, ἐπί τινι, upon any one, 8, 252. Od. 22, 203; ἔν τινι, 5, 161.

θρωσμός, ὁ (θρώσκω), a place springing up, as it were, above another, an elevation, a height. θρωσμὸς πεδίοιο, the heights of the plain, 10, 160. 11, 56. Thus the more elevated part of the Trojan plain is called, which stretched from the high shore of the Scamandrus to the camp; Voss, not with exact propriety, calls it 'the hill of the plain;' still less is it the hill of Callicolone, as Köppen, ad Il. 10, 160, has it.

θυγάτηρ, ἡ, gen. θυγατέρος and θυγατρός, dat. θυγατέρι and θυγατρί, accus. θύγατρα, 1, 13; nom. plur. θυγατέρες and θύγατρες, dat. θυγατέρεσσιν, 15, 197: H. uses both forms; a daughter. (υ is prop. short; but, in all cases which are more than trisyllabic, for metre's sake long.)

Θυέεσσιν, dat. plur. from θύος.

θύελλα, ἡ (θύω), a tempest, a whirlwind, a storm, a hurricane, often ἀνέμοιο, ἀνέμων θύελλα, 6, 346. πυρός τ' ὀλοοῖο θύελλα (V. a consuming fire-tempest), Od. 12, 68: mly spoken of a violent tempest, or of a storm-cloud rising with wind, 23, 366.

Θυέστης, ου, ὁ, Ep. and Æol. Θυέστα, 2, 107; (from θύω. Furius, Herm.) Thyestes, son of Pelops, grandson of Tantalus, brother of Atreus; he begot Ægisthus from his own daughter Pelopia. According to 2, 107, he succeeded Atreus in the government of Mycenæ. In Od. 4,

517, the abode of Thestes is mentioned, prob. in Midia, on the Argolic gulf; for here Thyestes dwelt, according to Apd. 2, 4. 6 ; see Nitzsch ad Od. l. c.

Θυεστιάδης, ου, ὁ, son of Thyestes = Ægisthus.

θύηεις, εσσα, εν (θύος), smoking with offerings, exhaling incense, sending forth vapour, epith. of βωμός, 8, 48. 23, 148. Od. 8, 363.

θυηλή, ἡ (θύω), the portion of victim burnt in honour of the gods (Schol. ὡς ἀπαρχαί), the offering of the first portion, [the consecrated morsel, Cp.], 9, 220;† see ἄργμα.

*θυίω = θύω, to rave, to be in a state of inspiration, of prophetic frenzy, h. Merc. 560.

θῦμαλγής, ές, gen. έος (ἄλγος), heart-paining, distressing, χόλος, λώβη, μῦθος, ἔπος, 4, 513. 9, 387. Od. 8, 272.

θυμαρής, ές, also θυμήρης (ἄρω), pleasing the mind, agreeable, delightful, pleasant, ἄλοχος, 9. 336. Od. 23, 232; σκῆπτρον, Od. 17, 199 (According to the Schol. ad Od. 23, 232, the accent of one form should be θυμαρής, of the other θυμήρης.)

Θυμβραῖος, ὁ, a Trojan slain by Diomedes, 11, 322.

Θύμβρη, ἡ, Thymbra, a plain (τόπος) in Troas, on the river Thymbrius, from which the camp of the Trojan allies extended to the sea. Later, this place was called Θυμβραῖον πεδίον, and there was the temple o' the Thymbrian Apollo, 10, 430.

θυμηγερέω (ἀγείρω), only partcp. pres. gathering courage, recovering one's spirits, Od. 7, 283.†

θυμηδής, ές (ἦδος), gen. έος, delighting the heart, grateful, Od. 16, 389.†

θυμῆρες, neut from θυμήρης, as an adv. agreeably, see θυμαρής.

θυμοβόρος, ον (βορά), heart-gnawing, soul-consuming, ἔρις, *7, 210. 16, 476. 20, 253.

θυμοδακής, ές (δάκνω), heart-biting, soul-stinging, μῦθος, Od. 8, 185.†

Θυμοίτης, ου, ὁ, Thymœtes, a distinguished Trojan, 3, 146.

θυμολέων, οντος (λέων). lion-hearted, epith. of heroes, 5, 639. Od. 4, 724. 814.

θυμοραϊστής, οῦ, ὁ (ῥαίω). life-destroying, deadly, θάνατος, 13, 544. 16, 414; δήϊοι, 16, 591.

θυμός, ὁ (θύω), prop. that which moves and animates in men, cf 7, 216; the heart, the soul, as the seat of feeling, will, and thought, but always regarded as in motion; chiefly the passions and desires; hence 1) the soul, as life, the vital powers, θυμὸν ἐξαίνυσθαι, ἀφελέσθαι, ὀλέσαι, Il. ἐξελέσθαι μελέων θυμόν, Od. 11, 201 : on the other hand, θυμὸν ἀγείρειν, to collect the vital powers, to recover, see ἀγείρειν; spoken also of the vital powers of beasts, 3, 294. 12, 150, etc. 2) the soul, as the seat of feeling, especially of the stronger passions, anger, courage, wrath, displeasure. ὀρίνειν θυμόν, to excite the soul, especially to pity, to fear, 4, 208. 5, 29; on the other hand, πᾶσιν κάππεσε θυμός the spirit of all fell, 15, 280; anger, displeasure, 2, 156. (Od. 4, 694. b) Sometimes a so spoken of the gentler emotions· ἐκ θυμοῦ φιλέειν, to love from the heart, 9. 486. ἀπὸ θυμοῦ μᾶλλον ἐμοὶ ἔσεαι, thou wilt be farther removed from my heart. 1, 561. 3) the soul, as the seat of willing or wishing. a) desire, inclination, esply for food and drink, appetite, 1, 468. 4, 263. πλήσασθαι θυμόν, to satisfy the appetite. Od. 19, 198; again, θυμὸς ἀνώγει, ἐποτρύνει, κελεύει, κέλεται, with infin., my heart prompts, commands me. b) will, resolution, thought. ἐδαίζετο θυμός, 9. 8. ἕτερος δέ με θυμὸς ἔρυκεν, another thought restrained me, Od. 9, 302. 3) Generally. mind, disposition, spirit. ἕνα or ἴσον θυμὸν ἔχειν, to have a like mind, 13. 487. 704 δόκησε δ᾽ ἄρα σφίσι θυμὸς ὡς ἔμεν, so seemed their heart to be (i. e. they seem to be affected, just as they would have been if, &c.), Od. 10. 415. 5) In many phrases we find the dat θυμῷ, 1, 24. Od. 19. 304; also κατὰ θυμόν, ἐν θυμῷ: and often κατὰ φρένα καὶ κατὰ θυμόν. a construction like mente animoque, in the inmost heart.

θυμοφθόρος, ον (φθείρω). prop. soul-wasting; hence, life-destroying, fatal; θυμοφθόρα πολλά, sc. σήματα, signs which commanded to put the bearer to death. 6, 169; φάρμακα, fatal poisons, or, with others, poisons destroying the understanding, infatuating, Od. 2. 329; ἄχος, κάματος, Od. 4, 716. 10, 363. 2) Generally, soul-harassing, Od. 19. 323.

*θυμόω (θυμός), to make angry, to enrage, in the aor. pass Batr. 242.

θύνω (θύω), intrans. to move oneself violently, to rush. to dash on, to run impetuously, ἂμ πεδίον, διὰ προμάχων, Il. κατὰ μέγαρον, Od., spoken esply of warriors in battle; ἄμυδις, to rush on in crowds, 10, 524; with partcp. 2, 446. (θύνω bears the same relation to θύω as δύνω to δύω.)

θυόεις, εσσα, εν (θύος), odoriferous, fragrant, νέφος, 15, 153; † and epith. of Eleusis, h. Cer. 97.

θύον, τό (θύω), a tree whose fragrant wood was used for incense. Plin. H. N. XIII. 16, understands by it citrus, the lemon-tree, or the pyramidal cypress. Theophrastus describes θύον as a shrub which Sprengel considers the thyia articulata. Billerbeck (Flor. Classic p. 234) thinks it the thyia cypressoides, Od. 5, 60. †

θύος, εος, τό, incense, and generally oblation, sacrifice, 6, 270. 9. 499. Od. 15, 261; only in the plur. (H. was not acquainted with incense see Nitzsch ad Od. 5, 60.)

θυοσκόος, ὁ (from θύος and κέω. καίω). prop. the sacrifice-burner, the sacrificial priest, the inspector of the sacrifice, who from the the flame, and especially from the vapour of the victim prophesied, Od.

21, 145. According to 24, 221, distinguished from μάντις and ἱερεύς (Eustath. ad Od. 21, 145, would rather derive it from κοέω, Ion. for νοέω.)

θυόω (θύος), fut. ώσω, to perfume by fumigation, to make fragrant; only partcp. of the perf. pass. τεθυωμένον ἔλαιον, fragrant, perfumed oil, 14, 172; † εἴματα, h. Ap. 184.

θύραζε, adv. out of the door, out of doors, 18, 29. 2) Generally, out, without. ἔκβασις ἁλὸς θύραζε, an egress out of the sea, a landing-place Od. 5, 410.

θυρεός, ὁ (θύρα), a door-stone, a stone placed before the entrance, *Od. 9, 240. 313. 340.

θύρετρον, τό (θύρα), a door, a gate, used only in the plur., 2, 415. Od. 18, 385.

θύρη, ἡ, Ion. for θύρα, a door, prop. an opening in the wall, whether of a single room or of the whole house; a gate, mly in the plur. folding-doors (i. q. σανίδες, θύραι δικλίδες. Od. 7, 267; ἐπί or παρὰ Πριάμοιο θύρῃσιν, at the doors of Priam, i e before the dwelling, 2, 788. 2) Generally, access, entrance, Od. 9, 243. 13, 109.

θύρηθε, adv. poet. for θύραθεν, out of the door, out, out of [the water, Bothe], Od. 14, 352. †

θύρηφι. Ep. dat. from θύρη, as adv. without, Od. 9, 238.

θυσανόεις, εσσα, εν, Ep. θυσσανόεις, fringed, furnished with tassels or fringes, epith. of the aegis, *5, 739. 15, 229: only in the Ep. form.

θύσανος, ὁ (θύω), a tuft, a tassel, a fringe, as an ornament on the shield of Agamemnon, the aegis, and the girdle of Hêrê, *2, 448. 14, 181.

θύσθλα, τά (θύω), the sacred things used in the festivals of Bacchus, accord. to the Gramm. esply the thyrsi, torches, etc., 6, 134 †

*θυσίη, ἡ (θύω), the act of sacrifice; the victim itself, h. Cer. 313. 369.

θύω, fut. θύσω, aor. ἔθυσα, I) Trans. to sacrifice, to slay or burn a victim, ἄργματα θεοῖς, Od. 14, 446; without accus. 9, 219. Od. 15, 222. 260; ἄλφιτα, h. Ap. 491; absol. τινί, to sacrifice to a god, Od. 9, 231. II) Intrans. to move violently, to rush on, to roar. To flow. a) Spoken of wind, Od. 12, 400. 408; of rivers and floods, 21, 324. 23, 230. δάπεδον αἵματι θύεν, the floor swam with blood, Od. 11, 420. 22, 309. b) Spoken of men, generally, to rage, to storm, to rush boisterously on, φρεσί, 1, 342; ἔγχεϊ, dat. instrum. 11, 180. 16, 669 (cf. θύνω. In the second signif. θύω has always ῠ, and in the first likewise, except in the trisyllabi cases of the partcp. pres. θύων, see Spitzner, § 52. 4).

θυώδης, ες (εἶδος), fragrant, perfumed, odoriferous, θάλαμος, Od. 4, 121; εἵματα, Od. 5, 264. 21, 52.

*Θυώνη, ἡ, an appellation of Semele, after she was received amongst the gods, h. 5, 21; (from θύω, accord. to Diod. 2-

62: ἀπὸ τῶν θυομένων αὐτῇ θυσιῶν καὶ θυηλῶν.)

θωή, ἡ (τίθημι), an imposed punishment, a fine, Od. 2, 192; ἀργαλέην θωὴν ἀλέεινε Ἀχαιῶν (he avoided the ignominious punishment of the Greeks, Voss), 13, 669. According to the Gramm. it here means blame, insult, reproach, and Nitzsch, ad Od. 2, 92, approves this; accord. to Od. 14, 239, χαλεπὴ δήμου φῆμις, the reproachful remarks of the people which compel one to go to war.

θῶκος, ὁ, Ep. for θόωκος, Od. 2, 26. 12, 318 (Att. θᾶκος), a seat. Od. 2, 14; θεῶν θῶκοι, 8, 439. 2) a sitting in council, an assembly, Od. 2, 26; θωκόνδε, to the council, at the council, Od. 5, 3.

Θὼν, ῶνος, ὁ, Thôn, husband of Polydamna, a noble Egyptian, at the Canopic mouth of the Nile, who received Menelaus, Od. 4, 228. Strab. XVII. p. 801, mentions a tradition, that not far from Canôpus there was a city Thonis, which received its name from the king Thon. This town is distinctly mentioned by Diodor. 1, 19. Heeren, however (Ideen II. 2. Absch. 3, p. 706), supposes that Diod. may have indicated the city Thonis, as the oldest port of Egypt, perhaps from the Thonis, which Herod. (II. 113) from the account of the Egyptian priests, calls a guard (φύλακος) of the Canopic mouth. Canopus itself, it is said, received its name from the pilot of Menelaus, who was buried there, Strab. (Θῶνος, according to Eustath. in the Od. stands for Θόωνος, or, rather by syncope, for Θώνιος.)

θωρηκτής, οῦ, ὁ (θωρήσσω), one who is armed with a cuirass, a cuirass-bearer; always in the plur. as adj. πύκα θωρηκταί, with closely fitted cuirasses, *12, 317; and often.

θώρηξ, ηκος, ὁ, Ion. for θώραξ, the coat of mail, the cuirass, a covering of metal for the upper part of the body from the neck to the abdomen, 3, 332; where the girdle (ζωστήρ) was attached to it. It was commonly of metal, for the most part of brass, and consisted of two curved plates (γύαλα), of which one covered the breast, and the other the back; at the sides they were fastened together by hooks; it is hence called διπλόος, 4, 133. cf. 15, 530. It was not only carefully polished but ornamented; hence, ποικίλος, πολυδαίδαλος, παναίολος, particularly the cuirass of Agamemnon, 11, 20—27. The edge was commonly encompassed with a border of tin. Besides metallic cuirasses there were also lighter ones, as the chain-cuirass, στρεπτὸς χιτών, q. v., and the linen corselet, 2, 529. 830. See Köpke, Kriegswes. der Griech., p. 95.

θωρήσσω (θώρηξ), aor. 1 ἐθώρηξα, Ep. θώρηξα, aor. 1 pass. ἐθωρήχθην, I) Act. to put on a cuirass, to arm, τινά. 2, 11; τινὰ σὺν τεύχεσιν, 16, 155. II) Mid. and

aor. pass. to put on one's cuirass, to arm oneself, often absol. in the Il.: once χαλκῷ, Od. 23, 368; mly τεύχεσιν, also σὺν τεύχεσιν, Il. δὸς δέ μοι ὤμοιϊν τὰ σὰ τεύχεα θωρηχθῆναι, permit me to put thine armour about my shoulders, 16, 40; præg. θωρήσσεσθαι Ἐφύρους μέτα, to march armed, 13, 301.

θώς, θωός, ὁ, a ravenous beast of prey, which, 11, 474, is named in connexion with the lion; in 13, 103, with panthers and wolves; in colour it is δαφοινός. Most critics understand by it the jackal, canis aureus, Linn., which in the shape of its body bears a great resemblance to the fox.

I.

I, Iota, the ninth letter of the Greek alphabet, and hence the index of the ninth rhapsody.

ἴα, ἰῆς, Ep. for μία, see ἴος.

ἰά, τά, heterog. plur. of ἰός.

ἰαίνω, aor. 1 ἴηνα, aor. 1 pass. ἰάνθην, 1) to warm, to make warm, to heat, ἀμφὶ πυρὶ χαλκόν, the kettle, Od. 8, 426; ὕδωρ, Od. 10, 359; hence, to make soft or liquid, κηρόν. Od. 12, 175. 2) Metaph. to warm, to enliven, θυμόν τινι, Od. 15, 379. h. Cer. 435; often pres. θυμὸς εὐφροσύνῃσιν ἰαίνεται, the heart is warmed with joy, Od. 6, 156; and generally, to rejoice, to gladden, 23, 598. Od. 4, 549. 840; μέτωπον ἰάνθη, the brow is cleared up, 15, 103: also θυμὸν ἰαίνομαι, I am become cheerful in heart, φρένας, Od. 23, 47. 24, 382; τινί. to delight in any one, Od. 19, 537. b) to soften, to mollify, θυμόν, 24, 119. 147. (Prop. ῐ, on account of aug., and for metre's sake also ῑ.)

Ἴαιρα, ἡ (ῐ). daughter of Nereus, 18, 42. (From ἰαίνω, gladdening.)

ἰάλλω, aor. ἴηλα, infin. ἰῆλαι (ἵημι), 1) to send, to send away, to shoot, διστὸν ἀπὸ νευρῆφιν, 8, 300. 309; χεῖρας ἐπ' ὀνείατα, to extend the hands to the food, 9, 91; περὶ χερσὶ δεσμόν, to put chains on the hands, 15, 19; ἑτάροις ἐπὶ χεῖρας ἰάλλειν, to lay hands upon the companions, Od. 9, 288; uncommon is: ἰάλλειν τινὰ ἀτιμίῃσιν, to wound any one with insults, like βάλλειν τινά τινι, Od. 13, 142.

Ἰάλμενος, ὁ (ῐ, the attacker. from ἰάλλω), son of Ares and Astyochê, leader of the Bœotians from Orchomenus and Aspledon; he is mentioned as an Argonaut, and as a suitor of Helen, Apd. 1, 9. 16. Il. 2, 512. 9, 83. According to Aristot. Epigr. Anth. he fell before Troy.

*Ἰάμβη. ἡ, (ῐ, fr. ἰάπτω, the female scoffer), an handmaid of Celeus and Metaneira, with whom Dêmêtêr tarried, when she was seeking her stolen daughter. Iambê forced the sad goddess to laugh by her jests, h. in Cer. 195. 203. [Apd. 1, 5. 1. According to the Schol. ad Orest. Eur. 662, daughter of Echo and Pan.

Ἰαμενός, ὁ (ῐ, partep. ἰάμενος), a Trojan hero, slain by Leonteus, 12, 139. 193.

Ἰάνασσα, ἡ, (ῐ, the warmer, fr. ἰαίνω), daughter of Nereus and Doris, 18, 47.

Ἰάνειρα (ῐ), Ianeira, 1) daughter of Nereus and Doris, 18, 47. 2) daughter of Oceanus and Tethys, h. in Cer. 421.

*Ἰάνθη, ἡ (ῐ = Ἰάνειρα), daughter of Oceanus and Tethys, h. in Cer. 418.

ἰάνθην, see ἰαίνω.

ἰάομαι, depon. mid. fut. ἰήσομαι, Ion. for ἰάσομαι, aor. 1 ἰησάμην, to heal, spoken only of external wounds. with accus. τινά, 5, 904; ὀφθαλμόν, Od. 9, 525; absol. 5, 899 (ῐ).

Ἰάονες, οἱ (ῐ), Ep. for Ἴωνες, the Ionians, in 13, 685.† h. Ap. 147; the inhabitants of Attica. In this appellation of the Athenians both ancient and modern critics have found difficulty, because the Ionians, almost 200 years before the Trojan war, emigrated from Attica to Ægialus, and not till eighty years after it in part returned. The name, however, with Heyne, Köppen, Bothe, may be very well defended, because the inhabitants of Attica still retained the name of Ionians, when Ion had taken possession of Ægialus, Hdt. 8, 44. The inhabitants of Ægialus, in distinction from the Attic Ionians, were called Αἰγιαλεῖς Ἴωνες, Paus. 7, 1. 2. Also the region of country from Sunium to the Isthmus was called Ionia, cf. Plut. Thes. 24.

Ἰαπετός (ῐ), a Titan, son of Uranus and Gæa (Tellus), husband of Clymenê, father of Atlas, Promêtheus, and Epimêtheus, see Τιτῆνες, 8, 479. (According to Heffter, motion upon the earth personified, in oppos. to Ὑπερίων.)

ἰάπτω (akin to ἵημι), 1) to send, to cast, to hurl, cf. προϊάπτω. 2) to touch, to hit, to wound, to injure, τί (Schol. διαφθείρειν, βλάπτειν), prop. καταϊάπτω, with tmesis; only. ὡς ἂν μὴ κλαίουσα κατὰ χρόα καλὸν ἰάπτῃ, that she should not injure [impair, Ὑ̅p.] her beautiful person by weeping, Od. 2, 376. 4, 749. (Some think it a separate verb, akin to ἴπτω, ἅπτω in the signif. to injure, Passow in Lex. supplies χεῖρας, and explains it, to lay hands upon, etc.)

Ἰάρδανος ὁ (ῐ), Iardanus, 1) A river in Elis near Pheia, 7, 135; according to Strab. VIII. p. 348, a tributary of the Arideon, which derived its name from the monument of the ancient hero Iardanus, near Chaa in Elis on the Arcadian borders: Paus. 5, 5. 5, says it is the Acidas or Acidon itself, but incorrectly, cf. Mannert, 8. p. 394. Otofr. Müll. Gesch. d. Hell. St. 1. p. 272. 2) a river in Crete, Od. 3, 292.

ἰᾶσι, see εἶμι.

Ἰασίδης, ου, ὁ (‾‾‾‾), son of Iasus, 1) = Amphion, Od. 11, 283. [2) = Dmetor, Od. 17, 443.]

Ἰασίων, ωνος, ὁ (‾‾‾), son of Zeus and Electra, according to Apd. 3, 12. 1, brother of Dardanus, a beautiful youth. He was killed by lightning, Od. 5, 125. Accord. to Hesiod. Th. 962, where he is called Ἰάσιος, he was the father of Plutus by Dêmêtêr.

Ἰασον Ἄργος, τό, for Ἰάσιον, the Iasian Argos. The city Argos received its name from king Iasus, q. v. Od. 18, 246. Accord. to the Schol. Peloponnesus is here to be understood.

Ἴασος, ὁ (ῐ from εἶμι, Egredus, Herm.) 1) king of Orchomenus, father of Amphion, Od. 11, 283. 2) son of Argos I. and Evadnê, father of Agênor, ruler of Peloponnesus. From him Argos derived the epith. Ἴασον, Apd. 2, 1. 2. 3) son of Sphelus, leader of the Athenians, slain by Æneas, 15, 332. 337. 4) Father of Dinetor in Cyprus, Od. 17, 443.

ἰαύω (αὔω), aor. 1 ἴαυσα, to sleep, and generally, to lie, to rest, νύκτας, 9, 325; and ἐν ἀγκοίνῃσίν τινος, 14, 213. Od. 10, 261: also of beasts, Od. 9, 184.

*ἰαχέω=ἰάχω, aor. ἰάχησα, h. Cer. 20; in the pres. obsol.

ἰαχή, ἡ (ῐ), 1) a cry, both the shout of warriors in making an attack, and the cry of suppliants and of the shades, 4, 456. Od. 11, 43. 2) Spoken of inanimate things, noise, uproar, h. 13, 3.

*Ἰάχη, ἡ, a nymph, the playmate of Persephônê, h. in Cer. 419.

ἰάχω (a word formed to imitate the sound, akin to ἄχω), aor. 1 ἰάχησα, h. Cer. 20; 1) to cry aloud, to cry out, spoken of the cry of applause, 2, 333. 394; partic. spoken of the battle-cry of warriors, Il., also of the lamentation of the wounded, 5, 343; and of mourners, 18, 29. 2) Spoken of inanimate things: to make a loud noise, to sound, to roar, spoken of waves and of flames, Il., to twang, spoken of the bow-string, 4, 125; to clang, spoken of the trumpet, 18, 219: to hiss, spoken of glowing iron immersed in water, Od. 9, 392.

Ἰάων, ονος, ὁ, see Ἴωνες.

Ἰαωλκός, ἡ, Ep. for Ἰωλκός (ῐ), Iolcus, a town in Magnesia (Thessaly), on the Pelasgic gulf, not far from the port Aphêtæ, the rendezvous of the Argonauts; later only a port of the new city Demetrias, now Volo, 2, 712. Od. 11, 255.

ἰγνύη, ἡ, the ham, poples, 13, 212.† (akin to γόνυ).

*ἰγνύς, ύος, ἡ = ἰγνύη, h. Merc. 152; παρ᾽ ἰγνύσι, but Herm. corrects παροιγνύς λαίφος.

Ἰδαῖος, αίη, αῖον (ῐ), Idæan, relating to Ida, in Phrygia. τὰ Ἰδαῖα ὄρεα, the Idæan mountains, on account of the different peaks=Ἴδη, 8, 170. 410. 12, 19. ὁ Ἰδαῖος, epith. of Zeus, because on the promontory Gargarus he had an altar and a grove, 16, 605. 24, 291.

Ἰδαῖος. ὁ (ῐ), 1) a herald of the Trojans, charioteer of Priam, 3, 248. 24, 325.

2) son of Dares, the priest of Hêphæstus, a Trojan, 5, 11; delivered from Diomêdê· by Hêphæstus, v 23.

ἰδέ, conj. Ep for ἠδέ, and. (The deriv. from ἰδέ. see, according to Thiersch. § 312. 12, cannot be proved.)

ἴδε, ἰδέειν, ἴδεσκον, see ΕΙΔΩ, A.

ἰδέω, Ep. see ΕΙΔΩ, B.

Ἴδη, ἡ, Dor. Ἴδα, Ida, (ῑ), a lofty and steep mountain-range, beginning in Phrygia and extending through Mysia. Its slope formed the plain of Troy, and it terminated in the sea, in the promontories of Gargarus, Lectum, and Phalacra. On the highest point, Gargarus, stood an altar of Zeus, now Ida, or Kas Daghi, 2. 821. From this, an adv. Ἴδηθεν. down from Ida. 3, 276. (Ἴδη, fr. εἰδεῖν, according to Herm. Gnarius, from which one can see far.)

ἴδηαι. see ΕΙΔΩ, A.

Ἴδης, εω, ὁ, Ep. and Ion. for Ἴδας, son of Aphareus, and brother of Lynceus from Messênê, father of Cleopatra. He was an excellent archer, see Εὔηνος, 9, 558. (Ἴδης, according to Etym. M. the seer.)

ἴδιος, ίη, ιον, own, proper. peculiar, private, πρῆξις ἰδίη. the private business of an individual, in opposition to δήμιος, •Od. 3, 82. 4, 314.

ἰδίω (ῑ long, from ἴδος), Ep. for ἱδρόω, to sweat, to perspire, only imperat. ἴδιον, Od. 20, 204.†

ἴδμεν, ἴδμεναι, see ΕΙΔΩ, B.

ἰδνόω, fut. ώσω, only aor. 1 pass. ἰδνώθην, to bend, to curve; plur. to bend oneself, to cringe, 2, 266. 12, 205. Od. 8, 375.

ἰδοίατο, Ep. for ἴδοιντο, see ΕΙΔΩ, A.

Ἰδομενεύς, ῆος and έος, accus. ῆα, and έα (ῑ), son of Deucalion, grandson of Minos, king of Crete, 13, 449—454. Before Troy he distinguished himself by his bravery, 2, 645. 4, 252, seq. According to Od 3, 191, he returned prosperously home. A later tradition says that, having been banished from Crete, he sailed to Italy.

ἰδρείη, ἡ (ἴδρις), knowledge, experience. 7, 198. 16, 359.

ἴδρις, ι, gen. ιος (ἴδμεν), intelligent, skilful, wise, Od. 6, 233. 23, 160; with infin. Od. 7, 108.

ἱδρός, ὁ, Ep. for ἱδρώς, q. v.

ἱδρόω (ἱδρός), fut. ἱδρώσω, aor. ἵδρωσα, to sweat, to perspire, esply from effort. 18, 372; from fear, 11, 119; with accus. ἱδρῷ ἱδρῶσαι, 4, 27. (On the forms ἱδρώοντα. ἱδρώουσα, see Thiersch, § 222, 85. 11. Rost, Dial. 71. 6.)

ἱδρύνω, an assumed form of ἱδρύω for the derivation of the aor. pass. ἱδρύνθην.

ἱδρύω, aor. 1 ἵδρυσα, aor. 1 pass. ἱδρύνθην, 1) Act. to cause to sit, to seat or bid to sit, with accus. λαούς. 2, 191; ἐν θρόνῳ, Od. 5, 86. Pass. to sit, to be seated, to seat oneself, 3, 78 (ἱδρύνθησαν. placed themselves, Buttm. Lex. p. 101]. 7, 56.

ἱδρώς, ῶτος, ὁ (ἴδος), sweat, often is the Il. On the accus. ἱδρῶ for ἱδρῶτα, and dat. ἱδρῷ for ἱδρῶτι, 4, 27. 17, 385, see Thiersch, § 188, 13 1. Buttm. § 56. 5. 6. Rost, Dial 31. Rem. Kühner, § 266.

ἰδυῖα, ἡ. Ep. see ΕΙΔΩ, B.

ἴδω, ἴδωμι, see ΕΙΔΩ, A.

ἰέ, ἰεν, Ep., see εἶμι.

ἰει, see ἵημι.

ἰείη, Ep. for ἴοι, 3 sing. optat. of εἶμι, 19, 209. πρὶν δ᾽ οὔπως ἂν ἔμοιγε φίλον κατὰ λαιμὸν ἰείη Οὐ πόσις, οὐδὲ βρῶσις, before there shall pass into my throat neither food nor drink. Thus Wolf correctly from MS. Townl. for ἰείη, see εἶμι.

ἴεμαι, pres. pass. and mid. from ἵημι.

ἵεμαι, pres. and ἰέμην, imperf. mid., poet. form of εἶμι, q. v., to go, also with the idea of haste, 12, 274. Od. 22, 304. In other places now ἵεμαι.

ἰέμεναι, Ep. for ἰέναι, see ἵημι.

ἴεν, see ἵημι.

ἱέρεια, ἡ, fem. of ἱερεύς, a priestess, 6, 300.†

ἱερεῖον, τό, Ep. and Ion. ἱερήιον. a victim, rare, spoken of sacrificing for the dead; elsewhere τόμιον or ἔντομον, Od. 11, 23. 2) Generally, cattle for killing. as an adage. οὐχ ἱερήιον, οὐδὲ βοείην ἀρνύσθην, they did not strive for a fat ox or a bull's hide (as was the case in combats), 22, 159. Od. 14, 250. H. always the Ion. form.

ἱερεύς. ῆος, ὁ, Ep. ἱρεύς, 5, 10 (ἱερός), a priest, one who sacrifices victims, the priest of a particular deity, who had the charge of the temple service in the presentation of victims, 1, 23. 370. Od. 9. 198. Besides, they explained the divine will from an examination of the entrails. 1, 62. 24, 221.

ἱερεύω (ἱερός), Ep. ἱρεύω, with ῑ, Od. 19, 198. 20, 3; fut. σω, prop. to make holy, to consecrate and slay a victim, to sacrifice, βοῦς, ταύρους, αἶγας θεῷ, Il. 2) Generally, to slay, because, of every thing prepared to eat. some portion was presented to the gods, Od.; ξείνῳ, in honour of a guest, Od. 14, 414.

ἱερήιον, τό, Ion. for ἱερεῖον.

ἱερόν, τό, Ep. ἱρόν (prop. neut. of ἱερός. but used entirely as a subst.). that which is consecrated; hence, a votive offering. ὄφρ᾽ ἱρὸν ἑτοιμασσαίατ᾽ Ἀθήνῃ, 10, 571; esply a victim for sacrifice: chiefly plur. τὰ ἱερά, 1, 147. Od. 1, 66; and ἱρά, 2, 420.

ἱερός, ή, όν, Ep. ἱρός, ή, όν, 1) consecrated to a deity, sacred, holy, divine, spoken of things which are above human power, and are the ordinances of higher beings. cf. Nitzsch ad Od. 3, 278; ἦμαρ, κνέφας. 8. 66. 11, 194; again, ῥόος Ἀλφειοῖο, 11, 726; ἄλφιτον, 11, 631; and also ἰχθύς, as a present from the gods, 16, 407; see no. 3. 2) holy, spoken of every thing which men consecrate to the gods: βωμός, δόμος. Il., esply often ἑκατόμβη. ἄλσος, ἐλαίη, Od. 13, 372; ἀλωή, the sacred threshing-floor (upon which the fruits of Dêmêtêr were cleansed), 5, 499; again, countries. cities, islands, etc. were called sacred, as being under the protection of some tutelary deity, as Troy, Thebes, etc. 3) *glorious, excellent, admirable,* spoken of men, like *divine;* ἰς Τελεμάχοιο, Od. 2, 409; τέλος φυλάκων, 10, 56; δίφρος, 17, 464. (ι is sometimes long in ἱερός: in ἱρός always.)

ἰζάνω (ἵζω), 1) Intrans. *to seat oneself, to sit,* Od. 24, 209; metaph. *to sink,* spoken of sleep, 10, 92. 2) Trans. *to cause to be seated,* with accus. ἀγῶνα, 23, 258.

ἵζω, imperf. ἷζον, I) Act. 1) Intrans. *to seat oneself, to sit down, to sit, to rest;* ἐπὶ θρόνου, 18, 422; ἐς θρόνον, Od. 8, 469. ἐπ᾽ ἀμφοτέρους πόδας ἵζει, he sits upon both feet, 13, 281; εἰν ἀγορῇ, 9, 13. βουλὴ ἵζε, 2, 53: spoken of warriors, to take their place, 2, 96. 2) Trans. *to cause to sit, to be seated,* once τινὰ ἐς θρόνον, 24, 553. II) Mid. like act. *to seat oneself, to place oneself in ambuscade,* 18, 522. Od. 22, 335 (only pres. and imperf.).

ἰηλα, infin. ἰῆλαι, see ἰάλλω.

Ἰηλυσός, ἡ, Ion. for Ἰαλυσός, a town on the island of Rhodes, in Strabo's time a village; now *Jaliso.* 2, 656; Strab. XIV. p. 653. (υ long in H.; hence in some editions Ἰηλυσσός, as Hdt. 1, 144; ῠ̆, Dion Per. 505.)

ἵημι (root ΕΩ), pres. 3 plur. ἰεῖσι, infin. ἱέναι, Ep. ἱέμεναι, 22, 206; partcp. ἱείς, imperat. ἵει, impf. ἵην (whence ἵεν, Æol. for ἵεσαν, 12, 331) and ἵουν (as if from ἱέω), often 3 sing. ἵει, fut. ἥσω, aor. 1 ἧκα, Ep. ἕηκα, except sing. only 3 plur. ἧκαν, Od 15, 458. Of the 2 aor. 3 sing. subj. ἥσιν, 15, 359. On ἕωμεν, see that word. Mid. only pres. and imperf. ἵεμαι, ἱέμην, and aor. 2 in tmesis, ἐξ ἕρον ἕντο, see ἐξίημι. (ι is in H. mly short.) I) Act. 1) Trans. *to put in motion,* hence *a) to send, to send away, to let go,* τινὰ ἐξ ἀδύτοιο, 5, 513; ἄγγελόν τινι, 18, 132), ἐν δὲ παρηορίησιν Πήδασον ἵει (for ἵεις), he attached Pêdasus with the side-rein, 16, 152; cf. παρηορίη; esply spoken of what is sent by a god: δράκοντα φόωσδε, 2, 309; of inanimate things: σέλας, ἀστέρα; ἵκμενον οὖρόν τινι, to send to any one a favorable wind, 1, 479; and metaph. ὄπα, to send out the voice, to utter, 3, 152. 221; ἔπεα. 3, 22. *b) to cast, to throw, to hurl, to shoot, to let fly,* spoken of lying bodies, περίσω. λάαν: esply of missiles: βέλος, ὄρον, ὀϊστόν τινος, to shoot an arrow at one. 13, 650; sometimes without accus. 2. 774. 15, 359. Od. 9, 499. *c)* Spoken of water: *to pour out, to let flow,* ῥόον ἐς τεῖχος, 12, 25; of a river: ὕδωρ, 21, 158. *d) to let down, to let fall.* ἐκ δὲ ποδοῖιν ἄκμονας ἧκα δύω, from thy feet I made two anvils hang down (since Zeus. after attaching them, let them fall), 15, 19; ἐκ χειρὸς φάσγανον, Od. 22, 84; δάκρυον, Od. 16, 191. 23, 33; metaph. spoken of

hair: *to let fall or roll down,* ἐθείρας, 18, 383. 22, 316; κόμας, Od. 6, 231. 2) Intrans. *a) to flow along,* spoken of a river; ἐπὶ γαῖαν, Od. 11, 239; from the fountain: *to gush forth,* Od. 7, 130. *b) to cease from,* with gen. ἐπεί χ᾽ ἕωμεν πολέμοιο, when we have retired from the war, 19, 402; see ἕωμεν. II) Mid. *to put oneself in motion, to move to,* often partcp. with gen. of the body only: ποταμοῖο ῥοάων, to turn oneself towards the current of the river, Od. 10, 529; absol. ἀκόντισαν ἱέμενοι, striving, they hurled their javelins, Od. 22, 256 (cf. Nitzsch ad Od. 1, 58); mly spoken of the mere direction of the mind: *to aspire to, to strive for, to desire, to wish,* with infin. 2, 589. 5, 434, seq. The partcp. ἱέμενος, striving for, also with gen. πόλιος, 11, 168; νόστοιο, Od. 15, 69; elsewhere with adv. οἴκαδε, πολεμόνδε. ἱέμενο κατὰ ὦλκα, struggling along the furrows, 13, 707 (another reading is ἱέμενο).

ἵηνα, see ἰαίνω.

*Ἰηπαιήων, ονος, ὁ, an appellation of Apollo, from the exclamation ἰὴ παιάν, h. Ap. 272. 2) a hymn.

ἰήσασθαι, see ἰάομαι.

ἵῃσι, Ep. for ἵῃ, see εἶμι.

Ἰησονίδης, ου, ὁ, son of Jason = *Euneus,* 7, 468, 469.

Ἰήσων, ονος, ὁ, Ep. and Ion. for Ἰάσων (the healer, from ἴασις), son of Æson and Polymêdê, leader of the Argonauts. He was sent by Pelias to Colchis, to bring the golden fleece. On the voyage thither he landed at Lemnos, and by Hypsipylê begat Euneus and Nebrophonus, 7, 468, 469. With the aid of Medêa, daughter of Aêtês, in Colchis, he obtained the golden fleece. He took her for his wife. Subsequently, however, he cast her off and married Cretûsa, Od. 12, 69 seq.; see Πελίης.

ἰητήρ, ῆρος, ὁ (ῑ), poet. for ἰητρός, 2, 732; κακῶν, Od. 17, 384; νόσων, h. 15, 1.

ἰητρός, ὁ, Ion. for ἰατρός (ἰάομαι), *a physician, a surgeon;* also with ἀνήρ, 11, 514, and Od.

ἰθαιγενής, ές, poet. for ἰθαγενής (ἰθύς, γένος), *straight-born,* i. e. *legitimately born,* born in lawful wedlock, Od. 14, 203.†

Ἰθαιμένης, εος, ὁ, a Lycian, 16, 586.

Ἰθάκη, ἡ (ῐ), *Ithaca,* a little island of the Ionian sea, between the coast of Epirus and the island Samos, the country of Odysseus (Ulysses); now *Theaki,* 2, 632. It extends from south-east to north-west, and is composed of two parts, which are connected by a small isthmus. It is called, Od. 9, 25, the most western island, and thus appears not to agree with the situation of the present Theaki, cf. Völcker, Hom. Geogr. § 32. (The poet may here be mistaken; still, in an age destitute of all the means for chart-drawing, it cannot be a matter of reproach.) It was very mountainous;

H. mentions the Nēritus, Neĭon, and the promontory Corax. It was therefore not adapted to horses, Od. 4, 605, seq.; but well suited for pasturing goats and cattle, Od. 13, 244; and fruitful in corn and wine. Besides the port Reithrum, he mentions only one town, Ithaca. 2) The town was situated at the foot of Neĭon, Od. 2, 154. The citadel of Odysseus (Ulysses) was connected with the town. According to most critics, as Voss, Kruse, the town was in the middle of the island, on the west side, under the northern mountain, Neĭon. By this mountain also was the port Reithrum formed, Od. 1, 185. At the town itself was also a port, Od. 16, 322. Völcker, Hom. Geogr. p. 70, strives to prove that the town must be placed on the eastern coast. From this, adv. Ἰθάκηνδε, to Ithaca, Od. 16, 322; and subst. Ἰθακήσιος, ὁ, an inhabitant of Ithaca.

Ἴθακος, ὁ (ῐ), an ancient hero, according to Eustath., son of Pterelāus, from whom the island of Ithaca had its name, Od. 17, 207.

ἴθι. prop. imperat. from εἶμι, go! come! often used as a particle, like ἄγε, up! on! come on! 4, 362. 10, 53.

ἴθμα, ατος, τό (εἶμι), a step, gait; and generally motion, 5, 778 † h. Ap. 114.

ἰθύντατα, see ἰθύς.

ἰθύνω (ἰθύς, Ion. and Ep. for εὐθύνω), I) Act. 1) to make straight, to regulate; τὶ ἐπὶ σταθμήν. to regulate or measure any thing by the carpenter's line, Od. 5, 245. 17, 341. Hence pass. ἵππω δ' ἰθυνθήτην, the steeds were made straight again, i. e. placed in a line by the pole, 16, 475. 2) to guide directly towards, to direct, to regulate, with accus. 4, 132; and with double accus. 5, 290. Ζεὺς πάντ' ἰθύνει, sc. βέλεα, 17, 632; in like manner, ἵππους, ἅρμα, νῆα, with the prep. ἐπί, παρά. II) Mid. to direct, with reference to the subject, with accus. Od. 22, 8. ἀλλήλων ἰθυνομένων δοῦρα, they directing the spears at each other, 6, 3; πηδαλίῳ νῆα, Od. 5, 270 (cf. ἰθύω).

ἰθυπτίων, ωνος, ὁ, ἡ (ῑ), epith. of the spear, 21, 169.† μελίην ἰθυπτίωνα ἐφῆκε. Most probably it is derived, according to Apoll., from ἰθύς and πέτομαι, as it were ἰθυπετίωνα, flying straight forward, straight to the mark, cf. 20. 99. Zenodotus read ἰθυκτίωνα, and derived it from κτείς, straight-grained, straight-fibred.

ἰθύς, ἰθεῖα, ἰθύ (ῑ), Ion. and Ep. for εὐθύς, 1) As adj. straight, direct; only the neut. τέτραπτο πρὸς ἰθύ οἱ, he was turned directly to him (others refer it to ἔγχος), 14, 403; with gen. ἰθύ τινος, directly to or at any one, 20, 99; metaph. straight, upright, just. ἰθεῖα ἔσται, subaud. δίκη or ὁδός, the sentence will be just, 23, 580. ἰθύντατα εἰπεῖν δίκην, 18, 508. 2) ἰθύς as an adv. like ἰθύ, directly towards, straight at, for the most part with the gen. Δαναῶν, 12, 106; προθύροιο, Od. 1, 119; with prep. ἰθὺς πρὸς

τεῖχος, straight to the wall, 12, 137. ἰθὺς μεμαώς, rushing straight upon, 11, 95. τῇ ῥ' ἰθὺς φρονέειν, to think right onward, with direct purpose, 13, 135 [ἰθὺς φρονέειν, like ἰθὺς μεμαώς, to stretch straight on, Passow]. τῇ ῥ' ἰθὺς φρονέων ἵππους ἔχε, 12, 124. In this passage, Spitzner after the Schol. connects ἰθὺς with ἔχειν, and translates φρονέων, of set purpose, with design, as 23, 343. ἰθὺς μάχεσθαι, to contend directly against, 17, 168. μένος χειρῶν ἰθὺς φέρειν, to bring straight on the strength of hands [i. e. to come into direct conflict], 5, 506. 16, 602.

ἰθύς, ύος, ἡ (ἰθύω) (ῑ), a straight direction in motion, hence ἀν' ἰθύν, directly up, 21, 303. Od. 8, 377; hence attack, an onset, an undertaking, a project, 6, 79. Od. 4, 434; and, in reference to the mind, a strong impulse, a desire, a longing, Od. 16, 304. h. Ap. 539.

ἰθύω (ἰθύς), aor. ἴθῡσα, 1) to rush directly upon, to attack, to run impetuously upon, to rage; limited by an adv. or prep. ἐπὶ τεῖχος, διὰ προμάχων, 12, 443. 16, 582; with gen. νέος, to rush against the ship, 15, 693. 2) to stretch after, to strive, to desire ardently, with infin. 17, 353. Od. 11, 591. 22, 408 (υ is short, but before σ long).

Ἰθώμη, ἡ, a fortress in Thessaly (Hestiæōtis), near the later Metropolis; subsequently also called Θούμαιον, 2, 729.

ἰκάνω, Ep. form of ἱκνέομαι (ἴκω, ῑ), to come, to reach, to arrive at, mly with accus., more rarely with ἐπί, ἐς, τί, 1, 431. 2, 17. 9, 354; prim., 1) Of living beings, 6, 370. Od. 13, 231. 2) Of inanimate things: φλὲψ ἣ αὐχέν' ἱκάνει, a vein which reaches the neck, 13, 547. 3) Of all sorts of conditions and situations: to attain, to come upon, to befall, 10, 96; μόρος, 18, 465; esply of human feelings: ἄχος, πένθος, ἱκάνει με, pain. grief came upon me; and with double accus., 2, 171. II) In like manner the Mid. ἱκάνομαι, 10, 118. 11, 610; and with accus., Od. 23, 7. 27.

Ἰκάριος, ὁ, Icarius, son of Periērēs and of Gorgophonê, brother of Tyndareus, and father of Penelopê. He dwelt in Lacedæmonia; he fled with his brother to Acarnania, and remained there after the return of his brother, cf. Strab. X. p. 461. Od. 1, 276. 329. Accord. to others, he lived in Cephalênia or Samos, Od. 2, 53; cf. Nitzsch ad loc. (The first ι long.)

Ἰκάριος, η, ον (ῑ), Icarian, belonging to Icarus or the island Icarus. ὁ πόντος Ἰκάριος, the Icarian sea, a part of the Ægean; accord. to tradition it received its name from Icarus, son of Dædalus, who was drowned in this sea. It was very stormy and dangerous, 2, 145. (The first ι long.)

*Ἰκάριος, ἡ, or Ἰκαρίη (ῑ), an island of the Ægean sea, which at an early period was called Δολίχη, and received its name from Icarus son of Dædalus; now *Nica-r·a.* h. Bacch. 26. 1.

ἴκελος, η, ον, (ῐ), poet. for εἴκελος, *similar, like,* with dat. 2, 478. Od. 4, 249.

Ἰκετᾱονίδης, ου, ὁ, son of Hiketaon = *Menalippus,* 15, 547.

Ἰκετᾱων, ονος, ὁ (ῐ, ἱκέτης), son of Laomedon, and brother of Priam, father of Melanippus, 3, 147. 20, 238.

ἱκετεύω (ἱκέτης), aor. ἱκέτευσα, *to come or go to any one as a supplicant,* εἴς τινα, 16, 574; or τινά, Od. and generally, *to beg suppliantly, to supplicate, to beseech,* Od. 11, 530.

ἱκέτης, ου, ὁ, *a suppliant,* one who comes to another for protection against persecution, or to seek purification from blood-guiltiness; the persons of such suppliants were inviolable, when they had once seated themselves before the altar of Zeus (ἱκετήσιος) or at the hearth, 24. 158. 570. Od 9, 270. 19, 134. According to the Schol. on Od. 16, 422, it denotes also the receiver of the suppliant, the same relation existing as in ξένοι. This signif. however ἱκέτης never has in H., and we may better understand here Penelopê and her son by ἱκέται.

ἱκετήσιος, ὁ (ἱκέτης), *the protector of suppliants,* epith. of Zeus, Od. 13, 213.†

ἱκραι, Ep. for ἵκῃ, see ἱκνέομαι.

Ἰκμάλιος. ὁ, an artist in Ithaca, Od. 19, 57. (According to Damm from ἐξικμαίνω = *Meister Trockenholz,* Mr. Drywood.)

ἰκμάς, άδος. ἡ. *the moisture,* which destroys all roughness, and yields smoothness and flexibility. ἄφαρ ἰκμὰς ἔβη. δύνει δέ τ᾽ ἀλοιφή, quickly a softness comes and the oil enters (spoken of leather which is rendered soft by oil), 17, 392. Cp., like Voss, translates (ἔβη = ἀπέβη), 'it *sweats The moisture out and drinks the unction in.'* See Nitzsch ad Od. 2, 419.

ἴκμενος, ὁ, always in connexion with οὖρος, *a favorable wind;* prob. for ἴκμενος from ἱκέσθαι, the wind which comes upon the ship, *secundus,* Eustath. Schol. Venet. Others (Hesych. Etym. M.) *a moist, gently blowing,* or, according to Nitzsch ad Od. 2, 419, *a uniform breeze,* (opp. one that drives the vessel about, &c.) from ἰκμάς, slipperiness, smoothness (cf. Od. 5, 478; ἄνεμοι ὑγρὸν ἀέντες), 1, 479. Od. 2, 420.

ἱκνέομαι, poet. depon. mid. (from ἵκω). fut. ἵξομαι, aor. ἱκόμην, *to come, to go, to attain, to reach,* with the accus. of the aim, or with εἴς τι; more rarely, with ἐπί, πρός. κατά, etc.; with dat. ἐπειγομένους δ᾽ ἵκοντο, 12. 374. 1) Spoken of any thing living; ἐς χεῖράς τινος, to fall into any one's hands, 10, 448; ἐπὶ νῆας, 6, 69; *eaply* to come to any one as a suppliant, 14, 260. 22, 123. 2) Spoken of any thing inanimate, conceived of as in motion; τινά, 11. 3) Of various states and conditions. Ἀχιλλῆος ποθὴ ἵξεται υἷας Ἀχαιῶν, regret for Achilles will at

length come upon the sons of the Greeks, 1, 240. κάματός μιν γούναθ᾽ ἵκετο, fatigue attacked his knees, 13, 711; in like manner, σέβας, πένθος etc., with double accus. 1, 362. 11, 88. (ι is short, except when long by augm.)

ἴκρια, τά, always in the plur., Ep. gen. ἰκριόφιν (from ἴκριον, a plank, a beam), *the deck,* which covered only the fore and hind part of the ship; the middle was open for the seats of the rowers, 15, 676. Od. 12, 229. 13, 74. In the difficult passage, Od. 5, 252, are commonly understood the ship's ribs, connected by cross-pieces, upon which the deck rested. Voss, more correctly, considers σταμίνες the *ribs;* 'he placed around it planks, fastening them to the frequent ribs;' see ἐπηγκενίδες. Nitzsch ad loc. understands by ἴκρια *the planks* which formed the inner coating, as it were, of the ship's sides, cf. Od. 5, 163. In a large vessel this *lining* of boards was confined to the prow and stern, the centre-portion being left with naked timbers to form the *hold.*

ἵκω, Ep. imperf. ἵκον, aor. 2 ἷξον, ἷξες, the root of ἱκάνω and ἱκνέομαι. (Upon the aor. see Buttm. § 96, note 9. Root. Dial. 52, d); *to go, to come, to reach, to arrive at, to attain,* with accus. of the aim, 1, 317. 9, 525. ὅ τι χρειὼ τόσον ἵκει, what so great need is come, 10, 142; often with a partcp. ἐς Ῥόδον ἷξεν ἀλώμενος, he came to Rhodes in his wandering, 2, 667. (ι is regularly long.)

ἰλαδόν, adv. (ἴλη), *in crowds, in troops, troop by troop,* 2, 93.†

*ἵλαμαι, mid. poet. form for ἱλάσκομαι, see ἵλημι, h. 20, 5.

ἱλάομαι, Ep. for ἱλάσκομαι, *to appease, to propitiate,* ἱλάονταί μιν ταύροισι. 2, 550† (viz. Erechtheus, say the Gramm. and Voss; others, as Heyne, refer it to Athênê).

ἵλαος (ῑ, ᾱ), *propitiated, favorable,* p l a c a t u s, spoken of the gods: *gracious, merciful,* 1. 583; of men: *gentle, kind,* *9, 639. h. Cer. 204.

ἱλάσκομαι, depon. mid. (ἱλάω, ῑ), fut. ἱλάσομαι, Ep. σσ. aor. ἱλασάμην, Ep. σσ. spoken only of gods, *to appease, to propitiate, to conciliate, to render gracious or favorable,* with accus. θεόν, Ἀθήνην, 1, 100. 147. 386. Od. 3, 419; τινὰ μολπῇ, 1, 472. cf. h. 20, 5. (Kindred forms, ἵλαμαι, ἱλάομαι; prop. ῑ, sometimes ῐ, 1, 100.)

ἵλημι, poet. (from root ἱλάω), only imperat ἵληθι and perf. subj. ἱλήκῃσι, optat. ἱλήκοι, *to be propitiated, gracious, favorable.* ἵληθι, be gracious, in addresses to the gods, *Od. 3, 380. 16. 184. The perf. with signif. of pres. with dat. Od. 21, 365. h. in Ap. 165.

Ἰλιάς, άδος, ἡ, prop. adj. *Trojan, of Troy;* as subst. subaud. ποίησις, *the Iliad.*

Ἰλήϊος, ον, Ep. for Ἴλειον, *Ilian, relating to Ilus.* τὸ πεδίον Ἰλήϊον, *the Ilian* plain; the Schol. says it was so called from the monument of Ilus, cf. Ἶλος, 2. But, in the first place, this region was never so called; in the next, Agênor would in that case have retired from Ida and gone back; more correctly. Lenz understands (Ebene von Troj. S. 226) the plain back of Troy towards Ida. Crates therefore has amended it to Ἰδή ιον, and Voss translates, the Idæan plain, 21, 558; cf. Köpke Kriegswes. d. Griech. S. 193.

Ἰλιονεύς, ῆος, ὁ (ῑ), son of Phorbas, a Trojan, slain by Peneleus, 14, 489. (The first ι long.)

Ἰλιόθεν, adv. from Ilium (Troy), 14, 251.

Ἰλιόθι, adv. at Ilium (Troy), always Ἰλιόθι πρό, before Ilium (Troy), 8, 561. Od. 8, 581.

Ἴλιον, τό = Ἴλιος, q. v.

Ἴλιος, ἡ, (ῑ) (τὸ Ἴλιον, 15, 71†), Ilios or Ilium, the capital of the Trojan realm, afterwards called Troja (Troy). It received its name from its founder, Ilus. This city, with its citadel (Πέργαμος), in which was the sanctuary of Athênê, and the temple of Zeus and Apollo (22, 191) called by the later Greeks τὸ παλαιὸν Ἴλιον, was situated upon an isolated hill in a great plain (20, 216), between the two rivers Simoeis and Scamandrus, where they approached each other. Their confluence was to the west of the city. It was thirty stadia beyond Novum Ilium, about six Roman miles from the sea. On the west side of the city, towards the Grecian camp, was the great gate, called the Σκαιαὶ πύλαι, also called Dardanian. Now the village Bunar-Baschi occupies its site. New Ilium lay near to the coast, only twenty stadia from the mouth of the Scamander; originally a village with a temple of Athênê, which under the Romans grew into a city; now Trojahi, cf. Lenz, die Ebene vor Troja, 1797. Ἴλιος is also applied to the whole Trojan realm, 1, 71. 18, 58. 13, 717. (The first ι long; the second also long in 21, 104.)

Ἰλιόφιν, Ep. for Ἰλίου, 21, 295.

ἱλλάς, άδος, ἡ (ἴλλω, εἴλω), prop. that which is twisted (of thongs or any thing flexible), a string, a rope, plur. 13, 572.†

Ἶλος, ὁ, Ilus, 1) son of Dardanus and Bateia, king of Dardania, who died without children, Apd. 3, 12. 2 2) son of Tros and Calirrhoê, father of Laomedon, brother of Ganymede, founder of Ilium, 20, 232. His monument was situated beyond the Scamandrus, midway between the Scæan gate and the battle-ground, 10, 415. 11, 166. 371. 3) son of Mermerus, grandson of Pheres, in Ephyra, Od. 1, 259.

ἰλύς, ύος, ἡ, prob. from εἰλύω, mud, mire, 21, 318.†

ἱμάς, άντος, ὁ (ῑ, rarely ῑ, from ἵημι), a leathern thong, 21, 30. 22, 397; hence 1) a thong or strap for harnessing horses,

8, 544. 10, 475: also a trace, 23, 324. 2) the straps with which the chariot-body was fastened, 5, 727. 3) the whip-thong, a whip, 23, 363. 4) the thong for fastening the helmet under the chin, 3, 371; also the thongs with which the helmet was lined for protection, 10, 2. 265) the magic-girdle, the cestus of Aphroditê, which, by its magic power, inspired every one with love, 14, 214. 219. 6) the thongs of pugilists, cæstus, which were made of undressed leather and wound around the hollow of the hand, 23, 684. 7) In the Od., the thong fastened to the bolt of the door, and drawn through a hole. To shut the door, the bolt (κληΐς) was drawn forward, and fastened to the κορώνη; to open the door, the thong was first untied, and then the bolt pressed back with a hook, Od. 1, 4. 424, 802.

ἱμάσθλη, ἡ (ἱμάσσω), prop. a whip-thong, then a whip, 8, 43, and Od.

ἱμάσσω (ἱμάς), aor. 1 ἵμασα, Ep. σσ, to whip, to lash, to strike, ἵππους, ἡμιόνους, Il. and Od.; πληγαῖς τινα, 15, 17; metaph. γαῖαν, to strike (lash) the earth with lightning spoken of Zeus), 2, 782. h. Ap. 340.

Ἰμβρασίδης, υυ, ὁ, son of Imbrasus = Peirus, 4, 520.

Ἴμβριος, ὁ, son of Mentor of Pedæon, husband of Medesicastê, son-in-law of Priam, slain by Teucer, 13, 171. 197. [2) As adj. of Imbrus, Imbrian, 21, 43.]

Ἴμβρος, ἡ, 1) an island on the coast of Thrace, famed for the worship of the Caberi and of Hermês; now Imbro, 13, 33. 24, 78. 2) a city on the above island, 14, 281. 21, 43.

ἱμείρω, poet. and Ion. ἵμερος (ῑ). 1) to long for, to desire ardently, with gen. κακῶν, Od. 10, 431. 555. 2) Mid. as depon. aor. 1 ἱμειράμην; more frequently with gen. αἶης, Od. 1, 41; and with infin. Il. 14, 163. Od. 1, 59.

ἴμεν and ἴμεναι, see εἶμι.

ἱμερόεις, εσσα, εν (ἵμερος). awakening desire or longing; enchanting, fascinating, lovely, agreeable, χορός, 18, 603; ἀοιδή Od. 1, 421; γόος, the lamentation of longing desire, Od. 10, 398; chiefly charming, exciting amorous passions. στήθεα, 3, 397; ἔργα γάμοιο, 5, 429. Neut. as adv. ἱμερόεν κιθάριζε, 18, 570.

ἵμερος, ὁ (ῑ), longing, ardent desire for a person or thing, τινός, 11, 89. 23, 14. 108, and also connected with a gen. of the object: πατρὸς ἵμερος γόοιο, a strong desire to mourn his father [Cp.], Od. 4. 113; esply amorous desire, love, 3, 140. 14, 198.

ἱμερτός, ή, όν (ἱμείρω), longed for, attractive, lovely. epith. of a river, 2, 751.† of the harp, h. Merc. 510.

ἴμμεναι, see εἶμι, cf. Thiersch, §229, a. ἵνα, 1) Adv. of place, where, in which place, 2, 558. Od. 6, 322; for ἐκεῖ, there, 10, 127. b) More rarely, whither, Od. 4, 821. 6, 55. In Od. 6, 27, it is explained as an adv. of time, *when;* and Od. 8, 313, *how;* in both places, however, the *local* signif. is predominant; in the first, we may translate ἵνα, *whereat* (on which occasion); and in the second, *how* —*there,* cf. Nitzsch ad Od. 4, 821. II) Conjunct. *that, in order to,* denoting purpose. 1) With the subj. after a primary tense (pres., perf., fut.), 1, 203. 3, 252. 11, 290; and after an aor. with pres. signif. 1, 410. 19, 347. Apparently the indicat. is often found here, since the Ep. subj. shortens the long vowel, 1, 363. 2, 232. 2) With the optat. after an historical tense (imperf., pluperf. aor.), Od. 3, 2. 77. 5, 492. As exceptions, notice *a)* The subj. stands with a preceding historical tense α) When the aor. has the signif. of the perf., Od 3, 15. 11, 93. β) In the objective representation of past events, 9, 495. *b)* The optat. follows a primary tense, when the declaration assumes the character of dependent discourse (in H. examples are wanting), cf. ὄφρα. Sometimes the subj. and optat. follow one after the other in two dependent clauses, 15, 596. 24, 584. Od. 3, 78. 3) ἵνα μή, that not, 7, 195. Od. 4, 70; construc. as in ἵνα, 1, 2: ἵνα μή, in Il. 7, 353, is explained by the Schol. by ἐὰν μή, if not: the verse is, however, suspected. 4) With other particles, ἵνα δή, ἵνα περ, 7, 26. 24, 382.

ἰνδάλλομαι (εἶδος, εἰδάλιμος), *to present oneself in view, to appear, to show oneself,* 23, 460. Od 3, 246. h. Ven. 179. The dat. τινί indicates him to whom any thing appears. ἰνδάλλετό σφισι πᾶσι τεύχεσι λαμπόμενος Πηλείωνος, he (viz. Patroclus) appeared to all, gleaming in the arms of Peleides, 17. 213 (As the sense appears to be ' he was like Achilles,' Heyne, Bothe, and Spitzner, after Aristarchus, have adopted Πηλείωνι. Commonly the nom. indicates the person who appears, or in whose character any one appears; the dat., however, is not unusual, cf. Od. 3, 246, where formerly stood ἀθανάτοις; h. Ven. 179. ὥς μοι ἰνδάλλεται ἦτορ, as he appears to me in my mind (= *recollection*), Od. 19, 224; for here Odysseus (Ulysses) is immediately described, as to his exterior. Damm takes it here as mid. = φαντάζεται, *conceives, imagines* [ἦτορ as *nom.*] ; so also Voss, ' so far as my mind remembers.'

ἴνεσι, see ἴς.

ἰνίον, τό (ῐ, ἴς), the back bone of the head, *the neck, the nape of the neck,* *5, 73. 14, 495.

Ἰνώ, όος, ἡ, see Λευκοθέα.

*Ἴνωπος, ὁ (ῑ, Ἰνωπός, Strab.), a fountain and rivulet in Delos, h. Ap. 18.

ἰξαλος, ον, epith. of αἴξ ἄγριος, prob. *fast-springing, climbing,* from ἄϊσσω or ἰκνεῖσθαι and ἄλλομαι, other say, *lascivious,* from ἰξύς, 4, 105.†

ἴξον, ες, ε, see ἴκω.

ἰξύς, ύος, ἡ, *the flank* or *side of the*

body, the region above the hips, ἰξυῖ, Ep. contr. dat. for ἰξύϊ, *Od. 5, 231. 20, 544.

Ἰξίων, ίωνος, ὁ, *Ixion,* king of Thessaly and husband of Dia, who bore Peirithous by Zeus; from this Ἰξιόνιος, ίη, ιον, *pertaining to Ixion;* ἄλοχος, 14, 317.

Ἰοβάτης, ου, ὁ, king of Lycia, father of Antia, and father-in-law of Proetus, who sent Bellerophontes to him, that he might put him to death. H., 6, 173, mentions not his name, but Apd. 2, 2. 1; cf. Ἄντεια and Προῖτος.

ἰοδνεφής, ές (ῐ, from ἴον, νέφος), *violet-coloured, purple,* and generally, *dark-coloured,* εἶρος, *Od. 4, 135. 9, 426.

ἰοδόκος, ον (ῐ, from ἰός, δέχομαι), *containing arrows, arrow-holding,* φαρέτρη, Od. 21, 12. 60.†

ἰοειδής, ές (ῐ, from ἴον, εἶδος), *violet-coloured,* and generally, *dark-coloured,* cf. πορφύρεος, epith. of the sea, 11, 298. Od. 5, 56

ἰόεις, εσσα, εν (ῐ, from ἴον), *violet-coloured, dark-coloured* (as πολιός), σίδηρος, 23, 850.

Ἰοκάστη, ἡ, see Ἐπικάστη.

ἰόμωρος, ον (ῐ), a reproachful epith. of the Argives, *4. 242. 14, 479; according to most critics, *skilled with the arrow, fighting with arrows,* from ἰός and μῶρος (=μόρος). Schol. οἱ περὶ τοὺς ἰοὺς μεμορημένοι), cf. ἐγχεσίμωρος; sense: ye, who only fight at a distance with missiles, but will not attack the enemy in close conflict with sword and spear. It indicates, therefore, cowardice; and from many passages in H., it appears that archery was little reputable. Köppen, without probability, takes it as an honorary epithet. But as the ι here is short, and the ι in ἰός is always long, consequently several other explanations have been sought Schneider derives it from ἰά, voice, and translates, ' ready with the voice, boastful, braggarts.' Others, from ἴον, explaining it, 'destined to the fate of the violet,' i. e. a short-lived fate, or, to a violet-coloured, i. e. a dark fate, etc.

ἴον, τό (ῐ), *a violet,* Od. 5, 72.† h. Cer. 6. There were, according to Theophr. Hist. Plant. 6, 6, white, purple, and black.

ἰονθάς, άδος. ἡ, *shaggy, hairy,* epith. of wild goats, Od. 14, 50.† (From ἴονθος, akin to ἄνθος.)

ἰός, ὁ (ῑ, from ἵημι), plur. οἱ ἰοί and once τὰ ἰά, 20, 68;† prop. that which is cast, *an arrow* cf. ὀϊστός.

ἴος, ἴη, ἴον, Ep. for εἷς, μία, ἕν, in gen. and dat. with altered accent, ἰῆς, ἰῷ, 6, 122; ἰῇ, one, 9, 319. τῇ δέ τ᾽ ἰῇ ἀναφαίνεται ὄλεθρος, supply βοΐ, to one (cow) death appeared, 11, 174. Od. 14, 435.

*ἰοστέφανος, ον (στέφανος), *violet-crowned,* h. 5, 18.

ἰότης, ητος, ἡ (ῐ, prob. from ἴς), only in the dat. and accus. *will, resolution, counsel, bidding, advice,* 15, 41; often θεῶν ἰότητι, by the will of the gods, 19, 9. Od. 7, 214. ἀλλήλων ἰότητι, the counsel of each other, 5. 874.

ἱέμεναι, Ep. for ἱέναι, see ἵημι.

Ἰησονίδης, ον, ὁ, son of Jason = Εὔνευς, 7, 468, 469.

ἴκμαι, Ep. for ἵκη, see ἱκνέομαι.

ἵμεν and ἵμεναι, see εἶμι.

ἵμερος, ὁ (ῑ), longing, ardent desire f a person or thing, τινός, 11, 89. 23, 1 108, and also connected with a gen. the object: πατρὸς ἵμερος γόοιο, a stron desire to mourn his father [Cp.], Od. 113; esply amorous desire, love, 3, 14 14, 198.

ἴξαλος, ον, epith. of αἴξ ἄγριος, prob. *fleet-springing, climbing,* from ἀΐσσω or ἰσκύσθαι and ἅλλομαι, other say, *lascivious,* from ἰξύς. 4. 105.†

ἴουλος, ὁ (οὖλος), the first down, the earliest appearance of beard only in the plur. Od. 11, 319.†

ἰοχέαιρα, ἡ (ῑ, from ἰός, χαίρω), delighting in arrows, arrow-loving, epith. of Artĕmis; as subst. mistress of the bow, huntress, 21, 480. Od. 11, 198.

ἱππάζομαι, depon. mid. (ἵππος), to guide horses, to drive a chariot, 23, 426.†

Ἱππασίδης, ου, ὁ, son of Hippasus = Charops, 11, 426: = Socus, 11, 431; = Hypsēnor, 13, 411: = Apisāon, 17, 348.

Ἵππασος, ὁ, 1) father of Charops and Sŏcus, a Trojan, according to Hyg. f. 90, son of Priam, 11, 425: 450. 2) father of Hypsēnor, 13, 411. 3) father of Apisāon, 17, 348.

ἵππειος, η, ον (ἵππος), of a horse, belonging to a horse, ζυγόν, φάτνη, ὁπλή, Il., κάπη, Od. 4, 40. ἵππειος λόφος, a crest of horse-hair, Il. 15. 537.

ἱππεύς, ῆος, ὁ (ἵππος), plur. once ἱππεῖς, 11, 151; a knight; in H. a charioteer, one who guides horses, 11, 51; = ἡνίοχος, for the most part, opposed to πεζός, one who fights from a chariot, 2, 810. 11, 529; also a combatant for a prize in a chariot, 23, 262. cf. ἡνίοχος, παραιβάτης.

ἱππηλάσιος, η, ον (ἐλαύνω), good for travelling with horses, passable for chariots. ἱππηλάσιος ὁδός, a chariot-road, 7, 340. 439.

ἱππηλάτα, ὁ, Ep. for ἱππηλάτης, only nom. sing. (ἐλαύνω), a charioteer, a horseman, epith. of distinguished heroes, 4, 387. Od. 3, 436; always in the Ep. form.

ἱππήλατος, ον (ἐλαύνω), suited to driving horses, convenient for travelling, νῆσος (convenient for a race-ground, V.), Od. 4, 607. 13, 242.

Ἱππημολγοί, οἱ, the Hippomolgi, prop. horse-milkers, from ἵππος and ἀμέλγω, Scythian nomades, who lived upon mare's milk; Strab., VII. p. 260, after Posidonius, places them in the north of Europe. H. calls them ἀγαυοί, from their simple mode of life, 13, 5.

ἱππιοχαίτης, ου, ὁ (χαίτη), of horse-hair, λόφος, 6, 469.

ἱππιοχάρμης, ου, ὁ (χάρμη), that practises fighting from a chariot, a charioteer, 24, 257. Od. 11, 259.

ἱππόβοτος, ον (βόσκω), pastured by horses, horse-nourishing, epith. of Argos, because the plain of this city, abounding in water, was suited to the pasturing of horses; also spoken of Tricca and Elis, 4, 202. Od. 21, 347.

Ἱπποδάμας, αντος, ὁ, a Trojan, slain by Achilles, 20, 401 (= ἱππόδαμος).

Ἱπποδάμεια, ἡ, Hippodameia. 1) daughter of Atrax, wife of Pirithous, mother of Polypœtes, 2, 742. 2) daughter of Anchises, wife of Alcathous, sister of Æneas, 13, 429. 3) prop. name of Briseïs, according to Schol. ad Il. 1, 184; see Βρισηΐς. 4) a handmaid of Penelopê, Od. 18 182.

ἱππόδαμος, ον (δαμάω), horse-subduing, horse-taming, epith. of heroes, and also of the Trojans and Phrygians, 2, 230. 10 431. Od. 3, 17.

Ἱππόδαμος, ὁ, Hippodamus, son of Merops, from Percôtê, a Trojan, slain by Odysseus (Ulysses), 11. 335.

ἱππόδασυς, εια, υ (δασύς), thickly covered with horse-hair, κόρυς, 3, 369; κυνέη, Od 22. 111.

ἱππόδρομος, ὁ (δρόμος), a race-course for chariots, 23, 330.†

ἱππόθεν, adv. (ἵππος from a horse), Od 8, 515. 11, 531.

Ἱππόθοος, ὁ, 1) son of Lethus from Larissa, grandson of Teutamus, leader of the Pelasgians, 2, 840, seq.; he is slain, 17, 217—318. 2) son of Priam, 24 251.

ἱππόκέλευθος, ον (κέλευθος, travelling by horses, fighting from a chariot, epith of Patroclus, in 16. 126. 584. 839; since being the charioteer of Achilles he fought not on foot. Thus the better Gramm. Eustath. Ven. Schol. The interpret. & ἵπποις κελεύεις, thou that commandest horses, is contrary to the usus loquendi. Bentley would write, ἱπποκελεύστης.)

ἱππόκομος, ον (κόμη), set with horse hair, crested with horse-hair, τρυφάλεια κόρυς, 12, 339. 13, 132, seq.

ἱπποκορυστής, ου, ὁ (κορύσσω), arming horses, or more correctly passive, furnished with horses for fighting, epith. of heroes fighting from war-chariots, 2, 1 16, 287. 21, 205.

Ἱπποκόων, ωντος, ὁ, a relative and comrade of the Thracian king, Rhesus, 10 518. (From κοεῖν = νοεῖν, acquainted with horses.)

Ἱππόλοχος, ὁ, 1) son of Bellerophontes father of Glaucus, 6, 119. 197; king of the Lycians, 17, 140. seq. 2) a Trojan son of Antimachus, slain by Agamemnon 11, 122.

Ἱππόμαχος, ὁ, son of Antimachus, Trojan, slain by Polypœtes, 12, 189.

Ἱππόνοος, ὁ (acquainted with horses 1) a Greek, slain by Hector, 11. 303. 2 prop. name of Bellerophontes, cf. Schol ad Il. 6, 155.

ἱπποπόλος, ον (πολέω), to go about with horses, horse-driving, epith. of the Thra cians, 13, 4. 14, 227.

ἵππος, ὁ, a horse, a steed; ἡ ἵππος, mare; also θήλεες ἵπποι, 5, 269; and ἵπποι θήλειαι, 11, 681. H. uses both genders, but chiefly the fem., since mares were regarded as better suited for tra velling and fighting, 2, 763. 5, 269. Od 4, 635. The heroes of the Trojan wa used horses only for drawing cha riots: though 10, 513, is mly unde stood of riding, but not with entire cer tainty. See κέλης and ἅρμα, Od 4. 590 hence, 2) In the plur., and rarely i the dual (5, 13. 237), a pair of horses, a team, in connexion with ἅρμα, 12, 120 and often ἵπποισιν καὶ ὄχεσφιν, 12, 114 119; hence also a) the chariot itself, 2

285. 5, 13, etc.; hence, ἁλὸς ἵπποι, the chariot of the sea, for a ship, Od. 4. 708. b) warriors fighting from a chariot, in opposition to πεζοί, Od. 14, 267. ἵπποι τε καὶ ἀνέρες, Il. 5, 554. 16, 1ι.7.

ἱπποσύνη, ἡ (ἵππος), the art of managing horses and of fighting from a chariot, 4, 403. 11, 503; also in the plur. 16, 776. Od. 24, 40.

ἱππότα, ὁ, Ep. for ἱππότης (ἵππος), a charioteer, a warrior fighting from a chariot, epith. of heroes, esply of Nestor, only Ep. form, often in the Il., and Od. 3, 68.

Ἱπποτάδης, ου, ὁ, a descendant of Hippŏtes = Æolus, Od. 10, 2. 36.

Ἱππότης, ου, ὁ, son of Poseidôn or of Zeus, father of Æolus, according to H. and Ap. Rh. 4, 778; others say grandfather of Æolus, through his daughter Arne, see Αἴολος.

Ἱπποτίων, ωνος, ὁ, a Mysian, father of Morys, 13, 392; slain by Meriones, 14, 514, or perhaps another.

ἱππουρις, ιδος, ἡ (οὐρά), as fem. adj. furnished with a horse-tail, κυνέη and κόρυς, 3, 337. 11, 42. Od. 22, 124.

ἵπταμαι, depon. mid. fut. ἵψομαι, aor. ἱψάμην, to press, to squeeze; but only in the metaph. sense, to oppress, to afflict (strike, V.) with accus. (spoken of Zeus and Apollo) λαόν, 1, 454. 16, 237; (of Agamemnon,) to chastise, to punish, 2, 193 (related to ἵπος, ἱπόω), *Il.

ἱραί, αἱ or ἱραι, different readings, 18, 551, for εἱραι, q. v.

ἱρεύς, Ep. and Ion. for ἱερεύς.

ἱρεύω, Ep. and Ion. for ἱερεύω.

Ἱρή, ἡ ed. Wolf, Ἱρη ed. Spitzner, a city in Messenia (different from Εἱρα), one of the towns promised by Agamemnon to Achilles as a dowry, 9, 150. Paus. calls it the later Ἀβία; Strab. VIII. 360, incorrectly, Ἱρα. on the way from Andania to Megalopŏlis. Spitzner has adopted Ἱρη, which was the common reading in Paus., and which the rule of accent requires. Aristarch., on the other hand, writes Ἱρη, cf. Spitzner.

ἱρηξ, ηκος, ὁ, Ion. and Ep. for ἱέραξ (ἱερός), a hawk or falcon, to which species also the κίρκος belonged, Od. 13, 86; prop. the sacred bird, because the soothsayers observed and divined from its flight, 13, 62. 16, 582 (only in the contr. form with ῑ).

Ἱρις, ιδος, ἡ, accus. Ἱριν, Iris, according to Hes. daughter of Thaumas and Electra; in the earlier rhapsodies of the Iliad only, she is the messenger of the gods, not only amongst each other, 8. 398. 15, 144; but also to men, 2, 786. She interposes of her own accord, 3, 122. 24, 74; and brings spontaneously the commands of Achilles to the winds, 23, 198. She commonly appears in a foreign form, e. g. as Polites, 2, 791; and Laodikê (Laodice), 3, 122. Her fleetness is compared to the fall of hail, or to wind, 15, 172; hence ἀελλόπος, ποδήνεμος. In the later poets

she is goddess of the rainbow. (According to Herm. Sertia, from εἴρω, to join.)

ἴρις, ιδος, ἡ, dat. plur. ἴρισσιν, 11, 27; the rainbow, which in ancient times passed with men as · a message from heaven, 17, 547.

ἱρός, ή, όν (ῑ), Ep. for ἱερός.

Ἱρος, a beggar in Ithaca, who was prop. called Arnæus, but was denominated Ἱρος, messenger (from Ἱρις), because the suitors thus employed him. He was large in person, but weak, and insatiably greedy; he was beaten by Odysseus (Ulysses), whom he insulted, Od. 18, 1—7. 73. 239.

ἴς, ἰνός, ἡ, dat plur. ἴνεσι (ῑ), 1) sinew, muscle, nerve; in the plur. Od. 11, 219. Il. 23, 191; esply the neck-sinews, 17, 522. 2) muscular power, bodily strength, vigour, strength, prim. of men, 5, 245. 7, 269; also of inanimate things, ἀνέμου and ποταμοῦ, 15, 383. 21, 356. 3) Since strength is the prominent trait of every hero, the strength of the hero is spoken of by a circumlocution for the hero himself. κρατερὴ ἲς Ὀδυσῆος, the vigorous strength of Odysseus (Ulysses), for the powerfully strong Odysseus. 23. 720; Τηλεμάχοιο, Od. 2, 409; cf. βίη, σθένος.

ἱσάζω (ἴσος), fut. ἱσάσω, aor. 1 mid. Ep. iterat. form ἱσάσκετο, 24, 607; act. to make equal, spoken of a woman weighing wool in scales, 12, 435; see ἔχω. 2) Mid. to make oneself equal, to esteem oneself equal, τινί, 24, 607.

ἴσαν, 1) 3 plur. imperf. from εἶμι. 2) Ep. for ἤδεσαν, see ΕΙΔΩ. B.

Ἴσανδρος, ὁ (man-like), son of Bellerophontes, slain by Ares in an engagement against the Solymi, 6, 197. 203.

ἴσασι, see ΕΙΔΩ, B.

ἱσάσκετο, see ἱσάζω.

ἴσθι imper. see ΕΙΔΩ, B.

ἴσθμιον, τό (ἰσθμός), prop. what belongs to the neck, a necklace, a neck-band, Od. 18, 300.†

ἴσκω, Ep. (from root ΙΚ, εἴκω), poet. form of εἴσκω, only pres. and imperf. to make equal, to make similar, to liken, τί τινι. φωνὴν ἀλόχοις (for φωνῇ ἀλόχων) ἴσκουσα, making the voice like the voices of the wives [i. e. imitating their voices], Od. 4, 279. 2) In thought: to deem like, to esteem equal or like. ἐμὲ σοὶ ἴσκοντες, esteeming me like thee (i. e. taking me for thee, V.), 16, 41. cf. 11, 799. 3) In two places, Od. 19, 203, and 22, 31, some critics explain ἴσκε and ἴσκεν, 'he spake,' as it occurs also in Ap. Rhod. But Eustath, with the more exact critics, interprets it by εἴκαζε, ὡμοίου, Od. 19, 203. ἴσκε ψεύδεα πολλὰ λέγων ἐτύμοισιν ὁμοῖα, prop. uttering many falsehoods, he made them like the truth [uttered many 'specious fictions,' Cp.]; and Od. 22, 31, ἴσκεν ἕκαστος ἀνήρ, each one imagined, i. e. was deceived in thinking as the following words show, cf. Buttm. Lex. p. 279, who

L

conjectures that ἴσπε should be the reading in Od. 22. 31.

Ἴσμαρος, ἡ. a city in Thrace, in the realm of the Ciconians, near Maronia, famed for its strong wine, Od. 9, 40. 198.

ἰσόθεος, ον (ῐ, θεός), godlike, equal to a god, epith. of heroes, 2, 565, and Od.

ἰσόμορος, ον (ῐ, μόρος), having an equal share, an equal lot. 15, 209.†

ἰσόπεδον, τό (πέδον), an equal bottom, level ground, a plain, 13, 142.†

ἴσος, ἴση, ἴσον, Ep. for ἶσος, Ep. also in fem. εἴση, q. v. 1) equal in quality, number, value, strength; sometimes also similar; absol. ἶσον θυμὸν ἔχειν, 13, 704; with dat. δαίμονι. 5, 884; Ἄρηῑ, 11, 295; and even often with the dat. of the pers., although the comparison concerns only something belonging to the person. οὐ μὲν σοί ποτε ἶσον ἔχω γέρας for γέρας τῷ σῷ γέραῑ ἶσον, I never receive a reward equal to thine, 1, 163. cf. 17, 51. 2) equally shared. ἴση μοῖρα μένοντι καὶ εἰ μάλα τις πολεμίζοι, there is an equal portion to him who remains behind (at the ships), and to him who fights ever so vigorously, 9, 318; often ἴση alone, 11, 705. 12, 423. Od. 9, 42. 3) The neut. sing. as adv. ἶσον and ἶσα. ἶσον κηρί, like death, 3, 454. 15, 50; oftener the neut. plur. ἶσα τεκέεσσι, 5, 71. 15, 439; and with prep. κατὰ ἶσα μάχην τανύειν, to suspend the fight in equipoise, to excite it equally, 11, 336. ἐπ' ἶσα, 12, 436. The passage Od. 2, 203, is variously explained. κρήματα δ' αὖτε κακῶς βεβρώσεται, οὐδέ ποτ' ἶσα ἔσσεται, thy possessions are consumed, and never will the like be to thee, i. e. that which is consumed will never be replaced. Thus Nitzsch, and this appears most natural. Eustath. says, 'they will never remain equal,' i. e. will continually decrease. Others, as Voss, 'there will be no equity.' Both are contrary to the Hom. usus loquendi.

Ἶσος, ὁ, son of Priam, slain by Agamemnon, 11, 101.

ἰσοφαρίζω (ῐ, from ἶσος and φέρω), to put oneself on an equality with any man, to liken, to compare oneself to in any thing; τινὶ μένος, to any man in strength, 6, 101; ἔργα Ἀθήνη, 9, 390; and with the dat. alone, 21, 194.

ἰσοφόρος, ον (φέρω), bearing a like burden, of equal strength, βόες, Od. 18, 373 †

ἰσόω (ἶσος), only optat. aor. ἰσωσαίμην, to make equal, mid. to become equal, with dat., Od. 7, 212.†

ἵστημι, imperf. ἵστην, 3 sing. Ep. iterat. form ἵστασκε, ἵστασχ', Od. 19, 574; fut. στήσω, aor. 1 ἔστησα, also Ep. 3 plur. ἔστασαν for ἔστησαν, 12, 55. 2, 525 (ἵστασαν, Spitzner). Od. 3, 182. 18, 307 (cf. ἔπρεσε); aor. 2 ἔστην, Ep. iterat. form στάσκον, and 3 plur. Ep. ἔσταν and στάν, subj. στῶ, 2 sing. στήῃς for στῇς, etc., 1 plur. Ep. στέωμεν and στείομεν for στῶμεν, infin. στήμεναι for στῆναι, perf.

ἕστηκα, and pluperf. ἑστήκειν; the dual and plur. only in the syncop. forms : dual ἔστατον, plur. ἔσταμεν, ἔστατε, and poet. ἔστητε, 4, 243. 246; 3 plur. ἑστᾶσι, subj. ἑστῶ, optat. ἑσταίην, infin. ἑστάμεναι, ἑστάμεν, partcp. only the obliq. case, ἑστάότος, etc., pluperf. dual ἑστάτον, 3 plur. ἔστασαν: mid. fut. στήσομαι, aor. ἐστησάμην, aor. pass. ἐστάθην, signif.: I) Trans. in the pres. imperf. fut. and aor. 1, to place, to cause to stand, of animate and inanimate objects, hence 1) to put up, to set up, to place erect, with accus. 2, 525; ἔγχος, 15, 126; τρίποδα, 18, 344. 2) to cause to rise, to raise, νεφέλας, 5, 523. Od. 12. 405; κονίης ὀμιχλήν, 13, 336; hence metaph. to excite, to stir up, φυλόπιδα, ἔριν, Od. 11, 314. 16, 292. 3) to cause to stand, to hinder, to bring to a stand, to check, to stop (in their course), ἵππους, 5, 368; νέας, to anchor the ships, Od. 2, 391. 3, 182; μύλην, to stop the mill, Od. 20, 111; hence, to cause to stand in the balance, i. e. to weigh, τάλαντα, 19, 247. 22, 350. II) Intrans. and reflex. in the aor. 2 perf. and pluperf. act. 1) to place oneself, to stand, perf. ἕστηκα, I have placed myself, or I stand; ἑστήκειν, I stood, in which signif. the mid. is used to supply the pres. imperf. and fut. both of animate and inanimate things. 2) to stand, of warriors, 4, 334; νῆες, σκόλοπες, 9, 44. 12, 64. 3) to stand up, to arise, 1, 535; to stand forth, to lift oneself, χρημνοί, 12, 55. ὀρθαὶ τρίχες ἔσταν, the hair stood erect, 24, 359. ὀφθαλμοὶ ὡσεὶ κέρα ἔστασαν, the eyes stood out like horns, Od. 19. 211; hence metaph. ἕβδομος ἑστήκει μείς, the seventh month had begun, 19, 117; hence ἵσταται, begins, Od. 14, 162. 4) to stand still, to keep one's place, κρατερῶς, 11, 410. 13, 56. III) Mid. esply aor. 1. 1) to place for oneself, to put up with accus. κρατῆρα θεοῖσι, 6, 528; ἱστόν to put up the loom-beam, Od. 2, 94 ἱστόν, to raise the mast, 1, 480. Od. 9 77. ἀγῶνα, to begin a combat, h. Ap 150. 2) Oftener intrans. and reflex., t place oneself, in the passages cited unde no. II. Il. 2, 473. πάντεσσιν ἐπὶ ξυροῑ ἵσταται ἀκμῆς [in balance hangs, poise on a razor's edge. Cp.], 10, 173; see ἀκμή δοῦρα ἐν γαίῃ ἵσταντο, the spears re mained sticking in the earth, 11, 574 metaph. νεῖκος ἵσταται, the contest be gins, 13, 333. Cf. on ἔστασαν, Buttm § 107. 6. Thiersch, § 223. Kühner, § 18

Ἱστίαια, ἡ, Ep. and Ion. for Ἑστίαια a town in Euboea, on the northern coas later Ὠρεός, 2, 537.

ἱστίη, ἡ, Ion. and Ep. for ἑστία, th domestic hearth, which at the same tin was a domestic altar of the househol gods; it was the asylum of all sup pliants, and an oath by it was peculiar sacred, *Od. 14, 159. 17, 156. 19, 30 (The middle syllable is always long.)

Ἱστίη, ἡ (Ἱστίη, ed. Henn.), Ep. f Ἑστία, Vesta, daughter of Kronus (Satur and Rhea, tutelary deity of the domestic hearth, of houses and cities, h. 23, 1. 28, 1.

ἰστίον, τό (dim. from ἰστός), prop. any thing woven, *cloth ;* in H. *a sail,* mly in the plur., 1, 480; sing., 15, 627. Od. 2, 427. The sails were commonly of linen (also called σπεῖρα). They were attached to the mast by yards. They were hoisted (πετανννύναι, ἀναπεταννύναι) in a favorable wind, and furled (στέλλεσθαι) in an unfavorable, 1, 433. Od. 3, 11.

ἰστοδόκη, ἡ (δέχομαι), *the receptacle of the mast,* the place in which it was stowed when lowered [its *crutch,* Cp.], 1, 434.†

ἰστοπέδη, ἡ (πέδη), *the mast-stay,* a transverse piece of timber, in which the mast of a vessel was fixed, *Od. 12, 51. 162.

ἰστός, ὁ (ἵστημι), 1) *the mast,* which stood in the middle of the ship, and was attached by two ropes (πρότονοι) to the bows and stern of the ship. The mast was taken down, and lay in the ship when at anchor, 1, 434; at departure it was raised (ἀείρειν, στήσασθαι), Od. 2, 424. 9, 77. 2) *a loom-beam,* the beam upon which the warp was drawn up perpendicularly, so that the threads hung down, instead of lying horizontally upon the warp-beam as with us; hence ἰστὸν στήσασθαι, to put up the loom-beam. Od. 2, 94. ἰστὸν ἐποίχεσθαι, to go around the loom in order to weave; for the weaver sat not before it, as with us, but went around, 1, 31. Od. 5, 62. This kind of weaving is still in partial use in India. 3) *the warp* itself, and generally *the web.* ἰστὸν ὑφαίνειν, 3, 125. Od. 2, 104. 109.

ἴστω, imperat. see ΕΙΔΩ, B.

ἴστωρ, ορος, ὁ (εἰδέναι), one who is intelligent, one who knows: esply like cognitor, *an umpire.* ἐπ' ἴστορι, before the judge, or rather witness (μάρτυρι ἢ κριτῇ, Schol.), *18, 501. 23, 486. ἴστωρ stands in ed. Heyne, and in h. 32, 2, ed. Wolf. The derivation favours the spiritus lenis.

ἰσχαλέος, η, ον, poet. for ἰσχνός, *dry, dried.* Od. 19, 233.†

ἰσχανάω, Ep. form of ἴσχω; ἰσχανάᾳ, ἰσχανόωσιν, Ep. for ἰσχανᾷ, ἰσχανῶσιν, Ep. iterat. imperf. ἰσχανάασκον, 1) Act. *to hold, to hold back,* with accus., 5, 89. 15, 723. 2) *to attach oneself to, to strive after, to be eager for,* with gen. δρόμου, φιλότητος, 23, 300. Od. 8, 288; and with infin. 17, 572. II) Mid. *to check oneself, to delay, to tarry,* ἐπὶ νηυσίν, 12, 38. Od. 7, 161. (Only pres. and imperf.)

ἰσχάνω, poet. form from ἴσχω = ἰσχανάω, *to hold, to hold back, to hinder,* with accus., 14, 387. 17, 747. Od. 19, 42; see κατισχάνω, h. 6, 13.

ἰσχίον, τό, 1) Prop. *the hip-joint, the hip-pan,* i. e. the cavity in the hip-bone in which the head of the thigh-bone

(μηρός) turns, 5, 305. 2) Mly *the hip, the loins,* exply the upper part, 11, 339. Od. 17, 234; plur. 8, 340. (Prob. from ἰσχύς, akin to ἰξύς.)

*Ἴσχυς, υος, ὁ, son of Elatus, the lover of Corônis, h Ap. 210.

*ἰσχύω (ἰσχύς), fut. ύσω, *to be strong, to be able,* Batr. 280.

ἴσχω, poet. form of ἔχω, only pres. and imperf. chiefly in the signif.: I) *to hold, to hold fast, to hold back,* τινά, 5, 812 ; ἵππους, 15, 546; metaph. θυμόν, *to restrain the spirit,* 9, 256 ; σθένος, 9, 352. II) Mid. *to hold oneself, to restrain oneself,* 2, 247; restrain yourself, i. e. be silent, Od. 11, 251. *b)* With gen. *to restrain oneself* from a thing, *to cease,* λώβης, πτολέμου, Od. 18, 347. 24, 531.

ἰτέη, ἡ, Ion. for ἰτέα, *willow,* 21, 350 ; *salix alba,* the common ozier, Od. 10, 510.

ἴτην, imperf. of εἶμι.

Ἴτυλος, ὁ, son of Zethus and Aêdon, whom his mother killed in a fit of frenzy, Od. 19, 522; cf. Ἀηδών.

Ἰτυμονεύς, ῆος, ὁ, son of Hyperôchus in Elis, who abstracted from Nestor a part of his herds, and was slain by him, 11, 671, seq.

ἴτυς, υος, ἡ, prop. any circle; in H. the *circumference* or *periphery* of a wheel, made of felloes of wood, 4, 486. 5, 724. (Prob. from ἰτέα.)

ἴτω, see εἶμι.

Ἴτων, ωνος, ἡ (ῑ), a town in Larissa, in Phthiô is (Thessaly), with a temple of Athênê, 2, 696. Ἴτωνος, ὁ, Strab.

ἰυγμός. ὁ (ἰύζω), *a cry, a cry of joy, a shout,* 18, 572.†

ἰύζω (ῑ), *to shout for joy, to cry aloud;* in H. to terrify an animal by loud crying and shrieking, 17. 66. Od. 15, 162.

Ἰφεύς, ῆος, ὁ (ῑ), see Ἴφις.

Ἰφθ'μη ἡ, daughter of Icarius and sister of Penelopê, wife of Eumêlus of Pheræ, Od. 4, 797.

ἴφθιμος, η, ον and ος, ον, 1) *highly honoured. greatly lauded,* and generally, *active, lively, noble,* 5, 415 ; spoken of women, ἄλοχος, 19, 116. Od. 10, 106. (Prob. from ἶφι and τιμή, greatly lauded. Schol.; so Wolf and Thiersch.) Hence, 2) *to be honored for one's strength, might,* &c., *strong, brave, mighty, powerful,* prim. as epith. of heroes possessing physical power, hence also spoken of head and shoulders, 3, 336. 11, 55.

ἶφι, adv. (prob. an old dat. from ἴς), *strongly, powerfully, with might, with power,* ἀνάσσειν, μάχεσθαι, 1, 38. 2, 720 ; δαμῆναι, Od. 18, 156.

Ἰφιάνασσα, ἡ (ῑ, ruling with power), daughter of Agamemnon and Klytæmnêstra (Clytæmnestra), called in the tragic writers Ἰφιγένεια, 9, 145.

Ἰφιδάμας, αντος. ὁ (ῑ), son of Antênor and Theäno, who was educated in Thrace with his grandfather Cisseus, 11, 221.

Ἰφικλήειος, η, ον, Ep. for Ἰφικλείος,

pertaining to Iphiclus. ἡ βίη Ἰφικληείη, Od. 11, 290.

Ἴφικλος, ὁ (ῑ in the beginning), son of Phylacus, from Phylacê in Thessaly, father of Protesilaus and Podarces, noted as a runner. His noble herds of cattle were demanded by Neleus of Bias as a price for his daughter of Pero, 2, 705. 23, 636. Od. 11, 289, seq. Cf. Βίας.

Ἰφιμέδεια, ἡ (ῑ in the beginning), daughter of Triops, wife of Alôeus, mother of Otus and Ephialtes by Poseidôn, Od. 11, 305 (from μέδομαι, the mighty ruler).

Ἰφίνοος, ὁ (the first ι long) son of Dexius, a Greek, slain by the Lycian, Glaucus, 7, 14.

Ἶφις, ιος, ὁ (not Ἰφεύς), accus. Ἶφεα, a Trojan, slain by Patroclus, 16, 417; see Buttm. Gr. Gram. § 51. Rem. 1. p. 192.

Ἶφις, ιος, ἡ, daughter of Enyeus, a slave of Patroclus, 9, 667.

ἶφιος, η, ον (ἶφι), or ἶφις, ἶφι, strong, explv robust, fat, fatted, only ἶφια μῆλα, 5, 556. Od. 11, 108 (the first ι long).

Ἰφιτίδης, ὁ, son of Iphitus = Archeptolemus, 8, 128.

Ἰφιτίων, ωνος, ὁ (ῑ in the beginning), son of Otrynteus of Hydê, slain by Achilles, 20, 382. (From τίω, avenging powerfully.)

Ἴφιτος, ὁ (ῑ in the beginning) 1) son of Eurytus, from Œchalia, brother of Iolê, an Argonaut. On the journey, when he was seeking the mares which had been concealed by Hêraclês, he gave his bow to Odysseus (Ulysses), in Messenia. When he found them with Hêraclês, he was slain by him, Od. 21, 14, seq. 2) son of Naubôlus, an Argonaut of Phocis, father of Schedius and Epistrôphus, 2, 518. 17, 306. 3) father of Archeptolemus, 8, 128.

ἰχθυάω (ἰχθύς), Ep. iterat. form, imperf. ἰχθύασκον, Od. 4, 368; to fish, to take fish, *Od. 12, 95.

ἰχθυόεις, εσσα, εν (ἰχθύς), fishy, abounding in fish, epith. of the sea, and of Hyllus, 9, 4. 360. 20, 392; κέλευθα, Od. 3, 177.

ἰχθύς, ύος, ὁ, nom. and accus. plur. ἰχθύες, ἰχθύας, contr. ἰχθῦς. Od. 5, 53. 12, 331; a fish; taking fish in nets was already customary, Od. 22, 384, seq. (υ in nom. and accus. sing. long, 21, 127; elsewhere short.)

Ἰχναῖος, αίη, αῖον (ἴχνος), tracing, tracking, epith. of Themis, who traces out the actions of men, h. in Ap. 94. According to the Gram. from the town Ichnæ in Thessaly, where she had a temple. The last derivation Herm. ad loc. prefers.

ἴχνιον, τό (prop. dimin. of ἴχνος), a trace, a track, a footstep, 18, 321. h. Merc. 220. μετ᾿ ἴχνιά τινος βαίνειν, to follow a man's steps, Od. 2, 406; tracks, Od. 19, 436. 2) Generally, gait, movement, 13, 71.

ἴχνος, τό, a track, a footstep, a trace, Od. 17, 317.†

ἰχώρ, ῶρος, ὁ, accus. ἰχῶ, Ep. for ἰχῶρα (Kühner, § 266, 1. Buttm. § 56, note 6, e); ichor, the blood of the gods,—a humour similar to blood, and which supplies its place in the gods, *5, 340. 416.

ἴψ, ἰπός, ὁ, nom. plur. ἶπες (ἴπτομαι), an insect which gnaws horn and vines, Od. 21, 395.†

ἴψαο, see ἴπτομαι.

ἰωγή, ἡ, a shelter, a protection. Βορέω. against the north wind, Od. 14, 533;† see ἐπιωγαί.

ἰωή, ἡ (ἰά, ῑ), a call, a voice, spoken of men, 10, 139; and generally. clamour, noise, of the lyre and the wind, Od. 17, 261. Il 4, 276; of fire, 16, 127.

ἰῶκα, see ἰωκή.

ἰωκή, ἡ (from δίω and διώκω), metaplast. accus. ἰῶκα, as if from ἰώξ, 11, 601;† prop. pursuit in battle; and generally, the tumult of battle, the noise of battle, plur. 5, 521. 2) Ἰωκή, personified, like Ἔρις, *5, 740.

ἰωχμός, ὁ (ἰωκή), pursuit, the tumult of battle, *8, 89. 158.

K.

K, the tenth letter of the Greek alphabet, and the sign of the tenth book.

κάββαλε, Ep. for κατέβαλε, see καταβάλλω.

Καβησός, ἡ, a town in Thrace on the Hellespont, or in Lycia, from which is Καβησόθεν, from K. (ἔνδον refers to Troy), 13, 363.

κάγ, Ep. for κατ᾿ before γ; κὰγ γόνυ, for κατὰ γόνυ (accord. to Bothe, καγγόνυ), 20, 458.†

κάκκανος, ον (καίω with a kind of redupl.), that may be burned, dry, ξύλα, 21, 364. Od. 18, 308. h. Merc. 136.

καγχαλάω (Ep. prcs. καγχαλόωσι, καγχαλόων for καγχαλῶσι, καγχαλῶν), to laugh aloud, to rejoice, 6, 514. Od. 23, 1. 59; to laugh to scorn, 3, 43. (From ΧΑΩ, χαλάω, cachinnor.)

κἀγώ, contr. from καὶ ἐγώ, 21, 108;† yet rejected by Spitzner.

κάδ, Ep. for κατά before δ, e. g. κὰδ δέ, κὰδ δώματα, Od. 4, 72.

καδδραθέτην, see καταδαρθάνω.

καδδῦσαι, see καταδύω.

Καδμεῖος, η, ον (Κάδμος), derived from Cadmus, Cadmêan, in Hom. plur. οἱ Καδμεῖοι, the inhabitants of the citadel Cadmeia, i. e. the Thebans, 4, 391. Od. 11, 276.

Καδμείων, ωνος, ὁ = Καδμεῖος, 4, 385. 5, 804.

Καδμηΐς, ΐδος, ἡ, peculiar fem. of Καδμεῖος, daughter of Cadmus = Semelê, h. 6, 57.

Κάδμος, ὁ (Herm. Instruus), Cadmus, son of the Phœnician king Agênor, brother of Eurôpa, husband of Harmonia. In his journeyings in quest of Europa, who had been seduced by Zeus, he came at last to Bœotia, and founded the fortress Cadmeia. H. mentions him only as the father of Ino, Od. 5, 334.

ΚΑΔ, see καίνυμαι.

Κάειρα, ἡ, fem. of Κάρ, a female Carian, prob. from the root Κάηρ, 4, 142.†

καήμεναι, see καίω.

καθαιρέω (αἱρέω), fut. ήσω, aor. καθεῖλον, subj. Ep 3 sing. καθέλῃσι, 1) to take (pull or let) down, τί; ἱστία, Od. 9. 149: ζυγόν, 24, 268; ὄσσε θανόντι, to close the eyes of a corpse, 11, 453; and in tmesis, Od. 11, 426. 2) Esply to take down with violence, to cast down, τινά, 21, 327; hence, to overpower, to carry off, spoken of Fate, Od. 2, 100; metaph. of sleep, Od. 9, 372, 373.

καθαίρω (καθαρός), aor. 1 ἐκάθηρα and Ep. κάθηρα, to purify, to cleanse, to wash, with accus. κρητῆρας, θρόνους, τραπέζας ὕδατι, Od. 20, 152. 22, 439. 453; ῥυπόωντα, Od. 6. 87; trop. κάλλεϊ προσώπατα καθαίρειν, to adorn with beauty, see κάλλος, Od. 18, 192. 2) to bring away by cleansing, to wash away; ἀπὸ χροὸς λύματα, 14, 171; ῥύπα, Od. 6, 93; with double accus. εἰ δ᾽ ἄγε—αἷμα κάθηρον Ἐλθὼν ἐκ βελέων Σαρπηδόνα, 16, 667. In this passage, which is variously explained, place with Spitzner a comma before and after ἐκ βελέων, so that it may signify extra jactum telorum. Thus Voss: 'Go, beloved Phœbus, to cleanse, beyond the reach of the enemy's spears, Sarpedon from his blood.' Instead of Σαρπηδόνα, Aristarchus reads Σαρπηδόνι; Eustath., however, defends the double accus. and compares 1, 236, 237. 18, 345. b) In a religious signif. θεείῳ δέπας, to purify a goblet by fumigation with brimstone, 16, 228.

καθάλλομαι, depon. mid. (ἄλλομαι), to leap down; metaph. to rush down, spoken of a tempest, 11, 298.†

καθάπαξ, adv. (ἅπαξ), once for all, entirely, Od. 21, 349.†

καθάπτομαι, depon. mid. (ἅπτω), to touch, to attack, always τινὰ ἐπέεσσιν, to approach any one with words, a) In a good sense: ἐπ. μαλακοῖσίν τινα, to address any one with kind words, 1, 582; or μειλιχίοις ἐπ., Od. 24, 393; absol. Od. 2, 39. 240, seq. b) In a bad signif. ἀντιβίοις ἐπ., to attack or assail with angry words, Od. 18, 415. 20, 323; absol. 15, 127. 16, 421. (The dat. depends upon κέκλετο cf. Od. 2, 39.)

καθαρός, ή, όν, clean, unspotted, εἵματα, Od. 2) clean. clear. ἐν καθαρῷ, subaud. τόπῳ, in a clear place (a place free from dead bodies), 8, 491. 10, 199. 3) Metaph. pur., blameless. καθαρῷ θανάτῳ, by an honorable death, i. e. not by the halter, Od. 22, 462. Adv. καθαρῶς, purely, h. Ap. 121.

καθέζομαι, depon. mid. (ἕζομαι), only pres. and imperf. to sit down, to sit, ἐπὶ

θρόνου, 1, 536; ἐπὶ λίθοισι, Od. 3, 406; to sit in council, to hold a session, Od. 1, 372. 2) to reside, to dwell, Od. 6, 295.

καθῆκα, see καθίημι.

καθείατο, see κάθημαι.

καθῖσα (εἷσα), defect. aor. to seat, to cause any one to be seated, τινὰ ἐπὶ θρόνου, 18, 389. 2) to set down, to place, to cause to remain, 2, 549. 3, 382; τινὰ σκοπόν, to place a man as a spy, Od. 4, 524.

καθέξει, see κατέχω.

καθεύδω, imperf. Ep. καθεῦδον, only pres. and imperf. to sleep, to rest, 1, 611; ἐν φιλότητι, Od. 8, 313. According to Eustath. [ἀναπίπτειν ὡς ἐπὶ ὕπνῳ], it signifies in ll. 1, 611, 'to lie down to sleep.' [This, however, is not the necessary sense, since the usual signif. does not conflict with 2, 2, where οὐκ ἔχε νήδυμος ὕπνος forms an antithesis with εὗδον παννύχιοι, cf. Schol. ad Il. 2, 2. Am. Ed.]

καθεψιάομαι, depon. mid. (ἐψιάομαι), to deride, to mock, τινός, Od. 19, 372.†

κάθημαι (ἧμαι), imperf. ἐκαθήμην, 3 sing. καθῆστο and ἐκάθητο, h. 6, 14; 3 plur. καθείατο, Ep. for κάθηντο, to sit down, παρά τινι, 7, 443; ἐν or ἐπί τινι, 11, 76. 14, 5; esply to sit at ease, to sit in state, to be throned, Od. 16, 264.

κάθηρα, see καθαίρω.

καθιδρύω (ἱδρύω), to seat, to cause to sit, τινά, Od. 20, 257.†

καθιζάνω (ἱζάνω), to seat oneself, θῶκόνδε, Od. 5, 3.†

καθίζω (ἵζω), imperf. κάθιζον, once ἐκάθιζον, Od. 16. 408 (Buttm. Lex. p. 122, would read δὲ κάθιζον), aor. ἐκάθισα, part. Ep. καθίσσας, 1) Trans. to seat, to cause to sit, with accus. ll.; ἀνδρῶν ἀγοράς, to constitute, to convoke assemblies of men, Od. 2, 69; proverbially, καθίζειν τινὰ ἐπ᾽ οὔδει, to seat any one upon the ground, i. e. to plunder him of his property, h. Merc. 284; see οὔδας. 2) Intrans. to seat oneself, to sit, ἐπί, παρά τινι, 8, 436; and alone, 3, 426. Od. Od. 4, 649.

καθίημι (ἵημι), aor. 1 καθῆκα, inf. aor. 2 καθέμεν, Ep. for καθεῖναι, 1) to send down, to cast down, with accus. οἶνον λαυκανίης, to send or pour wine down the throat, 24, 642; ἵππους ἐν δίναις, to sink the horses in the waters, in order to propitiate the river-god, 21, 132; κεραυνὸν χαμᾶζε, 8, 134 (by tmesis). 2) to let down, to lower, ἱστία ἐς νῆας. Od. 11, 72. h. Ap. 503. 481. (On the dual aor. 2 καθέτον, see Buttm. Ausf. Gram. § 33. 3. Rem. 3.)

καθικνέομαι (ἱκνέομαι) only aor. καθικόμην, to go to, to reach, to arrive at, to touch, to hit; only metaph.; spoken only of disagreeable things. ἐμὲ καθίκετο πένθος, Od. 1, 342. μάλα πώς με καθίκεο θυμὸν ἐνιπῇ, thou hast exceedingly touched (= wounded) my heart by reproach, 14, 104.

καθίστημι (ἵστημι), imperf. pres. Ep. καθίστα, aor. 1 κατέστησα, aor. 1 mid. κατεστησάμην, 1) Only trans. to put

H. mentions the Nêritus, Neïon, and the promontory Corax. It was therefore not adapted to horses, Od. 4, 605, seq.; but well suited for pasturing goats and cattle, Od. 13, 244; and fruitful in corn and wine. Besides the port Reithrum, he mentions only one town, Ithaca. 2) The town was situated at the foot of Neïon, Od. 2, 154. The citadel of Odysseus (Ulysses) was connected with the town. According to most critics, as Voss, Kruse, the town was in the middle of the island, on the west side, under the northern mountain, Neïon. By this mountain also was the port Reithrum formed, Od. 1, 185. At the town itself was also a port, Od. 16, 322. Völcker, Hom. Geogr. p. 70, strives to prove that the town must be placed on the eastern coast. From this, adv. Ἰθάκηνδε, to Ithaca, Od. 16, 322; and subst. Ἰθακήσιος, ὁ, an inhabitant of Ithaca.

Ἴθακος, ὁ (ῐ), an ancient hero, according to Eustath., son of Pterelāus, from whom the island of Ithaca had its name, Od. 17, 207.

ἴθι. prop. imperat. from εἶμι, go! come! often used as a particle, like ἄγε, up! on! come on! 4, 362. 10, 53.

ἴθμα, ατος, τό (εἶμι), a step, gait; and generally motion, 5, 778 † h. Ap. 114.

ἰθύντατα, see ἰθύς.

ἰθύνω (ἰθύς, Ion. and Ep. for εὐθύνω), I) Act. 1) to make straight, to regulate; τὶ ἐπὶ σταθμήν. to regulate or measure any thing by the carpenter's line, Od. 5, 245. 17, 341. Hence pass. ἵππω δ' ἰθυνθήτην, the steeds were made straight again, i. e. placed in a line by the pole, 16, 475. 2) to guide directly towards, to direct, to regulate, with accus. 4, 132; and with double accus. 5, 290. Ζεὺς πάντ' ἰθύνει, sc. βέλεα, 17, 632; in like manner, ἵππους, ἅρμα, νῆα, with the prep. ἐπί, παρά. II) Mid. to direct, with reference to the subject, with accus. Od. 22, 8. ἀλλήλων ἰθυνομένων δοῦρα, they directing the spears at each other, 6, 3; πηδαλίῳ νῆα, Od. 5, 270 (cf. ἰθύω).

ἰθυπτίων, ωνος, ὁ, ἡ (ῐ), epith. of the spear, 21, 169.† μελίην ἰθυπτίωνα ἐφῆκε. Most probably it is derived, according to Apoll., from ἰθύς and πέτομαι, as it were ἰθυπετίωνα, flying straight forward, straight to the mark, cf. 20, 99. Zenodotus read ἰθυκτίωνα, and derived it from κτείς, straight-grained, straight-fibred.

ἰθύς, ἰθεῖα, ἰθύ (ῐ), Ion. and Ep. for εὐθύς, 1) As adj. straight, direct; only the neut. τέτραπτο πρὸς ἰθύ οἱ, he was turned directly to him (others refer it to ἔγχος), 14, 403; with gen. ἰθύ τινος, directly to or at any one, 20, 99; metaph. straight, upright, just. ἰθεῖα ἔσται, subaud. δίκη or ὁδός, the sentence will be just, 23, 580. ἰθύντατα εἰπεῖν δίκην, 18, 508. 2) ἰθύς as an adv. like ἰθύ, directly towards, straight at, for the most part with the gen. Δαναῶν, 12, 106; προθύροιο, Od. 1, 119; with prep. ἰθὺς πρὸς

τεῖχος, straight to the wall, 12, 137. ἰθὺ μεμαώς, rushing straight upon, 11, 95. τῇ ῥ' ἰθὺς φρονεῖν, to think right onward, with direct purpose, 13, 135 [ἰθὺς φρονεῖν, like ἰθὺς μεμαώς, to stretch straight on, Passow]. τῇ ῥ' ἰθὺς φρονέων ἵππους ἔχε, 12, 124. In this passage, Spitzner after the Schol. connects ἰθὺς with ἔχειν, and translates φρονέων, of set purpose, with design, as 23, 343. ἰθὺς μάχεσθαι, to contend directly against, 17, 168. μένος χειρῶν ἰθὺς φέρειν, to bring straight on the strength of hands [i. e. to come into direct conflict], 5, 506. 16, 602.

ἰθύς, ύος, ἡ (ἰθύω) (ῑ), a straight direction in motion, hence ἀν' ἰθύν, directly up, 21, 303. Od. 8, 377; hence attack, an onset, an undertaking, a project, 6, 79. Od. 4, 434; and, in reference to the mind, a strong impulse, a desire, a longing, Od. 16, 304. h. Ap. 539.

ἰθύω (ἰθύς), aor. ἴθυσα, 1) to rush directly upon, to attack, to run impetuously upon, to rage; limited by an adv. or prep. ἐπὶ τεῖχος, διὰ προμάχων, 12, 443. 16, 582; with gen. νέος, to rush against the ship, 15, 693. 2) to stretch after, to strive, to desire ardently, with infin. 17, 353. Od. 11, 591. 22, 408 (υ is short, but before σ long).

Ἰθώμη, ἡ, a fortress in Thessaly (Hestiæōtis), near the later Metropolis; subsequently also called Θούμαιον, 2, 729.

ἱκάνω, Ep. form of ἱκνέομαι (ἵκω, ῐ), to come, to reach, to arrive at, mly with accus., more rarely with ἐπί, ἐς, τί, 1, 431. 2, 17. 9, 354; prim., 1) Of living beings, 6, 370. Od. 13, 231. 2) Of inanimate things: φλὲψ ἡ αὐχέν' ἱκάνει, a vein which reaches the neck, 13, 547. 3) Of all sorts of conditions and situations: to attain, to come upon, to befall, 10, 96; μόρος, 18, 465; esply of human feelings: ἄχος, πένθος, ἱκάνει με, pain, grief came upon me; and with double accus., 2, 171. II) In like manner the Mid. ἱκάνομαι, 10, 118. 11, 610; and with accus., Od. 23, 7. 27.

Ἰκάριος, ὁ, Icarius, son of Perierês and of Gorgophonê, brother of Tyndareus, and father of Penelopê. He dwelt in Lacedæmonia; he fled with his brother to Acarnania, and remained there after the return of his brother, cf. Strab. X. p. 461. Od. 1, 276. 329. Accord. to others, he lived in Cephalênia or Samos, Od. 2, 53; cf. Nitzsch ad loc. (The first ι long.)

Ἰκάριος, η, ον (ῑ), Icarian, belonging to Icarus or the island Icarus. ὁ πόντος Ἰκάριος, the Icarian sea, a part of the Ægean; accord. to tradition it received its name from Icarus, son of Dædalus, who was drowned in this sea. It was very stormy and dangerous, 2, 145. (The first ι long.)

#Ἰκάριος, ἡ, or Ἰκαρίη (ῑ), an island of the Ægean sea, which at an early period was called Δολίχη, and received its name from Icarus son of Dædalus; now *Nica-ria.* h. Bacch. 26. 1.

ἴκελος, η, ον, (ῑ), poet. for εἴκελος, *similar, like,* with dat. 2, 478. Od. 4, 249.

Ἱκετάονίδης, ου, ὁ, son of Hiketaon = *Menalippus,* 15, 547.

Ἱκετάων, ονος, ὁ (ῐ, ἱκέτης), son of Laomedon, and brother of Priam, father of Melanippus, 3, 147. 20, 238.

ἱκετεύω (ἱκέτης), aor. ἱκέτευσα, *to come* or *go to any one as a supplicant,* εἴς τινα, 16, 574; or τινά, Od. and generally, *to beg suppliantly, to supplicate, to beseech,* Od. 11, 530.

ἱκέτης, ου, ὁ, *a suppliant,* one who comes to another for protection against persecution, or to seek purification from blood-guiltiness; the persons of such suppliants were inviolable, when they had once seated themselves before the altar of Zeus (ἱκετήσιος) or at the hearth, 24, 158. 570. Od. 9, 270. 19, 134. According to the Schol. on Od. 16, 422, it denotes also the receiver of the suppliant, the same relation existing as in ξένοι. This signif. however ἱκέτης never has in H., and we may better understand here Penelopê and her son by ἱκέται.

ἱκετήσιος, ὁ (ἱκέτης), *the protector of suppliants,* epith. of Zeus, Od. 13, 213.†

ἵκμαι, Ep. for ἵκῃ, see ἱκνέομαι.

Ἱκμάλιος, ὁ, an artist in Ithaca, Od. 19, 57. (According to Damm from ἐξικμαίνω = *Meister Trockenholz,* Mr. Drywood.)

ἰκμάς, άδος, ἡ, *the moisture,* which destroys all roughness, and yields smoothness and flexibility. ἄφαρ ἰκμὰς ἔβη, δύνει δέ τ᾿ ἀλοιφή, quickly a softness comes and the oil enters (spoken of leather which is rendered soft by oil), 17, 392. Cp., like Voss, translates (ἔβη = ἀπέβη,) '*it sweats The moisture out and drinks the unction in.*' See Nitzsch ad Od. 2, 419.

ἴκμενος, ὁ, always in connexion with οὖρος, *a favorable wind;* prob. for ἱκμενος from ἱκέσθαι, the wind which comes upon the ship, *secundus,* Eustath. Schol. Venet. Others (Hesych. Etym. M.) *a moist, gently blowing,* or, according to Nitzsch ad Od. 2, 419, *a uniform breeze,* (opp. one that drives the vessel about, &c.) from ἰκμάς, slipperiness, smoothness (cf. Od. 5, 478; ἄνεμοι ὑγρὸν ἀέντες), 1, 479. Od. 2, 420.

ἱκνέομαι, poet. depon. mid. (from ἵκω). fut. ἵξομαι, aor. ἱκόμην, *to come, to go, to attain, to reach,* with the accus. of the aim, or with εἴς τι; more rarely, with ἐπί, πρός, κατά, etc.; with dat. ἐπειγομένοισι δ᾿ ἵκοντο, 12, 374. 1) Spoken of any thing living; ἐς χεῖράς τινος, to fall into any one's hands, 10, 448; ἐπὶ νῆας, 6, 69; eaply to come to any one as a suppliant, 14, 260. 22, 123. 2) Spoken of any thing inanimate. conceived of as in motion; τινά, 11. 3) Of various states and conditions. Ἀχιλλῆος ποθὴ ἵξεται υἷας Ἀχαιῶν, regret for Achilles will at

length come upon the sons of the Greeks, 1, 240. κάματός μιν γούναθ᾿ ἵκετο, fatigue attacked his knees, 13, 711'; in like manner, σέβας, πένθος etc., with double accus. 1, 362. 11, 88. (ι is short, except when long by augm.)

ἴκρια, τά, always in the plur., Ep. gen. ἱκριόφιν (from ἴκριον, a plank, a beam), *the deck,* which covered only the fore and hind part of the ship; the middle was open for the seats of the rowers, 15, 676. Od. 12, 229. 13, 74. In the difficult passage, Od. 5, 252, are commonly understood the ship's ribs, connected by cross-pieces, upon which the deck rested. Voss, more correctly, considers σταμίνες the *ribs;* 'he placed around it planks, fastening them to the frequent ribs;' see ἐπηγκενίδες. Nitzsch ad loc. understands by ἴκρια *the planks* which formed the inner coating, as it were, of the ship's sides, cf. Od. 5, 163. In a large vessel this *lining* of boards was confined to the prow and stern, the centre-portion being left with naked timbers to form the *hold.*

ἵκω, Ep. imperf. ἷκον, aor. 2 ἷξον, ἷξες, the root of ἱκάνω and ἱκνέομαι. (Upon the aor. see Buttm. § 96, note 9 Root. Dial. 52, d); *to go, to come, to reach, to arrive at, to attain,* with accus. of the aim, 1, 317. 9, 525. ὅ τι χρειὼ τόσον ἵκει, what so great need is come, 10, 142; often with a partcp. ἐς Ῥόδον ἷξεν ἀλώμενος, he came to Rhodes in his wandering, 2, 667. (ι is regularly long.)

ἰλαδόν, adv. (ἴλη), *in crowds, in troops, troop by troop,* 2, 93.†

*Ἴλαμαι, mid. poet. form for ἱλάσκομαι, see ἵλημι, h. 20, 5.

ἱλάομαι, Ep. for ἱλάσκομαι, *to appease, to propitiate,* ἱλάονταί μιν ταύροισι. 2, 550† (viz. Erechtheus, say the Gramm. and Voss; others, as Heyne, refer it to Athênê).

ἵλαος (ῑ, ᾱ), *propitiated, favorable,* placatus, spoken of the gods: *gracious, merciful,* 1. 583; of men: *gentle, kind,* 9, 639. h. Cer. 204.

ἱλάσκομαι, depon. mid. (ἱλάω, ῑ), fut. ἱλάσομαι, Ep. σσ. aor. ἱλασάμην, Ep. σσ. spoken only of gods, *to appease, to propitiate, to conciliate, to render gracious* or *favorable,* with accus. θεόν, Ἀθήνην, 1, 100. 147. 386. Od. 3, 419; τινὰ μολπῇ, 1, 472. cf. h. 20, 5. (Kindred forms, ἵλαμαι, ἱλάομαι; prop. ῑ, sometimes ῐ, 1, 100.)

ἵλημι, poet. (from root ἱλάω), only imperat. ἵληθι and perf. subj. ἱλήκῃσι, optat. ἱλήκοι, *to be propitiated, gracious, favorable.* ἵληθι, be gracious, in addresses to the gods, *Od. 3, 380. 16. 184. The perf. with signif. of pres. with dat. Od. 21, 365. h. in Ap. 165.

Ἰλιάς, άδος. ἡ, prop. adj. *Trojan, of Troy;* as subst. subaud. ποίησις, *the Iliad.*

Ἰλήϊος, ον, Ep. for Ἴλειον, *Ilian, relating to Ilus.* τὸ πεδίον Ἰλήϊον, the Ilian plain; the Schol. says it was so called from the monument of Ilus, cf. Ἶλος, 2. But, in the first place, this region was never so called; in the next, Agênor would in that case have retired from Ida and gone back; more correctly. Lenz understands (Ebene von Troj. S. 226) the plain back of Troy towards Ida. Crates therefore has amended it to Ἰδή ἴον, and Voss translates, *the Idæan plain*, 21, 558; cf. Köpke Kriegswes. d. Griech. S. 193.

Ἰλιονεύς, ῆος, ὁ (ῑ), son of Phorbas, a Trojan, slain by Peneleus, 14, 489. (The first ι long.)

Ἰλιόθεν, adv. *from Ilium* (*Troy*), 14, 251.

Ἰλιόθι, adv. *at Ilium* (*Troy*), always Ἰλιόθι πρό, before Ilium (*Troy*), 8, 561. Od. 8, 581.

Ἴλιον, τό = Ἴλιος, q. v.

Ἴλιος, ἡ, (ῑ) (τὸ Ἴλιον, 15, 71†), *Ilios* or *Ilium*, the capital of the Trojan realm, afterwards called *Troja* (*Troy*). It received its name from its founder, Ilus. This city, with its citadel (Πέργαμος), in which was the sanctuary of Athênê, and the temple of Zeus and Apollo (22, 191) called by the later Greeks τὸ παλαιὸν Ἴλιον, was situated upon an isolated hill in a great plain (20, 216), between the two rivers Simoeis and Scamandrus, where they approached each other. Their confluence was to the west of the city. It was thirty stadia beyond Novum Ilium, about six Roman miles from the sea. On the west side of the city, towards the Grecian camp, was the great gate, called the Σκαιαὶ πύλαι, also called Dardanian. Now the village *Bunar-Baschi* occupies its site. *New Ilium* lay near to the coast, only twenty stadia from the mouth of the Scamander; originally a village with a temple of Athênê, which under the Romans grew into a city; now *Trojahi*, cf. Lenz, die Ebene vor Troja, 1797. Ἴλιος is also applied to the whole Trojan realm, 1, 71. 18, 58. 13, 717. (The first ι long; the second also long in 21, 104.)

Ἰλιόφιν, Ep. for Ἰλίου, 21, 295.

ἰλλάς, άδος, ἡ (ἴλλω, εἴλω), prop. that which is twisted (of thongs or any thing flexible), *a string, a rope*, plur. 13, 572.†

Ἶλος, ὁ, *Ilus*, 1) son of Dardanus and Bateia, king of Dardania, who died without children, Apd. 3, 12. 2. 2) son of Tros and Calirrhoê, father of Laomedon, brother of Ganymede, founder of Ilium, 20, 232. His monument was situated beyond the Scamandrus, midway between the Scæan gate and the battle-ground, 10, 415. 11, 166. 371. 3) son of Mermerus, grandson of Pheres, in Ephyra, Od. 1, 259.

ἰλύς, ύος, ἡ, prob. from εἰλύω, *mud, mire*, 21, 318.†

ἱμάς, άντος, ὁ (ῑ, rarely ῐ, from ἵημι), a *leathern thong*, 21, 30. 22, 397; hence 1) *a thong* or *strap* for harnessing horses,

8, 544. 10, 475; also *a trace*, 23, 324. 2) the *straps* with which the chariot-body was fastened, 5, 727. 3) *the whip-thong*, a whip, 23, 363. 4) the *thong* for fastening the helmet under the chin, 3, 371; also the *thongs* with which the helmet was lined for protection, 10, 2. 265) *the magic-girdle, the cestus* of Aphroditê, which, by its magic power, inspired every one with love, 14, 214. 219. 6) *the thongs* of pugilists, cæstus, which were made of undressed leather and wound around the hollow of the hand, 23, 684. 7) In the Od., the *thong* fastened to the bolt of the door, and drawn through a hole. To shut the door, the bolt (κληΐς) was drawn forward, and fastened to the κορώνη; to open the door, the thong was first untied, and then the bolt pressed back with a hook, Od. 1, 4. 424, 802.

ἱμάσθλη, ἡ (ἱμάσσω), prop. *a whip-thong*, then *a whip*, 8, 43, and Od.

ἱμάσσω (ἱμάς), aor. 1 ἵμασα, Ep. σσ, to *whip, to lash, to strike*, ἵππους, ἡμιόνους, Il. and Od.; πληγαῖς τινα, 15, 17; metaph. γαῖαν, to strike (lash) the earth with lightning spoken of Zeus), 2, 782. h. Ap. 340.

Ἰμβρασίδης, ου, ὁ, son of Imbrasus = *Peirus*, 4, 520.

Ἴμβριος, ὁ, son of Mentor of Pedæon, husband of Medesicastê, son-in-law of Priam, slain by Teucer, 13, 171. 197. [2. As adj. *of Imbrus, Imbrian*, 21, 43.]

Ἴμβρος, ἡ, 1) an island on the coast of Thrace, famed for the worship of the Caberi and of Hermês; now *Imbro*, 13, 33. 24, 78. 2) a city on the above island, 14, 281. 21, 43.

ἱμείρω, poet. and Ion. ἵμερος (ῑ), 1) *to long for, to desire ardently*, with gen. κακῶν, Od. 10, 431. 555. 2) Mid. as depon. aor. 1 ἱμειράμην; more frequently with gen. αἴης, Od. 1, 41; and with infin. Il. 14, 163. Od. 1, 59.

ἴμεν and ἴμεναι, see εἶμι.

ἱμερόεις, εσσα, εν (ἵμερος), *awakening desire* or *longing; enchanting, fascinating, lovely, agreeable*, χορός, 18, 603; ἀοιδή, Od. 1, 421; γόος, the lamentation of longing desire, Od. 10, 398; chiefly *charming, exciting amorous passions*, στήθεα, 3, 397; ἔργα γάμοιο, 5, 429. Neut. as adv. ἱμερόεν κιθάριζε, 18, 570.

ἵμερος, ὁ (ῑ), *longing, ardent desire* for a person or thing, τινός, 11, 89. 23, 14. 108, and also connected with a gen. of the object: πατρὸς ἵμερος γόοιο, a strong desire to mourn his father [Cp.], Od. 4, 113; esply *amorous desire, love*, 3, 140. 14, 198.

ἱμερτός, ή, όν (ἱμείρω), *longed for, attractive, lovely*, epith. of a river, 2, 751; of the harp, h. Merc. 510.

ἴμμεναι, see εἶμι, cf. Thiersch, § 229, a.

ἵνα, 1) Adv. of place, *where, in which place*, 2, 558. Od. 6, 322; for ἐκεῖ, *there*, 10, 127. b) More rarely, *whither*, Od. 4, 821. 6, 55. In Od. 6, 27, it is explained as an adv. of time, *when*; and Od. 8, 313, *how*; in both places, however, the *local* signif. is predominant; in the first, we may translate ἵνα, *whereat* (on which occasion); and in the second, *how* —*there*, cf. Nitzsch ad Od. 4, 821. II) Conjunct. *that, in order to*, denoting purpose. 1) With the subj. after a primary tense (pres., perf., fut.), 1, 203. 3, 252. 11, 290; and after an aor. with pres. signif. 1, 410. 19, 347. Apparently the indicat. is often found here, since the Ep. subj. shortens the long vowel, 1, 363. 2, 232. 2) With the optat. after an historical tense (imperf., pluperf., aor.), Od. 3, 2. 77. 5, 492. As exceptions, notice *a*) The subj. stands with a preceding historical tense *a*) When the aor. has the signif. of the perf., Od 3, 15. 11, 93. β) In the objective representation of past events, 9, 495. *b*) The optat. follows a primary tense. when the declaration assumes the character of dependent discourse (in H. examples are wanting), cf. ὄφρα. Sometimes the subj. and optat. follow one after the other in two dependent clauses, 15, 596. 24, 584. Od. 3, 78. 3) ἵνα μή, that not, 7, 195. Od. 4, 70; construc. as in ἵνα, 1, 2; ἵνα μή, in Il. 7, 353, is explained by the Schol. by ἐὰν μή, if not; the verse is, however, suspected. 4) With other particles, ἵνα δή, ἵνα περ, 7, 26. 24, 382.

ἰνδάλλομαι (εἶδος, εἰδάλιμος), *to present one-self in view, to appear, to show oneself*, 23, 460. Od 3, 246. h. Ven. 179. The dat. τινί indicates him to whom any thing appears. ἰνδάλλετό σφισι πᾶσι τεύχεσι λαμπόμενος Πηλείωνος, he (viz. Patroclus) appeared to all, gleaming in the arms of Peleides, 17. 213 (As the sense appears to be 'he was like Achilles,' Heyne, Bothe, and Spitzner, after Aristarchus, have adopted Πηλείωνι. Commonly the nom. indicates the person who appears, or in whose character any one appears; the dat., however, is not unusual, cf. Od. 3, 246, where formerly stood ἀθανάτοις; h. Ven. 179. ὥς μοι ἰνδάλλεται ἦτορ, as h⸗ appears to me in my mind (= *recollection*), Od. 19, 224; for here Odysseus (Ulysses) is immediately described, as to his exterior. Damm takes it here as mid. = φαντάζεται, *conceives, imagines* [ἦτορ as nom.]; so also Voss, 'so far as my mind remembers.'

ἴνεσι, see ἴς.

ἰνίον. τό (ἴ, ἴς), the back bone of the head, *the neck, the nape of the neck*, *5, 73. 14, 495.

Ἰνώ, όος, ἡ, see Λευκοθέα.

*Ἴνωπος, ὁ (ἴ, Ἰνωπός, Strab.), a fountain and rivulet in Delos, h. Ap. 18.

ἴξαλος, ον, epith. of αἴξ ἄγριος, prob. *fast-springing, climbing*, from αἴσσω or ἰκνεῖσθαι and ἄλλομαι, other say, *lascivious*, from ἰξύς, 4, 105.†

Ἴξω, ες, ε, see ἴκω.

ἰξύς, ύος, ἡ, *the flank* or *side of the*

body, the region above the hips, ἰξυῖ, Ep. contr. dat. for ἰξύι, *Od. 5, 231. 20, 544.

Ἰξίων, ίωνος, ὁ, *Ixion*, king of Thessaly and husband of Dia, who bore Peirithous by Zeus; from this Ἰξιόνιος, ίη, ιον. *pertaining to Ixion*; ἄλοχος, 14, 317.

Ἰοβάτης, ου, ὁ, king of Lycia, father of Antia, and father-in-law of Prœtus, who sent Bellerophontes to him, that he might put him to death. H., 6, 173, mentions not his name, but Apd. 2, 2. 1; cf. Ἄντεια and Προῖτος.

ἰοδνεφής, ές (ἴ, from ἴον, νέφος), *violet-coloured, purple*, and generally, *dark-coloured*, εἶρος, *Od. 4, 135. 9, 426.

ἰοδόκος, ον (ἴ, from ἰός, δέχομαι), *containing arrows, arrow-holding*, φαρέτρη, Od. 21, 12. 60.†

ἰοειδής, ές (ἴ, from ἴον, εἶδος), *violet-coloured*, and generally, *dark-coloured*, cf. πορφύρεος, epith. of the sea, 11, 298. Od. 5, 56

ἰόεις, εσσα, εν (ἴ, from ἴον), *violet-coloured, dark-coloured* (as πολιός), σι δηρος, 23, 850.

Ἰοκάστη, ἡ, see Ἐπικάστη.

ἰόμωρος, ον (ἴ), a reproachful epith. of the Argives, *4, 242. 14, 479; according to most critics, *skilled with the arrow, fighting with arrows*, from ἰός and μώρος (= μόρος). Schol. οἱ περὶ τοὺς ἰοὺς μεμορημένοι), cf. ἐγχεσίμωρος; sense: ye, who only fight at a distance with missiles, but will not attack the enemy in close conflict with sword and spear. It indicates, therefore, cowardice; and from many passages in H., it appears that archery was little reputable. Köppen, without probability, takes it as an honorary epithet. But as the ι here is short, and the ι in ἰός is always long, consequently several other explanations have been sought. Schneider derives it from ἰά, *voice*, and translates, 'ready with the voice, boastful, braggarts.' Others, from ἴον, explaining it, 'destined to the fate of the violet,' i. e. a short-lived fate, or, to a violet-coloured, i. e. a dark fate, etc.

ἴον, τό (ἴ), *a violet*, Od. 5, 72.† h. Cer. 6. There were, according to Theophr. Hist. Plant. 6, 6, white, purple, and black.

ἰονθάς, άδος. ἡ, *shaggy, hairy*, epith. of wild goats, Od. 14, 50.† (From ἴονθος, akin to ἄνθος.)

ἰός, ὁ (ἴ, from ἵημι), plur. οἱ ἰοί and once τὰ ἰά, 20, 68;† prop. that which is cast, *an arrow*. cf. ὀϊστός.

ἰός, ἰή, ἰον, Ep. for εἷς, μία, ἕν, in gen. and dat. with altered accent, ἰῆς, ἰῷ, 6, 122; ἰῇ, one, 9, 319. τῇ δέ τ᾽ ἰῇ ἀναφαίνεται ὄλεθρος, supply βοΐ, to one (cow) death appeared, 11, 174. Od. 14, 435.

*ἰοστέφανος, ον (στέφανος), *violet-crowned*, h. 5, 18.

ἰότης, ητος, ἡ (ἴ, prob. from ἴς), only in the dat. and accus. *will, resolution, counsel, bidding, advice*, 15, 41; often θεῶν ἰότητι, by the will of the gods, 19, 9. Od. 7, 214. ἀλλήλων ἰότητι, the counsel of each other. 5. 874.

ἴουλος, ὁ (οὖλος), the first down, the earliest appearance of beard only in the plur. Od. 11, 319.†

ἰοχέαιρα, ἡ (ῑ, from ἰός, χαίρω), delighting in arrows. arrow-loving, epith. of Artĕmis; as subst. mistress of the bow, huntress, 21, 480. Od. 11, 198.

ἱππάζομαι, depon. mid. (ἵππος), to guide horses, to drive a chariot, 23, 426.†

Ἱππασίδης, ου, ὁ, son of Hippasus = Charops, 11, 426 : = Socus, 11, 431 ; = Hypsênor, 13, 411 : = Apisāon, 17, 348.

Ἵππασος, ὁ, 1) father of Charops and Sŏcus, a Trojan, according to Hyg. f. 90, son of Priam, 11, 425: 450. 2) father of Hypsênor, 13, 411. 3) father of Apisāon, 17, 348.

ἵππειος, η, ον(ἵππος), of a horse, belonging to a horse, ζυγόν, φάτνη, ὁπλή, Il., κάπη, Od. 4, 40. ἵππειος λόφος, a crest of horse-hair, Il. 15, 537.

ἱππεύς, ῆος, ὁ (ἵππος), plur. once ἱππεῖς, 11, 151 ; a knight; in H. a charioteer, one who guides horses, 11, 51 ; = ἡνίοχος, for the most part, opposed to πεζός, one who fights from a chariot, 2, 810. 11, 529; also a combatant for a prize in a chariot, 23, 262. cf. ἡνίοχος, παραιβάτης.

ἱππηλάσιος, η, ον (ἐλαύνω), good for travelling with horses, passable for chariots. ἱππηλάσιος ὁδός, a chariot-road, *7, 340. 439.

ἱππηλάτα, ὁ, Ep. for ἱππηλάτης, only nom. sing. (ἐλαύνω), a charioteer, a horseman, epith. of distinguished heroes, 4, 387. Od. 3, 436; always in the Ep. form.

ἱππήλατος. ον(ἐλαύνω), suited to driving horses, convenient for travelling, νῆσος (convenient for a race-ground, V.), *Od. 4, 607. 13, 242.

Ἱππημολγοί, οἱ, the Hippomolgi, prop. horse-milkers, from ἵππος and ἀμέλγω, Scythian nomades, who lived upon mare's milk; Strab., VII. p. 260. after Posidonius, places them in the north of Europe. H. calls them ἀγανοί, from their simple mode of life, 13, 5.

ἱππιοχαίτης, ου, ὁ (χαίτη), of horse-hair, λόφος, 6, 469.

ἱππιοχάρμης, ου, ὁ (χάρμη), that practises fighting from a chariot, a charioteer, 24, 257. Od. 11, 259.

ἱππόβοτος, ον (βόσκω), pastured by horses, horse-nourishing, epith. of Argos, because the plain of this city, abounding in water, was suited to the pasturing of horses; also spoken of Tricca and Elis, 4, 202. Od. 21, 347.

Ἱπποδάμας, αντος, ὁ, a Trojan, slain by Achilles, 20, 401 (= ἱππόδαμος).

Ἱπποδάμεια, ἡ, Hippodameia. 1) daughter of Atrax, wife of Pirithous, mother of Polypœtes, 2, 742. 2) daughter of Anchises, wife of Alcathous, sister of Æneas, 13, 429. 3) prop. name of Brisēis, according to Schol. ad Il. 1, 184; see Βρισηΐς. 4) a handmaid of Penelopê, Od. 18 182.

ἱππόδαμος, ον (δαμάω), horse-subduing, horse-taming, epith. of heroes, and also of the Trojans and Phrygians, 2, 230. 10, 431. Od. 3, 17.

Ἱππόδαμος, ὁ, Hippodamus, son of Merops, from Percôtê, a Trojan, slain by Odysseus (Ulysses), 11. 335.

ἱππόδασυς, εια, υ (δασύς), thickly covered with horse-hair, κόρυς, 3, 369 ; κυνέη, Od. 22. 111.

ἱππόδρομος, ὁ (δρόμος), a race-course for chariots, 23, 330.†

ἱππόθεν, adv. (ἵππος from a horse), *Od. 8, 515. 11, 531.

Ἱππόθοος, ὁ, 1) son of Lethus from Larissa, grandson of Teutamus, leader of the Pelasgians, 2, 840, seq.; he is slain, 17, 217—318. 2) son of Priam, 24 251.

ἱπποκέλευθος, ον (κέλευθος, travelling by horses, fighting from a chariot, epith. of Patroclus, in *16. 126. 584. 839; since being the charioteer of Achilles he fought not on foot. Thus the better Gramm. Eustath. Ven. Schol. The interpret. &c ἵπποις κελεύεις, thou that commandest horses, is contrary to the usus loquendi. Bentley would write, ἱπποκελεύστης.)

ἱππόκομος, ον (κόμη), set with horse-hair, crested with horse-hair, τρυφάλεια, κόρυς, *12. 339. 13, 132, seq.

ἱπποκορυστής, οῦ, ὁ (κορύσσω), arming horses, or more correctly passive, furnished with horses for fighting, epith. of heroes fighting from war-chariots, *2, 1. 16, 287. 21, 205.

Ἱπποκόων, ωντος, ὁ. a relative and comrade of the Thracian king, Rhesus, 10, 518. (From κοεῖν = νοεῖν, acquainted with horses.)

Ἱππόλοχος, ὁ, 1) son of Bellerophontes, father of Glaucus, 6, 119. 197; king of the Lycians, 17, 140, seq. 2) a Trojan, son of Antimachus, slain by Agamemnon. 11, 122.

Ἱππόμαχος, ὁ, son of Antimachus, a Trojan, slain by Polypœtes, 12, 189.

Ἱππόνοος, ὁ (acquainted with horses), 1) a Greek, slain by Hector, 11. 303. 2) prop. name of Bellerophontes, cf. Schol. ad Il. 6, 155.

ἱπποπόλος, ον (πολέω), to go about with horses, horse-driving, epith. of the Thracians, 13, 4. 14, 227.

ἵππος, ὁ, a horse, a steed; ἡ ἵππος, a mare; also θήλεες ἵπποι, 5, 269 ; and ἵπποι θήλειαι, 11, 681. H. uses both genders, but chiefly the fem., since mares were regarded as better suited for travelling and fighting, 2, 763. 5, 269. Od. 4, 635. The heroes of the Trojan war used horses only for drawing chariots : though 10, 513, is only understood of riding, but not with entire certainty. See κέλης and ἅρμα, Od 4. 590; hence, 2) In the plur., and rarely in the dual (5, 13. 237), a pair of horses, or a team, in connexion with ἅρμα, 12, 120; and often ἵπποισιν καὶ ὄχεσφιν, 12, 114. 119; hence also a) the chariot itself, 5.

265. 5, 13, etc. ; hence, ἁλὸς ἵπποι, the chariot of the sea, for a ship, Od. 4. 708. b) *warriors fighting from a chariot,* in opposition to πεζοί, Od. 14, 267. ἵπποι τε καὶ ἀνέρες, Il. 5, 554. 16, 1ι7.

ἱπποσύνη. ἡ (ἵππος), *the art of managing horses* and *of fighting from a chariot,* 4, 403. 11, 503; also in the plur. 16, 776. Od. 24, 40.

ἱππότα, ὁ, Ep. for ἱππότης (ἵππος), *a charioteer, a warrior fighting from a chariot,* epith. of heroes, esply of Nestor, only Ep. form, often in the Il., and Od. 3, 68.

Ἱπποτάδης, ου, ὁ, a descendant of Hippotes=Æolus, Od. 10, 2. 36.

Ἱππότης, ου, ὁ, son of Poseidon or of Zeus, father of Æolus, according to H. and Ap. Rh. 4, 778; others say grandfather of Æolus, through his daughter Arne, see Αἴολος.

Ἱπποτίων, ωνος, ὁ, a Mysian, father of Morys, 13, 392; slain by Meriones, 14, 514, or perhaps another.

ἱππουρις, ιδος, ἡ (οὐρά), as fem. adj. *furnished with a horse-tail,* κυνέη and κόρυς, 3, 337. 11, 42. Od. 22, 124.

ἵπταμαι, depon. mid. fut. ἴψομαι, aor. ἰψάμην, to press, to squeeze; but only in the metaph. sense, *to oppress, to afflict* (strike, V.) with accus. (spoken of Zeus and Apollo) λαόν, 1, 454. 16, 237 ; (of Agamemnon,) to chastise, to punish, 2, 193 (related to ἴπος, ἰπόω), *Il.

ἱραί, αἱ or Ἱραι, different readings, 18, 531, for εἱραι, q. v.

ἱρεύς, Ep. and Ion. for ἱερεύς.

ἱρεύω, Ep. and Ion. for ἱερεύω.

Ἱρή, ἡ ed. Wolf, Ἵρη ed. Spitzner, a city in Messenia (different from Εἴρα), one of the towns promised by Agamemnon to Achilles as a dowry, 9, 150. Paus. calls it the later Ἀβία; Strab. VIII. 360, incorrectly, Ἴρα, on the way from Andania to Megalopolis. Spitzner has adopted Ἵρη, which was the common reading in Paus., and which the rule of accent requires. Aristarch., on the other hand, writes Ἱρήν, cf. Spitzner.

ἱρηξ, ηκος, ὁ, Ion. and Ep. for ἱέραξ (ἱερός), *a hawk or falcon,* to which species also the κίρκος belonged, Od. 13, 86; prop. the sacred bird, because the soothsayers observed and divined from its flight, 13, 62. 16, 582 (only in the contr. form with ι̅).

Ἶρις, ιδος, ἡ, accus. Ἶριν, *Iris,* according to Hes. daughter of Thaumas and Electra; in the earlier rhapsodies of the Iliad only, she is the messenger of the gods, not only amongst each other, 8. 398. 15, 144; but also to men, 2, 786. She interposes of her own accord, 3, 122. 24, 74; and brings spontaneously the commands of Achilles to the winds, 23, 198. She commonly appears in a foreign form, e. g. as Polites, 2, 791; and Laodikè (Laodice), 3, 122. Her fleetness is compared to the fall of hail, or to wind, 15, 172; hence ἀελλόπος, ποδήνεμος. In the later poets

she is goddess of the rainbow. (According to Herm. *Sertia,* from εἴρω, to join.)

Ἶρις, ιδος, ἡ, dat. plur. ἴρισσιν, 11, 27; *the rainbow,* which in ancient times passed with men as a message from heaven, 17, 547.

ἱρός, ή, όν (ι̅), Ep. for ἱερός.

Ἶρος, a beggar in Ithaca, who was prop. called *Arnæus,* but was denominated Ἶρος, *messenger* (from Ἶρις), because the suitors thus employed him. He was large in person, but weak, and insatiably greedy; he was beaten by Odysseus (Ulysses), whom he insulted, Od. 18, 1—7. 73. 239.

ἴς, ἰνός, ἡ, dat plur. ἴνεσι (ι̅), 1) *sinew, muscle, nerve;* in the plur. Il. 11, 219. Il. 23, 191; esply the neck-sinews, 17, 522. 2) *muscular power, bodily strength, vigour, strength,* prim. of men, 5, 245. 7, 269; also of inanimate things, ἀνέμου and ποταμοῦ, 15, 383. 21, 356. 3) Since strength is the prominent trait of every hero, the strength of the hero is spoken of by a circumlocution for the hero himself. κρατερὴ ἲς Ὀδυσῆος, the vigorous strength of Odysseus (Ulysses), for the powerfully strong Odysseus, 23. 720; Τηλεμάχοιο, Od. 2, 409; cf. βίη, σθένος.

ἰσάζω (ἴσος), fut. ἰσάσω, aor. 1 mid. Ep. iterat. form ἰσάσκετο, 24, 607; act. *to make equal,* spoken of a woman weighing wool in scales, 12, 435; see ἔχω. 2) Mid. *to make oneself equal, to esteem oneself equal,* τινί, 24, 607.

ἴσαν, 1) 3 plur. imperf. from εἶμι. 2) Ep. for ᾔδεσαν, see ΕΙΔΩ. Β.

Ἴσανδρος, ὁ (man-like), son of Bellerophontes, slain by Ares in an engagement against the Solymi, 6, 197. 203.

ἴσασι, see ΕΙΔΩ, Β.

ἰσάσκετο, see ἰσάζω.

ἴσθι, imper. see ΕΙΔΩ, Β.

ἴσθμιον. τό (ἰσθμός), prop. what belongs to the neck, *a necklace, a neck-band,* Od. 18, 300.†

ἴσκω, Ep. (from root ΙΚ, εἴκω), poet. form of εἴσκω, only pres. and imperf. *to make equal, to make similar, to liken,* τί τινι. φωνὴν ἀλόχοις (for φωνῇ ἀλόχων) ἰσκουσα, making the voice like the voices of the wives [i. e. imitating their voices], Od. 4, 279. 2) In thought: *to deem like, to esteem equal* or *like.* ἐμὲ σοὶ ἴσκοντες. esteeming me like thee (i. e. taking me for thee, V.), 16, 41. cf. 11, 799. 3) In two places, Od. 19, 203, and 22, 31, some critics explain ἴσκε and ἴσκεν, ' he spake,' as it occurs also in Ap. Rhod. But Eustath. with the more exact critics, interprets it by εἴκαζα, ὡμοίου, Od. 19, 203. ἴσκε ψεύδεα πολλὰ λέγων ἐτύμοισιν ὁμοῖα, prop. uttering many falsehoods, he made them like the truth [uttered many 'specious fictions,' Cp.]; and Od. 22, 31, ἴσκεν ἕκαστος ἀνήρ. each one imagined, i. e. was deceived in thinking as the following words show, cf. Buttm. Lex. p. 279, who

L

conjectures that ἴσπε should be the reading in Od. 22. 31.

Ἴσμαρος, ἡ, a city in Thrace, in the realm of the Ciconians, near Maronia, famed for its strong wine, Od. 9, 40. 198.

ἰσόθεος, ον (ῑ, θεός), godlike, equal to a god, epith. of heroes, 2, 565, and Od.

ἰσόμορος, ον (ῑ, μόρος), having an equal share, an equal lot. 15, 209.†

ἰσόπεδον, τό (πέδον), an equal bottom, level ground, a plain, 13, 142.†

ἴσος, ἴση, ἴσον, Ep. for ἶσος, Ep. also in fem. ἐΐση, q. v. 1) equal in quality, number, value, strength; sometimes also similar; absol. ἶσον θυμὸν ἔχειν, 13, 704; with dat. δαίμονι, 5, 884; Ἄρηϊ, 11, 295; and even often with the dat. of the pers., although the comparison concerns only something belonging to the person. οὐ μὲν σοί ποτε ἶσον ἔχω γέρας for γέρας τῷ σῷ γέραϊ ἶσον, I never receive a reward equal to thine, 1, 163. cf. 17, 51. 2) equally shared. ἴση μοῖρα μένοντι καὶ εἰ μάλα τις πολεμίζοι, there is an equal portion to him who remains behind (at the ships), and to him who fights ever so vigorously, 9, 318; often ἴση alone, 11, 705. 12, 423. Od. 9, 42. 3) The neut. sing. as adv. ἶσον and ἶσα. ἶσον κηρί, like death, 3, 454. 15, 50; oftener the neut. plur. ἶσα τεκέεσσι, 5, 71. 15. 439; and with prep. κατὰ ἶσα μάχην τανύειν, to suspend the fight in equipoise, to excite it equally, 11, 336. ἐπ' ἶσα, 12, 436. The passage Od. 2, 203, is variously explained. κρήματα δ' αὖτε κακῶς βεβρώσεται, οὐδέ ποτ' ἶσα ἔσσεται, thy possessions are consumed, and never will the like be to thee, i. e. that which is consumed will never be replaced. Thus Nitzsch, and this appears most natural. Eustath. says, 'they will never remain equal,' i. e. will continually decrease. Others. as Voss, 'there will be no equity.' Both are contrary to the Hom. usus loquendi.

Ἶσος, ὁ, son of Priam, slain by Agamemnon, 11, 101.

ἰσοφαρίζω (ῑ, from ἶσος and φέρω), to put oneself on an equality with any man, to liken, to compare oneself to in any thing; τινὶ μένος, to any man in strength, 6, 101; ἔργα Ἀθήνῃ, 9, 390; and with the dat. alone, 21, 194.

ἰσοφόρος, ον (φέρω), bearing a like burden, of equal strength, βόες, Od. 18, 373 †

ἰσόω (ἶσος), only optat. aor. ἰσωσαίμην, to make equal, mid. to become equal, with dat., Od. 7, 212.†

ἴστημι, imperf. ἴστην, 3 sing. Ep. iterat. form ἴστασκε, ἴστασχ', Od. 19, 574; fut. στήσω, aor. 1 ἔστησα, also Ep. 3 plur. ἔστασαν for ἔστησαν, 12, 55. 2, 525 (ἴστασαν, Spitzner). Od. 3, 182. 18, 307 (cf. ἔπρεσε); aor. 2 ἔστην, Ep. iterat. form στάσκον, and 3 plur. Ep. ἔσταν and στάν, subj. στῶ, 2 sing. στήῃς for στῇς, etc., 1 plur. Ep. στέωμεν and στείομεν for στῶμεν, infin. στήμεναι for στῆναι, perf.

ἔστηκα, and pluperf. ἐστήκειν; the dual and plur. only in the syncop. forms: dual ἕστατον, plur. ἕσταμεν, ἕστατε, and poet. ἕστητε, 4, 243. 246; 3 plur. ἕστᾶσι, subj. ἑστῶ, optat. ἑσταίην, infin. ἑστάμεναι, ἑστάμεν, partcp. only the obliq. case, ἑστᾶότος, etc., pluperf. dual ἕστᾶτον, 3 plur. ἕστᾶσαν: mid. fut. στήσομαι, aor. ἐστησάμην, aor. pass. ἐστάθην, signif.: I) Trans. in the pres. imperf. fut. and aor. 1, to place, to cause to stand, of animate and inanimate objects, hence 1) to put up, to set up, to place erect, with accus. 2, 525; ἔγχος, 15, 126; τρίποδα, 18, 344. 2) to cause to rise, to raise, νεφέλας, 5, 523. Od. 12. 405; κονίης ὀμίχλην, 13, 336; hence metaph. to excite, to stir up, φυλόπιδα, ἔριν, Od. 11, 314. 16, 292. 3) to cause to stand, to hinder, to bring to a stand, to check, to stop (in their course), ἵππους, 5, 368; νέας, to anchor the ships, Od. 2, 391. 3, 182; μύλην, to stop the mill, Od. 20, 111; hence, to cause to stand in the balance, i. e. to weigh, τάλαντα, 19, 247. 22, 350. II) Intrans. and reflex. in the aor. 2 perf. and pluperf. act. 1) to place oneself, to stand, perf. ἕστηκα, I have placed myself, or I stand; ἑστήκειν, I stood, in which signif. the mid. is used to supply the pres. imperf. and fut. both of animate and inanimate things. 2) to stand, of warriors, 4, 334; νῆες, σκόλοπες, 9, 44. 12, 64. 3) to stand up, to arise, 1, 535; to stand forth, to lift oneself, χρημνοί, 12, 55, ὀρθαὶ τρίχες ἔσταν, the hair stood erect, 24, 359. ὀφθαλμοὶ ὡσεὶ κέρα ἕστασαν, the eyes stood out like horns, Od. 19. 211; hence metaph. ἕβδομος ἑστήκει μείς, the seventh month had begun, 19, 117; hence ἵσταται, begins, Od. 14, 162. 4) to stand still, to keep one's place, κρατερῶς, 11, 410. 13, 56. III) Mid. esply aor. 1. 1) to place for oneself, to put up, with accus. κρατῆρα θεοῖσι, 6, 528; ἱστόν, to put up the loom-beam, Od. 2, 94; ἱστόν, to raise the mast, 1, 480. Od. 9, 77. ἀγῶνα, to begin a combat, h. Ap. 150. 2) Oftener intrans. and reflex., to place oneself, in the passages cited under no. II. Il. 2, 473. πάντεσσιν ἐπὶ ξυροῦ ἵσταται ἀκμῆς [in balance hangs, poised on a razor's edge. Cp.], 10, 173; see ἀκμή. δοῦρα ἐν γαίῃ ἵσταντο, the spears remained sticking in the earth, 11, 574; metaph. νεῖκος ἵσταται, the contest begins, 13, 333. Cf. on ἕστασαν, Buttm. § 107. 6. Thiersch, § 223. Kühner, § 182.

Ἱστίαια, ἡ, Ep. and Ion. for Ἑστίαια, a town in Euboea, on the northern coast, later Ὠρεός, 2, 537.

ἱστίη, ἡ, Ion. and Ep. for ἑστία, the domestic hearth, which at the same time was a domestic altar of the household gods; it was the asylum of all suppliants, and an oath by it was peculiarly sacred, •Od. 14, 159. 17, 156. 19, 304. (The middle syllable is always long.)

•Ἱστίη, ἡ (Ἱστίη, ed. Herm.), Ep. for Ἑστία, Vesta, daughter of Kronus (Saturn) and Rhea, tutelary deity of the domestic hearth, of houses and cities, h. 23, 1. 23, 1.

ἱστίον, τό (dim. from ἱστός), prop. any thing woven, *cloth* ; in H. *a sail*, mly in the plur., 1, 480; sing., 15, 627. Od. 2,427. The sails were commonly of linen (also called σπεῖρα). They were attached to the mast by yards. They were hoisted (τετανύναι, ἀναπετανύναι) in a favorable wind, and furled (στέλλεσθαι) in an unfavorable, 1, 433. Od. 3, 11.

ἱστοδόκη, ἡ (δέχομαι), *the receptacle of the mast*, the place in which it was stowed when lowered [its *crutch*, Cp.], 1, 434.†

ἱστοπέδη, ἡ (πέδη), *the mast-stay*, a transverse piece of timber, in which the mast of a vessel was fixed, *Od. 12, 51. 162.

ἱστός, ὁ (ἵστημι), 1) *the mast*, which stood in the middle of the ship, and was attached by two ropes (πρότονοι) to the bows and stern of the ship. The mast was taken down, and lay in the ship when at anchor, 1, 434; at departure it was raised (ἀείρειν, στήσασθαι), Od. 2, 424. 9, 77. 2) *a loom-beam*, the beam upon which the warp was drawn up perpendicularly, so that the threads hung down, instead of lying horizontally upon the warp-beam as with us; hence ἱστὸν στήσασθαι, to put up the loom-beam. Od. 2, 94. ἱστὸν ἐποίχεσθαι, to go around the loom in order to weave; for the weaver sat not before it, as with us, but went around, 1, 31. Od. 5, 62. This kind of weaving is still in partial use in India. 3) *the warp* itself, and generally *the web*. ἱστὸν ὑφαίνειν, 3, 125. Od. 2, 104. 109.

ἴστω, imperat. see ΕΙΔΩ, B.

ἴστωρ, ορος, ὁ (εἰδέναι), one who is intelligent, one who knows: esply like cognitor, *an umpire*. ἐπ' ἴστορι, before the judge, or rather witness (μάρτυρ ἢ κριτῇ, Schol.), *18, 501. 23, 486. ἴστωρ stands in ed. Heyne, and in h. 32, 2, ed. Wolf. The derivation favours the spiritus lenis.

ἰσχαλέος, η, ον, poet. for ἰσχνός, *dry, dried*, Od. 19, 233.†

ἰσχανάω, Ep. form of ἴσχω; ἰσχανάᾳ, ἰσχανόωσιν, Ep. for ἰσχανᾷ, ἰσχανῶσιν, Ep. iterat. imperf. ἰσχανάασκον, 1) Act. *to hold, to hold back*, with accus., 5, 89. 15, 723. 2) *to attach oneself to, to strive after, to be eager for*, with gen. δρόμου, φιλότητος, 23, 300. Od. 8, 288; and with infin. 17, 572. II) Mid. *to check oneself, to delay, to tarry*, ἐπὶ νηυσίν, 12, 38. Od. 7, 161. (Only pres. and imperf.)

ἰσχάνω, poet. form from ἴσχω = ἰσχανάω, *to hold, to hold back, to hinder*, with accus., 14, 387. 17, 747. Od. 19, 42 ; see κατισχάνω, h. 6, 13.

ἰσχίον, τό, 1) Prop. *the hip-joint, the hip-pan*, i. e. the cavity in the hip-bone in which the head of the thigh-bone

(μηρός) turns, 5, 305. 2) Mly *the hip, the loins*, exply the upper part, 11, 339. Od. 17, 234; plur. 8, 340. (Prob. from ἰσχύς, akin to ἰξύς.)

*Ἴσχυς. νος, ὁ, son of Elatus, the lover of Corōnis, h Ap. 210.

ἰσχύω (ἰσχύς), fut. ὕσω, *to be strong, to be able*, Batr. 280.

ἴσχω, poet. form of ἔχω, only pres. and imperf. chiefly in the signif.: 1) *to hold, to hold fast, to hold back*, τινά, 5, 812; ἵππους, 15, 546; metaph. θυμόν, to restrain the spirit, 9, 256; σθένος, 9, 352. II) Mid. *to hold oneself, to restrain oneself*, 2, 247; restrain yourself, i. e. be silent, Od. 11, 251. b) With gen. *to restrain oneself* from a thing, *to cease*, λώβης, πτολέμου, Od. 18, 347. 24, 531.

ἰτέη, ἡ, Ion. for ἰτέα, *willow*, 21, 350 ; *salix alba*, the common ozier, Od. 10, 510.

ἴτην, imperf. of εἶμι.

Ἴτυλος, ὁ, son of Zethus and Aëdon, whom his mother killed in a fit of frenzy, Od. 19, 522; cf. Ἀηδών.

Ἰτυμονεύς, ῆος, ὁ, son of Hyperōchus in Elis, who abstracted from Nestor a part of his herds, and was slain by him, 11, 671, seq.

ἴτυς, νος, ἡ, prop. any circle; in H. the *circumference* or *periphery* of a wheel, made of felloes of wood, 4, 486. 5, 724. (Prob. from ἰτέα.)

ἴτω, see εἶμι.

Ἴτων, ωνος, ἡ (ῑ), a town in Larissa, in Phthiö is (Thessaly), with a temple of Athēnê, 2, 696. Ἴτωνος, ὁ, Strab.

ἰυγμός. ὁ (ἰύζω), *a cry, a cry of joy, a shout*, 18, 572.†

ἰύζω (ῑ), *to shout for joy, to cry aloud*; in H. to terrify an animal by loud crying and shrieking, 17. 66. Od. 15, 162.

Ἰφεύς, ῆος, ὁ (ῑ), see Ἴφις.

Ἰφθίμη ἡ, daughter of Icarius and sister of Penelopê, wife of Eumēlus of Pherae, Od. 4, 797.

ἴφθιμος, η, ον and ος, ον, 1) *highly honoured. greatly lauded*, and generally, *active, lively, noble*, 5, 415 ; spoken of women, ἄλοχος, 19, 116. Od. 10,106. (Prob. from ἴφι and τιμή, greatly lauded. Schol.; so Wolf and Thiersch.) Hence, 2) *to be honored for one's strength, might, &c., strong, brave, mighty, powerful*, prim. as epith. of heroes possessing physical power, hence also spoken of head and shoulders, 3, 336. 11, 55.

ἴφι, adv. (prob. an old dat. from ἴς), *strongly, powerfully, with might, with power*, ἀνάσσειν, μάχεσθαι, 1, 38. 2, 720 ; δαμῆναι, Od. 18, 156.

Ἰφιάνασσα, ἡ (ῑ, ruling with power), daughter of Agamemnon and Klytaemnêstra (Clytaemnestra), called in the tragic writers Ἰφιγένεια, 9, 145.

Ἰφιδάμας, αντος. ὁ (ῑ), son of Antênor and Theāno, who was educated in Thrace with his grandfather Cisseus, 11, 221.

Ἰφικλήειος, η, ον, Ep. for Ἰφικλεῖος,

pertaining to Iphiclus. ἡ βίη Ἰφικληείη, Od. 11, 290.

Ἴφικλος, ὁ (ῑ in the beginning), son of Phylacus, from Phylacē in Thessaly, father of Protesilaus and Podarces, noted as a runner. His noble herds of cattle were demanded by Neleus of Bias as a price for his daughter of Pero, 2, 705. 23, 636. Od. 11, 289, seq. Cf. Βίας.

Ἰφιμέδεια, ἡ (ῑ in the beginning), daughter of Triops, wife of Alōeus, mother of Otus and Ephialtes by Poseidōn, Od. 11, 305 (from μέδομαι, the mighty ruler).

Ἰφίνοος, ὁ (the first ι long) son of Dexius, a Greek, slain by the Lycian, Glaucus, 7, 14.

Ἶφις, ιος, ὁ (not Ἰφεύς), accus. Ἶφεα, a Trojan, slain by Patroclus, 16, 417; see Buttm. Gr. Gram. § 51. Rem. 1. p. 192.

Ἶφις, ιος, ἡ, daughter of Enyeus, a slave of Patroclus, 9, 667.

ἴφιος, η, ον (ἶφι), or ἶφις, ἶφι, *strong,* esply *robust, fat, fatted,* only ἴφια μῆλα, 5, 556. Od. 11, 108 (the first ι long).

Ἰφιτίδης, ὁ, son of Iphitus = *Archeptolemus,* 8, 128.

Ἰφιτίων, ωνος, ὁ (ῑ in the beginning), son of Otrynteus of Hydē, slain by Achilles, 20, 382. (From τίω, avenging powerfully.)

Ἴφιτος, ὁ (ῑ in the beginning) 1) son of Eurytus, from Œchalia, brother of Iolē, an Argonaut. On the journey, when he was seeking the mares which had been concealed by Hēraclēs, he gave his bow to Odysseus (Ulysses), in Messenia. When he found them with Hēraclēs, he was slain by him, Od. 21, 14, seq. 2) son of Naubŏlus, an Argonaut of Phocis, father of Schedius and Epistrŏphus, 2, 518. 17, 306. 3) father of Archeptolemus, 8, 128.

ἰχθυάω (ἰχθύς), Ep. iterat. form, imperf. ἰχθυάασκον, Od. 4, 368; *to fish, to take fish,* *Od. 12, 95.

ἰχθυόεις, εσσα, εν (ἰχθύς), *fishy, abounding in fish,* epith. of the sea, and of Hyllus, 9, 4. 360. 20, 392; κέλευθα, Od. 3, 177.

ἰχθῦς, ύος, ὁ, nom. and accus. plur. ἰχθύες, ἰχθύας, contr. ἰχθῦς, Od. 5, 53. 12, 331; *a fish;* taking fish in nets was already customary, Od. 22, 384, seq. (υ in nom. and accus. sing. long, 21, 127; elsewhere short.)

*ἰχναῖος, αίη, αῖον (ἴχνος), *tracing, tracking,* epith. of Themis, who traces out the actions of men, h. in Ap. 94. According to the Gram. from the town *Ichnæ* in Thessaly, where she had a temple. The last derivation Herm. ad loc. prefers.

ἴχνιον, τό (prop. dimin. of ἴχνος), *a trace, a track, a footstep,* 18, 321. h. Merc. 220. μετ᾽ ἴχνιά τινος βαίνειν, to follow a man's steps, Od. 2, 406; tracks, Od. 19, 436. 2) Generally, *gait, movement,* 13, 71.

ἴχνος, τό, *a track, a footstep, a trace,* Od. 17, 317.†

ἰχώρ, ῶρος, ὁ, accus. ἰχῶ, Ep. for ἰχῶρα (Kühner, § 266, 1. Buttm. § 56, note 6, e); *ichor,* the blood of the gods,—a humour similar to blood, and which supplies its place in the gods, *5, 340. 416.

ἴψ, ἰπός, ὁ, nom. plur. ἶπες (ἴπτομαι), an insect which gnaws horn and vines, Od. 21, 395.†

ἴψαο, see ἴπτομαι.

ἰωγή, ἡ, *a shelter, a protection.* Βορέω, against the north wind, Od. 14, 533; † see ἐπιωγαί.

ἰωή, ἡ (ἰά, ῑ), *a call, a voice,* spoken of men, 10, 139; and generally. *clamour, noise,* of the lyre and the wind, Od. 17, 261. Il 4, 276; of fire, 16, 127.

ἰῶκα, see ἰωκή.

ἰωκή, ἡ (from δίω and διώκω), metaplast. accus. ἰῶκα, as if from ἰώξ, 11, 601; † prop. *pursuit in battle;* and generally, *the tumult of battle, the noise of battle,* plur., 5, 521. 2) Ἰωκή, personified, like Ἔρις, *5, 740.

ἰωχμός, ὁ (ἰωκή), *pursuit, the tumult of battle,* *8, 89. 158.

K.

K, the tenth letter of the Greek alphabet, and the sign of the tenth book.

κάββαλε, Ep. for κατέβαλε, see καταβάλλω.

Καβησός, ἡ, a town in Thrace on the Hellespont, or in Lycia, from which is Καβησόθεν, from K. (ἔνδον refers to Troy), 13, 363.

κάγ, Ep. for κατ᾽ before γ; κὰγ γόνυ, for κατὰ γόνυ (accord. to Bothe, καγγόνυ), 20, 458.†

κάκκανος, ον (καίω with a kind of redupl.), *that may be burned, dry,* ξύλα, 21, 364. Od. 18, 308. h. Merc. 136.

καγχαλάω (Ep. prts. καγχαλόωσι, καγχαλόων for καγχαλῶσι, καγχαλῶν), *to laugh aloud, to rejoice,* 6, 514. Od. 23, 1. 59; to laugh to scorn, 3, 43. (From ΧΑΩ, χαλάω, *cachinnor.*)

κἀγώ, contr. from καὶ ἐγώ, 21, 108; † yet rejected by Spitzner.

κάδ. Ep. for κατά before δ, e. g. κὰδ δέ, κὰδ δώματα, Od. 4, 72.

καδδραθέτην, see καταδαρθάνω.

καδδῦσαι, see καταδύω.

Καδμεῖος, η, ον (Κάδμος), *derived from Cadmus, Cadmēan,* in Hom. plur. οἱ Καδμεῖοι, the inhabitants of the citadel Cadmeia, i. e. the Thebans, 4, 391. Od. 11, 276.

Καδμείων, ωνος, ὁ = Καδμεῖος, 4, 385. 5, 804.

*Καδμηΐς, ΐδος, ἡ, peculiar fem. of Καδμεῖος, daughter of Cadmus = Semelē, h. 6, 57.

Κάδμος, ὁ (Herm. *Instruus*), Cadmus, son of the Phœnician king Agēnor.

brother of Eurôpa, husband of Harmonia. In his journeyings in quest of Europa, who had been seduced by Zeus, he came at last to Bœotia, and founded the fortress Cadmeia. H. mentions him only as the father of Ino, Od. 5, 334.

ΚΑΔ, see καίνυμαι.

Κάειρα, ἡ, fem. of Κάρ, *a female Carian*, prob. from the root Κάηρ, 4, 142.†

κατμεναι, see καίω.

καθαιρέω (αἱρέω), fut. ήσω, aor. καθεῖλον, subj. Ep 3 sing. καθέλησι, 1) *to take* (*pull* or *let*) *down*, τί; ἱστία, Od. 9. 149: ζυγόν, 24, 268; ὄσσε θανόντι, *to close the eyes of a corpse*, 11, 453; and in tmesis, Od. 11, 426. 2) Esply *to take down with violence*, *to cast down*, τινά, 21, 327; hence, *to overpower*, *to carry off*, spoken of Fate, Od. 2, 100; metaph. of sleep, Od. 9, 372, 373.

καθαίρω (καθαρός), aor. 1 ἐκάθηρα and Ep. κάθηρα, *to purify*, *to cleanse*, *to wash*, with accus. κρητῆρας, θρόνους, τραπέζας ὕδατι, Od. 20, 152. 22, 439. 453; ῥυπόωντα, Od. 6, 87; trop. κάλλεϊ προσώπατα καθαίρειν, *to adorn with beauty*, see κάλλος, Od. 18, 192. 2) *to bring away by cleansing*, *to wash away*; ἀπὸ χροὸς λύματα, 14, 171; ῥύπα, Od. 6, 93; with double accus. αἱ δ᾽ ἄγε—αἷμα κάθηρον Ἐλθὼν ἐκ βελέων Σαρπηδόνα, 16, 667. In this passage, which is variously explained, place with Spitzner a comma before and after ἐκ βελέων, so that it may signify *extra jactum telorum*. Thus Voss: 'Go, beloved Phœbus, to cleanse, beyond the reach of the enemy's spears, Sarpêdon from his blood.' Instead of Σαρπηδόνα, Aristarchus reads Σαρπηδόνι; Eustath., however, defends the double accus. and compares 1, 236, 237. 18, 345. b) In a religious signif. θείῳ δέπας, *to purify a goblet by fumigation with brimstone*, 16, 228.

καθάλλομαι, depon. mid. (ἄλλομαι), *to leap down*; metaph. *to rush down*, spoken of a tempest, 11, 298.†

καθάπαξ, adv. (ἅπαξ), *once for all, entirely*, Od. 21, 349.†

καθάπτομαι, depon. mid. (ἅπτω), *to touch, to attack*, always τινὰ ἐπέεσσιν, *to approach any one with words*, a) In a good sense: ἐπ. μαλακοῖσίν τινα, *to address any one with kind words*, 1, 582; or μειλιχίοις ἐπ., Od. 24, 393; and Od. 2, 39. 240, seq. b) In a bad signif. ἀντιβίοις ἐπ., *to attack or assail with angry words*, Od. 18, 415. 20, 323; absol. 15, 127. 16, 421. (The dat. depends upon κέκλετο cf. Od. 2, 39.)

καθαρός, ή, όν, *clean, unspotted*, εἵματα, Od. 2) *clean, clear*. ἐν καθαρῷ, subaud. τόπῳ, *in a clear place* (a place free from dead bodies), 8, 491. 10, 199. 3) Metaph. pur-, *blameless*. καθαρῷ θανάτῳ, *by an honorable death*, i. e. not by the halter, Od. 22, 462. Adv. καθαρῶς, *purely*, h. Ap. 121.

καθέζομαι, depon. mid. (ἕζομαι), only pres. and imperf. *to sit down, to sit*, ἐπὶ θρόνου, 1, 536; ἐπὶ λίθοισι, Od. 3, 406; *to sit in council, to hold a session*, Od. 1, 372. 2) *to reside, to dwell*, Od. 6, 295.

καθέηκα, see καθίημι.

καθείατο, see κάθημαι.

καθεῖσα (εἶσα), defect. aor. *to seat, to cause any one to be seated*, τινὰ ἐπὶ θρόνου, 18, 389. 2) *to set down, to place, to cause to remain*, 2, 549. 3, 382; τινὰ σκοπόν, *to place a man as a spy*, Od. 4, 524.

καθέξει, see κατέχω.

καθεύδω, imperf. Ep. καθεῦδον, only pres. and imperf. *to sleep, to rest*, 1, 611; ἐν φιλότητι, Od. 8, 313. According to Eustath. [ἀναπίπτειν ὡς ἐπὶ ὕπνῳ], it signifies in Il. 1, 611, 'to lie down to sleep.' [This, however, is not the necessary sense, since the usual signif. does not conflict with 2, 2, where οὐκ ἔχε νήδυμος ὕπνος forms an antithesis with εὖδον παννύχιοι, cf. Schol. ad Il. 2, 2. Am. Ed.]

καθεψιάομαι, depon. mid. (ἐψιάομαι), *to deride, to mock*, τινός, Od. 19, 372.†

κάθημαι (ἥμαι), imperf. ἐκαθήμην, 3 sing. καθῆστο and ἐκάθητο, h. 6, 14; 3 plur. καθείατο, Ep. for κάθηντο, *to sit down*, παρά τινι, 7, 443; ἐν or ἐπί τινι, 11, 76. 14, 5; esply *to sit at ease, to sit in state, to be throned*, Od. 16, 264.

κάθηρα, see καθαίρω.

καθιδρύω (ἱδρύω), *to seat, to cause to sit*, τινά, Od. 20, 257.†

καθιζάνω (ἱζάνω), *to seat oneself*, θωκόνδε, Od. 5, 3.†

καθίζω (ἵζω), imperf. κάθιζον, once ἐκάθιζον, Od. 16, 408 (Buttm. Lex. p. 122, would read δὲ κάθιζον, aor. ἐκάθισα, part. Ep. καθίσσας, 1) Trans. *to seat, to cause to sit*, with accus. Il.; ἀνδρῶν ἀγοράς, *to constitute, to convoke assemblies of men*, Od. 2, 69; proverbially, καθίζειν τινὰ ἐπ᾽ οὐδεῖ, *to seat any one upon the ground*, i. e. to plunder him of his property, h. Merc. 284; see οὐδας. 2) Intrans. *to seat oneself, to sit*, ἐπί, παρά τινι, 8, 436; and alone, 3, 426. Od. Od. 4, 649.

καθίημι (ἵημι), aor. 1 καθῆκα, inf. aor. 2 καθέμεν, Ep. for καθεῖναι, 1) *to send down, to cast down*, with accus. οἶνον λαυκανίης, *to send or pour wine down the throat*, 24, 642; ἵππους ἐν δίναις, *to sink the horses in the waters*, in order to propitiate the river-god, 21, 132; κεραυνὸν χαμᾶζε, 8, 134 (by tmesis). 2) *to let down, to lower*, ἱστία ἐς νῆας. Od. 11, 72. h. Ap. 503. 481. (On the dual aor. 2 κάθετον, see Buttm. Ausf. Gram. § 53, 3. Rem. 3.)

καθικνέομαι (ἱκνέομαι) only aor. καθικόμην, *to go to, to reach, to arrive at, to touch, to hit*; only metaph.; spoken only of disagreeable things. ἐμὲ καθίκετο πένθος, Od. 1, 342. μάλα πώς με καθίκεο θυμὸν ἐνιπῇ, thou hast exceedingly *touched* (= wounded) my heart by reproach, 14, 104.

καθίστημι (ἵστημι), imperf. pres. Ep. καθίστα, aor. 1 κατέστησα, aor. 1 mid. κατεστησάμην, 1) Only trans. *to put* down, to set down, to put away; with accus. κρητῆρα, the mixer, 9, 202; νῆα, to direct the ship down, i. e. to shore [appelle navem], Od. 12, 185; hence Πύλονδε καταστῆσαί τινα, to convey any one to Pylos (connected with ἐφέσσαι, to put ashore [but Fäsi aft. Schol. to take him on board: a hysteron-proteron]), Od. 13, 274. II) Mid. = ací. to let down, λαῖφος βοεῦσιν, h. Ap. 407.

*καθοπλίζω (ὁπλίζω), to arm; mid. to arm oneself, Batr. 122.

καθοράω (ὁράω), aor. κατεῖδον, part. κατιδών, to look down, ἐξ Ἴδης, 11, 337; with accus. to survey, to inspect any thing, h. Ap. 136. Mid. as depon. ἐπ᾽ αἶαν, 13, 4.

καθύπερθε, and before a vowel καθύπερθεν, adv. (ὕπερθε), 1) from above, down from above, 3, 337; with gen. Od. 8, 279. 2) above, over, 2, 754. λαοῖσιν καθύπερθε πεποιθότες, trusting to the men who were above [i. e. on the walls], 12, 153; of the situation of places, 24, 545; with gen. Χίοιο, above Chios, i. e. north of it, Od. 3, 170. 15, 404.

καί, conjunc. and, even, marking connexion or heightened force. I) As a copulative conjunc. καί connects 1) Ideas and sentences of every kind, whilst the enclit. τέ connects only related ideas. 2) τε—καί, as well—as, both — and, shows that the connected ideas stand in close and necessary union; in H. the two words stand together, 1, 7. 17. Od. 3, 414. 3) καί τε, the Lat. atque, annexes something homogeneous and equal (in quantity, &c.): it often points to something special: and indeed, 1, 521. Od. 23, 13. In like manner we have ἠδὲ καί, Od. 1, 240; ἠμέν, ἠδὲ καί, 5, 128. 4) The original enhancing power shows itself, although feebly, in sentences which annex an action quickly following what precedes, ὡς ἄρ᾽ ἔφη, καὶ ἀναΐξας—τίθει. 1, 584. 5) In an anacoluthon καί connects a partcp and a finite verb, ὡς φαμένη, καὶ ἡγήσατο, 22, 247. In like manner in apodosis after temporal conjunctions, καὶ τότε, 1, 478. II) As an enhancing adverb: in the orig. signif. even, also, still, etiam, καί renders a single word or a sentence emphatic. According to the character of the antithesis, the augmenting force may be 1) Strengthening. a) With verbs, substantives, numerals: even. τάχα κεν καὶ ἀναίτιον αἰτιόωτο, he might easily blame even an innocent person, 12, 301. cf. 4, 161. b) Esply, καί with partcp. and adj. forms an antithesis to the main verb of the sentence; in which case it may be translated by although, however. Ἕκτορα, καὶ μεμαῶτα (however impetuous) μάχης σχήσεσθαι ὀΐω, 9, 655. καὶ ἐσσύμενον, 13. 787. 16, 627. c) With compar. still. θεὸς καὶ ἀμείνονας ἵππους δωρήσαιτο, 10, 556. d) With adverbs: καὶ λίην, καὶ μάλα, 13, 237. 19, 408. Od. 1, 46. 2) Diminishing: ἱέμενος καὶ καπνὸν—νοῆσαι, to see if but

the smoke, Od. 1, 58. III) καί in connexion with conjunctions: καὶ γάρ, since indeed, for indeed; καὶ γὰρ δή, for certainly, for really, καὶ — γε, and (indeed); καὶ δέ, and yet, but also; καὶ δή, and now, and certainly; καὶ εἰ, even if; καὶ μέν = καὶ μήν, and certainly, and surely, surely also, 23, 410; also (indeed), Od. 11, 582; καί τοι, and yet, although, etc. [To the above may be added καί as an expletive. κασίγνητος καὶ ὄπατρος, 12, 371; as also the use between numerals, sometimes=or. ἕνα καὶ δύο, 2, 346. cf. Od. 3, 115.]

Καινείδης, ὁ, son of Cæneus=Corönus, 2, 746.

Καινεύς, ῆος, ὁ, son of Elātus, king of the Lapithæ, father of the Argonaut Corönus, 1, 264. (From καίνυμαι, that overpowers.)

*καινός, ή, όν, new, strange, unknown, τέχνη, Batr. 116.

καίνυμαι, poet. depon. (root ΚΑΔ for καίδνυμαι), perf. κέκασμαι, pluperf. ἐκεκάσμην, 1) to excel, τινά, Od. 3, 282. More freq. the perf. and pluperf. in the signif. of the pres. and imperf. κεκάσθαι τινά τινι, to excel a man in any thing, 2, 530. 13, 431. Od 19, 395. Instead of the dat. the infin. stands in Od. 2, 159. 3. 283. 2) Alone with dat. without accus. of pers. to be distinguished in any thing, to be remarkable for any thing, to be adorned with, δόλοισι (for evil wiles renowned), 4, 339. c) With prep. accompanying the pers. and a dat. of the thing, παντοίης ἀρετῆσι ἐν Δαναοῖσι, Od. 4, 725: μετὰ δμωῇσι, Od. 19, 82; ἐπ᾽ ἀνθρώπους, 24, 535. (Others suppose a root ΚΑΖΩ.)

καίπερ, Ep. separated καί περ, except Od. 7, 224; although, however, however much; πέρ takes its place after the emphatic word. καὶ ἀχνύμενοί περ, however grieved they are, 2, 270. 24, 20. καὶ πρὸς δαίμονά περ. 17. 104.

καίριος, η, ον (καιρός), happening at the right time, seasonable, hitting the right place; in H. only in the neut. καίριον, the vital part of the body, where wounds are fatal. ὅθι μάλιστα καίριόν ἐστιν, where the blow is fatal, 8, 84 326. ἐν καιρίῳ, κατὰ καίριον, in a mortal part, 4, 185. 11, 439.

καιρόεις, εσσα, εν, well-woven, close-woven, from καῖρος, the threads which cross the chain or warp in weaving [the woof or filling], Lat. licia. καιροσέων ὀθονέων ἀπολείβεται ὑγρὸν ἔλαιον, Od. 7, 107,† from the close-woven linen flows off the liquid oil, i. e. the linen is wrought so thick that even the penetrating oil flows off; καιροσέων is the reading of Aristarchus, and is, according to the Schol., gen. plur. for καιροεσσῶν, καιροσσῶν, Ion. καιροσέων. Voss translates differently, 'and as the woven linen gleams with the dripping oil,' see Nitzsch ad loc. [Bright as with oil the new-wrought texture shone, Cp]

καιροσέων, see καιρόεις.

καίω, Ep. for κάω, aor. 1 ἔκηα and κῆα, plur. subj. κήομεν for κήωμεν, 3 sing. and plur. optat. κήαι, κήαιεν, infin. κῆαι, in the Od. also κεῖαι, κείομεν, κείαντες, aor. 1 mid. ἐκηάμην, partcp κηάμενος (in the Od. κείαντο, κειάμενος, Od. 16, 2. 23, 51); aor. pass. ἐκάην, infin. Ep. καήμεναι, 1) to kindle, to light up, to set in a blaze, πῦρ, Il. 2) to consume, to burn, μηρία, νεκρούς, Il.; hence pass. to burn, πυραὶ καίοντο, 1, 52. b) to be burnt, Od. 12. 13. II) Mid. only aor. 1, to enkindle for oneself, to kindle, with accus. πῦρ, πυρά, 9, 88. Od. 16, 2. (On the exchange of η and ει, see Buttm. p. 287. Rost. p. 308; Kühner, § 151. A. The forms κήω and κείω are doubtful.)

κάκ, abbreviated κατά before κ; mly κὰκ κεφαλήν, κὰκ κόρυθα, 11, 351. Others, κακκεφαλήν, etc.

κακίζω (κακός), to render bad. 2) Mid. to make oneself bad, to show oneself cowardly, 24, 214.†

κακκεῖαι, see κατακαίω, Od. 11, 74.

κακκείοντες, see κατακείω.

κακκεφαλῆς, see κάκ.

κακκόρυθα, see κάκ.

*κακοδαίμων, ον (δαίμων), wretched, unhappy, miserable, Ep. 14, 21.

κακοείμων, ον, gen. ονος (εἶμα), wretchedly clothed, ill-clad, πτωχοί, Od. 18, 41.†

κακοεργίη, ἡ (κακοεργός), a bad deed, a wicked act, Od. 22, 374.†

κακοεργός, όν, poet. (ἔργον), wicked; γαστήρ, the abominable stomach [=hunger always counsellor of ill. Cp.], Od. 18, 54.†

Κὰκοίλιος, ἡ ('Ίλιος), wretched Ilium, *Od. 19, 260. 23, 19.

*κακομηδής, ές (μῆδος), crafty, deceitful, h. Merc. 389.

κακομήχανος, ον (μηχανή), contriving evil, destructive, 6, 344. 9, 257. Od. 16, 418.

κακόξεινος, ον, Ion. and Ep. for κακόξενος (ξένος), inhospitable, having bad guests. Thus, Τηλέμαχ' οὔτις σεῖο κακοξεινώτερος ἄλλος, no other one has worse guests, is more unfortunate in his guests than thou, Od. 20, 376.†

κακορραφίη, ἡ (ῥάπτω), the machination of evil things, craftiness, treachery, trickery, malice, 15, 16. Od. 12, 26; plur. Od. 2, 236.

κακός, ή, όν, bad, evil, hence 1) Spoken of external qualities of animate and inanimate things: of the external appearance of a person or thing, ugly, homely. κακὸς εἶδος, 10, 316. κακὰ εἵματα, esply of persons, a) In point of rank, mean, vulgar, ignoble, 14, 126. Od. 1, 411. 4, 64. b) bad, worthless, miserable, νομῆες, Od. 17, 246. 2) Of conditions and circumstances: evil, bad, ruinous, injurious, wretched. Κῆρες, δόλος, νύξ, θάνατος, etc. 3) Spoken of the character: bad, mean, wicked; in H. esply of warriors, cowardly. κακὸς καὶ ἀνάλκις, 8, 153. 5, 643 Neut. κακόν and κακά as subst. badness, vileness, misfortune, mi-

sery, wretchedness, evil; spoken of Ares, τυκτὸν κακόν, an unnatural, monstrous evil, 5, 831, see τυκτός; as an exclamation, μέγα κακόν, a great evil (V. 'O shame!'), 11, 404. κακόν τι ποιεῖν, to do some harm, 13, 120. κακὸν or κακὰ ῥέζειν τινά, to do harm to any one, 2, 195. 4, 32; rarely τινί, Od. 14, 289. κακὰ φέρειν τινί, Il. 2, 304; also absol. κακὰ Πριάμῳ for εἰς κακά, to the ruin of Priam, 4, 28. 4) Adv. κακῶς, badly, wickedly, basely, insultingly, e. g. ἀφιέναι τινά, νοστεῖν, 1, 25. 2, 153. It often has a strengthening force. κακῶς ὑπερηνορέοντες, Od. 4, 766. 5) As a compar. in H. a) Regular: κακώτερος, η, ον, 19, 321. κακίων, ον, 9, 601; from which κακίους for κακίονας, Od. 2, 277. Superl. κάκιστος, η, ον, Il. and Od. b) Irregular: χερείων, together with the forms χέρηῐ, χέρηα, etc., χερειότερος, ἥσσων, q. v.

κακότεχνος, ον (τέχνη), practising evil arts, deceitful, wily, 15, 14.

κακότης, ητος, ἡ (κακός), badness, worthlessness, 1) moral vileness, baseness, wickedness, 3, 366. 13, 108. Od. 24, 455; spoken of warriors, cowardice, timidity, Il. 2, 368. 15, 721. 2) evil, harm, misfortune, 10, 71. Od. 3, 175; esply the sufferings of war, Il. 11, 382. 12, 332.

κακοφραδής, ές (φράζομαι), evil-minded, irrational, foolish, 23, 483.†

*κακοφραδίη, ἡ, evil intention, folly, indiscretion, plur. h. Cer. 227.

κακόω (κακός), aor. ἐκάκωσα, perf. pass. κεκάκωμαι, to do badly, to inflict evil upon, to make unhappy, to maltreat, to injure, τινά, 11, 690. Od. 16, 212. κεκακωμένοι ἦμεν, we were in a bad case, 11, 689. κεκακωμένος ἅλμῃ, disfigured by seawater, Od. 6, 137; metaph. μηδὲ γέροντα κάκου (imperat. for κάκοε) κεκακωμένον, do not afflict the afflicted old man, Od. 4, 754.

κάκτανε, see κατακτείνω.

κακώτερος, η, ον, see κακός.

καλάμη, ἡ. 1) a stalk or straw of corn, 19, 222. 2) the stubble (in harvesting only the ears were cut off); hence metaph. the rest, the remnant. ἀλλ' ἔμπης καλάμην γέ σ' ὀΐομαι εἰσορόωντα γιγνώσκειν, but still, I think, that on beholding, even the stubble, thou wilt recognize it, i. e. thou wilt recognize, in my still remaining strength, what I once was, Od. 14, 214. [But mark the stubble, and thou canst not much Misjudge the grain. Cp.]

*Καλαμίνθιος, ὁ (καλαμίνθη), the lover of calamint, a frog's name, Batr. 227.

*κάλαμος, ὁ, a reed, h. Merc. 47.

*καλαμοστεφής, ές (στέφω), crowned with reed, rush-covered; βυρσαί, coria calamis obducta, Batr. 127.

καλαῦροψ, οπος, ἡ, the herdsman's crook, which the herdsmen bore, and threw at the cattle to drive them, 23, 845.

καλέω, infin. Ep. καλήμεναι, 10, 125; fut. καλέσω, Ep. σσ, and καλέω, Od. 4, 532; aor. 1 ἐκάλεσα, Ep. σσ. aor. 1 mid.

L 4

ἐκαλεσάμην. Ep. σσ, perf. pass. κέκλη μαι, pluperf. 3 plur. κεκλήατο, fut. 3 κεκλήσομαι, Ion. iterative imperf. καλέεσκον and καλεσκόμην, I) to call, i. e. (1 to name. to call by name; τινὰ ἐπώνυμον or ἐπίκλησιν, to call one by a surname, 9, 562. 18, 487; hence pass. to be called, to be named, often, 2, 260. 684. 4, 61. ἐμὴ ἄλοχος κεκλήσεαι. h. Ven. 489. 2) to call, to call to; spoken of several, to call together, with accus. τινὰ εἰς ἀγορήν, εἰς Ὄλυμπόν Od. 1. 90. Il. 1, 402; also ἀγορήνδε, θάλαμόνδε οἰκόνδε; with accus. alone, ὅσοι κεκλήατο βουλήν, whosoever had been called to the council, 10, 195; and with infin. to call upon, to require, to challenge, καταβῆναι, 3, 250. 10, 197; to call, to invite to a repast, Od. 4, 532. 11, 187. II) Mid. in the aor. to call to oneself, to summon, 5, 427. h. Ven. 126; τινὰ φωνῇ, 3, 161; λαὸν ἀγορήνδε, 1, 54.

καλήμεναι. see καλέω.

Καλήσιος. ὁ, a comrade and charioteer of Axylus, from Arisbê in Thrace; slain by Diomêdês, 6, 18.

Καλητορίδης, ου, ὁ, son of Calêtor = Aphareus, 13. 541.

καλήτωρ, ορος, ὁ (καλέω), a crier, 24, 577.†

Καλήτωρ, ορος, ὁ (καλέω), pr. n. 1) son of Clytius, a kinsman of Priam, 15, 419. 2) father of Aphareus.

καλλείπω, Ep. for καταλείπω.

Καλλιάνασσα, ἡ, daughter of Nereus and Doris, 18, 46.

Καλλιάνειρα, ἡ, daughter of Nereus, 18, 44.

Καλλίαρος, ἡ, a town in Locris, in Strabo's time destroyed, 2, 531.

καλλιγύναιξ. αικος (γυνή), abounding in beautiful women or virgins, epith. of Hellas [Achaia] and Sparta, only in accus., 2, 683 [3, 75]. Od. 13, 412.

*Καλλιδίκη, ἡ, daughter of Keleos (Celeus) in Eleusis. h. in Cer. 109.

καλλίζωνος, ον (ζώνη), beautifully girdled or [rather having a beautiful girdle, cf. Od. 5, 231], epith. of noble women, 7, 139. Od 23, 147.

*Καλλιθόη, ἡ, daughter of Keleos (Celeus) in Eleusis, h. in Cer. 110.

καλλίθριξ, τριχος (θρίξ) having beautiful hair; epith. of horses: having beautiful manes, 5, 323; epith. of sheep: having beautiful wool, Od. 9, 936. 469.

Καλλικολώνη. ἡ (κολώνη), Mount Beauty, a beautiful hill in the Trojan plain, not far from Troy, on the right side of the Simoeis, 20, 53. 151. Not far from it was the valley Θύμβρη.

καλλίκομος, ον (κόμη), having beautiful hair, having beautiful tresses, epith. of handsome women, 9, 449. Od. 15, 58.

καλλικρήδεμνος, ον (κρήδεμνον), having a beautiful head-band or fillet (beautifully veiled, V.), ἄλοχοι, Od. 4, 623.†

κάλλιμος. ον, poet. for καλός, beautiful, *Od. 4, 130. Il. 529. 640.

κάλλιον, see καλός.

*Καλλιόπη, ἡ (from ὄψ, having a

beautiful voice), the eldest of the nine Muses, later the goddess of Epic song, h. 31, 2.

καλλιπάρηος, ον (παρειά), having fair cheeks, epith. of beautiful women, 1, 143. Od. 15, 123.

κάλλιπε, καλλιπέειν, see καταλείπω.

*καλλιπέδιλος, ον (πέδιλον,) having beautiful sandals, h. Merc. 57.

καλλιπλόκαμος, ον (πλόκαμος), having beautiful locks, having lovely tresses, epith. of fair women, Il. and Od.

καλλιρέεθρος, ον (ῥέεθρον). beautifully flowing, κρήνη, Od. 10, 107.† h. Ap. 240.

καλλίροος, ον, poet. for καλίρροος.

Καλλιρόη, ἡ, poet. for Καλιρρόη, daughter of Oceanus and Tethys, wife of Chrysâôr, h. in Cer. 419.

καλλίρροος, ον, Ep. καλλίροος, Od. 5, 441. 17, 206 (ῥόος), beautifully flowing, epith. of rivers and fountains, 2, 752. 21. 147.

*καλλιστέφανος, ον (στέφανος), beautifully crowned, epith. of Dêmêtêr, h. Cer. 252.

κάλλιστος, η, ον, see καλός.

καλλίσφυρος, ον (σφυρόν), prop. having beautiful ankles or feet, slender-footed, epith. of beautiful women, 9, 557. Od. 5, 333.

καλλίτριχες, see καλλίθριξ.

κάλλιφ' for κατέλιπε. see καταλείπω.

καλλίχορος, ον (χορός), having beautiful dancing-places, or having beautiful plains, Πανοπεύς, Od. 11, 581; Θῆβαι. h. 14, 2; see εὐρύχορος.

[Καλλίχορος. ὁ, a sacred fountain near Eleusis, h. Cer. 273.]

κάλλος, τό (καλός), beauty, both of men and women, 3, 392. 6, 156. Od. 6, 18. 8, 457; spoken of Penelopê, κάλλεϊ μέν οἱ πρῶτα πρόσωπα καλὰ κάθηρεν ἀμβροσίῳ, οἵῳ Ἀφροδίτη χρίεται, Athênê illuminated her lovely countenance with ambrosial beauty, such as Aphroditê adorns herself with, Od. 18, 191. (Here critics take it, unnecessarily, for 'fragrant ointment.' Beauty, as Passow remarks, is in H. something corporeal, which the gods put on and take off from men like a garment, cf. Od. 23, 156. 162.)

*κᾶλον, τό, wood, esply dry wood for burning, h. in Merc. 112.

κᾱλός, ή, όν, compar. καλλίων, superl. κάλλιστος, beautiful. 1) Spoken of the external form both of animals and inanimate objects: beautiful, fascinating, lovely, agreeable, spoken of men, καλός τε μέγας τε, Il.; often of women; of parts of the body, of clothes, arms, furniture, regions, etc.; λιμήν, a beautiful harbour. Od. 6. 263. 2) Of internal quality: beautiful, noble, glorious, excellent; in H. only neut. καλόν ἐστι, it is well. it is becoming. with infin., 9, 615. 17. 19. νῦν δὴ κάλλιον μεταλλῆσαι. now it is more fitting to ask, Od. 3. 69. οὐ μὴν οἱ τόγε κάλλιον, this is by no means well. Il. 24. 52. Od. 7, 159. The neut. sing. καλόν and plur. καλά are often used by

H. as adv. *well, fitly, beautifully*, καλόν, Od. 1, 155. 8, 266; in the Il. καλά, 6, 326. 8, 400. The adv. καλῶς, only Od. 2, 64, see διόλλυμι.

κάλος, ὁ, Att. κάλως, *a rope, a sailrope*, Od. 5, 260;† different from ὑπεραί and πόδες.

κάλπις, ιδος, ἡ, *a vessel for drawing or scooping up water, a pitcher, an urn*, Od. 7, 20.† h. Cer. 207.

*καλύβη, ἡ (καλύπτω), *a shelter, a hut, an harbour*, Batr. 30.

Κάλὔδναι, αἰ νῆσοι, *the Calydnæ islands*, according to Strab. X. p. 489, *the Sporades*, near the island of Cos, which received their name from the larger, afterwards called Καλύμνα, but in earlier times Καλύδνα. Others understood by the word, the two islands Leros and Calymna. According to Demetrius, the island was called Καλύδναι, like Θῆβαι, 2, 677.

Κᾰλὔδών, ῶνος, ἡ, *a very ancient town in Ætolia* on the Evênus, famed on account of the Calydonian boar, 2, 640. 9, 340. 13, 217.

*καλυκῶπις, ιδος, ἡ (ὤψ), *with a florid countenance, having a blooming face*, h. Cer. 420. Ven. 285.

κάλυμμα, ατος, τό (καλύπτω), *an envelopment*; esply the head-covering of the women, *a veil*=καλύπτρη. It is called κυάνεον, dark-coloured, as used in mourning, 24, 93.† It would seem, however, to be more correct to distinguish κάλυμμα from καλύπτρη, and, with Voss, to translate it 'mourning robe,' since it is followed by τοῦ δ᾽ οὔτι μελάντερον ἔπλετο ἔσθος, cf. h. Cer. 42.

κάλυξ, υκος, ἡ, 1) Prop. *an envelope*; hence *a bud*, esply *a flower-bud, a flowercup*, or *calyx*. 2) In H., 18, 401,† as a *female* ornament, perhaps *ear-pendants* in the form of a flower-cup. According to some Gramm. they are the σωληνίσκοι, σύριγγες (Voss, 'hair-pins'); al. small *tubes* to keep the hair in curl [*pipes*, Cp.], cf. h. Ven. 87. 164.

καλύπτρη, ἡ (καλύπτω), *a covering*, esply *a veil*, with which females cover the face upon going out, 22, 406. Od. 5, 232. 10, 543.

καλύπτω, fut. ψω, aor. 1 ἐκάλυψα, Ep. κάλυψα, aor. mid. ἐκαλυψάμην, perf. pass. κεκάλυμμαι, aor. pass. ἐκαλύφθην. 1) *to cover, to envelope, to wrap around*. πέτρον περὶ χεῖρ ἐκάλυψεν, the hand [just] covered the stone, i. e. it was as great as the hand could grasp, 16, 735. Mly constr. τί τινι, to cover something with something, 7, 462. 10, 29; more rarely, τί τινι, to (cover =) *spread* something over any one, 5, 315. 21, 321; ἀμφί τινι and πρόσθε τινός, e. g. σάκος, to hold a shield before any one, 17, 132. 22, 313. Pass. κεκάλυπτο ἦρι, 16, 790. ἀσπίδι κεκαλυμμένος ὤμους, having the shoulders covered with a shield, 16, 360. 2) Metaph. of *death*: τέλος θανάτοιο κάλυψεν αὐτόν, death enveloped him, 5, 553; with double

accus. τὸν δὲ σκότος ὄσσε κάλυψε, 4, 461; and often spoken also of swooning, οἱ ὄσσε νὺξ ἐκάλυψε μέλαινα, 14, 439. Spoken of a mental state, 11, 249. II) Mid. *to envelope oneself* with any thing, *to cover*, τινί; ὀθόνῃσιν, κρηδέμνῳ, 3, 141. 14, 184: with accus. πρόσωπα, h. Ven. 184.

Καλυψώ, οῦς, ἡ (*the concealer*, Occulina. Herm.), *daughter of Atlas*; she dwelt in the island Ogygia, remote from all intercourse with gods or men, Od. 1, 50, 52. She received the shipwrecked Odysseus (Ulysses) into her abode, and wished ever to retain him with her, promising to make him immortal, Od. 7, 244, seq. He spent here seven years, till at last, in the eighth, the gods pitied him, and Hermês was sent by Zeus with the command to Calypso to permit him to return home, Od. 5, 28—31. Unwillingly she obeyed the command of the gods. Odysseus (Ulysses) built a ship under her direction; and, after he was furnished by Calypso with the necessary implements and provisions, he departed with a favorable wind, which the goddess sent after him, Od. 7, 265, seq. 5, 160, seq. According to h. Cer. 422; Hes. Th. 1016, she was a daughter of Oceanus.

Κάλχας, αντος, ὁ, voc. Κάλχαν, son of Thestor, *a famous seer of the Greeks*, who by his art guided the Grecian enterprises before Troy, since he knew the present, the past, and the future, 1, 69—72. 2, 300. 13, 45.

κάμ, Ep. abbrev. κατά before μ. κὰμ μέσσον, 11, 172. κὰμ μέν, Od. 20, 2.

κάμαξ, ακος, ἡ, *a stake, a pole*; *a vine-prop*, to which the vines were bound, 18, 563.†

*καματηρός, ή, όν (κάματος), *wearisome, burdensome*, γῆρας, h. Ven. 247.

κάματος, ὁ, 1) *labour, toil, hardship*, 15, 365. ἄτερ καμάτοιο, Od. 7, 325. 2) *fatigue, weariness, exhaustion*, 4, 230. 13, 711 (see ΑΔΕΩ). Od. 6, 2. 12, 281. πολυάϊξ κάματος, fiercely assailing weariness, or the fatigue of impetuous battle, 5, 811. 3) *labour*, i. e. *the gains of labour*, Od. 14, 417.

κάμε, Ep. for ἔκαμε, see κάμνω.

Κάμειρος, ἡ, *Cameirus*, a town on the western coast of the island of Rhodes, now *Jerachio*, 2, 656.

*κάμινος, ὁ, *an oven* for baking; an oven for burning potters' ware, Ep. Hom. 14.

καμινώ, οῦς, ἡ, connected with γρῆυς, *an old oven-woman*, with the implied notion of loquacity, Od. 18, 27.†

καμμονίη, ἡ (Ep. for καταμονίη), prop. *endurance, perseverance in battle*; the victory thus obtained, *22, 257. 23, 661.

κάμμορος (Ep. for κακόμορος, according to Ap.), *ill-fated, miserable, unfortunate*, *Od. 2, 351. 5, 160.

*καμμῦσαι, see καταμύω.

κάμνω, fut. καμοῦμαι, aor. ἔκαμον

3 sing. κάμε, Ep. subj. κεκάμω with re-dupl., aor. mid. ἐκαμόμην, perf. κέκμηκα, partcp. κεκμηώς, gen. ῶτος, accus. plur. κεκμηότας, 1) Intrans. *to fatigue oneself with labour.* a) *to take pains, to toil, to suffer,* μάλα πολλά, 8, 22. 448; with part. οὐδὲ τόξον δὴν ἔκαμον τανύων, I did not long weary myself in drawing the bow [JN. δὴν τανύων, Fäsi], Od. 21, 426; of works of art, κάμε τεύχων, Il. 2, 101. 7, 220. 8, 195. b) *to become fatigued, to become weary, to become relaxed;* with accus. χεῖρα, in the hand, 2. 389 5, 797; γυῖα, ὦμον, often with a partcp. ἐπὴν κε-κάμω πολεμίζων, after I am fatigued in battle, 1, 168; so κάμνει θέων, ἐλαύνων, he is weary with running, rowing. 4, 244. 7, 5 κεκμηώς, a fatigued person, 6, 261. 11, 802; but οἱ καμόντες, the wearied ones; epith. of the dead who have escaped from their labours, 3, 278 (V. 'those who rest'). Od. 11, 476. According to Buttm , Lex. p. 371, 'the worn out, the *enfeebled*,' as a kind of euphemism for θανόντες, the word presenting, instead of the notion of non-existence, the lowest degree of life short of annihilation. 2) Trans. *to make with toil, to prepare,* with accus esp'ly works of art in brass, μίτρην, 4, 187. 18, 614; νῆας, Od. 9, 126. Mid. *to work upon with pains-taking for oneself, to cultivate,* with accus. νῆσον, Od. 9, 130. 2) *to earn by labour for oneself, to ac-quire,* δουρί τι, Il. 18, 341.

κάμπτω, fut. ψω, aor. ἔκαμψα, *to bend, to curve,* with accus. ἴτυν, 4, 486; esp'ly γόνυ, to bend the knee, in order to rest, 7, 118. 29, 72; γούνατα χεῖράς τε, Od. 5, 453.

καμπύλος, η, ον (κάμπτω). *curved, crooked, bent,* epith. of the bow, chariot and wheel, 5, 97. 231. 722. Od. 9, 156; ἄροτρον, h. Cer. 308.

*κάναστρον, τό (κάνη), a basket made of twisted osier; an earthen vessel, Ep. h. 14, 3.

καναχέω (καναχή), only aor. κανάχησε, *to resound, to make a noise, to rattle, to ring,* spoken of brass, Od. 19, 469.

καναχή, ἡ (καναζω), *noise, sound, rat-tling, ringing:* spoken of brass, 16, 105; of the stamping of mules, Od. 6, 82; of the gnashing of teeth, Il. 19, 365; of the lyre, h. Ap. 185.

καναχίζω = καναχέω, only imperf. *to rattle, to ring, to resound.* κανάχιζε δού-ρατα πύργων βαλλόμενα, the timbers of the towers being hit resounded, 12, 36. (The explanation 'δούρατα ἐπὶ τοὺς πύρ-γους ἀκοντιζόμενα' is contrary to the usus loquendi)

κάνειον, τό, Ep.=κάνεον, Od. 10, 355.†

κάνεον, τό, Ep. κάνειον (κάνη), prop. a *basket* make of twisted reeds; a *reed basket;* generally a *basket, a vessel, a dish* for bread and for the sacred barley in a sacrifice; spoken of brass, 11, 630; and of gold, Od. 10, 355.

καννεύσας, see κατανεύω.

κανών, όνος, ὁ (κάνη), prop. *a reed rod,*

any straight rule for measuring, etc.; in H. 1) κανόνες are two cross-bars (ῥάββοι, Hesych.) on the inside of a shield. The left arm was put through one of these, whilst the left hand grasped the other, when an attack was made upon the enemy; a *handle.* They were made of leather, and also of metal, 8, 193. 13, 407; later, ὄχανα. Others suppose these were two cross-bars to which the τελα-μών was attached, cf. Köpke, Kriegsw. d. Gr. S. 110. 2) A straight piece of wood, or spool, upon which the yarn of the woof was wound, in order to throw it through the warp; Voss, *the shuttle* (it is incorrectly explained as 'the great beam of the loom') ἐπὶ δ' ὤρνυτο δῖος 'Οδυσ-σεὺς "Αγχι μάλ'· ὡς ὅτε τίς τε γυναικὸς εὐζώνοιο Στήθεός ἐστι κανών. 23, 760. Here the gen. στήθεος depends upon ἄγχι, for the sense is, Odysseus (Ulysses) was as near Ajax, as the instrument with which the woof is inserted in the warp is to the breast of the woman. [Bothe sup-poses an hypallage: κανών τις γυναικ. for κανὼν γυναικός τινος.] [Cp. "Near as some cinctured maid Industrious holds the distaff to her breast."]

κάπ, Ep. abbreviated for κατά before π and φ. κὰπ πεδίον, κὰπ φάλαρα, 11, 167. 16, 106.

Καπανεύς, ῆος, ὁ, son of Hipponous and Laodicê. father of Sthenelus, one of the seven princes before Thebes, was killed by lightning as he was mounting the walls, 2, 564.

Καπανηϊάδης, ου, ὁ, and Καπανήϊος υἱός, son of Capaneus=Sthenelus, 5, 108, 109. 4, 367.

κάπετος, ἡ (σκάπτω), *a ditch, a foss* = τάφρος, 15, 356; *a pit, a vault,* 24, 797; and generally *a trench,* *18, 564.

κάπη, ἡ (κάπτω), *a crib, a manger* with the food, 18, 433. Od. 4, 40.

καπνίζω (καπνός), aor. ἐκάπνισα, Ep. σσ, *to make a smoke, to kindle a fire,* 2, 399.†

καπνός, ὁ (ΚΑΠΩ), *smoke, fume,* dis-tinct from κνίσση, 1, 317. Od. 1, 58; the vapour from waves, Od. 12, 219.

κάππεσον, see καταπίπτω.

κάπριος. for κάπρος, 11, 414. 12, 42; and σῦς κάπριος, 11, 293. 17, 282.

κάπρος, ὁ, *a boar, a wild swine.* The male swine was taken as an offering in forming a treaty, 19, 196.

καπύω (ΚΑΠΩ), aor. ἐκάπυσα, Ep. σσ, *to breathe, to breathe forth.* ἀπὸ δὲ ψυχὴν ἐκάπυσσεν, 22, 467.†

Κάπυς, υος, ὁ, son of Assaracus, father of Anchises, 20, 239.

ΚΑΠΩ, see ΚΑΦΩ.

κάρ, Ep. abbrev. κατά before ρ. κὰρ ρόον, 12, 33.

κάρ, according to the Schol. an ancient Ep. abbrev. form for κάρη: hence ἐπὶ κάρ, *upon the head, headlong,* 16, 392.† Later it was written ἐπίκαρ.

κάρ (ᾰ), a word of uncertain signif., prob. an ancient word for θρίξ, in the passage τίω δέ μιν ἐν καρὸς αἴσῃ, I value him equally with a hair, i. e. not at all, 9, 378.† According to Clarke and Heyne, probably of a common origin with ἀκαρής, Hesych. τὸ βραχύ, ὃ οὐδὲ κεῖραι οἷόν γε so that it has yielded a word κάρ (capillus rasus, from κείρω), like the Latin nec hilum or flocci facere. The ancients take it, some for κηρός, like death (cf. 3, 454); some for Καρός, like a' Carian, because the Carians were despised as soldiers. The quantity is at variance with both, and with the last also the state of things when H. lived. [Död. accepts the explanation of the Schol. Ven. = φθείρ, pediculus.]

Κάρ, Κᾶρός, ὁ, a Carian, an inhabitant of Caria, the south-western country in Asia Minor, 2, 867. 10, 428.

Καρδαμύλη, ἡ, a town near Leuctra, in Messenia, which Agamemnon promised to give Achilles as a dowry; now Scardamoula, 9, 150.

καρδίη,ἡ, Ep. κραδίη, the last the common Ep. form; καρδίη only 2, 452. 1) the heart, as a part of the human body, the seat of the circulation of the blood and of life, 10, 94. 13, 282. 2) Metaph. the heart, as the seat of the feelings, desires, impulses, and passions, 1, 225. 395. Od. 4, 293; connected with θυμός, 2, 171. Od. 4, 548. 3) As the seat of the faculty of thought, the soul, the mind, the understanding, 10, 244. 21. 441.

*κάρδοπος, ὁ, a kneeding-trough, a tray, Epigr. 15, 6.

κάρη, τό, Ion. and Ep. for κάρα, gen. κάρητος, καρήατος, dat. κάρητι, καρήατι, accus.κάρη,plur.nom.κάρα, h.Cer.12 (from κάρατα, κάραα), καρήατα, 17, 437; accus. κράατα. Here belong the forms ΚΡΑΣ, gen. κρατός, κράατος, dat. κρατί, κράατι, accus. κράτα, Od. 8, 92; plur. gen. κράτων (more correctly, κρατῶν), dat. κρασί; and from κάρηνον: καρήνου, κάρηνα, καρήνων, see Thiersch, § 197, 55. Rost, Dial. 39; the head, of men and of brutes, κάρη, only nom. and accus., Il. 2, 259. 6, 509; gen. κάρητος, Od. 6, 230; κάρητι, Il. 15, 75.

κάρηας, τό, a later nom., used of Antimachus, probably formed from the Ep. forms καρήατος, καρήατι, καρήατα, see κάρη.

καρηκομάω, only in the pres. partcp. καρηκομόωντες, Ep. for καρηκομόοντες (κομάω), long-haired, epith. of the Achæans, who wore the hair long; opposed to ὄπιθεν κομόωντες, 2, 542.

κάρηνον, τό, Ep. form of κάρη, q. v. 1) the head, καρήνου, h. 7, 12; often in periphr. ἀνδρῶν, ἵππων κάρηνα, 9, 407. 11, 500. νεκύων κάρηνα, Od. 10, 521. 2) Metaph. the top, the summit, of mountains, 1, 44. Od. 1, 102; citadels, the strong-holds of cities, Il. 2, 117. 9, 24.

Κάρησος, ὁ, a river in Mysia, which flowed into the Æsôpus; later Πίτυς,12,20.

καρκαίρω, to shake, to tremble, to quake, 20, 157.†

*καρκίνος, ὁ, a crab, Batr. 301.

Κάρπαθος, ἡ, Ep. Κράπαθος, an island between Crete and Rhodes, in the sea called from it the Carpathian; now Scarpanto, 2, 676. The first form is found in h. Ap. 43.

καρπάλιμος, ον (for ἁρπάλιμος from ἁρπάζω), fleet, rapid, hasty, πόδες, 16, 342. 809. Frequently the adv. καρπαλίμως, quickly, rapidly, hastily.

καρπός, ὁ, 1) fruit, both of trees and of the field, 6, 142. Od. 10, 242. 2) the wrist, the part of the hand near the wrist, 5, 458. 8, 328. Od. 18, 258.

καρρέζουσα, see καταρρέζω.

καρτερόθυμος, ον (θυμός), of strong spirit, steadfast, courageous, epith. of Heracles, Achilles, and the Mysians, 5, 277. 13, 350. Od. 21, 25.

καρτερός, ή, όν (κάρτος), Ep. for κρατερός, strong, mighty, powerful, powerful, for the most part spoken of men and human affairs; chiefly bold, brave, θυμός, 5, 806. καρτεραὶ φάλαγγες, the mighty or brave squadrons, 5, 592. b) Of things: ἔργα, mighty deeds, 5, 757; ὅρκος, 19, 105. Od. 4, 253. ἕλκος, 16, 517.

*καρτερόχειρ, ος, ὁ, strong-handed, powerful, epith. of Arês, h. 7, 3.

κάρτιστος, η, ον, Ep. for κράτιστος superl. from κρατύς or κράτος, the strongest, the mightiest, Il. and Od.

κάρτος, εος, τό, Ep. for κράτος, strength, might, power, 9, 254; and oftener connected with βίη and σθένος, see κράτος.

καρτύνω, Ep. for κρατύνω (κράτος), to make strong; only mid. to strengthen for oneself, always ἐκαρτύναντο φάλαγγας, *11, 215. 12, 415. 16, 563.

*κάρυον, τό, any kind of nut, esply walnut, Batr. 31.

Κάρυστος, ἡ, a city on the southern coast of Eubœa, famed for its marble; now Caristo, 2, 539.

καρφαλέος, η, ον (κάρφω), 1) dry, parched, ᾖα, Od. 5, 369. 2) Metaph. spoken of a sound, dull, hollow, ἀσπὶς καρφαλέον αὖσεν, 13, 409.

κάρφω, fut. κάρψω, aor. κάρψα, to draw together, to wrinkle, to wither; only χρόα, to wrinkle the skin, *Od. 13, 398. 430.

καρχαλέος, η, ον (κάρχαρος), rough, sharp; metaph. δίψῃ, rough (in the throat) from thirst, 21, 541.† (καρφαλέοι is a gloss.)

καρχαρόδους, όδοντος, ὁ, ἡ (ὀδούς), having sharp teeth, κύνες, *10, 360. 13, 198.

κασιγνήτη, ἡ (fem. from κασίγνητος), an own sister, a sister. 4, 441, and often.

κασίγνητος, ὁ (κάσις, γεννάω), 1) a brother, a full, an own brother, ὁπάτρος, 12, 371. 2) Generally a near kinsman, esply the child of a brother or sister, 15, 545. 16, 456. 3) As adj. for κασιγνητικός, πόλλ' ἀκέουσα κασιγνήτοιο φόνοιο, on account of the slaughter of her brothers; for Meleager slew several brothers of Althæa, Apd. 1, 8. 3. The poet, however, might mean Iphiclus, who cor

L 6 ἀνήρ

tested with Meleager the honour of victory; hence Voss, 'on account of the slaughter of an own brother,' 9, 567.

Κάσος, ἡ, an island of the Ægean Sea near Cos. now *Casso*, 2, 676.

Κασσάνδρη, ἡ, daughter of Priam, had received from Apollo the gift of prophecy; but, because she did not return his love, he laid a curse upon her prophecies. She prophesied only misfortune, and no one believed her, 13, 366. After the sack of Troy she became the slave of Agamemnon, and was slain by Klytæmnêstra (Clytæmnestra) in Mycenæ, Od. 11, 420.

κασσίτερος, ὁ, *tin*, plumbum album, different from lead, plumbum nigrum. H. mentions it as an ornament of cuirasses and shields, 11, 25. 34. 18, 565. 575; and of chariots, 23, 503. Also greaves were made of tin, or for ornament coated with tin, 21, 592. 18, 613. According to 18. 474, it was melted and over other metal. χεῦμα κασσιτέροιο, tin-casting, 23, 561. Probably, however, it was also beaten into plates with the hammer, 20, 271, and hence called ἑανός. Beckmann, Geschich. der Erfind. c. 4, 3, considers it the *stannum* of the Romans, a mixture of silver and lead, because soft tin would have afforded no protection in war. (Schneider in his Lex. agrees with this view). *Il.

Κασσιάνειρα, ἡ, *Castianeira*, mother of Gorgythion, 8, 305.

Κάστωρ, ορος, ὁ, son of King Tyndareus and of Leda, or, by mythology, of Zeus, brother of Polydeukês (Pollux) and Helen, 3, 238, famed for his skill in managing horses. According to later mythology, he took part in the Calydonian hunt and in the Argonautic expedition. He was born mortal, and, when he was killed by Idas, Polydeukês (Pollux) shared immortality with him. Alternately they spent a day in the upper and a day in the under world, 3, 237. Od. 11, 209, seq. Mly, Kastôr (Castor) and Polydeukês (Pollux) together are called *Dioscūri*, i. e. sons of Zeus, see Διόσκουροι. 2) *Castor*, son of Hylacus, a fictitious personage, Od. 14, 204.

*καστορνῦσα, see καταστορέννυμι.

κασχέθε, see κατέχω.

κατα, 1) Prep. with gen. and accus., prim. signif. *down from above* 1) With the gen. spoken only of place: *a*) To indicate a downward motion, *down from, down*. βῆ δὲ κατ᾿ Οὐλύμποιο καρήνων, 1, 44. καθ᾿ ἵππων ἆλτο; hence also with the implied notion of extension, *down from above*. κατ᾿ ὀφθαλμῶν κέχυτο νύξ, down over the eyes the night was poured; again, κατ᾿ ἄκρης, prop. from the summit down, i. e. entirely, 13, 772. cf. ἄκρος. *b*) To indicate direction to a place in a lower situation, *down upon, down to, under*. κατὰ χθονὸς ὄμματα πῆξαι, to fasten the eyes upon the ground, 3, 217.

υχὴ κατὰ χθονὸς ᾤχετο, under the earth,

23, 100: and generally of direction to an object, Od 9, 330. 2) With accus. *a*) Spoken of place (here it forms an antithesis with ἀνά, in reference to the commencing-point. but agrees with it in expressing expansion over an object). *a*) To indicate direction to an object, mostly one in a lower situation, *in, upon, into*. βάλλειν κατὰ γαστέρα; in like manner, νύσσειν, οὐτᾶν κατά τι, κατ᾿ ὄσσε ἰδών, looking into the eyes, 17, 167. β) To indicate extension from above downwards, *through, over, along upon*. κατὰ στρατόν, through the army, in the army. κατὰ λαόν, κατὰ γαῖαν. Thus often κατὰ θυμόν, in the heart. *b*) In reference to cause, manner, etc *a*) To denote design, purpose: πλεῖν κατὰ πρῆξιν, on business, Od. 3, 72. κατὰ χρέος ἐλθεῖν, Od. 11, 479. β) To denote suitableness, *according to*, secundum: κατὰ μοῖραν, according to propriety. κατὰ δύναμιν, according to a man's power. γ) To denote the manner, etc. κατα λοπὸν κρομύοιο, after the manner of an onion-skin, Od. 19, 233. κατὰ μέρος, part by part, h. Merc. 53. κατ᾿ ἐμ᾿ αὐτόν. by myself, Il. 1, 271. κατὰ σφέας, by themselves, 2, 366. κατὰ φῦλα, by tribes, 2. 362. II) Adv. without case. κατά as an adv. has the signif. *down, downward, down from above*, 1, 40. 436; again, *fully, utterly, entirely*. κατὰ πάντα φαγεῖν, Od. 3, 315. III) In composition it has the same signif., and often strengthens the notion. IV) κατά may be placed after the subst., and then the accent is retracted: δόμον κάτα. In the poets it is sometimes elided into κατ even before consonants. The accent is retracted and the τ assimilated to the following consonant: κὰδ δύναμιν. Others connect the prep. with the following word: καδδύναμιν

καταβαίνω (βαίνω), fut. καταβήσομαι, aor. 2 κατέβην, from this 1 plur. subj. καταβείομεν. Ep. for καταβῶμεν. aor. 1 mid. κατεβησάμην; also the Ep. forms καταβήσετο and imper. καταβήσεο, 1) *to descend, to come down, to alight*, ἔκ τινος, or with gen. alone, 5, 109; with the question whither, we have ἐς and ἐπί with the accus. 3, 252. 10, 541; or the accus. alone. κατεβήσατο θάλαμον, he descended to the chamber, Od. 2, 337. 2) With accus. *to descend* any thing. κλίμακα κατεβήσατο, he descended, went down, the stairs, Od. 1, 330. ξεστὸν ἐφόλκαιον καταβῆναι, to slide down by the smooth rudder (into the deep), Od. 14, 350; in a similar manner, ὑπερώια κατέβαινε, she descended the upper chamber, i. e. from the chamber, Od. 18, 206. 23, 85.

καταβάλλω (βάλλω), aor. 2 κατέβαλον. Ep. 3 sing. κάββαλε for κατέβαλε, 1) *to cast down, to tear down, to demolish*, with accus., 12, 206; *to dash into*, 15, 357; and κατὰ πρηνὲς βαλέειν μέλαθρον, i. e. καταβαλέειν, to demolish, 2, 414; *to cast upon* the land, Od. 6, 172. 2) *to lay down*, κρεῖον ἐν πυρὸς αὐγῇ. 9, 206. 3)

to cause to fall. 5, 343. 8, 249; hence
of a dog: οὔατα κάββαλεν, he dropt his
ears (on recognizing his master), Od. 17,
302.

καταβείομεν, see καταβαίνω.

καταβήσετο, see καταβαίνω.

*καταβιβρώσκω (βιβρώσκω), aor. 2 κατ-
έβρων, to devour, to consume, h. Ap.
127

*καταβλάπτω (βλάπτω), to hurt, to
injure, with accus. h. Merc. 93.

καταβλώσκω (βλώσκω), only pres. to go
or pass through, with accus. ἄστυ [to
range the city-streets Cp.], Od. 16, 466.

(καταβρόχω), only 3 sing. optat. aor.
act. καταβρόξειε, to swallow, to swallow
down, φάρμακον, Od. 4, 222;† see ἀναβρόχω.

καταγηράσκω and καταγηράω (γηράω),
from which κατεγήρα, to grow old, *Od. 9,
510. 19, 360.

καταγινέω, Ep. form of κατάγω, to bring
down, to convey, to bring, with accus.
ὕλην, Od. 10, 104.†

κατάγνυμι (ἄγνυμι), fut. κατάξω, aor.
κατέαξα, to break, to dash in pieces. with
accus. 8, 403. Od. 9, 283. τὸ κατεάξαμεν,
ὃ πρὶν ἔχεσκον. we broke this (spear)
which I was before accustomed to carry,
13, 257. That the plur. should be used
is surprising, since the sing. follows;
still it may be very well accounted for:
we (Idomeneus and Meriones), says the
latter, broke, in our conflict, the spear
which I used to bear, cf. Spitzner ad
loc.

κατάγω (ἄγω), fut. κατάξω, Ep. infin.
καταξέμεν, aor. act. κατήγαγον, aor. mid.
κατηγαγόμην, 1) to conduct down, to
bring down, with accus. τινὰ εἰς Ἀΐδαο,
Od. 11, 164. 24, 100. 2) Generally, to
lead away, to conduct, for the most part
from a higher to a lower region, as ἴπ-
πους ἐπὶ νῆας, 5, 26. 6, 53. τινὰ Κρήτηνδε,
to drive a man to Crete (of a wind), Od.
19, 186. Mid. to proceed from the high
sea into port, to put into harbour, opposed to ἀνάγεσθαι, spoken of ships, Od.
3, 10; ἐς Γεραιστόν, Od. 3, 178 ; Ἰθάκηνδε,
Od. 16, 322 ; spoken of seamen : νηὶ
κατάγεσθαι, Od. 10, 140.

καταδαίομαι (δαίω), fut. δάσομαι, to
tear in pieces, to devour, only in tmesis,
κατὰ πάντα δάσονται, 22, 354.†

*καταδάκνω (δάκνω), to bite severely,
Batr. 45.

*καταδάμναμαι, depon. mid. (δάμνα-
μαι, poet. for καταδαμάω, to tame, to
subdue, to overpower, h. Merc. 137.

καταδάπτω (δάπτω). aor. κατέδαψα, 1)
to tear in pieces, to lacerate, with accus.
spoken of dogs and birds of prey, 22,
339. Od. 3, 259. 2) Metaph. ἦτορ κατα-
δάπτεται, my (tortured) soul is rent=
wounded, distressed, Od. 16, 92.

καταδαρθάνω (δαρθάνω), aor. κατέδαρ-
θον, poet. κατέδραθον, 3 dual. Ep. καθ-
δραθέτην for κατεδραθέτην, Od. 15, 494;
subj. καταδραθώ, which aor. sometimes
passes into the pass. form ἐδάρθην, Od. 5,

471; only in the Ep. aor. to go to sleep,
to sleep. οὔπω τοιόνδε κατέδραθον, subaud.
ὕπνον, I never slept so soundly, *Od. 23,
18.

καταδέρκομαι, poet. (δέρκομαι), to look
down, τινά, upon any one, Od. 11, 16.†

καταδεύω (δεύω), aor. κατέδευσα, to
wet, to drench, χιτῶνα οἴνου, to deluge
my vest with wine [Cp.], 9, 490.†

καταδέω (δέω), aor. κατέδησα, 1) to
bind, to bind fast, ἵππους ἐπὶ κάπῃ 8,
434. Od. 4, 40 ; ἱστὸν προτόνοισιν, the
mast with ropes, Od. 2, 425. 2) to bind
together, to lock up, to obstruct, with
accus. ἀνέμων κελεύθους, Od 5, 383. 10, 20.

καταδημοβορέω (δημοβόρος), prop. to
consume the property of the people. 2)
to consume in common, 18, 301.†

καταδραθώ, see καταδαρθάνω.

*καταδύνω, a form of καταδύω, h. Merc.
237.

καταδύω (δύω), aor. 2 κατέδυν, partcp.
καταδύς, nom. plur. fem. καδδῦσαι for
καταδῦσαι, 19, 25 ; fut. mid. καταδύσο-
μαι. aor. 1 mid. κατεδυσάμην, with the
Ep. form καταδύσεο, only in an intrans.
signif. 1) to descend into, to go into, to
penetrate, εἰς Ἀΐδαο δόμους, Od. 10, 174 ;
κατὰ ὠτειλάς, to enter into the wounds,
Il. 19, 25 ; with accus. δόμον, to go into
a house; πόλιν, Od. 4, 246; often ὅμιλον, Il. 4, 86. 10, 517 ; in like manner
μάχην, μῶλον Ἄρηος, 18, 134. 2) to put
on, spoken of arms, τεύχεα. 7, 103. 3)
Absol. to set, to go down, spoken of the
sun. ἠέλιος κατέδυ, 1, 475. 592, and
often.

καταειμένος, η. ον, see καταέννυμι.

καταείνυον, see καταέννυμι.

καταείσατο, see κάτειμι.

καταέννυμι, poet. for καθέννυμι (ἕννυμι), imperf. καταείνυον, 23, 135 (as if
from εἰνύω); perf. pass κατειμένος, to
clothe, to cover. with accus. νέκυν, 23,
135; metaph. ὄρος καταειμένον ὕλῃ, a
mountain clothed with wood, Od. 13,
351. 19, 431.

καταζαίνω (ἀζαίνω), to wither up, to
cause to dry, with accus. Ep. iterat. aor.
καταζήνασκε, Od. 11, 587.†

καταθάπτω (θάπτω), aor. 1 infin. κατθάψαι, Ep. for καταθάψαι, 24, 611 ; to
bury, to inter. τινά, *19, 228.

καταθείομαι, καταθείομεν, see κατατίθημι.

καταθέλγω (θέλγω), aor. 1 κατέθελξα,
to charm, to transform, spoken of Circe
[Kirkê], who metamorphosed the companions of Odysseus (Ulysses) into brutes,
Od. 10, 213.† cf. θέλγω.

καταθνήσκω (θνήσκω), aor. κατέθανον,
Ep. κάτθανε, perf. κατατέθνηκα, infin.
κατατεθνάναι, Ep. κατατεθνάμεν, partcp.
κατατεθνηώς. to die, to expire, to decease;
chiefly the partcp. perf. dead, deceased.
ἀνήρ, 7, 89; plur. νεκροί and νέκυες κατατεθνηῶτες (the dead, the slain; the corpses
of the slain). 7, 409. Od. 22, 448.

καταθνητός, ή, όν (θνητός), mortal, ἀνήρ
and ἄνθρωπος, 6, 123. Od. 3, 114.

καταθρώσκω (θρώσκω), only in tmesis, κὰδ δ᾽ ἔθορε, to leap down, 4, 79. h. Cer. 28.

καταθύμιος, ον (θυμός), lying in the mind, in the heart. μηδέ τί τοι θάνατος καταθύμιος ἔστω, let not death come into thy mind, i. e. entertain no thought of it [Cp.], 10, 383. 17, 201. ἔπος, τό μοι καταθύμιόν ἐστιν, (such) order as is in my mind, as my mind suggests. Others (aft Eust., τὸ κατὰ νοῦν νόημα), transl. it according to my mind, as I wish, Od. 22, 392. [Cf. Jahr. Jahn und K. p. 269, where the last signif. is rejected.]

καταϊάπτω see ιάπτω.

καταιβατός, ή, όν. poet. καταβατός (βαίνω), descending, leading downwards, θύραι καταιβαταὶ ἀνθρώποισιν, doors, by which men descend, Od. 13, 110.†

καταικίζω (αἰκίζω), perf. pass. κατήκισμαι, to abuse, to disfigure, τεύχεα κατήκισται (by smoke and dirt), *Od. 16, 290. 19, 9.

καταισχύνω (αἰσχύνω), to shame, to insult, to disgrace, to dishonour, πατέρων γένος. Od. 24, 508. 512; δαῖτα, *Od. 16, 293.

καταΐσχω, poet. for κατίσχω=κατέχω: οὔτ᾽ ἄρα ποίμνῃσιν καταΐσχεται, it (the island) was not inhabited by shepherds, *Od. 9, 122.†

καταῖτυξ, υγος, ἡ. a head-piece, a low, light helmet [or casque, Cp.], without a cone or crest, 10, 258. (Prob. from κατά and τεύχω.)†

κατακαίω (καίω), infin. pres. κατακαιέμεν (κατακηέμεν ed. Wolf), 7, 408; aor. 1 κατέκηα, su j. 1 plur. Ep. κατακήομεν, infin. aor. κατακεῖαι, Od. 10, 533; Ep. κακκεῖαι, Od. 11, 74; aor. 2 pass. κατεκάην, to burn up, to consume, with accus. of victims and of the dead, Il. 1, 40. 6, 418. In the pass. intrans. κατὰ πῦρ ἐκάη, the fire burnt down [tne flame declined. Cp.], 9, 212. The infin. pres. κατακηέμεν or κατακειέμεν is doubtful, for which reason Spitzner has adopted κατακαιέμεν, see Thiersch, § 213, 38. Buttm, p. 287. Cf. καίω.

κατακαλύπτω (καλύπτω), aor. κατεκάλυψα, only in tmesis, to envelope entirely, to cover, with the accus. μηρούς κνίσῃ, to wrap the thigh-bones with fat, 1, 460. 2, 423. Od 3, 464.

κατακεῖαι, see κατακαίω.

κατακειέμεν or κατακηέμεν, see κατακαίω.

κατάκειμαι, depon. mid. (κεῖμαι), to lie down, to lay oneself down, 17, 677; metaph. to rest: ἄλγεα ἐν θυμῷ κατακεῖσθαι ἐάσομεν, we will permit the pangs to rest in the mind, 24, 523. 2) to lie, to be in store, 24, 527. Od. 19, 439.

κατακείρω (κείρω), prop. to cut off; hence to consume, to plunder, βίοτον, οἶκον, *Od. 4, 686. 22, 36; μῆλα, *Od. 23, 356.

κατακείω (κείω), partcp. κακκείοντες, Ep. for κατακείοντες, desider., to desire to lie down, to go to rest, 1, 606. Od. 1, 424 (see κείω).

κατακήομεν, see κατακαίω.

κατακλάω (κλάω), aor. 1 pass. κατεκλάσθην, to break in pieces, to break, with accus. 13, 608. 20, 227; metaph. ἔμοιγε κατεκλάσθη ἦτορ, my heart was broken, i e. overcome, distressed, Od. 4, 481. 9, 256.

κατακλίνω (κλίνω), aor. κατέκλινα, to bend down, to lay down, δόρυ ἐπὶ γαίῃ, Od. 10. 165.†

Κατακλῶθες, αἱ (κατακλώθω), according to Eustath. metaplast. plur. for Κατακλωθοί, from Κλωθώ, prop. the spinners, for the Parcæ, the Fates, Od. 7, 197.† πείσεται, ἅσσα οἱ Αἶσα Κατακλῶθές τε βαρεῖαι Γεινομένῳ νήσαντο, which Fate and the inexorable sisters spun for him. Plainly the Cataclothes are here annexed to Aisa, as the special to the generic, although we cannot refer them to the three post-Homeric Moiræ. The figurative expression to spin is current in H., see ἐπικλώθω. The other reading, καταλώθῃσι βαρεία, must be rejected, see Nitzsch ad loc.

κατακοιμάω (κοιμάω), only aor. pass. κατεκοιμήθην, to put to sleep. Pass. to go to sleep, to rest, παρά τινι, 2, 355. 9, 427; ἐν ἔτεσιν, *11, 730.

κατακοσμέω (κοσμέω), 1) to adjust, to put aright, with accus. ὀϊστὸν ἐπὶ νευρῇ, 4, 118. 2) Mid. to put in order, δόμον, Od. 22, 440.

κατακρεμάννυμι (κρεμάννυμι), aor. κατεκρέμασα, to hang up, to suspend, φόρμιγγα. Od. 8, 67; τόξα, h. 27, 16.

κατάκρηθεν, adv. according to Aristarch. κατὰ κρῆθεν, from above, down from the head, Od. 11. 588. h. Cer. 182, metaph. from the top to the bottom, entirely, thoroughly. Τρῶας κατάκρηθεν λάβε πένθος, grief took complete possession of the Trojans, 16, 548. (Prob. from κάρη, κάρηθεν, syncop. κρῆθεν, which is found as an Ep. gen. in Hes. sc. 7, on which account it is better written separately; others say from κατά and ἄκρηθεν, see Spitzner ad Il. 16, 548.)

*κατακρημνάω (κρημνάω), to hang down (trans.), only mid. to hang down (intrans.), κατεκρημνῶντο βότρυες, h. 6, 39.

*κατάκρημνος, ον (κρημνός), precipitous, steep, Batr. 154.

κατακρύπτω (κρύπτω), fut. ψω, to conceal, to hide, to dissemble. τί, 22, 120. οὔτι κατακρύπτουσιν, they (the gods) conceal nothing from him, Od. 7, 205; apparently intrans.: ἄλλῳ δ᾽ αὐτὸν (for ἑαυτὸν) φωτὶ κατακρύπτων ἤϊσκεν, disguising he made himself like another man, (αὐτόν is to be referred to both verbs,) Od. 4, 247.

κατακτάμεν and κατακτάμεναι, see κατακτείνω.

κατακτάς, see κατακτείνω.

κατακτείνω (κτείνω), fut. act. κατακτενῶ, 23, 412; κατακτανέω, Ep. for κτανῶ. 6, 409; aor. 1 κατέκτεινα, aor. 2 κατέκτανον, imperat. κάκτανε, Ep. for κατάκτανε, 6, 164; also the Ep. aor. κατέκταν, infin.

κατακτάμεν and κατακτάμεναι. partcp. κατακτάς, aor. 1 pass. κατεκτάθην, fut. mid. κατακτανέομαι, with pass. signif.—to kill, to slay, to slaughter, τινά ; ὧδε κατακτανέεσθε καὶ ὔμμες, thus will you also be slain, 14, 481 ; κατέκταθεν, Ep. for κατεκτάθησαν, Il. and Od.

κατακύπτω (κύπτω), aor. κατέκυφα, to stoop (bend or bow) the head forward, *16, 611. 17, 527.

καταλαμβάνω (λαμβάνω), to take possession of, to seize, only in tmesis, see λαμβάνω.

καταλέγω, Ep. (λέγω), fut. καταλέξω, aor. 1 κατέλεξα, fut. mid. καταλέξομαι, aor. 1 κατελεξάμην and Ep. aor. syncop. 3 sing. κατέλεκτο, infin. καταλέχθαι, Od. 15, 304 ; partcp. καταλέγμενος, prim. to lay down. I) Act. to lay down, to tell, to relate, to recount, τί τινι, often with ἀτρεκέως and εὖ, 9, 115. 10, 413 ; καταλέξαι τινά, to relate of any one, Od. 4, 831. II) Mid. to lay oneself down, to lie, to rest, 9, 662. Od. 3, 353. (On the deriv. see λέγω.)

καταλείβω (λείβω), to pour down. Mid. to drop down, to trickle down, 18, 109.†

καταλείπω, and Ep. καλλείπω (λείπω), fut. καταλείψω, Ep. καλλείψω, aor. 2 κατέλιπον, Ep. 3 sing. κάλλιπε and κάλλιφ', 6, 223 ; infin. καλλιπέειν, Od. 16, 296 ; 1) to leave, with accus. Il. 6, 223 ; of battle, 12, 226. Od. 13, 208. 2) to leave behind, to leave, spoken esply of persons dying and departing on a journey, τινὰ χήρην, 24, 726 ; εὐχωλήν τινι, to leave an oject of desire to any one, 4, 173 ; τινὶ ὀδύνας, Od. 1, 243. 3) to abandon, to give up, τινά, with infin. ἔλωρ γενέσθαι. 17, 151. Od. 3, 271.

καταλέω (ἀλέω), aor. κατήλεσα, Ep. σσ, to grind, τί, in tmesis, Od. 20, 109.†

καταλήθομαι (λήθομαι), Ep. for λανθάνομαι), to forget entirely, 22, 389.†

κατελλοφάδια, adv. (λόφος), on the neck, φέρειν, Od. 10, 169.† (a and ι are Ep. used as long.)

καταλύω (λύω), fut. καταλύσω, aor. 1 κατέλυσα, to dissolve ; hence, 1) to destroy, to demolish, πολέων κάρηνα, 2, 117. 9, 74. 2) to loose, to unyoke, ἵππους, Od. 4, 28.

καταλωφάω (λωφάω), to rest (from), to become free, τινός ; κὰδ δέ κ' ἐμὸν κῆρ λωφήσειε κακῶν [would lighter feel my wrong. Cp.], only in tmesis, Od. 9, 460.† cf. λωφάω.

καταμάρπτω (μάρπτω), aor. 1 κατέμαρψα, to seize, to overtake, to lay hold of, τινά, 5, 65. 16, 598 ; metaph. spoken of age, Od. 24, 390.

καταμάω (ἀμάω), only aor. 1 mid. καταμησάμην, to amass, to heap up, κόπρον, 24, 165.†

καταμίγνυμι and καταμίσγω (μίγνυμι), to mingle ; καμμίξας, 24, 529 ; for which Wolf has adopted κ' ἀμμίξας. Mid. to mingle themselves, h. 18, 26.

καταμύσσω (ἀμύσσω), aor. 1 mid. καταμυξάμην Ep. for κατήμ., to lacerate, to

scratch. Mid. to scratch oneself, χεῖρα, to scratch one's hand, 5, 425.†

*καταμύω, Ep. καμμύω (μύω), aor. Ep. infin. καμμῦσαι, to close the eyes, to sleep, Batr. 192.

κατανεύω (νεύω), fut. (once, 1, 524), κατανεύσομαι, aor. 1 κατένευσα, partcp. καννύσας, Ep. for κατανεύσας, to nod, to beckon, κεφαλῇ or κρατί, with the head, i. e. to assent, to grant, τινί τι, any thing to any one ; νίκην, κῦδος, 8, 175 ; with the infin. 2, 112. 10, 393.

κατάνομαι, Ep. for κατανύομαι (ἄνω), only pass. πολλὰ κατάνεται, much is finished, i. e. much is destroyed, consumed, *Od. 2, 58. 17, 537.

κάταντα, adv. (κατάντης), downwards, 23, 116.†

κατάντηστιν, adv. (ἀντάω), opposite, Od. 20, 387.† ed. Wolf, where others read κατ' ἄντηστιν or ἄντησιν According to Eustath. from κατάντητος with epenth. σ, as in προμνηστῖνοι.

καταντικρύ, adv. (ἀντικρύ), directly down, with gen. τέγεος, *Od.10, 539. 11, 64.

καταπάλλω (πάλλω), Ep. aor. sync. mid. κατέπαλτο, to hurl down. Pass. to hurl oneself down, to leap down, to descend, οὐρανοῦ ἐκ, 19, 351.† (The Schol. explain it: καθήλατο, and write κατέπαλτο, as if from κατεφάλλεσθαι), cf. πάλλω.

καταπατέω (πατέω), aor. κατεπάτησα, to tread down, to trample under foot, i. e. to despise, with accus. ὅρκια, in tmesis, 4, 157.†

κατάπαυμα, τό (καταπαύω), cessation, rest, alleviation. quiet, γόου, 17, 38.†

καταπαύω (παύω), fut. σω, aor. κατέπαυσα. 1) to cause to cease, to stop, to end, with accus. πόλεμον, 7, 36 ; μηνιθμόν, 16, 62 ; to appease, χόλον θεῶν, Od. 4, 583. 2) Spoken of persons : τινά, to stop any one, to check, to restrain, 16, 618. Od. 2, 618. ἡμέας ὀτρύνων καταπαυέμεν (Ep. infin.), Od. 2, 244 (construct : ὀτρ. [sc. Ἰθακησίους] ἡμ. κατ. exhorting [the people] to restrain us ; to put an end to our proceedings ;) τινά τινος, to restrain a man from any thing ; ἀγηνορίης, 22, 457 ; ἀφροσυνάων, Od. 24, 457.

καταπεδάω (πεδάω), aor. κατεπέδησα, prop. to bind with foot fetters ; hence, to fetter, to bind, τινά, only in tmesis, 19, 94. Od. 11, 292 ; see πεδάω.

καταπέσσω (πέσσω), aor. κατέπεψα, to boil down, to digest, with accus. χόλον, to restrain anger (V. to check), 1, 81.†

καταπετάννυμι (πετάννυμι), to spread over, to cover, only in tmesis. κατὰ λῖτα πετάσσας, 8, 441.†

(καταπέφνω), defect obsol. pres. to the aor. κατέπεφνον, to which belongs the irregularly accented partcp. καταπέφνων, to kill, to slay, τινά, 17, 539. (cf. ΦΕΝΩ.) Il. and Od.

καταπήγνυμι (πήγνυμι), aor. 1 κατέπηξα, Ep. aor. syncop. mid. 3 sing. κατέπηκτο, I) Act. to strike into the earth, to infix, ἔγχος ἐπὶ χθονί, 6, 213 ; σκόλοπας, 7, 441.

II) Mid. *to remain fixed, to stand firm,* Ep. aor. ἐν γαίῃ, *11, 378.

καταπίπτω (πίπτω), aor. κατέπεσον, Ep. κάππεσον, 1) *to fall down,* ἀπὸ πύργου, 12, 386; ἀπ' ἰκριόφιν, Od. 12, 414. 2) *to fall down,* ἐν Δήμνῳ, Il. 1, 593; ἐν κονίῃσιν, 4, 523; *to fall,* in battle, 15, 538; metaph. πᾶσιν παραὶ ποσὶ κάππεσε θυμός, the courage of all fell before their feet, i. e. sunk entirely, 15, 280.

καταπλέω (πλέω), *to sail down,* from the high sea to the coast, to make the land, Od. 9, 142.†

καταπλήσσω (πλήσσω), only aor. pass. κατεπλήγην, Ep. for κατεπλάγην, act. prop. *to strike down;* pass. metaph., *to be terrified, to be amazed* or *confounded,* 3, 31.†

*καταπνείω, poet. for καταπνέω (πνέω), *to breathe upon, to blow against,* h. Cer. 239.

καταπρηνής, ές (πρηνής), *prone downwards,* epith. only of χείρ, the flat hand (the palm downwards), to represent the action of striking [or *pressing* forcibly down], 15, 114. Od. 13, 164. h. Ap. 333.

καταπτήσσω (πτήσσω), aor. 1 κατέπτηξα, Ep. aor. 2 sync. κατέπτην (from ΠΤΑΩ). *to stoop down from fear, to conceal oneself,* Od. 8, 190; ὑπὸ θάμνῳ, Il. 22, 191; metaph. *to be terrified, to be frightened.* ἵππω καταπτήτην, the horses were terrified, 8, 136.

καταπτώσσω (πτώσσω) = καταπτήσσω, only pres. *to hide oneself fearfully, to cringe,* 4, 224. 340. 5, 254; metaph. *to be terrified, to be dismayed,* *5, 476.

καταπύθω (πύθω), aor. κατέπυσα, *to render putrid, to let putrefy,* with accus. h. Ap. 371. Mid. *to become putrid, to putrefy,* 23, 328.†

καταράομαι, depon. mid. (ἀράομαι), *to invoke any thing upon a man, esply evil, to imprecate:* ἄλγεά τινι, Od. 19, 330; absol. πολλὰ κατηρᾶτο, he cursed much, Il. 9, 454.

καταρέζω, poet. for καταρρέζω.

καταρίγηλός, ή, όν (ῥιγέω), *horrible, terrible, odious,* Od. 14, 226.†

καταρρέζω (ῥέζω), aor. 1 Ep. κατέρεξα, partcp. pass. καρρέζουσα, Ep. for καταρρέζουσα, 5, 424: to put down, to stroke down, and thus put down; metaph. *to caress, to soothe,* τινὰ χειρί, 1, 361. Od. 4, 610.

καταρρέω (ῥέω), *to flow down,* Od. 17, 209; ἐξ ὠτειλῆς, Il. 4, 149; and with gen. χειρός, 13, 539.

κατάρχομαι, mid. (ἄρχω), in a religious signif. *to begin a sacrifice,* spoken of the ceremony which precedes the proper act of sacrifice, rarely with accus. χέρνιβά τ' οὐλοχύτας, to begin the sacrifice with the lustral water and the sacred barley, Od. 3, 445.†

κατασβέννυμι (σβέννυμι), aor. 1 κατέσβεσα, *to extinguish, quench,* πῦρ, *21, 381; in tmesis, 16, 292.

κατασεύομαι, poet. (σεύω), only Ep.

aor. 2. mid. κατέσσυτο, *to rush down:* with accus. ῥέεθρα, to rush into the stream. 21. 382.†

κατασκιάω, poet. for κατασκιάζω (σκιάζω). *to shade, to cover,* with accus. Od. 12, 436.†

κατασμύχω (σμύχω), *to burn down,* only in tmesis, see σμύχω.

*καταστείβω (στείβω), *to tread upon,* with accus. h. 18, 4.

*καταστίλβω (στίλβω), *to beam down, to shine upon;* transit. πρηΰ σέλας, to send down mild beams, h. 7, 10.

καταστορέννυμι (στορέννυμι) and καταστόρνυμι, partcp. καστορνῦσα, Ep. for καταστορνῦσα, Od. 17, 32; aor. 1 κατεστόρεσα. 1) *to spread out, to spread upon, to lay down,* with accus. ῥῆγος, Od. 13, 73; κώεα, Od. 17, 32. 2) *to cover over:* κάπετον λάεσσιν, the pit with stones, Il. 24, 798.

καταστόρνυμι. see καταστορέννυμι.

*καταστρέφω (στρέφω). aor. 1 κατέστρεψα, *to turn about, to overturn;* ποσσί τι, pedibus evertere, h. Ap. 73.

καταστυγέω (στυγέω), aor. κατέστυγον. 1) *to be amazed, terrified, to start back terrified,* absol, 17, 694. 2) Transit. with accus. *to be terrified at,* Od. 10, 113.

καταστύφελος, ον (στυφελός), *very hard, firm,* πέτρη, h. Merc. 124.

κατασχεθεῖν, poet. for κατασχεῖν, see κατέχω.

κατασχεῖν, see κατέχω.

*κατατανύω (τανύω), poet. for κατατείνω, aor. 1 καττάνυσα, Ep. for κατετάνυσα, *to pull down, to draw down,* ὅπλα, h. 6, 34.

κατατείνω (τείνω), aor. κατέτεινα, prop. *to pull down;* in tmesis, κατὰ δ' ἡνία τείνεν ὀπίσσω, he drew the reins back, 3, 261. 19, 311.†

κατατήκω (τήκω), aor. 1 act. κατέτηξα, 1) Act. trans. *to melt,* with accus. χιόνα, Od. 19, 206. 2) Mid. intrans. *to melt, to dissolve;* metaph. *to consume oneself, to pine away:* ἦτορ, at heart, *Od. 19, 136.

κατατίθημι (τίθημι), fut. καταθήσω, aor. 1 κατέθηκα, aor. 2 only plur. in the Ep. forms κάθεμεν, κάθετε, κάθεσαν, for κατέθεμεν, κατέθετε, etc., subj. καταθείομεν, Ep. for καταθῶμεν, infin. καταθέμεν, Ep. for καταθεῖναι, aor. 2 mid. plur. καθθέμεθα, καθθέσθην, Ep. for κατεθέμεθα, κατεθέσθην, and 3 plur. κατέθεντο, subj. καταθείομαι, Ep. for καταθῶμαι, 21, 111; *to set down, to put down.* w lay down, to place in, to put away, with accus. ἐπὶ χθονός and ἐπὶ χθονί, 3, 293. 6, 473; τινὰ ἐν λεχέεσσι, 18, 233; τόξα ἐς μυχόν, Od. 16, 285; τί τινι, to propose as a combat-prize, 23, 267. 851; ἄεθλον, to propose a contest, Od. 19, 572 [cf. 576]; τινα εἰς Ἰθάκην, to land any one in Ithaca, Od. 16, 230. Mid. *to lay down for oneself* (with reference to the subject); τεύχεα ἐπὶ γαίῃ, Il. 3, 114. 22, 111; ὅπλα νηός, h. Ap. 457; of the dead, *to lay out, to inter,* Od. 24, 190. 2) to lay up, to keep, τὶ ἐπὶ δόρπῳ, Od. 18, 45.

*κατατρίζω (τρίζω), spoken of the piercing cry of birds, mice, etc., to squeak, to squeal; and generally, to wail, to lament, Batr. 88.

κατατρύχω (τρύχω), to wear out, to consume, to exhaust, λαοὺς δώροις, 17, 225. Od. 15, 309. 16, 84.

*κατατρώγω (τρώγω), aor. κατέτρωξα, to gnaw, to corrode, to consume, Batr. 126.

καταῦθι, adv. on the spot, there, 13, 253. Od. 10, 567; a false reading for κατ' αὖθι.

καταφαγεῖν, infin. aor. to κατεσθίω.

*καταφαίνω (φαίνω), to show; mid. to become visible, to show oneself, h. Ap. 431.

καταφέρω (φέρω), only fut. mid. κατοίσομαι, to bear down, to bring or conduct down. Mid. as depon. τινὰ Ἀΐδος εἴσω, any one to the realms of Hades, 22, 425.†

*καταφθινύθω, a form of καταφθίω, only pres. to destroy, to annihilate, τιμήν, h. Cer. 334.

καταφθίω (φθίω), fut. καταφθίσω, perf. pass. κατέφθιμαι, pluperf. κατεφθίμην, which is at the same time a syncop. aor. mid. infin. καταφθίσθαι, partcp. καταφθίμενος, 1) Act. trans. to destroy, to kill, to annihilate, τινά, Od. 5, 341. 2) Intrans. in the pass. and mid. to perish, to go to ruin, to vanish away. ἥϊα κατέφθιτο, the stores had vanished, Od. 4, 363; esply partcp. aor. destroyed, dead, Il. 22, 288; plur. subst. the dead, the shades, h. Cer. 347.

καταφλέγω (φλέγω), fut. ξω, to burn down, to consume, πάντα πυρί, 22, 512.†

καταφῦλαδόν, adv. (φυλή), by tribes, divided into tribes, 2, 668.†

καταχέω (χέω), Ep. aor. 1 κατέχευα, Ep. aor. syncop. mid. κατέχυντο, 1) Prop. spoken of fluids: to pour over, to pour upon, to pour out. ἔλαιον χαιτάων τινί, to pour oil upon any one's hair, 23, 282; ὕδωρ 14, 435. 2) Of dry things: to pour down, to let fall, χιόνα, νιφάδας, Od. 19, 206. Il. 12, 158; πέπλον ἐπ' οὔδει, to let the robe fall on the floor, 1. 734; θύσθλα χαμαί, to let the staves, the thyrsi, fall to the ground, 6, 134; τεῖχος εἰς ἅλα, 7, 461. 3) Metaph. to pour out, to spread out, τί τινι; ὀμίχλην τινί, 3, 10; ἀχλύν τινι, Od. 7, 42; χάριν τινί, Od. 2, 12. 8, 19; ἐλεγχείην, αἰσχός τινι, to pour reproach, insult upon any man, 23, 408. Od. 11, 433; πλοῦτόν τιν, Il. 2. 670. Mid. to flow down, to fall down, only Ep. sync. aor. εἰς ἄντλον, Od. 12, 411.

καταχθόνιος, ον (χθών), subterranean, Ζεύς = Hades (Pluto), 9, 457.†

κατέαξα, see κατάγνυμι.

κατέδω (ἔδω), Ep. for the prose κατεσθίω, fut. κατέδομαι, perf. act. κατέδηδα, in tmesis. 17, 542; to eat up, to devour, to consume, prim. spoken of brutes; with accus. Il. metaph. to consume, to waste,

οἶκον, κτήματα. Od. 2, 237. ὃν θυμὸν κατέδειν, to consume (devour, prey upon) one's own heart, to feed on grief [Cp.], Il. 6, 202.

*κατέργω (εἴργω), aor. κατέερξα, to drive in, to shut up, βοῦς, h. Merc. 356.

κατείβω (εἴβω), poet. = καταλείβω, 1) Act. to let flow down, to shed, δάκρυ, Od. 21, 86. 2) Mid. to flow down, to trickle down, with gen. παρειῶν, Il. 24, 794; spoken of the water of the Styx, 15, 37; metaph. κατείβετο αἰών, life flowed away, Od. 5, 152.†

κατεῖδον (ΕΙΔΩ), partcp. κατιδών, 4, 508. Batr. 11; defect. aor. 2 of καθοράω, to look down.

κατειλύω (εἰλύω), fut. ύσω, to surround, to cover, τινὰ ψαμάθοις, any one with sand, 21, 318.† in tmesis.

κάτειμι (εἶμι), partcp. pres. κατιών, Ep. and aor. mid. καταεισάμην for κατεισ., 1) to descend, to go down; δόμον Ἀΐδος, into the abode of Hades 14, 457. 2) Metaph. spoken of a river, to flow down, 11, 492; of a ship, to proceed, ἐς λιμένα, Od. 16, 472; of missiles: δόρυ καταείσατο γαίης, the spear entered the earth, Il. 11, 358.

κατέκταθεν, see κατακτείνω.

κατεναίρω (ἐναίρω), only aor. mid. κατενηράμην, to slay, to kill, τινὰ χαλκῷ, Od. 11, 519.†

κατεναντίον, adv. (ἐναντίον), over against, opposite, τινί, 21, 567.†

*κατενήνοθε (ἐνήνοθα), an old perf. with the signif. of the pres. and imperf., to lie upon, to be upon. κόμαι κατενήνοθεν ὤμους, hairs covered the shoulders, h. Cer. 280; the connexion of the subst. fem. plur. with a verb in the sing. is called schema Pindaricum, cf. Rost Gram. § 100, p. 478. Kühner, § 370.

κατενῶπα, adv. (ἐνωπή), directly before the face, opposite, with gen. Δαναῶν, 15, 320.† More correctly, κατ' ἐνῶπα, see ἐνώψ.

κατεπάλμενος, see κατεφάλλομαι.

κατέπαλτο, see καταπάλλω.

κατερείπω (ἐρείπω), prop. to snatch down; in the aor. and perf., aor. κατήριπον, perf. κατερήριπα, intrans. to fall down, to tumble down, spoken of a wall, 14, 55. Metaph. κατήριπεν ἔργα αἰζηῶν, the labours of the youths perished, Voss, Il. 5, 92.

κατερητύω (ἐρητύω), to restrain, to check, τινά, 9, 465. Od. 3, 31.

κατερυκάνω, poet. for κατερύκω, 24, 218 †

κατερύκω (ἐρύκω), 1) to stop, to check, τινά, 6, 190. Od. 3, 345. 2) to retard, to detain, to hinder; in a bad sense, τινά, 23, 734. Od. 2, 242; hence pass. to linger, Od. 1, 197. 4, 498.

κατερύω (ἐρύω), aor. 1 κατείρυσα, perf. pass. κατείρυσμαι, to pull down, to draw down, always of ships, which are drawn down from the shore into the sea, with accus. Od. 5, 261. Pass. *Od. 8, 151.

κατέρχομαι, depon. (ἔρχομαι), fut. κατελεύσομαι, aor. κατῆλθον, poet. κατ-

II) Mid. *to remain fixed, to stand firm,* Ep. aor. ἐν γαίῃ, *11, 378.

καταπίπτω (πίπτω), aor. κατέπεσον, Ep. κάππεσον, 1) *to fall down,* ἀπὸ πύργου, 12, 386; ἀπ' ἰκριόφιν, Od. 12, 414. 2) *to fall down,* ἐν Λήμνῳ, Il. 1, 593; ἐν κονίῃσιν, 4, 523; *to fall,* in battle, 15, 538; metaph. πᾶσιν παραὶ ποσὶ κάππεσε θυμός, the courage of all fell before their feet, i. e. sunk entirely, 15, 280.

καταπλέω (πλέω), *to sail down,* from the high sea to the coast, to make the land, Od. 9, 142.†

καταπλήσσω (πλήσσω), only aor. pass. κατεπλήγην, Ep. for κατεπλάγην, act. prop. *to strike down;* pass. metaph., *to be terrified, to be amazed or confounded,* 3, 31.†

*καταπνείω, poet. for καταπνέω (πνέω), *to breathe upon, to blow against,* h. Cer. 239

καταπρηνής. ές (πρηνής), *prone downwards,* epith. only of χείρ, the flat hand (the palm downwards), to represent the action of striking [or *pressing* forcibly down], 15, 114. Od. 13, 164. h. Ap. 333.

καταπτήσσω (πτήσσω), aor. 1 κατέπτηξα, Ep. aor. 2 sync. κατέπτην (from ΠΤΑΩ). *to stoop down from fear, to conceal oneself,* Od. 8, 190; ὑπὸ θάμνῳ, Il. 22, 191; metaph. *to be terrified, to be frightened.* ἵππω καταπτήτην, the horses were terrified, 8, 136.

καταπτώσσω (πτώσσω) = καταπτήσσω, only pres. *to hide oneself fearfully, to cringe,* 4, 224. 340. 5, 254; metaph. *to be terrified, to be dismayed,* *5, 476.

καταπύθω (πύθω), aor. κατέπυσα, *to render putrid, to let putrefy,* with accus. h. Ap. 371. Mid. *to become putrid, to putrefy,* 23, 328.†

καταράομαι, depon. mid. (ἀράομαι), *to invoke any thing upon a man, esply evil, to imprecate:* ἀλγεά τινι, Od. 19, 330; absol. πολλὰ κατηρᾶτο, he cursed much, Il. 9, 454.

καταρέζω, poet. for καταρρέζω.

καταρίγηλός, ή, όν (ῥιγέω), *horrible, terrible, odious,* Od. 14, 226.†

καταρρέζω (ῥέζω), aor. 1 Ep. κατέρεξα, partcp. pass. καρρέζουσα, Ep. for καταρρέζουσα, 5, 424: to put down, to stroke down, and thus put down; metaph. *to caress, to soothe,* τινὰ χειρί, 1, 361. Od. 4, 610.

καταρρέω (ῥέω), *to flow down,* Od. 17, 209; ἐξ ὠτειλῆς, Il. 4, 149; and with gen. χειρός, 13, 539.

κατάρχομαι, mid. (ἄρχω), in a religious signif. *to begin a sacrifice,* spoken of the ceremony which precedes the proper act of sacrifice, rarely with accus. χέρνιβά τ' οὐλοχύτας, to begin the sacrifice with the lustral water and the sacred barley, Od. 3, 445.†

κατασβέννυμι (σβέννυμι), aor. 1 κατέσβεσα, *to extinguish, quench,* πῦρ, *21, 381; in tmesis, 16, 292.

κατασεύομαι, poet. (σεύω), only Ep.

aor. 2. mid. κατέσσυτο, *to rush down* with accus. ῥέεθρα, to rush into the stream, 21, 382.†

κατασκιάω, poet. for κατασκιάζω (σκιάζω). *to shade, to cover,* with accus. Od. 12, 436.†

κατασμύχω (σμύχω). *to burn down,* only in tmesis, see σμύχω.

*καταστείβω (στείβω), *to tread upon,* with accus. h. 18, 4.

*καταστίλβω (στίλβω), *to beam down, to shine upon;* transit. πρηϋ σέλας, to send down mild beams, h. 7, 10.

καταστορέννυμι (στορέννυμι) and καταστόρνυμι, partcp. καστορνῦσα, Ep. for καταστορνῦσα, Od. 17, 32; aor. 1 κατεστόρεσα. 1) *to spread out, to spread upon, to lay down,* with accus. ῥῆγος. Od. 13, 73; κῶεα, Od. 17, 32. 2) *to cover over:* κάπετον λάεσσιν, the pit with stones, Il. 24, 798.

καταστόρνυμι. see καταστορέννυμι.

*καταστρέφω (στρέφω), aor. 1 κατέστρεψα, *to turn about, to overturn;* ποσσί τι, *pedibus evertere,* h. Ap. 73.

καταστυγέω (στυγέω). aor. κατέστυγον, 1) *to be amazed, terrified, to start back terrified,* absol , 17, 694. 2) Transit. with accus. *to be terrified at,* Od. 10, 113.

*καταστύφελος, ον (στυφελός), *very hard, firm,* πέτρη, h. Merc. 124.

κατασχεθεῖν, poet. for κατασχεῖν, see κατέχω.

κατασχεῖν, see κατέχω.

*κατατανύω (τανύω), poet. for κατατείνω, aor. 1 καττάνυσα, Ep. for κατετάνυσα, *to pull down, to draw down,* ὅπλα, h. 6, 34.

κατατείνω (τείνω), aor. κατέτεινα, prop. *to pull down;* in tmesis, κατὰ δ' ἡνία τεῖνεν ὀπίσσω, he drew the reins back, 3, 261. 19, 311.†

κατατήκω (τήκω), aor. 1 act. κατέτηξα, 1) Act. trans. *to melt,* with accus. χιόνα, Od. 19, 206. 2) Mid. intrans. *to melt, to dissolve;* metaph. *to consume oneself, to pine away;* ἦτορ, at heart, *Od. 19, 136.

κατατίθημι (τίθημι), fut. καταθήσω, aor. 1 κατέθηκα. aor. 2 only plur. in the Ep. forms κάτθεμεν. κάτθετε. κάτθεσαν, for κατέθεμεν, κατέθετε. etc., subj. καταθείομεν, Ep. for καταθῶμεν, infin. κατθέμεν, Ep. for καταθεῖναι, aor. 2 mid. plur. καθθέμεθα, καθθέσθην, Ep. for κατεθέμεθα, κατεθέσθην, and 3 plur. κάτθεντο, subj. καταθείομαι, Ep. for καταθῶμαι, 21, 111; *to set down, to put down. to lay down, to place in, to put away,* with accus. ἐπὶ χθονός and ἐπὶ χθονί, 3, 293. 6, 473; τινὰ ἐν λεχέεσσι, 18, 233; τόξα ἐς μυχόν, Od. 16, 285; τί τινι, to propose as a combat-prize, 23, 267. 851; ἄεθλον, to propose a contest, Od. 19, 572 [cf. 576]; τινὰ εἰς Ἰθάκην, to land any one in Ithaca, Od. 16, 230. Mid. *to lay down for oneself* (with reference to the subject); τεύχεα ἐπὶ γαίῃ, Il. 3, 114. 22, 111; ὅπλα νηός, h. Ap. 457; of the dead, *to lay out, to inter,* Od. 24, 190. 2) *to lay up*, *to keep*, τὶ ἐπὶ δόρπῳ, Od. 18, 45.

κατατρίζω (τρίζω), spoken of the piercing cry of birds, mice, etc., *to squeak*, *to squeal*; and generally, *to wail*, *to lament*, Batr. 88.

κατατρύχω (τρύχω), *to wear out*, *to consume*, *to exhaust*. λαοὺς δώροις, 17, 225. Od. 15, 309. 16, 84.

κατατρώγω (τρώγω), aor. κατέτρωξα, *to gnaw*, *to corrode*, *to consume*, Batr. 126.

κατ**αῦθι**, adv. *on the spot*, *there*, 13, 253. Od. 10, 567; a false reading for κατ' αὖθι.

κατα**φαγεῖν**, infin. aor. *to* κατεσθίω.

καταφαίνω (φαίνω), *to show*; mid. *to become visible*, *to show oneself*, h. Ap. 431.

κατα**φέρω (φέρω)**, only fut. mid. κατοίσομαι, *to bear down*, *to bring* or *conduct down*. Mid. as depon. τινὰ Ἀΐδος εἴσω, any one to the realms of Hades, 22, 425.†

καταφθινύθω, a form of καταφθίω, only pres. *to destroy*, *to annihilate*, τιμήν, h. Cer. 334.

κατα**φθίω (φθίω)**, fut. καταφθί σω, perf. pass. κατέφθιμαι, pluperf. κατεφθίμην, which is at the same time a syncop. aor. mid. infin. καταφθίσθαι, partcp. καταφθίμενος, 1) Act. trans. *to destroy*, *to kill*, *to annihilate*, τινά, Od. 5, 341. 2) Intrans. in the pass. and mid. *to perish*, *to go to ruin*, *to vanish away*. ἦα κατέφθιτο, the stores had vanished, Od. 4, 363; esply partcp. aor. *destroyed*, *dead*, Il. 22, 288; plur. subst. *the dead*, *the shades*, h. Cer. 347.

κατα**φλέγω (φλέγω)**, fut. ξω, *to burn down*, *to consume*, πάντα πυρί, 22, 512.†

κατα**φῦλαδόν**, adv. (φυλή), *by tribes*, *divided into tribes*, 2, 668.†

κατα**χέω (χέω)**, Ep. aor. 1 κατέχευα, Ep. aor. syncop. mid. κατέχυντο, 1) Prop. spoken of fluids: *to pour over*, *to pour upon*, *to pour out*. ἔλαιον χαιτάων τινί, to pour oil upon any one's hair, 23, 282; ὕδωρ 14, 435. 2) Of dry things: *to pour down*, *to let fall*, χιόνα, νιφάδας, Od. 19, 206. Il. 12, 158; πέπλον ἐπ' οὔδει, to let the robe fall on the floor, 1, 734; θύσθλα χαμαί, to let the staves, the thyrsi, fall to the ground, 6, 134; τεῖχος εἰς ἅλα, 7, 461. 3) Metaph. *to pour out*, *to spread out*, τί τινι; ὁμίχλην τινί, 3, 10; ἀχλύν τινι, Od. 7, 42; χάριν τινί, Od. 2, 12. 8, 19; ἐλεγχείην, αἰσχός τινι, *to pour reproach*, insult upon any man, 23, 408. Od. 11, 433: πλοῦτόν τινα, Il. 2, 670. Mid. *to flow down*, *to fall down*, only Ep. sync. aor. εἰς ἄντλον, Od. 12, 411.

κατα**χθόνιος**, ον (χθών), *subterranean*, Ζεύς = Hades (*Pluto*), 9, 457.†

κατ**έαξα**, see κατάγνυμι.

κατ**έδω (ἔδω)**, Ep. for the prose κατεσθίω, fut. κατέδομαι. perf. act. κατέδηδα, in tmesis. 17, 542; *to eat up*, *to devour*, *to consume*, prim. spoken of brutes; with accus. Il. metaph. *to consume*, *to waste*,

οἶκον, κτήματα, Od. 2, 237. ὃν θυμὸν κατέδων, *to consume* (devour, prey upon) one's own heart, *to feed on grief* [*Cp.*], Il. 6, 202.

κατέέργω (εἴργω), aor. κατέερξα, *to drive in*, *to shut up*, βοῦς, h. Merc. 356.

κατ**είβω (εἴβω)**, poet. = καταλείβω, 1) Act. *to let flow down*, *to shed*, δάκρυ, Od. 21, 86. 2) Mid. *to flow down*, *to trickle down*, with gen. παρειῶν, Il. 24, 794; spoken of the water of the Styx, 15, 37; metaph. κατείβετο αἰών, life flowed away, Od. 5, 152.†

κατ**εῖδον (ΕΙΔΩ)**, partcp. κατιδών, 4, 508. Batr. 11; defect. aor. 2 of καθοράω, *to look down*.

κατ**ειλύω (εἰλύω)**, fut. ύσω, *to surround*, *to cover*, τινὰ ψαμάθοις, any one with sand, 21, 318.† in tmesis.

κάτ**ειμι (εἶμι)**, partcp. pres. κατιών, Ep. and aor. mid. κατεισάμην for κατεισ., 1) *to descend*, *to go down*; δόμον Ἀΐδος, into the abode of Hades 14, 457. 2) Metaph. spoken of a river, *to flow down*, 11, 492; of a ship, *to proceed*, ἐς λιμένα, Od. 16, 472; of missiles: δόρυ κατεισατο γαίης, the spear entered the earth, Il. 11, 358.

κατ**έκταθεν**, see κατακτείνω.

κατ**εναίρω (ἐναίρω)**, only aor. mid. κατενηράμην, *to slay*, *to kill*, τινὰ χαλκῷ, Od. 11, 519.†

κατ**εναντίον**, adv. (ἐναντίον), *over against*, *opposite*, τινί, 21, 567.†

κατενήνοθε (ἐνήνοθα), an old perf. with the signif. of the pres. and imperf., *to lie upon*, *to be upon*. κόμαι κατενήνοθεν ὤμους, hairs covered the shoulders, h. Cer. 280; the connexion of the subst. fem. plur. with a verb in the sing. is called schema Pindaricum, cf. Rost Gram. § 100, p. 478. Kühner, § 370.

κατ**ένωπα**, adv. (ἐνωπή), *directly before the face*, *opposite*, with gen. Δαναῶν, 15, 320.† More correctly, κατ' ἐνῶπα, see ἐνώψ.

κατ**επάλμενος**, see κατεφάλλομαι.

κατ**έπαλτο**, see καταπάλλω.

κατ**ερείπω (ἐρείπω)**, prop. *to snatch down*; in the aor. and perf., aor. κατήριπον, perf. κατερήριπα, intrans. *to fall down*, *to tumble down*, spoken of a wall, 14, 55. Metaph. κατήριπεν ἔργα αἰζηῶν, the labours of the youths perished, Voss, Il. 5, 92.

κατ**ερητύω (ἐρητύω)**, *to restrain*, *to check*, τινά, 9, 465. Od. 3, 31.

κατ**ερυκάνω**, poet. for κατερύκω, 24, 218.†

κατ**ερύκω (ἐρύκω)**, 1) *to stop*, *to check*, τινά, 6, 190. Od. 3, 345. 2) *to retard*, *to detain*, *to hinder*; in a bad sense, τινά, 23, 734. Od. 2, 243; hence pass. *to linger*, Od. 1, 197. 4, 498.

κατ**ερύω (ἐρύω)**, aor. 1 κατείρυσα, perf. pass. κατείρυσμαι, *to pull down*, *to draw down*, always of ships, which are drawn down from the shore into the sea, with accus. Od. 5, 261. Pass. *Od. 8, 151.

κατ**έρχομαι**, depon. (ἔρχομαι), fut. κατελεύσομαι, aor. κατῆλθον, poet. κατ-

II) Mid. *to remain fixed, to stand firm*, Ep. aor. ἐν γαίῃ, *11, 378.

καταπίπτω (πίπτω), aor. κατέπεσον, Ep. κάππεσον, 1) *to fall down*, ἀπὸ πύργου, 12, 386; ἀπ' ἰκριόφιν, Od. 12, 414. 2) *to fall down*, ἐν Δήμνῳ, Il. 1, 593; ἐν κονίῃσιν, 4, 523; *to fall*, in battle, 15, 538; metaph. πᾶσιν παραὶ ποσὶ κάππεσε θυμός, the courage of all fell before their feet, i. e. sunk entirely, 15, 280.

καταπλέω (πλέω), *to sail down*, from the high sea to the coast, to make the land, Od. 9, 142.†

καταπλήσσω (πλήσσω), only aor. pass. κατεπλήγην, Ep. for κατεπλάγην, act. prop. *to strike down*; pass. metaph., *to be terrified, to be amazed* or *confounded*, 3, 31.†

*καταπνείω, poet. for καταπνέω (πνέω), *to breathe upon, to blow against*, h. Cer. 239.

καταπρηνής. ές (πρηνής), *prone downwards*, epith. only of χείρ, the flat hand (the palm downwards), to represent the action of striking [or *pressing* forcibly down], 15, 114. Od. 13, 164. h. Ap. 333.

καταπτήσσω (πτήσσω), aor. 1 κατέπτηξα, Ep. aor. 2 sync. κατέπτην (from ΠΤΑΩ). *to stoop down from fear, to conceal oneself*, Od. 8, 190; ὑπὸ θάμνῳ, Il. 22, 191; metaph. *to be terrified, to be frightened*. ἵππω καταπτήτην, the horses were terrified, 8, 136.

καταπτώσσω (πτώσσω) = καταπτήσσω, only pres. *to hide oneself fearfully, to cringe*, 4, 224. 340. 5, 254; metaph. *to be terrified, to be dismayed*, *5, 476.

καταπύθω (πύθω), aor. κατέπυσα, *to render putrid, to let putrefy*, with accus. h. Ap. 371. Mid. *to become putrid, to putrefy*, 23, 328.†

καταράομαι, depon. mid. (ἀράομαι), *to invoke* any thing upon a man, esply evil, *to imprecate*: ἄλγεά τινι, Od. 19, 330; absol. πολλὰ κατηρᾶτο, he cursed much, Il. 9, 454.

καταρέζω, poet. for καταρρέζω.

καταρίγηλός, ή, όν (ῥιγέω), *horrible, terrible, odious*, Od. 14, 226.†

καταρρέζω (ῥέζω), aor. 1 Ep. κατέρεξα, partcp. pass. καρρέζουσα, Ep. for καταρρέζουσα. 5, 424: *to put down, to stroke down, and thus put down*; metaph. *to caress, to soothe*, τινὰ χειρί, 1, 361. Od. 4, 610.

καταρρέω (ῥέω), *to flow down*, Od. 17, 209; ἐξ ὠτειλῆς, Il. 4, 149; and with gen. χειρός, 13, 539.

κατάρχομαι, mid. (ἄρχω), in a religious signif. *to begin a sacrifice*, spoken of the ceremony which precedes the proper act of sacrifice, rarely with accus. χέρνιβά τ' οὐλοχύτας, to begin the sacrifice with the lustral water and the sacred barley, Od. 3, 445.†

κατασβέννυμι (σβέννυμι), aor. 1 κατέσβεσα, *to extinguish, quench*, πῦρ, *21, 381; in tmesis, 16, 292.

κατασεύομαι, poet. (σεύω), only Ep.

aor. 2. mid. κατέσσυτο, *to rush down*; with accus. ῥέεθρα, to rush into the stream. 21. 382.†

κατασκιάω, poet. for κατασκιάζω (σκιάζω). *to shade, to cover*, with accus. Od. 12, 436.†

κατασμύχω (σμύχω), *to burn down*, only in tmesis, see σμύχω.

*καταστείβω (στείβω), *to tread upon*, with accus. h. 18, 4.

*καταστίλβω (στίλβω), *to beam down, to shine upon*; transit. πρηὺ σέλας, to send down mild beams, h. 7, 10.

καταστορέννυμι (στορέννυμι) and καταστόρνυμι, partcp. καστορνῦσα, Ep. for καταστορνῦσα, Od. 17, 32; aor. 1 κατεστόρεσα. 1) *to spread out, to spread upon. to lay down*, with accus. ῥῆγος, Od. 13, 73; κώεα, Od. 17, 32. 2) *to cover over*: κάπετον λάεσσιν, the pit with stones, Il. 24, 798.

καταστόρνυμι, see καταστορέννυμι.

*καταστρέφω (στρέφω), aor. 1 κατέστρεψα, *to turn about, to overturn*; ποσσί τι, *pedibus evertere*, h. Ap. 73.

καταστυγέω (στυγέω), aor. κατέστυγον, 1) *to be amazed. terrified, to start back terrified*, absol. 17, 694. 2) Transit. with accus. *to be terrified at*, Od. 10, 113.

*καταστύφελος, ον (στυφελός), *very hard, firm*, πέτρη, h. Merc. 124.

κατασχεθεῖν, poet. for κατασχεῖν, see κατέχω.

κατασχεῖν, see κατέχω.

*καταταντύω (τανύω), poet. for κατατείνω, aor. 1 καττάνυσα, Ep. for κατετάνυσα, *to pull down, to draw down*, ὅπλα, h. 6, 34.

κατατείνω (τείνω), aor. κατέτεινα, prop. *to pull down*; in tmesis, κατὰ δ' ἡνία τεῖνεν ὀπίσσω, he drew the reins back, 3, 261. 19, 311.†

κατατήκω (τήκω), aor. 1 act. κατέτηξα, 1) Act. trans. *to melt*, with accus. χιόνα, Od. 19, 206. 2) Mid. intrans. *to melt, to dissolve*; metaph. *to consume oneself, to pine away*; ἦτορ, at heart, *Od. 19, 136.

κατατίθημι (τίθημι), fut. καταθήσω, aor. 1 κατέθηκα. aor. 2 only plur. in the Ep. forms κάτθεμεν, κάτθετε, κάτθεσαν, for κατέθεμεν, κατέθετε, etc., subj. καταθείομεν, Ep. for καταθῶμεν, infin. κατθέμεν, Ep. for καταθεῖναι, aor. 2 mid. plur. καθθέμεθα, κατθέσθην, Ep. for κατεθέμεθα, κατεθέσθην, and 3 plur. κάτθεντο, subj. καταθείομαι, Ep. for καταθῶμαι, 21, 111; *to set down, to put down, to lay down, to place in, to put away*, with accus. ἐπὶ χθονός and ἐπὶ χθονί, 3, 293. 6, 473; τινὰ ἐν λεχέεσσι, 18, 233; τόξα ἐς μυχόν, Od. 16, 285; τί τινι, to propose as a combat-prize, 23, 267. 851; ἄεθλον, to propose a contest, Od. 19, 572 [cf. 576]; τινὰ εἰς Ἰθάκην, to land any one in Ithaca, Od. 16, 230. Mid. *to lay down for oneself* (with reference to the subject); τεύχεα ἐπὶ γαίῃ, Il. 3, 114. 22, 111; ὅπλα νηός, h. Ap. 457; of the dead, *to lay out, to inter*, Od. 24, 190. 2) *to* lay up, to keep, τὶ ἐπὶ δόρπῳ, Od. 18, 45.

*κατατρίζω (τρίζω), spoken of the piercing cry of birds, mice, etc., to squeak, to squeal; and generally, to wail, to lament, Batr. 88.

κατατρύχω (τρύχω), to wear out, to consume, to exhaust. λαοὺς δώροις, 17, 225. Od. 15, 309. 16, 84.

*κατατρώγω (τρώγω), aor. κατέτρωξα, to gnaw, to corrode, to consume, Batr. 126.

καταῦθι, adv. on the spot, there, 13, 253. Od. 10, 567; a false reading for κατ' αὖθι.

καταφαγεῖν, infin. aor. to κατεσθίω.

*καταφαίνω (φαίνω), to show; mid. to become visible, to show oneself, h. Ap. 431.

καταφέρω (φέρω), only fut. mid. κατοίσομαι, to bear down, to bring or conduct down. Mid. as depon. τινὰ Ἀϊδος εἴσω, any one to the realms of Hades, 22, 425.†

*καταφθινύθω, a form of καταφθίω, only pres. to destroy, to annihilate, τιμήν, h. Cer. 334.

καταφθίω (φθίω), fut. καταφθί σω, perf. pass. κατέφθιμαι, pluperf. κατεφθίμην, which is at the same time a syncop. aor. mid. infin. καταφθίσθαι, partcp. καταφθίμενος, 1) Act. trans. to destroy, to kill, to annihilate, τινά, Od. 5, 341. 2) Intrans. in the pass. and mid. to perish, to go to ruin, to vanish away. ἦια κατέφθιτο, the stores had vanished, Od. 4, 363; esply partcp. aor. destroyed, dead, Il. 22, 288; plur. subst. the dead, the shades, h. Cer. 347.

καταφλέγω (φλέγω), fut. ξω, to burn down, to consume, πάντα πυρί, 22, 512.†

καταφυλαδόν, adv. (φυλή), by tribes, divided into tribes, 2, 668.†

καταχέω (χέω), Ep. aor. 1 κατέχευα, Ep. aor. syncop. mid. κατέχυντο, 1) Prop. spoken of fluids: to pour over, to pour upon, to pour out. ἔλαιον χαιτάων τινί, to pour oil upon any one's hair, 23, 282; ὕδωρ, 14, 435. 2) Of dry things: to pour down, to let fall, χιόνα, νιφάδας, Od. 19, 206. Il. 12, 158; πέπλον ἐπ' οὔδει, to let the robe fall on the floor, 1. 734: θύσθλα χαμαί, to let the staves, the thyrsi, fall to the ground, 6, 134; τεῖχος εἰς ἅλα, 7, 461. 3) Metaph. to pour out, to spread out, τί τινι; ὁμίχλην τινί, 3, 10; ἀχλύν τινι, Od. 7, 42; χάριν τινί, Od. 2, 12. 8, 19: ἐλεγχείην, αἰσχός τινι, to pour reproach, insult upon any man, 23, 408. Od. 11, 433: πλοῦτόν τινι, Il. 2. 670. Mid. to flow down, to fall down, only Ep. sync. aor. εἰς ἄντλον, Od. 12, 411.

καταχθόνιος, ον (χθών), subterranean. Ζεύς = Hades (Pluto), 9, 457.†

κατέαξα, see κατάγνυμι.

κατέδω (ἔδω), Ep. for the prose κατεσθίω, fut. κατέδομαι, perf. act. κατέδηδα, in tmesis, 17, 542; to eat up, to devour, to consume, prim. spoken of brutes; with accus. Il. metaph. to consume, to waste, οἶκον, κτήματα. Od. 2, 237. ὃν θυμὸν κατέδειν, to consume (devour, prey upon) one's own heart, to feed on grief [Cp.], Il. 6, 202.

*κατέργω (εἴργω), aor. κατέερξα, to drive in, to shut up, βοῦς, h. Merc. 356.

κατείβω (εἴβω), poet. = καταλείβω. 1) Act. to let flow down, to shed, δάκρυ, Od. 21, 86. 2) Mid. to flow down, to trickle down, with gen. παρειῶν, Il. 24, 794; spoken of the water of the Styx, 15, 37; metaph. κατείβετο αἰών, life flowed away, Od. 5, 152.†

κατεῖδον (ΕΙΔΩ), partcp. κατιδών, 4, 508. Batr. 11; defect. aor. 2 of καθοράω, to look down.

κατειλύω (εἰλύω), fut. ύσω, to surround, to cover, τινὰ ψαμάθοις, any one with sand, 21, 318.† in tmesis.

κάτειμι (εἶμι), partcp. pres. κατιών, Ep. and aor. mid. κατεεισάμην for κατεισ., 1) to descend, to go down; δόμον Ἀϊδος, into the abode of Hades 14, 457. 2) Metaph. spoken of a river, to flow down, 11, 492; of a ship, to proceed, ἐς λιμένα, Od. 16, 472; of missiles: δόρυ κατεείσατο γαίης, the spear entered the earth, Il. 11, 358.

κατέκταθεν, see κατακτείνω.

κατεναίρω (ἐναίρω), only aor. mid. κατενηράμην, to slay, to kill, τινὰ χαλκῷ, Od. 11, 519.†

κατεναντίον, adv. (ἐναντίον), over against, opposite, τινί, 21, 567.†

*κατενήνοθε (ἐνήνοθα), an old perf. with the signif. of the pres. and imperf., to lie upon, to be upon. κόμαι κατενήνοθεν ὤμους, hairs covered the shoulders, h. Cer. 280; the connexion of the subst. fem. plur. with a verb in the sing. is called schema Pindaricum, cf. Rost Gram. § 100, p. 478. Kühner, § 370.

κατένωπα, adv. (ἐνωπή), directly before the face, opposite, with gen. Δαναῶν, 15, 320.† More correctly, κατ' ἐνῶπα, see ἐνώψ.

κατεπάλμενος, see κατεφάλλομαι.

κατέπαλτο, see καταπάλλω.

κατερείπω (ἐρείπω), prop. to snatch down: in the aor. and perf., aor. κατήριπον, perf. κατήριπα, intrans. to fall down, to tumble down, spoken of a wall, 14, 55. Metaph. κατήριπεν ἔργα αἰζηῶν, the labours of the youths perished, Voss, Il. 5, 92.

κατερητύω (ἐρητύω), to restrain, to check, τινά, 9, 465. Od. 3, 31.

κατερυκάνω, poet. for κατερύκω, 24, 218.†

κατερύκω (ἐρύκω), 1) to stop, to check, τινά, 6, 190. Od. 3, 345. 2) to retard, to detain, to hinder; in a bad sense, τινά, 23, 734. Od. 2, 242; hence pass. to linger, Od. 1, 197. 4. 498.

κατερύω (ἐρύω), aor. 1 κατείρυσα, perf. pass. κατείρυσμαι, to pull down, to draw down, always of ships, which are drawn down from the shore into the sea, with accus. Od. 5, 261. Pass. *Od. 8, 151.

κατέρχομαι, depon. (ἔρχομαι), fut. κατελεύσομαι, aor. κατῆλθον, poet. κατ-

ἤλυθον, infin. κατελθέμεν, Ep. for κατελθεῖν, 1) *to come down, to go down*, Od. 1, 304; esply Ἀϊδόσδε or Ἀΐδος εἴσω, *to descend to the realms of Hades*, 6, 284. 7, 330. Od. 10, 560. 2) Metaph. spoken of a fragment of rock, *to rush down*, Od. 9, 484. 511.

κατεσθίω (ἐσθίω), imperf. κατήσθιε, aor. κατέφαγον, only in tmesis, *to eat up, to devour*, 3, 25. Od. 1, 9.

κατέσσυτο, see κατασεύομαι.

κατευνάζω (εὐνάζω), also κατευνάω, fut. άσω, aor. 1 pass. κατευνάσθην, *to put in bed, to lull to sleep*, only pass. *to lie down, to go to sleep*, 3, 448.†

κατευνάω = κατευνάζω, from which the fut. ήσω, aor. κατεύνησα, aor. pass. κατευνήθην, *to put in bed, to lull to sleep*, τινά, 14, 245. 248. Pass. *to lie down*, Od. 4, 414.

κατεφάλλομαι (ἅλλομαι), Ep. partcp. aor. sync. κατεπάλμενος, *to leap down upon*, 11, 94.

κατέχω (ἔχω), fut. καθέξω, aor. 2 κάτεσχον, aor. 2 mid. κατεσχόμην, partcp. κατεσχόμενος, also the Ep. lengthened aor. 2 κατέσχεθον and 3 sing. κάσχεθε for κατέσχεθε, 11, 702. 1) Trans. *a) to hold down*, κεφαλήν, Od. 24, 242. *b) to stop, to restrain, to check, to hinder*, τινά, 11, 702. Od. 3, 284. ἤέρι κατέχοντο, they were checked by a cloud, 17, 368. 644. *c) to take possession of, to occupy*; ἀλαλητῷ πᾶν πεδίον, to fill the whole plain with shouting, 16, 79; hence *d) to hold concealed, to cover*, spoken esply of the grave, 3, 243. Od. 11, 301. 549; spoken of night, οὐρανόν, Od. 13, 269. σελήνη κατείχετο νεφέεσσι, Od. 9, 419. 2) Intrans. *to hold on, to proceed*. κατέσχεθον Θορικόνδε, h. Cer. 126. Mid. *to hold before oneself, to cover oneself*; ἑανῷ, with a veil, 3, 419; πρόσωπα χερσί, Od. 19, 361.

κατηπιάω (ἠπιάω), *to assuage, to soothe, to mitigate*; pass. ὀδύναι κατηπιόωντο, Ep. for κατηπιώντο. 5, 417.†

κατηρεφής, ές (ἐρέφω), prop. *roofed, covered over*, i. e. furnished with a roof, κλισίαι, 18, 589: hence *vaulted*, σπέος, Od. 13, 349; δάφνῃσι, shaded with laurels, Od. 9, 183. Metaph. κῦμα κατηρεφές, an overhanging wave, Od. 5, 367.

κατήριπε, aor. 2 of κατερείπω.

κατήφεια, ή, Ep. for κατήφεια (κατηφής), prop. the casting down of the eyes, *dejection, sadness, shame*, *3, 51. 16, 498.

κατηφέω (κατηφής), aor. 1 κατήφησα, prop. *to cast down the eyes, to be cast down, sad, dejected*, 22, 293. Od. 16, 342.

κατηφής, ές, *cast down, dejected, ashamed*, Od. 24, 432.† (Prob. from κατά and φάος, having the eyes cast down.)

κατηφών, όνος, ὁ. according to Aristarch. = κατήφεια, *sadness, shame*, probrum, dedecus; the abstract for the concrete, *causing dejection, sadness, shame*, 24, 253.† Thus Priam calls his sons κατηφόνες, ye who cause me shame.

κάτθανε, see καταθνήσκω.

κατθάψαι, see καταθάπτω.

κατθέμεν, κάτθεμεν, κάτθετε, κάτθεσαν, see κατατίθημι.

κατίμεν, Ep. for κατιέναι, see κάτειμι.

κατισχάνω = κατίσχω, *to hold back, to restrain*, only in tmesis. κατὰ τὸν σὸν νόον ἴσχανε, Od. 19, 42.†

κατίσχω (ἴσχω), a form from κατέχω, only pres. and imperf. 1) *to stop, to check*, ἵππους, 23, 321; metaph. θυμοῦ μένος, h. 7, 14. 2) *to take possession of, to occupy*, spoken of an island: οὐ ποίμνῃσιν καταίσχεται, it is not pastured by herds, Od. 9, 122. 3) *to hold towards, to direct* from the sea to the shore, νῆα, Od. 11, 456. Mid. *to retain, to hold for oneself, to hold back*, τινά, Il. 2, 233.

καταίσομαι, see καταφέρω.

κατόπισθε, before a vowel κατόπισθεν, adv. (ὄπισθε). 1) Of place : *behind, after*, with gen. νηός, Od. 12, 148. 2) Of time : *afterwards, in future*, Od. 22, 40. 24, 546. κατόπισθε λιπέσθαι, to remain behind, Od. 21, 116.

*κατόπτης, ον, ὁ (ὀπτής), *an observer, a spy*, h. Merc. 372.

*κατορούω (ὀρούω), *to rush down*, h. Cer. 342.

*κατουδαῖος, ον (οὖδας), *under the earth, subterranean*, h. Merc. 112.

*καττάνυσαν, see κατατανύω.

κάτω, adv. (κατά), *down, downwards*, ἕλκειν, 17, 136; ὁρόων, Od. 23, 91.

κατωθέω (ὠθέω), *to push* or *hurl down, to throw*, in tmesis, 16, 410.†

κατωμάδιος, η, ον (ὦμος), *from over the shoulder*, spoken of the discus, which is thrown with hand extended far from the shoulder. ὅσσα δὲ δίσκου οὖρα κατωμαδίοιο πέλονται, 23, 431.† (' As far as the discus flies from the sweep of the upraised arm,' Voss.)

κατωμαδόν (ὦμος), *from the shoulder*, ἐλαύνειν, according to Eustath. with reference to the driver, 'to strike with outstretched hand,' *15. 352. 23, 500; but most Gramm. refer it to the horses. ' to strike over the shoulders.' Thus Voss and Spitzner.

*κάτωρ, ορος. ὁ, a word of unknown origin in h. 6, 55; it is explained by deriving it from ΚΑΖΩ; *ruler*. Some would read κράτωρ or ἄκτωρ; cf. Herm.

κατωρυχής, ές, poet. for κατῶρυξ, υχος, ὁ, ἡ (κατορύσσω), *buried, deposited in the earth* κατωρυχέεσσι λίθοισι, Od. 6, 267. 9, 185.

Καύκωνες, οἱ, 1) a nation who were not of Hellenian origin, in Asia Minor: at a later date they inhabited Bithynia, from the Mariandyni to the river Parthenius, and were neighbours of the Paphlagonians, 10, 429. 20, 329. In Strabo's time they had disappeared. 2) a nation which dwelt in Triphylia, in the south-eastern part of Elis, Od. 3, 366. According to Strab. VIII. p. 345, there were different traditions, some of which made all the Epeans Caucônes, and others gave them a residence in lower Elis and Triphylia. Probably they were a remnant of the ancient Pelasgians, a part of whom migrated to Asia, Hdt. 1, 146. cf. Mannert. VIII. s. 352.

καυλός, ὁ, prop. *a stem, a handle;* in H. according to the Schol., the end of the shaft which was inserted into the socket of the spear's head, *the spear-shaft,* 13, 162. 16, 115; but 16, 338, *the hand-guard* of the sword. *Il.

καῦμα, τό (καίω). *a fire, heat,* esply *the heat of the sun,* 5, 865.†

καυστειρός, ή, όν (καίω), *burning, hot,* μάχη, *4, 342. 12, 316.

Κάϋστριος, ὁ, Ep. for Κάϋστρος, *Caÿster,* a river in Ionia, which rises in Lydia, and flows into the sea near Ephesus. 2, 461 (ὡς διὰ κεκαυμένης ῥέων).

ΚΑΦΩ. Ep. obsol. pres. akin to κάπτω and καπύω, *to gasp, to breathe forth,* from which only partcp. perf. in the accus. κακαφηότα θυμόν, the gasping soul, occurs 5, 698. Od. 5, 468.

κε, before a vowel κεν, an enclit. particle, Ep. and Ion. for ἄν, q. v.

Κεάδης, ου, ὁ, son of Keas = Trœzenius, 2, 847.

κεάζω (κέω), aor. 1 ἐκέασα, Ep. σσ, perf. pass. κεκέασμαι, aor. pass. ἐκεάσθην. *to split, to cleave,* prop. spoken of splitting wood, Od.; *to split in pieces, to crash,* spoken of lightning, Od. 5, 132. Pass. κεφαλὴ ἄνδιχα κεάσθην, the head was split in two pieces, 16, 412. 578. 20, 337.

*κέαρ, αρος, τό, contr. κῆρ, *the heart,* Batr. 212.

κέαται, κέατο, Ep. and Ion. for κεῖνται, ἔκειντο, from κεῖμαι.

*Κεβρήνιος, ίη, ιον, *Cebrenian, belonging to the town Kebrēn Cebren)* in Æolia; subst. the inhabitants of Kebrēn, Ep. 10.

Κεβριόνης, ου, ὁ, son of Priam, and charioteer of Hector, slain by Patroclus, 8, 318. 16, 738, seq.

κεδάννυμι, Ep. for σκεδάννυμι, aor. ἐκέδασα, Ep. σσ, aor. pass. ἐκεδάσθην, *to scatter, to disperse, to dissipate,* κύνας, φάλαγγας, 17, 283. 285. Od. 3, 131; pass. Il. 2, 398. κεδασθείσης ὑσμίνης, when the battle had scattered, i. e. when it was no longer fought in dense crowds, 15, 328. 16, 306. *b)* Of lifeless things, rare: *to tear away, to prostrate,* spoken of a torrent, γεφύρας, 5, 88. (H. has not the pres.)

κεδνός, ή. όν (κῆδος). superl. κεδνότατος, 9. 586. 1) Act. *careful, prudent, provident, trusty,* epith. of persons upon whom the conscientious attendance upon some duty rests, Od.; hence neut. plur. as adv. κέδν' εἰδυῖα, of a careful, faithful disposition, (Od. 1, 428. 2) Pass. worthy of care, *estimable, dear,* ἕταιροι, 9, 586; τοκέες. 17, 28. Od. 10, 225.

κέδρινος, η, ον (κέδρος), *of cedar,* θάλαμος. 24, 192.†

κέδρος, ἡ, *the cedar-tree,* whose fragrant wood was used for fumigation, and of which a species is yet produced

in Greece, Od. 5, 60; prob. *juniperus oxycedrus,* Linn.†

κειάμενος, κείαντες, see καίω.

κείαται, κείατο, see κεῖμαι.

κεῖθεν, adv. Ion. and Ep. for ἐκεῖθεν, *from there, thence,* Il. and Od. κεῖθεν φράσομαι ἔργον, then I will consider what is to be done, Il. 15, 234.

κεῖθι, adv. Ion. and Ep. for ἐκεῖθι, *there, in that place,* 3, 402. Od. 3, 116. κἀκεῖθι, another reading for καὶ κεῖθι, Il. 22, 390.

κεῖμαι (prop. perf. pass. from κέω), 2 sing. κεῖσαι. Ep. also κεῖαι, h. Merc. 254; 3 plur. κεῖνται, Ep. κέαται, κείαται and κέονται, 22, 510; subj. κέωμαι, 3 sing. κῆται, 19, 32. Od. 2, 102; for the earlier reading κεῖται (which Buttm. Gram. § 109, prefers), infin. κεῖσθαι, imperf. ἐκείμην, Ep. κείμην, 3 plur. ἔκειντο, Ep. κέατο and κείατο, 3 sing. iterat. κέσκετο, Od. 21, 41; fut. κείσομαι; primary signif. prop. to be laid; hence *to lie.* 1) Spoken of animate beings; of men : *to lie, to repose, to rest,* spoken of the sleeping, the inactive, the sick, the weak, the wounded, the miserable, and the dead; esply to lie unburied, 5, 685. 19, 32. 2) Spoken of inanimate things: *a)* Of regions, countries, islands : *to lie : to be situated,* Od. 7, 244. 9, 25. *b)* Of things : *to lie, to be,* esply of valuable objects, *to be treasured up, to be in store.* κτήματα, κειμήλια κεῖται ἐν δόμοις, 9, 382. 11, 132. κεῖται ἄεθλον, the prize is fixed, 23, 273: also spoken of chariots, ἅρματα κεῖτο, 2, 777 *c)* Metaph. spoken of conditions : πένθος ἐνὶ φρεσὶ κεῖται, sadness is in the soul, Od. 24, 423; and often ταῦτα θεῶν ἐν γούνασι κεῖται, see γόνυ.

κειμήλιον, τό (κεῖμαι). a valuable article which is laid aside and preserved, *a valuable, a jewel,* 6, 47. 9, 330; esply spoken of gifts of hospitality. Od. 1, 312. 4, 600. In the most general signif. it means property stored up, in opposition to herds and flocks. κειμήλιά τε πρόβασίς τε, stores and grazing animals, Voss, Od. 2, 75.

κεῖνος, κείνη, κεῖνο, *that one, he, she, it,* Ep. and Ion. for ἐκεῖνος, q. v.; κείνῃ, subaud. ὁδῷ, in that way, Od. 13, 111.

κεινός, κεινή, κεινόν, Ep. for κενός, *empty,* 3, 376. 4, 181. 11, 160. 15, 453.

κείρω, fut. κερῶ, infin. κερέειν, aor. 1 Ep. ἔκερσα, aor. 1 mid. ἐκειράμην, 1) *to cut off, to shear off.* κόμην τινί, 23, 146; δοῦρα, 24, 450. 2) *to consume, to devour, to graze,* spoken of brutes, λήϊον, 11, 560; δημόν, 21, 204; ἧπαρ, Od. 11, 578. 3) *to eat up, to waste, to destroy,* κτήματα, Od. 2, 312; in like manner βίοτον, Od. 1, 378. 2, 143: metaph. *to render void,* see ἐπικείρω. Mid. *to cut off a man's hair,* which the mourner consecrated to the dead. as an offering, κόμην, χαίτας, 23, 46. Od. 4, 198. 24, 46.

κεῖσε, adv. Ion. and Ep. for ἐκεῖσε,

which is not found in H., *thither*, 12, 356. Od. 4, 274.

κείω and κέω, Ep. fut. without the characteristic of the tense, from the obsolete root ΚΕΩ, *to wish to lie down, to desire to sleep* or *rest*, Od. 19, 340; often as partcp. βῆ δὲ κείων, Od. 14, 532. ἴομεν κείοντες, 14, 340 ὅρσο κείων Od. 7, 342; infin. κειέμεν, Od. 8, 315.

κείω, ground form of κεάζω, *I split*, Od. 14, 425.†

κεκαδήσομαι, see κήδω.
κεκαδήσω, see χάζομαι.
κεκάδοντο, aor. of χάζομαι.
κεκαδών, see χάζομαι.
κεκάμω, see κάμνω.
κέκασμαι, see καίνυμαι.
κεκαφηώς, see ΚΑΦΩ.
κέκλετο, see κέλομαι.
κέκληγα, see κλάζω.
κεκλήατο, see καλέω.
κεκλόμενος, see κέλομαι.
κέκλυθι, κέκλυτε, see κλύω.
κέκμηκα, see κάμνω.
κεκοπώς, see κόπτω.
κεκόρημαι and κεκορηότα, see κορέννυμι.
κεκορυθμένος, see κορύσσω.
κεκοτηώς, see κοτέω.
κεκράανται, κεκράαντο, see κραίνω.
κεκρύφαλος, ὁ (κρύπτω), a net, knit or twisted, with which women confined their hair, *a head-net, a net cap*, 22, 469.†

κεκύθωσι, see κεύθω, Od.
κελαδεινός, ή, όν (κέλαδος), *rushing, noisy*, Ζέφυρος, 23, 208. h. Merc. 95; chiefly an epith. of Artēmis, as goddess of the chase, 16, 183; as prop. name, 21, 511.

κελαδέω, poet. (κέλαδος), aor. 1 κελάδησα. *to rush, to make a noise, to cry, to make a tumult*, spoken of men, 23, 869.† see ἐπικελαδέω.

κέλαδος, ὁ, *a rushing noise, a tumult, a cry*, esply of the chase, Il.; spoken of the suitors, Od. 18, 402.

κελάδω = κελαδέω, poet. only partcp. pres. κελάδων, *rushing, roaring*, spoken of water, 18, 576. 21, 16; of wind, Od. 2, 421.

Κελάδων, οντος, ὁ, prop. name, a little river, in Elis or Arcadia, which flows into the Alpheus, 7, 133. According to Strab. VIII. p. 348, some critics would here read Ἀκίδων, cf. Ottfr. Müller, Orchom. p. 372.

κελαινεφής, ές, poet. (νέφος), *cloudy*, generally *black, dark*, αἷμα, 4, 140. 16, 667. 2) Freq. an epith. of Zeus, *enveloped in black clouds*, as the god of rain and tempest, 2, 412; as prop. name, Od. 13, 147. (Some Gramm. and the Etym. M., p. 501, explain it actively, *cloud-darkener*. Modern critics have even derived it from κέλλω, cloud-compeller, like νεφεληγερέτης.)

κελαινός, ή, όν. Ep. for μέλας (Buttm. Gram. § 16, 2), *black, dark*, often αἷμα, also δέρμα, νύξ, κῦμα, λαῖλαψ, *5, 310. 6, 117. 11, 747. κελαινὴ χθών, 16, 384; for

which Spitzner, far better, reads κελαινῇ. in reference to λαίλαπι.

κελαρύζω, poet. *to rush, to roar, to gush, to flow*, spoken of blood, 11, 813; of water, 21, 261. Od. 5, 523.

*Κελεός, ὁ, *Celeus*, son of Eleusis. father of Triptolemus, king of Eleusis, h. Cer. 105.

κέλευθος, ἡ (κέλλω), plur. οἱ κέλευθοι, and τὰ κέλευθα, in H., 1) *a way, a path. a course*, often ὑγρὰ and ἰχθυόεντα κέλευθα, the watery and fishy paths, spoken of the voyages of seamen, 1, 312. Od. 3, 71 177; also ἀνέμων, Od. 5, 383. ἐγγὺς νυκτός τε καὶ ἤματός εἰσι κέλευθοι, the paths of night and day are near, Od. 10, 86. The ancient critics in part understood it of place (τοπικῶς) in the sense, that the pastures of the night, (for the kine,) and of the day, (for the sheep,) were situated near the city; and in part of time, as a figurative representation of the short nights and long days, the rising of Helios, as it were, coinciding with the night; hence a sleepless man might earn double wages. This last explanation, proposed by Crates, seems to be required by the context, as Nitzsch ad loc. shows at large. The poet presupposes the well-known custom of driving out the kine very early, and folding the sheep very late. A man, therefore, who should renounce all sleep, might earn double wages, first with the kine, driving them out at day-break, and secondly, with the sheep, since it is scarcely dark before it becomes light again. The poet does not indeed here consider whether the herdsman is at home when the sheep must be driven out. It only occurred to him that the returning shepherd, if willing to forego sleep, might become the out-driving herdsman. 2) the act of *going*, the *course* which a man takes, *a journey* χάζεσθαι κελεύθου, to retire from one's course, i. e. place, 11. 504. 12. 262. 14, 282. 3) Metaph. *walk, course of life*, θεῶν, 3, 406; see ἀποειπεῖν.

κελευτιάω (frequentat. from κελεύω, only partcp. pres. κελευτιόων, Ep. for κελευτιῶν, *to command now here and now there, to exhort frequently*, *12, 265. 13. 125.

κελεύω (κέλομαι), fut. κελεύσω, aor. 1 ἐκέλευσα, Ep. κέλευσα, prop *to urge on. to drive*, μάστιγι, 23, 642; hence, 1) *to call to, to exhort, to order, to command. to demand*, spoken not only of rulers, but also 2) *Of equals: to desire, to wish*, 11 781 Od. 10, 17. It is construed a) With the dat. τινί, very often : *to call* to any one, *to command*, 2, 151. 442; or with dat. of pers. and accus. of the thing, ἀμφιπόλοισι ἔργα, 6, 324; and instead of the accus. with the infin. 2. 50. Od. 2, 9. b) More frequently with accus. of the pers. and infin. Il. 2, 114. 8. 318. 10, 242. 17, 30, seq.; more rarely with accus. of the pers. alone : τινά, *to exhort any one, to demand*, 13, 784. Od.

4, 274. 8, 204. 9, 278; and e) With
double accus., 7, 68. 349. 20, 87.

κέλης, ητος, ὁ (κέλλω), a racer, race-
horse, courser, a riding-horse for running-
races, ἵππος. Od. 5, 371.†

κελητίζω (κέλης), to ride upon a race-
horse, and generally, to ride, ἵπποισι, 15,
679.†

κέλλω [∾ pello; cf. κύαμος, πύαμος,
&c., or κίω as obsol. cillo ∾ cio. Lob.
Techn. 117], poet aor. 1 ἔκελσα, only in
the aor. 1) Trans. to drive, to urge on;
νῆα, to propel the ship to land, appellere,
Od. 9, 549. 10, 511. 12, 5. 2) Intrans. to
strike the ground [Cp.]. to run in to a low
sandy shore. ἡ νηῦς ἔκελσε, *Od. 9, 144.

κέλομαι. poet. (κέλλω), fut. κελήσομαι,
aor. 2 Ep. ἐκεκλόμην, κεκλόμην. partcp.
κεκλόμενος, 1) = κελεύω, to urge on, to
exhort, to command, to bid, to advise;
an unusual meaning is: ἐπεὶ κέλετο μα-
γάλη ἴς (the wax melted), since a great
force constrained it, Od. 12, 175; viz.
the wax became soft through the strong
pressure of the hands, since the following verse (176), which refers it to the sun,
is probably not genuine. Construct. as
with κελεύω. chiefly with accus. of pers.
and with accus. and infin. 2) to call to, to
call, chiefly in aor. with dat. of pers. 6,
66. 110. 8, 172; with accus. Ἥφαιστον,
18, 391.

κέλσαι, see κέλλω.

κεμάς, άδος, ἡ, poet. according to the
Gramm. a kind of deer or roe [hind. Cp.];
according to Aristot. Hist. A. 9. 6, 2, a
two-year old deer, Il. 10, 361.†

κέν, see κέ.

κενευχής, ές, poet. (αὐχή) empty-
boasting; vain-glorious [Cp.], 8, 230 †

κενεός, ή, όν, Ep. and Ion. for κενός,
empty, void, χείρ, Od. 10, 42. 2) κενεὸν
νίεσθαι, to return empty, i. e. with unaccomplished object [re infecta], 2, 298.
Od. 15, 214.

κενεών, ῶνος, ὁ (κενεός), prop. any void
space, esply the flank, the sides of the
abdomen between the hips and the ribs,
5, 284. 11, 381. Od. 22, 295.

κενός, ή, όν, empty, vain, metaph. idle,
groundless. κενὰ εὔγματα, Od. 22, 249.
Hom. uses elsewhere κενεός and κεινός,
q. v.

κένσαι, see κεντέω.

Κένταυροι, οἱ, the Centaurs. 1) In H.,
an ancient savage tribe in Thessaly, between Pelion and Ossa, who were expelled by the neighbouring Lapithæ.
According to H. 1, 268, they were rough
mountaineers of great stature (φῆρες
ὀρεσκῷοι), 11, 382. Od. 21, 295. 2) Later,
prob. in Pindar's age, they were fabu-
lously represented as possessing horses'
feet, prob. because they were good riders,
and gradually they were converted into
monsters, half man, half horse, Batr.
cf. Voss. Myth. Br. II. 33; Κενταύρου
for κεν ταύρου is the reading of Herm. h.
Merc. 224. (Prob. from ταῦρος and κεντέω, ox-hunter.)

κεντέω, Ep. aor. infin. κένσαι, to prick,
to goad, in order to urge on, ἵππον, 23,
337.†

κεντρηνεκής, ές (ἠνεκής). urged with a
goad, spurred, *5, 752. 8, 396.

κέντρον, τό (κεντέω). a goad with which
horses, oxen, and other draught-cattle
are urged on, 23, 387. 430; the horse
goad, or a whip ending in a goad (Voss).

κέντωρ, ορος, ὁ, poet. (κεντέω), a goader,
a driver, ἵππων, an honorable epith. of the
Cadmeans and Trojans, *4, 391. 5, 102.

κέομαι, Ep. and Ion. for κεῖμαι, from
which κέονται.

κεραΐζω (akin to κείρω), to destroy utterly, to lay waste, to raze, with accus.
πόλιν, σταθμούς, 5, 557. 24, 245. Od. 8,
516. 2) Of living beings: to kill, to
slay, 2, 861.

κεραίνω, κεραίρω, another form of κεραίω, in 9, 203.

*κεραϊστής, οῦ, ὁ (κεραΐζω), a destroyer,
a plunderer, h. Merc. 336.

κεραίω, Ep. for κεράννυμι, to mingle, to
mix, only imperat. κέραιε, 9, 203.†

κεραμεύς, έως, ὁ (κέραμος), a potter, 18,
601.†

*κεραμήϊος, ίη, ϊον (κέραμος), Ep. for
κεράμειος, of clay, earthern, Ep. 14.

κέραμος, ὁ (ἔρα), 1) potter's earth, potter's clay, Ep. 14. 2) all kinds of ware
burned of clay, a bowl, a vessel, a pitcher,
9, 469. 3) a prison, so called, according
to the Schol., amongst the Cyprians,
either from its form, or because any one
was kept in it, as it were in a jug, χαλκέῳ
ἐν κεράμῳ, 5, 387.

κεράννυμι, Ep. κεράω and κεραίω, also
the poet. forms κιρνάω and κίρνημι, aor.
1 act. ἐκέρασα, Ep. σσ, aor. 1 mid. ἐκε-
ρασάμην, Ep. σσ; H. uses in the pres.
act. κεράω, from which the partcp. κε-
ρῶντας, Od. 24, 364; imper. κέραιε, Il. 9,
203, and κίρνημι, q. v., subj. pres. mid.
κέρωνται, as if from κέραμαι, imperf.
ἐκίρνα and κίρνη, imperf. mid κερόωντο,
Ep. for ἐκερῶντο from κηράω, Od. 8, 470;
1) to mingle, to mix, esply spoken of the
mixing of wine and water, νέκταρ, οἶνον,
Od. 5, 93. 24, 364; ἐνὶ κρητῆρσι, Il. 4,
260. 2) to temper, to soften, by mixing,
spoken of bathing water, Od. 10, 362.
Mid. to mix for oneself, often οἶνον ἐν
κρητῆρσι,.to mingle wine for oneself in
the mixers, Il. 4, 260; οἶνον alone Od. 3,
332. 8, 47; also κρητῆρα οἴνου, to mingle
a mixer of wine, Od. 3, 393; and without
gen. Od. 7, 179. 13, 50.

κεραοξόος, ον (ξέω), smoothing or working horn, τέκτων, 4, 110.†

κεραός, ή, όν, horned, ἔλαφος, 3, 24. 11,
475; ἄρνες, Od. 4, 85.

κέρας, τό, gen. Ep. κέραος, dat. κέρᾳ,
plur. nom. κέρα, gen. κεράων, dat. κέρασι
Ep. κεράεσσι. The a in κέρα is mly
short. 1) a horn, chiefly of the bovine
genus, as an image of fixedness, Od. 19,
211. 2) horn, as a material for artificial
products, Od. 19, 563. 3) every thing
made of horn, esply the bow, Od. 21,

395. κέρᾳ ἀγλαέ, thou that shinest with the bow [naming the *material* in contempt], Il. 11, 385. Thus Köppen, Voss according to Aristarch. (The other explanation of a high dressing of hair, Schol. τρίχωσις, is foreign from H.) 4) the *horn*, on the fish-line, according to Aristarch. a horn tube above the hook, to prevent the fish from biting off the line, 24, 81. Od. 12, 251.

κεραυνός, ὁ, *a thunder-bolt*, i. e. a stroke of lightning which is immediately followed by thunder (cf. βροντή and ἀστεροπή), the common weapon of Zeus, 8, 133. Od. 5, 128.

κεράω, Ep. form from κεράννυμι, q. v.

*κερδαίνω (κέρδος), aor. ἐκέρδηνα, *to gain, to derive profit*, Ep. 14, 6.

κερδαλέος, η, ον, 1) *gainful, profitable*, βουλή, 10, 44; hence, *crafty, wise*, μῦθος, Od. 6, 148; νόημα, Od. 8, 548. 2) Of men: *eager for gain*; and in a good sense, *wise, intelligent*, Od. 13, 291. 15, 451.

κερδαλεόφρων, ον (φρήν), *whose mind is set upon gain, subtle, crafty, selfish*, *1, 149. 4, 339.

κερδίων, ον, Ep. compar., and κέρδιστος, η, ον, superl. derived from κέρδος; *more gainful, more advantageous, better*; compar. only neut. 3, 41. Od. 2, 74; superl. *most crafty*, Il. 6. 153.†

κέρδος, εος, τό (prob. from κείρω, prop. what is scraped off), *gain, profit, advantage*, 10, 225. Od. 16, 311. 2) *crafty counsel, cunning*, mly in the plur. κέρδεα εἰδέναι, to understand crafty counsels, 23, 709. κέρδεα νωμᾶν ἐνὶ φρεσί, to have crafty designs in the mind, Od. 18, 216. 23, 140; in a bad sense, *crafty devices, tricks*, Od. 2, 88; κακὰ κέρδεα, Od. 23, 217.

κερδοσύνη, ἡ (κέρδος), *craftiness, cunning, wiliness*, only dat. as adv. 21, 247. Od. 4, 251.

κερκίς, ίδος, ἡ, a rod or staff used in the ancient mode of weaving, for striking home the threads, now called *a weaver's reed-stay* or *comb*, later σπάθη. Thus Schneider in Lex. Il. 22, 448. Od. 5, 62. Some ancient Gramm. understand by it, *the shuttle*. (Prob. from κέρκω=κρέκω.)

κέρσας, see κείρω.

κερτομέω (κέρτομος), *to nettle, to goad, to jeer* or *mock, to deride*, with accus. τινά, Od. 16, 87. 18, 350; often with ἐπέεσσιν, and in the partcp. with ἀγορεύειν, 2, 251. Od. 8, 153; generally, *to provoke, to irritate*, σφῆκας, Il. 16, 261. h. Merc. 56.

κερτομίη, ἡ (κερτόμιος), *jeering, taunting, derision, sarcasm*, only plur. 20, 202. Od 20, 263.

κερτόμιος, ον (κέρτομος), *irritating, deriding, jeering, provoking, mocking*, only κερτ. ἔπεα, 4, 6. 5, 419; also κερτόμια, *abuse*, 1. 539. Od. 9, 474.

κέρτομος (κέαρ, τέμνω), prop. heartcutting; hence, *stinging, cutting, insulting*. 2) *deceitful, crafty*, h. Merc. 338.

κέρωνται, see κεράννυμι.

κέσκετο, see κεῖμαι.

κεστός, ή, όν (κεντέω), *stitched* (with a needle), *sowed, embroidered*; ἱμάς, an embroidered girdle, 14, 214.†

κευθάνω, poet. for κεύθω, 3, 453.†

κευθμός, ὁ = κευθμών; ἐκ κευθμῶν, 13, 28.†

κευθμών, ῶνος, ὁ (κεύθω), any concealed place, *a hiding-place, a hole*, Od. 13, 167. 2) *a lair* of animals. πυκινοὶ κευθμῶνες, (the close-locked sties of the swine, Voss), Od. 10, 283.

κεῦθος, εος, τό (κεύθω), poet. form of κευθμών, only dat. plur. κεύθεσι γαίης, in the depths of the earth, spoken of the dwelling of Hades (Pluto), 22, 482. Od. 24, 204.

κεύθω, fut. κεύσω, perf. κέκευθα, aor. 2 ἔκυθον and κύθον, and with Ep. redupl. subj. κεκύθω, Od. 6, 303. The perf. has the signif. of the pres. 1) *to hide, to conceal*, with accus. 22, 118; δάκρυα, Od. 19, 212; spoken of a residence in a place, τινά, Od. 6, 303. 9, 348; chiefly of the dead: ὅπου κύθε γαῖα, Od. 3, 16; hence pass. κεύθεσθαι Ἄϊδι, to be concealed in the realms of Hades, Il. 23. 244. 2) Esply *to conceal in oneself, to hide in one's bosom, to be silent*, with νόῳ, θυμῷ, ἐνὶ στήθεσσιν, absol. and with accus. μῆτιν, Od. 3, 318. οὐκέτι κεύθεν θυμῷ βρωτὸν οὐδὲ ποτῆτα, no longer conceal in your mind meat and drink. i. e. you show that you have eaten and drunk immoderately (Voss, 'your open hearts tell of meat and drink'), Od. 18, 404; κεύθειν, with accus. of pers. τινά, to conceal any thing from any one, Od. 3, 187.

κεφαλή ἡ, κεφαλῆφι, Ep. as gen. Il. 350; and dat. κεφαλῆφι, 10, 30. 1) *the head*, of men and brutes, 11, 72. 2) *the head*, as the noblest part, for the whole person, like κάρη, δέμας, 11, 55. τὸν τῖον ἴσον ἐμῇ κεφαλῇ, I honoured him as myself, 18, 82. cf. 16, 77. Od. 1, 343; hence, the oath by the head. 13, 39; as an address, φίλη κεφαλή, *dear head, dear soul*, 8, 281. 23, 94. 3) *the head*, as the seat of life: ἀποτίειν σὺν κεφαλῇσιν, to expiate with the heads, i. e. with their lives, 4, 162. 17, 242. παραθέσθαι κεφαλάς, to expose their heads, Od. 2, 237.

Κεφαλλήν, ῆνος, ὁ, plur. Κεφαλλῆνες, the *Cephallenians*, the subjects of Odysseus (Ulysses), the inhabitants of Samê, Ithaca, Zacynthus, Dulichium, and the main-land, 2, 631. Od. 20, 210. 24, 354. 377; later, the inhabitants of the island Cephallenia.

κέχανδα, see χανδάνω.

κεχαρησέμεν, κεχαρήσεται, κεχαρηώς, κεχάροιατο, κεχάροντο, Ep. forms from χαίρω

κεχαρισμένος, η, ον, see χαρίζομαι.

κεχηνώς, see χαίνω.

κεχόλωμαι, see χολόω.

κεχρημένος, η, ον, see χράομαι.

κέχυμαι, see χέω.

κέω 1) Ep. form of κείω, q. v. only ὄρσο κέων, go, in order to lie down to sleep, Od. 7, 342,† 2) as a form of καίω, it is doubtful, see Buttm. Gramm., § 114. p. 287.

κῆαι, κήαι (3 optat. aor.), κηάμενος, Ep. aor. forms from καίω

κήδειος, ον (κῆδος), Ep. also κήδεος, q. v. worth care, dear, beloved, 19, 224. (The other explanation : ' to be buried by us,' does not suit the connexion, 19, 294.) Superl. κήδιστος.

κηδεμών, όνος, ὁ (κηδέω), one who has the charge, a guardian, a protector, in *23, 163. 674, those who have charge of the interment of the dead.

κήδεος, ον, Ep. for κήδειος, οἷσι κήδεός ἐστι νέκυς, either generally, dear, or [less probably], according to Voss, ' upon whom devolves the care of the corpse,' 23, 160.† (Some Gramm. considered the word as gen. of κῆδος : ' to whom the dead is an object of care.')

κηδέω, absol. pres. of the fut. κηδήσω, see κήδω.

κήδιστος, η, ον (superl. formed from κῆδος, in signif. belonging to κήδειος), dearest, most beloved, 9, 642. Od. 10, 225. (In like manner, Od. 8, 583, without exactly indicating the nearest kindred.)

κῆδος, εος. τό, care, sadness, trouble, grief, τῶν ἄλλων οὐ κῆδος, about the others there is no care, i. e. there is no trouble with the others, Od. 22, 254. σ᾽ ἐμῷ ἐνὶ κήδεα θυμῷ. Il. 18, 53. κήδεα θυμοῦ, heart-troubles, Od. 14, 197 ; distinguished from ἄχος, Od. 4, 108 ; esply grief for the death of one dear to us, Il. 4, 270. 5, 156. 13, 464.-18, 8. 2) that which occasions care, need, misery, wretchedness; esply in the plur. l; 445. 9, 592. Od. 1, 244; and often. (The signif. relationship, Voss, Il. 13, 464, ' if relationship touches thy soul,' is justly rejected by Passow.)

κήδω (ΚΑΔΩ), fut. κηδήσω, fut. mid. κεκαδήσομαι, iterat. imperf. κηδέσκετο, 1) Act. only Ep. a) to render anxious, to sadden, to trouble, to distress, τινά, 9, 615; θυμόν, 5, 400. 11, 458. b) More frequently : to injure externally, to violate, to harass, θεοὺς τόξοισιν, 5, 404; μῆλα, 17, 550 ; οἶκον, Od. 23, 9. 2) Mid. to be anxious, sad, to trouble oneself, always partcp. 1, 196. Od. 3, 240. 3) to be anxious about any man, to care for any man, τινός, Il. 1, 56 ; Δαναῶν, 8, 353 ; βιότοιο, Ou. 14, 4. (The aor. 2 κέκαδον and fut. κεκαδήσω, in the signif. to deprive, belongs to χάζομαι.)

κῆεν, see καίω.

κηκίω, to gush forth, to stream (from), spoken of water, ἂν στόμα, out of the mouth. Od. 5, 455.† (from κίω, with reduplicat.)

κήλειος, ον, Ion. and Ep. for κήλεος, 15, 744.†

κήλεος. ον (κάω, καίω, like δαιδάλεος), burning, flaming, always πυρὶ κηλέῳ (the last dissyllabic), 8, 217. Od. 9, 328.

κηληθμός, ὁ (κηλέω), enchantment, pleasure, transport, *Od. 11, 334. 13, 2.

κῆλον, τό (καίω), prop. a dry stick of wood, esply the shaft of an arrow : an arrow itself in H. ; in the plur. κῆλα, missiles, shafts: used only of the gods, *l, 53. 12, 280. h. Ap. 444.

*Κηναῖον, τό, a promontory on the north-west coast of the island Euboea, now Cap Lithoda, h. in Ap. 219.

κήξ, κός. ἡ = κηϋξ, a sea-bird, the sea-hen. or sew-mew, Od. 15, 479.†

κήομεν, Ep. for κήωμεν, see καίω.

κῆπος, ὁ, a garden, and generally a piece of land, inclosed and set with trees or other vegetation, 8, 305. Od. 4, 737. 7, 129.

Κήρ, κηρός. ἡ, the goddess of death, (distinct from Μοῖρα and Αἶσα), the personified power of death, which brings death in a particular form : as death in battle, sickness, drowning in the sea, etc., hence, in sing. and plur. Κῆρες θανάτοιο, 2, 302. 11, 332; and Κήρ in connexion with φόνος, θάνατος. 2, 352. Od. 4, 273. 5, 387. 16, 169. He who was to die by a violent death had the Κήρ allotted him at birth, 23, 79. To Achilles were two Κῆρες allotted, 9, 411. Zeus laid the Κῆρες of Achilles and Hector in the scales, to determine which was to die first, 22, 210. The Κῆρες are μυρίαι, since one is allotted to each person who is destined to a violent death,12, 326, 327. 2) As an appell. fate, death, in Wolf's ed. only once : τὸ δέ τοι κὴρ εἴδεται εἶναι, that seems to thee to be death, 1, 228. Bothe has it in many passages beside, 2, 352. 3, 32. 5, 22. e c. which also Passow prefers. In 1, 97, Wolf, after a conjecture of Markland, has λοιμοῖο Κήρας ἀφέξει instead of the reading of the Cdd. χεῖρας (κήρ prob. from κέρω, κείρω).

κῆρ, κῆρος. τό, contr. from κέαρ, Batr. the heart, esply, 1) the soul, the mind, as the seat of the feelings and passions, 1, 44; chiefly the dative κῆρι as adv. in the heart, for the most part with περὶ preceding, (ed. Wolf) much at heart. 4, 46. 53. 13, 119. 430. Od. 5, 36, where περὶ is an adv. according to Passow. Spitzner rejects this and writes with the ancients περὶ κῆρι, in heart. That this is the true explanation is shown by the kindred phrases περὶ θυμῷ, περὶ φρεσίν, 22, 70. 16, 157. cf. περὶ, and Thiersch, § 264. p. 458. 2) As a periphrasis of the person, like βίη : Πυλαιμένεος λάσιον κῆρ, 2, 851. cf. Od. 4, 270.

κηρεσσιφόρητος, ον (φορέω), brought by the Fates, or impelled by the Fates [iniquo fato advectus. Db.], [these dogs, κύνες, whom Ilium's unpropitious fates Have wafted hither. Cp.], i. e. the Greeks sent by the Κῆρες for the destruction of Troy 8, 527.

Κήρινθος, ἡ. a town in Euboea, northeast of Chalcis, 2, 538.

*κηρίον, τό (κηρός), a cake of honey, a honey-comb, h. Merc. 559.

κηρόθι, adv. (κῆρ), in the heart, heartily,

strengthened by μᾶλλον, 9, 300. Od. 15, 369.

κηρός, ὁ, *wax.* *Od. 12, 48. 173. 175.

κῆρυξ, ῦκος, ὁ, *a herald.* The heralds were most respectable royal servants, and even of noble and often of royal blood, 1, 321. 3, 116. They receive as epithets, ἀγανοί, 3, 268: θεῖος, 4, 192. Their office was to convoke assemblies, and to preserve order in them, 2, 50. 280. In war they were employed to treat with the enemy, 7, 274, seq. Esply in time of peace all care of sacrifices and sacrificial feasts devolved upon them, Od. 1, 110. 3, 472. As an ensign of office they carried a sceptre, Il. 18, 505. Od. 2, 38. They were under the immediate protection of Zeus, Διὸς ἄγγελοι, Διὶ φίλοι, 1, 334. 8, 517. They placed the sceptre in the hand of one about to speak in the assembly, 24, 567, seq. Od. 2, 38; they waited at meals. Od. 1, 143. 146.

κηρύσσω (κῆρυξ), 1) *to be a herald, to hold the office of herald,* 17, 325. 2) *to proclaim as a herald, to cry out,* 2, 438; with accus. λαὸν ἀγορήνδε, 2, 51. Od. 2, 7; πόλεμόνδε. Il. 2, 443.

κῆται, for κέηται, see κεῖμαι.

Κήτειοι, οἱ, the *Ceteans,* an unknown tribe in Mysia, so called from the river Κητώεις in the region of the later Elea or Pergamus, Od. 11, 521. (The old Gramm. were uncertain about them: Aristarchus explains ἑταῖροι κήτειοι by μεγάλοι from κῆτος; others read κήδειοι)

κῆτος, εος, τό (according to Buttm., Lex. p. 378. from ΧΑΩ. χάσκω, prop. *a hollow, a chasm,* as appears in the deriv.). any large sea-animal, *a sea-monster,* 20, 147. Od. 5, 421; in Od. 4, 443. 446. 452 = φώκη.

κητώεις. εσσα, εν (κῆτος), only as an epith. of Lacedæmon, *having many chasms and hollows;* cf. Λακεδαίμων, 2, 581. Od. 4, 1: because it [the valley of the Eurotas] lies in a hollow, surrounded with mountains and narrow passes. Thus Buttm., Lex. p. 378, and Nitzsch; others, as Heyne, Voss, *spacious, vast, huge,* a definition less suited to fact.

Κηφισίς. ίδος, ἡ λίμνη, *the Cephisian lake,* 5, 709; elsewhere ἡ Κωπαῖς λίμνη, *the lake Copaïs,* in Bœotia, which was nine geographical miles in circumference, and often occasioned a flood, now the lake of *Livadia* or *Topolia.* (It received its name from the river Κηφισός, q v.)

Κηφισός. ὁ, a river in Phocis; it rises near Lilæa. and flows into the lake Copaïs, now *Mauro-Nero,* 2, 522. (Κηφισσός, a later form, cf. Buttm. Gram. § 21.)

κηώδης. ες (κάω, καίω), *exhaling vapour, sweet-scented. fragrant,* κόλπος, 6, 467.† (according to Passow from an old subst. κῆος = θύος.)

κηώεις, εσσα, εν = κηώδης, *fragrant,* always epith. of θάλαμος, 3, 382. Od. 15, 99.

κίδναμαι (intrans.), Ep. mid. from κίδνημι, poet. form of σκεδάννυμι, *to spread, to extend,* Ἠὼς ἐκίδνατο πᾶσαν ἐπ᾽ αἶαν, *8, 1. 24, 695. ὑπεὶρ ἅλα, 23, 227.

κιθάρα, ἡ = κίθαρις, a later form, h. Merc. 509. 515

κιθαρίζω (κίθαρις). *to play upon the harp,* and generally, *to play upon a stringed instrument,* φόρμιγγι, 18, 570;† λύρῃ, h. Merc. 433.

κίθαρις. ιος, ἡ, accus. κίθαριν, *a harp, a lute,* a stringed instrument which differed in form from the lyre. According to Buretti in the Mémoir. des Inscript. de l'Acad. des Sciences à Paris IV. p 116, the *cithara* had two curved horns, which at the top turned outwards and at the bottom inwards, and stood upon a hollow-sounding stand. Above and below were two cross-pieces for fastening the strings (ὑπολύριον and ζυγόν). The strings were strained above by pegs (κόλλοπες). The *cithara* had a soft tone, and was closely related to the φόρμιγξ. 3, 54. Od. 1, 153. 2) *the act of playing upon the harp, the tone of stringed instruments,* Il. 13, 731. Od. 8, 248.

κιθαριστύς. ύος. ἡ. *the art of playing upon the* cithara, *harp playing,* 2, 600.†

κιθαριστής, οῦ. ὁ (κιθαρίζω), *a harp-player, a harper,* h. 24, 3.

κικλήσκω, Ion. and Ep. form for καλέω in the pres. and imperf. 1) *to call,* τινά, 2, 404. 9, 11; *to call upon, to cry to,* Ἀΐδ,ν, 9, 569. 2) *to name,* with accus of the pers. and of the name, 2, 813. Od 4, 355; and ἐπίκλησιν κικλήσκειν, to call by surname, Il. 7, 139. Mid. Batr. 27.

Κίκονες, οἱ, sing. Κίκων, ονος, a people in Thrace, who dwelt along the southern coast of Ismarus to Lissus, 2, 846. Od. 9, seq.

κίκυς, ἡ, an ancient poet. word, *strength,* Od. 11, 393.† h. Ven. 238. (According to Eustath. from κίω, to go; others write κηκίς, and explain it, moisture, blood.)

Κίλικες, οἱ, sing. Κίλιξ; the *Cilicians* had their seat in H.'s time in greater Phrygia. Here they were governed in two kingdoms, of which one had its capit at Thebe, at mount Placus, the other at Lyrnessus, 6, 397. 415. cf. 2, 692. At a later date they emigrated to the country called by their name.

Κίλλα, ἡ, a small town in Troas or in Æolis in Asia Minor, having a temple of Apollo, 1, 38. 452.

Κιμμέριοι, οἱ, *Cimmerii,* in H. a fabulous people, who dwelt in the western part of the earth, on Oceanus, north of the entrance to the under world; they are wrapped in clouds and storms, and live in perpetual night, Od. 11, 14, seq. The ancient critics place them either in Italy, in the region of Baiæ, or in Spain, cf. Strab. That the Cimmerian night indicates the extreme north, cannot be denied; and we may certainly suppose that a dark rumour of a night lasting many months may have had a place in the poet's imagination, though he thought of no definite country. Völcker, Hom. Geogr. p. 154, derives the name from χειμέριος; Voss, on the other hand, from the Phœnician word *Kamar*, *Kimmer*.

*κίνδυνος, ὁ, peril, danger, Batr. 9.

κινέω (κίνω), poet. form, mid. κίνυμαι, fut. κινήσω, aor. 1 ἐκίνησα, aor. pass. ἐκινήθην, to put in motion, to move, to excite, to urge on; often κάρη, to move the head, 17, 200. Od. 5, 285; σφῆκας, to excite the wasps, Il. 16, 264; νεφέλην, 16, 297; κῦμα (spoken of wind), 2, 395; τινὰ λάξ, to thrust a man with one's foot (to awaken him), 10, 158; θύρην, Od. 22, 394. Mid. and pass. to move oneself, to move. κινήθη ἀγορή, ἐκίνηθεν φάλαγγες, Il. 2, 144. 16, 280; to move oneself forward, i. e. to go, 1, 47.

*κινητήρ, ῆρος, ὁ (κινέω), a mover, one who shakes; γαίης, a shaker of the earth, h. 21, 2.

κίνυμαι, mid. poet. form of κινέω, to be moved. κινύμενον ἔλαιον, 14, 173; often to move oneself, i. e. to go, ἐς πόλεμον, 4, 281. 332. 10, 280.

Κινύρης, αο, ὁ, Ion. for Κινύρας, ruler in Cyprus, 11, 20. Apd. 3, 14. 4; son of Sandacus, grandson of Phaëthon, at first king of Syria; he went afterwards to Cyprus and built Paphos, cf. Κινύρου πλουσιώτερος, Tyrt. III. 6.

κινυρός, ή, όν, wailing, moaning, plaintive, 17, 5.†

Κίρκη, ἡ, Kirkē (Circe), daughter of Helios and Persē, sister of Æêtês, a nymph, skilled in magic, who dwelt on the island Ææa. Od. 10, 136; see Αἶα. Odysseus (Ulysses), having escaped from the terrible Læstrygones, landed on her island. The enchantress metamorphosed his companions into swine; he compelled her to disenchant them, Od. 10, 230–364. He lived a year with Circe in perpetual feasting; and, in order to procure intelligence concerning his return, he visited, by her advice, the entrance of the infernal regions, Od. 10, 466, seq. 11, 1, seq. According to Hes. Th. 759, she bore two sons by Odysseus (Ulysses), Agrius and Latinus. (Herm. de Myth. Græc. Antiq. explains the name, navigatio in orbem facta.)

κίρκος, ὁ, a hawk, a kind of falcon, which describes circles in flying, 17, 757. 22, 139. Because his flight was regarded as ominous, he was called Ἀπόλλωνος ἄγγελος, Od. 15, 526; and also ἱρηξ κίρκος, the circling hawk, Od. 13, 87.

κιρνάω and κίρνημι, poet. form of κεράννυμι, to mingle, to mix, from which we have partcp κιρνάς, Od. 16, 14; imperf. ἐκίρνα, Od. 7, 182. 10, 356; and from κίρνημι, imperf. κίρνη, *Od. 14, 78. 16, 52.

Κισσηίς, ίδος, ἡ, daughter of Kissês

(Cisses)= Theāno, 6, 299.

Κισσῆς, οῦ, ὁ, contr. from Κισσεάς, later Κισσεύς, έως, king of Thrace, father of Theāno, 11, 223. (Κισσεύς, from κισσός, crowned with ivy.)

*κισσοκόμης, ου, ὁ (κομάω), having tresses of ivy, having the hair decorated with ivy, h. 25, 1.

*κισσός, ὁ, ivy, a plant sacred to Dionŷsos, h. 6, 40.

κισσύβιον, τό, a goblet, a cup, prop. made of ivy wood, *Od. 9, 346. 14, 78. 16, 52.

κίστη, ἡ, chest, a box, Od. 6, 76.†

κιχάνω and κιχάνομαι. Ep. imperf. ἐκίχανον, 2 sing. ἐκίχεις (cf. ἐτίθεις), dual ἐκιχήτην, 1 plur. ἐκίχημεν. fut. κιχήσομαι (as if from κιχέω), aor. 2 ἐκιχον, and aor. 1 mid. ἐκιχήσατο, partcp. pres. mid. κιχήμενος; also from an obsol. form κίχημι. pres. subj. κιχῶ, Ep. κιχείω, optat. κιχείην. inf. κιχῆναι, partcp. κιχείς, 1) to reach, to attain, to overtake; with accus. ποσσὶ τινά, to overtake a man with the feet, i. e. in running, 6, 228; δουρί, 10, 370; metaph. spoken of death and destruction, 9, 416. 11, 441. 451. κιχάνει δίψα τε καὶ λιμός, 19, 165. cf. κιχήμενον βέλος, a hitting arrow, with gen. of pers. 5, 187. 2) to hit, to meet with, to find, τινὰ παρὰ νηυσί, 1, 26. Od. 13, 228.

κίχλη, ἡ, the thrush, Od. 22, 468.†

*κίχρημι (χράω), fut. χρήσω, to lend, mid. to borrow, only χρησαμένη, Batr. 187.

κίω, poet. form from εἶμι, ΊΩ, in pres. indicat. obsol., only optat. κίοιμι, partcp. κιών, imperf. ἔκιον, κίον, to go, to go away, like εἶμι. spoken of living beings; only, 2, 509. κίον νῆες.

κίων, ονος, ἡ, and masc. ὁ, Od. 8, 66. 473. 17, 29. 19, 38; a pillar, a column, nly spoken of the pillars which supported the roof of the eating-room. Od. 1, 127. 6, 307. 19, 38, seq. 22, 466; metaph. spoken of Atlas, ἔχει κίονας μακράς, see Ἄτλας. *Od.

κλαγγή, ἡ (κλάζω), generally an inarticulate sound, produced by animate and inanimate objects; a sound, a noise, spoken of men; a cry, a tumult, spoken of warriors, 2, 100. 10, 523; of the dead, Od. 11, 604; of animals, esply of cranes, Il. 3, 2; of swine, Od. 14, 412; of the roar of lions, h. 13, 4; of the twang of the bow, Il. 1, 49.

κλαγγηδόν, adv. (κλαγγή), with a cry, with a clamour, 2, 463.†

κλάζω, aor. 1 ἔκλαγξα, Ep. perf. with pres. signif. κέκληγα, partcp. κεκληγώς, of this the plur. is κεκλήγοντες (as if from a pres. κεκλήγω), aor. 2 ἔκλαγον, spoken of any articulate sound, to resound, to clang, to ring, to cry, spoken of the cry of men, 2, 222. 12, 125; of the cry of the eagle, 12, 207. 16, 429; of herons and jackdaws, 10, 276. 17, 756; of the barking of dogs, Od. 14, 30; to resound, to whiz or hum, spoken of arrows, Il. 1,

46; *to roar or hiss*, spoken of the wind, Od. 12, 408. ἔκλαγεν οἶος. in h. 18, 14, according to Herm. ad loc. *solus sub vesperam fistula canit* (Pan).

κλαίω, fut. κλαύσομαι, aor. 1 ἔκλαυσα, Ep. κλαῦσα, Ep. iterat. imperf. κλαίεσκον, 1) *to weep, to wail, to lament*, absol. κλαίοντά σε ἀφήσω, I will send thee forth weeping, i. e. I will punish thee, 2, 263; esply *to weep for the dead*, 7, 427. 19, 75. 2) With accus. *to weep for* any man, *to bewail*, 22, 87. 210. Od. 1, 363, and often.

*Κλάρος, ἡ, a small town near Colophon in Ionia, upon a point of land, with a temple and oracle of Apollo; now *Zille*, h. Ap. 40.

κλαυθμός, ὁ (κλαίω), *the act of weeping* or *wailing, lamentation*, 24, 717, and often Od.

κλάω, aor. 1 Ep. κλάσε, aor. pass. ἐκλάσθην, *to break, to break off*, with accus. πτόρθον, Od. 6, 128. Pass. intrans. *to break in pieces*, Il. 11, 584.

κλεηδών, όνος, ἡ, once κληηδών, Od. 4, 317; Ion. and Ep. for κληδών (κλέος), 1) *report, rumour, fame; πατρός*, intelligence about one's father, Od. 4, 317. 2) Esply *a divine voice, an omen*, like ὄσσα, *Od. 18, 117. 20, 120.

Κλεισιδίκη, daughter of Keleos (Celeus), in Eleusis, h. in Cer. 109.

κλειτός, ή, όν (κλείω), *famous, glorious, excellent, illustrious*, spoken of persons, 3, 451. Od. 6, 54; of things: ἑκατόμβη. often Il.; Πανοπεύς, 17, 307.

Κλεῖτος, ὁ, *Clitus*, son of Pisênor, a Trojan, 15, 445, seq. 2) son of Mantius, grandson of Melampus, Od. 15, 249.

κλείω, poet. for κλέω (from κλέω; H. has only pres. pass. κλέομαι, imperf. ἔκλεο for ἐκλέεο, 24, 202; also fut. act. κλήσω, h. 31, 19); *to make known, to render famous; to praise*, with accus. ἔργα, Od. 1, 338. 17, 418. Pass. *to be made known, to be famous*, ἐπ' ἀνθρώπους, Il. 24, 202; whereby κέρδεσιν, Od. 13, 299.

Κλεόβουλος, ὁ, a Trojan, slain by Ajax, son of Oïleus, 16, 330.

Κλεοπάτρη, ἡ, daughter of Idas and Marpessa, wife of Meleagros (Meleager), see Ἀλκυόνη, 9, 556.

κλέος, εος, τό (κλέω), 1) *report, rumour, fame*, 2, 486; with gen. κλέος Ἀχαιῶν, the report of the Greeks, 11, 227; πολέμοιο, 13, 364; πατρός, Od. 2, 308. 3, 83; σὸν κλέος, intelligence of thee, Od. 13, 415; ἐμόν, Od. 18, 255. 2) *a good report, fame, glory, honour*, in connexion with ἐσθλόν, μέγα, εὐρύ, and alone Il. 4, 197; and often in the plur. κλέα ἀνδρῶν, for κλέεα, famous deeds, *laudes*, 9, 189. 524. Od 8, 73.

κλέπτης, ου, ὁ (κλέπτω), *thief, robber*, 3, 11.†

κλεπτοσύνη, ἡ, *thievery, knavery, deception*, Od. 19, 396.†

κλέπτω, aor. 1 ἔκλεψα, 1) *to steal, to procure by stealth*, 5, 268. 24, 24. 2)

Metaph. *to deceive, to cheat, to overreach*, νόον τινός, 14, 217; absol. μὴ κλέπτε νόῳ, cherish not deception in thy soul (Voss, 'meditate not deceit'), 1, 132.

κλέω, from which pass. κλέομαι, see κλείω.

Κλεωναί, αἱ, *Cleônæ*, a town in Argolis, south-west of Corinth, 2, 570.

*κλεψίφρων, ον (φρήν), *having deceitful purposes, cunning, crafty*, h. Merc. 413.

κληδήν, adv. (καλέω), *by name, namely*, 9, 11.†

κληηδών, όνος, Ep. form of κληδών, q. v.

κλήθρη, ἡ, Ion. for κλήθρα, *the alder*, alnus, *Od. 5, 64. 239.

κληΐζω, as a form of κλείω, κληΐω is incorrect, see Buttm. Ausführ. Gram. Th. 2, p. 169.

*κλήϊθρον, τό, Ion. and Ep. for κλῆθρον, *a lock, a bolt*, h. Merc. 146.

κληΐς, ῖδος(ῐ), ἡ, Ion. and Ep. for κλείς, (only in the Ion. form), 1) Prop. that which locks, a) *the bolt or bar*, which locks the door inside, and which from without is pulled forward with a thong; to unlock, after untying the thong, the bolt is pressed back with a hook. ἐπὶ κληῖδ'(ῐ) ἐτάνυσσεν ἱμάντι, Od. 1, 442. Il. 24, 455. This bolt is also called ἐπιβλής, 24, 453; and ὀχεύς, 12, 121. b) the bolt, which locked together two corresponding bars, 12, 456. 14, 168. c) Esply *a key*, of brass, with ivory handle, with which the door was locked and opened, Od. 21, 6. Il. 6, 89. It was a curved hook with which, in locking, the bolt was thrust forward; in opening, pushed back through a hole, into which the key was introduced, Od. 21, 6. 47. 241. d) the *hook* of a clasp, Od. 18, 294. 2) the *clavicle*, the bone between the neck and breast, Il. 5, 146. 8, 325. plur. 22, 324; (in the Od. it has not this signif. 3) κληῖδες(ῐ), only in the plur. the *rowers' seats* in the ship, i. e. the seats where the oars were worked in leather thongs in the manner of a key, Od. 2, 419. 4, 579. Il. 16, 170.† cf. Voss ad Arat. Phænom. 191.

κληϊστός, ή, όν (κληΐω), Ion. for κλειστός, *locked, that may be locked*. Od. 2, 344.†

κληΐω, Ion. and Ep. for κλείω (κληΐς), aor. 1 ἐκλήϊσα, *to shut up, to lock*, with accus. θύρας, Od. 19. 30. 24, 166 (κλήϊσσεν with σσ is incorrect, as ι is long), *Od.

*κληροπαλής, ές (πάλλω), *distributed by shaking lots*, by lot, h. Merc. 129.

κλῆρος, ὁ, 1) *a lot*, any thing used for casting lots; in the earliest times, stones, pieces of wood, etc., marked by those who were casting lots, 7, 175. In H. the lots are placed in a helmet, shaken, and he whose lot first leapt out of the helmet, was the individual destined by the lot, 3, 316. 325. Od. 10, 206. 2) that which is obtained by lot, esply as is

Κλητός.　　　　243　　　　Κλυταιμνήστρη.

heritance, Il. 15, 498. Od. 14, 64. (From κλάω, because a fragment was used for a lot.)

κλητός, ή, όν (καλέω), 1) called, called out, hence chosen, 9, 165. 2) summoned, invited, Od. 17, 386.

*κλήω = κλείω, to celebrate, to render famous, κλήω, h. 31, 16; κλῆσαι, Ep. 4, 9.

κλῖμαξ, ακος, ἡ (κλίνω), a ladder, a staircase, *Od. 1, 330. 10, 558. 21, 5.

κλιστήρ, ῆρος, ὁ (κλίνω), an easy chair, a couch, Od. 18, 190.†

κλίνω, aor. 1. ἔκλῖνα, perf. pass. κέκλιμαι. 3 plur. Ep. κεκλίαται, aor. pass. ἐκλίθην, Ep. ἐκλίνθην, ground signif., I) Act. to incline, to bend. 1) to incline, to lean, τί τινι, any thing against another: σάκεα ὤμοισι, 11, 593. 13, 488; ἅρματα πρὸς ἐνώπια, 8, 435; τόξον πρὸς ἐνώπια, Od. 22, 121. 2) to incline, to change the direction, τάλαντα, to bend the balances, so that one scale rises and the other falls, 19, 223: ὄσσε πάλιν, to turn back, 3, 427. Esply 3) to bend, to force to yield, to put to flight, μάχην Τρῶας, 14, 510. 5, 37. Od. 9, 59. 11) Mid. with aor. pass. to incline oneself to one side, to lie down, Od. 19, 470. Il. 10, 350; and perf. and pluperf. pass. a) to be inclined, to support oneself, τινί, on or against any thing. κεκλιμένος στήλῃ, inclined against a pillar, 11, 371. Od. 6, 307; ἀσπίσι, leaning upon the shields, Il. 3, 335. b) to lie, 10. 472. Od. 11, 194; spoken esply of places, to lie, to be situated, ἁλί, towards the sea, Od. 4, 608. 13, 215: also of persons, κεκλιμένος λίμνῃ, inclined to the lake, i. e. dwelling at, Il. 5, 709. 16, 68. 2) to bend oneself, to sink, esply in aor. pass. 3, 360. 7, 254. 13, 543.

κλισίη, ἡ (κλίνω), Ep. dat. κλισίηφι, 13, 168: prop. a place where a man may lie down or recline; hence 1) a lodge, a hut, a tent, made of posts, inwoven with ozier twigs and covered above with reeds. a) the huts of herdsmen, 18, 589. Od. 14, 45. 16, 1. b) Esply the lodges of warriors, which were in like manner built of wood, often in the plur. 1, 306. 2, 91, sq. The lodge of Achilles is described, 24, 450. Tents like those now used were probably of later invention, see Mitford's Greece, I. § iii. p. 147. 2) an easy-chair, an arm-chair, Od. 4, 123. 19 55: mly κλισμός, q. v.

κλισίηθεν, from the lodge, from the tent, *1, 391 11, 603; and often.

κλισίηνδε, adv. (κλισίη), to the lodge, to the tent, 9, 712. Od. 14, 45. 48.

κλίσιον, τό (κλισίη), the domestics' house, a dwelling for the servants of a family, Od. 24, 208.†

κλισμός, ὁ (κλίνω), an easy-chair, an arm-chair, distinct from θρόνος, Od. 3, 389: prob. somewhat lower, often elegantly wrought, and decked with shining ornaments, Od. 1, 132 Il. 8, 436; also sometimes with a foot-stool, Od. 4, 136.

κλῖτύς, ύος, poet. accus. plur. κλῖτύς, inclination, declivity, a descent, 16, 390. Od. 5, 470.

κλονέω, for the most part poet. only pres. and imperf. 1) Act. to put in violent motion, to drive before a man, to chase, with accus. φάλαγγας, 5, 96; spoken of lions: ἀγέλην, 15, 324; absol. to make a tumult, 11, 496. 526. 14, 14; metaph. of the wind: to drive, νέφεα, 23, 213; φλόγα, 20, 492. 2) Mid. and pass. to put oneself in disorderly motion, to be in confusion, to be tumultuous, 11, 148. 15, 448; ὁμίλῳ, 4, 302: ὑπό τινι, *5, 93.

Κλονίος, ὁ, son of Alector, and leader of the Boeotians before Troy, 2, 495.

κλόνος, ὁ, any violent motion, a press, a tumult, a confusion, esply of warriors, who are thrown into disorder, 16, 331. 713. 729; ἐγχειάων, a press of spears, *5, 167.

κλόπιος, η, ον (κλώψ), thievish, stolen, stealthy, crafty, Od. 13, 295.†

*κλόπος, ὁ κλώψ), a thief, h. Merc. 276.

κλοτοπεύω, 19, 149.† οὐ γὰρ χρὴ κλοτοπεύειν, from the connexion it seems to signify, 'it is not proper to employ fine words,' or 'to use plausible pretexts.' (The deriv. is uncertain, Hesych. and other Gramm. explain it by παραλογίζεσθαι, ἀπατᾶν, and derive it from κλέπτω, supposing it to be equivalent to κλοποπεύειν, to delay by plausible pretexts. One Schol. B. explains it: καλλιλογεῖν καὶ κλυτοῖς ἔπεσιν ἐνδιατρίβειν, 'to employ fine words,' and derives it from κλυτός and ὄψ, proposing to write κλυτοπεύειν or κλύτ' ὀπεύειν.)

κλύδων, ωνος (κλύζω), a wave, a dashing of the surge, Od. 12, 421.†

κλύζω, κλύσω, fut. Ep. aor. pass. ἐκλύσθην, prob. a word formed to imitate the sound of agitated water. 1) to dash upon, to plash, to beat, spoken of waves, ἐπ' ἠϊόνος, 23, 61. b) τινά, h. Ap. 74. 2) Pass. to roll in waves, to dash in waves. ἐκλύσθη θάλασσα ποτὶ κλισίας, 14, 392. Od. 9, 484. Batr. 76.

κλῦθι, see κλύω.

Κλυμένη, ἡ, 1) a Nereid, 18, 47. 2) a handmaid of Helen, 3, 144. 3) daughter of Minyas or Iphis, wife of Phylacus, mother of Iphiclus, Od. 11, 326.

Κλύμενος, ὁ, son of Presben, king of the Minyae in Orchomenos, father of Erginus and Eurydice, who was mortally wounded at Thebes, on a feast of Poseidon, Od. 3, 452. Apd. 2, 4. 11.

(κλῦμι), an assumed root of κλῦθι.

Κλυσώνυμος, ὁ, son of Amphidamas, slain by Patroclus, 23, 88.

Κλυταιμνήστρη, ἡ, daughter of Tyndareus and Leda, sister of Helen, wife of Agamemnon, q. v., 1, 113. Od. 3, 264. She lived in illicit intercourse with Ægisthus, who with her aid slew her husband upon his return from Troy. Orestes avenged his father's death, by the murder of his mother and her paramour, Od. 1, 300. 11, 409.

M 2

Κλυτίδης. ου, ὁ. son of Clytius, 1) =
Piræus, of Elis. Od. 15, 539. 16, 327. 2)
= Dolops, Il. 11, 302.

Κλυτίος, ὁ, 1) son of Laomĕdon, and
brother of Priam, father of Calêtor, one
of the counsellors, 3, 147. 15. 419. 2)
father of Piræus of Ithaca, Od. 16, 327.
15, 539. 3) a Greek, father of Dolops,
Il. 11, 302. The accentuation Κλύτιος is
incorrect, cf. Göttling, Lehre vom Accent,
§ 23.

κλυτοεργός, όν, poet. (ἔργον), famed by
works, illustrious by his products, an illustrious artist, epith. of Hephæstus,
Od. 8, 345.†

Κλυτομήδης, εος, ὁ, son of Enops from
Ætolia, whom Nestor conquered in a
pugilistic combat, 23, 634

*κλυτόμητις, ι. poet. (μῆτις), famed for
knowledge, intelligent, h. 19, 1.

Κλυτόνηος, ὁ, son of Alcinous, a fleet
runner, Od. 8, 119. 122.

κλυτόπωλος, ον, poet. (πῶλος), famed
for horses, or rather, having famous horses,
cf. Schol. ad Il. 5, 754, and κλυτότοξος ; in the Il. an epith. of Hades, *5,
654. 11, 445. 16, 625 ; of the country
Dardania, Fr. 38.

κλυτός, ή, όν, rarely ός, όν. poet. 2,
742 ; and Od. 5, 422 ; (κλύω), prop.
heard, hence : of which one hears much.
i. e. famed, famous, glorious, often an
epith. of gods and men ; κλυτὰ φῦλα
ἀνθρώπων in opposition to brutes, 14,
361 ; generally, spoken of animate and
inanimate objects : famed, glorious, splendid, μῆλα, τεύχεα, δώματα, ἄλσος. (The
signif. roaring, noisy, that makes itself
heard, has been given to the word, in
connexion with μῆλα, λιμήν, Od. 9, 308.
10, 87 ; although the signif. glorious is
suitable.)

κλυτοτέχνης, ον, ὁ, poet. (τέχνη), famous
for art, an illustrious artist, i, 571. Od. 8,
286.

κλυτότοξος, ον. poet. (τόξον), famed by
the bow, or, rather, having a famous bow,
cf. ἀργυρότοξος, ἀγκυλότοξοι : an illustrious archer, epith. of Apollo, 4, 101.
Od. 17, 494.

κλύω. poet. (akin to κλέω), imperf.
ἔκλυον with signif. of aor., also imperat.
aor. 2 κλῦθι. κλῦτε, and with redupl.
ἔκλυθι. κέκλυτε, 1) to hear, to apprehend, mly with accus. δοῦπον, αὐδήν, 4,
455. 13, 757 ; more rarely with gen. of
pers. and partcp. ἔκλυον αὐδήσαντος, I
heard him speaking, 10. 47 ; with gen. of
pers. and thing, 16, 76 ; ἐκύρης ὀπός, 22,
451 ; κέκλυτέ μευ μύθων, Od. 10, 189.
311. 481. 12, 271. 340 ; ἔκ τινος, to hear
of any man, Od. 19, 93 ; generally, to
learn, to become acquainted with, Od. 6,
185. 2) to hear, to listen to, mly with
gen. of pers. Il. 1, 43. 218 ; with dat.
after κλῦθι and κλῦτε, 5, 115. Od. 2, 262,
is rather dat. commod., yield to my desires ; in like manner, θεά οἱ ἔκλυεν ἀρῆς,
the goddess listened to her prayer, Od. 4,
767. 3) to hear to any man, to obey, in

connexion with πείθομαι, Il. 7, 379. 9,
79. Od. 3, 477.

κλωμακόεις, εσσα, εν (κλῶμαξ), stony,
rocky, poet. Ἰθώμη. 2, 729.†

κνάω, imperf. κνῆ, Ep. for ἔκνη, to
scrape, to rub, τυρόν, 11, 639.† (κνῆ is
not aor. cf. Buttm. Gram. § 105, note 5.
Rost, p. 234.)

κνέφας, αος, τό (akin to νέφος), darkness, gloominess, esply the obscurity of
evening twilight, 1, 475. Od. 5, 225; only
nomin. and accus.

κνῆ, see κνάω.

κνήμη, ἡ, the leg between the knee
and ankle, the shank, the tibia, 4, 147.
519. Od. 19, 469.

κνημίς, ῖδος, ἡ (κνήμη), armour for the
legs, greaves, a covering worn for protection in war. It consisted of two metallic plates, fastened together with
buckles or clasps (ἐπισφύρια). 3, 330;
prob. they were of tin or plated with tin,
18, 613. 21. 392. In Od. 24, 228, leathern
greaves or guiters are mentioned, a kind
of boots worn for a protection against
thorns.

κνημός, ὁ, a mountain height, a mountain forest, the Lat. saltus, Pass.: plur.
2, 281. 11, 105. Od. 4, 337; sing. h. Ap.
283.

κνῆστις, ιος, ἡ (κνάω), a scraping knife,
a scraper, a rasp, dat. κνήστι for κνήστιι,
11, 640.†

*Κνίδος, ἡ, Cnidus, a town on the pro-
montory Triopium, upon an isthmus,
with a temple of Aphrodite, h. in Apoll.
43.

κνίσση, ἡ, also κνίση, ed. Spitzn. and
Dindorf.) 1) vapour from the fat of burnt
meat, the odour or vapour of fat. esply the
sacrificial vapour, 1, 66. 317. 8, 549. 2) fat,
esply the fat of the kidneys, mly called
suet or tallow, in which the sacrifice was
enveloped, 1. 460. Od. 3, 457; see Voss.
mythol. Brief. 2. p. 316; according to
Heyne the fat caul about the stomach
and intestines, omentum, which is justly
rejected by Voss.

κνισσήεις. εσσα, εν (κνίσση). full of the
vapour of fat, full of sacrificial vapour,
Od. 10, 10.†

*κνισσοδιώκτης, ὁ (διώκω), fat-smeller,
that runs after roast meat, Batr. 231.

κνυζηθμός, ὁ (κνύζω). the whine, howl,
or growl of a dog, Od. 16, 163.+

κνυζόω, fut. ώσω, aor. ἐκνύζωσα (akin
to κνύω), to render obscure, to becloud,
τινὶ ὄσσε. *Od. 13, 401. 453.

κνώδαλον, τό. 1) any living thing
which is monstrous and dangerous of its
kind, a monster, a reptile. a wild beast,
Od. 17, 317.† 2) Adj. monstrous, horrible,
γέρων. h. Merc. 188. according to Voss.
and Passow. But this is not suitable,
hence Herm. conjectures νωχαλόν, i. e.
ῥάθυμον.

κνώσσω, poet. to sleep, to slumber, Od.
4, 809.†

Κνωσός, ἡ (also Κνωσσός), the chief
town of the island of Crete, on the Cæra-

tus, in H. the residence of Minos at a later period famous for its Labyrinth, 2. 646. Od. 19, 178. From this Κνώσιος, ίη, ιον, Cnossian, from Cnossus.

κοῖλος, η, ον (akin to κύω), 1) hollow, excavated, deep, often epith. of ships. κοῖλος δόμος, the hollow structure, spoken of a wasp's nest, 12, 169; κοῖλον δόρυ, the hollow wood; of the Trojan horse, Od. 8, 507; σπέος, a deep cave, Od. 2) Esp. of places which lie in the valleys between mountains: κοίλη ὁδός, a hollow pass, a defile, Il. 23, 419. κοίλη Λακεδαίμων, the hollow Lacedæmon (i. e. lying in a deep situation), 2, 581; metaph. λιμήν, a harbour encompassed by hills, Od. 10, 92.

κοιμάω (κεῖμαι), aor. ἐκοίμησα, aor. mid. ἐκοιμησάμην, partcp. aor. pass. κοιμηθείς, 1) Act. prop. to lay down. to lay to rest, to put to bed, τινά, Od. 3, 397: spoken of animals: e. g. of a hart laying her fawns to rest, Od. 4, 336. 17, 127. 2) to close in sleep, to lull, ὄσσε, Il. 14, 236; τινὰ ὕπνῳ, Od. 12, 372; metaph. to calm, to still, to hush, ἀνέμους, Il. 12, 281; κύματα, Od. 12, 169; to assuage, ὀδύνας, Il. 16, 524. II) Mid. and aor. pass., to go to bed, to lie down to sleep, to go to sleep, often in H. χάλκεον ὕπνον, to sleep the brazen sleep, i. e. the sleep of death, 11, 241: spoken of animals: to sleep, Od. 14, 411.

*Κοῖος, ὁ, Cœus, son of Uranus and Gæa (Tellus), husband of Phœbe, father of Latona, h. Ap. 62. (With οι shortened in Κοίοιο.)

κοιρανέω, poet. (κοίρανος), 1) to be ruler, to rule, to command, spoken both of war: κατὰ πόλεμον, ἀνὰ μάχην, 2, 207. 5, 824: πολέας διά, 4, 230. πόλεμον κάτα κοιρανέουσιν, 5, 332; and of peace, 12, 318; Ἰθάκην κάτα, Od. 1, 247. 2) to domineer, to play the master, spoken of the suitors, Od. 20, 234.

κοίρανος, ὁ (akin to κῦρος), ruler, commander, λαῶν, 7, 234. 2) Generally, lord, master, Od. 18, 106.

Κοίρανος, ὁ, 1) a Lycian, slain by Odysseus (Ulysses), 5, 677. 2) a Cretan, from Lyctus, 17, 611.

κοίτη, ἡ (κεῖμαι), a couch, a bed, Od. 19, 341.

κοῖτος, ὁ = κοίτη, 1) a couch, a bed. 2) the going to sleep, sleep, *Od. 19, 510. 5 5. [κοίτοιο μέδεσθαι, to think about going to bed, 2, 358.]

*κόκκος, ὁ, the kernel or stone [granum] of fruits; of the pomegranate, h. Cer. 373. 412.

κολεόν, τό, Ep. κουλεόν, a scabbard of a sword, made of metal, or decorated with it, 11, 29, seq. H. has it only as neut. κολεόν, Od. 8, 404. μέγα κουλεόν, Il. 3, 272. 11, 30. The nom. κολεός does not occur in H.

κολλήεις, εσσα, εν, poet. κολλάω, glued together, fastened together, ξυστά, 15, 389.†

κολλητός, ή, όν (κολλάω), glued together,

and generally, joined together, δίφρος, ἄρματα, ξυστόν, 15, 678; σανίδες. Od. 21, 137. 164.

κόλλοψ, οπος. ὁ, the key or peg of a lyre, to which the strings were attached, Od. 21, 407 † (Prop. the thick skin on the neck of oxen.)

κολοιός, ὁ, the jackdaw, graculus, *16, 583. 17. 755 (akin to κολῳός).

*κολοκύντη, ἡ (also κολοκύνθη), the round gourd, the pumpkin, Batr. 53.

κόλος, ον (akin to κυλλός). mangled, maimed; δόρυ, a spear with its head lopped off [his mutilated beam, Cp.], 16, 117.†

κολοσυρτός, ὁ poet. (akin to κολῳός), noise, tumult, uproar, hubbub, of men and dogs, *12, 147. 13, 472.

κολούω (κόλος), to maim, to cut short, to curtail; only metaph. τὸ μὲν τελέει (τό relates by synes. to μῦθος), τὸ δὲ καὶ μεσσηγὺ κολούει, one he fulfils, another he cuts short in the midst, i. e. leaves half accomplished, 20, 370. ἐὸ δ᾽ αὐτοῦ πάντα κολούει. Cp. 'he cripples his own interest,' Od. 8, 211; δῶρα, to curtail your gifts [scantily to impart, Cp.]. Od 11, 340.

κόλπος, ὁ, 1) the bosom of the human body. δέχεσθαι κόλπῳ, 6, 483. παῖδ᾽ ἐπὶ κόλπῳ ἔχειν, as an expression of tender maternal love, 6, 400. 2) the bosom, the swell of the garment formed by the girdle, 22, 80. Od. 15, 469; plur. Il. 9. 570. 3) any thing formed like a bosom. a gulf of the sea, 2, 560; the bosom of the deep, 18, 140. Od. 5, 52. h. Ap. 431.

κολῳάω (κολῳός), to screech, to cry, to clamour, to wrangle [in piercing accents stridulous, Cp.], spoken of Thersites, 2, 212.†

κολώνη, ἡ, a hill, an elevation, *2, 811. 11, 711.

*κολωνός, ὁ = κολώνη, h. Cer. 273.

κολῳός. οῦ, poet. a screech, a cry, scolding strife [prop. a shrill chattering, B.]. κολῳὸν ἐλαύνειν, to make an uproar, to quarrel, 1, 575.† (according to Buttm. Lex. p. 391, akin to κολοιός, κέλω, κέλομαι: but, according to Döderlein, L. Hom. Sp. 1. p. 4, κολῳάω is a collateral form of κέλλω).

κομάω (κόμη), fut. ήσω, to let the hair grow long, to have long hair, in Il. only partcp. Ἄβαντες ὄπιθεν κομόωντες, the Abantes, long-haired behind, 2, 542 (Strabo assigns as a reason, that no enemy might seize them by the hair); spoken of horses: furnished with manes, 8, 42. 13, 24. 2) Metaph. of fields and plants: to be overgrown, to be verdant, to wave, fut. ἀσταχύεσσι, h. Cer. 454, *II.

κομέω, poet. to take care of, to tend, to provide for, υἱούς, γέροντα, Od. 11, 250. 24, 212; ἵππους, Il. 8, 109. 113; κύνας, Od. 17, 310. 319.

κόμη. ἡ, the hair. the hair of the head, more rarely plur. κόμαι Χαρίτεσσιν ὁμοῖαι, 17, 51 (see ὅμοιος). Od. 6, 231. 2)

Metaph. κόμη ελαίης, the foliage of the olive-tree, Od. 23, 195.

κομιδή (κομίζω), care, attendance, the care of feeding, in the Il spoken of horses, 8. 186. 23, 411. in the Od spoken of men, and of the care of the garden, Od. 24, 245. 247. ἐπεὶ οὐ κομιδὴ κατὰ νῆα ἦεν ἐπηετανός, since I have not all along had (ample or) good accommodation in a ship: he had lost his ship and been obliged to swim, Od. 8, 232; see Damm and Nitzsch. Passow unnecessarily assumes here the signif. 'nourishment, provisions.' So also Cp.

κομίζω (κομέω), aor. ἐκόμισα, Ep. σσ. aor. mid. ἐκομισάμην, 1) to take care of, to attend upon, to provide for, like κομέω, spoken of things and persons: ἔργα, 6, 490. Od. 1, 356. 21, 350; κτήματα, to manage possessions, Od. 23, 355; τινά, to take care of any man, esply to entertain as a host, often in the Od. (in the Il. in this signif. only in the mid.). 2) to take up any thing, to bear away, to carry away, prim. to take care of, χλαῖναν, τρυφάλειαν, 2, 183. 13, 578; and generally, to bear off, to carry off, to take away, in a good and bad sense: νεκρόν, 13, 196; ἵππους, Il.; ἄκοντα κόμισε χροΐ, he bore off the spear in his body, i. e. he received it in the body, 14, 456 463. Mid. to provide for in a man's house, to attend upon, to entertain, τινά, 8, 284. Od. 6, 278. 14, 316. 2) to take up for oneself, to receive. Σίντιες ἐκόμισαντο αὐτόν, the Sintians took him up, 1, 594; τινα, to convey away (from the battle), 5, 359. ἔγχος ἐνὶ χροῒ κομίσασθαι, to receive a spear in the body, 22. 286. cf. Act. 2.

κομπέω (κόμπος), to resound, to rattle, to clash or clang, spoken of brass, 12, 151.†

κόμπος, ὁ, a rattling, a noise, a clashing, a sound arising from striking upon a body; spoken of the tread or stamping of dancers, Od. 8, 380; ὀδόντων, of the noise of the tusks of the wild boar, Il. 11, 417. 12, 149.

κοναβέω, kindr. from κοναβίζω, poet. (κόναβος), aor. 1 κονάβησα, to resound, to rattle, to ring, spoken of brass, 15, 648. 21, 593; to resound, to re-echo, νῆες, δῶμα, 2, 334. 16, 277. Od. 17, 542. (κοναβέω only in the aor.)

κοναβίζω = κοναβέω, only in the imperf. *2, 466. 13, 498. 21, 255.

κόναβος, ὁ, poet. a sound, a clashing, a noise, Od. 10, 122.† (Prob. from κόμπος)

κονίη, ἡ, poet. form κόνις, ἡ, 1) dust, esply the powdered dust of the earth, often in plur. ἐν κονίῃσι πίπτειν, Il. ἐν κονίῃσι βάλλειν τινά, to cast any one into the dust, i. e. to slay him, 8, 156. 2) sand, river-sand, 21, 271. 3) ashes, Od. 7, 153. 160 (ι in the arsis of the sixth foot is used by H. as long).

κόνις, ιος, ἡ = κονίη, dust, in connexion with ψάμαθος, to indicate infinity of number, 9, 385. (κόνι, Ep. dat. for κόνι, 24, 18. Od. 11, 191.) 2) ashes, κόνις αἰθαλόεσσα, Il. 18, 23.

κονίσαλος or κονίσσαλος, ὁ (κόνις), dust, a whirlwind of dust *3, 13. 5, 503. 22, 401.

κονίω (κόνις), fut. κονίσω, aor. ἐκόνισα, perf. pass. κεκόνῑμαι, 1) to fill with dust, to cover with dust, with accus. χαίτας, 21, 407; pass. 21, 405; πεδίον, to fill the plain with dust, spoken of the flying Trojans, 14, 145; hence κεκονιμένοι, covered with dust, 21, 541. 2) intrans. to excite dust, spoken of fleet horses and men; always κονίοντες πεδίοιο, raising a dust through the plain, 13, 820. 23, 372. Od. 8, 122.

κοντός, ὁ, a pole, a stick, Od. 9, 487.†

*κοπόω (κόπος), to weary, to fatigue; pass. to become weary. Batr. 190.

Κοπρεύς, ῆος, ὁ, son of Pelops, from Elis, a herald of Eurystheus, 15, 639, seq.

κοπρίζω (κόπρος), fut. ίσω, to manure with dung, Od. 17, 299.†

κόπρος, ὁ. 1) manure, dung, Od. 9, 329. 17, 297; and generally, dirt, filth, Il. 22, 414. 24, 164. 2) a stable, a yard for cattle, 18, 575. Od. 10, 411.

κόπτω, aor. 1 ἔκοψα, perf. κέκοφα, aor. mid. ἐκοψάμην, 1) to strike, to thrust, τινά, spoken of persons fighting, Od. 18. 28. 335. κώληπα, Il. 23, 726; with double accus. τινὰ παρήϊον, 23, 690; and with dat. instrum. ἵππους τόξῳ, with the bow, σκηπανίῳ, 10, 514. 13, 60; spoken of a serpent: κόψε αἰετὸν κατὰ στῆθος, it struck or bit the eagle in the breast, 12, 204; also spoken of the blow with which oxen were stunned when they were to be slaughtered, 17, 521. Od. 14, 425. 2) to strike off, to cut off, κεφαλὴν ἀπὸ δειρῆς, Il. 13, 203. Od. 22, 477. 3) to hammer, to forge, δεσμούς, Il. 18, 379. Od. 8, 274. Mid. to smite oneself, κεφαλὴν χερσίν, to beat a man's head, Il. 22. 23.

Κόρακος πέτρη, ἡ, the rock Korax, in Ithaca, near the fountain Arethusa, according to Gell, on the south east end of the island, still called Koraka Petra; according to Voss, in the middle of the island upon the east side, on Neion; Völcker, Hom. Geogr., places it on the west side as a part of Neritus, Od. 13, 408. It received its name, according to the Schol., from Korax, son of Arethusa, who in a hunt fell from this rock.

κορέννῦμι, fut. κορέσω, Ep. κορέω, 8. 379. 13, 831; aor. 1 ἐκόρεσα, Ep. σσ. aor. 1 mid. ἐκορεσάμην, perf. Ion. κεκόρημαι, also Ep. partcp. perf. act. with pass signif. κεκορηώς, Od 18, 372; aor. pass. ἐκορέσθην, to satiate, to satisfy, τινά, any man. Il. 16, 747: with any thing, τινί: κύνας, ἠδ᾽ οἰωνοὺς δημῷ καὶ σάρκεσσι, spoken of the corpses which lie unburied, Il. 8, 379. 13, 831. 17, 241 Mid. to satiate oneself, to be sated or satisfied, have (had) one's fill, also perf. pass. and αοτ. pass. 1) With gen. φορβῆς, 11, 562; σιτου, Od. 14, 46: also with θυμὸν δαιτός. Od. 8, 96; metaph. θυλόπιδος κορέσσασθαι, to be sated with battle, Il. 13, 635; also ἀέθλων, Od. 23, 350. 2) Often with partcp. κλαίουσα ἐκορέσσατο, she sated herself with weeping, Od. 20, 59. κλαίων ἐκορέσθην, Od. 4, 541. ἐκορέσσατο χεῖρας τάμνων, he was satiated in his hands with cutting, i. e. tired, Il. 11, 87. οὔπω κεκόρησθε ἐελμένοι: are ye not yet satisfied with being enclosed? 18, 287. (H. has not the pres. κορέννυμι.)

κορέω. fut. ήσω, to sweep, to take care of, to clean, δῶμα, Od. 20, 149.†

κόρη, ἡ, Ep. κούρη, q. v., h. Cer. 439.†

κορθύω (κόρθυς), to lift up, only mid. to lift oneself. κῦμα κορθύεται, the wave lifted itself up, 9 7.†

Κόρινθος, ἡ, Corinthus, mentioned 2, 570; afterwards, one of the most flourishing cities of the old world, situated on the isthmus According to Pausan. 2, 1. 1, built by Ephyra, daughter of Oceanus, of whom a descendant Corinthus changed the name; according to Apd 1, 9. 3, by Sisyphus, son of Æolus, cf. Ἐφύρη. In Hom. Κορ. is prob. fem., for ἀφνειός is common, as in Soph. and Herod. It is found masc. in an oracle, Herod. 5, 92. and in Strab. ὁ δὲ Κόρ. ἀφνειός, p. 580. From this the adv. Κορινθόθι, at Corinth, 13, 664.

κορμός, ὁ (κείρω), a piece cut off, a billet, a log, Od. 23, 196.†

κόρος, ὁ (κορέννυμι), satiety. the state of satiety, (one's) fill, φυλόπιδος, γοοῖο, 19, 221. Od. 4, 103. πάντων κόρος ἐστί, there is a satiety of all, Il. 13. 636.

κόρος, ὁ, Ep. and Ion. κοῦρος, q. v.

κόρση, ἡ, Ep. and Ion. for κόρρη, the temples, the temples of the head, *4, 502. 13. 574.

κορυθάϊξ, ἴκος, ὁ (ῖ, ἀΐσσω). helm-shaking, crest-waving, i. q. κορυθαίολος epith. of Arês, 22, 132.†

κορυθαίολος, ον (αἰόλος), helm-shaking, crest-waving, often an epith. of Hector, 2, 816: once of Arês, 20, 38. (Others explain it, 'with variegated helmet,' see αἰόλος.)

κόρυμβος, ὁ, plur. τὰ κόρυμβα (κορυφή), prop. the upper part of a thing, the point, the top, the peak, ἄκρα κόρυμβα νηῶν, the extreme points of the curved stern of the ships=ἄφλαστα (aplustria), which were commonly adorned with ornaments, 9. 241.† Thus Heyne after Hesych. Voss. on the other hand, 'the splendid beaks,' after Etym. M. ἄφλαστα μὲν λέγεται τὰ πρυμνήσια, κόρυμβα τὰ πρωρήσια; or the Schol. κάκροστόλια, the ships' beaks which were erected as trophies.' This was, however, a later custom. [our vessel-heads, Cp.]

κορύνη, ἡ, a club, a mace; σιδηρείη, iron or covered with iron, *7, 141. 143.

κορυνήτης, ου, ὁ, a mace-bearer, a warrior armed with a club, *7, 9. 138.

κόρυς, υθος, ἡ, accus. κόρυθα and κόρυν,

13, 131. 16, 215; the helmet; it was coated with brass, χαλκήρης, χαλκείη, and differed in this respect from the leathern κυνέη, although this difference is not always regarded, 12, 184. The helmet had a crest, λόφος. made of horse-hair (ἱπποδάσεια, ἵππουρις); this was put into a conical elevation (φάλος), and many helmets had several φάλοι, hence ἀμφίφαλος, τετράφαλος, etc. The helmet itself was fastened with a strap (ὀχεύς) under the neck.

κορύσσω (κόρυς), aor. 1 mid. Ep. κορυσσάμενος, perf. pass. Ep. κεκορυθμένος, 1) Prop. to put on a helmet, hence generally, to equip, to arm, τινά, Batr. 123. 2) to raise, to excite, πόλεμον, 2, 273; κῦμα, 21, 306. Mid. often: 1) to equip oneself, to arm oneself for war, absol. 10, 37. Od. 12, 121; with dat. instrum. χαλκῷ, τεύχεσι, Il. 7, 206. 17, 199; in the partcp. κεκορυθμένος χαλκῷ, 4, 495. 5, 562. Od. 21, 434; metaph. spoken of arms: δοῦρα κεκορυθμένα χαλκῷ, spears armed with brass, Il. 3, 18. 11, 43. 16, 802. 2) to raise oneself, to rise, prop. for battle, metaph. spoken of strife, 4, 442. κῦμα κορύσσεται, the wave swells, 4, 424; in the Od. rarely.

κορυστής, οῦ, ὁ (κορύσσω), prop. one wearing a helmet; then generally, one armed, ἀνήρ, 4, 457, and often. *Il.

κορυφή, ἡ (κόρυς), prop. the extreme part of any thing, hence 1) the crown of the head, 8, 83. h. Ap. 309. 2) the top, of a mountain, the summit, often plur. with ὄρεος or ὀρέων, Il. and Od.

κορυφόω (κορυφή), to carry any thing to the highest point, hence mid. to reach the highest point, to tower aloft; only κῦμα κορυφοῦται, the wave towers aloft [curls its head on high. Cp.], 4, 426.†

Κορώνεια, ἡ, a town in Bœotia on the west side of the lake Copaïs, now Diminia, 2, 503.

κορώνη (κορωνός), prop. any thing curved, hence 1) the crow (from the curved beak), always the sea-crow or cormorant, εἰναλίη, Od 5. 66. 12, 418. 14, 308. 2) the ring on the house-door with which it is shut, Od. 1, 441. 7, 90. 21, 46. 3) the curved end of a bow, which was furnished with a knob or ring to which the string was fastened, Il. 4, 111. Od. 21, 138. 4) the curved stern of a ship, see κορωνίς. [Död. thinks κορωνίζειν was=κρώζειν: cornix=coronix.]

κορωνίς, ίδος, ἡ (κορώνη), curved, beaked, epith. of ships, from the curved stern, Il. often, once Od. 19, 182.

*Κορωνίς. ίδος, ἡ, daughter of Phlegyas of Laceria in Magnesia, sister of Ixion, who bore Asklêpios (Æsculapius), to Apollo on the plain of Dotium, h. 15. cf. Apd. 3, 10, 3.

Κόρωνος, ὁ (appell. κορωνός), son of Cæneus, father of Leonteus. king of the Lapithæ, at Gyrton in Thessaly, 2, 746.

κοσμέω (κόσμος), aor. 1 Ep. κόσμησα,

M 4

aor. mid. ἐκοσμησάμην, aor. pass. ἐκοσμήθην, 1) *to put in order, to arrange, to draw up in line*, with accus. of warriors : ἵππους τε καὶ ἀνέρας, 2, 554. 704. 14, 379. πένταχα κοσμηθέντες, arranged in five troops, 12, 87. διὰ τρίχα κοσμηθέντες, see διακοσμέω. φθὰν μέγ' ἱππήων ἐπὶ τάφρῳ κοσμηθέντες, they were drawn up at the trench before the charioteers, Il. 51. (The gen. ἱππήων depends upon φθάνω, since this contains a notion of comparison, and not upon κοσμέω, cf. Thiersch, Gram. § 254, d.) δόρπον, to prepare a repast, Od. 7, 13 ; ἀοιδήν, h. 6, 59. 2) *to adorn, to deck*, χρυσῷ, h. Ven. 65 ; σῶμα ἐν ἔντεσι, Batr. 121. Mid. *to put in order*, with reference to the subject, with accus. πολιήτας, 2, 806.

κοσμητός. ή. όν (κοσμέω), *set in order, arranged.* πρασιαί, Od. 7, 127.†

κοσμήτωρ, ορος, ὁ, poet. for κοσμητήρ, one who orders, *a commander*, always with λαῶν, 1, 16. Od. 18, 152.

κόσμος, ὁ (prob. from κομέω), 1) *order, arrangement, suitableness, propriety.* κόσμῳ ἔρχεσθαι, to go in order, 12, 225 ; καθίζειν, Od. 13, 77 ; esply κατὰ κόσμον, in order ; and strengthened with εὖ, Il. 10, 472. 12, 85, according to propriety, as is befitting ; often οὐ κατὰ κόσμον, not according to propriety, contrary to propriety ; ἐρίζειν, εἰπεῖν ; hence, ἵππου κόσμος, the arrangement, the construction of the (wooden) horse. Od. 8, 492. 2) *ornament, decoration*, of women, Il. 14, 187. h Ven. 163 ; of horses, 4, 145.

κοτέω and κοτέομαι, poet. (κότος). Of the act. there occur : pres. indic. aor. II partcp. κοτέσας, h. Cer. 254 ; Ep partcp. perf. κεκοτηώς, always κεκοτηότι θυμῷ, only mid. pres., fut. κοτέσομαι, Ep. σσ. aor. I ἐκοτεσάμην, Ep σσ, *to be angry, enraged*, with dat. pers., 3, 345. 5, 177. 14. 143. τοῖσίντε κοτέσσεται for κοτέσηται. 5. 747. 8, 391. Od. 1, 101 (cf. Rost, p. 629. Kühner, § 661. 1) ; with gen. of the thing. ἀπάτης, on account of deception, Il. 4, 168 ; and with accus. κοτεσσαμένη τόγε θυμῷ, angry in mind at this, 14, 191.

κοτήεις, εσσα, εν, poet. (κοτέω), *wrathful, angry, enraged* θεός), 5. 191.†

κότος, ὁ, prop. *a grudge* ; then, *anger, hatred.* κότον ἔχειν τινί, to have a grudge against any man, 13, 517. κότον ἐντίθεσθαί τινι, Od. 11, 102. 13, 342

κοτύλη, ἡ (akin to κοῖλος), prop. any cavity ; hence 1) *a small vessel for fluids, a cup, a little goblet*, 22, 495. Od. 15, 312. 17, 12. 2) *the hip-pan*, the socket in which the head of the thigh-bone turns, Il. §. 306, 307.

κοτυληδών, όνος, ὁ (κοτύλη), any cavity ; esply, *a*) a little cavity in the arms of sea-polypi [like a small cupping-glass, with which they attached themselves to the rocks, Passow], *b*) the *branching arms* themselves. πουλύποδος πρὸς κοτυληδονόφιν (Ep. for κοτυληδόσι) πυκιναὶ λάιγγες ἔχονται, to the arms of the poly-

pus many pebbles attach themselves, Od. 5. 433 :† see πουλύπους.

κοτλήρυτος, ον (ἀρύω), that may be drawn with a cup, *gushing, copious*, ἔρρεεν αἷμα [*flowed by goblets full*], 23, 34.†

*κότυλος, ὁ=κοτύλη. *a cup*, Ep. 14, 3.

κουλεόν, τό, Ep. and Ion. for κολεόν, q. v.

κούρη, ἡ, Ion. for κόρη. *a maiden, a virgin*, 2, 872 ; *a daughter*, 1, 111 ; Διός, Il. 9, 536 ; mly with gen. of a prop. name, alone 6, 247. 2) *a bride*, Od. 18, 279 ; always the Ion. form, except h. Cer. 479.

*κουρήϊος, ίη, ἴον, Ion. for κόρειος (κούρη), *appertaining to virgins, youthful*, h. Cer. 108.

κούρητες, οἱ (κοῦρος), *youths*, Παναχαιῶν, *19, 193. 248.

Κουρῆτες, οἱ, *the Curētes*, the most ancient inhabitants of the south-eastern parts of Ætolia, about Pleuron, probably belonging to the Lelěges ; they were expelled by the Ætolians ; for which reason they attacked them in their chief town Calydon, 9, 532. (Prob. from κουρή, tonsure, because they wore short hair, cf. Eustath. ad Il. 19, 193.)

κουρίδιος, ίη, ιον, Ion. and poet. (κοῦρος), *conjugal, legitimate*, connected with πόσις, ἀνήρ, ἄλοχος or γυνή, in opposition to illicit concubinage ; as clearly appears from 19, 298, where Briseis says that it is forbidden her to become the κουριδίη ἄλοχος, the lawful wife of Achilles ; κουρίδιος πόσις, 5, 414. Od. 11, 430 ; also κουρίδιος φίλος, as subst beloved husband. Od. 15, 22 ; ἀνὴρ κουρ. Od. 19, 266 ; ἄλοχος, Il. 1, 114. Od. 14, 245 ; γυνή, Od. 13, 43 ; λέχος. the conjugal couch, Il. 15, 40 ; κουρ δῶμα, the house of the husband, Od. 19, 580. The common explanation *youthful*, after the Schol., a wife whom a man has married as κούρη is refuted by Buttm, Lex p. 393 ; although the derivation from κοῦρος, as denoting the bloom of life, or, of free, noble birth. is not rejected. According to Döderlein, κούριος is the Homeric form of the later κύριος.)

κουρίζω (κοῦρος), *to be young, juvenile,* only Od. 22, 185.†

κουρίξ, adv. (κουρά), *by the hair*, Od. 22, 118.†

κοῦρος, ὁ, Ion and Ep. for κόρος, 1) *a youth, a boy*, from the earliest age to the vigour of manhood ; hence often the young warriors are called κοῦροι Ἀχαιῶν, 1, 473 : spoken of one unborn, 6, 59 ; Καδμείων, 5. 807 ; also, *a son*, κοῦροι Ζήθοιο, Od. 19, 523. 2) the *servants at* sacrifices and entertainments, who were always free-born, and often of royal descent, Il. 1, 470. Od. 1, 148. 3. 339.

κουρότερος, η, ον, compar. of κοῦρος *younger*, and generally, *youthful*, ἀνήρ. Od. 21, 310 ; subst. Il 4, 316.

κουροτρόφος, ον (τρέφω), *nourishing boys or youth*, epith. of Ithaca, Od 9, 27 t.

κοῦφος, η, ον, light; [hence] feet: σάνδαλα, h. Merc. 83. The neut. plur. as adv. κοῦφα προβιβάς, lightly striding along. 13, 158; and compar. κουφότερον μετεφώνεε, he addressed them more lightly, i. e. more cheerfully, Od. 8, 201.

*κοχλίας, ου, ὁ, a snail with convoluted shell, Batr. 165.

Κόων, ωνος, ὁ, son of Antēnor, a Trojan, slain by Agamemnon, 11, 248—260.

Κόως, ἡ, Ep. for Κῶς q. v.

κράας, τό, obsol. nom. of the Ep. oblique cases, κράατος, κράατι, etc. see κάρη.

κραδαίνω, Ep. form of κραδάω, to brandish, to hurl; pass. αἰχμὴ κραδαινομένη, 13, 504. ἔγχος κραδαινόμενον, 17, ‑24.

κραδάω (κράδη), Ep. form κραδαίνω, only in pres. pass. partcp. to brandish, to swing, to shake, with accus. always κραδάων ἔγχος, δόρυ, 7, 213. Od. 19, 438.

κραδίη, η, Ep. for καρδίη.

κραιαίνω, Ep. length. form of κραίνω, q. v.

κραίνω, oftener the Ep. lengthened κραιαίνω (κάρη). imperf. ἐκραίαινον, fut. κρανέω, 9, 310, another reading for φρονέω, aor. 1 ἔκρηνα, Ep. ἐκρήηνα, imperat. κρήηνον, Il., κρῆνον, Od.; infin. κρηῆναι, Il., κρῆναι, Od.; perf. pass. κεκράανται, fut. mid. κρανέομαι, Il. 9, 626, with pass. signif.: 1) to finish, to end, to accomplish, to complete, to fulfil, to perform, with accus. ἐφετμάς, 5, 508; ἐέλδωρ τινί, to fulfil a wish for any man, 1, 41. Od. 3.418; ἔπος, Od. 20, 115; absol. Od. 5, 170 (antith. νοῆσαι); hence pass. οὔ μοι δοκέει τῇδε ὁδῷ κρανέεσθαι, it seems to be that it [our object] will not be attained in this way, Il. 9, 626. χρυσῷ ἐπὶ χείλεα κεκράανται, the lips are finished off with gold, i. e. gilded (spoken of a cup), Od. 4, 616. 15, 116; κεκράαντο, Od. 4, 133. 2) to be head, to rule, to reign, Od. 8, 391 (κραίνω in the Od., κραιαίνω in the Il. except κρανέεσθαι). κραίνων ἀθανάτους τε θεοὺς καὶ γαῖαν, h. Merc. 427. Passow explains: he completed the gods and the earth, i. e. he represented them in his song as coming into being, as they really did come. Math. and Herm. think κραίνων corrupt; the latter conjectures κλείων. [Bothe after Hesych. renders κραίνων, honorans, celebrans.]

κραιπνός, ή, όν, compar. κραιπνότερος. 1) sweeping, snatching away, Βορέης, Od. 5, 385. 2) rapid, fleet, swift, πόδες, πόμποι; metaph. κραιπνότερος νόος, a vehement spirit, Il. 23, 590. As adv. often neut. plur. κραιπνά, with κραιπνῶς. 13, 18. 5, 223. (Prob. from ΑΡΠΩ, ἁρπάζω.)

*κραιπνῶς, adv. (κραιπνός), quickly, swiftly, 10, 162. Od. 8, 247.

*κράμβη, ἡ, cabbage, Batr. 163.

*Κραμβοφάγος, ὁ (φαγεῖν), Cabbage-eater, name of a frog, Batr. 221.

Κρανάη, ἡ (appellat. κρανή), Cranaë, an island to which Paris first brought

Helen from Lacedæmon, 3, 445. According to the ancient critics, it is either the island Helena in Attica, Eur. Hel. 1690; or a small island in the Laconian gulf, now Marathonisi, Paus. 3, 22. 2. Ottfr. Müller, Orchom. p. 316, decides in favour of the latter. Others suppose it Cythera.

*κραναήπεδος. ον (πέδον), having a hard, rocky soil, h. Ap. 72.

κραναός, ή, όν, hard, rough, stony, rocky, epith. of Ithaca, 3, 201. Od. 1, 247.

κρανέεσθαι, see κραίνω.

κράνεια, ἡ, the cornel-tree, cornus, 16, 767. According to Od. 10, 242, swine were fed with the fruit [corn‑l‑fruit, Cp.].

*κρανέϊνος, η, ον, made of the cornel-tree, ἀκόντιον, h. Merc. 460.

κρανίον, τό (κρανον), the skull, 8, 84.†

Κράπαθος, ἡ, Ep. for Κάρπαθος, q. v.

ΚΡΑΣ, ὁ, used only in the oblique cases, gen. κρατός, dat. κρατί, as a form of κάρη, q. v., the head, the summit. ὑπὸ κράτεσφι, under the head, 10, 156.

κραταίγυαλος, ον, poet. (γύαλον), furnished with strong arched plates, strong-arched, θώρηξ, 19, 361 †

κραταιΐς, ἡ, Ep. (κράτος). τότ' ἀποστέψασκε κραταιῒς αὖτις, Od. 11, 597.† According to Schol. br. ἡ κραταιὰ δύναμις ὅ ἐστι τὸ βάρος, the overpowering force, the weight of the stone (for which also some of the ancients would write κραται'ῒς), rolled it back.' Aristarchus took it as an adv.: 'then rolled it violently back;' [cf. λικριφίς.] Nitzsch (and so Fäsi) thinks κραταιῒς is (as in the next article) a personification; a sort of sprite, 'Mastery;' or 'Force.'

Κραταιΐς, ἡ, the powerful, the mother of Scylla. a nymph, Od. 12. 124.

κραταιός, ή, όν, poet (κράτος), strong, powerful, mighty, Μοῖρα, 5, 83; θήρ, 11, 119; φώς, h. Merc. 265.

κραταίπεδος. ον, poet. (πέδον). having a firm, hard bottom or soil, οὔδας, Od. 23, 46.†

*κραταίπους, οδος, ὁ, ἡ, poet. (πούς), strong-footed, Ep. 15, 9.

κρατερός, ή, όν (κράτος), Ep. κάρτερος. strong, mighty, powerful. a) Spoken of persons: Ἄρης, Ἔρις, esply of warriors; brave, bold, courageous, Il. 2) Of things: βέλος. ὑσμίνη, Il.; φύλοπις. Od. 16, 268; μῦθος, a violent, harsh word, Il. 1, 25. 326; [aspera vox, Nägelsb.:] from this κρατερῶς, strongly, mightily, powerfully, μάχεσθαι, νεμεσσᾶν, Il. ἀγορεύειν, to speak powerfully, with emphasis, 8, 29.

κρατερόφρων, ον, gen. ονος, poet. (φρήν), of a firm, hard temper, spirited, courageous, unterrified, epith. of Heracles, 14, 524; of the Dioscuri, Od. 11, 298; of the lion, Il. 10, 184.

κρατερῶνυξ, υχος, ὁ, ἡ. poet. (ὄνυξ), strong-hoofed, ἵπποι, ἡμίονοι, 5. 329. 24, 277: strong-clawed, λύκοι [talon'd wolves, Cp.], λέοντες, Od. 10. 218.

κράτεσφι, see ΚΡΑΣ.

κρατευταί, αἱ, Ep. (κρατέω), the forked

supports upon which the spit rested
(Voss, *the supporting-forks*), according to
Aristarch., stones upon which the roast-
ing spit was laid, 9, 214.†

κρατέω (κράτος), fut. ήσω, 1) *to have
might, power: to exercise sway, to command,* absol. 5, 175. 16, 172. 2) *to rule,
to command,* with gen., over any man,
1, 79. 288. rarely with dat. νεκύεσσιν, to
have dominion amongst the dead, Od.
11, 485; ἀνδράσι, ἀθανάτοισι, Od. 16,
265. 3) With accus., to get any thing
into one's power, *to hold, to grasp,* Batr.
63. 2:6.

κράτιστος, η, ον. Ep. κάρτιστος, q. v.

κράτος, εος, τό. Ep. κάρτος. *strength,
might, power,* Od. 1, 70. 359; esply
spoken of bodily strength, Il. 7, 142. 9,
39. 13, 486; of iron : *strength, hardness,*
Od. 9, 393. 2) *mastery, superiority, victory,* Il. 1, 509. 6, 387; ἐγγυαλίζειν τινὶ
κράτος, Il, 192. 753, φέρεσθαι, to bear
away the victory, 13, 486

κράτός, gen. from ΚΡΑΣ, see κάρη.

κρατύς, ὁ, poet. (κράτος) = κρατερός,
powerful, mighty, epith. of Hermês, 16,
184. Od. 5, 49.

*Κραυγασίδης, ου, ὁ (κραύγασος), *Vo-
ciferator,* a frog's name, Batr. 216.

κρέας, ατος, τό, nom. and accus. plur.
κρέα. gen. κρεάων, h. 2, 130; κρεῶν, Od.
15, 98; Ep. κρειῶν, Il. 11, 551; dat.
κρέασιν, 8, 162; *meat, flesh,* in sing.
only accus. Od. 8, 477; plur. *pieces of
meat.* (The a in the last syllable in
κρέα is short, and in the Od. is also
elided, Od 3, 65. 470.) To be read with
synizesis, Od. 9, 347; (see Buttm. Gram.
§ 54. note 3. Thiersch, § 188. Rost, Dial.
38.)

κρεῖον, τό (κρέας), *a meat-table, a
dresser* [Cp.], upon which meat was cut
up, 9, 206.†

κρείσσων, ον, gen. ονος, irreg. compar.
of ἀγαθός, prop. from κρατύς or κράτος
for κράσσων, *stronger, more powerful,* 1,
80; esply *superior, victorious,* in connexion with νικᾶν, 3, 71. 92. Od. 18, 46;
sometimes with infin. Od. 21, 345.

Κρειοντιάδης, αο, ὁ, Ep. for Κρεοντιά-
δης, son of Creon, 19, 240.

κρείων, οντος, ὁ, fem. κρείουσα, ἡ,
(prob. from κρᾶς, κραίνω), *ruler, commander,* spoken of kings and gods: also
of Eteoneus, a servant of noble race, Od.
4, 22; κρείουσα, ἡ, only once, Il. 22,
48.

Κρείων, οντος, ὁ, Ep. for Κρέων, father
of Megara, ruler in Thebes, Od. 11, 269.
2) father of Lycomêdês, Il. 9, 84.

κρέμαμαι, depon. mid. *I hang,* see κρεμάννυμι

κρεμάννυμι, fut. κρεμάσω, contr. κρε-
μῶ, and expanded κρεμόω, 7, 83; aor. 1
ἐκρέμασα, mid. κρέμαμαι, imperf. ἐκρεμά-
μην, 2 sing. ἐκρέμω and κρέμω, which
has been falsely given as aor. 2 mid. 1)
to hang up, to suspend, to let hang, τεύχεα
προτὶ νηόν, 7, 83; σειρὴν ἐξ οὐρανόθεν,
to let a chain hang down from heaven,

8, 19. Mid. *to hang. to be suspended,* ὅτι
τ' ἐκρέμω ὑψόθεν, when thou wert suspended on high, *15, 18. 21.

κρεμβαλιαστύς, ύος, ἡ (κρέμβαλον), *a
rattling, a jingling,* h. Ap. 162.

κρέων, see κρέας, Od.

κρήγυος, ον, poet. *good, advantageous,
profitable,* τὸ κρήγυον εἰπεῖν, 1, 106.†
(According to Buttm., Lex. p. 395, from
χρήσιμος, others think from κέαρ, γαίω,
that which rejoices the heart, see
Thiersch, § 199. 7.)

κρήδεμνον. τό (κρᾶς. δέω), prob. *a head-
band, a veil,* a female head-covering,
with which the whole face could be
covered, and whose long ends were permitted to hang down over both cheeks,
14, 184. Od. 1, 334. Nitzsch, ad Od. 5,
346, thinks it perhaps differed from
the καλύπτρη, in being attached to the
head by a band, whereas the καλύπτρη
was thrown over it. Odysseus (Ulysses)
used the veil of the goddess Ino as a
girdle in swimming, Od 5, 346. 2)
Metaph. Τροίης ἱερὰ κρήδεμνα, the sacred
battlements of Troy, which, like a band
or fillet, encircled and protected the city,
Il. 16, 100. Od. 13, 388. b) *the lid of a
vessel,* since κάρη denotes the upper part
of a thing, Od. 3, 392; perhaps *a cover
tied over* the opening: cf. Od. 10, 23.

κρήῆναι, Ep. for κρῆναι, see κραίνω.

κρῆθεν, adv. (syncop. from κάρη, κάρτ
θεν), *from the head, from above,* 16, 548.
Od. 11, 588; see κατακρῆθεν.

Κρηθεύς. ῆος, ὁ, son of Æolus and Enaretê or Laodicê, founder of Iolcus in
Thessaly, husband of Tyro, brother of
Salmoneus, father of Æson, Amythaon,
and Pheres, Od. 11, 236, seq. 253—258.

Κρήθων, ωνος, ὁ, son of Diocles, brother
of Orsilochus of Pheræ in Messenia, slain
by Æneas, 5, 542, seq.

κρημνός, ὁ, *any overhanging edge: a
precipice,* or *cliff,* of a mountain, &c.;
or the *edge* of a deep trench, *12, 54. 21,
175. 234.

κρηναῖος, η, ον (κρήνη), *belonging to a
fountain.* (Νύμφαι κρηναῖαι, fountain-
nymphs, Od. 17, 240.†)

κρήνη, ἡ (akin to κάρη), *a fountain, a
spring, a well,* 9, 14; κρήνηνδε, Od. 20,
154.

Κρής, ὁ, gen. Κρητός, plur. οἱ Κρῆτες,
the Cretans, inhabitants of the island of
Crete, 2, 645. Their reputation as liars,
according to Damm, originated in the
fiction of Odysseus (Ulysses), Od. 14,
200, seq.

Κρήτη, ἡ, and poet. αἱ Κρῆται, Od. 14,
199, a large island in the Mediterranean
Sea, famed by the legislation of Minos
and by the fable of Zeus and Europa;
now *Candia.* Even in the time of Homer
it was very populous, for he speaks of it
as having a hundred cities, 2, 649; in
round numbers, however, as in Od. 19,
174, he mentions only ninety. From
this the adv. Κρήτηθεν, from Crete, Il. 3,
233. Κρήτηνδε, to Crete, Od. 19, 186

κρητήρ, ηρος, ὁ (κεράννυμι), a mixing-vessel, a mixer, the vessel in which the wine was tempered with water, and from which it was poured into the goblets, 3, 247. Od. 1, 110. 7, 179. 9, 9. 13, 50. The mixing-vessel stood upon a tripod, Od. 21, 141. 145. 22, 341; was of silver, Il. 23. 741. Od. 9. 203; and prob. also furnished with a golden rim, Od. 4, 615. Il. 23, 219.

κρῖ, τό, Ep. abbreviated form for κριθή, in nom. and accus. barley. [Prob. the original form, see Buttm. § 57, note 3.] [" Every fina· consonant that the Greek language did not admit as a termination is either rejected or changed into a permissible consorant of the same organ, or assimilated to the nearest vowel. The earliest form of the language had some neuters without suffix; hence by the changes just enumerated we get δῶ (= δόμ), κρῖ (= κριθ), βρῖ (= βριθ [βρίθος, βριθοσύνη]), γάλα (= γαλαγ, γλάγος), κτῦ (κτυθός, Hes.), &c.," Död., p. 231, note 163.]

κρίζω, aor. ἔκρικον (akin to κράζω), to crack, to snap, spoken of a breaking body, 16. 470.†

*κριθαίη, ἡ, prob. barley broth, Ep. 15, 7.

κριθή, ἡ, barley, only plur., 11, 69. Od. 9,110. Sing. Ep. abbrev. κρῖ λευκόν, Il. 8, 564. Od. 4, 604. 12, 358. It is mentioned as food for horses. Prob. hordeum vulgare, Linn.

κρίκε, Ep. for ἔκρικε, see κρίζω.

κρίκος, Ep. for κίρκος, a ring, placed upon or over the pin on the pole, in attaching the horses to the chariot, 24, 272;† see ἕστωρ.

κρίνω, aor. 1 ἔκρῖνα, aor. 1 mid. ἐκρῖνάμην, perf. pass. κέκρῐμαι, aor. pass. ἐκρίθην, partcp. κριθείς and κρινθείς, 13, 129. Od. 8, 48; 1) to separate, to divide, to sunder, with accus. Il. 2, 362; καρπόν τε καὶ ἄχνας, 5, 502. 2) to choose out, to select, φῶτας ἐκ Λυκίης, 6, 188. Od. 4, 666. 10, 102; hence partcp. κεκριμένος and κρινθείς, selected, chosen, Il. 10, 417, Od. 13, 182; but οὖρος κεκριμένος, a decided wind, which blows steadfastly to one point of the compass, 11. 14, 19. 3) to deride, to judge, νείκεα, Od. 12, 440. σκολιὰς θέμιστας κρίνειν, to give tortuous sentences, i. e. to pervert the laws in judging. Il. 16, 387; spoken also of war: νεῖκος πολέμου. to decide the contest of battle, Od. 18, 264; hence pass. ὁππότε μνηστῆρσι καὶ ἡμῖν μένος κρίνηται Ἄρηος, when between the suitors and us the strength of Ares is decided, i. e. when it comes to open conflict, Od. 16, 269. Mid. 1) to separate oneself, to withdraw oneself, Od. 8, 36. 24, 507; esply from battle: κρίνεσθαι Ἄρηϊ, according to Wolf: ' to get clear, as it were, of each other by fighting,' and generally, to contend in open battle, to decide any thing by fighting, Il. 2, 385. 18, 209. 2) to select for oneself, to choose for oneself,

ἑταίρους, Od. 4, 408. Il. 9, 521. 11, 697. 3) to decide, to judge, as depon. ὀνείρους, to explain dreams. 5, 150.

Κρῖσα, ἡ, later orthography Κρίσσα, h. Ap. 269, ed. Herm. and Ilgen; a very ancient city in Phocis. north of Cirrha, a colony of Cretans according to h. Ap. At a later day, it was destroyed by a decree of the Amphictyons, and its territory attached to Delphi; still it remained the port of Delphi; now Chriso, 2, 520. Whence ὁ Κρίσσης κόλπος, the Crisean Gulf, on the coast of Phocis, now Mare di Lipanto. Strabo distinguishes Κρῖσα and Κίρρα, but Pausanias, 10, 37. 4, considers them as one place. With him accords Ottfr. Müller, Orchom. S. 495.

κριός, ὁ, a ram, *Od. 9, 447. 461.

κριτός, ή, όν (κρίνω), separated, chosen, selected, 7, 434. Od. 8, 258. 12, 439.

κροαίνω (κρούω), to strike, to stamp, spoken of a horse, *6, 507. 15, 264.

Κροῖσμος, ὁ, a Trojan, slain by Meges, 15, 523.

*κροκήϊος, η, ον, poet. (κρόκος), saffron-coloured, ἄνθος, h. Cer 178.

κροκόπεπλος, ον (πέπλος), having a saffron-coloured robe, epith. of [the saffron-mantled Morn. Cp.] Aurora, 8, 1, and elsewhere.

κρόκος, ὁ, saffron, a flower which grows in the mountains of southern Europe, crocus vernus, Linn., Il. 14, 348.†

Κροκύλεια, τά, a place in Acarnania according to Strabo. or in Ithaca according to Steph., Il. 2, 633.

κρόμυον, τό, an onion (allium cepa, Linn.); it is spoken of as food 11, 630. Od. 19, 233 (later orthography κρόμμυον).

Κρονίδης, ου, ὁ [also αω and εω, h. Cer. 414. h. 32. 2], son of Kronus = Zeus, often, standing alone, or connected with Ζεύς. 2, 375. Od. 1, 45.

Κρονίων, ἴωνος and ἴονος, son of Kronus = Zeus, also Ζεὺς Κρονίων (ῑ in nom. and gen. Κρονίονος, 14, 247. Od. 11, 620; elsewhere ῐ.)

Κρόνος, ὁ, Saturnus, son of Uranus and Gaia or Gæa (Tellus), husband of Rhea, father of Zeus. Poseidôn, Hadês, Hêrê, Dêmêtêr, and Hestia (Vesta). Before Zeus, he governed the world, till he was dethroned by his sons, and confined with the Titans in Tartarus, 8, 479. The sons divided the kingdom of their father, 15, 157. The golden age was during his dominion, Hes. Op. 111. (Κρόνος from κραίνω, the finisher, Perficus, as the last of the Titans, Herm.)

κρόσσαι, αἱ (akin to κόρση), τῶν πύργων, the battlements [?] of towers, Schol. ἄκραι, στεφάναι, *12, 258. 484. They are distinct from ἐπάλξεις. Hdt. 2, 125, compares them with ἀναβαθμοί, projecting stones by which the wall could be ascended; hence κροσσάων ἐπέβαινον, 12, 444. Other critics incorrectly understand by it, scaling-ladders.

κροταλίζω (κρόταλον), to clatter, to

produce a rattling; with accus. ὄχεα, to hurry away the chariots with a rattling noise, 11, 160.†

κρόταλον, τό, a clapper, a bell, h. 13, 3.

κρόταφος, ὁ (κροτέω), *the temple* of the head, *the temples*, 4, 502; mly plur., 13, 188, and Od. 18, 378.

κροτέω (κρότος), *to cause to clatter* or *rattle*, ὄχεα, 15, 453.†

Κρουνοί, οἱ, κ fountain, not far from Chalcis, of a little river in the southern part of Elis, with a village of the same name, cf. Strab. VIII. p. 351. Od. 15, 295. h. Ap. 425. (Barnes has introduced the verse from Strabo into the Od; Wolf, on the other hand, has enclosed it in brackets.)

κρουνός, ὁ 1) *a fountain, a spring*, 22, 208. 2) *the basin* in which the water is collected; *the bed* of a stream, 4, 454.

κρύβδα, adv. (κρύπτω), *secretly, privately*: with gen. Διός, without the knowledge of Zeus, 18, 168.†

κρύβδην, adv. i. q. κρύβδα, *Od. 11, 455. 16, 153.

κρυερός, ή, όν (κρύος), *cold, chilling*; metaph. *terrific, horrible*, φόβος (*icy fear*), γόος, 13, 48. 24, 524. Od. 4, 103.

κρυόεις, εσσα, εν (κρυός), *cold, chilling; icy, terrific*. φόβος, Ἰωκή, *5, 740. 9, 2.

κρυπτάδιος, η, ον (κρύπτω), *concealed, secret*, φιλότης. 6, 161. κρυπτάδια φρονεῖν, to devise secret plans, *1, 542.

κρυπτός, ή, όν (κρύπτω), *concealed, secret*, κληΐς, 14. 168.†

κρύπτω. Ep. iterat. imperf. κρύπτασκε, 8, 272, for κρύπτεσκε, h. Cer. 239; fut. κρύψω, aor. 1 ἔκρυψα, perf. pass. κέκρυμμαι, aor. pass. ἐκρύφθην, 1) *to conceal, to hide*, with accus. 18, 397. Od. 11, 244; for protection, τινὰ σάκεϊ, to cover any one with a shield. Il. 8, 272. κεφαλὰς κορύθεσσιν, 14, 373. 2) Metaph. *to conceal, to be silent*, τινὶ ἔπος, Od. 4, 350. τὸ δὲ καὶ κεκρυμμένον εἶναι (for the imperat.), let the other remain unspoken, Od. 11, 443. Mid. with aor. pass. *to conceal oneself*, ὑπ᾽ ἀσπίδι, Il. 13, 405. κρύπτων Ἥρην, h. 26, 7, has been explained as reflexive, 'concealing oneself from Hêrê,' but unnecessarily; supply σέ from what precedes, and render, 'concealing thyself from Hêrê.'

κρύσταλλος, ὁ (κρύος), any transparent, congealed, or frozen substance, *ice*, 22, 152. 14, 477.

κρυφηδόν, adv. (κρύπτω), *secretly, in a concealed manner, clandestinely*, *Od. 14, 330. 19, 299.

Κρῶμνα, ἡ, a place in Paphlagonia; according to Strabo at a later day, with Sesamus and Cytôrus, it formed Amastris. 2, 885.

κτάμεν, κτάμεναι, κτάμενος, see κτείνω.

κτάομαι, aor. 1 ἐκτησάμην, perf. ἔκτημαι, only infin. ἐκτῆσθαι, *to gain, to acquire, to earn, to procure, to purchase*, with accus. 9, 400; also τινί τι, to obtain any thing for any one, Od. 20,

265; perf. *to have acquired, to possess*, Il. 9, 402.

ΚΤΑΩ, assumed ground form of the Ep. aor. ἔκταν, ἐκτάμην, see κτείνω.

κτέαρ, ατος, τό, only dat. plur. κτεά- τεσσι; poet. *that which is gained, property, possessions*, 5, 154. Od. 1, 218, and often.

κτεατίζω (κτέαρ), aor. 1 ἐκτεάτισα, Ep. σσ. perf. mid ἐκτεάτισμαι, 1) *to acquire for oneself, to procure*, with accus. πολλά, Od. 2, 102: δουρί, in war, Il. 16,57. Mid. *to acquire for oneself*. h. Merc. 522.

Κτέατος, ὁ, son of Actor and Molionê, or, according to fable, son of Poseidôn, twin brother of Eurytus; Heracles slew him, 2, 601. 13, 185; see Εὔρυτος.

κτείνω, fut. κτενῶ, κτενεῖ, Ep. κτενέω, έεις, and fut. partcp. κτανέοντα, 18, 309; aor. 1 ἔκτεινα, aor. 2 ἔκτανον, aor. 1 pass. 3 plur. ἔκταθεν for ἐκτάθησαν, Od. 4, 537; Ep. aor. act. ἔκταν, 3 plur. ἔκταν for ἔκτασαν. subj. κτῶ, Ep. 1 plur. κτώμεν, infin. κτάμεν, κτάμεναι for κτάναι, aor. 2 mid. ἐκτάμην, with pass. signif. infin. κτάσθαι, partcp. κτάμενος (akin to καίνω, θείνω) *to slay, to kill, to slaughter*, τινά, esply in battle, rarely spoken of the killing or slaughtering of a brute. 15, 587. Od. 12, 379. Pass. κτείνεσθαί τινι, to be slain by any one, Il. 5, 465; Ep. aor. 2 mid. with pass. signif. 3, 375. 5, 301. 15, 558.

κτέρας, τό = κτέαρ, Ep. *possessions, property*, only sing. nom., *10, 216. 24, 235.

κτέρεα, τά (the nom. sing. κτέρος, i. q. κτέαρ, does not occur), prop. *possessions*; then, every thing bestowed upon a dead person as property, and burned with the funeral pile; generally, *funeral obsequies, the last offices to the dead*, extremi honores; mly κτέρεα κτερείζειν, Od. 1, 291. 3, 285. Il. 24, 38.

κτερείζω, fut. κτερείξω, a lengthened form of κτερίζω, 23, 646. 24, 657. Od. 1, 291. 2, 222.

κτερίζω (κτέρεα), fut. κτερίσω, Ep. κτεριῶ, aor. ἐκτέρισα, originally = κτεαρίζω, confined in use to the funeral rites of the dead. 1) With accus. *to inter a man with funeral honours*, 11, 458. 18, 334. 22, 236. κτερείζειν τινὰ ἀέθλοις, to solemnize the interment of any one with funeral games, 23, 646. 2) with the accus. κτέρεα, to perform the obsequies, *justa facere*, 24, 38. Od. 1, 291.

κτῆμα, ατος, τό, *that which is gained, possessions, property, estate*, sing. only Od. 15, 19. Plur. in the Il. mly *treasures, valuables*, 9, 382. Od. 4, 127; in the Od. rather, *property, estate*, Od. 1, 375. 404.

*κτῆνος, εος, τό = κτῆμα, *possessions*, esply an *ox*, plur. *oxen, domestic animals*, h. 30, 10.

Κτήσιος, ὁ, son of Ormenus, father of Eumæus, of Syria, Od. 15, 414.

Κτήσιππος, ὁ (possessing horses), son of Polytherses of Samê, a suitor of Penelope, Od. 20, 288. 22, 279.

κτῆσις, ιος, ἡ, *that which is gained, possession, property*, 5, 158. Od. 4, 687.

κτητός, ἡ, όν (κτάομαι), gained. 2) *to be acquired, to be gained*, 9, 407.† cf. ἐλετός.

κτίδεος, έη, εον (κτίς), for ἰκτίδιος, *pertaining to a weasel.* κυνέη κτιδέη, a head-piece of weasel-skin [*of ferret's felt*, Cp.], *10, 335 458. (According to most critics, κτίς or ἰκτίς is *mustela putorius*, a polecat; some define it to be a ferret, *viverra.*)

κτίζω, fut. ίσω, aor. 1 ἔκτισα, Ep. σσ, *to make a country habitable, to settle, to people; to found to build a city*, with an ac. us 20, 216; Θήβης, ἄδος, Od. 11, 263. (Akin to κτάομαι.)

κτίλος, ὁ, prop adj *tame*; then subst. *a ram*, *3, 196. 13, 492.

Κτιμένη, ἡ, daughter of Laertes, sister of Odysseus (Ulysses); she was married and settled in Samê, Od. 15, 362, seq.

κτυπέω (κτύπος), aor. ἔκτυπον, *to crack, to rattle, to resound*, 13, 140. 23, 119; often Ζεὺς ἔκτυπε, Zeus thundered, 8, 75. Od. 21 413.

κτύπος, ὁ (τύπτω), a noise, crash, &c. produced by striking or stamping, *noise, rattling, uproar, hubbub*; ἴππων, the stamping of steeds, 10, 532. 535; ποδοῖιν (of men), Od. 16, 6. Il. 19, 363; of the tumult of battle, 12, 338; Διός, the thunder of Zeus, 15, 379. 20, 66.

κύαμος, ὁ, a bean, prob. *the field-bean*, 13, 589.† Batr. 125

κυάνεος, έη, εον (κύανος), *dark-blue, black blue*; and generally, *dark-coloured*, blackish ὀφρύες (of Zeus), 1, 528; of Hêrê, 15, 102; χαῖται, spoken of the hair of Hector and Odysseus (Ulysses), 22, 402. Od. 16, 176; δράκων, Il. 11, 26; κάλυμμα, 24, 94; νέφος, νεφέλη, 23, 188. 5, 345; trop. κυάνεον, Τρώων νέφος. 16, 66. κυάνεαι φάλαγγες, dark squadrons, which move on like dark clouds, 4, 282.

κυανόπεζα, ἡ (πέζα), *having dark-blue feet*, a table with dark-blue pedestal, V., Il. 629.

*κυανόπεπλος, ον (πέπλος), *having a dark-coloured robe, dark-robed* epith. of Dêmêtêr, h. in Cer. 320.

κυανοπρώρειος, ον and κυανόπρωρος, ον (πρώρα), *having a dark-blue or black prow, black-beaked* [*sable-prow'd*, Cp.], νηῦς. 15, 693. and often. (κυανοπρώρειος only Od. 3, 299.)

κύανος, ὁ, *a blue cast metal* (according to Voss, *blue cast steel*); Beckmann, Geschich. der Erfind. 4 B. p. 356, with Voss, takes it for *steel*; and according to Köpken Kriegswissensch. it cannot be denied that the ancients used steel, cf. 23. 850, and Od. 9, 391. As there is no other blue-black metal, whether produced by nature or by art, H. very probably intends this by κύανος. Millin (Mineralogie d'Homère) considers it as *tin or lead*, and several ancients (Hesych.) thought it a *dark colour*. or a kind of *mineral varnish or lacker*. Thus Schneider in

Lex. This metal was used for ornament, as upon the shield of Agamemnon ten strips. 11, 24; and in Od. 7, 87, in the hall of Alcinous, a cornice of κύανος is mentioned.

κυανοχαίτης, ου, ὁ (χαίτη), *having dark hair*, mly *having dark locks*, epith. of [the *azure-haired*, Cp.] Ποσειδῶν (once ἵππος, black-maned, 20, 144); as subst. *one having black locks*, 20, 144 Od. 9, 536.

κυανῶπις, ιδος, ἡ (ὤψ), *dark- or black-eyed*, epith. of Amphitritê, Od. 12, 60.†

κυβερνάω, aor. infin. κυβερνῆσαι, *to steer, to pilot, νῆα*, Od 3. 283.†

κυβερνητήρ, ῆρος, ὁ = κυβερνήτης, Od. 8, 557.†

κυβερνήτης, ου, ὁ (κυβερνάω), *a pilot*, gubernator, 19, 43. Od. 9, 78

κυβιστάω (κυβή), *to place or throw oneself upon the head, esply to plunge head foremost, to dive down*, 16, 745. 749; spoken of fish, *21, 354.

κυβιστητήρ, ῆρος, ὁ (κυβιστάω), *one who places himself upon his head, or who turns a somerset, a juggler, a tumbler*, 18, 605. Od. 4, 18. 2) *a diver*, Il. 16, 750.

κυδαίνω (κῦδος), poet. κυδάνω, fut. κυδανῶ, aor. 1 ἐκύδηνα. 1) Prop. *to render famous; to honour, to distinguish, to glorify*, τινά with τιμᾶν, 15, 612. 2) *to place any one in an enviable condition, to honour, to distinguish. to glorify*, spoken of the body (opposed to κακῶσαι) < Αἰνείαν ἀκέοντό τε κύδαινόν τε, they healed Æneas and restored his former beauty, 5, 448; [*him—they healed and glorified*, Cp.] cf. Od. 16, 212. The Schol. explain it: ἐδόξαζον, λόγῳ παρεμύθοντο: Damm; *honore afficiebant*, notions which do not suit ἀκέοντο. b) Spoken of the mind, *to rejoice*, θυμὸν ἄνακτος, Od. 14, 438.

κυδάλιμος, ον, poet. (κῦδος), *famous, renowned, lauded*, epith. of individual heroes and of entire people, 6, 184. 204. 2) ambitious, noble, κῆρ, 10, 16. Od. 21, 147; spoken of lions, 12, 45.

κυδάνω, poet. for κυδαίνω, *to honour*, τινὰ ὁμῶς θεοῖσιν, 14, 73.† 2) Intrans. = κυδιάω, *to vaunt oneself, to be proud*, imperf. κύδανον, 20, 42.

κυδιάνειρα, ἡ (κυδαίνω), poet. *man-honouring, man-ennobling*, μάχη. Il. and once ἀγορή, *1, 490. It is derived not from κῦδος, but from κυδαίνω, hence Hesych. justly: ἡ τοὺς ἄνδρας δοξάζουσα.

κυδιάω (κῦδος), intrans. *to boast, to be proud, to be puffed up, to stride proudly*, spoken of warriors, 2, 579. 21, 519. of steeds, 6, 509. 15, 266; for the most part, the Ep. partcp. κυδιόων (*glorying* [in]); only εὐφροσύνῃ κυδιόωσι, h. 30, 13.

*κύδιμος, ον (κῦδος) = κυδάλιμος, epith. of Hermês, only n. Merc. 46, and repeated nine times.

κύδιστος, η, ον (irreg superl. of κύδρος, as if formed from κῦδος), *most famous,* must honorable, most honoured, epith. of Zeus and Athênê, 4, 415; and of Agamemnon, 2, 434.

κυδοιμέω (κυδοιμός), fut. ήσω, 1) to make a noise, to raise a disturbance, to make an uproar, ἀν' ὅμιλον, 11, 324. 2) Trans. to throw into confusion, with accus. *15, 136.

κυδοιμός, ὁ, noise, tumult, the tumult of battle, Il., confusion, panic, 18, 218. 2) As a mythic being: the deity of the tumult of battle, as companion of Enyo (Bellona), 5, 593. 18, 535. (Bothe as appellat.) *Il.

κῦδος, εος, τό. 1) splendour, glory, honour, praise, dignity, often connected with τιμή, 16, 84. 17, 251; in the address, κῦδος Ἀχαιῶν, glory or pride of the Greeks, 9, 673. Od. 3, 79　2) that which gives glory and fame, prosperity, success, fortune. κῦδος ὀπάζειν τινί. Od. 3, 57. 15, 326; in the Il. success in war, the glory of victory, 5, 225. 8, 141; famous bodily strength, lofty courage, κῦδος καὶ ἀγλαΐην, Od. 15, 78. Il. 1, 405. 5, 906. Nitzsch ad Od. 3, 57.

κυδρός, ή. όν, poet. (κῦδος), famous, famed, glorious, always fem., epith. of Hêrê, Lêtô (Latona), Athênê, and of a mortal female, Od. 15, 26. The masc. h. Merc. 461.

Κύδων, ωνος, ὁ, plur. οἱ Κύδωνες, the Cydônes, a people who dwelt on the north-west side of the island of Crete. According to Strab. they were the aborigines of the island, and, according to Mannert, VIII. p. 679, prob. a division of the Etruscans. Their town Cydonia was prob. situated where stands the present Canea, Od. 3, 292. 19, 176.

κυέω. poet. old form for κύω, to become pregnant, to be pregnant with; to conceive, with accus. υἱόν, spoken of a woman, 19, 117; of a mare, 23, 266; mid. h. 26, 4.

κύθε, see κεύθω.

Κυθέρεια, ή, an appellation of Aphrodîtê, either from the island Cythêra, which was sacred to her, or from the town Cythera in Cyprus, Od. 8, 288. 18, 192. h. Ven. 6; with Κυπρογενής, h. 9, 8.

Κύθηρα, τά, an island on the Laconian coast, south-west (according to Strab. one mile) of the promontory of Malea, now Cerigo. According to later fable, Aphrodîtê landed upon it when she rose from the foam of the sea, 15. 432. Od. 8, 288. The chief town Cythêra, had a noted temple of Aphrodîtê. From this Κυθηρόθεν, from Cythera, Il. 15, 438; Κυθήριος, born in Cythera, 10, 268.

κυκάω, particp. pres. κυκόων, Ep. for κυκῶν, aor. 1 ἐκύκησα, aor. 1 pass. ἐκυκήθην, 1) to touch, to mingle, to stir in, 5, 903; with dat. instrum τυρὸν οἴνῳ, Od. 10, 235. Il. 11, 637. 2) Metaph. to confuse, to throw into confusion, to put into disorder; only pass. to be confused, to be thrown into disorder, 11, 129. 18. 229; of horses: to be terrified, 20, 489; of

rivers and waves: to be in uproar, to be turbid, 21, 235. Od. 12, 238. 241.

κυκείω and κυκέω, see κυκεών.

κυκεών, ῶνος, ὁ (κυκάω), Ep. accus. κυκειῶ and κυκεῶ, Ep. for κυκεῶνα, a mixture, a potion, draught (Cp.), or jelly which was prepared from barley-meal, goat's-milk cheese, and Pramnian wine, 11, 624. 638. 640. In Od. 10, 234. 290, Circê casts in honey. That it was somewhat thick appears from the Od.. where it is called σῖτος. In h. Cer. 208, it is prepared of barley-meal, water, and penny-royal. This jelly was taken to strengthen and recruit; and even in later times it was an article of food for the lower classes, Theoph. Char. 4, 1. (On the accus. see Thiersch, § 188, 15. Buttm. § 55, note.)

κυκλέω (κύκλος), fut. ήσω, to carry away on wheels, to convey away, νεκροὺς βουσί, 7, 332.†

κύκλος, ὁ, plur. οἱ κύκλοι and τὰ κύκλα, spoken of a chariot, 1) a circle, a ring, a circumference, esply the circular rim of a shield, κύκλοι. 11, 33. 12, 297; trop. b) a circle, spoken of men. ἱερὸς κύκλος, of a popular assembly, 18, 504. c) δόλιος κύκλος, the deceitful circle, which hunters form around wild animals, Od. 4, 792: κύκλῳ, in the circle, Od 8, 278. 2) any thing circular; in form, a wheel, which is the signif. of τὰ κύκλα. Il. 5, 722. 18, 375. b) the disc, the ball of a planet, h. 7, 6.

κυκλόσε, adv. (κύκλος), in a circle, round about, *4, 212. 17, 392.

κυκλοτερής, ές (κύκλος), round, circular, ἄλσος, Od. 17, 209. κυκλοτερὲς τείνειν τόξον, to send the bow to a circle, Il. 4, 124.

Κύκλωπες, οἱ, sing. Κύκλωψ, ὁ (prop. circular-eyed), the Cyclôpes, in the Od. are a rude, gigantic race, who live in a scattered, nomadic manner, without laws or cities, Od. 9, 106. seq. Polyphêmus, the most powerful amongst them, sprung from Poseidôn, Od. 1, 63, seq. That they were only one-eyed, appears from the circumstance that Polyphemus after losing his eye, saw no more, cf. Od 9, 397. 416. The ancients generally place them in Sicily, in the region of Ætna, Thuc. 6, 2. Some regard the Leontines as springing from them. Amongst the moderns Voss places them on the south side of Sicily; Völcker, Hom. Geogr. § 58, with great probability, on the southwest coast, near the promontory Lilybæum. Distinct from them are the Cyclopes mentioned by Hes. Th. 140, children of Uranus and Gaia (Tellus), who forge lightning and thunderbolts for Zeus.

κύκνος, ὁ, a swan, *2, 460. 15, 692.

κυλίνδω, only pres. and imperf. and aor. 1 pass. ἐκυλίσθην as if from κυλίω, to roll, to move by rolling, with accus. spoken of waves, ὀστέα, Od. 1, 162; or the wind, κῦμα, Od. 5, 296; metaph. πῆμά τινι, to bring a misfortune upon any one, Il. 17, 688. Mid. with aor. pass. *to roll oneself, to roll away.* spoken of a tempest and of waves, 5, 142. 11, 307; of a wounded horse: περὶ χαλκῷ, 8, 86; spoken of men, as an expression of vehement grief; κατὰ κόπρον, to roll (oneself) in the dirt, 22, 414. 24, 165 Od. 4, 541. Metaph. νῶϊν πῆμα κυλίνδεται, ruin is rolling upon us, Il. 11, 347. 17, 99. Od. 2, 163.

Κυλλήνη, ἡ, a mountain in northern Arcadia on the borders of Achaia, having a temple of Hermês, 2, 603. h. Merc. 2, a town in Elis, now *Chiarenza.*

Κυλλήνιος, ὁ, the *Cyllenian.* 1) epith. of Hermês, Od. 24, 1. 2) an inhabitant of the town of Cyllênê in Elis, Il. 15, 518. according to Schol. Venet. and Eustath.

Κυλλοποδ̄ίων, ονος, ὁ (κυλλός, πούς), voc. Κυλλοπόδιον, *having crooked feet, lame,* epith. of Hêphæstus, *18, 371. 21, 331.

κῦμα, ατος, τό (κύω), *a wave, a swell* of rivers and the sea, often plur. κύματα παντοίων ἀνέμων, the waves excited by winds from every direction (gen. origin.), 2, 397.

κυμαίνω (κῦμα), *to swell into waves, to undulate,* only partcp. πόντος κυμαίνων, 14, 229. Od. 4, 425. and often.

κύμβαχος, ον (κύπτω, κύβη, κύμβη), adj. *head forwards, head foremost, headlong.* 2) Subst. *the upper arch* or *head of the helmet,* in which the crest was inserted, *15, 536.

*Κύμη, ἡ, a town in Æolis (Asia), a colony of Ætolians, Ep. 1, 2. 4, 16.

κύμινδις, ὁ, *a night-hawk,* Plin. H. N. *nocturnus accipiter;* according to 14, 291,† it was called in the earlier language χαλκίς, in the later κύμινδις.

Κυμοδόκη, ἡ (δέχομαι), a Nereid, prop. the wave-receiver, 18, 39.

Κυμοθόη, ἡ (θοός), a Nereid, prop. wave-swift, 18, 41.

κυνάμυια, ἡ (μυῖα), *a dog-fly,* i. e. according to Voss, an impudent fly, a term of reproach used in regard to women, who like dogs and flies are shameless and impudent. Arês uses it to Athênê and Hêrê [*Wasp!* front of impudence! *Cp.*], 21, 394. 421. Others, as Bothe, read κυνό-μυια, as common in prose.

κυνέη, ἡ (prop. fem. from κύνεος, subaud. δορά), *a dog's-skin,* from which head-coverings were made; generally, *a helmet, a head-piece,* without regard to the derivation; the κυνέη was made of ox-hide, ταυρείη, 10, 258; of weasel's [or ferret's]-skin, κτιδέη, 10, 335; and set with metal, χαλκήρης, χαλκοπάρηος, also entirely of brass, πάγχαλκος, Od. 18, 378; κυνέη αἰγείη, a cap of goat's skin, is mentioned Od. 24, 231, which countrymen wore in labouring. • The κυνέη ῎Αϊδος rendered the wearer invisible (like the *Nebel-* or *Tarn-kappe* of the Niebelungenlied), 5, 845; it was made by the Cyclopes, Apd. 1, 2. 1.

κύνεος, έη, εον, *of a dog, canine, shameless, impudent,* 9, 373.†

κυνέω, aor. 1 ἔκυσα, Ep. σσ (from κύω), *to kiss,* with accus. υἱόν 6, 474. Od 16, 190; γούνατα, χεῖρας, Il. 8, 371. 24, 478; and with double accus. κύσσε μιν κεφαλήν, Od. 16, 15. 17, 39; (κυνέω only in the pres. and imperf. Od. 4, 522. 17, 35.)

κυνηγέτης, ου, ὁ (ἡγέτης), that leads dogs to the chase, *an hunter.* Od. 9, 120.†

*Κύνθιος, η, ον, *Cynthian,* ὄχθος=Κύνθος, h. Ap. 27.

*Κύνθος, ὁ, a mountain on the island of Delos, the birth-place of Apollo and Diana, h. Ap. 141; and Κύνθου ὄρος, for Κύνθος, according to an emend. of Hollstein ad Steph. cf. Herm. ad loc.

κυνοραιστής, ὁ (ῥαίω), *a dog-louse, a dog-tick,* acarus ricinus, Od. 17, 300.†

Κῦνος, ἡ, a city in Locris, on a peninsula of the same name, the port of Opus, now *Cyno,* 2, 531.

κύντερος, η, ον, compar. and κύντατος, η, ον, superl. formed from κύων: *more dog-like,* metaph. *more shameless, more impudent,* 8, 483. Od. 7, 216. Superl. κύντατον ἔρδειν, to act most impudently, 11 10, 503.

κυνώπης, ου, ὁ (fem. κυνῶπις, ιδος), *dog-eyed, dog-faced,* i. e. shameless, impudent; voc. κυνῶπα, spoken of Agamemnon, 1, 159.†

κυνῶπις, ιδος, ἡ, fem. of κυνώπης, *dog-eyed,* i. e. shameless, impudent, of Helen, 3, 180. Od. 4, 146; of Hêrê, Il. 18, 396; of Aphroditê, Od. 8, 319.

Κυπαρισσήεις, εντος, ἡ, a town in Triphylia in Elis, on the borders of Messenia, according to Strab. in the ancient Macistia, and in his time an uninhabited place, called ἡ Κυπαρισσία, 2, 593.

κυπαρίσσινος, η, ον (κυπάρισσος), *made of cypress-wood,* Od. 17, 340.†

Κυπάρισσος, ἡ, *cypress,* cupressus semper virens, which in Greece was very abundant, Od. 5, 64.†

Κυπάρισσος, ἡ, a little town in Phocis on Parnassus, not far from Delphi, or a cypress-grove: according to Steph. at an early period *Eranos,* later *Apollonias,* 2, 519.

κύπειρον, τό, a meadow-plant, *the cyperus,* cyperus longus, Linn. Heyne, ad Il. 21, 351, understands by it *the fragrant cyperus,* cyperus rotundus, Linn. Voss, on the other hand, *the galangal,* pseudo-cyperus, Plin.; it was used as food for horses, Od. 4, 603.

*κύπειρος, ὁ, prob.=κύπειρον, h. Merc. 107.

κύπελλον, τό (κύπτω), *a goblet, a beaker, a drinking-cup,* often the same with δέπας, mly of metal, χρύσεια κύπελλα, 3, 248; and Od. 1, 142.

Κύπρις, ιδος, ἡ, accus. Κύπριδα, 5, 458; and Κύπριν (Κύπρος), 5, 330; *Cypris,* an appellation of Aphroditê, because she was especially worshipt on the island Cyprus, or was supposed to have been born there, *5, 422.

*Κυπρογενής, οῦς, ἡ, one born in Cyprus, epith. of Aphroditê, h. 8, 9.

Κύπρος, ἡ, an island of the Mediterranean sea, on the coast of Asia Minor, noted for the worship of Aphroditê, for its fruitfulness, and its rich mines of metals, now Cipro, 11, 21. Od. 4, 83. 8, 362. (υ prop. short, but Ep. also long.)

κύπτω, aor. 1 ἔκυψα, to bow oneself, to bend forwards, 4, 468. 17, 621. Od. 11, 585.

*κυρβαίη μάζα, ἡ, a kind of paste or broth, Ep. 16, 6; where Suid. has κυρκαίη; Herm. would read : πυρκαῖῃ δ' αἰεὶ κατὰ καρδόπου ἕρπεο, μάζαν ἔμμεν, ignis mactram calefaciat, ut semper placenta suppetat.

κυρέω, Ion. and poet., rarely κύρω, imperf. κῦρε for ἔκυρε, 23, 821; aor. 1 ἔκυρσα (ἐκύρησα, Ep. 6, 6), pres. mid. κύρομαι=κυρέω, 1) with dat. to fall by chance upon any thing, to hit, to meet any thing, ἅρματι, 23, 428; κακῷ κύρεται, he is fallen into misfortune, 24, 530; ἐπὶ σώματι, spoken of a lion which meets with prey, 3, 23; αἰὲν ἐπ' αὐχένι κῦρε δουρὸς ἀκωκῇ, he aimed even at the neck with the spear's point, 23, 821. 2) With gen. to reach any point, to attain, to reach, Ep. 6, 6. (Pres. κυρέω is not found in H.)

κύρμα, ατος, τό, any thing which one falls upon and finds, a windfall, spoil, booty, plunder, in connexion with ἕλωρ, 5, 488. 17, 151. 272. Od. 3, 271. 5, 473.

κύρσας, see κυρέω.

κυρτός, ή, όν, bent, curved, crooked, κῦμα, 4, 426. 13, 799. ὤμω, *2, 218.

κυρτόω (κυρτός), fut. ὥσω, to bend, to curve, to arch; κῦμα οὔρεϊ ἶσον κυρτωθέν, arched like a mountain, Od. 11, 244.†

κύστις, ιος, ἡ (κύω), a bladder, *5, 67. 13. 652.

Κύτωρος, ἡ, a town in Paphlagonia, later the port of Amastris, now Quitros, 2, 853; Strab. τὸ Κύτωρον.

κυφός, ή, όν (κύπτος), bent forwards, bowed down, γήραϊ, Od. 2, 16.†

Κύφος, ἡ, a town in Perrhæbia (Thessaly), upon a mountain of the same name, 2, 748; elsewhere ἡ Κῦφος.

κύω, 1) a later form from κυέω, q. v. 2) the root of κυνέω.

κύων, gen. κυνός, ὁ, ἡ, dat. κυσί, Ep. κύνεσσι, 1) a dog, a bitch : κύνες θηρευταί, hunting dogs; hounds; τραπεζῆες, table-dogs. It was a heroic custom to take dogs into the assembly, Od. 2, 11. 17, 62. 2) As a term of reproach, to indicate shamelessness, impudence, as of Helen, Athênê, Hêrê, 6, 344. 356. 8, 423. 21, 481: used of a maid of Odysseus (Ulysses), Od. 18, 338, spoken of men it indicates rage, rashness; of Hector : κύων λυσσητήρ, a raging dog, Il. 8, 299; but also shameless cowardice, esply in the fem κακαὶ κύνες, ye dastardly dogs

(spoken of Trojans), 13, 623. 3) κύων Ἀΐδαο, the dog of Hades, is Cerberus, 8, 368. 4) κύων Ὠρίωνος. the dog of Orion (the dog-star, Σείριος, Hes.), which, with his master, was placed amongst the constellations. In hot regions it is the forerunner of fevers and epidemics, 22, 29. 5) a sea-dog, Od. 12, 96.

κῶας, τό, plur. κώεα, dat. κώεσιν, a soft, hairy skin; a sheep-skin, a fleece. Such skins were spread on the ground, or on chairs and beds, to sit or lie upon, 9, 661, once; Od. 3, 38. 16, 47, and often.

κώδεια, ἡ (κόττα), a head, esply, a poppy-head, 14, 499.† Cf. on the passage the word φή.

κωκυτός, ὁ (κωκύω), howling, lamentation, wailing. *22, 409. 447.

Κώκυτος, ὁ, Cocytus, a river in the under-world, which issued from the Styx, Od. 10, 514.

κωκύω, aor. 1 ἐκώκυσα, to howl, to lament, to wail, to groan, always spoken of women, 18, 37. 71. Od. 2, 361 (in the pres. and imperf. ὔ, Od. 4, 259. 8, 527).

κώληψ, ηπος, ἡ (κῶλον), the ham, 23, 726.†

κῶμα, τό (κοιμάω), a deep, sound sleep, 14, 359. Od. 18, 201.

*κῶμος, ὁ. a feast, a festal entertainment, h. Merc. 481.

*κώνωψ, ωπος, ὁ, ἡ, a gnat, Batr. 203.

Κῶπαι, αἱ, Copæ, an old town on the north side of the lake Copais in Bœotia, now Topolia, 2, 502.

κώπη, ἡ (ΚΑΠΩ, κάπτω), a handle, hence 1) the hilt of a sword, the hilt of a dagger, 1, 219. Od. 8, 403. 11, 531. b) the handle of an oar, Od 9, 489. 12, 214; also the oar itself. [For the last signif. there is no sufficient proof, see Jahrb. Jahn und K. p. 271.] c) the handle of a key, Od. 21, 7.

κωπήεις, εσσα, εν (κώπη), furnished with a handle or hilt; hilted, ξίφος, *15, 713. 16, 332. 20, 475.

κώρυκος, ὁ, a leathern sack or wallet, in which provisions were carried, *Od. 5, 267. 9, 213.

*Κώρυκος, ὁ, a steep mountain in Ionia (Asia Minor), which forms a promontory, according to Steph. near Troy and Erythræ, h. Ap. 39.

Κῶς, Ep. Κόως, gen. Κῶ, accus. Κῶν, 2, 677; a little island of the Icarian sea, with a town of the same name; it was inhabited by the Meropes, 2, 677. h. Ap. 43. Adv. Κόωνδε, to Cos, 14, 255. 15. 28.

κωφός, ή, όν (κόπτω, cf. tusus, obtusus), blunt, obtuse, powerless, βέλος, 11, 390; esply 1) obtuse in the senses, deaf, h. Merc. 92. 2) mute, still. κῦμα κωφόν, the mute [or still, Cp.] wave, as a pre-monitory sign of a coming tempest, 14, 16; κωφὴ γαῖα, the mute or dumb, i. e. the senseless earth, 24, 54.

Λ.

Λ, the eleventh letter of the Greek alphabet: hence the sign of the eleventh rhapsody.

λᾶας. contr. λᾶς, ὁ, gen. λᾶος, dat. λᾶϊ, accus. λᾶαν, dat. plur. λάεσσι, *a stone*, such as warriors hurl at one another in battle, 3, 12. 4, 521. 2) *a rock, a crag*, Od. 13, 163. [3) *a stone-seat*, Od. 6, 267.]

Λάας, contr. Λᾶς, ὁ, accus. Λάαν, an old town in Laconia, ten stadia from the sea; it was destroyed by the Dioscūri, who from this acquired the name Λακέρσαι, 2, 385. (Λᾶς, nom. in Scyl. and Paus. According to Eustath, and Steph. ἡ Λᾶ and ὁ Λᾶς were used in the nom.)

λαβραγόρης, ου, ὁ (ἀγορεύω), *prating boldly, pertly; forward with the tongue*, 23, 479.†

λαβρεύομαι, depon. mid. (λάβρος), *to speak in a bold, rash, or pert manner, to prate inconsiderately*, *23, 474; μύθοις, 478.

λάβρος, ον superl. λαβρότατος, *vehement, impetuous, violent, rapid*, spoken of wind, 2, 148. Od. 15, 293; κῦμα, Il. 15, 625; ποταμός, 21, 271; and of rain, λαβρότατον χέει ὕδωρ Ζεύς, 16, 385. (The deriv. is obscure; the Gramm. derive it from λα and βορά, very voracious, greedy; that is, however, a post-Hom. notion: according to Passow from ΛΑΩ)

λαγχάνω. aor. 2 ἔλαχον, subjunc. λάχω. Ep. λελάχω, 7, 350; perf. λέλογχα, Ep. for εἴληχα; (3 plur. λελόγχασ'. Od. 11, 304, is a conject. of Eustath. instead of the vulgar λελόγχασι, with a short, Thiersch, § 211. 26. Rem.) 1) *to receive by lot, to receive* by fate or the will of the gods, because, *to learn this*, recourse was had to lots, and generally, *to receive, to obtain*. a) With accus. γέρας, 4, 49; οὐρανόν, 15, 192; αἶσαν, Od. 5, 40: πολλά. Od. 14, 233. h. Merc. 420; also κλήρῳ λαχεῖν, Il. 23, 862; with infin. following, 23, 356. 357. cf. 15, 191; hence abso. ὅς τε λάχῃσιν, on whom the lot falls, 7, 171. 10, 430. cf. Od. 9, 334. In the perf *to be master of, to possess, to have*, τιμήν, Od. 11, 304. h. 18, 6. b) With gen. *to become partaker of a thing*, as it were, to obtain part of a thing, δώρων, Il 24, 76; κτερέων, Od. 5, 311. 2) *to cause to partake of*, to make one a partaker of a thing, τινά τινος; however, the subj. aor. with redupl. has this signif. only in the Il θανόντα πυρός, to yield the dead the honour of fire, 7, 80. 15, 350. 23, 76. 3) Intrans. *to fall by lot, to be allotted to*. ἐς ἑκάστην ἐννέα λάγχανον αἶγες, nine goats fell to the lot of each ship. Od. 9, 160.

*λαγών, όνος, ἡ, or ὁ, prop. a cavity. 2)

the *flank* (the space between the hips and the ribs), Batr. 225.

λαγωός. ὁ, Ion. and Ep. for λαγώς. *a hare*; its cry in mating-time is a hollow muttering; when distressed, it is like the crying of a child, 10, 361. Od. 17, 295.

Δαέρκης, ους, ὁ, 1) son of Αἵμων (Æmon), father of Alcimedon, a noble Myrmidon, 16, 197. 17, 467. 2) An artist in Pylos, Od. 3, 425. According to Eustath. ὁ λαοῖς ἐπαρκῶν, who aids the people.

Δαέρτης, αο, ὁ, son of Arcesius, father of Odysseus (Ulysses), king of Ithaca: in his youth he destroyed Nericus; he lived to an advanced age in the country, Od. 11, 186, seq. 24, 219, seq.; and fought with his son against the people of Ithaca, Od. 24, 498.

Δαερτιάδης, ου, ὁ, son of Laertes = Odysseus (Ulysses), Il. and Od.

λάζομαι. depon. only pres. and imperf. Ion. and Ep. for λαμβάνω, *to take, to seize, to grasp, to lay hold of*, with accus. ἡνία χερσί, 5, 365. Od. 3, 483: ἀγκὰς θυγατέρα, to take in the arms, to embrace, Il. 5, 371; γαῖαν ὀδάξ, to lay hold of the earth with the teeth, to bite the earth, to perish, 2, 418; metaph. μῦθον πάλιν, to take again the word, to answer, 4, 357. Od. 13, 255.

*λάζυμαι, a form of λάζομαι, h. Merc. 316.

λαθικηδής, ές (κῆδος), *that causes to forget trouble, soothing*, μαζός, 22, 83.†

λάθρη. Ion. and Ep. for λάθρα, adv. (λανθάνω), *secretly, unobserved*, 2, 515. Od. 4, 92; with gen. λάθρη τινός, without the knowledge of, Il. 5, 269. 24, 72. (λάθρα, h. Cer. 241.)

λᾶϊγξ, ιγγος, ἡ (dimin. of λᾶας), *a pebble, a stone*. *Od. 5, 433. 6, 95.

λαῖλαψ, απος. ἡ, *a tempest* with a whirlwind, rain, and darkness, *a hurricane*, 4, 278. To it H. compares his heroes, 1', 747. 12, 375; expl a sea-storm, Od. b, 68. 12, 314.

λαιμός, ὁ (λάω), *the throat, the gorge, the gullet*, 13, 388. Od. 22, 15.

λάϊνεος, ἑη, ἑον (only 22, 154), and λάϊνος, ον (λᾶας), *stony, of stone*, οὐδός, 9, 404 λάϊνος χιτών, 3, 57 (cf. ἕννυμι). πάντῃ περὶ τεῖχος ὀρ'ρει θεσπιδαὲς πῦρ λάϊνον. every where the dreadful fire arose around the wall of stone, 12, 177. Thus Damm explains this passage, constructing λάϊνον with τεῖχος by hyperbaton. Others (as Heyne and Voss) construct λάϊνον with πῦρ, and understand it in a trop. signif. 'around the wall arose the dreadful fire of rattling stones.' (Several Gramm. consider this verse as not genuine.)

λαισήϊον, τό (prob. from λάσιος), *the target, a kind of shield*. prob. of leather, and lighter than the ἀσπίς, hence πτερόεις, *5, 453. 12, 426. cf. Hdt. 7, 91.

Δαιστρῡγόνες, οἱ, sing. Δαιστρῡγών, όνος, the *Læstrygones*, an ancient rude race, who lived by grazing cattle. The ancients. Thuc. 6, 2, placed them on the east side of Sicily, where the city Leontini (afterwards called Lentini) was situated: Voss. and Völcker, with more probability, place them on the north-west coast. Some of the ancients supposed their place of abode was in Formiæ in lower Italy, Od. 10, 119, seq. cf. Cic. ad Atticum, 11. 13.

Λαιστρῡγόνιος. ίη, ιον, Læstrygonian, Od. 10, 82; in Wolf's ed. Λαιστρυγονίη stands as prop. name. and τηλέπυλος as adj. Even the ancients were not agreed about the name of the city; it is best to take Τηλέπυλος as the prop. name, as Voss translates it, and even Wolf in Od. 23, 318. Cf. Δάμος. Nitzsch, however, ad loc., prefers Λαιστρυγονίην as prop. name.

λαῖτμα, ατος, τό (λαιμός), the deep, an abyss; always with ἁλός or θαλάσσης, the abyss of the sea, 19, 267. Od. 4, 504; and generally, the depths of the sea; the Deep, often Od.

λαῖφος, εος, τό, a ragged garment, an old cloak (pl. tatters), *Od. 13, 399. 20, 206. 2) a sail, h. Ap. 206. (Akin to λῶπος.)

λαιψηρός, ή, όν, quick, rapid, fleet, esply γούνατα, 20, 358. (= αἰψηρός, cf. εἴβω and λείβω, see Thiersch, Gram., § 158. 12.) *Il.

λάκε, Ep. for ἔλακε, see λάσκω.

Λακεδαίμων, ονος, ἡ, Lacedæmon, 1) Prop. the name of the country, later Laconia, which in heroic times was settled only in country villages and residences. As it forms a wide basin between two mountains running down from Arcadia, it is called hollow, κοίλη: abounding in hollows, cavernous, κητώεσσα, 2, 581. 2) the chief town of Lacedæmon=Σπάρτη, Od. 4, 1; or, according to Buttm. Lex. p. 383, the country also, as a collection of villages.

λακτίζω (λάξ), to strike with the heel, and generally, to thrust, to strike, ποσὶ γαῖαν, Od 18, 99; to struggle, to writhe, *Od. 22, 88 Batr. 90.

*Λακωνίς, ίδος, ἡ, adj. Laconian, γαῖα, h. in Ap. 410.

λαμβάνω, aor. 2 ἔλαβον, Ep. ἔλλαβον and λάβον, aor. 2 mid. ἐλαβόμην, Ep. ἐλλαβόμην, infin. λελαβέσθαι, only in the aor. 1) to take, to grasp, to lay hold of, with accus. ἔγχος χειρί or χερσί, ἡνία ἐν χείρεσσι, 5, 853. 8, 116. The part taken hold of stands in the gen. τινὰ ποδῶν, by the feet, 4, 463; γούνων, by the knees, Od. 6, 142. The gen. often alone: ἑανοῦ, ποδῶν, γενείον; metaph. spoken of external and internal states: τρόμος ἔλλαβε γυῖα, Il. 8, 452; in like manner, χόλος, πένθος, with double accus. 4, 230 16, 335. 2) to take, to receive, to take possession of, τὶ ἐκ πεδίοιο, 17, 621; esply in a bad signif.: to take any one prisoner, 5, 159. 11, 126; to make booty of, ἵππους, 10, 545; κτήματα, Od. 9, 41; in a good signif.: to acquire, κλέος, Od. 1, 298. 3) to receive, to receive into one's house, Od.

7, 255. rarely. The partcp. λαβών apparently often stands superfluously. λαβὼν κύσε χεῖρα, he kissed his hand, prop. having taken it, Od. 24, 398. Mid. to take any thing for oneself. to seize upon any thing, with gen. σχεδίης, Od. 5, 325; with accus. Od. 4, 388.

Δάμος. ὁ (gorge), king of the Læstrygones, founder of the city Telepylos, according to Eustath. and the ancients generally, son of Poseidôn. cf. Ovid, Metam. 14. 23. (Some take Lamos for the name of the city Λάμου πτολίεθρον, like Ἰλίου πόλιν. 5, 642; cf. Τροίης πτολ. Od. 1. 2.) Od. 10, 81.

λαμπετάω, poet. = λάμπω, to shine. to blaze; only partcp. pres. λαμπετόωντι πυρί, 1, 104. Od. 4, 662.

Λαμπετίδης, ου, ὁ, Ep. for Λαμπίδης, son of Lampus=Dolops, 15, 526.

Λαμπετίη, ἡ (the shining), daughter of Helius and Neæra, who with her sister pastured the herds of her father in Trinacria, Od. 12, 132 cf. 374.

Λάμπος, ὁ, 1) son of Laomedon in Troy, father of Dolops, a counsellor, 3, 147. 20, 237. 15, 825. 2) a horse of Aurora, Od. 23, 246.

λαμπρός, ή, όν, superl. λαμπρότατος, η, ον (λάμπω), shining, gleaming, beaming, spoken of the heavenly bodies, Il. and Od.; of brass, 13, 132. The neut. sing. as adv. 5. 6. 13, 265.

λαμπτήρ, ῆρος, ὁ (λάμπω), a fire-vase, a lighter, a vessel in which dry wood was burned for a light, *Od. 8, 307. 343. cf. Od. 19, 63.

λάμπω and λάμπομαι, fut. ψω, 1) to give light, to shine, to glimmer, to beam, to flash, prop. spoken of fire, mly of brass, 10, 154. πᾶς χαλκῷ λάμφ' (=ἔλαμπε), κε. Hector, 11. 66; of the eyes: ὀφθαλμὼ οἱ πυρὶ λαμπετον, the eyes flashed with fire, 13, 474. Mid. in Il. and Od. only in the partcp. spoken of persons and things: λάμπετο δουρὸς αἰχμή, 6, 319; χαλκός. 20, 131; of Hector: λαμπόμενος πυρί. τεύχεσι, 15, 623. 20, 46; but also λαμπομένη κόρυς, δαΐς, Od. 19, 48. λάμπετο φλόξ, h. Merc. 113.

λανθάνω, Ep. and Ion. oftener λήθω, Ep. iterat λήθεσκε, 24, 13; fut. λήσω, aor. 2 ἔλαθον. Ep. λάθον, subj. Ep. λελάθω, mid. λανθάνομαι, only imperf. oftener Ep. and Ion. λήθομαι, aor. 2 ἐλαθόμην, Ep. λελαθόμην, perf. mid. λέλασμαι; λανθάνω in the imperf. only three times, 13, 721. Od. 8, 93 532; and imperf. mid. once, Od. 12, 227. 1) Act. 1) to be concealed, to remain concealed or unobserved, τινά, from any one: σὺ λῆθε Διὸς νόον, 15, 461. Oftener there stand with it, a) A partcp. οὔ σε λήθω κινύμενος, I do not moving remain concealed from thee, i. e. I do not move without being observed by you, 10, 279. 13. 273. Od. 8. 93. 12, 17. b) With ὅτι: οὐ με λήθεις, ὅττι θεῶν τίς σ' ἦγε, it was not concealed from me, that some one of the gods conducted thee, Il. 24, 563. c)

The partcp. aor. often stands as adv.
ἆλτο λαθών, he leapt down unobserved,
12, 390. 2) Trans. *to cause one to forget*
a thing, only in the subj. aor. 2 with redupl. τινά τινος. 15, 60. cf. ἐκλανθάνω.
II) Mid. *to forget*, with gen. often ἀλκῆς,
χάρμης. Il.; ἀθανάτων, Od. 14, 421. 2)
to neglect, to omit. Il. 9, 537.

λάξ, adv (*striking*) *with the heel*, or
(*thrusting*) *with the foot*, also λάξ ποδί, 10,
158. Od. 15. 45.

Λαόγονος. ὁ. 1) son of Onêtor, a Trojan. slain by Meriones, 16, 604. 2) son
of Bias, a Trojan, 20, 460.

Λαοδάμας, αντος. ὁ (subduer of the
people). 1) son of Antênor, a Trojan,
slain by Ajax. 15, 516. 2) son of king
Alcinous in Scheria, an excellent pugilist, Od. 8. 116. seq.

Λαοδάμεια, ἡ. daughter of Bellerophontes, who bore Sarpêdon by Zeus.
Artemis, being angry, slew her, 6, 197,
seq. 205.

Λαοδίκη, ἡ. 1) daughter of Priam in
Troy, wife of Helicâon, 6, 252. 2)
daughter of Agamemnon, 9, 145. 287 (on
account of her beauty, in the tragic poets
Electra).

Λαοδόκος or Λαόδοκος. ὁ (receiving the
people), 1) son of Antênor, a Trojan, 4,
87. 2) a Greek, a friend of Antilochus,
17, 699.

Λαοθόη, ἡ. daughter of Altes, king of
the Leleges. mother of Lycaon, 21, 85.
22, 48. (Damm, '*a concursu populi ad
eam spectandam.*')

Λαομεδοντιάδης, ου, ὁ. son of Laomedon = *Priam* or *Lampus*, 3, 250. 15, 527.

Λαομέδων, οντος. ὁ. son of Ilus, father
of Tithônus, Priam, Lampus, etc.. 5,
269. 20, 237. Poseidôn and Apollo
served him, at the command of Zeus.
for a year at wages. The former built
the walls of Troy; the latter kept his
herds. When they demanded their
wages. he refused to pay them, and
wished to sell them as slaves, 21, 441. cf.
7, 452. They left him in anger; Poseidôn sent a ravaging sea-monster, and
Apollo a pestilence. According to the
oracle. the anger of the gods could only
be appeased by exposing his daughter
Hesiônê, as a victim, to the monster.
This was done. Heracles delivered her,
but Laomedon did not give him the promised reward: therefore Heracles sacked
Troy and slew him, 5, 638, seq. 20, 145.
cf. Ἡρακλῆς.

Λαός. ὁ, *the people*, as a mass or collection of men 1) Esply plur. *troops,
army*, sometimes *infantry*. in opposition
to ἵπποι 7, 342. 9, 708. 18, 153; or the
army in the ships. 9, 424. 2) In the Od.
often λαοί, rarely λαός. people. λαοὶ
ἀγροιῶται. country people, Il. 11, 676.
λαοὶ ἑταροι, 13, 710.

Λαοσσόος. ον Ep (σεύω), *exciting the
people, urging the people to battle, exciting
the nations*, epith. of Arês. of Eris, 17,
398 20, 48; of Athênê, 13, 128. Od. 22,

210; of Apollo, 20, 79; of Amphiaraus,
Od. 15, 244.

λαοφόρος. ον, Ep. (φέρω), *bearing the
people;* ὁδός, the public road, 15, 682.†

λαπάρη, ἡ, *the flank* (between the ribs
and hips), 6, 64, and often.

Λαπίθαι, οἱ, *the Lapithæ*, an ancient
warlike race, about Olympus and Pelion
in Thessaly, known by their contest with
the Centaurs at the marriage of Pirithous,
1, 266. 12, 128. Od. 21, 295, seq.

λάπτω, ψω, poet. *to lap, to lick up*. as
cats and dogs drink; spoken of wolves:
γλώσσῃσιν ὕδωρ, 16, 161.†

Λάρισσα, ἡ (*fortress*. a Pelasg. word),
a town of the Pelasgians in Æolia, in
Cymê, afterwards called *Phryconis*, 2,
841. 17, 301.

λάρναξ, ακος, ἡ. *a chest, a box*, and
generally, a repository for keeping any
thing, 18, 413; *an urn* in which the
bones of Hector were placed, *24, 795.

λάρος, ὁ, a voracious sea-bird, *a sea-
mew*, larus, Linn., Od. 5, 51.†

λαρός, ἡ, όν. superl. irreg. λαρώτατος,
Od. 2, 350; *agreeable, palatable. delicious, sweet*, spoken of taste, δεῖπνον,
δόρπον, οἶνος. λαρόν οἱ αἷμ' ἀνθρώπου,
sweet to it (the gnat or musquito) is the
blood of man, Il. 17, 572 (λάω, *capio*,
hence *acceptus*; or from λάω, to wish.)

*λασιαύχην, ενος, ὁ (αὐχήν), *having a
hairy neck, shaggy-necked*, epith. of the
bull, h. Merc. 224; of the bear, h. 6, 46.

λάσιος, ίη, ιον, *thick-haired, shaggy,
hairy*, spoken of men: λάσια στήθεα,
λάσιον κῆρ, the hairy breast, the hairy
heart. as a mark of manhood and of
distinguished bodily vigour, 1, 189. 2,
851; *woolly*, ὄϊς, 24, 125; γαστήρ, Od. 9,
433.

λάσκω. poet. aor. 2 ἔλακον, Ep. λάκον,
perf. λέληκα. partcp. λεληκώς, fem. λε-
λακυῖα, aor. 2 mid. λελάκοντο, h. Merc.
145. 1) *to sound, to crack, to snap, to
creak*, spoken of hard bodies which are
struck; of brass, 14, 25. 20, 277. λάκε
ὀστέα, the bones cracked, 13, 616. 2) *to
cry, to bark*. spoken of the cry of the
falcon, 21. 141; of the barking of Scylla,
Od. 12. 85.

λαυκανίη, ἡ (λάω, λάβω), *the gorge, the
gullet*, *22, 325. 24, 642.

λαύρη, ἡ, *a lane, street, a way* between
houses, *Od. 22, 128. 137. (From λάω,
λάβω, a gorge-like opening.)

λαφύσσω (λάπτω), *to swallow greedily,
to devour*, αἷμα καὶ ἔγκατα. spoken of
lions, *11, 176. 17, 64. 18, 583.

λάχε, Ep. for ἔλαχε, see λαγχάνω.

λάχεια. ἡ, Od. 9, 116. 10, 509; as an
epith. of νῆσος, ἀκτή, Eustath. Apoll.
Etym. M. explain it by εὔγεως ἢ εὔσκα-
φος, and derive it from λαχαίνειν, having
good arable land. More correct is the
reading of Zenodotus: νῆσος ἔπειτ' ἐλάχεια and ἀκτή τ' ἐλάχεια, a little island,
a little coast. Thus Voss, cf. Thiersch,
Gram. § 201. 14. c.

λάχνη, ἡ, *wool, woolly hair*, spoken of

the human hair and beard, 2, 219. Od. 11, 320; of a mantle, Il. 10, 134.

λαχνήεις, εσσα, εν (λάχνη, *woolly, hairy, shaggy, φῆρες, στήθεα, Il λαχνῆεν δέρμα συός, the bristly skin, 9, 548; ὄροφος. the hairy reed, 24, 451.

λάχνος, ὁ=λάχνη. wool, Od. 9, 445 †

λάω, an ancient Ep. word found only in three places; according to the best Gramm. it signifies, *to see, to look at.* κύων ἔχε ἐλλόν, ἀσπαίροντα λάων, (a dog held a fawn, looking at it palpitating,) Od. 19, 229: and v. 230: ὁ μὲν λάε νεβρὸν ἀπάγχων, choking he looked at the fawn Clearer still is ἀιετὸς ὀξὺ λάων, h Merc. 360. It is the root of γλαύσσω, and of ἀλαός, blind. Some explain it as meaning *to seize,* from the root ΔΑΩ=λαμβάνω, ἀπολαύω.

λέβης, ητος. τό (λείβω), prop. a vessel for pouring, *a basin, a cauldron.* 1) a vessel for boiling, made of brass, often connected with τρίπους, and prob. smaller than the tripod, 9, 123. 21, 362. 23, 267. 2) *a basin* or *ewer,* on which, before eating, water (χέρνιψ) was carried to strangers, in a golden laver. It was frequently made of silver, and ornamented with artificial work, Od. 1, 137. 3, 440; also for bathing the feet, Od. 19, 386.

λέγω, fut. λέξω. aor. 1 ἔλεξα, fut. mid. λέξομαι, aor. 1 mid. ἐλεξάμην, Ep sync. aor. ἐλέγμην imperat. λέξο and λέξαι, aor. 1 pass. ἐλέχθην, I) Act. Ep. *to lay any one down,* to put to bed, τινά, only in the aor. 1 act. 24, 635; metaph. *to quiet, to soothe,* Διὸς νόον, 14, 252. 2) *to lay single things together, to pick up, to gather,* to collect, ὀστέα, 23, 239. 24, 72; αἱμασιάς, Od. 18, 359. 24, 224. 3) *to place single things in a row,* i. e. *to count, to count out.* ἐν δ' ἡμέας πρώτους λέγε κήτεσσιν. he counted us first amongst the sea-calves, Od. 4, 452; hence pass. ἐλέχθην μετὰ τοῖσιν, I was counted with these, Il. 3, 188. 13, 276. 4) *to recount, to relate,* τί, often, esply Od. τί τινι, only ὀνείδεά τινι, to utter reproaches against any one, Il. 2, 222. II) Mid. 1) *to lie down,* to place oneself, *to lie,* aor. 1 mid. and the sync. aor 2 and imperat. λέξο, λέξεο. a) *to lay oneself down to sleep,* 14, 350. Od. 10, 320. λέξασθαι ὕπνω, Il. 4, 131; εἰς εὐνήν, Od. 17, 102. b) *to place oneself, to lie down,* (in ambush,) περὶ ἄστυ ἐς λόχον, Il. 9, 67. Od. 4. 413. 453. 2) *to pick up for oneself, to gather,* ξύλα, Il. 8. 507. 547; hence, *to pick out for oneself, to select,* Τρῶας, 2, 125. 21. 27: ἄνδρας, Od 24, 108. 3) *to place oneself with,* to count oneself amongst, *to count for oneself.* ἐγὼ πέμπτος μετὰ τοῖσιν ἐλέγμην, I reckoned myself as the fifth amongst them, Od. 9, 335; but λέκτο ἀριθμόν, he counted over their number (for himself), Od. 4, 451. 4) *to recount* any thing, *to relate, to talk of,* μηκέτι ταῦτα λεγώμεθα, let us speak no more about these things, Il 2. 435 13, 292. cf. 275. Od. 3, 240. The Schol. explain μηκ.

ταῦτ. λεγ. by καθήμεθα, κείμεθα; hence Wolf, 'let us not lay our hands in the lap,' but cf. Buttm., Lex. p. 398. (Buttm., Lex. p. 403, takes for the signif. *to lay,* the theme ΛΕΧΩ [Germ. *legen*], hence λέχος, λόχος, and for the other signif. the theme λέγω.)

λειαίνω, Ep. for λεαίνω (λεῖος), fut. λειανέω, aor. 1 ἐλείηνα, *to make smooth, to smooth, to polish,* κέρα, 4, 111; κέλευθον, to smooth the way, 15, 261; χορόν, Od. 8, 260.

λείβω (akin to εἴβω), aor. 1 ἔλειψα, *to drop, to pour, to pour out, to shed,* δάκρυα, esply to pour out wine as a libation to a deity, οἶνόν τινι, 10, 579. Od. 2, 432; and absol. Il. 24, 285.

λειμών, ῶνος, ὁ (λείβω), any moist place, *a meadow, a field, a pasture,* 2, 461. Od. 4, 605.

λειμωνόθεν, adv. *from the meadow* or *pasture,* 24, 451.†

λεῖος, η, ον, *smooth, polished,* spoken of the trunk of a poplar, 4, 484; *level, plain,* of places: πεδίον, ὁδός, and with gen. χῶρος λεῖος πετράων. a place free from rocks, Od. 5, 443. ποιεῖν λεῖα θεμείλια, to level the foundation (of the wall). Il. 12, 30.

λείουσι, see λέων.

λείπω, fut. λείψω, aor. 2 ἔλιπον, perf. λέλοιπα, aor. mid. ἐλιπόμην, perf. pass. λέλειμμαι, aor. 1 pass. ἐλείφθην, h. Merc. 195; aor. 2 pass. ἐλίπην, 16, 507: fut. pass. λελείψομαι, 24, 742. I) Act. a) *to leave, to quit, to forsake, to leave behind,* with accus. of persons, things, and places, θάλαμον, Ἑλλάδα, Il. λείπειν φάος ἡελίοιο, to leave the light of the sun, i. e. to die, 18, 11; on the other hand, τὸν λίπε θυμός, ψυχή; ψυχὴ λέλοιπε, subaud. ὀστέα ('the soul left the bones,' Voss), Od. 14, 134; in like manner, v. 213; in πάντα λέλοιπε, supply the accus. ἐμέ, all things have left me. (Some Gramm. take λέλοιπα as intrans.: this, however, is foreign to the Homeric usus loquendi.) Again, τί τινι, to bequeath, to leave behind, any thing to any one, Il. 2, 106. 722, seq. b) *to abandon, to leave in the lurch,* 16, 368; ἔλιπον ἰοὶ ἄνακτα, the arrows left the king, i. e. failed him, Od 22, 119. II) Mid. and pass. 1) *to be left behind, to be forsaken,* spoken of persons and things, Il. 2, 700. 10, 256; hence, *to remain, to survive,* 5. 154. 12, 14. Od. 3, 196. 2) *to remain back* or *behind* (in the course), ἀπό τινος, far from any one, Il. 9, 437. 445; esply in foot and chariot races, 23, 407. 409. Od. 8, 125: with gen. of the person, *to remain behind any one,* Il. 23, 523. 529. δουρὸς ἐρωήν (a spear's cast), hence, λελειμμένος οἰῶν, remaining behind the sheep (the ewes), Od. 9, 448; ἀπ' ἄλλων, h. Ven. 76. (In Il. 16, 507, ἐπεὶ λίπεν ἅρματ' ἀνάκτων, λίπεν stands for ἐλίπησαν, aor. 2 pass. (Schol. Ven. ἐλείφθησαν). The Myrmidons held up the panting horses, which strove to fly, after the chariots were left by the kings. (The reading of Zenodot. which Voss follows, was λίπον, after they had left the chariots.)

λειριόεις. εσσα, εν (λείριον), lily(as adj.), having the colour of a lily, only metaph. χρώς lily-white, i. e. tender, delicate skin, 13, 830; ὄψ. the tender (clear-chirping, V) voice of the cicada [his slender ditty sweet, Cp.], 3, 152.

*λείριον, τό, a lily, esply the white, h. Cer. 427.

λαϊστός, ή, όν (λαΐζομαι), Ion. and poet. for ληϊστός, q. v.

*Δειχήνωρ, ορος, ὁ (ἀνήρ), Licker, name of a mouse, Batr. 205.

*Δειχομύλη, ἡ (μύλη), Lick-mill, one that licks up the flour in the mill, name of a mouse, Batr. 29.

*Δειχοπίναξ. ακος, ὁ (πίναξ), Plate-licker, name of a mouse. Batr. 106.

Δειώδης, ου, ὁ, son of Ænops, a prophet and suitor of Penelope. He was opposed to the impiety of the suitors; still Odysseus (Ulysses) slew him, Od. 21, 144. 22, 310.

Δείκριτος, ὁ, 1) son of Arisbas, a Greek, slain by Æneas, 17, 344. 2) son of Evenor. a suitor of Penelope, Od. 2, 242. 22, 294.

λείων, see λέων.

λέκτο, Ep. for ἔλεκτο, see λέγω.

Δεκτόν, τό (more correctly Δέκτον), a promontory on the Trojan coast, at the foot of Ida, opposite Lesbos. now Cap Baba, 14, 283 (h. Ap. 217, it stands incorrectly; hence Ilgen would read Δεύκος. Herm. Δύγκος).

λέκτρον, τό (λέγω), 1) a couch, a bed, mly in the plur. Il. and Od. λέκτρονδε, to bed, ἰέναι, Od. 8, 292.

λελαβέσθαι, λελάβησι, see λαμβάνω.

λελάθη, λελάθοντο, see λανθάνω.

λελάκοντο, λελακυία, see λάσκω.

λέλασμαι, see λανθάνω.

λελάχητε, λελάχωσι, see λαγχάνω.

Δάλεγες, οἱ, the Leleges, an ancient race of the southern coast of Troas, about Pedasus and Lyrnessus, opposite Lesb a, 10, 429 20, 96. After the destruction of Troy, they migrated to Caria. According to Mannert, they together with the Curētes were of Illyrian origin, and dwelt originally in Acarnania, Ætolia, etc. Prob. they were a Pelasgian race. having their earliest place of settlement in Greece.

λεληκώς, see λάσκω.

λελίημαι, an old perf. with pres. signif.: to strive, to hasten, only partcp.λελιημένος, used as an adj. eager. [= eagerly], impetuous, 12, 106. 16, 552; with ὄφρα, 4, 465. 5, 690. (From λιλάομαι (simpler form of λιλάομαι] for λελίλημαι, see Thiersch, Gram. § 233. 85.) *11. [Buttm., Lex. p. 77.]

λέλογχα, see λαγχάνω.

λέξεο and λέξο, see λέγω.

Δεοντεύς, ῆος, ὁ, son of Corōnus, one of the Lapithæ, a suitor of Helen; he went to Troy with twenty ships, 2, 745. 23, 841.

λέπαδνον, τό, the yoke-strap; mly in the plur., according to App. Lex. the leathern straps with which the yoke was fastened under the necks of the draught-animals, and connected with the girth; but in H., the straps with which the yoke was made fast to the end of the pole. These straps served perhaps also to govern the horses, 5, 730. 19, 393; cf. Köpke, Kriegsw. d. G. S. 137.

λεπταλέος. έη, έον, poet. (λεπτός), slender, weak, delicate, φωνή, 18, 571.†

λεπτός, ή, όν (λέπω, prop. peeled), 1) thin, fine, delicate, mly spoken of the products of the loom, 18, 595. Od. 2, 95; of brass, Il. 20, 275; of barley, trodden fine, 20, 497; εἰσίθμη, a narrow entrance, Od. 6, 264. 2) little, slender, weak, μῆτις, Il. 10, 226.

*λεπτουργής, ές (ἔργον), wrought finely, h. 31, 14.

*λέπυρον, τό (λέπος). a rind, a husk, a shell, καρύοιο, Batr. 131.

λέπω, aor. ἔλεψα, to peel off, to strip off, with accus. φύλλα, 1, 236.†

Δέσβος, ἡ, an island of the Ægean sea, opposite the Adramyttian gulf, having a town of the same name, now Mettellino, 24, 544. Od. 3, 169; from which 1) Adv. Δεσβόθεν, from Lesbos, Il. 9, 660. 2) Δεσβίς, ίδος, ἡ, Lesbian; subst. a Lesbian female. 9, 129.

λέσχη, ἡ (λέγω), 1) talk. 2) a place frequented for talk and gossip [the public portico, Cp.]; a rendezvous for idlers and loungers, Od. 18, 329.†

λευγαλέος. έη, έον (from λυγρός as πευκάλιμος from πυκνός), wretched, sad, miserable, lamentable, bad, miser. 1) Of persons: πτωχός, Od. 16, 273. 17, 202. 20, 203. λευγαλέοι ἐσόμεσθα, we shall be miserable, i. e. weak (Ntz.), Od. 2, 61. 2) Of things: miserable, wretched, θάνατος, a miserable death, in distinction from a natural death, Il. 21, 281. Od. 5, 312; πόλεμος, 13, 97. λευγ. ἔπεα, harsh words, 20, 109. λευγ. φρένες, an evil mind, 9, 119. (According to the Schol. act. hurtful; but see Nitzsch ad Od. 2, 61.)

λευγαλέως, adv. sadly, lamentably, 13, 723.†

λευκαίνω (λευκός), to whiten, ὕδωρ ἐλατῆσιν [to sweep the whit'ning flood, Cp.], Od. 12, 172†

Δευκάς, άδος, ἡ, πέτρη, the Leucas-rock, i. e. white-rock, is prop. a rock on the coast of Epirus. where the ancients placed the entrance into the under-world, also=Δευκαδία, now S. Maura. In H. Od. 24, 11, it is further west. near Occanus, but still to be regarded as this side of it, on the light-side of the earth.

λεύκασπις, ιδος, ὁ, ἡ (ἀσπίς), having a white shield, epith. of Deiphobus [white-shielded chief, Cp.], 22, 294.†

*Δευκίππη, ἡ, daughter of Oceanus and Tethys, h. Cer. 418.

*Δεύκιππος, ὁ, 1) son of Periêres,

brother of Aphareus. 2) son of Œnomaus in Elis, who loved Daphne, h. Ap. 212.

Λευκοθέη, ἡ, i. e. white-goddess, a name of Ino, after she was reckoned amongst the sea-deities. She was the daughter of Cadmus, king of Thebes, and, being pursued by her raging husband Athamas, she precipitated herself with her son Melicertes, from the rock Moluris on the Corinthian isthmus, into the sea, Od. 5, 334. Cf. Apd. 3, 4. 2.

λευκός, ή, όν (λάω, λεύσσω), compar. λευκότερος, 1) shining, gleaming, bright, clear, 14, 185; αἴγλη, λέβης, hence also: λευκὸν ὕδωρ, clear water, 23, 282. Od. 5, 70: esplv white-shining; πόλις, κάρηνα, ὀδόντες, Il. 2) Most mly: white, whitish, in manifold degrees. λευκότεροι χιόνος, spoken of steeds, 10, 437; γάλα, 5, 902; ὀστέα. Od. 1, 161; ἄλφιτα, Il. 11, 640; χρώς, 11, 573; λευκοὶ κονισάλῳ, with white dust, 5, 503.

Δεῦκος, ὁ, 1) a companion of Odysseus (Ulysses), 4, 491 2) a river in Macedonia, h. Ap. 217; according to Ilgen for Λέκτον.

*λευκοχίτων, ωνος, ὁ, ἡ (χιτών), white-clad, ἧπαρ, the liver wrapped in a white net, Batr. 37.

λευκώλενος, ον. Ep. (ὠλένη), having white elbows, white-armed, epith. of Hêrê, and of many women, Il. and Od.

λευρός ή, όν (λεῖος), Ion. level, smooth, χῶρος, Od. 7, 123.†

λεύσσω, poet. (λάω), prop. to emit light, then, to see, to look; ab·ol πρόσσω καὶ ὀπίσσω, forwards and backwards, i. e. to be prudent, wise, 3, 110; ἐπὶ πόντον, ἐς γαῖαν, 5, 771. Od. 9. 166. b) With accus. to see, to behold, Il. 1, 120. 16, 70. 127. Od. 6, 157. 23, 124.

λεχεποίης, ου, ὁ. fem. λεχεποίη, ἡ, Ep. only accus. λεχεποίην (ποία), overgrown with long grass, suitable for making beds, abounding in grass, grassy, as masc. epith. of the river Asôpos, 4, 383; as fem. of the towns Pteleus, Teumessus, and Onchestus, 2, 697, h. 224. It is incorrect to assume that λεχεποίην (with the names of cities) is an accus. fem. to λεχέποιος. Cf. Eustath. ad Il. 2, 679.

λέχος, εος, τό (λέγω, ΔΕΧ), 1) a couch, a bed, in the plur. a bedstead, 3, 391. Od. 1, 440, exply, a) the nuptial bed, Od. 8, 269. Il. 3, 411. 15, 39, hence. the nuptial embrace, in the construct. λέχος πορσύνειν, ἀντιᾶν, 1, 31. Od. 3, 403. b) a death-bed, for laying out a corpse, Il. 18, 233. 24. 589, and often.

λέχοσδε, adv. to bed, 3, 448.

λέων, οντος, ὁ, dat. plur. Ep. λείουσι, (Ep. form λῖς), a lion, often as a comparison for heroes, Il. once for λέαινα: Ζεύς σε λέοντα γυναιξὶ θῆκε, Zeus made thee a li ness, i. e. a destroyer, for women, spoken by Hêrê, of Artemis, because the sudden death of women was ascribed to the arrows of Artemis, 21, 483.

λήγω, fut. λήξω, aor. ἔληξα, Ep. λῆξα. 1) Intrans. to cease. to desist, to leave off. obsol 21, 218; ἐν σοὶ μὲν λήξω, σέο δ᾽ ἄρξομαι, in thee I will leave off and with thee begin, i. e I confine myself especially to thee. a) With gen. to desist from, to rest from, χόλοιο, ἔριδος, φόνοιο, χοροίο, ἀπατάων. b) With partcp. λήγω ἀείδων, I cease singing, 9, 191. Od. 8, 87; ἐναρίζων, Il. 21, 224. h. Ap. 177. 2) Transit. only poet. to cause to cease, to quiet, to allay, τί, any thing. μένος, 13, 424 21, 305. b) τί τινος: λήγειν χεῖρας φόνοιο, to stay the hands from slaughter, Od. 22, 63: (λήγω, akin to λέγω, to lay.)

Λήδη, ἡ, Ep. for Λήδα, daughter of Thestius, wife of Tyndareus; she bore to Zeus, who visited her in the form of a swan, Helen, Kastôr (Castor), and Polydeukês (Pollux), Od. 11, 298: (according to Damm. from λῆδος, a thin robe.)

ληθάνω, poet. form in tmesis, see ἐκλανθάνω.

λήθη, ἡ (λῆθος), forgetfulness, oblivion. 2, 33.†

Λῆθος, ὁ, son of Teutamus, king of the Pelasgians in Larissa, 2, 843. 17, 288.

λήθω, mid. λήθομαι, Ep. ancient form of λανθάνω. q. v

ληϊάς, άδος, ἡ, pecul. poet. fem. of ληΐδιος (ληΐς), a female captive, 20, 193.†

ληΐβότειρα, ἡ, fem. from ληϊβοτήρ, (βόσκω), crop-devouring, σῦς, Od. 18, 29.†

ληΐζομαι. depon. mid. (ληΐς), fut. ληΐσομαι, aor. 1 ἐληϊσάμην, Ep. 3 sing. ληΐσσατο. to lead away as booty, to plunder, to obtain in war, spoken of persons : τινά, 18, 28. Od. 1, 398; spoken of things : πολλά, Od. 23. 357.

λήϊον, τό, a crop, a harvest, standing in the field, 2, 147. Od. 9, 135.

ληΐς, ΐδος, ἡ, Ion. and Ep. for λεία, plunder, booty in war, spoken of men and cattle, 9, 138. 280. Od. 3, 106; (from λαός, as common property, divided amongst the warriors.)

ληϊστήρ, ῆρος, ὁ (ληΐζομαι), a spoiler, a plunderer, esply a sea-robber, a pirate. *Od. 3, 73. 9, 254. Piracy and coast-robbery, according to Homeric notions, were not disgraceful, cf. Thuc. 1, 5.

*ληϊστής. οῦ, ὁ=ληϊστήρ. h. 6, 7.

ληϊστός, ή, όν (ληΐζομαι), Ep. also λεϊστός, ή, όν. plundered, robbed; capable of being plundered, ληϊστοὶ βόες, 9, 406; ἀνδρὸς δὲ ψυχὴ πάλιν ἐλθεῖν οὔτε λεϊστή. οὔτε, κτλ, the soul of man cannot be seized (and constrained) to return again [ἐλθεῖν=ὥστε ἐλθεῖν], 9, 408; cf. ἑλετός.

ληΐστωρ, ορος, ὁ = ληϊστήρ, Od. 15. 427.†

λήϊτις, ιδος, ἡ (ληΐς), one who makes booty, the bestower of spoil, epith. of Athênê, 10, 460.†

Λήϊτος, ὁ, son of Alectryon, leader of the Bœotians before Troy, 2, 494; wounded by Hector, 17, 601.

λήκυθος, ἡ. an oil-flask, an oil-cruet, *Od 6, 79. 215.

*Δήλαντον πεδίον, τό, the Lelantian plain, a fruitful plain in the western part of the island of Euboea, near Eretria, on the river Lelantus, having warm baths and iron mines, h. Ap. 220.

Λῆμνος, ἡ, an island in the northern part of the Ægean sea, having in H.'s time perhaps a town of the same name, sacred to Hêphæstus on account of the volcano Mosychlus, now Stalimene, 1, 594. 2, 722. Od. 8, 283.

*ληρός, ἡ and ὁ, any tub-like vessel; esply a trough, for watering cattle, a watering-place, h. Merc. 104.

*λησίμβροτος, ον, poet.(βροτός), stealing unawares upon men, deceiver, thief, h. Merc. 339.

λήσω, λήσομαι, see λανθάνω.

*Λητοΐδης, ου, ὁ, son of Lêtô (Latona) =Apollo, h. Merc. 253.

Λητώ, οῦς, ἡ, voc. Λητοῖ, Lêtô (Latona), daughter of the Titan Koios (Cœus), and Phœbe, mother of Apollo and Artemis by Zeus, 1, 9. Od. 6, 318; she cures the wounded Æneas, Il. 5, 447. On the way to Delphi she was violently attacked by Tityus, Od. 11, 580. (According to Herm. Sopitia, akin to λήθειν.)

λιάζομαι, depon. pass. aor. 1 ἐλιάσθην, Ep. λιάσθην, prop. to bend, mly, 1) to bend sidewise, to bend outwards, to retire, to retreat, for the most part spoken of men, ὕπαιθα, 15, 520. 21, 255. δεῦρο λιάσθης, retiredst hither, 22, 12; and so also νόσφι λιασθείς (going or turning aside), 1, 349. 11, 80. ἐκ ποταμοῖο, ἀπὸ πυρκαῆς, to escape from the river, to go away from the funeral pile, Od. 5, 462. Il. 23, 231; and with the gen. alone, 21, 255. ἀμφὶ δ' ἄρα σφι λιάζετο κῦμα, 24, 96; absol. to retire, Od. 4, 838. 2) to bend down, to sink, to fall, to slip, only Ep. ποτὶ γαίῃ, Il. 20, 418. πρηνὴς ἐλιάσθη, 15, 243. πτερὰ πυκνὰ λίασθεν for ἐλιάσθησαν, the thick wings sank, dropt, 23, 879 (see Buttm., Lex. p. 404).

λιαρός, ἡ, όν (χλιαίνω, ἰαίνω), warm, tepid, αἷμα, ὕδωρ, 11, 477. 846. Od. 24, 25; οὖρος, a soft wind, Od. 5, 268. 2) Generally, mild, gentle, agreeable, ὕπνος, Il. 14. 164.

Λιβύη, ἡ, Libya, in H. the country west of Egypt as far as Oceanus; later entire North Africa, Od. 4, 85. 14, 295.

λίγα. adv. from λιγύς for λιγέα, loudly, clear-sounding, mly with κωκύειν, 19, 284; with ἀείδειν, only Od. 10, 254.

λιγαίνω (λιγύς), shrill-crying. to cry loudly, spoken of heralds, 11, 685.†

λίγγω, aor. λίγξε, see λίζω.

λίγδην. adv. poet. (λίζω). in the manner of grazing, scratching; βάλλειν χεῖρα, to wound the hand superficially [with a surface wound, Cp.], Od. 22, 278.†

λιγέως, adv. from λιγύς, q. v.

*λιγύμολπος, ον (μολπή), clear-singing, Νύμφαι, h. 18. 19.

λιγυπνείων, οντος, ὁ, poet. (πνέω), clear

or loud-blowing, roaring, ἀήτης, Od. 4, 567.†

*λιγύπνοιος, ον (πνοιή)=λιγυπνείων, h. Ap. 28.

λιγυρός, ή, όν (lengthened from λιγύς), clear-sounding, whistling, shrill, spoken of the wind, 5, 526. 13, 590; loud-cracking, spoken of a whip [shrill-sounding, Cp.], 11, 52; clear-sounding, of a bird, 14, 290; loud-singing, of the Sirens, Od. 12, 44. 183.

λιγύς, εῖα, ύ, Ep. and Ion. in fem. λίγεια, poet. clear or loud-sounding, spoken of any fine, sharp, and piercing sound. 1) Of inanimate things : clear-whistling, roaring, of the wind, 13. 334. Od. 3, 176 ; clear-ringing, of the lyre, Il. 9, 186. Od. 8, 67. 2) Of living beings : of the muse, Od. 24, 62. h. 13, 2; esply of Nestor, clear-voiced. ἀγορητής, Il. 1, 248; adv. λιγέως: aloud, loudly, often with κλαίειν, 19, 5; of wind: φυσᾶν, to blow loudly, 23, 218. λιγέως ἀγορεύειν, to speak impressively, emphatically, 3, 214. (On the accentuation λίγεια, Ion. for λιγεῖα, see Thiersch, Gram. § 201. c.)

λιγύφθογγος, ον, poet. (φθογγή), clear-sounding, clear-voiced, epith. of heralds, 2, 50, and once Od. 2, 6.

λιγύφωνος, ον, poet. (φωνή), clear-voiced, loud-crying, spoken of the eagle, 9, 350.†

λίζω, only aor. 1 λίγξε for ἔλιγξε, to twang, 4, 125.†

λίην, Ion. and Ep. for λίαν, adv. 1) too much, exceedingly, very much, for the later ἄγαν, with verbs and adject. 1, 553. Od. 3, 227. 4, 371; more rarely, much, greatly, οὔτι λίην, Il. 13, 284. 14, 368. 2) Frequently καὶ λίην stands at the beginning of a sentence with emphasis, for καὶ μάλα, certainly, by all means, yes certainly. καὶ λίην οὗτός γε μένος θυμόν τ' ὀλέσειεν, certainly he would have lost his strength and his life, 8, 357. καὶ λίην κεῖνός γε ἐοικότι κεῖται ὀλέθρῳ, Od. 1, 46. 3, 203. 9, 477. (ι is prop. short, but in καὶ λίην always long.)

λίθαξ, ακος, ὁ, ἡ (λίθος), stony, rocky, hard, πέτρη, Od. 5, 415.†

λιθάς, άδος, ἡ = λίθος, a stone, a rock, *Od. 14, 36. 23, 193.

λίθεος, η, ον (λίθος), of stone, 23, 202. Od. 13, 107.

*λιθόρρῖνος, ον (ῥῖνος), having a hard shell, stone-cased. χελώνη. h. Merc. 48.

λίθος, ὁ, twice ἡ, 12, 287. Od. 19, 494 ; a stone, as an image of what is hard and unfeeling, Il. 4, 510. Od. 23, 103 ; esply a field-stone thrown by warriors at each other, Il., in the plur. λίθοι, οἱ, stone seats, 18, 504. Od. 3, 406. b) a rock, Od. 3, 296. 13, 156. (In later writers ἡ λίθος, a precious stone.)

λικμάω (λικμός), to cleanse grain with the winnowing-fan, to winnow, καρπόν, 5, 500.†

λικμητήρ, ῆρος, ὁ, poet. (λικμάω), a winnower, a grain-cleaner, 13, 590.†

*λίκνον, τό, a winnowing-fan, probably of osier basket-work, h. Merc. 21, 63.

λικριφίς, adv. poet. from the side, sidewise, ἀΐσσειν, 14, 463. Od. 19, 451.

Λικύμνιος, ὁ, son of Electryon and Midea, uncle of Heracles; he was slain by the son of that hero, Tlepolemus, by mistake, 2, 663. (According to Herm. Subolescentius)

Λίλαια, ἡ, a city of Phocis, at the source of the Cephisus, now Lellen, 2, 523.

λιλαίομαι, depon. Ep. (λι—λάω), only pres. and imperf. to desire ardently. to strive for, to long for, to wish. 1) With infin. poet. also spoken of inanimate things, of the spear, 21, 168; uncommonly is λιλαιομένη πόσιν εἶναι, i. e. τοῦ εἶναι αὐτόν οἱ πόσιν, desiring that he might be her husband, Od. 1, 15; cf. Thiersch, § 296. 2. b. 2) to long for, to desire earnestly, with gen. πολέμοιο, ὁδοῖο, Il. 3, 133 Od. 1, 315. 12, 328. (From this the Ep. perf. λελίημαι.)

λιμήν, ένος, ὁ (λείβω), a haven, a bay, or harbour, in general ὅρμος, the inner portion of it, 1, 432. Od. 2, 391.

λίμνη, ἡ (λείβω), properly, water which washes a neighbouring shore; hence 1) a pool or lake, 2, 711. 865. 5, 709; also, water overflowing from a river or the sea, a marsh, or a sound (fretum), between two neighbouring shores, generally, the sea, 24, 79. 13, 21. 32. περικαλλὴς λίμνη, in Od 3, 1, according to ancient critics, is a part of Oceanus; according to Voss, from a fragment of Æschylus in Strab. I. p. 33, a pool in which Helius bathes his horses, and from which he mounts the heavens; Nitzsch ad Od. p. 131, explains it generally, as the water of Oceanus standing near the shore.

*Λιμνήσιος, ὁ, an inhabitant of the marsh, Fenman or " Marsh," a frog's name, Batr. 229.

*λιμνοχαρής, ές, gen. έος (χαίρω), delighting in a marsh, epith. of the frog, Batr. 13.

*Λιμνόχαρις, ὁ, Marshjoy, a frog's name, Batr. 211.

Λιμνώρεια, ἡ, daughter of Nereus and Doris, 18, 41.

λιμός, ὁ (prob. from λείπω, λέλειμμαι), hunger, famine, 17, 166. Od. 4, 369; as fem., h. Cer. 12; according to the Gramm. Doric.

Λίνδος, ἡ, a town on the island Rhodes, with a temple of Athênê, now Lindo, 2, 656.

λινοθώρηξ. ηκος, Ep. (θώραξ). wearing a linen cuirass (clad in thick-woven mail. Cp.], epith. of Ajax, son of Oïleus, and of Amphius, 2, 529. 830.

λίνον, τό. flax. 1) any thing made of flax: a) thread. yarn; esply an angling-line, 16, 408; metaph. the thread of life, which the Fates spin for men, 20, 128. 24, 210. Od. 7, 198. 2) a fisher's net, Il. 5, 487. 3) linen, λίνοιο ἄωτον. 9, 661. Od. 13, 73: see ἄωτον, plur. h. Ap. 104.

Λίνος, ὁ. an ancient hero or a country youth, slain by Apollo because he en-

gaged in a contest with him, Paus. 9, 29. 3. From this, as later, is distinguished the singer of Thebes, son of Apollo and a Muse (Calliope or Urania), teacher of Orpheus and Heracles, Hes. fr. 1. Apd. 1, 3. 2. From this,

Λίνος, ὁ, the Linus song, a song named after the hero of the famous mythic bard Linus (see Λίνος), which was originally serious and sad, but later of a joyful character, Hdt. 2, 79. Athen. XIV. p. 619. C; generally, singing, a song, spoken of a song in vintage, 18, 570.† λίνον δ᾽ ὑπὸ καλὸν ἄειδε, he sang beautifully the Linus song. Thus Aristarch. and, amongst the moderns, Voss, Heinrichs, Spitzner. Others, as Köppen, Heyne, take λίνον as the accus. from τὸ λίνον. thread, the string of a lyre (since these strings were first made of thread), and construe, ὑπὸ λίνον καλὸν ἄειδε, he sang beautifully to the string of the lyre. (This construction is not to be received, if only for the reason that thread does not make good lute strings.)

λίπα. Ep. λίπ᾽ ἐλαίῳ ἀλεῖψαι, 18, 350: and ἀλείψασθαι, 10, 577. 14, 171; χρῖσαι and χρίσασθαι, Od. 3, 466. 6, 96. 10, 364; to anoint oneself with oil. According to Herodian in Eustath. λίπα is origin. dat. from τὸ λίπα, oil, fat, gen. αος, dat. λίπαϊ, λίπᾳ; later, this dat. was by use shortened to λίπα (ἔλαιον is adj. from ἐλάα, olive; hence λίπ᾽ ἐλαίῳ, with olive oil), see Buttm. Gram. § 58, p. 90. Kühner, § 270. Others consider λίπα an adv. unctuously (as an abbrev. from λιπαρά), hence λίπα ἀλείφειν, to anoint with fat. see Thiersch, Gram. § 198. 2.

λιπαροκρήδεμνος. ον (κρήδεμνον), having a shining head-band, splendidly veiled, Χάρις, 18, 382.† h. Cer. 25.

λιπαροπλόκαμος, ον (πλόκαμος), having anointed or glossy tresses, 19, 126.†

λιπαρός ή. όν (λίπας), superl. λιπαρώτατος, h. Ap. 33; originally 1) fat. anointed. Wealthy persons anointed themselves after bathing, and also on festival occasions, esply the head, face, and hair; hence λιπαροὶ κεφαλὰς καὶ καλὰ πρόσωπα, spoken of the suitors. Od. 15, 332. 2) shining, beaming, bright, beautiful, nitidus, spoken of the external form, πόδες, nly of men, and of Hêrê, Il. 14, 186; κρήδεμνα, the splendid veil, Od. 1, 334. 16, 416; but, the gleaming battlements. Od. 13, 388. Λιπαραὶ θέμιστες, rich, splendid tributes, Il. 9, 156. b) agreeable, happy, esply spoken of age, Od. 11, 136. 19, 368; hence adv. λιπαρῶς, happily. γηράσκειν, Od. 4, 210.

λιπάω (λιπάς), Ep. λιπόω, to be fat, to shine, an old reading for ῥυπόω, Od. 19, 72.†

λίς or λῖς, Ep. for ὁ λέων, a lion, a defect. subst , of which except the nom n. we have only the accus., λῖν, 11, 480. Spitzner, ad Il. 15, 275, prefers λίς.

λῖ΄ς. ἡ, abbrev. form for λισσή. smooth. λὶς πέτρη, *Od. 12, 64. 79. 2) λίς, ὁ, for λίς, occurring only in the dat. sing. λιτί and accus. λῖτα, an old Ep. defect. =λίνον, *linen*; in the phrase ἑανῷ λιτὶ κάλυψαν, they covered him with costly linen, Voss, Il. 18, 352. 23, 254 (spoken of the linen with which the dead was shrouded); and accus. sing. ὑπὸ λῖτα πετάσσας καλόν, Od. 1, 130. cf. Od. 10, 353. Il. 8, 441; spoken of linen cloth spread upon seats and over a chariot. Thus Apoll., Heyne, Butim., Gram. p. 91. Thiersch, Gram. § 197. 60. Wolf, on the contrary, in Anal. IV. p. 501, Passow, Rost, and Nitzsch ad Od. 1, 130, take λῖτα as accus. plur. from an old neut. λί, Ep. for λισσόν, λεῖον, smooth cloth without embroidered figures=λεῖα, Thuc. 2, 97. In favour of this are the epithets καλόν. δαιδαλέον, Od. 1, 130, which are generally used with θρόνος, but never with λῖτα, Il. 18, 390. Od. 10, 314. 366.

λίσσομαι, more rarely λίτομαι, poet. depon. mid. Ep. imperf. ἐλλισόμην, and iterat. λισσέσκετο, fut. λίσσομαι, aor. 1 ἐλισάμην, Ep. ἐλλισάμην, Od. imperat. λίσαι, aor. 2 ἐλιτόμην, from the optat. λιτοίμην, Od. 14, 406: infin. λιτέσθαι, Il. 16, 47. 1) Absol. *to supplicate, to entreat*; ὑπέρ τινος, by any one, thus ὑπὲρ τοκέων, ὑπὲρ ψυχῆς καὶ γούνων, 15, 660. Od. 15, 261; and gen. alone, Od. 2, 68. 2) *to beg, to implore, to adjure*. a) With accus. of the person: τινά; the object of the entreaty stands a) In the infin. οὔ σε λίσσομαι μένειν, Il. 1, 174. 283. 4, 379; or in the accus. with the infin. 9, 511. Od. 8, 30; sometimes also ὅπως follows, Od. 3, 19. 327. β) In the accus. οἳ αὐτῷ θάνατον λιτέσθαι, to implore death for oneself, Il. 16, 47; and with double accus. ταῦτα οὐχ ὑμέας ἔτι λίσσομαι. these things I no longer entreat of you, Od. 2, 210. cf 4, 347. λίσσεσθαί τινα γούνων, Il. 9, 451, supplicating to embrace the knees, for the usual λαβὼν γούνων, 6, 45. (λίτομαι stands only h. 15, 5. 18, 48.)

λισσός, ή, όν, poet. form of λεῖος, *smooth*, always λισσή πέτρη, *Od. 3, 293. 5. 412. cf. λίς.

λιστρεύω (λίστρον), *to level, to dig, to dig about*. φυτόν, Od. 24, 227.†

λίστρον, τό, *a spade, a mattock*, for digging the earth; *a shovel* for cleaning the ground, Od. 22, 455.† (From λισσός.)

λῖτα, see λίς.

Λιταί, αἱ (cf. λιτή), *Prayers* personified as mythic beings, daughters of Zeus, and sisters of Atê. They are penitent and timorous deprecations after the commission of a fault; hence the poet describes them as lame, wrinkled, squint-eyed maidens, since it is unwillingly that a man forces his spirit to deprecation after the commission of a crime, 9, 502 sqq [they are also *wrinkled* from anxiety, and dare not *look one* in the face, Db.]

λιτανεύω (λιτή), fut. εύσω, 1) *to beseech, to entreat*, esply as a suppliant for protection, Od. 7, 145; γούνων, to entreat by one's knees, Od. 10, 481. cf. Il. 24, 357; with infin. following, 23, 196. 2) With accus. of the pers. *to beseech or supplicate* any one, 9, 581. 22, 414. (The λ is doubled with an augm. ἐλλιτάνευε.)

λιτή, ἡ, *the act of supplication, entreaty, prayer*, Od. 11, 34.†   Plur. αἱ Λιταί. q. v.

λιτί, see λίς.

*λίτομαι, a rare pres. for λίσσομαι, q. v.

λό' for λόε, see λοέω.

λοβός, ὁ (prob. from λέπω), the lower part of the ear, *the lobe of the ear*, 14, 182.† h. 5, 8.

λόγος, ὁ (λέγω), *a saying, a word*; plur. *words, discourse*, only twice, 15, 393. Od 1, 57; but also in the Hymn. and Batr.

*λόγχη, ἡ, *a lance. a spear*, Batr. 129.

λόε, Ep. for ἔλοε, see λούω.

λοέσσαι, λοεσσάμενος, see λούω.

λοετρόν, τό, ancient Ep. for λουτρόν (λοέω), *a bath, the act of bathing*, always plur.; mly θερμὰ λοετρά, warm bath, 14, 6; but λοετρὰ Ὠκεανοῖο, 18, 489. Od. 5, 275. The contr. form stands only in h. Cer. 50.

λοετροχόος, ον, old Ep. for λουτροχόος (χέω), prob. *pouring out water for bathing, bath-filling*; τρίπους, a bathing-kettle, i. e. a three-footed kettle, in which water for bathing was warmed, 18, 346. Od. 8, 435; subst. ἡ λοετροχόος, the maid who prepares a bath, Od. 20, 297.

λοέω, Ep. form of λούω, from which λοέσσαι, λοέσσασθαι, etc., see λούω.

λοιβή, ἡ (λείβω), *dropping, pouring out*; only in a religious sense, *that which is poured out. a libation*, mly with wine; connected with κνίσσα. 9, 500. Od. 9, 349.

λοίγιος, ον. poet. (λοιγός), *bad, sad, ruinous, mischievous*; ἔργα, pernicious things, 1, 518; οἴω λοίγι' ἔσεσθαι, I think it will be ruinous, *21, 533.

λοιγός, ὁ (akin to λυγρός), *destruction, mischief, ruin, death*, *1, 67. 5, 603. 9, 495; spoken of the destruction of the ships, *16, 80.

λοιμός, ὁ (akin to λύμη), *pestilence, a pestilential and deadly sickness, contagion*, *1, 61. 97.

λοισθήϊος, ον. Ep. for λοίσθιος (λοῖσθος), *relating to the last*, λοισθήϊον ἄεθλον, a prize for the last, 23, 785; also subst. τὰ λοισθήϊα. *23, 751.

λοῖσθος, ον (λοιπός), *the last, the extreme*, 23, 536.†

Δοκροί, οἱ. *the Locrians*, inhabitants of the district of Locris in Hellas, who were divided into two races: the *Epicnemidian* or *Opuntian* at Mount Cnemis, and the *Ozolæ*, on the Corinthian gulf. The first only are mentioned by H., 2, 527.

*λοξοβάτης, ον, ὁ, *going obliquely*,

N

slant-gaited, an epith. of the crab, Batr. 297.

λοπός, ὁ (λέπω), a shell, a rind, a skin; κρομύοιο, an onion-skin, Od. 19, 233.†

*λουέω, Ep. form of λούω, from which ἐλούεον, h. Cer. 290.

*λουτρόν, τό, contr. for λοετρόν.

λούω, Ep. resolved λοέω, λονέω, imperf. ἐλούεον, aor. 1 ἔλουσα, Ep. λοῦσα, infin. λοέσσαι, partcp. λούσας, Ep. λοέσσας, fut. mid. λοέσσομαι, aor. 1 ἐλουσάμην, Ep. λουσάμην, with this the infin. λοέσσασθαι, partcp. λοεσσάμενος, perf. pass. λέλουμαι, 5, 6. In the pres. and imperf. are found the common and shortened forms λούεσθαι and λοῦσθαι, Od. 6, 216; imperf. ἐλόεον, Od. 4, 252; also an old aor. 2 ἔλοον, from the root ΔΟΩ, from which λόε, Od. 10, 361; λόον, h. Ap. 120; to wash, to bathe, always spoken of human beings, τινὰ ποταμοῖο ῥοῇσιν, Il. 16, 669; of horses only, 23, 282. Mid. to wash or bathe oneself, very often ἐν ποταμῷ, Od. 6, 210; and ποταμοῖο, in the river, Il. 6, 508. 15, 265; spoken of Sirius: λελουμένος Ὠκεανοῖο, having bathed in Oceanus, i. e. when he rises, 5, 6.

λοφάδια, see καταλοφάδια.

λοφιή, ἡ (λόφος), the neck, with long, stiff hair, spoken of the boar: the bristles, Od. 19, 446.†

λόφος, ὁ (λέπω), 1) the neck, prim. of draught-animals, which was rubbed by the yoke in drawing, 23, 508; then, of men, 10, 573. 2) a crest, mly made of the mane of horses, which was placed in a conical elevation (φάλος) upon the helmet, 6, 469; having coloured hair, v. 537. Od. 22, 124. 3) a hill, an elevation, Od. 11, 596. 16, 471. h. Ap. 520. In this signif. it is not found in the Il.

λοχάω (λόχος), aor. infin. λοχῆσαι, fut. mid. λοχήσομαι, partcp. aor. 1 λοχησάμενος, 1) to lay an ambuscade, 18, 520. Od. 4, 487. b) With accus. to waylay any one, to lie in ambush for any one. Od. 14, 181. 15, 28. Mid. as depon. to place oneself in ambush, Od. 4, 388. 463. 13, 268; with accus. τινά, to waylay any one, only Od. 4, 670.

*λοχεύω (λόχος), fut. σω, to bring into the world, to bear, spoken of the mother, h. Merc. 230.

λόχμη, ἡ (λόχος), a lair, a thicket, Od. 19, 439.†

λόχονδε, adv. (λόχος), to an ambuscade, 1, 227. Od. 14, 217.

λόχος, ὁ (from λέγω or ΛΕΧΩ), 1) concealment, ambush, prim. spoken of place, 1, 227. 11, 379; of the Trojan horse: κοῖλος or πυκινὸς λόχος, Od. 4, 227. 8, 515. 11, 525. 2) ambuscade, as an action, the act of waylaying, 18, 513. 24, 779. Od. 4, 441; λόχος γέροντος, the way to seize the old man, Od. 4, 395. 3) ambuscade, spoken of the force composing it, Il. 4, 392. 6, 189. λόχον ἀνδρῶν ἐσίζεσθαι, to place oneself in the ambush of men, 13, 285. 8, 522; hence,

generally, 4) a troop, a company of warriors, Od. 20, 49.

*λύγξ, ὁ, gen. λυγκός, a lynx, h. 18, 24.

λύγος, ὁ, Abraham's balm, vitex agnus castus, Linn., a kind of shrub, like willow; and generally, a willow, a rod, an osier twig, Od. 9, 427. 10, 167; δίδη μόσχοισι λύγοισι, he bound them with tender willows: thus Heyne, Il. 11, 105; for Apoll. explains μόσχοι by ἀπαλαῖς καὶ νεαῖς. Others consider λύγοισι as an adj., and μόσχοισι as subst., as Köppen and Voss: with willow rods, cf. μόσχος. [Db. with flexible rods, sc. osiers.]

λυγρός, ή, όν (λύζω), that which causes sighs; sad, gloomy, lamentable, miserable, wretched. 1) Spoken prim. of human conditions: ὄλεθρος, γῆρας, δαίς, ἄλγος; τὰ λυγρά, sad things, 24, 531. Od. 14, 226; εἵματα, miserable garments, Od. 16, 457; apparently active, pernicious, destructive, φάρμακα, γαστήρ, Od. 4, 230. 17, 473. 2) Of men: sad, miserable, i. e. weak, cowardly, Il. 13, 119. Od. 18, 107; but = bad, destructive, Od. 9, 454. Adv. λυγρῶς, miserably, wretchedly, πλήσσειν, Il. 5, 763.† Cf. λευγαλέος.

λύθεν, Ep. for ἐλύθησαν, see λύω.

λύθρον, τό or λύθρος, ὁ (λύμα), prop a stain of blood; in H. the blood which flows from wounds, the life-blood as shed; according to the Gramm. blood mixed with dust, 11, 169; always dat. αἵματι καὶ λύθρῳ πεπαλαγμένος, defiled with blood and the dust of battle [or, battle-stains], 6, 268. Od. 22, 402. 23, 48.

λυκάβας, αντος, ὁ, the year, *Od. 14, 161. 19, 306 (probably from λύκη and βαίνω), the course of light, the progress of the sun; Eustath. strangely derives it from λύκος and βαίνω, because the days follow one another like wolves, which in passing over a river are said to seize one another by the tail.) [According to Ameis, walker-in-light, the composit. requiring an act. signif.]

Λύκαστος, ἡ, a town in the southern part of Crete, 2, 647.

Λυκάων, ονος, ὁ, 1) ruler of Lycia, father of Pandarus, Il. 2, 826. 4, 88. 2) son of Priam and Laothoë, Il. 3, 333. Achilles took him prisoner, and sold him to Lemnos; he escaped, and was finally slain by Achilles, 21, 35, seq.

λυκέη, ἡ, sc. δορά, prop. adj. from λύκος, a wolf-skin, 10, 459.†

Λυκηγενής, οὖς, ὁ (Λυκία, γένος), one born in Lycia (V. Lycian). Apollo was a national deity of the Lycians, 4, 101. 119. Another deriv. is from λύκη, light, the father of the light, in allusion to the rising sun. This contravenes the usu. loq. because γενής in compos. is always passive. [According to K. O. Müller, Λυκηγενής = light-born, not one born in Lycia, cf. h. Apoll. 440, seq. Light played a great part both symbolically in the cultus of Apollo, and in the poetic imagery connected with him.]

Λυκίη, ἡ. Lycia, 1) a district in Asia Minor, between Caria and Pamphylia, named by the Gramm. Great Lycia, 2, 877. 2) a district in the north of Asia Minor, at the foot of Ida. from the river Æsëpus to the city Zeleia. This the Gramm. call Lesser Lycia, 5, 173. Also adv. 1) Λυκίηθεν, from Lycia. 2) Λυκίηνδε, to Lycia.

Λύκιοι, οἱ, the Lycians, 1) the inhabitants of the district of Great Lycia, who were governed by Sarpêdon, 2, 876. 6, 194. 2) the inhabitants of the district of Little Lycia, led by Pandarus, 15, 486.

Λυκομήδης, ους, ὁ, son of Creon, a Bœotian, one of the seven heroes, who commanded the watch at the trench, 9, 84. 12, 366. 17, 345, 346.

Λυκόοργος, ὁ, Ep. for Λυκοῦργος, 1) son of Dryas, king of the Edônes in Thrace, the insulter of Dionÿsos. He persecuted the god, so that he fled to Thetis in the sea. The gods for a punishment made him blind, and he lived but a short time. 6, 130, seq. 2) son of Aleus, king of Arcadia, grandfather of Agapênor; he slew Areïthous, and presented his club to Ereuthalion, 7, 142, seq. (According to Damm, from λύκος and ὀργή, wolf-spirited; more correctly from ἔργω, wolf-slaying, cf. Hdt. 7, 76.)

λύκος, ὁ, a wolf. often used as a figure of ferocity and greediness, 4, 471. 16, 156. Od.

Λυκοφόντης, ου, ὁ, 1) a Trojan, slain by Teucer, 8, 275. 2) Another reading for Πολυφόντης, q. v.

Λυκόφρων, ονος, ὁ, son of Mastor, from Cythêra, a companion of the Telamonian Ajax, 15, 430, seq.

Λύκτος, ἡ, an ancient town in Crete, east of Cnossus. a colony of Lacedæmonians, 2, 647. 17, 611; in Polyb. Λύττος, (according to Herm Crepusca.)

Λύκων. ωνος, ὁ, a Trojan slain by Peneleus, 16, 335, seq.

λῦμα, ατος, τό (λύω, λούω), uncleanness, dirt, filth, defilement, 14, 171; the dirty water which is poured away after a purification, *1, 314.

λυπρός, ή, όν (λυπηρός), sad, wretched, miserable, epith. of Ithaca, Od. 13, 243.†

ʼλύρη, ἡ, a lyre; a seven-stringed instrument. said to have been invented by Hermês, h. Merc. 423. It had, like the cithara, two sides, which however were less curved. Its sounding-board was shaped like the turtle-shell, for which reason it did not stand upright, but was held between the knees. Its tone was stronger and sharper than that of the cithara, see Forkel's Gesch. der Mus. I. p. 250.

Λυρνησός, ἡ (Λυρνησσός), a town in Mysia (Troas), in the kingdom of Thebes, the residence of king Mynes, 2, 690. 19, 60. 20, 92.

Λύσανδρος, ὁ, Lysander, a Trojan wounded by Ajax, 11, 491.

λυσιμελής, ές (μέλος), relaxing the limbs, limb-relaxing, ὕπνος, *Od. 20, 57. 23, 343.

λῦσις, ιος, ἡ (λύω), the act of loosing, resolving; hence, setting free, liberating, θανάτου, from death, Od. 9, 421; esply ransoming from slavery, Il. 24, 655.

λύσσα, ἡ, frenzy, madness, always spoken of warlike rage, *9, 239. 21, 542.

λυσσητήρ, ῆρος, ὁ, one furious or frenzied, a raver, κύων, 8, 299.†

λυσσώδης, ες (εἶδος), like one raving or mad, spoken of Hector, 18, 53.†

λύχνος, ὁ (ΔΥΚΗ), a light, a lamp, Od. 19, 34,† and Batr.

λύω, fut. λύσω, aor. 1 ἔλῦσα, fut. mid. λύσομαι, aor. 1 ἐλῦσάμην, perf. pass. λέλῦμαι, 3 sing. optat. λελῦτο for λελῦῖτο, Od. 18, 238; aor. pass. ἐλύθην, and Ep. pass. aor. without a connective vowel ἐλύμην, from this: λύτο and λῦτο. 1) Act. to loose, i. e. 1) to unbind or loosen any thing from an object, with accus. θώρηκα, ζωστῆρα, ζωνήν, Od. 11, 245. cf. ζώνη, frequently, ἱστία, πρυμνήσια, Od. (not in the Il.) ἀσκόν, Od. 10, 47. b) Spoken of horses: to unyoke, to unharness, ἵππους ἐξ or ὑπὲξ ὀχέων, ὑπὸ ζυγοῦ, ὑφ' ἅρμασιν, Il. 5, 369. 8, 504. 543. 18, 244. c) to release, to free from fetters, 15, 22; metaph. τινὰ κακότητος, to release any man from misery, Od. 5, 397; esply to liberate, to release any one from imprisonment, τινὰ ἀποίνων, for a ransom, Il. 11, 106; without ἀποίνων, 1, 20. 29. 2) to dissolve, to dismiss, to loose, ἀγορήν, Il. 1, 305. Od. 2, 257; pass. λύτο δ' ἀγών, Il. 24, 1: νείκεα, to dismiss contest, 14, 205. Od. 7, 74; metaph. λύειν γυῖα, γούνατα, to loose the limbs, i. e. to relax them, to deprive them of power, Il. 4, 469. 5, 176. 16, 425, seq.; frequently = to kill, also λύειν μένος, Od. 3, 450; but spoken also of one fatigued, sleeping, terrified, pass., Il. 7, 16. 8, 123; λύθεν δέ οἱ ἄψεα πάντα (of sleep), Od. 4, 794; λύτο γούνατα καὶ ἦτορ, knees and heart trembled, Od. 4, 703; again: λύθη ψυχή, μένος, Il. 5, 296. 8. 315, hence generally: to dissolve, to destroy, to ruin; λέλυνται σπάρτα, the ropes are ruined, 2, 135; λύειν κάρηνα, κρήδεμνα πόλιος, to destroy the citadels, the battlements, 2, 118. 16, 100. Od. 13, 388. Il) Mid. 1) to unloose for oneself, ἱμάντα, Il. 14, 214; ἵππους, to unyoke his horses: 23, 7. 11; τεύχεα ἀπ' ὤμων, to take off the arms for themselves, viz. from the dead, 17, 318. 2) to ransom any one for oneself, θυγατέρα, 1, 13. 10, 378. Od. 10, 284. (ῠ is short, long only before σ, twice ῠ in the pres. and imperf. Od. 7, 74. Il. 23, 513.)

λωβάομαι, depon. mid. (λώβη), aor. 1 ἐλωβησάμην, to treat with insult or contempt, to dishonour; to insult, 1, 232. 2,

242; with accus. τινὰ λώβην, to offer an insult to any man, 13, 623.

λωβεύω (λώβη) = λωβάομαι, to insult, to deride, to revile, τινά, *Od. 23, 15. 26,.

λώβη, ἡ. insulting treatment, in word and deed, abuse, insult, injury, indignity. λώβην τῖσαι, to expiate the injury, 11, 142; and ἀποδοῦναι, 9, 387; in connexion with αἶσχος, mockery and insult, 13, 622. Od. 18, 225; an occasion of insult, Il. 3, 42. 7, 97.

λωβητήρ, ῆρος, ὁ (λωβάομαι), 1) a reviler, 2, 275. 2) a vile man, a villain, *24, 239.

λωβητός, ή, όν (λωβάομαι), shamefully treated, insulted. λωβητόν τινα τιθέναι, to overwhelm one with insult, 24, 531.†

λωΐτερος, η, ον, see λωΐον.

λωΐων, ον, gen. ονος (λάω), irreg. compar. of ἀγαθός, more desirable, more agreeable, better. only in the neut. 1, 229. 6, 339; from which a new compar. λωΐτερος, η, ον, with ἄμεινον, Od. 1, 376. :, 141.

λώπη, ἡ, poet. (λέπω), a covering, a woollen garment, a robe, Od. 13, 224.†

λωτεῦντα, see λωτόεις.

λωτόεις, εσσα, εν, poet. (λωτός), overgrown with lotus, πεδία λωτεῦντα, contr. for λωτοῦντα from λωτόεντα, plains full of lotus-trefoil, 12, 283.† Aristarch. here wrote λωτοῦντα; others consider it as a partcp. of a verb not elsewhere found, λωτέω = λωτίζω.

λωτός, ὁ. 1) the lotus, lotus-trefoil, a species of trefoil used as food for horses, growing in the moist low-lands of Greece and Troy; according to Voss, ad Virg. Georg. 2, 84, trifolium melilotus, Linn., Il. 2, 776. 14, 384. Od. 4, 603. 2) the lotus-tree, later also called the Cyrenian lotus, a kind of tree with a sweet fruit, on the African coast, upon which some of the inhabitants chiefly lived. According to H. Od. 9, 84, it was the food of the Lotophagi. This species of tree is described by Hdt. 2, 96; he compares its fruit in size with the berry of the mastich-tree, and in taste with the date. According to Sprengel. Antiq. Botan. p. 51, it is the rhamnus lotus, Linn., or Zizyphus lotus. It is now known in Tunis and Tripoli under the name jujuba. From the words ἄνθινον εἶδαρ, Od. 9, 84, it has been incorrectly concluded that H. intended a plant; cf. Miguel, Hom. Flor. p. 18.

Λωτοφάγοι, οἱ, the Lotophagi, i. e. the lotus eaters (see λωτός), a peaceable, hospitable people, to whom Odysseus (Ulysses) came from Cythêra, after a ten days' voyage, Od. 9, 84. Without doubt, they must be sought on the Libyan coast, according to Völcker's Hom. Geogr. p. 100, at the Syrtis Minor. According to Hdt. 4, 177, they were upon a cape not far from the Gindânĕs [an African tribe]; according to most of the old commentators, on the island Meninx, now Zerbi.

λωφάω (λόφος), fut. ήσω, prop. spoken of draught-cattle, which being unyoked, and having the neck at liberty, rest; generally, to rest, to recruit, 21, 292; κακῶν, to recruit oneself from miseries, Od. 9, 460; see καταλωφάω.

M.

M, the twelfth letter of the Greek alphabet; in H. the sign of the twelfth rhapsody.

μ', 1) With apostroph. for με. 2) Rarely and only Ep. for μοι, as 9, 673; cf. Thiersch. Gram. § 164. 2. Rem. 2.

μά, a particle of asseveration, connected with the accus. of the deity or thing by which one swore. It stands 1) Prim. in negative clauses: οὐ μὰ γὰρ Ἀπόλλωνα, no, by Apollo, 1, 86. 23, 43. Od. 20, 339. 2) Connected with ναί, it stands affirmatively: ναὶ μὰ τόδε σκῆπτρον, verily, by this sceptre, Il. 1, 234.

*μάγειρος, ὁ (μάσσω), a cook, Batr. 40.

Μάγνητες, οἱ, sing. Μάγνης, ητος. ὁ. the Magnêtes, inhabitants of a district of Thessaly, Magnesia, a Pelasgian race, deriving its origin from Magnes, son of Æolus, 2, 756.

*μάζα, ἡ (μάσσω), kneaded dough and barley-bread prepared from it, κυρβαίη μάζα, Ep. 15, 6.

μαζός, ὁ. a breast. a pap. distinct from στέρνον and στῆθος, 4, 528. 2) Chiefly of a woman, the (maternal-) breast, Il. 22, 80. 83. 24, 58. Od. 11, 448.

ΜΑΘΩ, obsol. root of μανθάνω.

μαῖα, ἡ, mother, a friendly mode of addressing aged women, *Od. 2, 349. 19, 16 (later, a wet-nurse), h. Cer. 147.

Μαῖα. ἡ. poet. also Μαιάς. άδος, ἡ, Od. 14, 435; Maja, Maia, daughter of Atlas and Pleïonê, mother of Hermês by Zeus. h. Merc. 3.

Μαίανδρος. ὁ. Meander, a river in Ionia and Phrygia, famed for its manifold sinuosities, which flows into the Icarian sea near the city Miletus, now Meinder, 2, 869.

Μαιάς, άδος, ἡ = Μαῖα, q. v.

Μαιμαλίδης, ου, ὁ, son of Mæmalus = Pisandrus, 16, 194.

μαιμάω (μαίω), poet. aor. 1 Ep. μαίμησα, often in the Ep. form μαιμώωσι, μαιμώωσα for μαιμῶσι, μαιμῶσα, to desire earnestly, to rush impetuously, to rage, 15, 742; αἰχμὴ μαιμώωσα, the rushing spear: the impetuous spear, 5, 661. 15, 542. περὶ δούρατι χεῖρες μαιμώσιν, 13, 78. cf. v. 75; metaph. μαίμησε οἱ ἦτορ, violently was his heart agitated, 5, 670.

μαιμώω, μαιμώωσα, see μαιμάω.

μαινάς, άδος, ἡ (μαίνομαι), a frenzied, raging female, 22, 460.† h. Cer. 386.

μαίνομαι, depon. pass. (ΜΑΩ), only pres. and imperf. 1) *to become frenzied, to rave, to be furious, to rage. a)* Mly spoken of the gods and men, with reference to an attack in battle, 5, 185. 6, 101. Od. 11. 537; also of anger, Il. 8, 360; of Dionysus *to be under the influence of divine enthusiasm, of prophetic frenzy,* 6, 132; of the drunken, Od. 18, 406. 22, 298. *b)* Of inanimate things; of hands and of the spear, Il. 16, 75. 245. 8, 111; of fire, 15, 606.

μαίομαι, dep. mid. (ΜΑΩ), *to touch [to will; to strice,* Död.], esply *to seek, to explore,* Od. 14, 356. h. Cer. 44; with acc. κευθμῶνας (*to explore* its secret nooks), Od. 13, 367; only pres. and imperf. (ἐπὶ χερσὶ μάσασθαι, Od. 11, 591, belongs to ἐπιμαίομαι.) *Od. [But cf. Död. p. 88.]

Μαῖρα, ἡ (the sparkling) 1) daughter of Nereus and Doris, 18, 48. 2) daughter of Proetus and Anteia (Antea), a companion of Artemis; at a later period, when she became the mother of Locrus by Zeus, she was slain by the goddess, Od. 11, 326.

Μαίων, ονος, ὁ, son of Hæmon, a Theban, leader of the ambuscade with Polyphontes, 4, 394, seq.

*μάκαιρα, h. Ap. 14; see μάκαρ.

μάκαρ, αρος, ὁ, ἡ, pecul. poet. fem. μάκαιρα, superl. μακάρτατος, η, ον, 1) *happy, blessed,* prim. spoken of the gods. θεοὶ μάκαρες, 1, 339; but οἱ μάκαρες, the happy dead, *the blest,* Od. 10, 299. 2) Spoken of men: *happy,* i. e. *rich, opulent,* Il. 3, 182. 11, 68. Od. 1, 217. 6, 158. σεῖο δ᾽, Ἀχιλλεῦ, οὔτις ἀνὴρ μακάρτατος, in comparison with thee was no one the most happy, or, no one was so entirely happy as thou, Od. 11, 483, where the compar. would naturally be expected; see Thiersch, Gram. § 282, 5.

Μάκαρ, αρος, ὁ, son of Æolus, king of Lesbos, 24, 544. h. Ap. 37.

μακαρίζω (μάκαρ), *to esteem happy,* τινά, any one, *Od. 15, 538. 17, 165.

μακεδνός, ή, όν, poet. μακεδανός, *tall, slender,* epith. of the poplar, Od. 7, 106.†

μάκελλα, ἡ (κέλλω), *a broad mattock, a shovel, a spade,* 21, 259.†

μακρός, ή, όν (μάκος=μῆκος), compar. μακρότερος, η, ον, poet. μάσσων, ον, Od. 8, 203; superl. μακρότατος, η, ον, Ep. μήκιστος; *long.* 1) Spoken of space: *long,* i. e. far-reaching, δόρυ, ἔγχος, but also of perpendicular distance: *high,* Ὄλυμπος, οὔρεα, ἐρινεός; μακρὰ φρείατα, deep wells, 21, 197; again: *far,* μακρὰ βιβάς, βιβῶν, far-striding, 3, 22. 7, 213; spoken of the voice: μακρὸν ἀϋτεῖν, to cry afar, i. e. aloud, 3, 81. 5, 101. 2) Spoken of time: *long-lasting,* = *long,* ἤματα, νύξ, Od.: ἐέλδωρ, a long-cherished wish, Od. 23, 54.

μάκων, see μηκάομαι.

μάλα, adv., compar. μᾶλλον, superl. μάλιστα, *A)* μάλα, *very, exceedingly, entirely. a)* Strengthening a single word (adv., adj., and verb): μάλα πάντες, all (without exception): μάλα πάγχυ, altogether; εὖ μάλα, very well; μάλ᾽ αἰεί, for ever and ever; with compar. μάλα πρότερος, much before or earlier, 10, 124. (*b*) With ἀλλά, having a compar. force=*sed potius,* but rather, Od. 6, 44.) *c)* Establishing and affirming an entire clause: *gladly, certainly, by all means,* μάλ᾽ ἕψομαι, gladly will I follow, Il. 10, 108. cf. Od. 4, 733. Often ἦ μάλα, yes, certainly, and ἦ μάλα δή. ἀλλὰ μάλα, but rather, Od. 4, 472; εἰ μάλα, εἰ καὶ μάλα, although greatly; though never so much, &c.; mly with optar., and μάλα πέρ, καὶ μάλα πέρ, with partcp. in the same signif. *B)* Compar. μᾶλλον, *more, more strongly, more vehemently.* It is often strengthened by πολύ, ἔτι, καί, also καὶ μᾶλλον, and rather, much more, Il. 8, 470. 13, 638. Od. 18, 154. *b) rather,* Il. 5, 231. Od. 1, 351. *c)* Also with compar. μᾶλλον ῥηίτεροι, still [much] more easy, Il. 24, 243. *d)* On the omission of μᾶλλον with βούλομαι, see this word. *C)* Superl. μάλιστα, *most, most strongly, for the most part, chiefly, especially, exceedingly,* with the positive as a periphrastic superl. 14, 460; it also stands for the purpose of strengthening it with a superl. ἔχθιστος μάλιστα, 2, 220. 24, 334.

μαλακός, ή, όν (μαλός), compar. μαλακώτερος, *soft, mild, gentle, tender.* 1) Spoken of corporeal things: εὐνή, κῶας. μαλακὴ νειός, a mellow fallow-field, 18, 541; λειμών, Od. 5, 72. 2) Metaph. *soft, mild, gentle,* θάνατος, ὕπνος, Il. 10, 2. Od. 18, 202; ἔπεα, 6, 337; of the slain Hector Achilles says: ἦ μάλα δὴ μαλακώτερος ἀμφαφάασθαι Ἕκτωρ, assuredly, Hector is now much more easy to be handled (is 'far more patient to the touch,' *Cp.*], Il. 22, 373. Adv. μαλακῶς, gently, softly, Od. 3, 350. 24, 255.

*μαλάχη, ἡ (μαλάσσω), *mallows,* Batr. 161.

Μάλεια, ἡ, Ep. for Μαλία, Od. 9, 80; and Μαλειάων ὄρος, Od. 3, 287; Μαλειῶν, Od. 14, 137; *Malea,* a promontory in the south-eastern part of Laconia, dangerous to navigators, now *Cap Malio di St. Angelo,* Od. and h. Ap. 409.

μαλερός, ή, όν (μάλα), *fierce, violent, strong,* epith. of fire, *9, 242. 20, 316. 21, 375.

μαλθακός, ή, όν (poet. for μαλακός), *soft, tender,* ἄνθος, h. 30, 15; metaph. *cowardly,* αἰχμητής, 17, 588.†

μάλιστα, μᾶλλον, superl. and compar. of μάλα.

μάν, Dor. and old Ep. for μήν, as a particle of asseveration: *truly, certainly, by all means, verily.* 1) Standing alone, 8, 373; ἄγρει μάν, up! on! 2) Strengthened: ἦ μάν, yea, verily; *assuredly,* 2, 370. 3) With negat. οὐ μάν, surely not, certainly not, 12, 318; μὴ μάν, 8, 512. Od. 11, 344; see μήν.

μανθάνω (ΜΑΘΩ), aor. 2 ἔμαθον, Ep. μάθον and ἔμμαθον, only in the aor. *to*

N 3

learn, to have learnt, i. e. to understand, κακὰ ἔργα, Od. 17, 226; 18, 362; and with infin. Il. 6, 444.

*μαντείη, ἡ (μαντεύομαι), prophecy, the act of prophesying, h. Merc. 533; plur. 472.

μαντεῖον, τό, Ion. and Ep. μαντήϊον, prophesying, a response, an oracle, Od. 12, 272.†

μαντεύομαι, depon. mid. (μάντις), to communicate an oracle, to prophesy, 2, 300; with accus. κακά, 1, 107; τινί τι, 16, 859; without accus. 19, 420; and generally, to predict, Od. 2, 170.

Μαντινέη, ἡ, Ep. and Ion. for Μαντίνεια, Mantinēa, a town in Arcadia on the river Ophis, north of Tegea, 2, 607.

Μάντιος, ὁ, son of Melampus and brother of Antiphātes, Od. 15, 242, seq.

μάντις, ιος, ὁ (from μαίνομαι), prop. one entranced, one inspired by a deity, who unveils the future; a seer, a prophet, who penetrates the future, both with and without external omens. This name also often comprehends those who divine by birds, dreams, and sacrifices, 1, 62. Od. 1, 201.

μαντοσύνη, ἡ, the art of prophecy, the art of divination, Il. and Od.; also plur. Il. 2, 832.

(μάομαι), see μαίομαι.

Μαραθών, ῶνος, ὁ and ἡ, a village and borough in Attica, on the eastern coast, later famed for the overthrow of the Persians, named from the fennel (μάραθον) growing there, Od. 7, 80.

μαραίνω, aor. 1 ἐμάρᾱνα, h. Merc. 140; aor. pass. ἐμαράνθην, 1) Act. to extinguish, ἀνθρακίην, h. Merc. 140. 2) Pass. to be extinguished, to burn out, to cease to burn, *9, 212. 23, 228.

μαργαίνω (μάργος), to rave, to be frantic, to be boisterous, ἐπί τινα, 5, 882.†

μάργος, η, ον, raving, raging, boisterous, Od. 16, 421; γαστήρ, Od. 18, 2; foolish, irrational, *Od. 23, 11.

Μάρις, ιος, ὁ, son of Amisodarus, a Lycian, wounded by Antilochus, 16, 319. 327.

μαρμαίρω (μαίρω), to glimmer, to twinkle, to shine, to sparkle, for the most part spoken of the splendour of metals, 12, 195. ὄμματα μαρμαίροντα, the sparkling eyes (of Aphroditê), *3, 397.

μαρμάρεος, έη, εον (μαρμαίρω), gleaming, shining, beaming, spoken of metals esply, αἰγίς, ἄντυξ, 17, 594. 18, 480. ἅλς, μαρ., the sparkling sea (in a calm), 14, 273.

μάρμαρος, ὁ (μαρμαίρω), in H. stone, a block of stone, with the notion of shining, 12, 380. Od. 9, 499; an adj., πέτρος, μάρμαρος, the gleaming stone, Il. 16, 735.

μαρμαρυγή, ἡ (μαρμαρύσσω), splendour, radiancy, twinkling, metaph. the quivering, rapid movements of the feet, spoken of dancers, Od. 8, 265.† h. Ap. 203.

μάρναμαι, depon. mid. Ion. and poet. infin. μάρνασθαι. only pres. and imperf. like ἴσταμαι, pres. optat. μαρνοίμην, Od. 11, 513 (prob. from μάρη), to fight, to do battle, to contend, a) Mly spoken of war: τινί, dat. of pers. with a man, mly, against a man, Il. 9, 327. Od. 22, 228; rarely ἐπί τινι, Il. 9, 317. 17, 148; and dat. instrum. χαλκῷ, ἔγχει; περί τινος, about or over a man, 16, 497; but περὶ ἔριδος, to contend from discord, 7, 301. b) to contend, to dispute, with words, 1, 257.

Μάρπησσα, ἡ, daughter of Evēnus, wife of Idas. She was carried away by Apollo, but Idas received her again, 9, 557; see Idas, Ἴδης, and Evenus. (From μάρπτω, one seized.)

μάρπτω, poet. fut. μάρψω, aor. 1 ἔμαρψα, 1) to lay hold of, to seize or grasp, to hold, with accus. Od. 9, 289; ἀγκάς τινα, to embrace any one with the arms, Il. 14, 346; χείρας σκαιῇ, 21, 489. 2) to touch, to overtake, τινὰ ποσί, 21, 564; χθόνα ποδοῖιν, to touch the earth with the feet, 14, 228; spoken of the lightning of Zeus: μάρπτειν ἕλκεα, to inflict (Cp. impress) wounds [= corripiendo infligere: of lightning], 8, 405. 519; metaph. ὕπνος ἔμαρπτε αὐτόν, sleep overtook him, 23, 62. Od. 20, 56; γῆρας, Od. 24, 390.

μαρτυρίη, ἡ (μάρτυρ), witness, testimony, Od. 11, 325.†

μάρτυρος, ὁ, Ep. for μάρτυς, a witness, in the sing. only Od. 16, 423; often in the plur. μάρτυροι ἔστων (plur. with dual), Il. 1, 338.

*μάρτυς, υρος, ὁ, a witness, h. Merc. 372.

Μάρων, ωνος, ὁ, son of Euanthês, priest of Apollo at Ismarus in Thrace, who presented Odysseus (Ulysses) with wine, Od. 9, 197, seq.

Μάσης, ητος, ἡ, a town in Argolis, later the port of Hermiōnē, 2, 562.

μάσσων, ὁ, ἡ, neut. μᾶσσον or μάσσον, irreg. compar. of μακρός, longer, greater, Od. 8, 203.

μάσταξ, ακος, ἡ (μαστάζω [which Död. connects with ἀμάω]), 1) that with which one chews, the mouth [i e. the interior mouth with its organs of mastication, Död.], Od. 4, 287. 23, 76. 2) food, esply that which a bird brings in its beak for its young ones. νεοσσοῖσι προφέρει μάστακ' for μάστακα (τροφήν. Schol.), Il. 9, 324. Al. μάστακι, in the beak.

μαστίζω (μάστιξ). aor. Ep. μάστιξα. to wield the whip, to whip, to lash, ἵππους, 5, 768; often with infin. μάστιξεν δ' ἐλάαν, he whipt, in order to drive, 5, 366. Od. 3, 484. (Another form is μαστίω.)

μάστιξ, ιγος, ἡ (μάσσω). Ep. also μάστις, from this dat. μάστι for μάστις, 23, 500; accus. μάστιν, Od. 15, 182; a whip, a scourge, for driving horses, 5, 226. 748. 2) Metaph. strife, punishment, Διός, 12, 37. 13, 812.

μαστις, ἡ, Ion. and Ep. for μάστιξ, q. v.

μαστίω, poet. for μαστίζω, to lash, 17, 622. Mid. spoken of lions: οὐρῇ πλευρὰς μαστίεται, he lashes his sides with his tail, *20, 171.

Μαστορίδης, ου, ὁ, son of Mastor = Halitherses, Od. 2, 158; = Lycophron, Il. 15, 430. 438.

Μάστωρ, ορος. ὁ, 1) father of Lycophron from Cythêra, Il. 2) father of Halitherses, Od.

*μασχάλη, ἡ, the shoulder, and the armpit, h. Merc. 242.

ματάω (μάτην), aor. 1 ἐμάτησα, to be inactive, to delay, to loiter, 16, 474. 23, 510; spoken of horses: μὴ—ματήσετον for ματήσητον, *5, 233.

ματεύω (ΜΑΩ), poet. = μαστεύω, to seek, to look up, 14, 110.†

*μάτην, adv. in vain, to no purpose, h. Cer. 309.

ματίη, ἡ (μάτην), a vain undertaking, a fruitless attempt, levity, folly, Od. 10, 79.†

μάχαιρα, ἡ (akin to μάχη), a large knife, a dagger, a sabre, which hung beside the sword, and which was used particularly in slaughtering victims, a sacrificial knife, 3, 271. 18, 597; Machaon also used it for cutting out an arrow, *11, 844.

Μαχάων, ονος, ὁ, voc. Μαχάον, son of Asklepios (Æsculapius), ruler of Tricca and Itbômê in Thessaly, distinguished for his medical skill, 2, 732. Cheiron had given his father healing remedies, 4, 219.

μαχειόμενος, Ep. see μάχομαι.

μαχεσύμενος, see μάχομαι.

μάχη, ἡ, [referred by Död. to ἀμάν, mactare, &c.], a battle, a combat, a contest, a fight, mly a battle between heroes. μάχεσθαι μάχην, to fight a battle, 15, 673. 18, 533; also of a duel, 7, 263. 11, 542. 2) contest, quarrel, dispute, with words, 1, 177. H. mentions four contests in particular: the first between the Simoïs and Scamandrus, 4, 446. 7, 305; the second between the city of Troy and the Grecian ships, 8, 53—488; the third on the Scamandrus, from 11—18, 242; the fourth embraces the deeds of Achilles, and ends with Hector's death, 20—22. Il. and Od.

μαχήμων, ον (μαχέομαι), eager for battle, warlike, κραδίη, 12, 247.†

μαχητής, οῦ, ὁ (μαχέομαι), a warrior, combatant, Il.; with ἀνήρ, Od. 18, 261.

μαχητός, ή. όν (μάχομαι), to be attacked, to be combated, that may be vanquished, κακόν, Od. 12, 119.†

μαχλοσύνη, ἡ (μάχλος), incontinence, luxury, voluptuousness, sensuality, 24, 30, spoken of Paris. Aristarchus wished to strike out the word, because it is elsewhere used only of women; but without reason; on the contrary, it suits Paris very well, cf. 3, 39.

μάχομαι, Ion. and Ep. (μαχέομαι,) do-

pon. mid. fut. μαχέσομαι and μαχήσομαι (the Att. fut. μαχοῦμαι is not Homeric), aor. ἐμαχεσάμην, ἐμαχησάμην, pres. μαχέομαι, 2, 366; μαχεῖται, 20, 26. μαχέοιτο, μαχέοιντο, 2, 72. 344; in pres. partcp. for metre's sake, μαχειόμενος and μαχεουμενος. The fut. and aor. Wolf always writes with η; only in the infin. aor. 1, for metrical reasons, stands μαχέσασθαι, 3, 20. 433. 7, 40; and optat. μαχέσαιο, 6, 329. According to Buttm. Gram. p. 291, in the aor. ἐμαχεσσάμην, not ἐμαχησάμην, agrees with the MSS., a reading which Spitzner follows. 1) to contend, to fight, to war, to battle, a) Esply in a contest both between whole armies and between single warriors, 3, 91. 435. 19, 153; mly τινί, with or against any man, ἐπί τινι, 5, 124. 244; ἀντία τινός, 20, 80. 88; ἐναντίον τινός, 3, 433; πρός τινα, 17, 471; but σύν τινι, with any man, i. e. with any man's aid, Od. 13, 391. Of the thing for which a man fights we have mly περί τινος, also περί τινι, Il. 16, 568. Od. 2, 245; ἀμφί τινι, Il. 8, 70. 16, 565; and εἵνεκά τινος, 2, 377; sometimes a dat. instrum. is added: τόξοις, ἀξίνῃσι. 2) Generally, to contend, to fight, without reference to war: ἀνδράσι περὶ δαιτί, about a repast, Od. 2, 245: spoken of a contest with beasts, Il. 16, 429. 758. b) Spoken of a prize-combat: πύξ, to contend with the fist, 23, 621. c) Spoken of contest of words, with ἐπέεσι, 1, 304. 5, 875; and without ἐπ. 1, 8.

μάψ, adv. poet. = μάτην, 1) in vain, fruitlessly, to no purpose, 2, 120. μὰψ ὀμόσαι, 15, 40. 2) without reason, foolishly, inconsiderately, often μάψ, ἀτὰρ οὐ κατὰ κόσμον, foolishly and indecently, 2, 214. Od. 3, 138. (Prob. from μάρπω, μάπω.)

μαψιδίως, adv. poet.=μάψ, 5, 374. Od. 3, 72. 7, 310.

*μαψιλόγος, ον, poet. (λέγω), speaking in vain or without sense, h. Merc. 546.

ΜΑΩ, an obsolete root, of which some forms remain. Perf. μέμαα, with pres. signif. Sing. obsol. for which μέμονα, ας, ε (cf. γέγονα with γέγαα) is used, dual μέματον, plur. 1 μέμαμεν, 3 plur. μεμάασι. Imperat. μεμάτω, partcp. μεμαώς, gen. μεμαῶτος and μεμαότος, 3 plur. pluperf. μέμασαν, to strive for, 1) to rush eagerly to any thing, to dash impetuously on, 8, 413; πρόσσω, 11, 615; ἐγχείῃσι, 2, 818; ἐπί τινι, 8, 327. 20, 326. Often the partcp. μεμαώς, as an adj. or connected with another verb: in haste, impetuously, zealously, earnestly. 2) to desire ardently, to long for. a) Mly with the infin. pres., 1, 590. 2, 543. b) With gen. of thing: ἔριδος, αὐτῆς, 5, 732. 13, 197. 20, 256; μέμονα, mly with infin., 5, 482. 7, 36. 3) It also gives tenses to μαίομαι, q. v.

Μεγάδης, ου, ὁ, son of Megas=Perimus, 16, 695.

μεγάθυμος, ον, poet. (θυμός), high-

N 4

souled, noble-hearted; esp'ly brave, courageous, epith. of brave men and nations, 2, 541; of a bull, 16, 488; of Athênê, Od. 8, 520. 13, 121.

μεγαίρω (μέγας), aor. 1 ἐμέγηρα, prop. to regard any thing as too great, with the notion of vexation, envy; hence, 1) to envy, to grudge, to deny any thing to any man. as too great for him, τινί τι, 23, 865. Od. 3, 55. Δαναοῖσι μεγήρας (sc. βίον), 15, 473; and with infin. μηδὲ μεγήρῃς ἡμῖν τελευτῆσαι τάδε ἔργα, deem it not too great for us to accomplish this work, Voss, Od. 3, 55; with accus. and infin. Od. 2, 235; and generally, to refuse, to deny. κατακαιέμεν (to refuse permission to burn the dead), Il. 7, 408. οὔτι μεγαίρω, I hinder it not, Od. 8, 207. Il. 8, 54. Also with gen. τί τινος, any thing from any man; spoken of Poseidôn: αἰχμὴν βιότοιο μεγήρας, diverting the spear from the life (viz. of Antilochus: refusing it the life = refusing to permit it to take the life) of Antilochus: according to Buttm, Lex. p. 409, Il. 13, 563 (refusing the life, V.)

μεγακήτης, ες (κῆτος), prob. that which has a great hollow or belly, and generally, vast, very great, prodigious, νηῦς, 8, 222; πόντος, Od. 3, 158; δελφίν, Od. 21, 22.

μεγαλήτωρ, ορος, ὁ, ἡ (ἦτορ), great-hearted, high-minded, magnanimous, courageous, epith. of heroes and of whole nations, 13, 302. Od. 19, 176; spirited, proud, θυμός, Il. 9, 109. Od. 5, 298.

μεγαλίζομαι, mid. (μέγας), to make oneself great, to elevate oneself, to be proud, θυμῷ, 10, 69. Od. 23, 174.

*μεγαλοσθενής, ές (σθένος), very strong, Ep. 6.

μεγάλως, adv. (μέγας), greatly, very. μάλα μεγάλως, very greatly, 17, 723. Od. 16, 432.

μεγαλωστί, adv. (μέγας), in a great space, always μέγας μεγαλωστί, great and long, 16, 776. Od. 24, 40.

Μεγαμηδείδης. ου, ὁ, son of Megamêdês. So is the father of Pallas called, h. Merc. 100.

Μεγαπένθης, εος, ὁ (sorrowful), son of Menelaus by a female slave; he was married to the daughter of Elector, Od. 4. 10. 15, 100. He received his name from his father's feelings on account of the rape of Helen.

Μεγάρη, ἡ, Megara, daughter of King Creon, in Thebes, wife of Heracles, Od. 11, 268. 269.

μέγαρον, τό (μέγας), a large room, a hall, hence esp'ly, 1) the assembling-room of the men, the men's hall. It was the main room, situated in the middle of the house, and in which the meals were taken. The roof was supported by pi 'ars, and it was lighted by a front and side door, Od. 1, 270. 22, 127. cf. Od. 1, 127—130. 133. 2) Generally, any large room, as that of the mistress, of the maids. Il. 3, 125. Od. 18, 98. 19, 60. 3)

in plur. a house, a dwelling, a palace, 1, 396. 5, 805. Od. 2, 400.

μεγαρόνδε, adv. to the house, to the dwelling, *Od. 16, 413. 21, 58.

μέγας, μεγάλη, μέγα, compar. μείζων, ον, superl. μέγιστος, η. ον, 1) great, spoken of extension in various ways: high, long, wide, broad, of animate and inanimate things, thus Ὄλυμπος, οὐρανός, αἰγιαλός. πέλαγος, etc. 2) great, i. e. strong, powerful, mighty, spoken of the gods; also, ἄνεμος, κράτος, κλέος. μέγα ἔργον, a great, i. e. a difficult work, Od. 3, 261. 3) too great, immoderate. λίην μέγα εἰπεῖν, to say something too great, Od. 3, 227. The neut. sing. and plur. μέγα and μεγάλα as adv. greatly, very, strongly, powerfully; μέγα with verbs and adj. μέγα ἔξοχος, very conspicuous; also with compar. and superl. μέγ' ἀμείνων, far better, Il. 2, 239. 23, 315; and μέγ' ἄριστος, by far the best, 2, 82. 763; plur. μεγάλα with κτυπεῖν, εὔχεσθαι, etc.

Μέγας, ὁ, a noble Lycian, 16, 695.

μέγεθος, εος, τό (μέγας), size, height, always spoken of the size of the body, mly with εἶδος and κάλλος, 2, 58. Od. 6, 152. 18, 219.

Μέγης, ητος, ὁ, son of Phyleus, sister's son of Odysseus (Ulysses), commander of the Dulichians and of the inhabitants of the Echinädes, 2, 625. 13, 692. 15, 302.

μέγιστος, η. ον, see μέγας.

μεδέων, οντος, ὁ, fem. μεδέουσα, ἡ, poet. for μέδων, a ruler, a sovereign, masc. spoken of Zeus: Ἰδῆθεν, Δωδώνης. *16, 234. Fem. a female ruler, Σαλαμῖνος, h. 9, 4.

Μεδεών, ῶνος, ὁ, a city in Bœotia, near mount Phœnicius, 2, 501.

μέδομαι, depon. (prop. mid. of μέδω), fut. μεδήσομαι, 9, 650.† 1) to take care of, to have charge of, to think of, to consider about, with gen. πολέμοιο, κοίτου, 2, 384. Od. 2. 358; δόρποιο, Il. 18, 245; νόστοιο, 9, 622. Od. 11, 110; often ἀλκῆς, to think of defence, Il. 2) to prepare any thing for any man, to invent, to plot, κακά τινι, 4, 21. 8, 458.

μέδων, οντος, ὁ, prop. partcp. pres. from μέδω, as subst. one who cares for, ruler, sovereign, sing. only ἁλὸς μέδων. Od. 1, 72; elsewhere always ἡγήτορες ἠδὲ μέδοντες,

Μέδων, οντος, ὁ, 1) son of Oïleus and Rhênê (2, 727), step-brother of Ajax: he dwelt in Phylacê, whither he had fled, because he had slain his step-mother's brother. He was the leader of the warriors from Methônê when Philoctêtês remained behind in Lemnos. Æneas slew him, 2, 727. 13, 693, seq. 15. 332. 2) a Lycian, 17, 216. 3) a herald of Ithaca in the train of the suitors; he disclosed to Penelope the danger of her son Telemachus, and was on that account afterwards saved by him. Od. 4, 677. 22, 357.

μεθαιρέω (αἱρέω), aor. μεθεῖλον, Ep.
iterat. form μεθέλεσκον, to take, to catch,
spoken of a ball: ὁ δ' ἀπὸ χθονὸς ὑψόσ'
ἀερθείς, ῥηιδίως μεθέλεσκε, subaud. σφαῖραν, the other, springing high from the
earth, caught it with ease, Od. 8, 374.†
(Damm [e contrario capio] and Voss.)

μεθάλλομαι (ἅλλομαι), only partcp aor.
sync. μετάλμενος, to leap over, to spring
upon or to, absol. 5, 336. 11, 538; to leap
after, *23, 345.

μεθείω, Ep. for μεθῶ, see μεθίημι.

μεθέλεσκε, see μεθαιρέω.

μεθέμεν, Ep. for μεθεῖναι, see μεθίημι.

μεθέπω (ἔπω), partcp. aor. 2 act. μετασπών and mid. μετασπόμενος, I) Act.
intrans. to be behind, to go after, hence
1) to pursue, to follow, τινὰ ποσσί, 17,
190. Od. 14, 33. b) to seek, to seek
for, with accus. Il. 8, 126; spoken of
regions: to visit, absol. to arrive, Od. 1,
175. 2) Trans. with double accus. to
cause to go after, to drive after; ἵππους
Τυδείδην, to drive the horses after Tydides [κατόπιν ἤλαυνε, Schol.], Il. 5,
329. II) Mid. to follow, to pursue; τινά,
only, 13, 567.

μέθημαι (ἧμαι), to sit in the midst;
with dat. μνηστῆρσι, in the midst of the
suitors, Od. 1, 118.†

μεθημοσύνη, ἡ (μεθήμων), negligence,
remissness, *13, 108. 121.

μεθήμων, ον (μεθίημι), negligent, remiss, lazy, supine, 2, 241. Od. 6, 25.

μεθίημι (ἵημι), infin. pres. Ep. μεθιέμεναι and μεθιέμεν, fut. μεθήσω, aor. 1
μεθῆκα, μεθέηκα. Of the aor. 2 subj.
μεθῶ, Ep. μεθείω: optat. μεθείην, infin.
μεθέμεν for μεθεῖναι. Of the pres. indic.
μεθείω, 2 and 3 sing. μεθιεῖς, μεθιεῖ: of
the imperf. 2, 3 sing. μεθίεις, μεθίει; but
3 plur. μεθίειν for μεθίεσαν, to neglect,
I) Trans. with accus. 1) to let loose, to
let go (any thing bound or detained);
τινά, to let a prisoner go, 10, 449. cf. 16,
762; spoken of missiles: ἰόν, 5, 48; τι
ἐς ποταμόν, to let any thing fall into the
river, Od. 5, 460; metaph. χόλον τινός,
to give up anger about any man, Il. 15,
138; Ἀχιλλῆι, to remit his wrath against
Achilles, 1, 283; κῆρ ἄχεος, to free the
heart from care, 17, 539. 2) to abandon,
τινά, 3, 414. Od. 15, 212. εἰ με μεθείη
ῥῖγος, Od. 5, 471. 3) to give, to permit,
to yield, νίκην τινί, Il. 14, 364; and
with infin. ἐρύσαι, to permit to draw, 17,
418. II) Intrans. 1) Absol. to be negligent, to relax, to become weary, to loiter,
to linger, often absol. 6, 523. 10, 121,
also Od. 4, 372; βίη, in strength, Il. 21,
177. 2) to neglect, to desist, to cease
from; with gen. πολέμοιο, from war, 4,
240. 13, 97; in like manner ἀλκῆς, μάχης, βίης. Od. 21, 126; χόλοιο Τηλεμάχῳ
(against Telem.), Od. 21, 377. b) With
infin. and partcp. rarely in H. μάχεσθαι,
to cease to fight, Il. 13, 234. 23, 434.
κλαύσας μεθέηκε, he ceased weeping, 24,
48. (On quantity, see ἵημι.)

μεθίστημι (ἵστημι), fut. μεταστήσω,

1) Act. transit. to transfer, to transpose,
to change, to exchange, τινί τι, Od. 4, 612.
2) Mid. intrans. to transfer oneself, i. e.
to go elsewhere, with dat. ἑτάροισι, 5,
514.

μεθομιλέω (ὁμιλέω), to have intercourse, to associate; τινί, with any man,
1, 269.†

μεθορμάω (ὁρμάω), only partcp. aor.
pass. μεθορμηθείς, to drive after. 2)
Pass. to follow, to pursue, Od. 5, 325. Il.
20, 192.

μέθυ, νος, τό, any strong, intoxicating
drink, esply wine, 7, 471. Od. 4, 796.

μεθύστερος, η, ον (ὕστερος), after,
later, the neut. as adv. h. Cer. 205.

μεθύω (μέθυ), only pres. and imperf
drink unmixed wine, Od. 18, 240
Metaph. to be thoroughly soaked or saturated (with). βοείη μεθύουσα ἀλοιφῇ,
an ox-hide soaked with fat [drunken
with slippery lard, Cp.], Il. 17, 390.

μειδάω, only in aor. 1 ἐμείδησα, Ep.
μείδασα; and μειδιάω, from which only
partcp. pres. μειδιόων, Ep. for μειδιῶν,
to smile; on the other hand, γελᾶν, to
laugh aloud, h. Cer. 204; βλοσυροῖσι
προσώπασι, 7, 212; Σαρδάνιον, Od. 20,
303; see this word.

μειδιάω, see μειδάω.

μείζων, ον, irreg. compar. of μέγας.

μείλας, Ep. μέλας, 24, 79; † only μείλανι πόντῳ, see ὁ Μέλας πόντος.

μείλια, τά (μέλι, μειλίσσω), any thing
gladdening, rejoicing, esply gratifying
presents, *9, 147. 289; spoken of the gifts
which a father gives to his daughter as a
portion; marriage presents; dower.

μείλιγμα, ατος, τό (μειλίσσω), any thing
which serves to soothe or please. μειλίγματα θυμοῦ, dainties, which the master
takes for his dogs, Od. 10, 216.†

μείλινος, η, ον, poet. for μέλινος, q. v.
*Il.

μειλίσσω, only pres. (akin to μέλι,
prop. to make sweet), hence 1) Act. to
please, to rejoice, esply to soothe, to calm;
νεκρὸν πυρός, to appease the dead by
fire (the funeral pile), 7, 408. The dead,
according to the views of the ancients,
were angry if their obsequies were not
soon performed. 2) Mid. to enjoy oneself,
to rejoice, h. Cer. 291. b) to be gentle, to
use gentle words, to address kindly, Od. 3,
96. 4, 326.

μειλιχίη, ἡ (μειλίχιος), gentleness, mildness; πολέμοιο, slackness in battle [i. e.
the dealing gentle blows; or making little
exertion], 15, 741.†

μειλίχιος, η, ον and μείλιχος, ον (μειλίσσω), prop. sweet; hence mild, gentle,
kind, affectionate. a) Spoken of persons
(of whom alone μείλιχος is used, except
Od. 15, 374), Il. 17, 671. 21, 300. b)
μειλίχιος μῦθος, 10, 288; and μύθοισιν,
ἐπέεσσι μειλιχίοις προσαυδᾶν, to address
any man with friendly words, 6, 343.
Od. 6, 143; and μειλιχίοις alone, Il.
4, 256; αἰδώς, Od. 8, 172.

μείρομαι, from which ἔμμορε as 3 sing.

N 5

souled, *noble-hearted*; esp.ly *brave, courageous*, epith. of brave men and nations, 2. 541; of a bull, 16, 488; of Athênê, Od. 8, 520. 13, 121.

μεγαίρω (μέγας), aor. 1 ἐμέγηρα, prop. to regard any thing as too great, with the notion of vexation, envy: hence, 1) *to envy, to grudge, to deny* any thing to any man. as too great for him, τινί τι, 23, 865. Od. 3, 55. Δαναοῖσι μεγῆρας (sc. βίόν), 15, 473; and with infin. μηδὲ μεγήρῃς ἡμῖν τελευτῆσαι τάδε ἔργα, deem it not too great for us to accomplish this work, Voss, Od. 3, 55; with accús. and infin. Od. 2, 235; and generally, *to refuse, to deny.* κατακαιέμεν (*to refuse permission to burn the dead*), Il. 7, 408. οὔτι μεγαίρω, I hinder it not, Od. 8, 207. Il. 8, 54. Also with gen. τί τινος, any thing from any man; spoken of Poseidôn: αἰχμὴν βιότοιο μεγῆρας, diverting the spear from the life (viz. of Antilochus: refusing it the life = refusing to permit it to take the life) of Antilochus: according to Buttm, Lex. p. 409, Il. 13, 563 (refusing the life, V.)

μεγακήτης, ες (κῆτος), prob. that which has a great hollow or belly, and generally, *vast, very great, prodigious*, νηῦς, 8, 222; πόντος, Od. 3, 158; δελφίν, Od. 21, 22.

μεγαλήτωρ, ορος, ὁ, ἡ (ἦτορ), *great-hearted, high-minded, magnanimous, courageous*, epith. of heroes and of whole nations, 13, 302. Od. 19, 176; *spirited, proud*, θυμός, Il. 9, 109. Od. 5, 298.

μεγαλίζομαι, mid. (μέγας), *to make oneself great, to elevate oneself, to be proud*, θυμῷ, 10, 69. Od. 23, 174.

*μεγαλοσθενής, ές (σθένος), *very strong*, Ep. 6.

μεγάλως, adv. (μέγας). *greatly, very*. μάλα μεγάλως, very greatly, 17, 723. Od. 16, 432.

μεγαλωστί, adv. (μέγας), *in a great space*, always μέγας μεγαλωστί, great and long, 16, 776. Od. 24, 40.

Μεγαμηδείδης, ου, ὁ, son of Megamêdês. So is the father of Pallas called, h. Merc. 100.

Μεγαπένθης, εος, ὁ (sorrowful), son of Menelaus by a female slave; he was married to the daughter of Elector, Od. 4, 10. 15, 100. He received his name from his father's feelings on account of the rape of Helen.

Μεγάρη, ἡ, Megara, daughter of King Creon, in Thebes, wife of Heracles, Od. 11, 268. 269.

μέγαρον, τό (μέγας), *a large room, a hall*, hence esp.ly, 1) the assembling-room of the men, *the men's hall*. It was the main room, situated in the middle of the house, and in which the meals were taken. The roof was supported by pi 'ars, and it was lighted by a front and side door, Od. 1, 270. 22, 127. cf. Od. 1, 127—130. 133. 2) Generally, *any large room*, as that of the mistress, of the maids. Il. 3, 125. Od. 18, 98. 19, 60. 3)

in plur. *a house, a dwelling*, a 396. 5, 805. Od. 2, 400.

μεγαρόνδε, adv. *to the hous dwelling*, *Od. 16, 413. 21, 58.

μέγας, μεγάλη, μέγα, compar. ον, superl. μέγιστος, η. ον, spoken of extension in various high, long, wide, broad, of ani inanimate things, thus Ὄλυμ νός, αἰγιαλός, πέλαγος, i. e. *strong, powerful, mighty*, the gods; also, ἄνεμος, κρατ μέγα ἔργον, a great, i. e. a diffic Od. 3, 261. 3) *too great, im λίην μέγα εἰπεῖν*, to say somet great, Od. 3, 227. The neut. si plur. μέγα and μεγάλα as adv. *very, strongly, powerfully*; μεγ verbs and adj. μέγα ἔξοχος, very spicuous; also with compar. and μέγ᾽ ἀμείνων, far better, Il. 2, 315; and μέγ᾽ ἄριστος, by far the 2, 82. 763; plur. μεγάλα with εὔχεσθαι, etc.

Μέγας, ὁ, a noble Lycian, 16, 695.

μέγεθος, εος, τό (μέγας), *size, he* always spoken of the size of the b mly with εἶδος and κάλλος, 2, 58. Od 152. 18, 219.

Μέγης, ητος, ὁ, son of Phyleus, si son of Odysseus (Ulysses), comm of the Dulichians and of the inhabit of the Echinádes, 2, 625. 13, 692. 302.

μέγιστος, η. ον, see μέγας.

μεδέων, οντος, ὁ, fem. μεδέουσα. poet. for μέδων, *a ruler, a sovere* masc. spoken of Zeus: Ἰδηθεν, Δωδών *16, 234. Fem. *a female ruler*, Σαλ ρος, h. 9, 4.

Μεδεών, ῶνος, ὁ, a city in Bœotia, ne mount Phœnicius, 2, 501.

μέδομαι, depon. (prop. mid. of μέδω fut. μεδήσομαι, 9, 650.† 1) *to take ca of, to have charge of, to think of, to con sider about*, with gen. πολέμοιο, κοίτοι 2, 384. Od. 2. 358; δόρποιο, Il. 18, 245 νόστοιο, 9, 622. Od. 11, 110; often ἀλκῆ to think of defence, Il. 2) *to prepar any thing for any man, to invent, to plot κακά τινι, 4, 21. 8, 458.

μέδων, οντος, ὁ, prop. partcp. pres from μέδω, as subst. *one who cares for, ruler, sovereign*, sing. only ἁλὸς μέδων, Od. 1, 72; elsewhere always ἡγήτορες ἠδὲ μέδοντες,

Μέδων, οντος, ὁ, 1) son of Oïleus and Rhênê (2, 727), step-brother of Ajax; he dwelt in Phylacê, whither he had fled, because he had slain his step-mother's brother. He was the leader of the warriors from Methônê when Philoctêtês remained behind in Lemnos. Æneas slew him, 2, 727. 13, 693, seq. 15. 332. 2) a Lycian, 17, 216. 3) a herald of Ithaca in the train of the suitors; he disclosed to Penelopa the danger of her son Telemachus, and was on that account afterwards saved by him, Od. 4, 677. 22, 357.

μεθαιρέω (αἱρέω), aor. μεθεῖλον, Ep. iterat. form μεθέλεσκον, to take, to catch, spoken of a ball: ὁ δ' ἀπὸ χθονὸς ὑψόσ' ἀερθείς, μεθέλεσκε subaud. σφαῖραν, the other, springing high from the earth, caught it with ease, Od. 8, 374.† (Damm [e contrario capio] and Voss.)

μεθάλλομαι (ἅλλομαι), only partcp aor. μεταλμένος, to leap over, to spring upon or to, absol. 5, 336. 11, 538; to leap after, *21, 345.

μεθέω, Ep. for μεθῶ, see μεθίημι.

μεθέλεσκε, see μεθαιρέω.

μεθέμεν, Ep. for μεθεῖναι, see μεθίημι.

μέθεπω (ἕπω), partcp. aor. 2 act. μετασπών and mid. μετασπόμενος, I) Act. intrans. to be behind, to go after, hence 1. to pursue, to follow, τινὰ ποσσί, 17, 190. Od. 14, 33. b) to seek, to seek for, with accus. Il. 3, 126; spoken of τόπους: to visit, absol. to arrive, Od. 1, 175. 2) Trans. with double accus. to cause to go after, to drive after; ἵππους Τυδείδην, to drive the horses after Tydides [ἐλαύνειν ἤλαυνε, Schol.], Il. 5, 329. li) Mid. to follow, to pursue; τινά, only, 13, 567.

μεθέρπω [impol.] to set in the midst; with μετὰ ἀριστερῶν, in the midst of the van, ... ii, 114.†

μεθημοσύνη, ἡ (μεθήμων), negligence, remissness, *13, 108. 121.

μεθήμων, ον (μεθίημι), negligent, remiss, lazy, supine, 2, 241. Od. 6, 25.

μεθίημι (ἵημι), infin. pres. Ep. μεθιέμεναι and μεθιεῖν, fut. μεθήσω, aor. 1 μεθῆκα, μεθέηκα. Of the aor. 2 subj. μεθῶ, Ep. μεθείω: optat. μεθείην, infin. μεθεῖναι for μεθεῖναι. Of the pres. indic. μεθίεις, 2 and 3 sing. μεθιεῖς, μεθιεῖ: of the imperf. 2, 3 sing. μεθίεις, μεθίει; but 3 plur. μεθίεν for μεθίεσαν, to neglect, I, Trans. with accus. 1) to let loose, to let go (any thing bound or detained); τινὰ, to let a prisoner go, 10, 449. cf. 16, 762; spoken of missiles: ἰόν, 5, 48; τι ἐς ποταμόν, to let any thing fall into the river, Od. 5, 460; metaph. χόλον τινός, to give up anger about any man, Il. 15, 138; Ἀχιλληι, to remit his wrath against Achilles, 1, 283; κῆρ ἄχεος, to free the heart from care, 17, 539. 2) to abandon, τινί, 3, 414. Od. 15, 212. εἴ με μεθείη μένος, Od. 5, 471. 3) to give, to permit, to yield, νίκην τινί, Il. 14, 364; and with infin. ἐρύσσαι, to permit to draw, 17, 36. II) Intrans. 1) Absol. to be negligent, to relax, to become weary, to loiter, to linger, often absol. 6, 523. 10, 121, also Od. 4, 372; βίῃ, in strength, Il. 21, 177. 2) to neglect, to desist, to cease from; with gen. πολέμοιο, from war, 4, 240. 13, 97; in like manner ἀλκῆς, μάχης, βίης. Od. 21, 126; χόλοιο Τηλεμάχῳ (against Telem.), Od. 21, 377. b) With infin. and partcp. rarely in H. μάχεσθαι, to cease to fight, Il. 13, 234. 23, 434. κλαίουσα μεθέηκε, he ceased weeping, 24, 48. (On quantity, see ἵημι.)

μεθίστημι (ἵστημι), fut. μεταστήσω,

1) Act. transit. to transfer, to transpose, to change, to exchange, τινί τι, Od. 4, 612. 2) Mid. intrans. to transfer oneself, i. e. to go elsewhere, with dat. ἑτάροισι, 5, 514.

μεθομιλέω (ὁμιλέω), to have intercourse, to associate; τινί, with any man, 1, 269.†

μεθορμάω (ὁρμάω), only partcp. aor. pass. μεθορμηθείς, to drive after. 2) Pass. to follow, to pursue, Od. 5, 325. Il. 20, 192.

μέθυ, υος, τό, any strong, intoxicating drink, esply wine, 7, 471. Od. 4, 796.

*μεθύστερος, η, ον (ὕστερος), after, later, the neut. as adv. h. Cer. 205.

μεθύω (μέθυ), only pres. and imperf. drink unmixed wine, Od. 18, 240. Metaph. to be thoroughly soaked or saturated (with). βοείη μεθύουσα ἀλοιφῇ, an ox-hide soaked with fat [drunken with slippery lard, Cp.], Il. 17, 390.

μειδάω, only in aor. 1 ἐμείδησα, Ep. μείδασα, and μειδιάω, from which only partcp. pres. μειδιόων, Ep. for μειδιῶν, to smile; on the other hand, γελᾶν, to laugh aloud, h. Cer. 204; βλοσυροῖσι προσώπασι, 7, 212; Σαρδάνιον, Od. 20, 803; see this word.

μειδιάω, see μειδάω.

μείζων, ον, irreg. compar. of μέγας.

μείλας, Ep. μέλας, 24, 79; † only μείλανι πόντῳ, see ὁ Μέλας πόντος.

μείλια, τά (μέλι, μειλίσσω), any thing gladdening, rejoicing, esply gratifying presents, *9, 147. 289; spoken of the gifts which a father gives to his daughter as a portion; marriage presents; dower.

μείλιγμα, ατος, τό (μειλίσσω), any thing which serves to soothe or please. μειλίγματα θυμοῦ, dainties, which the master takes for his dogs, Od. 10, 216.†

μείλινος, η, ον, poet. for μέλινος, q. v. *Il.

μειλίσσω, only pres. (akin to μέλι, prop. to make sweet), hence 1) Act. to please, to rejoice, esply to soothe, to calm; νεκρὸν πυρός, to appease the dead by fire (the funeral pile), 7, 408. The dead, according to the views of the ancients, were angry if their obsequies were not soon performed. 2) Mid. to enjoy oneself, to rejoice, h. Cer. 291. b) to be gentle, to use gentle words, to address kindly, Od. 3, 96. 4, 326.

μειλιχίη, ἡ (μειλίχιος), gentleness, mildness; πολέμοιο, slackness in battle [i. e. the dealing gentle blows; or making little exertion], 15, 741.†

μειλίχιος, η, ον and μείλιχος, ον (μειλίσσω), prop. sweet; hence mild, gentle, kind, affectionate. a) Spoken of persons (of whom alone μείλιχος is used, except Od. 15, 374), Il. 17, 671. 21, 300. b) μειλίχιος μῦθος, 10, 288; and μύθοισι, ἐπέεσσι μειλιχίοις προσαυδᾶν, to address any man with friendly words, 6, 343. Od. 6, 143; and μειλιχίοις alone, Il. 4, 256; αἰδώς, Od. 8, 172.

μείρομαι, from which ἔμμορε as 3 sing.

souled, noble-hearted; esply brave, courageous, epith. of brave men and nations, 2, 541; of a bull, 16, 488; of Athênê, Od. 8, 520. 13, 121.

μεγαίρω (μέγας), aor. 1 ἐμέγηρα, prop. to regard any thing as too great, with the notion of vexation, envy; hence, 1) to envy, to grudge, to deny any thing to any man. as too great for him, τινί τι, 23, 865. Od. 3, 55. Δαναοῖσι μεγήρας (sc. βίον), 15, 473; and with infin. μηδὲ μεγήρης ἡμῖν τελευτῆσαι τάδε ἔργα, deem it not too great for us to accomplish this work, Voss, Od. 3, 55; with accus. and infin. Od. 2, 235; and generally, to refuse, to deny. κατακαιέμεν (to refuse permission to burn the dead), Il. 7, 408. οὔτι μεγαίρω, I hinder it not, Od. 8, 207. Il. 8, 54. Also with gen. τί τινος, any thing from any man: spoken of Poseidôn: αἰχμὴν βιότοιο μεγήρας, diverting the spear from the life (viz. of Antilochus: refusing it the life = refusing to permit it to take the life) of Antilochus: according to Buttm , Lex. p. 409, Il. 13, 563 (refusing the life, V.)

μεγακήτης, ες (κῆτος), prob. that which has a great hollow or belly, and generally, vast, very great, prodigious, νηῦς, 8, 222; πόντος, Od. 3, 158; δελφίν, Od. 21, 22.

μεγαλήτωρ, ορος, ὁ, ἡ (ἦτορ), great-hearted, high-minded, magnanimous, courageous, epith. of heroes and of whole nations, 13, 302. Od. 19, 176; spirited, proud, θυμός, Il. 9, 109. Od. 5, 298.

μεγαλίζομαι, mid. (μέγας), to make oneself great, to elevate oneself, to be proud, θυμῷ, 10, 69. Od. 23, 174.

*μεγαλοσθενής, ές (σθένος), very strong, Ep. 6.

μεγάλως, adv. (μέγας). greatly, very. μάλα μεγάλως, very greatly, 17, 723. Od. 16, 432.

μεγαλωστί, adv. (μέγας), in a great space, always μέγας μεγαλωστί, great and long, 16, 776. Od. 24, 40.

Μεγαμηδείδης. ου, ὁ, son of Megamêdês. So is the father of Pallas called, h. Merc. 100.

Μεγαπένθης, εος. ὁ (sorrowful), son of Menelaus by a female slave; he was married to the daughter of Elector, Od. 4, 10. 15, 100. He received his name from his father's feelings on account of the rape of Helen.

Μεγάρη, ἡ, Megara, daughter of King Creon, in Thebes, wife of Heracles, Od. 11, 268. 269.

μέγαρον, τό (μέγας), a large room. a hall, hence esply, 1) the assembling-room of the men, the men's hall. It was the main room, situated in the middle of the house, and in which the meals were taken. The roof was supported by pi 'ars, and it was lighted by a front and side door, Od. 1, 270. 22, 127. cf. Od. 1, 127—130. 133. 2) Generally, any large room, as that of the mistress, of the maids. Il. 3, 125. Od. 18, 98. 19, 60. 3)

in plur. a house, a dwelling, a palace, 1, 396. 5, 805. Od. 2, 400.

μέγαρόνδε, adv. to the house, to the dwelling, *Od. 16, 413. 21, 58.

μέγας, μεγάλη, μέγα, compar. μείζων, ον, superl. μέγιστος, η. ον, 1) great, spoken of extension in various ways: high, long, wide, broad, of animate and inanimate things, thus Ὄλυμπος, οὐρανός, αἰγιαλός, πέλαγος, etc. 2) great, i. e. strong, powerful, mighty, spoken of the gods; also, ἄνεμος, κρατος, κλέος. μέγα ἔργον, a great, i. e. a difficult work. Od. 3, 261. 3) too great, immoderate. λίην μέγα εἰπεῖν, to say something too great, Od. 3, 227. The neut. sing. and plur. μέγα and μεγάλα as adv. greatly, very, strongly, powerfully; μέγα with verbs and adj. μέγα ἔξοχος, very conspicuous; also with compar. and superl. μέγ᾽ ἀμείνων, far better, Il. 2, 239. 23, 315; and μέγ᾽ ἄριστος, by far the best, 2, 82. 763; plur. μεγάλα with κτυπεῖν, εὔχεσθαι, etc.

Μέγας, ὁ, a noble Lycian, 16, 695.

μέγεθος, εος, τό (μέγας), size, height, always spoken of the size of the body, mly with εἶδος and κάλλος, 2, 58. Od. 6, 152. 18, 219.

Μέγης, ητος, ὁ, son of Phyleus, sister's son of Odysseus (Ulysses), commander of the Dulichians and of the inhabitants of the Echinâdes, 2, 625. 13, 692. 15, 302.

μέγιστος, η. ον, see μέγας.

μεδέων, οντος, ὁ, fem. μεδέουσα. ἡ, poet. for μέδων, a ruler, a sovereign, masc. spoken of Zeus: Ἰδηθεν, Δωδώνης, *16, 234. Fem. a female ruler, Σαλαμῖνος, h. 9, 4.

Μεδεών, ῶνος, ὁ, a city in Bœotia, near mount Phœnicius, 2, 501.

μέδομαι, depon. (prop. mid. of μέδω), fut. μεδήσομαι, 9, 650.† 1) to take care of, to have charge of, to think of, to consider about, with gen. πολέμοιο, κοίτου, 2, 384. Od. 2, 358; δόρποιο, Il. 18, 245; νόστοιο, 9, 622. Od. 11, 110; often ἀλκῆς. to think of defence, Il. 2) to prepare any thing for any man, to invent, to plot, κακά τινι, 4, 21. 8, 458.

μέδων, οντος, ὁ, prop. partcp. pres. from μέδω, as subst. one who cares for, ruler, sovereign, sing. only ἁλὸς μέδων. Od. 1, 72; elsewhere always ἡγήτορες ἠδὲ μέδοντες,

Μέδων, οντος, ὁ, 1) son of Oïleus and Rhênê (2, 727), step-brother of Ajax; he dwelt in Phylacê, whither he had fled, because he had slain his step-mother's brother. He was the leader of the warriors from Methônê when Philoctêtês remained behind in Lemnos. Æneas slew him, 2, 727. 13, 693, seq. 15, 332. 2) a Lycian, 17, 216. 3) a herald of Ithaca in the train of the suitors; he disclosed to Penelope the danger of her son Telemachus, and was on that account afterwards saved by him, Od. 4, 677. 22, 357.

μεθαιρέω (αἱρέω), aor. μεθεῖλον, Ep.
iterat. form μεθέλεσκον, to take, to catch,
spoken of a ball : ὁ δ' ἀπὸ χθονὸς ὑψόσ'
ἀερθείς, ῥηϊδίως μεθέλεσκε, subaud. σφαῖραν, the other, springing high from the
earth, caught it with ease, Od. 8, 374.†
(Damm [e contrario capio] and Voss.)

μεθάλλομαι (ἅλλομαι), only partcp aor.
sync. μετάλμενος, to leap over, to spring
upon or to, absol. 5, 336. 11, 538; to leap
after, *23, 345.

μεθείω, Ep. for μεθῶ, see μεθίημι.

μεθέλεσκε, see μεθαιρέω.

μεθέμεν, Ep. for μεθεῖναι, see μεθίημι.

μεθέπω (ἕπω), partcp. aor. 2 act. μετασπών and mid. μετασπόμενος, I) Act.
intrans. to be behind, to go after, hence
1) to pursue, to follow, τινὰ ποσσί, 17,
190. Od. 14, 33. b) to seek, to seek
for, with accus. Il. 8, 126; spoken of
regions : to visit, absol. to arrive, Od. 1,
175. 2) Trans. with double accus. to
cause to go after, to drive after ; ἵππους
Τυδείδην, to drive the horses after Tydides [κατόπιν ἤλαυνε, Schol.], Il. 5,
329. II) Mid. to follow, to pursue ; τινά,
only, 13, 567.

μέθημαι (ἧμαι), to sit in the midst;
with dat. μνηστῆρσι, in the midst of the
suitors, Od. 1, 118.†

μεθημοσύνη, ἡ (μεθήμων), negligence,
remissness, *13, 108. 121.

μεθήμων, ον (μεθίημι), negligent, remiss, lazy, supine, 2, 241. Od. 6, 25.

μεθίημι (ἵημι), infin. pres. Ep. μεθιέμεναι and μεθιέμεν, fut. μεθήσω, aor. 1
μεθῆκα, μεθέηκα. Of the aor. 2 subj.
μεθῶ, Ep. μεθείω : optat. μεθείην, infin.
μεθέμεν for μεθεῖναι. Of the pres. indic.
μεθίεις, 2 and 3 sing. μεθιεῖς, μεθιεῖ : of
the imperf. 2, 3 sing. μεθίεις, μεθίει ; but
3 plur. μεθίεν for μεθίεσαν, to neglect,
I) Trans. with accus. 1) to let loose, to
let go (any thing bound or detained) ;
τινά, to let a prisoner go, 10, 449. cf. 16,
762; spoken of missiles : ἰόν, 5, 48 ; τὶ
ἐς ποταμόν, to let any thing fall into the
river, Od. 5, 460; metaph. χόλον τινός,
to give up anger about any man, Il. 15,
138; Ἀχιλλῆϊ, to remit his wrath against
Achilles, 1, 283; κῆρ ἄχεος, to free the
heart from care, 17, 539. 2) to abandon,
τινά, 3, 414. Od. 15, 212. εἴ με μεθείη
ῥῖγος, Od. 5, 471. 3) to give, to permit,
to yield, νίκην τινί, Il. 14, 364; and
with infin. ἐρύσαι, to permit to draw, 17,
418. II) Intrans. 1) Absol. to be negligent, to relax, to become weary, to loiter,
to linger, often absol. 6, 523. 10, 121,
also Od. 4, 372; βίῃ, in strength, Il. 21,
177. 2) to neglect, to desist, to cease
from ; with gen. πολέμοιο, from war, 4,
240. 13, 97; in like manner ἀλκῆς, μάχης, βίης. Od. 21, 126; χόλοιο Τηλεμάχῳ
(against Telem.), Od. 21, 377. b) With
infin. and partcp. rarely in H. μάχεσθαι,
to cease to fight, Il. 13, 234. 23, 434.
κλαίουσα μεθέηκε, he ceased weeping, 24,
48. (On quantity, see ἵημι.)

μεθίστημι (ἵστημι), fut. μεταστήσω,

1) Act. transit. to transfer, to transpose,
to change, to exchange, τινί τι, Od. 4, 612.
2) Mid. intrans. to transfer oneself, i. e.
to go elsewhere, with dat. ἑτάροισι, 5,
514.

μεθομιλέω (ὁμιλέω), to have intercourse, to associate ; τινί, with any man,
1, 269.†

μεθορμάω (ὁρμάω), only partcp. aor.
pass. μεθορμηθείς, to drive after.) 2)
Pass. to follow, to pursue, Od. 5, 325. Il.
20, 192.

μέθυ, υος, τό, any strong, intoxicating
drink, esply wine, 7, 471. Od. 4, 796.

*μεθύστερος, η, ον (ὕστερος), after,
later, the neut. as adv. h. Cer. 205.

μεθύω (μέθυ), only pres. and imperf '
drink unmixed wine, Od. 18, 240,
Metaph. to be thoroughly soaked or saturated (with). βοείη μεθύουσα ἀλοιφῇ,
an ox-hide soaked with fat [drunken
with slippery lard, Cp.], Il. 17, 390.

μειδάω, only in aor. 1 ἐμείδησα, Ep.
μείδησα; and μειδιάω, from which only
partcp. pres. μειδιόων, Ep. for μειδιῶν,
to smile; on the other hand, γελᾶν, to
laugh aloud, h. Cer. 204 ; βλοσυροῖσι
προσώπασι, 7, 212; Σαρδάνιον, Od. 20,
303 ; see this word.

μειδιάω, see μειδάω.

μείζων, ον, irreg. compar. of μέγας.

μείλας, Ep. μέλας, 24, 79 ;† only μείλανι πόντῳ, see ὁ Μέλας πόντος.

μείλια, τά (μέλι, μειλίσσω), any thing
gladdening, rejoicing, esply gratifying
presents, *9, 147. 289; spoken of the gifts
which a father gives to his daughter as a
portion ; marriage presents ; dower.

μείλιγμα, ατος, τό (μειλίσσω), any thing
which serves to soothe or please. μειλίγματα θυμοῦ, dainties, which the master
takes for his dogs, Od. 10, 216.†

μείλινος, η, ον, poet. for μέλινος, q. v.
*II.

μειλίσσω, only pres. (akin to μέλι,
prop. to make sweet), hence 1) Act. to
please, to rejoice, esply to soothe, to calm ;
νεκρὸν πυρός. to appease the dead by
fire (the funeral pile), 7, 408. The dead,
according to the views of the ancients,
were angry if their obsequies were not
soon performed. 2) Mid. to enjoy oneself,
to rejoice, h. Cer. 291. b) to be gentle, to
use gentle words, to address kindly, Od. 3,
96. 4, 326.

μειλιχίη, ἡ (μειλίχιος), gentleness, mildness ; πολέμοιο, slackness in battle [i. e.
the dealing gentle blows ; or making little
exertion], 15, 741.†

μειλίχιος, η, ον and μείλιχος, ον (μειλίσσω), prop. sweet ; hence mild, gentle,
kind, affectionate. a) Spoken of persons
(of whom alone μείλιχος is used, except
Od. 15, 374), Il. 17, 671. 21, 300. b)
μειλίχιος μῦθος, 10, 288; and μύθοισι,
ἐπέεσσι μειλιχίοις προσαυδᾶν, to address
any man with friendly words, 6, 343.
Od. 6, 143; and μειλιχίοις alone, Il.
4, 256 ; αἰδώς, Od. 8, 172.

μείρομαι, from which ἔμμορε as 3 sing.

N 5

λίς, occurring only in the dat. sing. λιτί and accus. λῖτα, an old Ep. defect. =λίνον, *linen*; in the phrase ἑανῷ λιτί κάλυψαν, they covered him with costly linen, Voss, Il. 18, 352. 23, 254 (spoken of the linen with which the dead was shrouded): and accus. sing. ὑπὸ λῖτα πετάσσας καλόν, Od. 1, 130. cf. Od. 10, 353. Il. 8, 441; spoken of linen cloth spread upon seats and over a chariot. Thus Apoll., Heyne, Buttm., Gram. p. 91. Thiersch, Gram. § 197. 60. Wolf, on the contrary, in Anal. IV. p. 501, Passow, Rost, and Nitzsch ad Od. 1, 130, take λῖτα as accus. plur. from an old neut. λί, Ep. for λισσόν, λεῖον, smooth cloth without embroidered figures=λεῖα, Thuc. 2, 97. In favour of this are the epithets καλόν, δαιδαλέον, Od. 1, 130, which are generally used with θρόνος, but never with λῖτα, Il. 18, 390. Od. 10, 314. 366.

λίσσομαι, more rarely λίτομαι, poet. depon. mid. Ep. imperf. ἐλλισόμην, and iterat. λισσέσκετο, fut. λίσσομαι, aor. 1 ἐλισάμην, Ep. ἐλλισάμην, Od. imperat. λῖσαι, aor. 2 ἐλιτόμην, from the optat. λιτοίμην, Od. 14, 406: infin. λιτέσθαι, Il. 16, 47. 1) Absol. *to supplicate, to entreat*; ὑπέρ τινος, by any one, thus ὑπὲρ τοκέων, ὑπὲρ ψυχῆς καὶ γούνων, 15, 660. Od. 15, 261; and gen. alone, Od. 2, 68. 2) *to beg, to implore, to adjure.* a) With accus. of the person: τινά; the object of the entreaty stands a) In the infin. οὔ σε λίσσομαι μένειν, Il. 1, 174. 283. 4, 379; or in the accus. with the infin. 9, 511. Od. 8, 30; sometimes also ὅπως follows, Od. 3, 19. 327. β) In the accus. οἱ αὐτῷ θάνατον λιτέσθαι, to implore death for oneself, Il. 16, 47; and with double accus. ταῦτα οὐχ ὑμέας ἔτι λίσσομαι. these things I no longer entreat of you, Od. 2, 210. cf 4, 347. λίσσεσθαι τινα γούνων, Il. 9, 451, supplicating to embrace the knees, for the usual λαβὼν γούνων, 6, 45. (λίτομαι stands only h. 15, 5. 18, 48.)

λισσός, ή, όν, poet. form of λεῖος, *smooth*, always λισσὴ πέτρη, *Od. 3, 293. 5. 412. cf. λίς.

λιστρεύω (λίστρον), *to level, to dig, to dig about.* φυτόν, Od. 24, 227.†

λίστρον, τό, *a spade, a mattock, for digging* the earth; *a shovel for cleaning the ground,* Od. 22, 455.† (From λισσός.)

λῖτα, see λίς.

Λιταί, αἱ (cf. λιτή), *Prayers* personified as mythic beings, daughters of Zeus, and sisters of Atê. They are penitent and timorous deprecations after the commission of a fault; hence the poet describes them as lame, wrinkled, squinteyed maidens, since it is unwillingly that a man forces his spirit to deprecation after the commission of a crime, 9, 502 (they are also *wrinkled* from anxiety, and dare not *look one* in the face, Db.]

λιτανεύω (λιτή), fut. εύσω, 1) *to beseech, to entreat,* esply as a suppliant for

protection, Od. 7, 145; γούνων, to entreat by one's knees, Od. 10, 481. cf. Il. 24, 357; with infin. following, 23. 196. 2) With accus. of the pers. *to beseech* or, *supplicate* any one, 9, 581. 22, 414. (The λ is doubled with an augm. ἐλλιτάνευε.)

λιτή, ἡ, *the act of supplication, entreaty, prayer,* Od. 11, 34.† Plur. αἱ Λιταί. q. v.

λιτί, see λίς.

*λίτομαι, a rare pres. for λίσσομαι, q. v.

λῶ for λόε, see λοέω.

λοβός, ὁ (prob. from λέπω), the lower part of the ear, *the lobe of the ear,* 14, 182.† h. 5, 8.

λόγος, ὁ (λέγω), *a saying, a word*; plur. *words, discourse,* only twice, 15, 393. Od 1, 57; but also in the Hymn. and Batr.

*λόγχη, ἡ, *a lance, a spear,* Batr. 129.

λόε, Ep. for ἔλοε, see λούω.

λοέσσαι, λοεσσάμενος, see λούω.

λοετρόν, τό, ancient Ep. for λουτρόν (λοέω), *a bath, the act of bathing,* always plur.: mly θερμὰ λοετρά, warm bath, 14, 6; but λοετρὰ Ὠκεανοῖο, 18, 489. Od 5, 275. The contr. form stands only in h. Cer. 50.

λοετροχόος, ον, old Ep. for λουτροχόος (χέω), prob. *pouring out water for bathing, bath-filling*; τρίπους, a bathing-kettle, i. e. a three-footed kettle, in which water for bathing was warmed, 18, 346. Od. 8, 435; subst. ἡ λοετροχόος, the maid who prepares a bath, Od. 20, 297.

λοέω, Ep. form of λούω, from which λοέσσαι, λοέσσασθαι, etc., see λούω.

λοιβή, ἡ (λείβω), *dropping, pouring out*; only in a religious sense, *that which is poured out. a libation,* mly with wine: connected with κνίσσα, 9, 500. Od. 9, 349.

λοίγιος, ον. poet. (λοιγός), *bad, sad, ruinous, mischievous*; ἔργα, pernicious things, 1, 518; οἴω λοίγι᾽ ἔσεσθαι, I think it will be ruinous, *21, 533.

λοιγός, ὁ (akin to λυγρός), *destruction, mischief, ruin, death,* *1, 67. 5, 603. 9, 495; spoken of the destruction of the ships, *16, 80.

λοιμός, ὁ (akin to λύμη), *pestilence, a pestilential and deadly sickness, contagion,* *1, 61. 97.

λοισθήϊος, ον, Ep. for λοίσθιος (λοῖσθος), *relating to the last,* λοισθήϊον ἄεθλον, a prize for the last, 23, 785; also subst τὰ λοισθήϊα, *23, 751.

λοῖσθος, ον (λοιπός), *the last, the extreme,* 23, 536.†

Λοκροί, οἱ, *the Locrians,* inhabitants of the district of Locris in Hellas, who were divided into two races: the *Epicnemidian* or *Opuntian* at Mount Cnemis, and the *Ozolæ,* on the Corinthian gulf. The first only are mentioned by H., 2, 527.

*λοξοβάτης, ον, ὁ, *going obli*

the cultus of Apollo, and in the poetic imagery connected with him.]

Λυκίη,-η. Lycia, 1) a district in Asia Minor, between Caria and Pamphylia, named by the Gramm. Great Lycia, 2, 877. 2) a district in the north of Asia Minor, at the foot of Ida. from the river Æsëpus to the city Zeleia. This the Gramm. call Lesser Lycia, 5, 173. Also adv. 1) Λυκίηθεν, from Lycia. 2) Λυκίηνδε, to Lycia.

Λύκιοι, οἱ, the Lycians, 1) the inhabitants of the district of Great Lycia, who were governed by Sarpêdon, 2, 876. 6, 194. 2) the inhabitants of the district of Little Lycia, led by Pandarus, 15, 486.

Λυκομήδης, ους, ὁ, son of Creon, a Bœotian, one of the seven heroes, who commanded the watch at the trench, 9, 84. 12, 366. 17, 345, 346.

Λυκόοργος, ὁ, Ep. for Λυκούργος, 1) son of Dryas, king of the Edônes in Thrace, the insulter of Dionȳsos. He persecuted the god, so that he fled to Thetis in the sea. The gods for a punishment made him blind, and he lived but a short time, 6, 130, seq. 2) son of Aleus, king of Arcadia, grandfather of Agapênor; he slew Areïthous, and presented his club to Ereuthalion, 7, 142, seq. (According to Damm, from λύκος and ὀργή, wolf-spirited; more correctly from ἔργω, wolf-slaying, cf. Hdt. 7, 76.)

λύκος, ὁ, a wolf, often used as a figure of ferocity and greediness, 4, 471. 16, 156. Od.

Λυκοφόντης, ου, ὁ, 1) a Trojan, slain by Teucer, 8, 275. 2) Another reading for Πολυφόντης, q. v.

Λυκόφρων, ονος, ὁ, son of Mastor, from Cythéra, a companion of the Telamonian Ajax, 15, 430, seq.

Λύκτος, ἡ, an ancient town in Crete, east of Cnossus. a colony of Lacedæmonians, 2, 647. 17, 611; in Polyb. Λύττος, (according to Herm Crepusca.)

Λύκων, ωνος, ὁ, a Trojan slain by Peneleus, 16, 335. seq.

λῦμα, ατος, τό (λύω, λούω), uncleanness, dirt, filth, defilement, 14, 171; the dirty water which is poured away after a purification, *1, 314.

λυπρός, ή, όν (λυπηρός), sad, wretched, miserable, epith. of Ithaca, Od. 13, 243.†

*λύρη, ἡ. a lyre; a seven-stringed instrument. said to have been invented by Hermês, h. Merc. 423. It had, like the cithara, two sides, which however were less curved. Its sounding-board was shaped like the turtle-shell, for which reason it did not stand upright, but was held between the knees. Its tone was stronger and sharper than that of the cithara, see Forkel's Gesch. der Mus. I. p. 250.

Λυρνησσός, ἡ (Λυρνησσός), a town in Mysia (Troas), in the kingdom of Thebes, the residence of king Mynes, 2, 690. 19, 60. 20, 92.

Λύσανδρος, ὁ, Lysander, a Trojan wounded by Ajax, 11, 491.

λυσιμελής, ές (μέλος), relaxing the limbs, limb-relaxing, ὕπνος, *Od. 20, 57. 23, 343.

λύσις, ιος, ἡ (λύω), the act of loosing, resolving; hence, setting free, liberating, θανάτου, from death, Od. 9, 421; esply ransoming from slavery, Il. 24, 655.

λύσσα, ἡ, frenzy, madness, always spoken of warlike rage, *9, 239. 21, 542.

λυσσητήρ, ῆρος, ὁ, one furious or frenzied, a raver, κύων, 8, 299.†

λυσσώδης, ες (εἶδος), like one raving or mad, spoken of Hector, 13, 53.†

λύχνος, ὁ (ΛΥΚΗ), a light, a lamp, Od. 19, 34.† and Batr.

λύω, fut. λύσω, aor. 1 ἔλῦσα, fut. mid. λύσομαι, aor. 1 ἐλῦσάμην. perf. pass. λέλῦμαι, 3 sing. optat. λελῦτο for λελύοιτο, Od. 18, 238; aor. pass. ἐλύθην, and Ep. pass. aor. without a connective vowel ἐλύμην, from this: λύτο and λύντο. 1) Act. to loose, i. e. 1) to unbind or loosen any thing from an object, with accus. θώρηκα, ζωστῆρα, ζώνην, Od. 11, 245. cf. ζώνη, frequently, ἱστία, πρυμνήσια, Od. (not in the Il.) ἀσκόν, Od. 10, 47. b) Spoken of horses: to unyoke, to unharness, ἵππους ἐξ or ὑπὲξ ὀχέων, ὑπὸ ζυγοῦ, ὑφ' ἅρμασιν, Il. 5, 369. 8, 504. 543. 18, 244. c) to release, to free from fetters, 15, 22; metaph. τινὰ κακότητος, to release any man from misery, Od. 5, 397; esply to liberate, to release any one from imprisonment, τινὰ ἀποίνων, for a ransom, Il. 11, 106; without ἀποίνων, 1, 20. 29. 2) to dissolve, to dismiss, to loose, ἀγορήν, Il. 1, 305. Od. 2, 257; pass. λύτο δ' ἀγών, Il. 24, 1: νείκεα, to dismiss contest, 14, 205. Od. 7, 74; metaph. λύειν γυῖα, γούνατα, to loose the limbs, i. e. to relax them, to deprive them of power, Il. 4, 469. 5, 176. 16, 425, seq.: frequently = to kill, also λύειν μένος, Od. 3, 450; but spoken also of one fatigued, sleeping, terrified, pass., Il. 7, 16. 8, 123; λύθεν δέ οἱ ἅψεα πάντα (of sleep), Od. 4, 794; λύτο γούνατα καὶ ἦτορ, knees and heart trembled, Od. 4, 703; again: λύθη ψυχή, μένος, Il. 5, 296. 8. 315, hence generally: to dissolve, to destroy, to ruin; λέλυνται σπάρτα, the ropes are ruined, 2, 135: λύειν κάρηνα, κρήδεμνα πόλιος, to destroy the citadels. the battlements, 2, 118. 16, 100. Od. 13, 388. II) Mid. 1) to unloose for oneself, ἱμάντα, Il. 14, 214; ἵππους, to unyoke his horses: 23, 7. 11; τεύχεα ἀπ' ὤμων, to take off the arms for themselves, viz. from the dead, 17, 318. 2) to ransom any one for oneself, θυγατέρα, 1, 13. 10, 378. Od. 10, 284. (υ is short, long only before σ, twice ῡ in the pres. and imperf. Od. 7, 74. Il. 23, 513.)

λωβάομαι, depon. mid. (λώβη), aor. 1 ἐλωβησάμην, to treat with insult or contempt, to dishonour; to insult, 1, 232. 2,

μαίνομαι, depon. pass. (ΜΑΩ), only pres. and imperf. 1) to become frenzied, to rave, to be furious, to rage. a) Mly spoken of the gods and men, with reference to an attack in battle, 5, 185. 6, 101. Od. 11, 537; also of anger, Il. 8, 360; of Dionȳsus to be under the influence of divine enthusiasm, of prophetic frenzy, 6, 132; of the drunken, Od. 18, 406. 22, 298. b) Of inanimate things; of hands and of the spear, Il. 16, 75. 245. 8, 111; of fire, 15, 606.

μαίομαι, dep. mid. (ΜΑΩ), to touch [to will; to strice, Död.], esply to seek, to explore, Od. 14, 356. h. Cer. 44; with acc. κευθμῶνας (to explore its secret nooks), Od. 13, 367; only pres. and imperf. (ἐπὶ χερσὶ μάσασθαι. Od. 11, 591, belongs to ἐπιμαίομαι.) *Od. [But cf. Död. p. 88.]

Μαῖρα, ἡ (the sparkling) 1) daughter of Nereus and Doris, 18, 48. 2) daughter of Prœtus and Anteia (Antēa), a companion of Artĕmis; at a later period, when she became the mother of Locrus by Zeus, she was slain by the goddess, Od. 11, 326.

Μαίων, ονος, ὁ, son of Hæmon, a Theban, leader of the ambuscade with Polyphontes, 4, 394, seq.

*μάκαιρα, h. Ap. 14; see μάκαρ.

μάκαρ, αρος, ὁ, ἡ, pecul. poet. fem. μάκαιρα, superl. μακάρτατος, η, ον, 1) happy, blessed, prim. spoken of the gods. θεοὶ μάκαρες, 1, 339; but οἱ μάκαρες, the happy dead, the blest, Od. 10, 299. 2) Spoken of men: happy, i. e. rich, opulent, Il. 3, 182. 11, 68. Od. 1, 217. 6, 158. σεῖο δ', Ἀχιλλεῦ, οὔτις ἀνὴρ μακάρτατος, in comparison with thee was no one the most happy, or, no one was so entirely happy as thou, Od. 11, 483, where the compar. would naturally be expected; see Thiersch, Gram. § 282, 5.

Μάκαρ, αρος, ὁ, son of Æolus, king of Lesbos, 24, 544. h. Ap. 37.

μακαρίζω (μάκαρ), to esteem happy, τινά, any one, *Od. 15, 538. 17, 165.

μακεδνός, ή, όν, poet. μακεδανός, tall, slender, epith. of the poplar, Od. 7, 106.†

μάκελλα, ἡ (κέλλω), a broad mattock, a shovel, a spade, 21, 259.†

μακρός, ή, όν (μάκος=μῆκος), compar. μακρότερος, η, ον, poet. μάσσων, Od. 8, 203; superl. μακρότατος, η, ον, Ep. μήκιστος; long. 1) Spoken of space: long, i. e. far-reaching, δόρυ, ἔγχος, but also of perpendicular distance: high, Ὄλυμπος, οὔρεα, ἐρινεός; μακρὰ φρείατα, deep wells, 21, 197; again: far, μακρὰ βιβάς, βιβῶν, far-striding, 3, 22. 7, 213; spoken of the voice: μακρὸν ἀΰτειν, to cry afar, i. e. aloud, 3, 81. 5, 101. 2) Spoken of time: long-lasting, = long, ἤματα, νύξ, Od.: ἐέλδωρ, a long-cherished wish, Od. 23, 54.

μάκων, see μηκάομαι.

μάλα, adv., compar. μᾶλλον, superl. μάλιστα, A) μάλα, very, exceedingly, entirely. a) Strengthening a single word

(adv., adj., and verb): μάλα πάντες, all (without exception): μάλα πάγχυ, altogether; εὖ μάλα, very well; μάλ' αἰεί, for ever and ever; with compar. μάλα πρότερος, much before or earlier, 10, 124. (b) With ἀλλά, having a compar. force=sed potius, but rather, Od. 6, 44.) c) Establishing and affirming an entire clause: gladly, certainly, by all means, μάλ' ἕψομαι, gladly will I follow, Il. 10, 108. cf. Od. 4, 733. Often ἦ μάλα, yes, certainly, and ἦ μάλα δή. ἀλλὰ μάλα, but rather, Od. 4, 472; εἰ μάλα, εἰ καὶ μάλα, although greatly; though never so much, &c.; mly with optat., and μάλα πέρ, καὶ μάλα πέρ, with partcp. in the same signif. B) Compar. μᾶλλον, more, more strongly, more vehemently. It is often strengthened by πολύ, ἔτι, καί, also καὶ μᾶλλον, and rather, much more, Il. 8, 470. 13, 638. Od. 18, 154. b) rather, Il. 5, 231. Od. 1, 351. c) Also with compar. μᾶλλον ῥηΐτεροι, still [much] more easy, Il. 24, 243. d) On the omission of μᾶλλον with βούλομαι, see this word. C) Superl. μάλιστα, most, most strongly, for the most part, chiefly, especially, exceedingly, with the positive as a periphrastic superl. 14, 460; it also stands for the purpose of strengthening it with a superl. ἔχθιστος μάλιστα, 2, 220. 24, 334.

μαλακός, ή, όν (μαλός), compar. μαλακώτερος, soft, mild, gentle, tender. 1) Spoken of corporeal things: εὐνή, κῶας. μαλακὴ νειός, a mellow fallow-field, 18, 541; λειμών, Od. 5, 72. 2) Metaph. soft, mild, gentle, θάνατος, ὕπνος, Il. 10, 2. Od. 18, 202; ἔπεα, 6, 337; of the slain Hector Achilles says: ἦ μάλα δὴ μαλακώτερος ἀμφαφάασθαι Ἕκτωρ, assuredly, Hector is now much more easy to be handled (is 'far more patient to the touch,' Cp.], Il. 22, 373. Adv. μαλακῶς, gently, softly, Od. 3, 350. 24, 255.

*μαλάχη, ἡ (μαλάσσω), mallows, Batr. 161.

Μάλεια, ἡ, Ep. for Μαλέα, Od. 9, 80; and Μαλειάων ὄρος, Od. 3, 287; Μαλειῶν, Od. 14, 137; Malea, a promontory in the south-eastern part of Laconia, dangerous to navigators, now Cap Malio di St. Angelo, Od. and h. Ap. 409.

μαλερός, ή, όν (μάλα), fierce, violent, strong, epith. of fire, *9, 242. 20, 316. 21, 375.

μαλθακός, ή, όν (poet. for μαλακός), soft, tender, ἄνθος, h. 30, 15; metaph. cowardly, αἰχμητής, 17, 588.†

μάλιστα, μᾶλλον, superl. and compar. of μάλα.

μάν, Dor. and old Ep. for μήν, as a particle of asseveration: truly, certainly, by all means, verily. 1) Standing alone, 8, 373; ἄγρει μάν, up! on! 2) Strengthened: ἦ μάν, yea, verily; assuredly, 2, 370. 3) With negat. οὐ μάν, surely not, certainly not, 12, 318; μὴ μάν, 8, 512. Od. 11, 344; see μήν.

μανθάνω (ΜΑΘΩ), aor. 2 ἔμαθον, Ep. μάθον and ἔμμαθον, only in the aor. to

μαστις, ἡ, Ion. and Ep. for μάστιξ, q. v.

μαστίω, poet. for μαστίζω, to lash, 17, 622. Mid. spoken of lions: οὐρῇ πλευρὰς μαστίεται, he lashes his sides with his tail, •20, 171.

Μαστορίδης, ου, ὁ, son of Mastor = Halitherses, Od. 2, 158; = Lycophron, Il. 15, 430. 438.

Μάστωρ, ορος. ὁ, 1) father of Lycophron from Cythêra, Il. 2) father of Halitherses, Od.

•μασχάλη, ἡ, the shoulder, and the armpit, h. Merc. 242.

ματάω (μάτην), aor. 1 ἐμάτησα. to be inactive, to delay, to loiter, 16, 474. 23, 510; spoken of horses: μὴ—ματήσετον for ματήσητον, •5, 233.

ματεύω (ΜΑΩ), poet. = μαστεύω, to seek, to look up, 14, 110.†

•μάτην, adv. in vain, to no purpose, h. Cer. 309.

ματίη, ἡ (μάτην), a vain undertaking, a fruitless attempt, levity, folly, Od. 10, 79 †

μάχαιρα, ἡ (akin to μάχη), a large knife, a dagger, a sabre, which hung beside the sword, and which was used particularly in slaughtering victims, a sacrificial knife, 3, 271. 18, 597; Machaon also used it for cutting out an arrow, •11, 844.

Μαχάων, ονος, ὁ, voc. Μαχάον, son of Asklepios (Æsculapius), ruler of Tricca and Ithômê in Thessaly, distinguished for his medical skill, 2, 732. Cheiron had given his father healing remedies, 4, 219.

μαχειόμενος, Ep. see μάχομαι.

μαχεούμενος, see μάχομαι.

μάχη, ἡ, (referred by Död. to ἀμάν, mactare, &c.), a battle, a combat, a contest, a fight, mly a battle between heroes. μάχεσθαι μάχην, to fight a battle, 15, 673. 18, 533; also of a duel, 7, 263. 11, 542. 2) contest, quarrel, dispute, with words, 1, 177. H. mentions four contests in particular: the first between the Simois and Scamandrus, 4, 446. 7, 305; the second between the city of Troy and the Grecian ships, 8, 53—488; the third on the Scamandrus, from 11—18, 242; the fourth embraces the deeds of Achilles, and ends with Hector's death, 20—22. 11. and Od.

μαχήμων, ον (μαχέομαι), eager for battle, warlike, κραδίη, 12, 247.†

μαχητής, οῦ, ὁ (μαχέομαι), a warrior, combatant, Il.; with ἀνήρ, Od. 18, 261.

μαχητός, ή. όν (μάχομαι), to be attacked, to be combated, that may be vanquished, κακόν, Od. 12, 119.†

μαχλοσύνη, ἡ (μάχλος), incontinence, luxury. voluptuousness, sensuality, 24, 30, spoken of Paris. Aristarchus wished to strike out the word, because it is elsewhere used only of women; but without reason; on the contrary, it suits Paris very well, cf. 3, 39.

μάχομαι, Ion. and Ep. (μαχέομαι,) de-

pon. mid. fut. μαχέσομαι and μαχήσομαι (the Att. fut. μαχοῦμαι is not Homeric), aor. ἐμαχεσάμην and ἐμαχησάμην, pres. μαχέομαι, μαχέονται, 2, 366; μαχεῖται, 20, 26. μαχέοιτο, μαχέοιντο, 2, 72. 344; in pres. partcp. for metre's sake, μαχειόμενος and μαχεούμενος. The fut. and aor. Wolf always writes with η; only in the infin. aor. 1, for metrical reasons, stands μαχέσασθαι, 3, 20. 433. 7, 40; and optat. μαχέσαιο, 6, 329. According to Buttm. Gram. p. 291, in the aor. ἐμαχεσσάμην, not ἐμαχησάμην, agrees with the MSS., a reading which Spitzner follows. 1) to contend, to fight, to war, to battle, a) Esply in a contest both between whole armies and between single warriors, 3, 91. 435. 19, 153; mly τινί, with or against any man, ἐπί τινι, 5, 124. 244; ἀντία τινός, 20, 80. 88; ἐναντίον τινός, 3, 433; πρός τινα, 17, 471; but σύν τινι, with any man, i. e. with any man's aid, Od. 13, 391. Of the thing for which a man fights we have mly περί τινος, also περί τινι, Il. 16, 568. Od. 2, 245; ἀμφί τινι, Il. 3, 70. 16, 565; and εἵνεκά τινος, 2, 377; sometimes a dat. instrum. is added: τόξοις, ἀξίνῃσι. 2) Generally, to contend, to fight, without reference to war: ἀνδράσι περὶ δαιτί, about a repast, Od. 2, 245: spoken of a contest with beasts, Il. 16, 429. 758. b) Spoken of a prize-combat: πύξ, to contend with the fist, 23, 621. c) Spoken of contest of words, with ἐπέεσσι, 1, 304. 5, 875; and without ἐπ. 1, 8.

μάψ, adv. poet. = μάτην, 1) in vain, fruitlessly, to no purpose, 2, 120. μὰψ ὀμόσαι, 15, 40. 2) without reason, foolishly, inconsiderately, often μάψ, ἀτὰρ οὐ κατὰ κόσμον, foolishly and indecently, 2, 214. Od. 3, 138. (Prob. from μάρπω, μάπω.)

μαψιδίως, adv. poet.=μάψ, 5, 374. Od. 3, 72. 7, 310.

•μαψιλόγος, ον, poet. (λέγω), speaking in vain or without sense, h. Merc. 546.

ΜΑΩ, an obsolete root, of which some forms remain. Perf. μέμαα, with pres. signif. Sing. obsol. for which μέμονα, ας, ε (cf. γέγονα with γέγαα) is used, dual μέματον, plur. 1 μέμαμεν, 3 plur. μεμάασι. Imperat. μεμάτω, partcp. μεμαώς, gen. μεμαῶτος and μεμάότος, 3 plur. pluperf. μέμασαν, to strive for, 1) to rush eagerly to any thing, to dash impetuously on, 8, 413; πρόσσω, 11, 615; ἐγχείῃσι, 2, 818; ἐπί τινι, 8, 327. 20, 326. Often the partcp. μεμαώς, as an adj. or connected with another verb: in haste, impetuously, zealously, earnestly. 2) to desire ardently, to long for. a) Mly with the infin. pres., 1, 590. 2, 543. b) With gen. of thing: ἔριδος, αὐτῆς, 5, 732. 13, 197. 20, 256; μέμονα, mly with infin., 5, 482. 7, 36. 3) It also gives tenses to μαίομαι, q. v.

Μεγάδης, ου, ὁ, son of Megas = Perimus, 16, 695.

μεγάθυμος, ον, poet. (θυμός), high-

N 4

μεθαιρέω (αἱρέω), aor. μεθεῖλον, Ep. iterat. form μεθέλεσκον, to take, to catch, spoken of a ball : ὁ δ᾽ ἀπὸ χθονὸς ὑψόσ᾽ ἀερθείς, ῥηιδίως μεθέλεσκε, subaud. σφαῖραν, the other, springing high from the earth. caught it with ease, Od. 8, 374.† (Damm [e contrario capto] and Voss.)

μεθάλλομαι (ἅλλομαι), only partcp aor. sync. μετάλμενος, to leap over, to spring upon or to, absol. 5, 336. 11, 538 ; to leap after, *23, 345.

μεθείω, Ep. for μεθῶ, see μεθίημι.

μεθέλεσκε, see μεθαιρέω.

μεθέμεν, Ep. for μεθεῖναι, see μεθίημι.

μεθέπω (ἔπω), partcp. aor. 2 act. μετασπών and mid. μετασπόμενος, I) Act. intrans. to be behind, to go after, hence 1) to pursue, to follow, τινὰ ποσσί, 17, 190. Od. 14, 33. b) to seek, to seek for, with accus. Il. 8, 126 ; spoken of regions : to visit, absol. to arrive, Od. 1, 175. 2) Trans. with double accus. to cause to go after, to drive after ; ἵππους Τυδεΐδην, to drive the horses after Tydides [κατόπιν ἤλαυνε, Schol.], Il. 5, 329. II) Mid. to follow, to pursue ; τινά, only, 13, 567.

μέθημαι (ἧμαι), to sit in the midst ; with dat. μνηστῆρσι, in the midst of the suitors, Od. 1, 118.†

μεθημοσύνη, ἡ (μεθήμων), negligence, remissness, *13, 108. 121.

μεθήμων, ον (μεθίημι), negligent, remiss, lazy, supine, 2, 241. Od. 6, 25.

μεθίημι (ἵημι), infin. pres. Ep. μεθιέμεναι and μεθιέμεν, fut. μεθήσω, aor. 1 μεθῆκα, μεθέηκα. Of the aor. 2 subj. μεθῶ, Ep. μεθείω : optat. μεθείην, infin. μεθέμεν for μεθεῖναι. Of the pres. indic. μεθείω, 2 and 3 sing. μεθιεῖς, μεθιεῖ : of the imperf. 2, 3 sing. μεθίεις, μεθίει ; but 3 plur. μεθίεν for μεθίεσαν, to neglect, I) Trans. with accus. 1) to let loose, to let go (any thing bound or detained), τινά, to let a prisoner go, 10, 449. cf. 16, 762 ; spoken of missiles : ἰόν, 5, 48 ; τι ἐς ποταμόν, to let any thing fall into the river, Od. 5, 460 ; metaph. χόλον τινός, to give up anger about any man, Il. 15, 138 ; Ἀχιλλῆϊ, to remit his wrath against Achilles, 1, 283 ; κῆρ ἄχεος, to free the heart from care, 17, 539. 2) to abandon, τινά, 3, 414. Od. 15, 212. εἴ με μεθείη ῥῖγος, Od. 5, 471. 3) to give, to permit, to yield, νίκην τινί, Il. 14, 364 ; and with infin. ἐρύσαι, to permit to draw, 17, 418. II) Intrans. 1) Absol. to be negligent, to relax, to become weary, to loiter, to linger, often absol. 6, 523. 10, 121, also Od. 4, 372 ; βίῃ, in strength, Il. 21, 177. 2) to neglect, to desist, to cease from ; with gen. πολέμοιο, from war, 4, 240. 13, 97 ; in like manner ἀλκῆς, μάχης, βίης. Od. 21, 126 ; χόλοιο Τηλεμάχῳ (against Telem.), Od. 21, 377. b) With infin. and partcp. rarely in H. μάχεσθαι, to cease to fight, Il. 13, 234. 23, 434. κλαίουσα μεθέηκε, he ceased weeping, 24, 48. (On quantity, see ἵημι.)

μεθίστημι (ἵστημι), fut. μεταστήσω,

1) Act. transit. to transfer, to transpose, to change, to exchange, τινί τι, Od. 4, 612. 2) Mid. intrans. to transfer oneself, i. e. to go elsewhere, with dat. ἑτάροισι, 5, 514.

μεθομιλέω (ὁμιλέω), to have intercourse, to associate ; τινί, with any man, 1, 269.†

μεθορμάω (ὁρμάω), only partcp. aor. pass. μεθορμηθείς, to drive after. 2) Pass. to follow, to pursue, Od. 5, 325. Il. 20, 192.

μέθυ, υος, τό, any strong, intoxicating drink, esply wine, 7, 471. Od. 4, 796.

*μεθύστερος, η, ον (ὕστερος), after, later, the neut. as adv. h. Cer. 205.

μεθύω (μέθυ), only pres. and imperf. drink unmixed wine, Od. 18, 240 , Metaph. to be thoroughly soaked or saturated (with). βοείη μεθύουσα ἀλοιφῇ, an ox-hide soaked with fat [drunken with slippery lard, Cp.], Il. 17, 390.

μειδάω, only in aor. 1 ἐμείδησα, Ep. μείδησα ; and μειδιάω, from which only partcp. pres. μειδιόων, Ep. for μειδιῶν, to smile ; on the other hand, γελᾶν, to laugh aloud, h. Cer. 204 ; βλοσυροῖσι προσώπασι, 7, 212 ; Σαρδάνιον, Od. 20, 303 ; see this word.

μειδιάω, see μειδάω.

μείζων, ον, irreg. compar. of μέγας.

μείλας, Ep. μέλας, 24, 79 ;† only μείλανι πόντῳ, see ὁ Μέλας πόντος.

μείλια, τά (μέλι, μειλίσσω), any thing gladdening, rejoicing, esply gratifying presents, *9, 147. 289 ; spoken of the gifts which a father gives to his daughter as a portion ; marriage presents ; dower.

μείλιγμα, ατος, τό (μειλίσσω), any thing which serves to soothe or please. μειλίγματα θυμοῦ, dainties, which the master takes for his dogs, Od. 10, 216.†

μείλινος, η, ον, poet. for μέλινος, q. v. *Il.

μειλίσσω, only pres. (akin to μέλι, prop. to make sweet), hence 1) Act. to please, to rejoice, esply to soothe, to calm ; νεκρὸν πυρός, to appease the dead by fire (the funeral pile), 7, 408. The dead, according to the views of the ancients, were angry if their obsequies were not soon performed. 2) Mid. to enjoy oneself, to rejoice, h. Cer. 291. b) to be gentle, to use gentle words, to address kindly, Od. 3, 96. 4, 326.

μειλιχίη, ἡ (μειλίχιος), gentleness, mildness ; πολέμοιο, slackness in battle [i. e. the dealing gentle blows ; or making little exertion], 15, 741.†

μειλίχιος, η, ον and μείλιχος, ον (μειλίσσω), prop. sweet ; hence mild, gentle, kind, affectionate. a) Spoken of persons (of whom alone μείλιχος is used, except Od. 15, 374), Il. 17, 671. 21, 300. b) μειλίχιος μῦθος, Od. 10, 288 ; and μύθοισιν, ἐπέεσσι μειλιχίοις προσαυδᾶν, to address any man with friendly words, 6, 343. Od. 6, 143 ; and μειλιχίοις alone, Il. 4, 256 ; αἰδώς, Od. 8, 172.

μείρομαι, from which ἔμμορε as 3 sing.

N 5

censed by the imprecations of his mother, withdrew, then the Curêtes besieged Calydon itself. At, last, upon the prayer of his wife, he took part again in the contest, and repulsed the Curêtes, 9, 541. see 'Αλθαία.

μελέδημα, ατος, τό, poet. (μελέδη), care, anxiety, always plur., 23, 62. μελεδήματα πατρός, anxieties about one's father, Od. 15, 8.

*μαλεδών, ῶνος, ἡ = μελεδώνη, h. Ap. 532.

μελεδώνη, ἡ, poet. care, trouble, Od. 18, 517.†

μέλει, see μέλω.

μελεϊστί, adv. (μέλος), limb by limb, 24, 409.† [Bothe and Nitzsch read διὰ μελεϊστί for διαμελεϊστί, Od. 9, 291.]

μέλεος, έη, εον, idle, vain, unprofitable, αὖτος, 23, 795. ὁρμή, Od. 5, 416; inactive, 10, 480. Neut. as adv. vainly, 16, 336. 21, 473.

*μελετάω (μέλω), aor. 1 ἐμελέτησα, 1) to care. 2) to take care of, to practise, with accus. h. Merc. 557.

*Μέλης, ητος, ὁ, a river in Ionia near Smyrna, where H. is said to have been born, h. 8, 3. Ep. 4, 7.

μέλι, ιτος, τό, honey, 1, 249; vessels of honey and fat were placed upon the funeral piles, 23, 170. Od. 24, 68.

Μελίβοια, ἡ, a town in Magnesia (Thessaly), at Mount Othrys, 2, 717.

μελίγηρυς, υ (γῆρυς), sweet-voiced, sweet-toned, ὄψ, Od. 12, 187.† ἀοιδή, h. Ap. 519.

μελίη, ἡ, the ash, fraxinus excelsior, 13, 178. 16, 767. 2) the ashen shaft of a spear, and often the spear itself, 2, 543. Od. 14, 281.

μελιηδής, ές (ἡδύς), sweet as honey, honey-sweet, οἶνος, πυρός, often metaph. sweet, lovely, θυμός, 10, 495; νόστος, ὕπνος, Od. 11, 100. 19, 551.

μελίκρητος, ον, Ion. for μελίκρατος (κεράννυμι), mixed with honey; τὸ μελίκρητον, a honey-mixture, a drink of milk and honey, which was presented to the souls of the dead and to the infernal deities, *Od. 10, 519. 11, 27.

μείλινος, ίνη, ινον, Ep. μείλινος (μελίη), ashen, made of ash, μέλινος οὐδός, Od. 17, 339; in the Il. always μείλινος, as epith. of ἔγκος. δόρυ.

μέλισσα, ἡ (μέλι), a bee, 2, 87. Od. 13, 106.

Μελίτη, ἡ, daughter of Nereus and Doris, 18, 42. [2) a companion of Persephône, h. Cer. 419.]

*μελίτημα, ατος, τό (μελιτόω), honey-cake, Batr. 39.

μελίφρων, ον (φρήν), by its sweetness delighting the soul, heart-refreshing, οἶνος, πυρός, σῖτος, Il. and Od., metaph. ὕπνος, Il. 2, 34.

μέλλω, only pres. and imperf. prim. signif. to consider, in eo esse, ut, an auxiliary verb, which for the most part stands with the infin. fut., more rarely with pres and aor. It must be ren-

dered, shall, will, should, would, must, may, according as it expresses the purpose of a man, or something dependent upon the will of another, or upon the condition of things; hence, 1) to will, to purpose, to design, to think, to be about to do, to indicate the human will. ἔμελλε διεξίμεναι πεδίονδε, he was about to go out, 6, 393; ἔμελλε στρέψεσθαι ἐκ χώρης, he designed, was on the point of, going away, 6, 515. cf. 6, 52. 10, 336. Od. 11, 553 rarely with infin. pres. Il. 10, 454. Od. 6, 110. 19, 94; and aor. Il. 23, 773. 2) to be destined, to be about, a) According to the will of a deity or of fate: οὐ τελέεσθαι ἔμελλε, it should not be, i. e. was not to be fulfilled, 2, 36. cf. Od. 2, 156. Il. 5, 686; with infin. pres. 17, 497; with infin. aor. ἔμελλε—λιτέσθαι, he was about to supplicate, 16, 46. b) According to human arrangement, 11, 700. c) According to the situation of things, 11, 22. Od. 6, 135; οὐκ ἄρ' ἔμελλες ἀνάλκιδος ἀνδρὸς ἑταίρους ἔδμεναι, it was to be [ἄρα = ut nunc apparet] no timid chief whose companions thou devouredst, &c. (ironical), Od. 9, 475. 3) to be obliged, must. a) According to right and duty: καὶ λίην σέγ' ἔμελλε κιχήσεσθαι κακὰ ἔργα, vengeance was sure to overtake thee (could not but overtake thee), Od. 9, 477. b) According to probable consequence, i. e. may, might, must, sometimes to seem, οὕτω που Διὶ μέλλει φίλον εἶναι, thus it seemed pleasing to Zeus, Il. 2, 116. μέλλω που ἀπέχθεσθαι Διΐ, 21, 83. τὰ δὲ μέλλετ' ἀκουέμεν, this you will have heard, 14, 125. μέλλεν ποτὲ οἶκος ἀφνειὸς ἔμμεναι, once the house may (or must) have been rich, Od. 1, 232. 4, 181; with infin. aor. 24, 46. Od. 14, 133. [So also πολλάκι που μέλλεις ἀρήμεναι, you must or will often have prayed (of a probable inference), Od. 22, 322.]

μέλος, εος, τό, a limb, always in the plur. Il. and Od. 2) an air, a melody, h. 18, 16.

μέλπηθρον, τό (μέλπω), diversion, play, sport. μέλπηθρα κυνῶν and κυσὶν γενέσθαι, to be a sport (refreshment, V.) of the dogs; spoken of the corpses of enemies, lying unburied, *13, 233. 17, 255. 18, 179.

μέλπω, 1) Prop. to sing, with dance and sports, to sing, to celebrate in song, Ἑκάεργον, 1, 474. 2) Mid. as depon. a) to sing, ἐμέλπετο θεῖος ἀοιδὸς φορμίζων, 18, 604. Od. 4, 17. 13, 27. 3) to sing and dance, to lead a choir of dancers, Il. 16, 182; Ἄρηϊ, to dance in honour of Arês, i. e. to fight bravely, 7, 241.

μέλω, rarely personal, mly impersonal, pres. μέλει, μέλουσι, fut. μελήσει, perf. Ep. μέμηλα, partcp. μεμηλώς, mid. Ep. fut. μελήσεται, perf. mid. μέμβλεται, and pluperf. μέμβλετο, Ep. for μεμήληται, μεμήλητο, 1) Active. a) Personal, only one sing. to be an object of care, to lie on the heart, ἀνθρώποισι μέλω, I am prized amongst men, V., Od. 9, 20, cf.

Μενέσθης, ους, ὁ, a Greek, slain by Hector, 5, 609.

Μενέσθιος, ὁ, 1) son of Areïthous, sovereign of Arnæ in Bœotia, slain by Paris, 7, 9. 2) son of the Spercheius, or Borus and Polydôra, a leader of the Myrmidons, 16, 173—178.

μενοεικής, ές (εἴκω), prop. *gratifying the desire*; hence: *sufficient, plentiful, abundant*, spoken of food and drink, δαίς, ἐδωδή, οἶνος, τάφος, 23, 29; also θήρη, ληίς, Od. and ὕλη, abundant wood. Il. 23, 139. 2) Generally: *agreeable, pleasing, wished for*, 9, 227. Od. 16, 429.

μενοινάω (μένος), Ep. μενοινώω, Ion. μενοινέω, aor. 1 ἐμενοίνησα, *to have in mind, to think, to consider, to wish, to will*, τί, or with infin. 10, 101. Od. 2, 36; and τινί τι, to purpose any thing against any man, κακά, Od. 11, 532. μενοίνεον (sc κέ), αἴ τελέουσιν (fut.), they considered whether they should accomplish it, Il. 12, 59. [Bth. says: *deliberare et dubitare solent;* but Schol. προεθυμοῦντο (not supplying κε) and so Cowper and Voss.]

μενοινώω, Ep. for μενοινάω, q. v.

Μενοιτιάδης, ου [also εω, 18, 93], ὁ, son of Menœtius = *Patroclus*, Il.

Μενοίτιος, ὁ, son of Actor, father of Patroclus, an Argonaut, 11, 765. 16, 14. 23, 85, seq

μένος, εος, τό (μένω), prop. perseverance in a thing, hence 1) any vehement manifestation of spirit, and particularly a) *impetuosity, fierceness, rage, anger*, 1, 103. 9, 679: esply *warlike spirit, bravery*, μένος ἀνδρῶν, 2, 387; also plur. μένεα πνείοντες, the courage-breathing, 2, 536. 11, 508; connected with θυμός, ἀλκή, θάρσος, 5, 2. 470. 9, 706. b) *desire, longing, wish, purpose*, 13, 634; also plur. 8, 361. 2) *animation, life, vigour*, since this manifests itself in ardent desires, 3, 294; hence ψυχή τε μένος τε, life and strength, 5, 296. 8, 123. 3) *strength, force, power* of body, as a manifestation of a resolute will: to bear strength of hands against one another, 5, 506; thus also μένος καὶ χεῖρες, 6, 502. μένος καὶ γυῖα, 6, 27. b) Of animals, 17, 20. Od. 3, 450. c) Of inanimate things: of the spear, Il. 13, 444: of the wind, 5, 524; of fire, Od. 11, 220: of the sun, Il. 23, 190; of streams, 12, 18. 4) It is often used periphrastically, as βίη, ἴς. μένος Ἀτρείδαο, 11, 268. ἱερὸν μένος Ἀλκινόοιο, the blessed strength (Nitzsch), Od. 7, 167.

Μέντης, ου, ὁ, 1) leader of the Kikōnes (Ciconians), 17, 73. 2) king of the Taphians, a friend of Odysseus (Ulysses) in Ithaca, under whose form Athênê came to Telemachus, Od. 1, 105. 180.

μέντοι, Od. 4, 157, ed. Wolf; better separate, see μέν.

Μέντωρ, ορος, ὁ, 1) father of Imbrius, 13, 171. 2) son of Alcimus, an intimate friend of Odysseus (Ulysses) in Ithaca, to whom, on his departure, he entrusted his domestic affairs. Athênê assumed

his form when she accompanied Telemachus to Pylos, Od. 2, 225. 4, 654. 17, 68.

μένω, poet. μίμνω, fut. Ep. μενέω for μενῶ, aor. 1 ἔμεινα, 1) Intrans. *to remain, to abide;* esply a) In battle: *to maintain one's ground, to remain firm*, with τλῆναι. b) Generally, *to remain, to continue, to abide*, αὖθι, αὐτόθι, 3, 291. 14, 119; with prep. ἀπό τινος, παρά τινι, etc., spoken of inanimate things: *to remain standing*, 17, 434. c) *to wait*, with accus. and infin. 4, 247. μένον δ᾽ ἐπὶ ἕσπερον ἐλθεῖν, they waited till the evening came on, Od. 1, 422; or εἰσόκε with subj., Il. 9, 45. 2) Transit. with accus. *to await, to wait for*, esply spoken of an attacking enemy: *to resist, to withstand, to stand against*, τινά, Il.; δόρυ, Il. 13, 830; spoken of beasts and lifeless things, 13, 472. 15, 620. b) Generally, *to wait for, to await*, Ἡῶ, 11, 723; τινά, 20, 480. Od. 4, 847. (The perf. 2 μέμονα belongs in signif. to μέμαα, see ΜΑΩ.)

Μένων. ωνος, ὁ, a Trojan, 12, 93.

***Μεριδάρπαξ**, αγος, ὁ (ἅρπαξ), *Crumb-snatcher*, name of a mouse in Batr. 265.

***μαρίζω** (μέρος), perf. pass. μεμέρισμαι, *to divide*, Batr. 61.

***μέρμινα**, ἡ, *care, solicitude, anxiety*, h. Merc. 44. 160. (From μερίς, μαρίζω.)

μέρμερος, ον, poet. (from μέρμηρα, Hes. poet. = μέριμνα), *exciting care, causing trouble*, spoken of actions: *wearisome, difficult, terrible, dreadful*, spoken only of warlike deeds, in the plur. μέρμερα ἔργα, 8, 453; and μέρμερα alone, *10, 48. 11, 502.

Μερμερίδης, αο, ὁ, son of Mermerus = *Ilus*, Od. 1, 259.

Μέρμερος, ὁ, 1) a Mysian, slain by Antilochus, 14, 513. 2) father of Ilus, Od.

μερμηρίζω (μέρμερος), aor. 1 Ep. μερμήριξα, 1) Intrans. *to be anxious, to be troubled, to revolve anxiously in the mind, to ponder;* esply δίχα and διάνδιχα, *to be irresolute, to be doubtful*, to hesitate between two courses, *to delay*, Od. 16, 73. Il. 1, 169. 8, 167. There follows it ὡς, 2, 3; ὅπως, 14, 159. Od. 20, 8; often ἤ—ἤ, whether—or, Il. 5, 672. 10, 503; also infin. ἐλθεῖν ἠδὲ πυθέσθαι, Od. 10, 152. 438. 24, 235; περί τινος, Il. 20, 17. 2) Trans. with accus. *to devise, to plot, to resolve upon*, δόλον, Od. 2, 93; πολλά, Od. 1, 427; φόνον τινί, Od. 2, 325. 19, 52.

μέρμις, ιθος, ἡ (prob. from εἴρω), a *bond, a cord, a rope*, Od. 20, 23.†

***μέρος**, εος, τό, *a part, a share*. κατὰ μέρος, each in his part, h. Merc. 53.

μέροψ, οπος, ὁ (μείρομαι, ὄψ), *endowed with (articulate) speech, discoursing, speaking*, epith. of men, who are distinguished from brutes by uttering articulate, instead of inarticulate sounds, 1, 250. 9, 340. Od. 20, 49. (Voss, 'the speaking tribes of men,' but in h. Cer. 'manytoned,' or speaking many tongues.)

***Μέροπες**, οἱ, the ancient name of the

subsequence: *after*, Il. 8, 261. 18, 96. 23, 27. μετὰ κλέος, after the news, report, 11, 227. μετὰ ταῦτα, h. Merc. 126; often with partcp. μετὰ Πάτροκλον θανόντα, 24, 575. *c*) Spoken of cause, manner, etc. *a*) To indicate the object: *for, after*, 7, 418. ἰέναι μετὰ δόρυ, to go to bring a spear, 13, 247. βῆναι μετὰ πατρὸς ἀκουήν, to go in quest of intelligence from a father, Od. 2, 308. β) To indicate suitableness: *according to, after*. μετὰ σὸν κῆρ, Il. 15, 52. Od. 8, 583. II) Adv. without cases. 1) *together, moreover, besides*, 2, 446. 2) *behind, hereafter*, of space and of time, 23, 133. Od. 15, 400. Frequently it is separated from the verb by tmesis. III) In composition, it has, in addition to the definitions already given, this, that it indicates a change from one condition to another.

μέτα. with anastrophe for μετά, 1) When it follows the subst. 13, 308. 2) For μέτεστι, Od. 21, 93.

μεταβαίνω (βαίνω), μεταβήσομαι, aor. μετέβην, perf. μεταβέβηκα, to go elsewhere, to go over. 1) Spoken of the stars: μετὰ δ᾽ ἄστρα βεβήκει, the stars had gone over, viz. *had traversed the mid sky* (Cp.), Od. 12, 312. 14, 483. 2) Spoken of singers: *to go over* from one subject to another, *to proceed*, *Od. 8, 492; with ἔς τι, h. 8, 9.

μεταβάλλω (βάλλω), aor. 2 μεταβαλών only in tmesis, *to cast around*, hence *to turn around*; νῶτα, to turn the backs (in flight), 8, 94.†

μεταβουλεύω (βουλεύω), *to change a resolution, to alter one's mind*, μετεβούλευσαν, Od. 5, 286.†

μετάγγελος, ὁ (ἄγγελος), one who bears intelligence from one to another, *a messenger* [internuncius], *15, 144. 23, 199. In 15, 144, Wolf reads μετ᾽ ἄγγελος.

μεταδαίνυμαι, mid. (δαίνυμαι), fut. μεταδαίσομαι, *to eat with, to feast with*; ἱρῶν, to participate in the sacrificial feast, 23, 207; τινί, with any one, 22, 498. Od. 14, 48.

μεταδήμιος, η, ον (δῆμος), *existing amongst the people*. κακὸν μεταδήμιον, evil amongst the people, Od. 13, 46; spoken of an individual: *domestic, native*, at home, *Od. 8, 293.

μεταδόρπιος. ον (δόρπον), *in the midst of or during supper*, Od. 4, 194.†

μεταδρομάδην, adv. *running after, pursuing*, 5, 80.†

μεταίζω, poet. for μεθίζω (ἴζω), *to seat oneself with*, Od. 16, 362.†

μεταίσσω (ἀίσσω), partcp. aor. μεταίξας, *to leap after, to pursue, to rush after*, only absol. in the partcp. aor. 15, 293. Od. 17, 236.

μετακιάθω, Ep. (κιάθω), only imperf. μετεκίαθον, 1) *to go after*, 11, 52; in a hostile signif. *to pursue*, τινά, 16, 685. 18, 581. 2) *to go to some other place, to visit*; τινά, any man, Od. 1, 22; πεδίον, to reach the plain, Il. 11, 714.

μετακλαίω, *to weep after, to deplore*, 11, 764.†

μετακλίνω (κλίνω), aor. pass. μετεκλίνθην, *to bend to another quarter*. πολέμοιο μετακλινθέντος, when the battle has turned, i. e. is yielding, 11, 509.†

μεταλήγω (λήγω), Ep. aor. 1 optat. μεταλλήξειε, partcp. μεταλλήξας, *to cease, to desist from*; with gen. χόλοιο, from anger, *9, 157. 261. h. Cer. 340.

μεταλλάω (μετ᾽ ἄλλα), aor. 1 μετάλλησα, prop. to search after other things, hence 1) *to search after, to seek after, to inform oneself about*, with accus. τινά or τί, 10, 125. Od. 3, 243. 2) *to inquire for, to ask after*; τινά, any man, and τινά τι, to ask a man about any thing, Il. 3, 177. Od. 1, 231; also ἀμφί τινι, Od. 17, 554. [Herm. Op. vii. 141, is dissatisfied with Buttmann's explanation, Lex. 412.]

μεταλλήγω Ep. for μεταλήγω.

μετάλμενος, partcp. aor. 2 from μεθάλλομαι.

μεταμάζιος, ον (μαζός), *between the breasts*; στῆθος, the middle of the breast, 5, 19.†

*μεταμέλπομαι, mid. (μέλπω), *to sing or dance amongst*, with dat. h. Ap. 197.

μεταμίγνυμι (μίγνυμι), Ep. μεταμίσγω, fut. μεταμίξω, *to mix with, to mingle amongst*, τί, Od. 18, 310; τινί τι, *Od. 22, 221.

μεταμώλιος, ον=μεταμώνιος.

μεταμώνιος. ον, poet. (ἄνεμος), prop. with the wind, i. e. *idle, vain, profitless*, νήματα, Od. 2, 98. πάντα μεταμώνια τιθέναι, to render all vain, Il. 4, 363; μεταμώνια βάζειν, to prate idly, Od. 18, 332. (Wolf has μεταμώνιος for μεταμώλιος, after the best MSS.)

μετανάστης, ον, ὁ (ναίω), one who goes from one place to another, *a stranger, a settler, a new-comer*, *9, 648. 16, 59.

Μετάνειρα, ἡ, wife of Celeüs, mother of Demophon, h. Cer. 161. 206.

μετανίσσομαι, poet. (νίσσομαι), *to go over, to go to the other side*, spoken of Helios: μετενίσσετο βουλυτόνδε, Helios went to the unyoking of oxen. i. e. descended to his setting, 16, 779. Od. 9, 58.

*μετάνοια, ἡ (νοέω), *a change of mind, repentance*, Batr. 10.

μεταξύ, adv. (μετά), *in the midst*, 1, 156.†

μεταπαύομαι, mid. (παύω), *to cease in the midst, to take rest*, 17, 373.†

μεταπαυσωλή, ἡ (παύω), *intermediate rest, refreshment*, πολέμοιο, 19, 201. According to Heyne and Nägelsb. ad Il. 2, 386, to be written μετὰ παυσωλή.

μεταπρεπής, ές, poet. (πρέπω), *distinguished amongst*; with dat. ἀθανάτοισιν, amongst immortals, 18, 370.†

μεταπρέπω, poet. (πρέπω), *to distinguish oneself, to be eminent amongst*; with dat. of pers. ἡρώεσσιν, amongst the heroes, Il. and Od.; with dat. of the thing, γαστέρι, Od. 18, 2. *b*) With double dat.

μετρέω (μέτρον), aor. 1 ἐμέτρησα, to *measure*; hence poet. πέλαγος, to measure the sea, i. e. to navigate, to sail over, Od. 3, 179.†

μέτρον, τό, *a measure*. 1) the instrument for measuring, *a measure*, 12, 422. 2) Esply a measuring vessel for liquids and dry goods, οἴνου, 7, 471. 23, 268. ἀλφίτου, Od. 2, 355. (How much it held is not known.) 3) *that which is measured*, i. e. *space, length*, μέτρα κελεύθου, Od. 4, 389. 10, 539. ὅρμου μέτρον ἱκέσθαι, the space of the harbour, Od. 13, 101; metaph. μέτρον ἥβης, the full measure of youth, i. e. the bloom of life, Il. 11, 225. Od. 11, 317.

μετώπιον, τό = μέτωπον, *the forehead*, Il. 15. 16, 739; prop. neut. of the adj. μετώπιος.

μέτωπον, τό (ὤψ), *the forehead*, mly of men, plur., Od. 6, 107; once of a horse, Il. 23, 454. 2) Metaph. *the front, the fore-part*, κόρυθος, 16, 70.

μεῦ, Ion. for μοῦ, see ἐγώ.

μέχρι, poet. before vowel μέχρις, prep. with gen. *until, as for as*. 1) Spoken of place : θαλάσσης, 13. 143. 2) Of time : τέο-μέχρις; till when, how long? 24, 128.

μή, adv. and conj. *not, that not*. 1) Adv. μή, *not*; it never denies independently and directly (cf. οὐ), but always indirectly, and in reference to a preced. representation. It is found, therefore, only in a really dependent denial, or in one conceived of as dependent; and esply in such main and subordinate clauses as express a wish, will, command, a case or condition, a fear or anxiety. (The same holds true of the compounds : μηδέ, μηδείς, etc.) A) In main clauses : 1) In such as express a command, the sort of forbidding or warning, where mly the imperat. pres. stands, 1. 32. 363; or instead of it the infin., 7, 413. 17, 501; or the subj. aor. μὴ δή με ἕλωρ ἐάσῃς κεῖσθαι, do not, do not let me lie as a prey [*hoc tantum te rogo . . . ne*], 5, 684; often with an implied threat, μή σε παρὰ νηυσὶ κιχείω, let me not meet thee at the ships, 1, 26. 21. 563. Rare and mly Ep. is the imperat. aor. 4, 410. Od. 16, 301; and the fut., 15, 115. 2) In sentences expressing a wish, either with the optat. or the indic. histor. tenses : μὴ τοῦτο φίλον Διὶ πατρὶ γένοιτο! may this not please father Zeus! Od. 7. 316. μὴ ὄφελες λίσσεσθαι, would that thou hadst not supplicated, Il. 9, 698. 22, 481; also with infin. μὴ πρὶν ἐπ᾽ ἠέλιον δῦναι. 2, 413. 3) In sentences which contain an exhortation with the subj. μὴ ἴομεν for ἴωμεν. let us not go, Il. and Od. 4) In oaths, sometimes instead of the direct negative οὐ, Il. 10, 330. B) In subordinate clauses : 1) In all clauses expressing design or a condition; therefore with the conjunct. ἵνα, ὡς, ὅπως, ὄφρα, εἰ, ἤν, etc. On the construct. see these conjunct. (οὐ stands only when

the negation is limited to a single word, 24, 296.) 2) With infin. only in dependent discourse in H. : ὄμνυθι, μὴ μὲν ἑκὼν τὸ ἐμὸν δόλῳ ἅρμα πεδῆσαι, swear to me, that thou didst not wittingly by craft obstruct my chariot, 23, 585. cf. 19, 261. I) Conjunct. *that not*: 1) After the primary tenses or an aor. with pres. signif. with subjunct., 1, 522. 17, 17; after a historical tense with optat., 10, 468. 2) After verbs to fear, to avoid, to beware, to prevent, etc., μή like the Lat. *ne* signifies *that*: δείδω μὴ τὸ χθιζὸν ἀποστήσωνται Ἀχαιοὶ χρέος, I fear that the Greeks will pay yesterday's debt, 13, 745. cf. 1, 553. 14, 261; after ἰδεῖν, to take heed, 10, 98. Such clauses with μή are often elliptical, so that δέδοικα or φοβοῦμαι must be supplied before them (cf. A 1), μήτι χολωσάμενος ῥέξῃ κακὸν υἷας Ἀχαιῶν, that in anger he may inflict some evil upon the sons of the Achaians, 2, 195. 5, 487. 17, 93. *b*) If οὐ is added, it is thereby shown that the apprehended event will not ensue, μή νύ τοι οὐ χραίσμῃ, lest haply it should avail thee nothing, 1, 28. μὴ οὔτις, 10, 39. and with indicat., Od. 5, 300, is to be taken as an interrogative particle. III) An interrogative particle : μή as such stands, 1) In a direct question, when a negative answer is expected : ἦ μή πού τινα δυσμενέων φάσθ᾽ ἔμμεναι ἀνδρῶν, you did not surely suppose it to be one of the enemy, Od. 6, 200. cf. Od. 9, 405. 2) In an indirect question; *whether not*, after ἰδεῖν, φράζεσθαι, mly with subjunct. and optat., Il. 10, 98. 101. 15, 164. Od. 24, 291; rarely with the indicat. when a man is convinced that the apprehended act will happen or is true : δείδω, μὴ δὴ πάντα θεὰ νεμερτέα εἶπεν, I have my fears whether the goddess did not speak all things truly, Od. 5, 300.

μηδέ, adv. connects two clauses, prop. adversatively : *but not*, 4, 302. 10, 37. mly merely annexing : *also not, and not*, 2, 260. Od. 4, 752. 2) *also not, not even*, and repeated for the sake of emphasis, 6, 38. 10, 239. 2) Doubled μηδέ, μηδέ, *neither, nor*, 4, 303.

Μηδείδης, ου, ὁ, h. Bacch. 6, 43. ed. Wolf, after the conjec of Barnes for μὴ δείδειν, the name of a pilot. Herm. amends : νῆ᾽ ἤδη, which Frank has adopted.

μηδείς, μηδεμία. μηδέν (μηδέ and εἰς), *no one, none*, in H. μηδέν, 18, 500.†

Μηδεσικάστη, ἡ (adorned with wisdom), daughter of Priam, wife of Imbrius, 13, 173.

μήδομαι, depon. mid. (μῆδος), fut. μήσομαι, aor. ἐμησάμην, *to have in mind*, like *parare*, not merely to devise, but also to execute: hence, 1) Absol. *to devise, counsel*, 2, 360. 2) *to devise, to plot, to prepare*, τί, Od. 5, 173. νόστον, Od. 3, 160. κακά, Od. 3, 166. τί τινι, Od. 5, 189. κακά τινι, Il. 6, 157. 7, 478. ὄλεθρόν τινι, Od. 3, 249. 9, 92; also with

They were then covered with pieces of flesh from the other parts, enveloped with a doubled covering of caul, and thus burnt as a sacrifice to the gods, Il. 1, 460. Od. 3, 456; hence often πίονα μηρία, 1, 40; thus Nitzsch ad Od. 3, 456. Voss, Myth. Brief. I. 39, explains μηρία as the hip-bones, with the flesh belonging to them.

Μηριόνης, ους, ὁ, son of Molus of Crete, charioteer of Idomeneus, 2, 651. 7, 166.

μηρός, ὁ, the upper fleshy part of the hip. the thigh, spoken of men, 5, 305. 12, 162. ἄορ ἐρύσασθαι παρὰ μηροῦ, to draw the sword from the thigh, Il. 2) Spoken of beasts, only in the connexion, μηροὺς ἐξέταμον, see μηρίον, 1, 460. Od. 12. 360.

μηρύομαι, depon. mid. aor. Ep. μηρῡσάμην, to draw in, to take in, to furl, ἱστία, Od. 12, 170.†

μήστωρ, ωρος, ὁ (μήδομαι), 1) an adviser, a counsellor, spoken of Zeus (governor of the world, V.), 8, 22; of heroes: μήστωρες μάχης, αὔτῆς, counsellors in battle (Voss: 'exciters of battle'), 4, 328. 17, 339. 2) which occasions any thing: φόβοιο, the occasion or cause of flight, 6, 97. 12, 39; but of horses, skilled in flying (impetuous steeds, V.), 5, 272. 8, 108.

Μήστωρ, ορος, ὁ, son of Priam, 24, 257.

μήτε (τε), and not, and that not. μήτε—μήτε, neither—nor, also with τε in the second member, 13, 230. On the construc. see μή.

μήτηρ, μητέρος, ἡ, contr. μητρός, a mother, spoken of animals, 2, 313. 17, 4. Od. 10, 414. 2) Metaph. spoken of regions in which any thing especially flourishes: μήτηρ μήλων, θηρῶν, mother of sheep; of wild beasts, i. e. abounding in sheep, etc., Il. 2, 696. 8, 47, and elsewhere.

μήτῑ, neut. of μήτις, q. v.

μήτῑ, see μήτις.

μητιάω (μήτις), Ep. μητιόω, only pres. and imperf. 1) to have in mind, to devise, to plan, βουλάς, 20, 153; absol. 7, 45. 2) to devise prudently, to plan, to p ot. τί, 10, 208; κακά, 15, 27. 18, 312; νόστον τινί, Od. 6, 14. Mid. to conclude by oneself, to deliberate, Il. 22, 174; with infin. 12, 17.

μητίετα, ὁ, Ep. for μητιέτης (μητίομαι) counsellor, counselling (ruling, V.), epith. of Zeus, 1, 175. Od. 14, 243, and often.

μητιόεις, εσσα, εν (μήτις), 1) rich in counsel, wise, h Ap. 344. 2) wisely prepared or devised, φάρμακα, Od. 4, 227.†

μητίομαι, depon. mid. (μήτις), fut. μητίσομαι, aor. 1 ἐμητισάμην; the pres. is not found in H.:=μητιάω, 1) to have in mind, to deliberate upon. Od. 9, 262. 2) to invent, to devise, to plot, ἔχθεα, Il. 3, 417; μέρμερα, to practise dreadful deeds, 10, 48; θάνατόν τινι, 15, 349; κακά τινα,

Od. 18, 27. (In the earlier edd. we find incorrectly μητίσσομαι)

μητιόω, Ep. for μητιάω.

μῆτις, ιος, ἡ, dat. μήτῑ, Ep. for μήτιι, 1) prudence, understanding, intelligence, the ability to counsel, often Il. and Od. 2) counsel, advice, plan, expedient, esply μῆτιν ὑφαίνειν, Il. 7, 324. 10, 19. Od. 4, 678.

μῆτις or μή τις, neut. μήτι, gen. μήτινος (τίς), that none, (that no) that no one, constr. of μή. 2) μήτι, frequently, as adv. that not perhaps, indeed not perhaps, 4, 42. 5, 567. Od. 2, 67.

μητροπάτωρ, ορος, ὁ, poet. (πατήρ), a mother's father, a maternal grandfather, 11, 224.†

μητρυιή, ἡ, a step-mother, *5, 389. 13, 697.

μητρώϊος, ίη, ἴον. poet. for μητρῷος (μήτηρ). maternal, δῶμα, Od. 19, 410.†

μήτρως, ωος, ὁ (μήτηρ), a mother's brother, an uncle, *2, 662. 16, 717.

μηχανάομαι, depon. mid. (μηχανή), only pres. and imperf., 3 plur. imperf. μηχανόωντο, Ep. for ἐμηχανῶντο, 1) Prop. to prepare with art, to build, machinor, τείχεα, 8, 177. 2) to invent, to devise, to purpose, to practise, mly in a bad signif.: κακά, ἀτάσθαλα, to practise wickedness, 11, 695; τινί and ἐπί τινι, Od. 4, 822.

μηχανάω, Ep. μαχανόω = μηχανάομαι, from this the partcp. μηχανόωντας, Od. 18, 143.†

*μηχανιώτης, ου, ὁ, poet. for μηχανητής, machinator, one who practises cunning or prudence, crafty, h. Merc. 436.

μῆχος, εος, τό, poet. for μηχανή, means, remedy, counsel, 2, 342. οὐδέ τι μῆχός ἐστι, there is no remedy, i. e. it is impossible, 9, 249. cf. ἄκος, Od. 14, 238.

Μῄων, ονος, ὁ [5, 43], see Μῄονες.

μιαίνω, aor. 1 ἐμίηνα, aor. 1 pass. ἐμιάνθην, Ep. 3 plur. for ἐμιάνθησαν, 4, 146; according to Buttm. 3 dual aor. 2 sync. for ἐμιάνσθην, 1) to stain, to colour, ἐλέφαντα φοίνικι, 4, 141. 2) to stain, to defile, to foul, αἵματι, κονίῃσι, *16, 797. 17, 439.

μιαιφόνος, ον (μιαίνεσθαι φόνος), defiled with slaughter, stained with slaughter, reeking with gore [gore-tainted, Cp.], epith. of Arês, *5, 31. 455. 844. Lobeck and Buttm. read μιαίφονος from μιαίνεσθαι and φόνος, and its connexion with βροτολοιγέ and τειχεσιπλῆτα requires an act. signif. accustomed to stain oneself with blood (Schol. μιαινόμενος (Mid.) φόνοις). Ameis.

μιαρός, ή, όν (μιαίνω), stained, defiled, fouled, 24, 420.†

μιγάζομαι, poet. for μίγνυμαι, mid. Od. 8, 271.†

μίγδα, adv. (μίγνυμι), mixed, mingled together, Od. 24, 77; with dat. θεοῖς, mixed among the gods, Il. 8, 437.

*μίγδην, adv. = μίγδα, h. Merc. 494.

μίγνῡμι, Ep. μίσγω, fut. μίξω, aor. 1 ἔμιξα, fut. mid. μίξομαι, Ep. aor. 2 sync.

little, for a time, mly of time, 4, 466. Od. 15, 494.

μινυνθάδιος, ον (μίνυνθα), compar. μινυνθαδιώτερος, *lasting but a short time,* αἰών, 4, 778; *short-lived,* 1, 352. Od. 11, 307.

μινυρίζω (μινυρός), *to moan, to whimper, to lament, to wail,* prop. spoken of women, 5, 859. Od. 4, 719.

Μινώϊος, ον, Ep. for Μινῷος, *Minoian,* h. Ap. 393.

Μίνως, ος, ὁ, accus. Μίνωα and Μίνω ed. Wolf, Μίνων ed. Spitzner after Aristarch., Il. 14, 322; son of Zeus and Europa, king of Crete, famed as a wise ruler and lawgiver, 13, 450. 451. 14, 322. His wise laws he had received from Zeus himself, since he had for nine years intercourse with Zeus, Od. 19, 178. His daughter is Ariadne and his son Deucalion, Od. 11, 321 19, 178. He also appears in the realm of shades as ruling king, Od. 11, 567. Later tradition alone makes him a judge in the under world.

μισγάγκεια, ἡ (ἄγκος), *a dell, glen, gulley, a defile, a ravine,* in which the mountain torrents meet, 4, 455.†

μίσγω, a form of μίγνυμι, q. v.

μισέω (μῖσος), aor. 1 ἐμίσησα, *to hate, to abominate, to detest.* μίσησέ μιν κυσὶ κύρμα γενέσθαι, it was an abhorrence to him to become a prey to the dogs, Voss, Il. 17, 272.

μισθός, ὁ, *a reward, wages, hire,* 10, 304. 21, 445. 450; plur., Od. 10, 84.

μιστύλλω (akin to μίτυλος), *to cut in small pieces, to cut up,* spoken of carving flesh, with accus., 1, 465. 2, 428. Od. 3, 462.

μίτος, ὁ, *the cord, the thread,* a single thread introduced into the warp (πηνίον), 23, 762.† (Others understand *the warp* by it, stamen. Cp. translates, 'she tends the flax, drawing it to a thread.')

μίτρη, ἡ, *a belt, a girdle,* a woollen belt worn by warriors about the abdomen, furnished with metallic plates as a defence against missiles, and distinct from ζωστήρ, *5, 857. 4, 137.

μιχθείς, see μίγνυμι.

μνάομαι, ground form of μι-μνήσκομαι, *to remember,* contr. μνῶμαι, which occurs in the Ep. expanded forms of the pres. and imperf. see μιμνήσκω.

μνάομαι, contr. μνῶμαι, depon. mid. iterat. imperf μνάσκετο, *to court, to woo, to seek in marriage,* with ἄκοιτιν, γυναῖκα, etc. 1, 39. 16, 431; and absol. *Od. 16, 77. 19, 529. (Only in the pres. and imperf sometimes in the contract and sometimes in the expanded forms.)

ΜΝΑΩ, root of μιμνήσκω.

μνῆμα, ατος, τό (ΜΝΑΩ), *a memorial, a monument,* χειρῶν, Od. 15, 126. 21, 40; τάφον, a tomb, 23, 619.

μνημοσύνη, ἡ (μνήμων), *remembrance, memory.* μνημοσύνη τις ἔπειτα πυρὸς γενέσθω, then let there be some remembrance of the fire, 8, 181.†

*Μνημοσύνη, ἡ (Moneta, Herm.),

daughter of Uranus, mother of the Muses by Zeus, h. Merc. 429.

μνήμων, ον, gen. ονος (μνήμη), *mindful, remembering,* Od. 21, 95; with gen. φόρτου, mindful of the lading [i. e. careful of the goods stowed in his ship], Od. 8, 163.

μνῆσαι, μνησάσκετο, see μιμνήσκω.

Μνῆσος, ὁ, a noble Pæonian, 21, 210.

μνηστεύω (μνηστός), fut. μνηστεύσω, *to woo, to solicit in marriage,* absol. Od. 4, 684; and with accus. γυναῖκα, a woman, Od. 18, 276.

μνηστήρ, ῆρος, ὁ (μνάομαι), *a suitor, a wooer,* often spoken of the suitors of Penelope; the number of them, *Od. 16, 245.

μνῆστις, ιος, ἡ. poet. for μνῆμα, *remembrance, memory.* οὐδέ τις ἡμῖν δόρπου μ., = we thought not of supper, Od. 13, 280.†

μνηστός, ή, όν (μνάομαι), *wooed,* who is won by presents, and hence *a lawful wife,* always as fem. with ἄλοχος, κουριδίη, 6, 246. Od. 1. 36.

μνηστύς, ύος, ἡ, Ion. for μνηστεία, *the act of wooing, soliciting in marriage,* *Od. 2, 199. 19, 13.

μνωόμενος, μνώοντο, Ep. for μνώμενος, ἐμνῶντο from μνάομαι, q. v.

μογέω (μόγος), aor. 1 ἐμόγησα. 1) Intrans. *to weary oneself, to fatigue oneself, to exert oneself, to suffer pain,* mly as part. with another verb, 11, 636. 12, 29. 2) Trans. with accus. *to endure, to bear, to suffer,* ἄλγεα, Od. 2, 343. πολλά, Il. 23, 607. ἀέθλους, Od. 4, 170. ἐπί τινι, about any thing, Il. 1, 162. Od. 16, 19.

μόγις, adv. (μόγος), *with difficulty, scarcely.* (22, 412. ι is long in the arsis,) 9, 355. Od. 3, 119.

μόγος, ὁ, *pains, labour, exertion,* 4, 27.†

μογοστόκος, ον (μόγις, τίκτω), *exciting pains* (dolorum creatrix, Ern.), that causes the woman to bear with pain. Thus according to Aristarchus. Others, 'aiding those that bring forth with difficulty,' but such paroxytones have an active signification (cf. θεοτόκος), epith. of Ilithyia (Eileithyia), *11, 270. 16, 187. 19, 103.

μόθος, ὁ, poet. (akin to μόγος), *the tumult of battle, battle,* 7, 117. 18, 159; ἵππων, a tumult of horses, the battle-fray of cavalry, 7, 240.

μοῖρα, ἡ (μείρομαι), 1) *a part,* in opposition to the whole, 10, 253. Od. 4, 97; esply *a share* in any thing, Od. 11, 534; in a repast, *a portion,* Od. 3, 40. 66; and often metaph. οὐδ' αἰδοῦς μοῖραν ἔχειν. to have no particle of shame, Od. 20, 171; hence *fitness, propriety*; κατὰ μοῖραν, suitably, properly, often with εἰπεῖν, also ἐν μοίρῃ, Il. 19, 186; and παρὰ μοῖραν, contrary to propriety, Od. 15, 509. 2) Esply *the portion of life, the lot of life,* Od. 19, 192; in full, μοῖρα βιότοιο, the measure of life, Il. 4, 175; generally, *fate, destiny,* with infin. Od. 4, 475. Il 7, 52, μοχθέω (μόχθος), fut. ήσω, like μογέω, to take pains, to trouble oneself, to be distressed, κήδεσιν, 10, 106.†

μοχθίζω=μοχθέω, to suffer, to be sick, ἕλκεϊ, with a wound, 2, 723.†

μοχλέω (μοχλός), to move with levers; στήλας, to turn over the pillars, 12. 259.†

μοχλός, ὁ, 1) a lever, Od. 5, 261. 2) any long, strong stake, *Od. 9, 332.

Μυγδών, όνος, ὁ, king of Phrygia, in whose time the Amazons attacked Phrygia. 3, 186.

μυδαλέος, η, ον (μυδάω), wet through, moist, damp; αἵματι, sprinkled with blood, 11, 54.†

Μύδων, ωνος, ὁ (appell. μυδών), 1) son of Atymnius, charioteer of Pylæmĕnes, a Trojan, slain by Antilochus, 5, 580. 2) a Trojan slain by Achilles, 21, 209.

μυελόεις, εσσα, εν (μυελός), full of marrow, marrowy, ὀστέα, Od. 9, 293.†

μυελός, ὁ. marrow, 20, 482; metaph. μυελὸς ἀνδρῶν, the marrow of men, spoken of nourishing food, Od. 2, 291. 20, 108.

μυθέομαι, depon. mid. (μῦθος), fut. μυθήσομαι, aor. 1 ἐμυθησάμην, Ep. form 2 sing. μυθέαι and μυθεῖαι, Ep. iterat. imperf. μυθέσκοντο, 1) to discourse, to speak, to tell, absol. and with accus. and infin. 21, 462. 2) Trans. to tell, to narrate, to call, τινί τι, 11, 201. πάντα κατὰ θυμόν, to speak every thing according to one's mind [agreeably to me], 9, 645. ἀληθέα, νημερτέα, 6, 376. 382. ἐναίσιμα, Od. 2, 159. πόλιν πολύχρυσον, to call the city rich in gold, Il. 18, 289. ποτὶ ὃν θυμόν, to speak to a man's heart, i. e. to consider, 17, 200. Od. 5, 285; hence to counsel, Od. 13, 191. [3) to explain, to indicate, to interpret, Il. 1, 74.]

μυθολογεύω, fut. σω, to relate, to tell, τί τινι, *Od. 12, 450. 453.

μῦθος, ὁ, 1 discourse, word, as opposed to ἔργον 9, 443. Od. 4, 777; in special applications: a) a public discourse, Od. 1, 358. b) narration, conversation. μῦθος παιδός, the narration of the son, Od. 11, 492. 2, 314. 4, 324. c) bidding, command, commission, counsel, Il. 2, 282. 5, 493. 7, 358. 2) a resolve, plan, project, since it is presented in words, undertaking, 14, 127. Od. 3, 140. 22, 288. 3) Od 21, 70, 71 is explained as Æol. for μόθος, noise, confusion, but unnecessarily: it signifies project, purpose, as no. 2. οὐδέ τιν' ἄλλην μύθου ποιήσασθαι ἐπισχεσίην ἐδύνασθε, you could not make any pretext for your undertaking, Voss.

μυῖα, ἡ. a fly, an image of unblushing impudence. a) a house-fly, 4, 131. b) a mosquito, 2, 469. 17, 570. c) a carrion-fly, 19, 25.

Μυκάλη, ἡ, a mountain in Ionia (Asia Minor), opposite Samos, which formed a promontory; also called Trogilium, 2, 869.

Μυκαλησσός, ἡ (Μυκαλησσός, Herm. h.

Ap. 224), a city in Bœotia, near Tanagra, 2, 498.

μυκάομαι, depon. (μύ), aor. ἔμυκον, perf. μέμῡκα, 1) to bellow, spoken of cattle, Od. 10, 413. Il. 18, 580. 2) to crack, to rattle, to buzz, to roar, spoken of doors and of a spear, 5, 749. 20, 260; of a river, 12, 460. 21, 237.

μύκηθμός, ὁ, bellowing, roaring, 18, 575. Od. 12, 265.

Μυκήνη, ἡ, 1) daughter of Inachus, wife of Arestor, who gave name to the city Mycēne, Od. 2, 120. 2) Plur. Μυκῆναι, Mycēnæ, a town in Argolis, the residence of Agamemnon, at the time of the Trojan war famous esply for the treasury of Atreus, and by the Cyclopæan walls; its ruins are near the village Krabata; plur. 2, 569; sing. 4, 52. From this 1) adv. Μυκήνηθεν, from Mycēnæ. 2) Μυκηναῖος, η, ον, Mycenian, 15, 638.

μύκον, see μυκάομαι.

μύλαξ, ακος, ὁ (μύλη), prop. a millstone; and generally, any large stone, 12, 161.†

μύλη, ἡ (μύλλω), a mill, *Od. 7, 104. 20, 106. The mills of the ancients were hand-mills, which were turned by maids; or rather mortars, in which the grain was broken.

μυλήφατος, ον (πέφαμαι), broken or ground in a mill, Od. 2, 355.†

μυλοειδής, ές (εἶδος), similar to a millstone, πέτρος, 7, 270.† Batr. 217.

μυνή, ἡ (akin to ἀμύνω), a pretext, an excuse, a tarrying, plur. Od. 21, 111.†

Μύνης, ητος, ὁ, son of Evenus, husband of Briseis, ruler in Lyrnessus, 2, 692. 19, 296.

*μυοκτόνος, ον (κτείνω). mouse-slaying, μυοκτ. τρόπαιον, a trophy on account of the slaughter of the mice, Batr. 159.

μυρίκη, ἡ, a tamarisk, according to Miquels, Hom. Flora. p. 39, the French tamarisk, tamarix Gallica, a shrub common in southern marshy regions, *10, 466. h. Merc. 81. (ῑ in the arsis, 21, 350.)

μυρίκινος, η, ον, of the tamarisk; ὄζος, a tamarisk branch, 6, 39.†

Μυρίνη, ἡ, daughter of Teucer, wife of Dardanus, according to Strab. an Amazon, who lay buried here. The tradition of the Pelasgians called a mound the monument of Myrina, which the men of that day called thorn-hill, 2, 814; see Βατίεια.

μύριος, η, ον, very much, infinite, innumerable. μυρίον χέραδος, immense rubbish, 21, 320; frequently in the plur. 1, 2. 12, 326. 2) infinitely great, illimitable, a thousand-fold, ἄχος, 20. 282; ἄνος, Od. 15, 452; often plur. ἄλγεα, κήδεα (μυρίοι, countless; but μύριοι, ten thousand, according to the Granim.).

Μυρμιδόνες, οἱ, sing. Μυρμιδών, όνος, the Myrmidons, an Achaian race in Thessaly, Phthiôtis, under the dominion of Achilles, whose chief towns were Phthia

ναύλοχος, ον (ΛΕΧΩ), *offering a secure anchorage, a convenient station for ships*; λιμήν (Cp. *a commodious haven*; Voss, 'a ship-protecting harbour'), *Od. 4, 846. 10, 141.

ναύμαχος, ον (μάχη), *employed in naval battles*, ξυστά [*naval poles ... for conflict maritime prepared*, Cp.], *15, 389. 677.

Ναυσίθοος, ὁ (ship-swift), son of Poseidôn and Periboea, father of Alcinous and Rhexênor, sovereign of the Phæaces in their new abode at Scheria, Od. 7, 56, seq. cf. 6, 7—11.

Ναυσικάα, ἡ, the beautiful daughter of the Phæacian sovereign Alcinous in Scheria, who conducted the ship-wrecked Odysseus (Ulysses) to the house of her father, Od. 6, 17, seq.

ναυσικλειτός, ή, όν (κλειτός), poet. *renowned in naval affairs*, Od. 6, 22.† Εὔβοια, h. Ap. 31. 219.

ναυσικλυτός, ή, όν (κλυτός). = ναυσικλειτός, epith. of Phæaces, Od. 7, 39; of the Phœnicians, *Od. 15, 415.

ναυτεύς. ῆος, ὁ (= ναύτης), a noble Phæacian, Od. 8, 112.

ναύτης, ου, ὁ (ναῦς), *a sailor, a seaman, a mariner*, 4, 76. Od. 1, 171.

ναυτιλίη, ἡ (ναυτίλος), *navigation*, Od. 8, 253.†

ναυτίλλομαι, depon. only pres. and imperf. *to navigate, to go by ship*, *Od. 4, 672. 14. 246.

ναῦφι, ναῦφιν, Ep. see νηῦς.

νάω and ναίω, Ep. only pres. and imperf. ναῖον, *to flow*, κρήνη νάει, Od. 6, 292. κρῆναι νάουσι, Il. 21, 197. ναῖον ὀρῷ ἄγγεα, the vessels flowed with whey, Od. 9, 222. (ᾱ, Od. 6, 292. ᾰ, Il. 21, 197.) 2) Root of ναίω.

Νέαιρα, ἡ (the *younger*), a nymph, who bore to Helios Lampetiê and Phaetūsa, Od. 12, 133.

νεαρός, ή, όν (νέος), *young, tender*, παῖδες, 8, 289.†

νέατος, η, ον, Ep. νείατος (prob. old superl. of νέος), always in the Ep. form. except 9, 153. 295. 11, 712: *the last, the extreme, the lowest*, always spoken of p ace: τοῦς, ἀνθερεών, κενεών, Il. b) with gen. νείατος ἄλλων, the lowest of them all, Il. 6, 295. πόλις νεάτη Πύλου, the last city of Pylos, 11, 712; and plur νέαται Πύλου (not for νενέαται from ναίω), 9, 153.

νεβρός, ὁ (akin to νεαρός), the young of the stags, *a fawn*, also *a deer*, 4, 243. Od. 4, 336.

νέες, νέεσσι, see νηῦς.

νέηαι, Ep. for νέη, see νέομαι.

νεηγενής, ές, Ep. for νεαγ. (γένος), *new-born*, *Od. 4, 336. 17, 127.

νεήκης, ες, Ep. for νεάκ. (ἀκή), *newly-sharpened, whetted*, πέλεκυς [*a new-edged axe*, Cp.], *13, 391. 16, 484.

νεήλυς. υδος, ὁ, ἡ (ἤλυθον), *newly* or *just arrived*, *10, 434. 558.

νεηνίης, ου, ὁ, Ep. for νεανίας (νέος), *young, juvenile*, always as adj. ἀνήρ, *Od. 10, 278. 14, 524. h. 7, 3.

νεῆνις. ιδος, ἡ, Ep. for νεᾶνις (νέος), adj. *youthful*, παρθενική, Od. 7, 20. 2) Subst. *a virgin, a maiden*, 18, 418.

νεήφατος, ον (φημί), *newly-said, new-resounding*, h. Merc. 443.

νεῖαι, Ep. for νέεαι, see νέομαι.

νείαιρος, only in the fem. νείαιρα, irreg. compar. of νέος, *the latter, the outer, the lower*, mly νειαίρη γαστήρ, the lower belly, the abdomen, *5, 539. 616, and elsewhere.

νείατος, η, ον, Ep. for νέατος, q. v.

νεικέω (νεῖκος), and according to the necessity of the metre νεικείω: as subj. νεικείῃσι, infin. νεικείειν, imperf. νείκειον and νεικείεσκον, fut. νεικέσω, aor. 1 ἐνείκεσα, Ep νείκεσα, and σσ. 1) Intrans. *to quarrel, to dispute, to wrangle*, τινί, with any one, Od. 17, 189. ἀλλήλῃσιν, Il. 20, 254. εἵνεκά τινος, 18, 498. νείκεα νεικεῖν, 20, 251. 2) *to provoke, to irritate, to blame, to scold, to accuse*, with accus. αἰσχροῖς ἐπέεσσιν. 3, 38; χολωτοῖσιν, 15, 210. Od. 22, 525: spoken of Paris: νείκεσσε θεάς — τὴν δ' ᾔνησε, *to slight*, in antith. to αἰνεῖν, since he gave Aphroditê the preference to Hêrê and Athênê, Il. 24, 29.

νεῖκος, τό, 1) *quarrelling, contention, disputation*, esply with words: the act of blaming, reproaching, abusing, 7, 95. 9, 448. Od. 8, 75; also in the assembly, Il 18, 497.. 2) Often also, *contest* in deed: *fight, battle*, Il. νεῖκος πολέμοιο, contest of war. 13, 271. Od. 18, 264; thus also φυλόπιδος, ἔριδος, Il. 17, 384. 20, 140.

νεῖμα, Ep. for ἔνειμα, see νέμω.

νειόθεν, Ion. for νεόθεν, adv. (νέος), *from beneath*. νειόθεν ἐκ κραδίης, deep from the heart, 10, 10.†

νειόθι, Ion. for νεόθι, adv. (νέος), *in the lowest part*; with gen. λίμνης, deep down in the lake, 21, 317.†

νειός, ἡ, subaud. γῆ (νέος), *new land, fallow ground*; also *newly-ploughed land*, which has lain for a season untilled, and is now fresh ploughed. νειὸς τρίπολος, thrice-plowed fallow, Od. 5, 127. Il. 18, 541.

νεῖται, contr. for νέεται, see νέομαι.

νεκάς. άδος, ἡ (νέκυς), *a heap of corpses*, 5, 886.†

νεκρός, ὁ, 1) Subst. *a dead body, a corpse*; also Ep. νεκροὶ τεθνηῶτες and κατατεθνηῶτες. the departed dead, 6, 71. b) *the dead, the departed*, as inhabitants of the under-world, 23, 51. Od. 10, 526. 2) Adj. perhaps, Od. 12, 11.

νέκταρ, αρος, τό, *nectar*, the drink of the gods, which was conceived of as the noblest wine, of red colour and fragrant smell, 19, 38. Od. 5, 93. h. Ap. 124. Also Thetis uses it to guard the corpse of Patroclus from putrefaction, Il. 19, 38.

νεκτάρεος, η, ον (νέκταρ), *nectarean, resembling nectar, fragrant like nectar*, ἑανός, χιτών, *3. 335. 18, 25.

νέκυς. υος, ὁ, like νεκρός, dat. plur. νεκύεσσι, rarely νέκυσσι, Od. 11, 569.

O

μετρέω (μέτρον), aor. 1 ἐμέτρησα, to measure; hence poet. πέλαγος, to measure the sea, i. e. to navigate, to sail over, Od. 3, 179.†

μέτρον, τό, a measure. 1) the instrument for measuring, a measure, 12, 422. 2) Esply a measuring vessel for liquids and dry goods, οἴνου, 7, 471. 23, 268. ἀλφίτου, Od. 2, 355. (How much it held is not known.) 3) that which is measured, i. e. space, length, μέτρα κελεύθου, Od. 4, 389. 10, 539. ὅρμου μέτρον ἱκέσθαι, the space of the harbour, Od. 13, 101; metaph. μέτρον ἥβης, the full measure of youth, i. e. the bloom of life, Il. 11, 225. Od. 11, 317.

μετώπιον, τό = μέτωπον, the forehead, Il. 95. 16, 739; prop. neut. of the adj. μετώπιος.

μέτωπον, τό (ὤψ), the forehead, mly of men, plur., Od. 6, 107; once of a horse, Il. 23, 454. 2) Metaph. the front, the fore-part, κόρυθος, 16, 70.

μεῦ, Ion. for μοῦ, see ἐγώ.

μέχρι, poet. before vowel μέχρις, prep. with gen. until, as far as. 1) Spoken of place: θαλάσσης, 13. 143. 2) Of time: τέο μέχρις; till when, how long? 24, 128.

μή, adv. and conj. not, that not. 1) Adv. μή, not: it never denies independently and directly (cf. οὐ), but always indirectly, and in reference to a preced. representation. It is found, therefore, only in a really dependent denial, or in one conceived of as dependent; and esply in such main and subordinate clauses as express a wish, will, command, a case or condition, a fear or anxiety. (The same holds true of the compounds: μηδέ, μηδείς, etc.) A) In main clauses: 1) In such as express a command, the act of forbidding or warning, where mly the imperat. pres. stands, 1. 32. 363; or instead of it the infin., 7, 413. 17, 501; or the subj. aor. μὴ δή με ἕλωρ ἐάσῃς κεῖσθαι, do not, do not let me lie as a prey [hoc tantum te rogo ... ne]. 5, 684; often with an implied threat, μή σε παρὰ νηυσὶ κιχείω, let me not meet thee at the ships, 1, 26. 21, 563. Rare and mly Ep. is the imperat. aor. 4, 410. Od. 16, 301; and the fut., 15, 115. 2) In sentences expressing a wish, either with the optat. or the indic. histor. tenses: μὴ τοῦτο φίλον Διὶ πατρὶ γένοιτο! may this not please father Zeus! Od. 7, 316. μὴ ὄφελες λίσσεσθαι, would that thou hadst not supplicated, Il. 9, 698. 22, 481; also with infin μὴ πρὶν ἐπ' ἠέλιον δῦναι, 2, 413. 3) In sentences which contain an exhortation with the subj. μὴ ἴομεν for ἴωμεν, let us not go, Il. and Od. 4) In oaths, sometimes instead of the direct negative οὐ, Il. 10, 330. B) In subordinate clauses: 1) In all clauses expressing design or a condition: therefore with the conjunct. ἵνα, ὡς, ὅπως, ὄφρα, εἰ, ἤν, etc. On the construct. see these conjunct. (οὐ stands only when

the negation is limited to a single word, 24, 296.) 2) With infin. only in dependent discourse in H.: ὄμνυθι, μὴ μὲν ἑκὼν τὸ ἐμὸν δόλῳ ἅρμα πεδῆσαι, swear to me, that thou didst not wittingly by craft obstruct my chariot, 23, 585. cf. 19, 261. II) Conjunct. that not: 1) After the primary tenses or an aor. with pres. signif. with subjunct., 1, 522. 17, 17; after a historical tense with optat., 10, 468. 2) After verbs to fear, to avoid, to beware, to prevent, etc., μή like the Lat. ne signifies that: δείδω μὴ τὸ χθιζὸν ἀποστήσωνται Ἀχαιοὶ χρέος, I fear that the Greeks will pay yesterday's debt, 13, 745. cf. 1, 553. 14, 261; after ἰδεῖν, to take heed, 10, 98. Such clauses with μή are often elliptical, so that δέδοικα or φοβοῦμαι must be supplied before them (cf. A 1), μήτι χολωσάμενος ῥέξῃ κακὸν υἷας Ἀχαιῶν, that in anger he may inflict some evil upon the sons of the Achaians, 2, 195. 5, 487. 17, 93. b) If οὐ is added, it is thereby shown that the apprehended event will not ensue, μή νύ τοι οὐ χραίσμῃ, lest haply it should avail thee nothing. 1, 28. μὴ οὔτις, 10, 39. μή with indicat., Od. 5, 300, is to be taken as an interrogative particle. III) An interrogative particle: μή as such stands, 1) In a direct question, when a negative answer is expected: ἦ μή πού τινα δυσμενέων φάσθ' ἔμμεναι ἀνδρῶν, you did not surely suppose it to be one of the enemy, Od. 6, 200. cf. Od. 9, 405. 2) In an indirect question; whether not, after ἰδεῖν, φράζεσθαι, mly with subjunct. and optat., Il. 10, 98. 101. 15, 164. Od. 24, 291; rarely with the indicat. when a man is convinced that the apprehended act will happen or is true: δείδω, μὴ δὴ πάντα θεὰ νημερτέα εἶπεν, I have my fears whether the goddess did not speak all things truly, Od. 5, 300.

μηδέ, adv. connects two clauses, prop. adversatively: but not, 4, 302. 10, 37. mly merely annexing: also not, and not, 2, 260. Od. 4, 752. 2) also not, not even, and repeated for the sake of emphasis, 6, 38. 10, 239. 2) Doubled μηδέ, μηδέ, neither, nor, 4, 303.

Μηδείδης, ου, ὁ, h. Barch. 6, 43. ed. Wolf, after the conjec. of Barnes for μὴ δείδειν, the name of a pilot. Herm. amends: νηῒ ἤδη, which Frank has adopted.

μηδείς, μηδεμία. μηδέν (μηδέ and εἷς), no one, none, in H. μηδέν, 18, 500.†

Μηδεσικάστη, ἡ (adorned with wisdom), daughter of Priam, wife of Imbrius, 13, 173.

μήδομαι, depon. mid. (μῆδος), fut. μήσομαι, aor. ἐμησάμην, to have in mind, like parare, not merely to devise, but also to execute: hence, 1) Absol. to devise, counsel, 2, 360. 2) to devise, to plot, to prepare, τί, Od. 5, 173. νόστον, Od. 3, 160. κακά, Od. 3, 166. τί τινι, Od. 5, 189. κακά τινι, Il. 6, 157. 7, 478. ὄλεθρόν τινι, Od. 3, 249. 9, 92; also with

They were then covered with pieces of flesh from the other parts, enveloped with a doubled covering of caul, and thus burnt as a sacrifice to the gods, Il. 1, 460. Od. 3, 456; hence often πίονα μηρία, 1, 40; thus Nitzsch ad Od. 3, 456. Voss, Myth. Brief. I. 39, explains μηρία as the *hip-bones*, with the flesh belonging to them.

Μηριόνης, ους, ὁ, son of Molus of Crete, charioteer of Idomeneus, 2, 651. 7, 166.

μηρός, ὁ, the upper fleshy part of the hip. *the thigh,* spoken of men, 5, 305. 12, 162. ἄορ ἐρύσασθαι παρὰ μηροῦ, to draw the sword from the thigh, Il. 2) Spoken of beasts, only in the connexion, μηροὺς ἐξέταμον, see μηρίον, 1, 460. Od. 12. 360.

μηρύομαι, depon. mid. aor. Ep. μηρῡσάμην, *to draw in, to take in, to furl,* ἱστία, Od. 12, 170.†

μήστωρ, ωρος, ὁ (μήδομαι), 1) *an adviser, a counsellor,* spoken of Zeus (governor of the world, V.), 8, 22; of heroes: μήστωρες μάχης, ἀϋτῆς, counsellors in battle (Voss: 'exciters of battle'), 4, 328. 17, 339. 2) which occasions any thing: φόβοιο, the occasion or cause of flight, 6, 97. 12, 39; but of horses, skilled in flying (impetuous steeds, V.), 5, 272. 8, 108.

Μήστωρ, ορος, ὁ, son of Priam, 24, 257.

μήτε (τε), *and not, and that not.* μήτε —μήτε, *neither—nor,* also with τε in the second member, 13, 230. On the construc. see μή.

μήτηρ, μητέρος, ἡ, contr. μητρός, *a mother,* spoken of animals, 2, 313. 17, 4. Od. 10, 414. 2) Metaph. spoken of regions in which any thing especially flourishes: μήτηρ μήλων, θηρῶν, mother of sheep; of wild beasts, i. e. abounding in sheep, etc., Il. 2, 696. 8, 47, and elsewhere.

μήτῑ, neut. of μήτις, q. v.

μήτι, see μήτις.

μητιάω (μήτις), Ep. μητιόω, only pres. and imperf. 1) *to have in mind, to devise. to plan,* βουλάς, 20, 153; absol. 7, 45. 2) *to devise prudently, to plan, to plot,* τί, 10, 208; κακά, 15, 27. 18, 312; νόστον τινί, Od. 6, 14. Mid. *to conclude by oneself, to deliberate,* Il. 22, 174; with infin. 12, 17.

μητίετα, ὁ, Ep. for μητιέτης (μητίομαι) *counsellor, counselling* (ruling, V.), epith. of Zeus, 1, 175. Od. 14, 243, and often.

μητιόεις, εσσα, εν (μήτις), 1) *rich in counsel, wise,* h Ap. 344. 2) *wisely prepared* or *devised,* φάρμακα, Od. 4, 227.†

μητίομαι, depon. mid. (μήτις), fut. μητίσομαι, aor. 1 ἐμητῑσάμην; the pres. is not found in H.:=μητιάω, 1) *to have in mind, to deliberate upon.* Od. 9, 262. 2) *to invent. to devise, to plot,* ἔχθεα, Il. 3, 417; μέρμερα, to practise dreadful deeds, 10, 48; θάνατόν τινι, 15, 349; κακά τινα,

Od. 18, 27. (In the earlier edd. we find incorrectly μητίσσομαι)

μητίω, Ep. for μητιάω.

μῆτις, ιος, ἡ, dat. μήτῑ, Ep. for μήτι, 1) *prudence, understanding, intelligence,* the ability to counsel, often Il. and Od. 2) *counsel, advice, plan, expedient,* esply μῆτιν ὑφαίνειν, Il. 7, 324. 10, 19. Od. 4, 678.

μήτις or μή τις, neut. μήτι, gen. μήτινος (τις), *that none,* (that no) *that no one,* constr. of μή. 2) μήτι, frequently, as adv. *that not perhaps, indeed not perhaps,* 4, 42. 5, 567. Od. 2, 67.

μητροπάτωρ, ορος, ὁ, poet. (πατήρ), *a mother's father, a maternal grandfather,* 11, 224.†

μητρυιή, ἡ, *a step-mother,* °5, 389. 13, 697.

μητρώιος, ιη, ἰον. poet. for μητρῷος (μήτηρ), *maternal,* δῶμα, Od. 19, 410.†

μήτρως, ωος, ὁ (μήτηρ), *a mother's brother,* an uncle, °2, 662. 16, 717.

μηχανάομαι, depon. mid. (μηχανή), only pres. and imperf., 3 plur. imperf. μηχανόωντο, Ep. for ἐμηχανῶντο, 1) Prop. *to prepare with art, to build,* machinor, τείχεα, 8, 177. 2) *to invent, to devise, to purpose, to practise,* mly in a bad signif.: κακά, ἀτάσθαλα, to practise wickedness, 11, 695; τινί and ἐπί τινι, Od. 4, 822.

μηχανάω, Ep. μαχανόω = μηχανάομαι, from this the partcp. μηχανόωντας, Od. 18, 143.†

°μηχανιώτης, ου, ὁ, poet. for μηχανητής. machinator, one who practises cunning or prudence, *crafty,* h. Merc. 436.

μῆχος, εος, τό, poet. for μηχανή, *means, remedy, counsel,* 2, 342. οὐδέ τι μῆχός ἐστι, there is no remedy, i. e. it is impossible, 9, 249. cf. ἄκος, Od. 14, 238.

Μήων, ονος, ὁ [5, 43], see Μήονες.

μιαίνω, aor. 1 ἐμίηνα, aor. 1 pass. ἐμιάνθην, Ep. 3 plur. for ἐμιάνθησαν, 4, 146; according to Buttm. 3 dual aor. 2 sync. for ἐμιάνσθην, 1) *to stain, to colour,* ἐλέφαντα φοίνικι, 4, 141. 2) *to stain, to defile, to foul,* αἵματι, κονίησι, °16, 797. 17, 439.

μιαιφόνος, ον (μιαίνεσθαι φόνος), *defiled with slaughter, stained with slaughter, reeking with gore* [gore-tainted, Cp.], epith. of Arês, °5, 31. 455. 844. Lobeck and Buttm. read μιαίφονος from μιαίνεσθαι and φόνος, and its connexion with βροτολοιγῷ and τειχεσιπλῆτα requires an act. signif. *accustomed to stain oneself with blood* (Schol. μιαινόμενος (Mid.) φόνοις). Ameis.

μιαρός, ή, όν (μιαίνω), *stained, defiled, fouled,* 24, 420.†

μιγάζομαι, poet. for μίγνυμαι, mid. Od. 8, 271.†

μίγδα, adv. (μίγνυμι), *mixed, mingled together,* Od. 24, 77; with dat. θεοῖς, mixed among the gods, Il. 8, 437.

°μίγδην, adv. = μίγδα, h. Merc. 494.

μίγνῦμι, Ep. μίσγω, fut. μίξω, aor. 1 ἔμιξα, fut. mid. μίξομαι, Ep. aor. 2 sync.

little, for a time, mly of time, 4, 466. Od.
15, 494.

μινυνθάδιος, ον (μίνυνθα), compar. μινυνθαδιώτερος, lasting but a short time,
αἰών, 4, 778; short-lived, 1, 352. Od. 11,
307.

μινυρίζω (μινυρός), to moan, to whimper,
to lament, to wail, prop. spoken of women,
5, 889. Od. 4, 719.

*Μινώιος, ον, Ep. for Μινῷος, Minoian,
h. Ap. 393.

Μίνως, ος, ὁ, accus. Μίνωα and Μίνω
ed. Wolf, Μίνων ed. Spitzner after Aristarch., Il. 14, 322; son of Zeus and
Europa, king of Crete, famed as a wise
ruler and lawgiver, 13, 450. 451. 14, 322.
His wise laws he had received from
Zeus himself, since he had for nine years
intercourse with Zeus, Od. 19, 178. His
daughter is Ariadne and his son Deucalion, Od. 11, 321 19, 178. He also
appears in the realm of shades as ruling
king, Od. 11, 567. Later tradition alone
makes him a judge in the under world.

μισγάγκεια, ἡ (ἄγκος·, a dell, glen,
gulley, a defile, a ravine, in which the
mountain torrents meet, 4, 455.†

μίσγω, a form of μίγνυμι, q. v.

μισέω (μῖσος), aor. 1 ἐμίσησα, to hate,
to abominate, to detest. μίσησέ μιν κυσὶ
κύρμα γενέσθαι, it was an abhorrence to
him to become a prey to the dogs, Voss,
Il. 17, 272.

μισθός, ὁ, a reward, wages, hire, 10,
304. 21, 445. 450; plur., Od. 10, 84.

μιστύλλω (akin to μίτυλος), to cut in
small pieces, to cut up, spoken of carving
flesh, with accus., 1, 465. 2, 428. Od. 3,
462.

μίτος, ὁ, the cord, the thread, a single
thread introduced into the warp (πηνίον),
23. 762.† (Others understand the warp
by it. stamen. Cp. translates, 'she
tends the flax. drawing it to a thread.')

μίτρη, ἡ, a belt, a girdle, a woollen belt
worn by warriors about the abdomen,
furnished with metallic plates as a defence against missiles, and distinct from
ζωστήρ. *5, 857. 4, 137.

μιχθείς, see μίγνυμι.

μνάομαι, ground form of μιμνήσκομαι,
to remember. contr. μνῶμαι, which occurs
in the Ep. expanded forms of the pres.
and imperf. see μιμνήσκω.

μνάομαι, contr. μνῶμαι, depon. mid.
iterat. imperf μνάσκετο, to court, to woo,
to seek in marriage, with ἄκοιτιν, γυναῖκα,
θ... 1, 39. 16, 431; and absol. *Od. 16,
77. 19, 529. (Only in the pres. and imperf, sometimes in the contract and
sometimes in the expanded forms.)

ΜΝΑΩ, root of μιμνήσκω.

μνῆμα, ατος, τό (ΜΝΑΩ), a memorial,
a monument, χειρῶν, Od. 15, 126. 21, 40;
τάφον, a tomb, 23, 619.

μνημοσύνη, ἡ (μνήμων), remembrance,
memory. μνημοσύνη τις ἔπειτα πυρὸς γενέσθω, then let there be some remembrance
of the fire, 8, 181.†

*Μνημοσύνη, ἡ (Moneta, Herm.),

daughter of Uranus, mother of the Muses
by Zeus, h. Merc. 429.

μνήμων, ον, gen. ονος (μνήμη), mindful, remembering, Od. 21, 95; with gen.
φόρτου, mindful of the lading [i. e. careful
of the goods stowed in his ship], Od. 8,
163.

μνήσαι, μνησάσκετο, see μιμνήσκω.

Μνῆσος, ὁ, a noble Pæonian, 21. 210.

μνηστεύω (μνηστός), fut. μνηστεύσω,
to woo, to solicit in marriage, absol. Od.
4, 684; and with accus. γυναῖκα, a woman,
Od. 18, 276.

μνηστήρ, ῆρος, ὁ (μνάομαι), a suitor,
a wooer, often spoken of the suitors of
Penelope; the number of them, *Od.
16, 245.

μνῆστις, ιος, ἡ, poet. for μνῆμα, remembrance, memory, οὐδέ τις ἡμῖν δόρπου μ., = we thought not of supper, Od.
13, 280.†

μνηστός, ή, όν (μνάομαι), wooed, who
is won by presents, and hence a lawful
wife, always as fem. with ἄλοχος, κουριδίη,
6, 246. Od. 1. 36.

μνηστύς, ύος, ἡ, Ion. for μνηστεία, the
act of wooing, soliciting in marriage,
*Od. 2, 199. 19, 13.

μνωόμενος, μνώοντο, Ep. for μνώμενος,
ἐμνῶντο from μνάομαι, q. v.

μογέω (μόγος), aor. 1 ἐμόγησα. 1) Intrans. to weary oneself, to fatigue oneself,
to exert oneself, to suffer pain, mly as
part. with another verb, 11, 636. 12, 29.
2) Trans. with accus. to endure, to bear,
to suffer, ἄλγεα, Od. 2, 343. πολλά, Il. 23,
607. ἀέθλους, Od. 4, 170. ἐπί τινι, about
any thing, Il. 1, 162. Od. 16, 19.

μόγις, adv. (μόγος), with difficulty,
scarcely. (22, 412. ι is long in the arsis,)
9, 355. Od. 3, 119.

μόγος, ὁ, pains, labour, exertion, 4,
27.†

μογοστόκος, ον (μόγις, τίκτω), exciting
pains (dolorum creatrix, Ern.), that
causes the woman to bear with pain.
Thus according to Aristarchus. Others,
'aiding those that bring forth with difficulty,' but such paroxytones have an
active signification (cf. θεοτόκος), epith.
of Ilithyia (Eileithyia), *11, 270. 16, 187.
19, 103.

μόθος, ὁ, poet. (akin to μόγος), the tumult of battle, battle, 7, 117. 18. 159;
ἵππων, a tumult of horses, the battle-
fray of cavalry, 7, 240.

μοῖρα, ἡ (μείρομαι), 1) a part, in opposition to the whole, 10, 253. Od. 4, 97;
esply a share in any thing, Il, 15, 534;
in a repast, a portion, Od. 3, 40. 66; and
often metaph. οὐδ' αἰδοῦς μοῖραν ἔχειν,
to have no particle of shame, Od. 20, 171;
hence fitness, propriety; κατὰ μοῖραν,
suitably, properly, often with εἰπεῖν, also
ἐν μοίρῃ, (Il. 19. 186; and παρὰ μοῖραν,
contrary to propriety, Od. 15, 509. 2)
Esply the portion of life, the lot of life,
Od. 19, 192; in full, μοῖρα βιότοιο, the
measure of life, Il. 4, 175; generally, fate,
destiny, with infin. Od. 4, 475. Il 7, 52,

Μενέσθης, ους, ὁ, a Greek, slain by Hector, 5, 609.

Μενέσθιος, ὁ, 1) son of Areïthous, sovereign of Arnæ in Bœotia, slain by Paris, 7, 9. 2) son of the Spercheius, or Borus and Polydôra, a leader of the Myrmidons, 16, 173—178.

μενοεικής, ές (εἴκω), prop. gratifying the desire; hence: sufficient, plentiful, abundant, spoken of food and drink, δαίς, ἐδωδή, οἶνος, τάφος, 23, 29; also θήρη, ληίς, Od. and ὕλη, abundant wood. Il. 23, 139. 2) Generally: agreeable, pleasing, wished for, 9, 227. Od. 16, 429.

μενοινάω (μένος), Ep. μενοινώω, Ion. μενοινέω, aor. 1 ἐμενοίνησα, to have in mind, to think, to consider, to wish, to will, τί, or with infin. 10, 101. Od. 2, 36; and τινί τι, to purpose any thing against any man, κακά, Od. 11, 532. μενοίνεον (sc κέ), εἰ τελέουσιν (fut.), they considered whether they should accomplish it, Il. 12, 59. [Bth. says: deliberare et dubitare solent; but Schol. προεθυμοῦντο (not supplying κε) and so Cowper and Voss.]

μενοινώω, Ep. for μενοινάω, q. v.

Μενοιτιάδης, ου [also εω, 18, 93], ὁ, son of Menœtius=Patroclus, Il.

Μενοίτιος, ὁ, son of Actor, father of Patroclus, an Argonaut, 11, 765. 16, 14. 23, 85, seq

μένος, εος, τό (μένω), prop. perseverance in a thing, hence 1) any vehement manifestation of spirit, and particularly a) impetuosity, fierceness, rage, anger, 1, 103. 9, 679: esply warlike spirit, bravery. μένος ἀνδρῶν, 2, 387; also plur. μένεα πνείοντες, the courage-breathing, 2, 536. 11, 508; connected with θυμός, ἀλκή, θάρσος, 5, 2. 470. 9, 706. b) desire, longing, wish, purpose, 13, 634; also plur. 8, 361. 2) animation, life, vigour, since this manifests itself in ardent desires, 3, 294; hence ψυχή τε μένος τε, life and strength, 5, 296. 8, 123. 3) strength, force, power of body, as a manifestation of a resolute will: to bear strength of hands against one another, 5, 506; thus also μένος καὶ χεῖρες, 6, 502. μένος καὶ γυῖα, 6, 27. b) Of animals, 17, 20. Od. 3, 450. c) Of inanimate things: of the spear, Il. 13, 444: of the wind, 5, 524; of fire, Od. 11, 220: of the sun, Il. 23, 190; of streams, 12, 18. 4) It is often used periphrastically, as βίη, ἴς. μένος Ἀτρείδαο, 11, 268. ἱερὸν μένος Ἀλκινόοιο, the blessed strength (Nitzsch), Od. 7, 167.

Μέντης, ου, ὁ, 1) leader of the Kikónes (Ciconians), 17, 73. 2) king of the Taphians, a friend of Odysseus (Ulysses) in Ithaca, under whose form Athênê came to Telemachus, Od. 1, 105. 180.

μέντοι, Od. 4, 157, ed. Wolf; better separate, see μέν.

Μέντωρ, ορος, ὁ, 1) father of Imbrius, 13, 171. 2) son of Alcimus, an intimate friend of Odysseus (Ulysses) in Ithaca, to whom, on his departure, he entrusted his domestic affairs. Athênê assumed

his form when she accompanied Telemachus to Pylos, Od. 2, 225. 4, 654. 17, 68.

μένω, poet. μίμνω, fut. Ep. μενέω for μενώ, aor. 1 ἔμεινα, 1) Intrans. to remain, to abide; esply a) In battle: to maintain one's ground, to remain firm, with τλῆναι. b) Generally, to remain, to continue, to abide, αὖθι, αὐτόθι, 3, 291. 14, 119; with prep. ἀπό τινος, παρά τινι, etc., spoken of inanimate things: to remain standing, 17, 434. c) to wait, with accus. and infin. 4, 247. μένον δ' ἐπὶ ἕσπερον ἐλθεῖν, they waited till the evening came on. Od. 1, 422; or εἰσόκε with subj., Il. 9, 45. 2) Transit. with accus. to await, to wait for, esply spoken of an attacking enemy: to resist, to withstand, to stand against, τινά, Il.; δόρυ, Il. 13, 830; spoken of beasts and lifeless things, 13, 472. 15, 620. b) Generally, to wait for, to await, Ἠῶ, 11, 723; τινά, 20, 480. Od. 4, 847. (The perf. 2 μέμονα belongs in signif. to μέμαα, see ΜΑΩ.)

Μένων. ωνος, ὁ, a Trojan, 12, 93.

*Μεριδάρπαξ, αγος, ὁ (ἅρπαξ), Crumb-snatcher, name of a mouse in Batr. 265.

*μερίζω (μέρος), perf. pass. μεμέρισμαι, to divide, Batr. 61.

*μέριμνα, ἡ, care, solicitude, anxiety, h. Merc. 44. 160. (From μερίς, μερίζω.)

μέρμερος, ον, poet. (from μέρμηρα, Hes. poet. = μέριμνα), exciting care, causing trouble, spoken of actions: wearisome, difficult, terrible, dreadful, spoken only of warlike deeds, in the plur. μέρμερα ἔργα, 8, 453; and μέρμερα alone, *10, 48. 11, 502.

Μερμερίδης, αο, ὁ, son of Mermerus = Ilus, Od. 1, 259.

Μέρμερος, ὁ, 1) a Mysian, slain by Antilochus, 14, 513. 2) father of Ilus, Od.

μερμηρίζω (μέρμερος), aor. 1 Ep. μερμήριξα, 1) Intrans. to be anxious, to be troubled, to revolve anxiously in the mind, to ponder; esply δίχα and διάνδιχα, to be irresolute, to be doubtful, to hesitate between two courses, to delay, Od. 16, 73. Il. 1, 189. 8, 167. There follows it ὡς, 2, 3; ὅπως, 14, 159. Od. 20, 8; often ἤ—ἤ, whether—or, Il. 5, 672. 10, 503; also infin. ἐλθεῖν ἠδὲ πυθέσθαι, Od. 10, 152. 438. 24, 235; περί τινος, Il. 20, 17. 2) Trans. with accus. to devise, to plot, to resolve upon, δόλον, Od. 2, 93; πολλά, Od. 1, 427; φόνον τινί, Od. 2, 325. 19, 52.

μέρμις, ιθος, ἡ (prob. from εἴρω), a bond, a cord, a rope, Od. 20, 23.†

*μέρος, εος, τό, a part, a share. κατὰ μέρος, each in his part, h. Merc. 53.

μέροψ, οπος, ὁ (μείρομαι, ὄψ), endowed with (articulate) speech, discoursing, speaking, epith. of men, who are distinguished from brutes by uttering articulate, instead of inarticulate sounds, 1, 250. 9, 340. Od. 20, 49. (Voss, 'the speaking tribes of men,' but in h. Cer. 'many-toned,' or speaking many tongues.)

*Μέροπες, οἱ, the ancient name of the

subsequence: *after*, Il. 8, 261. 18, 96. 23, 27. μετὰ κλέος, after the news, report, 11, 227. μετὰ ταῦτα, h. Merc. 126; often with partcp. μετὰ Πάτροκλον θανόντα, 24, 575. c) Spoken of cause, manner, etc. α) To indicate the object: *for, after*, 7, 418. ἰέναι μετὰ δόρυ, to go to bring a spear, 13, 247. βῆναι μετὰ πατρὸς ἀκουήν, to go in quest of intelligence from a father, Od. 2, 308. β) To indicate suitableness: *according to, after*. μετὰ σὸν κῆρ, Il. 15, 52. Od. 8, 583. II) Adv. without cases, 1) *together, moreover, besides*, 2, 446. 2) *behind, hereafter*, of space and of time, 23, 133. Od. 15, 400. Frequently it is separated from the verb by tmesis. III) In composition, it has, in addition to the definitions already given, this, that it indicates a change from one condition to another.

μέτα, with anastrophe for μετά, 1) When it follows the subst. 13, 308. 2) For μέτεστι, Od. 21, 93.

μεταβαίνω (βαίνω), μεταβήσομαι, aor. μετέβην, perf. μεταβέβηκα, to go elsewhere, to go over. 1) Spoken of the stars: μετὰ δ᾽ ἄστρα βεβήκει, the stars had gone over, viz. *had traversed the mid sky* (Cp.), Od. 12, 312. 14, 483. 2) Spoken of singers: *to go over* from one subject to another, to proceed, *Od. 8, 492; with ἔς τι, h. 8, 9.

μεταβάλλω (βάλλω), aor. 2 μεταβαλών only in tmesis, to *cast around*, hence to *turn around*; νῶτα, to turn the backs (in flight), 8, 94.†

μεταβουλεύω (βουλεύω), to change a resolution, to alter one's mind, μετεβούλευσαν, Od. 5, 286.†

μετάγγελος, ὁ (ἄγγελος), one who bears intelligence from one to another, *a messenger* [internuncius], *15, 144. 23, 199. In 15, 144, Wolf reads μετ᾽ ἄγγελος.

μεταδαίνυμαι, mid. (δαίνυμαι), fut. μεταδαίσομαι, *to eat with, to feast with*; ἱρῶν, to participate in the sacrificial feast, 23, 207; τινί, with any one, 22, 498. Od. 18, 48.

μεταδήμιος, η, ον (δῆμος), *existing amongst the people*. κακὸν μεταδήμιον, evil amongst the people, Od. 13, 46; spoken of an individual: *domestic, native*, at home, *Od. 8, 293.

μεταδόρπιος, ον (δόρπον), *in the midst of or during supper*, Od. 4, 194.†

μεταδρομάδην, adv. *running after, pursuing*, 5, 80.†

μεταίζω, poet. for μεθίζω (ἵζω), to *seat oneself with*, Od. 16, 362.†

μεταίσσω (ἀΐσσω), partcp. aor. μεταΐξας, to *leap after, to pursue, to rush after*, only absol. in the partcp. aor. 15, 398. Od. 17, 236.

μετακιάθω, Ep. (κιάθω), only imperf. μετεκίαθον, 1) *to go after*, 11, 52; in a hostile signif. *to pursue*, τινά, 16, 685. 18, 581. 2) *to go to some other place, to visit*; τινά, any man, Od. 1, 22; πεδίον, to reach the plain, Il. 11, 714.

μετακλαίω, to *weep after, to deplore*, 11, 764.†

μετακλίνω (κλίνω), aor. pass. μετεκλίνθην, to *bend to another quarter*. πολέμοιο μετακλινθέντος, when the battle has turned, i. e. is yielding, 11, 509.†

μεταλήγω (λήγω), Ep. aor. 1 optat. μεταλλήξειε, partcp. μεταλλήξας, *to cease, to desist from*; with gen. χόλοιο, from anger, *9, 157. 261. h. Cer. 340.

μεταλλάω (μετ᾽ ἄλλα), aor. 1 μετάλλησα, prop. to search after other things, hence 1) *to search after, to seek after, to inform oneself about*, with accus. τινά or τί, 10, 125. Od. 3, 243. 2) to *inquire for, to ask after*; τινά, any man, and τινά τι, to ask a man about any thing, Il. 3, 177. Od. 1, 231; also ἀμφί τινι, Od. 17, 554. [Herm. Op. vii. 141, is dissatisfied with Buttmann's explanation, Lex. 412.]

μεταλλήγω Ep. for μεταλήγω.

μετάλμενος, partcp. aor. 2 from μεθάλλομαι.

μεταμάζιος, ον (μαζός), *between the breasts*; στῆθος, the middle of the breast, 5, 19.†

*μεταμέλπομαι, mid. (μέλπω), to *sing or dance amongst*, with dat. h. Ap. 197.

μεταμίγνυμι (μίγνυμι), Ep. μεταμίσγω, fut. μεταμίξω, to *mix with, to mingle amongst*, τί, Od. 18, 310; τινί τι, *Od. 22, 221.

μεταμώλιος, ον = μεταμώνιος.

μεταμώνιος, ον, poet. (ἄνεμος), prop. with the wind, i. e. *idle, vain, profitless*, νήματα, Od. 2, 98. πάντα μεταμώνια τιθέναι, to render all vain, Il. 4, 363; μεταμώνια βάζειν, to prate idly, Od. 18, 332. (Wolf has μεταμώνιος for μεταμώλιος, after the best MSS.)

μετανάστης, ου, ὁ (ναίω), one who goes from one place to another, *a stranger, a settler, a new-comer*, *9, 648. 16, 59.

Μετάνειρα, ἡ, wife of Celeüs, mother of Demophon, h. Cer. 161. 206.

μετανίσσομαι, poet. (νίσσομαι), to *go over, to go to the other side*, spoken of Helios: μετενίσσετο βουλυτόνδε, Helios went to the unyoking of oxen, i. e. descended to his setting, 16, 779. Od. 9, 58.

*μετάνοια, ἡ (νοέω), *a change of mind, repentance*, Batr. 10.

μεταξύ, adv. (μετά), *in the midst*, 1, 156.†

μεταπαύομαι, mid. (παύω), to *cease in the midst, to take rest*, 17, 373.†

μεταπαυσωλή, ἡ (παύω), *intermediate rest, refreshment*, πολέμοιο, 19, 201. According to Heyne and Nägelsb. ad Il. 2, 386, to be written μετὰ παυσωλή.

μεταπρεπής, ές, poet. (πρέπω), *distinguished amongst*; with dat. ἀθανάτοισιν, amongst immortals, 18, 370.†

μεταπρέπω, poet. (πρέπω), to *distinguish oneself, to be eminent amongst*; with dat. of pers. ἡρώεσσιν, amongst the heroes, Il. and Od.; with dat. of the thing, γαστέρι, Od. 18, 2. b) With double dat.

μετρέω (μέτρον). aor. I ἐμέτρησα, *to measure*; hence poet. πέλαγος, to measure the sea, i. e. to navigate, to sail over, Od. 3, 179.†

μέτρον, τό, *a measure*. 1) the instrument for measuring, *a measure*, 12, 422. 2) Esply a measuring vessel for liquids and dry goods, οἴνου, 7, 471. 23, 268. ἀλφίτου, Od. 2, 355. (How much it held is not known.) 3) *that which is measured*, i. e. *space*, *length*, μέτρα κελεύθου, Od. 4, 389. 10, 539. ὅρμου μέτρον ἱκέσθαι, the space of the harbour, Od. 13, 101; metaph. μέτρον ἥβης, the full measure of youth, i. e. the bloom of life, Il. 11, 225. Od. 11, 317.

μετώπιον, τό = μέτωπον, *the forehead*, 11, 95. 16, 739; prop. neut. of the adj. μετώπιος.

μέτωπον, τό (ὤψ), *the forehead*, mly of men, plur., Od. 6, 107; once of a horse, Il. 23, 454. 2) Metaph. *the front*, *the fore-part*, κόρυθος, 16, 70.

μεῦ, Ion. for μοῦ, see ἐγώ.

μέχρι, poet. before vowel μέχρις. prep. with gen. *until*, *as far as*. 1) Spoken of place: θαλάσσης, 13. 143. 2) Of time: τέο μέχρις; till when, how long? 24, 128.

μή, adv. and conj. *not*, *that not*. 1) Adv. μή, *not*; it never denies independently and directly (cf. οὐ), but always indirectly, and in reference to a preced. representation. It is found, therefore, only in a really dependent denial, or in one conceived of as dependent: and esply in such main and subordinate clauses as express a wish, will, command, a case or condition, a fear or anxiety. (The same holds true of the compounds: μηδέ, μηδείς, etc.) A) In main clauses: 1) In such as express a command, the act of forbidding or warning, where mly the imperat. pres. stands, 1. 32. 363; or instead of it the infin., 7, 413. 17, 501; or the subj. aor. μὴ δή με ἕλωρ ἐάσῃς κεῖσθαι, do not, do not let me lie as a prey [hoc tantum te rogo … se], 5, 684; often with an implied threat, μή σε παρὰ νηυσὶ κιχείω, let me not meet thee at the ships, 1, 26. 21. 563. Rare and mly Ep. is the imperat. aor. 4, 410. Od. 16, 301; and the fut., 15. 115. 2) In sentences expressing a wish, either with the optat. or the indic. histor. tenses: μὴ τοῦτο φίλον Διὶ πατρὶ γένοιτο! may this not please father Zeus! Od. 7. 316. μὴ ὄφελες λίσσεσθαι, would that thou hadst not supplicated, Il. 9, 698. 22, 481; also with infin. μὴ πρὶν ἐπ' ἠέλιον δῦναι. 2, 413. 3) In sentences which contain an exhortation with the subj. μὴ ἴομεν ὕδωρ, let us not go, Il. and Od. 4) In oaths, sometimes instead of the direct negative οὐ, Il. 10, 330. B) In subordinate clauses: 1) In all clauses expressing design or a condition; therefore with the conjunct. ἵνα, ὡς, ὅπως, ὄφρα, εἰ, ἤν, etc. On the construct. see these conjunct. (οὐ stands only when

the negation is limited to a single word, 24, 296.) 2) With intin. only in dependent discourse in H.: ὄμνυθι, μὴ μὲν ἑκὼν τὸ ἐμὸν δόλῳ ἅρμα πεδῆσαι, swear to me, that thou didst not wittingly by craft obstruct my chariot, 23, 585. cf. 19, 261. II) Conjunct. *that not*: 1) After the primary tenses or an aor. with pres. signif. with subjunct., 1, 522. 17, 17; after a historical tense with optat., 10, 468. 2) After verbs to fear, to avoid, to beware, to prevent, etc., μή like the Lat. *ne* signifies *that*: δείδω μὴ τὸ χθιζὸν ἀποστήσωνται Ἀχαιοὶ χρέος, I fear that the Greeks will pay yesterday's debt, 13, 745. cf. 1, 553. 14, 261; after ἰδεῖν, to take heed, 10, 98. Such clauses with μή are often elliptical, so that δέδοικα or φοβοῦμαι must be supplied before them (cf. Α 1), μήτι χολωσάμενος ῥέξῃ κακὸν υἷας Ἀχαιῶν, that in anger he may inflict some evil upon the sons of the Achaians, 2, 195. 5, 487. 17, 93. b) If οὐ is added, it is thereby shown that the apprehended event will not ensue. μή νύ τοι οὐ χραίσμῃ, lest haply it should avail thee nothing, 1, 28. μὴ οὔτις, 10, 39. μή with indicat., Od. 5, 300, is to be taken as an interrogative particle. III) An interrogative particle: μή as such stands, 1) In a direct question, when a negative answer is expected: ἦ μή πού τινα δυσμενέων φάσθ᾽ ἔμμεναι ἀνδρῶν, you did not surely suppose it to be one of the enemy, Od. 6, 200. cf. Od. 9, 405. 2) In an indirect question; *whether not*, after ἰδεῖν, φράζεσθαι, mly with subjunct. and optat., Il. 10, 98. 101. 15, 164. Od. 24, 291; rarely with the indicat. when a man is convinced that the apprehended act will happen or is true: δείδω, μὴ δὴ πάντα θεὰ νημερτέα εἶπεν, I have my fears whether the goddess did not speak all things truly, Od. 5, 300.

μηδέ, adv. connects two clauses, prop. adversatively: *but not*, 4, 302. 10, 37. mly merely annexing: *also not*, *and not*, 2, 260. Od. 4, 752. 2) *also not*, *not even*, and repeated for the sake of emphasis, 6, 38. 10, 239. 2) Doubled μηδέ, μηδέ, *neither*, *nor*, 4, 303.

Μηδείδης, ου, ὁ, h. Bacch. 6, 43. ed. Wolf, after the conjec. of Barnes for μὴ δείδειν, the name of a pilot. Herm. amends: νῇ᾽ ἤδη, which Frank has adopted.

μηδείς, μηδεμία. μηδέν (μηδέ and εἷς), *no one*, *none*, in H. μηδέν, 18, 500.†

Μηδεσικάστη, ἡ (adorned with wisdom), daughter of Priam, wife of Imbrius, 13, 173.

μήδομαι, depon. mid. (μῆδος), fut. μήσομαι, aor. ἐμησάμην, *to have in mind*, like *parare*, not merely to devise, but also to execute: hence, 1) Absol. *to devise*, *counsel*, 2, 360. 2) *to devise*, *to plot*, *to prepare*, τί, Od. 5, 173. νόστον, Od. 3, 160. κακά, Od. 3, 166. τί τινι, Od. 5, 189. κακά τινι, Il. 6, 157. 7, 478. ὄλεθρόν τινι, Od. 3, 249. 9, 92; also with

They were then covered with pieces of flesh from the other parts, enveloped with a doubled covering of caul, and thus burnt as a sacrifice to the gods, Il. 1, 460. Od. 3, 456; hence often πίονα μηρία, 1, 40; thus Nitzsch ad Od. 3, 456. Voss, Myth. Brief. I. 39, explains μηρία as the *hip-bones*, with the flesh belonging to them.

Μηριόνης, ους, ὁ, son of Molus of Crete, charioteer of Idomeneus, 2, 651. 7, 166.

μηρός, ὁ, the upper fleshy part of the hip. *the thigh*, spoken of men, 5, 305. 12, 162. ἄορ ἐρύσασθαι παρὰ μηροῦ, to draw the sword from the thigh, Il. 2) Spoken of beasts, only in the connexion, μηροὺς ἐξέταμον, *seu* μηρίον, 1, 460. Od. 12. 360.

μηρύομαι, depon. mid. aor. Ep. μηρύσάμην, *to draw in, to take in, to furl,* ἱστία, Od. 12, 170.†

μήστωρ, ωρος, ὁ (μήδομαι), 1) *an adviser, a counsellor*, spoken of Zeus (governor of the world, V.), 8, 22; of heroes: μήστωρες μάχης, ἀϋτῆς, counsellors in battle (Voss: 'exciters of battle'), 4, 328. 17, 339. 2) which occasions any thing: φόβοιο, the occasion or cause of flight, 6, 97. 12, 39; but of horses, skilled in flying (impetuous steeds, V.), 5, 272. 8, 108.

Μήστωρ, ορος, ὁ, son of Priam, 24, 257.

μήτε (τε), *and not, and that not.* μήτε—μήτε, *neither—nor*, also with τε in the second member, 13, 230. On the construc. see μή.

μήτηρ, μητέρος, ἡ, contr. μητρός, *a mother*, spoken of animals, 2, 313. 17, 4. Od. 10, 414. 2) Metaph. spoken of regions in which any thing especially flourishes: μήτηρ μήλων, θηρῶν, mother of sheep; of wild beasts, i. e. abounding in sheep, etc., Il. 2, 696. 8, 47, and elsewhere.

μήτι, neut. of μήτις, q. v.

μήτι. see μήτις.

μητιάω (μῆτις), Ep. μητιόω, only pres. and imperf. 1) *to have in mind, to devise, to plan,* βουλάς, 20, 153; absol. 7, 45. 2) *to devise prudently, to plan,* to p ot, τι, 10, 208; κακά, 15, 27. 18, 312; νοστον τινί, Od. 6, 14. Mid. *to conclude by oneself, to deliberate,* Il. 22, 174; with infin. 12, 17.

μητίετα, ὁ, Ep. for μητιέτης (μητιόωαι). *counsellor, counselling* (ruling, V.). epith. of Zeus, 1, 175. Od. 14, 243, and often.

μητιόεις, εσσα, εν (μῆτις), 1) *rich in counsel, wise,* h Ap. 344. 2) *wisely prepared* or *devised*, φάρμακα, Od. 4, 227.†

μητίομαι, depon. mid. (μῆτις), fut. μητίσομαι, aor. 1 ἐμητῑσάμην; the pres. is not found in H. :=μητιάω, 1) *to have in mind, to deliberate upon.* Od. 9, 262. 2) *to invent. to devise, to plot,* ἔχθεα, Il. 3, 417; μέρμερα, to practise dreadful deeds, 10, 48; θανατόν τινι, 15, 349; κακά τινα,

Od. 18, 27. (In the earlier edd. we find incorrectly μητίσσομαι)

μητίω, Ep. for μητιάω.

μῆτις, ιος, ἡ, dat. μήτῑ, Ep. for μήτῑι, 1) *prudence, understanding, intelligence,* the ability to counsel, often Il. and Od. 2) *counsel, advice, plan, expedient,* esply μῆτιν ὑφαίνειν, Il. 7, 324. 10, 19. Od. 4, 678.

μήτις or μή τις, neut. μήτι, gen. μήτινος (τὶς), *that none,* (that no) *that no one,* constr. of μή. 2) μήτι, frequently, as adv. *that not perhaps, indeed not perhaps,* 4, 42. 5, 567. Od. 2, 67.

μητροπάτωρ, ορος, ὁ, poet. (πατήρ), *a mother's father, a maternal grandfather,* 11, 224.†

μητρυιή, ἡ, *a step-mother,* *5, 389. 13, 697.

μητρώϊος, ίη, ίον. poet. for μητρῷος (μήτηρ). *maternal.* δῶμα, Od. 19, 410.†

μήτρως, ωος, ὁ (μήτηρ), *a mother's brother,* an uncle, *2, 662. 16, 717.

μηχανάομαι, depon. mid. (μηχανή). only pres. and imperf., 3 plur. imperf. μηχανόωντο, Ep. for ἐμηχανῶντο, 1) Prop. *to prepare with art, to build,* machinor, τείχεα, 8, 177. 2) *to invent, to devise, to purpose, to practise,* mly in a bad signif.: κακά, ἀτάσθαλα, to practise wickedness, 11, 695; τινί and ἐπί τινι, Od. 4, 822.

μηχανάω, Ep. μαχανόω = μηχανάομαι, from this the partcp. μηχανόωντας, Od. 18, 143.†

*μηχανιώτης, ου, ὁ, poet. for μηχανητής. machinator, one who practises cunning or prudence, *crafty*, h. Merc. 436.

μῆχος, εος, τό, poet. for μηχανή, *means, remedy, counsel,* 2, 342. οὐδέ τι μῆχός ἐστι, there is no remedy, i. e. it is impossible, 9, 249. cf. ἄκος, Od. 14, 238.

Μήων, ονος, ὁ [5, 43], see Μήονες.

μιαίνω, aor. 1 ἐμίηνα, aor. 1 pass. ἐμιάνθην, Ep. 3 plur. for ἐμιάνθησαν, 4, 146; according to Buttm. 3 dual aor. 2 sync. for ἐμιάνθην, 1) *to stain, to colour,* ἐλέφαντα φοίνικι, 4, 141. 2) *to stain, to defile, to foul,* αἵματι, κονίῃσι, *16, 797. 17, 439.

μιαιφόνος, ον (μιαίνεσθαι φόνος), *defiled with slaughter, stained with slaughter, reeking with gore* (gore-tainted, Cp.), epith. of Ares, *5, 31. 455. 844. Lobeck and Buttm. read μιαίφονος from μιαίνεσθαι and φόνος, and its connexion with βροτολοιγέ and τειχεσιπλήτα requires an act. signif. *accustomed to stain oneself with blood* (Schol. μιαινόμενος (Mid.) φόνοις). Ameis.

μιαρός, ή, όν (μιαίνω), *stained, defiled, fouled,* 24, 420.†

μιγάζομαι, poet. for μίγνυμαι, mid. Od. 8, 271.†

μίγδα, adv. (μίγνυμι), *mixed, mingled together,* Od. 24, 77; with dat. θεοῖς, mixed among the gods, Il. 8, 437.

*μίγδην, adv. = μίγδα, h. Merc. 494.

μίγνυμι, Ep. μίσγω, fut. μίξω, aor. 1 ἔμιξα, fut. mid. μίξομαι, Ep. aor. 2 sync.

little, for a time, mly of time, 4, 466. Od. 15, 494.

μινυνθάδιος, ον (μίνυνθα), compar. μινυνθαδιώτερος, lasting but a short time, αἰών, 4, 778; short-lived, 1, 352. Od. 11, 307.

μινυρίζω (μινυρός), to moan, to whimper, to lament, to wail, prop. spoken of women, 5, 889. Od. 4, 719.

*Μινώϊος, ον, Ep. for Μινῷος, Minoian, h. Ap. 393.

Μίνως, ος, ὁ, accus. Μίνωα and Μίνω ed. Wolf, Μίνων ed. Spitzner after Aristarch., Il. 14, 322; son of Zeus and Europa, king of Crete, famed as a wise ruler and lawgiver, 13, 450. 451. 14, 322. His wise laws he had received from Zeus himself, since he had for nine years intercourse with Zeus, Od. 19, 178. His daughter is Ariadne and his son Deucalion, Od. 11, 321. 19, 178. He also appears in the realm of shades as ruling king, Od. 11, 567. Later tradition alone makes him a judge in the under world.

μισγάγκεια, ἡ (ἄγκος), a dell, glen, gulley, a defile, a ravine, in which the mountain torrents meet, 4, 455.†

μίσγω, a form of μίγνυμι, q. v.

μισέω (μῖσος), aor. 1 ἐμίσησα, to hate, to abominate, to detest. μίσησέ μιν κυσὶ κύρμα γενέσθαι, it was an abhorrence to him to become a prey to the dogs, Voss, Il. 17, 272.

μισθός, ὁ, a reward, wages, hire, 10, 304. 21, 445. 450; plur., Od. 10, 84.

μιστύλλω (akin to μίτυλος), to cut in small pieces, to cut up, spoken of carving flesh, with accus., 1, 465. 2, 428. Od. 3, 462.

μίτος, ὁ, the cord, the thread, a single thread introduced into the warp (πηνίον), 23, 762.† (Others understand the warp by it, stamen. Cp. translates, 'she tends the flax, drawing it to a thread.')

μίτρη, ἡ, a belt, a girdle, a woollen belt worn by warriors about the abdomen, furnished with metallic plates as a defence against missiles, and distinct from ζωστήρ, *5, 857. 4, 137.

μιχθείς, see μίγνυμι.

μνάομαι, ground form of μι-μνήσκομαι, to remember. contr. μνῶμαι, which occurs in the Ep. expanded forms of the pres. and imperf. see μιμνήσκω.

μνάομαι, contr. μνῶμαι, depon. mid. iterat. imperf. μνάσκετο, to court, to woo, to seek in marriage, with ἄκοιτιν, γυναῖκα, Od. 1, 39. 16, 431; and absol. *Od. 16, 77. 19, 529. (Only in the pres. and imperf sometimes in the contract and sometimes in the expanded forms.)

ΜΝΑΩ, root of μιμνήσκω.

μνῆμα, ατος, τό (ΜΝΑΩ), a memorial, a monument, χειρῶν, Od. 15, 126. 21, 40; τάφον, a tomb, 23, 619.

μνημοσύνη, ἡ (μνήμων), remembrance, memory. μνημοσύνη τις ἔπειτα πυρὸς γενέσθω, then let there be some remembrance of the fire, 8, 181.†

*Μνημοσύνη, ἡ (Moneta, Herm.),

daughter of Uranus, mother of the Muses by Zeus, h. Merc. 429.

μνήμων, ον, gen. ονος (μνήμη), mindful, remembering, Od. 21, 95; with gen. φόρτου, mindful of the lading [i. e. careful of the goods stowed in his ship], Od. 8, 163.

μνῆσαι, μνησάσκετο, see μιμνήσκω.

Μνῆσος, ὁ, a noble Pæonian, 21. 210.

μνηστεύω (μνηστός), fut. μνηστεύσω, to woo, to solicit in marriage, absol. Od. 4, 684; and with accus. γυναῖκα, a woman, Od. 18, 276.

μνηστήρ, ῆρος, ὁ (μνάομαι), a suitor, a wooer, often spoken of the suitors of Penelope; the number of them, *Od. 16, 245.

μνῆστις, ιος, ἡ, poet. for μνῆμα, remembrance, memory, οὐδέ τις ἡμῖν δόρπου μ., = we thought not of supper, Od. 13, 280.†

μνηστός, ή, όν (μνάομαι), wooed, who is won by presents, and hence a lawful wife, always as fem. with ἄλοχος, κουριδίη, 6, 246. Od. 1. 36.

μνηστύς, ύος, ἡ, Ion. for μνηστεία, the act of wooing, soliciting in marriage, *Od. 2, 199. 19, 13.

μνώμενος, μνώοντο, Ep. for μνώμενος, ἐμνῶντο from μνάομαι, q. v.

μογέω (μόγος), aor. 1 ἐμόγησα. 1) Intrans. to weary oneself, to fatigue oneself, to exert oneself, to suffer pain, mly as part. with another verb, 11, 636. 12, 29. 2) Trans. with accus. to endure, to bear, to suffer, ἄλγεα, Od. 2, 843. πολλά, Il. 23, 607. ἀέθλους, Od. 4, 170. ἐπί τινι, about any thing, Il. 1, 162. Od. 16, 19.

μόγις, adv. (μόγος), with difficulty, scarcely. (22, 412. ι is long in the arsis,) 9, 355. Od. 3, 119.

μόγος, ὁ, pains, labour, exertion, 4, 27.†

μογοστόκος, ον (μόγις, τίκτω), exciting pains (dolorum creatrix, Ern.), that causes the woman to bear with pain. Thus according to Aristarchus. Others, 'aiding those that bring forth with difficulty,' but such paroxytones have an active signification (cf. θεοτόκος), epith. of Ilithyia (Eileithyia), *11, 270. 16, 187. 19, 103.

μόθος, ὁ, poet. (akin to μόγος), the tumult of battle, battle, 7, 117. 18, 159; ἵππων, a tumult of horses, the battle-fray of cavalry, 7, 240.

μοῖρα, ἡ (μείρομαι), 1) a part, in opposition to the whole, 10, 253. Od. 4, 97; esply a share in any thing, Od. 11, 534; in a repast, a portion, Od. 3, 40. 66; and often metaph. οὐδ' αἰδοῦς μοῖραν ἔχειν, to have no particle of shame, Od. 20, 171; hence fitness, propriety; κατὰ μοῖραν, suitably, properly, often with εἰπεῖν, also ἐν μοίρῃ, Il. 19. 186; and παρὰ μοῖραν, contrary to propriety, Od. 15, 509. 2) Esply the portion of life, the lot of life, Od. 19, 192; in full, μοῖρα βιότοιο, the measure of life, Il. 4, 175; generally, fate, destiny, with infin. Od. 4, 475. Il. 7. 52,

μοχθέω (μόχθος), fut. ήσω, like μογέω, to take pains, to trouble oneself, to be distressed, κήδεσιν, 10, 106.†

μοχθίζω=μοχθέω, to suffer, to be sick, έλκεϊ, with a wound, 2, 723.†

μοχλέω (μοχλός), to move with levers; στήλας, to turn over the pillars, 12, 259.†

μοχλός, ὁ, 1) a lever, Od. 5, 261. 2) any long, strong stake, *Od. 9, 332.

Μυγδών, όνος, ὁ, king of Phrygia, in whose time the Amazons attacked Phrygia, 3, 186.

μυδαλέος, η, ον (μυδάω), wet through, moist, damp; αἵματι, sprinkled with blood, 11, 54.†

Μύδων, ωνος, ὁ (appell. μυδών), 1) son of Atymnius, charioteer of Pylæmenes, a Trojan, slain by Antilochus, 5, 580. 2) a Trojan slain by Achilles, 21, 209.

μυελόεις, εσσα, εν (μυελός), full of marrow, μurrowy, ὀστέα, Od. 9, 293.†

μυελός, ὁ, marrow, 20, 482; metaph. μυελὸς ἀνδρῶν, the marrow of men, spoken of nourishing food, Od. 2, 291. 20, 108.

μυθέομαι, depon. mid. (μῦθος), fut. μυθήσομαι, aor. 1 ἐμυθησάμην, Ep. form 2 sing. μυθέαι and μυθεῖαι, Ep. iterat. imperf. μυθέσκοντο, 1) to discourse, to speak, to tell, absol. and with accus. and infin. 21, 462. 2) Trans. to tell, to narrate, to call, τινί τι, 11, 201. πάντα κατὰ θυμόν, to speak every thing according to cne's mind [agreeably to me], 9, 645. ἀληθέα, νημερτέα, 6, 376. 382. ἐναίσιμα, Od. 2, 159. πόλιν πολύχρυσον, to call the city rich in gold, Il. 18, 289. ποτὶ ὃν θυμόν, to speak to a man's heart, i. e. to consider, 17, 200. Od. 5, 285; hence to counsel, Od. 13, 191. [3) to explain, to indicate, to interpret, Il. 1, 74.]

μυθολογεύω, fut. σω, to relate, to tell, τί τινι, *Od. 12, 450. 453.

μῦθος, ὁ, 1 discourse, word, as opposed to ἔργον 9, 443. Od. 4, 777; in special applications: a) a public discourse, Od. 1, 358. b) narration, conversation. μῦθος παιδός, the narration of the son, Od. 11, 492. 2, 314. 4, 324. c) 'bidding, command, commission, counsel, Il. 2, 282. 5, 493. 7, 358. 2) a resolve, plan, project, since it is presented in words, undertaking, 14, 127. Od. 3, 140. 22, 288. 3) Od 21, 70, 71 is explained as Æol. for μόθος, noise, confusion, but unnecessarily: it signifies project, purpose, as no. 2. οὐδέ τιν' ἄλλην μύθου ποιήσασθαι ἐπισχεσίην ἐδύνασθε, you could not make any pretext for your undertaking, Voss.

μυῖα, ἡ, a fly, an image of unblushing impudence. a) a house-fly, 4, 131. b) a squito, 2, 469. 17, 570. c) a carrion-fly, 19, 25.

Μυκάλη, ἡ, a mountain in Ionia (Asia Minor), opposite Samos, which formed promontory; also called Trogilium, 2, 869.

Μυκαλησός, ἡ (Μυκαλησσός, Herm. h.

Ap. 224), a city in Bœotia, near Tanagra, 2, 498.

μυκάομαι, depon. (μύ), aor. ἔμυκον, perf. μέμυκα, 1) to bellow, spoken of cattle, Od. 10, 413. Il. 18, 580. 2) to crack, to rattle, to buzz, to roar, spoken of doors and of a spear, 5, 749. 20, 260; of a river, 12, 460. 21, 237.

μύκηθμός, ὁ, bellowing, roaring, 18, 575. Od. 12, 265.

Μυκήνη, ἡ, 1) daughter of Inachus, wife of Arestor, who gave name to the city Mycēne, Od. 2, 120. 2) Plur. Μυκῆναι, Mycēnæ, a town in Argolis, the residence of Agamemnon, at the time of the Trojan war famous esply for the treasury of Atreus, and by the Cyclopean walls; its ruins are near the village Krabata; plur. 2, 569; sing. 4, 52. From this 1) adv. Μυκήνηθεν, from Mycēnæ. 2) Μυκηναῖος, η, ον, Mycenian, 15, 638.

μύκον, see μυκάομαι.

μύλαξ, ακος, ὁ (μύλη), prop. a millstone; and generally, any large stone, 12, 161.†

μύλη, ἡ (μύλλω), a mill, *Od. 7, 104. 20, 106. The mills of the ancients were hand-mills, which were turned by maids; or rather mortars, in which the grain was broken.

μυλήφατος, ον (πέφαμαι), broken or ground in a mill, Od. 2, 355.†

μυλοειδής, ές (εἶδος), similar to a millstone, πέτρος, 7, 270.† Batr. 217.

μύνη, ἡ (akin to ἀμύνω), a pretext, an excuse, a tarrying, plur. Od. 21, 111.†

Μύνης, ητος, ὁ, son of Evenus, husband of Briseis, ruler in Lyrnessus, 2, 692. 19, 296.

*μυοκτόνος, ον (κτείνω), mouse-slaying, μυοκτ. τρόπαιον, a trophy on account of the slaughter of the mice, Batr. 159.

μυρίκη, ἡ, a tamarisk, according to Miquels, Hom. Flora. p. 39, the French tamarisk, tamarix Gallica, a shrub common in southern marshy regions, *10, 466. h. Merc. 81. (ῑ in the arsis, 21, 350.)

μυρίκινος, η, ον, of the tamarisk; ὄζος, a tamarisk branch, 6, 39.†

Μυρίνη, ἡ, daughter of Teucer, wife of Dardanus, according to Strab. an Amazon, who lay buried here. The tradition of the Pelasgians called a mound the monument of Myrina, which the men of that day called thorn-hill, 2, 814; see Βατίεια.

μυρίος, η, ον, very much, infinite, innumerable. μυρίον χέραδος, immense rubbish, 21, 320; frequently in the plur. 1, 2. 12, 326. 2) infinitely great, illimitable, a thousand-fold, ἄχος, 20, 282; ὄνος, Od. 15, 452; often plur. ἄλγεα, κήδεα (μυρίοι, countless; but μύριοι, ten thousand, according to the Gramm.).

Μυρμιδόνες, οἱ, sing. Μυρμιδών, όνος, the Myrmidons, an Achaian race in Thessaly, Phthiōtis, under the dominion of Achilles, whose chief towns were Phthia

ναύλοχος, ον (ΛΕΧΩ), *offording a secure enchorage, a convenient station for ships;* λιμήν (Cp. *a commodious haven;* Voss, 'a ship-protecting harbour'), *Od. 4, 846. 10, 141.

ναύμαχος, ον (μάχη), *employed in naval battles,* ξυστά [*naval poles . . . for conflict maritime prepared,* Cp.], *15, 389. 677.

Ναυσίθοος, ὁ (ship-swift), son of Poseidôn and Periboea, father of Alcinous and Rhexênor, sovereign of the Phæaces in their new abode at Scheria, Od. 7, 56, seq. cf. 6, 7—11.

Ναυσικάα, ἡ, the beautiful daughter of the Phæacian sovereign Alcinous in Scheria, who conducted the ship-wrecked Odysseus (Ulysses) to the house of her father, Od. 6, 17, seq.

ναυσικλειτός, ή, όν (κλειτός), poet. *renowned in naval affairs,* Od. 6, 22.† Εὔβοια, h. Ap. 31. 219.

ναυσικλυτός, ή, όν (κλυτός). =ναυσικλειτός, epith. of Phæaces, Od. 7, 39; of the Phœnicians, *Od. 15, 415.

Ναυτεύς, ῆος, ὁ (= ναύτης), a noble Phæacian, Od. 8, 112.

ναύτης, ου, ὁ (ναῦς), *a sailor, a seaman, a mariner,* 4, 76. Od. 1, 171.

ναυτιλίη, ἡ (ναυτίλος), *navigation,* Od. 8, 253.†

ναυτίλλομαι, depon. only pres. and imperf. *to navigate, to go by ship,* *Od. 4, 672. 14. 246.

ναῦφι, ναῦφιν, Ep. see νηῦς.

νάω and ναίω, Ep. only pres. and imperf. ναῖον, *to flow,* κρήνη νάει, Od. 6. 292. κρῆναι νάουσι, Il. 21, 197. ναῖον ὀρῷ ἄγγεα, the vessels flowed with whey, Od. 9, 222. (ā, Od. 6, 292. ă, Il. 21, 197.) 2) Root of ναίω.

Νέαιρα, ἡ (the younger), a nymph, who bore to Helios Lampetiê and Phaetûsa, Od. 12, 133.

νεαρός, ή, όν (νέος), *young, tender,* παῖδες, 8, 289.†

νέατος, η. ον, Ep. νείατος (prob. old superl. of νέος), always in the Ep. form, except 9, 153. 295. 11, 712; *the last, the extreme, the lowest,* always spoken of place: τοῦς, ἀνθερεών, κενεών, Il. 5) With gen. νείατος ἄλλων, the lowest of them all, Il. 6, 295. πόλις νεάτη Πύλου, the last city of Pylos, 11, 712; and plur νέαται Πύλου (not for νενέαται from ναίω), 9, 153.

νεβρός, ὁ (akin to νεαρός), the young of the stags, *a fawn,* also *a deer,* 4, 243. Od. 4. 336.

νέες, νέεσσι, see νηῦς.

νέηαι, Ep. for νέῃ, see νέομαι.

νεηγενής, ές, Ep. for νεαγ. (γένος), *new-born,* *Od. 4. 336. 17, 127.

νεήκης, ες, Ep. for νεάκ. (ἀκή), *newly-sharpened, whetted,* πέλεκυς [*a new-edged axe,* Cp.], *13, 391. 16, 484.

νήλυς. υδος, ὁ, ἡ (ἤλυθον), *newly* or *just arrived,* *10. 434. 558.

νεηνίης, ου, ὁ, Ep. for νεανίας (νέος), *young, young, juvenile,* always as adj. ἀνήρ, *Od. 10, 278. 14, 524. h. 7, 3.

νεῆνις. ιδος. ἡ, Ep. for νεᾶνις (νέος), adj. *youthful,* παρθενική, Od. 7, 20. 2) Subst. *a virgin, a maiden,* 18, 418.

νεήφατος, ον (φημί), *newly-said, new-resounding,* h. Merc. 443.

νείαι, Ep. for νέεαι, see νέομαι.

νείαιρα, only in the fem. νείαιρα, irreg. compar. of νέος, *the latter, the outer, the lower,* mly νειαίρη γαστήρ, the lower belly, the abdomen, *5, 539. 616, and elsewhere.

νείατος, η. ον, Ep. for νέατος, q. v.

νεικέω (νεῖκος), and according to the necessity of the metre νεικείω: as subj. νεικείησι, infin. νεικείειν, imperf. νείκειον and νεικείεσκον, fut. νεικέσω, aor. 1 ἐνείκεσα, Ep νείκεσα, and σσ. 1) Intrans. *to quarrel, to dispute, to wrangle,* τινί, with any one, Od. 17, 189. ἀλλήλησιν, Il. 20, 254. εἵνεκά τινος, 18, 498. νείκεα νεικεῖν, 20, 251. 2) *to provoke, to irritate, to blame, to scold, to accuse,* with accus. αἰσχροῖς ἐπέεσσιν. 3, 38; χολωτοῖσιν, 15, 210. Od. 22, 525; spoken of Paris: νείκεσσε θεὰς — τὴν δ᾽ ἤνησε, *to slight,* in antith. to αἰνεῖν, since he gave Aphroditê the preference to Hêrê and Athênê, Il. 24, 29.

νεῖκος, τό, 1) *quarrelling, contention, disputation,* esply with words: the act of *blaming, reproaching, abusing,* 7, 95. 9, 448. Od. 8, 75; also in the assembly, Il 18, 497.. 2) Often also, *contest in deed: fight, battle,* Il. νεῖκος πολέμοιο, contest of war, 13, 271. Od. 18, 264; thus also φυλόπιδος, ἔριδος, Il. 17, 384. 20, 140.

νεῖμα, Ep. for ἔνειμα, see νέμω.

νειόθεν, Ion. for νεόθεν, adv. (νέος), *from beneath.* νειόθεν ἐκ κραδίης, deep from the heart, 10, 10.†

νειόθι, Ion. for νεόθι, adv. (νέος), *in the lowest part;* with gen. λίμνης, deep down in the lake, 21, 317.†

νειός, ἡ, subaud. γῆ (νέος), *new land, fallow ground;* also *newly-ploughed land,* which has lain for a season untilled, and is now fresh ploughed. νειὸς τρίπολος, thrice-plowed fallow, Od. 5, 127. Il. 18, 541.

νεῖται, contr. for νέεται, see νέομαι.

νεκάς, άδος, ἡ (νέκυς), *a heap of corpses,* 5, 886.†

νεκρός, ὁ, 1) Subst. *a dead body, a corpse;* also Ep. νεκροὶ τεθνηῶτες and κατατεθνηῶτες. the departed dead, 6, 71. b) *the dead, the departed,* as inhabitants of the under-world, 23. 51. Od. 10, 526. 2) Adj. perhaps, Od. 12, 11.

νέκταρ, αρος, τό, *nectar,* the drink of the gods, which was conceived of as the noblest wine, of red colour and fragrant smell, 19, 38. Od. 5, 93. h. Ap. 124. Also Thetis uses it to guard the corpse of Patroclus from putrefaction, Il. 19, 38.

νεκτάρεος, η. ον (νέκταρ), *nectarean, resembling nectar, fragrant like nectar,* ἑανός, χιτών, *3. 335. 18, 25.

νέκυς. υος, ὁ, like νεκρός, dat. plur. νεκύεσσι, rarely νέκυσσι, Od. 11, 569,

Myrmidons back to Phthia, and then married Hermionē, daughter of Menelaus, Od. 3, 188. 4, 9. 11, 506. According to other traditions, he emigrated to Epirus, and was slain in Delphi, Pind.

νέος, η, ον, compar. νεώτερος, superl. νεώτατος, *new*, i. e. 1) Spoken of things: *fresh, new*, ἄλγος, ἀοιδή. 2) Of persons : *young, juvenile, youthful*, παῖς (opposed to παλαιός), 14, 108; κοῦρος, γυνή. οἱ νέοι, the youth, in opposition to the γέροντες, 2, 789. 9, 36. Adv. νέον, *newly, fresh, lately, just now*. νέον γεγαώς, just born, Od. 4, 144.

νεός, see νηῦς.

νεόσμηκτος, ον (σμήχω), *newly-rubbed, newly-burnished*, θώρηξ, 13, 342. †

νεοσσός, ὁ (νέος), *a young one*, esply of animals, *2, 311. 9, 323.

νεόστροφος, ον (στρέφω), *newly-twisted*, 15, 469. †

*Νεοτειχεύς, έως, ὁ, an inhabitant of the Æolian town Neonteichus in Mysia, Epigr. 1.

νεότευκτος, ον (τεύχω), *newly made, newly-wrought*, κασσίτερος, 21, 592. †

νεοτευχής, ές = νεότευκτος, δίφρος, 5, 194. †

νεότης, ητος, ἡ (νέος), prop. *newness*; esply *youth, the age of youth*, 23, 445. ἐκ νεότητος, from youth up, *14, 86.

νεούτατος, ον (οὐτάω), *newly* or *just wounded*, *13, 539. 18, 536.

νέποδες, ων, οἱ, Od. 4, 404; † epith. of seals. The ancient Gramm. explain, 1) By ἄποδες, *footless* (from νή and πούς, in which case νη is shortened to νε; thus Apion). 2) By νηξίποδες, *having feet suited to swimming*: *web-footed* (from νέω πούς, according to Etym. Mag. Apoll. Lex.) 3) By ἀπόγονοι, *the young*, according to Ap. Lex. and Eustath. The last signif. was rejected by Apoll.; the second is most probable. Voss, ' web-footed.'

νέρθε. before a vowel νέρθεν, adv. poet. for ἔνερθε, *under, from beneath*. 2) Prep. *under, beneath*, with gen. γαίης νέρθεν, 14, 204. νέρθεν γῆς, Od. 11, 302.

Νεστόρεος, η, ον, *Nestorean*, appertaining to Nestor, νηῦς, 2, 54.

Νεστορίδης, ου, ὁ, son of Nestor, Od. 3, 482.

Νέστωρ, ορος, ὁ, son of Nēleus and Chlōris, king of Pylos (see Πύλος), engaged when an old man in the Trojan war, as he was reigning over the third generation, 1, 247 — 252; and distinguished himself by his wisdom and eloquence, 2, 370, seq. Of his former exploits, he relates, that he slew Ereuthalion, 4, 319; fought against the Epeans, 11, 669, seq.; took part in the war of Peirithous against the Centaurs, 1, 262, seq. ; and at the funeral games of Amarynceus contended with Phyleus, 23, 630. He returned prosperously home from Troy, and was visited by Telemachus, Od. 3, 17, seq. According to H. he had seven sons, Od. 3, 412, seq. From his birth-place he was called Γερήνιος.

νεῦμαι, see νέομαι.

νευρή, ἡ, Ep. gen. νευρῆφι, νευρῆφιν, 8, 300; Ep. dat. νευρῆφι, Od. 11, 607; always *the bow-string;* in Il. 8, 328, ῥῆξε δέ οἱ νευρήν, he broke the string of the bow (not the cord of the hand : Teucer stood ready to shoot ; the stone burst the string, and then grazed the hand).

νεῦρον, τό. 1) *a sinew, a tendon, the muscular cords*, only once, plur. 16, 316. 2) *a cord, a ligament, a thong;* the cord with which the point of the arrow was bound to the shaft, 4, 151 ; but νεῦρα βόεια, v. 122, seems to mean the bow-string, *Il.

νευστάζω (νεύω), *to nod*, κεφαλῇ, Od. 18, 154 ; ὀφρύσι, to make signs with the eyes, Od. 12, 194 ; κόρυθι, to nod with the crest (as the consequence of a firm step), Il. 20, 162.

νεύω, fut. νεύσω, aor. always Ep. νεῦσα, 1) *to nod, to beckon, to give the wink*, τινί, 9, 223 ; and εἰς ἀλλήλους, h. 6, 9. *b*) *to nod to*, i. e. to promise, to assure, τί τινι, h. Cer. 445 ; mly with accus. and infin. *c*) *to nod, to incline*, i. e. to bend forwards, 13, 132 ; often spoken of the crest, 3, 337. 2) Trans. *to incline, to droop*, κεφαλάς, Od. 18, 237.

νεφέλη, ἡ (νέφος), *a cloud, mist, vapour;* often metaph. νεφ. κυανέη, spoken of the darkness of death, 20, 417 ; ἄχεος, cloud of grief, 17, 591. Od. 24, 315.

νεφεληγερέτα, αο, ὁ. Ep. for νεφεληγερέτης (ἀγείρω), *the cloud-collecter* [*cloud-assembler*, Cp.], who drives the clouds together, epith. of Zeus, 1, 511. Od. 1, 63.

νέφος, εος. τό, *cloud, mist*, often in the plur.; generally, *darkness*, νέφος θανάτοιο, 16, 350 ; ἀχλύος, 15, 668. *b*) Metaph. *a dense multitude, a troop*, that looks like a *cloud*, Τρώων, πεζῶν, ψαρῶν, 16, 66. 4, 274. 17, 755 ; πολέμοιο, the cloud of battle, i. e. the dense tumult of battle, 17, 243.

νέω, only pres. and imperf. ἔννεον, Ep. for ἔνεον, 21, 11 ; *to swim*, Od. 4, 344. 442.

νέω, later νήθω, *to spin*, only aor. 1 mid. νήσαντο, Od. 7, 198 ; τινί τι, to spin a man any thing. †

νή, Ep. inseparable particle, which in composition denies the notion contained in the word.

νῆα, see νηῦς.

νηγάτεος, έη, εον, poet. (for νεήγατος from νέος and γάω [γείνω, γέγαα· cf. τατός from τείνω. B.]), *newly-made, newly-wrought*, χιτών, κρήδεμνον, 2, 43. 14, 185. h. Ap. 122 ; cf. Buttm., Lex. p. 413.

νήγρετος, ον, poet. (νή. ἐγείρω), *from which one cannot be awaked, deep*, not to be broken, ὕπνος, Od. 13, 80 ; neut. sing. as adv. *Od. 13, 74.

νήδυια, τά, poet. (νηδύς), *the intestines*, 17, 524. †

νήδυμος, ον, an epith. of sleep (which occurs twelve times in Il. and Od.), of uncertain derivation, prob. = ἥδυμος and

2, 145. Neut. as adv. νήποινον, Od. 1, 160. 377; and often. *Od.

νηπύτιος, ίη, ιον (νή — ἀπύω), young, 20. 200; metaph. childish, foolish, simple, *13, 292. [According to Ameis, a lengthened form of νήπιος, found only in the three books, 13. 20. 21.]

Νηρεύς. ῆος, ὁ (from νή and ῥέω, Neμus, Herm.), Nereus, son of Pontus and Gæa (Tellus), husband of Doris, father of the Nereids; he ruled in the Ægean sea, under Poseidôn. The poet calls him ὁ γέρων. 18, 141. The name occurs first h. Ap. 319.

Νηρηίς, ίδος, ἡ, Ion. for Νηρεΐς, a Nereid, daughter of Nereus and Doris; in the Il. only plur. αἱ Νηρηΐδες, 18, 38, 52.

Νήρικος, ἡ, an ancient city on the island Leucas, according to Strab, where the isthmus formerly was connected with the main-land, Od. 24, 377. At a later day, the isthmus was pierced by the Corinthians, and the town Leucas founded, now St. Maura.

Νήριτον, neut. τό, Od. 13, 351; ὁ Νήριτος, Strab. a mountain in the southern part of Ithaca, according to Ged, now Anoi, Il. 2, 632. Od. 9, 22; see Ἰθάκη.

Νήριτος, ὁ, son of Pterelăus, brother of Ithacus, 17, 207.

Νησαίη, ἡ (belonging to an island), a Nereid, 18, 40.

νῆσος, ἡ (νάω), prop. floating land, an island, 2, 108. Od. 1, 50.

νῆστις, ιος, ὁ, ἡ (νή, ἐσθίω), not eating, fasting, abstaining from food, 19, 207. Od. 18, 370.

νητός, ή, όν (νέω), heaped, accumulated, Od. 2, 338.†

νηῦς, Ion. for ναῦς, gen. νηός and Ep. shortened νεός, dat. νηΐ, accus. νῆα, νέα, plur. νῆες, νέες, gen. νηῶν, νεῶν, ναῦφιν, dat. plur. νηυσί, νήεσσι, νέεσσιν, ναῦφιν, accus. νῆας, νέας, a ship. H. mentions two kinds: 1) ships of burden, φορτίδες Od. 9, 322. 2) ships of war, called by way of eminence, νῆες. According to the Catalogue of ships, they bore 50, and some even 150 men, and could not have been very small. As parts of the ships, are mentioned τρόπις, πρώρη, πρύμνη, ἴκρια, πηδάλιον, ἱστός, ζυγά; to the tackle belong ἱστία, ἐρετμά, πείσματα, πρυμνήσια; see these words. The station of the Greeks was between the two promontories Rhœteum and Sigeum; see 14, 30, seq. According to Strab. these promontories are sixty stadia apart. As the space could not contain the large number of ships (by the catalogue 1186), they probably lay in several rows, cf. 14, 31. Achilles held with his ships the right wing near Sigeum, Odysseus (Ulysses) the middle, and the Telamonian Ajax the left near Rhœteum. Between the rows of ships were the huts or lodges; towards Troy was the encampment surrounded by a ditch and wall. An exact description has been given by

K. G. Lenz, in a work entitled: die Ebene von Troja, 1797, p. 189. Köpke in der Kriegsw. der Gr. 184, seq.

νήχω and νήχομαι, depon. mid. fut. νήξομαι, to swim, the act. Od. 5, 375. 7, 276; mid. *Od. 6, 364. 14, 352.

νίζω, takes the tenses of νίπτω (which in H. occurs only in the pres. ἀπονίπτεσθαι, Od. 18, 179.), fut. νίψω, aor. 1 Ep. νίψα, mid. aor. 1 ἐνιψάμην, perf. νένιμμαι, 1) to bathe, to wash, with accus. δέπα, τραπέζας, with double accus. νίψαι τινὰ πόδας, ' d. 19, 376. 2) to wash off or away, ἱδρῶ ἀπό τινος, Il. 10, 572; αἷμα, 11, 830. Mid. to wash oneself, with accus. χεῖρας (before a libation and generally before eating the Greeks were accustomed to wash the hands), 16, 230. Od. 12, 336; (as a religious service) χεῖρας ἁλός, from the sea, Od. 2. 261; with double accus. ἐκ ποταμοῦ χρόα ἅλμην, to wash the sea-water from the body, Od. 6, 224. b) With accus. to wash oneself, to bathe, Il. 24, 305. Od. 1, 138.

νικάω (νίκη), fut. νικήσω, aor. 1 ἐνίκησα and νίκησα, partcp. aor. 1 pass. νικηθείς, 1) Intrans. to conquer, to vanquish, to have the mastery, to be superior, 3, 71; hence νικήσας, the victor, 3, 178; metaph. dat. instrum. μύθοισιν, ἔγχεϊ, 18, 252; δόλοισι, Od. 3, 121; absol. τὰ χερείονα νικᾷ, the worse prevails, Il. 1, 576. βουλὴ κακὴ νίκησεν, Od. 10. 46. b) In judicial language: to be acquitted, to gain the cause, Od. 11, 548. 2) Trans. to conquer, to vanquish, with accus. τινὰ μάχη, Il. 16, 79; πόδεσσι, 20, 410; metaph. to excel, to surpass, τινα ἀγορῇ, κάλλεϊ, 2, 370. 9, 130; νόον νεοίη, 23, 604. b) to gain, to bear off; νίκην, to gain a victory, Od. 11, 545. πάντα ἐνίκα, he bore off all the prizes, subaud. ἄεθλα, Il. 4, 389.

νίκη, victory, mly in battle, 3, 457. 7, 26. b) victory, in a civil cause, Od. 11, 545. 2) Prop. name, the goddess of victory, daughter of Arês, h. 7, 4.

Νιόβη, ἡ, daughter of Tantalus and Dia, wife of King Amphīon of Thebes. Proud of her twelve children, and boasting over Lêtô (Latona), she was first deprived of her children, and then converted to a stone, 24, 602. 606.

νίπτω, see νίζω.

Νιρεύς, ῆος, ὁ, son of Charopos and Aglaia, from the island Symê, the handsomest Greek before Troy except Achilles, 2, 671, seq.

Νίσα, ἡ (otherwise Νίσσα), a town in Bœotia, 2, 508. According to Strab, there was no town of this name; hence, he understands Νῦσα, a village near Helicon; cf. Ottf. Müller, Orchomen. p. 381.

Νῖσος, ὁ, son of Arêtus, a Dulichian, father of Amphinŏmus, Od. 16, 395.

νίσσομαι, poet. (akin to νέομαι), fut. νίσομαι, 23, 76. 1) to go, πόλεμόνδε, 13, 186. 2) Esply to go away, to return, οἴκαδε, Od. 5, 19. ἐκ πεδίον, Il. 12, 119.

gen. πατρός, from one's father, Od. 23, 98; absol. aor. pass. Od. 11, 73. b) With accus. to leave, to forsake any thing, παῖδα, δῶμα, Od. 4, 264. 21, 104. ὄρεα. Od. 19, 339. 2) Metaph. spoken of the mind: to separate oneself, to turn from any one, from hatred or contempt, Il. 2, 81. 24, 222. N. B. νοσφισθεῖσα, in the signif. of the aor. mid. with accus. θεῶν ἀγορήν, h. Cer. 92.

νοτίη, ή, poet. (νότιος), subst. prop. moisture, then rain, plur. 8, 307.†

νότιος, ίη, ιον (νότος), wet, moist, ἱδρώς, 11, 811. ἐν νοτίῳ τήνγε ὥρμισαν, subaud. ναῦν, they anchored the ship high in the water (not the deep water, but the shore water), Od. 4, 785. 8, 55; see Nitzsch ad Od. 2, 414.

Νότος, ὁ, the south wind, or, more precisely, the south-west wind, 2, 145. It brings wet weather, 3, 10. 11, 306; and with the zephyr is the most stormy wind, Od. 12, 289.

νοῦσος, ή, Ion. for νόσος, h. 15, 1†; sickness, disease, and generally, evil, wretchedness, Od. 15, 408.

νύ, νύν, mly Ep. enclitic particle (shortened from νῦν), it marks, 1) The progress of the action or discourse (see νῦν 2), now, then, thereupon often at the same time moderately illative, 1, 382. Od. 4, 363; rarely Ep. in a temporal signif. Il. 10, 105. 2) It has a strengthening force, a) In exhortations, now, then, δεῦρό νυν, 23, 485. b) In other clauses: then, therefore, now, 10, 165. 17, 469; often with irony, certainly, οὔ νύ τι, not surely, Od. 1, 347. c) In interrogations, now, Il. 1, 414. 4, 31. Od. 2, 320. 4, 110.

νυκτερίς, ίδος, ή (νύξ), a night-bird, esply a bat, *Od. 12, 433. 24, 6.

νυμφᾶ, see νύμφη.

νύμφη, ή, vocat. poet. νύμφα, only 3, 130. Od. 4, 743 (perhaps from the obsol. νύβω, nubo, to envelope), a bride (who was conducted to the bridegroom, with the face veiled), Il. 18, 493; generally, a) a young wife, a married woman, 3, 130. Od. 4, 743. b) a virgin, a maiden, of nubile age, Il. 9, 560.

Νύμφη, ή, a nymph, a female deity of inferior rank. The nymphs inhabited islands, mountains, forests, fountains, etc. 20, 8, 9. H mentions Νύμφη Νηΐς, a fountain nymph, Il. Νύμφαι ὀρεστιάδες, mountain nymphs, 6, 420; ἀγρονόμοι, country nymphs, as companions of Artĕmis, Od. 6, 105. They are daughters of Zeus, Il. 6, 420; springing from fountains, groves, and streams, Od. 10, 350; the handmaids of other goddesses, Od. 6, 105. 10, 348; and were worshipt in sacred grottoes with sacrifices, Od. 14, 435.

νύμφιος, ὁ (νύμφη) a bridegroom, an affianced husband (newly married, V.), 23, 223. Od. 7, 65.

νῦν, adv. 1) now, immediately, at once, nunc, prop. spoken of the immediate present, opposed to ὕστερον, 1, 27. Od. 4, 727. νῦν δή, Il. 2, 82. καὶ νῦν,

ἤτοι, and just now, Od. 4, 151. Sometimes like the English now, a) Spoken of the past, Il. 3, 439. Od. 1, 43. b) Of the future, Il. 5, 279. 2) Frequently metaph. for νύν, now, then, thereupon, esply with the imperat. 10, 175. 15, 115. cf. νύ, νύν.

νύν, see νύ.

νύξ, νυκτός, ή, 1) night, both generally, and spoken of individual nights. H. divides the night into three parts, 10, 253. Od. 12, 312. νυκτός, by night, Od. 13, 278. νύκτα = διὰ νύκτα, through the night, Od. 3, 151. νυκτὶ πείθεσθαι, to obey the night, i. e. to cease, Il. 7, 282. 2) the darkness of night, and generally, darkness, obscurity, 5, 23. 13, 425; esply a) the night of death, the darkness of death, 5, 659. 13, 580. b) As an image of terrour, spoken of Apollo: νυκτὶ ἐοικώς, 1, 47. τάδε νυκτὶ ἐΐσκει, the things he esteemed as the night, Od. 20, 362.

Νύξ, κτός, ή, the goddess of night, 14, 78. 259; according to Hes. Th. 123, daughter of Chaos, who with Erebus begat Æther and Day. [In 14, 78, it should be appellat. νύξ, cf. Jahrb. Jahn und K., p. 275.]

νυός, ή, poet. a daughter-in-law, 22, 65. Od. 3, 451. 2) Generally, one related by marriage, a sister-in-law, Il. 3, 49. h. Ven. 136.

*Νῦσα, ή (akin to νύσσα), a name given to mountains and cities, whither Dionўsus was said to have come, perhaps a mountain in Arabia, τηλοῦ Φοινίκης, h. 26, 8. cf. 25, 5.

Νυσήϊον ὄρος, τό, the Nyseïan mountain, perhaps in Thrace, according to V. an Edonian mountain, 6, 133; others suppose it a mountain in Arabia or India.

*Νύσιον πεδίον, τό (Νῦσα), the Nyseïan plain, according to Creuzer in Asia, h. Cer. 17. cf. Apd. 3, 4. 3. Voss regards it as the Bœotian village Nysa, others still as Phocis.

νύσσα, ή (νύσσω), 1) a pillar on the race-ground, around which the runners were obliged to turn, the goal, μετά, 23, 332. 338. 2) the point of starting, the barriers, 23, 758. Od. 8, 121.

νύσσω, aor. 1 Ep. νύξα, 1) to prick, to thrust; absol. with dat. instrum. ξίφεσιν καὶ ἔγχεσιν, 13, 147; with accus. τινά, to pierce, to wound any one, 5, 46. 12, 395; to pierce, to thrust through, σάκος 11, 561; τινὰ κατα χεῖρα, to wound any one in the hand, 11, 252; also with double accus. 11, 96. 2) Generally, to thrust, ἀγκῶνι νύσσειν τινά, to thrust any one with the elbow, Od. 14, 485.

νώ, see νῶϊ.

νωθής, ές, poet. (perhaps from νή, ὠθέω), slow, lazy, dull, epith. of the ass, 11, 559.†

νῶϊ, nom. dual, gen. dat. νῶϊν, accus. νῶϊ and νώ, the last only, 5, 219. Od. 15, 475. 16, 306; both of us, we two. (νῶϊν as nom. or accus. is to be rejected, and νῶϊ

ception and entertainment, Od. 1, 313. This bond descended by inheritance; hence ξεῖνος πατρώϊος, a paternal table-friend, a guest by inheritance, Il. 6, 215. Od. 1, 187. The ξεῖνος is both the guest who is entertained, Od. 8, 543, and the host who provides the entertainment, Il. 15, 532. 21, 42: =ξεινοδόκος.

ξεινοσύνη, Ion. for ξενοσύνη, hospitality, rights of hospitality, Od. 21, 35.†

ξεινήη, ἡ (ξεῖνος), hospitality, hospitable reception and entertainment, guest-friendship. *Od. 24, 286. 314.

ξείνιος, ίη, ιον, for the Ion. ξείνιος, q. v.

ξερός, ή, όν, Ion. for ξηρός, dry. ξερὸν ἠπείροιο, the dry ground of the mainland, Od. 5, 402.†

ξέσσα, Ep. for ἔξεσε, see ξέω.

ξεστός, ή, όν (ξέω), shaved, smoothed, polished, spoken of wood, δίφρος, 24, 322; ἵππος, the artificial horse, Od. 4, 272; spoken of stones: ξεστοὶ λίθοι, hewn stones, for benches or seats before the door, Il. 18, 504. Od. 3, 406; in like manner αἴθουσα, portico, Il. 6, 243; spoken of horn, Od. 19, 566.

ξέω, aor. 1 ἔξεσα, always Ep. ξέσσα, to shave, to scrape; esply to work any thing carefully with fine tools, to smooth, to polish, to plane, *Od. 5, 245. 17, 341. 23, 199.

ξηραίνω (ξηρός), aor. pass. ἐξηράνθην, to dry up, to make dry, only ἐξηράνθη πεδίον, *21, 345. 348.

ξίφος, εος, τό (akin to ξύω), a sword; it seems to be not materially different from the φάσγανον, q. v.; and is spoken of as large and two-edged, 21, 118. It had a straight blade (τανύηκης), was carried in a sheath (κουλεόν), hung upon a belt (τελαμών). The handle (κώπη) was often decorated. ξίφος Θρήϊκιον, a Thracian sword; according to the Gramm. ad Il. 13, 576. it was large and broad.

*ξουθός, ή, όν, poet. yellow, brownish, h. 33, 3.

*ξύλινος, η, ον, of wood, wooden, δόλος, Batt. 116.

ξύλον, τό (ξύω), wood which is cut and split: only in the plur. wood, fire-wood, logs, sing. 23, 327.

ξύλοχος, ἡ (ἔχω), ground covered with wood; a wood, a thicket, as a lurking-place of wild animals, 11, 415. Od. 4, 335.

ξυμβλήμεναι, ξυμβλήτην, ξύμβλητο, ξύμβληντο, see συμβάλλω.

ξύμπας, ασα, αν, see σύμπας.

ξύν, Ep. and earlier form for σύν, which H. rarely uses, and then, for the most part, to support the metre. H. 'as the following compounds: ξυναγεί-ρω, ξυνάγω, ξυνδέω, ξυνελαύνω, ξυνέχω, ξύνιεμαι, which are to be found under συν.

ξυνέαξε, see συνάγνυμι.

ξυνείκοσι, Ep. for συνείκοσι, Od.

ξυνέηκα, see συνίημι.

ξυνεοχμός, ὁ, see συνεοχμός.

ξύνεσις, ιος, ἡ, see σύνεσις.

ξυνήϊος, η, ον, Ep. and Ion. for ξυνός, common, public. ξυνήϊα, common property, belonging to the whole army, *1, 124. 23, 809.

ξυνίει, see συνίημι.

ξύνιον, Ep. for ξυνίεσαν, see συνίημι.

ξυνιόντος, ξύνισαν, see σύνειμι.

ξυνός, ή, όν, Ion. and poet. for κοινός, common, in common, public; κακόν, 16, 262. ξυνὸς Ἐνυάλιος, common is the god of war, i. e. he helps now this, now that party [Mars his favour deals impartial, Cp.], 18, 309: with gen. γαῖα ξυνὴ πάντων, *15, 193.

ξυρόν, τό (ξύω), a razor; proverbial: ἐπὶ ξυροῦ ἵσταται ἀκμῆς, it stands upon the edge of the razor, i. e. this is the decisive instant, 10, 173.† (Cf ἵσταμαι.) The met., according to Köppen and Passow, is derived from the notion, that any thing resting upon a razor's edge must instantly incline to one of the two sides.

ξυνοχή, ἡ, see συνοχή.

ξυστόν, τό (ξύω), prop. a smoothed stake; a spear-shaft, a spear, 4, 269. 11, 260. ξυστὸν ναύμαχον, the pike or pole used in naval engagements, which, according to 15, 677, was twenty-two cubits long, and pointed with iron.

ξύω (akin to ξέω), aor. 1 ἔξυσα, to shave, to rub, to smooth; δάπεδον λίστροισιν, to clean the floor with shovels, Od. 22, 456. 2) Generally, to do fine work. ἑανὸν ἔξυσε ἀσκήσασα, she had woven the garment delicately with art, Voss, Il. 14, 179. Others: she had smoothed or polished it.

Ο.

Ο, the fifteenth letter of the Greek alphabet; and hence the sign of the fifteenth rhapsody.

ὁ, ἡ, τό, Ep. forms are: sing. gen. τοῖο, masc. and neut.; plur. nomin. τοί and ταί: gen. fem. τάων for τῶν; dat. τοῖσι, ταῖσι, τῇσι, and τῆς: ταῖς is not Homeric. (Some ancient Gramm. would write the unaccented cases ὁ, ἡ, οἱ, αἱ, with the acute; when standing alone, they are used as demonstrative, cf. Thiersch, § 284. 16, and Spitzner ad Il. 1, 9, who follows this in his ed. The opposite view is held by Buttm., Gr. Gram. § 75. Rem. 5. p. 305.) It has, like the German article der, die, das, in H. the signif. both of a demonstrative and of a relative pronoun.

I) ὁ, ἡ, τό, as a demonstrative pronoun, it points out an object, and indicates it as something known and already spoken of. Often, however, the demonstrative force is so weakened, that the transition to the Attic article clearly shows itself. 1) The pure demonstrative

ception and entertainment, Od. 1, 313. This bond descended by inheritance; hence ξεῖνος πατρώϊος, a paternal table-friend, a guest by inheritance, Il. 6, 215. Od. 1, 187. The ξεῖνος is both the guest who is entertained, Od. 8, 543, and the host who provides the entertainment, Il. 15, 532. 21, 42:=ξεινοδόκος.

ξεινοσύνη, Ion. for ξενοσύνη, hospitality, rights of hospitality, Od. 21, 35.†

ξενίη, ἡ (ξένος), hospitality, hospitable reception and entertainment, guest-friendship. *Od. 24, 286. 314.

ξένιος, ίη, ιον, for the Ion. ξείνιος, q. v.

ξερός, ή, όν, Ion. for ξηρός, dry. ξερὸν ἠπείροιο, the dry ground of the mainland, Od. 5, 402.†

ξέσσε, Ep. for ἔξεσε, see ξέω.

ξεστός, ή, όν (ξέω), shaved, smoothed, polished, spoken of wood, δίφρος, 24, 322; ἵππος, the artificial horse, Od. 4, 272; spoken of stones: ξεστοὶ λίθοι, hewn stones, for benches or seats before the door, Il. 18, 504. Od. 3, 406; in like manner αἴθουσα, portico, Il. 6, 243; spoken of horn, Od. 19, 566.

ξέω, aor. 1 ἔξεσα, always Ep. ξέσσα, to shave, to scrape; esply to work any thing carefully with fine tools, to smooth, to polish, to plane, *Od. 5, 245. 17, 341. 23, 199.

ξηραίνω (ξηρός), aor. pass. ἐξηράνθην, to dry up, to make dry, only ἐξηράνθη πεδίον, *21, 345. 348.

ξίφος, εος, τό (akin to ξύω), a sword; it seems to be not materially different from the φάσγανον, q. v.; and is spoken of as large and two-edged, 21, 118. It had a straight blade (τανύηκης), was carried in a sheath (κουλεόν), hung upon a belt (τελαμών). The handle (κώπη) was often decorated. ξίφος Θρήϊκιον, a Thracian sword; according to the Gramm. ad Il. 13, 576. it was large and broad.

*ξουθός, ή, όν, poet. yellow, brownish, h. 33, 3.

*ξύλινος, η, ον, of wood, wooden, δόλος, Batr. 116.

ξύλον. τό (ξύω), word which is cut and split; mly in the plur. wood, fire-wood, logs, sing. 23, 327.

ξύλοχος, ἡ (ἔχω), ground covered with wood; a wood, a thicket, as a lurking-place of wild animals, 11, 415. Od. 4, 335.

ξυμβλήμεναι, ξυμβλήτην, ξύμβλητο, ξύμβληντο, see συμβάλλω.

ξύμπας, ασα, αν, see σύμπας.

ξύν. Ep. and earlier form for σύν, which H. rarely uses, and then, for the most part, to support the metre. H. 'as the following compounds: ξυναγείρω, ξυνάγω, ξυνδέω, ξυνελαύνω, ξυνέχω, ξυνιέναι, which are to be found under συν.

ξυνέαξε, see συνάγνυμι.

ξυνείκοσι, Ep. for συνείκοσι, Od.

ξυνέηκα, see συνίημι.

ξυνεοχμός, ὁ, see συνεοχμός.

ξύνεσις, ιος, ἡ, see σύνεσις.

ξυνήϊος, η, ον, Ep. and Ion. for ξυνός, common, public. ξυνήϊα, common property, belonging to the whole army, *1, 124. 23, 809.

ξυνίει, see συνίημι.

ξύνιον, Ep. for ξυνίεσαν, see συνίημι.

ξυνιόντος, ξύνισαν, see σύνειμι.

ξυνός, ή, όν, Ion. and poet. for κοινός, common, in common, public; κακόν, 16, 262. ξυνὸς Ἐννάλιος, common is the god of war, i. e. he helps now this, now that party [Mars his favour deals Impartial, Cp.], 18, 309; with gen. γαῖα ξυνὴ πάντων, *15, 193.

ξυρόν, τό (ξύω), a razor; proverbial: ἐπὶ ξυροῦ ἵσταται ἀκμῆς, it stands upon the edge of the razor, i. e. this is the decisive instant, 10, 173.† (Cf ἵσταμαι.) The met., according to Köppen and Passow, is derived from the notion, that any thing resting upon a razor's edge must instantly incline to one of the two sides.

ξυνοχή, ἡ, see συνοχή.

ξυστόν, τό (ξύω), prop. a smoothed stake; a spear-shaft, a spear, 4, 269. 11, 260. ξυστὸν ναύμαχον, the pike or pole used in naval engagements, which, according to 15, 677, was twenty-two cubits long, and pointed with iron.

ξύω (akin to ξέω), aor. 1 ἔξυσα, to shave, to rub, to smooth; δάπεδον λίστροισιν, to clean the floor with shovels, Od. 22, 456. 2) Generally, to do fine work. ἑανὸν ἔξυσε ἀσκήσασα, she had woven the garment delicately with art, Voss, Il. 14, 179. Others: she had smoothed or polished it.

O.

O, the fifteenth letter of the Greek alphabet; and hence the sign of the fifteenth rhapsody.

ὁ, ἡ, τό, Ep. forms are: sing. gen. τοῖο, masc. and neut.; plur. nomin. τοί and ταί: gen. fem. τάων for τῶν; dat. τοῖσι, ταῖσι, τῇσι, and τῆς: ταῖς is not Homeric. (Some ancient Gramm. would write the unaccented cases ὁ, ἡ, οἱ, αἱ, with the acute; when standing alone, they are used as demonstrative, cf. Thiersch, § 284. 16, and Spitzner ad Il. 1, 9, who follows this in his ed. The opposite view is held by Buttm., Gr. Gram. § 75. Rem. 5. p. 305.) It has, like the German article der, die, das, in H. the signif. both of a demonstrative and of a relative pronoun.

I) ὁ, ἡ, τό, as a demonstrative pronoun, it points out an object, and indicates it as something known and already spoken of. Often, however, the demonstrative force is so weakened, that the transition to the Attic article clearly shows itself. 1) The pure demonstrative

row, eaply, 1) *the furrow* in ploughing, 18, 546; or *the swath* which mowers or reapers cut and leave in rows, 11, 68. 18, 552; metaph. πίονες ὄγμοι, rich (*furrows*=) fields, h. Cer. 455. · 2) *the path* (of the heavenly bodies, h. 32, 11.

Ὀγχηστός, ὁ, a town in Bœotia, on the lake Copaïs, having a grove, sacred to Poseidôn; now the convent *Mazaraki*, 2, 506; from this the adv. Ὀγχηστόνδε, to O., h. Merc. 186.

ὄγχνη, ἡ. *a pear-tree*, Od. 11, 589. 2) *the pear itself*, *Od. 7, 120.

ὀδαῖος, η, ον (ὀδός), *belonging to the way*. τὰ ὀδαῖα, prop. that on account of which a journey is undertaken, according to the Schol. *merchandise* (V. *wares*), Od. 8, 163; and *provisions for a journey*, Od. 15, 445, Eustath. Better, according to Nitzsch, *the back freight*, or the wares received in exchange for those carried, hence ὦνος ὀδαίων, the gain in the back freight.

ὀδάξ, adv. (δάκνω, ὀδούς), *biting with the teeth*, λάζεσθαι γαῖαν, Il.; ἑλεῖν οὖδας, 11, 749. ὀδάξ ἐν χείλεσσι φῦναι, to bite oneself in the lips, Od. 1, 381. 20, 268; see φύω.

ὅδε, ἥδε, τόδε, demonstr. pron. with the enclitic δέ, which strengthens its demonstrative force, in the dat. plur. Ep. τοῖσδεσσι and τοῖσδεσσιν, both parts being inflected; *this here, that there, this*. It indicates primar. the nearness of the subject. οὐκ ἔρανος τάδε γ' ἐστίν, Od. 1, 226; but is also often 1) To be referred to what immediately succeeds, Il. 1, 41. 504. 2) It also points emphatically to a near or remote place, esply in connexion with personal and other pronouns, and is then translated only by *here, there*. ὅδ' ἐγώ, I here, Od. 16, 205. ἡμεῖς οἵδε, Od. 1, 76; δῶρα δ' ἐγὼν ὅδε (εἰμὶ) πάντα παρασχεῖν, I am here, to present—to thee, Il. 19, 140. ἀνδρὶ ὅστις ὅδε κρατέει, who here governs, Il. 3, 175. νηῦς δέ μοι ἥδ' ἕστηκεν ἐπ' ἀγροῦ, there in the field, Od. 1, 185. Absol. use of single cases: 1) τῇδε, *here, there*, Il. 12, 345. Od. 6, 173. 2) τόδε, accus. *hither*, Il. 14, 298. Od. 1, 409. δεῦρο τόδε, Il. 14, 309. b) *therefore, for that reason*, Od. 20, 217. 23, 213.

ὁδεύω (ὁδός), *to go, to journey*, ἐπὶ νῆας, 11, 569.†

Ὀδίος, ὁ (Ion. for Ὀδῖος = adj. ὀδῖος), 1) leader of the Halizones, slain by Agamemnon, 2, 856. 5, 39. 2) a herald of the Greeks, 9, 170.

ὁδίτης, ου, ὁ (ὁδός). *a traveller, a wayfaring man*, also with ἄνθρωπος, 16, 263. Od. 13. 123.

ὀδμή, ἡ (ὄζω), Ion. and poet. *odour, fragrance*, Il., also *vapour, stench*, Od. 4, 406.

*ὁδοιπορίη, ἡ, *a journey, a way*, h. Merc. 85.

ὁδοιπόριος, ον (πόρος), *relating to a journey*. τὸ ὁδοιπόριον, recompense for a journey, passage-money for a voyage, Od. 15, 506.†

ὁδοιπόρος, ον (πόρος), *travelling:* subst. *a traveller, a travelling companion*, 24, 375.†

ὁδός, ἡ, Ion. οὐδός, Od. 17, 196; † *the way*. 1) Spoken of place: *a path, a street*, ὁδ. ἱππηλασίη, Il. 7, 340; ὁδ. λαοφόρος, 15, 682. πρὸ ὁδοῦ γενέσθαι, to go forwards, 4, 382. 2) Spoken of the act: *progress, travel, journeying*, 9, 626; also by sea, Od. ὁδὸν ἔρχεσθαι, generally, to go a journey, according to Voss, Il. 1, 151; (in distinction from ἴφι μάχεσθαι, Bothe: *embassy*.) It is not with the ancients to be explained by λόχος, but means any *journey* or *mission* (though by *implication*, it would usually have a warlike object).

ὀδούς, ὀδόντος, ὁ (ἔδω), d e n s ; *a tooth*; in the boar, *a tusk*, 11, 416. Od. 19, 393; on ἔρκος ὀδόντων, see ἔρκος.

ὀδύνη, ἡ, *pain, pang*, a) Spoken of the body, always in the plur. 4, 117. 5, 397. 766, and often. b) Spoken of the soul: *grief, sadness*, Od. 2, 79; connected with γόοι, Od. 1, 242; sing. only ὀδύνη Ἡρακλῆος, pain about Heracles, Il. 15, 25.

ὀδυνήφατος, ον, poet. (φάω), *pain-destroying, pain-quieting, soothing, assuasive*. φάρμακα, *5, 401. 900. 11, 847.

ὀδύρομαι, depon. mid. partcp. aor. ὀδυράμενος, 24, 48. 1) Intrans. *to lament, to wail aloud, to complain, to grieve*, spoken of men; once of birds, 2, 315: often absol. and a) With gen. τινός, about any one, 22, 424. Od. 4, 104; ἀμφί τινα, Od. 10, 486. b) With dat. τινί, for any one, Od. 4, 740; ἀλλήλοισι, mutually to complain to each other, Il. 2, 290. 2) Trans. *to bewail, to lament for, to deplore*, with accus. of the person, 24, 740. Od. 1, 243; of the thing: νόστον, Od. 5, 153. 13, 219.

Ὀδυσήϊος. ίη, ιον, Ep. for Ὀδύσσειος, relating to Odysseus (Ulysses), Od. 18, 353.

Ὀδυσσεύς, ὁ, Ep. Ὀδυσεύς, gen. Ὀδυσσῆος, Ὀδυσῆος, Ὀδυσσείος, and Æol. and Ep. Ὀδυσεῦς, Od. 24, 398; dat. Ὀδυσῆϊ and Ὀδυσεῖ, accus. Ὀδυσσῆα, Ὀδυσσέα and Ὀδυσῆ, Od. 19, 136; *Odysseus (Ulysses, Ulixes)*, son of Laertes and Ctimene, Od. 16, 117, seq., king of the Cephallenes, i. e. of the islands Ithaca, Same, Zacynthus, and of the neighbouring continent, husband of Penelope and father of Telemachus; he received this name from his grandfather Autolychus, because he came angry with many (ὀδυσσάμενος), Od. 19, 407. In him the poet presents to us a hero, who distinguished himself as much by spirit and bravery as by cunning, prudence, and steadfastness. He sailed to Troy with twelve ships, Il. 2, 631; and, after the destruction of this city, he made sail first with Menelaus to return to Ithaca, Od. 3, 162. He spent ten years in wanderings, so that he reached home in the twentieth year. His wanderings are described in the Odyssey. After he was landed in Ithaca by the Phæaces, Athênê communi-

of a family, 5, 413: as early as in the Od. *servant, slave*, 14, 4. 4, 245.

οἰκέω (οἶκος), fut. -ήσω, aor. 1 pass. 3 plur. ᾤκηθεν, Ep. for ᾠκήθησαν. 1) Intrans. *to dwell, to live,* mly with ἐν, 14, 116. Od. 9, 200. 2) Trans. *to inhabit,* with accus. ὑπωρείας, Il. 20. 218; hence pass. a) *to be inhabited,* οἰκέοιτο πόλις, 4. 18. b) *to be settled, to keep house,* as οἰκίζεσθαι: τριχθὰ ᾤκηθεν, they dwelt in three divisions, 2, 668.

οἰκίον, τό (dimin. only in form from οἶκος), *a house, an abode, a dwelling, a habitation,* always in the plur. mly spoken of men. b) Spoken of animals: *an abode, a nest,* of wasps, bees, 12, 168; of the eagle, 12, 221. c) Spoken of the underworld, 20, 64.

Ὀϊκλέης, έους, ὁ, poet. Ὀϊκλείης, Od. 15, 244: accus. Ὀϊκλῆα, son of Antiphātes, father of Amphiaräus, Od. 15, 243. cf. Apd. 2, 6. 4.

οἴκοθεν, adv. (οἶκος), *from a house,* i. e. a) from a dwelling, 11, 632. b) from a man's own property, *7, 364. 391. 23, 558.

οἴκοθι, adv. (οἶκος), poet. =οἴκοι, *in the house, at home,* domi, 8, 513. Od. 3, 303.

οἴκοι, adv. (οἶκος), *to the house, to home,* 1, 113. Od. 1, 12, and often.

οἴκόνδε, adv. (οἶκος), poet. = οἴκαδε, *to one's house, home.* a) to the dwelling, 3, 390. b) to one's country, φεύγειν, 2, 158; ἄγειν), to conduct home, Od. 6, 159.

οἶκος, ὁ. 1) *a house,* i. e. *an abode, a dwelling* of any kind; the tent of Achilles, 24, 471; the cave of the Cyclops, Od. 9, 478. b) single parts of a house, *a chamber, a room,* Od. 1, 356. 362; also plur. οἶκοι, like *ædes,* spoken of a house, Od. 24, 417. 2) *house,* i. e. *household, family,* Od. 1, 232. 2, 64. 6, 181. Il. 15, 498.

οἰκτείρω (οἶκτος), aor. 1 ᾤκτειρα, *to pity, to commiserate, to grieve for,* τινά, 11, 814. πολιόν τε κάρη, πολιόν τε γένειον, *24. 516. h. Cer. 137.

οἴκτιστος, η, ον, see οἰκτρός.

οἶκτος, ὁ (οἴ), *compassion; sorrow (for), commiseration, pity,* *Od. 2, 81. 24, 438.

οἰκτρός, ή, όν (οἶκτος), compar. οἰκτρότερος, superl. οἰκτρότατος, Od. 11, 421; oftener οἴκτιστος, *lamentable, deplorable, pitiable,* Il. and Od. neut. plur. οἴκτρα, as adv. ὀλοφύρεσθαι, to wail or complain piteously, Od. 4, 719; also superl. οἴκτιστα θανεῖν, Od. 22, 472.

οἰκωφελίη, ἡ (ὀφέλλω), *advantage for a house, domestic economy, domestic life,* Od. 14, 223.†

Ὀϊλεύς, ῆος, ὁ, king of Locris, husband of Eriopis, father of the Locrian Ajax, and of Medon, 2, 527. 727. 13, 694. 2. a Trojan charioteer, of Bianor, 11, 93.

Ὀϊλιάδης, ου, ὁ, son of Oïleus = Ajax, 12, 365.

αἷμα, ατος, τό, poet. (οἴω), *an assault,*

an attack, 16, 752; spoken of lions, and plur. of the eagle, *21, 252.

οἰμάω, poet. (οἶμα), aor. 1 οἴμησε, *to assault, to rush upon,* spoken of an attack, 22, 308. Od. 24, 538; of the hawk, μετὰ πέλειαν, to pounce upon a dove, Il. 22, 140.

οἴμη, ἡ = οἶμος, poet. prop. *a way, a path,* metaph. spoken of the course which a narration takes; hence, *a narrative, a lay, a song,* *Od. 8, 74. 481. 22, 347.

οἶμος, ὁ, poet. (οἴω = φέρω), *a way, a path,* metaph. a) *a strip,* οἶμοι κυάνοιο, strips of steel (upon the shield), 11, 24.† b) *the course of a song, an air, a melody,* h. Merc. 450.

οἰμωγή, ἡ (οἰμώζω), *lamentation, wailing, a cry of distress,* as of persons dying, 4, 450. Od. 20, 353.

οἰμώζω (οἴμοι), aor. 1 ᾤμωξα, partcp. οἰμώξας, prop. to cry οἴμοι (ah me); hence, *to lament, to wail, to howl,* often in the partcp. aor. with κάππεσεν, πέσεν, 5, 68. Od. 18, 398.

Οἰνείδης, ου, ὁ, son of Œneus = Tydeus, 5, 813.

Οἰνεύς, ῆος, ὁ (the vintner, from οἶνος), son of Portheus, king of Calydon, husband of Althæa, father of Tydeus. Meleager, etc. 14, 117. Bellerophon was his table-friend, 6, 215. He once forgot Artemis in an offering of first-fruits; incensed thereat, she sent a wild boar upon him as a punishment, 9, 529, seq.

οἰνίζομαι, only mid. (οἶνος), imperf. without augm. *to procure wine for oneself, to purchase wine,* χαλκῷ, for brass, 7, 472; οἶνον, to fetch wine, *8, 506. 546. (The act. is not found in H.)

οἰνοβαρέω, Ep. οἰνοβαρείων, *to be heavy, or drunken with wine,* only partcp pres. in the Ep. form, *Od. 9, 374. 21, 304.

οἰνοβαρής, ές, poet. (βάρος), *heavy with wine, intoxicated, drunken with wine,* 1, 225.†

Οἰνόμαος, ὁ (Vindemius, Herm.), 1) an Ætolian, 5, 706. 2) a Trojan, slain by Idomeneus, 12. 140.

οἰνόπεδος, ον (πέδον), *having vineyards, producing wine, abounding in wine,* ἀλωή, Od. 1, 193. 11, 193; neut. subst. τὸ οἰνόπεδον, *a vineyard,* Il. 9, 579.

Οἰνοπίδης, ου, ὁ, son of Œnopion = Helenus, 5, 707.

οἰνοπληθής, ές, poet. (πλῆθος), *full of wine, abounding in wine,* Συρίη, Od. 15, 406.†

οἰνοποτάζω, poet. for οἰνοποτέω (πότης), *to drink wine,* 20. 84. Od. 6, 309.

οἰνοποτήρ, ῆρος *a wine-drinker, a wine-bibber,* Od. 8, 456.†

οἶνος, ὁ, *wine;* the Homeric heroes were wont to drink it mingled with water; the red wine seems to have been most common (μέλας, ἐρυθρός), Od. 12, 19. No other wine is mentioned in H. Andromache sprinkled with wine the wheat given as food to the horses, Il. 8,

as, in comparisons, Od. 3, 73. 9, 128. 3) *as indeed, because indeed, since indeed,* cf. 2, b. Il. 17, 587. Od. 14, 392. (The first syllable is sometimes used as short, Il. 13, 275. Od. 7, 312.)

οἰός and ὄϊος, see ὄϊς.

οἰοχίτων, ωνος, ὁ, ἡ, poet. (χιτών), *simply in the tunic* (clad thus sparely, Cp.), Od. 16, 489.†

οἰόω (οἶος), only aor. pass. Ep. οἰώθη, *to leave alone;* pass. *to be left alone, to remain alone,* *6, 1. 11, 401.

ὄϊς, ὁ, ἡ, Ion. for οἶς, gen. ὄϊος, οἰός, accus. ὄϊν, plur. gen. ὀΐων, οἰῶν, dat. ὀΐεσσιν, οἴεσιν, ὄεσσιν, accus. ὄϊς, contr. for ὄϊας, *a sheep;* ὁ ὄϊς, the ram, also ὄϊς ἄρσην, 12, 451.

ὀΐσατο, Ep. see ὀΐομαι.

ὄϊσε, οἰσέμεν, οἰσέμεναι, see φέρω.

οἴσθα, 2 sing. of οἶδα, see ΕΙΔΩ.

ὀϊσθείς, see ὀΐομαι.

ὀϊστεύω, poet. (ὀϊστός) aor. 1 ὀΐστευσα, *to shoot with an arrow;* τινός, at any one, 4, 100: often absol. with βάλλειν, 4, 196; τόξῳ, with the bow, Od. 12, 84.

ὀϊστός, ὁ, Ep. for οἰστός (οἴω), *an arrow;* it consisted of wood or reed; had a metallic point with barbs, 4, 139. cf. 151; sometimes three-pointed, 5, 393. Poisoned arrows are also mentioned, Od. 1, 261.

οἶστρος, ὁ, *a gad-fly,* œstrus, Od. 22, 300.†

οἰσύϊνος, η, ον (οἰσύα), *willow, osier,* made of willow, Od. 5, 256.†

οἴσω, see φέρω.

οἶτος, ὁ, Ep. (οἴω = φέρω, as *fors* from *fero*), *lot, destiny, fate,* mly in a bad signif.: *misfortune, death,* for the most part κακὸς οἶτος, 3, 417. 8, 554; without κακός, 9, 563. Od. 8, 489.

Οἴτυλος, ἡ, a town in Laconia, on the coast, now *Vitylo,* 2, 385; ὁ Οἴτ., Strab.

Οἰχαλίη, ἡ, a town in Thessaly on the Pēneius, the residence of Eurytus, according to 2, 730. 596. cf. Εὔρυτος. According to later tradition, Heracles destroyed it, because he refused him his daughter Iole, cf. O. Müller, Dorians, vol. i. 2) a city in Messenia, called at a later day *Carnesion,* to which is also transferred the story of Eurytus. Thus it appears, Od. 8, 214. cf. Paus. 4, 2. 1. Strab. understood also this, Il. 2, 596. 3) At a still later day, the story of Eurytus was transferred also to Œchalia in Eubœa, from which Οἰχαλίηθεν, from Œch., 2, 596; from this the subst. Οἰχαλιεύς, ἦος, ὁ, the Œchalian, 2, 596.

οἰχνέω, poet. for οἴχομαι, Ion. iterat. imperf. οἴχνεσκον, 5, 790; *to go, to come,* 3 plur. pres. οἰχνεῦσιν, Od. 3, 322.

οἴχομαι, depon. mid. imperf. ᾠχόμην, only pres. and imperf. prop. *to be away, rarely, to go away, to depart,* and the latter mostly in the imperf., also simply *to go, to come.* 1) Spoken of animate beings: with prep. ἐς, ἐπί, κατά, μετά,

with accus.; chiefly as an euphemism for *to die.* οἴχεται ἐς Ἀΐδαο [sc. δῶμα], he has departed to Hades, 22, 213. 2) Of inanimate things: of storms and missiles, *to fly, to travel,* 1, 53. 13, 505. Od. 20, 64. 3) Of other things: πῇ σοι μένος οἴχεται, where is thy courage gone, Il. 5, 472. ποῦ τοι ἀπειλαὶ οἴχονται, where are thy threats gone, 13, 220. cf. 24, 201. Often it is connected with a partcp., when it can be translated by *away.* οἴχεται φεύγων, he flew away, Od. 8, 356. οἴχεται προφέρουσα, the tempest bore away, Il. 6, 346; ἀνάγων, 13, 627. h. Cer. 74.

οἴω and οἴω, Ep. for ὀΐομαι, q. v.

οἰωνιστής, οῦ, ὁ (οἰωνίζομαι), *a diviner by birds,* one who presages the future by the voice or the flight of birds, *an augur,* 13, 70; as adj. skilled in augury by birds, *2, 858.

οἰωνοπόλος, ον (πολέω), one who concerns himself about the ominous flight of birds: subst. *an augur,* *1, 69. 6, 76; see οἰωνός.

οἰωνός, ὁ (οἴος), 1) Prop. a bird which flies by itself, esply *a bird of prey,* as *an eagle, a vulture, a hawk,* 11, 453. Od. 16, 216. These were sacred birds, whose flight was especially observed, in order to predict the prosperous or disastrous issue of an undertaking. The flight to the right, i. e. to the east, indicated prosperity; to the left, i. e. to the west, on the other hand, adversity, Il. 12, 239. Other circumstances also, as the voice, were ominous, 12, 200; hence 2) Generally, *an omen, an augury.* εἷς οἰωνὸς ἄριστος, ἀμύνεσθαι, etc., one omen is the best, to fight for the country, 12, 243; see Nitzsch ad Od. 2, 146.

ὀκνέω, Ep. ὀκνείω, 5, 255: *to delay, to loiter, to be slow, to hesitate,* with infin. *20, 155.

ὄκνος, ὁ (from ἔχω), prop. *delay, slowness, dilatoriness,* spoken esply of bodily exhaustion: *slothfulness,* 5, 817. ὄκνῳ εἴκων, evercome by slothfulness, *10, 122.

ὀκριάω, poet. (ὄκρις), prop. *to make sharp,* metaph. *to irritate;* pass. *to be irritated* or *made angry:* 3 plur. imperf. Ep. ὀκριόωντο for ὀκριῶντο, Od. 18, 33.†

ὀκρόεις, εσσα, εν, poet. (ὄκρις = ἄκη), having several points, *pointed, ragged, sharp-pointed;* χερμάδιον, μάρμαρος, 4, 518. 12, 380. Od. 9, 499. (In other places now ὀκρυόεις.)

ὀκριόωντο, see ὀκριάω.

ὀκρυόεις, εσσα, εν, poet. (for κρυόεις with o prosthetic, from κρύος), *cold, making cold;* metaph. *awful, horrible. dreadful,* κύων, 6, 344; (Helen) and πόλεμος, *9, 64.

ὀκτάκνημος, ον (κνήμη), *having eight spokes,* κύκλα, 5, 723.†

*ὀκτάπους, ποδος (πούς), *eight-footed,* Batr. 299.

ὀκτώ, indeclin. *eight,* Il. and Od. often

ὀκτωκαιδέκατος, η, ον, *the eighteenth*

stone). The other form, with the spiritus asper, is supposed to be derived from ὅλος, whole, a completely round stone; a rolling-stone. This form is adopted by Spitzner after Cod. Ven., and Herod. 5, 92. 8, 52, sanctions it, cf. Nitzsch ad Od. 1, 52.

ὀλοός, ή, όν (ὀλῶ, ὄλλυμι), compar. ὀλοώτερος, ὀλοώτατος, Ep. form ὀλοιός, οὖλος, destructive, ruinous, mischievous, cruel, spoken of persons: Κήρ, Μοῖρα. θεῶν ὀλοώτατος, of Apollo, 22, 15: of Zeus, ὀλοώτερος Od. 20, 201. b) Of things: πόλεμος, λύσσα, πῦρ. Il. 3. 133. 9, 305. 13, 629. (We must remark ὀλοώτατος ὀδμή, Od. 4, 422, as fem., and ὀλοῇσιν, with lengthened o, Il. 1, 342.) ὀλοὰ φρονέων, 16, 701.

Ὀλοσσών, όνος, ή, a town in Perrhæbia (Thessaly), on the Eurotas, later Elasson, now Alassona, 2, 739.

ὀλοόφρων, ονος, ὁ, ή, Ep. (ὀλοός, φρήν), plotting destruction, savage, deadly-minded (fell, Cp.), epith. of the serpent, the lion, and the boar, 2, 723. 15, 630. 17, 21. b) Spoken of persons: devising mischief (evil-minded, ill-disposed), epith. of Atlas, Æêtês, Minos, Od. 1, 52. 10, 137. 11, 322. Thus Voss and Nitzsch translate; Wolf and Spitzner on the contrary take it with Eustath. and App. in the Od. for τῶν ὅλων φροντιστικός, all-wise, see Spitzner on Köppens Anm. ad Il. 15, 630. Passow, on the other hand, justly remarks, that in the earliest language any one might be denominated evil-minded, in so far as by superior power or intelligence he could become dangerous to others. [Herm. Opusc. VII. p. 250: Ut Æetes ut Minos ὀλοόφρονες, quod est perniciosa meditati, ab Homero appellantur, sic etiam Atlas, fragilem truci committens pelago ratem.]

ὀλοφυδνός, ή, όν, poet. (ὀλοφύρομαι), wailing, plaintive, complaining, ἔπος, 5, 683. Od. 19, 362.

ὀλοφύρομαι, depon. mid. aor. Ep. ὀλοφυράμην, 1) Intrans. to complain, to wail, to lament, to be troubled, often absol. in partcp. 5, 871; with infin. πῶς ὀλοφύρεαι ἄλκιμος εἶναι, how lamentest thou to be brave, Od. 22, 232. b) With gen. τινός, to complain about any one, i. compassionate any one, Il. 8, 33. 202. 15, 17. 2) Trans. with accus. to lament, to bewail, to deplore any one, 8, 245. 17, 648; to pity any one, Od. 4, 364. 10, 157; (it is derived from ὀλοός.)

ὀλοφώιος, ον, Ep. destructive, mischievous, frightful, only in the neut. plur. ὀλοφ. δήνεα, pernicious artifices, Od. 10, 289; and ὀλοφώια without a subst. artifices, according to the Schol. Od. 4, 410; ὀλοφώια εἰδώς, devising pernicious things, Od. 4, 460. 17, 248; (prob. from ὀλοός and ΦΑΩ = φαίνω, showing destruction; not from ὀλῶ and φώς, mandestroying.)

Ὀλυμπιάς, άδος, ή, pecul. fem. of

Ὀλύμπιος, Olympian, epith. of the Musea, 2, 491. h. Merc. 450.

Ὀλύμπιος, η, ον, Olympian, dwelling in Olympus, epith. of the gods, esply of Zeus, who is also called Ὀλύμπιος alone, 2, 309. Od. 1. 60. Ὀλύμπια δώματα, the dwellings of the gods in Olympus, Il. 1, 18.

Ὄλυμπος, ὁ, poet. and Ion. Οὔλυμπος, prop. a lofty mountain on the border of Thessaly and Macedonia, with several snow-capped peaks, now Elimbo, cf. 14, 225. Od. 11, 315. According to the popular belief, which the poet followed, Olympus was the abode of the gods, Il. 2, 30. 5, 360. In the Iliad, however, it is expressly distinguished from the broad heavens (οὐρανός), 5, 867, 868. 15, 192. Upon the highest point is the palace of Zeus, where the gods assemble in council, 1, 498. 8, 3. 44. Od. 1, 27. In the neighbourhood, upon the inferior peaks, the other gods have their palaces, Il. 11, 76. 18, 186. Od. 3. 377. The notion of the mountain is often confounded with the heavenly residence of the gods, since its heights lifted themselves into heaven, high above the clouds, cf. Il. 8, 18—26; the description of it, Od. 6, 42—46. Still Olympus as a mountain always remains the residence of the gods; from it the gods descend to earth, and to it they return, Il. 14, 225. Od. 1, 103. 6, 41. Voss supposes, without necessity, that the highest point pierces through an opening, into the brazen vault of heaven, cf. Mythol. Br. I. p. 170. Völcker, Hom. Geogr. p. 4, seq.

ὀλύρα, ή, only plur. a kind of grain, used as food for horses, and mentioned in connexion with barley, *5, 196. 8, 564; according to Schneider, perhaps triticum monococcum, Linn., St. Peter's corn; or, according to Sprengel, Geschich. Botan. triticum spelta, spelt, Od. 4, 41; ζειά is mentioned in its stead.

ὄλωλα, see ὄλλυμι.

ὁμαδέω, Ep. (ὅμαδος), aor. 1 ὁμάδησα, without augm. to make a noise or tumult, always spoken of the suitors, *Od. 1, 365. 4, 768. 17, 360.

ὅμαδος, ὁ, poet. (ὁμός), noise, uproar, tumult, disturbance, spoken of a tumultuous assemblage, 2, 96. 9, 573. 10, 13. Od. 10, 556 (where it is distinguished from δοῦπος), metaph. the roaring of a tempest, Il. 13, 797. 2) a crowd itself, a throng, 7, 3 7. 15, 689.

ὁμαλός. ή, όν (ὁμός), like, even, smooth, Od. 9, 327.†

ὁμαρτέω, poet. (ὁμός, ἀρτάω), aor. optat. ὁμαρτήσειεν, partcp. aor. ὁμαρτήσας. imperf. ὁμαρτήτην, Ion. for ὁμαρτείτην, to coincide in a thing, to do the same thing, 12, 400. 13, 584. 2) Esply to go together, 24, 438; in the partcp. for the adv. ἁμαρτῇ, in common, together, Od. 21, 188; to be equally swift, spoken of the hawk, Od. 13. 87. (According to Ameis, this verb never governs the accus., and with infin. to exhort to do any thing, 16, 714.

ὁμοκλή, ἡ, poet. (καλέω), prop. the act of calling together several persons, the threatening call of enemies (V. a call of derision), 16, 147. 2) Mly, calling to, encouraging, threatening (a threatening cry, V.), 6, 137. 12, 413. Od. 17, 189.

ὁμοκλητήρ, ῆρος, ὁ, poet. (ὁμοκλάω), one who calls to, encourages or threatens, *12, 273. 23, 452.

*ὁμοργάζω, a form of ὁμόργνυμι, h. Merc. 361.

ὁμόργνυμι, poet. aor. mid. ὠμορξάμην, to wipe off, to dry up, only mid. to wipe away, in reference to the subject, to dry up, δάκρυα, Od. 8, 88; δάκρυα παρειάων, the tears from the cheeks, Il. 18, 124. Od. 11, 530.

ὁμός, ή, όν, poet. (akin to ἅμα), prop. 1) equal, similar, the same, γένος, often. 2) common, in common, spoken of space, νεῖκος, 13, 333; λέχος, 8, 291; ὀϊζύς, Od. 17, 563.

ὁμόσαι, see ὄμνυμι.

ὁμόσε, adv. (ὁμός), to one and the same place, *12, 24. 13, 337.

ὀμόσσαι, Ep. see ὄμνυμι.

ὁμοστιχάω (στιχάω), to go with, to go together, with dat. βόεσσιν, to walk among the cattle, 15, 635.†

ὁμότιμος, ον (τιμή), equally honoured, equal in worth, 15, 186.†

*ὁμότροφος, ον (τρέφω), brought up together, educated or grown up together, h. Ap. 199.

ὁμοῦ, adv. (ὁμός), 1) together, in the same place (ἅμα, relating to time), ἔχειν, 11, 127; always spoken of space, so also 1, 61, where it seems to stand for ἅμα. 2) together with, along with, with dat. Od. 4, 723. 15, 364; and ὁμοῦ νεφέεσσιν, with the clouds, Il. 5, 867.

ὁμοφρονέω (ὁμόφρων), to be like-minded, to have similar thoughts, to agree. Od. 9, 456; also νοήμασιν, *Od. 6, 183.

ὁμοφροσύνη, ἡ (ὁμόφρων), similarity in disposition, harmony, agreement, Od. 6, 181. plur. *Od. 15, 198.

ὁμόφρων, ονος, ὁ, ἡ (φρήν), like-minded, harmonious, united, θυμός, 22, 263.†

ὁμόω, poet. (ὁμός), aor. pass. infin. ὁμωθῆναι, to unite; pass. to be united, to unite. φιλότητι, 14, 209.†

ὀμφαλόεις, εσσα, εν, poet. (ὀμφαλός), having a navel, having a boss like a navel in the middle: ἀσπὶς ὀμφαλόεσσα [his bossy shield, Cp.], 4, 448. Od. 19, 32, and often; ζυγόν, Il. 24, 269.

ὀμφαλός, ὁ (akin to ἄμβων), 1) a navel, 4, 525. 2) any navel-shaped elevation in the middle of a surface: a) the boss of a shield, 11, 34. cf. ἀσπίς. b) a knob on the yoke for fastening the reins, 24, 273. c) Generally, the centre, the middle, θαλάσσης, as the island of Calypso, Od. 1, 50.

ὄμφαξ, ακος, ἡ, an unripe wine-grape, Od. 7, 125.†

ὀμφή, ἡ, poet. (ἔπω, with ej enthetic μ),

a voice, in H. always the voice of the gods, the voice of destiny, which was thought to be recognized in dreams, in the flight of birds, and in other omens, 2, 41. 20, 129; θεοῦ, Od. 3, 215.

ὁμώνυμος, ον (ὄνομα), having the same name, 17, 720.†

ὁμῶς, adv. (ὁμός), 1) together, at once, equally, in like manner, frequently between two substantives, which are already connected by τὲ καί, 8, 214. 24, 73. 2) alike, in the same way, 1, 196. Od. 11, 565; with dat. ὁμῶς Πριάμοιο τέκεσσιν, like the sons of Priam, 5, 535. 9, 312.

ὅμως, conj. (ὁμός), however, still, notwithstanding, 12, 393.†

ὄναρ, τό, only nom. and accus. sing. a dream, a dreaming vision, in the nom. 1, 63. 10, 496; in opposition to ὕπαρ, Od. 19, 547. 2)=ὄνειαρ, in h. Cer. 269; according to a conjecture of Herm. (From ὄναρ are formed ὀνείρατα, ὄνειρος, see the latter.)

ὄνειαρ, ατος, τό, poet. (ὀνίνημι), 1) Prop. every thing profitable, help, aid, profit, advantage, 22, 433. 486; refreshment, Od. 4, 444. 15, 78. 2) In the plur. pleasing things; hence, valuables, Il. 24, 367; elsewhere always food, a refreshing repast, 9, 91. Od. 1, 149. (In h. Cer. 270, ει in ὄνειαρ is shortened.)

*ὀνείδειη, ἡ, poet. for ὄνειδος, Ep. 4, 12.

ὀνείδειος, ον (ὄνειδος), insulting, blaming, chiding, reproaching, often with ἔπεα, also μῦθος, *21, 393.

*ὀνειδείω, poet. for ὀνειδίζω, Fr. I. 18, ed. Wolf.

ὀνειδίζω (ὄνειδος), aor. 1 ὠνείδισα, partcp. ὀνειδίσας, 1) Absol. to vituperate, to insult, to reproach, ἔπεσιν, 1, 211. 2) to cast reproach, τινί, 2, 255; τινί τι, to allege any thing as a reproach against any one, to reproach him with—, Od. 18, 380. Il. 9, 34.

ὄνειδος, εος, τό, insult, abuse. a) Esply in words: reproach, blame, vituperation, often in the plur. ὀνείδεα μυθεῖσθαι, λέγειν, 1, 291. Od. 22, 463. b) that which brings reproach to others: σοὶ κατηφείη καὶ ὄνειδος ἔσσομαι, I shall be to thee a reproach and shame, Il. 16, 498. 17, 556. Od. 6, 285.

ὀνείρατα, τά, see ὄνειρον.

ὀνείρειος, η, ον (ὄνειρος), of a dream, belonging to a dream. ἐν ὀνειρείῃσι πύλῃσι, in the gates of dreams, Od. 4, 809.†

ὄνειρον, τό, see ὄνειρος.

ὀνειροπόλος, ον (πολέω), conversant with dreams, i. e. expounding dreams, γέρων, 5, 149. Subst. an expounder of dreams, *1, 63.

ὄνειρος, ὁ (from ὄναρ), a rare form is ὄνειρον, Od. 4, 841; irreg. nom. plur. ὀνείρατα [cf. ὄναρ], Od. 20, 87.† 1) a dream, a vision, mly sent by Zeus. According to Od. 19, 562 seq., dreams come from the under-world, cf. Od. 24, 12; δῆμος Ὀνείρων, through two gates: the true come through a gate of horn, and the false through one of ivory; a

οπ, 5, 334. Pass. χειμάρρους ὀπαζόμενος Διὸς ὄμβρῳ, a torrent urged or driven on by the ra n of Zeus, swollen, 11, 493. Mid. to cause to follow oneself, to associate to oneself, to take any man as a companion, τινά, 10. 238. 19, 238. Od. 10, 59.

ὀπαῖος, αίη, αῖον (ὀπή), see ἀνοπαῖα.

ὄπατρος, ὁ, poet. for ὁμόπατρος, by the same father. κασίγνητος καὶ ὄπατρος, a brother, and sprung from the same father, *11, 257. 12, 371.

ὀπάων, ονος, ὁ (ὀπάζω), a companion, a comrade, an associate in war, esply an armour-bearer, 7, 165; also fem. a female companion, h. Cer. 440.

ὄπερ. Ep. for ὅσπερ.

ὄπῃ, Ep. ὄππῃ, adv. (πῇ), 1) Spoken of place: where, in which place, prop. dat. local. 22. 321. Od. 1, 347; for the most part with reference to direction. whither, Il. 12, 48. Od. 3, 106. 2) Spoken of manner, etc.: how, in what way, Il. 20, 25. Od. 1, 347. 8, 45.

ὀπηδέω, poet. (ὀπηδός), Ion. for ὀπαδέω, only pres. and imperf. ὀπηδεῖ and ὀπήδει, to follow, to attend or accompany, to go with, τινί, spoken of persons, also ἅμα τινί, Od. 7, 181; to help, h. Ap. 530. b) Spoken of things, Il. 5, 216. ἐκ Διὸς τιμὴ ὀπηδεῖ, honour and fame come from Zeus, 17, 251.

*ὀπηδός, ὁ, ἡ, following, accompanying, τινί, h. Merc. 450.

ὀπίζομαι, depon. poet. (ὄπις), only pres. and imperf. to dread, to fear, to regard, always from fear of guilt and punishment, with accus. μητρὸς ἐφετμήν, 18, 216; also τινά, to dread any one, 22, 332; in the Od. only in reference to the gods: Διὸς μῆνιν, θυμόν, Il. 14, 283. 13, 148.

ὄπιθε and ὄπιθεν, poet. for ὄπισθεν.

ὀπιπτεύω (ὄπτω), fut. σω, aor. ὀπίπτευσας, to look about oneself at any thing, to observe with curiosity, to spy out, to look out for, with accus. πολέμοιο γεφύρας, 4, 371; γυναῖκας, to gaze at the women, Od. 19, 67; absol. λάθρῃ, to watch for secretly, Il. 7, 243.

ὄπις, ιδος, ἡ, poet. (ἔπω), accus. ὄπιδα, according to Apoll. prop. the consequence of human actions, in H. for the most part, of bad actions: θεῶν, punishment, vengeance of the gods, 16, 388. Od. 20, 215: without θεῶν, Od. 14, 82. 88. (According to others, from ὄψ, the monitory inspection of the gods; thus Nitzsch ad Od. 5, 146, and Köppen, contrary to the Gramm., cf. Spitzner ad Il. 16, 388.)

ὄπισθε, before a vowel ὄπισθεν, adv. Ep. also ὄπιθε, 16. 791; ὄπιθεν, 1) Spoken of place: behind, from behind, backwards. ὄπισθε μένειν, to remain behind, 9, 332. οἱ ὄπισθε, those behind, Od. 11, 66. τὰ ὄπισθεν, the hinder parts, the back, Il. 11, 613. b) As prep. with gen. behind. ὄπ. μάχης, Il. 13, 538. 2) Spoken of time: hereafter, henceforth, in future, 9, 519. Od. 2, 270. h. Merc. 75.

ὀπίσσω, Ep. for ὀπίσω, q. v.

ὀπίστατος, η, ον, superl. from ὄπισθε, the hindmost, the last, *8, 342. 11, 178.

ὀπίσω, Ep. ὀπίσσω, adv. (ὄπις), 1) Spoken of place: backwards, back; also strengthened, πάλιν ὀπίσσω, Od. 11, 149. ὀπίσσω χάζεσθαι, Il. 5, 443; νεκρῶν, 13, 193. 2) Spoken of time: henceforth, hereafter, in future, prop. that which is yet in the background, which cannot be seen, 3, 411. Od. 1, 222 ἅμα πρόσσω καὶ ὀπίσσω νοεῖν, λεύσσειν, ὁρᾶν, to see that which lies before and the following, i. e. the present and the future, Il. 1, 343. 3, 109. Od. 24, 452 (according to Heyne, Voss, and Nägelsbach, 'forwards and backwards,' i. e. into the future and the past, contrary to the usus loquendi).

Ὀπίτης, ου, ὁ, a Greek, slain by Hector. Il. 11, 301.

ὁπλέω, poet. for ὁπλίζω, only imperf. ὥπλεον, to harness, to prepare, ἄμαξαν, Od. 6, 73.†

ὁπλή, ἡ (akin to ὅπλον), a hoof, of a horse, *11, 536. 20, 501; spoken of bovine cattle, h. Merc. 77.

ὁπλίζω (ὅπλον), aor. 1 ὥπλισα, Ep. σσ, aor. pass. ὡπλίσθην, without augm. ὁπλισάμεσθα and ὅπλισθεν for ὡπλίσθησαν, to put right, to fit out, hence 1) to prepare, with accus. of food: κυκειώ, 11, 641; ἠῖα, Od. 2, 289. 2) to harness, spoken of a chariot, Il. 24, 190. 3) Of ships: to fit out, Od. 17, 288. Mid. 1) to equip oneself, to adapt oneself to an employment, with infin. Il. 7, 417. ὅπλισθεν γυναῖκες, the women prepared or adorned themselves (for the dance), Od. 23, 143; esply to arm oneself, Il. 8. 55; ἐπὶ πόλεμον, Batr. 140. 2) to prepare for oneself, (sibi), with accus. δεῖπνον, δόρπον; ἵππους, to harness one's horses, 23, 301.

ὁπλομαι, poet. for ὁπλίζομαι, mid. to prepare for oneself, δεῖπνον, *19, 172. 23, 159.

ὅπλον, τό, mostly in the plur., sing. only Od. Batr. equipment, instruments, furniture in general and in particular. 1) the tools of a forge, 18, 409. Od. 3, 433. 2) a ship's gear, tackle, every thing belonging to the equipment of a ship, a cable, a sail, in the last signif. twice in the sing. Od. 14, 346. 21, 390. 3) implements of war, esply arms, equipment, *Il. Sing. spoken of the lightning of Zeus, Batr. 282.

ὁπλότερος, η, ον and ὁπλότατος. η, ον, poet. compar. and superl. without positive, younger, later, the youngest, the latest; γενεῇ, younger in birth, 2, 707. Od. 19, 184. ὁπλότατος, γενεῆφιν, Il. 9, 58. ὁπλοτάτη, Od. 3, 465. (Originally from ὅπλον, capable of bearing arms, cf. Il. 3, 108. Ep. 4, 5.)

Ὀπόεις, εντος, ὁ, Ep. for Ὀποῦς, the chief city of the Locrians, not far from the sea, founded by Opus, son of Locrus, and the native city of Patroclus, 2, 531. 18, 326.

ὁπόθεν, Ep. ὁππόθεν, adv. (πόθεν).

design or purpose. 1) With subjunct. without ἄν after a primary tense, 3, 110. Od. 1, 77. If ἄν or κέ is annexed, the expressed or implied condition is alluded to, Od. 4, 545. 2) With optat. after a historical tense, Il. 1, 344. Od. 3, 129. 3) With indic. fut. to indicate a certain expectation of the result, only Od. 1, 57 ; cf. Kühner, § 690. Thiersch, § 341. 7. § 342. Rost, § 122.

*ὄραμα, ατος, τό (ὀράω), a thing seen, a sight, Batr. 83.

ὀράω, Ep. ὀρόω, imperf. without augment. ὅρων, fut. ὄψομαι, aor. εἶδον, perf. Ep. ὄπωπα. H. uses partly the contr. forms, as ὀρῶ, ὀρᾷς, etc. partly the Ep. expanded, as ὀρόω, ὀράᾳς, ὀράαν, ὀρόωσα, 2 plur. optat. ὀρόῳτε for ὀρῷτε, etc. The mid. is depon. ; rare forms are 2 sing. pres. ὄρηαι for ὀρᾷ, and 3 sing. imperf. ὄρητο, for which others write ὄρηαι, ὄρητο, as if from ὄρημαι. Also the aor. εἰδόμην, infin. ἰδέσθαι, to gaze, to look. a) Absol. with the prep. εἴς τι or τινα, at any thing, or any one, 10, 238. Od. 5, 439 ; again, ἐπὶ πόντον, 1, 350 ; κατά τινα, 16, 646. b) Trans. with accus. to see, to behold, to observe, to perceive, 23, 323 ; with the adjunct ὀφθαλμοῖσιν, Od. 3, 94. ὀρᾶν φάος Ἠελίοιο, to behold the light of the sun, for to live, 5, 120 ; with ὅτι, 7, 448 ; with partcp. 9, 359. 2) Mid. as depon. to see, to behold, τινά, 1, 56. Od. 4, 226.

*ὀργή, ἡ (ἘΡΓΩ), prop. impulse, emotion, passion = θυμός, h. Cer. 205.†

*ὄργια, τά, secret religious usages, mysteries, orgies, spoken of the secret worship of Dēmētēr, h. Cer. 274. 476 ; (from ὀργάω, ὀργή, because these usages were solemnized with enthusiastic movements;) the sing. does not occur.

*ὀργιών, ἴονος, ὁ, one initiated, a priest, h. Ap. 389.

ὄργυια, ἡ (ὀρέγω), in H. ἄ (in the later language ὀργυιά with ᾱ), a fathom, the space between the hands when the arms are extended, 23, 327. Od. 9, 325.

ὀρέγνυμι, poet. form of ὀρέγω, from which partcp. ὀρεγνύς, •1, 351. 22, 37.

ὀρέγω. fut. ὀρέξω, aor. ὤρεξα, mid. aor. 1 ὠρεξάμην, Ep. ὀρεξάμην, perf. mid. ὀρώρεγμαι, 3 plur. ὠρωρέχαται, pluperf. 3 sing. ὀρώρεχατο, 1) to stretch, to reach, to extend, with accus. χεῖρα εἰς οὐρανόν (spoken of suppliants), 15, 371. cf. 1. 351 ; χεῖράς τινι, to stretch out the hands towards any one, Od. 12, 257. 2) to reach, to present, to give, often κῦδός or εὖχός τινι, κοτύλην καὶ πύρνον, Od. 15, 312. Mid. 1) to stretch oneself, to extend oneself, with dat. χερσί, with the hands, i. e. to reach to any thing, Il. 23, 99. ἵπποι ποσσὶ ὀρωρέχαται, the steeds stretched themselves with their feet, i. e. took long strides, stept out, 16, 834. τρὶς ὀρέξατ' ἰών, thrice he strode forth (spoken of Poseidōn), 13, 20 ; ἔγχει ὀρεξά, to stretch oneself with the spear, i. e. to thrust with the spear, 4, 307. 13,

190. 2) With gen. to stretch oneself towards any thing, to reach after, παιδός, 6, 466. 3) With accus. trans. to reach any thing, to attain, Od. 11, 392 ; to hit, σκέλος, Il. 16, 314. 322. 4)=act. ἀνδρὸς ποτὶ στόμα χεῖρ' ὀρέγεσθαι, i. e. (according to the Schol. Vict.), χεῖρε ἀνδρὸς ποτὶ στόμα, to press the hands of the man (viz. of Achilles) to the mouth. This explanation is followed by Voss. It is confirmed also by v. 478, where Priam kisses Achilles' hand, 24, 506.

*ὀρείχαλκός, ὁ (ὄρος, χαλκός), orichalcum, mountain brass, a metal of uncertain composition ; according to Beckmann, copper-brass, h. 5, 9.

ὀρεκτός, ή, όν (ὀρέγω), stretched out, extended, μελίαι, 2, 543.†

ὀρέομαι=ὄρνυμαι, only 3 plur. imperf. ὀρέοντο, they hastened, •2, 398. 20, 140. 23, 212.

'Ορέσβιος, ὁ (living on mountains), a rich Bœotian of Hylē, 5, 707.

ὀρεσίτροφος, ον, poet. (τρέφω), raised or nourished upon the mountains, epith. of the lion, 12, 299. Od. 6, 130.

ὀρεσκῷος, ον, poet. (κέω), lying in the mountains, dwelling in the mountains, wild, 1, 268. Od. 9, 155.

ὀρέστερος, η, ον, poet. (ὄρος), for ὄρειος, living upon mountains, in mountains, epith. of the serpent, of wolves, 22, 93. Od. 19, 212.

'Ορέστης, αο, ὁ (mountaineer, Herm. Excitus), son of Agamemnon and Klytæmnêstra (Clytemnestra), 9, 142 ; he was brought by his sister to his uncle Strophius in Phocis, where he entered into the well-known bond of friendship with his son Pylades. H. does not mention this, unless Od. 11, 458—462 refers to it. According to Od. 3, 305, he returned in the eighth year of the reign of Ægisthus to Mycênæ, slew him and his mother Klytæmnêstra (Clytemnestra), in order to avenge the death of his father, and then reigned in Mycenæ, Od. 11, 457, seq. Because all the traditions point to Phocis, Zenodot. wrote, Od. 3, 307 : ἀπὸ Φωκήων for ἀπ' 'Αθηνάων. 2) A Greek [slain by Hector], Il. 5, 705. 3) [A Trojan, 12, 139. 193.]

ὀρεστιάς, άδος, ἡ (ὄρος), inhabiting mountains, Νύμφαι, the mountain nymphs, 6, 420.

ὀρεσφι, see ὄρος.

ὀρεχθέω, poet. strengthened form of ὀρέγω, intrans. only βόες ὀρέχθεον ἀμφὶ σιδήρῳ σφαζόμενοι, 23, 30 ; the oxen stretched themselves about the iron, according to the Schol. ἀπετείνοντο ἀναιρούμενοι, 23, 30.† Others : palpitated, struggled, thus Suid. κινεῖν, and Bothe. Others. with Hesych. : bellowed, ἐμυκῶντο, ἐρρόχθουν. Thus Voss, cf. Spitzner, Excurs. XXXIV. [According to others it is akin to ὀργή, ὀργάω, and means intumescere, so Ameis, in Jahrb. Jahn und K., p. 276. Am. Ed.]

ὀρθαι, see ὄρνυμι.

founder of Ormenion, 9, 448. 2) a Trojan, 8. 274. 3) a Trojan, 12, 187. 4) father of Ctesius, Od. 15, 414.

ὄρμενος, see ὄρνυμι.

ὁρμή ἡ (ὄρνυμι), a vehement assault, an attack, a fierce onset, fury, spoken of a warrior, 9, 355; of a beast, 11, 119. h. Cer. 382; often spoken of inanimate things: of the waves, Od 5, 320; of fire (the fierceness of it), Il. 11, 157. ἐς ὁρμὴν ἔγχεος ἐλθεῖν, to come within the reach of a man's spear, 5, 118. 2) the beginning of an undertaking, 4, 466; the commencement of a journey, Od. 2, 403. 3) Generally, impulse, inclination, effort, Od 5, 416; ψυχῆς, h. 7, 13.

ὅρμημα, ατος. τό (ὁρμάω), of uncertain signif. occurring only twice, in the plur. *2, 356. 590; in the verse: τίσασθαι Ἑλένης ὁρμήματά τε στοναχάς τε, Eustath. explains: ὅρμιμα (ἡ ἐξ ἀρχῆς ἱκουσία ἔλευσις), therefore : ʻ the undertaking of Helen and her groans,' i. e. her repentance afterwards; so also Bothe: Helenae ausa et gemitus. Most ancient critics take ὁρμήματα for troubles, cares, hence Voss. translates: ʻ before he has avenged the troubles and groans of Helen,' and Buttm. [deriving it fm ὁρμάω] follows him, Lex. p. 439. More probable, according to Rost in Damm's Lex., is the first signif. the undertaking, and the gen. is explained as gen. object.: ʻ their toils and groans on Helen's account.'

ὁρμίζω (ὅρμος), prop. to bring into port; then, to anchor, νῆα, Od. 3, 11. 12, 317; and generally, to make fast, to render secure, ὕψι ἐπ᾽ εὐνάων or ὑψοῦ νῆα ἐν νοτίῳ, a ship upon the sea, Il. 14, 77. Od. 8, 55; by means of a large stone, see εὐνή. Cf. Nitzsch ad Od. II. p. 118 who thinks the ship was drawn partly up upon the moist, overflowed sand of the shore. Am. Ed.]; see νότιος.

ὅρμος, ὁ (εἴρω). 1) a string, a chain, esply a necklace, a neck-chain. as an ornament of women, 18, 401. Od. 15, 460. 2) an anchorage, a harbour, a road, a basen, Il. 1, 435. Od. 13, 101 Batr. 67. For the second signif. ὄρνυμι is taken as the theme.)

Ὄρνειαί, αἱ, Ep. for Ὄρνεαι, a city in Argolis, with a temple of Priāpus, 2, 571.

ὄρνεον, τό, poet. for ὄρνις, a bird. 13, 64.†

ὄρνις, ἴθος, ὁ and ἡ, plur. ὄρνιθες, dat. ὀρνίθεσσι (ὄρνυμι), 1) a bird, both wild and tame. 2) a bird from whose flight and voice omens were taken; hence generally, σημα, 24, 219. (ι in the disyllabic cases is double-timed, 9, 323. Il. 218; in the trisyllabic always long.)

ὄρνυμι, poet. Ep. form ὀρνύω (from this imperf. ὤρνυον), imperat. ὄρνυθι, infin. Ep. ὀρνύμεν, fut. ὄρσω, aor. 1 ὦρσα. iterat. form ὄρσασκε. Ep. aor. 2 ὤρορον, mly trans.=ὦρσα. only for perf. intrans. 13, 78. Od. 8, 539. Mid. ὄρνυμαι, imperf. ὠρνύμην, fut. ὀροῦμαι, 3 sing. ὀρεῖται, aor. ὠρόμην, Ep. 3 sing.

ὦρτο, 3 plur. ὄροντο, Od. 3, 471; subj. ὄρηται, imperat. ὄρσο and ὄρσεο [contr ὄρσευ, Il. 4, 264], infin. Ep. ὄρθαι, 8, 474; partcp. ὄρμενος, η, ον, perf. act. intrans. only sing. ὄρωρε, subj. ὀρώρῃ, pluperf. ὀρώρει and ὠρώρει, 18, 498 (to be distinguished from aor. 2 ὤρορε). Of like signif is the perf. mid. ὀρώρεται, subj. ὀρώρηται. 13, 271; Ep. ὀρέοντο, see ὄρσομαι. 1) Trans. in the act. to excite, to move, to arouse, with accus. 1) Spoken of persons, and generally of animate beings : α) to put in motion bodily. to urge on, to make to go, τινὰ κατὰ μέσον, 5, 8; esply in a hostile signif. τινὰ ἐπί τινι, 5, 629; ἀντία τινός, 20, 79. β) to cause to rise, to make to lift oneself, Ἠριγένειαν ἀπ᾽ Ὠκεανοῦ, Od. 23, 348 ; to awaken, Il. 10, 518; spoken of beasts, to drive up, to rouse, αἶγας, Od. 9, 154. b) Frequently in reference to the mind: to excite, to impel, to encourage, to inflame, τινά, spoken esply of excitement by the gods, Il. 5, 105. Od. 4, 712; with infin following, Il. 12, 142. 13, 794. 2) Spoken of things, to excite, to move, to cause, πόλεμον, μάχην, νοῦσον: spoken of states of mind, ἵμερον, γόον, φόβον: of natural objects, ἄνεμον, θύελλαν, κύματα. II) Intrans. in the mid. together with perf. 2 ὄρωρα, to rouse oneself, to move oneself, to stir. 1) Spoken of persons in reference to the body: to more, to hasten, 4, 421; with infin. Od. 2, 397; esply to raise oneself, to arise, ἐξ εὐνήφιν, Od. 2, 2; ἐκ λεχέων, Il. 11, 2; ἀπ᾽ Ὠκεανοῖο ῥοάων, 19, 2; ἀπὸ θρόνον, 11, 645; absol. esply in imperat. pres. and aor. ὄρσο and ὄρσεο, stand up! rouse up! hence in a hostile signif. to leap upon, to rush upon, to run upon, χαλκῷ, with the spear, 3, 349. 5, 17; ἐπί τινα, 5, 590; also with infin. to raise oneself, to begin to do any thing: νιφέμεν, ἴμεν, 12, 279; and with partcp. ὄρσο κέων, up, to go to sleep, Od. 7, 342. 2) Spoken of things, to rise, to be excited. to begin, to arise, esply in perf. 2, I have arisen: spoken of bodily and mental states, εἰσόκε μοι φίλα γούνατ᾽ ὀρώρῃ, as long as my limbs move (prop. have raised themselves), Il. 9, 610. 10, 90: spoken of events in life, πόλεμος, μάχη, νεῖκος: of states of nature, νύξ, φλόξ, ἄνεμος. πῦρ ὄρμενον, the fire which has arisen, 17, 738. δοῦρα ὄρμενα πρόσσω, spears flying forwards, 11, 572; and with infin. πῦρ ὤρετο καιέμεν ὕλην, 14, 397. ὦρτο—οὖρος ἀήμεναι, the wind rose to blow, Od. 3, 176.

ὀρνύω, poet. form of ὄρνυμι, q. v.

ὀροθύνω, poet. lengthened form of ὄρνυμι, only act. to excite, to arouse, to put in motion, to stimulate, to encourage, only spoken of persons, τινά. b) Of things, ἐναύλους, to raise the mountain streams, 21, 312; ἀέλλας, Od 5, 292.

ὅρομαι (akin to οὖρος, ὁράω), to watch, ὄρονται, Od. 14, 104.†

ὄρος εος, τό, Ion. οὖρος, dat. ὄρεσι, ὄρεσσι, Ep. gen. and dat. ὄρεσφιν, 4,

with certainty, Ep. also with indicat. fut. and κέ, Il. 9, 155. b) With indicat. of the historical tenses and ἄν or κέ, Od. 5, 39. 14, 62; cf. ἄν. 2) With subjunct. with ἄν, κέ, and Ep. also without ἄν, after a primary tense, when the declaration is given as supposed or possible [hypothetical use], or can be resolved by ἐάν or τίς, Od. 1, 352. Il. 2, 231; hence also a) To indicate an often-recurring case, 2, 391. b) In comparisons, 13, 63. 17, 110. 3) With optat. without ἄν after a historical tense, 10. 20. 489; as with subjunct. again: b) As part of a wish, 14, 107. Also ἄν or κέ is added, 15, 738. 7) Absol. use of single cases, a) Gen. sing. οὗ, always ἐξ οὗ, since. b) Dat. sing. ᾗ, q. v. c) Accus. neut. ὅ very mly for ὅτι, that, 1, 120; for δι᾽ ὅ, thereat, that, Od. 1, 382; because, Il. 9, 493. 17, 207.

II) As a demonstrative pronoun, for οὗτος, this, and he, she, it, esply with οὐδέ, μηδέ, γάρ, καί, 6, 59. 21, 198. Od. 1, 286. οἱ—οἱ, these—those, Il. 21,353. 354.

ὅς, ἥ, ὅν, a possessive pronoun of the third person for ἑός, ἑή, ἑόν, his, her, its; it has in the gen. sing. οἷο, 20, 235; without subst. ὄν, 15, 112. 2) Ep. it stands instead of the pronoun of the second and third person, Od. 1, 402. 13, 320. Doubtful is Od. 9, 28. Other places have been altered by Aristarch. Il. 19, 174. cf. Buttm. Lex. p. 251.

ὁσάκι and ὁσάκις, Ep. ὁσσάκι, how many times, how often, as often as, always in the Ep. form, 21, 265. Od. 11, 585.

ὁσάτιος, η, ον, Ep. ὁσσάτιος, poet. for ὅσος, λαός, 5, 587.†

ὁσίη, ἡ (prop. fem. of ὅσιος, holy), 1) divine or natural right, and every thing which in accordance with it is consecrated or permitted: hence οὐχ ὁσίη, with infin. it is not right, permitted. Od. 16, 423. 32, 412. 2) a sacred service, a holy usage, in sacrifices and the worship of the gods, h. Ap 237. ὁσίη κρεάων, the sacred use of the sacrificial flesh, h. Merc. 130. ὁσίης ἐπιβῆναι, to go to a sacred service, h. Cer. 211. Merc. 173.

ὅσιος, η, ον. prop. consecrated by divine laws; spoken of persons: pious, devout, Ep. 6, 6.

ὅσος, ὅση, ὅσον, Ep. ὅσσος, 1) how great, how wide, how long, how much, how many, spoken of space, time, number, and degree; if the correlative demonstrative τόσος precedes, ὅσος is translated as [cf. 3, 12. 6, 450]; with the gen. it stands periphrastically: ὅσον πένθεος for ὅσον πένθος, 11, 658. cf. 5, 267. c) In the plur. all who, as many as, with preceding τοσοῦδε, 14. 94. οὔτις—ὀνόσσεται ὅσσοι Ἀχαιῶν for οὗτις Ἀχαιῶν, 9, 55. ὅσσαι νύκτες καὶ ἡμέραι ἐκ Διός εἰσιν, all the days and nights, which come from Zeus, Od. 14, 93. 2) Frequently the neut. plur. and sing. as adv. as greatly, as much, as far, so greatly, so much, so far, with τόσον, 5, 786. Od. 4,

356; and without τόσον: ὅσσον, as far as, Il. 5, 860; absol. ἀλλ᾽ ὅσον ἐς Σκαιὰς πύλας ἵκανεν, he came only, 9, 354. b) When with ὅσον τε the limitation of space stands in the accus. it signifies about. ὅσον τε ὄργυιαν, Od. 9, 322 325. 10, 167; prop. an attraction, cf. Kühner, § 656, and Od. 10, 113. c) ὅσσον ἐπι and ὅσσον τ᾽ ἐπί for ἐφ᾽ ὅσον, as far as, Il. 2, 616. 3, 12. a) With compar and superl. by how much, how much. ὅσσον ἐγώ — ἀτιμοτάτη εἰμί, how much I am the most dishonoured, 1, 516. On ὅσος τε and ὅσος περ, see τέ and πέρ.

ὅσπερ, Ep. also ὅπερ, ἥπερ, ὅπερ; the strengthening πέρ indicates, a) That the relative clause has equal compass with the main clause: entirely, the very same, the very—who. θεὸς ὅσπερ ἔφηνεν, the very god, who, 2, 318. cf. 4, 524. b) Or that the clauses oppose each other. ὑπόσχεσις, ἥνπερ ὑπέσταν, i. e. ὑποστάντες, πέρ, which they nevertheless promised, although having promised, 2, 286. 6, 100. Od. 20, 46. Frequently, however, it can be translated only by the simple relative who, which, cf. πέρ.

ὄσσα, ἡ (akin to ὄψ, ἔπος), 1) Generally, a voice, sound, a tone, as of the cithara, h. Merc. 443. 2) fame, report, rumour, esply that of which the author is not known; it is therefore, as every thing for which a reason cannot be given, derived from the deity, Od. 1, 282.

Ὄσσα, ἡ, as pr. n. Ossa, a messenger of Zeus, 2, 93. Od. 24, 413.

Ὄσσα, ἡ, a mountain in Thessaly, famed as the abode of the centaurs, now Kissavos, Od. 11. 315.

ὅσσα, Ep. for ὅσα.

ὁσσάκι, Ep. for ὁσάκι.

ὁσσάτιος, η, ον, Ep. for ὁσάτιος.

ὄσσε, τώ, only nom. and accus. dual neut. in Il. and Od.; later also plur. ὄσσοις, h. 31, 9; the two eyes, also (in two passages), with adj. neut. plur. φαεινά, αἱματόεντα, Il. 13, 435. 617.

ὄσσομαι (from ὄσσε), depon. mid. only pres. and imperf. 1) Prop. to look with the eyes, to see, cf. Od. 7, 31; esply 2) to see with the mind, to foresee, to surmise, to think upon any thing, κακά or κακόν, Od. 10, 374. 18, 154; ἄλγεα θυμῷ, Il. 18, 224; πατέρα ἐνὶ φρεσίν, Od. 1, 115; and without θυμῷ, φρεσί, Od. 20, 81. 3) to indicate any thing by the countenance or aspect, to foretoken, to look, κακά (Vnas, 'with threatening look'), Il. 1, 105; ὄλεθρον, to threaten destruction, Od. 2, 152; spoken of the sea, Il. 14, 17; and generally, τινί τι, to predict any thing to any one, 24, 172.

ὅσστε, η, ον, Ep. for ὅσος.

ὅστε, ἥτε, ὅ, τε, he who, she who, that which; τέ indicates the mutual internal relation of the main and adjunct clauses, 2, 365. Od. 3, 73. Plur. ἅτε [τά τ᾽] after a sing. like those which [= οἶά τε, qualia, with ref. to the collective notion. F.]. Od. 5, 438; hence also such as.

any thing is denied positively, whether it is expressed as something certain by the indicat. or as something possible by the optat. In H. οὐ also stands in connexion with the subjunct. when it has the signif. of the future, 1, 262. Od. 6, 201. 2) In interrogative sentences, as *non, nonne*, when the speaker expects an affirmative answer, Il. 10, 165. 3) In sentences which imply a command, by the optat. with ἄν, with and without a question: οὐκ ἂν δὴ τόνδ᾽ ἄνδρα μάχης ἐρύσαιο, wilt thou not—save? 5, 456. Od. 7, 22. II) In subordinate clauses: 1) In such as are introduced by ὅτι, ὡς, *that;* because they have the character of independent principal clauses. 2) In subordinate clauses showing the time and reason, commencing with ἐπεί, ἐπειδή, ὅτε, etc. Il. 21, 95. 3) In relative clauses, when the thought contained in them is positively denied. III) The negation is repeated: 1) For emphasis' sake, Od. 3, 27; thus also οὐ—οὐδέ, Il. 17, 641. Od. 8, 280. 2) When a whole which is denied is distributed into parts: οὐ—οὔτε—οὔτε, Il. 6, 450. 3) Indefinite pronouns and adverbs in a negative sentence (as any one, any where, etc.) are expressed negatively, 1, 86. 88.

οὗ, gen. sing. of the defect. pronoun of the third pers. masc. and fem. Ep. ἕο, εὗ, εἶο, ἔθεν, dat. οἷ, accus. ἑέ (εὗ and ἔθεν are enclitics), prop. reflexive: *of himself, of herself, of itself;* but often a personal pron. *his, her, to him, to her, she, it;* the accus. ἕ as neut. 1, 236; and for the plur. h. Ven. 268.

οὖας, ατος, τό, Ep. and poet. for οὖς.

οὖδας, τό (akin to οὐδός), poet. gen. οὔδεος, dat. οὔδει and οὔδει, 1) *the floor* or *pavement* in chambers or houses, Od. 23, 46. Il. 5, 734. 2) *the ground, the earth,* Od. 9, 135. 13, 395. οὖδας ὀδὰξ ἑλεῖν. to seize the earth with the teeth, i. e. to fall, Il. 11, 749. ὕπτιος οὔδει ἐρείσθη. he sank backwards to the earth, 7, 145; οὐδάσδε, to the ground, 17, 457.

οὐδέ, conjunc. (δέ), *but not, and not; nor (yet).* οὐδέ unites 1) Entire sentences, and expresses prop. an antithesis: *not however, but not,* 24, 25. Od. 3, 143. Often οὐδέ stands, when the same notion is expressed first affirmatively and then negatively: μνήσομαι οὐδὲ λάθωμαι, h. Apoll. 1. Od. 9, 408. 2) Mly it serves to annex a new sentence: *and not, also not, nor yet,* Il. 9, 372; often οὐ, οὐδέ. 3) οὐδέ—οὐδέ, when occurring in one sentence it is a strengthened οὐδέ: *not at all, certainly not,* 5, 22. Od. 8, 32. οὐδέ—οὐδέ at the beginning of two clauses signifies: *also not—and not* (never: *neither—nor*), Il. 9, 372. Sometimes we have also οὐδέ—οὔτε, h. Cer. 22. 4) οὐδέ in the middle of a sentence also stands in an adverbial signif. and means: *also not, not even (ne .. quidem);* often οὐδ᾽ ἠβαιόν, οὐδὲ τυτθόν.

οὐδείς, οὐδεμία, οὐδέν, gen. οὐδενός,

etc. (οὐδέ, εἷς), *also not one,* i. e. *no one, nothing.* The neut. οὐδέν often stands as an adv. *not at all, not in the least,* 1, 412. Od. 4, 195. [A still stronger form of speech is οὐχ εἷς, found only once, h. Merc. 284. *Am. Ed.*]

οὐδενόσωρος, ον, ὁ (οὐδείς, ὤρα) *not to be esteemed, contemptible, worthless,* τείχεα. 8, 178.†

οὐδέπη or οὐδέ πη, adv. *in no wise,* i. e. *not at all;* in H. separated, Od. 12, 433; οὐδέ πη ἔστιν, with infin., it is by no means possible, h. 6, 58.

οὐδέποτε or οὐδέ ποτε, adv., *also not ever,* i. e. *never,* spoken of the past and future. Wolf writes at one time οὐδέποτε, 5, 789; at another divided, οὐδέ ποτε, Od. 2, 203.

οὐδέπω or οὐδέ πω, adv. *not yet,* mly *not at all, in no wise,* in H. mly separated by a word or more, 1, 108.

οὐδετέρωσε, adv. (οὐδέτερος), *on neither side, in neither direction,* 14, 18.†

οὐδός, ὁ, Ion. and Ep. for ὁδός. *the threshold of a house;* then also used of any other entrance, 6, 375. Od. 1, 104; of the under-world, Il. 8, 15. *b)* Metaph. γήραος οὐδός, the threshold of old age, i. e. its commencement. Thus Voss and Heyne; according to the ancient Gramm. = ἔξοδος γήρως, extreme old age, 22, 60. 24, 487. Od. 15, 246.

οὐδός, ἡ, Ion. for ὁδός, *a way,* Od. 17, 196.†

οὖθαρ, ατος, τό, *the udder, the breast,* prop. of animals, Od. 9, 440. *b)* Metaph. *fruitfulness, fertility.* οὖθαρ ἀρούρης. the fruitfulness of the land, i. e. blessed land, a land of milk and honey, Il. 9, 141. 283.

οὐκ, before a vowel for οὐ.

Οὐκαλέγων, οντος, ὁ (οὐκ, ἀλέγω), *Ucalegon,* a Trojan counsellor, 3, 148.

οὐκέτι, adv. (ἔτι), *no more, no longer, not again.* strengthened by οὐδέ, 12, 73. οὐκέτι πάγχυ. no more at all, 19, 343.

οὐκί, adv. Ep. and Ion. for οὐκ, *not,* mly at the close of a sentence, 15, 137, Od. 11, 493.

οὐλαί, αἱ [according to Eustath. ad Il. 1, 449; and Et. Mag. οἱ], Att. ὀλαί, *coarsely ground barley-corn,* (Voss: 'sacred barley,') which was strewn between the horns of the victim before the sacrifice, Od. 3, 441.† The Gramm. derive οὐλή from ὅλος, *whole,* and supply κριθαι, *whole barley-corns:* more prob. according to Buttm., Lex. p. 455, ὀλή comes from ΕΛΩ, ἀλέω, as τομή from τέμω, and signifies prop. *that which is ground;* then plur. οὐλαί, *bruised barley-corns, barley-grits,* the simplest treatment of grain. This was retained in sacred rites as a memorial of the earliest kind of food. Perhaps it was first roasted and mixed with salt (*mola salsa,* amongst the Romans).

οὐλαμός, ὁ (εἴλω), *a press, a tumult, a crowd,* ἀνδρῶν, *4, 251. 20, 113.

οὖλε, see οὖλω.

P 3

seq. The clouds cover the heavens, and hide from the inhabitants of the earth the view of it, of the æther and the constellations, Od. 5. 293. Il. 8, 555; hence 2) *the atmospheric space above the earth*, which was distinguished from the αἰθήρ, 2, 458. 8, 558. 15, 192. Since Olympus extends into the upper air, οὐρανός is called, 3) *the abode of the gods*, 6, 108. Od. 1, 67. (We nowhere, however, find in the poems of Hom. the observation of Voss confirmed, that the arch of heaven has an opening directly over Olympus.) 4) Metaph. *heaven*, to denote the highest region : οὐρανὸν ἱκάνειν, to reach, to pierce to heaven, Il. 2, 153. Od. 12, 73, and often ; cf. Völcker's Hom. Geogr. p. 5—14.

Οὐρανός, ὁ, prop. name, son of Erebus and of Gæa (Tellus), husband of Gæa (Tellus), by whom he begat the Titans and Titanides, the Cyclôpes, the Hecatoncheires, Hes. Th. 125. Il. 15, 36. Od. 5, 184.

οὔρεα, τά, Ion. for ὄρεα, see ὄρος.

*οὔρειος, η, ον, Ion. and Ep. for ὄρειος (ὄρος), *mountainous*, h. Merc. 244.

οὐρεύς, ῆος, ὁ, Ion. for ὀρεύς (probably from ὄρος), *a mule*, 1, 50. 24, 716; see ἡμίονος.

οὐρεύς, ῆος, ὁ, Ion. for οὖρος, *a watch, a guard*, 10, 84;† in the gen. οὐρήων. This verse was rejected by the ancients because οὐρεύς was here made to signify *a watch*. Voss translates it *mule*, and Menelaus might be supposed looking for a mule that had strayed.

οὐρή, ἡ, Ion. for οὐρά, *the tail*, 20, 170. Od. 17, 302.

οὐρίαχος, ὁ (οὐρά), *the extreme end*; always with ἔγχεος, *13, 443. 16, 612.

οὖρον, τό, Ep. for ὄρος, *a boundary, extent, space*, plur. οὖρα. ὅσσον τ' ἐν νειῷ οὖρον πέλει ἡμιόνοιϊν, as far in the fallow field as is the limit to the mules, i. e. as much as is required of a pair of mules in the same time in which Cytoneus ran; as oxen accomplish less, Od. 8. 124. ὅτε δή ῥ' ἀπέην ὅσσον τ' ἐπὶ οὖρα (thus Spitzner after the Schol. instead of the common ἐπίουρα), πέλονται ἡμιόνων, when he was so far removed as the space of mules extends. Il. 10, 350. The sense is : Dolon ran so far forward as a pair of mules could plough, viz. in the time that Odysseus (Ulysses) and Diomedes remain standing. The words αἳ γάρ τε βοῶν προφερέστεραί εἰσιν are added by Hom. to show that the distance between Dolon and the two heroes was considerable. Thus Heyne and Spitzner, Excurs. XX, correctly explain the passage. Less natural seems the explanation of Aristarchus followed by Voss. Aristarchus namely supposes two teams, and finds the point of comparison in the space by which a pair of mules in ploughing outstrips a yoke of oxen : (*for as mules surpass Slow oxen furrowing the fallow field*, Cp.); ὅσ ι δίσκου οὖρα πέλονται, as far as

are the limits of the discus, i. e. as far as it flies, 23, 431.

οὖρος, ὁ, poet. *a favorable wind*, often ἱκμενος οὖρος (*secundus ventus*), 7, 5. Od. 2, 420 ; plur. Od. 4, 360. (From ὄρνυμι, or prob. akin to αὔρη.)

οὖρος, ὁ, Ion. for ὄρος, Ep. also οὖρον, τό, *a boundary, a limit*, dat. plur. 12, 421; accus. sing. *21, 405.

οὖρος, εος, τό, Ion. for ὄρος, q. v. *a mountain*.

οὖρος, ὁ, poet. (from ὁράω), *a watcher, a guard*, Od. 15, 89. Thus esply Nestor, οὖρος Ἀχαιῶν, guardian or protector of the Greeks, Il. 8, 80. Od. 3, 411. Damm derives it fm ὥρα, *cura*.

οὐρός, ὁ (ΟΡΩ, *moveo*), *the trench* or canal (ὄρυγμα), by which the ships were drawn into the sea. These canals must have been easily choked up, since they were cleaned out when the ships were to be run into the sea, 2, 153.†

οὖς, τό, gen. ὠτός, dat. plur. ὠσίν, Ep. and Ion. οὔας, ατος [dat. plur. οὔασι, 12, 442]. (Of the comm. form only accus. sing. and dat. plur. 11, 109. 20, 473. Od. 12, 200.) 1) *the ear*. ἀπ' οὔατος, far from the ear, Il. 22, 454. 2) *an ear, i. e. a handle*, 11, 633. 18, 378.

οὐτάζω, fut. άσω ; and οὐτάω, fut. ήσω. Of the first form H. has pres. and imperf. aor. οὔτασα, perf. pass. οὔτασμαι, 11, 661; and from οὐτάω only aor. 1 οὔτησα, aor. pass. οὐτηθείς. Besides the Ep. iterat. imperf. οὔτασκε and the aor. 1 οὐτήσασκε, we find the Ep. aor. 2 οὖτα, infin. οὐτάμεν and οὐτάμεναι, and partcp. aor. 2 mid. οὐτάμενος, *to wound, to hit, to strike*, with any kind of weapon, χαλκῷ, ἔγχεϊ, δουρί, ξίφεϊ : but spoken esply of weapons used with the hand, 11, 661. Od. 11, 536 ; with accus. of the pers. or the part wounded, and with double accus. τινὰ πλευρά, Il. 4, 469. 13, 438; also τινὰ κατὰ λαπάρην, κατ' ἀσπίδα, 6, 64. 11, 434; and spoken of things : οὐτάζειν σάκος, to injure the shield, 7, 258; also ἕλκος, to strike a wound, 5, 361; hence οὐταμένη ὠτειλή, 14, 518.

οὔτασκε, see οὐτάω.

οὐτάω, see οὐτάζω.

οὔτε, adv. *and not*, mly doubled : οὔτε, οὔτε, *neither, nor*, to connect negative members of a sentence. We also find the following constructions : οὐ—οὔτε, 6, 450. 22, 265 ; οὐδὲ—οὔτε, h. Cer. 22. A negative sentence is connected with a positive by οὔτε—τέ, *not—and*, 24, 185.

οὐτήσασκε, see οὐτάζω.

οὔτι, neut. of οὔτις, q. v.

οὐτιδανός, ή, όν (οὔτις), *profitless, worthless, good for nothing, naught*, 1, 231. Od. 9, 460.

οὔτις, neut. οὔτι (τίς), *no one, no man*. The neut. οὔτι, stands after adv. *not at all, by no means*, Od. 4, 199; often separate, Od. 1, 202.

Οὖτις, ὁ, accus. Οὖτιν, *a feigned name* of Odysseus (Ulysses), which he assumed

ὄχα, adv. Ep. (ἔχω, ὄχος), prop. *prominently*; then, *by far, far*, always in connexion with the superl. ὄχ' ἄριστος, 1, 69. Od. 3, 129.

ὄχεσφι, poet. dat., see ὄχος.

ὀχετηγός, όν, poet. (ἄγω), *cutting a trench* or *canal; cutting channels* or *water-courses for irrigation*. ἀνήρ [*a peasant conducting a rill* (through his garden), Cp.], 21, 257.†

ὀχεύς, ῆος, ὁ, poet. (ὀχέω), *a holder*, an instrument for carrying or fastening; hence, 1) the strap or thong with which the helmet was bound under the chin, 3, 372; the clasps of the girdle, 4, 132. 2) Frequently the *bolts* or *bars* which fastened the gate, 12, 121. 291. Od. 21, 47.

ὀχέω (ὄχος), iterative imperf. ὀχέεσκον, fut. mid. ὀχήσομαι, 24, 731; aor. ὀχησάμην. 1) *to carry, to convey, to conduct*, hence metaph. νηπιάας, to practise puerilities, Od. 1. 297. 2) *to endure, to bear*, ὀϊζύν, μόρον, Od. 7, 211. 11, 619. Mid. *to be borne, to suffer oneself to be borne*, κύμασιν, Od. 5, 54; chiefly by ships, chariots, and beasts; *to travel, to ride*, νηυσίν, Il. 24, 731; ἵπποισιν, h. Ven. 218; ἵπποι ἀλεγεινοὶ ὀχέεσθαι, horses difficult to manage, 10, 403. 17, 77.

Ὀχήσιος, ὁ, an Ætolian, 5, 843.

ὀχθέω, Ep. (akin to ἄχθεσθαι), *to be heavy at heart*, from pain, anger, despondency; hence *to be displeased, sad, dispirited, troubled;* often μέγ' ὀχθήσας ἔφη or εἶπε, 4, 30. Od. 4, 332.

ὄχθη, ἡ (ἔχω), prop. prominence; *an elevation of earth, a wall of earth;* esply *a shore, a coast*, 4, 475. Od. 6, 97; spoken of a trench, Il. 15, 356.

*ὄχθος, ὁ=ὄχθη, *a mound of earth, a hill*, h. Ap. 17.

ὀχλέω, Ion. for ὀχλεύω (ὀχλεύς), prop. to move forward with a lever, *to roll on*, only pass. ὑπὸ ψηφῖδες ἅπασαι ὀχλεῦνται, 21, 261.

ὀχλίζω (ὀχλεύς), = ὀχλέω, only optat. aor. 1 ὀχλίσσειαν, prop. to remove with a lever, *to convey away, to roll away*, τὶ ἀπ' οὔδεος ἐπ' ἄμαξαν, something from the ground to the carriage, 12, 448. Od. 9, 242.

ὄχος, εος, τό (ἔχω), always in the plur. τὰ ὄχεα, Ep. dat. ὀχέεσσιν and ὀχεσφιν, *a chariot*, often παρ' ἵπποισι καὶ ὀχεσφιν, 5, 794. 12, 114; also ὑπ' ὀχεσφι τιτύσκεσθαι, 13, 23.

ὄχος, ὁ (ἔχω), *a holder, a bearer;* νηῶν ὄχοι, a holder or protector of ships, spoken of a port, Od. 5, 404.† 2) *a carriage, a chariot*=τὸ ὄχος, h. Cer. 19.

ὄψ, ὀπός, ἡ (ἔπος), accus. ὄπα, *the voice* of men and of animals, 2, 182; spoken of the shriek of Cassandra, Od. 11, 421; of the weeping of Penelope, Od. 20, 92; of the voice of the cicāda, Il. 3, 152; of the bleating of lambs, 4, 435. 2) *utterance, discourse*, 7, 53; ὄπ' for ὄφ', h. 27, 18.

ὀψέ, adv. (akin to ὄπις), *late, long after,*

esply *late in the day, at evening*, 21, 232. Od. 5, 272.

ὀψείω (ὄψομαι), desiderat. *to wish to see*, with gen. αὐτῆς καὶ πολέμοιο, 14, 37.†

ὀψίγονος, ον (γόνος), *late-born, born after*, h. Cer. 141; ἄνθρωποι, posterity, 3, 353. Od. 1, 302.

ὄψιμος, ον, poet. (ὀψέ), *late, late-fulfilled*, τέρας, 2, 325.†

ὄψις, ιος, ἡ (ὄψομαι), dat. ὄψει, *the sight*, i. e. *the aspect, the appearance, the countenance*, 6, 468. Od. 23, 94. h. 18, 29.

ὀψιτέλεστος, ον (τελέω), *late-fulfilled*, or *to be fulfilled*, τέρας, 2, 325.† [Like ὄψιμος, Passow. The emphasis lies not merely in the synonym, but also in the asyndeton; see Nägelsbach ad Il. 1, 99.]

ὄψομαι, fut. of ὁράω.

ὄψον, τό (from ἔψω, prop. any thing cooked), esply any thing eaten with bread, particularly *meat*, Od. 3, 480; generally, *viands*, Il. 11, 630; the onion is called ὄψον ποτῷ, a luncheon with drink. Later, fish were so called, but these in the Homeric age were eaten only in case of necessity.

Π.

Π, the sixteenth letter of the Greek alphabet; hence in Hom. the sign of the sixteenth rhapsody.

πάγεν, Ep. for ἐπάγησαν, see πήγνυμι.

πάγη, Ep. for ἐπάγη, see πήγνυμι.

*παγίς, ίδος, ἡ (πήγνυμι), *a trap, a snare*, Batr. 50.

*παγκράτιον, τό (κρατέω), the pancratium, a kind of combat including at once wrestling and boxing, prop. *the all-combat*, Batr. 95.

πάγος, ὁ (πήγνυμι), *a point of rock, a cliff of rock, a rocky summit*, *Od. 5, 405 [*a craggy mass*, Cp.]. 411.

παγχάλκεος, ον (χαλκός), *all of brass, entirely brazen*, 20, 102; ἄορ, Od. 8, 403; ῥόπαλον, Od. 11, 575.

πάγχαλκος, ον = παγχάλκεος, *Od. 18, 378. 22, 102.

παγχρύσεος, ον (χρυσός), *all of gold, entirely golden*, 2, 448.† h. 8, 4.

πάγχυ, adv. (πᾶς), poet. for πάνυ, *altogether, entirely*, with augment. μάλα πάγχυ, 14, 143. Od. 17; 217; once πάγχυ λίην, Od. 4, 825.

πάθε, Ep. for ἔπαθε, see πάσχω.

παθέειν, Ep. for παθεῖν, see πάσχω.

παιδνός, ή, όν (shortened from παιδικός), *childish, childlike*, in H. as subst. for παῖς, a boy, *Od. 21, 21. 24, 338.

παιδοφόνος, ον (φονεύω), *slaying children* or *boys*, 24, 506.†

παίζω (παῖς), fut. σω, mly in pres. and imperf., imperat. aor. only Od. 8, 251, παίσατε, prop. to behave like a child, hence 1) *to play, to trifle, to sport, to amuse oneself*, Od. 6, 106. 7, 291. h. Cer. 5, 425. 2) Esply *to dance*, Od. 8, 251.

θυγατέρος, 21, 504; sometimes strength-ened. πάλιν αὖτις, back again, 5, 257. ἄψ πάλιν and πάλιν ὀπίσσω, 18, 280. Od. 11, 149. 2) back, with the notion of opposition: πάλιν ἐρέειν, to contradict, Il. 9, 56. πάλιν λάζεσθαι μῦθον, to take back the word, i. e. to speak otherwise than before, 4, 357. Od. 13, 254. 3) Later: again, anew, Batr. 115.

παλινάγρετος, ον, poet. (ἀγρέω), prop. taken back; then to be taken back, to be re-called. τέκμωρ οὐ παλινάγρετον, an irrevocable pledge, 1, 526.†

παλινόρμενος, ον, poet. (ὄρνυμι), turn-ing back, hastening back, 11, 326.†

παλίνορσος, ον, poet. (ὄρνυμι), turning back, hastening back, 3, 33.†

παλίντιτος, ον, poet. (τίνω), paid back, requited, hence punished, avenged. πα-λίντιτα ἔργα γίγνονται, the deeds were avenged, *Od. 1, 379. 2, 144.

παλίντονος, ον (τείνω), stretched back, epith. of the bow, which can be drawn back, hence a general epith. in reference to its elasticity; flexible, elastic, 8, 266. Od. 21, 11. Thus Köppen and Spitzner ad Il. 15, 443. Some critics take it in a double sense: a) stretched back, spoken of the bow, whose string is drawn back when an arrow is to be shot, 8, 266. 15, 443. b) loosed, unbent, spoken of the bow in a state of rest, 10, 459. Others, with Eustath. ad Il. 8, 266, understand by παλίντονον τόξον, a bow which has a repeated curvature, as the Scythian bow, or which was bent upwards at both ends.

παλιρρόθιος, ον (ῥόθος), rushing back, flowing back, κῦμα, *Od. 5, 430. 9, 485.

*παλίσκιος, ον, poet. (σκιά), deeply-shaded, dark, ἄντρον, h. 17, 6.

παλίωξις, ιος, ἡ, poet. (ἰωκή), the act of turning and driving back, when the flying party turns and repels the pursuer, and in turn becomes the pursuer, *12, 71. 15, 69.

παλλακίς, ίδος, ἡ, a concubine, 9, 449. 452. Od. 14, 203.

Παλλάς, άδος, ἡ, epith. of Athênê, from πάλλω, as brandishing the spear, or on account of the expertness of her hands in certain arts, mly Παλλὰς Ἀθήνη or Ἀθηναίη, Il.

Παλλάς, αντος, ὁ, father of Selene, h. Merc. 100.

πάλλω, aor. 1 ἔπηλα, Ep. sync. aor. masc. 3 sing. πάλτο, 15, 645. 1) to brandish, to hurl, to cast; with accus. τινὰ χερσίν, to toss (a child) in one's hands, 6, 474. Esply a) Spoken of weap-ons: δοῦρα, ἔγχος, λίθον. b) Spoken of lots: κλήρους, to shake the lots, viz. in the helmet till one should fly out whose owner was destined, 3, 316; and without κλήρους: to cast lots, 3, 324. 7, 181. Mid. to leap, to spring. ἐν ἀσπίδος ἄντυγι πάλτο, he sprang upon the rim of the shield, 15, 645 (cf. Spitzner, Excurs. XVI.); metaph. to tremble, to palpitate, with fear or joy. πάλλεται ἦτορ ἀνὰ στό-

μα, my heart leaps up to my mouth, 22, 451; δείματι, h. Cer. 294. 2) to cast lots, μετά τινος, with any man, 24, 400. παλλομένων. subaud. ἡμῶν, 15, 191; spoken of those casting lots, not pass. as explained by Heyne, κληρῶν being un-derstood.

Πάλμυς, υος, ὁ (the brandisher), an ally of the Trojans from Ascania, 13, 792. πάλτο, Ep. for ἔπαλτο, see πάλλω.

παλύνω (akin to πάλλω), to strew, to strew upon, ἄλφιτα, 18, 560. Od. 4, 77. b) to bestrew, to cover; with accus. τὶ ἀλφίτου ἀκτῇ, any thing with barley flour, Od. 14, 429; spoken of snow: ἀρούρας, Il. 10, 7.

*παμβώτωρ, ορος, ὁ (βώτωρ), all-nou-rishing, Fr. 25.

παμμέλας, αινα, αν (μέλας), entirely black, ταῦροι, *Od. 3, 6. 10, 525.

*παμμήτειρα, ἡ (μήτηρ), mother of all, all-mother, universal mother, epith. of the earth, h. 30, 1.

Πάμμων, ονος, ὁ (the wealthy, from πᾶμα), son of Priam and Hecabê (Hecu-ba), 24, 250.

πάμπαν, adv. (πᾶς), entirely, altogether, 12, 406. Od. 2, 49.

παμποίκιλος, ον (ποικίλος), exceedingly variegated, beautifully wrought, πέπλοι, 6, 289. Od. 15, 105.

πάμπρωτος, ον (πρῶτος), the very first, Il. 7, 324. The neut. sing. and plur. as adv. first of all, Il. and Od.

παμφαίνω, poet. (from φαίνω, formed by reduplic.), only pres. and imperf., whence παμφαίνῃσι, 3 sing. pres. indic. as if from παμφαίνημι (where, however, with Spitzner, the subj. παμφαίνῃσι should stand), 5, 6; to shine brightly, to beam, to gleam brightly, spoken of stars, l. c. 11, 63; and of brass, with pres. partcp.; sometimes with dat. χαλκῷ, 14, 11. στή-θεσσι παμφαίνοντας, v. 100; Ep. παμ-φανόων.

παμφανόων, gen. ωντος, fem. παμφανό-ωσα, Ep. partcp. from παμφαίνω, as if from παμφανάω, resolved from παμφαι-νῶν, always as adj. brightly shining, gleaming, beaming, flashing, epith. of arms and of brass; ἐνώπια, beaming walls, because they were on the sunny side, 8, 435. Od. 4, 42.

Πάν, gen. Πανός, ὁ, Pan, son of Hermês, by the daughter of Dryops, according to h. 18, 28; or son of Zeus and Thymbris, Apd.; a field, forest, and pastoral divinity of the Greeks, esply of the Arcadians. Particularly sa-cred to him was the mountain Lycaon, in Arcadia. He was represented as hav-ing a rough, hairy form, goat's ears, short goat's horns, and goat's feet. He mly bears a pipe, cf. h. Pan. 2, seq. Ac-cording to h. 18, 47, his name is derived from πᾶς, ὅτι φρένα πᾶσιν ἔτερψεν.

πάναγρος, ον (ἄγρα), all catching, all embracing, λίνον, 5, 487.†

πάναιθος, η, ον, poet. (αἴθω), all burn-ing, all radiant, κόρυς, 14, 372.†

P 6

333. 18, 84; πάντη. Od. 12, 233. 2) With accus. to look around for any one who is missed, Il. 4, 200. 17, 115.

πάρ. poet. shortened: 1) for παρά. 2) for πάρεστι, 9, 43.

παρά, Ep. παραί, and shortened πάρ, I) Prep. with gen., dat., and accus., primar. signif. by, near, at [apud]. A) With gen. 1) spoken of space: a) to indicate withdrawment from the vicinity of a place or person, prop. from the side, mly from : φάσγανον παρὰ μηροῦ ἐρύσσασθαι, to draw the sword from his side [lit. thigh], 1, 190; ἐλθεῖν παρὰ Διός. to come from Zeus, like de chez qin, 21, 444; φέρειν τεύχεα παρὰ Ἡφαίστοιο, to bring arms from Hêphæstus, 18, 137; φθέγξασθαι παρὰ νηός, 11, 585; ἀπονοστεῖν παρὰ νηῶν, 12, 114. 15, 69; ἔρχεσθαι παρὰ ναῦφιν, 12, 225; more rarely spoken of a state of rest: at, by, παρ' ἀσπίδος, 4, 468. 19, 253. 2) To indicate a causal relation in naming the author, still closely bordering on the signif. of place: δέχεσθαι τεύχεα παρά τινος, to receive from any man, 19, 10. 24, 429; τυχεῖν παρά τινος, Od. 6, 290; φράζειν τι παρὰ Ζηνός, 11, 795. B) With dat. 1) spoken of space: a) In marking continuance with an object or person: by, near, at, before: ἧσθαι παρὰ κλισίῃ, to sit by the tent, 1, 329; μένειν παρ' ἀλλήλοισιν, to remain near one another, 5, 577; ἀείδειν παρὰ μνηστήρσιν, to sing by or before the suitors, Od. 1, 154. 2) In a causal signif. perhaps. also φιλέεσθε παρ' αὐτῇ, Il. 13, 627, where however it may be taken in the local sense: to be hospitably entertained with or by any one, cf. Od. 1, 123. C) With accus. 1) spoken of space: a) In indicating an aim. a) Spoken of motion or direction to the vicinity of a person or thing, to, towards: παρὰ νῆας ἰέναι, to go to the ships, 1, 347; ἔρχεσθαι παρὰ Μενέλαον, Od. 1, 185. β) Of motion or direction by a place: by, along: βῆναι παρὰ θῖνα, to go along the shore, Il. 1, 34; οἱ δὲ — παρ' ἐρινεὸν ἐσσεύοντο, they hastened along by the fig-tree hill, 11. 167. b) To indicate an extension in the vicinity of an object without special reference to the motion of it : along, a round. οἱ δὲ κοιμήσαντο παρὰ πρυμνήσια νηός. Od. 12, 32; cf. Il. 1, 463. 16, 312. 2) Metaph. spoken of immaterial states, prop. along by. i. e. without touching; hence, against, contrary to, πὰρ δύναμιν, beyond a man's power, 13, 787: often παρὰ μοῖραν, against fate. Od. 14, 509; opposed to κατὰ μοῖραν. Note: παρά in all three cases can be placed after the nouns, but is then in anastrophe [i. e. cum accentu retracto], Il. 4, 97. II) As adv. only Ep. thereby, by the side, thereupon, 1, 611. 2, 279. III) In composition it has all the significations cited, and, in addition to this, it denotes a transformation or change, as the German um, ver [vors].

πάρα, in anastrophe stands 1) for

παρά. when it is placed after the case governed, 6, 177. 2) for πάρεστι, 5, 603. Od. 3, 324. πάρα σοί, it rests with thee, Il. 19, 148.

παραβαίνω (βαίνω), partcp. perf. παρβεβαώς, Ep. for παραβεβαώς, to mount beside, hence in the perf. to stand in the chariot beside any one, with τινί, 11, 522. 13, 708; see παραβάτης.

παραβάλλω (βάλλω), aor. παρέβαλον, prop. to cast beside; to cast before, τινί τι, any thing to any one, spoken of food, 5, 369. Od. 4, 41: always in tmesis. Mid. prop. to throw, or put down by one-self, as the stm one stakes; hence, to hazard or stake upon, to venture, ψυχήν, 9. 322.

παραβάσκω (βάσκω), Ep. form of παραβαίνω, only imperf. 3 sing. παρέβασκε, he stood by him, 11, 104.†

παραβάτης, ου, ὁ, Ep. παραιβάτης (παραβαίνω), one who stands beside the warrior, i. e. the hero who stands beside the charioteer in the chariot, 23, 132.† in Ep. form.

παραβλήδην, adv. (παραβάλλω), properly, in the manner of being thrown beside; hence metaph. in an ironical signif. παραβ. ἀγορεύειν. to speak covertly, allusively, 4, 6.† According to Schol. 'to speak deceitfully or in reply;' or, according to Wolf, 'falling into the discourse,' interrupting; = ὑποβλήδην.

παραβλώσκω (βλώσκω), perf. Ep. παρμέμβλωκα, to go to the side, to help, τινί, any one. *4, 11. 24, 73.

παραβλώψ, ῶπος, ὁ, ἡ, Ep. (παραβλέπω), looking sidewise, looking askance [slant-eyed, Cp. It is of the Λιταί], 9, 503.†

*παράβολος, ον, poet. παραίβολος: only παραίβολα κερτομεῖν like παραβλήδην, to rebuke in a sly covert manner, to teaze by oblique insinuations, to make side-thrusts at, h. Merc. 56.

παραγίγνομαι (γίγνομαι), to be beside or at, with dat. δαιτί, Od. 17, 173.†

παραδαρθάνω (δαρθάνω), aor. παρέδαρθον, Ep. παρέδραθον, infin. παραδραθέειν, to sleep beside or with any one, τινί, Od. 20. 88; τινὶ φιλότητι, Il. 14, 163.

παραδέχομαι, depon. mid. (δέχομαι), aor. παρεδεξάμην. to take, to receive, τί τινος, any thing from any one, 6, 178.†

παραδραθέειν, see παραδαρθάνω.

παραδραμέτην, see παρατρέχω.

παραδράω (δράω), 3 plur. pres. παραδρώωσι, Ep. resolved for παραδράουσι, to serve, to render service, τινί, to any one, Od. 15, 324.†

παραδύω (δύω), infin. aor. 2 παραδύμεναι, poet. for παραδῦναι, only intrans. to glide along, to creep by, 23, 416.†

παραείδω (ἀείδω), to sing by or before; τινί, to sing before any one, Od. 22, 348.†

παραείρω (ἀείρω), aor. pass. παρηέρθην, to raise beside, pass. to hang beside, 16, 341.†

παραί, poet. for παρά.

παραιβάτης, ου, ὁ, Ep. for παραβάτης, q. v.

subj. παραθείω. Ep. for παραθῶ, optat. 3
plur. παραθεῖεν, imperat. παραθές, mid.
aor. 2 optat. 3 sing. παραθεῖτο, partcp.
παρθέμενος for παραθ., 1) to sit by or
near, to place beside, τινί τι; τράπεζαν,
δίφρον, Od. 5, 92. 20, 259; spoken esply
of food: to place before, δαῖτα, Il. 9, 90;
βρῶσίν τε, πόσιν τε, Od. 1, 192. b) Generally, to present, to give, to bestow,
ξεινιά τινι, Il. 11, 779. 18, 408; δύναμιν
τινι, Od. 3, 205. Mid. to set or put before
oneself, δαῖδας, Od. 2, 105. 19, 150. 2)
to place upon (prop. spoken of a stake),
to venture upon, to peril, κεφαλάς, Od. 2,
237; ψυχάς, Od. 3, 74.

παρατρέπω (τρέπω), aor. 1 παρέτρεψα,
in turn sidewise, to turn aside, to guide
away. παρατρέψας εἶχεν ἵππους, turned
(a little) out of his course and guided
his horses by, *23, 398; ἐκτὸς ὁδοῦ, 423;
other forms, παρατροπέω, τρωπάω.

παρατρέχω (τρέχω), only aor. 2 παρέδρα-
μον, Ep. παραδραμέτην. to run by, 10,
350. 2) to outrun, to outstrip any one,
τινὰ πόδεσσιν, 23, 636. h. 18, 16.

παρατρέω (τρέω), aor. 1 παρέτρεσα, Ep.
σσ, to tremble at the side, to start ti-
morously aside, 5, 295.†

παρατροπέω (τροπέω), poet. for παρατρέπω, only partcp. metaph. τί με ταῦτα
παρατροπέων ἀγορεύεις, wherefore sayest
thou these things to me turning aside,
i. e. dissembling (Prôteus well knew the
design of Menelaus, but dissembled,
pretending not to know), Od. 4, 465.†

παρατρωπάω, poet. = παρατρέπω, only
pres. to turn about; θεοὺς θύεσσι, to prevail on the gods by the vapour of sacrifice, 9, 500.†

παρατυγχάνω (τυγχάνω), to be close by,
to come to, τινί. 11, 74.†

παραυδάω (αὐδάω), partcp. aor. παραυ-
δήσας, 1) to address, to comfort, Od. 15,
53; θάνατόν τινι, to comfort any one
concerning death, Od. 11, 488. 2) to say
or tell, Od. 18, 178.

παράφασις, ἡ, Ep. παραίφασις and
πάρφασις, 1) the act of addressing, per-
suading, encouraging, 11, 793. 15, 404.
b) allurement, 14, 217; in the girdle of
Aphroditē; according to the Schol. to
be taken as adj. with ὀαριστύς; ὁμιλία
παραινετική, intimate intercourse.

παραφεύγω (φεύγω). aor. 2 Ep. infin.
παρφυγέειν, to flee by, with dat. Od. 12, 99.†

παράφημι (φημί). to which aor. παρεί-
πον, mid. παράφαμαι, partcp. παρφάμε-
νος for παραφάμ., infin. παρφάσθαι for
παραφ., 1) to persuade, to counsel, τινί,
1, 577; mly mid. with accus. τινὰ ἐπέεσσιν, to persuade any one by words, to
wheedle, with the notion of craft, 12,
249. Od. 2, 189.

παραφθάνω (φθάνω), only aor. optat.
παραφθαίησι, partcp. παραφθάς, and aor.
2 mid. παραφθάμενος to outstrip, to surpass, τινὰ πόδεσσι, 10, 346. Mid. = act.
τινὰ τάχει. 23, 515.

παρβεβαώς, see παραβαίνω.

παρδαλέη, ἡ, poet. for παρδαλῆ, subaud.

δορά, a leopard-skin [cf. πάρδαλις], 3, 17.
10, 29; prop. fem. of παρδάλεος, έη, εον
(πάρδαλις), belonging to a leopard.

*πάρδαλις, ιος, ἡ, a leopard or panther
[animals then undistinguished], 13, 103.
21, 573, where Spitzner has adopted this
form as approved by Aristarch. for πορ-
δαλίων, πόρδαλις, cf. πόρδαλις, h. Ven.
71.

παρέζομαι, depon. mid. (ἔζομαι), to sit
by, to seat oneself; absol, τινί, by any
man, 1, 557; esply to converse with him,
Od. 4, 738.

παρειά, ἡ, a cheek, prop. spoken of
human beings; rarely of the eagle, Od.
2, 153. 2) the cheek-pieces of the
helmet, h. 31, 11.

παρείθη, see παρίημι.

πάρειμι (εἰμί), pres. 3 plur. πάρεασι,
imperf. 3 plur. πάρεσαν, infin. παρέμμε-
ναι, poet. for παρεῖναι, fut. παρέσομαι,
Ep. σσ, 1) to be beside, present, near,
absol. 2, 485. 14, 299; with dat. τινί, to
be near any one; often for support or
assistance; hence to aid, 11, 75. 18, 472;
also spoken of things: μάχῃ. to be present in the battle. Od. 4, 497; and ἐν
δαίτῃσι, Il. 10, 217. 2) Generally, to be
there, to be ready, to be in store; hence
τὰ παρεόντα, property, stores, Od. 1, 140.
εἴ μοι δύναμίς γε παρείη, if I had the
power, Od. 2, 62. ὅση δύναμίς γε πάρεστι,
as much as is in my power, Il. 8, 294.
13, 786.

πάρειμι (εἶμι), partcp. παριών, to go
near or by, to pass by, *Od. 4, 527. 17,
233. Ep. 3, 6.

παρεῖπον (εἶπον), defect. aor. 2 to παρα-
φημι, 1) to persuade, to address, to
wheedle, τινά, 1, 555. 2) With accus. of
the thing: to advise, to counsel, αἴσιμα,
6, 62. 7, 121; absol. 11, 793.

παρέκ, before a vowel παρέξ, also before consonants, 11, 486. Od. 12. 216.
14, 168 (in later writers πάρεξ), I) Prepos. 1) With gen. without, out of. (ἐκ
with the notion of παρά), παρὲξ ὁδοῦ, Il.
10, 349. h. in Merc. 188; παρὲκ λιμένος,
not far from the harbour. Od. 9, 116. 2)
With accus. near by, without, out of,
beyond, aside from. (παρά with the notion of ἐκ). παρὲξ ἅλα, Il. 9, 7. παρὲκ
μίτον, 23, 762 Od. 12, 443. 16, 165. 343;
along by. παρὲξ τὴν νῆσον ἐλαύνειν νῆα,
Od. 12, 276. 15, 199. h. Ap. 410. In Il.
24, 349, the prep. stands after the accus.
when, according to Spitzner, παρέξ would
better be connected with the verb and
the accus. depend upon it, cf. Od. 12,
53. b) Metaph. παρὲκ νόον, beyond
reason, i. e. without reason, foolishly,
Il. 10, 391. 20, 133. h. Merc. 547. β)
without, except. παρὲξ Ἀχιλῆα, without
Achilles's knowledge, 24, 134. II) Adv.
1) near, near by, along by; στῆναι, 11,
486; νηχεῖν, Od. 5, 439; ὠθεῖν, Od. 9,
488. νῆα παρὲξ ἐλάαν, Od. 12, 109. cf. v.
53. 2) Metaph. aside, i. e. contrary to
right and truth. hence a) ἀλλὰ παρὲξ
εἰπεῖν, παρακλιδόν, turning aside from

come to, to approach, τινι, any one, esply in the pres. and imperf. mid. in a good sense, hence to help, to aid, to stand by, Il. 5, 809. 10, 290. Od. 13, 301; and in a bad sense, Il. 3, 405. 20, 472; often the partcp. aor. 2 παραστάς. 2) to stand by, to be near, esply in the perf. and pluperf. τινί, any one, 15, 255. 17, 563; also spoken of things: νῆες παρέστασαν, the ships were there, 7, 467. b) Metaph. to be near, to be before. ἀλλά τοι ἤδη ἄγχι παρέστηκεν θάνατος, but now death stands immediately before thee, is at hand, 16, 853. αἶσα παρέστη ἡμῖν, Od. 9, 52.

παρίσχω (ἴσχω), poet. form from παρέχω, infin. Ep. παρισχέμεν, 1) to hold near, ἵππους, 4, 229. 2) to reach to, to present. τί τινι, 9, 638.

παρκατέλεκτο, see παρακαταλέγομαι.

παρμέμβλωκε, see παραβλώσκω.

παρμένω, Ep. for παραμένω.

Παρνησός, ὁ Ion. for Παρνασσός, a large mountain in Phocis on the borders of Locris, at the foot of which lay Delphi; now Japara, Od. 19, 431; with σσ, h. Ap. 269. Adv. Παρνησόνδε, to Parnassus, Od. 19, 394. On the orthography, see Buttm., Ausf. Gram. § 21, p. 86.

*παροέγνυμι (οἴγνυμι), to open at the side, to open a little, h. Merc. 152, according to Herm. conject.

πάροιθε, before a vowel πάροιθεν, adv. (πάρος), a) Spoken of place: before, in front [20, 473, of a javelin; = at the point], 8, 494. οἱ πάροιθεν (ἵπποι), the first, or foremost (in the race), opp. οἱ δεύτεροι. 23, 498. b) Of time: before, previously, formerly, 15, 227. τὸ πάροιθεν, οἱ πάροιθεν, those before, Il. 23, 498. 2) Prep. with gen. before, in view, opposite, τινός. 1, 360. 14, 428.

παροίτερος, η, ον, compar. of πάροιθε, the former, the earlier, *23, 459. 480.

παροίχομαι (οἴχομαι), perf. παρώχηκα, to go by, to pass beyond, 4, 272; spoken of time: to pass away, *10, 252.

πάρος, adv. of time: a) before, formerly; in like manner: τὸ πάρος, with the pres. at other times. πάρος οὔτι θαμίζεις, t' ou dost not at other times come often; thou hast hitherto not been a frequent visitor, 18, 386. Od. 5, 88. cf. Il. 12, 346: with πρίν γε following: before, 5. 218. Od. 2, 127. b) As relat. partcp. with infin. before, ere. πάρος τάδε ἔργα γενέσθαι, ere these deeds occurred, 6, 348. Od. 1, 21. c) rather, Il. 8, 166; according to Damm: πάρος τοι δαίμονα δώσω, where it likewise signifies 'before.' 2) As prep. before, for πρό only 8, 254 †

*Πάρος, ἡ, one of the Cyclades, an island in the Ægean sea, famed for its white marble, h. Ap. 44; now Paro.

παρπεπιθών, see παραπείθω.

Παρρασίη. ἡ, a town in Arcadia according to 2, 608; later, a district in the south-western part of Arcadia.

παρσταίην. παρστάς. see παρίστημι.

παρστήσετον, see παρίστημι.

παρτιθεῖ, see παρατίθημι.

πάρφαμαι, see παράφημι.

πάρφασις, ἡ, see παράφασις.

παρώχηκα, see παροίχομαι.

πᾶς, πᾶσα, πᾶν, gen. παντός, πάσης, παντός, dat. plur. Ep. πάντεσσι for πᾶσι, and gen. plur. fem. πασέων for πασῶν, 1) every one, in sing. 16, 265. Od. 13, 313. Plur. all; when the notion of union or exclusion is expressed: ἐννέα πάντες, nine all of them = nine together or all nine [al. nine in all], Il. 7, 161. Od. 8, 258. 2) (the) whole, including all the parts. πᾶσα ἀλήθεια, Il. 24, 407. Od. 11, 507: οἶκος, Od. 2, 48. 3) Pecul. uses = παντοῖος, of every kind, δαίδαλα πάντα. οἰωνοῖσι πᾶσι, Il. 1, 5. γίγνεσθαι πάντα, to become all things, i. e. to assume every form, Od. 4, 417. 4) The neut. plur. as adv. entirely, altogether, Il. and Od.

Πασιθέη, ἡ, one of the Graces, whom Hêrê promised to the god of sleep for a bride, 14, 269. 276.

πασιμέλουσα, ἡ (μέλω), an appellation of the ship Argo, prop. which is a care to all, known to all, Od. 12, 70.†

πάσσαλος, ὁ (πήγνυμι), Ep. dat. πασσαλόφι, a wooden pin, a peg, to hang any thing upon, Il. ἀπὸ πασσαλόφι αἱρεῖν, to take down from the pin, 24, 268.

πάσασθαι, see πατέομαι.

πάσσω, only pres. and imperf. to strew, lay, or sprinkle upon, spoken of dry and of liquid things, prop. with accus. φάρμακα, also with gen. ἁλός, to strew some salt upon, *9, 214; see ἐμπάσσω.

πάσσων, ον, compar. of παχύς.

πάσχω, fut. πείσομαι. aor. 2 ἔπαθον, perf. πέπονθα, also πέποσθε for πέπονθτε, πεπόνθατε, see Buttm., Gram. § 110, note 5 (according to Thiersch, perf. pass. § 212. 26); also Ep. partcp. perf. fem. πεπαθυῖα, Od. 17, 555 (prop. to receive an impression, both good and bad); in H. always in a bad sense: 1) to suffer, to endure, to bear, to sustain, spoken both of the body and the soul, with accus. κακόν, κακά, ἄλγεα, πήματα, often ἀλγέα θυμῷ, κατὰ θυμόν, Il. 9, 321. Od. 1, 4; ἔκ τινος, Od. 2, 134. b) Often absol. μήτι — πάθῃ, = lest any thing should happen to him, i. e. lest he should die, Il. 5, 567. 10, 538. Od. 17, 596. 2) In the interrogation τί πάθω; what am I to do? as an expression of the greatest embarrassment, Il. 11, 404. Od. 5, 465; and in like manner in the partcp. aor. τί παθόντε λελάσμεθα ἀλκῆς; what has happened to us, that we have forgotten our strength? Il. 11, 313. cf. Od. 24, 106.

πάταγος, ὁ, any loud noise arising from the collision of bodies, cracking or breaking trees, 16, 769; the chattering of the teeth, 13, 282; the dashing of the waves, *21, 9.

πατάσσω (akin to πάταγος), to strike, to beat, to knock, to palpitate, spoken of the heart, *7, 216. 13, 282.

πατέομαι. Ep. depon. mid. aor. ἐπασάμην, Ep. πασσάμην, pluperf. πεπάσμην,

hinder, to hold, to stop, with accus. ἅρμα, νῆα, Il. 23, 585 Od. 13, 168; with double accus. τινὰ βλέφαρα, to blind any one's eyes, Od. 23, 17. 2) Spoken esply of the supposed influence of a deity, who obstructs men in the accomplishment of their purposes: to restrain, to entangle, to ensnare, spoken of Atē, Moira, Διώρεα Μοῖρ' ἐπέδησαν, Il. 4, 517; ἀπὸ πατρίδος αἴης, to hold back from one's country, Od. 23, 353; and simply gen. κελεύθου, from the way, Od. 4, 380; with infin. Ἕκτορα μεῖναι Μοῖρα ἐπέδησε, Fate compelled Hector to remain, Il. 22, 5. Μοῖρά μιν ἐπέδησε δαμῆναι, Fate entangled him to be slain, Od. 3, 269. (Nitzsch and Bothe correctly refer μίν to the singer; the following ἀοιδόν is not superfluous, but opposed to ἐθέλουσαν. Eustath., and amongst the moderns Passow and Voss refer it to (Clytemnestra) Klytæmnestra; Voss translates, 'after the fate of the gods had ensnared her for destruction;' and Passow, 'that she was overcome,' i. e. that she yielded to his will. But H. uses this phrase always of one who is about to die, Il. 16, 434. 17, 421; cf. δαμάω. Others [so the most recent editor, Fäsi] refer it, with equal incorrectness, to Ægisthus.)

πέδη, ἡ (πέδον), a foot-fetter for horses, the tether with which horses pasturing in the field were bound; in the plur. 13, 36.†

πέδιλον, τό, a sandal; these were bound upon the feet in going out, Od. 15, 550. They were made of ox-hide, Od 14, 23; and sometimes ornamented. With the gods they are ambrosial and golden, and have a motive power of their own, Il. 24, 340; see Voss, Myth. Br. I. p. 128.

πεδίον, τό (πέδον), plain, field, level surface, Il. and Od.; plur. πεδία with ā, Il. 12, 283.

πεδίονδε, adv. to the plain, 6, 693. Od. 3, 421.

πεδόθεν, adv. (πέδον), from the ground; metaph. fundamentally, thoroughly, φίλος, Od. 13, 295.†

*πέδον, τό, the ground, the floor, the earth, h. Cer. 455.

πέδονδε, adv. down to the ground, to the earth, 13, 796. Od. 11, 598.

πέζα, ἡ (akin to πούς), the foot, mly the end, the extremity, of the pole, 24, 272.†

πέζος, ὁ (πέζα), going on foot, one who walks, in opposition to one who rides, 4, 231. 5, 13. 2) by land, in distinction from those who go by ship, 9, 329. Od. 1, 173. 11, 58.

πείθω, fut. πείσω, aor. 1 ἔπεισα, only optat. πείσειε, Od. 14, 123; aor. 2 Ep. πέπιθον, subj. πεπίθω, optat. πεπίθοιμι, infin. πεπιθεῖν, partcp. πεπιθών, imperat. πέπιθε, h. Ap. 275; fut. mid. πείσομαι, aor. 2 ἐπιθόμην with redupl. optat. πεπίθοιτο, only Il. 10, 204; perf. 2 πέποιθα, I trust, pluperf. πεποίθεα, Od. 4, 434; also the syncop. form ἐπέπιθμεν, Il. 2,

341. Also an Ep. form from aor. 2, fut. πιθήσω, ἐπίθησα, see ΠΙΘΕΩ, and fut. πεπιθήσω, trans. 22, 223. I) Act. to move by representations and friendly means; hence a) By words or prayers, to persuade, to induce, to convince, to influence by entreaty, with accus. τινά, 1, 132. Od. 14, 363; often with φρένας τινί, Il. 4, 104; θυμόν τινος, 9, 587; and with infin. 22, 223; primar. in a good sense, but also to persuade, to wheedle, through craft, 1, 132. Od, 2, 106. b) By presents: to persuade, to appease, to conciliate, Il. 1, 100. 9, 181. c) to induce to obedience, τινά, 9, 345; poet. θυέλλας. to excite storms, 15, 26. II) Mid. to move oneself, to let oneself be persuaded, won over, hence 1) to be convinced, to believe, to trust, often absol. 8, 154. 2) to obey, to follow, to yield to, τινί, any one, with double dat. τινὶ ἔπεσι, 1, 150; γέραϊ, to obey or give up to age, i. e. to accommodate oneself to the disabilities of age, 23, 645; νυκτί, to obey the night, i. e. to take rest, 7, 182; πάντα, to obey in every thing, Od. 17, 21. ἅ τιν' οὐ πείσεσθαι ὀίω, in which I do not think any one will obey him, Il. 1, 289. cf 20, 466. Od. 3, 146. 3) The perf. πέποιθα, to trust in, to confide in, to rely, to be confident, esply often in the partcp. with dat. ποδωκείῃσι, ἱπποσύνῃ, ἀλκί, Il. 2, 792; absol. 1, 524; and with infin. following, 13, 96. Od. 16, 71.

πείκω, see πέκω.

πεινάω (πεῖνα), contr. πεινῶ, hence infin. πεινήμεναι. Od. 20, 137. elsewhere uncontr. to be hungry, to hunger, Il. 3, 25; τινός, to hunger for a thing. Od. 20, 137.

πείνη, ἡ, Ep. for πεῖνα, hunger, famine, Od. 15, 407.†

πειράζω = πειράω, to tempt, to put to the proof, absol. Od. 9, 281; τινός, *Od. 16, 319.

Πειραΐδης, ου, ὁ, son of Piræus = Ptolemaus, 4, 228.

Πείραιος, ὁ, son of Clytius, Od. 15, 539, 540.

πειραίνω, poet. for περαίνω, aor. 1 ἐπείρηνα, perf. pass. πεπείραμαι. 1) to bring to an end, to accomplish. πάντα πεπείρανται, Od. 12, 37. 2) to pierce through, to transfix. πειρήνας διὰ νῶτα χελώνης, sc. δόνακας, h. Merc. 48. 3) to bind to, to attach, prop. opposite ends (πείρατα), to fasten with a knot; σειρὴν ἔκ τινος, *Od. 22, 175.

πεῖραρ or πεῖρας, ατος, τό, Ep. for πέρας, 1) an end, a limit, a boundary, γαίης, πόντου, 14, 200. 8, 478. 2) termination, completion, issue. πεῖραρ ἑλέσθαι, to receive the issue (viz. of the contest), to bring the contest to an end, 18, 501. πείρατα νίκης ἔχονται ἐν θεοῖσιν, the end, i. e. the attainment of victory depends upon the gods, 7, 102. πείρατα ὀλέθρου ἱκνεῖσθαι, to reach the limit of destruction, 6, 143; in like manner πειρ. ὀλ. ἐφῆπται, the end of destruction depends over the Trojans, 7, 402. 12, 79

high sea, in the plur. ἁλὸς ἐν πελάγεσσιν (in the gulfs of ocean, Cp.), Od. 5, 335. h. Ap. 73.

Πελάγων, οντος, ὁ, a leader of the Pylians, Od. 4, 295. 2) a Lycian, a companion of Sarpêdon, Il. 5, 695.

πελάζω (πέλας), aor. 1 ἐπέλασα, Ep. πέλασα (σσ), mid. aor. 1 ἐπελασάμην, aor. pass. ἐπελάσθην, Ep. syncop. aor. mid. ἐπλήμην, from which πλῆτο, plur. πλῆτο, perf. pass. πεπλημένος, Od. 12, 108; also Ep. form πελάω, infin. πελάαν, h. 6, 44. 1) Act. 1) Trans. to bring near, to cause to approach, spoken of things animate and inanimate: τινά, or τί τινι, Il. 2, 744. Od. 3, 300; νευρὴν μαζῷ, to bring (draw) the string to the breast, Il. 4, 123; τινὰ χθονί or οὔδει, to stretch a man upon the earth, 8, 277; ἱστὸν ἱστοδόκῃ, to let down the mast into its receptacle, 1, 434; metaph. τινὰ ὀδύνῃσι, to put any one in pangs, 5, 766; sometimes absol. without dat. and accus. 15, 418. 21, 93. b) Instead of the dat. in Od. εἴς τι, ἔν τινι, Od. 7, 254. 10. 404: τινὰ οὔδασδε, Od. 10, 440; τινὰ δεῦρο, Od. 5, 111. 2) Intrans. to near, to approach, Od. 12, 41; with dat. νήεσσι, Il. 12, 112. II) Mid. 1) Intrans. esply in the aor. 1 pass. and Ep. aor. mid. to approach, to come near, to go to, absol. 12, 420: with dat. 5, 282. πλῆτο χθονί, he sank to the earth, 14, 438; οὔδει, v. 467. ἀσπίδες ἔπληντ᾽ ἀλλήλῃσι, the shields pressed upon one another, 4. 449. 2) Trans. to bring near, to cause to approach, only in the aor. τινὰ νηυσίν, to convey any one to the ships, 17, 341.

πέλας, adv. near, close by, Od. 10, 516, with gen. Τηλεμάχου πέλας, *Od. 15, 257.

Πελασγικός, ή, όν, Pelasgian. τὸ Πελασγικὸν Ἄργος, the Pelasgian Argos in Thessaly, 2, 681 (see Ἄργος). 2) ὁ Πελασγικός, an appell. of Zeus in Dôdôna, 16, 233.

Πελασγοί. οἱ, the Pelasgi, one of the oldest and greatest of the tribes of Greece. They dwelt originally in the Peloponnesus, in Thessaly and Epīrus, 2, 681. 16, 234. Thence they spread themselves to Asia Minor, esply about Larissa, 2, 840: to Crete, Od. 19, 177. According to Hdt. 1, 56, 57, they were the aboriginal inhabitants of the country. They were probably a different race from the Hellēnes, and migrated from Asia into Greece. The name is derived from πελάζειν; it signifies, therefore, one approaching, a stranger, and according to Strab. V. p. 221, it is equivalent to Πελαργοί.

*πελάω, poet. form of πελάζω, q. v.

πέλεθρον, τό, poet. for πλέθρον, an acre, a piece of land, prob. as much as one can plough in a day with a team, 21, 407. Od. 11, 577.

πέλεια, ἡ (πελός, πέλιος), the wild dove, of a bluish colour, 21, 493. Od. 15, 527.

πελειάς. άδος. ἡ = πέλεια, only in the plur. Il. 634. 5, 775.

πελεκάω (πέλεκυς), aor. 1 ἐπελέκησα Ep. πελέκκησα, to cut with an axe, to hew, χαλκῷ δοῦρα, Od. 5, 244;† in the Ep. form.

πελέκκησε, see πελεκάω.

πέλεκκον, τό, Ep. πέλεκκον (πέλεκυς), the helve or handle of an axe, 13, 612.†

πέλεκυς, εος, ὁ, dat. plur. πελέκεσσι, a hatchet, an axe, for carpenter's work and for the slaughter of victims, 13, 391. Od. 3, 499; a battle-axe, only Il. 15, 711.

πελεμίζω, Ep. aor. 1 πελέμιξα, aor. pass. Ep. πελεμίχθην, 1) to put in violent motion, to wave, to cause to tremble, to shake, with accus. οὐρίαχον, 13, 443: σάκος, 16, 108; ὕλην, 16, 766; τόξον, to shake a bow, spoken of one who begins or attempts to draw it, Od. 21, 125. Pass. to put oneself in violent motion, to tremble, to shake, spoken of Olympus, Il. 8, 413; often aor. to be violently repulsed, πελεμίχθη χασσάμενος, 4, 535. 5, 626.

πελάσκεο, see πέλομαι.

πέλευ, see πέλομαι.

Πελίης, ον, ὁ, Ion. for Πελίας, son of Crêtheus, or, according to fable, of Poseidôn and Tyro, sovereign of Iolcos. He wrested from his brother Æson the dominion of Iolcos, and also banished his other brother, Nêleus. Jason, the son of Æson, he compelled to undertake the expedition to Colchis, Od. 11, 254, seq

πέλλα, ἡ. a milk-pail, a vessel for milking, 16, 642 †

Πελλήνη, ἡ, a city in Achaia. between Sicyon and Ægeira, in the time of Strabo a village; now, the ruins near Trikala, 2, 574.

*Πελοπόννησος, ἡ, the Peloponnesus, Pelops's island. It received this name from the Phrygian Pelops; earlier it was called Ἀπία, Πελασγία, Ἄργος, h. Ap. 250. 290.

Πέλοψ, οπος, ὁ, son of Tantalus, husband of Hippodameia, father of Atreus, Thyestès, etc. Expelled from Phrygia, he went with a colony to Elis, to king Œnomäus; whose daughter Hippodameia he won in a race, together with the kingdom of Elis. He extended his dominion over the greater part of the Peloponnêsus, so that this peninsula received a name from him, 2, 104, seq.

πέλω, mly πέλομαι, depon. mid. poet. only pres. and imperf. Of the act. 3 sing. pres. πέλει, imperf. 3 sing. πέλεν and ἔπλε. More frequently the mid. in the imperf. also syncop. forms: 2 sing. ἔπλεο, contr. ἔπλευ, 3 sing. ἔπλετο, Ep. iterat. πελέσκεο, 22, 433; Ep. imperat. πέλευ for πέλου. 1) Prop. to be in motion, to stir oneself, to move oneself, rarely: πέλει κλαγγὴ οὐρανόθι πρό. the cry rose to heaven, 3, 3. cf. Od. 13, 60. Il. 11, 392. 2) Mly to be, like versari, with the implied notion of motion. a) With subst. οἰμωγὴ καὶ εὐχωλὴ πέλεν, 4, 450. ἔπλετ᾽ ἔργον ἅπασιν, now was a work for all 12, 271. b) With adj. τοῦτο δὴ οἴκτιστον πέλεται βροτοῖσι, this is most piable to

πέπων, ονος, ὁ, ἡ (πέσσω), prop. cooked by the sun; hence, *ripe, mellow, tender;* spoken of fruits, in H. always metaph. in an address: 1) In a good sense, ὦ πέπον, *friend, companion, beloved,* 5, 109. 15, 437; and κριὲ πέπον, Od. 9, 447. 2) In a bad sense: *dastard, coward,* Il. 2, 235; (according to Voss, also Il. 13, 120.)

περ, an enclitic particle, shortened from περί, signifies prop. *through and through, throughout;* it strengthens the word to which it is annexed, in respect to the *compass* of the notion. It signifies hence: 1) *very, entirely [valde]*, when it stands by itself, without reference to another thought; a rare and only Ep. use is with adj. and adv.: ἀγαθός περ ἐών, very good, 1, 131; cf. Od. 1, 315. φράδμων περ, Il. 16. 638. ἐπεί μ' ἔτεκές γε μινυνθάδιόν περ ἐόντα, being very short-lived, 1. 352. μίνυνθά περ, for a very short time, 1, 416. ὀλίγον περ, 11, 391. 2) More frequently in the Ep. language it is used in reference to another thought: a) If the two corresponding notions, of which one is to be supplied, be concordant, περ has an enhancing force: *entirely, indeed, by all means.* καὶ αὐτοί περ πονεώμεθα, let us work ourselves' (not merely others), 10, 70; οἴκαδέ περ νεώμεθα, let us by all means return home', 2, 236. b) If the two notions are antithetical, περ signifies *by all means yet, at least.* ἐπεί μ' ἔτεκές γε μινυνθάδιόν περ ἐόντα, τιμήν πέρ μοι ὄφελλεν Ὀλύμπιος ἐγγυαλίξαι, Zeus should yet have by all means accorded honour to me, 1, 353. cf. 9, 301. c) Esply it then stands with partcp. and signifies, *how much soever, although, though:* ἱέμενός περ, however much thou desirest; ἀχνύμενός περ, a'though grieved; οὐτάμενός περ. 3) Very often πέρ stands after conjunct. or relatives: 1) If the two members of a sentence, or the sentences relating to each other are concordant, πέρ signifies, *entirely, by all means, throughout;* ὅσπερ, *the very same, who,* in like manner οἷός περ; ὅπου περ, *wheresoever:* ὅθεν περ, *whencesoever,* etc. 2) In antithetic members πέρ signifies *still, also;* ὅσπερ, *who yet;* εἴ περ, *although,* q. v.; cf. Kühner, § 595. Rost, § 133.

περάαν, see περάω.

Περαιβοί, οἱ, poet. for Περραιβοί, the *Perrhæbi,* inhabitants of Perrhæbia in Thessaly. They dwelt first on the Peneus, as far as the sea; subsequently being driven back by the Lapithæ, further in the interior, 2, 749. The comm. form h. Apoll. 218.

περαιόω (περαῖος), aor. pass. περαιωθέντες, 1) *to convey over, to bring over;* pass. *to pass over, to travel over,* Od. 24, 437.†

περάτη, ἡ, fem. from πέρατος, subaud. γῆ or χώρα, *the region beyond, the country opposite,* esply the opposite quarter of the heavens, ἐν περάτῃ, as opposed to

Ἡώς, in the western sky (V. 'at the end of the path'), Od. 23, 243.†

περάω (πέρα), pres. infin. περάαν, Ep. for περᾶν, iterat. imperf. περάασκε, fut. περήσω, 1) Intrans. *to pierce through, to go through, to pass through,* spoken of missiles, absol. 21, 594; διὰ κροτάφοιο, 4, 563; of the rain, Od. 5, 480; with accus. of the place, ὀδόντας, Il. 5, 291 ὀστέον εἴσω, 4, 460. 6, 10; hence generally. *to go through, to pass through, to steer through,* spoken of persons: πόντον, Od. 24, 118; τάφρον, to pass over the ditch, Il 12, 63; πύλας Ἀΐδαο, to pass through the gates of Hades, 5, 646; also absol. with prep: διὰ Ὠκεανοῖο, through Oceanus, Od. 10, 508; ἐπὶ πόντον, to sail over the sea, Il. 2, 613. 2) Trans. only poet. *to convey through, to conduct through,* τὶ κατὰ δειρῆς, h. Merc. 133; perhaps also Il. 5, 291.

περάω (πέρα), aor. ἐπέρασα, Ep. σσ, perf. pass. πεπέρημαι, 21, 58; =the later πιπράσκω, prop. *to bring over for sale;* hence, *to sell,* with accus. 21, 102. h. Cer. 132: τινὰ Λῆμνον, to sell any one to Lemnos, 21, 40; or ἐς Λῆμνον, v. 58, and πρὸς δώματα, Od. 15, 387. The pres. περάω does not occur; for which we have the poet. form πέρνημι.

Πέργαμος, ἡ (among later writers τὸ Πέργαμον and τὰ Πέργαμα), the citadel of Ilium, see Ἴλιος, 4, 508. 5, 446. 460.

Περγασίδης, ου, ὁ, son of Pergasus = Deïcoon, 5, 535.

πέρην, Ep. and Ion. for πέραν, prep. with gen. 1) *beyond,* on the other side, 24, 752. 2) *opposite to;* Εὐβοίης, *Il. 2, 535.

περησέμεναι, see περάω.

πέρθαι, see πέρθω.

πέρθω, fut. πέρσω, aor. 1 ἔπερσα, aor. 2 ἔπραθον, mid. fut. with pass. signif. πέρσομαι. infin. of the syncop. aor. 2 πέρθαι, 1) *to lay waste, to destroy, to desolate,* spoken only of cities and countries, with accus. πόλιν. 2, 660. Od. 1, 2. οὐ νύ τοι αἶσα, πόλιν πέρθαι Τρώων, it is not appointed to thee by fate to destroy the city of the Trojans, 16, 708. Pass. 2, 374. 4, 291. πόλις πέρσεται. 24, 729. 2) *to pillage, to plunder,* τὶ ἐκ πολίων, 1, 125.

περί, I) Prep. with gen. dat. and accus. primar. signif *round about,* spoken both of the full circumference of an object, as also of only that part embraced by one view. A) With gen. 1) Spoken of place: a) To indicate existence about an object, poet. and rare: *around.* τετάνυστο περὶ σπείους ἡμερίς, around the cave, Od. 5, 68. περὶ τρόπιος βεβαώς, riding upon the keel, Od. 5, 130. 2) In a causal relation, in manifold applications: a) In presenting an object, about which as a centre the action moves, almost like ἀμφί, *around, about, concerning, for, over, before.* a) Almost local, still with verbs signif. to fight, to contend in order to plunder, to defend,

lying open, κολώνη, 2, 812; αὐλή, Od. 14, 7.

περιδρύπτω (δρύπτω), Ep. aor. pass. περιδρύφθην, to tear round about; pass. to b·torn or lacerated: ἀγκῶνας περιδρύφθη, his elbows were lacerated, 23, 395.†

περιδύω (δύω), aor. 1 Ep. περιδῦσα, to draw off round about, to pull or strip off (elsewhere ἀπέδυσε), with accus χιτῶνας, 11, 100.†

περιδώμεθον, see περιδίδωμι.

περιειδον (ΕΙΔΩ), defect. aor. 2 in. H. only perf. περίοιδα, infin. περιΐδμεναι, Ep. for περιειδέναι, pluperf. περιῄδειν, 3 sing. περιῄδη, with pres. signif. to know or understand better [than others, or than most], with infin. [= to know well how to—],10, 247; with accus. of the thing and gen. of the pers. τινός, than another, Od. 3, 244. b) to be more intelligent in any thing, to be wiser in any thing, τινί, Od. 17, 317. βουλῇ περιΐδμεναι ἄλλων, to excel others in counsel, Il. 13, 728.

περίειμι (εἰμί), 1) to be above, i. e. to be more excellent than any one, to excel, to be superior, with gen. of the pers. and accus. of the thing: φρένας, νόον, in intelligence, wisdom, Od. 18, 248. 19, 326. Il. 1, 258; in tmesis.

περιέπω, only in tmesis, see ἕπω, 15, 555.

περιέχω (ἔχω), only aor. 2 Ep. mid. περισχόμην, imperat. περίσχεο, to encompass, to embrace. Mid. to hold oneself around anything, i. e. to embrace any one protectingly, to protect, to shelter any one, with gen. of pers. 1, 393; with accus. Od. 9, 199.

Περιήρης, ους, ὁ, father of Borus, 16, 177.

περιζαμενῶς, poet. adv. (ζαμενής), very powerfully, very vehemently. h. Merc. 495.

περιηχέω (ἠχέω), aor. περιήχησα, to resound round about, to ring, to rattle, 7, 267.†

περιΐδμεναι. see περιειδον.

περιΐστημι (ἵστημι). aor. 2 περίστην, Ep. for περιέστην, subj. περιστήωσι for περιστῶσι, optat. περισταίεν, aor. 1 mid. περιστησάμην, aor. pass. περιστάθην. H. only intrans. aor. 2 act. mid. and aor. pass.: 1) to place oneself about, to stand about, 4, 532; also aor pass. Od. 11, 243. 2) to place oneself about any one or any thing, to surround him, to encircle, with accus. βοῦν περιστήσαντο, they placed themselves around the ox, Il. 2, 410; τινά, 17, 95. Od. 20, 50.

περικαλλής, ές (καλός), very beautiful, exceedingly beautiful, fascinating, mly epith. of things; more rarely spoken of persons, 5, 389. Od. 11, 281. h. Merc. 323.

περικαλύπτω, only in tmesis, see καλύπτω.

περίκειμαι, depon. mid. (κεῖμαι), to lie around any thing, to surround, to embrace, with dat. τόξῳ, Od. 21, 54; τινί, to hold any one encompassed, Il. 19, 4; metaph. οὐδέ περίκειται μοί τι, nor have I any advantage or benefit [any thing

peculiar in store, or reserved, for me], 9, 321.

περικήδομαι, mid. (κήδω), to be very anxious, to be troubled, τινός, about any one, Od. 3, 219; τινὶ βιότου, to be anxious for any one concerning property, *Od. 14, 527.

περίκηλος, ον, poet. (κῆλον), parched, very dry, *Od. 5, 240. 18, 309.

Περικλύμενος, ὁ, son of Neleus and Perô; he had received from Poseidôn the gift of metamorphosing himself into many forms, Od. 11, 286.

*περίκλυστος, η, ον (κλύζω), washed on all sides by the waves, sea-girt, Δῆλος, h. Ap. 181.

περικλυτός, όν (κλυτός), heard on all sides, hence: speaking loud, singing loud: it is thus explained as an epith. of ἀοιδός, Od. 1, 325. (V. on the other hand 'far celebrated'), mly. 2) heard of round about, i. e. celebrated, famous, glorious, epith. of persons and things, Il. 1, 607. 7, 299.

περικτείνω, only in tmesis, see κτείνω.

περικτίονες, οἱ (κτίζω), only plur. those dwelling round about, neighbours, 19, 104; also as adj. with ἄνθρωποι, Od. 2, 65; ἐπίκουροι, Il. 17, 220.

περικτίται, ων, οἱ, Ep. = περικτίονες, Od. 11, 288.†

περιλέπω, only in tmesis, see λέπω.

περιμαιμάω, Ep. (μαιμάω), only pres. partcp. Ep. περιμαιμώωσα for περιμαιμάουσα, to seek eagerly round about, to be in eager quest of, with accus. σκόπελον, Od. 12, 95.†

περίμετρος, ον (μέτρον), immensely great, ἱστόν, *Od. 2, 95. 19, 140.

Περιμήδης, εος, ὁ (very wise, see μῆδος), 1) a companion of Odysseus (Ulysses), Od. 11, 23. 2) father of Schedius, Il. 15, 515.

περιμήκετος, ον. poet. = περιμήκης; ἐλάτη, 14, 287; Τηΰγετον, Od. 6, 103.

περιμήκης, ες (μῆκος), very long, very high, spoken of mountains, 13, 65. Od. 13, 183; of the wand of Kirkê (Circe), Od. 10, 293; of the neck of Scylla, Od. 12, 90.

περιμηχανάομαι, depon. mid. (μηχανάω), 3 plur. pres. περιμηχανόωνται, Ep. resolved: to prepare craftily on all sides: generally, to resolve upon craftily, to devise or contrive, τί, Od. 7, 200; δούλιον ἦμάρ τινι, *Od. 14, 340.

Πέριμος, ὁ, son of Meges, a Trojan, slain by Patroclus, 16, 695.

περιναιετάω, poet. (ναιετάω), to dwell round about, *Od. 2, 66. 8, 551. 2) Intrans. to be inhabited, to lie, spoken of cities, Od 4, 177.

περιναιέτης, ον, ὁ, poet. (ναίω), one of those dwelling round about, a neighbour, 24, 488.†

περιξεστός, ή, όν (ξεστός), hewed round about, smoothed, smooth, πέτρη, Od. 12, 79.†

περίοιδα, see περιειδον.

περιπέλομαι, depon. mid. poet. (πέλο-

9. 465: with accus. φῦλα ἀνθρώπων, to have commerce or intercourse with the tribes of men, h. Merc. 542.

περίτροχος, ον (τρέχω), *running around in a circle*, hence *circular*, 23, 455.†

περιφαίνομαι, pass. (φαίνω), *to appear round about, to be visible round about*, only partcp. περιφαινόμενον: ὄρος, a far-seen mountain, 13, 179. h. Ven. 100. ἐν περιφαινομένῳ, in a conspicuous place, Od. 5, 476.

Περίφας, αντος, ὁ, 1) son of Ochesius, an Ætolian, who was slain by Arês, 5, 842. seq. 2) son of Epytus, a herald of the Trojans, 17, 323.

Περιφήτης, ου, ὁ, son of Copreus of Mcênæ, slain by Hector, 15, 639. 2) a Mysian, 14, 515.

περιφραδής, ές (περιφράζομαι), *very considerate, prudent, wise*, h. Merc. 464; often adv. περιφραδέως, *thoughtfully, considerately*, 2, 466. Od. 14, 431.

περιφράζομαι, mid (φράζω), *to consider on all sides, carefully to ponder*, νόστον, Od. 1, 76.†

περίφρων, ον (φρήν) *very considerate, prudent, intelligent*, epith. of women, 5. 412. Od. 1, 329; and often.

περιφύω (φύω), only aor. 2 infin. περιφῦναι and partcp. περιφύς, intrans. *to grow round about*; hence περιφῦναί τινι, *to intwine oneself about any one, to embrace*, Od. 19, 416; mly with accus. Od. 24, 236. 320; without case, *Od. 16, 21.

περιχέω (χέω), aor. 1 περιχεῦα, Ep. for περιέχεα, aor. 1 mid. subj. περιχεύεται with shortened vowel, Od. 6, 232. cf. Od. 3, 426; *to pour around, to pour upon*, τί, Il. 21, 319: esply spoken of workers in metal: χρυσὸν κέρασι, to put gold about the horns, spoken of a victim adorned for sacrifice by putting gold plates about the horns, or gilding them, Od. 3, 426. Il. 10, 294; metaph. χάριν τινί. to pour grace over any one, Od. 23, 162. Mid. 1) *to pour about oneself*; χρυσὸν ἀργύρῳ, to put gold about silver, i e. to gild it, Od. 6, 232. 23, 159. 2) *to spread or extend over any thing*, metaph. ἀχλύεσις, Il. 2, 19.

περιχώομαι (χώομαι), aor. Ep. περιχωσάμην without augm. *to be violently angry*, τινί τινος, at any one on account of some one, *9, 449. 14, 266.

περιωπή, ἡ (ὤψ), a place from which one can have a wide observation, *an election, a height*, 14, 8. Od. 10, 146.

περιώσιος, ον, poet. for περιούσιος, *excessive, very great*; neut. as adv. *excessively, too much*, 4, 359. Od. 16, 203. Fur. h. 18, 41; with gen. περιώσιον ἄλλων, far beyond the others, h. Cer. 74.

πελιδνός, ή, όν, poet. *blackish, dark, dusky, sable*(V. b'ack-winged), epith. of the eagle, 24, 316.† Schol. μέλας, cf. μόρφνος.

Περκώσιος, ὁ, *of Percôte*, 2, 831. 6, 30.

Περκώτη, ἡ, a city in Asia Minor on the Hellespont, between Abȳdos and Lampsacus, 2, 835. 11, 229; in the time

of Strabo, a village near Parion: Παλαιπερκώτη. (Περκώπη is a false reading.)

πέρνασχ' for πέρνασκε, see πέρνημι.

πέρνημι, Ep. form of περάω, partcp. περνάς, iterat. imperf. 3 sing. πέρνασχ' for πέρνασκε, *to lead out and sell*, τινά, any one, 22, 45. 24, 752. κτήματα περνάμενα, goods (brought) for sale, *18, 292.

περονάω (περόνη), aor. Ep. περόνησα, aor. mid. περονησάμην always without augment, 1) *to pierce with a clasp or buckle*, generally, *to pierce through*, τινὰ δουρί, 7, 145. Mid. *to fasten any thing (for oneself) with a clasp* or *buckle*, with accus. χλαῖναν, 10, 133; τί ἐνετῇσι, with buckles, *14, 180.

περόνη, ἡ (πείρω), prop. *the tongue of a buckle*; generally. *a buckle, a brooch*, for fastening a cloak, 5, 425. Od. 18, 293. 19, 226.

περόωσι, see περάω.

Πέρραιβοί, see Περαιβοί, h. Ap. 218.

*Περσαῖος, ὁ (Πέρσης, Hes. Th. 377), son of the Titan Kriŏs (Crius) and Eurybia, father of Hecate, h. Cer. 24.

πέρσα, Ep. for ἔπερσα, see πέρθω.

Περσεύς, έως, Ion. and Ep. ῆος (Herm. *Penetrius*), 1) son of Zeus and Danaê, daughter of king Acrisius in Argos. His grandfather caused him with his mother to be cast in a chest into the sea; he was, however, rescued by king Polydectes in Serïphus. When he had grown up, Polydectes, in order to remove him, commissioned him to bring the head of Medūsa. He accomplished the task prosperously, and upon his return liberated Andromĕda, daughter of Cepheus, who was bound to a rock and destined to be the prey of a sea-monster. Andromeda became his wife and bore to him Alcæus and Electryon, 14, 320. 2) son of Nestor and Anaxibia, Od. 3, 414. 445.

Περσεφόνεια, ἡ, Ep. for Περσεφόνη, daughter of Zeus and Dēmētēr, 14, 326; wife of Hades, who bore her off from her mother. She rules with her husband the shades, and generally the underworld, Od. 10, 491. 11, 47. Il. 9, 457. Her sacred groves are on the western margin of the earth, on the borders of the realms of shades, Od. 10, 509. (According to Eustath. ad Od. 10, 491, from φέρειν and φόνος, who brings death, prop. Φερσεφόνη. Ion. Περσεφόνη.)

Πέρση, ἡ, daughter of Oceanus, wife of Helios, mother of Æetes and Kirkê (Circe), Od. 10, 139. Περσηίς, ἴδος, ἡ, Hes. Th. 356.

Περσηϊάδης, ου, ὁ, poet. for Περσεΐδης, son or descendant of Perseus = *Sthenelus*, 19, 116.

πεσέειν and πεσέεσθαι, see πίπτω.

πεσσός, ὁ, Att. πεττός, *a stone* used in playing draughts, Od. 1, 107.† πεσσοῖσι θυμὸν τέρπειν. Eustath. ad loc. and Etym. M. mention the following games: 1) Two persons play, each with five stones. For this purpose a surface of

Q 2

πεφυνῖα, Ep. see φύω.

πέφυρμαι, see φύρω.

πῆ or πῆ (ed. Spitzner), adv. interrog.
1) how, in what way, wherefore, why,
10, 385. Od. 2, 364. 2) Spoken of place:
whither, Il. 5, 472. 6, 377. Od. 17, 219;
where, 13, 307.

πή or πή (ed. Spitz.), enclit. adv. 1)
in any way, in some way, perchance.
οὕτω πη, thus perhaps [tali quodam
modo], 24, 373. 2) to any place. οὕτε πη
ἀλλῃ, Od. 2, 127; any where, Od. 22,
25.

πηγεσίμαλλος, ον (μαλλός), thick-
woolled, having a thick fleece, ἀρνειός, 3,
197.†

πηγή, ἡ, a fountain, a spring, 2, 523.

πήγνῦμι, fut. πήξω, aor. ἔπηξα, Ep.
πῆξα, perf. II. πέπηγα, pluperf. 3 sing.
ἐπεπήγει, pass. aor. 2 ἐπάγην, Ep. πάγην,
aor. 1 pass. only πῆχθεν, Ep. for ἐπήχθη-
σαν, 8, 298. I) Act. prop. to make firm,
hence 1) to stick in firmly, to stick in,
to thrust in, to drive in, τί, any thing;
the place is accompanied by a prep.
ἔγχος, δόρυ ἐν μετώπῳ, γαστέρι, 4, 460.
13. 372; ἐρετμον ἐπὶ τύμβῳ, to fix an oar
upon the grave, Od. 11, 77: and dat. alone,
Od. 11. 129; κεφαλὴν ἀνὰ σκολόπεσσι,
to fix his head upon stakes [to impale it],
18, 177; metaph. ὄμματα κατὰ χθονός, to
fasten one's eyes upon the ground, 3, 217.
2) to join together, to construct, to build,
νῆας, 2, 664. II) Mid. and aor. 1 and 2
pass. and perf. 2. 1) Intrans. to become
firm, hence a) to remain infixed, to
stick fast, 4, 185. 5, 616. δόρυ δ' ἐν κραδίῃ
ἐπεπήγει, the spear remained infixed in
the heart, 13, 442. cf. 16, 772. 2) to become
firm, hard. γοῦνα πήγνυται, the limbs
become stiff, 22, 453. 3) Trans. in aor.
1, to join together, to construct, to build,
ἴκρια ἐπ' αὐτῆς (sc. νηός), Od. 5. 163.

πηγός, ή, όν, poet. (πήγνυμι)=εὐπηγής,
thick, firm, compressed; hence ἵπποι,
well-fed, powerful horses, Schol. εὐτρα-
φεῖς, 9, 124. 266. κῦμα πηγόν, a dense,
i. e. huge, mighty wave, Od. 5, 388. 23,
235 (On the critics, who explain it now
'white,' and now 'black,' see Nitzsch ad
Od. 5, 388.)

πηγυλίς, ίδος, ἡ, poet. (πήγνυμι), frosty,
cold, freezing, νύξ, Od. 14, 476.†

Πήδαιον, τό, according to Eustath. an
unknown place in Troy, or a river of the
island Cyprus, in Ptolem. Pediæus, cf.
Mannert VI. 1. v. 442. Il. 13, 172.

Πηδαῖος, ὁ, son of Antênor, who was
slain by Meges, 5, 69.

πηδάλιον, τό (πηδόν), the rudder, the
helm, in the stern of a ship, *Od. 3, 281.
h. Ap. 418.

Πήδασος, ἡ, 1) a city of the Leleges
in Troas, on the Satnioeis, the residence
of king Altes, which Achilles destroyed,
6, 35. 21, 85; according to Pliny=Adra-
myttium. 2) a town in Messene, according to Strab. VIII. p. 369, the later
Mothône, 9, 152. 294.

Πήδασος, ὁ, 1) son of Bucolion, brother

of Æsêpus of Troy, 6, 21, seq. 2) a
steed of Achilles, 16, 152.

πηδάω, imperf. 3 sing. ἐπήδα, aor. 1
ἐπήδησα, to spring, to leap, ποσσίν, 21,
269; spoken of missiles: to go, to fly,
*14, 455.

πηδόν, τό (πέζα), prop. the lower part
of an oar, an oar-blade, generally, a rudder, *Od. 7, 328. 13, 78.

πηκτός, ή, όν (πήγνυμι), joined together,
bound fast, firm, ἄροτρον, 10, 353. 13,
703. Od. 13, 32. h. Cer. 196.

πῆλαι, πῆλε, see πάλλω.

Πηλεγών, όνος, ὁ, son of the river-god
Axius and the nymph Peribœa, 21, 141,
seq.

Πηλείδης, ao and εω, ὁ, Ep. Πηληϊάδης,
ao, son of Peleus=Achilles, 1, 146. (Gen.
Πηληϊάδεω, 1, 1, is pentesyllabic with
synizesis.)

Πηλείων, ωνος, ὁ = Πηλείδης, I) 1,
188. Od. 5, 310. 2) Mud-dweller, the
name of a frog, Batr. 209.

Πηλειωνάδε, adv. to Pelides, 24, 338.†

Πηλεύς, ῆος and έος, ὁ (Herm. Pul-
santius), son of Æacus, sovereign of the
Myrmidons at Phthia in Thessaly, 2,
188, 189. He fled, on account of the
slaughter of his brother Phocus, to
Phthia, to Eurytion, whose daughter
Antigône he married. She bore him
Polydôra, 16, 175. He then took part in
the Argonautic expedition and in the
Calydonian hunt. After the death of
Antigône, he married the Nereïd Thetis,
who bore him Achilles, 16, 33. 20. 206.
In the marriage festival the gods took
part and made him presents, 24, 59, seq.
16, 143. 2) the mud-dweller, the name
of a frog (from πηλός), Batr. 29.

Πηληϊάδης, Ep. for Πηλείδης, q. v.

Πηλήϊος, η, ον, Ep. for Πήλειος Πηλεύς), Peleïan, δόμος, 18, 60. 441.

πήληξ, ηκος, ἡ (πάλλω), a helmet, so
called from the waving crest, *8, 308.
15, 608. Od. 1, 256.

Πηλιάς, άδος, ἡ, Pelian, from the
mountain Pelion; ἡ μελίη, the Pelian
spear, which was presented to Peleus by
Chiron, *16, 143. 19, 390.

Πήλιον, τό, a high, woody mountain
in Thessaly, lying over against Ossa,
which terminated in the promontory
Sep as; now Zagora, 2, 744. 16. 144.

*Πηλοβάτης, ον, ὁ (βαίνω), the mud-
walker, a frog's name, Batr. 240.

*πηλός, ὁ, mud, mire, clay, Batr. 240.

πῆμα, ατος, τό (πέπηθα, πάσχω), evil,
wretchedness, misfortune, injury, ruin,
often plur. πήματα πάσχειν. πῆμα κακοῖο
(V. the punishment of wickedness), Od.
3, 152. δύης πῆμα, Od. 14, 318. Often
spoken of persons instead of evil-bring-
ing: ἔτρεφε πῆμα Τρωσί, Zeus nourished
him as a great pest to the Trojans Il. 8,
282. cf. 3, 50. 10, 453. 11, 347. Od. 12,
125. 17, 446. h. Ap. 304.

πημαίνω (πῆμα), fut. πημανῶ, Ep.
-ανέω, aor. 1 ἐπήμηνα, aor. pass. Ep. πη-
μάνθην, 1) Intrans. to devise mischief,

generally, *disagreeable, odious*, Od. 17, 448. cf. Buttm., Lex. p. 319.

πίλναμαι, Ep. form of πελάζω, *quickly to approach a thing, to touch, io rush upon* or *to*, with dat. χθονί, 23, 368. h. Cer. 115; also ἐπ' οὐδεί, 19, 93; absol. ἀμφὶ δὲ χαῖται πίλναντο, round about the hair fluttered, 22, 402.

πῖλος, ὁ, *felted wool, felt*; a kind of helmet was made of it, 10, 265.†

πιμπλάνω, Ep. form of πίμπλημι; 3 pres. mid. πιμπλάνεται, 9, 679.

πίμπλημι, pres. 3 plur. πιμπλᾶσι, fut. πλήσω, aor. ἔπλησα. Ep. πλῆσα, mid. πίμπλαμαι, aor. mid. ἐπλησάμην, aor. pass. ἐπλήσθην, 3 plur. πλῆσθεν for ἐπλήσθησαν, also Ep. aor. II. ἐπλήμην, only 3 sing. and plur. πλῆτο and πλῆντο, 1) *to fill, to make full, to fill up*, τί, 14, 35: τινός, with any thing; ἐναύλους νεκύων, τινὰ μένεος, 16, 72. 13, 60; τινί, 16, 374. Mid. with aor. 1, 1) *to fill for oneself, to satiate oneself, to satisfy*, with accus. δέπας οἴνοιο, 9, 224; θυμὸν ἐδητύος καὶ ποτῆτος, to satisfy the desire with food and drink, Od. 17, 603. 19, 198. 2) Intrans. in aor. pass. and Ep. aor. 2. *to fill oneself, to be full*, μένεος, of rage, Il. 1, 104: ἀλκῆς, 17, 211. h. Cer. 281. τῶν δὲ πλῆτο σπέος, the cave was full, 18, 50. cf. Od. 8, 57; Ep. form πιμπλάω and πλήθω.

πίμπρημι, not found in Hom., see πρήθω.

πίναξ, ακος, ὁ, *a board*, Od. 12, 67; generally, a wooden table, esply 1) a *writing-table*, prob. made of two small boards, which were laid together, and fastened with a seal. b) *a plate, a vessel*, small boards upon which meat was laid, Od. 1, 141.

πινύσσω (from πνέω, πέπνυμαι), *to make wise, to instruct, to inform*, τινά, 14, 249.†

πινυτή, ἡ (πινύσσω), poet. *understanding, wisdom*, 7, 289. Od. 20, 71.

πινυτός, ή, όν (πινύσσω, πινύω), *intelligent, prudent, wise*, *Od. 1, 229. 4, 211; and often.

πίνω, pres. infin. πινέμεναι, imperf. iterat. πίνεσκε, fut. πίομαι, aor. 2 ἔπιον, imperat. πίε, Od. 9, 347; infin. πιεῖν, Ep. πιέειν, πιέμεν, perf. pass. *to drink*, spoken of men and animals, mly with a cus. οἶνον, Il. 5, 341; also κρητῆρας οἴνοιο, to drink jars of wine, 8, 232; κύπελλα, 4, 346. b) Rarely with gen. Od. 11. 96. 15, 373. (Iota is in the fut. long; in the aor. short; long by the arsis in the infin. πιέμεν, Od. 18, 3.)

πίομαι, see πίνω.

πιότατος, η, ον, superl. of πίων.

πίπτω (for πιπέτω from root πέτω), fut. πεσέομαι, aor. 2 ἔπεσον, Ep. πέσον, perf. partcp. πεπτεώς, with synizesis of εω: accus. plur. πεπτεῶτας, Od. 22, 384; *to fall*, i. e. *to fall down, to plunge, to fall* from a higher to a lower place, spoken of persons with prep. showing whence, ἐξ ἵππων, ὀχέων, Il. 7, 16. 16, 379; of

things: of missiles, of snow, fire, 17, 633. 12, 156; whither by prep. ἐν, ἐπί, παρά, with dat. or dat. alone πεδίῳ, 5, 82; or by adv. ἔραζε, χαμαί. Esply 1) *to fall out, to drop*, spoken of reins: ἐκ χειρῶν, 5, 583. μετὰ ποσσὶ γυναικός, to fall from the lap of the mother, i. e. to be born, 19, 110. ἐκ θυμοῦ τινι, to fall from any one's heart, i. e. to lose his favour, 23, 595. 2) *to fall down, to fall around*, often spoken of trees, harvests, etc. 11, 69. 18, 552. 3) In the constructio praegnans: *to fall dying, to fall, to perish*, spoken of men who are slain in battle, ὑπό τινος and τινι, 6, 453. 17, 428; in full: θνήσκοντες πίπτουσι, 1, 243. 4) *to fall*, i. e. *to rush upon, to cast oneself upon*; ἐν νηυσί, upon the ships, 9, 235. 11, 311. 823. 12, 107. 126. 15, 63. 17, 639; cf. ἔχω. (Voss. incorrectly translates, 11, 823, ἐν νηυσὶ πεσέονται, they were stretched about the ships): of wind, Od. 14, 475; metaph. spoken of discord. Il. 21. 385. 5) *to fall, to sink*, i. e. to become weak and faint, spoken of courage, 14, 418; of the wind, Od. 19, 202.

πῖσος, εος, τό, poet. (πίνω), *a moist place, a meadow, a meadow-pasture, marshy land*, 20, 9. Od. 6, 124. h. Ven. 99; (less correct is πεῖσος.)

πίσσα, ἡ (πίτυς), *pitch*, 4, 277.†

πιστός, ή, όν (πείθω), superl. πιστότατος, who is believed or trusted: *credible, faithful, trusty, trustworthy*, ἑταῖρος, 16, 147; ὅρκια, 2, 124; οὐκέτι πιστὰ γυναιξίν, no confidence can be placed in the women, Od. 11, 456.

πιστόω (πιστός), aor. mid. ἐπιστωσάμην, aor. pass. ἐπιστώθην, to make trusty, true; hence, pass. *to be assured, to believe, to trust*, Od. 21, 218. Mid. *to give mutual security, to become security, to promise fidelity*, Il. 6, 233; ἐπέεσσιν, by words, 21, 286; also in the aor. pass. ὅρκῳ πιστωθῆναί τινι, to give security to any one upon oath, Od. 15, 436.

πίσυνος, η, ον, poet. (πείθω), *trusting to, confiding in* any thing, with dat. τόξοισι, Διί, 5, 205. Od. 18, 140.

πίσυρες, οἱ, αἱ, πίσυρα, τά, Æol. and Ep. for τέσσαρες, *four*, 15, 680. Od. 5, 70.

Πιτθεύς, ῆος, ὁ, the well-known Pittheus was son of Pelops, king of Trœzène, father of Æthra; but from 2, 105, seq. it would appear that the son of Pelops and the father of the Æthra mentioned in 3, 144, were probably distinct persons; hence Damm, s. v. Alius erat filius Pelopis.

πιτνάω and πίτνημι, poet. form of πετάννυμι, *to spread out, to stretch out*, ἠέρα πίτνα for ἐπίτνα, 21, 7; πιτνὰς εἰς ἐμὲ χεῖρας, Od. 11, 392.

Πιτύεια, ἡ, Ep. for Πιτύα, a town in Asia Minor, between Parion and Priāpus, 2, 829 (prop. the *fir-town*).

πίτυς, υος, ἡ, *a fir, a pitch-pine*, pinus abies, 13, 390; dat. plur. πίτυσσιν, Od. 9, 186.

Q 4

Ætolia, on the river Evênus, the abode of the Curêtes, with a temple of Athênê, 2, 639. 13, 217; from which Πλευρώνιος, η, ον, Pleuronian; subst. a Pleuronian.

πλέω, Ep. form πλείω; from which πλείειν, πλείοντες, fut. πλεύσομαι, Od. 12, 25. (Ep. form πλώω,) to sail, to travel by sea; to voyage, ἐπὶ πόντω, Il. 7, 88; ἐνὶ πόντω, Od. 16, 367; with accus. of place: ὑγρὰ κέλευθα, to navigate the watery paths, Od. 3, 71. 9, 252. (πλέων, Od. 1, 183, monosyllabic.)

ΠΛΕΩ, falsely assumed root for some of the tenses of πίμπλημι.

πλέων, πλέον, see πλείων.

πληγή, ἡ (πλήσσω), a stroke, a blow, a lash, Od. 4, 244; esply the cut of a whip, Il. 11, 532. 2) Διὸς πληγή, ἡ, a blow of Zeus=lightning, 14, 414.

πλῆθος, εος, τό (πλήθω), dat. πλήθεϊ, prop. fulness; mly multitude, crowd; *17, 330. 23, 639.

πληθύς, ύος, ἡ, Ion. for πλῆθος, dat. πληθυΐ, 22, 458. Od. 16, 105; prop. fulness, multitude; mly a crowd of men, with verb plur. Il. 2, 278. 15, 305. Od. 11, 514; esply spoken of great multitudes, the people, in distinction from the leader, Il. 2, 143.

πλήθω, only pres. and imperf. to be full, to fill oneself, to become full, with gen. ἵππων καὶ ἀνδρῶν, 8, 214; σίτου, Od. 9, 8; spoken of rivers: to rise, to swell, Il. 5, 87. 11, 492. πάντες ποταμοὶ πλήθουσι ῥέοντες, the flowing rivers rise, 16, 389; metaph. spoken of the moon: πλήθουσα Σελήνη, the full moon, 18, 484. cf. h. 32, 11.

Πληϊάδες, αἱ, Ion. for Πλειάδες, the Pleiades, the seven daughters of Atlas and Pleïône; they were placed by Zeus amongst the stars and formed the constellation of the seven stars in Taurus. Their rising brought summer, their setting winter, and so the beginning and end of navigation, 18, 486. Od. 5, 272. h. 7, 7. (The name is derived by some from πλέω, as the stars of navigation; by others, as Voss ad Arat. from πέλομαι, versari; according to others still = πελειάδες, a flight of wild doves, cf. Nitzsch ad Od. 5, 272.)

πληκτίζομαι, depon. mid. (πλήκτης), to strike, to fight, to contend, τινί, 21, 499.†

*πλῆκτρον, τό, prop. an instrument for striking: the plectrum, for playing upon the lyre, h. Ap 185.

πλημμυρίς, ίδος, ἡ, the flow or flux of the sea, in opposition to the ebb, Od. 9, 486.† In Hom. ῠ, in Eurip. ῡ, in like manner, πλήμυρα. (According to Buttm., Gr. Gram. § 7, 17, note, from πλήν and μύρω, according to others, from πλῆμα.)

πλήμνη, ἡ (πλήμη), prop. the filling; then, the nave of the wheel, in which the axle runs, and into which the spokes are inserted, *5, 726. 23, 339.

πλήν, as prep. besides, except, with gen. Od. 8, 207.†

πλῆντο, 1) Ep. 3 plur. aor. sync. pass. of πίμπλημι, Od. 8, 57. 2) 3 plur. aor. sync of πελάζω, Il. 14, 468.

πλῆξα, see πλήσσω.

πλήξιππος, ον (ἵππος), horse-spurring, horse-taming, *2, 104.

πλησίος, η, ον (πέλας), near, neighbouring, mly with gen. 6, 249. Od. 5, 71; with dat. Il. 23, 732. Od. 2, 149; as subst. a neighbour, the nearest person, πλησίος ἄλλος, Il. 2, 271. Neut. as adv. near, in the vicinity, with gen. 3, 115; rarely with dat. 23, 732.

πλησίστιος, ον (ἱστίον), filling or swelling the sails, οὖρος, *Od. 11, 7. 12, 149.

πλήσσω, aor. 1 ἔπληξα, always Ep. πλῆξα, Ep. aor. 2 πέπληγον and ἐπέπληγον, perf. πέπληγα, always in act signif. Mid. aor. 1 ἐπληξάμην. Ep. aor. 2 πεπληγόμην, aor. pass. ἐπλήγην, 1) to strike, to smite, to thrust, any one: πληγῆσιν, to punish any one with blows, 2, 264: σκήπτρω μετάφρενον, 2, 266. ποδὶ πλῆξαι, to strike with the foot, Od. 22, 20; χορὸν ποσίν, Od. 8, 264; ἵππους ἐς πόλεμον, to drive the steeds to the battle, Il. 16, 728; hence, b) Esply spoken of arms, for the most part of the sword: to smite, to wound, to hit; often with double accus. τινὰ κληΐδα, to strike any one upon the clavicle, 5, 147; τινὰ αὐχένα, 11, 240. Pass. in aor. 1, to be struck, 23, 694; esply to be struck by lightning, κεραυνῷ, 8, 455 (here stands πληγέντε masc. instead of πληγείσα), Od. 12, 416. b) Metaph. to be violently attacked, Il. 13, 394. 16, 203; see ἐκπλήττω. Mid. to strike oneself, with accus. στήθεα, upon the breast, 18, 51; μηρώ, 12, 162. 16, 125. h. Cer. 218.

πλῆτο, Ep. aor. sync. from πίμπλημι. 2, 3 sing. Ep. aor. sync. from πελάζω, 14, 438.

πλίσσομαι (from πλίξ. Dor. = βλῆμα), mid. (elsewhere also πλίσσω), to stride, prop. according to the Gramm. to weave the legs, by putting one foot before the other; or, generally, to stride with extended legs, spoken of running mules: εὖ πλίσσοντο πόδεσσιν, well strode they forward with the legs, Od. 6, 318.†

πλόκαμος, ὁ (πλέκω), curled hair, a curl, a lock, in the plur. 14, 176.†

πλόκιος. η, ον (πλέκω), curled, entangled, for κλόπιος, Od. 13, 295.†

πλόος, ὁ (πλέω), the act of sailing, navigation, Od. 3, 169.† h. 33, 16.

*πλούσιος, η, ον (πλοῦτος), rich, h. Merc. 171.

πλοῦτος, ὁ (πλέος, not from πολύ, ἔτος), abundance, wealth, property, connected with ἄφενος, 1, 171; ὄλβος, Il., and Od. 14, 206.

†Πλοῦτος, ὁ, son of Jasion and Dêmêter, god of wealth, h. Cer. 489

*Πλουτώ, οῦς, ἡ, daughter of Oceanus and Tethys, companion of Proserpina, h Cer. 422.

πλοχμός, ὁ, poet. (πλέκω) = πλόκαμος, twisted hair, a curl, 17, 52.†

7, 339: σάκος ταύρων (gen. mater.), a shield of ox-hide, 7, 222; τύμβον to cast up a sepulchral mound, 7, 435. εἴδωλον, Od. 4, 796. b) Spoken of states and of things, to which esply mental action belongs: τελευτήν, to make an end, Od. 1, 250; φόβον, to excite fear, Il. 12, 432; νόημά τινι ἐν φρεσίν, to put a thought into any one's mind, Od. 14, 274; ἀθύρματα, to pursue pastimes, Il. 15, 363; κακὸν μεῖζον, to prepare a greater evil, 13, 120; γαλήνην, Od. 5, 452; pass. ἦ σοι ἄριστα πεποίηται κατὰ οἶκον πρὸς Τρώων (ironical), truly, excellent things have been done to thee in thy house by the Trojans, Il. 6, 57. 2) to make, i. e. to place a man in a condition; a) With double accus. to convert, to render: with subst. τινὰ βασιλέα, to make a man a king, Od. 1, 387; κεῖνον ταμίην ἀνέμων, Od. 10, 21; λαοὺς λίθους, the people to stones, Il. 24, 611; θεὰν ἄκοιτιν θνητῷ, to make a goddess bride to a mortal, 24, 537; with adj. τινὰ ἄφρονα, to render a man senseless, Od. 23, 12; ἄϊστον, Od. 5, 235; θεμείλια λεῖα, to make the ground smooth, i. e. level, Il. 12, 30; cf. δίπτυχα. Mid. 1) to make any thing for oneself, like the act. a) With a more or less distinct reference to the subj.: οἰκία, to build houses or dwellings for oneself, 12, 168; τεῖχος, νηόν, 12, 5. h. Ap. 286; σχεδίην, Od. 5, 251. b) ἀγορήν, to make an assembly, Il. 8, 2; κλέος αὐτῇ ποιεῖται, she acquired glory for herself, ῥήτρην ποιεῖσθαι, Od. 14, 393. 2) With double accus. τινὰ ἄλοχον, to make any one a wife, Il. 3, 409; τινὰ ἀκοίτην, Od. 5, 120; τινὰ υἱόν, to take any one as a son, Il. 9, 495.

ποίη, ἡ, Ion. for πόα, grass, herbage, pasturage, 14, 347.† Od. 9, 499; and often.

ποιήεις, εσσα, εν (ποίη), grassy, verdant, green, epith. of towns and islands, 2, 503: πίσεα, 20, 9; ἄγκεα, Od. 4, 337.

ποιητός, ή, όν (ποέω), made, prepared; in H. well-wrought or built, spoken of dwellings, 5, 198. Od. 1, 333; of arms and vessels, Il. 10. 262.

ποικίλλω (ποικίλος), to variegate, spoken of embroidering and painting; especially to adorn with various colours, to work or form with skill, χορόν, 18, 590.†

ποίκιλμα, ατος, τό (ποικίλλω), variegated work, esply painting, embroidery, ποικίλμασι κάλλιστος, spoken of a robe, 6, 294. Od. 15, 107.

ποικιλομήτης, ου, ὁ (μῆτις), full of manifold devices, abounding in expedients, cunning, epith. of Odysseus (Ulysses), 11, 482. Od. 3, 163; of Zeus and Hermês, h. Ap. 322. Merc. 155.

ποικίλος, η, ον, 1) variegated, having divers colours, παρδαλέη, 10, 30. 2) adorned, painted, embroidered, spoken of garments, 6, 735. Od. 18, 293; and gen. wrought with art, beautifully formed, epith. of arms, chariots, etc. ποικίλα χαλκῷ ἅρματα, chariots adorned with

brass, Il. 4, 226; in like manner τεύχεα, 3, 327; δεσμός, Od. 8. 448.

ποιμαίνω (ποιμήν), to pasture, to drive to pasture, spoken of shepherds; μῆλα, Od. 9, 188; also absol. ἐπ' οἴεσσι, to be a shepherd with sheep, Il. 6, 25. Mid. pasture, to graze, spoken of flocks, 11, 244.

ποιμήν, ένος, ὁ (πάομαι), a herdsman, esply a shepherd, 5, 137; then metaph. ποιμὴν λαῶν, a shepherd of the people, frequently an epith. of princes, Il. and Od.

ποίμνη, ἡ (ποιμαίνω), a flock or herd of cattle pasturing, Od. 9, 122.†

ποιμνήϊος, η, ον (ποίμνη), Ion. for ποιμνεῖον, belonging to the flock or herd, σταθμός, the fold of the flock or herd, 2, 470.†

ποινή, ἡ (akin to ΦΕΝΩ), prop. compensation for a committed homicide, the money with which a man redeems himself from blood-guiltiness; hence, 1) penalty, vengeance (which I take or which is taken of me), with gen. for or on account of any one, παιδός, 13, 659; κασιγνήτοιο, 14, 483; cf. 16, 398. 9, 633; and generally, recompense, requital, 5, 266. Od. 23, 312: τῶν ποινήν, ὁ, as appos. Il. 17, 207; cf. 21, 28.

ποῖος, η, ον (πός), what sort of, of what kind (qualis). ποῖον τὸν μῦθον ἔειπες! what a word hast thou spoken, and neut. ποῖον ἔρεξας! 23, 570. With infin. ποῖοί κ' εἶτ' Ὀδυσῆϊ ἀμυνέμεν, how would you be able to defend Odysseus (Ulysses), Od. 21, 195.

ποιπνύω, partcp. aor. ποιπνύσας (prob. from πνέω, πέπνυμαι, with redupl.), prop. to be out of breath from haste; hence, 1) to be hasty, active, to move hastily, ἀνὰ μαχήν, 14, 155. 8, 219; in a sacrifice, Od. 3, 430. Esply 2) to serve with assiduity, to wait upon assiduously, Il. 1, 600. 18, 421. Od. 20,149 (υ is in the pres. and imperf. short, with a following short syllable, long with a following long, Il. 1, 601. 24, 475).

πόκος (πέκω), wool shorn off, a fleece, 12, 451.†

πολέες, Ep. for πολλοί, see πολύς.

πολεμήϊος, ον, Ion. for the unusual πολέμειος, warlike; ἔργα, 2, 338. Od. 12, 116; τεύχεα, Il. 7, 193.

πολεμίζω, Ep. for πτολεμίζω (πόλεμος), fut. πολεμίξω, 1) to war, to fight, to contend, τινί, with any one: ἄντα τινός, against any one, 8, 428; τινὸς ἐναντίβιον, 20, 85; μετ' Ἀχαιοῖσιν, 9, 352; also πόλεμον, to wage a war. 2, 121. 2) to make war upon, to invade. ῥηΐτεροι πολεμίζειν, more easy to assail, 18, 258.

πολεμιστά, ὁ, Ep. for πολεμιστής.

πολεμιστής, οῦ, ὁ, Ep. πτολεμιστής (πόλεμος), a warrior, a combatant, 5, 289; and often; Od. 24. 499.

*πολεμόκλονος, ον (κλόνος), making a warlike noise or tumult, Batr. 4. 276.

πόλεμόνδε, adv. Ep. πτόλεμόνδε, to the war, 8, 313, and often.

7, 339: σάκος ταύρων (gen. mater.), a shield of ox-hide, 7, 222; τύμβον to cast up a sepulchral mound, 7, 435. εἴδωλον, Od. 4, 796. *b)* Spoken of states and of things, to which esply mental action belongs: τελευτήν, to make an end, Od. 1, 250; φόβον, to excite fear, Il. 12, 432; νόημά τινι ἐν φρεσίν, to put a thought into any one's mind, Od. 14, 274; ἀθύρματα, to pursue pastimes, Il. 15, 363; κακὸν μεῖζον, to prepare a greater evil, 13, 120; γαλήνην, Od. 5, 452; pass. ἦ σοι ἄριστα πεποίηται κατὰ οἶκον πρὸς Τρώων (ironical), truly, excellent things have been done to thee in thy house by the Trojans, Il. 6, 57. 2) *to make*, i. e. to place a man in a condition; *a)* With double accus. *to convert, to render :* with subst. τινὰ βασιλέα, to make a man a king, Od. 1, 387; κεῖνον ταμίην ἀνέμων, Od. 10, 21; λαοὺς λίθους, the people to stones, Il. 24, 611; θεὰν ἄκοιτιν θνητῷ, to make a goddess bride to a mortal, 24, 537; with adj. τινὰ ἄφρονα, to render a man senseless, Od. 23, 12; ἄϊστον, Od. 5, 235; θεμείλια λεῖα, to make the ground smooth, i. e. level, Il. 12, 30; cf. δίπτυχα. Mid. 1) *to make any thing for oneself*, like the act. *a)* With a more or less distinct reference to the subj. : οἰκία, to build houses or dwellings for oneself, 12, 168; τεῖχος, νηόν, 12, 5. h. Ap. 286; σχεδίην, Od. 5, 251. *b)* ἀγορήν, to make an assembly, Il. 8, 2; κλέος αὐτῇ ποιεῖται, she acquired glory for herself, ῥήτρην ποιεῖσθαι, Od. 14, 393. 2) With double accus. τινὰ ἄλοχον, to make any one a wife, Il. 3, 409; τινὰ ἀκοίτην, Od. 5, 120; τινὰ υἱόν, to take any one as a son, Il. 9, 495.

ποίη, ἡ, Ion. for πόα, grass, herbage, pasturage, 14, 347.† Od. 9, 499; and often.

ποιήεις, εσσα, εν (ποίη), grassy, verdant, green, epith. of towns and islands, 2, 503: πίσεα, 20, 9; ἄγκεα, Od. 4, 337.

ποιητός, ή, όν (ποιέω), made, prepared; in H. well-wrought or built, spoken of dwellings, 5, 198. Od. 1, 333; of arms and vessels, Il. 10, 262.

ποικίλλω (ποικίλος), to variegate, spoken of embroidering and painting; especially to adorn with various colours, to work or form with skill, χορόν, 18, 590.†

ποίκιλμα, ατος, τό (ποικίλλω), variegated work, esply painting, embroidery, ποικίλμασι κάλλιστος, spoken of a robe, 6, 294. Od. 15, 107.

ποικιλομήτης, ου, ὁ (μῆτις), full of manifold devices, abounding in expedients, cunning, epith. of Odysseus (Ulysses), 11, 482. Od. 3, 163; of Zeus and Hermes, h. Ap. 322. Merc. 155.

ποικίλος, η, ον, 1) variegated, having divers colours, παρδαλέη, 10, 30. 2) adorned, painted, embroidered, spoken of garments, 5, 735. Od. 18, 293; and gen. wrought with art, beautifully formed, epith. of arms, chariots, etc. ποικίλα χαλκῷ ἅρματα, chariots adorned with

brass, Il. 4, 226; in like manner τεύχεα, 3, 327; δεσμός, Od. 8. 448.

ποιμαίνω (ποιμήν), to pasture, to drive to pasture, spoken of shepherds; μῆλα, Od. 9, 188; also absol. ἐπ' οἴεσσι, to be a shepherd with sheep, Il. 6, 25. Mid. pasture, to graze, spoken of flocks, 11, 244.

ποιμήν, ένος, ὁ (πάομαι), a herdsman, esply a shepherd, 5, 137; then metaph. ποιμὴν λαῶν, a shepherd of the people, frequently an epith. of princes, Il. and Od.

ποίμνη, ἡ (ποιμαίνω), a flock or herd of cattle pasturing, Od. 9, 122.†

ποιμνήϊος, η, ον (ποίμνη), Ion. for ποιμνεῖον, belonging to the flock or herd, σταθμός, the fold of the flock or herd, 2, 470.†

ποινή, ἡ (akin to ΦΕΝΩ). prop. compensation for a committed homicide, the money with which a man redeems himself from blood-guiltiness; hence, 1) penalty, vengeance (which I take or which is taken of me), with gen. for or on account of any one, παιδός, 13, 659; κασιγνήτοιο, 14, 483; cf. 16, 398. 9, 633; and generally, recompense, requital, 5, 266. Od. 23, 312; τῶν ποινήν, ὁ, as appos. Il. 17, 207; cf. 21, 28.

ποῖος, η, ον (πός), what sort of, of what kind (qualis). ποῖον τὸν μῦθον ἔειπες! what a word hast thou spoken, and neut ποῖον ἔρεξας! 23, 570. With infin. ποιοί κ' εἶτ' Ὀδυσῆϊ ἀμυνέμεν, how would you be able to defend Odysseus (Ulysses), Od. 21, 195.

ποιπνύω, partcp. aor. ποιπνύσας (prob. from πνέω, πέπνυμαι, with redupl.), prop. to be out of breath from haste; hence, 1) to be hasty, active, to move hastily, ἀνὰ μαχήν, 14, 155. 8, 219; in a sacrifice, Od. 3, 430. Esply 2) to serve with assiduity, to wait upon assiduously, Il. 1, 600. 18, 421. Od. 20,149 (υ is in the pres. and imperf. short, with a following short syllable, long with a following long, Il. 1, 601. 24, 475).

πόκος (πέκω), wool shorn off, a fleece, 12, 451.†

πολέες, Ep. for πολλοί. see πολύς.

πολεμήϊος, ον, Ion. for the unusual πολεμείος, warlike; ἔργα, 2, 338. Od. 12, 116; τεύχεα, Il. 7, 193.

πολεμίζω. Ep. πτολεμίζω (πόλεμος), fut. πολεμίξω), 1) to war, to fight, to contend, τινί, with any one: ἄντα τινός, against any one, 8, 428; τινὸς ἐναντίβιον, 20, 85; μετ' Ἀχαιοῖσιν, 9, 352; also πόλεμον, to wage a war. 2, 121. 2) to make war upon, to invade: ῥηίτεροι πολεμίζειν, more easy to assail, 18, 258.

πολεμιστά, ὁ, Ep. for πολεμιστής.

πολεμιστής, οῦ, ὁ, Ep. πτολεμιστής (πόλεμος), a warrior, a combatant, 5, 289; and often; Od. 24. 499.

*πολεμόκλονος, ον (κλόνος), making a warlike noise or tumult, Batr. 4, 276.

πολεμόνδε. adv. Ep. πτολεμόνδε, to the war, 8, 313, and often.

embracing, epith. of Hades, =Πολυδέγμων h. Cer. 9.

πολυδένδρεος, ον (δένδρον), abounding in trees, woody, *Od. 4, 737. 23, 139. h. Ap. 475.

πολύδεσμος, ον, poet. (δεσμός), well-bound, well-joined. σχεδίη, *Od. 5, 33. 7, 264.

Πολυδεύκης. ους, ὁ, accus. Πολυδεύκεα, Pulydeukês (Pollux), son of Zeus and Leda, brother of Kastôr (Castor), one of the Dioscûri, famous as a pugilist; he alone as the son of Zeus was immortal, see Κάστωρ, 3, 237. Od. 11, 299, seq.

πολυδίψιος, ον (δίψα), very thirsty, destitute of water, epith. of Argos, 4, 171. It refers to the tradition that the realm of Argos was once destitute of water, cf. Apd. 2, 1. 4. According to others, long looked for, Fr. 2, 1.

Πολυδώρη. ἡ, daughter of Peleus and Antigone, wife of Borus and mother of Menesthius, 16, 175.

πολύδωρος, ον (δῶρον). richly gifted, i. e. πολύεδνος, epith. of ἄλοχος, who on account of her beauty had received many presents, 6, 394. 22, 88. Od. 24, 293 In the last passage it has been translated well-portioned. [Cf. Lenz Gesch. d. Weiber, 8. 170. Am. Ed.]

Πολύδωρος, ὁ, son of Priam and Laothoë. Because he was the youngest and most beloved of his sons, Priam would not permit him to take part in the battle. Disobedient to the command, he exposed himself in the fight and was slain by Achilles, 20, 407, seq. 21, 85, seq. (2) One of the Epigoni, conquered by Nestor, 23, 637.

Πολύειδος, ὁ, see Πολύϊδος.

*πολυεύχετος, ον (εὔχομαι), much wished. much prayed for, h. Cer. 165.

πολύζυγος, ον, poet. 'ζυγόν), having many banks of rowers, well-oared, νηῦς, 2, 293.†

πολυήρατος, ον (ἐράω), much beloved, greatly wished for, dear, Θήβη, γάμος, *Od. 11, 275. 15, 126. 366. h. Ven. 226.

πολυηχής, ές (ἠχή), loud sounding, i. e. 1) loud singing, full-voiced, spoken of the nightingale, Od. 19, 521. 2) loud echoing, loud resounding, spoken of a shore. 4. 422.

πολυθαρσής, ές (θάρσος), very bold, very courageous, spirited, 17, 156. Od. 13, 387.

Πολυθερσείδης, ου, ὁ, son of Polytherses, =Ctesippus, Od. 22, 287.

Πολύϊδος, ὁ (ῑ). (who knows much, from πολύς and ἰδεῖν, according to Wolf. Heyne, on the other hand, writes Πολύειδος, according to Etym. M. and also Eustath. mentions this orthography, so also Paus. Plat.) son of Cœranus, a prophet of Corinth. of the family of Melampus, father of Euchênor, 13, 663. 2) son of Eurydamas, a Trojan, 5, 148.

πολυϊδρείη. ἡ, poet. (πολύϊδρις), much knowledge; hence, wisdom, intelligence, plur. *Od. 2, 346. 23, 77.

πολύϊδρις, ιος, ὁ, ἡ, poet. (ἴδρις), much knowing; hence, wise, intelligent, crafty, *Od. 15, 459. 23, 82.

πολύϊππος, ον (ἵππος), having many horses, abounding in horses, 13, 171.†

*πολυΐχθυος. ον (ἰχθύς), abounding in fish, h. Ap. 417.

πολυκαγκής, ές, poet. (κάγκανος), very parching; δίψα, burning thirst. 11. 642†.

πολύκαρπος, ον (καρπός), abounding in fruits, ἀλωή, *Od. 7, 122. 24, 221.

Πολυκάστη, ἡ (the much adorned), daughter of Nestor and Anaxibia, Od. 3, 46†. According to Eustath. wife of Telemachus.

πολυκέρδεια, ἡ (πολυκερδής). great craftiness, cunning, in the plur. Od. 24, 167.*

πολυκερδής, ές (κέρδος), very crafty, cunning, νόος, Od. 13, 255.†

πολύκεστος. ον (κεστός), much embroidered, richly embroidered, ἱμάς, 3, 371.†

πολυκηδής, ές, poet. (κῆδος), full of care, causing trouble (νόστος), *Od. 9, 37. 23, 351.

*πολύκλαυτος, ον, poet. for πολύκλαυστος (κλαίω), much wept, greatly lamented, Ep. 3, 5.

πολυκλήϊς, ῖδος, ἡ, poet. (κλίς), furnished with many benches of oars, well-oared epith. of ships, 2, 74. 20, 382. Od. (Iota long in all the cases.)

πολύκληρος, ον (κλῆρος), prop. of a great lot; having a great inheritance, very rich, wealthy, Od 14, 211.†

πολύκλητος, ον (καλέω), called from many places, called from far, epith. of allies, *4, 438. 10, 420.

πολύκλυστος, ον, poet. (κλύζω), prop. much washed; heaving, rolling great waves, πόντος, *Od. 4, 354. 6, 204.

πολύκμητος, ον (κάμνω), wrought with much toil and effort, prepared with toil, prop. spoken of iron which was hard for the ancients to work (V. beautifully wrought), 6, 48. 10, 379; and often; θάλαμος only Od. 4, 718.

πολύκνημος, ον, poet. (κνημός), having many wooded hills, abounding in woods, 2, 497.†

πολυκοιρανίη, ἡ (κοίρανος), a multiplicity of rulers, 2, 204.†

*πολύκροτος, ον (κρότος), very noisy, loud-resounding, h. 18, 37.

πολυκτήμων, ον (κτῆμα), having great possessions, wealthy, 5, 613.†

Πολυκτορίδης, ου, ὁ, son of Polyctor = Pisander, Od. 18, 299.

Πολύκτωρ. ορος, ὁ wealthy, (from κτέαρ), 1) son of Pterelaus, one of the oldest heroes of Ithaca, Od. 17, 207. 2) father of Pisander, Od. 22, 243. [3) a fictitious Myrmidon, feigned by Hermês as his father, Il. 24, 397.]

πολυλήϊος, ον (λήϊον), rich in harvests, rich in fields, 5, 613.† h. Merc. 171.

πολύλλιστος, ον, Ep. for πολύλιστος, poet. (λίσσομαι), much prayed for, Od. 5, 445;† νηός, a temple in which the deity

expression, observe 1) It stands often
with the gen. to express the notion of a
part. πολλοὶ Τρώων, many of the Trojans, Il. 18. 271. Also the neut. sing.
πολλὸν σαρκός, βίης, Od. 19, 450. 21,
185. 2) Mly πολύς is treated as a complete predicate, and hence is connected
with another adj. by καί, Ep. τὲ καί.
πολλοὶ καὶ ἄλλοι, many others. πολλὰ
καὶ ἐσθλά, many valuables, Od. 4, 96.
πολέες τε καὶ ἐσθλοί, Il. 6, 452. 21, 586;
or τέ, τέ, in which case πολύς takes the
second place. παλαιά τε πολλά τε, Od. 2,
188 2) Often it stands alone as subst.
in H., very rarely with article. τὰ πολλά,
the many, i. e. the most, Od. 2, 58. 17,
537; so also πολλά, Il. 9, 333; πολλοί
also stands sometimes for οἱ πολλοί, the
most, the multitude, 2, 483. 21, 524. 3)
The neut. sing. and plur. as adv. much,
greatly, very, strongly, long, often, πολλόν,
9, 506. 20, 178; πολλά, often μάλα πολλά, Il. 1, 35. Od. 2, 151. b) It enhances
also the compar. and superl. πολὺ μᾶλλον, much more. πολλὸν ἀμείνων, much
better. πολλὸν ἄριστος, by much the
bravest.

*πολυσημάντωρ, ορος, ὁ, poet. who
rules many, epith. of Hades, h. Cer. 31.
84. 377.

πολύσκαρθμος, ον, poet. (σκαίρω),
leaping strongly, springing actively, epith.
of the Amazon Myrina, 2, 814,† in reference to dancing; or, according to some,
hastening away with steeds.

πολυσπερής, ές, poet (σπείρω), wide-
sowed, widely-scattered, ἄνθρωποι, 2, 804.
Od. 11, 365.

πολυστάφυλος, ον (σταφυλή), abounding in grapes, abounding in wine, *2,
507.† h. 25, 11.

πολύστονος, ον (στένω), much-groaning,
unfortunate, Od. 19, 118. b) Act. causing
many groans, epith. of Strife, of the arrow, Il. 1, 445. 11, 73.

πολύτλας, αντος, ὁ, poet. (τλῆναι), that
has endured much, much-enduring, much-
suffering, epith. of Odysseus (Ulysses),
only nom. 8, 97. Od. 5, 171; and often.

πολυτλήμων, ονος, ὁ, ἡ (τλήμων), much-
enduring, much-sustaining, epith. of
Odysseus (Ulysses), Od. 18, 319; θυμός,
the much-enduring spirit, Il. 7, 152.

πολύτλητος, ον, poet. (τλῆναι), that
has suffered much, much-enduring, γέροντες, Od. 11, 38.†

πολυτρήρων, ωνος, ὁ, ἡ (τρήρων), abounding in doves, epith. of regions, *2, 502.
582.

πολύτρητος, ον (τρητός), much-pierced,
much-perforated, σπόγγος, *Od. 1, 111.
22, 439.

πολύτροπος, ον (τρέπω), that has endured much, far-travelled, epith. of Odysseus (Ulysses), Od. 1, 1. 10, 230. Thus
Voss, Myth. Br. p. 102, and Nitzsch ad
loc., as also the epexegesis shows; on
the contrary, Damm and Wolf: very ver-
satile, crafty, and so also h. Merc. 13,
439.

*πολύυμνος, ον, poet. (ὑμνέω), much-
sung, highly celebrated, h. 25, 7.

πολυφάρμακος, ον (φάρμακον), acquainted with many remedies or magic
drugs, ἰητροί, 16, 28: Κίρκη, Od. 10,
276.

Πολυφείδης, ους, ὁ, son of Mantius,
grandson of Melampus, Od. 15, 249.

πολύφημος, ον (φήμη), many-toned,
much-speaking; ἀοιδός, abounding in
songs, Od. 22, 376; βάτραχος, the much-
croaking frog, Batr. 12; ἀγορή, the
many-voiced, noisy market-place, Od. 2,
150.

Πολύφημος, ὁ, 1) son of Poseidôn
and of the nymph Thoôsa, one of the
Cyclôpes in Trinacria, Od. 1, 70. After
he had devoured six of the companions
of Odysseus (Ulysses), the latter avenged
himself by making him drunk and then
putting out his eye with a glowing stake,
Od. 9, 371, seq. cf. Κύκλωψ. 2) son of
Elatus, brother of Cæneus, a Lapithe of
Larissa, who took part in the Argonautic
expedition. Having been left in Mysia,
he founded the city Cios, Il. 1, 264.

πολύφλοισβος, ον, poet. (φλοῖσβος),
much-roaring, loud-resounding, epith. of
the sea, 1, 34; and Od. 13, 85.

Πολυφήτης, ου, ὁ, a Mysian of Ascania, 13, 791; it should prob. be read
Περιφήτης, according to Strab. XIV. p.
511.

Πολυφόντης, ου, ὁ, son of Autophônus,
who was slain by Tydeus before Thebes
in an ambush, 4, 395.

πολύφορβος, ον, poet. (φορβή), much-
nourishing, abounding in nourishment,
epith. of the earth, 14, 200. 301; also
πολυφορβή, *9, 365.

πολύφρων, ονος, ὁ, ἡ, poet. (φρήν),
very intelligent, very wise, very crafty,
epith. of Odysseus (Ulysses), Od. 14,
424; and of Hêphæstus, Il. 21, 367. Od.
8, 297.

*πολύφωνος, ον (φωνή), many-voiced,
loud-croaking, Batr. 216.

πολύχαλκος, ον, poet. (χαλκός), abounding in brass or copper, spoken of persons
and places, having many copper utensils,
10, 315. 18, 289. Od. 15, 424. 2) made
of much brass, adorned with much brass,
brazen, epith. of heaven, 5, 504. Od. 3,
2. According to Voss, Myth. Br. 1, 27,
in the literal sense; on the other hand,
Völcker, Hom. Geogr. p. 5, metaph. imperishable, enduring.

*πολυχρόνιος, ον (χρόνος), long-en-
during, lasting, h. Merc. 123.

πολύχρυσος, ον (χρυσός), abounding in
gold, rich in gold, epith. of persons and
places, 7, 180. 10, 315. Od. 3. 305;
adorned with gold, epith. of Aphroditê,
h. Merc. 1.

*πολυώνυμος, ον (ὄνομα), 1) having
many names, epith. of Hades, h. Cer. 18,
32. 2) having a great name, much-re-
nowned, h. Ap. 82.

πολυωπός, όν (ὀπή), having many holes,
having meshes, δίκτυον, Od. 22, 386.†

ὁδός: πόροι ἁλός, *the paths* of the sea, Od. 12, 259.

πόρπη, ἡ (πείρω), *the ring* of a buckle, upon which the tongue (περόνη) lies, hence *a buckle, a brooch, a clasp*, 18, 401.†
h. Ven. 164.

*πορσαίνω = πορσύνω, fut. πορσανέουσα. Ep. for πορσανοῦσα, ed. Spitzner, according to Cod. Ven. Il. 3, 411. h. Cer. 156.

πορσύνω (ΠΟΡΩ), poet. fut. πορσυνέω, *to bring to pass, to further, to prepare*, only λέχος, εὐνήν τινι, to prepare a bed, a couch for any one, always spoken of the wife who herself shares the couch with the husband, 3, 411 (cf. Nitzsch ad Od l. c.), Od. 3, 403.

πόρταξ, ακος, ἡ = πόρτις, *a calf, a heifer*, 17, 4.†

πόρτις, ιος, ἡ, another form πόρις, Od. 10, 410: *a calf, a heifer*, Il. 5, 162.† h. Cer. 174.

*πορτιτρόφος, ον, *nourishing calves* or *young cattle*, h. Ap. 21.

πορφύρεος, η, ον (πορφύρα), *purple, purple-coloured*. a) coloured with purple, dark red in different degrees; spoken of garments and carpets, φᾶρος, 8, 221. Od. 4, 115; αἷμα, Il. 17, 361. 2) Metaph. spoken of the sea: πόρφ. κῦμα, *the purple wave*, spoken of the sea disturbed by the wind or the stroke of the oar, 1, 482. Od. 2, 428. πόρφ. ἅλς, Il. 16, 391; νεφέλη, a dark cloud, 17, 351. πόρφ. θάνατος, dark death, like μέλας, 5, 85. 16, 334 (according to Passow also *blood-red, bloody*).

πορφύρω, poet. (πορφύρα), only pres. *to become purple, to be purpled* or *darkened* [Cp.], spoken of the disturbed sea, which assumes a dark colour, 14, 16. b) Metaph. spoken of the heart: *to swell, to be restless*. πολλά οἱ κραδίη πόρφυρε, his heart was greatly agitated, spoken of the unquiet spirit of one who cannot come to a resolution, 21, 551. Od. 4, 427.

ΠΟΡΩ (πόρος), obsol pres. poet. from which aor. ἔπορον, Ep. πόρον, partcp. πορών. perf. pass. πέπρωται, partcp. πεπρωμένος, prop. to bring to pass. hence *to procure, to give, to grant, to bestow*, τινί τι, for the most part spoken of things and states: δῶρα, φάρμακα, πένθος: of persons: τινὶ υἱόν, 16, 185. ἀνδρὶ παράκοιτιν, to give a wife to a man, 24, 60. b) For the accus. constr. with infin. πόρε καί σὺ Διὸς κούρῃσιν ἕπεσθαι τιμήν, grant also thou, that to the daughter of Zeus honour be yielded, 9. 513. 2) The perf. pass. is impers.; prop. *it is divided* or *distributed to*; then *it is fated, allotted by destiny*, τινί, to any one, with accus. and infin. 18, 329. The partcp. πεπρωμένος, *fated, destined*, and with dat. of the thing, ὀμῇ αἴσῃ, to the same fate, 15, 209. 16, 441.

πόσε, adv. (πός), *whither?* 16, 422. Od. 6, 199.

Ποσειδάων, ωνος, ὁ, voc. Ποσείδαον, Ep. for Ποσειδῶν (according to Herm.

from πόσις and εἴδεσθαι, *quod potabilis videtur*), *Poseidôn*, son of Kronus (Saturn) and Rhea, brother of Zeus, of Hades, etc., husband of Amphitrite, 15, 187. He is ruler of the sea, esply of the Mediterranean sea, which fell to him by lot, 14, 156. 15, 189. Although he reigns independently in his vast dominion, yet he recognizes the precedence of Zeus as the elder, 8, 210. 13, 355; and even unharnesses his steeds, 8, 440. He has his dwelling in the depths of the sea near Ægæ (see Αἰγαί), 13, 21. Od. 5, 381. Here stand his steeds; but he also comes to the assemblies of the gods in Olympus, Il. 8, 440. 15, 161. As sovereign of the sea he sends storms, Od. 5, 291; he gives also favorable winds and a prosperous voyage, Il. 9, 362. Od. 4, 500. He shakes the earth (ἐνοσίχθων, ἐννοσίγαιος), but he also holds it firm by his element (γαιήοχος). As the creator of the horse, he is the inventor and overseer of horses-races, Il. 23, 307. 584; and as such he is the god of the house and country of the horseman Nestor, see Nitzsch ad Od. 3, 7. In the Iliad he appears as the enemy of the Trojans, Æneas excepted, Il. 21, 442, seq., since Laomedon refused him the promised reward, when he and Apollo built the walls of Troy (see Λαομέδων). In the Od. he persecutes Odysseus (Ulysses) because he had blinded his son Polyphêmus, Od. 1, 20. 5, 286, seq. The symbol of his power is the trident; with this he excites and subdues the sea, Il. 12, 27. Od. 4, 506. He was worshipt at Onchêstus, Helicæ (see Ἑλικώνιος). Black bulls were sacrificed to him, Od. 3, 6. Il. 20, 404; also boars and rams, Od. 11, 130. Of his numerous progeny Homer mentions Eurytus and Cteatus, Nausithòus, Polyphêmus, Peleus, and Neleus.

Ποσιδήϊον, τό, *a temple of Poseidôn*, Od. 6, 266 †

Ποσιδήϊος, η, ον, Ion. for Ποσείδειος, *sacred to Poseidôn*, ἄλσος, 2, 506.†

πόσις, ιος, ὁ, poet. dat. πόσει and πόσει, 5, 71; *a husband*, Il. and Od.

πόσις, ιος, ἡ (πίνω), *drink*, often connected with ἐδητύς, 1, 469; and βρῶσις, 19, 210. Od. 1, 191.

ποσσῆμαρ, adv. Ep. for ποσῆμαρ (ἦμαρ), *in how many days?* 24, 657.†

πόστος, η, ον (πόσος), *how much?* Od. 24, 288.†

ποταμόνδε, adv. *into the river*, 21, 13. Od. 10, 150.

ποταμός, ὁ, *a river, a stream*, spoken also of Oceanus, 14, 245. 2) *a river-god*, 5, 544. 20, 7. 73. To the river deities were sacrificed bulls and horses, 21, 131. (From πίνω, πόω, prop. potable water.)

ποτάομαι, Ep. form of πέτομαι, *to fly*, pres. ποτῶνται, 2, 462. h. Merc. 558; perf. πεποτήαται, Ion. for πεπότηνται, 2 29; sing. πεπότηται, Od 11, 321.

°πρεσβηΐς, ΐδος, ἡ, poet. fem.=πρέσβα; τιμή, worthy honour, h. 29, 3.

°πρέσβις, ἡ, poet.=πρεσβεία, age, h. Merc 4 1.

πρέσβιστος, η, ον. see πρέσβυς.

πρεσβυγενής. ές (γένος), elder in years, first-born, 11, 249.†

πρέσβυς, ὁ, poet. for πρεσβύτης, not occurring in Hom., but the fem. Ep. πρέσβα, πρέσβειρα, πρεσβηΐς, compar. πρεσβύτερος, η, ον, 11, 787; superl. πρεσβύτατος, η, ον and πρέσβιστος, h. 30, 2; old, venerable. πρεσβύτατος γενεῇ, eldest in birth, 6, 24. Od. 13, 142.

πρήθω, poet. form of πίμπρημι, which is not found in Hom.; aor. 1 ἔπρησα, Ep. πρῆσα, 1) to burn, to inflame, τί, with gen. mater. (cf. Kühner, § 455. Rem.); θύρετρα πυρός, with fire, 2, 415; cf ἐνιπρήθω. 2) to blow upon, to swell, spoken of wind, τί; μέσον ἱστίον, Od. 2, 427. b) to cast out, to breathe out, to blow out, αἷμα ἀνὰ στόμα, Il. 16, 350. (According to Buttm., Lex. in voc., akin to πρίω and πέρθω; it is uncertain whether its prop. signif. is to kindle, to inflame, or to spout out, to emit; according to Rost it is to rattle, to crack.)

πρηκτήρ, ῆρος, ὁ (πρήσσω), Ion. for πρακτήρ, 1) a performer, a doer, an author. ἔργων, 9, 443. 2) Esply a tradesman, Od. 8, 162.

πρηνής. ές, Ion. for πρανής (akin to πρό), bent forwards, headlong, κατά (adv.) πρηνὲς βάλλειν τι, to cast any thing down, 2, 414; πρηνὴς ἤριπε, he fell forwards. 5, 58. ἔπεσε, ἐλιάσθη, also πρηνὴς ἐν κονίῃσι, 2, 418.

πρῆξις, ιος, ἡ (πράσσω), 1) doing, an action, business, undertaking, κατὰ πρῆξιν, on business, in opposition to μαψιδίως, Od. 3, 72. esply traffic, h. Ap. 398. 2) the produce of it, gain, advantage, οὔτις πρῆξις πέλεται γοόιο, there is no advantage from lamentation (V. 'we effect nothing'), Il. 24, 524; or οὔτις πρ. ἐγίγνετο μυρομένοισιν, there was no help to them complaining, Od. 10, 202.

πρήσσω, Ion. for πράσσω, fut. πρήξω, aor. ἔπρηξα, prop. to do, to act; hence, 1) to effect, to accomplish, to attain, with accus. Od. 16, 88; ἔργον, Od. 19, 324; absol. Il. 18, 357; esply partcp. πρήξας, Od. 3, 60; often with οὔτι, Il. 1, 562. 11, 552. Od. 2, 191. 2) Esply spoken of a way: to finish, to pass over, with accus. κέλευθον, Il. 14, 282. Od. 13, 83; ἅλα, to sail over the sea, Od. 9, 491; with gen. ὁδοῖο, Il. 24, 264. Od. 3, 476. 3) to collect, to gather, τινὰ τόκους, usury from any one, Batr. 186.

°πρηΰνω, Ion. for πραΰνω (πραΰς), to render mild. to calm, to appease, with accus. h. Merc. 417.

πρηΰς, ύ, Ion. for πραΰς, mild, gentle, h. 7, 10. cf. Gramm.

πρίασθαι, mid. defect. verb, of which only aor. 2 is in use, 3 sing. πρίατο, to buy, τί. any thing, κτεάτεσσιν, for treasures, °Od. 1, 430. 14, 115. 452.

Πριαμίδης, ου, ὁ, son of Priam (the first ι long by the arsis).

Πρίαμος, ὁ, son of Laomedon, king of Troy, husband of Hecuba (Hekabê). According to H. he had fifty sons, nineteen of them by Hecuba. Hector was the dearest of them all, 24, 493, seq. Of the time before the Trojan war, it is mentioned that he aided the Phrygians against the Amazons, 3, 184, seq. At the beginning of the siege of Troy he was already at an advanced age, and took no part in the contest, 24, 487. He appears only once on the battle field, to conclude the treaty concerning the duel of Paris and Menelaus, 3, 261. After Hector's death, he went, under the conduct of Hermês, into the tent of Achilles, and redeemed the corpse of his son, 24, 470, seq. According to later tradition he was slain by Neoptolemus, son of Achilles. (On the name Πρίαμος, cf. Apd. 2, 6, 4.)

πρίν, adv. and conjunct. I) Adv. of time: in independent sentences, before, ere, first, sooner, and, generally, earlier, at an earlier time; mly opposed to νῦν, 2, 112. 344; πολὺ πρίν, long before, Od. 2, 167. 2) Often with the article, τοπρίν or τὸ πρίν, ed. Spitzner, Il. 6, 125. 16, 373; but Od. τὸ πρίν, Od. 3, 265. 4, 32; formerly (olim). 3) As adv. it stands also with indicat. πρίν μιν καὶ γῆρας ἔπεισιν, first (i. e. sooner) shall old age come upon her, Il. 1, 29; cf. Thiersch, § 292. 2. Il. 18, 283; with optat. πρίν κεν ἀνιηθεὶς σὴν πατρίδα γαῖαν ἵκοιο, thou wouldst be wearied out and return to thy native land before [the tale was ended], Od. 3, 117. II) Conjunct. in relative clauses of time: before, ere; in this signif. πρίν—πρίν, πρίν—πρίν γε, πάρος—πρίν γε, etc., often stand in Hom. 1) With indicat. in the H. poems alone only in h. Ap. 357; but πρίν γ' ὅτε, as long as, until, Il. 9, 588. 12, 437. Od. 4, 180. 13, 322. h. Ap. 47. 2) With the future only in conceived actions, when the main clause is always denied. a) With subjunct. after a primary tense in the main clause, Il. 24, 551. Od. 10, 175; with πρίν γε, Il. 18, 135. Od. 13, 336; with πρίν γ' ὅτ' ἄν, Od. 2, 374. b) With optat. after an historical tense in the main clause, Il. 21, 580; after πρίν γ' ὅτε, 9, 488. 3) Most frequently with infin. aor. when the action of the subordinate clause appears as a temporal consequence of the main clause: οὐδ' ὅγε πρίν—Κήρας ἀφέξει, πρίν γ' ἀπὸ πατρὶ δομέναι — κουρήν, 1, 98. 9, 387; and often. The infin. with accus. occurs when the dependent clause has a new subject, 6, 82. 22, 156. Od. 23, 138. Also πρίν γ' ἤ (cf. priusquam), Il. 5, 288. 22, 266. 4) In H. passages also occur where the infin. is exchanged with the optat, 17, 504, seq. 5) πρίν stands elliptically, Od 15, 394; πρίν ὥρη, subaud. ῆ. before it is time. (ι is short, but is used as long Ep.)

προέμεν, see προίημι.

προερέσσω (ἐρέσσω), aor. 1 προέρεσα, Ep. σσ, to row forwards, onwards, ἐς λιμένα, Od. 13, 279; trans. τὴν (νῆα) δ' εἰς ὅρμον προέρεσσαν ἐρετμοῖς, Il. 1, 435; a reading adopted by Spitzner for προρύσσαν, because προερύειν signifies 'to draw forward,' and hence cannot be spoken of oars. Also in Od. 9, 73; αὐτὰς —προερέσσαμεν ἠπειρόνδε.

προερύω, poet. (ἐρύω), aor. 1 προέρυσα, Ep. σσ, to draw forwards, onwards; spoken always of ships, a) From the shore into the sea, ἅλαδε, 1, 308. b) From the open sea to propel by rowing to the land, ἠπειρόνδε, Od. 9, 73. Il. 1, 435; but cf. προερέσσω.

πρόες, see προίημι.

προέχω, contr. προὔχω (ἔχω), always in the contr. form, except imperf. 3 sing. πρόεχε, Od. 12, 11. 2) Intrans. to be before, to come before, spoken of persons: προύχων, the prominent man, Il. 23, 325. 453; δῆμον, to be eminent among the people, h. Cer. 151; spoken of things: to project, to be prominent, Od. 12, 11. Mid. to have or hold before oneself, ταύρους, Od. 3, 8 (where others read, προύθεντο).

προήκης, ες (ἀκή), pointed before, Od. 12, 205.†

*προθαλής, ές, poet. (θάλλω), growing well, h. Cer. 241.

προθέλυμνος, ον, poet. (θέλυμνον), by the roots, utterly, entirely (Schol. πρόρριζος), προθελύμνους ἕλκετο χαίτας, he tore his hair out by the roots, 10, 15. προθέλυμνα χαμαὶ βάλε δένδρεα ["trees he cast on earth Uprooting them," Cp.], 9, 541; φράσσειν σάκος σάκεϊ, shield pressed on shield compactly, densely, in close array, 13, 130. They locked the shields so closely together that no space remained between. (Others take it in reference to τετραθέλυμνος, with close layers. The derivation from θέλυμνον = θεμέλιον, from the foundation, is most probable; the signif. close, one upon another (Schol. ἐπ' ἀλλήλοις), seems borrowed from the last passage; still Voss follows it, and Köppen ad Il. 13, 130.)

προθέουσι, 1, 291; see προτίθημι.

προθέω (θέω), Ion. iterat. imperf. προθέεσκε, to run before, 10, 362. 22, 459. Od. 11, 515.

Προθοήνωρ, ορος, ὁ, son of Areïlycus, leader of the Bœotians, 2, 495.

Πρόθοος, ὁ, son of Tenthredon, leader of the Magnetæ, 2, 756.

προθορών, see προθρώσκω.

Προθόων, ωνος, ὁ, a Trojan, slain by Teucer, 14, 515.

προθρώσκω (θρώσκω), partcp. aor. προθορών, to leap before, to spring before, *14, 363. 17, 522.

προθυμίη, ἡ (θυμός), readiness, good will, good courage, plur. 2, 588.† (Poet. with ἰ.)

*προθύραιος, ον (θύρα), before the door, τὰ προθύραια = πρόθυρα, h. Merc. 384.

πρόθυρον, τό (θύρα), mly plur. the doorway to the court, Il. and Od. 2) the place before the door, a porch, Od. 20, 355. 21, 299. 22. 474.

προϊάλλω (ἰάλλω), poet. only imperf. to send forth, to send away, τινὰ ἀπ' οὐρανόθεν, 8, 365; ἐπὶ νῆας, 11, 3; ἀγρόνδε, Od. 5, 369.

προϊάπτω (ἰάπτω), fut. προϊάψω, aor. προΐαψα (ῑ), prop. to thrust forth; then, to send away, to send, τινὰ Ἄϊδι, any one to Hades, 1, 3. 6, 487; Ἀϊδωνῆϊ, *5, 190.

προΐειν, see προίημι.

προΐημι (ἵημι), imperf. Ion. and Att. προΐειν, aor. 1 προῆκα or προέηκα, 2 aor. 3 plur. πρόεσαν, imperat. πρόες, προέτω, infin. προέμεν, Ep. for προεῖναι, prop. to send forwards; hence, 1) Spoken of persons: to send forth, to send away, to let go, τινά, 1, 326; with infin. following, καλήμεναι, in order to call, 10, 125. cf. v. 388. 563. b) Of things: νῆας, 7, 468; of missiles: to let fly, to cast, to hurl, ὀϊστούς, βέλος, ἔγχος, 8, 297. 17, 516; of a river: ὕδωρ ἐς Πηνειόν, it sends out, i. e. pours its water into the Peneus, 2, 752. 2) to let go, to let fall, πηδάλιον ἐκ χειρῶν, Od. 5, 316; ἔπος, to let a word drop, Od. 14, 466. πόδα προέηκε φέρεσθαι, Od. 19, 468; φήμην, Od. 20, 105. 3) to send to, τινά or τί τινι, Il. 1, 127; ἀγγελίας, to send an embassy, Od. 2, 92; and generally, to give, to bestow, like διδόναι; κῦδός τινι, Il. 16, 241. ἐμοὶ πνοιὴν Ζεφύρου προέηκεν, he let the breath of the Zephyr blow upon me, Od. 10, 25; οὖρον, Od. 3, 183. [But πρό cannot signify to; it rather means forth, and these citations may better be referred to no. 2.]

προΐκτης, ου, ὁ (προΐξ). a beggar, a mendicant, Od. 17, 449. ἀνὴρ προΐκτης, *Od. 17, 347. 352.

προΐξ, contr. προΐξ, gen. προικός, a gift, a present. γενέσθαι προικός, to enjoy his present [to taste his mendicated mess, Cp.], Od. 17, 413; then προικός, as adv. gratuitously, i. e. without a (present in) return, χαρίζεσθαι, Od. 13. 15 (cf. Thiersch, § 198. 6). Another Schol. connects προικός as a subst. with χαρίσασθαι; hence Voss and Passow: 'to bestow generous gifts.' Cf. Od. 1, 140.

προΐστημι (ἵστημι), aor. 1 partcp. προστήσας, trans. to place before, to put before; τινὰ μάχεσθαι, any one to fight, 4, 156.†

Προῖτος, ὁ, son of Abas. king of Tiryns, husband of Antia. Being expelled by his brother Acrisius, he fled to king Iobätes in Lycia. He gave him his daughter Antia, and restored him to his kingdom, 6, 157, seq.

προκαθίζω (ἵζω), to sit down before, to settle, spoken of cranes, 2, 463.†

προκαλέω (καλέω), only mid. aor. 1, Ep. προκαλεσσάμην, subj. προκαλέσσεται with shortened vowel. 7, 39, 1) to call forth to oneself, to challenge, τινά, absol. Od. 8, 142; and χάρμῃ, to battle,

only once with gen. 11, 831. 22, 198.
4) With gen. 1) Spoken of place: a)
Prop. to indicate motion from an object:
from. ἵκετο—ἠὲ πρὸς ἠοίων ἢ ἑσπερίων
ἀνθρώπων, from eastern or western men,
Od. 8, 29; mly πρός indicates only
motion, hence to a point, to, towards.
πρὸς ἁλός, to the sea, Il. 10, 428. 430.
πρὸς νηῶν, 15, 670. πρὸς Βορέαο, to the
north, Od. 13, 110. 21, 347, cf. 3) With
accus. b) In indicating near approach
to an object: close upon, near by, before
(coram). ποτὶ πτόλιος πέτετ' ἀεί, he
flew always close by the city, Il. 22, 198.
τοῦτό σοι πρὸς Τρώων κλέος ἔσται, this
shall redound to thy glory before the
Trojans, 22, 514. cf. 16, 85. 2) In
causative relations, as indicating any
thing which proceeds from or is effected
by a person or thing: from, through, by
means of, by virtue of. a) Spoken of the
author: ἔχειν τιμὴν πρὸς Ζηνός, Od. 11,
302. ἀκούειν τι πρός τινος, from any
man, i. e. from his mouth, Il. 6, 525.
οἵτε θέμιστας πρὸς Διὸς εἰρύαται, from
Zeus (auctore Jove), 1, 339; and with
the pass. διδάσκεσθαι πρός τινος, to be
taught by any one, 11, 831. cf. 6, 57. b)
Spoken of the possessor: πρὸς Διός εἰσι
ξεῖνοι, strangers belong to Zeus, Od. 6,
207. 14, 57. c) In oaths and asseverations: πρὸς θεῶν, by the gods (for the
sake of the gods), 1, 339. 19, 188. Od.
11, 67. 13, 324. B) With dat. spoken
only of place in indicating continuance
with an object: before, by, near, beside,
upon, at. πρὸς ἀλλήλῃσι ἔχονται, by one
another, Od. 5, 329. Often with the implied notion of motion: λιάζεσθαι ποτὶ
γαίῃ, βάλλεσθαι προτὶ γαίῃ, Il. 20, 420.
22, 64. 2) In indicating approach: to,
towards, Od. 10, 68. c) With accus. 1)
Spoken of place: a) In indicating motion or direction to an object: to, towards, against. ἰέναι πρὸς Ὀλυμπον, φέρειν τι προτὶ ἄστυ; also εἰπεῖν, μυθήσασθαι πρός τινα, to speak to any one;
spoken also of the situation of places:
πρὸς Ἠῶ τ' Ἠέλιόν τε, Il. 12, 239. Od.
9, 26. cf. Il. 8, 364. b) In a hostile
signif.: μάχεσθαι πρὸς Τρῶας, to fight
against the Trojans, 17, 471; metaph.
πρὸς δαίμονα, against the deity, i. e.
against the will of the deity, 17, 98. 104.
2) Spoken of time: towards, ποτὶ ἔσπε-
ρα, Od. 17, 191. 3) In causative relations; only of exchange: ἀμείβειν τι
πρός τινα. to exchange any thing with
any one, Il. 6, 235. II) Adv. without
cases: mly πρὸς δέ, besides, moreover, in
addition, 1, 245. 5, 307. III) In composition, πρός has the signif. already
given: to, towards, etc.
πρσάγω (ἄγω), aor. 2 προσήγαγον, to
lead to, to bring to, to procure for, τί
τινι, Od. 17, 446 †; δῶρά τινι, to present
gifts to any one, h. Ap. 272.
*προσαΐσσω (ἀΐσσω), partcp. aor.
προσαΐξας, to rush upon, to leap or spring
to, *Od. 22, 337. 342. 365.

προσαλείφω (ἀλείφω), to rub on, to
anoint; φάρμακόν τινι, to anoint one
with a drug, Od. 10, 392.†
προσαμύνω (ἀμύνω), infin. aor. προσαμῦναι, 1) to repel, to avert, τινά, 5,
139. 2) With dat. τινί, to come to protect, to aid, *2, 238. 16, 509.
*προσαναγκάζω (ἀναγκάζω), aor. προσ-
ηνάγκασα, poet. σσ, to constrain still further, to compel, with infin. h. Cer. 413.
προσάπτω, Dor. and Ep. προτιάπτω
(ἅπτω), to attach; metaph. to dispense, to
grant, κῦδός τινι, 24, 110.†
προσαραρίσκω (ΑΡΩ), only partcp.
perf. προσαρηρώς, iutrans. to fit to, to
suit; ἐπίσσωτρα προσαρηρότα, close fitting tires, 5, 725.†
προσαρηρότα, see προσαραρίσκω.
προσαυδάω (αὐδάω), poet. 3 sing. imperf. προσηύδα, 3 dual προσαυδήτην, to
speak to, to address, often absol. and
with accus. τινά, ἐπέεσσιν, 11, 136. Od.
15, 440; and μειλιχίοισιν, sc. ἐπέεσσιν,
to address with friendly words, Il. 4,
256; κερτομίοισι, 1, 539. b) Most frequently with double accus. τινὰ ἔπεα,
to speak words to any one.
προσβαίνω (βαίνω), partcp. aor. 2 προσβάς, aor. mid. Ep. προσεβήσατο, 1) to
go to, to step to; λὰξ προσβάς, treading
upon any thing with the heel, 5, 620. 2)
With accus. Ὀλυμπον, to mount Olympus, 2, 48; κλίμακα, Od. 21, 5; πρὸς
δειράδα, h. Ap. 281.
προσβάλλω (βάλλω), Ep. and Dor.
προτιβάλλω, aor. 2 προσέβαλον, mid.
προτιβάλλεαι, Ep. for προσβάλλῃ, 1)
Prop. to cast to; generally, to cast, τὶ
γαίῃ, only in tmesis, 1, 245. b) With
accus. to cast upon any thing, to hit or
touch any one, or any thing, thus Ἠέλιος προσέβαλλεν ἀρούρας, Helios touched
the fields, i. e. illuminated them, 7, 421.
Od. 19, 433. Mid. to cast oneself upon
any one, to attack any one, τινὰ ἔπεϊ,
ἔργῳ, any one with words, in act, Il. 5,
879.
προσδέρκομαι, Dor. and Ep. ποτιδέρκομαι, poet. (δέρκομαι), to look upon, to behold, τινά, Od. 20, 385; ποτιδ., Il. 16,
10. Od. 17, 518.
προσδέχομαι, depon. mid. Dor. and
Ep. ποτιδέχ. (δέχομαι), only partcp. aor.
sync. ποτιδέγμενος, prop. to receive, to
take up; only metaph. to expect, to await,
τινά or τί, 10, 123. 19, 234 Od. 2, 403;
absol. to wait, to stay, with ὁππότ' ἄν or
εἰ, Il. 7. 415. Od. 23, 91.
προσδόρπιος, ον, Ep. ποτιδόρπ. (δόρπον),
pertaining to eating, or serving for eating;
for supper, *Od. 9, 234. 249.
προσειλέω, Ep. προτιειλέω (εἰλέω),
infin. προτιειλεῖν, to press on, to drive,
τινὰ προτὶ νῆας, 10, 347.†
πρόσειμι (εἶμι), only partcp. pres.
προσιών, to go to, to come to, to rush
upon, 5, 515. 7, 308. Od. 16, 5.
προσεῖπον (εἶπον), aor. of πρόσφημι,
always Ep. προσέειπον. optat. Dor. and
Ep. ποτιείποι. 22, 329 prop. to speak

only once with gen. 11, 831. 22, 198. *A.* With gen. 1) Spoken of place: *a*) Prop. to indicate motion from an object: *ἵ π.* ἵκετο—ἠὲ πρὸς ἠοίων ἢ ἐσπερίων ἀνθρώπων, from eastern or western men, Od. 8, 29; mly πρός indicates only motion, hence to a point, *to, towards.* πρὸς ἁλός, to the sea, Il. 10, 428. 430. πρὸς ἠῶν, 15, 670. πρὸς Βορέαο, to the north, Od. 13, 110. 21, 347, cf. 3) With accus. *b*) In indicating near approach to an object: *close upon, near by, before* (coram). ποτὶ πτόλιος πέτετ' ἀεί, he flew always close by the city, Il. 22, 198. τοῦτό σοι πρὸς Τρώων κλέος ἔσται, this shall redound to thy glory before the Trojans, 22, 514. cf. 16, 85. 2) In causative relations, as indicating any thing which proceeds from or is effected by a person or thing: *from, through, by means of, by virtue of.* *a*) Spoken of the author: ἔχειν τιμὴν πρὸς Ζηνός, Od. 11, 302. ἀκούειν τι πρός τινος, from any man, i. e. from his mouth, Il. 6, 525. αἵτε θέμιστας πρὸς Διὸς εἰρύαται, from Zeus (*auctore Jove*), 1, 339; and with the pass. διδάσκεσθαι πρός τινος, to be taught by any one, 11, 831. cf. 6, 57. *b*) Spoken of the possessor: πρὸς Διός εἰσι ξεῖνοι, strangers belong to Zeus, Od. 6, 207. 14, 57. *c*) In oaths and asseverations: πρὸς θεῶν, by the gods (for the sake of the gods), 1, 339. 19, 188. Od. 11, 67. 13, 324. *B*) With dat. spoken only of place in indicating continuance with an object: *before, by, near, beside, upon, at.* πρὸς ἀλλήλῃσι ἔχονται, by one another, Od. 5, 329. Often with the implied notion of motion: λιάζεσθαι ποτὶ γαίῃ, βάλλεσθαι προτὶ γαίῃ, Il. 20, 420. 22, 64. 2) In indicating approach: *to, towards,* Od. 10, 68. *c*) With accus. 1) Spoken of place: *a*) In indicating motion or direction to an object: *to, towards, against.* ἰέναι πρὸς Ὄλυμπον, φέρειν τι προτὶ ἄστυ; also εἰπεῖν, μυθήσασθαι πρός τινα, to speak to any one; spoken also of the situation of places: πρὸς Ἠῶ τ' Ἠέλιόν τε. Il. 12, 239. Od. 9. 26. cf. Il. 8, 364. *b*) In a hostile signif.: μάχεσθαι πρὸς Τρῶας, to fight against the Trojans, 17, 471; metaph. πρὸς δαίμονα, against the deity, i. e. against the will of the deity, 17, 98. 104. 2. Spoken of time: *towards,* ποτὶ ἕσπερα, Od. 17, 191. 3) In causative relations; only of exchange: ἀμείβειν τι πρός τινα, to exchange any thing with any one, Il. 6, 235. II) Adv. without cases: mly πρὸς δέ, *besides, moreover, in addition,* 1, 245. 5, 307. III) In composition, πρός has the signif. already given: *to, towards,* etc.

προσάγω (ἄγω), aor. 2 προσήγαγον, *to lead to, to bring to. to procure for,* τί τινι, Od. 17, 446†; δῶρά τινι, to present gifts to any one, h. Ap. 272.

*προσαΐσσω (ἀΐσσω), partcp. aor. προσαΐξας, *to rush upon, to leap or spring* to, *Od. 22, 337. 342. 365.

προσαλείφω (ἀλείφω), *to rub on, to anoint;* φάρμακόν τινι, to anoint one with a drug, Od. 10, 392.†

προσαμύνω (ἀμύνω), infin. aor. προσαμῦναι, 1) *to repel, to avert,* τινά, 5, 139. 2) With dat. τινί, *to come to protect, to aid,* *2, 238. 16, 509.

*προσαναγκάζω (ἀναγκάζω), aor. προσηνάγκασε, poet. σσ, *to constrain still further, to compel,* with infin. h. Cer. 413.

προσάπτω, Dor. and Ep. προτιάπτω (ἅπτω), *to attach;* metaph. *to dispense, to grant,* κῦδός τινι, 24, 110.†

προσαραρίσκω ('ΑΡΩ), only partcp. perf. προσαρηρώς, intrans. *to fit to, to suit;* ἐπίσσωτρα προσαρηρότα, close fitting tires, 5, 725.†

προσαρηρότα, see προσαραρίσκω.

προσαυδάω (αὐδάω), poet. 3 sing. imperf. προσηύδα, 3 dual προσαυδήτην, *to speak to, to address,* often absol. and with accus. τινά, ἐπέεσσιν, 11, 136. Od. 15, 440; and μειλιχίοισιν, sc. ἐπέεσσιν, to address with friendly words, Il. 4, 256; κερτομίοισι, 1, 539. *b*) Most frequently with double accus. τινὰ ἔπεα, to speak words to any one.

προσβαίνω (βαίνω), partcp. aor. 2 προσβάς, aor. mid. Ep. προσεβήσατο, 1) *to go to, to step to;* λὰξ προσβάς, treading upon any thing with the heel, 5, 620. 2) With accus. Ὄλυμπον, to mount Olympus, 2, 48; κλίμακα, Od. 21, 5; πρὸς δειράδα, h. Ap. 281.

προσβάλλω (βάλλω), Ep. and Dor. προτιβάλλω, aor. 2 προσέβαλον, mid. προτιβάλλεαι, Ep. for προσβάλλῃ, 1) Prop. to cast to; generally, *to cast,* τὶ γαίῃ, only in tmesis, 1, 245. *b*) With accus. to cast upon any thing, *to hit or touch* any one, or any thing, thus Ἠέλιος προσέβαλλεν ἀρούρας, Helios touched the fields, i. e. illuminated them, 7, 421. Od. 19, 433. Mid. *to cast oneself upon* any one, *to attack* any one, τινὰ ἔπει, ἔργῳ, any one with words, in act, Il. 5, 879.

προσδέρκομαι, Dor. and Ep. ποτιδέρκομαι, poet. (δέρκομαι), *to look upon, to behold,* τινά, Od. 20, 385; ποτιδ., Il. 16, 10. Od. 17, 518.

προσδέχομαι, depon. mid. Dor. and Ep. ποτιδέχ. (δέχομαι), only partcp. aor. sync. ποτιδέγμενος, prop. to receive, to take up; only metaph. *to expect, to await,* τινά or τί, 10, 123. 19, 234 Od. 2, 403; absol. *to wait, to stay,* with ὁππότ' ἄν or εἰ, Il. 7, 415. Od. 23, 91.

προσδόρπιος, ον, Ep. ποτιδόρπ. (δόρπον), *pertaining to eating,* or *serving for eating; for supper,* *Od. 9, 234. 249.

προσειλέω, Ep. προτιειλέω (εἰλέω) infin. προτιειλεῖν, *to press on, to drive,* τινὰ προτὶ νῆας, 10, 347.†

πρόσειμι (εἰμι), only partcp. pres. προσιών, *to go to, to come to, to rush upon,* 5, 515. 7, 308. Od. 16, 5.

προσεῖπον (εἶπον), aor. of πρόσφημι, always Ep. προσέειπον, optat. Dor. and Ep. ποτιείποι. 22, 329 prop. to speak

προτέμνω (τέμνω), aor. 2 προταμών, optat. aor. mid. προταμοίμην, 1) to cut off before, to carve (for), 9, 489. 2) to cut off in front, at the end, with accus. κορμὸν, ἐκ ῥίζης, to cut off the trunk at the root, Od. 23, 196. Mid. to cut off for oneself; metaph. ὦλκα διηνεκέα, to cut a straight furrow, Od. 18, 375.

πρότερος, η, ον (πρό), compar. without posit. the former, the earlier, prior, 1) Spoken of time: former, earlier, elder, γενεῇ, 15, 166. πρότεροι ἄνθρωποι, men of former times, ancestors, forefathers, 5, 637; also πρότεροι alone: πρ. παῖδες, children of a former marriage. Od. 15, 22. τῇ προτέρῃ sc. ἡμέρᾳ, on the former day, Od. 16, 50; with gen. ἐμέο πρότερος, earlier than I, Il. 10, 124. 2) Of place: before, fore-, that is before, 16, 569. πόδες πρότεροι, the fore-feet, Od. 19, 228.

προτέρω, adv. (πρότερος), further, further forwards. πρ. ἔπεο, step nearer, Od. 5, 91; ἄγειν, Il. 3, 400. Od. 5, 91; metaph. forward, more violent. ἔρις προτέρω γένετο, the contest went forward, waxed more violent, 23, 490.

*προτέρωσε, adv. (πρότερος), forwards, h. 32, 10.

προτεύχω (τεύχω), perf. pass. προτέτυγμαι, to make or to prepare before. τὰ μὲν προτετύχθαι ἐάσομεν, these things we will allow to have happened, i. e. what is past we will let alone, 16, 60. 18, 112. 19, 65.

προτί, Dor. for πρός.

προτιάπτω, see προσάπτω.

Προτιάων, ονος, ὁ, a Trojan, father of Astynoüs, 15, 455.

προτιβάλλεαι, see προσβάλλω.

προτιειλεῖν, see προσειλέω.

προτιείποι, see προσεῖπον.

προτίθημι (τίθημι), 3 plur. pres. προθέουσι for προτιθέασι, 1, 291; as if from the theme ΘΕΩ, cf. Thiersch, § 224. Kühner I. § 202. 2. aor. 1 προὔθηκα, 1) to place before, to put before, to lay before, τὶ κυσίν, to devour, 24, 409. 2) to put out, to expose publicly for sale, for use; hence metaph. to allow, to permit, τινί, with infin. 1, 291. Mid. to place before oneself, τραπέζας. Od. 1, 112.

προτιμυθήσασθαι, see προσμυθέομαι.

προτιόσσομαι, Dor. for προσόσσομαι (ὄσσομαι), 1) to look upon, to behold, τινά, Od. 7, 31. 23, 365. ἦ σ' εὖ γιγνώσκων προτιόσσομαι οὐδ' ἄρ' ἔμελλον πείσειν, indeed knowing thee well, I behold thee, i. e. indeed, I see thee now as I have ever known thee (and I was not about to persuade thee), Il. 22, 356. Thus Passow and Bothe. Krause takes it as a pres. perf.: 'I anticipated it and anticipate it still.' 2) to foresee, to anticipate, ὄλεθρον, θάνατον, Od. 5, 389. 14, 219.

προτμησις, ιος, ἡ (τέμνω), 1) the part cut off. 2) Metaph. spoken of the human figure: the region about the loins and navel, the waist, 11, 424.†

πρότονος, ὁ (τείνω), in the plur.; α

rope, primar. the two great ropes that extend from the top of the mast, the one to the bow and the other to the stern of a ship, to support the mast and also to lower it, 1, 434. Od. 12, 409. h. Ap. 504.

προτρέπω (τρέπω), only mid. aor. 2 Ep. προτραπόμην, 1) to turn forwards. 2) Mid. to turn oneself forward, to betake oneself, to turn in flight, ἐπὶ νηῶν, 5, 700; spoken of Helios: ἐπὶ γαῖαν, to turn to the earth, Od. 11, 18. 2) Metaph. to turn oneself to, to yield to; ἄχεϊ, to grief, Il. 6. 336.

προτροπάδην, adv. (προτρέπω), prop. turned forwards; φοβέοντο, they fled ever forward. i. e. on and on, without stopping, 16, 304.†

προτύπτω (τύπτω). aor. προὔτυψα, prop. trans. to strike forwards; in Hom. only intrans. to press forwards, to push forward, 13, 136. 15, 306. 17, 262. ἀνὰ ῥῖνάς οἱ δριμὺ μένος προὔτυψε, fierce wrath pressed into his nose, Od. 24, 319.

προὔθηκε, see προτίθημι.

προὔπεμψε, see προπέμπω.

προὔφαινε, see προφαίνω.

προὔχω, for προέχω.

προφαίνω (φαίνω), imperf. προὔφαινον, perf. pass. 3 plur. προπέφανται, aor. 2 pass. partep. προφανείς, 1) Act. trans. to exhibit. to cause to appear, with accus. τέραα, Od. 12, 394. b) Intrans. like mid. to appear, to shine forth, spoken of the moon. Od. 9, 145. II) Mid. with aor. pass. to shine forth, to show oneself, to become visible, Od. 13, 169. οὐδὲ προὐφαίνετο ἰδέσθαι, nothing appeared so that one could behold it, or to the sight, Od. 9, 143. προπέφανται ἅπαντα, every thing is visible at a distance, is exposed to view (Cp.), Il. 14, 332. b) Esply of persons: to appear, to step forth, Od. 24, 160; ἀνὰ γεφύρας πολέμοιο, Il. 8, 378; ἐς πόλεμον for ἐν πολέμῳ Il. 17, 487; ἐς πεδίον, 24, 332.

πρόφασις, ιος, ἡ (πρόφημι), a pretext, a pretence, appearance; absol. πρόφασιν, in appearance, in pretence, *19, 262. 302.

προφερής, ές (προφέρω), compar. προφερέστερος, η, ον; superl. προφερέστατος, η, ον, Od.; prop. borne before, placed before: then generally, eminent, distinguished, excellent, with dat. of the thing, ἅλματι, βίῃ, Od. 8, 128. 221. 21, 134; with infin., Il. 10, 352.

προφέρω (φέρω), only pres. and imperf. to bring forward; hence 1) to bear onward, to carry forward. to bear away, spoken of a storm, τινὰ εἰς ὄρος, 6, 346. Od. 20, 64. 2) to bear to, to convey to, τινί τι. Il. 9, 323. 17, 121: metaph. in a bad sense (nearly = our to bring up against any body; or cast in his teeth), ὀνείδεά τινι, to cast reproaches upon any one, δῶρά τινι, 3, 64, to reproach with. 3) to bring forward, i. e. to bring to light, to present, to show, μένος, 10, 479; ἔριδα, to exhibit emulation, Od. 6, 92. II) Mid. with reference to the subject: ἔριδά

He was, according to the Cypr. Carm., soon after slain by Hector. After his death, he was worshipt as a hero in the Chersonêsus, 2, 698, seq. 13, 681.

Πρωτεύς, έος, ὁ, a fabulous sea-god; according to Od. 4, 385. He was father of Εἰδοθέη (Idothea), servant of Poseidôn, and attended his sea-calves in the Ægyptian sea. He had the gift of prophecy, and of changing himself into every possible form, Od. 4, 456, seq. Upon the advice of Idothea, Menelaus bound him, and forced him to inform him how he could return home. The later tradition made him king of Egypt, Hdt. 2, 112, seq.; or represented him as coming from Thrace to Egypt, Ap. 2, 5, 9.

πρώτιστος, η. ον, poet. superl. from πρῶτος, the first of all; also of two endings, κατὰ πρώτιστον ὀπωπήν, upon the very first look, h. Cer. 157. The neut. sing. and plur. πρώτιστον and πρώτιστα, as adv. first of all, 1, 105. Od. 8, 57. τὰ πρώτιστα, h. Ap. 407.

πρωτόγονος, ον (γόνος), first-born, *4, 102. 23, 864.

πρωτοπαγής, ές (πήγνυμι), now first constructed, just or newly made, new, ἅρμα, *Il. 5, 194. 24, 267.

πρωτόπλοος, ον (πλόος), sailing for the first time, newly made, νηῦς, Od. 8, 35.†

πρῶτος, η, ον (πρό), superl. contr. from πρόατος, the first, the foremost, often with ὕστατος, 2, 281. 11, 299; then the most distinguished, the noblest, hence a) οἱ πρῶτοι = πρόμαχοι, the first, the front warriors, 5, 536. 12, 306. 321; also pleonast. πρῶτοι πρόμαχοι, Od. 18, 279. b) τὰ πρῶτα, sc. ἄθλα, the first prizes, Il. 23, 275. The neut. sing. and plur. as adv. πρῶτον, πρῶτα, in like manner with the article, τοπρῶτον, ταπρῶτα, Il. (also separate, τὸ πρῶτον, τὰ πρῶτα, ed. Spitz. and in Od.) 1) first, at first, for the first time, Il. 9, 32; often πρῶτον καὶ ὕστατον. 2) too early. ἥ τ᾽ ἄρα καὶ σοὶ πρῶτα παραστήσεσθαι ἔμελλε Μοῖρα, truly fate was destined to approach thee too early, Od. 24, 28. 3) After an adv. of time: once. ἐπεὶ and ἐπειδὴ πρῶτον or πρῶτα, quum primum, when once, as soon as, 6, 489. Od. 3, 183. ἐξ οὗ δὴ πρῶτα, Il. 1, 6. Also aft. a relat. cf. Il. 1, 319.

πρωτοτόκος, ον (τίκτω), bearing for the first time, μήτηρ, 17, 5.†

Πρωτώ, οῦς, ἡ, daughter of Nereus and Doris, 18, 43.

πρώονος, ονι, etc. see πρών.

πταίρω, aor. 2 ἔπταρον, to sneeze, as a sign of good omen, Od. 17, 541.†

πτάμενος, πτάτο, see πέτομαι.

πτελέη, ἡ, an elm, ulmus campestris, *Il. 6, 419. 21, 242.

Πτελεός, ἡ [rather ὁ or τό, see λεχεποίης (πτελέη, an elm), 1) a place in Elis, a colony from the Thessalian Pteleos; in Strabo's time ruinous, 2, 594. τὸ Πτελεόν, Strabo. 2) an Achæan town in Thessaly, between Antrum and Pyraeus, with a port, 2, 697.

πτέρνα or πτέρνη, ἡ, the heel, 22, 397.† 2) Poet. for πέρνα, the ham, Batr. 37.

*Πτερνογλύφος, ὁ (γλύφω), Ham-hollower, name of a mouse, Batr. 227.

*Πτερνοτρώκτης, ου. ὁ (τρώγω), Hamgnawer, name of a mouse, Batr. 29.

*Πτερνοφάγος, ὁ (φαγεῖν), Ham-eater, name of a mouse, Batr. 230

πτερόεις, εσσα, εν, poet. (πτέρον), prop. feathered, winged, epith. of an arrow. since it was furnished with feathers at the upper end, 4, 117. 5, 171. 2) Metaph. πτερόεντα λαισήϊα, easily-brandished shields (as if feather-light), 5, 453; often πτερόεντα ἔπεα, winged words, which escape quickly from the lips, Il. and Od.

πτέρον, τό (πέτομαι), a feather, a wing, a pinion, mly in plur. πτέρα βάλλειν, to strike the wings, 11, 454; as an image of swiftness, Od. 7, 36. 2) Metaph. an oar or sail of a ship, Od. 11, 125. 23, 272.

πτέρυξ, υγος, ἡ (πτέρον), a wing, a pinion, 2, 316. 462. Od. 2, 149. ὑπὸ πτερύγων, under the stroke of the wings, h. 20, 1.

πτήσσω (πίπτω, πέτω), aor. 1 ἔπτηξα, Ep. perf. πεπτηώς, ῶτος, intrans. to creep away for fear, to crouch, to cringe, to shrink. κείμην πεπτηώς, I lay crouched together, Od. 14, 354. 22, 362. ὑπὸ τεύχεσι πεπτηῶτες, Od. 14, 474; generally, to be in fear, hence 2) Trans. in the aor. 1, to put in fright. to terrify. πτῆξε θυμὸν Ἀχαιῶν, he terrified the hearts of the Achæans, Il. 14, 40; πτήσσω as trans. is uncommon, hence some read πῆξε from πήγνυμι; others consider the verse not genuine, as Bothe. (Spitzner ad loc. defends πτῆξε.)

πτοέω, Ep. πτοιέω, poet. (akin to πτήσσω), aor. pass. Ep. 3 plur. ἐπτοίηθεν, to put in terrour, to terrify. Pass. to be terrified, to fear, Od. 22, 298.†

Πτολεμαῖος, ὁ (a warrior), son of Piræus, father of Eurymedon, 4, 228.

πτολεμίζω, Ep. for πολεμίζω.

πτολεμιστής, οῦ, ὁ, Ep. for πολεμιστής.

πτολεμόνδε, adv. for πολεμόνδε.

πτόλεμος, ὁ, Ep for πόλεμος.

πτολίεθρον, τό. Ep. for πολ. (πόλις). a city; always with the name in the gen. Ἰλίου πτολίεθρον, 2, 133. Od. 1, 2. (The form πολίεθρον is not used.) [It cannot, with Passow, be regarded as a dimin. of πόλις, for H. knows nothing of diminutives.]

πτολιπόρθιος, ὁ = πτολίπορθος, *Od. 9, 504. 530.

πτολίπορθος, ὁ, ἡ, Ep. for πολίπορθος (πέρθω), city-destroying, the destroyer of cities, epith. of Arês, Odysseus (Ulysses), Achilles, and of heroes, 2, 278. 8, 372; as fem. epith. of Enÿo (Bellona), 5, 333. (The form πολίπορθος is not used.)

πτόλις, ιος, ἡ, Ep. for πόλις.

πτόρθος, ὁ (πείρω), a sprout, a twig, a branch, Od. 6, 128.†

πτύγμα, ατος, τό (πτύσσω), a fold, a

*πρεσβηῖς, ίδος, ἡ, poet. fem.=πρέσβα; τιμή, worthy honour, h. 29, 3.

*πρέσβις, ἡ, poet.=πρεσβεία, age, h. Merc 4 1.

πρέσβιστος, η, ον. see πρέσβυς.

πρεσβυγενής. ές (γένος), elder in years, β. si-born, 11, 249.†

πρέσβυς, ὁ, poet. for πρεσβύτης, not occurring in Hom., but the fem. Ep. πρέσβα, πρέσβειρα, πρεσβηῖς, compar. πρεσβύτερος, η, ον, 11, 787; superl. πρεσβύτατος, η, ον and πρέσβιστος, h. 30, 2; old, venerable. πρεσβύτατος γενεῇ, eldest in birth, 6, 24. Od. 13, 142.

πρήθω, poet. form of πίμπρημι, which is not found in Hom.; aor. 1 ἔπρησα, Ep. πρῆσα, 1) to burn, to inflame, τί, with gen. mater. (cf. Kühner, § 455. Rem.); θύρετρα πυρός, with fire, 2, 415; cf ἐνιπρήθω. 2) to blow upon, to swell, spoken of wind, τί; μέσον ἱστίον, Od. 2, 427. b) to cast out, to breathe out, to blow out, αἷμα ἀνὰ στόμα, Il. 16, 350. (According to Buttm., Lex. in voc., akin to πρώ and πέρθω; it is uncertain whether its prop. signif. is to kindle, to inflame, or to spout out, to emit; according to Rost it is to rattle, to crack.)

πρηκτήρ. ῆρος, ὁ (πρήσσω), Ion. for πρακτήρ, 1) a performer, a doer, an author, ἔργων, 9, 443. 2) Esply a tradesman, Od. 8, 162.

πρηνής. ές, Ion. for πρανής (akin to πρό), bent forwards, headlong, κατὰ (adv.) πρηνὴς βάλλειν τι, to cast any thing down, 2, 414; πρηνὴς ἤριπε, he fell forwards. 5, 58. ἔπεσε, ἐλιάσθη, also πρηνὴς ἐν κονίῃσι, 2, 418.

πρῆξις. ιος, ἡ (πράσσω), 1) doing, an action, business, undertaking, κατὰ πρῆξιν, on business, in opposition to μαψιδίως, Od. 3, 72. esply traffic, h. Ap. 398. 2) the produce of it, gain, advantage, οὔτις πρῆξις πέλεται γοοῖο, there is no advantage from lamentation (V. 'we effect nothing'), Il. 24, 524; or οὔτις πρ. ἐγίγνετο μυρομένοισιν, there was no help to them complaining, Od. 10, 202.

πρήσσω, Ion. for πράσσω, fut. πρήξω, aor. ἔπρηξα, prop. to do, to act; hence, 1) to effect, to accomplish, to attain, with accus. Od. 16, 88; ἔργον, Od. 19, 324; absol. Il. 18, 357; esply partcp. πρήξας, Od. 3. 60; often with οὔτι, Il. 1, 562. 11, 552. Od. 2, 191. 3) Esply spoken of a way: to finish, to pass over, with accus. κέλευθον, Il. 14, 282. Od. 13, 83; ἅλα, to sail over the sea, Od. 9, 491; with gen. ὁδοῖο, Il. 24, 264. Od. 3, 476. 3) to collect, to gather, τινὰ τόκους, usury from any one, Batr. 186.

*πρηΰνω, Ion. for πραΰνω (πραΰς), to render mild, to calm, to appease, with accus. h. Merc. 417.

πρηΰς, ύ. Ion. for πραΰς, mild, gentle, h. 7, 10. cf. Gramm.

πρίασθαι, mid. defect. verb, of which only aor. 2 is in use, 3 sing. πρίατο, to buy, τι. any thing, κτεάτεσσιν, for treasures, *Od. 1, 430. 14, 115. 452.

Πρῖαμίδης, ου, ὁ, son of Priam (the first ι long by the arsis).

Πρίαμος, ὁ, son of Laomedon, king of Troy, husband of Hecuba (Hekabê). According to H. he had fifty sons, nineteen of them by Hecuba. Hector was the dearest of them all, 24, 493, seq. Of the time before the Trojan war, it is mentioned that he aided the Phrygians against the Amazons, 3, 184, seq. At the beginning of the siege of Troy he was already at an advanced age, and took no part in the contest, 24, 487. He appears only once on the battle field, to conclude the treaty concerning the duel of Paris and Menelaus, 3, 261. After Hector's death, he went, under the conduct of Hermês, into the tent of Achilles, and redeemed the corpse of his son, 24, 470, seq. According to later tradition he was slain by Neoptolemus, son of Achilles. (On the name Πρίαμος, cf. Apd. 2, 6, 4.)

πρίν, adv. and conjunct. I) Adv. of time: in independent sentences, before, ere, first, sooner, and, generally, earlier, at an earlier time; mly opposed to νῦν, 2, 112. 344; πολὺ πρίν, long before, Od. 2, 167. 2) Often with the article, τοπρίν or τὸ πρίν, ed. Spitzner, Il. 6, 125. 16, 373; but Od. τὸ πρίν, Od. 3, 265. 4, 32: formerly (olim). 3) As adv. it stands also with indicat. πρίν μιν καὶ γῆρας ἔπεισιν, first (i. e. sooner) shall old age come upon her, Il. 1, 29; cf. Thiersch, § 292. 2. Il. 18, 283; with optat. πρίν κεν ἀνιηθεὶς σὴν πατρίδα γαῖαν ἵκοιο, thou wouldst be wearied out and return to thy native land before [the tale was ended], Od. 3, 117. II) Conjunct. in relative clauses of time: before, ere; in this signif. πρίν—πρίν, πρίν—πρίν γε, πάρος—πρίν γε, etc., often stand in Hom. 1) With indicat. in the H. poems alone only in h. Ap. 357; but πρίν γ' ὅτε, as long as, until, Il. 9, 588. 12, 437. Od. 4, 180. 13, 322. h. Ap. 47. 2) With the future only in conceived actions, when the main clause is always denied. a) With subjunct. after a primary tense in the main clause, Il. 24, 551. Od. 10, 175; with πρίν γε, Il. 18, 135. Od. 13, 336; with πρίν γ' ὅτ' ἄν, Od. 2, 374. b) With optat. after an historical tense in the main clause, Il. 21. 580; after πρίν γ' ὅτε, 9, 488. 3) Most frequently with infin. aor. when the action of the subordinate clause appears as a temporal consequence of the main clause: οὐδ' ὅγε πρίν—Κῆρας ἀφέξει. πρίν γ' ἀπὸ πατρὶ δομέναι — κουρήν, 1, 98. 9, 387; and often. The infin. with accus. occurs when the dependent clause has a new subject, 6, 82. 22, 156. Od. 23, 138. Also πρίν γ' ἤ (cf. priusquam), Il. 5, 288. 22, 266. 4) In H. passages also occur where the infin. is exchanged with the optat, 17, 504, seq. 5) πρίν stands elliptically, Od 15, 394; πρὶν ὥρη, subaud. ᾖ, before it is time. (ι is short, but is used as long Ep.)

προέμεν, see προίημι.

προερέσσω (ερέσσω), aor. 1 προέρεσα, Ep. σσ, to row forwards, onwards, ἐς λιμένα. Od. 13, 279; trans. τὴν (νῆα) δ᾽ εἰς ὅρμον προέρεσσαν ἐρετμοῖς, Il. 1, 435; a reading adopted by Spitzner for προρύσσαν, because προερύειν signifies 'to draw forward,' and hence cannot be spoken of oars. Also in Od. 9, 73; αὐτὰς —προερέσσαμεν ἤπειρόνδε.

προερύω, poet. (ἐρύω), aor. 1 προέρυσα, Ep. σσ, to draw forwards, onwards; spoken always of ships, a) From the shore into the sea, ἅλαδε, 1, 308. b) From the open sea to propel by rowing to the land, ἤπειρόνδε, Od. 9, 73. Il. 1, 435; but cf. προερέσσω.

πρόες, see προίημι.

προέχω, contr. προύχω (ἔχω), always in the contr. form, except imperf. 3 sing. πρόεχε, Od. 12, 11. 2) Intrans. to be before, to come before, spoken of persons: προύχων, the prominent man, Il. 23, 325. 453; δήμου, to be eminent among the people, h. Cer. 151; spoken of things: to project, to be prominent, Od. 12, 11. Mid. to have or hold before oneself, ταύρους, Od. 3, 8 (where others read, προύθεντο).

προήκης, ες (ἀκή), pointed before, Od. 12, 205.†

*προθαλής, ές, poet. (θάλλω), growing well, h. Cer. 241.

προθέλυμνος, ον, poet. (θέλυμνον), by the roots, utterly, entirely (Schol. πρόρριζος), προθελύμνους ἕλκετο χαίτας, he tore his hair out by the roots, 10, 15. προθέλυμνα χαμαὶ βάλε δένδρεα ["trees he cast on eurth Uprooting them," Cp.], 9, 541; φράσσειν σάκος σάκεϊ, shield pressed on shield compactly, densely, in close array, 13, 130. They locked the shields so closely together that no space remained between. (Others take it in reference to τετραθέλυμνος, with close layers. The derivation from θέλυμνον = θεμέλιον, from the foundation, is most probable; the signif. close, one upon another (Schol. ἐπ᾽ ἀλλήλοις), seems borrowed from the last passage; still Voss follows it, and Köppen ad Il. 13. 130.)

προθέουσι, 1, 291; see προτίθημι.

προθέω (θέω), Ion. iterat. imperf. προθέεσκε, to run before, 10, 362. 22, 459. Od. 11. 515.

Προθοήνωρ, ορος, ὁ, son of Areïlycus, leader of the Bœotians, 2, 495.

Πρόθοος, ὁ, son of Tenthrêdon, leader of the Magnetæ, 2, 756.

προθορμω, see προθρώσκω.

Προθόων, ωνος, ὁ, a Trojan, slain by Teucer, 14, 515.

προθρώσκω (θρώσκω), partcp. aor. προθορών, to leap before, to spring before, *14, 363. 17, 522.

προθυμίη, ἡ (θυμός), readiness, good will, good courage, plur. 2, 588.† (Poet. with ι.)

*προθύραιος, ον (θύρα), before the door, τὰ προθύραια = πρόθυρα, h. Merc. 384.

πρόθυρον, τό (θύρα), mly plur. the doorway to the court, Il. and Od. 2) the place before the door, a porch, Od. 20, 355. 21, 299. 22, 474.

προϊάλλω (ἰάλλω), poet. only imperf. to send forth, to send away, τινὰ ἀπ᾽ οὐρανόθεν, 8, 365; ἐπὶ νῆας, 11, 3; ἀγρόνδε, Od. 5, 369.

προϊάπτω (ἰάπτω), fut. προϊάψω, aor. προΐαψα (ἴ), prop. to thrust forth; then, to send away, to send, τινὰ Ἄϊδι, any one to Hades, 1, 3. 6, 487; Ἀϊδωνῆϊ, *5, 190.

προΐειν, see προίημι.

προΐημι (ἵημι), imperf. Ion. and Att. προΐειν, aor. 1 προῆκα or προέηκα, 2 aor. 3 plur. πρόεσαν, imperat. πρόες, προέτω, infin. προέμεν, Ep. for προεῖναι, prop. to send forwards; hence, 1) Spoken of persons: to send forth, to send away, to let go, τινά, 1, 326; with infin. following, καλήμεναι, in order to call, 10, 125. cf. v. 388. 563. b) Of things: νῆας, 7, 468; of missiles: to let fly, to cast, to hurl, ὀϊστούς, βέλος, ἔγχος, 8, 297. 17, 516; of a river: ὕδωρ ἐς Πηνειόν, it sends out, i. e. pours its water into the Peneus, 2, 752. 2) to let go, to let fall, πηδάλιον ἐκ χειρῶν, Od. 5, 316; ἔπος, to let a word drop, Od. 14, 466. πόδα προέηκε φέρεσθαι, Od. 19, 468; φήμην, Od. 20, 105. 3) to send to, τινά or τί τινι, Il. 1, 127; ἀγγελίας, to send an embassy, Od. 2, 92; and generally, to give, to bestow, like δίδόναι: κῦδός τινι, Il. 16, 241. ἐμοὶ πνοιὴν Ζεφύρου προέηκεν ἀῆναι, he let the breath of the Zephyr blow upon me, Od. 10, 25; οὖρον, Od. 3, 183. [But πρό cannot signify to; it rather means forth, and these citations may better be referred to no. 2.]

προΐκτης, ου, ὁ (προΐξ). a beggar, a mendicant, Od. 17, 449. ἀνὴρ προΐκτης, *Od. 17, 347. 352.

προΐξ, contr. προΐξ, gen. προικός, a gift, a present. γενέσθαι προικός, to enjoy his present [to taste his mendicated mess, Cp.], Od. 17, 413; then προικός, as adv. gratuitously, i. e. without a (present in) return, χαρίζεσθαι, Od.13. 15 (cf. Thiersch, § 198. 6). Another Schol. connects προικός as a subst. with χαρίσασθαι; hence Voss and Passow: 'to bestow generous gifts.' Cf. Od. 1, 140.

προΐστημι (ἵστημι), aor. 1 partep. προστήσας, trans. to place before, to put before; τινὰ μάχεσθαι, any one to fight, 4, 156.†

Προῖτος, ὁ, son of Abas, king of Tiryns, husband of Antia. Being expelled by his brother Acrisius, he fled to king Iobâtes in Lycia. He gave him his daughter Antia, and restored him to his kingdom, 6, 157, seq.

προκαθίζω (ἵζω), to sit down before, to settle, spoken of cranes, 2, 463.†

πρόκαλέω (καλέω), only mid. aor. 1, Ep. προκαλεσσάμην, subj. προκαλέσσεται with shortened vowel. 7, 39, 1) to call forth to oneself, to challenge, τινά, absol. Od. 8, 142; and χάρμῃ, to battle, only once with gen. 11, 831. 22, 198. *A*) With gen. 1) Spoken of place : *a*) Prop. to indicate motion from an object : *from.* ἵκετο—ἠὲ πρὸς ἠοίων ἢ ἑσπερίων ἀνθρώπων, from eastern or western men, Od. 8, 29; mly πρός indicates only motion, hence to a point, *to, towards.* πρὸς ἁλός, to the sea, Il. 10, 428. 430. πρὸς νηῶν, 15, 670. πρὸς Βορέαο, to the north, Od. 13, 110. 21, 347, cf. 3) With accus. *b*) In indicating near approach to an object : *close upon, near by, before* (curam). ποτὶ πτόλιος πέτετ᾽ ἀεί, he flew always close by the city, Il. 22, 198. τοῦτό σοι πρὸς Τρώων κλέος ἔσται, this shall redound to thy glory before the Trojans, 22, 514. cf. 16, 85. 2) In causative relations, as indicating any thing which proceeds from or is effected by a person or thing : *from, through, by means of, by virtue of.* *a*) Spoken of the author : ἔχειν τιμὴν πρὸς Ζηνός, Od. 11, 302. ἀκούειν τι πρός τινος, from any man, i. e. from his mouth, Il. 6, 525. οἵτε θέμιστας πρὸς Διὸς εἰρύαται, from Zeus (*auctore Jove*), 1, 339; and with the pass. διδάσκεσθαι πρός τινος, to be taught by any one, 11, 831. cf. 6, 57. *b*) Spoken of the possessor : πρὸς Διός εἰσι ξεῖνοι, strangers belong to Zeus, Od. 6, 207. 14, 57. *c*) In oaths and asseverations : πρὸς θεῶν, by the gods (for the sake of the gods), 1, 339. 19, 188. Od. 11, 67. 13, 324. *B*) With dat. spoken only of place in indicating continuance with an object : *before, by, near, beside, upon, at.* πρὸς ἀλλήλῃσι ἔχονται, by one another, Od. 5, 329. Often with the implied notion of motion : λιάζεσθαι ποτὶ γαίῃ, βάλλεσθαι προτὶ γαίῃ, Il. 20, 420. 22, 64. 2) In indicating approach : *to, towards,* Od. 10, 68. *c*) With accus. 1) Spoken of place : *a*) In indicating motion or direction to an object : *to, towards, against.* ἰέναι πρὸς Ὄλυμπον, φέρειν τι προτὶ ἄστυ; also εἰπεῖν, μυθήσασθαι πρός τινα, to speak to any one ; spoken also of the situation of places : πρὸς Ἠῶ τ᾽ Ἠέλιόν τε, Il. 12, 239. Od. 9. 26. cf. Il. 8, 364. *b*) In a hostile signif. : μάχεσθαι πρὸς Τρῶας, to fight against the Trojans, 17, 471; metaph. πρὸς δαίμονα, against the deity, i. e. against the will of the deity, 17, 98. 104. 2) Spoken of time : *towards,* ποτὶ ἕσπερα, Od. 17, 191. 3) In causative relations ; only of exchange : ἀμείβειν τι πρός τινα, to exchange any thing with any one, Il. 6, 235. II) Adv. without cases : mly πρὸς δέ, *besides, moreover, in addition,* 1, 245. 5, 307. III) In composition, πρός has the signif. already given : *to, towards,* etc.

προσάγω (ἄγω), aor. 2 προσήγαγον, *to lead to, to bring to, to procure for,* τί τινι, Od. 17, 446 †; δῶρά τινι, to present gifts to any one, h. Ap. 272.

*προσαίσσω (αἴσσω), partep. aor. προσαΐξας, *to rush upon, to leap or spring to,* *Od. 22, 337. 342. 365.

προσαλείφω (ἀλείφω), *to rub on, to anoint ;* φάρμακόν τινι, to anoint one with a drug, Od. 10, 392.†

προσαμύνω (ἀμύνω), infin. aor. προσαμῦναι, 1) *to repel, to avert,* τινά, 5, 139. 2) With dat. τινί, *to come to protect, to aid,* *2, 238. 16, 509.

*προσαναγκάζω (ἀναγκάζω), aor. προσηνάγκασε, poet. σσ, *to constrain still further, to compel,* with infin. h. Cer. 413.

προσάπτω, Dor. and Ep. προτιάπτω (ἅπτω), *to attach ;* metaph. *to dispense, to grant,* κῦδός τινι, 24, 110.†

προσαραρίσκω (ΆΡΩ), only partep. perf. προσαρηρώς, intrans. *to fit to, to suit :* ἐπίσσωτρα προσαρηρότα, close fitting tires, 5, 725.†

προσαρηρότα, see προσαραρίσκω.

προσαυδάω (αὐδάω), poet. 3 sing. imperf. προσηύδα, 3 dual προσαυδήτην, *to speak to, to address,* often absol. and with accus. τινά, ἐπέεσσιν, 11, 136. Od. 15, 440; and μειλιχίοισιν, sc. ἐπέεσσιν, to address with friendly words, Il. 4, 256 ; κερτομίοισι, 1, 539. *b*) Most frequently with double accus. τινὰ ἔπεα, to speak words to any one.

προσβαίνω (βαίνω), partep. aor. 2 προσβάς, aor. mid. Ep. προσεβήσατο, 1) *to go to, to step to ;* λὰξ προσβάς, treading upon any thing with the heel, 5, 620. 2) With accus. Ὄλυμπον, to mount Olympus, 2, 48; κλίμακα, Od. 21, 5; πρὸς δειράδα, h. Ap. 281.

προσβάλλω (βάλλω), Ep. and Dor. προτιβάλλω, aor. 2 προσέβαλον, mid. προτιβάλλεαι, Ep. for προσβάλλῃ, 1) Prop. to cast to; generally, *to cast,* τὶ γαίῃ, only in tmesis, 1, 245. *b*) With accus. to cast upon any thing, *to hit* or *touch* any one, or any thing, thus Ἥλιος προσέβαλλεν ἀρούρας, Helios touched the fields, i. e. illuminated them, 7, 421. Od. 19, 433. Mid. *to cast oneself upon* any one, *to attack* any one, τινὰ ἔπεἳ, ἔργῳ, any one with words, in act, Il. 5, 879.

προσδέρκομαι, Dor. and Ep. ποτιδέρκομαι, poet. (δέρκομαι), *to look upon, to behold,* τινά, Od. 20, 385 ; ποτιδ., Il. 16, 10. Od. 17, 518.

προσδέχομαι, depon. mid. Dor. and Ep. ποτιδέχ. (δέχομαι), only partep. aor. sync. ποτιδέγμενος, prop. to receive, to take up ; only metaph. *to expect, to await,* τινά or τί, 10, 123. 19, 234 Od. 2, 403 ; absol. *to wait, to stay,* with ὁππότ᾽ ἄν or εἰ, Il. 7. 415. Od. 23, 91.

προσδόρπιος, ον, Ep. ποτιδόρπ. (δόρπον), *pertaining to eating,* or *serving for eating ; for supper,* *Od. 9, 234. 249.

προσειλέω, Ep. προτιειλέω (εἰλέω), infin. προτιειλεῖν, *to press on, to drive,* τινὰ προτὶ νῆας, 10, 347.†

πρόσειμι (εἰμι), only partep. pres. προσιών, *to go to, to come to, to rush upon,* 5, 515. 7, 308. Od. 16. 5.

προσεῖπον (εἶπον), aor. of πρόσφημι, always Ep. προσέειπον optat. Dor. and Ep. προτιείποι, 22, 329 prop. to speak

προτέμνω (τέμνω), aor. 2 προταμών, optat. aor. mid. προταμοίμην, 1) *to cut off before, to carve (for)*, 9, 489. 2) *to cut off in front, at the end*, with accus. κορμόν, ἐκ ῥίζης, to cut off the trunk at the root, Od. 23, 196. Mid. *to cut off for oneself;* metaph. ὦλκα διηνεκέα, to cut a straight furrow, Od. 18, 375.

πρότερος, η, ον (πρό), compar. without posit. *the former, the earlier, prior,* 1) Spoken of time: *former, earlier, elder,* γενεῇ, 15, 166. πρότεροι ἄνθρωποι, men of former times, ancestors, forefathers, 5, 637; also πρότεροι alone: πρ. παῖδες, children of a former marriage. Od. 15, 22. τῇ προτέρῃ sc. ἡμέρᾳ, on the former day, Od. 16, 50; with gen. ἐμέο πρότερος, earlier than I, Il. 10, 124. 2) Of place: *before, fore-, that is before,* 16, 569. πόδες πρότεροι, the fore-feet, Od. 19, 228.

προτέρω, adv. (πρότερος), *further, further forwards.* πρ. ἔπεο, step nearer, Od. 5, 91; ἄγειν. Il. 3, 400. Od. 5, 91; metaph. *forward, more violent.* ἔρις προτέρω γένετο, the contest went forward, waxed more violent, 23, 490.

*προτέρωσε, adv. (πρότερος), *forwards,* h. 32, 10.

προτεύχω (τεύχω), perf. pass. προτέτυγμαι, *to make or to prepare before.* τὰ μὲν προτετύχθαι ἐάσομεν, these things we will allow to have happened, i. e. what is past we will let alone, 16, 60. 18, 112. 19, 65.

προτί, Dor. for πρός.

προτιάπτω, see προσάπτω.

Προτιάων, ονος, ὁ, a Trojan, father of Astynoüs, 15, 455.

προτιβάλλεαι, see προσβάλλω.

προτιειλεῖν, see προσειλέω.

προτιείποι, see προσεῖπον.

προτίθημι (τίθημι), 3 plur. pres. προθέουσι for προτιθέασι, 1, 291; as if from the theme ΘΕΩ, cf. Thiersch, § 224. Kühner I. § 202. 2. aor. 1 προὔθηκα, 1) *to place before, to put before, to lay before,* τί κυσίν, to devour, 24, 409. 2) *to put out, to expose publicly* for sale, for use; hence metaph. *to allow, to permit,* τινί, with infin. 1, 291. Mid. *to place before oneself,* τραπέζας, Od. 1, 112.

προτιμυθήσασθαι, see προσμυθέομαι.

προτιόσσομαι, Dor. for προσόσσομαι (ὄσσομαι), 1) *to look upon, to behold,* τινά, Od. 7, 31. 23, 365. ᾗ σ᾽ εὖ γιγνώσκων προτιόσσομαι οὐδ᾽ ἄρ᾽ ἔμελλον πείσειν, indeed knowing thee well, I behold thee, i. e. indeed, I see thee now as I have ever known thee (and I was not about to persuade thee), Il. 22, 356. Thus Passow and Bothe. Krause takes it as a pres. perf.: 'I anticipated it and anticipate it still.' 2) *to foresee, to anticipate,* ὄλεθρον, θάνατον, Od. 5, 389. 14, 219.

πρότμησις, ιος, ἡ (τέμνω), 1) *the part cut off.* 2) Metaph. spoken of the human figure: *the region about the loins and navel, the waist,* 11, 424.†

πρότονος, ὁ (τείνω), in the plur.; a rope, primar. the two great ropes that extend from the top of the mast, the one to the bow and the other to the stern of a ship, to support the mast and also to lower it, 1, 434. Od. 12, 409. h. Ap. 504.

προτρέπω (τρέπω), only mid. aor. 2 Ep. προτραπόμην, 1) *to turn forwards.* 2) Mid. *to turn oneself forward, to betake oneself, to turn in flight,* ἐπὶ νηῶν, 5, 700; spoken of Helios: ἐπὶ γαῖαν, to turn to the earth, Od. 11, 18. 2) Metaph. *to turn oneself to, to yield to;* ἄχεϊ, to grief, Il. 6, 336.

προτροπάδην, adv. (προτρέπω), prop. *turned forwards;* φοβέοντο, they fled ever forward. i. e. on and on, without stopping, 16, 304.†

προτύπτω (τύπτω), aor. προὔτυψα, prop. trans. *to strike forwards;* in Hom. only intrans. *to press forwards, to push forward,* 13, 136. 15, 306. 17, 262. ἀνὰ ῥῖνάς οἱ δριμὺ μένος προὔτυψε, fierce wrath pressed into his nose, Od. 24, 319.

προὔθηκε, see προτίθημι.

προὔπεμψε, see προπέμπω.

προὔφαινε, see προφαίνω.

προὔχω, for προέχω.

προφαίνω (φαίνω), imperf. προὔφαινον, perf. pass. 3 plur. προπέφανται, aor. 2 pass. partcp. προφανείς, 1) Act. trans. *to exhibit, to cause to appear,* with accus. τέραα, Od. 12, 394. b) Intrans. like mid. *to appear, to shine forth,* spoken of the moon, Od. 9, 145. II) Mid. with aor. pass. *to shine forth, to show oneself, to become visible,* Od. 13, 169. οὐδὲ προὐφαίνετο ἰδέσθαι, nothing appeared so that one could behold it, or to the sight, Od. 9, 143. προπέφανται ἅπαντα, every thing is visible at a distance, is exposed to view (Cp.), Il. 14, 332. b) Espid of persons: *to appear, to step forth,* Od. 24, 160; ἀνὰ γεφύρας πολέμοιο, Il. 8, 378; ἐς πόλεμον for ἐν πολέμῳ Il. 17, 487; ἐς πεδίον, 24, 332.

πρόφασις, ιος, ἡ (πρόφημι), *a pretext, a pretence, appearance;* absol. πρόφασιν, in appearance, in pretence, *19, 262. 302.

προφερής, ές (προφέρω), compar. προφερέστερος, η, .ον; superl. προφερέστατος, η. ον, Od.; prop. borne before, placed before; then generally, *eminent, distinguished, excellent,* with dat. of the thing, ἅλματι, βίῃ, Od. 8, 128. 221. 21, 134; with infin., Il. 10, 352.

προφέρω (φέρω), only pres. and imperf. *to bring forward;* hence 1) *to bear onward, to carry forward, to bear away,* spoken of a storm, τινὰ εἰς ὄρος, 6, 346. Od. 20, 64. 2) *to bear to, to convey to,* τινί τι, Il. 9, 323. 17, 121; metaph. in a bad sense (nearly = our *to bring up against* any body; or *cast in his teeth*), ὀνείδεά τινι, to cast reproaches upon any one, δῶρά τινι, 3, 64, to reproach with. 3) *to bring forward,* i. e. *to bring to light, to present, to show,* μένος, 10, 479; ἔριδα, to exhibit emulation, Od. 6, 92. II) Mid. with reference to the subject: ἔριδά

R

He was, according to the Cypr. Carm., soon after slain by Hector. After his death, he was worshipt as a hero in the Chersonêsus, 2, 698, seq. 13, 681.

Πρωτεύς, έος, ὁ, a fabulous sea-god; according to Od. 4, 385. He was father of Εἰδοθέη (Idothea), servant of Poseidôn, and attended his sea-calves in the Ægyptian sea. He had the gift of prophecy, and of changing himself into every possible form, Od. 4, 456, seq. Upon the advice of Idothea, Menelaus bound him, and forced him to inform him how he could return home. The later tradition made him king of Egypt, Hdt. 2, 112, seq.; or represented him as coming from Thrace to Egypt, Ap. 2, 5, 9.

πρώτιστος, η, ον, poet. superl. from πρῶτος, the first of all; also of two endings, κατὰ πρώτιστον ὀπωπήν, upon the very first look, h. Cer. 157. The neut. sing. and plur. πρώτιστον and πρώτιστα, as adv. first of all, 1, 105. Od. 8, 57. τὰ πρώτιστα, h. Ap. 407.

πρωτόγονος, ον (γόνος), first-born, °4, 102. 23, 864.

πρωτοπαγής, ές (πήγνυμι), now first constructed, just or newly made, new, ἅρμα, °Il. 5, 194. 24, 267.

πρωτόπλοος. ον (πλόος), sailing for the first time, newly made, νηῦς, Od. 8, 35.†

πρῶτος, η, ον (πρό), superl. contr. from πρόατος, the first, the foremost, often with ὕστατος, 2, 281. 11, 299; then the most distinguished, the noblest, hence a) οἱ πρῶτοι = πρόμαχοι, the first, the front warriors, 5, 536. 12, 306. 321: also pleonast. πρῶτοι πρόμαχοι, Od. 18, 279. b) τὰ πρῶτα, sc. ἆθλα, the first prizes, Il. 23, 275. The neut. sing. and plur. as adv. πρῶτον, πρῶτα, in like manner with the article, τοπρῶτον, ταπρῶτα, Il. (also separate, τὸ πρῶτον, τὰ πρῶτα, ed. Spitz. and in Od.) 1) first, at first, for the first time, Il. 9, 32; often πρῶτον καὶ ὕστατον. 2) too early. ἤ τ᾽ ἄρα καὶ σοὶ πρῶτα παραστήσεσθαι ἔμελλε Μοῖρα, truly fate was destined to approach thee too early, Od. 24, 28. 3) After an adv. of time: once. ἐπεὶ and ἐπειδὴ πρῶτον or πρῶτα, quum primum, when once, as soon as, 6, 489. Od. 3, 183. ἐξ οὗ δὴ πρῶτα, Il. 1, 6. Also aft. a relat. cf. Il. 1, 319.

πρωτοτόκος, ον (τίκτω), bearing for the first time, μήτηρ, 17, 5.†

Πρωτώ, οῦς, ἡ, daughter of Nereus and Doris, 18, 43.

πρώωσιν, ονι, etc. see πρών.

πταίρω, aor. 2 ἔπταρον, to sneeze, as a sign of good omen, Od. 17, 541.†

πτάμενος, πτάτο, see πέτομαι.

πτελέη, ἡ, an elm, ulmus campestris, °Il. 6, 419. 21, 242.

Πτελεός, ἡ [rather ὁ or τό, see λεχεποίη] (πτελέη, an elm), 1) a place in Elis, a colony from the Thessalian Pteleos; in Strabo's time ruinous, 2, 594. τὸ Πτελεόν, Strabo. 2) an Achæan town in Thessaly, between Antrum and Pyrasus, with a port, 2, 697.

πτέρνα or πτέρνη, ἡ, the heel, 22, 397.† 2) Poet. for πέρνα, the ham, Batr. 37.

*Πτερνογλύφος, ὁ (γλύφω), Ham-hollower, name of a mouse, Batr. 227.

*Πτερνοτρώκτης, ου. ὁ (τρώγω), Hamgnawer, name of a mouse, Batr. 29.

*Πτερνοφάγος, ὁ (φαγεῖν), Ham-eater, name of a mouse, Batr. 230.

πτερόεις, εσσα, εν, poet. (πτέρον), prop. feathered, winged, epith. of an arrow. since it was furnished with feathers at the upper end, 4, 117. 5, 171. 2) Metaph. πτερόεντα λαισήϊα, easily-brandished shields (as if feather-light), 5, 453; often πτερόεντα ἔπεα, winged words, which escape quickly from the lips, Il. and Od.

πτέρον, τό (πέτομαι), a feather, a wing, a pinion, mly in plur. πτέρα βάλλειν, to strike the wings, 11, 454; as an image of swiftness, Od. 7, 36. 2) Metaph. an oar or sail of a ship, Od. 11, 125. 23, 272.

πτέρυξ, υγος, ἡ (πτέρον), a wing, a pinion, 2, 316. 462. Od. 2, 149. ὑπὸ πτερύγων, under the stroke of the wings, h. 20, 1.

πτήσσω (πίπτω, πέτω), aor. 1 ἔπτηξα, Ep. perf. πεπτηώς, ῶτος, intrans. to creep away for fear, to crouch, to cringe, to shrink. κείμην πεπτηώς, I lay crouched together, Od. 14, 354. 22, 362. ὑπὸ τεύχεσι πεπτηῶτες, Od. 14, 474; generally, to be in fear, hence 2) Trans. in the aor. 1, to put in fright. to terrify. πτῆξε θυμὸν Ἀχαιῶν, he terrified the hearts of the Achæans, Il. 14, 40; πτήσσω as trans. is uncommon, hence some read πτῆξε from πήγνυμι; others consider the verse not genuine, as Bothe. (Spitzner ad loc. defends πτῆξε.)

πτοέω, Ep. πτοιέω, poet. (akin to πτήσσω), aor. pass. Ep. 3 plur. ἐπτοίηθεν, to put in terrour, to terrify. Pass. to be terrified, to fear, Od. 22, 298.†

Πτολεμαῖος, ὁ (a warrior), son of Piræus, father of Eurymedon, 4, 228.

πτολεμίζω, Ep. for πολεμίζω.

πτολεμιστής, οῦ, ὁ, Ep. for πολεμιστής.

πτόλεμόνδε, adv. for πόλεμόνδε.

πτόλεμος, ὁ, Ep for πόλεμος.

πτολίεθρον, τό. Ep. for πολ. (πόλις). a city; always with the name in the gen. Ἰλίου πτολίεθρον, 2, 133. Od. 1, 2. (The form πολίεθρον is not used.) [It cannot, with Passow, be regarded as a dimin. of πόλις, for H. knows nothing of diminutives.]

πτολιπόρθιος, ὁ = πτολίπορθος, °Od. 9, 504. 530.

πτολίπορθος, ὁ, ἡ, Ep. for πολίπορθος (πέρθω), city-destroying, the destroyer of cities, epith. of Arês, Odysseus (Ulysses), Achilles, and of heroes, 2, 278. 8, 372; as fem. epith. of Enyo (Bellona), 5, 333. (The form πολίπορθος is not used.)

πτόλις. ιος, ἡ, Ep. for πόλις.

πτόρθος, ὁ (πείρω), a sprout, a twig, a branch, Od. 6, 128.†

πτύγμα, ατος, τό (πτύσσω), a fold, a

R 2

because the dragon slain by Apollo decayed there; according to others, from πυθέσθαι, to enquire of the oracle, but the short first syllable is unfavorable to this notion.)

Πυθώδε, adv. to Pytho, Od. 11, 581.

πύκα, adv. poet. 1) thickly, firmly, βάλλειν, 9, 588; ποιητός. 18, 608. Od. 1, 333. 2) Metaph. carefully, intelligently, τρέφειν. Il. 5, 70: φρονείν, 9, 554.

πυκάζω (πύκα), aor. ἐπύκασα, Ep. πύκασα, partcp. perf. pass. πεπυκασμένος, η, ον, 1) to make close, firm, to press closely together ἐντὸς σφέας αὐτούς, Od. 12, 225. 2) to cover closely, to veil, to conceal, τινὰ νεφέλη, Il. 17, 551; νέκυν, 24, 581; spoken of a helmet: πύκασε κάρη, 10, 271: in the pass. 2, 777: dat. instrum. ὄζοισιν, χρυσῷ. 14, 289. 23, 503. 3) Metaph. to envelope, to overshadow, to encompass; spoken of pain, τινὰ φρένας, 8, 124. 17, 83.

πυκιμήδης or πυκιμηδής, ές (μῆδος), of a considerate mind, careful, prudent, wise, Od. 1, 438; † h. Cer. 153.

πυκινά, adv. prop. neut. plur. from πυκινός = πυκνός.

πυκινός, ή, όν, Ep. for πυκνός, q. v.

πυκινόφρων, ον (φρήν), intelligent, wise, h. Merc. 538.

πυκνός, ή, όν, poet. πυκινός, ή, όν (πύκα), 1) thick, firm. a) In respect of the mass: firm, strong, θώρηξ, ἀσπίς, χλαῖνα. b) in respect of single parts: close, pressed together, λέχος, 9, 621 (because several coverings were laid one upon another); νέφος, 5, 751; φάλαγγες, στίχες, dense phalanxes, columns, 4, 281. 7, 61; πτερά, thickly feathered wings, 11, 454; βέλεα, λᾶες, thick arrows or stones, which were thrown in great numbers, Il.; c) also spoken of time: frequent, 10, 9. d) Spoken of something done: thick, strong, δόμος, 10, 267. Od. 6, 134; close-locked, θύρα, Il. 14, 167. 2) Generally, great, strong, ἄχος, ἄτη. 16, 599. 24, 480; πυκινὸν ἀχεύων, Od. 11, 88. b) Spoken of the mind: considerate, prudent, wise, intelligent, φρένες, νόος, μήδεα, βουλή, ἔπος: also ἐρετμή, μῦθος. The neut. πυκνόν and πυκνά, πυκινόν and πυκινά, as adv., as also πυκνῶς, 1) thickly, firmly, θύραι πυκινῶς ἀραρυίαι, closely fitted doors, Od. 2, 344. 2) Metaph. strongly, greatly, exceedingly, πυκινῶς ἀκάχημαι, Il. 19, 312; considerate, intelligent, Od. 1, 279. πυκινὰ φρονείν, to be wise of heart, Od. 9, 445.

Πυλαιμένης, ους, ὁ, king of the Paphlagonians, who came to the aid of Priam. Menelaus slew him, 2, 831. 5, 576. In 13, 643, seq., Pylæmĕnes, prince of the Paphlygonians, appears accompanying the corpse of his son Harpalion. The ancient critics attempted to remove the contradiction, by supposing two persons of this name. Modern critics imagine themselves to have found in the circumstance a proof that the Iliad was put together at a later period.

Πύλαιος, ὁ (adj. πυλαῖος), son of Lethus, leader of the Pelasgians, 2, 842.

πυλάρτης, αο, ὁ (ἄρω), who locks fast the gates of the under world, the door-keeper, epith. of Hades, 8, 367. Od. 11, 276.

Πυλάρτης, αο, ὁ, prop. name of a Trojan, slain by Patroclus, 11, 491. 16, 696.

πυλαωρός, ὁ (ὤρα), Ep. for πυλωρός, door-keeper, door-watch, 21, 530. 24, 681; spoken of dogs, *22, 69.

πύλη, ἡ, a door, a gate, of a chamber, a house, or a town, mly in the plur. Ἀΐδαο πύλαι, the gates of Hades, as a periphrasis for death, 5, 646. 9, 312; poet. also πύλαι οὐρανοῦ, Ὀλύμπου, 5, 749. 8, 411; ὀνείρων, Od. 19, 562. In Hom. always in the plural; with reference to the two wings or leaves (valvæ); hence, a folding-door.

Πυληγενής, ές, see Πυλοιγενής.

πυληδόκος, ὁ (δέχομαι), one who receives at the door, a door-keeper, h. Merc. 15.

Πυλήνη, ἡ, a town in Ætolia, later Proschium, 2, 639. Strab.

Πύλιος, η, ον (Πύλος), of Pylos, Pylian, ὁ Πύλιος γέρων = Nestor. Subst. the Pylian, 1, 248. Od. 3, 59.

Πυλόθεν, adv. from Pylos, Od. 16, 323.†

Πυλοιγενής, ές (γίγνομαι), born in Pylos, epith. of Nestor, 2, 54. 23, 303. The form Πυληγενής, h. Ap. 398. 424.

Πυλόνδε, adv. to Pylos, Od. 13, 274.

πύλος, ἡ = πύλη, a door, a gate; however only ἐν πύλῳ, which reading Wolf has adopted after Aristarch. 5, 397.† Ἀΐδου (Voss. 'at the gate Hades') is supplied, and it is referred to the fable, that Heracles, when he wished to bring up Cerberus, fought with Hades; cf. 8, 367. But as πύλος for πύλη does not occur elsewhere; and as we do not know who the νέκυες are, the reading ἐν Πύλῳ is adopted by Heyne. He refers it to the contest of Heracles with Neleus, in which he wounded Hades himself, cf. Apd. 2, 7. 3. Paus. 2, 7. 3, who quotes vs. 395—397; and Pind. Ol. 9, 31. cf. Ottf. Müller, Orchomen. I. p. 364.

Πύλος, ἡ (ὁ Strab.). According to Strabo and the well-known verse: Ἔστι Πύλος πρὸ Πύλοιο, Πύλος γε μέν ἐστι καὶ ἄλλη, Arist. Eq. 1059, there were in the Peloponnesus three cities of this name: 1) a town in the north of Elis on the Peneus, ὁ Ἠλειακός in Strab. 2) a town in Triphylia (Elis), south of the Alpheus, near Lepreon and Samicon: ὁ Τριφυλιακός, Λεπρεατικός in Strab. 3) a town in Messenia, on the coast (hence called sandy) on the Pamisus, upon an elevation on the promontory Coryphasium, a city founded by Neleus, cf. Apd. 1, 9. 9. Strabo calls it ὁ Μεσσηνιακός, now the port Old Navarino. Even in anti-

('sowed with wheat,' V.), ἄρουρα, πεδίον, *Il. 12, 314. 14, 123. 21, 602.

*πυρπαλαμάω (παλάμη), elsewhere depon. prop. to work with fire; according to Eustath. = κακοτεχνέω, to practise crafty devices. διὰ πυρπαλάμησεν ὁδοῦ, h. Merc. 157. ed. Wolf and Herm. But others διαπυρπαλάμησαν, cf. Frank.

πυρπολέω (πυρπόλος), to kindle a fire, to keep a watch-fire, Od. 10, 30.†

πυρσός, ὁ (πῦρ), a fire-brand, a torch, 18, 211.†

πώ, enclitic particle, somehow, in some way, yet; always in connexion with a negative, often compounded οὔπω, μήπω, not yet, or separately: οὔτε τί πω, 1, 108. Od 3, 23; οὐ γάρ πω, Il. 1, 262; μὴ δή πω, 15, 426.

πωλέομαι, depon. mid. (Ep. frequentat. of πέλομαι,) pres. 2 sing. πωλέ', i. e. πωλέεαι, partcp. Ion. πωλεύμενος, iterat. imperf. πωλέσκετο, fut. πωλήσομαι (versor), to be frequently in a place, to frequent, to have intercourse, to come or go anywhere frequently, εἰς ἀγορήν, πόλεμον, 1, 490. 5, 788; εἰς ἡμέτερον, sc. δῶμα, Od. 2, 55; ἐς εὐνήν, h. Ap. 170; μετ' ἄλλους, Od. 9, 189.

πωλέσκετο, see πωλέομαι.

*πωλέω, ήσω, to sell, Ep. 14, 5.

πῶλος, ὁ, a young horse, a foal, a colt, 11, 681. Od. 23, 246. h. in Ap. 231.

πῶμα, τό, the cover of a quiver, of a chest and a cup, 4, 116. Od. 2, 353.

πώποτε, adv. (ποτέ), at some time, at any time, mly after a negat.: οὐ πώποτε, not at any time, never yet, 1, 106. 3, 442.

πῶς, adv. interrog. how? in what way? and often connected with other particles: πῶς γάρ; for how? πῶς δή; how indeed? πῶς γὰρ δή; πῶς ἄρα; πῶς νῦν; how now? i. e. what thinkest thou? Od. 18, 223. It stands a) With indicat. Il. 1, 123. 10, 61. b) With subj. 18, 188. Od. 3, 22. c) With optat., Il. 11, 838. d) πῶς ἄν and πῶς κε, with optat. 9, 437. Od. 1, 65.

πώς, enclitic particle (πός), in some way, somehow, in any way, after another particle: αἴ κέν πως, if by any means, 1, 66; οὐ μέν πως. in no way, 4, 158; οὐκ ἄν πως, Od. 20, 392.

πωτάομαι, poet. form of πέτομαι, to fly. λίθοι πωτῶντο, 12, 287.† h. Ap. 442. 30, 4.

πῶυ, εος, τό, dat. plur. poet. πώεσι, a flock, always spoken of sheep; hence, ὄιων πῶυ and πώεα μήλων, 3, 198. 11, 678. Od. 4, 413.

P.

P, the seventeenth letter of the Greek alphabet; hence the sign of the seventeenth rhapsody.

ῥα, an enclitic particle, Ep. for ἄρα, often before a vowel, ῥ', see ἄρα.

ῥάβδος, ἡ (ῥάπις), = rod, a staff, a wand; in the plur. rods for fastening the leather to the shield, 12, 297; esply, 1) the wand of Hermês, the magic-rod, to compose to sleep and to awaken men, 24, 343. Od. 5, 47. 24, 2. h. Merc. 210. 526. 2) the magic wand of Kirkê (Circe), Od. 10, 238. 319; of Athênê, Od. 13, 429. 3) an angling rod, Od. 12, 251.

ῥαδαλός, ή, όν, a reading of Zenodot. for ῥοδανός, 18, 576; which is explained as a form of κραδαλός, easily moved.

ῥαδανός, a false reading in 18, 576; see ῥοδανός.

'Ραδάμανθυς, υος, ὁ, son of Zeus and Eurōpa, brother of Minos, 14, 321, 322. According to Od. 4, 565, he was translated, as being the son of Zeus, to Elysium. The Phæaces conveyed him at one time to Eubœa, Od. 7, 322. According to a later tradition, he was expelled by his brother from Crete, and fled to Bœotia. On account of his justice he was made judge in the under world, Apd. 3, 1. 2.

ῥαδινός, ή, όν, poet. slender, flexible; ἱμάσθλη, 23, 585;† hence, agile, active, fleet, πόδες, h. Cer. 183. [From this was derived the false reading ῥαδανός, in 18, 576.]

ῥαθάμιγξ, ιγγος, ἡ, poet. (ῥαθαμίζω), a drop. plur. 11, 536; metaph. κονίης ῥαθάμιγγες, drops, i. e. particles of dust, 23, 502.

ῥαίνω, from theme 'ΡΑΖΩ, Ep. aor. imperat. ῥάσσατε, Od. 20, 150; perf. pass. 3 plur. Ion. ἐῤῥάδαται, pluperf. ἐῤῥάδατο, see Buttm. § 103. IV. 3. Rost, Dial. § 52. c, to sprinkle, to besprinkle, to bestrew, τί τινι, any thing with another, κονίῃ, with dust, αἵματι δ' ἐῤῥάδαται τοῖχοι, the walls are drenched with blood, Od. 20, 354; ἐῤῥάδατο. Il. 12, 431.

ῥαιστήρ, ῆρος, ἡ, poet. (ῥαίω), a hammer, 18, 477;† elsewhere masc.

ῥαίω, poet. fut. Ep. infin. ῥαισέμεναι for ῥαίσειν, aor. 1 ἔῤῥαισα, aor. pass. ἐῤῥαίσθην, to break in pieces, to strike in pieces, to destroy, to dash in pieces, νῆα, Od. 13, 151; τινά, to dash about any one, esply spoken of shipwrecked persons, Od. 5, 221. 6, 326. Pass. to burst asunder, to fly in pieces, Il. 16, 339. τῷ κέ οἱ ἐγκέφαλος διὰ σπέος θεινομένου ῥαίοιτο πρὸς οὔδει, then should the brain of him dashed in pieces, fly through the cave over the ground, Od. 9, 459. The gen. of the partcp. comes from the circumstance that Hom uses the dat. of the pron. instead of the gen. Kühner II. § 587.

ῥάκος, εος. τό (ῥήγνυμι), prop. a piece torn off, a rag, a shred, a fragment of cloth; an old garment, a frock, Od. 14. 342.

ῥαπτός, ή, όν (ῥάπτω), sewed together, patched, *Od. 24, 228, 229.

ῥάπτω, αor. 1 Ep. ῥάψα, 1) to sew

together, to join together, to stitch. τί, any
thing. βοείας θαμειὰς χρυσείης ῥάβδοισι
διηνεκέσιν, to fasten the numerous hides
with golden rods running quite around
(that the leather might not warp), 12,
296. 2) Metaph. to plot, to machinate, to
derise craftily, κακά τινι, 18, 367. Od.
3, 718 ; φόνον, Od. 16, 379. 422.

'Ράριος, ίη, ιον, Rharian ; τὸ 'Ράριον,
the Rharian plain, in Eleusis, which
was sacred to Dēmētēr. and upon which
the first grain is said to have been sown,
h. Cer. 350. 'Ράριος is to be written
without the spiritus asper, cf. Herm. ad
l. c.

ῥάσσατε, see ῥαίνω.
*ῥαφάνη, ἡ, radish. Batr. 53.
ῥαφή, ἡ (ῥάπτω), a seam, Od. 22, 186.†
ῥάχις, ιος. ἡ (ῥάσσω), a back-bone, a
back-piece, 9, 208.†
ῥαψῳδία, ἡ (ῥάπτω, ᾠδή), prop. a
poem chanted by a rhapsodist: esply a
single book of the Hom. poems, a rhapsody.

'Ρέα, ἡ, mly Ep and Ion. 'Ρείη, h. Ap.
93 ; gen. 'Ρείης, 14, 203. 'Ρέα, monosyllabic, 15, 187.† 'Ρέη, h. Cer. 459 ;
daughter of Uranus and Gæa, wife and
sister of Kronus (Saturn), mother of
Zeus, Poseidôn, Hades, Hestia (Vesta),
Dēmētēr, and Hêrê, 14, 203. 15, 187.
h. Cer. 60, 442. (According to Plat.
Cratyl. p. 402, from ῥεῖν, to flow, Herm.
Fluonia, quod ex ea omnia effluxerint;
according to others, ἔρα, the earth by
metathesis.)

ῥέα and ῥεῖα, adv. poet. of ῥάδιος,
easily, without trouble, θεοὶ ῥεῖα ζώοντες,
the gods who live without labour or
trouble, 6, 138. Od. 4, 805. (ῥέα is used
by Hom. as monosyllabic, Il. 5, 304. 12,
381 ; and often)

ῥέεθρον, τό, Ion. and poet. for ῥεῖθρον
(ῥέω), a current, a stream; always plur.
ῥέεθρα, the floods, the waves, 2, 461. Od.
6, 317 ; once ῥεῖθρα, h. 18, 9.

ῥέζω, poet. fut. ῥέξω, aor. 1 ἔρρεξα,
and ἔρεξα, pass. only aor. pass. infin.
ῥεχθῆναι, partcp. ῥεχθείς, cf. ἔρδω, from
which it is formed by metathesis. 1) to
do, to make, to effect, with adv. or with
accus. αἴσυλα, to practise impiety, 5,
403 ; with double accus. τινά τι, to do
any thing to any one : κακόν or κακά
τινα, 2, 195. 4, 32 ; rarely τί τινι. Od. 20,
314 ; εὖ ῥέζειν τινά, to benefit any one, Il.
5, 650 ; on the other, κακῶς τινα. to abuse
any one, Od. 23, 56 ; pass. ῥεχθὲν κακόν,
9, 250. ῥεχθὲν δέ τε νήπιος ἔγνω, even a
simpleton knows what has happened, Il.
17, 32. 2) Esply to sacrifice ; prop. ἱερά,
to offer sacrifices, θεῷ, to a god, 8, 250;
ἑκατόμβην, to offer a hecatomb, θαλύσια,
to present the first fruits, 9, 535 ; βοῦν
θεῷ, 10, 292.

ῥέθος, εος, τό, poet. a limb, only plur.
*16, 856. 22, 68. 362.
ῥεῖα, adv. = ῥέα, q. v.
'Ρείη, ἡ, see 'Ρέα.
ῥεῖθρον, τό, poet. for ῥέεθρον, q. v.

'Ρεῖθρον, τό, a port in Ith
the city, Od. 1, 186 ; see '1θ
ῥέπω (akin to ῥέω), to b
sink ; esply spoken of a bal
and thereby give the prep
decision. ῥέπε αἴσιμον ἦμαρ
fated day of the Greeks pr
i. e. the misfortune of the
decided, 8, 72 ; spoken of
212.

ῥερυπωμένος, see ῥυπόω.
ῥεχθείς, see ῥέζω.
ῥέω, imperf. ἔρρεον, Ep
ἐρρύην, Ep. ῥύη, Od. 3,
flow, to run, spoken of
and sweat: also of brains
with dat. πηγὴ ῥέει ὕδατι,
runs with water. 22, 149 ;
γαῖα, the ground flows with
2) metaph. to flow, to s
spoken of discourse: ἀπὸ
αὐδή, 1, 249 ; of missiles
issue from the hands, 12,
μελέων τρίχες ἔρρεον, the h
their limbs, Od. 10, 393.

'ΡΕΩ, from this the aor.
ῥηθείς : ἐπὶ ῥηθέντι δικαίω
tence,' V.). Od. 18, 414. :
εἴρω and φημί.

ῥηγμίν, ῖνος, ὁ (ῥήγνυμι),
not used: 1) a high shore,
the waves break, a breaker,
430. 2) breaking waves th
dashing waves, Il. 20, 229.
Voss maintains that it neve
(as the Scholiasts assert), b
waves breaking upon the sho

ῥήγνυμι, another form ῥ
imperf. ῥήγνυσκα, fut. ῥήξω
Ep. ῥῆξα, mid. aor. 1 ἐρ
ῥηξάμην, 1) to tear, to tea
break in pieces, to dash in
accus. χαλκόν, ἱμάντα, νευρ
break through gates, 13, 12
in war: to break throug
φάλαγγας, ὅμιλον, στίχας,
15, 615. 2) Absol. to sta
prop. πέδον ποσί, to stam
with the feet, in the form ῥ
h. Ap. 516. Mid. 1) to
of the sea, ῥήγνυτο κῦμα
425. 2) to break throug
for oneself, to dash throug
τεῖχος, φάλαγγας, 12, 90. 44
to let break out, with accus
ῥῆγος, εος, τό (ῥήγνυμι).
torn off, a rug, a cover
prob. of wool, in oppos. to
73 ; often in the plur. cover
which were spread over b
24, 644. Od. 3, 349 ; or ov
10, 352.

ῥηΐδιος. η, ον, Ion. and I
compar ῥηΐτερος, η, ον, su
and ῥήϊστος, η, ον (from
without pains, with infin. π
ῥηϊδίη, a ditch easy to pas
the pers. and infin. 20, 26
[ῥητ. ἔπος, an easy respο
complied with, Od. 11,]

πολεμάζειν ἦσαν Ἀχαιοί for ῥηΐτερον ἦν πολεμ. τοῖς Ἀχαιοῖς, the Greeks were more easy to war against, Il. 18, 258. cf. 24, 243.

ῥηϊδίως, adv. *easily, without trouble*, 4, 390. Od. 8, 376.

ῥήϊστος, η, ον, superl. of ῥηΐδιος.

ῥήϊτατος, η, ον, superl. of ῥηΐδιος.

ῥηΐτερος, η, ον, compar. of ῥηΐδιος.

ῥηκτός, ή, όν (ῥήγνυμι), *torn, that may be torn*, poet. spoken of a man : χαλκῷ ῥηκτός, *that may be injured by the brass (weapon)*, (*vulnerable by it*, V. " *Whose flesh the spear can penetrate*," Cp.), 13, 323.†

Ῥήναια, ἡ, Ep. (more correctly Ῥήναια), for Ῥήνεια (Ῥηνέη, Hdt. Ῥηνία, Plut.), an island, one of the Cyclades (separated from Delos only by a strait), where all the dead of Delos were buried, now *Great Delos*, h. Ap. 44.

Ῥήνη, ἡ, concubine of Oïleus, mother of Medon, 2, 728.

ῥηξηνορίη, ἡ (ῥηξήνωρ), *the valour that breaks through troops or ranks of men* (" *phalanx-breaking might*," Cp.), Od. 14, 217.†

ῥηξήνωρ, ορος, ὁ (ἀνήρ), *dashing men in pieces; breaker of the ranks of war* (Cp.), epith. of Achilles, 7, 228. Od. 4. 5.

Ῥηξήνωρ, ορος, ὁ, son of Nausithöus, brother of Alcinöus, Od. 7, 63.

ῥῆσις, ιος, ἡ (ΡΕΩ), *the act of telling, speaking; discourse, speech*, Od. 21, 291.†

Ῥῆσος, ὁ, 1) son of Eïoneus, king of the Thracians, 10, 435, seq. ; or, according to Apd. 1. 3. 3, son of Strymon and a Muse; Diomēdes and Odysseus (Ulysses) slew him and seized his famous horses, Il. 1. c. 2) a river in Troas which flowed into the Granīcus, 12, 20.

ῥήσσω, a form of ῥήγνυμι, q. v.

ῥητήρ, ῆρος, ὁ, poet. (ΡΕΩ), *an orator, a speaker*, μύθων, 9, 443.†

ῥητός, ή, όν (ΡΕΩ), *said, spoken;* esply *expressly mentioned, definite*, μισθός, 21, 445.†

ῥήτρη, ἡ (ΡΕΩ), *a speech, a sentence;* hence, *an agreement, a convention*, Od. 14, 393.†

ῥιγεδανός, ή, όν (ῥιγέω), *shivering, that inspires shuddering, horrible, odious*, epith. of Helen, 19, 326.†

ῥιγέω, poet. (ῥῖγος), fut. ῥιγήσω, aor. ἐρρίγησα, perf. ἔρριγα, prop. to shiver with cold, to be cold, in H. always metaph. 1) Intrans. *to shudder, to be terrified, to be struck with fear*, mly absol. 3, 259; with partcp. 4, 279. 12, 331 ; or with a particle of time, 12, 108. 2) Trans. *to shudder before, to shrink trembling before*, τί; *to fear*, πόλεμον, 5, 351. 17, 175. Instead of the accus. the infin. 3, 353; or with μή following, Od. 23, 216. The perf. has a pres. signif. Il. 7, 114.

ῥίγιον, poet. compar. of ῥῖγος, used only in the neut. ; also superl. ῥίγιστος,

ῃ, εω, 1) *more chilly, more cold*, Od. 17, 191. 2) Metaph. *more terrible, more fearful, more horrible*. τὸ δὲ ῥίγιον, Il. 1, 325. Od. 20, 220. τὰ ῥίγιστα, *the most terrible things, most horrible*, Il. 5, 873.†

Ῥῖγμος, ὁ, son of Peirous, from Thrace, an ally of the Trojans, 20, 485, seq.

ῥῖγος, εος, τό, *cold, chilliness*, Od. 5, 472.†

ῥιγόω (ῥῖγος), fut. infin. Ep. ῥιγωσέμεν, *to be cold, to feel chilly*, Od. 14, 481.†

ῥίζα, ἡ, *a root* of plants ; also as a remedy, 11, 846; metaph. spoken of the eye, Od. 9, 390.

ῥιζόω (ῥίζα), aor. ἐρρίζωσα, perf. pass. ἐρρίζωμαι, *to cause to take root, to plant*, ἀλωήν, Od. 7, 122. 2) *to root, to fasten*, spoken of a ship which Poseidön changes to stone, *Od. 13, 163.

*ῥικνός, ή, όν (ῥῖγος), *stiff*, contracted with cold ; generally, *bent, crooked*, πόδας, h. Ap. 317.

ῥίμφα, adv. (ῥίπτω), prop. *hurled*, hence *quickly, fleetly, swiftly*, 6, 511. Od. 8, 193.

ῥίν, better ῥίς, q. v.

ῥινόν, τό = ῥινός, *a shield*. εἴσατο δ᾽ ὡς ὅτε ῥινὸν ἐν—πόντῳ, it appeared to him as a shield in the sea (spoken of Phæacia). The neut. is the later form, Od. 5, 281.†

ῥινός, ἡ, 1) *the skin* of the human body, 5, 308; also plur. Od. 5, 426. 14, 134. 2) *the skin* of an animal drawn off, *the hide*, Il. 7, 474. ῥινὸς λύκοιο, a wolf's skin, 10, 334 ; esply of horned cattle, 10, 155; hence 3) *a shield* which was made of ox-hide, with βοῶν, 12, 263; and often alone, 4, 447. ῥινοῦ τε, βοῶν τ᾽ εὐποιητάων seems, according to Aristarch., a case of hendiadys, like πόλεμόν τε μάχην (V. leather and well-prepared ox-hide), 16, 636.

ῥινοτόρος, ὁ (τορέω), *piercing the skin or the shield, shield-breaking*, epith. of Arês, 21, 392.†

ῥίον, τό, *the projecting point of a mountain;* hence 1) *a peak, a mountain-summit*, 8, 25 ; *a rock*. h. Ap. 383. 2) Esply *a promontory*, Od. 3, 295.

ῥιπή, ἡ (ῥίπτω), *a cast, a thrust, a throw, violence, force* with which any thing is thrown, 8, 355. h. Ap. 447. *b*) the force which any thing thrown has. ῥ. λᾶος, a stone's cast, 12, 462. Od. 8, 192 ; αἰγανέης, the cast of a spear, Il. 16, 589; and generally, *force, violence* of the wind and of fire, 15, 171. 21, 12.

Ῥίπη, ἡ, a town in Arcadia near Stratus, 2, 606.

*ῥιπίζω (ῥιπίς), partcp. aor. ῥιπίσσας, *to put in motion, to excite*, ἔριν, Fr. Hom. 26.

*ῥιπτάζω (frequent. from ῥίπτω), *to fling hither and thither, to hurl about*, as abuse, θεοὺς κατὰ δῶμα, 14, 257.† · 2) Intrans. *to move convulsively, to twitch*, ῥιπτάζεσκεν ὀφρύσι, h. Merc. 279.

ῥίπτασκον, see ῥίπτω.

ῥίπτω, Ep. iterat. imperf. ῥίπτασκον,

15, 23. cf. Thiersch, § 210. 22; fut.
ῥίψω, aor. ἔρριψα, Ep. ῥίψα, to cast, to
sling, to hurl, τινὰ ἀπὸ βηλοῦ, 1, 591; ἐς
Τάρταρον, 8, 13. Batr. 97; τὶ μετά τινα,
to cast any thing at any one, 3, 378. Od.
6, 115; ἔριψεν (Matthiæ ἔραψεν), h. Merc.
79.

ῥίς, ῥινός, ἡ, later ῥίν, the nose, plur.
ῥίνες the nostrils, 14, 467. 19, 39. Od.
5, 456.

ῥίψ, ῥιπός. ἡ, dat plur. ῥίπεσσι, a reed,
a rush; plur. osier-work, a hurdle, a mat,
Od. 5, 256.†

*ῥοδάνη, ἡ, the thread of the woof, the
woof, Batr. 186.

ῥοδανός, ή, όν, pliant, flexible [= εὐκί-
νητος], 18, 576. παρὰ ῥοδανὸν δονακῆα,
by a waving thicket of reeds. This is
the reading of Wolf after Aristarch.,
which Damm after Eustath. strangely
derives from ῥοή, whence ῥοανός, ῥοδανός; it is akin to κραδάω. Other readings are: ῥαδαλός, ῥαδανός, ῥαδινός, the
last according to Apoll. from ῥᾳδίως δο-
νεῖσθαι.

*Ῥόδεια, ἡ (the rosy), daughter of
Oceanus and Tethys, companion of Per-
sephōnē, h. Cer. 419.

Ῥόδιος, η, ον, see Ῥόδος.

Ῥοδίος, ὁ, or Ῥοδιός (with accent
changed), a river in Troas, north of cape
Dardanis, 12, 20.

ῥοδοδάκτυλος, ον, poet. (δάκτυλος), rosy-
fingered, epith. of (Eos) Aurora, since she
was conceived of as youthful, or according to Eustath. from the colour of the
dawning east, 6, 175. Od. 2, 5.

ῥοδόεις, εσσα, εν, poet. (ῥόδον), of roses,
rosy; ἔλαιον, oil of roses, which in the
opinion of the ancients prevented putrefaction, 23, 186.†

*ῥόδον, τό, a rose, h. Cer. 6.

*Ῥοδόπη, ἡ (having a rosy counte-
nance), daughter of Oceanus and Tethys,
h. Cer. 422.

*ῥοδόπηχυς, ὁ, ἡ, poet. (πῆχυς), rosy-
armed, h. Cer. 31. 6.

Ῥόδος, ἡ, Rhodus, Rhodes, a famous
island in the Carpathian sea, on the
coast of Asia, with three cities, Lindus,
Ialysus, and Cameirus; now Rhodis, 2,
655. The chief city, Rhodus, was built
at a later date, whose harbour is famed
on account of the Colossus, Strabo; from
this Ῥόδιος, η, ον, Rhodian; subst. a
Rhodian, 2, 654.

ῥοή, ἡ (ῥέω), a flowing, a current,
always in the pur. the floods, the waves,
spoken of Oceanus and of rivers, 2, 869.
Od 6, 216.

ῥόθιος, η, ον (ῥόθος), roaring, resounding, esply spoken of water, κῦμα, Od. 5,
412.†

ῥοιά, ἡ, the pomegranate, both fruit
and tree, Od. 7, 15. 11, 589. h. Cer. 373.
412.

ῥοιβδέω (ῥοῖβδος), aor. optat. ῥοιβδή-
σειεν, prop. to sup or gulp up, to swallow
with noise, spoken of Charybdis, Od. 12,
106.†

ῥοιζέω (ῥοῖζος), aor. 1 Ep.
whizz, to kiss, and generally
any sharp sound, to whistle, 1(

ῥοῖζος, ὁ, Ion. and Ep. ἡ,
whizzing, hissing, spoken of
spears in rapid motion, 16, 3
whistling of the Cyclops, (
(Akin to ῥέω.)

ῥόος, ὁ (ῥέω), flowing; a rive
a current; only sing often
Ἀλφειοῖο, Ὠκεανοῖο, 11, 726
κὰρ (Ep. for κατὰ) ῥόον, down
12, 33. κατὰ ῥόον, Od. 14, 254
up stream, Il. 12, 33.

ῥόπαλον, τό (ῥέπω), a st
thicker towards the top, a cu
11, 559. 561; of the Cyclops,
παγχάλκεον, the brazen club
Od. 11, 575.

ῥοχθέω, poet. (ῥόχθος), to
sound, spoken of the waves
upon the shore, *Od. 5, 402.

ῥύατο, see ῥύομαι.

ῥυδόν, adv. (ῥέω, ῥυῆναι), i
abundantly, immoderately, a
15, 426.†

ῥύη, Ep. for ἐρρύη, see ῥέω.

ῥυμός, ὁ (ἐρύω), the pole
draught-animals draw the c
729. 10, 505. cf. ἅρμα.

ῥύομαι, depon. mid. (pro
ἐρύω, but only in the signif.
aor. 1 ἐρρῦσάμην, Ep. ῥυσάμ
form of the pass. infin. ῥῦσ
imperf. 3 plur. ῥύατ' for ἐ
515; iterat. imperf. 2 sing.
to deliver, to rescue, to libera
ἐκ κακοῦ, any one from evil, (
ὑπ' ἤέρος, Il. 17, 645. cf. Oc
Generally, to deliver, to prot
ter, to preserve, to defend,
a) Spoken of gods and men,
ὑπό τινος, from any one, 1
Spoken of things, esply of v
259. 12, 8: μήδεα φωτός, to
to cover the man's shame,
3) to have under guard, to a
strain, Ἠώ, Od. 23, 246. (υ h
quantity in the pres. and i
the other hand, it is long in
tenses before σ, cf. Spitzner
6. According to Buttm., Le
is short in the fut. and ac
Gram. p. 302.)

ῥύπα, τά, see ῥύπος.

ῥυπάω, Ep. ῥυπόω, to be
Od. 19, 72. 23, 115. Partcp
*Od. 13, 435. 6, 87. 24, 227.

ῥύπος, ὁ, metaplast. plu
filth, foulness, Od. 6, 93.†
ῥύπον or ῥύπος is doubtful.)

ῥυπόω, partcp. perf. Ep.
for ἐρρύπ., to defile, to soil,
2) Ep. for ῥυπάω, q. v.

ῥῦσθαι, see ῥύομαι.

ῥύσιον, τό (ἐρύω, ΡΥΩ),
which is dragged away, boo
esply τὰ ῥύσια, that which is
from one who injures us,
compel satisfaction, a pledg

a *reprisal*. ῥύσια ἐλαύνεσθαι, to drive off booty as a reprisal, 11, 674.†

ῥύσκεν, Ep. for ῥύσκου, see ῥύομαι.

ῥυσός, ή, όν (ἐρύω), prop. drawn together, hence *shrivelled, wrinkled*, epith. of the Litæ, 9, 503.†

ῥυστάζω (frequent. from 'ΡΥΩ, ἐρύω), Ep. iterat. imperf. ῥυστάζεσκεν, poet. *to draw hither and thither, to drag, to trail*, with accus. of the corpse of Hector, 24, 755. 2) Generally, *to pull about, to abuse*, γυναῖκας, Od. 16, 109. 20, 319.

ῥυστακτύς, ύος, ή, poet. (ῥυστάζω), the act of *dragging around, pulling about*, generally, *abusing*, Od. 18, 224.†

ῥυτήρ, ῆρος, ὁ ('ΡΥΩ, ἐρύω), prop. one drawing; hence 1) *a drawer* of the bow, Od. 21, 173; ὀϊστῶν, the shooter of arrows, Od. 18, 262. 21, 173. 2) *the strap* on the bit of horses in which they draw, or *a rein*. ἐν δὲ ῥυτῆρσι τάννυσθεν, they ran in the reins, see τανύω, Il. 16, 475. 3) (ῥύομαι), *a protector, a watch*, σταθμῶν, Od. 17, 187. 223.

'Ῥύτιον, τό, a town in Crete, later prob. 'Ριθυμνία, now *Retimo*, 2, 648.

ῥυτός, ή, όν, poet. ('ΡΥΩ, ἐρύω), drawn on, *drawn to, dragged on*, spoken of large stones, *Od. 6, 267. 14, 10.

ῥωγαλέος, η, ον (ῥώξ), *torn asunder, split, cut apart*, 2, 417. Od. 13, 435. 17, 198.

ῥώξ, ῥωγός, ὁ and ή, poet. (ἔρρωγα, perf. from ῥήγνυμι), *a rent, a fissure*. ῥῶγες μεγάροιο are according to Eustath. δίοδοι, passages; Apoll. θυρίδες, side-doors of the hall; Etym. Mag. ἀναβάσεις; and Voss translates: ἀνὰ ῥῶγ. μεγ., up the stairs of the house; Wiedasch [and *Cp.*] correctly. the galleries of the house, Od. 22, 143.†

ῥώομαι. depon. mid. only 3 plur. imperf. ἐρρώοντο and ῥώοντο, and aor. ἐρρώσαντο, 1) *to move oneself violently and rapidly*. γούνατα δ' ἐρρώσαντο, Od. 23, 3. cf. Il. 18, 411. χαῖται ἐρρώοντο, the manes fluttered, 23, 367. 2) Esply *to go rapidly, to hasten, to run, to rush*, 11, 60; ἀμφί τινα, 16, 166. 24, 616; πυρὴν πέρι, Od. 24, 69. ὑπὸ δ' ἀμφίπολοι ῥώοντο ἄνακτι, the handmaids hastened with the king, Köppen; or, they exerted themselves for the king (supported the king, V.), Il. 18, 417. 3) Trans. with accus. χορόν, to speed the dance i. e. to dance, h. Ven. 262.

ῥωπήϊον, τό, Ion. for ῥωπεῖον (ῥώψ), a place grown up with bushes, *a thicket, a coppice*, mly plur. πυκνὰ ῥωπήϊα, 13, 199. 21, 559. Od. 14, 473. h. 18, 8.

ῥωχμός, ὁ (ῥώξ), *a rent, a fissure, a cleft*. 23, 420.†

ῥώψ, ῥωπός, ή, poet. (akin to ῥίψ), a low bush, *bushes, shrubbery, brambles*, plur. *Od. 10, 166. 14, 49. 16, 47.

Σ.

Σ, the eighteenth letter of the Greek alphabet; the sign, therefore, of the eighteenth book.

σ', apostroph. for σέ. 2) More rarely for σοί [perhaps in 1, 170, but cf. φύσσω, *Am. Ed.*]. 3) For σά, Od. 1, 356.

*Σαβάκτης, pr. n. a domestic goblin, Ep. 14, 9.

Σαγγάριος, ὁ, the largest river in Bithynia, rising near the village Sangia at the mountain Didymus, flowing through Phrygia and falling into the Pontus, now *Sakarja*, 3, 187. 16, 719.

*Σαιδήνη, ή, a lofty mountain in Asia Minor, near Cymê, Ep. 1, 3.

σαίνω (akin to σείω), aor. ἔσηνα, *to wag, to move*, prop. spoken of dogs, Od. 10, 217. 219. 16, 6; οὐρῇ, with the tail, *Od. 17, 302; of wolves, h. Ven. 70.

σακέσπαλος, ὁ (πάλλω), *shield-shaking*, (shield-brandishing), epith. of Tydeus, 15, 126.†

σάκος, εος, τό, *a shield*; prop. distinct from ἀσπίς, prob. larger than that. It was made of several ox-hides stretched one over another; the largest shield mentioned by Homer consisted of seven layers of ox-hide, above which was a plate of beaten brass, 7, 219, seq. It was besides variously adorned, see 11, 32, seq., and esply the description of the shield of Achilles received from Hêphæstus, 18, 478, seq.

Σαλαμίς, ῖνος, ή, later Σαλαμίν, 1) an island off the coast of Attica, which at an earlier period constituted a state, but afterwards came under the dominion of Athens, now *Koluri*; from it Aἴας (Ajax) conducted twelve ships to Troy, 2, 557. 2) a town in Cyprus, founded by the Salaminian Teucros (Teucer), now *Porto Constanza*, h. 9, 4.

Σαλμωνεύς, ῆος, ὁ, son of Æolus and Enaretê, father of Tyrô; he reigned first in Thessaly, migrated to Elis, and built the city Salmônê. In his pride he wished to be equal to Zeus, and imitated thunder and lightning by riding in a brazen chariot upon a copper floor and hurling down blazing torches. Zeus struck him with lightning, Od. 11, 236.

σάλπιγξ, γγος, ή, *a trumpet* with which the signal of attack was given, 18, 219.† This is the only passage in which this instrument is mentioned; perhaps it was used as a signal in sieges.

σαλπίζω, fut. σαλπίγξω, *to sound a trumpet*, Batr. 203; metaph. *to resound like a trumpet*. ἀμφὶ δὲ σάλπιγξεν οὐρανός (the heaven round about resounded like a trumpet, V.), spoken of thunder, 21, 388.† 2) Trans. with accus. *to peal forth, to trumpet*, Batr. 202.

Σάμη, ή, or Σάμος, 2, 634. Od. 4, 671;

an island near Ithaca, which belonged to the kingdom of Odysseus (Ulysses), later *Cephallenia*, now *Cephallonia*. It is separated from Ithaca by a narrow strait, Od. 1, 246. 9, 24. h. Ap. 429.

Σάμος, ἡ 1) = Σάμη, q v. 2) Σάμος Θρηϊκίη, later Σαμοθράκη, *Samothrace*, an island of the Ægean sea, on the coast of Thrace, opposite the mouth of the river Hebrus, later famed by the mysteries of the Cabeiri, having a town of the same name, now *Samothraki*, 13, 12; also simply Σάμος, 24, 78. 753. 3) an island in the Ægean sea, on the coast of Ionia, having a town of the same name, famed for its splendid temple of Hêrê, h. Ap. 41.

*σάνδαλον, τό, *a sole of wood*, which was bound to the feet by thongs, *a sandal*, h. Merc. 79. 83.

σανίς, ίδος, ἡ. 1) *a board, a plank.* 2) *any thing made of boards*; hence a) *doors*, always plur. σανίδες, *folding doors* [*valvæ*]. 9, 583. Od. 2, 344. b) *a scaffold of boards, a stage*, sing. Od. 21, 51.

ΣΑΟΣ, obsol. ground form of σῶς, σόος, from which the compar. σαώτερος, η, ον. σαώτερος ὥς κε νέηαι, that thou mayest return the more safely home, 1, 32; † prop. compar. with only a slight degree of augmentation (cf. Thiersch, § 202. 10). On the other hand, Buttm., Gr. Gram. § 69. N. 8, considers it as a simple positive.

σαοφροσύνη, ἡ, Ep. for σωφροσύνη (φρήν), prop. a sound understanding, *discretion, prudence*, *Od. 23, 13. 30.

σαόφρων, ονος, ὁ, ἡ, Ep. for σώφρων (φρήν), *discreet, intelligent, prudent*, 21, 462 Od. 4, 158 (later, *temperate, abstinent*).

σαόω, contr. σῶ. from which poet. σώω and σόω, Ep. form of σώζω (which occurs only once, Od. 5, 490, in the partcp. pres., but where prob. the reading should be σώων). Hom. has 1) From σαόω, fut. σαώσω, aor. ἐσάωσα, fut. mid. σαώσομαι, Od. 21, 309; aor. pass. ἐσαώθην, also imp. pres. act. σάω for σάοε, contr. σῶ, and extended by α, σάω, cf. ναιετάωσα, Od. 13, 230. 17, 595; 3 sing. imperf. σάου for ἐσάοε, contr. σῶ, and extended σάω, Il. 16, 363. 2) The contracted form σῶ does not occur; but the extended forms, a) σόω (from which σώζω), whence partcp. σώοντες and imperf. σώεσκον. b) σόω, from this subj. pres. σόῃ, σόῃς, σόωσι, 1) *to sustain in life, to save, to keep unconsumed, to preserve, to deliver*, τινά, also ζωούς. 21, 238; hence pass. *to be saved, to remain alive*, 15, 503; in oppos. to ἀπολέσθαι, 17, 228. b) Spoken of things: νῆας, πόλιν; also σπέρμα πυρός [*semina flammæ*, Virg.], to preserve the seeds of fire, Od. 5, 490. 2) *to rescue, to deliver, to bring safely*, with accus. from what? ἐκ φλοίσβοιο, πολέμου, Il. 5, 469. 11, 752; ὑπό τινος, 8, 363. b) to what? ἐς προχοάς, Od. 5, 452; ἐπὶ νῆα, Il. 17, 692;

πόλινδε, 5. 224; μεθ᾽ ὅμιλον, : this, cf. Thiersch, § 222.

σαπήῃ, Ep. for σαπῇ, see σ

Σαρδάνιος, η, ον, ed. Wolf, f μείδησε δὲ θυμῷ Σαρδάνιον he laughed in his heart a laugh, Od. 20, 302.† Voss 'with horrible laughter he c anger;' Wiedasch, 'he con forced laughter, anger in used of Odysseus (Ulysses), the missile of Ctesippus by ar of the head. Σαρδάνιον is sing. and used as an adv., sing. and γέλων is to be sup δάνιος γέλως, signifies, accor ancients, 'the scornful lau enraged man' (σαρκαστικός). word is to be derived from tath. Apoll. ἀπὸ τοῦ σεσηρέν σι or ἄκροις χείλεσι), hence a and signifies prop. *showing grinning*. Others write σαρ derive it from σαρδόνιον, : plant, which distorted the to an involuntary laugh. to grow chiefly in Sardi Eustath. quotes still other e. [*Sardonic*, Cowper, whose from the Schol., see ad Od. 2 *Ed.*]

σάρξ, σαρκός, ἡ, dat. plur *flesh*, the sing. only Od. 19 where plur. of men and beas Od. 9, 293.

Σαρπηδών, όνος, ὁ, Ep. f δοντος, 12, 379; Σαρπηδόν· voc. Σαρπῆδον, 5, 633; from Σαρπηδών, son of Zeus an 198, seq. (According to a la son of Evander and Didami of an elder Sarpêdon, Apd.), the Lycians, an ally of the 876; he was slain by Patro seq. Upon the command of : cleansed the dead body fror dust, and anointed it with a 667.

*σατίνη, ἡ, *a chariot, a w Ven. 13.

Σατνιόεις, εντος, ὁ, a lar Mysia, 6, 34. 14, 445; Σαφν

Σάτνιος, ὁ, son of Enops nymph, slain by Ajax, 14, 4

σαῦλος, η, ον (akin to ε mincing, affected. σαῦλα βαί 28.

σαυρωτήρ, ῆρος, ὁ, *the lo spear*; elsewhere οὐρίαχος. *spike of the shaft*, which w with iron, that it might be the ground, 10, 153 † (prob. a kind of snake or perhaps t

σάφα, adv. (from σαφ *clearly, certainly, definitely* with εἰδέναι, ἐπίστασθαι, 2, 730. σάφα εἰπεῖν, to speak speak truly, Il. 4, 404.

*σαφέως, adv. = σαφῶς fr Cer. 149.

*σαφής, ές, clear, certain, sure, h. Merc. 208.

σάω, for σάον, see σαόω.

σαῶσαι, σάωσε, etc., see σαόω.

σαώτερος, η, ον, Ep. compar. from ΣΑΟΣ.

σβέννυμι, only aor. 1 ἔσβεσα. Ep. infin. σβέσσαι, aor. 2 ἔσβην. 1) Trans. in the aor. 1, to extinguish, to quench, to put out, with accus. πυρκαιήν, 23, 237. 24, 791. b) Metaph. to moderate, to check, to restrain, χόλον, 9, 678; μένος, 16, 621. 2) Intrans. in the aor. 2, to go out, spoken of fire, 9, 471. b) Metaph. to become calm, spoken of wind, Od. 3, 182.

σεβάζομαι, depon. mid. (σέβας), aor. 1 only Ep. 3 sing. σεβάσσατο, to stand in awe, to be afraid of, τὶ θυμῷ. *6, 167. 417.

σέβας, τό (σέβομαι), only used in nom. and accus. 1) reverential fear, awe, that respect for the opinion of gods and men which restrains a person from doing any thing; fear, shame, with infin. 18, 178. h. Cer. 10. 2) astonishment, wonder, admiration, at uncommon occurrences; σέβας μ' ἔχει, Od. 3, 123. 4, 75.

σέβομαι, depon. (akin to σεύω), to stand in awe, to be ashamed, absol. 4, 240.†

σέθεν, Ep. for σοῦ, see σύ.

σεῖ', abbreviated for σεῖο, see σύ.

*Σειληνός. ὁ (later orthography Σιληνός), Silenus, foster-father and companion of Dionȳsus (Bacchus), who followed him always drunk and riding upon an ass. In the plur. οἱ Σειληνοί, generally, the ancient Satyrs, companions of Dionȳsus. h. Ven. 263.

σεῖο. Ep. for σοῦ, see σύ.

σειρή, ἡ (εἴρω), a rope, a cord, a string, 23, 115. Od. 22, 175; σ. χρυσείη, a golden chain, Il. 8, 19.

Σειρήν, ῆνος, ἡ, mly plur. αἱ Σειρῆνες (from σειρή, the entangling, the enticing), the Sirens, mythic virgins, who, according to Homer, dwelt between Ææa and the rock of Scylla, and by their sweet voices allured passengers and put them to death, Od. 12, 39. 52. Hom. knows but two, for v. 56, we have the dual Σειρήνοιιν. At a later day there were supposed to be three or four, cf. Eustath. ad loc. They were in antiquity, for the most part, placed in the Sicilian sea, on the south-west coast of Italy, hence also the three small dangerous rocks not far from the island of Caprea, were called Σειρηνοῦσαι, Strab. They are the daughters of the river god Achelôus and a muse, Ap Rh. 4, 895. Apd. 1, 34. At a still later period they were represented as birds with the faces of virgins.

σεύω (akin to σεύω), aor. 1 Ep. σεῖσα, aor mid. Ep. σεσάμην always without augm., to shake, to brandish, with accus. ἐγχείας, 3, 345; and pass. 13. 135: θύρας, to shake the doors, i. e. to knock at the doors, 9, 583; ζυγόν, to shake the yoke, spoken of running horses, Od. 3, 486. Mid. to move oneself, to shake, to

quake, Il. 14, 285. 20, 59; σείσατο εἰνὶ θρόνῳ, she was violently agitated, 8, 199.

σέλα for σέλαι, see σέλας.

Σέλαγος, ὁ, father of Amphius from Pæsus, 5, 612.

σέλας, αος, τό (akin to εἴλη), dat. σέλαϊ and σέλᾳ. light, splendour, brightness, a beam, spoken of fire, 8, 509. Od. 21, 246; of constellations and meteors, Il. 8, 76. h. Ap. 442. b) a torch, h. Cer. 52.

σελήνη, ἡ (σέλας), the moon, 8, 555; πλήθουσα, the full moon, 18, 484; an image of splendour, Od. 4, 45.

Σελήνη, ἡ, prop. name, Luna, the goddess of the moon; in the Il. and Od. we find nothing of her origin or of her rising and setting. In h. 31, 6, seq., she is called the daughter of Hyperion and Euryphaëssa (of Theia, Hes. Th. 375); in h. Merc. 94, daughter of Pallas, cf. h. 32.

Σεληπιάδης, ου, ὁ, son of Selēpius = Evēnus, 2, 693.

σέλινον, τό, parsley, a plant which belongs to the family of celery, and grows chiefly in depressed situations, 2, 776. Od 5, 72. Batr. 54. According to Billerbeck, Flor. Class. p. 70, hipposelinum s. Smyrnium olus atrum, Linn.; according to Heyne, apium graveolens, Linn.; also ἐλειοσέλινον; it is mentioned as a food of horses.

Σελλήεις, εντος, ὁ, 1) a river in Elis between the Penēus and the Alphēus, now Pachinta, 2, 659. 15, 531. 2) A river in Troas near Arisbe, 2, 839. 12, 97.

Σελλοί, οἱ (Ἑλλοί, in a Frag. Pind. in Strab. VII. c. 7), the Selli, priests of Zeus in Dodōna, who communicated or explained oracles, 16, 234. They appear, perhaps in accordance with a priestly vow, to have led a very austere life, hence they were called ἀνιπτόποδες. According to Strab. VII., the original inhabitants of Dodona.

*σέλμα, ατος, τό (akin to σελίς), a rower's bench, generally the upper deck (transtrum), h. 6, 47. cf. ζυγόν.

Σεμέλη, ἡ (according to Diod. Sic. 3, 61, from σεμνός), daughter of Cadmus, mother of Dionȳsus by Zeus. She implored Zeus that he would show himself to her in the full glory of his divinity. He fulfilled her request, but she was destroyed by his lightning, 14, 323; h. in Bacch. 6, 57. (According to Heffter from σύω, Bœot. = θέω, the frantic, Herm. solsequa from σέβειν and ἔλη = vitis.)

*σεμνός, ή, όν (σέβομαι), venerable, honoured, holy, prop. spoken of the gods, h. 12,]. Cer. 486.

σέο, Ep. for σοῦ, see σύ.

σεῦ and σεν, see σύ.

σεῦα, Ep. for ἔσσευα, see σεύω.

*Σευτλαῖος, ὁ (σεῦτλον), Beet-eater, a frog's name, Batr. 212.

*σεῦτλον, τό, a beet, a soft culinary

vegetable, *beta vulgaris*, Linn. Batr. 162.

σεύω, poet. (akin to θέω), aor. Ep. ἔσσευα and σεῦα, aor. mid. ἐσσευάμην, perf. pass. ἔσσυμαι, pluperf. ἐσσύμην. The perf. pass. often has a pres. signif. hence partcp. ἐσσύμενος, η, ον, with retracted accent. The pluperf. is at the same time Ep. aor. 2 ἐσσύμην, ἔσσυο, ἔσσυτο, Ep. σύτο, 21, 167. The pres. act. not found in Hom., the augment. tenses have double Sigma. 1) Act. trans. prop. *to put in violent motion, to drive;* hence, according to the prepos. *a) to drive, to urge, to chase,* τινὰ κατὰ Νυσσήϊον, 6, 133; τινὰ ἐπί τινι, any one against any one, 11, 293, 294; ἵππους, 15, 681. *b) to drive away, to chase away,* κύνας, Od. 14, 35; κατὰ ὀρέων, to drive down from the mountains, Il. 20, 189. *c)* Spoken of inanimate things: *to cast, to hurl,* κεφαλήν, 11, 147. 14, 413; αἷμα, to drive out the blood, i. e. to cause to flow, to draw, 5, 208. II) Mid. with Ep. aor. 2 and perf. pass. 1) Intrans. *to move oneself violently, to run, to hasten, to rush,* ἀνὰ ἄστυ, 6, 505; ἐπί τι, 14, 227. ψυχὴ κατ' ὠτειλὴν ἔσσυτο, the soul rushed to the wound, i. e. escaped through the wound, 14, 519; with infin. σεύατο διώκειν, he hastened to pursue, 17, 463. *b)* Metaph. spoken of the mind: *to desire ardently, to long for.* θυμός μοι ἔσσυται, Od. 10, 484; esply partcp. ἐσσύμενος, ardently desiring, *longing for, desirous,* with gen. ὁδοῖο, of the journey, Od. 4, 733; and with infin. πολεμίζειν, Il. 11, 717. Od. 4, 416. 2) With accus. trans. *a) to drive, to chase, c) to hunt.* esply wild beasts, with accus. κάπριον, λέοντα, 11, 415. *b) to chase away, to drive,* 3, 26; τινὰ πεδίονδε, 20, 148; metaph. κακότητα, h. 7, 13.

σηκάζω (σηκός). aor. pass. 3 plur. σηκάσθεν for ἐσηκάσθησαν, prop. to drive into the fold, *to fold,* spoken of sheep; generally, *to shut up, to enclose,* 8, 131.†

σηκοκόρος, ὁ (κορέω), one that cleans the stall, *a stable-cleanser, a stall-boy,* Od. 17, 224† [*a sweeper of my stalls,* Cp.].

σηκός, ὁ, an inclosed place: *a fold, a stall,* 18, 589. Od. 9, 219.

σῆμα, ατος, τό, *a sign,* to point out any thing; *a token,* of a lot, 7, 188; of theft, h. Merc. 136; esply 1) a sign sent by the deity, *an atmospheric sign, an aerial token,* such as thunder and lightning, which were regarded as omens and indications of the will of the gods, 2, 253. 351. 4, 381. 13, 244. · 2) *a monumental sign, a mound;* hence σῆμα χεῦαι, 2, 814. 7, 68. Od. 1, 291; generally, *a monument.* 3) *a written sign.* σήματα λυγρά, characters of fatal import [but not *alphabetical*], Il. 6, 168. Od. 1, 291; see γράφω. 4) *a mark,* 23, 843. Od. 8, 192.

σημαίνω (σῆμα), fut. σημανέω, aor. Ep. σήμηνα, aor. mid. ἐσημηνάμην. 1) *to give a sign* to do any thing; hence, *to*

command, *to order,* τινί, 1, 289 rarely with gen. τινός, Il. 14, ἐπί τινι, about any one, Od. 22, Trans. with accus. *to mark, to* τέρματα, Il. 23, 358. 757. Od Mid. *to mark* any thing *for one* ρον, one's lot, Il. 7, 175.

σημάντωρ, ορος, ὁ, poet. (prop. one who gives a signal, *commander, sovereign,* 4, 431 *driver of horses,* 8, 127; βοῶν, of cattle, a herdsman, 15, 315.

σήμερον, adv. (from τήμερα), 30. Od. 17, 186.

σήπω, perf. σέσηπα, aor. 2 from which Ep. 3 sing. subj. σαπῇ, 19, 27. Act. *to cause to* rot. Pass. and perf. intrans. putrid, *to rot, to moulder* aw σήπεται, 14, 27. 24, 414. 2 the timbers are decayed, *2, 13

σησαμόεις, εσσα, εν (σῆσα of sesame, Ep. 15, 8.

Σήσαμος, ἡ, a town in Pa later the citadel of Amastris, 2,

*σησαμότυρος, ὁ (τυρός), ses i. e. a kind of food made of se cheese, Batr. 36.

Σηστός, ἡ, a little town on lespont. in the Thracian Ch opposite the city of Abydos in rendered famous by the love o and Hero, now *Ialowa,* 2, 836.

σθεναρός, ή, όν, poet. (σθένο powerful, mighty,* epith. of Ἀτέ

Σθενέλαος, ὁ, son of Ithæme by Patroclus, 16, 586.

Σθένελος, ὁ (abbrev. from Σ 1) son of Capaneus and Evadi the Epigŏni and a leader be 2, 564. 23, 511; a companion des, 9, 48. 2) son of Perseu drŏmĕda, husband of Nicippe, Eurystheus, king of Argos and 19, 116.

σθένος, εος, τό, poet. *streng might,* primar. spoken of the men and beasts, 5, 139. Od more rarely of inanimate thin 751. 18, 607; esply of strengt *courage* in war: μέγα σθένος καρδίη, 2, 451. 14, 151. 2) *power, might,* 16, 542; *force* esply in periphrasis with gen. son (like βίη): σθένος Ἑκ might of Hector, i. e. the migh 9, 351; Ἰδομενῆος, 13, 248.

σίαλος, ὁ, prop. *fat, fattened* λος, a fat swine, 9, 208. Od. 1 Subst. *a fat hog,* Il. 21, 363.

σιγαλόεις, εσσα, εν. poet. (ἀ λος), (nitidus,) *shining, white, right, splendid* ('magnificent, c 1) Spoken of costly variegat broidered clothing, χιτών, εἵμα δέσματα, Il. and Od. 2) Οἱ horses, polished and perhap with metal, Il. 5, 226. Od. Spoken of household furnitu the dwelling, Od. 5, 86. 16, 44

significations, as *tender. soft, covered with foam*, are not proved.)

σῑγάω (σιγή), *to be silent, to be still*, only the imperat. σίγα, 14, 90. Od. 14, 493; σιγᾶν, h. Merc. 93.

σιγή, ἡ (σίζω), *silence*, only σιγῇ, dat. as adv. *in silence, still, quietly*. σιγῇ ἐφ' ὑμείων, *still before you*, 7, 195. σιγῇ νῦν, Od. 15, 391 (false reading σιγὴ νῦν).

σιδήρειος, η, ον, poet. for σιδήρεος, 7, 141. 8, 15, etc.

σιδήρεος, η, ον (σίδηρος), 1) *of iron, iron*, κορύνη, δέσματα; ὀρυμαγδός, the iron tumult, i. e. of iron arms, 17, 424; οὐρανός, the iron heaven, like χάλκεος, because the ancients conceived of it as made of iron. Od 15, 329. 17, 565; or, more correctly, in a metaph. sense. 2) Trop. *hard as iron, firm, strong*; θυμός, an iron mind, i. e. inexorable, Il. 22, 357; thus ἦτορ, κραδίη. σοίγε σιδήρεα, πάντα τέτυκται, to thee every thing is iron, Od. 12, 280. σιδ. πυρὸς μένος, the iron, i. e. the unwasting strength of fire, Il. 23, 177. (The forms with ει or ε change with the necessity of the metre.)

σίδηρος, ὁ, 1) *iron*; this metal is often mentioned in Homer; he calls it πολιός, αἴθων, ἰόεις; this last epithet, 'violet-coloured,' seems to indicate iron hardened to steel and become blue; also the method of hardening iron by immersing it in water was known to Hom., Od. 9, 391; as an image of hardness, Il. 4, 510. Od. 19, 211. 2) Metonym. *every thing made of iron, arms, furniture*, hence πολύμηκτος, Il. 6, 48; and often.

Σιδονίηθεν, adv. *from Sidon*, 6, 291.

Σιδόνιος, η, ον (Σιδών), Ep. for Σιδώνιος, *Sidonian, of Sidon*, 6, 289; from which, 1) ἡ Σιδονίη, the district of Sidonia in Phœnicia, or the entire coast of the Phœnicians, with the chief town, Sidon, Od. 13, 285. 2) ὁ Σιδόνιος, a Sidonian, Od. 4, 84. 618.

Σιδών, ῶνος, ἡ, the famous capital of the Phœnicians, situated on the sea, with a double port, now *Seida*, Od. 15, 425.

Σιδών, όνος. a Sidonian, an inhabitant of the city of Sidon, 23, 743.

σίζω, a word formed to imitate the sound; *to hiss*, primar. the sound of red-hot bodies immersed in water, hence also spoken of the eye of the Cyclops in which Odysseus (Ulysses) twisted the burning stake; only imperf. Od. 9, 394

Σικανίη, ἡ, the original name of the island of *Sicelia*, which it received from the Sicani, according to Thucyd. 6, 2. Diodor. 5, 6. When, at a later period, the Sicani were pressed by the Siceli immigrating from Italy, and confined to the region about Agragas, the latter was called Sicania, and the whole island Sicelia, Od. 24, 307.

Σικελός, ή, όν, *Sicelian* or *Sicilian*, elsewhere Θρινακίη. γυνὴ Σικελή, Od. 24, 211. 366. 389. Subst. οἱ Σικελοί, the *Siceli*, according to Thuc. 6, 2, an Italian

people, who, being pressed by the Pelasgi, emigrated to Italy, and first settled near Catana. Hence they dwelt on the eastern coast of the island, Od. 20, 383.

Σικυών, ῶνος, ὁ and ἡ, a town in the country Sicyonia, in the Peloponnesus, at an earlier day Αἰγιαλοί and Μηκώνη, famed for its traffic, and later the chief seat of Grecian art; now *Vasilika*, 2, 572.

Σιμόεις, εντος, ὁ, *Simois*, a small river in Troas, which rises in Ida, and flows north from the city of Troy and unites in the Trojan plain with the Scamander; now *Simas*, 4, 475. 5, 774. cf. Τρωϊκός. 2) the river-god of the Simois, 20, 53.

Σιμοείσιος, ὁ, son of the Trojan Anthemion, slain by Ajax, 4, 474, seq.

σίνομαι, depon. mid. only pres. and imperf. iterat. form σινέσκοντο, Od. 6, 6. 1) Prop. *to carry off, to plunder*, with accus. ἑταίρους τινί, Od. 12, 114. b) *to attack in order to plunder, to rob*, τινά, Od. 6, 6; spoken of herds, Od. 11, 112. 2) Generally, *to hurt, to injure, to harm*. αἰδὼς ἄνδρας σίνεται, shame injures men, Il. 24, 45.

σίντης, ὁ, poet. (σίνομαι), a *robber, a murderer*, as adj. *plundering, ravaging*, λῖς, λύκος, *11, 481. 16, 353. 20, 165.

Σίντιες, οἱ (=σίνται, robbers), *the Sinties*, the earliest inhabitants of the island of Lemnos, who received Hêphæstus when hurled down by Zeus, 1, 594. Od. 8, 294.

Σίπυλος, ὁ (Dor. for Θεόπυλος), a branch of mount Tmôlus, on the borders of Lydia and Phrygia, now *Mimas*, 24, 615.

Σίσυφος, ὁ (Æol. for σόφος). son of Æolus and Enarêtê, husband of Meropê, father of Glaucus, founder of Ephŷra or Corinth, noted for his cunning and propensity to robbery, 6, 153. He was doomed to roll a stone up a mountain in the under world, which always rolled back, because he betrayed to Asôpus that Zeus had seized his daughter, or because he had betrayed the secrets of the gods in general to men, Od. 11, 593. Apd. 1, 9, 3.

σιτέω (σῖτος), imperf. mid. σιτέσκοντο; act. *to give to eat, to feed*. Mid. *to give oneself food, to eat, to feed upon*, Od. 24, 209.

σῖτος, ὁ, only sing, *wheat*, generally, *grain*, and esply 1) *flour, bread*, prepared from it; in opposition to flesh. σῖτος καὶ κρέα, Od. 9, 9. 12, 19. 2) Generally, *food, victuals, nourishment*, hence often σῖτος καὶ οἶνος, Il. 9, 706. Od. 3, 479. σῖτος ἠδὲ ποτής, Il. 19, 306. Od. 9, 87. (It never appears as neut. in Hom.; but clearly as masc., Od. 13, 244. 16, 83. 17, 533.)

σιτοφάγος, ον (φαγεῖν), *eating grain or bread*, Od. 9, 191 Batr. 244.

σιφλόω (σιφλός [πόδα σιφλός = πηρός, Ap. Rhod. 1, 204]), aor. optat. σιφλώσειεν, prop. *to deform*, hence generally *to bring into disgrace, to destroy, to ruin,* τινά, 14, 142 † [al., less well, *to bring to shame.*]

σιωπάω (σιωπή), aor. optat. σιωπήσειαν, infin. σιωπῆσαι, *to be silent, to be still,* 2, 280. 23, 560. Od. 17, 513.

σιωπή, ή, *silence, stillness,* Hom. only dat. as adv. σιωπῆ, *in silence, still,* 6, 404. Od. 1, 325. ἀκὴν ἐγένοντο σιωπῇ, they were entirely still, Il. 3, 95. Od. 7, 154. σιω. ἐπινεύειν, to give the nod in silence, Il. 9, 616; and often.

σκάζω (akin to σκαίρω), *to limp, to hobble,* 19, 47; ἐκ πολέμου, 11, 811. Batr. 251.

Σκαιαί, αἱ, πύλαι, *the Scæan gate,* also called *the Dardanian* (Δαρδάνιαι); it was upon the west side of the city of Troy, hence the name *west gate* (σκαιός); it was the main gate, and led to the Grecian camp. From its turret were to be seen the oak, the watch-station, the fig-tree, and the monument of Ilus, 3, 145. 6, 237. 11, 170. cf. Τρωϊκὸν πεδίον.

σκαιός, ή, όν, *left.* ἡ σκαιή, sc. χείρ, the left hand; hence σκαιῇ, with the left, 1, 501. 16, 734. 2) *western,* perhaps σκαιὸν ῥίον, Od. 3, 295.

σκαίρω (akin to σκάζω), *to leap, to spring,* Od. 10, 412; ποσί, *to dance,* Il. 18, 572. h. 31, 18.

*σκαλμός, ὁ, *the pin,* a block upon the ship, upon which the oar rests, h. 6, 42.

Σκαμάνδριος, η, ον, *Scamandrian,* on the Scamander. τὸ Σκαμάνδριον πεδίον, the Scamandrian plain, = τὸ Τρωϊκὸν πεδίον, q. v., 2, 465; also λειμὼν Σκαμάνδριος, 2, 467. 2) Subst. name of Astyănax, which his father gave him, 6, 402; see Ἀστυάναξ. b) son of Strophius, a Trojan, 5, 49, seq.

Σκάμανδρος, ὁ (σκ never forms posit., cf. Thiersch, § 146. 8), *Scamander,* a river in Troas, called by the gods *Xanthus;* it rises, according to 22, 147, seq., near the city of Troy, from two fountains, of which the one had cold, the other warm water; it then flows south-west from the city through the plain, unites with the Simoeis, 5, 774, and falls into the Hellespont somewhat north of Sigeum, 21, 125. Il. 12, 21 seems to clash with the origin of the Scamander in 22, 147, according to which passage it rises upon Ida, as says also Strabo XIII. p. 602. [Lechevalier, and others maintain that both sources still exist, but that the *steam* of the warm one is only visible in winter.] Now the river is called *Mendere-Su.* 2) the river-god *Xanthus.* His contest with Achilles is found 20, 74. 21, 136, seq.

Σκάνδεια, ἡ, a harbour on the southern coast of the island Cythēra, now *Cerigo,* 10, 268.

*σκάπτω, fut. ψω, *to dig,* φυτά, h. Merc. 90, 207.

*σκαπτήρ, ῆρος, ὁ (σκάπτω), *a digger,* Fr. 2.

Σκάρφη, ἡ (Σκάρφεια, Strab.), a small town in Locris, not far from Thermopy-

læ, 2, 532. (According to St already, 400 years before C stroyed by a earthquake.)

σκαφίς, ίδος, ἡ (σκάπτω), a s for preserving any thing, *a b* Od. 9. 123.†

σκεδάννυμι, aor. 1 ἐσκέδασα δασα, only aor. as pres. the *to scatter,* to *drive apart* or *l* accus. λαόν, 19, 171. 23, 162 649. Od. 13, 352. ἀχλὺν ἀπ' ὀφ scatter the darkness from any Il. 20, 341; metaph. αἷμα, to 7, 330.

σκέδασις, ιος, ἡ (σκεδάννυμι) *scattering, dispersion,* *Od. 1, 1

σκέλλω (or σκελέω), Ep. aor. sing. σκήλειε, *to dry, to parch,* χρόα, 23. 191.†

σκέλος, εος, τό, in the broa the entire leg from the hip to in the narrower, *the shank* (t the calf; hence πρυμνὸν σκέλ (Schol. γαστροκνημίαν), 16, 31

σκέπαρνον, τό (prob. from c *double-edged axe,* for hewing *carpenter's axe* [used also for *Od. 5, 237. 9, 391.

σκέπας, αος, τό (σκεπάω), *covering, a shelter;* ἀνέμοιο, from the wind, *Od. 5, 443. 6.

σκεπάω, poet. (σκέπας), 3 σκεπόωσι, Ep. for σκεπῶσι, *protect;* spoken of the coa κῦμα ἀνέμων. the wave or th the winds, Od. 13, 99.†

σκέπτομαι, depon. mid. aoι ψάμην, to look at a distanc hand held over the eyes, *to lo to look around,* ἔς τι; μετά τ 247; with αἴ κεν, Il. 17, 652; ἐ h. Cer. 245. 2) Trans. *to c contemplate,* with accus. ὄϊστ 16, 361. h. Merc. 360.

*σκευάζω (σκεῦος), *to prepa ready:* absol. *to arrange dome κατ' οἶκον, in the house, h. M

σκηπάνιον, τό (σκῆπτω), = c *staff, a sceptre,* the ensign dignity; of Poseidōn, 13, 59; *24, 247.

σκηπτοῦχος (σκῆπτρον, ἔχ *bearing,* holding the sceptr kings, 2, 86. Od. 5, 9.

σκῆπτρον, τό (σκῆπτω), 1 *cane* to support oneself up 437. 14, 31. 17, 199. 2) Es *reign's sceptre, the sceptre,* a out a metallic point, and, acc 1, 246, adorned with golden st an ensign of imperial digni Kings early bore it, 1, 234. also priests and prophets, I 11, 91; heralds, Il. 7, 277; 18, 505. It was generally a public action; whoever spok sembly was obliged to hold in his hand, and received herald, 23, 568. Od. 2, 37; i oath the sceptre was raised,

10. 327. 3) **Metaph.** *the royal power, the imperial dignity*, 6, 259. σκῆπτρον καὶ θέμιστες, marks the union of the imperial and judicial power, 2, 206. 9, 99.

σκῆπτω, act., a false reading, '17, 437, from ἐπισκίμπτειν; now only mid. *to support oneself, to lean* upon a staff, spoken of old men and beggars, Od. 17, 203. 338; with dat. καί μιν ὀΐω αὐτῷ ·ἄκοντι) σκηπτόμενον· κατίμεν δόμον ᾿Αΐδος εἴσω, and I think that he will descend to the abode of Hades, supporting himself on the spear [will 'lean on it in his descent to Hell,' Cp.], sarcastic for 'he will die pierced through by my spear,' Il. 14, 457.

σκηρίπτω (σκήπτω), only mid. *to support oneself, to lean upon*, Od. 17, 196; spoken of Sisyphus rolling the stone, χερσίν τε ποσίν τε, to resist or push against it with hands and feet [to shove it, Cp.], *Od. 11, 595.

σκιάζω, poet. form σκιάω, aor. subj. σκιάσῃ, *to shade* or *overshadow, to envelope with shade, to veil*, with accus. of the night, ἄρουραν, 21, 232.†

σκιάω, poet. σκιάζω, only mid. *to become shady, to be darkened*, σκιόωντο, Ep. for ἐσκιῶντο πᾶσαι ἀγυιαί, all the streets were *dark*, *Od. 2, 388. 3, 487.

σκίδναμαι, mid. poet. a form of σκεδάννυμι, in the pres. and imperf. *to scatter, to separate*, spoken of men: κατὰ κλισίας, 1, 487; ἐπὶ ἔργα, Od. 2, 252; πρὸς δώματα, Od. 2, 258; ἐπὶ νῆα, Il. 19, 277; with infin. 24, 2; spoken of the foam of the sea: ὑψόσε, to dash on high, 11, 308; of dust: ὑπὸ νεφέων, to whirl upward, 16, 375; of a fountain: ἣ ἀνὰ κῆπον σκίδναται, is distributed through the garden, Od. 7, 130.

σκιερός, ή, όν, poet. (σκιή), *shadowy, shady, dark*, νέμος, 11, 480; ἄλσος, Od. 20, 278.

σκιή, ἡ, Ion. for σκιά, *a shadow, a shade*, spoken of the souls in Hades, *Od. 10, 495. 11, 207. h. Cer. 100.

σκιόεις, εσσα, εν, poet. (σκιά) *shady, shaded*, i. e. by trees, ὄρεα, 1, 157; *dark, gloomy*, μέγαρα, Od. 1, 365. 4, 768. (There were no windows in the hall, and it received light through the door; or, according to Eustath., because it protected from the heat.) νέφεα, Il. 5, 525. Od. 8, 374.

σκιρτάω, optat. pres. σκιρτῷεν, aor. 1 infin. σκιρτῆσαι, Batr. 60; *to leap, to spring*, ἐπὶ ἄρουραν, upon the earth, *20, 226; and v. 228, ἐπὶ νῶτα θαλάσσης.

σκολιός, ή, όν, *crooked, curved, tortuous, oblique*: metaph. σκολιὰς κρίνειν θέμιστας, to give perverse judgements, 16, 387.†

σκόλοψ, οπος, ὁ (from κόλος), a body having a sharp point, *a spit*, 18, 177. 2) Esply *a stake, a pale* for fortifying the walls of towns and encampments, 8, 343. 15, 1. Od. 7, 45.

σκόπελος, ὁ (σκοπός, prop. = σκοπιή), *a mountain peak, a rock, a cliff*, 2, 396; often Od. 12, 73. 95, 101.

σκοπιάζω (σκοπιά), prop. *to look abroad from a lofty place; generally, to spy, to watch, to observe*, 14, 58. Od. 10, 260. 2) Trans. *to spy out, to explore*, τινά, Il. 10, 40.

σκοπιή, ἡ, Ion. for σκοπιά (σκοπός), any elevated place from which observations can be taken, *a watch-station*, in Hom. always *a hill-top* [' a rocky point,' Cp.], 4, 275. Od. 4, 524; esply *a place* near Troy, Il. 22, 145. 2) *the act of spying*, observation, Od. 8, 302. h. Merc. 99.

σκοπός, ὁ (σκέπτομαι), 1) *a looker-out*, who from an elevated position surveys the region, *a watch*, Od. 4, 524; spoken of Helios, h. Cer. 63; also, *a scout*, = ἐπίσκοπος, Il. 10, 324. 526. 561; generally, *an overseer*, 23, 359; also *a female superintendent*, δμωάων, Od. 22, 396; in a bad sense, *a lier in wait*, Od. 22, 156. 2) In the Od. *the point* to which one looks, Od. 22, 6; metaph. *aim, purpose*. ἀπὸ σκοποῦ, contrary to the design, Od. 11, 344.

σκότιος, η, ον (σκότος), *dark, gloomy*; metaph. *secret, clandestine*, 6, 23.†

σκοτομήνιος, ον (μήνη), *in which the moon is obscured, dark, moonless*, νύξ, Od. 14, 457.†

σκότος, ὁ (akin to σκιά), *darkness, obscurity*, Od. 19, 389; esply metaph. *the darkness of death*, often spoken of the dying, τὸν δὲ σκότος ὄσσε κάλυψεν, Il. 4, 461. h. Ap. 370. In the Il. always in the metaph. signif.; in the Od. only once in the literal.

σκυδμαίνω, poet. form of σκύζομαι, Ep. infin. σκυδμαινέμεν, *to be angry at*, τινί, 24, 592.†

σκύζομαι, depon. only pres. and imperf. poet. (from κύων, to snarl like a dog), *to mutter, to be angry, to be displeased*, absol. 8, 483; τινί, at any one, 4, 23. 8, 460. Od. 23, 209.

σκύλαξ, ακος, ὁ, ἡ (κεύω, κύων), a young animal, esply *a young dog, whelp, puppy*, *Od. 9, 289. 12, 86. 20, 14; in Hom. always fem.

Σκύλλα, ἡ, mly in Hom. Σκύλλη (the nom. Σκύλλα, only Od. 12, 235; *that tears in pieces*, from σκύλλω), a sea-monster of the Italian coast in the Sicilian straits, opposite Charybdis, dwelling in a cavern, Od. 12, 85, seq. She is called the daughter of Crataïs, Od. 12, 124 (according to Ap. Rh. 4, 828, daughter of Phorcys and Hecatē). She had six dragon throats and twelve sharp claws, and her body was surrounded with half-projecting dogs and other horrible objects. She tore in pieces every living thing which approached her. She robbed Odysseus (Ulysses) of six of his companions. According to mythology, she was afterwards changed into a rock. This rock, named Scyllæum, lies opposite the promontory of Pelōrum, on whose east side there lies at this day a small town Scilla or Sciglio.

σκύμνος, ὁ (κύω), like σκύλαξ, *a young*

animal; esply the young of the lion, (lion's) whelp, 18, 319.†

Σκῦρος, ἡ, an island of the Ægean sea, north-west of Chios, with a town of the same name, birth-place of Neoptolemus, now Skyro, 9, 668. Od. 11, 509; from which Σκύροθεν, from Scyros, Il. 19, 332.

σκῦτος, εος, τό (cutis), the skin; esply dressed skin, leather, Od. 14, 34.†

σκυτοτόμος, ὁ (σκῦτος, τέμνω), prop. cutting leather; hence, a worker in leather [often = armourer, fm the use made of leather in the ancient shields, &c.], 7, 221.†

σκύφος, ὁ, (akin to κυφός), a goblet, a cup, Od. 14, 112.† (Aristoph. Byz. read σκύφος as neut.)

σκώληξ, ηκος, ὁ, an earth-worm, lumbricus, 13, 654.†

σκῶλος, ὁ = σκόλοψ, a pointed stake, or, according to Etym. Mag., a kind of thorn, 13, 564.†

Σκῶλος, ἡ, a village of the Theban dominions in Bœotia, 2, 497.

σκώψ, σκωπός, ὁ, an owl, the woodowl, strix aluco, Linn. According to Schneider ad Arist. H. A. 9, 19. 11, the small horned-owl, strix scops, Linn., Od. 5, 66.† (Either from σκέπτομαι, on account of its staring eyes, or from σκώπτω, from its droll form.)

σμαραγέω (akin to μαράσσω), aor. subj. σμαραγήσῃ, to resound, to roar. spoken of the sea and of thunder, 2, 210. 21, 199; spoken of the meadow, which resounded with the cry of the cranes, *2, 463.

*Σμάραγος, ὁ, the blusterer, a divinity, Ep. 14, 9.

σμερδαλέος, έη, έον, lengthened from σμερδνός, ή, όν, poet. frightful, fearful, terrific, odious, horrible, spoken esply of the appearance, δράκων, 2, 309. Od. 6, 137; κεφαλή. Od. 12, 91; hence spoken of brass and of weapons: χαλκός, αἰγίς, σάκος, Il. 12, 464. 20, 260. 21, 401. Od. 11, 609; the neut. sing. and plur. σμερδαλέον, σμερδαλέα, as adv. once of the look, δέδορκεν, 22, 95; elsewhere spoken with verbs of sound, βοᾶν, κοναβίζειν, κτυπεῖν, τινάσσεσθαι, 15, 609.

σμερδνός, ή, όν = σμερδαλέος, and much more rarely used; Γοργείη κεφαλῆς, 5, 742; the neut. σμερδνόν, as adv. 15, 687. h. 31, 9.

σμήχω, Ep. Ion. for σμάω, to wipe off, to rub off, χνόον ἐκ κεφαλῆς, Od. 6, 226.†

σμικρός, ή, όν. Att. for μικρός, small; in H. on account of the metre, 17, 757. h. Ven. 115.

Σμινθεύς, ῆος, ὁ, epith. of Apollo, according to Aristarch. from Σμίνθη, a town in Troas, because he had a temple there, or from the Æolic σμίνθος, a mouse, because these as well as other animals living under the earth, were a symbol of prophecy. 1, 39. According to other critics, as Apion, Eustath., it signifies, mouse-killer, because he once freed one of the priests from a plague

of mice in Chrysa, or becau cated to the Teucri, on the Troy, the place of their set mice, Strab. XIII. p. 604.

*Σμύρνη, ἡ, Ion. and Ep. a noted town in Ionia, on the with an excellent harbour, Ep. 4, 6.

σμύχω, poet. aor. ἔσμυξα, any thing by a smothered f down. κατά τε σμύξαι πυρὶ Pass. to be consumed by fire, π

σμῶδιγξ and σμῶδιξ, ιγγος or weal, a tumour, a stripe, blood, nom. σμῶδιξ, 2, 267 σμώδιγγες, *23, 716.

σόη, see σαόω.

σοιο, see σός.

σόλος, ὁ (σέλλω), a mass of for throwing; according to and Apoll. a spherical quoit Cp. an iron clod). Accordir and Tryphon, the same with except that this was always m the σόλος of iron; cf. Valken. de differ. voc. p. 60. *Il. 23, 8

Σόλυμοι, οἱ, the Solymi, nation, in the country of Ly Minor, 6, 184. According to they were neighbours of Æthiopians. According to H they were the original inh Lycia, and according to Str habited the points of the Lycia or Pisidia.

σόος, η, ον, Ep. shortened which is expanded from σό form of ΣΑΟΣ. 1) healthy, 7, 310; spoken of the moon alive, preserved, delivered, ὀλέσθαι, 1, 117. 5, 331; unhu 382. Od. 13, 364.

σορός, ὁ (akin with σωρός), preserving the bones of the d 23, 91.†

σός, ή, όν (σύ), Ep. gen. σ Od. 15, 511; thy, thine, mly article: with an art. τὸ σὸν 185. 18, 457: the neut. as σοῖσι, with thy friends, Od. form, τεός, ή, όν.)

Σούνιον, τό, the southern tica, with a temple of A Capo Colonni, Od. 3, 278.

σοφίη, ἡ (σοφός), dexterit telligence, wisdom, spoken of tect, 15, 412;† of music, h. 511.

*σοφός, ή, όν. expert, exp telligent, Fr. 1, 3.

σόω, Ep. form from σαόω σόῃς, σόῃ, and σόωσι, see σα

*σπαργανιώτης, ου, ὁ, a ch dling-clothes, h. Merc. 301.

*σπάργανον, τό (σπάργω), clothes, h. Merc. 151. 237.

*σπάργω, fut. ξω, to wrap, τί ἐν φάρεϊ, h. Ap. 121.

Σπάρτη, ἡ, the chief town mon, the residence of Mene

Eurôtas, in a valley almost entirely surrounded by mountains, the ruins now near Magula, see Λακεδαίμων. 2, 582. Od. 1, 93; from which adv. Σπάρτηθεν, from Sparta, Od. 2, 327.

σπάρτον, τό, a rope made of spartum (a kind of broom); generally, a rope, a cable. σπάρτα λέλυνται, Ep. (see Rost, § 100. 4. a. Kühner, § 369.), Il. 2. 135.† ὁ, ἡ σπάρτος is a shrub with tough branches, spartium scoparium, Linn.: genista in Pliny. (The reference is prob. not to the Spanish Spartos; and Varro ad Gell. 17, 3, doubts whether in Hom. the shrub gave the name.)

σπάω, aor. 1 ἔσπασα, aor. 1 mid. ἐσπασάμην, Ep. σπασάμην and with σσ, imperat. σπάσσασθε, partcp. σπασσάμενος. aor. 1 pass. ἐσπάσθην, to draw, to draw out, τι. h. Merc. 85; in tmesis, 5, 859; hence pass. σπασθέντος, sc. ἔγχεος, when the spear was drawn out, 11, 458. 2) Mid. to draw out for oneself, to snatch, ῥῶπας, Od. 10, 166; χεῖρα ἐκ χειρός τινος, Od. 2, 321. ἄορ παρὰ μηροῦ, to draw the sword from the thigh, Il. 16, 473; φάσγανον, Od. 22, 74; ἐκ σύριγγος ἔγχος, Il. 19, 387.

σπεῖος, see ἔπομαι

σπεῖος, τό, Ep. for σπέος, q. v.

σπεῖρον, τό (σπείρα), prop. cloth for a covering; a cover, a cloth; a robe, a garment, Od. 4, 245. 6, 179; esply linen cloth for shrouding the dead, Od. 2, 102. 19, 147. 2) Generally cloth, a sail = ἱστία, °Od. 6, 269. 5, 318.

σπεῖσαι, σπείσασκε, see σπένδω.

Σπειώ, οῦς, ἡ (from σπέος, a dweller in a cave), daughter of Nêreus and Dôris, 18, 43.

σπένδω, fut. σπείσω, aor. ἔσπεισα, Ep. σπεῖσα, 2 sing. subj. pres. σπένδῃσθα, Od. 4, 591; iterat. imperf. σπένδεσκε, Il. 16, 227; aor. σπείσασκε, to sprinkle, to pour out; prop. a word used of sacred rites, since a portion of the wine was poured out in honour of the gods upon the earth, the table or the altar, Lat. libare; mly absol. (make a libation) or with a dat. of the deity to whom the offering is made: Διΐ, to present a drink-offering to Zeus. 6, 259; θεοῖς, Od. 3, 334. 7, 137. b) Sometimes with an accus. of that which is offered: οἶνον, Il. 11, 775. Od. 14, 447; or with dat. ὕδατι, to sprinkle with water, Od. 12, 363. c) With dat. of the vessel: δέπαϊ, to pour out of a cup, Il. 23, 196. Od. 7, 137.

σπέος, τό, Ep. σπεῖος, gen. σπείους, dat. σπῆϊ, 24, 83; accus. σπεῖος, Od. 5, 194; plur. gen. σπείων, h. Ven. 264; dat. σπέσσι, Od. 1, 15; σπήεσσι, Od. 9, 400; a cave, a grotto, a cavern. σπέος appears to be more comprehensive than ἄντρον. cf. h. Merc. 228; and Nitzsch ad Od. 5, 57. [According to Ameis, σπέος is used when speaking of the exterior, and ἄντρον of the interior of a hollow space, cf. Od. 9, 182. 216. Am. Ed.]

σπέρμα, ατος, τό (σπείρω), seed, seed-corn, prop. spoken of plants, h. Cer. 208. 2) Metaph. σπέρμα πυρός, the seed of fire, Od. 5, 490.†

Σπερχειός, ὁ (that hastens, from σπέρχω), Sperchîus, a river in Thessaly, which flows from Mount Tymphrêstus into the Malean gulf, now Agramela, Il. 23, 142. 2) a river-god, father of Menesthius, 16, 174.

σπέρχω, poet. only pres. and imperf. Act. prop. trans. to drive on, to press, once intrans. like the mid. ὅθ᾽ ὑπ᾽ ἀνέμων σπέρχωσιν ἄελλαι, when the storms hasten on before the winds, 13, 334. h. 33, 7. Mid. to move oneself violently, i. e. to hasten, to run, to rush, spoken of men, with infin., 19, 317; absol. often in the partcp. hastening, fleet, 11, 110. Od. 9, 101; ἐρετμοῖς, to hasten with oars, i. e. to row swiftly, Od. 13, 22; spoken of a ship, to hasten, Od, 13, 115; of storms, Od. 3, 283.

σπέσθαι, see ἔπομαι.

σπεύδω, aor. ἔσπευσα, from this subj. σπεύσομεν for σπεύσωμεν, 17, 121; fut. mid. σπεύσομαι, 18, 402; mly in partcp. pres. 1) Intrans. to hasten, to speed, to make haste, often absol. ἐς μάχην, 4, 225; ὑπό τινος, before any one, 11, 119; εἰς τινα, 15, 402; with partcp., Od. 9, 250. b) to take pains, to strive, περὶ Πατρόκλοιο θανόντος, about the fallen Patroclus, i. e. to fight about him, Il. 17, 121. 2) Trans. with accus. to hasten any thing, to accelerate, to urge zealously, τι, 13, 237; γάμον, Od. 19, 137. (Of the mid. only the fut.)

σπῆϊ, σπήεσσι, see σπέος.

σπιδής, ές (σπίζω), extended, wide. διὰ σπιδέος πεδίοιο, through the wide plain, 11, 754;† the reading of Zenodotus; others read incorrectly δι᾽ ἀσπιδέος π., assuming an adj. ἀσπιδής, similar to a shield. According to Apoll. Etym. Mag. σπιδής is from σπίζω = ἐκτείνω, and accord. to the Gramm. Æschylus and Antimachus used σπίδιος and σπιδόθεν for μακρός, μακρόθεν.

σπιλάς, άδος, ἡ, a rocky cliff, a rock in the sea, °Od. 3. 298. 5, 401.

°σπινθαρίς, ίδος, ἡ = σπινθήρ, h. Ap. 442

σπινθήρ, ῆρος, ὁ, a spark, 4, 77.†

σπλάγχνον, τό, only in the plur., τὰ σπλάγχνα, entrails, esply the more important, the heart, liver, and lungs. These were immediately cut out after the victim was slain, roasted and eaten, whilst the offering was burning. Afterwards followed the sacrificial feast, 1, 464. Od. 3, 9. 40, 461.

σπόγγος, ὁ, Att. σφόγγος, a spunge (fungus), for cleaning the hands, 18, 414; the table and chairs, Od. 1, 111.

σποδιή, ἡ, Ion. for σποδιά, a heap of ashes, generally = σποδός, ashes, Od. 5, 488.†

σποδός, ἡ, ashes, Od. 9, 375.† h. Merc. 258. (Akin to σβέννυμι.)

σπονδή, ἡ (σπένδω), a libation, a drink-

Σεληπιάδης. ον, ὁ, son of Selêpius = Evênus, 2, 693.

σκεδάννῡμι, aor. 1 ἐσκέδασα,
δασα, only aor. as pres. the p
to scatter, to drive apart or le
accus. λαόν, 19, 171. 23, 162;
649. Od. 13, 352. ἀχλὺν ἀπ' ὀφθ
scatter the darkness from any c
Il. 20, 341; metaph. αἷμα, to sl
7, 330.

σκηπτοῦχος (σκῆπτρον, ἔχι
bearing, holding the sceptre
kings, 2, 86. Od. 5, 9.

σμύχω, poet. aor. ἔσμυξα, to any thing by a smothered fire down. κατά τε σμύξαι πυρὶ νῆ[...] Pass. *to be consumed by fire*, πυρί[...]

σόος, η, ον, Ep. shortened f[...] which is expanded from σῶς[...] form of ΣΑΟΣ. 1) *healthy, so[...] 7, 310; spoken of the moon. [...] *alive, preserved, delivered*, a [...] ὀλέσθαι, 1, 117. 5, 331; *unhur[...] 382. Od. 13, 364.

σός, ή, όν (σύ), Ep. gen. σοῦ[...] Od. 15, 511; *thy, thine*, mly v[...] article: with an art. τὸ σὸν γ[...] 185. 18, 457: the neut. as [...] σοῖσι, with thy friends, Od. 2, [...] form, τεός, ή, όν.

offering (libatio), of unmixed wine, which was poured out in honour of the gods at feasts and esply in making treaties; hence in the plur. σπονδαί, a solemn *league*, *a covenant*, 2. 341. 4, 159.

*σπουδαίος, η, ον (σπουδή), *hasty, zealous, important*. χρῆμα, h. Merc. 332.

σπουδή, ἡ (σπεύδω), 1) *haste, zeal, care, diligence*, ἄτερ σπουδῆς, without care, Od. 21, 409. 2) *earnestness*. ἀπὸ σπουδῆς, in earnest. Il. 7, 359. 12, 235. 3) Esply often in the dat. σπουδῇ, as adv. *in haste*, Od. 13, 279. 15, 209. b) With zeal, with pains; hence, *scarcely, with great difficulty*, Il. 2, 99. 11, 562. Od. 3, 297. 24, 119.

σταδίη, ἡ, see στάδιος.

στάδιος, η, ον (ἵστημι), *standing, firm*. ἡ σταδίη ὑσμίνη, a standing-fight, *a close battle*, i. e. a pitched-battle, in which man and man fought with spears or swords, or hand to hand, in distinction from a skirmish, cf. αὐτοσταδίη, 13, 314. 713; also ἐν σταδίῃ alone: in close conflict, *7, 241. 13, 514.

στάζω, aor. Ep. στάξα, *to drop, to trickle*; τινί τι κατὰ ῥινῶν, ἐν στήθεσσι, *19, 39. 348. 354. Batr. 232.

στάθμη, ἡ (ἵστημι), *a marking-cord, a carpenter's cord*, for making a straight line, or a *level* or *line*, for making an even surface, 15, 410; δόρυ ἐπὶ στάθμην ἰθύνειν, to hew the wood straight by the line, Od. 5, 245. 17, 341. 23, 197 [squaring it by line, Cp.].

σταθμόνδε, adv. *into the pen*, into the stall, Od. 9, 451.†

σταθμός, ὁ (ἵστημι), 1) a place of stopping for men and beasts; *a station, a stall, a stable, a pen, an enclosure*, 2, 470. 5, 140. Od. 16, 45. 2) *a post, a pillar*, often in the Od., 1, 333. 6, 19. 3) *a weight* in the scales, Il. 12, 434.

στάμεν, στάμεναι, Ep. for στῆναι.

σταμίν, ῖνος, ἡ (ἵστημι), *that stands upright*, the ribs or side-timbers of a ship, which rise from the keel; ἴκρια ἀραρὼν θαμέσι σταμίνεσσι, 'fitting the *deck* or *deck-planks* (ἴκρια, vid.) to the numerous ribs,' V., Od. 5, 252.† Others, as Eustath., understand by it the *cross-pieces*, the *side-boards*, by which the upright timbers were connected, see Nitzsch ad loc. (ι short from Ep. licence.)

στάν, see ἵστημι.

στάξ, Ep. for ἔσταξε, see στάζω.

στάς, see ἵστημι.

*στάσις, ιος, ἡ (ἵστημι), *sedition, strife, contention*, Batr. 135.

στατός, ή, όν (verbal adj. from ἵστημι), *placed, standing*; ἵππος, a horse standing in the stall, *6, 506. 15, 263.

σταυρός, ὁ (ἵστημι), *a stake, a pale*, 24, 453. Od. 14. 11.

σταφυλή, ἡ, the *wine-grape, the vine*, a shoot of a vine, 18, 561. Od. 7, 120. 9, 358. (In Od. 7, 120. 121. Franke ad Callim. p. 167, as also Bothe, rejects the words: μῆλον δ' ἐπὶ—σταφυλή.)

σταφύλη, ἡ, *the plummet*, in the car-

penter's *level*; then, *a plumb-line* ἵπποι σταφύλῃ ἐπὶ νῶτον ἐΐσαι (ἶ equal on the back by the level (actly matched in height), 2, 765.

στάχυς, υος, ἡ, Ep. also ἄστ ear of grain, 23, 598.†

ΣΤΑΩ, ground form of ἵστημι.

στέαρ, ατος, τό (ἵστημι), *conge tallow*, *Od. 21, 178. 183. (στέα be read as a dissyllable.)

στείβω, only pres. and imperf. *to trample, to tread in pieces*, wi spoken of horses, νέκυας, 11, 499; εἵματα ἐν βόθροισι, to trea in a cistern in order to cleanse tl 6, 92.

στεῖλα, Ep. for ἔστειλα, see σ

στειλειή, ἡ (στέλλω), *the hole* an axe for inserting the helve 422.†

στειλειόν, τό (στέλλω), *the h* an axe, Od. 5, 236.†

στεῖνος, εος, τό, poet. (στε *narrowness, a narrow space*, 8 66. 15, 426. Od. 22, 460. στε a narrow way, a narrow pass, I 2) Metaph. *pressure, distress*, ti Ap. 533.

στείνω, Ep. for στένω (στ *make narrow, to contract*; in pass. στείνομαι, *to become nar* tracted, θυρετρὰ φεύγοντι στεί gate is too narrow to one flyin 386; λαοὶ στείνοντο, the peo contracted, i. e. pressed togeth 34; hence, *a) to be oppressed*, τινί, by any thing, νεκύεσσιν, λαχνῇ, Od. 9, 445. b) *to be f* oneself, ἀρνῶν, Od. 9, 219.

στεινωπός, όν, Ion. for (στενός, ὤψ), *narrow, contr* στειν. ὁδός, a narrow way, a na a gorge, 7, 143. 23, 416; and ὁδός, Od. 12, 234.

στείομεν, Ep. for στῶμεν, see

στείρη, ἡ, Ion. for στεῖρα (στ main timber in the bottom of keel, 1, 482. Od. 2, 228.

στεῖρος, η, ον, Ion. form o prop. *stiff, hard*; hence me *fruitful*, unsuitable for cultiv *rilis*). βοῦς στεῖρη, *Od. 10, 5 20, 186.

στείχω, poet. aor. 2 ἔστιχο *enter in ranks, to march in*, 258; generally, *to go, to proceed* ἐς πόλεμον, to go to the war, 2 ἄστυ, Od. 7, 72; spoken of the 11, 17.

στέλλω, fut. στελέω, Ep. aor. ἔστειλα, Ep. στεῖλα, m λάμην, 1) *to place*; esply to a becoming condition, with accu to arrange the companions, 4, to prepare, to fit out, νῆα, Od. 248. 2) *to send*, τινὰ ἐς μάχη 325; ἀγγελίην ἐπί, to send up bassy, 4, 384. 3) *to take in*, ι ἱστία, Od. 3, 11. 16, 353. I either to take down or *to furl* here the latter, because ἀείραντες follows; the sails were drawn up to the sail-yard and tied fast to it. They were often let down with the yard. Mid. *to place oneself*, i. e. to prepare oneself, to fit oneself, Il. 23, 285. 2) *to draw in*, ἱστία (with reference to the subject [*vela contrahere*, Db.]), 1, 433.

στέμμα, ατος, τό (στέφω), prop. *a garland*; and plur. στέμμα Ἀπόλλωνος, the garland or wreath (laurel-wreath) of Apollo. According to Eustath. and the best critics, a garland, sacred to Apollo, wound with woollen cords; this the priest bears, as a suppliant, upon his staff, 1, 14. 28. Heyne incorrectly rejects this explanation, and understands by it, 'the holy priestly fillet' (*infula*), h. in Ap. 179.

στενάχεσχ' for στενάχεσκε, see στενάχω.

στεναχίζω, poet. form = στενάζω, *to sigh, to groan*, 19, 304. Od. 1, 243. Mid. with like signif., Il. 7, 95; metaph. spoken of the earth; ὑπὸ ποσσὶ στεναχίζετο γαῖα. the earth resounded, groaned under their feet, 2, 84. (Only pres. and imperf. The form στοναχίζω is rejected by Wolf, after the Cod. Ven., cf. Buttm. Lex. s. v., who defends it.)

στενάχω, poet. form of στενάζω; iterat. imperf. στενάχεσκε, only pres. and imperf. 1) *to sigh, to groan*, spoken of men, 8, 334. 13, 423; of beasts, *to pant*, 16, 393. 489. b) Metaph. spoken of the sea and of rivers: *to resound, to roar*, 16, 391. Od. 4, 516; *to bemoan, to bewail*, τινά, Il. 19, 392. Mid. = act. intrans. 19, 301; and trans., Od. 9, 467.

Στέντωρ, ορος, ὁ, a herald of the Greeks before Troy, who could cry as loud as fifty others; according to the Schol. an Arcadian, who contended with Herês in shouting and lost his life, 5, 785.

στένω, Ion. στείνω, only pres. and imperf. for the most part poet. to make narrow, to contract; then, *to sigh, to groan*. in which signif. H. uses the form στείνω, 10, 16. 18, 33; metaph. spoken of the sea: *to roar, to resound*, 23, 230. Cf. στείνω.

στερεός, ή, όν (ἵστημι), compar. στερεώτερος. 1) *stiff, rigid, hard*, λίθος, σίδηρος. Od. 19, 494; βοέη. Il. 17, 493. 2) Metaph. *hard, severe*, ἔπεα. 12, 267; κραδίη. Od. 23, 103. The adv. στερεῶς, *fast, firmly*, Il. 10, 263. Od. 14, 346; metaph *firmly, severely*, ἀποειπεῖν, Il. 9, 510. h. Ven. 25.

στερέω, aor. 1 infin. στερέσαι, Ep. for στερῆσαι, *to plunder*, τινά τινος, Od. 13, 262.

στέρνον, τό (στερεός), *the breast*, prop. the upper long part of it, 2, 479. 7, 224. Od. 5, 346; also spoken of beasts, Il. 4, 106. 23, 365. Od. 9, 443.

στεροπή, ἡ, poet. = ἀστεροπή (ἀστράπτω), 1) *lightning*, 11, 66. 184. 2) splendour similar to lightning, *a flash, a gleam, a beam, brightness*, spoken of metals, 19, 363. Od. 4, 72.

στεροπηγερέτα, αο, ὁ, Ep. for στεροπηγερέτης, epith. of Zeus, who collects the lightning (ἀγείρω), or according to Apoll. who excites (ἀγείρω) the lightning, *the lightning-sender*, 16, 298.†

(στεῦμαι), poet. akin to ἵσταμαι, only 3 sing. pres. στεῦται, and 3 sing. imperf. στεῦτο, prop. *to stand* in order to begin any thing; hence, 1) to assume the air of being about to do something, to place oneself, *to strive*. στεῦτο διψάων, thirsting he strove [*to drink*; πιέειν, to be borrowed fm the following clause, Fäsi]. Od. 11, 584; according to Eustath. ἵστατο. thirsting he stood. 2) *to promise, to assure, to boast, to threaten*, with infin. fut., Il. 2, 597 3, 83. 9, 241; and infin. aor., Od. 17, 525. According to Eustath. it arose from a contraction of the form στέομαι into στεῦμαι, the resulting diphthong passing into the other persons also, Kühner, § 242. Anm. Thiersch § 223, f.

στεφάνη, ἡ (στέφω), prop. any thing encompassing the upper part of a body; hence a) *a garland, a crown*, as a female head-ornament, 18. 597. b) *a rim, a brim, a border*, of the helmet, 7, 12. 11, 96; also the helmet itself, 10, 30. c) *the brow* of a mountain, *13, 138.

στέφανος, ὁ (στέφω), *a garland, a crown*, h. 6, 42. 2) Generally any thing which encompasses; hence metaph. [spoken of a company or circle of warriors, κύκλος πολεμούντων, Schol.] πάντη στέφανος πολέμοιο δέδηε περί σε, the crown of battle burns every where around thee [War, like a fiery circle, all around Environs thee. Cp.]. *13, 736.†

στεφανόω (στέφανος). perf. pass. ἐστεφάνωμαι, in H. only mid. to encompass a thing as a border, *to wind oneself*. ἣν περὶ πάντη φόβος ἐστεφάνωται, round about which fear wound itself (which fear encompassed), 5, 739. 11, 36. ἀμφὶ δέ μιν νέφος ἐστεφάνωτο. a cloud wound itself about him, enveloped him; 15, 153. περὶ νῆσον πόντος ἐστεφάνωτο, Od. 10, 195. h. Ven. 120. 2) With accus. *to surround, to encompass* any thing τά τ' (τείρεα) οὐρανὸς ἐστεφάνωται, Il. 18, 485; or pass. with which the heaven is crowned. accus. of object with the pass. Cf. Kühner, § 485. Anm. 2. (The act. is not found at all in H.)

στέφω, 1) *to surround, to encompass, to encircle*; τὶ ἀμφί τινι, to put any thing around any man, 18. 205; 2) Metaph. *to adorn, to ornament*; μορφὴν ἔπεσσι, his form with the gift of words [better, *formam addit sermoni*; crowns his discourse with beauty], Od. 8, 170.

στέωμεν, Ep. for στῶμεν, see ἵστημι.

στῆ, Ep. for ἔστη; στήη, Ep. for στῇ. see ἵστημι.

στῆθος, εος, τό (στῆναι, prop. that which projects), Ep. gen. and dat. στήθεσφι, *the breast*, both male and female, in the sing. and plur. 2, 218. 544. 23, 761; also spoken of beasts, 11, 282. 2) Metaph. *the breast* as the seat of the feelings, passions, and thoughts, 3, 68. 6, 51. Od. 2. 304.

στήλη, ἡ (ἵστημι), a column, 13, 437; exply a) a pillar, a buttress for the support of walls, 12, 259. b) a monumental pillar, a grave-stone, 11, 371. 16, 457. Od. 12, 14; and often.

στήμεναι, see ἵστημι.

*στήμων, ονος, ὁ, the warp in the loom, Batr. 83.

στηρίζω (ἵστημι), aor. 1 ἐστήριξα, and Ep. στήριξα, aor. mid. infin. στηρίξασθαι, 3 sing. pluperf. mid. ἐστήρικτο, 1) Trans. to support, to place firmly, to sustain, with accus. ἴριδας ἐν νέφεϊ, 11, 28; κάρη οὐρανῷ, to sustain the head in the clouds, i. e. to extend, 4, 443. 2) to support oneself, to stand firmly, ποσίν, Od. 12, 434; in like manner mid. intrans. πόδεσσιν. to stand firmly with the feet, l . 21, 242. b) With dat. κακὸν κακῷ ἐστήρικτο, evil pressed upon evil, 16, 111. δεκατὸς μεὶς οὐρανῷ ἐστήρικτο, the tenth month ascended the heavens, h. Merc. 11.

στιβαρός, ή, όν (στείβω), compar. στιβαρώτερος, η, ον, prop. firmly trodden; hence pressed, thick, firm, stout, strong, spoken of human limbs and of arms, 3, 335. 5, 400. 746. Od. 8, 187.

στιβαρῶς, adv. thick, firmly, 12, 454.†

στίβη, ἡ (στείβω), prop. condensed vapour), rime, hoar-frost, exply morning frost, *Od. 5, 467. 17, 25.

*στίβος, ὁ (στείβω), a trodden path, a way, a foot-path, h. Merc. 353.

στίλβω, to gleam, to shine, to beam, ἐλαίῳ, with evil, 18, 596; metaph. spoken of the shining of the skin, κάλλεϊ, χάρισιν, 3, 892. Od. 6, 237; ἀπό τινος, h. 31, 11.

στιλπνός, ή, όν, poet. (στίλβω), shining, gleaming, beaming, ἔερσαι, 14, 351.†

ΣΤΙΞ, Ep. in the nom. absol. for the prose στίχος, from which gen. sing. στιχός, and nom. and accus. plur. στίχες and στίχας, a row, a rank, exply a rank in battle, sing. 20, 362; mly plur. στίχες ἀνδρῶν, the ranks of men Il. and Od. κατὰ στίχας, in close ranks, by ranks, also ἐπὶ στίχας, 18, 602.

στιχάομαι, mid. poet. (στίχος), only 3 plur. imperf. ἐστιχόωντο for ἐστιχῶντο, to proceed in a line, generally, to march, to advance, spoken of warriors, εἰς ἀγορήν, 2, 92; ἐς μέσσον, 3, 266; of ships, *2, 516. 602.

Στιχίος, ὁ, leader of the Athenians before Troy, slain by Hector, 13, 195. 15, 329, seq.

*στοιχεῖον, τό (prop. dimin. from στοῖχος), prop. a small pole, a pin. 2) a letter; and as these are the simplest component parts of speech, hence in the plur. 3) στοιχεῖα, the simplest component parts of things, the elements, Batr. 61.

στόμα, ατος, τό, 1) the mouth of animals, the jaws, hence metaph. στόμα πολέμοιο, ὑσμίνης, the jaws of war, of the battle, poet. for the desolating

war, 10, 8. 19, 313. 20, 359. planation of Heyne, 'the first van,' belongs to a later peri verbial, ἀνὰ στόμα ἔχειν, διὰ σ σθαι, to carry in the mouth utter, 14, 91. ἀπὸ στόματος speak out freely, Batr. 77. 2) the opening of rivers, 12, 24. (στ. ἠϊόνος (V. an inlet of the 14, 36. (It was a coast stret into the sea [rather, into t bounded on both sides by pron λαύρης, the termination of t Od. 22, 137. 3) Generally, the spicuous part; hence the face 16, 410. b) Spoken of a sp στόμα. at the point, 15, 389. cers of a crab, Batr. 300.

στόμαχος, ὁ (στόμα). a mou in Hom. the gorge, the throat 17, 47. 19, 266.

στοναχέω, poet. (στοναχή), c aor. στοναχῆσαι, to sigh, to l 124.† cf. Buttm., Lex. p.

στοναχή, ἡ, poet. (στένω), sighing, groaning, a sigh, oft plur. 2, 356. Od. 5, 83.

στοναχίζω, see στεναχίζω.

στονόεις, εσσα, εν, poet. (στ of sighs, i. e. causing many sig lamentable, mournful, κήδεα, βέ Od. 17, 102; ἀοιδή, a dirge, Il

στόνος, ὁ, poet. (στένω), tl sighing, groaning. the rattlin throat of the dying, 4, 445. 10 23, 40.

στορέννυμι, aor. 1 ἐστόρεσα, ρεσα from στρώννυμι, perf. pa μαι, 3 sing. pluperf. pass. ἐστ pres. does not occur), 1) to lay down any thing (sternere); prepare a couch, 9, 621. Pas 158: also δέμνια, τάπητας, Ο 13, 73; ἀνθρακιήν, to spread Il. 9, 213. 2) to make level, passable, prop. spoken of a r πόντον, Od. 3, 158.

Στρατίη, ἡ (appell. στρατιή, a town in Arcadia, in Strabo's stroyed, 2, 606.

Στρατίος, ὁ (appell. στρατιή son of Nestor and Anaxibia. O

στρατός, ὁ (στράω = στορέν gen. στρατόφιν, 10, 347; a can camped army, and generally, a 10. Od. 2, 30.

στρατόομαι, mid. (στρατός), perf. ἐστρατόωντο, Ep. for ἐ to be encamped, 3, 187; πρὸς 377. cf. Buttm., Gr. Gram. I.

*στρεβλός, ή, όν (στρέφω), twisted, crooked. 2) Spoken o squint, Batr. 297.

στρεπτός, ή, όν (στρέφω), twisted, wound. στρ. χιτών, a of mail, which was formed o rings, according to Aristarch. hape we are to understand with which the two plates of t were united, 5, 113. (Pass

Schol. Ven.: a tunic of twisted work.) 2) that may be easily turned, pliable, voluble, γλῶσσα, 20, 248; hence tractable, manageable, φρένες, 15, 203; θεοί, 9, 497.

στρεύγομαι, depon. pass. poet. (akin to στράγγω), prop. to be expressed drop by drop, hence to become gradually enfeebled, exhausted, to become weary, ἐν αἰνῇ δηϊοτῆτι, 15, 512; ἐν νήσῳ, Od. 12, 351.

στρεφεδινέω, poet. (στρέφω, δινέω), to whirl around in a circle; pass. to turn oneself round in a circle. στρεφεδίνηθεν (Ep. for ἐστρεφεδινήθησαν) δέ οἱ ὄσσε, his eyes ['swam dizzy at the stroke,' Cp.], Il. 16, 792.† [According to Meiring, from στρέφεσθαι δίνῃ. Am. Ed.]

στρέφω, fut. στρέψω, aor. Ep. στρέψα, iterat. στρέψασκον, fut. mid. στρέψομαι, perf. pass. ἔστραμμαι, aor. 1 pass. ἐστρέφθην. 1) Act. intrans. to turn, to turn about, to bend, with accus. οὖρον, Od. 4, 520; esply ἵππους, to turn the horses, Il. 8. 168. Od. 15, 205; pass. στρεφθείς, firmly twisted, Od. 9, 435. 2) Intrans. to turn oneself, to turn about, Il. 18, 544; ἀνὰ ὄγμους, v. 546. εἰς Ἔρεβος στρέψας, Od. 10, 528. Mid. with aor. pass. 1) to turn oneself, to turn, Il. 18, 488. ἔνθα καὶ ἔνθα στρέφεται, to turn oneself hither and thither, 24, 5; hence 1) to turn oneself to, 12, 42. ἐστραμμέναι ἀλλήλῃσιν, h. Merc. 411; or to turn oneself from; ἐκ χώρης, to go from the region. 6, 516. 15, 645. 2) Like versari, to turn oneself about, to have intercourse with, with accus. h. Ap. 175.

στρέψασκον, see στρέφω.

στρόμβος, ὁ (στρέφω), prop. a twisted body, hence a whirlwind, 14, 413.†

στρουθός, ἡ, a sparrow, *2, 311. 317 (elsewhere also ὁ στρ.)

στροφάλιγξ, ιγγος, ἡ (στροφαλίζω), a whirlwind, esply κονίης, of dust, 16, 775. 21, 503. Od. 24, 39.

στροφαλίζω, poet. (στρέφω), a strengthened form, to turn, ἠλάκατα, Od. 18, 315.†

Στρόφιος, ὁ (dexterous, from στροφή), father of Scamandrius, 5, 49.

στρόφος, ὁ (στρέφω), a twisted cord, a string, a rope, a girdle, the band of a wallet, *Od. 13, 438. 17, 198. 2) a swathing-band, h. Ap. 123.

στρώννυμι, see στορέννυμι.

στρωφάω, poet. form of στρέφω, to turn, ἠλάκατα, Od. 6, 53. 17, 97. Mid. to turn oneself, κατά τινα, to any one, Il. 13. 557. b) to turn oneself hither and thither, i. e. to abide, to remain, κατὰ μέγαρα, 9, 463; ἀκάς, 20, 422. h. Cer. 48.

στυγερός, ή, όν, adv. στυγερῶς (στυγέω), prop. hated, abhorred; generally, hateful, abominable, horrible. a) Spoken of persons: Ἀΐδης, 8, 368; στυγερὸς δέ οἱ ἔπλετο θυμῷ, he was odious to her in the soul, 14, 158. b) Of things: πόλεμος, σκότος, γάμος, πένθος, 4, 240. Od.

1, 249. 16, 126. Adv. στυγερῶς, terribly, horribly, Il. 16, 123. Od. 21, 374. 23, 23.

στυγέω, aor. 2 ἔστυγον, aor. 1 ἔστυξα, causat. 1) Pres. with aor. 2 to hate, to abhor, to fear, τινά, 7, 112. Od. 13, 400. b) to stand in awe of, to fear, with infin., Il. 1, 186. 8, 515. 2) In the aor. 1 to render odious, frightful, τῷ κέ τεῳ στύξαιμι μένος, Od. 11, 502.

Στύμφηλος, ἡ, Ion. for Στύμφαλος, a town in Arcadia on the Stymphalian lake, 2, 608; famous in mythology on account of the Stymphalian birds.

Στύξ, Στυγός, ἡ (the horrible). 1) A river in the under world, by which the gods swore the most dreadful and sacred oath, 2, 755. Od. 8, 369. The Cocÿtus is a branch of it, Od. 10, 514. 2) As a nymph, daughter of Oceanus and Tethys, Hes. Th. 361. h. Cer. 424. She dwelt, according to Hes. Th. 778, at the entrance of the under world; her stream is a branch of Oceanus, and, as a part of it, flows from the world above to the world below, Il. 15, 37. Zeus granted to her, Hes. Thes. 383, the honour to be the most sacred oath of the gods, 14, 271. Od. 5, 183. According to Hes. Th. 783, seq., any one of the immortals, who had sworn a false oath, was obliged to lie down a full year breathless in sickness. Perhaps the fable was derived from the Arcadian fountain near Nonakris, whose water was said to be deadly, Hdt. 6, 74.

Στύρα, τά, a town on the island of Eubœa, 2, 539.

στυφελίζω (στυφελός), fut. στυφελίξω, aor. ἐστυφέλιξα, Ep. στυφέλιξα, 1) to strike, to thrust, to shake, with accus. ἀσπίδα, 5, 437; τινά, 7, 261; νέφεα, to scatter the clouds, 11, 305. b) to thrust away, to chase away, τινὰ ἐξ ἐδέων, ἐκ δαιτύος, ἐκτὸς ἀταρπιτοῦ, 1, 581. Od. 17, 234. 2) Generally, to push hither and thither, to abuse, to insult, τινά, Il. 21, 380. 512; pass., Od. 16. 108. 20, 318.

σύ, person. pron. of the second person, nom. Ep. τύνη. gen. Ep. σέο, σεῦ, σεῖο, τεοῖο, 8, 37; σέθεν, dat. σοί, τοί, accus. σέ (σε). The common gen. σοῦ is not found in Hom., σοί is always orthotone, τοί always enclitic: thou, gen. thine. σύγε, σύπερ, and connected with αὐτός, in which case it always retains the accent, 3, 51. 19, 416; hence we should write σοὶ αὐτῷ for σοι αὐτῷ, Od. 4, 601. 5, 187. 6, 39; cf. Thiersch, § 204, 205. Rost, Dial 44. Kühner, § 301.

συβόσιον, τό (βόσις), a herd of swine, with συῶν, 11, 679. Od. 14, 101 (with ι lengthened).

συβώτης, αο, ὁ (βόσκω), a swine-herd; often, *Od. 4, 640.

σύγε, see σύ.

συγκαλέω (καλέω), partcp. aor. συγκαλέσας, to call together, to collect, with accus. *2, 55. 10, 302.

συγκλονέω, poet. (κλονέω), to confound, to put in confusion, with accus. 13, 722.†

vegetable, *beta vulgaris*, Linn. Batr. 162.

σεύω, poet. (akin to θέω), aor. Ep. ἔσσευα and σεῦα, aor. mid. ἐσσευάμην, perf. pass. ἔσσυμαι, pluperf. ἐσσύμην. The perf. pass. often has a pres. signif. hence partcp. ἐσσύμενος, η, ον, with retracted accent. The pluperf. is at the same time Ep. aor. 2 ἐσσύμην, ἔσσυο, ἔσσυτο, Ep. σύτο, 21, 167. The pres. act. not found in Hom., the augment. tenses have double Sigma. 1) Act. trans. prop. *to put in violent motion, to drive;* hence, according to the prepos. a) *to drive, to urge, to chase,* τινὰ κατὰ Νυσσήϊον, 6, 133; τινὰ ἐπί τινι, any one against any one, 11, 293, 294; ἵππους, 15, 681. b) *to drive away, to chase away,* κύνας, Od. 14, 35; κατὰ ὀρέων, to drive down from the mountains, Il. 20, 189. c) Spoken of inanimate things: *to cast, to hurl,* κεφαλήν, 11, 147. 14, 413; αἷμα, to drive out the blood, i. e. to cause to flow, to draw, 5, 208. II) Mid. with Ep. aor. 2 and perf. pass. 1) Intrans. *to move oneself violently, to run, to hasten, to rush,* ἀνὰ ἄστυ, 6, 505; ἐπί τι, 14, 227. ψυχὴ κατ' ὠτειλὴν ἔσσυτο, the soul rushed to the wound, i. e. escaped through the wound, 14, 519; with infin. σεύατο διώκειν, he hastened to pursue, 17, 463. b) Metaph. spoken of the mind: *to desire ardently, to long for.* θυμός μοι ἔσσυται, Od. 10, 484; esply partcp. ἐσσύμενος, *ardently desiring, longing for, desirous,* with gen. ὁδοῖο, of the journey, Od. 4, 733; and with infin. πολεμίζειν, Il. 11, 717. Od. 4, 416. 2) With accus. trans. a) *to drive, to chase,* c) *to hunt,* esply wild beasts, with accus. κάπριον, λέοντα, 11, 415. b) *to chase away, to drive,* 3, 26; τινὰ πεδίονδε, 20, 148; metaph. κακότητα, h. 7, 13.

σηκάζω (σηκός), aor. pass. 3 plur. σηκάσθεν for ἐσηκάσθησαν, prop. to drive into the fold, to fold, spoken of sheep; generally, *to shut up, to enclose,* 8, 131.†

σηκοκόρος, ὁ (κορέω), one that cleans the stall, *a stable-cleanser, a stall-boy,* Od. 17, 224† [*a sweeper of my stalls,* Cp.].

σηκός, ὁ, an inclosed place: *a fold, a stall,* 18, 589. Od. 9, 219.

σῆμα, ατος, τό, *a sign,* to point out any thing; *a token,* of a lot, 7, 188; of theft, h. Merc. 136; esply 1) a sign sent by the deity, *an atmospheric sign, an aerial token,* such as thunder and lightning, which were regarded as omens and indications of the will of the gods, 2, 253. 351. 4, 381. 13, 244. · 2) *a monumental sign, a mound;* hence σῆμα χεῦαι, 2, 814. 7, 68. Od. 1, 291; generally, *a monument.* 3) *a written sign.* σήματα λυγρά, characters of fatal import [but not *alphabetical*], Il. 6, 168. Od. 1, 291; see γράφω. 4) *a mark,* 23, 843. Od. 8, 192.

σημαίνω (σῆμα), fut. σημανέω, aor. Ep. σήμηνα, aor. mid. ἐσημηνάμην. 1) *to give a sign* to do any thing; hence, *to*

command, *to order,* τινί, 1, 289. rarely with gen. τινός, Il. 14, 85 ἐπί τινι, about any one, Od. 22, 42 Trans. with accus. *to mark, to in* τέρματα, Il. 23, 358. 757. Od. Mid. *to mark* any thing *for onesel* ρον, one's lot, Il. 7, 175.

σημάντωρ, ορος, ὁ, poet. (σηι prop. one who gives a signal, *a commander, sovereign,* 4, 431; (*driver of horses,* 8, 127; βοῶν, a .of cattle, a herdsman, 15, 315.

σήμερον, adv. (from τήμερα), to 30. Od. 17, 186.

σήπω, perf. σέσηπα, aor. 2 (from which Ep. 3 sing. subj. σαι σαπῇ, 19, 27. Act. *to cause to d rot.* Pass. and perf. intrans. *to putrid, to rot, to moulder away* σήπεται, 14, 27. 24, 414. δοῦρα (the timbers are decayed, •2, 135.

*σησαμόεις, εσσα, εν (σήσαμο *of sesame,* Ep. 15, 8.

Σήσαμος, ἡ. a town in Paphl later the citadel of Amastris, 2, 8:

*σησαμότυρος, ὁ (τυρός), sesam i. e. a kind of food made of sesa cheese, Batr. 36.

Σηστός, ἡ, a little town on tl lespont. in the Thracian Chers opposite the city of Abydos in A: rendered famous by the love of I and Hero, now *Ialowa,* 2, 836.

σθεναρός, ή, όν, poet. (σθένος), *powerful, mighty,* epith. of Atê, 9

Σθενέλαος, ὁ, son of Ithæmene by Patroclus, 16, 586.

Σθένελος, ὁ (abbrev. from Σθε 1) son of Capaneus and Evadne, the Epigŏni and a leader befor 2, 564. 23, 511; a companion of des, 9, 48. 2) son of Perseus ε dromĕda, husband of Nicippe, f Eurystheus, king of Argos and N 19, 116.

σθένος, εος, τό, poet. *strength might,* primar. spoken of the b men and beasts, 5, 139. Od. l more rarely of inanimate things 751. 18, 607; esply of strength (*courage* in war: μέγα σθένος ἐι καρδίη, 2, 451. 14, 151. 2) Gε *power, might,* 16, 542; *forces,* esply in periphrasis with gen. of son (like βίη): σθένος Ἕκτοι might of Hector, i. e. the mighty 9, 351; Ἰδομενῆος, 13, 248.

σίαλος, ὁ, prop. *fat, fattened.* λος, a fat swine, 9, 208. Od. 14, Subst. *a fat hog,* Il. 21, 363. Oc

σιγαλόεις, εσσα, εν. poet. (akir λος), (n i t i d u s,) *shining, white, g right, splendid* ('magnificent, cor 1) Spoken of costly variegated broidered clothing, χιτών, εἵματε δέσματα, Il. and Od. 2) Of ι horses, polished and perhaps with metal, Il. 5, 226. Od. 6, Spoken of household furnitur the dwelling, Od. 5, 86. 16, 449.

significations, as *tender. soft, covered with foam*, are not proved.)

σιγάω (σιγή), *to be silent, to be still*, only the imperat. σίγα, 14, 90. Od. 14, 493; σιγᾶν, h. Merc. 93.

σιγή, ἡ (σίζω), *silence*, only σιγῇ, dat. as adv. *in silence, still, quietly*. σιγῇ ἐφ' ὑμείων, still before you, 7, 195. σιγῇ νῦν, Od. 15, 391 (false reading σιγὴ νῦν).

σιδήρειος, η, ον, poet. for σιδήρεος, 7, 141. 8, 15, etc.

σιδήρεος, η, ον (σίδηρος), 1) *of iron, iron*, κορύνη, δέσματα; ὀρυμαγδός, the iron tumult, i. e. of iron arms, 17, 424; οὐρανός, the iron heaven, like χάλκεος, because the ancients conceived of it as made of iron, Od 15, 329. 17, 565; or, more correctly, in a metaph. sense. 2) Trop. *hard as iron, firm, strong;* θυμός, an iron mind, i. e. inexorable, Il. 22, 357; thus ἦτορ, κραδίη. σοίγε σιδήρεα, πάντα τέτυκται, to thee every thing is iron, Od. 12, 280. σιδ. πυρὸς μένος, the iron, i. e. the unwasting strength of fire, Il. 23, 177. (The forms with ει or ε change with the necessity of the metre.)

σίδηρος, ὁ. 1) *iron;* this metal is often mentioned in Homer; he calls it πολιός, αἴθων, ἰόεις; this last epithet, 'violet-coloured,' seems to indicate iron hardened to steel and become blue; also the method of hardening iron by immersing it in water was known to Hom., Od. 9, 391; as an image of hardness, Il. 4. 510. Od. 19, 211. 2) Metonym. *every thing made of iron, arms, furniture*, hence πολύμηκτος, Il. 6, 48; and often.

Σιδονίηθεν, adv. *from Sidon*, 6, 291.†

Σιδόνιος, η, ον (Σιδών), Ep. for Σιδόνιος, *Sidonian, of Sidon*, 6, 289; from which, 1) ἡ Σιδονίη, the district of Sidonia in Phœnicia, or the entire coast of the Phœnicians, with the chief town, Sidon, Od. 13, 285. 2) ὁ Σιδόνιος, a Sidonian, Od. 4, 84. 618.

Σιδών, ῶνος, ἡ, the famous capital of the Phœnicians, situated on the sea, with a double port, now *Seida*, Od. 15, 425.

Σιδών, όνος, *a Sidonian*, an inhabitant of the city of Sidon, 23, 743.

σίζω, a word formed to imitate the sound; *to hiss*, primar. the sound of red-hot bodies immersed in water. hence also spoken of the eye of the Cyclops in which Odysseus (Ulysses) twisted the burning stake; only imperf. Od. 9, 394.†

Σικανίη, ἡ, the original name of the island of *Sicelia*, which it received from the Sicani, according to Thucyd. 6, 2. Diodor. 5, 6. When, at a later period, the Sicani were pressed by the Siceli immigrating from Italy, and confined to the region about Agragas, the latter was called Sicania, and the whole island Sicelia, Od. 24, 307.

Σικελός, ή, όν, *Sicelian or Sicilian*, elsewhere Θρινακίη. γυνὴ Σικελή, Od. 24, 211. 366. 389. Subst. οἱ Σικελοί, *the Siceli*, according to Thuc. 6, 2. an Italian

people, who, being pressed by the Pelasgi, emigrated to Italy, and first settled near Catana. Hence they dwelt on the eastern coast of the island, Od. 20, 383.

Σικυών, ῶνος, ὁ and ἡ, a town in the country Sicyonia, in the Peloponnesus, at an earlier day Αἰγιαλοί and Μηκώνη, famed for its traffic, and later the chief seat of Grecian art; now *Vasilika*, 2, 572.

Σιμόεις, εντος, ὁ, *Simois*, a small river in Troas, which rises in Ida, and flows north from the city of Troy and unites in the Trojan plain with the Scamander; now *Simas*, 4, 475. 5, 774. cf. Τρωικός. 2) the river-god of the Simois, 20, 53.

Σιμοείσιος, ὁ, son of the Trojan Anthemion, slain by Ajax, 4, 474, seq.

σίνομαι, depon. mid. only pres. and imperf. iterat. form σινέσκοντο, Od. 6, 6. 1) Prop. *to carry off, to plunder*, with accus. ἑταίρους τινί, Od. 12, 114. b) *to attack in order to plunder, to rob*, τινά, Od. 6, 6; spoken of herds, Od. 11, 112. 2) Generally, *to hurt, to injure, to harm*. αἰδὼς ἄνδρας σίνεται, shame injures men, Il. 24, 45.

σίντης, ὁ, poet. (σίνομαι), *a robber, a murderer*, as adj. *plundering, ravaging*, λῖς, λύκος, *11, 481. 16, 353. 20, 165.

Σίντιες, οἱ (=σίνται, robbers), *the Sinties*, the earliest inhabitants of the island of Lemnos, who received Hêphæstus when hurled down by Zeus, 1, 594. Od. 8, 294.

Σίπυλος, ὁ (Dor. for Θεόπυλος), a branch of mount Tmôlus, on the borders of Lydia and Phrygia, now *Mimas*, 24, 615.

Σίσυφος, ὁ (Æol. for σόφος), son of Æolus and Enarêtê, husband of Meropê, father of Glaucus, founder of Ephŷra or Corinth, noted for his cunning and propensity to robbery, 6, 153. He was doomed to roll a stone up a mountain in the under world, which always rolled back, because he betrayed to Asôpus that Zeus had seized his daughter, or because he had betrayed the secrets of the gods in general to men, Od. 11, 593. Apd. 1, 9. 3.

σιτέω (σῖτος), imperf. mid. σιτέσκοντο; act. *to give to eat, to feed*. Mid. *to give oneself food, to eat, to feed upon*, Od. 24, 209.†

σῖτος, ὁ, only sing, *wheat*, generally, *grain*. and esply 1) *flour, bread*, prepared from it; in opposition to flesh. σῖτος καὶ κρέα, Od. 9, 9. 12, 19. 2) Generally, *food, victuals, nourishment*. hence often σῖτος καὶ οἶνος, Il. 9, 706. Od. 3, 479. σῖτος ἠδὲ ποτής, Il. 19, 306. Od. 9, 87. (It never appears as neut. in Hom.; but clearly as masc., Od. 13, 244. 16, 83. 17, 533.)

σιτοφάγος, ον (φαγεῖν), *eating grain or bread*, Od. 9, 191 † Batr. 244.

σιφλόω (σιφλός [πόδα σιφλός = πηρός, Ap. Rhod. 1, 204]), aor. optat. σιφλώσειεν, prop. *to deform*, hence generally to bring into disgrace, to destroy, to ruin, τινά, 14, 142 † [al., less well, to bring to shame.]

σιωπάω (σιωπή), aor. optat. σιωπήσειαν, infin. σιωπῆσαι, to be silent, to be still, 2, 280. 23, 560. Od. 17, 513.

σιωπή, ἡ, silence, stillness, Hom. only dat. as adv. σιωπῇ, in silence, still, 6, 404. Od. 1, 325. ἀκὴν ἐγένοντο σιωπῇ. they were entirely still, Il. 3, 95. Od. 7, 154. σιω. ἐπινεύειν, to give the nod in silence, Il. 9, 616; and often.

σκάζω (akin to σκαίρω), to limp, to hobble, 19, 47; ἐκ πολέμου, 11, 811. Batr. 251.

Σκαιαί, αἱ, πύλαι, the Scæan gate, also called the Dardanian (Δαρδάνιαι); it was upon the west side of the city of Troy, hence the name west gate (σκαιός): it was the main gate, and led to the Grecian camp. From its turret were to be seen the oak, the watch-station, the fig-tree, and the monument of Ilus, 3, 145. 6, 237. 11, 170. cf. Τρωϊκὸν πεδίον.

σκαιός, ἡ, όν, left. ἡ σκαιή, sc. χείρ, the left hand; hence σκαιῇ, with the left, 1, 501. 16, 734. 2) western, perhaps σκαιὸν ῥίον, Od. 3, 295.

σκαίρω (akin to σκάζω), to leap, to spring, Od. 10, 412; ποσί, to dance, Il. 18, 572. h. 31, 18.

*σκαλμός, ὁ, the pin, a block upon the ship, upon which the oar rests, h. 6, 42.

Σκαμάνδριος, η, ον, Scamandrian, on the Scamander. τὸ Σκαμάνδριον πεδίον, the Scamandrian plain, = τὸ Τρωϊκὸν πεδίον, q. v., 2, 465; also λειμὼν Σκαμάνδριος, 2, 467. 2) Subst. name of Astyănax, which his father gave him, 6, 402; see Ἀστυάναξ. b) son of Strophius, a Trojan, 5, 49, seq.

Σκάμανδρος, ὁ (σκ never forms posit., cf. Thiersch, § 146. 8), Scamander, a river in Troas, called by the gods Xanthus; it rises, according to 22, 147, seq., near the city of Troy, from two fountains, of which the one had cold, the other warm water; it then flows south-west from the city through the plain, unites with the Simoeis, 5, 774, and falls into the Hellespont somewhat north of Sigeum, 21, 125. Il. 12, 21 seems to clash with the origin of the Scamander in 22, 147, according to which passage it rises upon Ida, as says also Strabo XIII. p. 602. [Lechevalier, and others maintain that both sources still exist, but that the steam of the warm one is only visible in winter.] Now the river is called Mendere-Su. 2) the river-god Xanthus. His contest with Achilles is found 20, 74. 21, 136, seq.

Σκάνδεια, ἡ, a harbour on the southern coast of the island Cythēra, now Cerigo, 10, 268.

*σκάπτω, fut. ψω, to dig, φυτά, h. Merc. 90, 207.

*σκαπτήρ, ῆρος, ὁ (σκάπτω), a digger, Fr. 2.

Σκάρφη, ἡ (Σκάρφεια, Strab.), a small town in Locris, not far from Thermopy-

læ, 2, 532. (According to Strab already, 400 years before Chr stroyed by a earthquake.)

σκαφίς, ίδος, ἡ (σκάπτω), a sma for preserving any thing, a bow Od. 9, 123.†

σκεδάννυμι, aor. 1 ἐσκέδασα, ἐ δασα, only aor. as pres. the po to scatter, to drive apart or let accus. λαόν, 19, 171. 23, 162; 649. Od. 13, 352. ἀχλὺν ἀπ' ὀφθα scatter the darkness from any on Il. 20, 341; metaph. αἷμα, to she 7, 330.

σκέδασις, ιος, ἡ (σκεδάννυμι), t scattering, dispersion, *Od. 1, 116.

σκέλλω (or σκελέω), Ep. aor. 1 sing. σκήλειε, to dry, to parch, t χρόα, 23, 191.†

σκέλος, εος, τό, in the broade the entire leg from the hip to t In the narrower, the shank (tib the calf; hence πρυμνὸν σκέλος, (Schol. γαστροκνημίαν), 16, 314.†

σκέπαρνον, τό (prob. from σκ double-edged axe, for hewing carpenter's axe [used also for sm *Od. 5, 237. 9, 391.

σκέπας, αος, τό (σκεπάω), a covering, a shelter; ἀνέμοιο, from the wind, *Od. 5, 443. 6, 2

σκεπάω, poet. (σκέπας), 3 plu σκεπόωσι, Ep. for σκεπῶσι, to protect; spoken of the coast, κῦμα ἀνέμων. the wave or the the winds, Od. 13, 99.†

σκέπτομαι, depon. mid. aor. ψάμην, to look at a distance hand held over the eyes, to look to look around, ἔς τι; μετά τιν 247; with αἱ κεν, 11. 17, 652; ἐκ θ h. Cer. 245. 2) Trans. to exa contemplate, with accus. ὀϊστῶ 16, 361. h. Merc. 360.

*σκευάζω (σκεῦος), to prepare, ready: absol. to arrange domesti κατ' οἶκον, in the house, h. Merc

σκηπάνιον, τό (σκῆπτω), = σκ staff, a sceptre, the ensign of dignity; of Poseidôn, 13, 59; c *24, 247.

σκηπτοῦχος (σκῆπτρον, ἔχω), bearing, holding the sceptre, kings, 2, 86. Od. 5, 9.

σκῆπτρον, τό (σκῆπτω), 1) cane to support oneself upon, 437. 14, 31. 17, 199. 2) Espl reign's sceptre, the sceptre, a sp out a metallic point, and, accor 1, 246, adorned with golden stud an ensign of imperial dignity Kings easily bore it, 1, 234. also priests and prophets, Il. 1 11, 91; heralds, Il. 7, 277; al 18, 505. It was generally an public action; whoever spoke sembly was obliged to hold t in his hand, and received it herald, 23, 568. Od. 2, 37; in oath the sceptre was raised,

10, 327. 3) Metaph. *the royal power, the imperial dignity*, 6, 259. σκῆπτρον καὶ θέμιστες, marks the union of the imperial and judicial power, 2, 206. 9, 99.

σκήπτω, act., a false reading, 17, 437, from ἐνισκίμπτειν; now only mid. *to support oneself, to lean* upon a staff, spoken of old men and beggars, Od. 17, 203. 338; with dat. καί μιν ὀΐω αὐτῷ (ἄκοντι) σκηπτόμενον· κατίμεν δόμον Ἀΐδος εἴσω, and I think that he will descend to the abode of Hades, supporting himself on the spear [will 'lean on it in his descent to Hell,' Cp.], sarcastic for 'he will die pierced through by my spear,' Il. 14, 457.

σκηρίπτω (σκήπτω), only mid. *to support oneself, to lean upon*, Od. 17, 196; spoken of Sisyphus rolling the stone, χερσίν τε ποσίν τε, to resist or push against it with hands and feet [to shove it, Cp.], *Od. 11, 595.

σκιάζω, poet. form σκιάω, aor. subj. σκιάσῃ, *to shade* or *overshadow, to envelope with shade, to veil*, with accus. of the night, ἄρουραν, 21, 232.†

σκιάω, poet. σκιάζω, only mid. *to become shady, to be darkened*. σκιόωντο, Ep. for ἐσκιῶντο πᾶσαι ἀγυιαί, all the streets were dark, *Od. 2, 388. 3, 487.

σκίδναμαι, mid. poet. a form of σκεδάννυμι, in the pres. and imperf. *to scatter, to separate*, spoken of men: κατὰ κλισίας, 1, 487; ἐπὶ ἔργα, Od. 2, 252; πρὸς δώματα, Od. 2, 258; ἐπὶ νῆα, Il. 19, 277; with infin. 24, 2; spoken of the foam of the sea: ὑψόσε, to dash on high, 11, 308; of dust: ὑπὸ νεφέων, to whirl upward, 16, 375; of a fountain: ἡ ἀνὰ κῆπον σκίδναται, is distributed through the garden, Od. 7, 130.

σκιερός, ή, όν, poet. (σκιή), *shadowy, shady, dark*, νέμος, 11, 480; ἄλσος, Od. 20, 278.

σκιή, ἡ, Ion. for σκιά, *a shadow, a shade*, spoken of the souls in Hades, *Od. 10, 495. 11, 207. h. Cer. 100.

σκιόεις, εσσα, εν, poet. (σκιά), *shady, shaded*, i. e. by trees, ὄρεα, 1, 157; *dark, gloomy*, μέγαρα, Od. 1, 365. 4, 768. (There were no windows in the hall, and it received light through the door; or, according to Eustath., because it protected from the heat.) νέφεα, Il. 5, 525. Od. 8, 374.

σκιρτάω, optat. pres. σκιρτῷεν, aor. 1 infin. σκιρτῆσαι, Batr. 60; *to leap, to spring*, ἐπὶ ἄρουραν, upon the earth, *20, 226; and v. 228, ἐπὶ νῶτα θαλάσσης.

σκολιός, ή, όν, *crooked, curved, tortuous, oblique*: metaph. σκολιὰς κρίνειν θέμιστας, to give perverse judgements, 16, 387.†

σκόλοψ, οπος, ὁ (from κόλος), *a body having a sharp point, a spit*, 18, 177. 2) Esply *a stake, a pale* for fortifying the walls of towns and encampments, 8, 343. 15, 1. Od. 7, 45.

σκόπελος, ὁ (σκοπός, prop. = σκοπιή), *a mountain peak, a rock, a cliff*, 2, 396; often Od., 12, 73. 95, 101.

σκοπιάζω (σκοπιά), prop. *to look abroad from a lofty place*; generally, *to spy, to watch, to observe*, 14, 58. Od. 10, 260. 2) Trans. *to spy out, to explore*, τινά, Il. 10, 40.

σκοπιή, ἡ, Ion. for σκοπιά (σκοπός), *any elevated place from which observations can be taken, a watch-station*, in Hom. always *a hill-top* ['a rocky point,' Cp.], 4, 275. Od. 4, 524; esply *a place near Troy*, Il. 22, 145. 2) *the act of spying*, observation, Od. 8, 302. h. Merc. 99.

σκοπός, ὁ (σκέπτομαι), 1) *a looker-out*, who from an elevated position surveys the region, *a watch*, Od. 4, 524; spoken of Helios, h. Cer. 63; also, *a scout*, = ἐπίσκοπος, Il. 10, 324. 526. 561; generally, *an overseer*, 23, 359; also *a female superintendent*, δμωάων, Od. 22, 396; in a bad sense, *a lier in wait*, Od. 22, 156. 2) In the Od. *the point* to which one looks, Od. 22, 6; metaph. *aim, purpose*. ἀπὸ σκοποῦ, contrary to the design, Od. 11, 344.

σκότιος, η, ον (σκότος), *dark, gloomy*; metaph. *secret, clandestine*, 6, 23.†

σκοτομήνιος, ον (μήνη), *in which the moon is obscured, dark, moonless*, νύξ, Od. 14, 457.†

σκότος, ὁ (akin to σκιά), *darkness, obscurity*, Od. 19, 389; esply metaph. *the darkness of death*, often spoken of the dying, τὸν δὲ σκότος ὄσσε κάλυψεν, Il. 4, 461. h. Ap. 370. In the Il. always in the metaph. signif.; in the Od. only once in the literal.

σκυδμαίνω, poet. form of σκύζομαι, Ep. infin. σκυδμαινέμεν, *to be angry at*, τινί, 24, 592.†

σκύζομαι, depon. only pres. and imperf. poet. (from κύων, to snarl like a dog), *to mutter, to be angry, to be displeased*, absol. 8, 483; τινί, at any one, 4, 23. 8, 460. Od. 23, 209.

σκύλαξ, ακος, ὁ, ἡ (κύω, κύων), *a young animal*, esply *a young dog, whelp, puppy*, *Od. 9, 289. 12, 86. 20, 14; in Hom. always fem.

Σκύλλα, ἡ, mly in Hom. Σκύλλη (the nom. Σκύλλα, only Od. 12, 235; *that tears in pieces*, from σκύλλω), a sea-monster of the Italian coast in the Sicilian straits, opposite Charybdis, dwelling in a cavern, Od. 12, 85, seq. She is called the daughter of Cratais, Od. 12, 124 (according to Ap. Rh. 4, 828, daughter of Phorcys and Hecatê). She had six dragon throats and twelve sharp claws, and her body was surrounded with half-projecting dogs and other horrible objects. She tore in pieces every living thing which approached her. She robbed Odysseus (Ulysses) of six of his companions. According to mythology, she was afterwards changed into a rock. This rock, named Scyllæum, lies opposite the promontory of Pelorum, on whose east side there lies at this day a small town Scilla or Sciglio.

σκύμνος, ὁ (κύω), like σκύλαξ, *a young*

animal; esply the young of the lion, (*lion's*) *whelp*, 18, 319.†

Σκῦρος, ἡ, an island of the Ægean sea, north-west of Chios, with a town of the same name, birth-place of Neoptolemus, now *Skyro*, 9, 668. Od. 11, 509; from which Σκύροθεν, from Scyros, Il. 19, 332.

σκῦτος, εος, τό (cutis), *the skin;* esply dressed skin, *leather*, Od. 14, 34.†

σκυτοτόμος, ὁ (σκύτος, τέμνω), prop. cutting leather; hence, *a worker in leather* [often = *armourer*, fm the use made of leather in the ancient *shields*, &c.], 7, 221.†

σκύφος, ὁ, (akin to κυφός), *a goblet, a cup*, Od. 14, 112.† (Aristoph. Byz. read σκύφος as neut.)

σκώληξ, ηκος, ὁ, *an earth-worm*, lumbricus, 13, 654.†

σκῶλος, ὁ = σκόλοψ, *a pointed stake*, or, according to Etym. Mag., a kind of thorn, 13, 564.†

Σκῶλος, ἡ, a village of the Theban dominions in Bœotia, 2, 497.

σκώψ, σκωπός, ὁ, *an owl*, the wood-owl, *strix aluco*, Linn. According to Schneider ad Arist. H. A. 9, 19. 11, the *small horned-owl, strix scops*, Linn., Od. 5, 66.† (Either from σκέπτομαι, on account of its staring eyes, or from σκώπτω, from its droll form.)

σμαραγέω (akin to μαράσσω), aor. subj. σμαραγήσῃ, *to resound, to roar*, spoken of the sea and of thunder, 2, 210. 21, 199; spoken of the meadow, which resounded with the cry of the cranes, *2, 463.

*Σμάραγος, ὁ, *the blusterer*, a divinity, Ep. 14, 9.

σμερδαλέος, έη, έον, lengthened from σμερδνός, ή, όν, poet. *frightful, fearful, terrific, odious, horrible*, spoken esply of the appearance, δράκων, 2, 309. Od. 6, 137; κεφαλή. Od. 12, 91; hence spoken of brass and of weapons: χαλκός, αἰγίς, σάκος, Il. 12, 464. 20, 260. 21, 401. Od. 11, 609; the neut. sing. and plur. σμερδαλέον, σμερδαλέα, as adv. once of the look, δέδορκεν, 22, 95; elsewhere spoken with verbs of sound, βοᾶν, κοναβίζειν, κτυπεῖν, τινάσσεσθαι, 15, 609.

σμερδνός, ή, όν=σμερδαλέος, and much more rarely used; Γοργείη κεφαλῆς, 5, 742: the neut. σμερδνόν, as adv. 15, 687. h. 31, 9.

σμήχω, Ep. Ion. for σμάω, *to wipe off, to rub off*, χνόον ἐκ κεφαλῆς, Od. 6, 226.†

σμικρός, ή, όν, Att. for μικρός, *small;* in H. on account of the metre, 17, 757. h. Ven. 115.

Σμινθεύς, ῆος, ὁ, epith. of Apollo, according to Aristarch. from Σμίνθη, a town in Troas, because he had a temple there, or from the Æolic σμίνθος, a *mouse*, because these as well as other animals living under the earth, were a symbol of prophecy, 1, 39. According to other critics, as Apion, Eustath., it signifies, mouse-killer, because he once freed one of the priests from a plague

of mice in Chrysa, or because cated to the Teucri, on the m Troy, the place of their settle mice, Strab. XIII. p. 604.

*Σμύρνη, ἡ, Ion. and Ep. for a noted town in Ionia, on the riv with an excellent harbour, no Ep. 4, 6.

σμύχω, poet. aor. ἔσμυξα, to any thing by a smothered fire, *down*. κατά τε σμῦξαι πυρὶ νῆα Pass. *to be consumed by fire*, πυρί

σμῶδιγξ and σμῶδιξ, ιγγος, ι or *weal, a tumour, a stripe*, l blood, nom. σμῶδιξ, 2, 267; σμώδιγγες, *23, 716.

σόῃ. see σαόω.

σοίο, see σός.

σόλος, ὁ (σέλλω), a mass of ir for throwing; according to tl and Apoll. *a spherical quoit* (V Cp. *an iron clod*). According and Tryphon, the same with th except that this was always made the σόλος of iron; cf. Valken. ad de differ. voc. p. 60. *Il. 23, 826

Σόλυμοι, οἱ, the *Solymi*, a nation, in the country of Lyci Minor, 6, 184. According to C they were neighbours of th Æthiopians. According to Her they were the original inhab Lycia, and according to Strab. habited the points of the T Lycia or Pisidia.

σόος, η, ον, Ep. shortened fr which is expanded from σῶς, form of ΣΑΟΣ. 1) *healthy*, so 7, 310; spoken of the moon, 7 *alive, preserved, delivered*, a ὀλέσθαι, 1, 117. 5, 331; *unhuri 382. Od. 13, 364.

σορός, ὁ (akin with σωρός), a preserving the bones of the dea 23, 91.†

σός, ή, όν (σύ), Ep. gen. σοῖο Od. 15, 511; *thy, thine*, mly w article: with an art. τὸ σὸν γ 185. 18, 457; the neut. as σοῖσι, with thy friends, Od. 2, form, τεός, ή, όν.

Σούνιον, τό, the southern ca tica, with a temple of Ath Capo Colonni, Od. 3, 278.

σοφίη, ἡ (σοφός), *dexterity, telligence, wisdom*, spoken of a tect, 15, 412; † of music, h. l 511.

*σοφός, ή, όν, *expert, experie telligent*, Fr. 1, 8.

σόω, Ep. form from σαόω, σόῃς, σόῃ, and σόωσι, see σαόω.

*σπαργανιώτης, ου, ὁ, a chil dling-clothes, h. Merc. 301.

*σπάργανον, τό (σπάργω), clothes, h. Merc. 151. 237.

*σπάργω, fut. ξω, *to wrap, t τί ἐν φαρεῖ, h. Ap. 121.

Σπάρτη, ἡ, *the chief town* mon, the residence of Menela

Eurôtas, in a valley almost entirely surrounded by mountains, the ruins now near Magula, see Λακεδαίμων. 2, 582. Od. 1, 93; from which adv. Σπάρτηθεν, from Sparta, Od. 2, 327.

σπάρτον, τό, a rope made of spartum (a kind of broom); generally, a rope, a cable. σπάρτα λέλυνται. Ep. (see Rost, § 100. 4. a. Kühner, § 369.), Il. 2. 135.† ὁ, ἡ σπάρτος is a shrub with tough branches, spartium scoparium, Linn.: genista in Pliny. (The reference is prob. not to the Spanish Spartos; and Varro ad Gell. 17, 3, doubts whether in Hom. the shrub gave the name.)

σπάω, aor. 1 ἔσπασα, aor. 1 mid. ἐσπασάμην, Ep. σπασάμην and with σσ, imperat. σπάσσασθε, partcp. σπασσάμενος, aor. 1 pass. ἐσπάσθην, to draw, to draw out, τί. h. Merc. 85; in tmesis, 5, 859; hence pass. σπασθέντος, sc. ἔγχεος, when the spear was drawn out, 11, 458. 2) Mid. to draw out for oneself, to snatch, ῥῶπας, Od. 10, 166; χεῖρα ἐκ χειρός τινος, Od. 2, 321. ἄορ παρὰ μηροῦ, to draw the sword from the thigh, Il. 16, 473; φάσγανον, Od. 22, 74; ἐκ σύριγγος ἔγχος, Il. 19, 387.

σπεῖο, see ἕπομαι

σπεῖος, τό, Ep. for σπέος, q. v.

σπεῖρον, τό (σπεῖρα), prop. cloth for a covering; a cover, a cloth; a robe, a garment, Od. 4, 245. 6, 179; esply linen cloth for shrouding the dead, Od. 2, 102. 19, 147. 2) Generally cloth, a sail = ἱστία, *Od. 6, 269. 5, 318.

σπεῖσαι, σπεῖσασκε, see σπένδω.

Σπειώ, οῦς, ἡ (from σπέος, a dweller in a cave), daughter of Nêreus and Dôris, 18, 43.

σπένδω, fut. σπείσω, aor. ἔσπεισα, Ep. σπεῖσα, 2 sing. subj. pres. σπένδῃσθα, Od. 4, 591; iterat. imperf. σπένδεσκε, Il. 16, 227; aor. σπεῖσασκε, to sprinkle, to pour out; prop. a word used of sacred rites, since a portion of the wine was poured out in honour of the gods upon the earth, the table or the altar, Lat. libare; mly absol. (make a libation) or with a dat. of the deity to whom the offering is made: Διί, to present a drink-offering to Zeus, 6, 259; θεοῖς, Od. 3, 334. 7, 137. b) Sometimes with an accus. of that which is offered: οἶνον, Il. 11, 775. Od. 14, 447; or with dat. ὕδατι, to sprinkle with water, Od. 12, 363. c) With dat. of the vessel: δέπαϊ, to pour out of a cup, Il. 23, 196. Od. 7, 137.

σπέος, τό, Ep. σπεῖος, gen. σπείους, dat. σπῆϊ, 24, 83; accus. σπεῖος, Od. 5. 194; plur. gen. σπείων, h. Ven. 264; dat. σπέσσι, Od. 1, 15; σπήεσσι, 9, 400; a cave, a grotto, a cavern. σπέος appears to be more comprehensive than ἄντρον. cf. h. Merc. 228; and Nitzsch ad Od. 5, 57. [According to Ameis, σπέος is used when speaking of the exterior, and ἄντρον of the interior of a hollow space, cf. Od 9, 182. 216. Am. Ed.]

σπέρμα, ατος, τό (σπείρω), seed, seed-corn, prop. spoken of plants, h. Cer. 208. 2) Metaph. σπέρμα πυρός, the seed of fire, Od. 5, 490.†

Σπερχειός, ὁ (that hastens, from σπέρχω), Sperchīus, a river in Thessaly, which flows from Mount Tymphrêstus into the Malean gulf, now Agramela, Il. 23, 142. 2) a river-god, father of Menesthius, 16, 174.

σπέρχω, poet. only pres. and imperf. Act. prop. trans. to drive on, to press, once intrans. like the mid. ὄφ᾽ ὑπ᾽ ἀνέμων σπέρχωσιν ἄελλαι, when the storms hasten on before the winds, 13, 334. h. 33, 7. Mid. to move oneself violently, i. e. to hasten, to run, to rush, spoken of men, with infin., 19, 317; absol. often in the partcp. hastening, fleet, 11, 110. Od. 9, 101; ἐρετμοῖς, to hasten with oars, i. e. to row swiftly, Od. 13, 22; spoken of a ship, to hasten, Od, 13, 115; of storms, Od. 3, 283.

σπέσθαι, see ἕπομαι.

σπεύδω, aor. ἔσπευσα, from this subj. σπεύσομεν for σπεύσωμεν, 17, 121; fut. mid. σπεύσομαι, 18, 402; mly in partcp. pres. 1) Intrans. to hasten, to speed, to make haste, often absol. ἐς μάχην, 4, 225; ὑπό τινος, before any one, 11, 119; εἰς τινα, 15, 402; with partcp., Od. 9, 250. b) to take pains, to strive, περὶ Πατρόκλοιο θανόντος, about the fallen Patroclus, i. e. to fight about him, Il. 17, 121. 2) Trans. with accus. to hasten any thing, to accelerate, to urge zealously, τί, 13, 237; γάμον, Od. 19, 137. (Of the mid. only the fut.)

σπῆϊ. σπήεσσι, see σπέος.

σπιδής, ές (σπίζω), extended. wide. διὰ σπιδέος πεδίοιο, through the wide plain, 11, 754;† the reading of Zenodotus; others read incorrectly δι᾽ ἀσπιδέος π., assuming an adj. σπιδέος π., assuming an adj. ἀσπιδής, similar to a shield. According to Apoll. Etym. Mag. σπιδής is from σπίζω = ἐκτείνω, and accord. to the Gramm. Æschylus and Antimachus used σπίδιος and σπιδόθεν for μακρός, μακρόθεν.

σπιλάς, άδος, ἡ, a rocky cliff, a rock in the sea, *Od. 3. 298. 5, 401.

*σπινθαρίς, ίδος, ἡ = σπινθήρ, h. Ap. 442

σπινθήρ, ῆρος, ὁ, a spark, 4, 77.†

σπλάγχνον, τό. only in the plur. τὰ σπλάγχνα, entrails, esply the more important, the heart, liver, and lungs. These were immediately cut out after the victim was slain, roasted and eaten, whilst the offering was burning. Afterwards followed the sacrificial feast, 1, 464. Od. 3, 9. 40, 461.

σπόγγος, ὁ, Att. σφόγγος, a spunge (fungus), for cleaning the hands, 18, 414; the table and chairs, Od. 1, 111.

σποδιή, ἡ, Ion. for σποδιά, a heap of ashes, generally = σποδός, ashes, Od. 5, 488.†

σποδός, ἡ, ashes, Od. 9, 375.† h. Merc. 258. (Akin to σβέννυμι.)

σπονδή, ἡ (σπένδω), a libation, a drink-offering (libatio), of unmixed wine, which was poured out in honour of the gods at feasts and esply in making treaties; hence in the plur. σπονδαί, a solemn *league, a covenant*, 2, 341. 4, 159.

*σπουδαῖος, η, ον (σπουδή), *hasty, zealous, important*. χρῆμα, h. Merc. 332.

σπουδή, ἡ (σπεύδω), 1) *haste, zeal, care, diligence*. ἄτερ σπουδῆς, without care, Od. 21, 409. 2) *earnestness*. ἀπὸ σπουδῆς, in earnest. Il. 7, 359. 12, 235. 3) Esply often in the dat. σπουδῇ, as adv. *in haste*, Od. 13, 279. 15, 209. b) With zeal, with pains; hence, *scarcely, with great difficulty*, Il. 2, 99. 11, 562. Od. 3, 297 24, 119.

σταδίη, ἡ, see στάδιος.

στάδιος, η, ον (ἵστημι), *standing, firm*. ἡ σταδίη ὑσμίνη, a *standing-fight, a close battle*, i. e. a pitched-battle, in which man and man fought with spears or swords, or hand to hand, in distinction from a skirmish, cf. αὐτοσταδίη, 13, 314. 713; also ἐν σταδίη alone: in close conflict, *7, 241. 13, 514.

στάζω, aor. Ep. στάξα, *to drop, to trickle*; τινί τι κατὰ ῥινῶν, ἐν στήθεσσι, *19, 39. 348. 354. Batr. 232.

στάθμη, ἡ (ἵστημι), a *marking-cord, a carpenter's cord*, for making a straight line, or a *level* or *line*, for making an even surface, 15, 410; δόρυ ἐπὶ στάθμην ἴθυνειν, to hew the wood straight by the line, Od. 5, 245. 17, 341. 23, 197 [squaring it by line, Cp.].

σταθμόνδε, adv. *into the pen*, into the stall, Od. 9, 451.†

σταθμός, ὁ (ἵστημι), 1) a place of stopping for men and beasts; a *station, a stall, a stable, a pen, an enclosure*, 2, 470. 5, 140. Od. 16, 45. 2) a *post, a pillar*, often in the Od., 1, 333. 6, 19. 3) a *weight* in the scales, Il. 12, 434.

στάμεν, στάμεναι, Ep. for στῆναι.

σταμίν, ῖνος, ἡ (ἵστημι), that stands upright, the *ribs* or *side-timbers* of a ship, which rise from the keel; ἴκρια ἀραρὼν θαμέσι σταμίνεσσι, 'fitting the *deck* or *deck-planks* (ἴκρια, vid.) to the numerous ribs,' V., Od. 5, 252.† Others, as Eustath., understand by it the *cross-pieces*, the *side-boards*, by which the upright timbers were connected, see Nitzsch ad loc. (ι short from Ep. licence.)

στάν, see ἵστημι.

στάξ, Ep. for ἔσταξε, see στάζω.

στάς, see ἵστημι.

*στάσις, ιος, ἡ (ἵστημι), *sedition, strife, contention*, Batr. 135.

στατός, ή, όν (verbal adj. from ἵστημι), *placed, standing*; ἵππος, a horse standing in the stall, *6, 506. 15, 263.

σταυρός, ὁ (ἵστημι), a *stake, a pale*, 24, 453. Od. 14, 11.

σταφυλή, ἡ, *the wine-grape, the vine*, a shoot of a vine, 18, 561. Od. 7, 120. 9, 358. (In Od. 7, 120. 121. Franke ad Callim. p. 167, as also Bothe, rejects the words: μῆλον δ' ἐπὶ—σταφυλή.)

σταφύλη, ἡ, *the plummet*, in the car-penter's *level*; then, a pl... ἵπποι σταφύλῃ ἐπὶ νῶτον ... equal on the back by the ... actly matched in height ...

στάχυς, υος, ἡ, Ep. a... ear of grain, 23, 598.†

ΣΤΑΩ, ground form of ...

στέαρ, ατος, τό (ἵστημι)... *tallow*, *Od. 21, 178. 183. be read as a dissyllable.)

στείβω, only pres. and ... *to trample, to tread in pi...* spoken of horses, νέκυα... 499; εἵματα ἐν βόθροισι, ... in a cistern in order to cl... 6, 92.

στεῖλα, Ep. for ἔστειλα...

στειλειή, ἡ (στέλλω), ... an axe for inserting the ... 422.†

στειλειόν, τό (στέλλω)... an axe, Od. 5, 236.†

στεῖνος, εος, τό, poet... *narrowness, a narrow s...* 66. 15, 426. Od. 22, 460... a narrow way, a narrow p... 2) Metaph. *pressure, dist...* Ap. 533.

στείνω, Ep. for στένω... *make narrow, to contrac...* pass. στείνομαι, *to becom... tracted*; θυρετρὰ φεύγοντ... gate is too narrow to one ... 386; λαοὶ στείνοντο, th... contracted, i. e. pressed t... 34; hence, a) *to be oppre...* τινί, by any thing, νεκύε... λαχνῷ, Od. 9, 445. b) *to ... oneself*, ἀρνῶν, Od. 9, 219.

στεινωπός, όν, Ion. ... (στενός, ὤψ), *narrow,* στειν. ὁδός, a *narrow way,* a gorge, 7, 143. 23, 416 ... ὁδός, Od. 12, 234.

στείομεν, Ep. for στῶμ...

στείρη, ἡ, Ion. for στεί... main timber in the bottom ... *keel*, 1, 482. Od. 2, 228.

στεῖρος, η, ον, Ion. f... prop. *stiff, hard*; henc... *fruitful*, unsuitable for ... rilis). βοῦς στείρη, *Od... 20, 186.

στείχω, poet. aor. 2 ... *enter in ranks, to marc...* 258; generally, *to go, to p...* ἐς πόλεμον, to go to the ... ἄστυ, Od. 7, 72; spoken ... 11, 17.

στέλλω, fut. στελέω... aor. ἔστειλα, Ep. στεῖ... λάμην, 1) *to place*; esp... a becoming condition, wit... to arrange the companio... to prepare, *to fit out*, νῆα ... 248. 2) *to send*, τινὰ ἐ... 325; ἀγγελίην ἔπι, to se... bassy, 4, 38†. 3) *to tak...* ἱστία, Od. 3, 11. 16, 3 ... either to take down or t...

it the latter, because ἀείραντες fol-
so; the sails were drawn up to the
yard and tied fast to it. They were
let down with the yard. Mid. *to
see oneself*, i. e. to prepare oneself, to
. oneself, Il. 23, 285. 2) *to draw in,*
(with reference to the subject [*vela
brakere*, Db.]), 1, 433.

στέμμα, ατος, τό (στέφω), prop. *a garland*; and plur. στέμμα Ἀπόλλωνος, the
band or wreath (laurel-wreath) of
Apollo. According to Eustath. and the
critics, a garland, sacred to Apollo,
bound with woollen cords; this the
priest bears, as a suppliant, upon his
staff, 1, 14. 28. Heyne incorrectly rejects
his explanation, and understands by it,
'the holy priestly fillet' (*infula*), h. in
Ap. 179.

στενάχεσχ' for στενάχεσκε, see στενάχω.
στεναχίζω, poet. form = στενάζω, *to
sigh, to groan*, 19, 304. Od. 1, 243. Mid.
with like signif., Il. 7, 95; metaph.
spoken of the earth; ὑπὸ ποσσὶ στεναχίζετο γαῖα. the earth resounded, groaned
under their feet, 2, 84. (Only pres. and
imperf. The form στοναχίζω is rejected
by Wolf, after the Cod. Ven., cf. Buttm.
Lex. s. v., who defends it.)
στενάχω, poet. form of στενάζω; iterat.
imperf. στενάχεσκε, only pres. and imperf. 1) *to sigh, to groan*, spoken of
men. 8, 334. 13, 423; of beasts, *to pant*,
16, 393. 489. b) Metaph. spoken of the
sea and of rivers: *to resound, to roar*,
16, 391. Od. 4, 516; *to bemoan, to bewail*,
τινά, Il. 19, 392. Mid. = act. intrans.
19, 301; and trans., Od. 9, 467.
Στέντωρ, ορος, ὁ, a herald of the Greeks
before Troy, who could cry as loud as
fifty others; according to the Schol. an
Arcadian, who contended with Herês in
shouting and lost his life, 5, 785.
στένω. Ion. στείνω, only pres. and imperf. for the most part poet. to make
narrow, to contract; then, *to sigh, to
groan*. in which signif. H. uses the form
στείνω, 10, 16. 18, 33; metaph. spoken
of the sea: *to roar, to resound*, 23, 230.
Cf. στείνω.
στερεός, ή. όν (ἵστημι), compar. στερεώτερος. 1) *stiff, rigid, hard*, λίθος, σίδηρος. Od. 19, 494; βοέη, Il. 17, 493. 2)
Metaph. *hard, severe*, ἔπεα, 12, 267;
κραδίη, Od. 23, 103. The adv. στερεῶς,
fast, firmly, Il. 10, 263. Od. 14, 346;
metaph *firmly, severely*, ἀποειπεῖν, Il. 9,
510. h. Ven. 25.
στερέω, aor. 1 infin. στερέσαι, Ep. for
στερῆσαι, *to plunder*, τινά τινος, Od. 13,
262.
στέρνον, τό (στερεός), *the breast*, prop.
the upper long part of it, 2, 479. 7, 224.
Od. 5, 346; also spoken of beasts, Il. 4,
106. 23, 365. Od. 3, 443.
στεροπή. ή, poet. = ἀστεροπή (ἀστράπτω), 1) *lightning*, 11, 66. 184. 2) splendour similar to lightning, *a flash, a gleam,
a beam, brightness*, spoken of metals, 19,
363. Od. 4, 72.

στεροπηγερέτα, αο, ὁ, Ep. for στεροπηγερέτης, epith. of Zeus, who collects
the lightning (ἀγείρω), or according to
Apoll. who excites (ἐγείρω) the lightning,
the lightning-sender, 16, 298.†
(στεῦμαι), poet. akin to ἵσταμαι, only
3 sing. pres. στεῦται, and 3 sing. imperf.
στεῦτο. prop. *to stand* in order to begin
any thing; hence, 1) to assume the air
of being about to do something, to place
oneself, *to strive*. στεῦτο διψάων, thirsting he strove [*to drink;* πιέειν, to be
borrowed fm the following clause, Fäsi],
Od. 11, 584; according to Eustath. ἵστατο. thirsting he stood. 2) *to promise, to
assure. to boast, to threaten*, with infin.
fut., Il. 2, 597 3, 83. 9, 241; and infin.
aor., Od. 17, 525. According to Eustath.
it arose from a contraction of the form
στέομαι into στεῦμαι, the resulting diphthong passing into the other persons also,
Kühner, § 242. Anm. Thiersch § 223, f.
στεφάνη, ἡ (στέφω), prop. any thing
encompassing the upper part of a body;
hence a) *a garland, a crown*, as a female
head-ornament, 18. 597. b) *a rim, a
brim, a border*, of the helmet, 7, 12. 11,
96; also the helmet itself, 10, 30. c) *the
brow* of a mountain. *13, 138.
στέφανος, ὁ (στέφω), *a garland, a
crown*, h. 6, 42. 2) Generally any thing
which encompasses; hence metaph.
[spoken of a company or circle of warriors, κύκλος πολεμούντων, Schol.] πάντη
στέφανος πολέμοιο δέδηε περὶ σε, the
crown of battle burns every where around
thee [War, like a fiery circle, all around
Environs thee, Cp.], *13, 736.†
στεφανόω (στέφανος). perf. pass. ἐστεφάνωμαι, in H. only mid. to encompass
a thing as a border, *to wind oneself*. ἦν
περὶ πάντη φόβος ἐστεφάνωται, round
about which fear wound itself (which
fear encompassed), 5, 739. 11. 36. ἀμφὶ
δέ μιν νέφος ἐστεφάνωτο, a cloud wound
itself about him, enveloped him; 15,
153. περὶ νῆσον πόντος ἐστεφάνωτο, Od.
10, 195. h. Ven. 120. 2) With accus. *to
surround, to encompass* any thing. τά τ'
(τείρεα) οὐρανὸς ἐστεφάνωται, Il. 18, 485;
or pass. with which the heaven is crowned. accus. of object with the pass. Cf.
Kühner, § 485. Anm. 2. (The act. is not
found at all in H.)
στέφω, 1) *to surround, to encompass,
to encircle;* τὶ ἀμφί τινι, to put any thing
around any man, 18, 205; 2) Metaph.
to adorn, to ornament; μορφὴν ἔπεσσι,
his form with the gift of words [better,
formam addit sermoni; crowns his discourse with beauty], Od. 8, 170.
στέωμεν, Ep. for στῶμεν, see ἵστημι.
στῆ, Ep. for ἔστη; στήῃ, Ep. for στῇ,
see ἵστημι.
στῆθος, εος, τό (στῆναι, prop. that
which projects), Ep. gen. and dat. στήθεσφι, *the breast*, both male and female,
in the sing. and plur. 2, 218. 544. 23,
761; also spoken of beasts, 11, 282. 2)
Metaph. *the breast* as the seat of the feel-

ings, passions, and thoughts, 3, 63. 6, 51. Od. 2. 304.

στήλη, ἡ (ἴστημι), a column, 13, 437; esply a) a pillar, a buttress for the support of walls, 12, 259. b) a monumental pillar, a grave-stone, 11, 371. 16, 457. Od. 12, 14; and often.

στήμεναι, see ἴστημι.

*στήμων, ονος, ὁ, the warp in the loom, Batr. 83.

στηρίζω (ἴστημι), aor. 1 ἐστήριξα, and Ep. στήριξα, aor. mid. infin. στηρίξασθαι, 3 sing. pluperf. mid. ἐστήρικτο, 1) Trans. to support, to place firmly, to sustain, with accus. ἴριδας ἐν νέφεϊ, 11, 28; κάρη οὐρανῷ, to sustain the head in the clouds, i. e. to extend, 4, 443. 2) to support oneself, to stand firmly, ποσίν, Od. 12, 434; in like manner mid. intrans. πόδεσσιν, to stand firmly with the feet, 1 . 21, 242. b) With dat. κακὸν κακῷ ἐστήρικτο, evil pressed upon evil, 16, 111. δεκατὸς μεὶς οὐρανῷ ἐστήρικτο, the tenth month ascended the heavens, h. Merc. 11.

στιβαρός, ή, όν (στείβω), compar. στιβαρώτερος, η, ον, prop. firmly trodden; hence pressed, thick, firm, stout, strong, spoken of human limbs and of arms, 3, 335. 5, 400. 746. Od. 8, 187.

στιβαρῶς, adv. thick, firmly, 12, 454.†

στίβη, ἡ (στείβω), prop. condensed vapour), rime, hoar-frost, esply morning frost, *Od. 5, 467. 17, 25.

*στίβος, ὁ (στείβω), a trodden path, a way, a foot-path, h. Merc. 353.

στίλβω, to gleam, to shine, to beam, ἐλαίῳ, with evil, 18, 596; metaph. spoken of the shining of the skin, κάλλεϊ, χάρισιν, 3, 392. Od. 6, 237; ἀπό τινος, h. 31, 11.

στιλπνός, ή, όν, poet. (στίλβω), shining, gleaming, beaming, ἔερσαι, 14, 351.†

ΣΤΙΞ, Ep. in the nom. absol. for the prose στίχος, from which gen. sing. στιχός, and nom. and accus. plur. στίχες and στίχας, a row, a rank, esply a rank in battle, sing. 20, 362; mly plur. στίχες ἀνδρῶν, the ranks of men Il. and Od. κατὰ στίχας, in close ranks, by ranks, also ἐπὶ στίχας, 18, 602.

στιχάομαι, mid. poet. (στίχος), only 3 plur. imperf. ἐστιχόωντο for ἐστιχῶντο, to proceed in a line, generally, to march, to advance, spoken of warriors, εἰς ἀγορήν, 2, 92; ἐς μέσσον, 3, 266; of ships, *2, 516. 602.

Στιχίος, ὁ, leader of the Athenians before Troy, slain by Hector, 13, 195. 15, 329, seq.

*στοιχεῖον, τό (prop. dimin. from στοῖχος), prop. a small pole, a pin. 2) a letter; and as these are the simplest component parts of speech, hence in the plur. 3) στοιχεῖα, the simplest component parts of things, the elements, Batr. 61.

στόμα, ατος. τό, 1) the mouth of animals, the jaws, hence metaph. στόμα πολέμοιο, ὑσμίνης, the jaws of war, of the battle, poet. for the desolating

war, 10, 8. 19, 313. 20, 359. planation of Heyne, 'the first van,' belongs to a later peri verbial, ἀνὰ στόμα ἔχειν, διὰ σ σθαι, to carry in the mouth utter, 14, 91. ἀπὸ στόματος speak out freely, Batr. 77. 2) the opening of rivers, 12, 24. στ. ἠϊόνος (V. an inlet of the 14, 36 (It was a coast stret into the sea [rather, into t bounded on both sides by pron λαύρης, the termination of t Od. 22, 137. 3) Generally, the spicuous part; hence the face 16, 410. b) Spoken of a sp στόμα. at the point, 15, 389. cers of a crab, Batr. 300.

στόμαχος, ὁ (στόμα). a mou in Hom. the gorge, the throat 17, 47. 19, 266.

στοναχέω, poet. (στοναχή), aor. στοναχῆσαι, to sigh, to l 124.† cf. Buttm., Lex. p.

στοναχή, ἡ, poet. (στένω), sighing, groaning, a sigh, oft plur. 2, 356. Od. 5, 83.

στοναχίζω. see στεναχίζω.

στονόεις, εσσα, εν, poet. (στ of sighs, i. e. causing many si lamentable, mournful, κήδεα, β Od. 17, 102; ἀοιδή, a dirge, Il

στόνος, ὁ, poet. (στένω), t sighing, groaning, the rattli throat of the dying, 4, 445. 1 23, 40.

στορέννυμι, aor. 1 ἐστόρεσα ρεσα from στρώννυμι, perf. pα μαι, 3 sing. pluperf. pass. ἐσ pres. does not occur), 1) to lay down any thing (sternere); prepare a couch, 9, 621. Pa 158: also δέμνια, τάπητας, Ο 13, 73; ἀνθρακιήν, to spread Il. 9, 213. 2) to make level, passable, prop. spoken of a πόντον, Od. 3, 158.

Στρατίη, ἡ (appell. στρατιή, a town in Arcadia, in Strabo stroyed, 2, 606.

Στρατίος, ὁ (appell. στρατιή, son of Nestor and Anaxibia. (

στρατός, ὁ (στράω = στορέ gen. στρατόφιν, 10, 347; a ca camped army. and generally, 10. Od. 2, 30.

στρατόομαι, mid. (στρατός), perf. ἐστρατόωντο, Ep. for to be encamped, 3, 187; πρὸς 377. cf. Buttm., Gr. Gram. I.

*στρεβλός, ή, όν (στρέφω), twisted, crooked. 2) Spoken squint, Batr. 297.

στρεπτός, ή, όν (στρεφω), twisted, wound. στρ. χιτών, a of mail, which was formed rings, according to Aristare haps we are to understand with which the two plates of were united, 5, 113. (Pa

Schol. Ven.: a tunic of twisted work.) 2) that may be easily turned, *pliable, voluble*, γλῶσσα, 20, 248; hence *tractable, manageable*, φρένες, 15, 203; θεοί, 9, 497.

στρεύγομαι, depon. pass. poet. (akin to στράγγω), prop. *to be expressed drop by drop*, hence *to become gradually enfeebled, exhausted, to become weary*, ἐν αἰνῇ δηϊοτῆτι, 15, 512; ἐν νήσῳ, Od. 12, 351.

στρεφεδινέω, poet. (στρέφω, δινέω), *to whirl around in a circle*; pass. *to turn oneself round in a circle*. στρεφεδίνηθεν (Ep. for ἐστρεφεδινήθησαν) δέ οἱ ὄσσε, his eyes ['*swam dizzy* at the stroke,' *Cp.*], Il. 16, 792.† [According to Meiring, from στρέφεσθαι δίνῃ. *Am. Ed.*]

στρέφω, fut. στρέψω, aor. Ep. στρέψα, iterat. στρέψασκον, fut. mid. στρέψομαι, perf. pass. ἔστραμμαι, aor. 1 pass. ἐστρέφθην, 1) Act. intrans. *to turn, to turn about, to bend*, with accus. οὖρον, Od. 4, 520; esply ἵππους, *to turn the horses*, Il. 8, 168. Od. 15, 205; pass. στρεφθείς, *firmly twisted*, Od. 9, 435. 2) Intrans. *to turn oneself, to turn about*, Il. 18, 544; ἀνὰ ὄγμους. v. 546. εἰς Ἔρεβος στρέψας, Od. 10, 528. Mid. with aor. pass. 1) *to turn oneself, to turn*, Il. 18, 488. ἔνθα καὶ ἔνθα στρέφεται, *to turn oneself hither and thither*, 24, 5; hence 1) *to turn oneself to*, 12, 42. ἐστραμμέναι ἀλλήλῃσιν, h. Merc. 411; or *to turn oneself from*, ἐκ χώρης, *to go from the region*, 6, 516. 15, 645. 2) Like *versari, to turn oneself about, to have intercourse with*, with accus. h. Ap. 175.

στρέψασκον, see στρέφω.

στρόμβος, ὁ (στρέφω), prop. *a twisted body*. hence *a whirlwind*, 14, 413.†

στρουθός, ἡ, *a sparrow*, *2, 311. 317 (elsewhere also ὁ στρ.)

στροφάλιγξ, ιγγος, ἡ (στροφαλίζω), *a whirlwind*, esply κονίης, of dust, 16, 775. 21, 503. Od. 24, 39.

στροφαλίζω, poet. (στρέφω), a strengthened form, *to turn*, ἠλάκατα, Od. 18, 315.†

Στρόφιος, ὁ (dexterous, from στροφή) father of Scamandrius, 5, 49.

στρόφος, ὁ (στρέφω), *a twisted cord, a string, a rope, a girdle*, the band of a wallet, *Od. 13, 438. 17, 198. 2) *a swathing-band*, h. Ap. 123.

στρώννυμι, see στορέννυμι.

στρωφάω, poet. form of στρέφω, *to turn*, ἠλάκατα, Od. 6, 53. 17, 97. Mid. *to turn oneself*, κατά τινα, *to any one*, Il. 13. 557. b) *to turn oneself* hither and thither, i. e. *to abide, to remain*, κατὰ μέγαρα, 9, 463; ἑκάς, 20, 422. h. Cer. 48.

στυγερός, ή, όν, adv. στυγερῶς (στυγέω), prop. *hated, abhorred*; generally, *hateful, abominable, horrible*. a) Spoken of persons: Ἀΐδης, 8, 368; στυγερὸς δέ οἱ ἔπλετο θυμῷ, he was odious to her in the soul, 14, 158. b) Of things: πόλεμος, σκότος, γάμος, πένθος, 4, 240. Od.

1, 249. 16, 126. Adv. στυγερῶς, *terribly, horribly*, Il. 16, 123. Od. 21, 374. 23, 23.

στυγέω, aor. 2 ἔστυγον, aor. 1 ἔστυξα, causat. 1) Pres. with aor. 2 *to hate, to abhor, to fear*, τινά, 7, 112. Od. 13, 400. b) *to stand in awe of, to fear*, with infin., Il. 1, 186. 8, 515. 2) In the aor. 1 *to render odious, frightful*, τῷ κέ τεῳ στύξαιμι μένος. Od. 11, 502.

Στύμφηλος, ἡ, Ion. for Στύμφαλος, a town in Arcadia on the Stymphalian lake, 2, 608; famous in mythology on account of the Stymphalian birds.

Στύξ, Στυγός, ἡ (the horrible). 1) A river in the under world, by which the gods swore the most dreadful and sacred oath, 2, 755. Od. 8, 369. The Cocÿtus is a branch of it, Od. 10, 514. 2) As a nymph, daughter of Oceanus and Tethys, Hes. Th. 361. h. Cer. 424. She dwelt, according to Hes. Th. 778, at the entrance of the under world; her stream is a branch of Oceanus, and, as a part of it, flows from the world above to the world below, Il. 15, 37. Zeus granted to her, Hes. Thes. 383, the honour to be the most sacred oath of the gods, 14, 271. Od. 5, 183. According to Hes. Th. 783, seq., any one of the immortals, who had sworn a false oath, was obliged to lie down a full year breathless in sickness. Perhaps the fable was derived from the Arcadian fountain near Nonakris, whose water was said to be deadly, Hdt. 6, 74.

Στύρα, τά, a town on the island of Eubœa, 2, 539.

στυφελίζω (στυφελός), fut. στυφελίξω. aor. ἐστυφέλιξα, Ep. στυφελίξα, 1) *to strike, to thrust, to shake*, with accus. ἀσπίδα, 5, 437; τινά, 7, 261; νέφεα, *to scatter the clouds*, 11, 305. b) *to thrust away, to chase away*, τινὰ ἐξ ἑδέων, ἐκ δαιτύος, ἐκτὸς ἀταρπιτοῦ, 1, 581. Od. 17, 234. 2) Generally, *to push hither and thither, to abuse, to insult*, τινά, Il. 21, 380. 512; pass., Od. 16. 108. 20, 318.

σύ, person. pron. of the second person, nom. Ep. τύνη. gen. Ep. σέο, σεῦ, σεῖο, τεοῖο, 8, 37; σέθεν, dat. σοί, τοί, accus. σέ (σε). The common gen. σοῦ is not found in Hom., σοί is always orthotone, τοί always enclitic: *thou*, gen. *thine*. σύγε, σύπερ, and connected with αὐτός, in which case it always retains the accent, 3, 51. 19, 416; hence we should write σοὶ αὐτῷ for σοι αὐτῷ, Od. 4, 601. 5, 187. 6, 39; cf. Thiersch, § 204, 205. Rost, Dial 44. Kühner, § 301.

συβόσιον, τό (βόσις). *a herd of swine*, with συῶν, 11, 679. Od. 14, 101 (with ι lengthened).

συβώτης, αο, ὁ (βόσκω), *a swine-herd*; often, *Od. 4, 640.

σύγε, see σύ.

συγκαλέω (καλέω), partcp. aor. συγκαλέσας, *to call together, to collect*, with accus. *2, 55. 10, 302.

συγκλονέω, poet. (κλονέω), *to confound, to put in confusion*, with accus. 13, 722.†

συγκυρέω, poet. (κυρέω), aor. 1 optat.
συγκύρσειαν, to strike together, to meet,
to justle (of chariots), 23, 435.†

συγχέω (χέω), aor. 1 συνέχευα, infin.
συγχεύαι, partcp. συγχέας, Ep. syncop.
aor. 2 mid. σύγχυτο, 1) to pour together, esply with the ruling notion of
disorder. to confound, to confuse, to
blend, to cast together, ψάμαθον, 15, 364;
and pass. 16, 471. 2) Metaph. a) Spoken
of things: to render null, to make void,
ὅρκια, 4, 269; κάματον, ἰούς, 15, 366.
473. b) In a mental respect, to confuse,
to sadden, to disquiet, θυμόν. νόον, 9,
612. 13, 808; ἄνδρα, Od. 8, 139. (V. 'to
destroy.')

συκέη, ἡ, contr. συκῆ, a fig-tree, Od.
7, 116. 11, 590; only once the longer
form, which is to be pronounced as a
monosyllable, *Od. 24, 341.

σῦκον, τό, a fig, Od. 7, 121. †Batr. 31.

συλάω, fut. σω, aor. optat. συλήσειε,
subj. συλήσω, partcp. συλήσας, also often
3 sing. imperf. ἐσύλα, and dual συλήτην,
13, 202. 1) to take away, to take down,
with accus. πῶμα φαρέτρης, 4, 116; τόξον,
to take out (of the case), 4, 105. 2) Esply
spoken of despoiling slain enemies, to
take away, to plunder, to strip, τεύχεα
ἀπ' ὤμων, 6, 28; and τεύχεα, alone, 4,
466. b) With accus. of the pers. to rob,
to plunder, to despoil, νεκρούς, 10, 343;
and τινὰ τεύχεα, to despoil any one of
arms, 6, 71. 15, 428. 16, 499; poet. form
συλεύω, *Il.

συλεύω, poet. form of συλάω, *5, 48.
24, 436.

συλλέγω, Ep. and Att. ξυλλέγω (λέγω),
partcp. aor. συλλέξας, aor. 1 mid. συν-
ελεξάμην, Ep. συλλεξάμην, fut. mid. συλ-
λέξομαι. 1) to put together, to bring together, to collect, τί, 18, 301. Mid. to
lay together for oneself, ὅπλα ἐς λάρνακα
(his implements), 18, 413. b) Spoken of
persons, to assemble, with accus., Od. 2,
292. (Bothe in his ed. has always ξυλλ.)

συμβάλλω or ξυμβάλλω (βάλλω), aor. 2
συνέβαλον, Ep. σύμβαλον, aor. mid. συν-
εβαλόμην; of the Ep. syncop. aor. act.
ξυμβλήτην (as if from βλῆμι), Od. 21,
15; infin. ξυμβλήμεναι, Il. 21, 578; Ep.
syncop. aor. mid. ξύμβλητο, 14, 39;
ξύμβληντο, 14, 27; subj. ξύμβληται, Od.
7, 204; partcp. ξυμβλήμενος, Od. 11,
127; from which Ep. fut. συμβλήσομαι,
Il. 20, 335. 1) Trans. to cast together. to
bring together, with accus. spoken of
rivers, ὕδωρ, to unite the water, 4, 453;
ῥόας, 5, 774; esply in war, ῥινούς, ἔγχεα,
to clash spears and shields together, 4,
447. 8, 61; metaph. πόλεμον, to begin a
battle, 12, 181. b) Spoken of persons:
to bring together, to put together, to set
together, in battle, ἀμφοτέρους, 20, 55;
with infin. μάχεσθαι. 3, 70. 2) Intrans.
like the mid. to fall in with, to meet.
τινί, Od. 21, 15; esply, to meet in battle,
to fall upon another, with infin., Il. 16,
565; Ep. aor. 21, 578. Mid. to fall in
with, to meet, with any one, τινί, often in

the Ep. aor. 2. Il. 14. 27. 231.
esply to meet, in battle, to con
conflict, Il. 16, 565.

Σύμη, ἡ, an island betwee
and Cnidus, on the coast of (
Symi; from which Σύμηθεν, f
2, 671.

συμμάρπτω. poet. (μάρπτω
aor. συμμάρψας, to grasp u
break off, τί, 10, 467.†

συμμητιάομαι, depon. mid. (μ
infin. pres. συμμητιάασθαι, Ep
μητιᾶσθαι, to consult togethe
berate, 10, 197.†

συμμίγνυμι, Hom. συμμίσγω
aor. συνέμιξα, aor. pass. συνεμ
to mingle together, to unite, τ
81; esply spoken of love, θεα
h. Ven. 80. Mid. to mingle
(with reference to the subje
of rivers, with dat. Πηνειῷ, 2
pugilistic combat, in tmesis, 2
μίγνυμι.

συμμίσγω, Hom. for συμμίγ
συμμύω, in tmesis, see μύω.

σύμπᾶς, ᾱσα, ᾱν, Ep. and A
(πᾶς strengthened by σύν), o
plur. all together, 1, 241. (Th
πάντα stands, Od. 7, 214. 14,
out metrical necessity; cf.
§ 175, 4)

συμπήγνυμι (πήγνυμι), aor. 1
to join together, to cause to ca
curdle or concrete, γάλα, 5, 90?

συμπίπτω (πίπτω), to fall i
meet in battle, only aor. 2 in
256. 21, 687; spoken of the w
295; cf. πίπτω.

συμπλαταγέω (πλαταγέω),
πλατάγησα, Ep. for συνεπλατ
together, χερσί, to clap the
192.†

συμφερτός, ἡ, όν (συμφέρω
together; hence, united, conn
φερτὴ δ' ἀρετὴ πέλει ἀνδρῶν,
λυγρῶν, the united force, ev
weak men, avails somewhat
(Thus Köppen, Spitzner, aft
πέλει must then be rendered
effects [Arist. καὶ σφόδρα κα
πων εἰς ταυτὸν συνελθόντων
ἀρετή]. The other explana
φερτὴ for συμφέρουσα, i. e
does not suit the context.)

συμφέρω (φέρω), fut. mid.
prop. to bring together, on
meet with, like congredi,
conflict, to engage in combat,
8, 400; μάχη, *11, 736.

συμφράδμων, ονος, ὁ, ἡ,
μων), deliberating with, aidi
sel, 2, 372.†

συμφράζομαι. mid. (φράζ
συνεφρασάμην, Ep. συμφρα
to consult, τινί, with any α
202; βουλάς τινι, to give cou
one, Il. 1, 537. 9, 374. 2)
by oneself, to ponder, θυμῷ, C

*σύμφωνος, ον (φωνή), con
monious, h. Merc. 51.

σύν, Ep. and old Att. ξύν, the latter rarely used, and only for some metrical reason. I) Prep. with dat. primary signif. with (cum). 1) Spoken of place, in indicating coexistence of persons: with, together with, in company with; σὺν ἑταίροις, often with the implied notion of assistance, σὺν θεῷ, with the help of the deity, 3, 439. 9, 49; σὺν 'Αθήνῃ, 10, 290. Od. 8, 493. b) Spoken of things: σὺν νηυσί, σκήπτρῳ, Il. 1, 179. 2, 187; σὺν τεύχεσι, ἔντεσι, ἄνεμος σὺν λαίλαπι. 17, 57. 2) Spoken of causal relations: a) In indicating the means, by which any thing is produced: with, by means of. σὺν νεφέεσσιν, Od. 5, 293. b) In assigning the measure by which the action is limited, σύν τε μεγάλῳ ἀπέτισαν, Il. 4, 161. II) As adv. at once, at the same time, together, 1, 579. 4, 269. 23, 879; σὺν δύο. two together, 10, 224. III) In composition it has the signif. of the adv., with, at once, together, and also that of accomplishing.

συναγείρω, Ep. and Att. ξυναγείρω (ἀγείρω). aor. 1 Ep. ξυνάγειρα, aor. 1 mid. Ep. ξυναγείρατο, Od. 14, 323; Ep. aor. 2 mid. συναγρόμενος, to bring together, to collect, spoken of persons and things, Il. 20, 21; βίοτον, Od. 4, 90. Mid. to collect or bring together for oneself, with accus. κτήματα, Od. 14, 323; ἵππους. Il. 15, 680 (συναγείρεται, shortened subj. aor. 1 mid. where Spitzner has adopted συναείρεται, after the Schol. A.). b) Intrans. to assemble, in partcp. aor. 2 mid. 11, 687. 24, 802.

συνάγνυμι, Ep. and Att. ξυνάγνυμι (ἄγνυμι), aor. 1 Ep. ξυνέαξα, to break in pieces, to shiver, to shatter, with accus. ἔγχος, 13, 166; νῆας, Od. 14. 383; τέκνα [breaks in pieces, Cp. (of a lion)], Il. 11, 114. (Hom. employs the form with ξ even without metrical necessity.)

συνάγω, Ep. and Att. ξυνάγω (ἄγω), fut. ξω, aor. 2 συνήγαγον, to lead together, to bring or gather together, with accus. γεραιὰς νηόν, to collect the matrons into the temple, 6, 87; ὅρκια θεῶν, 3. 269; φόρτον τινί, Od. 14, 291. b) Metaph. as συμβάλλειν 'Αρηα, to join or begin a battle, Il. 2, 381; also ἔριδα 'Αρηος, 6, 861; ὑσμίνην, 16, 764; πόλεμον. h. Cer. 267.

συναείρω, poet. (ἀείρω), aor. συνήειρα, prop. 1) to lift up together, in tmesis, 24, 590. 2) to take together, σὺν δ' ἤειρεν ἱμᾶσι, viz. ἵππους ('he bound them together with straps,' V.), 10, 499. Mid. τίσυρας συναείρεται ἵππους. ed. Spitzner, to harness together, cf. συναγείρω, *15, 680. (Eustath. explains it in the two last passages, by συμπλέκειν, συζευγνύειν; ἀείρειν is compounded of ἀ (ἅμα) and εἴρω, and thus equivalent to ὁμοῦ εἴρειν; but cf. παρήορος and συνήορος.)

συναίνυμαι, poet. (αἴνυμαι), to take together, to collect, with accus. 21, 502.†

συναίρω (αἱρέω), aor. 2 συνεῖλον, to take together, to gather together (with

violence and haste), with accus. χλαῖναν Od. 20, 25. 2) to take away, to tear away to crush (Schol. συνέτριψε), ὀφρῦς [dashed both his brows In pieces, Cp.]. Il. 16, 740

συναντάω, poet. ἀντέω (ἀντάω), imperf. dual. συναντήτην, aor. 1 mid. συνηντησά-μην, to meet with any one, Od. 16, 333. Mid. = act. to come against, to meet, τινί, Il. 17, 134.

συνάντομαι, poet. form of ἀντάω, in the pres. and imperf. 7, 22. 21, 34. Od. 4, 367. 15, 538.

συναράσσω (ἀράσσω), fut. ξω, aor. Ep. συνάραξα, to strike together, to dash in pieces, with accus. 12, 384. Od. 12, 412; only in tmesis.

*συναραρίσκω ('ΑΡΩ), only in the perf. συνάρηρα, intrans. to be joined together, to be united, h. Ap. 164.

*συναρωγός, ὁ (ἀρωγός), an assistant, an aid, h. 7, 4.

συνδέω, Ep. and Att. ξυνδέω (δέω), aor. 1 Ep. συνέδησα and ξυνέδ., infin. ξυνδῆσαι. 1) to bind together, to bind fast, to fetter, τινά, 1, 399; πόδας, Od. 10, 168. h. Merc. 82. 2) to bind up, spoken of a wound, Il. 13, 599. (In the Il. always the Att. form.)

*συνδύο, as dual (δύο). two and two, two together, h. Ven. 74 (in Il. separate).

συνέδραμον, see συντρέχω.

συνεεργάθω, Ep. form for συνεέργω (εἴργω), to enclose, to shut up, 14, 36.†

συνέεργω, Ep. for συνείργω, prop. to enclose together: then, to bind together, τὶ λύγοισιν Od. 9, 427. 12, 424; χιτῶνα ζωστῆρι, to bind together the tunic with the girdle, *Od. 14, 72.

συνείκοσι, Ep. and Att. ξυνεείκοσι, twenty together, Od. 14, 98.†

σύνειμι (εἰμί). fut. infin. Ep. and Att. ξυνέσεσθαι, to be together, to live with, ὀϊζύϊ πολλῇ, Od. 7, 270.†

σύνειμι (εἶμι), Ep. and Att. imperf. 3 plur. ξύνισαν, partcp. ξυνιόντες; on the other hand, συνίτην, 6, 120. 16, 476 (Bothe with ξ), to go or come together, ἐς χῶρον ἕνα, 4, 446. 8, 60; ἐς μέσον, 6, 120; esply in a hostile signif to meet together, to fall upon one another, 14, 393; with μάχεσθαι, 20, 159; or ἔριδι, 20, 66; absol. to fight; περὶ ἔριδος, from a spirit of strife (præ ira), *16, 476.

συνελαύνω, Ep. and Att. ξυνελαύνω (ἐλαύνω), aor. 1 συνήλασα, Ep. συν έλασσα, infin ξυνελάσσαι. to drive together, with accus. ληΐδα ἐκ πεδίων, 11, 677; βοῦς, h. Merc. 106; to draw together, κάρη χείράς τε, h. Merc. 240; ὀδόντας, to chatter with the teeth, in tmesis. Od. 18, 98: esply to bring toge ther in battle, to urge to engage in contest, θεοὺς ἔριδι, Il. 20, 134. Od. 18, 39. 2) Intrans. to meet, to engage in battle, Il. 22, 129.

σύνελον, Ep. for συνεῖλον, see συναιρέω.

συνεοχμός, ὁ (Att. ξυνεοχμός, Bth.), poet. for συνοχμός (συνέχω), a joining. κεφαλῆς τε καὶ αὐχένος [where neck and spine unite, Cp.], 14, 465.†

συνερείδω (ἐρείδω), *to press together*, in tmesis, στόμα, Od. 11, 426.†

συνέρίθος, ὁ, ἡ (ἔριθος), *a coadjutor*, Od. 6, 32.†

συνέσευε. see συσσεύω.

σύνεσις, ἡ, Ep. and Att. ξύνεσις (συνίημι), prop. *the act of meeting, uniting*, confluence, ποταμῶν, Od. 10, 515.†

συνεχής, ές (συνέχω), *holding together*. 2) spoken of time : *perpetual, unceasing*. The neut. sing συνεχές as adv., *perpetually, unceasingly* (continenter), 12, 26; also συνεχὲς αἰεί, Od. 9, 74.

συνέχω, Ep. and Att. ξυνέχω (ἔχω), Ep. perf. συνόχωκα, prop. *to hold together*, i. e. intrans. *to strike together, to unite*, 4, 133. 20, 415. 478. τὼ δὲ ὤμω ἐπὶ στῆθος συνοχωκότε, his shoulders were curved together towards the breast [*were o'er his breast contracted*, Cp.], 2, 218. (Perf. simple ὄχα, ὦχα, and with Att. redupl. ὄκωχα, see Thiersch, § 232, 6‡. Buttm., p. 283. Kühner, § 168.

*συνήθεια, ἡ (ἦθος), 1) *dwelling together*. 2) *custom, a customary manner*. συνήθειαι μαλακαί, consuetudines molles, = consuetudo leniter tangendi fides. Franke, h. Merc. 485.

συνημοσύνη, ἡ (συνήμων), *connexion, union*, hence *a promise, an agreement*, 22, 261.†

συνήορος, ον (συνείρω), *associated, united*. φόρμιγξ δαιτὶ συνήορος ('*the seasonable companion of a banquet*'), Od. 8, 99.†

συνθεσίη, ἡ, poet. (συντίθημι), *an agreement, contract, covenant*, 2, 339; in the plur. *a commission*, *5, 319.

συνθέω (θέω), fut. συνθεύσομαι, *to run together*; metaph. *to run happily, to go well*, Od. 20, 245.†

συνίημι. Ep. and Att. ξυνίημι (ἵημι), pres. imperat. ξυνίει. Od. 1, 271: imperf. 3 plur. ξύνιον for ξυνίεσαν (but Spitzner, with Aristarch., ξύνιεν), Il. 1, 273; aor. 1 ξυνέηκα, Ep. for ξυνῆκα, aor. 2 imperat. ξύνες, aor. 2 mid. ξύνετο. subj. 1 plur. συνώμεθα. I) Act. 1) Prop. *to send together, to bring together*, spoken of battle: *to cause to engage*, with accus. ἔριδι μάχεσθαι, to contend in strife [rather ἔριδι ξυνέηκεν (commisit) (ὥστε) μάχεσθαι (ἔριδι), N.], 1, 8. 7, 210. 2) *to understand, to observe, to hear* (cf. conjicere); mly with accus. of the thing and gen. of the pers. ὄπα θεᾶς, ἔπος τινός, 2, 182. Od. 6, 289. b) With gen. pers. ll. 2, 26; rei, 1, 273. II) Mid. 1) *to unite, to come together, to agree*, ἀμφί τινι. 13, 282. 2) Like act. *to perceive, to observe*, τοῦ ξύνετο, Od. 4, 76.

συνίστημι (ἵστημι), only intrans in the perf. partcp. *to stand together*. b) *to arise, to begin*, πολέμοιο συνεσταότος, 14, 96.†

συνοίσομεθα, see συμφέρω.

συνορίνω, poet. (ὀρίνω), *to move with* or *together*, act. only in tmesis, 24, 467. Mid. *to move oneself, to put oneself in motion*, spoken of warlike forces, 4, 332.†

συνοχή, ἡ, Ep. and Att. ξυνοχή (συν-

έχω), the act of *holding together*, m ἐν ξυνοχῆσιν ὁδοῦ (V., with the S in the narrow part of the way), 23,

συνοχωκότε. see συνέχω.

συνταράσσω (ταράσσω), *to throw confusion*, only in tmesis, 1, 579 [' with confusion mar the feast,' Cp.. ταράσσω.

συντίθημι (τίθημι), only aor. 2 ɪ sing. σύνθετο, imperat. often σ act. *to put together*. Mid., which Hom. uses, prop. *to put any thing ther for oneself*; hence with and out θυμῷ (animo componere), *serve, to notice, to perceive, to stand*, with accus. βουλήν, ἀοιδήν, Od. 1, 328. 16, 259. b) Absol. *to tentire, to attend*, Il. 1, 76. Od. 15

σύντρεις, neut. σύντρια, *three to* Od. 9, 429.†

συντρέχω (τρέχω), aor. 2 συνέδ *to run together*, in a hostile se: *rush upon each other*, *16, 335. 337 the constr. of the dual with the pl Rost, § 100. 4. e. Kühner, § 371.)

*Σύντριψ, ιβος, ὁ, ἡ (τρίβω), ℂ prop. name of a domestic gobli breaks vessels, Ep. 14.

συνώμεθα, see συνίημι.

Σύρίη, ἡ, Ep. for Σύρος, an is the Ægean sea, between Delos a ros, now *Sira*, according to Strat 487; see Ottfr. Müller's Orchon 326, and τροπή, Od. 15, 403. T derns seek it on the eastern c Sicily, see Ὀρτυγίη; cf. Voss alt kund. II. p. 295. Völcker, Hom. p. 24.

σῦριγξ, γος, ἡ, prop. any reed 1) *a pipe*, esply *a shepherd's pipe of Pan*, 10, 13. 18, 526. h. Merc. *a spear's case, a spear-sheath* (proɪ spear's head), *19, 387.

*σῦρίζω (σῦριγξ), *to whistle*, sp a spear, Fr. 72.

συρρήγνῦμι (ῥήγνυμι), fut. *strike together, to strike in pɪ break in pieces*, metaph. κακοῖσι: ῥήκται (he is *battered* with troublɪ Od. 8, 137.†

*σύρω, *to draw, to pull, to dr accus. Batr. 87.

σῦς, συός, ὁ and ἡ dat. συΐ, plɪ σύες, always uncontr. dat. σῦ σύεσσι, accus. σύας and σῦς, a boar, a sow, mly masc. σῦς κάπ κάπριος, 5, 783. 7, 257; also ᾱ 338. cf. ὗς.

*συσσεύω (σεύω), aor. συνέ drive together. βοῦς. h. Merc. 94.

σῦτο, Ep. for ἔσσυτο, see σεύω

συφειός and συφεός, ὁ (σῦς), hog-pen, Od. 10, 234. 14, 13; α to the sty, *Od. 10, 320.

συφορβός, ὁ (φέρβω), *a sw often Od. παῖς συφ., the youn herd, Il. 21, 282. cf. ὑφορβός.

σφάζω, aor. 1 ἔσφαξα and Eɪ perf. pass. ἔσφαγμαι, *to slay*, wɪ βοῦν, 9, 466; frequently spoken fires: to cut off the neck after they were slain, *to slaughter*, 1, 459. Od. 3, 454. Pass. Il. 23, 31. Od. 10, 532.

σφαῖρα, ἡ, a *sphere;* and generally, any round body, a ball. σφαίρῃ παίζειν, to play at ball, *Od. 6, 100. 115. 8, 372.

σφαιρηδόν, adv. in the form of a sphere, 13, 204.†

σφάλλω, aor. 1 Ep. σφῆλα, infin. σφῆλαι, *to cause to fall*, esply by striking out a leg (*suppiantare*); generally, *to throw* a man, τινά, 23, 719. Od. 17, 469.

σφαραγέομαι, mid. poet. = σμαραγέω, *to rattle, to roar, to hiss*, Od. 9, 390. 2) *to be filled, to be full*. οὔθατα σφαραγεῦντο, Od. 9, 440.

σφάς, enclit. for σφέας, see σφεῖς.

σφέ, enclit. accus. plur. of σφεῖς.

σφεδανός, ἡ, όν, poet. *violent, impetuous, terrible*, only neut. adv. κελεύειν, *11, 165. 16, 372. (It is mly derived from σπεύδειν, as if σπεδανός; others from σφαδᾶν, akin to σφοδρός.)

σφεῖς, plur. of the pron. of the third person. gen. σφῶν. Ep. σφέων (always monosyllabic), σφείων, dat. σφίσι (ν), Ep. and Ion. σφί(ν), accus. σφέας (monosyllabic and dissyllabic), Ep. σφάς and rarely σφέ, 19, 265. The nom. and the neut. are not found in Hom. at all; all the forms except σφείων are enclitic; σφάς and σφέ always; σφέ, according to Buttm., in Lexil., is shortened from σφωέ, and prop. dual. 1) *they, their*, in Hom. always personal, cf. Od. 10, 355; strengthened, σφέας αὐτούς, Od. 12, 225. 2) Rare and poet. is the use of this pronoun for ὑμεῖς, Il. 10, 398; cf. Thiersch, § 204, 205. Rost, Dialect. 44. p. 204. Kühner, § 301.

σφείων, see σφεῖς.

σφέλας, αος, τό, plur. Ep. σφέλα, Od. 17, 231; a *footstool*, Od. 18, 394. cf. Buttm., Gram. § 54. Rem. 3.

σφενδόνη, ἡ, a *sling*, esply the string of the sling, spun of wool, which later was made of leather, 13, 600.† It was an unusual weapon with the Greeks; only the Locrians are mentioned as slingers, 13, 712—721.

σφέτερος, η, ον (σφεῖς), pron. of the third pers. plur. *their*, as it now stands, with Aristarch., everywhere in Hom. 4, 409; strengthened by αὐτός, Od. 1, 7. ἐπὶ σφέτερα, substantively (*ad sua*), Od. 1, 274. 14, 9.

σφηκόω, poet. (σφήξ), perf. pass. ἐσφήκωμαι, *to draw closely together*, into the form of wasps; generally, *to bind fast*, πλοχμοὶ χρυσῷ τε καὶ ἀργύρῳ ἐσφήκωντο, the locks were wound about With twine of gold and silver (*Cp.*), 17, 52.†

Σφῆλος, ὁ (adj. σφηλός, easy to shake), son of Bucolus of Athens, 15, 338.

σφῆλεν, Ep. for ἔσφηλε, see σφάλλω.

σφήξ, σφηκός, ὁ, a *wasp*, *12, 167. 16, 259. According to Bothe we are not here to understand common wasps (*vespæ vulgares*), but *hornets* (*vespæ crabrones*). Linn.

σφί and σφίν, see σφεῖς.

*σφίγγω, *to contract, to draw together* πόδας κατὰ γαστέρος, to draw the legs to the body, Batr. 71, 88.

σφοδρῶς, adv. (from σφοδρός), *vehemently, violently, impetuously*, Od. 12, 124.†

σφονδύλιος, ὁ, Ep. for σφόνδυλος, a *vertebra* of the back-bone; plur. *the vertebræ*, 20, 483.†

σφός, σφή, σφόν (σφεῖς), sing. *his, her, it* (*suus*), plur. *their*, like σφέτερος, 1, 534. Od. 2, 237. σὺν σφοῖσιν τεκέεσσι. h. Ap. 148. Herm. reads: αὐτοῖς σὺν τεκέεσσι.

σφῦρα, ἡ, a *hammer, a mallet*, Od. 3, 434; where in ed. Wolf, σφύραν stands incorrectly, see Buttm., Ausf. Gram. § 33, 4. p. 142.

σφῦρόν, τό, the *ankle*, 4, 518; plur. *6, 117.

σφώ, 1) Abbrev. for σφῶι. 2) For σφωέ, Ep.

σφωέ, see σφωίν.

σφώ, Ep. σφῶιν and σφῶι, gen. and dat. σφῶιν, contr. σφῶν, Od. 4, 62; cf. Thiersch, Gram. § 204, 6; accus. σφῶι and σφώ, dual of the second personal pronoun, *ye two;* often ἀμφοτέρω σφῶι, Il. 7, 280; see Thiersch, § 204. Rost, Dial. 44. p. 412. Kühner, § 301.

σφωίν, dat. dual of the third personal pronoun, accus. σφώ, Ep. σφωέ; the nom. is not in use; all the forms are enclitic: *of them both, to them both;* strengthened: σφῶιν ἀμφοτέροιιν, Od. 20, 327. σφω' for σφωέ stands Il. 17, 531; σφώ, on the other hand, is found in Bothe, cf. Thiersch, Gram. § 204, 6. Rem.

σφωίτερος, η, ον (σφῶι), *your two, belonging to you two*, Il. 1, 216.†

σχεδίη, ἡ, prop. fem. of σχέδιος, subaud. νηῦς, a *vessel built in haste*, by Odysseus (Ulysses) for a shift: a *raft*, *Od. 5, 33. 163. According to Nitzsch ad loc. a *hand-boat*, which one man can manage alone. [According to Ameis. it is derived from σχεῖν, akin to σχεδόν; cf. the German *Gebünde*, contignatio. Am.]

σχεδίην, Ep. adv. (prop. fem. of σχέδιος), *near, in the vicinity*, 5, 830.†

Σχεδίος, ὁ (adj. σχέδιος), 1) son of Iphitus and Hippolytē, leader of the Phocians, slain by Hector, 2, 517. 2) son of Perimides, another leader of the Phocians, 15, 515.

σχεδόθεν, adv. poet. *from the vicinity*, 16, 807. 17, 359. 2) *in the vicinity, near*, with gen. Od. 19, 447; and dat. Od. 2, 267.

σχεδόν, adv. poet. (σχεῖν, ἔχω). *in the vicinity, near*, absol. οὐτάζειν, ἐλαύνειν, εἶναι, 5, 458. 11, 488. *b*) As prep. with gen. ἐλθεῖν τινος, to come near any one, 5, 607. Od. 4, 439; with dat. Od. 2, 284. οὐ σχεδὸν ἦν ὑπερθορέειν, it was not near to leap over, i. e. the other side of the ditch was not so near that the horses could reach it, Il. 12, 53. 2) *near*, spoken of time: σοὶ δ' αὐτῷ φημι σχεδὸν ἔμμεναι, 13, 817.

σχεθεῖν, Ep. σχεθέειν, infin. of a poet. lengthened aor. ἔσχεθον for ἔσχον, in the sigmif. *to hold, to restrain* ; see ἔχω.

σχεῖν, σχέμεν, see ἔχω.

σχέο, see ἔχω.

Σχερίη, ἡ (prob. from σχερός, the land), *Scheria*, the blessed land of the Phæaces, Od. 5, 34. 280. According to the local indications furnished Od. 6, 204. 279, it may be considered as the island furthest north of Ithaca, near the land of the Thesprotians ; according to the ordinary explanation of the ancients, the later Κέρκυρα, now *Corfu*, cf. Thuc. I, 25. Strab. These are followed amongst the moderns by Voss and Völcker: others place it towards Thesprotia or Campania (cf. Nitzsch ad Od. 7, 129). Others still regard it as a fabulous land in the vicinity of Elysium, as F. G. Welker in the treatise : *die homerischen Phäaken u. die Inseln der Seligen*, in the Rhein. Museum, St. 2, 1833, attempts to prove at large. Not inappropriately has the German *Schlaraffenland* (Pays de Cocagne), been compared with it.

σχέτλιος, η. ον (σχεῖν, ἔχω), the fem. only 3, 414. Od. 23, 150; that sustains or abides any thing; hence, 1) *strong, powerful, impetuous, bold, rash* ; mly spoken in a bad sense, of those who from impetuous courage, or from a bad use of their strength, are terrible, as Heracles, Achilles, Hector, Il. 5, 403. 9, 630. 16, 203. 17, 150. Od. 9, 351. 478. The fem. σχετλίη, Il. 3, 414; plur. Od. 4, 729. It stands in a more favorable sense in Il. 10, 164, where Nestor, on account of his restless activity, is called σχέτλιος by Diomedes. Here and in 18, 13. Od. 12, 279, expositors endeavour to apply the meaning, *miserable, wretched* ; it is, however, an expression like the Latin *improbus*, to be translated *wicked* or *prodigious, astonishing. b*) Often spoken of gods, and esply of Zeus, *harsh, severe, cruel*, 2, 111. 9, 19. Od. 3, 161 ; spoken of the gods generally. Il. 24, 133. Od. 5, 118. 2) Spoken of things, *violent, cruel, impious*, always with ἔργα, Od. 9, 295. 14, 83. 22, 413.

σχέτο, Ep. for ἔσχετο, see ἔχω.

ΣΧΕΩ, obsol., another form of ἔχω, q. v.

σχίζη, ἡ (σχίζω), *split wood, a billet of wood*, 1, 462. Od. 14, 425.

σχίζω, aor. 1 ἔσχισα, *to split, to cleave*, with accus. in tmesis, Od. 4, 507; generally, *to separate, to divide*, h. Merc. 128.

σχοίατο, Ion. for σχοῖντο, see ἔχω.

σχοῖνος, ὁ, *a rush, a bulrush*, also a place overgrown with rushes, Od. 5, 463.† Batr. 213.

Σχοῖνος, ἡ, a town in Bœotia, on the river Schœnus, not far from Thebes, 2, 497 Strabo calls it χώρα; the region

received the name from the rushes ing thereabouts.

σχόμενος, η, ον, see ἔχω.

σώεσκον, see σαόω.

σώζω, the comm. form instead Ep. σαόω, only σώζων, Od. 5, 490 σαόω.

σῶκος, η, ον, Ep. (σωκέω), *powerful* (V. 'that blesses'), e Hermês, 20, 72. (The derivatio σάοκος, that preserves the hou cording to Apion, is fanciful.

Σῶκος, ὁ, a Trojan, son of Hi slain by Odysseus (Ulysses), 11, 4

σῶμα, ατος, τό, *a body*, spoke of men and beasts; in Hom. *body, a corpse*, 7, 79. 23, 169. 53. [According to Aristot., san by Passow and Anieis, it is spoken of a dead body in Hom., v of men or beasts. According to brev. ad Il. 3, 23, it is there spo a living animal, cf. Eustath. ad I.

σῶς, contr from σάος, occurs i only in the nom. sing. *safe, unh* 332. Od. 15, 42. 2) *sure, cer* according to the Schol. comple ὄλεθρος, Il. 13, 773. Od. 5, 3ι σόος.

°σωτήρ, ῆρος, ὁ (σώζω), *a deli preserver*, h. 21, 5. 33, 6.

Σῶχ', poet. shortened from Σῶ from Σῶκος.

σώω, see σαόω.

T.

T, the nineteenth letter of the alphabet, hence in Hom. the sigi nineteenth rhapsody.

τ', with an apostrophe 1) for More rarely in Hom. doubtful in μέντ' according to Bothe. Il Wolf μέν τ', and in ταρ, see this

ταγός, ὁ (τάσσω), *an arranger*, a commander, 23. 160.† (Mly a Bothe and Spitzner have adopted which is the ancient reading.)

ΤΑΓΩ, obsol. theme of the partcp. aor. 2 with Ep. redupl. *to seize, to grasp, to lay hold* τεταγών, seizing by the foot, *1, 23. According to the Schol. = and akin to ΤΑΩ, τείνω, cf. Butt p.

ταθείς, τάθη, see τείνω.

*Ταίναρον, τό (also ὁ Ταίναρι Scylax ; ἡ Ταίναρος, Pind.). *T. a promontory in Laconia, the n the southern capes of the Pelop now *Cap Matapan*. Upon it the famous temple of Poseidôn, cave, where was the entrance t h. Ap. 412.